REFERENCE

D1163556

TOURO COLLEGE LIBRARY
Boro Park 53rd Street

Encyclopedia of
Psychological Assessment

Volume 1
A–L

REFERENCE

Encyclopedia of Psychological Assessment

Volume 1
A–L

Edited by Rocío Fernández-Ballesteros

Editorial Board

Dave Bartram
Gian Vittorio Caprara
Ronald K. Hambleton
Lutz F. Hornke
Jan ter Laak

Lilianne Manning
Rudolf Moos
Charles D. Spielberger
Irving B. Weiner
Hans Westmeyer

TOURO COLLEGE LIBRARY
Boro Park 53rd Street

SAGE Publications
London • Thousand Oaks • New Delhi

BP53

© Rocío Fernández-Ballesteros 2003

First published 2003
Reprinted 2003

Apart from any fair dealing for the purposes of research or
private study, or criticism or review, as permitted under the
Copyright, Designs and Patents Act, 1988, this publication
may be reproduced, stored or transmitted in any form, or by
any means, only with the prior permission in writing of the
publishers, or in the case of reprographic reproduction, in
accordance with the terms of licences issued by the Copyright
Licensing Agency. Inquiries concerning reproduction outside
those terms should be sent to the publishers.

SAGE Publications Ltd
6 Bonhill Street
London EC2A 4PU

SAGE Publications Inc
2455 Teller Road
Thousand Oaks, California 91320

SAGE Publications India Pvt. Ltd
32, M-Block Market
Greater Kailash-I
New Delhi 110 048

British Library Cataloguing in Publication data

A catalogue record for this book is available from
the British Library

ISBN 0 7619 5494 5

Library of Congress Control Number: 2002104967

Typeset by Keyword Publishing Services, Barking, Essex
Printed in Great Britain by The Alden Press, Oxford

7/31/07

Contents

List of Entries

Volume 1

Volume 2

Reader's Guide

This list is provided to assist readers in locating entries on related topics. It classifies entries into nine general categories: (1) Theory and Methodology; (2) Methods, Tests and Equipment; (3) Personality; (4) Intelligence; (5) Clinical and Health; (6) Educational and Child Assessment; (7) Work and Organizations; (8) Neurophysiopsychological Assessment; and (9) Environmental Assessment. Some entry titles appear in more than one category.

1. Theory and Methodology

Ambulatory Assessment
Assessment Process
Assessor's Bias
Automated Test Assembly Systems
Classical and Modern Item Analysis
Classical Test Theory
Classification (General, including Diagnosis)
Criterion-Referenced Testing: Methods and Procedures
Cross-Cultural Assessment
Decision (including Decision Theory)
Diagnosis of Mental and Behavioural Disorders
Diagnostic Testing in Educational Settings
Dynamic Assessment (Learning Potential Testing, Testing the Limits)
Ethics
Evaluability Assessment
Evaluation: Programme Evaluation (General)
Explanation
Factor Analysis: Confirmatory
Factor Analysis: Exploratory
Formats for Assessment
Generalizability Theory
History of Psychological Assessment
Intelligence Assessment through Cohort and Time
Item Banking
Item Bias
Item Response Theory: Models and Features
Latent Class Analysis
Multidimensional Item Response Theory
Multidimensional Scaling Methods
Multimodal Assessment (including Triangulation)
Multitrait–Multimethod Matrices
Needs Assessment
Norm-Referenced Testing: Methods and Procedures
Objectivity
Outcome Assessment/Treatment Assessment
Person/Situation (Environment) Assessment
Personality Assessment through Longitudinal Designs
Prediction (General)
Prediction: Clinical vs. Statistical
Qualitative Methods
Reliability
Report (General)
Reporting Test Results in Education
Self-Presentation Measurement
Self-Report Distortions (including Faking, Lying, Malingering, Social Desirability)
Test Adaptation/Translation Methods
Test User Competence/Responsible Test Use
Theoretical Perspective: Cognitive
Theoretical Perspective: Cognitive-Behavioural
Theoretical Perspective: Constructivism
Theoretical Perspective: Psychoanalytic

Contributors

Phillip L. Ackerman, School of Psychology, Georgia Institute of Technology, Atlanta, Georgia, USA

Icek Ajzen, Department of Psychology, University of Massachusetts, Amherst, Massachusetts, USA

Avi Allalouf, National Institute for Testing and Evaluation, Jerusalem, Israel

Manfred Amelang, Psychology Institute, Heidelberg University, Heidelberg, Germany

Craig A. Anderson, Department of Psychology, Iowa State University, Ames, Iowa, USA

María Teresa Anguera Argilaga, Faculty of Psychology, University of Barcelona, Barcelona, Spain

Alvaro de Ansorena, Euroresearch, Madrid, Spain

Alessandro Antonietti, Department of Psychology, Catholic University of Sacred Heart, Milan, Italy

Toni C. Antonucci, Institute for Social Research, University of Michigan, Ann Arbor, Michigan, USA

Carmen Armengol de la Miyar, ABPP, Counseling and Applied Educational Psychology, Northeastern University, Boston, Massachusetts, USA

Erik Arntzen, Akershus University College, Sadvika, Norway

Jens B. Asendorpf, Institute of Psychology, Humboldt University, Berlin, Germany

Jo-Anne Bachorowski, Department of Psychology, Vanderbilt University, Nashville, Tennessee, USA

Ruth A. Baer, Department of Psychology, University of Kentucky, Lexington, Kentucky, USA

Eva L. Baker, University of California, Los Angeles, California, USA

Marian J. Bakermans-Kranenburg, Center for Child and Family Studies, Leiden University, Leiden, The Netherlands

Albert Bandura, Department of Psychology, Stanford University, Stanford, California, USA

Claudio Barbaranelli, Department of Psychology, University of Rome 'La Sapienza', Rome, Italy

Pilar Barreto Martin, Faculty of Psychology, University of Valencia, Valencia, Spain

María Victoria del Barrio, Faculty of Psychology, UNED, Madrid, Spain

Dave Bartram, SHL Group plc, Thames Ditton, Surrey, UK

André Beauducel, Dresden University of Technology, Dresden, Germany

Robert B. Bechtel, Department of Psychology, University of Arizona, Arizona, USA

Mercedes Belinchón, Faculty of Psychology, Autónoma University of Madrid, Madrid, Spain

Giray Berberoğlu, Faculty of Education, Middle East Technical University, Ankara, Turkey

José Bermudez, Faculty of Psychology, UNED, Madrid, Spain

German E. Berrios, Addenbrooke's Hospital (Box 189), University of Cambridge and Robinson College, Cambridge, UK

David T.R. Berry, Department of Psychology, University of Kentucky, Kentucky, USA

Heather Biggar, Center for Research for Mothers and Children, National Institute of Child Health and Human Development, Rockville, Maryland, USA

Gerhard Blickle, University Koblenz-Landau, Landau, Germany

Robert H. Bodholt, Bastrop, Texas, USA

Anna Silvia Bombi, Department of Psychology, University of Rome 'La Sapienza', Rome, Italy

Katrin Borcherding, Institute of Psychology, Darmstadt University of Technology, Darmstadt, Germany

Rainer Bösel, Department of Psychology, Free University of Berlin, Berlin, Germany

Jason Z. Bowman, Department of Psychology, University of Florida, Gainesville, Florida, USA

John N. Boyd, Department of Psychology, Stanford University, Stanford, California, USA

K. Robert Bridges, Penn State University, New Kensington, Philadelphia, USA

Richard S. Brown, School of Education, University of California, Irvine, California, USA

G. Brugman, Department of Developmental Psychology, University of Utrecht, Utrecht, The Netherlands

Eric E.J. De Bruyn, Nijmegen Institute for Cognition and Information, University of Nijmegen, Nijmegen, The Netherlands

Barbara M. Byrne, School of Psychology, University of Ottawa, Ottawa, Ontario, Canada

Zinta S. Byrne, Department of Psychology, Colorado State University, Fort Collins, Colorado, USA

Wayne J. Camara, The College Board, New York, New York, USA

Gian Vittorio Caprara, Department of Psychology, University of Rome 'La Sapienza', Rome, Italy

Heliodoro Carpintero, Faculty of Psychology, Complutense University, Madrid, Spain

Maria Martina Casullo, Faculty of Psychology, Buenos Aires University, Buenos Aires, Argentina

Antonio Cepeda-Benito, Department of Psychology, Texas A&M University, College Station, Texas, USA

Daniel Cervone, Department of Psychology, University of Illinois, Chicago, Illinois, USA

Salvador Chacón-Moscoso, Department of Experimental Psychology, University of Seville, Seville, Spain

Gregory J. Cizek, School of Education, University of North Carolina, North Carolina, USA

Allison Collins, Department of Psychology, Bowling Green State University, Bowling Green, Ohio, USA

Roberto Colom, Faculty of Psychology, Autónoma University of Madrid, Madrid, Spain

John D. Cone, California School of Professional Psychology, Alliant International University, San Diego, California, USA

Cesare Cornoldi, Department of Psychology, University of Padova, Padova, Italy

José Antonio Corraliza, Faculty of Psychology, Autónoma University of Madrid, Madrid, Spain

Mark L. Davison, Department of Educational Psychology, University of Minnesota, Minneapolis, Minnesota, USA

Günter Debus, Department of Psychology, Aachen University of Technology, Aachen, Germany

Ana R. Delgado, Department of Psychology, Salamanca University, Salamanca, Spain

Ed Diener, Department of Psychology, University of Illinois, Champaign, Illinois, USA

Juan Díez Medrano, Department of Sociology, University of California, San Diego, La Jolla, California, USA

Juan Díez Nicolas, Faculty of Political Science and Sociology, Complutense University, Madrid, Spain

Mohamed Dirir, Connecticut Department of Education, Hartford, Connecticut, USA

Filip Dochy, Department EDIT Educational Innovarion & IT, University of Maastricht, Maastricht, The Netherlands

Levent Dumenci, Depatment of Psychiatry, University of Vermont, Vermont, USA

Stephen B. Dunbar, Iowa Testing Programs, University of Iowa, Iowa City, Iowa, USA

Riley E. Dunlap, Department of Sociology, Washington State University, Pullman, Washington, USA

Daniel R. Eignor, Educational Testing Service, Princeton, New Jersey, USA

Norman S. Endler, Department of Psychology, York University, Toronto, Ontario, Canada

Gary W. Evans, Departments of Design and Environmental Analysis and of Human Development, Cornell University, Ithaca, New York, USA

Lorraine Dittrich Eyde, U.S. Office of Personnel Management, Arlington, Virginia, USA

Babette Fahlbruch, Institute of Psychology, Technological University, Berlin, Germany

Jochen Fahrenberg, Department of Psychology, University of Freiburg, Freiburg, Germany

Hubert Feger, Department of Psychology, Free University of Berlin, Berlin, Germany

Guillem Feixas, Faculty of Psychology, University of Barcelona, Barcelona, Spain

Simeon Feldstein, School of Psychology, Georgia Institute of Technology, Atlanta, Georgia, USA

Fabio Ferlazzo, Department of Psychology, University of Rome 'La Sapienza', Rome, Italy

Francisco Fernández Ballesteros, Quality and Training, Javea, Alicante, Spain

Rocío Fernández-Ballesteros, Department of Psychobiology and Health Psychology, Autónoma University of Madrid, Madrid, Spain

José-Miguel Fernández-Dols, Faculty of Psychology, Autónoma University of Madrid, Madrid, Spain

Alfredo Fierro, Faculty of Psychology, University of Málaga, Málaga, Spain

Edwin A. Fleishman, George Mason University, Potomac, Maryland, USA

Maria Forns, Faculty of Psychology, University of Barcelona, Barcelona, Spain

Donata Francescato, Department of Psychology, University of Rome 'La Sapienza', Rome, Italy

Sarah L. Friedman, Center for Research for Mothers and Children, Bethesda, Maryland, USA

Svein Friis, Department of Research and Education, Division of Psychiatry, Ulleval University Hospital, Oslo, Norway

María Xesús Froján Parga, Department of Psychobiology and Health Psychology, Autónoma University of Madrid, Madrid, Spain

Carl B. Gacono, Austin, Texas, USA

Marco Gemignani, Department of Psychology, University of Florida, Gainesville, Florida, USA

Maria Gerbino, Department of Psychology, University of Rome 'La Sapienza', Rome, Italy

Jennifer M. Gillis, Center for Educational Partnerships, University of California, Irvine, California, USA

Cees A.W. Glas, Department of Educational Measurement and Data Analysis, University of Twente, Enschede, The Netherlands

Antonio Godoy, Faculty of Psychology, University of Málaga, Málaga, Spain

M.P.M. de Goede, Department of Methodology and Statistics, University of Utrecht, Utrecht, The Netherlands

Georg Goldenberg, Neuropsychological Department, Bogenhausen Hospital, Munich, Germany

Reginald G. Golledge, Department of Geography and Research Unit on Spatial Cognition and Choice, University of California, Santa Barbara, California, USA

Juana Gómez-Benito, Faculty of Psychology, University of Barcelona, Barcelona, Spain

Héctor González-Ordi, Faculty of Psychology, Complutense University of Madrid, Madrid, Spain

Jerry Gorham, CTB McGraw-Hill, New York, New York, USA

Linda S. Gottfredson, School of Education, University of Delaware, Newark, Delaware, USA

Benjamin H. Gottlieb, Department of Psychology, University of Guelph, Guelph, Ontario, Canada

Jaques Gregoire, Faculty of Psychology, Catholic University of Louvain, Louvain-la-Neuve, Belgium

Siegfried Greif, Department of Psychology, University of Osnabrück, Osnabrück, Germany

Gary Groth-Marnat, School of Psychology, Curtin University of Technology, Perth, WA, Australia

Dato N.M. de Gruijter, School of Education, Leiden, The Netherlands

Jon Randolph Haber, V.A. Medical Center, Menlo Park, California, USA

Ronald K. Hambleton, University of Massachusetts, Amherst, Massachusetts, USA

Terry Hartig, Institute for Housing and Urban Research, Uppsala University, Gävle, Sweden

Stephen N. Haynes, Department of Psychology, University of Hawaii, Honolulu, Hawaii, USA

Elaine M. Heiby, Department of Psychology, University of Hawaii, Honolulu, Hawaii, USA

Hubert J. M. Hermans, Department of Clinical Psychology and Personality, Catholic University of Nijmegen, Nijmegen, The Netherlands

José Manuel Hernández, Department of Psychobiology and Health Psychology, Autónoma University of Madrid, Madrid, Spain

Peter Herriot, CSA/Empower Management Consultants, Bromley, Kent, UK

Christopher Hertzog, School of Psychology, Georgia Institute of Technology, Atlanta, Georgia, USA

Robert M. Hessling, Department of Psychology, University of Wisconsin, Milwaukee, Wisconsin, USA

Richard E. Heyman, Department of Psychology, State University of New York, Stony Brook, New York, USA

Rebecca J. Hill, Department of Psychology, University of Arizona, Tucson, Arizona, USA

John M. Hintze, School of Education, University of Massachusetts at Amherst, Amherst, Massachusetts, USA

Robert Hogan, Hogan Assessment Systems, Tulsa, Oklahoma, USA

Charles J. Holahan, Department of Psychology, University of Texas, Austin, Texas, USA

Francisco Pablo Holgado Tello, Department of Methodology, UNED, Madrid, Spain

Lutz F. Hornke, Department of Industrial Psychology, Aachen University of Technology, Aachen, Germany

Anita M. Hubley, Department of ECPS, University of British Columbia, Vancouver, BC, Canada

José Manuel Igoa, Faculty of Psychology, Autónoma University of Madrid, Madrid, Spain

Marinus Van Ijzendoorn, Center for Child and Family Studies, Leiden University, Leiden, The Netherlands

Theodore Jacob, V.A. Palo Alto Health Care System, Palo Alto, California, USA

Arthur R. Jensen, School of Education, University of California, Berkeley, California, USA

Michael Jodoin, University of Massachusetts, Amherst, Massachusetts, USA

Robert Emmet Jones, Department of Sociology, University of Tennessee, Knoxville, Tennessee, USA

Joseph K. Kaholokula, Department of Psychology, University of Hawaii, Honolulu, Hawaii, USA

Velma A. Kameoka, School of Social Work, University of Hawaii, Honolulu, Hawaii, USA

Anil Kanjee, Human Sciences Research Council, Pretoria, South Africa

Edith Kaplan, Department of Psychology, Suffolk University, Boston, Massachusetts, USA

Mary Kaplar, Department of Psychology, Bowling Green State University, Bowling Green, Ohio, USA

Alan S. Kaufman, Department of Psychology, Yale University School of Medicine, New Haven, Connecticut, USA

James C. Kaufman, Educational Testing Service, Princeton, New Jersey, USA

Martin Kersting, Institute of Psychology, Aachen Technical University, Aachen, Germany

Thomas J. Kiresuk, Center for Addiction and Alternative Medicine Research, Minneapolis, Minnesota, USA

James H. Kleiger, Bethesda, Maryland, USA

Uwe Kleinbeck, Organizational Psychology, University of Dortmund, Dortmund, Germany

Reinhold Kliegl, Department of Psychology, University of Potsdam, Potsdam, Germany

Marie-Luise Kluck, Institute of Psychology, Bonn University, Bonn, Germany

Annette Kluge, Institute of Psychology, Aachen Technical University, Aachen, Germany

Nancy L. Kocovski, Department of Psychology, York University, Toronto, Ontario, Canada

Richard Koestner, Psychology Department, McGill University, Montreal, Quebec, Canada

Anita Konachoff, Department of Psychology, Temple University, Philadelphia, Pennsylvania, USA

William J. Korotitsch, Department of Psychology, University of North Carolina at Greensboro, Greensboro, North Carolina, USA

Jane Kroger, Psychology Department, University of Tromsø, Tromsø, Norway

Andreas Kruse, Institute of Gerontology, University of Heidelberg, Heidelberg, Germany

Patrick C. Kyllonen, Educational Testing Service, Princeton, New Jersey, USA

J. ter Laak, Department of Developmental Psychology, University of Utrecht, Utrecht, The Netherlands

Ángel Lara-Ruiz, Faculty of Psychology, University of Seville, Seville, Spain

Fiona Lee, Department of Psychology, University of Michigan, Michigan, USA

Judy H. Lee, Department of Psychology, University of Hawaii, Honolulu, Hawaii, USA

Ursula Lehr, The German Centre for Research on Ageing, Heidelberg, Germany

José León-Carrión, Department of Experimental Psychology, University of Seville, Seville, Spain

Nurit Levi, Beit-Berl College, Beit-Berl, Israel

Heidi Levitt, Department of Psychology, University of Memphis, Memphis, Tennessee, USA

Carol S. Lidz, Touro College, New York, New York, USA

Wim van der Linden, Department of Educational Measurement and Data Analysis, University of Twente, Enschede, The Netherlands

Friedrich Lösel, Institute of Psychology, University of Erlangen-Nuremberg, Nuremberg, Germany

Rodney L. Lowman, College of Organizational Studies, Alliant International University, San Diego, California, USA

Nicola Mammarella, Department of General Psychology, University of Padova, Padova, Italy

Lilianne Manning, Behavioural and Cognitive Neurosciences Laboratory, Louis Pasteur University, Strasbourg, France

María Oliva Márquez, Department of Psychobiology and Health Psychology, Autónoma University of Madrid, Madrid, Spain

Ignacio Martin, Institute of Social Sciences, Oporto, Portugal

Rosario Martínez Arias, Faculty of Psychology, Complutense University, Madrid, Spain

Vicente Martinez-Tur, Faculty of Psychology, University of Valencia, Valencia, Spain

Mark E. Maruish, United Behavioral Health, Minnetonka, Minnesota, USA

Christina Maslach, Department of Psychology, University of California, Berkeley, California, USA

Gerald Matthews, Department of Psychology, University of Cincinnati, Cincinnati, Ohio, USA

John D. Mayer, Department of Psychology, University of New Hampshire, Durham, New Hampshire, USA

Jessica M. McIlvane, Institute for Social Research, University of Michigan, Ann Arbor, Michigan, USA

Francisco Xavier Méndez Carrillo, Faculty of Psychology, University of Murcia, Murcia, Spain

Peter F. Merenda, Department of Psychology, Kingston, Rhode Island, USA

Peter G. Mezo, Department of Psychology, University of Hawaii, Honolulu, Hawaii, USA

Juan José Miguel-Tobal, Department of Basic Psychology II, Complutense University, Madrid, Spain

Elisabeth J. Moes, Psychology Department, Suffolk University, Boston, Massachusetts, USA

Rudolf H. Moos, Stanford University Medical Center, Veterans Affairs Health Care System, Palo Alto, California, USA

Leslie C. Morey, Department of Psychology, Texas A&M University, College Station, Texas, USA

Manolete S. Moscoso, Morton Plant Hospital, Cancer Center, Clearwater, Florida, USA

José Muñiz, Faculty of Psychology, University of Oviedo, Oviedo, Spain

Kevin R. Murphy, Department of Psychology, Pennsylvania State University, University Park, Pennsylvania, USA

Robert A. Neimeyer, Department of Psychology, University of Memphis, Memphis, Tennessee, USA

Greg J. Neimeyer, Department of Psychology, University of Florida, Gainesville, Florida, USA

Karl Nelson, Department of Psychology, University of Hawaii, Honolulu, Hawaii, USA

Rosemery O. Nelson-Gray, Department of Psychology, University of North Carolina at Greensboro, Greensboro, North Carolina, USA

William H. O'Brien, Department of Psychology, Bowling Green State University, Bowling Green, Ohio, USA

Julio Olea, Department of Methdology and Social Psychology, Autónoma University of Madrid, Madrid, Spain

Piotr K. Oles, Department of Clinical and Personality Psychology, Catholic University of Lublin, Lublin, Poland

José Olivares, Faculty of Psychology, University of Murcia, Spain

Maike Oppe, Institute of Psychology, University of Aachen, Aachen, Germany

Virginia L. Ordman, Lindquist Center, University of Iowa, Ames, Zowa, USA

Concetta Pastorelli, Department of Psychology, University of Rome 'La Sapienza', Rome, Italy

Constança Paúl, Institute of Biomedical Sciences Abel Salazar, University of Oporto, Oporto, Portugal

Delroy L. Paulhus, Department of Psychology, University of British Columbia, Vancouver, BC, Canada

William Pavot, Department of Psychology, University of Illinois, Champaign, Illinois, USA

Kurt Pawlik, Institute of Psychology, University of Hamburg, Hamburg, Germany

José María Peiró, Faculty of Psychology, University of Valencia, Valencia, Spain

José Antonio Pérez-Gil, Faculty of Psychology, University of Seville, Seville, Spain

Miguel Angel Pérez-Nieto, Madrid, Spain

Marco Perugini, Department of Psychology, University of Essex, Colchester, Essex, UK

Christopher Peterson, Department of Psychology, University of Pennsylvania, Philadelphia, Pennsylvania, USA

Robin L. Phaneuf, School of Education, University of Massachusetts, Amherst, Massachusetts, USA

Doris Philipp, Department of Psychology, University of Potsdam, Potsdam, Germany

Pierre Pichot, Paris, France

Marc Pilisuk, Saybrook Institute, San Francisco, California, USA

Barbara S. Plake, Buros Center for Testing, University of Nebraska-Lincoln, Lincoln, Nebraska, USA

Vicente Ponsoda, Department of Methodology and Social Psychology, Autónoma University of Madrid, Madrid, Spain

Ype H. Poortinga, Department of Psychology, Tilburg University, Tilburg, The Netherlands

Gerardo Prieto, Faculty of Psychology, University of Salamanca, Salamanca, Spain

George P. Prigatano, Barrow Neurological Institute, St. Joseph's Hospital and Medical Center, Phoenix, Arizona, USA

Boele De Raad, Department of Psychology, University of Groningen, Groningen, The Netherlands

William Randall, Department of Gerontology, St. Thomas University, Fredericton, New Brunswick, Canada

Abilio Reig-Ferrer, Department of Health Psychology, University of Alicante, Alicante, Spain

Britta Renner, Department of Psychology, University of Greifswald, Greifswald, Germany

Christian Rietz, Department of Psychology/Centre of Evaluation and Methodology (CEM), University of Bonn, Bonn, Germany

Jason C. Rinaldo, Department of Psychology, University of Kentucky, Kentucky, USA

Richard D. Roberts, Department of Psychology, Sydney University, Sydney, NSW, Australia

Shlomo Romi, School of Education, Bar-Ilan University, Ramat-Gan, Israel

Jan H. Rosenvinge, Psychology Department, University of Tromsø, Tromsø, Norway

Jürgen Rost, Institute for Science Education, Kiel, Germany

Victor J. Rubio, Department of Psychobiology and Health Psychology, Autónoma University of Madrid, Madrid, Spain

Georg Rudinger, Department of Psychology, Bonn University, Bonn, Germany

José María Ruiz Vargas, Faculty of Psychology, Autónoma University of Madrid, Madrid, Spain

Daniel W. Russell, Department of Psychology, Iowa State University, Ames, Iowa, USA

Torleif Ruud, Department of Health Care Research in Mental Health, SINTEF Unimed, Norway

Jocelyn Saferstein, Department of Psychology, University of Florida, Gainesville, Florida, USA

Carmina Saldaña, Faculty of Psychology, University of Barcelona, Barcelona, Spain

Stan Scarpati, School of Education, University of Massachusetts, Amherst, Massachusetts, USA

David Scheffer, Organisational Psychology, University of Bundeswehr Hamburg, Hamburg, Germany

Günter Schiepek, University Clinic, RWTH Aachen, Aachen, Germany

Martin Schmucker, Institute of Psychology, University of Erlangen-Nuremburg, Nuremburg, Germany

Ralf Schwarzer, Department of Health Psychology, Free University of Berlin, Berlin, Germany

Michael Scriven, Department of Psychology, Claremont Graduate University, Claremont, USA

Lee Sechrest, Department of Psychology, University of Arizona, Tucson, Arizona, USA

Martin E.P. Seligman, Department of Psychology, University of Pennsylvania, Philadelphia, Pennsylvania, USA

William G. Shadel, Department of Psychology, University of Pittsburg, Pittsburg, Pennsylvania, USA

Danilo R. Silva, Faculty of Psychology, Lisbon University, Lisbon, Portugal

Dean Keith Simonton, Department of Psychology, University of California, Davis, California, USA

Stephen G. Sireci, School of Education, University of Massachusetts, Amherst, Massachusetts, USA

Amy M. Smith Slep, Department of Psychology, State University of New York, Stony Brook, New York, USA

Douglas K. Snyder, Department of Psychology, Texas A&M University, College Station, Texas, USA

Will A.C. Spijkers, Institute of Psychology, RWTH Aachen, Aachen, Germany

Arthur W. Staats, Department of Psychology, University of Hawaii, Honolulu, Hawaii, USA

Ursula M. Staudinger, Department of Psychology, Dresden University, Dresden, Germany

Manfred Steffen, Educational Testing Service, Princeton, New Jersey, USA

Robert J. Sternberg, Centre for the Psychology of Abilities, Competencies, and Expertise, Yale University, New Haven, Connecticut, USA

Rolf Steyer, Institute of Psychology, Friedrich-Schiller University, Jena, Germany

Rolf-Dieter Stieglitz, University Psychiatric Outpatients Department, Basel, Switzerland
Martha Stocking, Educational Testing Service, Princeton, New Jersey, USA
Gary Stoner, School of Education, University of Massachusetts, Amherst, Massachusetts, USA
Jan Strelau, School of Social Psychology, University of Warsaw, Warsaw, Poland
Timo Suutama, Department of Psychology, University of Jyväskylä, Jyväskylä, Finland
Torbjörn Svensson, Gerontology Research Center, Lund, Sweden
H. Lee Swanson, School of Education, University of California, Riverside, California, USA
Sascha Tamm, Department of Psychology, Free University of Berlin, Berlin, Germany
Lydia R. Temoshok, Institute of Human Virology, University of Maryland, Baltimore, Maryland, USA
Christine Temple, Department of Psychology, University of Essex, Colchester, Essex, UK
Robert Tett, Department of Psychology University of Tulsa, Tulsa, Oklahoma, USA
Warren W. Tryon, Department of Psychology, Fordham University, Bronx, New York, USA
Graham Turpin, Department of Psychology, University of Sheffield, Sheffield, UK
Miguel Angel Verdugo, Faculty of Psychology, University of Salamanca, Salamanca, Spain
Fons van de Vijver, Department of Psychology, Tilburg University, Tilburg, The Netherlands
Jaime Vila, Faculty of Psychology, University of Granada, Granada, Spain
Carmen Vizcarro Guarch, Department of Psychobiology and Health Psychology, Autónoma University of Madrid, Madrid, Spain
Ajay Wagle, Queen Elizabeth Hospital, Kings Lynn, UK
Suvarna Wagle, Julian Hospital, Norwich, UK
Richard K. Wagner, Department of Psychology, Florida State University, Tallahassee, Florida, USA
Hans-Werner Wahl, The German Centre for Research on Ageing, Heidelberg, Germany
Howard Wainer, Educational Testing Service, Princeton, New Jersey, USA
Susan B. Watson, Department of Psychology, University of Hawaii, Honolulu, Hawaii, USA
Walter D. Way, Educational Testing Service, Princeton, New Jersey, USA
Hannelore Weber, Department of Psychology, University of Greifswald, Greifswald, Germany
Irving B. Weiner, Department of Psychology, University of South Florida, Tampa, Florida, USA
Nancy M. Wells, School of Social Ecology, University of California, Irvine, California, USA
Richard Wener, Polytechnic University, Brooklyn, New York, USA
Karl Westhoff, Department of Psychology, Dresden University of Technology, Dresden, Germany
Hans Westmeyer, Department of Psychology, Free University of Berlin, Berlin, Germany
Elaine Wethington, Department of Human Development, Cornell University, Ithaca, New York, USA
Mark Wilson, Department of Education, University of California, Berkeley, California, USA
David A. Winter, Barnet Healthcare NHS Trust, Edgware, Middlesex, UK
Angela Wong, University of California, Berkeley, California, USA
Orli Yazdi-Ugav, The Zinman College of Physical Education and Sport Sciences, Wingate Institute, Netania, Israel
James L. Zazzali, Department of Health Administration, Virginia Commonwealth University, Richmond, Virginia, USA
Moshe Zeidner, University of Haifa, Haifa, Israel
April L. Zenisky, School of Education, University of Massachusetts, Amherst, Massachusetts, USA
Fred R.H. Zijlstra, School of Human Sciences, University of Surrey, Guildford, Surrey, UK
Philip G. Zimbardo, Department of Psychology, Stanford University, Stanford, California, USA
Marvin Zuckerman, Department of Psychology, Delaware University, Newark, Delaware, USA
Bruno D. Zumbo, Department of ECPS, University of British Columbia, Vancouver, BC, Canada

Preface

Psychological assessment is the discipline of scientific psychology devoted to the study of a given human subject (or group of subjects) in a specific applied field (clinical, educational, work, etc.), by means of scientific tools (tests and other measurement instruments), with the purpose of answering clients' demands that require scientific operations such as describing, diagnosing, predicting, explaining or changing the behaviour of that subject (Fernández-Ballesteros et al., 2001). Therefore, from this perspective, psychological assessment cannot be reduced to any of its applied fields (it has sometimes been reduced to the clinical field: e.g. Meyer et al., 2001; Fernández-Ballesteros, 2002) or to specific scientific tools (it has been reduced to psychological testing: e.g. Anastasi, 1988) or to a scientific operation (in the past it was usually reduced to diagnosis and prediction).

Psychological assessment is one of the key disciplines of psychology, being an ever-present applied task in the activity of any psychologist (Bomholt, 1996; Greenberg, Smith & Muenzen, 1995). Researchers and professionals of all kinds (in the clinical, work, educational, etc., fields) are faced with the task of assessing, in one way or another, relevant variables in the particular individual or group of individuals that constitute the object of study. Whether this assessment is made by means of sophisticated equipment in the laboratory, through psychological tests, or through non-structured interviews and other qualitative techniques, the same condition applies: any type of psychological assessment device requires methodological evaluation and scientific guarantees.

The *Encyclopedia of Psychological Assessment* (EPA) will cover the following objectives:

1 To present the reader with a comprehensive network for psychological assessment as a conceptual and methodological discipline, and as a professional activity.
2 To make the reader aware of the complexity of assessment, which involves not only testing, but also a process of decision-making for answering relevant questions (diagnostic, prediction, personnel selection, treatment, etc.) that arise in the different applied fields.
3 To present relevant issues from basic theory (theoretical perspectives, ethics, etc.), methodology (validity, reliability, item response theory, etc.) to technology (tests, instruments and equipment for measuring behavioural operations, etc.).
4 To congregate the diverse applied field form in a comprehensive text: from the most traditional such as clinical, educational, and work and organizational psychology to the most recent applications linked to health, gerontology, neuropsychology and psychophysiology, and environmental assessment.

The Encyclopedia will be oriented to the psychology community, from psychology students to academics and practitioners. It may also be of interest to other professionals, such as health professions, educators, sociologists and other social scientists involved in assessment and measurement.

The Encyclopedia might be considered as supplementary reading for psychological assessment courses, as well as for courses related to theory, methodology, psychometrics, measurement, and areas such as counselling, programme evaluation or personnel selection.

The two volumes of the *Encyclopedia of Psychological Assessment* contain a series of 234 entries (of different lengths depending on their importance), organized alphabetically, and covering a variety of fields: theoretical, epistemological, methodological, technological, basic psychological constructs (personality and intelligence), and applied. Each entry includes a general conceptual and methodological overview, a section on relevant assessment devices and a list of references. Every entry provides a list of cross-references for entries and related concepts.

The *Encyclopedia of Psychological Assessment* has four main characteristics:

1 The EPA presents a semantic network for improving communication, serving as a useful epistemological tool for students, academics and practitioners.
2 The EPA attempts to offer an international perspective, both in terms of the selected authors (from twenty countries and five continents) and of the entries (which will require authors to give a cross-cultural panorama of a given topic).
3 The EPA aims to provide an integrated view of assessment, bringing together knowledge dispersed throughout several basic, methodological and applied fields, but united in its relevance for assessment.
4 The EPA can be considered as a source of information about psychological instruments for the collection of both qualitative and quantitative data from basic and widely used tests to other procedures for data collection.

Rocío Fernández-Ballesteros
Editor-in-Chief

References

Anastasi, A. (1988). *Psychological Testing* (6th ed.). New York: Macmillan.
Bomholt, N. (1996). A tale of two surveys: comparison between results of two opinion surveys. *European Journal of Psychological Assessment, 12,* 169–173.
Fernández-Ballesteros, R. (2002). Psychological assessment is not only clinical. *American Psychologist, 57,* 138–139.
Fernández-Ballesteros, R., de Bruyn, E.E.J., Godoy, A., Hornke, L.F., ter Laak, J., Vizcarro, C., Westhoff, K., Westmeyer, H. & Zaccagnini, J.L. (2001). Guidelines for the assessment process (GAP): a proposal for discussion. *European Journal of Psychological Assessment, 17,* 187–200.
Greenberg, S., Smith, I.L. & Muenzen, P.M. (1995). *Executive Summary: Study of the Licensed Psychologists in the United States and Canada.* New York: Professional Examination Services.
Meyer, G.J., Finn, S.E., Eyde, L.D., Kay, G.G., Moreland, K.L., Dies, R.R., Eisman, E.J., Kubiszyn, T.W & Reed, M. (2001). Psychological testing and psychological assessment: a review of evidence and issues. *American Psychologist, 56,* 128–165.

About the Editor

Rocío Fernández-Ballesteros is Professor of Psychological Assessment and Evaluation at the Autónoma University of Madrid (UAM) since 1980, Editor-in-Chief of the *European Journal of Psychological Assessment*, founder and former President of the European Association of Psychological Assessment (1992–9), President of the Division of Psychological Assessment and Evaluation of the International Association of Psychological Assessment (1994–8), programme evaluator of UNESCO and the EU, and a UN expert on ageing. She has served as Chair of the Department of Diagnostic and Measurement and Dean of the Faculty of Psychology (UAM). She is the author of twenty books and more than 200 scientific articles published in Spanish, English, Russian and Italian in the fields of assessment, evaluation and ageing.

Editorial Board

Dave Bartram (*SHL Group plc, UK*)
Research Director for SHL Group plc, President of the International Test Commission (ITC), and Honorary Professor at the University of Hull, UK. He is a Chartered Occupational Psychologist, Fellow of the British Psychological Society (BPS) and Fellow of the Ergonomics Society. He is heading ITC projects on international guidelines for standards in test use and standards for computer-based testing and the Internet. He is also a member of the British Psychological Society's Steering Committee on Test Standards and of the European Federation of Psychologists Association's Standing Committee on Tests and Testing. He has specialized in the design, implementation and validation of assessment procedures and personnel selection systems at all levels. His specialist area is computer-based testing and Internet assessment systems.

Gian Vittorio Caprara (*La Sapienza University, Rome, Italy*)
Professor of Personality at the University of Rome 'La Sapienza'. Has served as President of the European Association of Personality and on the editorial boards of several scientific journals. Fellow of NIAS and SCASSS. Member of the Academia Europaea. Author of twenty books and over 200 scientific articles in international journals.

Ronald K. Hambleton (*University of Massachussetts at Amherst, USA*)
Distinguished University Professor, Chairperson of the Research and Evaluation Methods Program and Co-Director of the Center for Educational Assessment; received his Ph.D. from the University of Toronto in 1969; received the National Council on Measurement in Education's Career Achievement Award in 1993 for contributions and leadership in the field of psychometric methods and an honorary doctorate in 1997 from the University of Umea in Sweden; research interests are in the areas of item response theory, criterion-referenced testing, test translation methodology and large-scale assessment; co-author or co-editor of seven books, including *Item Response Theory: Principles and Applications* and *Fundamentals of Item Response Theory*.

Lutz F. Hornke (*Aachen University of Technology, Germany*)
Head of Department and Professor of Industrial and Organizational Psychology at Aachen University of Technology, Aachen, Germany, since 1986, after having served at the University of Düsseldorf, Marburg University and Mannheim University. Since 1999 he has been President of the European Association of Psychological Assessment. He also chairs the DIN-33430 committee on quality assurance guidelines for professional assessment. In the past he has acted as co-editor of the *Zeitschrift für Differentielle und Diagnostische Psychologie*. He has published some 200 articles, tests and research reports, mainly on computerized adaptive testing. In his field of research and consultancy activities in industry and organizations he has led projects to evaluate and improve human relations in the workplace.

Jan ter Laak (*Utrecht University, The Netherlands*)
Associate Professor in Psychological Assessment and Personality Development at Utrecht University.

He is Associate Editor of the *European Journal of Psychological Assessment*. He graduated in Developmental, General and Educational Psychology, and has a B.A. in Philosophy. He was chairman of the Children and Youth Division of the Dutch Psychological Association, and also chaired the Test Committee of the Dutch Psychological Association. He was co-editor of two Dutch editions of *Test and Test Research in the Netherlands*. He has written more than 100 books, articles and book reviews published in Dutch, English, Spanish, Russian and Chinese on assessment and developmental and personality psychology.

Lilianne Manning (*Université Louis Pasteur, France*)

Professor of Neuropsychology in charge of the Cognitive Neuropsychology group within the Laboratory of Behavioural and Cognitive Neuroscience. Her current research deals with autobiographical memory and fMRI in normal subjects and brain-damaged patients. She is the author of several publications in English, French and Spanish.

Rudolf Moos (*Center for Health Care Evaluation, Stanford University, VA, USA*)

Research Career Scientist and Director of the Center for Health Care Evaluation at the Veterans Affairs Health Care System, and Professor in the Department of Psychiatry and Behavioral Sciences at Stanford University. He has developed a set of environmental assessment procedures and has conducted research on the outcome of psychiatric treatment and on the influence of life stressors, social resources and coping skills on adaptation. He has won awards for his research from several professional organizations, including the American Psychiatric Association, the American Psychological Association, the American Evaluation Association and the Department of Veterans Affairs.

Charles D. Spielberger (*University of South Florida, USA*)

Distinguished Research Professor of Psychology and Director of the Center for Research in Behavioral Medicine and Health Psychology at the University of South Florida, where he has been a faculty member since 1972. He previously directed the USF Doctoral Program in Clinical Psychology, and was a tenured faculty member at Duke University (1955–62), Vanderbilt University (1962–6) and at Florida State University (1967–72), where he was also Director of Clinical Training. He is author, co-author or editor of more than 400 professional publications. During 1991–2 he served as the hundredth President of the American Psychological Association and he is currently President of the International Association of Applied Psychology (1998–2002) and the International Stress Management Association (1993–2000), Chair of the National Academy of Science's International Psychology Committee (1996–2000) and a member of the APA Policy and Planning Board.

Irving B. Weiner (*University of South Florida, USA*)

Clinical Professor of Psychiatry and Behavioral Medicine at the University of South Florida. He is a Past President of the Society for Personality Assessment, and he has served as editor of the *Journal of Personality Assessment* (1985–93) and as editor of *Rorschachiana: Yearbook of the International Rorschach Society* (1990–7). He is the current President of the International Rorschach Society and the author of twelve books and numerous articles and chapters published in English, Danish, Japanese, Polish, Portuguese and Spanish.

Hans Westmeyer (*Free University of Berlin, Germany*)

Professor of Psychological Assessment and Intervention and Differential and Personality Psychology at the Department of Psychology of the Free University of Berlin (since 1976). Editor-in-Chief of *Diagnostica* (1979–94). Associate Editor of the *European Journal of Psychological Assessment* (1992–8). Consulting Editor of *Psychological Assessment* (since 1997). Co-founder and former Vice-President (1992–6) of the European Association of Psychological Assessment. Author or editor of twelve books and more than 150 scientific contributions published in German, English and Spanish in the fields of psychological assessment, clinical psychology, personality psychology and theoretical psychology.

ACHIEVEMENT MOTIVATION

INTRODUCTION

Human life can be described as a continuous work at tasks. Individuals may or may not be successful in facing these tasks. The psychology of achievement motivation is engaged to run research projects aiming at a better understanding of individual performance and the nature of human resources as well as at the development of assessment and intervention techniques to increase achievement motivation. Tasks in industrial settings and in service organizations become more and more complex and underlie dynamic changes arising from changing market demands. To keep individuals highly achievement motivated while doing their jobs, tasks have to be designed with high motivating potentials.

From a motivational perspective the action process is divided into two parts. The first part describes the development of achievement motivation as a consequence of a fit between the achievement motive and the achievement-oriented motivating potentials of the situation. *Achievement motivation* initiating action arises through interaction of achievement-oriented *motivating potentials* of the task in its situational context and the strength of the *achievement motive* on the side of the performing person. Personal goals controlling actions result directly from the strength of this achievement motivation (Figure 1). The second

part of the motivation process responsible for the translation of motivation into action is often called the volitional phase in the control of behaviour (Heckhausen, 1989); during this phase, goal-oriented action turns into outcomes controlled by the degree of *goal commitment*. Goal commitment affects the way persons choose to reach their goals and the selection of strategies they pursue (Brandtstädter & Renner, 1990). Examples for such strategies are to pursue a goal persistently even in cases of hindrance or to adapt flexibly to changing aspects of the situation. The translation process works better when more specific and concrete goals are set; the higher the goal commitment the more effective the chosen strategies of goal pursuit (Vroom, 1964; Locke & Latham, 1990; Kleinbeck, 2001).

A goal-oriented course of action immune to disturbances is especially supported by specific and concrete goals (goal characteristics; Figure 1).

Because of the many single concepts subsumed under the label of achievement motivation, it is necessary to develop as many measurement tools as possible to differentiate between the concepts. Outside current research projects, measures of achievement motivation are principally used in industrial settings, in service organizations and in educational fields. Here achievement motivation measurement is used to investigate the motivating

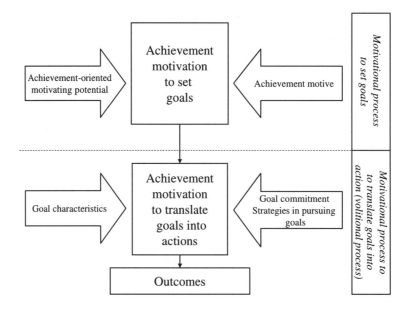

Figure 1.   Components of achievement motivation.

potentials of work tasks and work contexts to make full use of individual resources.

INSTRUMENTS TO ASSESS ACHIEVEMENT MOTIVATION

The theory of achievement motivation describes performance as multidimensional and as influenced by many different factors. The main personal factor is the achievement motive; the main task-specific factor is the motivating potential of the situation. For diagnostic information about mode and strength of the achievement motive there are three different sources (see Schneider & Schmalt, 2000: 50–56):

1   Self-judgement
2   Judgement by others
3   Behavioural indices

Assessing the strength of the achievement motive, different strategies are used according to these sources: operant procedures (e.g. the Thematic Apperception Test – TAT) and respondent procedures (e.g. questionnaires), and the grid technique that according to Schmalt (1999) lies in its methodological background between the first two types of measurement. Due to this fact, one can differentiate implicit and explicit components of the achievement motive. Using the material of the

TAT with pictorial presentations of situations it becomes possible to penetrate implicitly into the achievement motive system, because this kind of measurement allows one to approach materials of memory relevant for the motive system. Filling out questionnaires requires ego involvement, self-insight and self-reflection, and also explicit memory, because the answers to the questions can only be given with the help of conscious reflection to earlier experiences (Graf & Schacter, 1985: 501).

Schmalt and Sokolowski (2000) discuss the quality of the different techniques to measure the achievement motive and conclude that all available instruments work reliably. TAT and the grid technique have comparable and widely diversified validity ranges that are related to respondent and operant behaviour. Questionnaires used to diagnose motives seem to be specialized to predict respondent behaviour and conscious experiences (Spangler, 1992).

To measure the achievement-oriented motivating potentials of tasks, Hackman and Oldham (1975) developed and presented an instrument, the Job Diagnostic Survey (JDS), that has well proven its validity (Fried & Ferris, 1987). The JDS measures the motivating potentials of tasks in work situations and also of tasks that students are confronted with in learning situations (Schmidt & Kleinbeck, 1999). Measuring the achievement motive and the motivating potentials of tasks allows one to determine the strength of achievement motivation.

Rheinberg, Vollmeyer and Burns (2001) present an instrument to measure achievement motivation as a comprehensive construct. With 18 items, four components of the current state of achievement motivation are measured: (1) fear of failure; (2) probability of success; (3) interest; (4) challenge. In its German and English version, the instrument shows satisfying consistencies and according to the first validation data, the measured components of current achievement motivation correlate positively with learning behaviour and performance. Schuler and Prochaska (2000) define achievement motivation as a general behavioural orientation. The instrument they developed – the Hohenheim Test of Achievement Motivation (HTML) – allows measuring achievement motivation with 17 scales in a highly differentiated way. The results of the HTML measures correlate significantly with neuroticism and conscience in the five-factor model of personality (Costa & McCrae, 1989). Measures in HTML are positively related to success at school, university and work so that one can expect a successful application in personality research and in educational and occupational testing.

To measure goal characteristics (e.g. goal specificity and goal difficulty) that influence the achievement-oriented process of translating goals into action, Locke and Latham (1990) present a questionnaire that has been used mainly in research settings. Other questionnaires try to measure clarity of tasks and goals (Sawyer, 1992), clarity of methods (Breaugh & Colihan, 1994; Schmidt & Hollmann, 1998) and also clarity of performance judgements (Breaugh & Colihan, 1994; Kleinbeck & Fuhrmann, 2000). These components of achievement motivation measured by the mentioned questionnaires affect the motivation to translate goals into action and as a consequence performance outcome.

Recently researchers began to measure goal commitment (Hollenbeck et al., 1989). They invested considerable effort because goal setting is no homogeneous construct. As Tubbs (1993) could show there are three different components of goal commitment: the first component has to do with processes of weighing and evaluating the potential goals. During these processes, one calculates mainly values and expectancies that affect the strength of motivational tendencies for specific goals. The second component contains the result of these evaluative processes focussing on calculations of values and expectancies and leading to setting a personal goal. This component is also related to the decision to attain this

Table 1. Instruments for measuring components of achievement motivation

Instruments	Author	Concepts measured	Method used
TAT	Murray, 1943; McClelland et al., 1953	Achievement motive and other motives	Content analysis of stories (operant)
OMT	Kuhl & Scheffer, 2000	Achievement motive	Content analysis of written stories (operant)
MARPS	Mehrabian, 1968	Achievement motive	Questionnaire (respondent)
Grid-technique	Schmalt & Sokolowski, 2000	Achievement motive	Judgement of fit between pictures and motive-related statements
Questionnaire for current motivational states	Rheinberg et al., 2001	Current motivation for learning and performance	Questionnaire (respondent)
AVEM	Schaarschmidt & Fischer, 1996	Current work motivation	Questionnaire (respondent)
HLMT	Schuler & Prochaska, 2000	Achievement motivation	Questionnaire (respondent)
JDS	Hackman & Oldham, 1975	Motivating potential of tasks	Questionnaire (self-judgement and judgement by others)
Fragebogen für Zielcharakteristika	Locke & Latham, 1990	Goal specificity and others	Questionnaire (respondent)
Goal commitment	Hollenbeck et al., 1989	Goal commitment	Questionnaire (respondent)
Strategies of goal pursuit	Brandtstädter & Renner, 1990	Strategies of goal pursuit	Questionnaire (respondent)

particular goal. The third component of goal commitment is characterized by maintaining the set goal and by staying persistent even when faced with hindrances. Future research will show whether it will be possible to develop differentiated measurement procedures on the basis of these considerations.

With respect to goal commitment in goal-oriented action, people seem to be able to use stable dispositions. They either persist tenaciously in pursuing their goals or they adjust flexibly to new or other goals. Brandtstädter and Renner (1990) described two scales to measure 'tenacious goal pursuit' and 'flexible goal adjustment'. Their results show relations between these different strategies and age. Older people adapt more often flexibly instead of pursuing their goals tenaciously against hindrances. Table 1 summarizes the instruments for measuring components of achievement motivation.

FUTURE PERSPECTIVES

The current state of research can be described as presenting a set of different measurement approaches for the central components of achievement motivation. Future tasks for research and applications mainly in work and educational settings will be to determine the range of validity for the different measures more exactly. This can help to decide under what circumstances specific instruments can be used profitably. Although there are now some reliable and valid instruments to measure single components of achievement motivation, it would be helpful to have new instruments and procedures to relate them to each other.

CONCLUSIONS

A high achievement motivation in people guarantees success and wealth in human societies. To produce adequate conditions for the development of a high achievement motivation it is necessary to understand how achievement motivation is formed and how it can be translated into successful action. In accordance with the importance of this kind of motivation, a series of instruments have been designed to measure the different components of achievement motivation

reliably, validly and practically. The existing instruments can be used in research and practical settings.

References

Brandtstädter, J. & Renner, G. (1990). Tenacious goal pursuit and flexible goal adjustment: explications and age-related analysis of assimilative and accommodative strategies of coping. *Psychology and Aging, 5,* 58–67.

Breaugh, J.A. & Colihan, J.P. (1994). Measuring facets of job ambiguity: construct validity evidence. *Journal of Applied Psychology, 79,* 191–202.

Costa, P.T. & McCrae, R.R. (1989). *The NEO PI/FFI Manual Supplement.* Odessa, FL: Psychological Assessment Resources.

Fried, Y. & Ferris G. (1987). The validity of the job characteristics model: a review and meta analysis. *Personnel Psychology, 40,* 287–322.

Graf, P. & Schacter, D.L. (1985). Implicit and explicit memory for new associations in normal and amnesic subjects. *Journal of Experimental Psychology: Learning, Memory, and Cognition, 11,* 501–518.

Hackman, J.R. & Oldham, G.R. (1975). Development of the Job Diagnostic Survey. *Journal of Applied Psychology, 60,* 159–170.

Heckhausen, H. (1989). *Motivation und Handeln.* Berlin: Springer.

Hollenbeck, J.R., Klein, H.J., O'Leary, A.M. & Wright, P.M. (1989). Investigation of the construct validity of a self-report measure of goal commitment. *Journal of Applied Psychology, 74,* 951–956.

Kleinbeck, U. (2001). Das Management von Arbeitsgruppen. In Schuler, H. (Ed.), *Lehrbuch der Personalpsychologie.*

Kleinbeck, U. & Fuhrmann, H. (2000). Effects of a psychologically based management system on work motivation and productivity. *Applied Psychology: An International Review, 49,* 596–610.

Kuhl, J. & Scheffer, D. (2000). Auswertungsmanual für den Operanten Multi-Motiv-Test (OMT). Osnabrück, Unpublished Manuscript.

Locke, E.A. & Latham, G.P. (1984). *Goal-Setting: A Motivational Technique that Works.* Englewood Cliffs, NJ: Prentice Hall.

Locke, E.A. & Latham, G.P. (1990). *A Theory of Goal Setting and Task Performance.* Englewood Cliffs, NJ: Prentice Hall.

McClelland, D.C., Atkinson, J.W., Clark, R.A. & Lowell, E.L. (1953). *The Achievement Motive.* New York: Appleton-Century-Crofts.

Mehrabian, A. (1968). Male and female scales of the tendency to achieve. *Educational and Psychological Measurement, 28,* 493–502.

Murray, H.A. (1943). *Thematic Apperception Test Manual.* Cambridge: Harvard University Press.

Rheinberg, F., Vollmeyer, R. & Burns, B.D. (2001). FAM: Ein Fragebogen zur Erfassung aktueller Motivation in Lern- und Leistungssituationen. *Diagnostica, 2,* 57–66.

Sawyer, J.E. (1992). Goal and process clarity: specification of multiple constructs of role ambiguity and a structural equation model of their antecedents and consequences. *Journal of Applied Psychology*, 77, 130–142.

Schaarschmidt, U. & Fischer, A. (1996) *AVEM – Arbeitsbezogenes Verhaltens- und Erlebensmuster* (Manual). Frankfurt am Main: Swets Testservices.

Schmalt, H.-D. (1999). Assessing the achievement motive using the grid technique. *Journal of Research in Personality*, 33, 109–130.

Schmalt, H.-D. & Sokolowski, K. (2000). Zum gegenwärtigen Stand der Motivdiagnostik. *Diagnostica*, 46, 115–123.

Schmidt, K.-H. & Hollmann, S. (1998). Eine deutschsprachige Skala zur Messung verschiedener Ambiguitätsfacetten bei der Arbeit. *Diagnostica*, 44, 21–29.

Schmidt, K.-H. & Kleinbeck, U. (1999). Job Diagnostic Survey (JDS – deutsche Fassung). In Dunckel, H. (Ed.), *Handbuch psychologischer Arbeitsanalyseverfahren* (pp. 205–230). Zürich: vdf.

Schneider, K. & Schmalt, H.-D. (2000). *Motivation* (3rd ed.). Stuttgart: Kohlhammer.

Schuler, H. & Prochaska, M. (2000). Entwicklung und Konstruktvalidierung eines berufsbezogenen Leistungsmotivationstests. *Diagnostica*, 46, 61–72.

Spangler, W.D. (1992). Validity of questionnaire and TAT measures of need for achievement: two meta-analyses. *Psychological Bulletin*, 112, 140–154.

Tubbs, M.E. (1993). Commitment as a moderator of the goal-performance relation: a case of clearer construct definition. *Journal of Applied Psychology*, 78, 86–97.

Vroom, V.H. (1964). *Work and Motivation*. New York: Wiley.

Uwe Kleinbeck

RELATED ENTRIES

ACHIEVEMENT TESTING

INTRODUCTION

Achievement testing plays a central role in education, particularly given the current context of high-stakes educational reform seen in countries like the United States. This entry provides a brief overview of achievement testing beginning with a description of its role in education. Different types of achievement tests, commonly used derived scores, recent advances such as performance assessments, and future directions are described (Hambleton & Zaal, 1991).

ACHIEVEMENT TESTING AND ITS ROLE

Achievement tests are designed to measure the knowledge and skills that individuals learn in a relatively well-defined area through formal or informal educational experiences. Thus, achievement tests include tests designed by teachers for use in the classroom and standardized tests developed by school districts, states, national and international organizations, and commercial test publishers.

Achievement tests have been used for: (a) summative purposes such as measuring student achievement, assigning grades, grade promotion and evaluation of competency, comparing student achievement across states and nations, and evaluating the effectiveness of teachers, programmes, districts, and states in accountability programmes; (b) formative purposes such as identifying student strengths and weaknesses, motivating students, teachers, and administrators to seek higher levels of performance, and informing educational policy; and (c) placement and diagnostic purposes such as selecting and placing students, and diagnosing learning disabilities, giftedness, and other special needs.

The most controversial uses of achievement testing have been in high-stakes accountability programmes and minimum competency testing (MCT). Accountability practices vary and may include financial rewards for improved performance to providing remediation for students who perform poorly to sanctions such as public hearings, staff dismissals, and dissolution of districts. Two negative consequences that have been associated with high-stakes accountability include a pattern of inflated achievement results as highlighted by Cannell's (1988) finding that all states were reporting that their students were scoring above the national norm (Lake Wobegon effect), and the narrowing of instruction or 'teaching to the test' so that student scores compare favourably to norms.

MCT programmes were implemented in response to concerns about high levels of illiteracy and innumeracy and subsequent poor 'work force readiness' among high school graduates. In addition to course completion requirements, such programmes require students to pass tests of minimal basic skills (usually in reading, writing, and arithmetic) to graduate from high school. Legal cases such as *Debra P. vs. Turlington* raised questions about what constitutes minimum competency, whether the skills assessed are reflected in school curriculum, and whether students have been given adequate opportunity to learn the skills required (Anastasi & Urbina, 1997).

STANDARDIZED ACHIEVEMENT TESTS

Standardized tests may be classified using the overlapping categories of purpose, breadth, administration, item format, and interpretation.

Purpose

Screening tests tend to be relatively brief with only one subtest covering each subject area. These tests are useful in determining if more expensive comprehensive testing is warranted. Screening tests include the *Wechsler Individual Achievement Test* (WIAT) – *Screener, Wide Range Achievement Test – 3*, and *Basic Achievement Skills Individual Screener* (BASIS). Comprehensive or diagnostic tests typically include more than one subtest per subject area so each can be explored in depth. Examples of these tests include the *WIAT – Comprehensive Test, Woodcock–Johnson Complete Battery III, Gates–McKillop–Horowitz Reading Diagnostic Test, Comprehensive Tests of Basic Skills*, and *Terra Nova*.

Breadth

Single-subject tests include a number of subtests ranging from lower to higher skill levels to assess different aspects of a subject area. Single-subject tests include the *Woodcock Reading Mastery Tests – Revised* and *KeyMath – Revised*. Multiple-subject tests assess at least the three commonly taught subject areas of reading, mathematics, and written language. Such tests include the *Iowa Tests of Basic Skills, California Achievement Test, SRA Achievement Series, Stanford Achievement Test Series*, and *Tests of Achievement and Proficiency*.

Administration

Group administered achievement tests are usually multiple-subject tests that contain comparable subtests for students in different grades. These tests usually are administered within the classroom and are used throughout school districts or states. Examples include the *Iowa Tests of Basic Skills, Metropolitan Achievement Test 8, Iowa Tests of Educational Development, Gray Oral Reading Test – 3*, and *Sequential Tests of Educational Progress – III*. Individually administered achievement tests may include single- or multiple-subject tests and typically are administered in clinical and educational settings. Such tests include the *Kaufman Test of Educational Achievement, Wide Range Achievement Test – III, Gates–MacGinitie Reading Test*, and *Peabody Individual Achievement Test – Revised*.

Item Format

Fixed-response items include multiple-choice, true–false, matching, and stem completion items. A key advantage of fixed-response items is that considerable material can be covered in a relatively short period of time. Criticisms of these items are that they emphasize recall of facts over higher order thinking and problem-solving, they are susceptible to guessing and testwiseness, and they discourage creative thinking. They also tend to be difficult items to prepare. Nonetheless, multiple-choice items are the most common item format used in standardized achievement tests.

Constructed items include short answer and essay responses. The advantages of constructed items are that they require students to construct a response rather than simply recognize the correct answer, they assess students' ability to organize, connect ideas, and problem-solve, they reduce the impact of guessing, and preparation of questions is relatively quick and easy. Disadvantages of constructed items are that relatively few questions can be asked and thus adequate coverage of the subject area may not occur, they are susceptible to bluffing, and scoring is time-consuming, requires considerable subjective judgement, and is less reliable than scoring of fixed-response items.

Interpretation

When achievement test results are interpreted with reference to a normative group, the test is referred to as a norm-referenced test (NRT). Students' NRT scores usually are expressed in age- or grade-equivalent scores, standard scores, or percentiles. NRTs are designed to discriminate among students' performance; they do not provide information on the amount of information learned. Most of the tests discussed already are NRTs. When test results are interpreted in terms of whether each student has mastered specific knowledge and skills without reference to other students or a normative group, the test is said to be criterion-referenced (CRT). Students' CRT scores are usually expressed as per cent correct or by descriptors such as mastery/non-mastery. Most CRTs are developed by schools or states. Examples are the *Basic Skills Assessment Program*, *Kentucky Instructional Results Information System*, and *Louisiana Educational Assessment Program* (LEAP 21). Some NRT tests also provide CRT interpretations such as *BASIS*.

DERIVED SCORES ASSOCIATED WITH ACHIEVEMENT TESTS

Raw scores obtained on achievement tests typically are converted to derived scores, so we can make comparisons among test scores. Commonly found derived scores include age- or grade-equivalent scores, standard scores, and percentile scores. Age- or grade-equivalent scores ('developmental scores') reflect average performance at different age and grade levels. These scores are often (a) misinterpreted when individual performance is compared to the wrong reference group, and (b) inappropriately used as standards of performance when teachers and parents expect all students in a particular age group or grade to achieve age- or grade-equivalent scores.

Standard scores provide an indication of a student's relative performance on a test in terms of how far his/her score is from the mean in standard deviation units. Common types of standard scores are z-scores, T-scores, deviation IQ scores, and stanines. Standard scores are the most highly recommended derived scores.

Percentiles (percentile ranks) indicate the point in a distribution at or below which the scores of a given percentage of students fall and should not be confused with percentages or per cent correct. Percentiles are the most easily interpreted derived scores. However, percentiles do not represent equal intervals across the distribution, which means that they magnify small differences near the mean and minimize large differences in the upper and lower ends of the distribution.

RECENT ADVANCES IN ACHIEVEMENT TESTING

Computer Adaptive Testing

Computer adaptive testing (CAT) attempts to match the difficulty of test items to the knowledge and skill level of the student being assessed by tailoring the test so that a pre-selected sequence of items is administered based on whether or not the response to the previous item is correct. The advantages of CAT over traditional achievement tests include reduced testing time, the need for fewer items at a given level of measurement error, minimized frustration for students who perform poorly, and more precise estimates of achievement across the entire distribution.

Large-Scale Assessments

Large-scale assessments are conducted by the district, state, or nation(s) to examine the educational achievement of groups. The best-known large-scale assessments today are the *National Assessment of Educational Progress* (NAEP) in the United States and the surveys conducted by the International Association for the Evaluation of Educational Achievement (IEA). The purpose of NAEP, which was first introduced in 1969, was 'to improve the effectiveness of our Nation's schools by making objective information about student performance in selected learning areas available to policymakers at the national, State and local levels' (Public Law 100-297, Section 3401). The IEA has conducted numerous international achievement surveys since its first cross-national survey in 1959 and is best known for the longitudinal *Third International Mathematics and Science Study* (TIMSS) first conducted in 1995.

Performance Assessments

Increasing attention has been paid to performance assessments (also known as authentic or alternative assessments), which consist of students' constructed responses to 'real world' (authentic) tasks and problems and the cognitive skills and processes involved in the construction of those responses. Examples of performance assessments include portfolios of students' work over time, poetry, science experiments, conversations in a foreign language, and open-ended mathematics problems. The students' work is judged using an agreed-upon set of criteria. The advantages of these assessments are that they are meant to measure processes involved in the acquisition of knowledge and skills in ways that make the link between learning and instruction clearer. Disadvantages are that fewer tasks can be included given time constraints, creating agreed-upon criteria for scoring is time-consuming, and judgement of students' work is highly subjective, all of which make performance assessment expensive and open to bias.

Standards-Based Assessments

Standards-based reform describes efforts to improve education for all students through the setting of high standards. Its beginnings rest with the 1983 National Commission on Excellence in Education report, *A Nation at Risk: The Imperative for Educational Reform*, and it has culminated in the passing of 'Goals 2000: Educate America Act' by the U.S. Congress in 1994.

Standards-based approaches include content and performance standards, assessments that are aligned with these standards, and accountability measures. Content standards define what a student should know and be able to do and thus drive curriculum. Performance standards define how much a student should know and be able to do, and thus set the benchmarks or expected levels of achievement to be used for accountability. Standards-based assessments (also known as standards-referenced testing) are based on content and performance standards, involve multiple measures of student performance, and apply to all students. A critical aspect of such assessments is to produce and use 'better tests' such as performance assessments. Accountability measures focus on strengthening standards-based reform initiatives by rewarding teachers and schools whose students meet performance standards and sanctioning those who do not.

FUTURE PERSPECTIVES AND CONCLUSIONS

Current and future advances in achievement testing appear to be focussed on the development, improvement, and evaluation of standards-based and performance assessments. Five areas for future development include: (1) best practices for developing, and methods for evaluating, performance assessment scoring rubrics, (2) comparisons of the various types of data to be used in accountability models such as mean scores, value-added data, and residual scores adjusted for socio-economic status, (3) longitudinal research examining the impact of performance and standards-based assessments on student achievement, instructional practices, and student learning, (4) comparisons of traditional standardized testing (including multiple-choice formats) and performance assessments as measures of student achievement, and (5) exploration of computer-based, and notably Internet, delivery and scoring of performance assessments for large scale assessment.

References

Anastasi, A. & Urbina, S. (1997). *Psychological Testing*. Upper Saddle River, NJ: Prentice-Hall, Inc.

Cannell, J.J. (1988). Nationally normed elementary achievement testing in America's public schools: how all 50 states are above the national average. *Educational Measurement: Issues and Practice*, 7, 5–9.

Hambleton, R.K. & Zaal, J.N. (1991). *Advances in Educational and Psychological Testing: Theory and Applications.* Boston, MA: Kluwer Academic Publishers.

National Commission on Excellence in Education (1983, April). *A Nation at Risk: The Imperative for Educational Reform* (Doc. 20402). Washington, DC: U.S. Government Printing Office.

Anita M. Hubley

RELATED ENTRIES

APPLIED FIELDS: EDUCATION, ACHIEVEMENT TESTING, CRITERION-REFERENCED TESTING: METHODS AND PROCEDURES, NORM-REFERENCED TESTING: METHODS AND PROCEDURES, ITEM RESPONSE THEORY: MODELS AND FEATURES, ADAPTIVE AND TAILORED TESTING

A ADAPTIVE AND TAILORED TESTING (INCLUDING IRT AND NON-IRT APPLICATION)

INTRODUCTION

In computerized adaptive testing (CAT), a computer administers the items and gathers the examinee's responses, but its most distinctive feature is that the items finally administered depend on the examinee's ability. The test then adapts to the examinee's performance on the items. The idea of adaptive measurement can be traced back to Binet, but it never became a reality until the appearance of the item response theory (IRT) and the development of the computer. However, adaptive testing is also possible without IRT, as will be seen later. The first ideas on CAT appeared in the early 1970s (Lord, 1970). CAT has spent in the laboratory the greater part of the elapsed time since then, because the main concern of the researchers has been to obtain the most efficient, precise and possible strategies for item selection. They have become operational only in the last decade. Computerized adaptive tests were administered to more than a million people in 1999 (Wainer, 2000). Its main applications are to the areas of personnel selection, educational assessment, certification and licensure. Due to its practical applications, new concerns such as test security, profitability and social impact have arisen.

BASIC PRINCIPLES

The basic principles of a CAT are well established. Its aim is to apply to each examinee only the items that best serve to assess his/her level of ability. Its main advantage is that more efficient measurements are obtained. It needs fewer items (sometimes, less than half) than conventional tests to achieve the same level of precision as a full-length test. The elements that make up a CAT are: an item pool with known properties, a heuristic to choose the items, a method to evaluate ability and a criterion to end the application. Though they are all important, the efficiency of a CAT mostly depends on two closely related complementary processes: the statistical method of estimating ability and the criterion for item selection. This explains the great amount of procedures known and why they are two of the most studied aspects of CAT.

ITEM BANK

A CAT chooses items from a database (item bank) containing the available items and various information about each item, such as its stem, correct and incorrect options, item parameter estimates under an appropriate IRT model, classical item difficulty and discrimination indices, information on the specific domain the item measures, the proportion of times the item has been administered, etc. The bank has to be calibrated and its unidimensionality and acceptable fitting to an IRT model should be checked and accepted. Item banking and IRT are specific entries in this encyclopedia, and further details can be found there.

A CAT does not need a specific item format. A CAT may be developed both for dichotomous and polytomous items, and for multiple-choice or open-ended items. Items may be visual, auditory and also multimedia items. It is also possible to consider a testlet (cluster of related items) instead of single items as the analysis unit.

An important question to pay attention to is bank size. Well-known high-stake CATs, such as CAT-ASVAB (Sands et al., 1997), have more than one thousand items, but CATs for other uses ordinarily have smaller banks (even below 150 or 200 items). The number of items also depends on the restrictions the item-selection algorithm has implemented and the IRT model in use.

An item bank should also consider the ability prospective examinees have and the intended test use. It should contain discriminative items for the entire range of ability. The information function of the item bank should match these requirements.

Banks should be updated, both in the information on each item, as this information changes after each item administration, and also in the items themselves, because as the CAT is increasingly administered, new items should be added and old ones removed. Online calibration deals with effective procedures to carry-out bank updating.

ADAPTIVE HEURISTICS

A CAT needs four components in order to measure an examinee: (a) a procedure to select the first item to administer; (b) a method to estimate the examinee's ability and precision after each administered item; (c) an algorithm for selecting the remaining items; and (d) a criterion to end the test administration.

There are some alternatives available for selecting the first item. If we know the examinee's grade on other variables, and his/her course, this information may be used to predict the examinee's ability by linear regression. The first item is then selected to match the predicted ability. If no information on the examinee is available, the first item will then match a random ability selected from the central values of the ability distribution.

After each item is administered the examinee gives his/her response. The CAT needs to obtain the ability estimation from the observed responses to the set of administered items. The examinee's

test score will be his/her ability estimate when the test is over. The most widely used methods of estimation are based on the principle of maximum likelihood or Bayesian procedures. These methods have good properties when the number of items is high. Nevertheless, CATs are far from this ideal situation because they use very few items. This circumstance gives place to biased estimations, especially in the early stages of the test. So, a problem with CAT is to find a method that provides accurate estimations, which are unbiased and computationally efficient. Wang and Vispoel (1998) and Cheng and Liou (2000) have compared the characteristics (standard error, bias, efficiency, etc.) of the IRT estimation methods to determine when they are advisable in CAT. Since one of the problems that has been paid the most attention is the bias of the estimations, several strategies have been proposed for its control. Other questions, like the initial estimation and the effects of non-model fitting responses, have generated interest from researchers.

Once some items have been administered and an ability estimate for the examinee obtained, a new item has to be selected from the unused items remaining in the item pool. Two common principles are used to guide item selection. Under the *maximum information* principle, the information provided for each unused item for the last ability estimate is computed. The item with the highest information value is selected and administered. In other words, the more helpful item in order to increase precision is selected. The maximum information principle faces some difficulties when the ability estimate is biased or inaccurate, which is often the case when the test is short. If the estimate separates appreciably from the final estimation, the more informative items for these provisional estimations will be less informative for the final estimation. As a result, some items will have been of little use in the test. Cheng and Liou (2000) have proposed the use of alternative information measures in order to circumvent this difficulty. Under the *maximum expected precision* criterion, the item selected will minimize the expected value of the variance of the Bayesian posterior distribution of ability. Several item-selection criteria based on this principle have been proposed (van der Linden, 1998).

Both the procedures share a problem derived from choosing in each test the best items in the pool: some items are administered in most tests (even in more than 50% of the tests), risking test security and validity, whereas others are never shown (in one particular CAT, 80% of the items were never selected). To sort-out this difficulty, control exposure methods have been implemented. These methods trade-off precision with security. When a CAT has in use an exposure control method, such as the Sympson–Hetter method (Sympson & Hetter, 1985), precision of measurement is not as high, but the exposure rate of the most useful items is held under control, and the smaller exposure rates are obtained. Experimental CATs may have implemented one of the two pure item-selection procedures indicated above, but if a CAT has to give valid measures it needs to attend to other considerations in order to select items, such as the appropriate representation of the content or subject areas, the guarantee that the composition of the test is similar for all examinees, the control of the presence of items that should not appear together in the same test, etc. Item-selection rules should then consider not only the basic principles indicated above, but also item-control exposure and other restrictions. Linear programming techniques are often used to make item selection feasible when different restrictions have to be simultaneously considered.

The administration of items ends when either the test length or ability precision reach their preset values. In the second case, all the examinees will be measured with the same precision, but the number of items administered and testing time will differ. Sometimes the stopping criterion is mixed: the test stops after presenting a preset number of items if it does not reach the targeted precision.

PSYCHOMETRIC PROPERTIES

As in a conventional test, reliability and validity studies have to be carried out in a CAT. Besides traditional reliability methods, such as test–retest, simulation may be used to obtain information on test functioning. Indices such as RSME, bias and efficiency can be easily computed. Concerning validity, the procedures in use for conventional tests are applicable to CATs. For further details on this, see Chapters 7 and 8 of Wainer et al. (2000).

OTHER RESEARCH TOPICS

New Types of CATs

Most of the CATs have been elaborated to measure intelligence, aptitudes or achievement, and they are based on IRT models for unidimensional dichotomous items. However, other alternatives have been considered in the past few years. The need to measure other constructs such as attitudes, whose items have the format of ordered categories, and the possibility of using the incorrect options of the multiple-choice items to improve the estimation of ability, started a new line of work interested in elaborating CATs based on diverse types of polytomous models. Also, the acknowledgement that more than one trait intervenes in almost all the tasks has led to the use of multidimensional CATs (Segall, 2000).

CATs in Intelligent Tutoring Systems

The use of IRT in CATs imposes a few important constraints (Almond & Mislevy, 1999): (a) IRT has a simple way of representing knowledge and skills that intervene in complex tasks (unidimensionality); (b) it establishes strong assumptions that can be violated on some occasions (conditional independence); (c) it requires large samples to estimate the item parameters; and (d) it offers a score to express the level of ability, which does not exactly indicate what the subjects know or can do (diagnosis). All these aspects reduce their use in measuring domains that require multiple knowledge, skills and abilities, as in educational and job performance assessment. There is a tendency in education to integrate measurement, assessment, diagnosis, teaching and learning. This means that it is necessary to know in detail the knowledge and skills dominated by the students, the kinds of mistakes they make, the strategies they use, etc. to be able to adapt the contents and pedagogic strategies to them. To what extent can this be achieved by available CATs? Hardly at all, unfortunately.

This orientation in performance assessment is creating the need to introduce important changes in CATs, most of them coming from the literature on intelligent tutoring systems (ITS). In computerized teaching, since the ITS appeared, there has been a growing interest in giving it more capacity of accommodation for the candidates, including a CAT in its module of assessment. Most of these systems do not use IRT, they are based instead on other methodologies, such as the rule-space methodology (Tatsuoka & Tatsuoka, 1997), the knowledge spaces (Hockemeyer & Albert, 1999), Bayesian networks, or graphical models (Almond & Mislevy, 1999), etc.

Conditions of Application

Lastly, many practical problems emerge when CATs become operative instruments used in real life. One main concern is how to guarantee the security of the item pool against attempts at illegitimate appropriation of its contents as well as the complexity and high costs of the elaboration process, maintenance and renewal. A second topic of interest tries to make the conditions of test administration better psychologically for the candidates, such as obtaining optimum adjustment in the difficulty of the test, allowing review of the answers, and controlling the difficulty of the items to reduce anxiety.

FUTURE PERSPECTIVES AND CONCLUSIONS

From a technical perspective, there have been significant steps made in ability estimation methods. Likewise, the item-selection heuristics have reached a level of sophistication that makes it capable of guaranteeing the elaboration of tests that meet multiple requirements. In the next generation of CATs, new models will be used. Very soon we will be able to see comparative studies that analyse these new models that are multidimensional and can handle polytomous response data. However, the CATs elaborated from these models have yet to prove that their advantages are worth the additional effort their elaboration requires. This is especially true for multidimensional models.

Many practical problems have emerged with CAT going operational (Wise & Kingsbury, 2000), especially those related to test security and costs. Wainer (2000) provided a critical discussion of the supposed advantages attributed to CATs in the 1980s, from the experience accumulated on their massive use in the 1990s. His conclusion, though not very favourable, is not discouraging. Wainer argues for more focus on areas where CATs will be useful: (a) when the construct cannot be measured easily without a computer, (b) when the test has to be continuously administered, and (c) when it is important for everyone involved to get the right measurement.

In the past few years, a growing tendency to extend the use of CATs to the Internet, using its Web service (CAT-Web), has been appreciated. This tendency basically responds to the interest of having the distance learning system also offering an individualized assessment. In this way, more ITS destined to the Internet are continuously being released, and some of them already include a CAT-Web.

Finally, two challenges that CATs will face in the future will be to offer diagnostic information of quality on multiple abilities and to substantially reduce the costs associated with the elaboration of the item pool. In the first place, CATs have to go further than the unidimensional dichotomous IRT models, and especially to solve in an efficient way the problem of multidimensionality. Moreover, according to the objectives of the test, offering quantitative scoring may not be enough. The solution could be far from the IRT. The possibilities offered by the models of measurement based on knowledge, like the Bayesian inference network or the knowledge space theory, would have to be seriously considered. In the second place, an alternative to *online* calibration and the automatic generation of items that could serve to reduce costs is to elaborate *instruments of measurement that learn to measure*. The necessary elements would be a theoretical model of the construct that is well supported, a psychometric model, a group of experts on the subject to obtain the initial parameters and an algorithm of learning. The test will modify the initial estimates of the experts from the empirical information collected, and from its execution in activities in which it could be trained through simulation. The algorithm of learning would bring the values of the parameters up to date so they would adapt to the predictions of the theoretical model and the available empirical evidence. The uses of the scoring would be conditioned to the degree of competence achieved by the test. Although it may seem far-fetched, some attempts are being made in this direction in CATs of some ITS.

References

Almond, R.G. & Mislevy, R.J. (1999). Graphical models and computerized adaptive testing. *Applied Psychological Measurement, 23*(3), 223–237.

Cheng, P.E. & Liou, M. (2000). Estimation of trait level in computerized adaptive testing. *Applied Psychological Measurement, 24*(3), 257–265.

Hockemeyer, C. & Albert, D. (1999). The adaptive tutoring system RATH: a prototype. In Auer, M.E. & Ressler, U. (Eds.), *ICL99 Workshop Interactive Computer Aided Learning: Tools and Applications.* Austria: Willach.

Lord, F.M. (1970). Some test theory for tailored testing. In Holtzman, W.H. (Ed.), *Computer Assisted Instruction, Testing and Guidance* (pp. 139–183). New York: Harper and Row.

Sands, W.A., Waters, B.K. & McBride, J.R. (1997). *Computerized Adaptive Testing: From Inquiry to Operation.* Washington: American Psychological Association.

Segall, D.O. (2000). Principles of multidimensional adaptive testing. In van der Linden, W.C. & Glas, C.A.W. (Eds.), *Computerized Adaptive Testing: Theory and Practice* (pp. 53–73). Boston, MA: Kluwer-Nijhoff.

Sympson, J.B. & Hetter, R.D. (1985). *Controlling Item Exposure Rates in Computerized Adaptive Testing.* Paper presented at the meeting of the Military Testing Association, San Diego, CA.

Tatsuoka, K.K. & Tatsuoka, M. M. (1997). Computerized cognitive diagnostic adaptive testing: effect on remedial instruction as empirical validation. *Journal of Educational Measurement, 34*(1), 3–20.

van der Linden, W.J. (1998). Bayesian item selection criteria for adaptive testing. *Psychometrika, 63*(2), 201–216.

Wainer, H. (2000). CATS: whither and whence. *Psicológica, 21,* 121–133.

Wainer, H., Dorans, N.J., Flaugher, R., Green, B.F., Mislevy, R.J., Steinberg, L. & Thissen, D. (2000). *Computerized Adaptive Testing: A Primer* (2nd ed.). Hillsdale, NJ: Lawrence Erlbaum Associates.

Wang, T. & Vispoel, W.P. (1998). Properties of ability estimation methods in computerized adaptive testing. *Journal of Educational Measurement, 35,* 109–135.

Wise, S.L. & Kingsbury, G.G. (2000). Practical issues in developing and maintaining a computerized adaptive testing program. *Psicológica, 21,* 135–155.

Vicente Ponsoda and Julio Olea

RELATED ENTRIES

COMPUTER-BASED TESTING, ITEM BANKING, ITEM RESPONSE THEORY: MODELS AND FEATURES, AUTOMATED TEST ASSEMBLY SYSTEMS, THEORETICAL PERSPECTIVE: PSYCHOMETRICS

AMBULATORY ASSESSMENT

INTRODUCTION

Ambulatory assessment designates a new orientation in behavioural and psychophysiological assessment. This approach relates to everyday life ('naturalistic' observation) and claims the ecological validity of research findings. Methods of recording psychological data in everyday life have a long history in differential psychology and clinical psychology. Event recorders for the timed registration of stimuli and responses, 'beeper' studies in which a programmable wristwatch prompts the subject to respond to a questionnaire, self-ratings on diary cards, and electronic data loggers have all been used for this purpose. The arrival of pocket-sized (hand-held, palm-top) computers has eased the acquisition of data considerably. Computer-assisted methodologies facilitate investigations in real-life situations where relevant behaviour can be much more effectively studied than in the artificial environment of laboratory research. Such field studies are essential, for example, in research on stress–strain or in research on mechanisms that trigger off psychological and psychophysiological symptoms.

Ambulatory assessment originated from a number of previously rather independent research orientations with specific objectives. *Clinical (bedside) monitoring* was introduced as a means of continuously observing a patient's vital functions, e.g. respiratory and cardiovascular parameters under anaesthesia, during intensive care and in perinatal condition. If relevant changes occur, i.e. if certain critical values are exceeded, an alarm is set off. *Biotelemetry* employs transmitter–receiver systems (radio-telemetry) in order to measure physical functions in real life, e.g. cardiovascular changes during intense strain at the workplace or during athletic performance. Radio equipment basically makes two-sided communication possible, i.e. feedback, telestimulation and telecommand, in addition to telemetry. *Ambulatory monitoring* means continuous observation of free-moving subjects (patients) in everyday life as compared to stationary, bedside ('wired') monitoring. Ambulatory monitoring can be conducted either by biotelemetry or by a portable recording system. This methodology is appropriate for patients who exhibit significant pathological symptoms which, for a number of reasons, cannot be reliably detected in the physician's office or hospital as compared to a prolonged observation in everyday life. Such cases include ventricular arrhythmia, ischaemic episodes, sleep apnea, and epileptic seizures. Here, ambulatory monitoring furthers valid diagnoses as well as the stabilization of medication. *Field research* comprises observation in natural settings in contrast to the laboratory. Field research is an essential methodology in cultural anthropology, social research, and ethology. Likewise, in psychology and psychophysiology some research issues require field studies to obtain valid data (see Kerlinger & Lee, 2000; Patry, 1982). *Behavioural assessment* methods include, besides laboratory observation, a variety of in-vivo (in-situ) tests, simulated and quasi-naturalistic settings, such as behavioural approach/avoidance tests (BATs) which were designed to assess behaviour disorders and clinical symptoms.

Ambulatory assessment brings together those research orientations that correspond to each other in their basic ecological perspective. Ambulatory assessment involves the acquisition of psychological data and/or physiological measures in everyday life according to an explicit assessment strategy which relates data, theoretical constructs, and empirical criteria specific to the given research issue. Such field studies are not solely concerned with the ambulatory monitoring of patients, but rather include a wide spectrum of objectives and applications. Common features

are: recordings in everyday life, computer-assisted methodology, attempts to minimize method-dependent reactivity, maintaining ecological validity and, therefore, outstanding practical utility for various objectives – such as monitoring and self-monitoring, screening, classification and selection, clinical diagnosis, and evaluation – in many areas of psychology and psychophysiology (de Vries, 1992; Fahrenberg & Myrtek, 1996, 2001a, 2001b; Littler, 1980; Miles & Broughton, 1990; Pawlik & Buse, 1982, 1996; Pickering, 1991; Suls & Martin, 1993).

ACQUISITION OF PSYCHOLOGICAL DATA BY HAND-HELD PC

In psychology the hand-held PC so far has been predominantly used for recording self-reports on mood and other aspects of subjective state, including physical complaints and symptoms; that is, as an 'electronic diary' (e.g. job stress diary, pain diary). There are other kinds of data, which can be obtained in field studies: objective features of a behaviour setting, behaviour observations, behaviour and performance measures (psychometric testing), self-measurements of various kinds, for example blood pressure data, and, possibly, ratings of environmental aspects. Potential contents of a computer-assisted protocol may further include, for example, individual comments or self-evaluation in connection with events.

Advantages and Limitations

The application of a programmable pocket PC in ambulatory assessment has many advantages:

- alarm functions for prompting the subject at predefined intervals and a built-in reminder signal;
- reliable timing of input, delay of input, and duration of input;
- flexible layout of questions and response categories;
- branching of questions and tailor-made sequential or hierarchical strategies;
- concealment of previously recorded responses from the subjects;
- convenience and ease of transfer of data to a stationary PC for statistical analysis.

A higher technical reliability and ecological validity of computer-assisted recordings can be generally assumed compared with paper-and-pencil questionnaires and diaries that lack flexibility in data acquisition and exactness when timing responses. The versatility and wide acceptance of computer-assisted data acquisition is evident, although there are limitations and obvious restrictions. All participants of such studies will need sufficient practical training in at least the basic features of the PC and the program, to avoid malfunctions and missing data. In spite of the obvious increase in computer literacy within the general population, there are sub-populations which are less familiar with such devices or may experience problems.

Following the progress made in pocket-sized computers, software to facilitate the use of hand-held PCs in field studies has been developed in many institutions, more or less geared to the needs of certain studies. More flexible software systems suited to the requirements of a variety of applications are still an exception (AMBU for in-field performance testing, *cf.* Buse and Pawlik, Hogrefe Verlag, Göttingen, Germany; MONITOR, a flexible software system for ambulatory assessment, Psychology Department, University of Freiburg, Germany). The OBSERVER (Behaviour Observation System, Noldus Information Technology, AG Wageningen, NL, Noldus, 1991) was introduced to ease the recording of behaviour observations in field studies in animal and human ethology.

Computer-assisted self-reports require a hand-held PC with certain features: a large display, easy handling of basic controls, clock, beeper with volume control, sufficient capacity of storage, low power consumption, and a low weight. For many applications, a comparatively large alphanumeric keyboard (complete QWERTY) is also preferable in order to ease recording and, especially, to record verbal responses. The latter may involve, for example, recording reports and comments about specific events, or reporting more precisely the occurrence of physical and psychological symptoms, which in either case hardly fit pre-defined categories. For some applications it may suffice to record only 'yes' or 'no' responses or numbers. In this case, a smaller hand-held PC, e.g. the Palm™ series, may be preferable, although small keys or a stylus may present a problem for some subjects or patients.

PHYSIOLOGICAL MEASUREMENT AND MONITORING

A wide selection of physiological variables have been measured in daily life, using mostly non-invasive methods. The ECG and blood pressure enjoy by far the largest number of references in the literature to ambulatory monitoring. The application is predominantly in the medical field and only to a much smaller extent in the behavioural sciences; for example, in psychophysiology or behavioural medicine. The advances in microprocessor technology and storage capacity paved the way for multi-channel recordings and – another innovative step – led to the on-line analysis of medically important changes; for example, the immediate detection of ST-depression in the ECG.

The recording of posture and motion is another basic issue in the methodology of behaviour observation and performance measurement. Piezoresistive sensors (multi-site calibrated accelerometry) allow for:

- continuous recording and automatic detection of changes in posture and movement;
- assessment of movement disorders, such as hand tremor, restless legs syndrome;
- detection of head movement, e.g. nodding during a conversation, measured by a small accelerometer placed beneath the chin;
- estimation of gross physical activity and energy expenditure.

To assist in objective behaviour analysis, a range of interesting variables could be measured continuously:

- voice signal recorded via a throat sensor (micro);
- the temporal pattern of speech;
- ambient conditions recorded via suitable sensors for light, noise, and temperature.

Some hand-held PCs allow for audio recordings up to a number of minutes, depending on storage capacity. Digital dictating systems have a capacity up to 240 minutes in long play mode. In psychological and psychophysiological research, so far, little use has been made of digital mini-cams or web-cams for recordings of the videostream of behaviour.

Recorder–Analyser

Today, more than a dozen recorder–analyser systems are available from international manufactures – not to mention the even greater number of long-term ECG recorders–analysers and the long-term-BP recorders. Only a few systems have a multi-channel design, the advantage of which is that they can be applied to a variety of research questions that require different recording channels (for an overview of selected multi-purpose recorder systems, see Fahrenberg, 2001). Besides the devices suitable for ambulatory recordings and their use in 24-h or long-term monitoring, a wide range of portable (mobile) equipment designed for in-field measurement does exist.

ISSUES IN AMBULATORY ASSESSMENT

Assessment strategies, designs, and data analysis

In psychological research various designs for computer-assisted ambulatory assessment have already been employed, whereby some of these assessments lasted for many days or weeks. In psychophysiology and in medicine, the restriction to a single 24-h recording appears to be the preferred format due to the costly equipment. Ambulatory assessment requires the elaboration of specific designs and strategies, for example the strategic use and integration of time and event sampling, and the development of appropriate statistical models for multi-level analyses and for rather short time series (for a discussion, see Fahrenberg & Myrtek, 2001a; Schwarz & Stone, 1998; Stemmler, 1996). It would be oversimplified to state methodological advantages of the laboratory experiment as obstacles in field studies and vice versa, i.e. to retain the notion of basically different research strategies instead of a wider perspective that includes laboratory and field as complementary approaches.

Laboratory–field comparisons are designed to examine the validity of findings obtained in the laboratory to predict performance in real life. In the development of psychological tests such empirical validation studies play an important role. More recently, it has been questioned whether certain diagnostic techniques and measurements in the physician's office or in the psychophysiological laboratory, e.g. blood pressure measurement, reliably predict individual differences in real life. Laboratory–field comparisons revealed significant discrepancies. Office hypertension is a good example of how certain features of the setting and their meaning to the subject may play an important role in assessing individual differences: blood pressure readings are elevated if the measurement is made by the physician, but normal readings are obtained in everyday life.

Laboratory–field comparisons were valuable in the evaluation of methodological issues as well as practical aspects. Field studies, apparently, are more suited for prolonged observation that may extend over days and weeks. Accordingly, there is more chance for the detection of rare events and symptoms that occur at low frequencies or only in certain settings. Generally, larger response magnitudes and more realistic effect sizes may be expected in natural settings. Prolonged observation periods make the averaging/aggregation of measurements possible so that reliability and stability of measures may increase substantially. But field studies can be seriously threatened by the confounding of multiple effects which tend to produce 'noise' and, eventually, require relatively large subject samples in order to obtain valid estimates for main effects.

Psychophysiological monitoring. Multi-modal psychophysiological 24-h monitoring methodologies were developed in many fields, especially in research on blood pressure reactivity. This method consists of multi-channel recordings of blood pressure, heart rate, physical activity, and – concurrent to each blood pressure measurement – obtained a computer-assisted self-report on setting, behaviour, emotional state, and experience.

Controlled monitoring. Recordings obtained in everyday life will often include multiple effects. Therefore, investigators may wish to control for unwanted variance, such as blood pressure changes caused by physical activity. Concurrent recordings of physical activity provided means for a segmentation of recordings according to high or low activity. Furthermore, standardized or semi-standardized measurement periods were included which served as a reference for inter- and intra-individual comparison. As part of the standard protocol in 24-h monitoring, the subjects performed specific tasks: climbing a staircase, performing a mental test, and participating in a short interview.

Interactive monitoring. The development of recorder equipment suitable for physiological and psychophysiological recordings and on-line (real-time) analysis led to innovative research strategies. Contingent to changes of certain physiological parameters, a patient can be prompted by a beeper signal to record specific events, activities, or symptoms. Myrtek et al. (1988) developed a new methodology for interactive monitoring of 'additional heart rate' indicative for emotional states.

Acceptance, Compliance, and Reactivity

From the beginning, there have been concerns raised about the acceptance of hand-held PCs, and the validity of monitoring in daily life has been questioned. Ambulatory assessment with a pocket PC or recorder depends on the favourable attitude of the participating subjects. It is essential that the equipment is readily accepted and that good compliance to instructions is established and sustained. If the ambulatory monitoring is part of a diagnostic process or a treatment programme, the patient's compliance may be higher than in research projects. The ambulatory assessment should, of course, not cause major problems with the social environment.

The method of observation and measurement itself may cause unwanted variance because of specific interactions such as awareness, adaptation, sensitization, and coping tendencies. Three aspects of reactivity appear to be specific to ambulatory assessment. Subjects may: (1) tend to steer clear of certain settings during the recording in order to avoid being monitored there; (2) tend to unintentionally or deliberately manipulate the recording systems, shift settings of the PC and may even try to get access to the program; and (3) try to test their capacities or the equipment by unusual patterns of behaviour, exercise or vigorous movements. A comprehensive post-monitoring interview is recommended in order to obtain information on these essential aspects.

Ethical issues that are specific to ambulatory monitoring studies have hardly been discussed yet. Appropriate data protection is but one aspect, as ambulatory assessment may violate privacy more easily than other methods. Furthermore, significant others and bystanders may become involved when the observation and the evaluation of settings are demanded. Obtaining the subject's informed consent before the recording starts is essential, but may be problematic since the exact course of daily activities and events cannot be anticipated.

Acceptance and impact of computer-assisted monitoring methodology in psychophysiology and psychology. The ambulatory monitoring of BP and ECG are now indispensable routine methods in medicine. The ever more widespread application of the new methodology can be attributed to its practical usefulness which was evident in the increased validity of diagnosis and in the external validity of therapy outcome evaluation. In contrast, computer-assisted monitoring and assessment still appear to have had little impact in psychophysiology and psychology. Standard textbooks on behavioural research methods and assessment in clinical psychology hardly refer to the new methodologies based on computer-assisted data acquisition and monitoring in the natural environment.

FUTURE PERSPECTIVES

Computer-assisted ambulatory assessment is an emerging new methodology. Progress is obvious not only in instrumentation, but in assessment strategies as well. Ambulatory assessment, like any other method, has problematic aspects, in particular how to account for multiple effects in the recordings, but the benefits are evident:

- *recording* of relevant data in natural settings;
- *real-time measurement* of behavioural and physiological changes;
- *real-time assessment and feedback* by reporting physiological changes to the subject;
- *concurrent assessment* of psychological and physiological changes (detection of events, episodes);
- *correlation and contingency (symptom–context) analysis* across systemic levels as suggested in triple-response models (multimodal assessment);
- *ecological validity* of findings and suitability for direct application.

Genuine research findings in relevant fields suggest further development and application of ambulatory assessment methodology. The expectation is that the hand-held PCs and the recorder–analyser for physiological measures will in future become smaller, cheaper and more refined. Such developments may include new strategies in controlled or interactive monitoring and on-line feedback, monitoring and concurrent recording of audio and video signals (intelligently pre-processed before stored), setting-dependent sampling, new strategies in self-monitoring and self-management in chronic illness.

A hand-held PC may be useful in the diagnostic assessment of a variety of behaviour disorders, for example the assessment and self-management of drinking, smoking, and of eating disorders, and in facilitating self-management in chronic illness. Computer programs that are based on a hand-held PC can be used as a component of behavioural therapy (cf. a pilot study by Burnett et al., 1985).

There are noticeable developments which probably exert an essential influence on the computer-assisted methods in medicine and the behavioural sciences: the arrival of the wireless application protocol (WAP), the mobile phone short message systems (SMS), the web-based mobile telecommunication (IMT-2000 and UMTS) and the new patient monitoring equipment, which appears to revolutionize the way in which patient information is transmitted and used in the healthcare system. At present, we may only speculate about the consequences of such developing information technologies for the healthcare system and, to some extent, on subsequent developments in applied fields of psychology.

CONCLUSIONS

During the last two decades, a fast development in microprocessor technology has enabled the design of new instrumentation and, accordingly, new methodologies in medicine and the behavioural sciences. Multi-channel recorders–analysers and special purpose devices for physiological measures and convenient hand-held PCs for acquisition of psychological data are available. Such systems allow innovative research and

practical application in many fields and essential findings have been obtained.

References

Burnett, K.F., Taylor, C.B. & Agras, W.S. (1985). Ambulatory computer assisted therapy for obesity: a new frontier for behavior therapy. *Journal of Consulting and Clinical Psychology*, 53, 698–703.

de Vries, W. (Ed.) (1992). *The Experience of Psychopathology. Investigating Mental Disorders in Their Natural Settings*. Cambridge: Cambridge University Press.

Fahrenberg, J. (2001). Origins and developments of ambulatory monitoring and assessment. In Fahrenberg, J. & Myrtek, M. (Eds.), *Progress in Ambulatory Assessment: Computer-Assisted Psychological and Psychophysiological Methods in Monitoring and Field Studies* (pp. 587–614). Seattle, WA: Hogrefe and Huber.

Fahrenberg, J. & Myrtek, M. (Eds.) (1996). *Ambulatory Assessment: Computer-Assisted Psychological and Psychophysiological Methods in Monitoring and Field Studies*. Seattle, WA: Hogrefe and Huber.

Fahrenberg, J. & Myrtek, M. (Eds.) (2001a). *Progress in Ambulatory Assessment: Computer-Assisted Psychological and Psychophysiological Methods in Monitoring and Field Studies*. Seattle, WA: Hogrefe and Huber.

Fahrenberg, J. & Myrtek, M. (2001b). Ambulantes Monitoring und Assessment. In Rösler, F. (Ed.), *Enzyklopädie der Psychologie. Serie Biologische Psychologie. Band 4: Grundlagen und Methoden der Psychophysiologie* (pp. 657–798). Göttingen: Hogrefe.

Kerlinger, F.N. & Lee, H.B. (2000). *Foundations of Behavioral Research*. Fort Worth, TX: Harcourt.

Littler, W.A. (Ed.) (1980). *Clinical and Ambulatory Monitoring*. London: Chapman and Hall.

Miles, L.E. and Broughton, R.J. (Eds.) (1990). *Medical Monitoring in the Home and Work Environment*. New York: Raven Press.

Myrtek, M., Brügner, G., Fichtler, A., König, K., Müller, W., Foerster, F. & Höppner, V. (1988). Detection of emotionally induced ECG changes and their behavioral correlates: a new method for ambulatory monitoring. *European Heart Journal*, 9 (Supplement N), 55–60.

Noldus, L.P.J.J. (1991). The Observer: a software system for collection and analysis of observational data. *Behavior, Research Methods, Instruments & Computers*, 23, 415–429.

Patry, J.L. (Ed.) (1982). *Feldforschung. Methoden und Probleme sozialwissenschaftlicher Forschung unter natürlichen Bedingungen*. Bern: Huber.

Pawlik, K. & Buse, L. (1982). Rechnergestützte Verhaltensregistrierung im Feld: Beschreibung und erste psychometrische Überprüfung einer neuen Erhebungsmethode. *Zeitschrift für Differentielle und Diagnostische Psychologie*, 3, 101–118.

Pawlik, K. & Buse, L. (1996). Verhaltensbeobachtung in Labor und Feld. In Pawlik, K. (Ed.), *Enzyklopädie der Psychologie. Differentielle Psychologie und Persönlichkeitsforschung. Band 1. Grundlagen und Methoden der Differentiellen Psychologie* (pp. 359–394). Göttingen: Hogrefe.

Pickering, T. G. (1991). *Ambulatory Monitoring and Blood Pressure Variability*. London: Science Press.

Schwarz, J.E. & Stone, A.A. (1998). Strategies for analysing ecological momentary assessment data. *Health Psychology, 17*, 6–16.

Stemmler, G. (1996). Strategies and designs in ambulatory assessment. In Fahrenberg, J. and Myrtek, M. (Eds.), *Ambulatory Assessment: Computer-Assisted Psychological and Psychophysiological Methods in Monitoring and Field Studies* (pp. 257–268). Seattle, WA: Hogrefe and Huber.

Suls, J. & Martin, R.E. (1993). Daily recording and ambulatory monitoring methodologies in behavioral medicine. *Annals of Behavioral Medicine, 15*, 3–7.

Jochen Fahrenberg

RELATED ENTRIES

PSYCHOPHYSIOLOGICAL EQUIPMENT AND MEASUREMENTS, APPLIED FIELDS: PSYCHOPHYSIOLOGY, EQUIPMENT FOR ASSESSING BASIC PROCESSES, FIELD SURVEY: PROTOCOLS DEVELOPMENT, OBSERVATIONAL METHODS (GENERAL), SELF-OBSERVATION (SELF-MONITORING)

ANALOGUE METHODS

INTRODUCTION

Analogue behavioural observation (ABO) involves a situation designed by, manipulated by, or constrained by an assessor that elicits a measured behaviour of interest. Observed behaviours comprise both verbal and non-verbal emissions (e.g. motor actions, verbalized attributions, observable facial reactions).

ABO exists on a continuum of naturalism, ranging from highly contrived situations (e.g. How quickly do people walk down the hallway after being exposed to subconsciously presented words about ageing? Bargh et al., 1996) to naturalistic situations arranged in unnatural ways or settings (e.g. How do couples talk with one another when asked to discuss their top problem topic? Heyman, 2001) to naturalistic situations with some (but minimal) experimenter-dictated restrictions (e.g. family observations in the home; Reid, 1978).

WHY USE ABO?

ABO is used as a hypothesis-testing tool for three purposes: (a) to observe otherwise unobservable behaviours, (b) to isolate the determinants of behaviour, and (c) to observe dynamic qualities of social interaction. Although naturalistic observation might be preferable (i.e. generalizability inferences are minimized), the first two purposes require controlled experimentation, necessitating ABO; for the third purpose, ABO is often preferable because it allows the observer to 'stack the deck' to make it more likely that the behaviours (and/or functional relations) of interest will occur when the assessor can see them.

DOMAINS

ABO comprises two main assessment domains: individual/situation interactions and social situations. The goals of individual/situation interaction experiments are to manipulate the setting and test individual differences in response. This domain comprises a wide variety of tasks in developmental psychology (e.g. strange situation experiments; Ainsworth et al., 1978), social psychology (e.g. emotion regulation experiments; Tice et al., 2001) and clinical psychology (e.g. functional analysis of self-injurious behaviour; Iwata et al., 1994; social anxiety assessment; Norton & Hope, 2001).

The social situation domain employs ABO mostly as a convenience in assessing quasi-naturalistic interaction. The goal of such assessment is typically to understand behaviour and its determinants in dynamic, reciprocally influenced systems (e.g. groups, families, couples). Understanding generalizable factors that promote or maintain problem behaviours in such systems typically requires more naturalistic approaches than those used in the other domain. Thus, although experimentation is often extremely useful in understanding causal relations in social situations (e.g. whether maternal attributions affect mother–child interactions; Slep & O'Leary, 1998), most such ABO investigations aim for quasi-naturalism.

CLINICAL ASSESSMENT

ABO is a useful tool in clinical assessment, although relatively few ABO paradigms have been developed specifically with this application in mind. To be clinically useful, ABO must efficiently provide reliable, valid, and non-redundant (but cost-effective) information.

An apt analogy for research-protocol based assessment vs. field-realistic assessment might be found in the treatment literature. In recent years, a distinction has evolved between efficacy studies (i.e. those studying interventions under tightly controlled, idealized circumstances, such as a trial of treatment for major depressive disorder that eliminates all potential participants with co-morbid disorders) and effectiveness studies (i.e. those studying interventions under real-world conditions). Because we do not have an adequate research body of effectiveness studies, clinicians in the field, urged to use empirically validated treatments, are expected to adapt such protocols to meet real-world demands. Similarly, clinicians should be urged to use empirically validated ABO when it would be appropriate, but should be expected to adapt ABO protocols in a cost-effective but still clinically informative manner.

ABO Protocols

Space limitations preclude a summary of the wide variety of ABO protocols. We note, however, literatures on parent–child interaction (e.g. Roberts, 2001), couple interaction (e.g. Heyman, 2001), social anxiety and social interaction skills (Norton & Hope, 2001), fear (e.g. McGlynn & Rose, 1998), self-injurious behaviour in those with developmental disabilities (e.g. Iwata et al., 1994), the effect of alcohol consumption on family

interaction (e.g. Leonard & Roberts, 1998), cooperation and competition (e.g. the prisoner's dilemma paradigm; Sheldon, 1999), and aggression (e.g. Bandura, 1986).

Psychometric Considerations

Each ABO paradigm and its accompanying coding systems must be separately considered for reliability, validity, and utility. Like all psychological assessments, ABO psychometrics depend 'on the goals of assessment, the assessment settings, the methods of assessment, the characteristics of the measured variable, and the inferences that are drawn from the obtained measures' (Haynes & O'Brien, 2000: 201).

The psychometrics of ABO paradigms and coding systems has received little direct attention (see a special issue of *Psychological Assessment*, March 2001, for a notable exception). The validity of the ABO paradigms is implied by the results of studies using that paradigm. As such, ABO paradigms and their coding systems often have excellent validity and reported inter-rater agreement.

Coding

Although we have described ABO as a hypothesis testing tool, in reality it is a hypothesis testing setting; coding the observed behaviours turns ABO into a true tool. Creation or use of a coding system is a theoretical act, and the following questions should be answered before proceeding: Why are you observing? What do you hope to learn? How will it impact your hypotheses (i.e. either research questions or case-conceptualization questions)? This is especially true because coding of many ABO target behaviours is difficult to do in a reliable, valid, and cost-effective manner. Interested readers should consult several excellent resources for more complete coverage (e.g. Bakeman & Gottman, 1997; Haynes & O'Brien, 2000).

Sampling

The major sampling strategies are event sampling (the occurrence of behaviour is coded, ideally in sequential fashion), duration sampling (the length of each behaviour is recorded), interval sampling (the ABO period is divided into time blocks; during each time block, the occurrence of each code is noted), and time sampling (intermittent observations are made, typically in a duration or interval sampling manner). Advantages and disadvantages of each are discussed in Bakeman and Gottman (1997) and Haynes and O'Brien (2000).

Choosing What to Code

Some behaviours are so concrete that the observer serves more as a recorder than a coder (e.g. duration of a discrete behaviour). Other behaviours require at least some degree of inference. Such coding necessitates the use of culturally sensitive raters, using specified decision rules, to infer that a combination of situational, linguistic, paralinguistic, or contextual cues amounts to a codeable behaviour. Concrete codes are not necessarily better than social informant-inferred codes; sometimes one allows for a more valid measurement of a construct, sometimes the other does. In accord with Occam's razor, coding should be as simple as possible to reliably capture the behavioural constructs of interest.

Global (i.e. molar) coding systems make summary ratings for each code over the entire ABO (or across large time intervals). Codes tend to be few, representing behavioural classes (e.g. negativity). Microbehavioural (i.e. molecular) systems code behaviour as it unfolds over time, and tend to have many fine-grained behavioural codes (e.g. eye contact, criticize, whine).

Topographical coding systems measure the occurrence of a behaviour (including, potentially, its duration). Dimensional coding systems measure the intensity of the behaviour. Microbehavioural systems tend to be topographical; although global systems tend to be use-rating scales, they may summarize frequency rather than intensity. Dimensional coding of intensity, especially on a point-by-point basis, has been used sparingly in ABO.

Analyses

ABO frequently uses single subject multiple baseline designs. Data are plotted and visually inspected for trends.

Statistical analysis of ABO data uses standard statistical tools. Between-groups hypotheses about behavioural frequencies are tested with ANOVA, continuous association hypotheses are tested with correlations or regressions.

When functional relations are of interest, testing how interactions unfold across time becomes important. Functional relation hypotheses can be addressed with conditional probabilities or with sequential analysis, which is similar to conditional probability analysis but which allows for significance testing. Dimensional data assessed continuously would use time-series analysis instead of sequential analysis.

CONCLUSIONS

ABO can be a good theory-testing tool because (depending on exactly how it is employed) it minimizes inferences needed to assess behaviour, it can facilitate formal or informal functional analysis, provide the assessor with experimental control of situational factors, facilitate the observation of otherwise unobservable behaviours, and provide an additional mode of assessment in a multimodal strategy (e.g. questionnaires, interviews, observation). Finally, because the assessor can set up a situation that increases the probability that behaviours of interest will occur during the observation period, ABO can be high in clinical utility and research efficiency.

Like any tool, however, ABO's usefulness depends on its match to the resources and needs of the person considering using it. ABO can be a time, labour, and money-intensive assessment strategy. The use of research-tested protocols/coding is often impractical in clinical settings; adaptations of empirically supported ABO methodology in clinical settings may render them unreliable and of dubious validity. The conditional nature of validity may make it difficult to generalize ABOs to the broad variety of real-world settings. Finally, the less naturalistic the ABO situation, the more nagging the concerns about external validity.

Acknowledgements

Preparation of this entry was supported by the National Institutes of Mental Health (Grant R01MH57779) and National Center for Injury Prevention and Control, Centers for Disease Control and Prevention (Grant R49CCR218554-01).

References

Ainsworth, M.D.S., Blehar, M.C., Waters, E. & Wall, S. (Eds.) (1978). *Patterns of Attachment: A Psychological Study of the Strange Situation*. Hillsdale, NJ: Erlbaum.

Bakeman, R. & Gottman, J.M. (1997). *Observing Interaction: An Introduction to Sequential Analysis* (2nd ed.). New York: Cambridge University Press.

Bandura, A. (1986). *Social Foundations of Thought and Action: A Social Cognitive Theory*. Englewood Cliffs, NJ: Prentice-Hall.

Bargh, J.A., Chen, M. & Burrows, L. (1996). Automaticity of social behaviour: direct effects of trait construct and stereotype activation on action. *Journal of Personality and Social Psychology, 71*, 230–244.

Haynes, S.N. & O'Brien, W.H. (2000). *Principles and Practice of Behavioural Assessment*. New York: Kluwer.

Heyman, R.E. (2001). Observation of couple conflicts: clinical assessment applications, stubborn truths, and shaky foundations. *Psychological Assessment, 13*, 5–35.

Iwata, B.A., Pace, G.M., Dorsey, M.F., Zarcone, J.R., Vollmer, B. & Smith, J. (1994). The functions of self-injurious behaviour: an experimental-epidemiological analysis. *Journal of Applied Behaviour Analysis, 27*, 215–240.

Leonard, K.E. & Roberts, L.J. (1998). The effects of alcohol on the marital interactions of aggressive and nonaggressive husbands and their wives. *Journal of Abnormal Psychology, 107*, 602–615.

McGlynn, F.D. & Rose, M.P. (1998). Assessment of anxiety and fear. In Bellack, A.S. & Hersen, M. (Eds.), *Behavioural Assessment: A Practical Handbook* (4th ed., pp. 179–209). Needham Heights, MA: Allyn & Bacon.

Norton, P.J. & Hope, D.A. (2001). Analogue observational methods in the assessment of social functioning in adults. *Psychological Assessment, 13*, 59–72.

Reid, J.B. (Ed.) (1978). *A Social Learning Approach, Vol. 2: Observation in Home Settings*. Eugene, OR: Castalia.

Roberts, M.W. (2001). Clinic observations of structured parent–child interaction designed to evaluate externalizing disorders. *Psychological Assessment, 13*, 46–58.

Sheldon, K.M. (1999). Learning the lessons of tit-for-tat: even competitors can get the message. *Journal of Personality and Social Psychology, 77*, 1245–1253.

Slep, A.M.S. & O'Leary, S.G. (1998). The effects of maternal attributions on parenting: an experimental analysis. *Journal of Family Psychology, 12*, 234–243.

Tice, D.M., Bratslavsky, E. & Baumeister, R.F. (2001). Emotional distress regulation takes precedence over impulse control: if you feel bad, do it! *Journal of Personality and Social Psychology, 80*, 53–67.

Richard E. Heyman and Amy M. Smith Slep

RELATED ENTRIES

OBSERVATIONAL METHODS (GENERAL), OBSERVATIONAL TECHNIQUES IN CLINICAL SETTINGS, APPLIED FIELDS: CLINICAL

A ANGER, HOSTILITY AND AGGRESSION ASSESSMENT

INTRODUCTION

Over the last 25 years, interest in measuring the experience, expression, and control of anger has been stimulated by evidence that anger, hostility and aggression were associated with hypertension and cardiovascular disease (Williams, Barefoot & Shekelle, 1985; Dembroski, MacDougall, Williams & Haney, 1984). While definitions of anger-related constructs are often inconsistent and ambiguous, the experience and expression of anger are typically encompassed in definitions of hostility and aggression. Clearly, anger is the most fundamental of these overlapping constructs.

On the basis of a careful review of the research literature on anger, hostility and aggression, the following definitions of these constructs were proposed by Spielberger et al. (1983: 16):

Anger usually refers to an emotional state that consists of feelings that vary in intensity, from mild irritation or annoyance to intense fury and rage. Although hostility involves angry feelings, this concept has the connotation of a complex set of attitudes that motivate aggressive behaviours directed toward destroying objects or injuring other people. The concept of aggression generally implies destructive or punitive behaviour directed towards other persons or objects.

The physiological and behavioural manifestations of anger, hostility and aggression have been investigated in numerous studies, but until recently angry feelings have been largely ignored in psychological research. Consequently, psychometric measures of anger, hostility and aggression generally do not distinguish between feeling angry, and the expression of anger and hostility in aggressive behaviour. Most measures of anger-related constructs also fail to take the state–trait distinction into account, and confound the experience and expression of anger with situational determinants of angry behaviour. A coherent theoretical framework that recognizes the difference between anger, hostility and aggression as psychological constructs, and that distinguishes between anger as an emotional state and individual differences in the experience, expression and control of anger as personality traits, is essential for guiding the construction and cross-cultural adaptation of anger measures.

ASSESSMENT OF ANGER: MEASURING STATE–TRAIT AND THE EXPRESSION AND CONTROL OF ANGER

The State–Trait Anger Expression Inventory (STAXI) was developed to measure the experience, expression and control of anger (Spielberger et al., 1985; Spielberger, Krasner & Solomon, 1988). The State–Trait Anger Scale (STAS) was constructed to assess the intensity of anger as an emotional state, and individual differences in anger proneness as a personality trait (Spielberger et al., 1983). State anger was defined as '. . . an emotional state marked by subjective feelings that vary in intensity from mild annoyance or irritation to intense fury or rage, which is generally accompanied by muscular tension and arousal of the autonomic nervous system'. Trait Anger refers to individual differences in the disposition to experience angry feelings. The STAS Trait-Anger Scale evaluates how frequently State Anger is experienced.

Recognition of the importance of distinguishing between the experience and expression of anger stimulated the development of the Anger Expression (AX) Scale (Spielberger et al., 1985). The AX Scale assesses how often anger is suppressed (anger-in) or expressed in aggressive behaviour (anger-out). The instructions for responding to the AX Scale differ markedly

from the traditional trait-anger instructions. Rather than directing subjects to respond according to how they generally feel, they are instructed to report on how often they react or behave in a particular manner when they feel 'angry or furious' (e.g. 'I say nasty things'; 'I boil inside, but don't show it') by rating themselves on the same 4-point frequency scale that is used with the Trait-Anger Scale.

The identification of anger control as an independent factor stimulated the construction of a scale to assess the control of angry feelings (Spielberger et al., 1988). The content of three of the 20 original AX Scale items (e.g. control my temper, keep my cool, calm down faster), which were included to assess intermediate levels of anger-expression as a unidimensional bipolar scale, guided the generation of additional anger control items (Spielberger et al., 1985).

The last stage in the construction of the STAXI was stimulated by the research of psycholinguists, who identified English metaphors for anger, which called attention to the need to distinguish between two different mechanisms for controlling anger expression (Lakoff, 1987). The prototype of the anger metaphor was described as a hot liquid in a container, where blood was the hot liquid and the body was the container. The intensity of anger as an emotional state is considered analogous to the variations in the temperature of the hot liquid. The metaphor, boiling inside, has the connotation of an intense level of suppressed anger; blowing off steam connotes the outward expression of angry feelings; keeping the lid on implies controlling intense anger by preventing the outward expression of aggressive behaviour. Thus, Lakoff's (1987) anger metaphors suggested two quite different mechanisms for controlling anger: keeping angry feelings bottled up to prevent their expression, and reducing the intensity of suppressed anger by cooling down.

In the original STAXI scale, the content of all but one of the eight Control items was related to controlling anger-out (e.g. 'I control my temper'). Therefore, a number of new items were constructed to assess the control of anger-in by reducing the intensity of suppressed anger (Sydeman, 1995). The content of these items described efforts to calm down, cool off or relax when a person feels angry or furious. Factor analyses of the responses of large samples of male and female adults to the anger-control items identified two anger-control factors for both sexes: Anger Control-In and Control-Out.

OTHER MEANS OF MEASURING ANGER

(a) *Novaco Anger Inventory* (Novaco, 1975, 1977): this inventory is made up of 80 anger-provoking situations. Its reliability coefficient is rather high at 0.96, within a sample of 353 students (Biaggio, Supplee & Curtis 1981). This inventory has shown remarkable differences between psychiatric patients with anger problems and normal population (Novaco, 1977).

(b) *Multidimensional Anger Inventory – MAI* (Siegel, 1985): it is made up of 38 items, with a five-point 'Likert' scale. It measures anger-in with ruminations, anger-out with ruminations, anger-incited situations and hostile attitudes. It also provides a comprehensive index of anger in all its manifestations.

(c) *Harburg Anger In/Anger Out Scale* (Harburg, Erfurt, Chape, Hauenstein, Schull & Schork, 1973): this scale consists of a series of hypothetical interpersonal situations which may generate anger. It is a two-dimensional scale: it measures anger-in and anger-out, whereas at the same time it also provides a means of measuring resentment and reasoning.

(d) *Anger Self-Report Scale – ASR* (Zelin, Adler & Myerson, 1972): it consists of 74 items with a six-point 'Likert' scale. It measures anger awareness and anger expression. The anger expression scale makes a distinction between different sub-scales or levels of expression. This test has shown an average reliability coefficient in samples of psychiatric patients and students.

(e) *Anger Control Inventory*: this test consists of 134 items combining ten anger-provoking situations and six scales of anger response which describe cognitive, physiological and behavioural characteristics. Its reliability coefficient varies from 0.55 to 0.89 (Hoshmand & Austin, 1987).

(f) *Framingham Anger Scale*: these are self-report scales developed during the Framingham Project (Haynes, Levine, Scotch, Feinleib & Kannel, 1978). These scales are used to measure anger symptoms, anger-in and anger-out, and anger expression.

(g) *Subjective Anger Scale – SAS* (Knight, Ross, Collins & Parmenter, 1985): it measures the patient's proneness to experience anger by means of nine different situations and four scales of anger response.

(h) The *Anger Situation Scale* and the *Anger Symptom Scale* (Deffenbacher, Demm & Brander, 1986). They describe in detail the two worst, ongoing angering situations, and also, the two most salient physical signs of anger.

ASSESSMENT OF HOSTILITY

1 *Cook–Medley Ho Scale* (Cook & Medley, 1954). The Ho scale is a part of the MMPI. This scale, which has been widely used to measure hostility, is used in research on Health Psychology. However, its development has been shaped through research on rapport between teachers and students. Barefoot, Dodge, Peterson, Dahlstrom and Williams (1989) identified two subsets of items, which represent cognitive, affective and behavioural manifestations of hostility. Another subset of items reflects the tendency to elicit hostile intent from other people's behaviour. The remaining subset of items identifies social avoidance. Its test–retest reliability has been of 0.84 in a four-year interval (Shekelle, Gale, Ostfeld & Paul, 1983).

2 *The Buss–Durkee Hostility Inventory – BDHI* (Buss & Durkee, 1957): This scale consists of 75 items, with a true–false response scheme. It is one of the most comprehensive instruments to measure hostility. It is made up of seven sub-scales: Assault, Indirect Hostility, Irritability, Negativity, Resentment, Suspicion and Verbal Hostility. The factorial analysis of these scales reveals two well-defined factors. One of them reflects hostile expression and the other experiential aspects of hostility. Its test–retest reliability, given a two-week interval, is 0.82 for the total hostility measurement (Biaggio, Supplee & Curtis, 1981).

3 *Factor L*: It is a sub-scale of a more general personality inventory – Cattell's 16 P.F. (Cattell, Eber & Tatsuoka, 1970). It is

described as a measure of suspiciousness versus trust.

CROSS-CULTURAL ASSESSMENT OF ANGER, HOSTILITY AND AGGRESSION: THE SPANISH MULTICULTURAL STATE–TRAIT ANGER EXPRESSION INVENTORY

Spanish is spoken not only in Spain, but also in more than 20 countries in Central and South America and the Caribbean, and by more than 25 million native speakers of Spanish who reside in the United States. Although Spanish is the primary language in most of Latin America and for many Hispanic residents in the US, the indigenous cultures of these people often have profound effects on the Spanish they speak, and on the development of personality characteristics that influence their behaviour. Therefore, it is important to recognize the exceptionally complex social and cultural diversity of Hispanic populations, and the fact that language differences between these groups may outweigh the similarities. Consequently, in adapting English measures of emotion and personality for use in Spanish-speaking cultures, care must be taken to ensure that the key words and idiomatic expressions used for assessing anger-related concepts have essentially the same meaning in different Hispanic cultural groups.

The STAXI-2 (Spielberger, 1999) was adapted to measure the experience, expression and control of anger in culturally diverse populations in Latin America, and in Spanish-speaking sub-cultures in the United States (Moscoso & Spielberger, 1999a). Toward achieving this goal, the Spanish Multicultural State–Trait Anger Expression Inventory (STAXI-SMC) was designed to measure essentially the same dimensions of anger that are assessed with the revised STAXI-2. Scales and sub-scales were constructed to assess the following dimensions with the STAXI-SMC: (a) State Anger, with sub-scales for assessing Feeling Angry and Feel Like Expressing Anger; (b) Trait Anger, with sub-scales for measuring Angry Temperament and Angry Reaction; and (c) trait scales for measuring four dimensions of anger expression and control: anger-in, anger-out, and the control of anger-in and anger-out (Moscoso & Spielberger, 1999b).

Factor analyses of responses to the 56 preliminary STAXI-SMC items confirmed the hypothesized structural properties of the inventory. The eight factors that were identified corresponded quite well with similar factors in the STAXI-2. These included two S-Anger factors, two T-Anger factors, and four anger expression and control factors (Moscoso & Spielberger, 1999a). In separate factor analyses of the S-Anger items, two distinctive factors were identified for both males and females: 'Feeling Angry' and 'Feel Like Expressing Anger'. However, gender differences in the strength of the item loadings on these factors raised interesting questions with regard to how Latin American men and women may differ in the experience of anger. For females, the 'Feeling Angry' factor accounted for 73% of the total variance, while this factor accounted for only 19% of the variance for males. In contrast, the 'Feel Like Expressing Anger' factor accounted for 70% of the total variance of the males, but only 13% for females.

The factor analyses of the T-Anger STAXI-SMC items also identified separate Angry Temperament and Angry Reaction factors, providing strong evidence that the factor structure for this scale was similar to that of the STAXI-2. Factor analyses of the STAXI-SMC anger expression and control items identified the same four factors as in the STAXI-2. The items designed to assess anger-in and anger-out, and the control of anger-in and anger-out, had high loadings on the corresponding anger expression and control factors, which were similar for both sexes. The alpha coefficients for the STAXI-SMC State and Trait Anger scales and sub-scales, and the anger expression and anger control scales, were reasonably high, indicating that the internal consistency of these scales was satisfactory.

In summary, the results of the factor analyses of responses of the Latin American subjects to the STAXI-SMC items of the Latin American subjects identified eight factors that were quite similar to those found for the STAXI-2. Factor analyses of the anger expression and control items also identified the same four factors that are found in the STAXI-2. Thus, the multi-dimensional factor structure of the STAXI-SMC for the Latin American respondents was remarkably similar to the factor structure of the English STAXI-2. The adaptation of the STAXI-2 test carried out in

Spain, using Spanish mainland natives (Miguel-Tobal, Cano-Vindel, Casado & Spielberger, 2001), is made up of 49 items with a similar factorial structure and the same sub-scales.

FUTURE PERSPECTIVES AND CONCLUSIONS

Over the last quarter century, interest in measuring the experience, expression and control of anger has been stimulated by evidence that anger, hostility and aggression were associated with health problems and life-threatening disease. While definitions of anger-related constructs are often inconsistent and ambiguous, the experience and expression of anger are typically encompassed in definitions of hostility and aggression. Clearly, anger is the most fundamental of these overlapping constructs.

A sound theoretical framework that recognizes the difference between anger, hostility and aggression, and that distinguishes between anger as an emotional state and hostility in the experience, expression and control of anger as personality traits, is essential for guiding the construction of anger measures and cross-cultural adaptation.

In the cross-cultural adaptation of anger measures, it is essential to have equivalent conceptual definitions in the source and target languages that distinguish between the experience of anger as an emotional state, and hostility in the expression and control of anger as personality traits. The construction and development of the Spanish Multicultural State–Trait Anger Expression Inventory was guided by definitions of state and trait anger and anger-expression and anger-control as these constructs were conceptualized in the STAXI-2.

Factor analyses of the items constructed for the STAXI-SMC identified eight factors that were quite similar to the factor structure of the STAXI-2. Research on the STAXI-2 and the STAXI-SMC clearly indicates that anger and hostility as psychological constructs can be meaningfully defined as emotional states that vary in intensity, and as complex personality traits with major components that can be measured empirically.

The importance anger and hostility have within the fields of Psychology, and particularly of Health, asks for precise means of assessment and measurement. Nowadays, there are some remarkable self-report tests available, which provide evidence of cross-cultural validity. However, in order to develop more accurate means of anger assessment, it is advisable to use and develop lesser known techniques of behavioural observation, such as self-monitoring (e.g. Meichenbaum & Deffenbacher, 1988) and interviewing. Also, research in the fields of physiological measurement and cognitive variables of anger (appraisals, attributions etc.) needs to be given a further boost. Measurement issues are a fundamental part of the research and the study of the hostility and the anger.

Table 1.   Summary table of anger assessment scales

Scales	Assessment of					
	Anger	Expression of Anger	Anger-In	Anger-Out	Anger-Control	Hostility
STAXI	Yes	Yes	Yes	Yes	Yes	
Novaco Anger Inventory	Yes					
Multidimensional Anger Inventory	Yes		Yes	Yes		Yes
Harburg Anger-in/Anger-out	Yes		Yes	Yes		
Anger Self-Report Scale	Yes	Yes				
Anger Control Inventory	Yes					
Framingham Anger Scale	Yes	Yes	Yes	Yes		
Subjective Anger Scale	Yes					
Anger Situation Scale	Yes					
Anger Symptom Scale	Yes					
Cook–Medley Ho						Yes
Buss–Durkee Hostility Inventory						Yes
Factor L						Yes

References

Barefoot, J.C., Dodge, K.A., Peterson, B.L., Dahlstrom, W.G. & Williams, R.B. (1989). The Cook–Medley hostility scale: item content and ability to predict survival. *Psychosomatic Medicine, 51,* 46–57.

Biaggio, M.K., Supplee, K. & Curtis, N. (1981). Reliability and validity of four anger scales. *Journal of Personality Assessment, 45,* 639–648.

Buss, A.H. & Durkee, A. (1957). An inventory for assessing different kinds of hostility. *Journal of Consulting Psychology, 42,* 155–162.

Cattell, R.B., Eber, H.W. & Tatsuoka, M.M. (1970). *Handbook for the Sixteen Personality Factor Questionnaire (16PF).* Champaign, IL: Institute for Personality and Ability Testing.

Cook, W.W. & Medley, D.M. (1954). Propose hostility and pharasaic-virtue scales for the MMPI. *Journal of Applied Psychology, 38,* 414–418.

Deffenbacher, J.L., Demm, P.M. & Brander, A.D. (1986). High general anger. *Behaviour Research and Therapy, 24,* 481–489.

Dembroski, T.M., MacDougall, J.M., Williams, R.B. & Haney, T.L. (1984). Components of type A, hostility, and anger-in: relationship to angiographic findings. *Psychosomatic Medicine, 47,* 219–233.

Harburg, E., Erfurt, J.C., Chape, C., Hauenstein, L.S., Schull, W.J. & Schork, M.A. (1973). Socio-ecological stressor areas and black–white blood pressure: Detroit. *Journal of Chronic Disease, 26,* 595–611.

Haynes, S.N., Levine, S., Scotch, N., Feinleib, M. & Kannel, W.B. (1978). The relationship of psychological factors to coronary heart disease in the Framingham study: I. Methods and risk factors. *American Journal of Epidemiology, 107,* 362–363.

Hoshmand, L.T. & Austin, G.W. (1987). Validation studies of a multifactor cognitive-behavioural Anger Control Inventory. *Journal of Personality Assessment, 51,* 417–432.

Knight, R.G., Ross, R.A., Collins, J.I. & Parmenter, S.A. (1985). Some norms, reliability and preliminary validity data for an S-ROS: inventory of anger: the Subjective Anger Scale (SAS). *Personality and Individual Differences, 6,* 331–339.

Lakoff, G. (1987). *Women, Fire, and Dangerous Things*: What categories reveal about the mind. Chicago: The University of Chicago Press.

Meichenbaum, D.H. & Deffenbacher, J.L. (1988). Stress inoculation training. *The Counselling Psychologist, 16,* 69–90.

Miguel-Tobal, J.J., Cano-Vindel, A., Casado, M.I. & Spielberger, C.D. (2001). *Inventario de Expresión de Ira Estado Rasgo – STAXI – 2: Spanish Adaptation.* Madrid: TEA.

Moscoso, M.S. & Spielberger, C.D. (1999a). Evaluación de la experiencia, expresión y control de la cólera en Latinoamerica. *Revista Psicología Contemporánea, 6*(1), 4–13.

Moscoso, M.S. & Spielberger, C.D. (1999b). Measuring the experience, expression, and control of anger in Latin America: the Spanish multi-cultural State–Trait Anger Expression Inventory. *Interamerican Journal of Psychology, 33*(2), 4–13.

Novaco, R.W. (1975). *Anger Control: The Development and Evaluation of an Experimental Treatment.* Lexington: D.C. Health.

Novaco, R.W. (1977). Stress inoculation: a cognitive therapy for anger and its application to a case of depression. *Journal of Consulting and Clinical Psychology, 45,* 600–608.

Shekelle, R.B., Gale, M., Ostfeld, A.M. & Paul, O. (1983). Hostility, risk of coronary heart disease, and mortality. *Psychosomatic Medicine, 45,* 109–114.

Siegel, S.M. (1985). The multidimensional anger inventory. In Chesney, M.A. & Rosenman, N.H. (Ed.), *Anger and Hostility in Cardiovascular and Behavioural Disorders.* Washington, DC: Hemisphere.

Spielberger, C.D. (1999). *State–Trait Anger Expression Inventory – 2.* Odessa, FL: Psychological Assessment Resources.

Spielberger, C.D., Jacobs, G.A., Russell, S.F. & Crane, R.S. (1983). Assessment of anger: the State–Trait Anger Scale. In Butcher, J.N. & Spielberger, C.D. (Eds.), *Advances in Personality Assessment* (Vol. 2, pp. 159–187). Hillsdale, NJ: Erlbaum.

Spielberger, C.D., Johnson, E.H., Russell, S.F., Crane, R.J., Jacobs, G.A. & Worden, T.J. (1985). The experience and expression of anger: construction and validation of an anger expression scale. In Chesney, M.A. & Rosenman, R.H. (Eds.), *Anger and Hostility in Cardiovascular and Behavioural Disorders.* New York: McGraw-Hill/Hemisphere.

Spielberger, C.D., Krasner, S.S. & Solomon, E.P. (1988). The experience, expression and control of anger. In Janisse, M.P. (Ed.), *Health Psychology: Individual Differences and Stress* (pp. 89–108). New York: Springer Verlag.

Sydeman, S.J. (1995). *The Control of Suppressed Anger.* Unpublished Master's Thesis, University of South Florida, Tampa.

Williams, R.B., Barefoot, J.C. & Shekelle, R.B. (1985). The health consequences of hostility. In Chesney, M.A. & Rosenman, R.A. (Eds.), *Anger and Hostility in Cardiovascular and Behavioural Disorders* (pp. 173–185). New York: Hemisphere/McGraw-Hill.

Zelin, M.I., Adler, G. & Myerson, P.G. (1972). Anger self-report: an objective questionnaire for the measurement of aggression. *Journal of Consulting and Clinical Psychology, 39,* 340.

Manolete S. Moscoso and
Miguel Angel Pérez-Nieto

RELATED ENTRIES

A ANTISOCIAL DISORDERS ASSESSMENT

INTRODUCTION

Using a broad definition, Antisocial Disorders may be defined as pervasive, maladaptive behaviours that violate the norms and rules of a group or society, causing social impairment or distress to others. Currently, the classification and assessment of antisocial disorders may follow (a) the medical model or (b) the dimensional model:

- The medical model uses a categorical approach in which the presence of a variety of diagnostic criteria, such as persistent violations of social norms (including lying, stealing, truancy, inconsistent work behaviour and traffic arrests), is evaluated by experts (clinicians). This model relies on diagnostic criteria as outlined in the DSM-IV (Diagnostic and Statistic Manual of Mental Disorders: APA, 1994) and ICD (International Classification of Diseases: WHO, 1993).
- The dimensional model evaluates antisocial disorders along a continuum of development, from normal to pathological, focusing on behavioural and trait dimensions, and identifying clusters of highly interrelated behaviours and traits.

There is agreement among researchers about the development of antisocial behaviour: it begins early in life (infancy) with aggressive and oppositional behaviours (e.g. conduct problems), gradually advances toward more significant expressions of antisocial acts (e.g. vandalism, stealing, truancy, lying, substance abuse) during adolescence, and lastly, progresses to extreme forms of delinquency in adult life. The most recent longitudinal and retrospective studies (Patterson, Reid & Dishion, 1992) suggest that the 'early starters' (childhood and preadolescence) are at greater risk for adult involvement in delinquent acts and are more likely to move toward more serious offences that lead to a 'criminal career' compared to the 'later starters' (adolescence).

A variety of methods are used for assessing antisocial disorders; these include: self-report instruments, others' ratings, clinical interviews (structured and semi-structured), and direct behavioural observation (see Table 1).

CHILD AND ADOLESCENT ASSESSMENT

In order to establish the severity of antisocial behaviours during childhood and adolescence, it is important (a) to determine the *age of onset*; (b) to evaluate the *frequency* of aggressive acts; (c) to establish the *variety* of antisocial behaviours; and (d) to observe them in *multiple settings* (family, peers, school and community). As a necessary complement to this assessment, it is also important to evaluate other aspects of the individual's functioning in order to rule out the co-occurrence of other psychological disturbances.

For children and adolescents, the terms *conduct disorders* and *conduct problems* (aggressive and oppositional behaviours) may be used interchangeably. It is important to note that conduct disorders have different prevalence rates for boys and girls: 6 to 16% for boys, and 2 to 9% for girls.

In recent years, more complete assessment procedures have been developed to cover a full range of childhood and adolescent behaviours directly and indirectly linked to antisocial behaviours in different contexts. The advantages of these assessment procedures are (a) to have a complete picture of child and adolescent functioning for the purpose of differential diagnosis and (b) to collect data to provide empirical and theoretical support of the instruments used.

Instruments for Child and Adolescent Assessment

Here we present only a few of the numerous instruments that can be used for measuring antisocial behaviour. We included those that

Table 1. Assessment of antisocial disorder

Target	Informant	Model	Measure		
			Scale	Clinical Interviews	Observation
	Self	Dimensional	– Youth Self-Report (Achenbach, 1991c) – Behaviour Assessment System of Children–Self-Report of Personality Scale (Reynolds & Kamphaus, 1992)		– Direct Observation Form (Achenbach, 1986) – Behaviour Assessment System of Children – Student observation system (Reynolds & Kamphaus, 1992) – Family Interaction Coding System (Reid, 1978) – Observation of Peer Interactions (Dodge, 1983)
Children/ Adolescents	Others	Dimensional	– Revised Behaviour Problem Checklist (Quay & Peterson, 1983) – Child Behaviour Checklist (Achenbach, 1991a) – Teacher Report Form (Achenbach, 1991b) – Behaviour Assessment System of Scale (Reynolds & Kamphaus, 1992)		
Children/ Adolescents	Self	Categorical	– Devereux Scales of Mental Disorders (Naglieri, Lebuffe & Pfeiffer, 1994) – Eysenck Personality Questionnaire (Eysenck & Eysenck, 1993) – Minnesota Multiphasic Personality Inventory – II (Butcher et al., 1989)		

(continued)

Table 1. Continued

Target	Informant	Model	Measure		
			Scale	Clinical Interviews	Observation
Adults	Self	Dimensional	– Millon Clinical Multiaxial Inventory III (Millon, 1994) – Assessment of DSM-IV Personality Disorder Questionnaire – Antisocial Personality Questionnaire (Blackburn & Fawcett, 1999)	– Hare Psychopathy Checklist – Revised (Hare, 1991)	
		Categorical		– International Personality Disorder Examination (Loranger, Sartorius & Janca, 1996) – Structured Clinical Interview for DSM-IV (First et al., 1997) – Structured Interview for DSM-IV Personality Disorder (Pfohl, Blum & Zimmerman, 1995)	

provide a comprehensive assessment of different psycho-social domains and those that are in some way representative of the field of antisocial behaviour, both at the level of research and intervention.

Revised Behaviour Problem Checklist (RBPC)

The RBPC (Quay & Peterson, 1983) represents one of the first attempts to empirically classify childhood and adolescent disorders. The Revised Behaviour Problem Checklist covers the ages 5 to 17 years, and is available in two versions, one for teachers and one for mothers. It represents a revision of the original Behaviour Problems Checklist and now comprises six scales: Conduct Disorder, Socialized Aggression, Attention Problems–Immaturity, Anxiety–Withdrawal, Psychotic Behaviour, Motor Tension Excess. It allows one to distinguish between 'socialized' and 'undersocialized' conduct disorders. Socialized makes reference to antisocial behaviour within deviant peer group, unsocialized refers to impulsivity and irritability.

Child Behaviour Checklist (CBCL)

The CBCL (Achenbach, 1991a) (parent form), together with Youth Self-Report (YSR; Achenbach, 1991c), Teacher Report Form (TRF; Achenbach, 1991b) and Direct Observation Form (DOF; Achenbach, 1986), is one of the most comprehensive evaluation systems for childhood and adolescent psychopathology. It was developed by Achenbach in order to derive syndromes empirically and to allow for comparisons among different informants and cultures. The four forms share item content and can be used together to establish cross-contexts consistency.

They cover an age range of 4 to 18 years. The CBCL includes problem behaviour and social competence scales. Problem behaviour scales are: Aggressive Behaviours, Delinquency, Anxiety/Depression, Somatic Complaints, Attention Problems, Thought Problems and Social Withdrawal. In addition, there is a Sexual Problem Behaviour scale for children between 4 and 11 years old. It is also possible to derive two broader dimensions: Internalizing and Externalizing.

Behaviour Assessment System of Children (BASC)

The BASC (Reynolds & Kamphaus, 1992) is a multi-method, multidimensional assessment instrument aimed at evaluating the behaviours and self-perceptions of children aged 4 to 18 years old. Similar to the CBCL, it has several different versions: self-report, teacher rating scale, parent rating scale, student observation system and structured developmental history. The *Self-Report of Personality Scale* (6–18 years) is comprised of the following subscales: Anxiety, Attitude to School, Attitude to Teachers, Atypicality, Depression, Interpersonal Relations, Locus of Control, Relations with Parents, Self-Esteem, Self-Reliance, Sensation Seeking, Sense of Inadequacy, Social Stress, and Somatization. The *Teacher and Parent Rating Scales* (different forms for 4–5 years, 6–11 years, and 12–18 years) are comprised of the following subscales: Aggression, Conduct Problems, Attention Problems, Hyperactivity, Anxiety, Atypicality, Depression, Somatization, Withdrawal, Learning Problems, Leadership, Social Skills, Study Skills, Adaptability. The *Student Observation System* assesses a student's behaviour in the classroom such as inappropriate movement, inappropriate attention and work on school subjects.

Devereux Scales of Mental Disorders (DSMD)

The DSMD (Naglieri, Lebuffe & Pfeiffer, 1994) is designed to measure the risk for emotional and behavioural disorders in children between 5 and 18 years (5–12 years; 13–18 years). It relies on the DSM-IV, and has both teacher and parent forms. It includes scales to assess Problem Behaviours, Delinquency, Attention, Depression and Anxiety, Autism and Acute Problems. It provides three different composites: Internalizing, Externalizing and Critical Pathology.

Diagnostic Interview Schedule for Children – Child Interview (DISC-C)

The DISC-C (Costello, Edelbrock, Kalas, Kessler & Klaric, 1982) is a structured diagnostic interview that covers a broad range of DSM-IV diagnoses in children. Child, parent and teacher forms are available. Areas covered include: Behaviour/Conduct Disorder, Attention Deficit Disorder, Affective/Neurotic Anxiety, Fears and Phobias, Obsessive-Compulsive Disorder, Schizoid/Psychotic Disorders, Affective (depression) Disorders.

Family Interaction Coding System (FICS)

The FICS (Reid, 1978) is an assessment instrument used to register interactions between family members. This coding system enables researchers and family therapists to monitor clinical cases, systematically assess the outcome of family intervention programmes, and builds a database for studying aggressive antisocial behaviours exhibited by children. It is composed of 29 categories, but the Total Aversive Behaviour score (such as physical negative, tease, noncompliance, destructiveness etc.) is mostly used (Reid, 1978).

Observation of Peer Interactions

This instrument (Dodge, 1983) is used to register interactions among peers between the ages of 5 to 8 years. It has five categories: solitary active, interactive play, verbalizations, physical contacts with peers, and interactions with adult leaders within the group. This system is associated with dimensions of social status (rejection, popularity), and therefore may be useful to obtain a more complete assessment of peer interactions.

ADULT ASSESSMENT

Albeit with some differences, antisocial disorders may correspond with the Antisocial Personality Disorder (APD) classification of DSM-IV and the Dissocial Personality Disorder classification of ICD-10. APD is characterized by criminal and antisocial behaviour, and also by deceitfulness, lack of remorse, disregard for the safety of others (DSM-IV: APA, 1994), low tolerance for frustration and a low threshold for discharge of aggression (ICD-10: WHO, 1993). The emphasis is placed on a failure to conform to social norms, and on impulsivity and irresponsibility. Although it was excluded from recent classifications of mental disorders, the assessment of Psychopathy in adults with antisocial

disorders may be informative for differential diagnosis and treatment purposes. Psychopathy corresponds partially to the criteria of APD, but also includes emotional/interpersonal characteristics such as glibness, superficiality, egocentricity, grandiosity, lack of empathy, manipulativeness, and shallow emotions. When assessing antisocial disorders, it is also important to evaluate the co-occurrence of substance abuse, anxiety disorders and depression.

Instruments for Adult Assessment

As for children and adolescents, numerous instruments have been developed for the assessment of adult antisocial disorders. We have selected to present instruments that combine personality assessment (dimensional model) with classic diagnostic assessment (medical or categorical model), including interviews, checklists and questionnaires aimed at identifying the criteria for Antisocial Personality Disorders as presented in the DSM-IV and the ICD-10.

Eysenck Personality Questionnaire (EPQ-R)

The EPQ-R (Eysenck & Eysenck, 1993) is designed to measure the three traits of Eysenck's personality model: Extraversion (E), Neuroticism (N) and Psychoticism (P). This model links types, traits and behaviour into a hierarchical system. The P trait is the primary trait implicated in the development of antisocial behaviour, with elevations on E and N being secondary. In serious antisocial behaviour, the P trait has a primary role. When E is combined with high P, poor impulse control and a weakened association between behaviour and its consequences will exacerbate the P trait predisposition. Elevated E is more frequent among juvenile delinquents, and elevated N appears in adult criminals. The Eysenck Personality Inventory is also available in a form for adolescents.

Minnesota Multiphasic Personality Inventory – II (MMPI-II)

The MMPI-II (Butcher et al., 1989) is the most frequently used clinical test. It is the revised version of the MMPI. It was originally intended for use with an adult population. The MMPI-II has 10 clinical scales, 3 validity scales and 15 content scales. The clinical scales are Hypochondriasis, Depression, Hysteria, Psychopathic Deviate, Masculinity–Femininity, Paranoia, Psychasthenia, Schizophrenia, Hypomania, and Social Introversion. The clinical scales do not discriminate clinical groups from normal groups, as the labels might suggest. Subjects who score high on specific scales show particular behaviours and tendencies. For example, subjects scoring high on the Psychopathic Deviate Scale show disregard for social custom, shallow emotions, and an inability to learn from experience. Content scales include internalizing symptoms (somatic disorder, strange beliefs and dysfunctional ways of thinking), aggressive tendencies (dysfunctional control of behaviour, cynicism), low self-esteem, family problems, work interference and negative treatment indicators. The content scales offer behavioural descriptions that are easier to interpret than the clinical scales.

The interpretation of subject profiles must be done by experienced clinicians. Recently, an adolescent version has been developed.

Antisocial Personality Questionnaire (APQ)

The APQ (Blackburn & Fawcett, 1999) is a recently developed, short, multi-trait, self-report inventory aimed at measuring intrapersonal and interpersonal aspects of emotional dysfunction, impulse control, deviant beliefs about the self and others, and interpersonal problem behaviours related to antisocial behaviours. It was derived from another instrument previously developed for mentally disordered offenders. It comprises the following measures: Self-Control, Self-Esteem, Avoidance, Paranoid Suspicion, Resentment, Aggression, Deviance and Extraversion. It is possible to derive two second-order scales: Hostile-Impulsivity and Social Withdrawal. These two scales reflect orientations towards others and the self, respectively.

Hare Psychopathy Checklist – Revised (PCL-R)

PCL-R (Hare, 1991) is a single construct rating scale that uses a semi-structured interview, case-history information and specific diagnostic criteria to provide a reliable and valid estimate of the degree to which an offender or forensic psychiatric patient matches the traditional (prototypical) conception of a psychopath. The PCL-R evaluates emotional and interpersonal characteristics of psychopathy and social deviance.

Millon Clinical Multiaxial Inventory II (MCMI-II)

The MCMI-II (Millon, 1994) is composed of 24 self-administered scales, and is designed to measure 14 personality styles, grouped into (a) Clinical Personality Patterns (schizoid, avoidant [depressive], dependent, histrionic, narcissistic, antisocial [sadistic], compulsive and negativistic [masochistic]) and (b) Severe Personality Pathology (schizotypal, borderline and paranoid). The instrument was developed to match the DSM-IV personality disorder classifications. It also comprises 10 scales measuring other clinical syndromes (such as anxiety, depression, drug-dependence and thought disorders). This instrument also has an adolescent version.

International Personality Disorder Examination (IPDE)

The IPDE (Loranger, Sartorius & Janca, 1996) is a semi-structured interview designed for the assessment of both DSM-IV and ICD-10 Personality Disorders (PD). The IPDE also combines the categorical and dimensional models. Questions are arranged in sections (e.g. background information, work, self, interpersonal relationships).

Other Clinical Interviews for DSM-IV

The most frequently used clinical interviews for the diagnosis of Antisocial Personality Disorder are:

- Structured Clinical Interview for DSM-IV (Scid II; First et al., 1997)

  The SCID II is a semi-structured diagnostic interview organized by disorder which includes all DSM-IV personality disorders. A computerized administration and scoring program is available.

- Structured Interview for DSM-IV (SIDP-IV) Personality Disorder (Pfohl, Blum & Zimmerman, 1995)

The SIDP-IV consists of 160 questions grouped under 16 thematic sections, such as relationships, emotions and reactions to stressful situations. Questions are asked regarding behaviours in the last five years.

FUTURE PERSPECTIVES AND CONCLUSIONS

The assessment and diagnosis of antisocial disorders should be done by experienced mental health professionals. The assessment process should include multiple methods and informants, and use standardized instruments or structured diagnostic interviews, including complete information related to the ecology of the individual (family and social context) and individual functioning.

Based on the most relevant clinical research in the area of antisociality, we may conclude that in the future the assessment must focus more on both dysfunction and skills and try to integrate the two models, dimensional and categorical, in order to better direct the diagnostic process (screening, identification and placement for intervention).

References

American Psychiatric Association (1994). *Diagnostic and Statistical Manual of Mental Disorders* (4th ed.). Washington, DC: APA.

Achenbach, T.M. (1986). *Manual for the Child Behaviour Checklist – Direct Observation Form*. Burlington, VT: University of Vermont Department of Psychiatry.

Achenbach, T.M. (1991a). *Manual for the Child Behaviour Checklist/4–18 and 1991 Profile*. Burlington, VT: University of Vermont Department of Psychiatry.

Achenbach, T.M. (1991b). *Manual for Teacher Report's Form and 1991 Profile*. Burlington, VT: University of Vermont Department of Psychiatry.

Achenbach, T.M. (1991c). *Manual for the Youth Self-Report and 1991 Profile*. Burlington, VT: University of Vermont Department of Psychiatry.

Blackburn, R. & Fawcett, D. (1999). The Antisocial Personality Questionnaire: an inventory for assessing personality deviation in offenders. *European Journal of Psychological Assessment*, 15, 14–24.

Butcher, J.N., Dahlstrom, W.G., Graham, J.R., Tellegen, A. & Kaemmer, B. (1989). *Minnesota Multiphasic Personality Inventory-2 (MMPI-2), Manual for Administration and Scoring*. Minneapolis: University of Minnesota Press.

Costello, A.J., Edelbrock, C.S., Kalas, R., Kessler, M. & Klaric, S. (1982). *Diagnostic Interview Schedule for Children–Child Interview*. Bethesda, MD: National Institute of Mental Health.

Dodge, K. (1983). Behavioural antecedents of peer social status. *Child Development*, 54, 1386–1399.

Eysenck, H.J. & Eysenck, S.B.G. (1993). *Eysenck Personality Questionnaire – Revised*. San Diego: Educational and Industrial Testing Service.

First, M.B., Gibbon, M., Spitzer, R.L. & Williams, J.B.W. (1997). *User's Guide for the Structured Clinical Interview for DSM-IV Axis II Personality Disorders*. Washington, DC: American Psychiatric Press.

Hare, R.D. (1991). *Manual for the Hare Psychopathy Checklist – Revised*. Toronto: Multi Health System.

Loranger, A.W., Sartorius, N. & Janca, A. (Eds.) (1996). *Assessment and Diagnosis of Personality Disorders: The International Personality Disorder Examination* (IPDE). New York, NY: Cambridge University Press.

Millon, T. (1994). *Manual for the Millon Clinical Multiaxial Inventory – III*. Minneapolis: National Computer Systems.

Naglieri, J.A., Lebuffe, P.A. & Pfeiffer, S.I. (1994). *Devereux Scales of Mental Disorders*. New York: The Psychological Corporation.

Patterson, G.R., Reid, J.B. & Dishion, T.J. (1992). *Antisocial Boys: A Social Interactional Approach*, Vol. 4. Eugene, OR: Castalia.

Pfohl, B., Blum, N. & Zimmerman, M. (1995). *Structured Interview for DSM-IV Personality* (SIDP-IV). Iowa City, IA: The University of Iowa.

Quay, H.C. & Peterson, D.R. (1983). *Interim Manual for the Revised Behaviour Problem Checklist*. Coral Gables, FL: Author.

Reid, J.B. (1978). *A Social Learning Approach, Observation in Home Settings*. Vol. 2: Eugene, OR: Castalia Publishing Company.

Reynolds, C.R. & Kamphaus, R.W. (1992). *BASC Manual*. Circle Pines, MN: American Guidance Service.

World Health Organization (1993). *The ICD-10 Classification of Mental and Behavioural Disorders: Diagnostic Criteria for Research*. Geneva: WHO.

Concetta Pastorelli and Maria Gerbino

RELATED ENTRIES

APPLIED FIELDS: CLINICAL, DANGEROUS/VIOLENCE POTENTIAL BEHAVIOUR, CLASSIFICATION

ANXIETY ASSESSMENT

INTRODUCTION

The first assessment of individual differences is reported in the Bible in the Book of Judges, Chapter 7 on Gideon. God asked Gideon, who was battling the Midianites, to thin out his troops by rejecting individuals who were both fearful and afraid of battle. However, too many men were left, so God instructed Gideon to lead his men down to the water and used the following selection procedure. Out of 10,000 persons, 300 lapped with water from their hands, with their tongues. They were selected. The ones who knelt to drink were not.

This entry will focus on the assessment of anxiety as an individual differences variable; the dimensional conceptualization of anxiety. Dimensionality arises from a personality psychology tradition, in which traits and behaviours are measured psychometrically. Traits are viewed as existing on a continuum, with low levels of a trait (e.g. anxiety) at one end and high levels of the trait at the opposite end of the same continuum. In contrast to the dimensional approach is the typological or categorical conceptualization of anxiety, consistent with the medical model (Endler & Kocovski, 2001). Another entry in this encyclopedia covers the assessment of anxiety disorders.

Definition of Anxiety

Anxiety has been conceptualized as a stimulus, as a trait, as a motive, and as a drive and has been defined 'as an emotional state, with the subjectively experienced quality of fear as a closely related emotion' (Lewis, 1970: 77). Lewis notes that the emotion is unpleasant, future-oriented, disproportional to the threat and includes both subjective and manifest bodily disturbances. There are physiological, cognitive, and behavioural components to anxiety. These give rise to the various methods of the assessment of anxiety. It is important to first distinguish between state anxiety and trait anxiety.

State vs. Trait Anxiety

State anxiety is the momentary experience of anxiety. Trait anxiety is a predisposition or proneness to be anxious. The distinction between state and trait anxiety was first suggested by Cicero (Before the Common Era). Spielberger (1983) suggested that conceptual clarity could be achieved in the anxiety literature by distinguishing between state and trait anxiety. There are various methods to assess state anxiety. The assessment of trait anxiety has been conducted primarily through the use of self-report measures.

Multidimensionality of State and Trait Anxiety

Trait anxiety and state anxiety are both multidimensional constructs (Endler, 1997; Endler, Edwards & Vitelli, 1991). There are at least six facets of trait anxiety: social evaluation, physical danger, ambiguous, self-disclosure, separation and daily routines; and two facets of state anxiety: cognitive-worry and autonomic emotional (Endler & Flett, 2001). These facets of state and trait anxiety are presented in Table 1.

Interaction Model of Anxiety

The distinction between state and trait anxiety has achieved wide recognition in the interaction

Table 1.   Anxiety assessment techniques

Anxiety	Assessment Technique
State anxiety	Self-report
	Behavioural
	Cognitive
	Physiological
Trait anxiety	Self-report

model of anxiety, a subset of the interaction model of personality (Endler, 1997). According to the interaction model, increases in state anxiety will result only when a situational stressor is congruent with the facet of trait anxiety under investigation. Over 80% of the tests of the multidimensional interaction model of anxiety have yielded support for the model (Endler, 1997).

Assessment Techniques

The use of questionnaire measures has been the primary assessment technique for trait anxiety. There are multiple techniques that can be used for the assessment of state anxiety. The assessment techniques are shown in Table 1 and include self-report, behavioural, cognitive, and physiological measures. The most comprehensive method of assessing state anxiety is through a combination of the available techniques as there are individual differences in the experience of anxiety.

SELF-REPORT MEASURES

The majority of research in the area of personality is based on self-report measures,

despite the fact that personality theory also refers to observable behaviours. Self-report questionnaires have the following advantages: they are easy to administer, results are easy to analyse, results can be compared to normative data, and results can be subjected to factor analytic techniques (as well as other advanced statistical techniques).

Commonly used self-report measures are presented in Table 2. One of the first self-report anxiety measures is the Taylor Manifest Anxiety Scale (Taylor, 1953). Since then, numerous other scales have been developed. One commonly used self-report measure of anxiety is the State–Trait Anxiety Inventory (STAI; Spielberger, 1983). The STAI assesses both state and trait anxiety as unidimensional constructs. The state and the trait scales consist of 20 items each. These scales have been shown to have high internal consistency (approximately 0.90 for both the state and trait scales) and test–retest validity for the trait scale (Spielberger, 1983).

The Endler Multidimensional Anxiety Scales (EMAS) assess both state anxiety and trait anxiety as multidimensional constructs and assess the perception of the situation (Endler, Edwards & Vitelli, 1991). Cognitive-worry and autonomic-emotional are the two components of state anxiety assessed by the EMAS-State

Table 2. Self-report measures of anxiety

Name of scale	Author/year	Psychometric properties
Anxiety Sensitivity Index	Reiss et al. (1986)	Alpha reliability = 0.88; test–retest reliability ranges from 0.75 to 0.85 (2 week interval)
Beck Anxiety Inventory	Beck et al. (1988)	Alpha reliability = 0.92; test–retest reliability = 0.75 (1 week interval)
Endler Multidimensional Anxiety Scales (EMAS)	Endler et al. (1991)	Alpha reliabilities range from 0.89 to 0.95; test–retest reliabilities for the trait scales range from 0.60 to 0.79 (2 week interval)
EMAS–Social Anxiety Scales (EMAS-SAS)	Endler & Flett (2001)	Alpha reliabilities range from 0.92 to 0.93; test–retest reliabilities range from 0.69 to 0.77 (1 week interval)
State–Trait Anxiety Inventory (STAI)	Spielberger (1983)	Alpha reliabilities range from 0.91 to 0.93; test–retest reliabilities range from 0.71 to 0.75 for the trait scale (30 day interval)
Taylor Manifest Anxiety Scale	Taylor (1953)	Test–retest reliability = 0.88 (4 week interval)

measure (20 items in total). The EMAS-Trait measures assess a predisposition to experience anxiety in the following four situational domains (15 items each): social evaluation, physical danger, ambiguous, and daily routines. Recent research has resulted in the addition of the following two situational domains: self-disclosure (to family or to friends) and separation anxiety (Endler & Flett, 2001). The alpha reliabilities of these measures have been found to be highly acceptable (ranging from 0.89 to 0.95; Endler et al., 1991). Numerous studies have been conducted which have found support for the validity of the EMAS-State, Trait, and Perception scales (Endler et al., 1991; see Endler, 1997 for a review).

Another self-report instrument commonly used to assess anxiety is the Beck Anxiety Inventory (BAI; Beck, Epstein, Brown & Steer, 1988). The BAI consists of 21 items representing two factors: somatic symptoms and subjective anxiety symptoms. It has been shown to have a high internal consistency (alpha = 0.92). A weakness is that the BAI does not distinguish between state and trait anxiety. Respondents are asked to report the degree to which they have been bothered by the symptoms assessed over the past week. The BAI is primarily used in clinical settings. Finally, the Anxiety Sensitivity Index consists of 16 items and assesses the fear of experiencing anxiety (Reiss, Peterson, Gursky & McNally, 1986).

BEHAVIOURAL MEASURES

Another anxiety assessment technique is the measurement of various behaviours. The presence and frequency of certain behaviours are rated by others (e.g. clinicians, experimenters). A review of ratings by others for the purposes of clinical evaluation is beyond the scope of this entry. The behaviours used to represent an indication of the level of anxiety an individual is experiencing depend upon the situational domain. For example, behavioural measures of social anxiety include measurement of the maintenance of eye contact, the number of conversations initiated or amount spoken during a social encounter, hand tremors, and fidgeting (Leary, 1986). Not all of these behavioural measures are relevant for other situational domains.

Types of interaction used in behavioural observation can be classified as either artificial (i.e. a role-play situation) or naturalistic (i.e. *in vivo* observation; Glass & Arnkoff, 1989). Behaviours are often recorded in role-play situations due to the impracticality of rating people in naturalistic environments. Even within the naturalistic category, waiting-room type interactions are often used (especially for the assessment of social anxiety).

Behavioural observation techniques are less subjective on the part of the examinee than the use of self-report measures. However, the presence of the examiner in an evaluative role may affect the level of anxiety, and additionally, the examiner is responsible for determining whether the examinee's actual behaviour constitutes the behaviour being assessed. Furthermore, in an interaction type behavioural observation assessment, the behaviour of the partner (or confederate) may represent a confound. The partner may respond differently to different participants depending on variables such as the social skill level of the participant (Glass & Arnkoff, 1989). Despite these criticisms, behavioural assessment techniques for performance situations have been shown to be highly reliable.

COGNITIVE MEASURES

Anxiety also has a cognitive component. Cognitive measures examine the thoughts an individual has. This can be done through thought-listing procedures (Cacioppo & Petty, 1981) or via a questionnaire approach. Thought-listing techniques ask participants to record thoughts in paper and pencil format while they are in an anxious situation (Cacioppo & Petty, 1981). Participants are asked not to concern themselves with spelling or grammar and not to edit the thoughts as they arise. The list of thoughts is then analysed according to such indices as content or frequency. Variations of this technique include: (i) having participants state their thoughts aloud rather than recording them and (ii) having participants watch a video of their performance and state their thoughts during the viewing.

PHYSIOLOGICAL MEASURES

Anxiety has a physiological component, which is largely determined by the septo-hippocampal system (behavioural inhibition system; Gray & McNaughton, 1996), thus allowing for the assessment of anxiety through physiological means. Among the physiological measures are the measurement of heart rate, electrodermal activity, and respiration. Additionally, blushing, assessed with a photoplethysomograph, has been used to assess social anxiety. The different physiological measures do not, however, correlate well with one another or with self-report measures (Leary, 1986).

Heart Rate

Heart rate is the most commonly used physiological measure of anxiety. It is assessed either via electrodes (which can be attached to the patient's skin to the right and left of the sternum) or via sensors. The unit of measurement typically used is the number of beats per minute. This can be determined by (i) counting the number of beats per minute or, alternatively, (ii) using equipment to determine the length of the interval between heart beats and then calculating beats per minute based on that figure. These two approaches typically yield different results; however, both are used in the assessment of heart rate as an indicator of state anxiety. Heart rate has been found to be strongly correlated with self-report state anxiety in a competitive sports situation and moderately correlated with self-report state anxiety (and one item in particular which assesses heart rate) in a performance anxiety situation (Kantor, Endler, Heslegrave & Kocovski, 2001).

Finger Pulse Volume

Finger pulse volume is a measure of digital vasoconstriction (Bloom & Trautt, 1977). The use of finger pulse volume to assess anxiety is based on the premise that one of the responses of the sympathetic nervous system is decreased blood flow to peripheral areas of the body. Finger pulse volume has been shown to be a valid physiological measure in social-evaluation situations.

Electrodermal Activity

Another physiological measure of anxiety is sweat gland activity. The eccrine sweat glands are innervated by the sympathetic nervous system and are located throughout the surface of the body. The primary concentration of eccrine sweat glands is in the palms of the hands and the soles of the feet. Changes in the degree of sweat gland activity can be a result of state anxiety; however, there are other variables that also play a role. For example, room temperature affects the activity of the eccrine glands, as do person variables (e.g. gender). There are, therefore, numerous variables that can affect the internal validity of a study that uses sweat gland activity as an indication of anxiety as the dependent variable. These need to be considered both in research studies and in the assessment of an individual.

Clements and Turpin (1996) assessed the sweat gland activity of participants while giving a presentation and while being a member of the audience. Sweat gland activity was found to increase prior to and during the presentation and decrease upon completion of the presentation. Levels of state anxiety were also found to be elevated during the presentation. There was, however, no relationship found between the physiological measure (sweat gland activity) and each of state and trait anxiety.

Respiration

Respiration rate can also be used as a tool in the assessment of anxiety. To measure respiration rate, a stretchable device attached to equipment capable of measuring strain is placed around the chest and the abdomen. Respiration rate has been shown to be positively related to self-reported anxiety.

Correlations among the various physiological measures of anxiety are generally found to be low. There are many factors that can account for this difference, including individual differences in the experience of anxiety and temporal factors. For example, Bloom and Trautt (1977) found that, initially, participants were more anxious according to the finger pulse volume measure. However, according to heart rate, participants were more anxious later on. This provides support for the view that any measure of anxiety should be used along with other measures of anxiety. Various psychological, behavioural, and physiological processes are involved in the experience of anxiety and there are individual differences.

FUTURE PERSPECTIVES AND CONCLUSIONS

1 Most of the research has used self-report measures. Additional research can further investigate the reliability and validity of the various techniques in the assessment of anxiety.

2 Considerably more research has been conducted on the assessment of anxiety in the social evaluation situational domain (e.g. presentation situations, interaction situations) compared to other areas. This is especially the case with respect to the use of behavioural observation, cognitive measures, and physiological measures.

3 Future research can focus on the use of these techniques for the assessment of anxiety in situations other than social evaluation situations (i.e. physical danger situations, self-disclosure situations, separation situations, and ambiguous situations).

4 There are various techniques to assess state anxiety, the momentary experience of anxiety. Included among these are self-report instruments, behavioural observation methods, cognitive assessment techniques and physiological measures.

5 Trait anxiety, the predisposition to be anxious in different situations, is assessed through self-report instruments.

6 The reliability and validity of some techniques have been demonstrated to be higher than for other techniques.

7 There are individual differences in the qualitative experience of anxiety. It is therefore important to use diverse sets of assessment techniques that tap at the various facets of anxiety.

8 Self-report measures may be the most convenient method of anxiety assessment in terms of the time required for administration, the cost of administration, and data analyses. However, other factors (i.e. the validity of the assessment) are also important to consider.

Acknowledgements

This entry was supported, in part, by Grant No. 410-94-1473 from the Social Sciences and Humanities Research Council of Canada (SSHRC) to the first author and a SSHRC doctoral fellowship to the second author.

References

Beck, A.T., Epstein, N., Brown, G. & Steer, R.A. (1988). An inventory for measuring clinical anxiety: psychometric properties. *Journal of Consulting and Clinical Psychology, 56,* 893–897.

Bloom, L.J. & Trautt, G.M. (1977). Finger pulse volume as a measure of anxiety: further evaluation. *Psychophysiology, 14,* 541–544.

Cacioppo, J.T. & Petty, R.E. (1981). Social psychological procedures for cognitive response assessment: the thought-listing technique. In Merluzzi, T.V., Glass, C.R. & Genest, M. (Eds.), *Cognitive Assessment* (pp. 309–342). New York: Guilford.

Clements, K. & Turpin, G. (1996). Physiological effects of public speaking assessed using a measure of palmar sweating. *Journal of Psychophysiology, 10,* 283–290.

Endler, N.S. (1997). Stress, anxiety and coping: the multidimensional interaction model. *Canadian Psychology, 38,* 136–153.

Endler, N.S., Edwards, J.M. & Vitelli, R. (1991). *Endler Multidimensional Anxiety Scales (EMAS): Manual.* Los Angeles, CA: Western Psychological Services.

Endler, N.S. & Flett, G.L. (2001). *Endler Multidimensional Anxiety Scales – Social Anxiety Scales: Manual.* Los Angeles, CA: Western Psychological Services.

Endler, N.S. & Kocovski, N.L. (2001). State and trait anxiety revisited. *Journal of Anxiety Disorders, 15,* 231–245.

Glass, C.R. & Arnkoff, D.B. (1989). Behavioural assessment of social anxiety and social phobia. *Clinical Psychology Review, 9,* 75–90.

Gray, J.A. & McNaughton, N. (1996). The neuropsychology of anxiety: reprise. In Hope, D.A. (Ed.), *Nebraska Symposium on Motivation, 1995: Perspectives on Anxiety, Panic, and Fear. Current Theory and Research in Motivation,* Vol. 43 (pp. 61–134). Lincoln, NE: University of Nebraska Press.

Kantor, L., Endler, N.S., Heslegrave, R.J. & Kocovski, N.L. (2001). Validating self-report measures of state and trait anxiety with a physiological measure. *Current Psychology: Developmental, Learning, Personality, Social, 20,* 207–215.

Leary, M.R. (1986). Affective and behavioural components of shyness: implications for theory, measurement, and research. In Jones, W.H., Cheek, J.M. & Briggs, S.R. (Eds.), *Perspectives on Shyness: Research and Treatment* (pp. 27–38). New York: Plenum.

Lewis, A. (1970). The ambiguous word 'anxiety'. *International Journal of Psychiatry, 9,* 62–79.

Reiss, S., Peterson, R.A., Gursky, D.M. & McNally, R.J. (1986). Anxiety sensitivity, anxiety frequency, and the prediction of fearfulness. *Behaviour Research and Therapy, 24,* 1–8.

Spielberger, C.D. (1983). *Manual for the State–Trait Anxiety Inventory (Form V)*. Palo Alto, CA: Consulting Psychologists Press.

Taylor, J.A. (1953). A personality scale of manifest anxiety. *Journal of Abnormal and Social Psychology*, 48, 285–290.

Norman S. Endler and Nancy L. Kocovski

Norman S. Endler and Nancy L. Kocovski

ANXIETY DISORDERS ASSESSMENT

INTRODUCTION

Anxiety is one of the most common and universal emotions. This emotional reaction to the perception of threatening or dangerous stimuli occurs throughout an individual's lifetime. In fact, anxiety elicited by stimuli or situations such as animals, physical danger and separation is an early biological acquisition, whose function is to protect the child from potential dangers. In this sense, anxiety is undoubtedly of value in relation to the preservation of the human being.

The conceptualization of anxiety has varied considerably over recent decades. On the one hand, critics of the unidimensional view of anxiety have proposed a new multidimensional approach. From this perspective, anxiety is a combination of responses, including cognitive, physiological and behavioural (motor) reactions. These responses are provoked by identifiable cognitive-subjective, physiological or environmental stimuli. In spite of the lack of an accurate explanation of the contents of each system, and there being some discrepancies among authors on what might be understood by the responses of the cognitive system or, to a lesser extent, those of the physiological system (Cone & Hawkins, 1977; Fernández-Ballesteros, 1983), this classification of the different anxiety responses in three systems is widely accepted and used.

In addition, since the seminal works of Cattell or Spielberger in the 1960s, the differentiation between state and trait anxiety has become a classic one. State anxiety is conceptualized as a transitory emotional reaction to the individual's perception of a threatening or dangerous situation, while trait anxiety is defined as a relatively stable tendency to interpret situations as threatening or dangerous, and to react to them with anxiety. Recent works by Endler and his co-workers propose a multidimensional nature for trait anxiety, highlighting the existence of different facets (social evaluation, physical danger, etc.) closely related to specific situational areas.

With the aim of integrating the above-mentioned aspects, anxiety must be considered as an emotional response, or pattern of responses, that includes unpleasant cognitive aspects, physiological aspects characterized by high arousal of the Autonomous Nervous System, and inaccurate and less adaptive motor or behavioural reactions. The anxiety response may be provoked both by situational external and internal stimuli such as thoughts, ideas, images, etc., perceived by the individual as threatening or dangerous. Such anxiety-eliciting stimuli (external or internal) will be mainly determined by the subject's characteristics; thus, there are remarkable individual differences in relation to the tendency to manifest anxiety reactions in different situations (Miguel-Tobal, 1990).

ANXIETY AS DISORDER

Up to now, we have considered anxiety as a normal emotional response of an individual to different situations or circumstances. However, when its frequency, intensity and duration are excessive, producing serious limitations in different facets of individuals' lives and reducing their ability to adapt to the environment, we must talk about pathological anxiety.

Anxiety is closely related to anxiety disorders, depression, disorders traditionally labelled as neurotic, many psychotic disorders, and a wide

RELATED ENTRIES

PERSONALITY ASSESSMENT (GENERAL), EMOTIONS, ANXIETY DISORDERS ASSESSMENT, TEST ANXIETY, MULTIMODAL ASSESSMENT, APPLIED FIELDS: CLINICAL, APPLIED FIELDS: HEALTH, TRAIT–STATE MODELS variety of psychophysiological problems such as cardiovascular disorders, peptic ulcers, headaches, premenstrual syndrome, asthma, skin disorders, and so on. It is also involved in sexual disorders, addictive behaviour and eating disorders; more recently, there are findings that relate anxiety to weakness of the immune system.

Due to the wide variety of problems in which this emotion plays an important role, anxiety must be considered a central aspect of psychopathology and health psychology. In fact, thousands of persons with anxiety problems seek attention in hospitals, health centres, etc., and this results in an important economic cost to public health services.

Anxiety Disorders

Anxiety disorders constitute the most common psychopathology, followed by affective disorders and drugs and alcohol consumption. The life-prevalence rate accounts for 19.5% of females and 8% of males (Robins, Helzer & Weissman, 1984).

The classifications of anxiety disorders have varied over recent years. The most widely used are the ICD-10 (World Health Organization, 1992), the DSM-IV (American Psychiatric Association, 1994) and the DSM-IV-TR (American Psychiatric Association, 2000). The DSM-IV and DSM-IV-TR will be used as reference sources, and are shown in Table 1.

Anxiety Disorders Assessment

Changes in the theoretical frameworks of anxiety research that occurred in the late 1960s have not been accurately reflected in assessment procedures which are instruments, especially for self-report measures, the most widely used. This has impeded the consolidation of a systematic research line focused on different aspects of anxiety in several anxiety disorders.

The works of Lacey (1967) and Lang (1968) proposed the multidimensional nature of anxiety responses and the existence of three relatively independent response systems (cognitive, physiological, and motor responses), while the interactive model (Endler, 1973) stressed the multidimensionality of trait anxiety (Endler & Magnusson, 1974, 1976). Finally, the discovery of individual

Table 1. DSM-IV–DSM-IV-TR classification

Codes	Anxiety Disorders
300.01	Panic disorder without agoraphobia
300.21	Panic disorder with agoraphobia
300.22	Agoraphobia without history of panic disorder
300.29	Specific phobia
300.23	Social phobia (Social Anxiety Disorder, added in DSM-IV-TR)
300.3	Obsessive-compulsive disorder
309.81	Post-traumatic stress disorder
308.3	Acute stress disorder
300.02	Generalized anxiety disorder (includes overanxious disorder of childhood in DSM-IV-TR)
293.84	Anxiety due to a medical condition
Variable	Substance-induced anxiety disorder
300.00	Anxiety disorder not otherwise specified

differences in relation to the tendency to experience anxiety in some situations, but not in others, led to theoretical advances that have not yet been sufficiently applied in research on anxiety disorders.

With the aim of including all of these theoretical advances in an assessment instrument, we developed the *Inventory of Situations and Responses of Anxiety* (ISRA, Miguel-Tobal & Cano Vindel, 1986, 1988, 1994). The ISRA is a self-report instrument for a multidimensional and interactive assessment of anxiety that permits the evaluation of the three response systems (cognitive, physiological and motor responses), trait anxiety, and four situational areas or specific traits (test anxiety, interpersonal anxiety, phobic anxiety and daily life anxiety).

Several studies have explored differential anxiety characteristics, in both anxiety disorders and psychophysiological disorders, through the ISRA. Such studies indicate that there are characteristic profiles in different pathologies that can be relevant in both the research and clinical practice contexts (see Miguel-Tobal & Cano Vindel, 1995).

INSTRUMENTS AND PROCEDURES

A large number of procedures and instruments have been used for the assessment of anxiety, including self-reports, physiological procedures and behavioural methods. More information on this issue can be found in Endler and Kocovski's entry 'Anxiety Assessment' in this same volume. Here we shall focus especially on the instruments developed for the assessment of different anxiety disorders. It should be noted that procedures for the assessment of general anxiety are also commonly used in clinical practice.

Broad Screening

Several structured interviews have been used in order to determine the onset of an anxiety disorder or to make a more accurate diagnosis. Two good examples are the *Anxiety Disorder Interview Schedule – Revised* (Di Nardo et al., 1985), and the *Structured Clinical Interview for DSM-IV Axis I disorders* (Spitzer, Gibbon & Williams, 1996).

With regard to specific disorders, some widely used instruments and procedures are:

Panic Disorder Assessment

The most widely-used self-report instrument for the assessment of panic attacks is the *Panic Attack Questionnaire* (PAQ, Norton, 1988).

Agoraphobia Assessment

In the assessment of agoraphobia, both self-reports and behavioural measures have been used. Among self-reports, the *Agoraphobic Cognitions Questionnaire* (ACQ), along with its companion measure, the *Body Sensations Questionnaire* (BSQ), were devised to assess 'fear of fear' (Chambless, Caputo, Bright & Gallagher, 1984). Among behavioural measures, there are two kinds of devices: one type that measures avoidance behaviours, an example of which is the *Individualized Behavioural Avoidance Test* (IBAT, Agras, Leitenberg & Barlow, 1968), and another type for measuring the time and distance walked away from a 'safe' place as a cue for the intensity of agoraphobic reactions (see Emmelkamp, 1982). It should be noted that assessment instruments designed for phobia, social phobia, and panic attacks are also used in the evaluation of agoraphobia.

Specific Phobia Assessment

The most frequently used instruments are self-reports, such as the *Fear Survey Schedule I* (Lang & Lazovik, 1963) and *Fear Survey Schedule III* (Wolpe & Lang, 1964), for measuring the type and intensity of irrational fears and fear-eliciting stimuli. Also used are behavioural avoidance measures, such as the *Behavioural Avoidance Test* (Lang & Lazovik, 1963) and the *Behavioural Avoidance Slide Test* (Burchardt & Levis, 1977). It should be noted that some of these instruments are also used for the assessment of social phobia and agoraphobia.

Social Phobia Assessment

The *Social Avoidance and Distress Scale* (SADS), the *Fear of Negative Evaluation Scale* (FNE, Watson & Friend, 1969), the *Suinn Test Anxiety Behaviour Scale* (STABS, Suinn, 1969) and the *Social Reaction Inventory – Revised* (SRI-R, Curran, Corriveau, Monti & Hagerman, 1980) are used for assessing social skills, while the *Social Phobia and Anxiety Inventory* (SPAI, Turner, Beidel, Dancu & Stanley, 1989) is also employed. Among behavioural measures, the *Social Interaction Test* (SIT, Trower, Bryant & Argyle, 1978) is designed for measuring social skills in a test anxiety-provoking situation by means of role-play procedures.

Obsessive-Compulsive Disorder Assessment

The most important self-report measures used are the *Leyton Obsessional Inventory* (LOI, Cooper, 1970), the *Compulsive Activity Checklist* (CAC, Philpott, 1975) and the *Maudsley Obsessional-Compulsive Inventory* (MOCI, Hodgson & Rachman, 1977).

Post-Traumatic Stress Disorder Assessment

There are several methods for the assessment of PTSD disorder, including clinical interviews, self-report instruments and psychophysiological measures. For the purpose of this entry we consider general-oriented instruments rather than special populations-oriented ones (combat survivors, rape victims, etc.), except for psycho-physiological measures. Two good examples of clinical interviews are the *Clinical-Administered PTSD Scale* (CAPS-1, Blake, Weathers, Nagy, Kaloupek, Klauminzer, Charney & Keane, 1990), and the *PTSD Symptom Scale Interview* (PSS-I, Foa, Riggs, Dancu & Rothbaum, 1993). Two other good examples of self-report instruments are the *Revised Impact of Events Scale* (RIES, Horowitz, Wilner & Alvarez, 1979), and the *PTSD Diagnostic Scale* (PDS, Foa, 1995). Finally, data from laboratory studies provide evidence that psychophysiological measurement is a valuable tool in the assessment of PTSD. Studies with combat populations reveal that *cardiovascular measures* (heart rate and blood pressure) have generally shown good specificity and sensitivity in PTSD classification (see Lating & Everly, 1995; Miguel-Tobal, González Ordi & López Ortega, 2000).

Generalized Anxiety Disorder (GAD) Assessment

Given the lack of specificity of GAD general anxiety assessment instruments, including the *State–Trait Anxiety Inventory* (STAI, Spielberger, Gorsuch & Lushene, 1970), the *Beck Anxiety Inventory* (BAI, Beck, Epstein, Brown & Steer, 1988), the *Anxiety Sensitivity Index* (ASI, Reiss, Peterson, Gursky & McNally, 1986), the *Endler Multidimensional Anxiety Scales* (EMAS, Endler, Edwards & Vitelli, 1991) and, in Spain, the *Inventory of Situations and Responses of Anxiety* (ISRA, Miguel-Tobal & Cano Vindel, 1986, 1988, 1994), have been used for its evaluation.

As can be seen, there are very few references to physiological measures in this review since, though commonly used in clinical research, they have not generally shown enough specificity to discriminate between different anxiety disorders, except, as mentioned earlier, in the case of PTSD.

Finally, we should stress the appropriateness of using multiple instruments that allow the assessment of general anxiety on the one hand and the evaluation of a specific disorder or disorders on the other. Clinical practice reveals that it is hard to find a pure disorder, since, as Wittchen (1987) points out, the comorbidity rate for anxiety disorders is 68%: in other words, two out of every three patients also present another anxiety disorder.

FUTURE PERSPECTIVES AND CONCLUSIONS

Anxiety disorder assessment has mainly been carried out using self-reports, and to a lesser extent behavioural measures. Physiological measures do not provide sufficient specificity to delimit or evaluate specific disorders; however, there is a promising line of research in relation to PTSD.

In addition to this lack of specificity with regard to anxiety disorders, due to the overlapping of their symptoms, it is also important to consider the problem of their high comorbidity (68% for anxiety disorders and 50% for depression). Taking these aspects into account, it is necessary to carry out a wide-spectrum assessment that includes general anxiety measures, specific disorder measures and measures of depression.

Theoretical advances in the study of anxiety and research on measurement procedures have fostered the multisystem–multimethod assessment, but such advances have been weakly reflected in anxiety disorder assessment research, and have had even less impact on clinical practice. This is one of the challenges for the future, which it is to be hoped will see the development of new multidimensional instruments through the integration of data derived from self-reports, physiological records and behavioural measures.

References

Agras, W.S., Leitenberg, H. & Barlow, D.H. (1968). Social reinforcement in the modification of agoraphobia. *Archives of General Psychiatry*, 19, 423–427.

American Psychiatric Association (1994). *Diagnostic and Statistical Manual of Mental Disorders (DSM-IV)* (4th ed.). Washington, DC: APA.

American Psychiatric Association (2000). *Desk Reference to the Diagnostic Criteria from DSM-IV-TR*. Washington, DC: APA.

Beck, A.T., Epstein, N., Brown, G. & Steer, R.A. (1988). An inventory for measuring clinical anxiety: psychometric properties. *Journal of Consulting and Clinical Psychology*, 56, 893–897.

Blake, D.D., Weathers, F.W., Nagy, L.M., Kaloupek, D.G., Klauminzer, G., Charney, D. & Keane, T.M. (1990). A clinical rating scale for assessing current and lifetime PTSD: the CAPS-1. *Behaviour Therapist*, 18, 187–188.

Burchardt, C.J. & Levis, D.J. (1977). The utility of presenting slides of a phobic stimulus in the context of a behavioural avoidance procedure. *Behaviour Therapy*, 8, 340–346.

Chambless, D.L., Caputo, G.C., Bright, P. & Gallagher, R. (1984). Assessment of fear of fear in agoraphobics: the Body Sensations Questionnaire and the Agoraphobic Cognitions Questionnaire. *Journal of Consulting and Clinical Psychology*, 52, 1090–1097.

Cone, J.D. & Hawkins, R.P. (1977). *Behavioural Assessment: New Directions in Clinical Psychology*. New York: Brunner-Mazel.

Cooper, J. (1970). The Leyton Obsessional Inventory. *Psychological Medicine*, 1, 48–64.

Curran, J.P., Corriveau, D.P., Monti, P.M. & Hagerman, S.B. (1980). Social skill and social anxiety. *Behaviour Modification*, 4, 493–512.

Di Nardo, P.A., Barlow, D.H., Cerny, J.A., Vermilyea, B.B., Vermilyea, J.A., Himadi, W.G. & Wadell, M.T. (1985). *Anxiety Disorders Interview Schedule–Revised (ADIS-R)*. Albany, NY: Center for Stress and Anxiety Disorders.

Emmelkamp, P.M.G. (1982). *Phobic and Obsessive-Compulsive Disorders: Theory, Research and Practice*. New York: Plenum Press.

Endler, N.S. (1973). The person versus the situation: a pseudo issue? A response to others. *Journal of Personality*, 41, 287–303.

Endler, N.S., Edwards, J.M. & Vitelli, R. (1991). *Endler Multidimensional Anxiety Scales (EMAS): Manual*. Los Angeles, CA: Western Psychological Services.

Endler, N.S. & Magnusson, D. (1974). Interactionism, trait psychology, psychodynamics, and situationism. Report from the Psychological Laboratories. University of Stockholm, No 418.

Endler, N.S. & Magnusson, D. (Eds.) (1976). *Interactional Psychology and Personality*. Washington, DC: Hemisphere Publishing Co.

Fernández-Ballesteros, R. (1983). *Psicodiagn Óstico*. Madrid: UNED.

Foa, E.B. (1995). *PSD (Posttraumatic Stress Diagnostic Scale). Manual*. Minneapolis: National Computer System.

Foa, E.B., Riggs, D.S., Dancu, C.V. & Rothbaum, B.O. (1993). Reliability and validity of a brief instrument for assessing post-traumatic stress disorder. *Journal of Trauma Stress*, 6, 459–473.

Hodgson, R.J. & Rachman, S. (1977). Obsessional-compulsive complaints. *Behaviour Research and Therapy*, 15, 389–395.

Horowitz, M.J., Wilner, N. & Alvarez, W. (1979). Impact of Event Scale: a measure of subjective distress. *Psychosomatic Medicine*, 41, 207–218.

Lacey, J.I. (1967). Somatic responses patterning and stress: some revisions of the activation theory. In Appley, M.H. & Trumbull, R. (Eds.), *Psychological Stress: Issues in Research* (pp. 14–42). New York: Appleton-Century-Crofts.

Lang, P.J. (1968). Fear reduction and fear behaviour: problems in treating a construct. In Shilen, J.M. (Ed.), *Research in Psychotherapy*; Vol. III (pp. 90–103). Washington, DC: American Psychological Association.

Lang, P.J. & Lazovik, A.D. (1963). Experimental desensitization of a phobia. *Journal of Abnormal and Social Psychology*, 66, 519–525.

Lating, J.M. & Everly, G.S. (1995). Psychophysiological assessment of PTSD. In Everly, G.S. & Lating, J.M. (Eds.), *Psychotraumatology: Key Papers and Core Concepts in Post-Traumatic Stress* (pp. 129–145). New York: Plenum Press.

Miguel-Tobal, J.J. (1990). La ansiedad. In Mayor, J. & Pinillos, J.L. (Eds.), *Tratado de Psicología General. Vol. 8: Motivación y Emoción* (pp. 309–344). Madrid: Alhambra.

Miguel-Tobal, J.J. & Cano Vindel, A.R. (1986). *Inventario de Situaciones y Respuestas de Ansiedad (Inventory of Situations and Responses of Anxiety)* (1988 & 1994, 2nd and 3rd revisions, respectively). Madrid: TEA Ediciones.

Miguel-Tobal, J.J. & Cano Vindel, A. (1995). Perfiles diferenciales de los trastornos de ansiedad. *Ansiedad y Estrés*, 1, 37–60.

Miguel-Tobal, J.J., González Ordi, H. & López Ortega, E. (2000). Estrés postraumático: hacia una integración de aspectos psicológicos y neurobiológicos. *Ansiedad y Estrés*, 6, 255–280.

Norton, G.R. (1988). Panic Attack Questionnaire. In Hersen, M. & Bellack, A.S. (Eds.), *Dictionary of Behavioural Assessment Techniques* (pp. 332–334). New York: Pergamon Press.

Philpott, R. (1975). Recent advances in the behavioural measurement of obsessional illness: difficulties common to these and other instruments. *Scottish Medical Journal*, 20, 33–40.

Reiss, S., Peterson, R.A., Gursky, D.M. & McNally, R.J. (1986). Anxiety sensitivity, anxiety frequency, and the prediction of fearfulness. *Behaviour Research and Therapy*, 24, 1–8.

Robins, L.N., Helzer, J.E. & Weissman, M.M. (1984). Lifetime prevalence of specific psychiatric disorders in three sites. *Archives of General Psychiatry*, 41, 949–958.

Spielberger, C.D., Gorsuch, R.L. & Lushene, R.E. (1970). *STAI. Manual for the State–Trait Anxiety Inventory (Self-Evaluation Questionnaire)*. Palo Alto, CA: Consulting Psychologists Press.

Spitzer, R.L., Gibbon, M. & Williams, J.B.W. (1996). *Structured Clinical Interview for DSM-IV Axis I Disorders*. New York: New York State Psychiatric Institute, Biometrics Research Department.

Suinn, R. (1969). The STABS, a measure of test anxiety for behaviour therapy: normative data. *Behaviour Research and Therapy*, 7, 335–339.

Trower, P., Bryant, B. & Argyle, M. (1978). *Social Skills and Mental Health*. Pittsburgh: University of Pittsburgh Press.

Turner, S.M., Beidel, D.C., Dancu, C.V. & Stanley, M.A. (1989). An empirically derived inventory to measure social fears and anxiety: the Social Phobia and Anxiety Inventory. *Psychological Assessment, 1,* 35–40.

Watson, D. & Friend, R. (1969). Measurement of social-evaluative anxiety. *Journal of Consulting and Clinical Psychology, 33,* 448–457.

Wittchen, H.U. (1987). Epidemiology of panic attacks and panic disorder. In Hand, I. & Wittchen, H.U. (Eds.), *Panic and Phobias (1). Empirical Evidence of Theoretical Models and Long-Term Effects of Behavioural Treatments.* New York: Springer-Verlag.

Wolpe, J. & Lang, P.J. (1964). A fear survey schedule for use in behaviour therapy. *Behaviour Research and Therapy, 2,* 27–30.

World Health Organization (1992). *International Classification of Diseases and Related Health Problems. ICD-10.* Geneva: WHO.

Juan José Miguel-Tobal and
Héctor González-Ordi

RELATED ENTRIES

APPLIED BEHAVIOURAL ANALYSIS

INTRODUCTION

Applied behaviour analysis is a branch of science in which procedures derived from the principles of behaviour are systematically applied to improve socially meaningful behaviour that could be rigorously defined and objectively detected and measured (Cooper et al., 1987). As pointed out by Moore (1999), behaviour analysis has developed three components, as well as a philosophy of science: (1) the *experimental analysis of behaviour*, the basic science of behaviour, (2) *applied behaviour analysis*, the systematic application of behavioural technology, and (3) the *conceptual analysis of behaviour*, the philosophical analysis of the subject matter of behaviour analysis. The philosophy of science that guides behaviour analysis is called *radical behaviourism*. Even though the link between the experimental and applied component of behaviour analysis is not as united as it should be, bridges are being built between basic and applied work, such as the work being conducted in the areas of establishing fluency and building momentum (Mace, 1996). The impact of bridge studies has been especially pronounced in functional analysis methodologies on aberrant behaviour (Wacker, 2000). This entry will focus on important aspects of functional assessment.

CHARACTERISTICS AND AREAS OF INTEREST

Baer, Wolf, and Risley (1968) list seven defining characteristics of applied behaviour analysis: behaviour or stimuli studied are selected because of their significance to society rather than their importance to theory (*applied*). The behaviour chosen must be the behaviour in need of improvement and it must be measurable (*behavioural*). It requires a demonstration of the events that can be responsible for the occurrence or non-occurrence of that behaviour (*analytic*). The interventions must be completely identified and described (*technological*). The procedure for behaviour change is described in terms of the relevant principles from which they are derived (*conceptual systems*). The behavioural techniques must produce significant effects for practical value (*effective*). The behavioural change must be stable over time, appear consistently across situations, or spread to untrained responses (*generality*).

The writings of B. F. Skinner have inspired behaviour analysts to develop basic concepts of reciprocal behaviour–environment interactions. Over fifty years of research and application have shown the usefulness of these basic concepts in understanding many forms of behaviour, as well as in guiding effective behaviour-change strategies. The knowledge of *stimulus control* (when the presentation of a stimulus changes some measures of behaviour) and *reinforcement* (the process by which the frequency of an operant [class of responses] is increased) has been useful in the analysis and treatment of human behaviour problems, as well as creating novel behaviour since the inception of applied behaviour analysis. Applied behaviour analysis has played a prominent role in the treatment of individuals with autism and/or developmental disabilities. Though, the areas of interest have been expanding, e.g. school settings, treatment of habit disorders, paediatrics, troubled adolescent runaways, brain-injury rehabilitation, behavioural psychotherapy, organizational management, performance analysis, consultation, sport psychology, college teaching, and behavioural medicine (e.g. Austin and Carr, 2000).

ASSESSMENT

The role of assessment in applied behaviour analysis has been described as the process of identifying a problem and identifying how to alter it for the better. Furthermore, it involves selecting and defining the behaviour (target behaviour) to be changed. Two questions have been essential in behavioural assessment: '(a) What types of assessment methodologies provide reliable and valid data about behavioural function, and how can they be adapted for use in a particular situation? and (b) How might the results of such assessments improve the design and selection of treatment procedures?' (Neef & Iwata, 1994: 211). As we shall examine further, behaviour is assumed to be a function of current environmental conditions – antecedent and consequent stimuli – and it is predicted to be stable as long as the specific environmental conditions remain stable. On the contrary, traditional approaches or non-behavioural therapies assume that the behaviour is a function of enduring, underlying mental states or personal variables. One premise is that the client's verbal behaviour (what people talk about, what they do and why they do it) is considered important because it is believed to be reflective of a person's inner state and the mental processes that govern a person's behaviour (Cooper et al., 1987). This is quite different from a behaviour analytic view where a distinction is made between what people say they do and what they do (Skinner, 1953), and the focus is on behaviour for its own sake.

Function versus Structure

Behaviour could be classified either structurally or functionally. When we talk about a structural approach, behaviour is classified or analysed in terms of its form. For example within developmental psychology, the structural approach is a prominent approach in which researchers investigate what children do at specific stages of development, e.g. the behaviour is studied to draw inferences about cognitive abilities and so-called hypothetical structures, as object permanence or Piagetian schemes. In behaviour analysis, the topography or structure of a response is determined by the contingencies of this behaviour. Instead of inferring such cognitive abilities, the researchers consider the history of reinforcement to be responsible for the child's capability (Pierce & Epling, 1999). Structural approaches to assessment are exemplified by diagnostic, personality and psychodynamic approaches to human behaviour, while functional explanations focus on the relationships between what happens to the organism (i.e. stimuli) and the behaviour of the organism (responses) (Sturmey, 1996). The controversy between functional and structural approach is quite similar to debate in biology on the separation of physiology and anatomy, and also to Skinner's treatment of verbal behaviour (function; without regard to modality [vocal, gestures etc.], the field of verbal behaviour is concerned with the behaviour of individuals and the functional units of their verbal behaviour function) versus language (structure; the consistencies of vocabulary and grammar) (Catania, 1998).

Functional Assessment

Early in the development of behaviour analysis, Skinner (1938) argued that behaviour did not take place in a vacuum and a response must have a function. Empirical demonstrations of 'cause–effect relationships' between environment and behaviour have been rendered possible by functional analysis (Skinner, 1953). Since then comprehensive methods to systematically assess particular functions of different types of behaviour have been developed, and functional assessment is one of the most intense research areas in our field (see for example Iwata et al., 2000; Repp & Horner, 1999).

Functional assessment is an umbrella term and encompasses: (1) indirect assessments, which are characterized by interviews and questionnaires and behavioural functions. They are based on subjective verbal reports in absence of direct observation. Two recognized indirect methods are the *Motivation Assessment Scale* (Durand & Crimmins, 1988) and the *Motivation Analysis Rating Scale* (Wieseler et al., 1985); (2) descriptive assessments involve no manipulation of relevant variables and are based on direct observation, e.g. the antecedent–behaviour–consequence assessment (ABC) or scatter plot assessment; (3) functional experimental analyses or analogue functional assessment involve manipulation of suspected maintaining variables using experimental methodology to demonstrate control over responding (Desrochers et al., 1997). The first two approaches are approximations compared to the third because they do not elucidate functional relationships, and both are characteristically non-experimental. Furthermore, the functional experimental analysis is most effective in identifying the function of problem behaviour (Carr et al., 1999).

Experimental Functional Analysis or Analogue Functional Assessment

Since the prominent publication by Iwata et al. (1982) there has been a remarkable increase of publications concerning experimental functional analysis (see *Journal of Applied Behaviour Analysis*). Experimental functional analysis represents a simulation of the natural environment and will be the primary tool for demonstrating causal relationships (Carr et al., 1999). Experimental functional analysis methodologies can be used to identify: (1) antecedent conditions (setting events, establishing operations and/or discriminative stimuli) under which behaviour occurs, and these conditions may then be altered so that problem behaviours are less likely, (2) reinforcement contingencies that must be changed, (3) whether the same reinforcer that currently maintains the

behaviour problem may be used in establishing and strengthening alternative behaviours, and (4) those reinforcers and/or treatment components that are relevant (Iwata et al., 2000).

Results from the research on functional analysis methodologies have shown that functional analyses are effective in identifying environmental determinants of self-injurious behaviour (SIB), and subsequently, in guiding the process of treatment selection (Iwata et al., 1994). Furthermore, results have shown that the growing use of functional assessment based interventions have increased the number of studies using non-aversive procedures (Carr et al., 2000).

Recording Techniques

In applied behaviour analysis it is important to demonstrate that a particular intervention has been responsible for a particular behaviour change. Therefore, measurement is very important with respect to designing successful interventions and evaluating treatment changes. Automatic recording, permanent products, and direct observational recording are procedures used for measuring and recording behaviour. Direct observational recording include frequency or event, duration, or latency recording, and the recording could either be continuous, time sampling or interval (Cooper et al., 1987). Objectivity, clarity and completeness have been set forth as three criteria of an adequate response definition (Kazdin, 1982).

Experimental Designs

In experimental functional analyses various experimental designs have been used to rule out the possibility that changes in extraneous variable(s) other than in the independent variable could be responsible for the change in dependent variable, e.g. eliminating rival explanations. Thus, these experimental designs have been used to study the functional relationships between environmental changes and changes in target behaviour. Typical experimental design $N=1$ designs (within-subject manipulation, single-case research design) have been used in applied behaviour analysis, and the designs have been categorized as ABAB designs, multiple baseline designs, multiple treatment designs and changing criterion designs (Kazdin, 1982). The multi-element design (multiple treatment designs) has typically been used in experimental functional analysis (e.g. Iwata et al., 1982).

In single-case research, replication, either direct or systematic, is crucial for evaluating generality of intervention effects across subjects. The term direct replication has been used when the same procedures have been used across a number of different subjects, while systematic replication indicate that features (e.g. types of subjects, intervention, target behaviour) of the original experiment vary. By replicating in this way, knowledge will be accumulated, and behaviourists will be pyramid builders.

FUTURE PERSPECTIVES AND CONCLUSIONS

Different aspects regarding behavioural assessment as indirect assessment, descriptive assessment and experimental functional analysis have been discussed. Extension and refinement of behavioural assessment and functional analysis technologies will, hopefully, provide for even more effective methods in establishing behaviour and treating maladaptive behaviour. In addition, the advancement of computer technology allows for more simplified assessment techniques. Until now functional assessment technologies have primarily focused on non-compliance and self-injurious and aggressive behaviour in persons with disabilities and autism, but advancements in these procedures will include their applications on other types of behaviour and a larger diversity of problem behaviour in populations other than persons with autism and disabilities.

References

Austin, J. & Carr, J.E. (Eds.) (2000). *Handbook of Applied Behaviour Analysis*. Reno, Nevada: Context Press.

Baer, D.M., Wolf, M.M. & Risley, T.R. (1968). Some current dimensions of applied behaviour analysis. *Journal of Applied Behaviour Analysis*, 1, 91–97.

Carr, E.G., Langdon, N.A. & Yarbrough, S.C. (1999) Hypothesis-based intervention for severe problem behaviour. In Repp, A.C. & Horner, R.H. (Eds.), *Functional Analysis of Problem Behaviour* (pp. 9–31). Belmont, CA: Wadsworth Publishing Company.

Carr, J.E., Coriaty, S. & Dozier, C.L. (2000). Current issues in the function-based treatment of aberrant behaviour in individuals with developmental disabilities. In Austin, J. & Carr, J.E. (Eds.), *Handbook of Applied Behaviour Analysis* (pp. 91–112). Reno, Nevada: Context Press.

Catania, A.C. (1998). *Learning* (4th ed.). Englewood Cliffs, New Jersey: Prentice-Hall.

Cooper, J.O., Heron, T.E. & Heward, W.L. (1987). *Applied Behaviour Analysis*. Merrill Publications: Columbus.

Desrochers, M.N., Hile, M.G. & Williams-Moseley, T.L. (1997). Survey of functional assessment procedures used with individuals who display mental retardation and severe problem behaviours. *American Journal on Mental Retardation*, 5, 535–546.

Durand, M. & Crimmins, D.B. (1988). Identifying the variables maintaining self-injurious behaviour in a psychotic child. *Journal of Autism and Developmental Disorders*, 18, 99–117.

Iwata, B.A., Dorsey, M.F., Slifer, K.J., Bauman, K.E. & Richman, G.S. (1982). Toward a functional analysis of self-injury. *Analysis and Intervention in Developmental Disabilities*, 2, 3–20.

Iwata, B.A., Kahng, S.W., Wallace, M.D. & Lindberg, J.S. (2000). The functional analysis model of behavioural assessment. In Austin, J. & Carr, J.E. (Eds.), *Handbook of Applied Behaviour Analysis* (pp. 61–89). Reno, Nevada: Context Press.

Iwata, B.A., Pace, G.M., Dorsey, M.F., Zarcone, J.R., Vollmer, T.R., Smith, R.G., Rodgers, T.A., Lerman, D.C., Shore, B.A., Mazelski, J.L., Goh, H.-L., Cowdery, G.E., Kalsher, M.J., McCosh, K.C. & Willis, K.D. (1994). The functions of self-injurious behaviour: an experimental-epidemiological analysis. *Journal of Applied Behaviour Analysis*, 27, 215–240.

Kazdin, A.E. (1982). *Single-Case Research Designs*. New York: Oxford University Press.

Mace, F.C. (1996). In pursuit of general behavioural relations. *Journal of Applied Behaviour Analysis*, 29, 557–563.

Moore, J. (1999). The basic principles of behaviourism. In Thyer, B.A. (Ed.), *The Philosophical Legacy of Behaviourism* (pp. 41–68). Dordrecht: Kluwer Academic Publishers.

Neef, N.A. & Iwata, B.A. (1994). Current research on functional analysis methodologies: an introduction. *Journal of Applied Behaviour Analysis*, 27, 211–214.

Pierce, W.D. & Epling, W.F. (1999). *Behaviour Analysis and Learning* (2nd ed.). Englewood Cliffs, NJ: Prentice Hall, Inc.

Repp, A.C. & Horner, R.H. (Eds.) (1999). *Functional Analysis of Problem Behaviour*. Belmont, CA: Wadsworth Publishing Company.

Skinner, B.F. (1938). *The Behaviour of Organisms*. Acton, Massachusetts: Copley Publishing Group.

Skinner, B.F. (1953). *Science and Human Behaviour*. New York: Free Press.

Sturmey, P. (1996). *Functional Analysis in Clinical Psychology*. Baffins Lane, Chichester, UK: John Wiley & Sons.

Wacker, D.P. (2000). Building a bridge between research in experimental and applied behaviour analysis.

In Leslie, J.C. & Blackman, D.E. (Eds.), *Experimental and Applied Analysis of Human Behaviour* (pp. 205–234). Reno, Nevada: Context Press.

Wieseler, N.A., Hanzel, T.E., Chamberlain, T.P. & Thompson, T. (1985). Functional taxonomy of stereotypic and self-injurious behaviour. *Mental Retardation, 23*, 230–234.

Erik Arntzen

APPLIED FIELDS: CLINICAL

INTRODUCTION

Psychological assessment is utilized in clinical psychology primarily for purposes of differential diagnosis, treatment planning, and outcome evaluation. Differential diagnosis involves drawing on assessment information to describe an individual's psychological characteristics and adaptive strengths and weaknesses. These descriptions provide a basis for determining (a) what type of disorder an individual may have, (b) the severity and chronicity of this disorder and the circumstances in which it is likely to be manifest, and (c) the kinds of treatment that are likely to provide the individual relief from this disorder. With respect to further treatment planning, adequate assessment information helps to guide treatment strategies and anticipate possible obstacles to progress in therapy. As for outcome evaluation, pre-treatment assessments establish an objective baseline against which treatment progress can be monitored in subsequent evaluations, and by which the eventual benefits of the treatment can be judged at its conclusion. These clinical contributions of psychological assessment can be implemented during each of four sequential phases in delivering psychological treatment: deciding on therapy, planning therapy, conducting therapy, and evaluating therapy.

DECIDING ON THERAPY

The first step in the clinical utilization of assessment information consists of deciding whether a patient needs treatment and is likely to benefit from it. Accurate differential diagnosis identifies pathological conditions (e.g. depression, paranoia) and maladaptive characteristics (e.g. passivity, low self-esteem) for which treatment is usually indicated, and adequate psychological evaluation helps to distinguish such conditions and characteristics from normal range functioning that does not call for professional mental health intervention. Assessment methods also provide valuable information concerning two factors known to predict whether people are likely to become involved in and profit from psychotherapy: their motivation for treatment and their accessibility to being treated (Garfield, 1994; Greencavage & Norcross, 1990).

Motivation for treatment usually corresponds to the amount of subjectively felt distress that people are experiencing. Accessibility to psychological treatment typically depends on how willing people are to examine themselves, to express their thoughts and feelings openly, and to make changes in their customary beliefs and preferred ways of conducting their lives. Information derived from appropriate assessment procedures can provide clinicians with objective indices of each of these variables, and these assessment data can in turn be used as a basis for determining whether to recommend and proceed with some form of treatment.

PLANNING THERAPY

Planning therapy for patients who need and want to receive psychological treatment involves

(a) deciding on the appropriate setting in which to deliver the treatment, (b) estimating the duration of the treatment, and (c) selecting the particular type of treatment to be given. With respect to deciding on the treatment setting, assessment data provide reliable information concerning the severity of a patient's disturbance, the patient's ability to distinguish reality from fantasy, and his or her likelihood of becoming suicidal or dangerous to others, all of which bear on whether the person requires residential care or can be treated safely and adequately as an outpatient. The more severely disturbed people are, the farther out of touch with reality they are, and the greater their risk potential for violence, the more advisable it becomes to care for them in a protected environment.

Regarding treatment duration, clinical experience and research findings consistently indicate that mild and acute problems of recent onset can usually be treated successfully in a shorter period of time than severe and chronic problems of long-standing duration. A variety of psycho-diagnostic measures provide clues to the chronicity as well as the severity of symptomatic and characterological mental and emotional problems, and pretreatment data obtained with these measures can accordingly help clinicians formulate some expectation of how long a treatment is likely to last. Having available such assessment-based information on expected duration in turn assists clinicians in presenting treatment recommendations to prospective patients (Hurt, Reznikoff & Clarkin, 1991).

As for treatment selection, people who are relatively psychologically minded, self-aware, and interested in gaining fuller self-understanding are relatively likely to respond positively to an uncovering, insight-oriented, and conflict-focused treatment approach. Patients whose preference is to feel better without having to examine themselves closely, on the other hand, are more likely to become actively engaged in supportive and symptom-focused approaches to treatment than in exploratory psychotherapy. Psychologically minded people are inclined to feel dissatisfied with supportive treatment, because it does not get at the root of their problems, whereas relief-minded people tend to feel uncomfortable in uncovering treatment, because it makes unwelcome demands on them. Additionally, there is reason to believe that some kinds of conditions and difficulties, especially in people who are problem-oriented, respond relatively well to cognitive-behavioural forms of treatment, whereas other kinds of disorders and maladaptive tendencies, especially in people who are interpersonally oriented, respond better to psychodynamic-interpersonal than cognitive-behavioural therapy (Beutler & Harwood, 1995; Hayes, Nelson & Jarrett, 1987).

Psychological mindedness and preferences for problem-oriented or interpersonally oriented approaches to life situations are among a vast array of personality characteristics that can be measured with assessment methods. Accordingly, adequately conceived pretherapy psychological assessment can facilitate treatment planning by differentiating among psychological states and orientations of the individual that have known implications for successful response to particular treatment approaches.

CONDUCTING THERAPY

Psychological assessment can play a key role in conducting therapy by helping to identify in advance: (a) treatment targets on which the therapy should be focused and (b) possible obstacles to progress towards these treatment goals. Appropriately collected assessment data, and particularly the results of a multimethod test battery, typically contain many normal range findings and often some indications as well of notably good personality strengths and especially admirable personal qualities. At the same time, especially in people who are being evaluated for symptoms or difficulties that have led them to seek professional help, test data are likely to reveal specific adaptive shortcomings and coping limitations. One person may show a penchant for circumstantial reasoning and poor judgement; another person may give evidence of poor social skills and interpersonal withdrawal; a third may exhibit considerable emotional inhibition with restricted capacity to express feelings and feel comfortable in emotionally charged situations. In short, any assessment findings that fall outside of an established normal range and are known to indicate specific types of cognitive dysfunction, affective distress, coping deficit, personal dissatisfaction, or interpersonal inadequacy in turn assist therapists and their patients in deciding on the objectives of their work together and directing their efforts accordingly.

Some psychological characteristics of patients that constitute targets in their treatment may also pose obstacles to their becoming effectively engaged in therapy and making progress toward their goals. For example, people who are set in their ways and characteristically rigid and inflexible in their views often have difficulty reframing their perspectives or modifying their behaviour in response even to well-conceived and appropriately implemented treatment interventions. People who are interpersonally aversive or withdrawn may be slow or reluctant to form the kind of working alliance with their therapist that facilitates progress in most forms of therapy. People who are relatively satisfied with themselves and not experiencing much subjectively felt distress may have little tolerance for the demands of becoming seriously engaged in a course of psychological treatment (Blatt & Ford, 1994; Horvath & Greenberg, 1994; Shectman & Smith, 1984). Characteristics of these kinds do not preclude effective psychotherapy, but they can result in slow progress, and they may cause patients and therapists to become discouraged and terminate prematurely a treatment that does not appear to be going well. Pretreatment assessment data serve to alert therapists in advance to possible treatment obstacles, which can help them understand and be patient with initially slow progress and also guide them in dealing directly with these obstacles, as by concentrating in the early phases of therapy on encouraging flexibility and open-mindedness, building a comfortable and trusting treatment relationship, or generating some motivation for the patient's involvement in the therapy.

EVALUATING THERAPY

Psychological assessment provides valuable data for monitoring the progress of therapy and measuring its eventual benefit (Maruish, 1999; Weiner & Exner, 1991). For this potential benefit of assessment to be realized, it is vital for assessment data to be collected from patients prior to their beginning treatment. In addition to helping to identify treatment targets and the long-term objectives of therapy, pre-treatment data

provide an objective baseline for comparison with the results of subsequent assessments. Periodic re-evaluations can then shed light on whether the treatment is making a difference, how close it has come to meeting its aims, in what way the focus of continued treatment should be adjusted, and whether a termination point has been reached.

For example, if a reliable test index shows abnormally high anxiety, low self-esteem, poor self-control, or excessive anger, and a retest during treatment shows the same or a worse result for any of these treatment targets, there is objective evidence that no progress has been made on this front. Such results can then lead to an informed decision to alter the type or focus of the treatment, change the therapist, or await the next re-assessment before making any change. On the other hand, should retesting show an index closer to an adaptive range than initially, there is reason to conclude that progress is being made on the treatment target related to that index but that further improvement remains to be made in that area. When an initially abnormal test result is found on retesting to be in an adaptive range, then therapists and their patients can conclude with confidence that they have achieved the objective to which this result relates and do not need to address it further. At the point when retesting indicates that most or all of the treatment targets have reached or are approaching as much resolution as could realistically be expected, then the assessment process helps to indicate that an appropriate termination point has been reached.

Assessments conducted at the conclusion of psychotherapy, when compared with initial baseline evaluations, provide an objective basis for evaluating the overall benefit of the treatment that has been provided. Evaluations of treatment benefit made possible by pre-therapy and post-therapy assessments serve important research and practical purposes in clinical psychology. With respect to research issues, assessment data bearing on treatment benefit facilitates comparison studies of the relative effectiveness of different types and modalities of therapy. For practical purposes, retest findings demonstrating treatment benefit bear witness to the value of psychological interventions, particularly as weighed against the financial cost of these services (Kubiszyn et al., 2000).

WIDELY USED INSTRUMENTS

Surveys of clinical psychologists and the contents of standard handbooks concerning psychological assessment identify several instruments as being among those most widely used by clinicians in the United States for purposes of differential diagnosis, treatment planning, and outcome evaluation. Four of these measures are relatively structured self-report inventories on which conclusions are derived from what respondents are able and willing to say about themselves: the *Minnesota Multiphasic Personality Inventory*, the *Millon Clinical Multiaxial Inventory*, the *Sixteen Personality Factors Questionnaire*, and the *Personality Assessment Inventory*. Four of them are relatively unstructured performance-based measures in which the key data consist not of what respondents say about themselves but how they deal with various kinds of somewhat ambiguous tasks that are assigned to them: the Rorschach Inkblot Method, the Thematic Apperception Test, several types of figure drawing tasks, and some alternative sentence completion methods (Camara, Nathau & Puente, 2000; Maruish, 1999).

FUTURE PERSPECTIVES AND CONCLUSIONS

Psychological assessment has been an integral part of clinical psychology since its inception and continues to the present day to provide practitioners with valuable information to guide their evaluation and treatment of persons who seek their help. At times, failure to appreciate the benefits of preceding treatment with thorough assessment has led to insufficient teaching and learning of psychodiagnostic methods by clinical psychologists, as has the regrettable and short-sighted devaluing of diagnostic procedures by health insurance providers. However, the future application of psychodiagnostic methods in clinical psychology appears to rest safely in the hands of practitioners and researchers who know from their experience and data how useful assessment can be in facilitating good clinical decisions.

References

Beutler, L.E. & Harwood, T.M. (1995). How to assess clients in pre-treatment planning. In Butcher, J.N. (Ed.), *Clinical Personality Assessment* (pp. 59–77). New York: Oxford.

Blatt, S.L. & Ford, R.Q. (1994). *Therapeutic Change*. New York: Plenum.

Camara, W., Nathau, J. & Puente, A. (2000). Psychological test usage: implications in professional use. *Professional Psychology, 31*, 141–154.

Garfield, S.L. (1994). Research on client variables in psychotherapy. In Bergin, A.E. & Garfield, S.L. (Eds.), *Handbook of Psychotherapy and Behaviour Change* (4th ed.; pp. 190–228). New York: Wiley.

Greencavage, L.M. & Norcross, J.C. (1990). What are the commonalities among the therapeutic factors? *Professional Psychology, 21*, 372–378.

Hayes, S.C., Nelson, R.O. & Jarrett, R.B. (1987). The treatment utility of assessment. *American Psychologist, 42*, 963–974.

Horvath, O. & Greenberg, L.S. (Eds.) (1994). *The Working Alliance*. New York: Wiley.

Hurt, S.W., Reznikoff, M. & Clarkin, J.F. (1991). *Psychological Assessment, Psychiatric Diagnosis, & Treatment Planning*. New York: Brunner/Mazel.

Kubiszyn, T.W., Meyer, G.J., Finn, S.E., Eyde, L.D., Kay, G.G., Moreland, K.L., Dies, R.R. & Eisman, E.J. (2000). Empirical support for psychological assessment in clinical health care settings. *Professional Psychology, 31*, 119–130.

Maruish, M.E. (Ed.) (1999). *The Use of Psychological Testing for Treatment Planning and Outcome Assessment* (2nd ed.). Mahwah, NJ: Lawrence Erlbaum Associates.

Shectman, F. & Smith, W.H. (Eds.) (1984). *Diagnostic Understanding and Treatment Planning*. New York: Wiley.

Weiner, I.B. & Exner, J.E. (1991). Rorschach changes in long-term and short-term psychotherapy. *Journal of Personality Assessment, 56*, 453–465.

Irving B. Weiner

RELATED ENTRIES

A APPLIED FIELDS: EDUCATION

INTRODUCTION

The role of assessment and evaluation in education has been crucial, probably since the earliest approaches to formal education. However, change in this role has been dramatic in the last few decades, largely due to wider developments in society. The most dramatic change in our views of assessment is represented by the notion of assessment as a tool for learning. Whereas in the past, we have seen assessment only as a means to determine measures and thus certification, there is now a realization that the potential benefits of assessing are much wider and impinge on in all stages of the learning process. In this entry, we will outline some of the major developments in educational assessment, and we will reflect on the future of education within powerful learning environments, where learning, instruction and assessment are more fully integrated.

Consequences of the Developments in Society

Economic and technological change, which brings significant changes in the requirements of the labour market, poses increasing demands on education and training. For many years, the main goal of education has been to make students knowledgeable within a certain domain. Building a basic knowledge store was the core issue. Students taking up positions in modern organizations nowadays need to be able to analyse information, to improve their problem-solving skills and communication and to reflect on their own role in the learning process. People increasingly have to be able to acquire knowledge independently and use this body of organized knowledge in order to solve unforeseen problems. As a consequence, education should contribute to the education of students as lifelong learners.

Paradigm Change: From Testing towards Assessment

Many authors (Mayer, 1992; De Corte, 1990) have pointed to the importance of instruction to promote students' abilities as thinkers, problem-solvers and inquirers. Underlying this goal is the view that meaningful understanding is based on the active construction of knowledge and often involves shared learning. It is argued that a new form of education requires reconsideration about assessment (Dochy, Segers & Sluijsmans, 1999). Changing towards new forms of learning, with a status quo for evaluation, undermines the value of innovation. Students do not invest in learning that will not be honoured. Assessment is the most determining factor in education for the learning behaviour of students. Traditional didactic instruction and traditional assessment of achievement are not suited to the modern educational demands. Such tests were generally designed to be administered following instruction, rather than to be integrated with learning. As a consequence, due to their static and product-oriented nature, these tests not only lack diagnostic power but also fail to provide relevant information to assist in adapting instruction appropriately to the needs of the learner (Campione & Brown, 1990; Dochy, 1994). Furthermore, standard test theory characterizes performance in terms of the difficulty level of response choice items and focuses primarily on measuring the amount of declarative knowledge that students have acquired.

This view of performance is at odds with current theories of cognition. Achievement assessment must be an integral part of instruction, in that they should reflect, shape, and improve student learning. Assessment procedures should not only serve as a tool for crediting students with recognized certificates, but should also be used to monitor progress and, if needed, to direct students to remedial learning activities. The view that the evaluation of students' achievements is something which happens at the end of the process of learning is no longer widespread; assessment is now represented as a tool for learning (Dochy & McDowell, 1997).

The changing learning society has generated the so-called assessment culture as an alternative to the testing culture. The assessment culture strongly emphasizes the integration of instruction and assessment. Students play far more active roles in the evaluation of their achievement. The construction of tasks, the development of criteria for the evaluation of performance, and the scoring of the performance may be shared or negotiated among teachers and students. The assessment takes all kinds of forms such as observations, text- and curriculum-embedded questions and tests, interviews, performance assessments, writing samples, exhibitions, portfolio assessment, and project and product assessments. Several labels have been used to describe subsets of these alternatives, with the most common being 'direct assessment', 'authentic assessment', 'performance assessment' and 'alternative assessment'.

New Methods of Assessment

Investigations of new approaches (e.g. Birenbaum & Dochy, 1996; Nitko, 1995; Shavelson et al., 1996) illustrate the development of more 'in context' and 'authentic' assessment (Archbald & Newmann, 1992; Hill, 1993). Nisbet (1993) defines the term authentic assessment as 'methods of assessment which influence teaching and learning positively in ways which contribute to realizing educational objectives, requiring realistic (or "authentic") tasks to be performed and focusing on relevant content and skills, essentially similar to the tasks involved in the regular learning processes in the classroom' (p. 35).

Assessment of such 'authentic' tasks is highly individual and contextualized. The student gets feedback about the way he or she solved the task and about the quality of the result. Evaluation is given, on the basis of different 'performance tasks', performed and (reviewed) assessed at different moments. The evaluation criteria have to be known in advance. When students know the criteria and know how to reach them, they will be more motivated and achieve better results. This form of evaluation gives a more complete

and realistic picture of the student's ability (achievement). It evaluates not only the product, but also the process of learning. Students get feedback about their incorrect thinking strategies.

Within the new forms of 'new assessment', much attention is paid to authentic problem-solving, case-based exams, portfolios and the use of co-, peer-, and self-assessment (Birenbaum, 1996).

In traditional education, the question 'Who takes up the exam and who defines the criteria?' is seldom asked. Most of the time, it is the teacher. New forms of education do pose this question. Students themselves, other students or the teacher and students together are responsible for assessment. The type of student self-assessment referred to most frequently in the literature is a process, which involves teacher-set criteria and where students themselves carry out the assessment and marking. Another form of student self-assessment is the case where a student assesses herself or himself, on the basis of criteria which she or he has selected, the assessment being either for the student's personal guidance or for communication to the teacher or others. According to Hall (1995) there are two critical factors for genuine self-assessment: the student not only carries out the assessment, but also selects the criteria on which the assessment is based. Similarly, peer-assessment can indicate that fellow students both select the criteria and carry out the assessment. Any situation where the tutor and students share in the selection of criteria and/or the carrying-out of the assessment is more accurately termed co-assessment (Hall, 1995). However, it is still frequently the case that teachers control the assessment process, sometimes assisted by professional bodies or assessment experts, whereas students' assessments and criteria are taken seriously but considered to be additional to the assessment undertaken by the teacher or professor rather than replacing it (Rogers, 1995). Implementing forms of self-, peer- and co-assessment may decrease the time-investment professors would otherwise need to make in more frequent assessment. In addition to that advantage, using these assessment forms assists the development of certain skills for the students, e.g. communication skills, self-evaluation skills, observation skills, self-criticism.

ASSESSING NEW ASSESSMENT FORMS: DEVELOPMENTS IN EDUMETRICS

Judgements regarding the cognitive significance of an assessment begin with an analysis of the cognitive requirements of tasks as well as the ways in which students try to solve them (Glaser, 1990). Two criteria by which educational and psychological assessment measures are commonly evaluated are validity and reliability. One can say that based on these criteria, the results above are not yet consistent and depending upon the assessment form there is a larger or smaller basis to state that the evaluation is acceptable.

It is however important to note that Birenbaum (1996) mentions that the meaning of validity and reliability has recently expanded. Dissatisfaction with the available criteria, which were originally developed to evaluate indirect measures of performance, is attributed to their insensitivity to the characteristics of a direct assessment of performance.

The most important element of new assessment models is the reflection of the competencies required in real-life practice. The goal is to ensure that the success criteria of education or training processes are the same as those used in the practice setting. Hence, as notions of fitness of purpose change, and as assessment of more qualitative areas are developed, the concepts of validity and reliability encompassed within the instruments of assessment must also change accordingly. This means that we should widen up our view and search for other and more appropriate criteria. It should not be surprising that a new learning society and consequently a new instructional approach and a new assessment culture cannot be evaluated on the basis of the pre-era criteria solely.

Validity Related Issues

Although performance assessment appears to be a valid form of assessment, in that it resembles meaningful learning tasks, this measure may be no more valid than scores derived from response choice items (Linn et al., 1991). Evidence is needed to assure that assessment requires the high-level thought and reasoning processes that they were intended to evoke.

The authors of the 1985 Standards define *test validity* as 'a unitary concept, requiring multiple lines of evidence, to support the appropriateness, meaningfulness, and usefulness of the specific inferences made from test scores' (AERA, APA, NCME, 1985: 9). All validity research should be guided by the principles of scientific inquiry reflected in *construct validity*.

Within the construct validity framework, almost any information, gathered in the process of developing and using an assessment, is relevant, when it is evaluated against the theoretical rationale underlying the proposed interpretation and inferences, made from test scores (Moss, 1995). Thus, validation embraces all the experimental statistical and philosophical means by which hypotheses are evaluated. Validity conclusions, then, are best presented in the form of an *evaluative argument*, which integrates evidence to justify the proposed interpretation against plausible alternative interpretations.

Kane's *argument-based approach* is in line with Cronbach's view on validity. According to Kane (1992), to validate a test-score interpretation is to support the plausibility of the corresponding interpretative argument with appropriate evidence: (1) for the inferences and assumptions, made in the proposed interpretative argument, and (2) for refuting potential counter arguments. The core issue is not that we must collect data to underpin validity, but that we should formulate transparent, coherent, and plausible arguments to underpin validity.

Authors like Kane and Cronbach use validity principles from interpretative research traditions, instead of psychometric traditions, to assist in evaluating less-standardized assessment practices.

Other criteria suggested for measuring validity of new assessment forms are the transparency of the assessment procedure, the impact of assessment on education, directness, effectiveness, fairness, completeness of the domain description, practical value and meaningfulness of the tasks for candidates, and authenticity of the tasks (Haertel, 1991). According to Messick (1994), these validation criteria are, in a more sophisticated form, already part of the unifying concept of validity, which he expressed in 1989. He asserted that validity is an evaluative summary of both evidence for and the actual as well as potential consequences of score interpretation and use. The more traditional conception of validity as 'evidence for score interpretation and use' fails to take into account both evidence of the value implications of score interpretation and the social consequences of score use.

Messick's unifying concept of validity encompasses six distinguishable parts – content, substantive, structural, external, generalizability, and consequential aspects of construct validity – that conjointly function as general criteria for all educational and psychological assessment. The *content* aspect of validity means that range and type of tasks, used in assessment, must be an appropriate reflection (*content* relevance, representativeness) of the construct-domain. Increasing achievement levels in assessment tasks should reflect increases in expertise of the construct-domain. The *substantive* aspect emphasizes the consistency between the processes required for solving the tasks in assessment, and the processes used by domain-experts in solving tasks (problems). Further, the internal *structure* of assessment – reflected in the criteria, used in assessment tasks, the interrelations between these criteria and the relative weight placed on scoring these criteria – should be consistent with the internal structure of the construct-domain. If the content aspect (relevance, representativeness of content and performance standards) and the substantial aspect of validity is guaranteed, score interpretation, based on one assessment task, should be *generalizable* to other tasks, assessing the same construct. The *external* aspect of validity refers to the extent that the assessment scores' relationship with other measures and non-assessment behaviours reflect the expected high, low, and interactive relations. The *consequential* aspect of validity includes evidence and rationales for evaluating the intended and unintended consequences of score interpretation and use (Messick, 1994).

In line with Messick's conceptualization of consequential validity, Frederiksen and Collins (1989) proposed that assessment has 'systematic validity' if it encourages behaviours on the part of teachers and students that promote the learning of valuable skills and knowledge, and allows for issues of transparency and openness, that is to access the criteria for evaluating performance. Encouraging deep approaches to learning is one aspect, which can be explored in considering the consequences. Another is the impact which assessment has on teaching. Dochy

and McDowell (1997) argue that assessing high-order skills by means of authentic assessment will lead to the teaching of such high-order knowledge and skills.

With today's emphasis on high-stakes assessment, two threats to test validity are worth mentioning: construct under-representation and construct-irrelevance variance. In the case of *construct-irrelevance variation*, the assessment is too broad, containing systematic variance that is irrelevant to the construct being measured. The threat of *construct-underrepresentation* means that the assessment is too narrow and fails to include important dimensions of the construct being measured.

Special Points of Attention for New Assessment Forms

The above implies in our view that other criteria suggested for measuring validity of new assessment forms will need to be taken into account, i.e. the transparency of the assessment procedure, the impact of assessment on education, directness, effectiveness, fairness, completeness of the domain description, practical value and meaningfulness of the tasks for candidates, and authenticity of the tasks.

In addition, predictable difficulties will have to be taken into account, such as those outlined in the following paragraphs.

Authentic assessment tasks are more sensitive to construct-underrepresentation and construct-irrelevance variation, because they are often loosely structured, so that it is not always clear to which construct-domain inferences are drawn. Birenbaum (1996) argues that it is important to specify accurately the domain and to design the assessment rubrics so they clearly cover the construct-domain. Messick (1994) advises to adopt a construct-driven approach to the selection of relevant tasks and the development of scoring criteria and rubrics, because it makes salient the issue of construct-underrepresentation and construct-irrelevance variation.

Another difficulty with authentic tasks, with regard to validity, is concerning rating authentic problems. Literature reveals that there is much variability between raters in scoring the quality of a solution. Construct-underrepresentation in rating is manifested as omission of assessment criteria or idiosyncratic weighting of criteria such that some aspects of performance do not receive sufficient attention. Construct-irrelevance variance can be introduced by the rater's application of extraneous, irrelevant or idiosyncratic criteria (Heller et al., 1998). Suggestions for dealing with these problems in literature include constructing guidelines, using multiple raters and selecting and training raters.

Reliability Related Issues

Reliability in classical tests is concerned with the degree in which the same results would be obtained on a different occasion, in a different context or by a different assessor. Inter- and intrarater agreement is used to monitor the technical soundness of performance assessment rating. However, when these conventional criteria are employed for new assessments (for example using authentic tasks), results tend to compare unfavourably to traditional assessment, because of a lack of standardization of these tasks.

The unique nature of new forms of assessment has affected the traditional conception of reliability, resulting in the expansion of its scope and a change in weights attached to its various components (Birenbaum, 1996). In new assessment forms, it is not about achieving a normally distributed set of results. The most important question is to what extent the decision 'whether or not individuals are competent' is dependable (Martin, 1997). Differences between ratings sometimes represent more accurate and meaningful measurement than would absolute agreement. Measures of interrater reliability in authentic assessment, then, do not necessarily indicate whether raters are making sound judgement and do not provide bases for improving technical quality. Measuring the reliability of new forms of assessment stresses the need for more evidence in a doubtful case, rather than to rely on making inferences from a fixed and predetermined set of data (Martin, 1997).

In line with these views on reliability is Moss' idea (1992) about reliability. She asserts that a hermeneutic approach of 'integrative interpretations based on all relevant evidence' is more appropriate for new assessment, because it includes the value and contextualized knowledge of the reader, than the psychometric approach that limits human judgement 'to single performances', results of which are then aggregated and compared with performance standards.

FUTURE PERSPECTIVES AND CONCLUSIONS

The assessment culture leads to a change in our instructional system from a system that transfers knowledge into students' heads to one that tries to develop students who are capable of learning how to learn. The current societal and technological context requires education to make such a change. The explicit objective is to interweave assessment and instruction in order to improve education. A number of lessons can be learned from the early applications of new assessment programmes.

First, one should not throw the baby out with the bath water. Objective tests are very useful for certain purposes, such as high-stake summative assessment of an individual's achievement, although they should not dominate an assessment programme. Increasingly, measurement specialists recommend the so-called balanced or pluralistic assessment programmes, where multiple assessment formats are used. There are several motives for these pluralistic assessment programmes (Birenbaum, 1996; Messick, 1984): a single assessment format cannot serve several different purposes and decision-makers; and each assessment format has its own method variance, which interacts with persons.

There is a need to establish a system of assessing the quality of new assessment and implement quality control. Various authors have recently proposed ways to extend the criteria, techniques and methods used in traditional psychometrics. Others, like Messick (1995), oppose the idea that there should be specific criteria, and claim that the concept of construct validity applies to all educational and psychological measurements, including performance assessment.

References

American Educational Research Association, American Psychological Association, National Council on Measurement in Education (1985).

Standards for Educational and Psychological Testing. Washington, DC: American Psychological Association.

Archbald, D.A. & Newmann, F.M. (1992). Approaches to assessing academic achievement. In Berlak, H., Newmann, F.M., Adams, E., Archbald, D.A., Burgess, T., Raven, J. & Roberg, T.A. (Eds.), *Toward a New Science of Educational Testing and Assessment* (pp. 139–180). Albany: State University of New York Press.

Birenbaum, M. (1996). Assessment 2000: towards a pluralistic approach to assessment. In Birenbaum, M. & Dochy, F. (Eds.), *Alternatives in Assessment of Achievements, Learning Processes and Prior Knowledge*. Boston: Kluwer Academic.

Birenbaum, M. & Dochy, F. (Eds.) (1996). *Alternatives in Assessment of Achievements, Learning Processes and Prior Knowledge*. Boston: Kluwer Academic.

Campione, J.C. & Brown, A.L. (1990). Guided learning and transfer: implications for approaches to assessment. In Frederiksen, N., Glaser, R., Lesgold, A.A. & Shafto, M.G. (Eds.), *Diagnostic Monitoring of Skill and Knowledge Acquisition* (pp. 141–172). Hillsdale, NJ: Lawrence Erlbaum Associates.

De Corte, E. (1990). Toward powerful learning environments for the acquisition of problem solving skills. *European Journal of Psychology of Education*, 5(1), 519–541.

Dochy, F. (1994). Prior knowledge and learning. In Husén, T. & Postlethwaite, T.N. (Eds.), *International Encyclopedia of Education* (2nd ed., pp. 4698–4702). Oxford/New York: Pergamon Press.

Dochy, F. & McDowell, L. (1997). Introduction: assessment as a tool for learning. *Studies in Educational Evaluation*, 23(4), 279–298.

Dochy, F., Segers, M. & Sluijsmans, D. (1999). The use of self-, peer- and co-assessment in higher education: a review. *Studies in Higher Education*, 24(3), 331–350.

Frederiksen, J.R. & Collins, A. (1989). A system approach to educational testing. *Educational Researcher*, 18(9), 27–32.

Glaser, R. (1990). *Testing and Assessment; O Tempora! O Mores!* Horace Mann Lecture, University of Pittsburgh, LRDC, Pittsburgh, Pennsylvania.

Haertel, E.H. (1991). New forms of teacher assessment. In Grant, G. (Ed.), *Review of Research in Education*, 17, 3–29.

Hall, K. (1995). *Co-assessment: Participation of Students with Staff in the Assessment Process. A Report of Work in Progress*. Paper given at the 2nd European Electronic Conference on Assessment and Evaluation, EARLI-AE list, European Academic & Research Network (EARN) (listserv.surfnet.nl/archives/earli-ae.html).

Heller, J.I., Sheingold, K. & Myford, C.M. (1998). Reasoning about evidence in portfolios: cognitive foundations for valid and reliable assessment. *Educational Assessment*, 5(1), 5–40.

Hill, P.W. (1993). *Profiles and the VCE: Authentic Assessment in a High Stakes Environment*. Paper presented to the VCTA Comview Conference, Melbourne, 1 December.

Kane, M. (1992). An argument-based approach to validity. *Psychological Bulletin*, 112, 527–535.

Linn, R.L., Baker, E. & Dunbar, S. (1991). Complex, performance-based assessment: expectations and validation criteria. *Educational Researcher*, 20(8), 15–21.

Martin, S. (1997). Two models of educational assessment: a response from initial teacher education: if the cap fits. *Assessment and Evaluation in Higher Education*, 22(3), 337–343.

Mayer, R.E. (1992). *Thinking, Problem Solving, Cognition* (2nd ed.). New York: Freeman.

Messick, S. (1984). The psychology of educational measurement. *Journal of Educational Measurement*, 21, 215–238.

Messick, S. (1994). The interplay of evidence and consequences in the validation performance assessments. *Educational Researcher*, 23(2), 13–22.

Messick, S. (1995). Validity of psychological assessment. *American Psychologist*, 50(9), 741–749.

Moss, P.A. (1992). Shifting conceptions of validity in educational measurement: implications for performance assessment. *Review of Educational Research*, 62(3), 229–258.

Moss, P.A. (1995). Themes and variations in validity theory. *Educational Measurement*, 2, 5–13.

Nisbet, J. (1993). Introduction. In *OECD-Curriculum Reform: Assessment in Question*, 25–38. Paris: Organisation for Economic Cooperation and Development.

Nitko, A. (1995) Curriculum-based continuous assessment: a framework for concepts, procedures and policy. *Assessment in Education*, 2, 321–337.

Rogers, P. (1995). *Validity of Assessments*. Contribution to the 2nd EECAE Conference (European Electronic Conference on Assessment and Evaluation), EARLI-AE list, March 10–14.

Shavelson, R.J., Xiaohong, G. & Baxter, G. (1996). On the content validity of performance assessments: centrality of domain-specifications. In Birenbaum, M. & Dochy, F. (Eds.), *Alternatives in Assessment of Achievements, Learning Processes and Prior Knowledge* (pp. 131–142). Boston: Kluwer Academic.

Filip Dochy

RELATED ENTRIES

A

APPLIED FIELDS: FORENSIC

INTRODUCTION

Psychological forensic assessment aims to contribute to rational problem-solving in a forensic context when judgements have to be made about conditions or consequences of human behaviour brought to (criminal or civil) court. We describe a decision-oriented model of the process of psychological assessment that can serve as a general framework for psychological assessment concerning forensic questions. Frequently asked forensic questions relate to (1) psychological problems of parental custody and contact with children after divorce, (2) credibility of witness statements, and (3) prognosis of offence recidivism.

GENERAL CONCEPT

Modern psychological forensic assessment is conceived as an aid for optimizing forensic problem solving in a scientific process of hypotheses-testing. The assessment process can be regarded as a sequence of decisions. Decisions during planning have a crucial impact on assessment results: mistakes in planning may cause invalid results. Additionally, many decisions must be made while realizing the assessment plan and combining the data into results. Explicit rules to aid these decisions are explained and compiled in checklists by Westhoff and Kluck (1998).

This approach is in contrast to the – outdated – trait-oriented comprehensive 'portraying' of the personality. According to this general concept, it is not the personality that has to be evaluated, but the conditions and the course of a person's actions, or the relations between individuals, in the past, present and in the future. There are six sets of conditions influencing human behaviour: (1) environment; (2) organism; (3) cognition; (4) emotion; (5) motivation; and (6) social variables; and their interactions.

In a single case, all empirically relevant conditions and behavioural variables are checked for their contributions to the forensic question put to the psychological expert. In order to test the resulting hypotheses, different sources of information have to be selected, e.g. according to their psychometric properties. Data can be gathered from systematically planned interviews, observation of behaviour, biographical files and standardized procedures (e.g. tests or questionnaires). Assessors balance the costs of a special assessment procedure, e.g. a test, and its benefits. Of course, they take into consideration not only material, but also immaterial costs and benefits for each participant in the assessment process. A competent realization of the assessment plan requires the up-to-date knowledge and skills of a well-trained psychologist. This expert will use the most objective methods of documentation, e.g. tape recording of interviews.

Data from all relevant sources of information are weighted according to the single case and combined in order to reach a decision about each of the initial hypotheses. In a second step the outcomes of these decisions are integrated, in order to answer the forensic question(s) posed by the judicial system. The conclusions are always stated as probabilistic 'if–then'-statements.

The structure of a psychological report according to this assessment process corresponds to the international scientific publication standards and the Guidelines for the Assessment Process (GAP) of the European Association of Psychological Assessment (Fernández-Ballesteros et al., 2001):

1   Client's question (and client)
2   Psychological questions (= hypotheses)
3   Plan and sequence of the investigation (including the names of all investigators, all appointments, duration and locations of meetings)
4   Data

5   Results
6   Recommendations and suggestions (if asked for in the client's question)
7   References
8   Appendix (including psychometric calculations)
9   Signature (of the responsible psychologist)

JUDICIAL SYSTEM AND FORENSIC QUESTIONS PUT TO THE PSYCHOLOGICAL EXPERT

The roles and the tasks of all the participants in legal proceedings differ according to the different judicial systems in Western societies. Consequently, the questions put to forensic psychological experts, and their working conditions, differ as well. Nevertheless, there are common basic forensic-psychological concepts and methods. The following sections will deal with them. They will be illustrated by sketches of the forensic questions most frequently put to psychological experts.

Psychological Reports in Family Law

Writing a psychological report on questions of parental custody and contact of parents with their children after divorce is a very complex task which, primarily, needs thorough planning. Preparation of such a report aims to support the parents' readiness of communication with each other and their educational competence. The results of the psychological expert's work help the judge at the family court to decide in the 'best interest of the child'. Psychological experts optimize this assessment process by using explicit rules. Westhoff, Terlinden-Arzt, and Klueber (2000) explain every single decision that has to be made in this process. Additionally they give checklists containing rules to help avoid errors and mistakes and to minimize judgement biases.

To enable the parents and/or the judge to decide in the 'best interest of the child' requires the operationalization of this hypothetical construct. The psychological expert has to test the following sets of (psychological) variables:

1   the personal attachments of the child;
2   the continuity of personal care and the continuity environment of the child;
3   fostering the development of the child;
4   the attitudes of the child to possible solutions;
5   parents' readiness for communication with each other regarding the child;
6   their readiness to support the personal attachments of the child;
7   strategies of the family to cope with their divorce-related problems.

The psychological expert has to select the most useful, objective, reliable, and valid instruments for gathering the necessary data. There are only very few standardized procedures that match the questions asked by the family court. Most of the relevant data for psychological assessment in family court problems are obtained from systematic, partly standardized interviews and from the systematic observation of relevant behaviour (e.g. 'the strange situation' designed by Ainsworth et al. [1978] for the assessment of attachment quality). The Family Relations Test by Bene and Anthony (1985) can be very useful as a supporting instrument for the systematic interviewing of even young children: it helps the children to verbalize their incoming and outgoing emotions about each member of their family. The still widely used projective techniques as well as trait-oriented personality questionnaires are not validated for answering family court questions: the constitutional right to have or to rear children is not limited by a particular degree of any personality trait. Therefore, personality trait scores cannot be meaningful criteria in deciding with which of the parents the children should live or whether they should have contact with the other party.

Statement Credibility

In criminal investigation, psychological experts may be asked to assess the credibility of statements by witnesses of a crime. Expert knowledge is mainly required in cases of sexual abuse and maltreatment or other violent crimes, especially when children are victims and/or witnesses of such offences and where there is no other evidence than the victim's/witness's statement. Nevertheless, the principal logic and the basic procedure of conducting an expert assessment is not limited to minors or to particular kinds of crime.

The assessment process here is again a hypothesis-testing procedure: starting with the assumption that the statement is not based on a real-life experience of the witness, the expert has to look out for data that rule out this hypothesis. Only if there is strong evidence for the alternative hypothesis, 'the statement is based on an experienced real-life event', can this alternative hypothesis be accepted. In contrast to this, the presupposition that the alleged event has actually occurred would only need very weak supporting evidence to be accepted and would therefore lead to an extremely false-positive bias.

Assessing the credibility of a witness's statement does not rely on 'general trustworthiness' as a kind of personality construct, but refers only to the assessment of the veracity of the specific testimony in a particular case. The general question of credibility assessment can, therefore, be stated as follows: 'Is this individual witness, under the given conditions of the investigation and the possible influences of other people, capable of making this particular statement even if it is not based on real-life experience?' (translated from Steller & Volbert, 1999).

The basic working hypothesis for analysing the content of a witness's statement was developed by Undeutsch (1967); it says that a statement that is based on real-life experience differs systematically from one that lacks this experience. For credibility assessment, this means that the witness's statement has to be analysed according to quality criteria applied to its content, which differentiate between reality-based statements and others. Reality criteria have been described since the beginning of the 20th century in German psychological and juridical literature. Undeutsch (1967) was the first to describe a comprehensive set of reality criteria. Steller and Koehnken (1989) refer to former approaches proposed by several authors and describe a system of five categories of reality criteria (p. 221); these are:

1   general characteristics: logical structure, unstructured production, quantity of details;
2   specific contents: contextual embedding; descriptions of interactions; reproduction of conversation, unexpected complications during the incident;
3   peculiarities of content: unusual details, superfluous details, accurately reported

details misunderstood, related external associations, accounts of subjective mental state; attribution of perpetrator's mental state;
4   motivation-related contents: spontaneous corrections, admitting lack of memory, raising doubts about one's own testimony, self-deprecation; pardoning the perpetrator;
5   elements specific to the offence: details characteristic of the offence.

This integrative expert system has experienced-enhanced theoretical foundation (Ceci & Bruck, 1995). During the last fifteen years many studies of empirical validation of the system have been conducted in field studies and as well as in experimental studies. The criteria system has turned out to be a useful assessment instrument for scientific research and for practical use in assessing the credibility of a witness's statement.

Criteria Based Content Analysis (CBCA) can only lead to a valid credibility assessment if it takes into account certain characteristics of the witness as preconditions for a reliable and valid testimony. These are perception parameters, memory conditions and verbalization. In addition, there are motivational aspects to be considered like readiness to testify, goals, expectations, desires and fears connected with giving true or false testimony.

Furthermore there must be a test of whether there are or ever have been situational conditions that influence the statements so that they can even be made without that particular experience in real life. Statements by very young children in particular are susceptible to inductive and suggestive influences and questions, whether these are intentional or unintentional. Therefore, the 'history' of the statement and its development has to be explored, as well as the cognitive, emotional, and social developmental status of a young child witness.

The complete process of credibility assessment described here is called Statement Validity Assessment (SVA). In 1999, the Federal Supreme Court of Germany decided that expert opinions on the credibility of (child) witnesses are not acceptable in forensic contest unless they meet the standards of an SVA (Bundesgerichtshof, 1999).

Appropriate data for testing the above hypotheses for SVA are mainly obtained from biographical interviews; psychometric tests would have to be selected with regard to their ecological validity for the special aspects of the abilities in the forensic context mentioned above. While severe limitations of sensory perception and developmental delays can be easily observed or assessed by psychometric or otherwise standardized methods, an appropriate test of 'memory' for SVA would have to test 'episodic' memory; a test of 'logical thinking' would have to refer to 'understanding social context'. Special tests of this kind are not yet available.

Consequently, the most important procedure for gathering data to run an SVA is therefore a non-suggestive, systematic interview of the witness (for interviewing strategies, see Milne & Bull, 1999). Observation of overt behaviour can be helpful in certain aspects, but most non-verbal cues (e.g. facial expression or illustrators during speaking) are ambiguous with regard to the veracity of a witness's statement (Koehnken, 1990).

Prognosis of Offender Recidivism

Predicting the risk of recidivism of criminal offenders can very much influence the sentence and – in the case of mentally disordered offenders – the kind and duration of correctional treatment. This prediction task has to balance the severe consequences of false positive and of false negative judgements, both from the viewpoint of the individual offender and of the community.

Prognoses of offender recidivism are fraught with many specific and difficult problems: absolute certainty cannot be achieved by logical reason; the available data for prediction are incomplete; the only data about recidivism risks are those obtained about the individual offender; the important situational conditions can only be vaguely rated.

The process of psychological (and/or psychiatric) prognosis requires four steps of assessment (Rasch, 1999; Dahle, 1999): (1) analysis of the former criminal offences of the individual; (2) assessment of his present mental state (including possible mental disorders or illnesses); (3) analysis of the psychological development of the offender since the latest offence; (4) the general framework (situations, persons, chances) of his prospective living conditions. All these criteria are assessed according to the base rate of

individuals, where a similar constellation of conditions is observed.

Data for this prognosis task come from prison, hospital or therapy records, from some standardized psychodiagnostic questionnaires which have proven themselves as being reliable and valid predictors for criminal recidivism (such as the HCR-20 by Webster et al., 1994 and the Level of Service Inventory [LSI-R] by Andrews et al., 1995). Nevertheless, the most important method is the systematic interview with the offender based on the topics of the prognosis criteria.

CONCLUSIONS

The three topics of forensic assessment described here are only examples. In different countries there are many other forensic questions that are put to the psychological expert. These concern for example: (1) assessment of criminal responsibility, (2) 'lie detection' by psychophysiolgial methods, (3) assessment of the effects of victimization (4) and (other) special problems in civil law. The structure of the assessment process described above does not differ, however, for any forensic question whatsoever put to the forensic psychological expert.

References

Ainsworth, M.D.S., Blehar, M.C., Waters, E. & Wall, S. (1978). *Patterns of Attachment: A Psychological Study of the Strange Situation.* Hillsdale, NJ: Erlbaum.

Andrews, D.A. (1995). The psychology of criminal conduct and effective treatment. In McGuire, J. (Ed.), *What Works: Reducing Reoffending* (pp. 35–62). Chichester: Wiley.

Bene, E. & Anthony, J. (1985). *Family Relations Test, Children's Version, 1985 Revision.* Windsor: The NFER – Nelson Publishing Co. Ltd.

Bundesgerichtshof (1999). Wissenschaftliche Anforderungen an aussagepsychologische Begutachtungen (Glaubhaftigkeitsgutachten). BGH, Urteil vom 30.7.1999 – 1 StR 618/98 (LG Ansbach). *Neue Juristische Wochenschrift,* 2746–2751.

Ceci, S.J. & Bruck, M. (1995). *Jeopardy in the Courtroom.* Washington, DC: APA.

Dahle, K.-P. (1999). Psychologische Begutachtung zur Kriminalprognose. In Kröber, H.-L. & Steller, M. (Eds.), *Psychologische Begutachtung im Strafverfahren* (pp. 77–111). Darmstadt: Steinkopff.

Fernández-Ballesteros, R., De Bruyn, E.E.J., Godoy, A., Hornke, L.F., Ter Laak, J., Vizcarro, C., Westhoff, K., Westmeyer, H. & Zaccagnini, J.L. (2001). Guidelines for the assessment process (GAP): a proposal for discussion. *European Journal of Psychological Assessment, 17*(3), 178–191.

Koehnken, G. (1990). *Glaubwürdigkeit.* München: Psychologie Verlags Union.

Milne, R. & Bull, R. (1999). *Investigative Interviewing – Psychology and Practice.* New York: Wiley.

Rasch, W. (1999). *Forensische Psychiatrie* (2nd ed.). Stuttgart: Kohlhammer (1st ed., 1986).

Steller, M. & Koehnken, G. (1989). Criteria-based statement analysis. Credibility assessment of children's statements in sexual abuse cases. In Raskin, D.C. (Ed.), *Psychological Methods for Investigation and Evidence* (pp. 217–245). New York: Springer.

Steller, M. & Volbert, R. (1999). Forensisch-aussage-psychologische Begutachtung (Glaubwürdigkeitsbegutachtung), Gutachten für den BGH. *Praxis der Rechtspsychologie, 9,* 46–112.

Undeutsch, U. (1967). Beurteilung der Glaubhaftigkeit von Aussagen. In Undeutsch, U. (Ed.), *Handbuch der Psychologie. Forensische Psychologie*, Band 11 (pp. 26–181). Göttingen: Hogrefe.

Webster, C., Harris, G., Rice, M., Cormier, C. & Quinsey, V. (1994). *The Violence Prediction Scheme: Assessing Dangerousness in High Risk Men.* Toronto: Centre of Criminology, University of Toronto.

Westhoff, K. & Kluck, M.-L. (1998). *Psychologische Gutachten schreiben und beurteilen* (3rd ed.). Berlin: Springer (1st ed., 1991).

Westhoff, K., Terlinden-Arzt, P. & Klueber, A. (2000). *Entscheidungsorientierte Psychologische Gutachten für das Familiengericht.* Berlin: Springer.

Marie-Luise Kluck and Karl Westhoff

RELATED ENTRIES

ASSESSMENT PROCESS, CHILD CUSTODY, ANTISOCIAL DISORDERS ASSESSMENT

APPLIED FIELDS: GERONTOLOGY

INTRODUCTION

Older adults and particularly those frequently described as the 'oldest old' (85+) represent the fastest growing population subgroup in most (industrialized) countries around the world. Although high competence characterizes the majority of today's elders (Lehr & Thomae, 2000), a whole gamut of critical situations related to ageing, and particularly to very old age, underscores the need for psychological assessment in older adults. Psychological assessment provides a rational, scientific means for making decisions in these situations, prototypical examples of which are residential decisions (e.g. relocation to an institution or within institutions), treatment decisions (e.g. early diagnosis of dementia coupled with a promising cognitive training intervention), or rehabilitation decisions (e.g. the estimation of an individual's rehabilitation potential and remaining plasticity).

In order to define the content of this article, we first draw from Lawton and Storandt (1984), who suggested a broad conception of assessment: 'An attempt to evaluate the most important aspects of the behaviour, the objective, and the subjective worlds of the person [...]' (p. 258). Second, we argue for a theoretical framework to organize the different types of assessment and numerous instruments found in this rapidly evolving field of gerontology. Our suggestion is to roughly distinguish between three assessment approaches: (1) Person-oriented (P) assessment is aimed to address the older person's cognitive and behavioural competence, personality, and psychological aspects of health. (2) Environment-oriented (E) assessment addresses the social and the physical environment of the ageing person. (3) Finally, the assessment of P×E outcomes evaluates the impact of person–environment transactions on major domains of life quality such as subjective well-being, affect, and mental health. Below, we use this line of thinking to review psychological assessment in gerontology. The challenges of assessing older persons in terms of application and theoretical-methodological issues are discussed shortly thereafter. We end this entry with some general conclusions and the consideration of future perspectives.

MAIN APPROACHES IN THE ASSESSMENT OF OLDER PERSONS AND THEIR ENVIRONMENTS

The following overview draws from both old and new treatments of the assessment of older adults (e.g. Kane & Kane, 2000; Lawton & Storandt, 1984; Lawton & Teresi, 1994). Due to space limitations, each theoretical domain is illustrated using a small number of prototypical instruments that essentially reflect the construct or family of constructs in question (see also Table 1).

Person-Oriented Assessment

Cognitive and Behavioural Competence

Cognition is a major aspect of behavioural competence which undergoes particular decline in the later years. However, two reservations are warranted: first, this is true only for speed-dependent cognitive abilities ('fluid intelligence' in contrast to 'crystallized' intelligence); second, pronounced interindividual variability in performance is characteristic for old age. To test an individual's intellectual ability against the norm, the well-known *Wechsler Adult Intelligence Scale* (WAIS) is a classic in the field of ageing (Wechsler, 1981). Also, while there is a high correlation between cognitive functioning and the so-called 'Activities of Daily Living' (ADL; basic activities such as eating, washing, or dressing) as well as the 'Instrumental Activities of Daily Living' (IADL; more complex activities such as preparing meals, using the phone, or shopping), a separate assessment of ADL and IADL is nevertheless recommended to afford a comprehensive picture of the everyday competence of the older person. Respective assessment procedures (e.g. the classic scale proposed by Lawton & Brody, 1969) have proven to be powerful predictors of institutionalization and mortality. To further complement the evaluation of everyday competence, an additional assessment of leisure activities using an activity list or diary is helpful (Mannell & Dupuis, 1994).

Personality

There has been some debate in psychological gerontology regarding the question of whether personality traits such as the 'Big Five'

(neuroticism, extraversion, openness to experience, agreeableness, conscientiousness; Costa & McCrae, 1985) remain stable across the adult lifespan. Moderate stability has been widely confirmed, with a tendency toward lower stability over correspondingly longer observation periods. From a practical perspective, a recurring question is whether so-called 'problem behaviours' (such as antisocial behaviour, health-related risk behaviours, or the non-use of existing competencies) may be better explained by individual differences in personality. In this regard, the *NEO Personality Inventory* (Costa & McCrae, 1985) is a classic assessment device that has been used intensively with elders. Reservations have to be made regarding the practical utility of these and other personality instruments with respect to the very old and those suffering from mild cognitive impairments; short scales with easily understood items are still rare. Besides standardized testing, a careful semi-structured exploration of the biography and major (and often critical) turning points therein is essential for an in-depth understanding of an older person's current strengths and weaknesses (Lehr & Thomae, 2000).

In a process-oriented perspective of personality, two constructs are particularly useful to explain situation-specific outcomes such as subjective well-being: coping and control. A classic coping instrument is the *Ways of Coping Checklist*, which has also been proved as useful in a shortened version, helpful for assessing the very old (Folkman, Lazarus, Pimley & Novacek, 1987). For measurement of perceived control, we recommend a short instrument newly developed within the context of the Berlin Aging Study (Smith & Baltes, 1999; Smith, Marsiske & Maier, 1996).

Health

Gaining clarity on the influences of health impairments is important for psychological assessment in any age group. However, this is particularly true for older persons. Chronic conditions and multimorbidity occur frequently in later life and are among the most influential explanations of subjective well-being, depression, and the loss of independence. From a psychological perspective, the subjective evaluation of health based on a single-item assessment ('How would you rate your overall health at the present

Table 1. Recommendation of assessment instruments for use with older adults[a]

Assessment domain	Prototypical instrument	Application issues and selected psychometric information[b]
Person-oriented assessment		
Cognitive and behavioural competence	Wechsler Adult Intelligence Scale (WAIS) (Wechsler, 1981)	Very widely used; takes about 1.5 hours to administer;[c] Cronbach's alpha of all subscales >0.70; broad evidence underlining validity.
	Activities/Instrumental Activities of Daily Living Scale (ADL/IADL) (Lawton & Brody, 1969)	Very widely used; takes about 5 minutes to administer; Cronbach's alpha of both scales >0.80; inter-rater r 0.61 (ADL) and 0.91 (IADL); broad evidence underlining validity.
Personality	NEO Personality Inventory (Costa & McCrae, 1985)	Very widely used; takes about 20 minutes to administer; Cronbach's alpha of all subscales >0.70; broad evidence underlining validity.
	Ways of Coping Checklist (Short) (Folkman et al., 1987)	Frequently used; takes about 10 minutes to administer; Cronbach's alpha of subscales 0.47–0.74; some evidence underlining validity.
	Perceived Control (Smith et al., 1996)[d]	Instrument introduced in the Berlin Aging Study; takes about 10 minutes to administer; some evidence underlining reliability and validity.
Health (psychological aspects)	SF-36 (Ware & Sherbourne, 1992)	Frequently used; takes about 10 minutes to administer; Cronbach's alpha of subscales 0.57–0.94; some evidence underlining validity.
Environment-oriented assessment		
Social environment	Social Networks in Adult Life Survey (Kahn & Antonucci, 1980)	Frequently used; administration time depends on persons nominated as social network members; on an average about 30 minutes; reasonable degree of convergence between respondents' and significant others' report; some evidence underlining validity.
	UCLA Loneliness Scale (Russell et al., 1980)	Frequently used; takes about 10 minutes to administer; Cronbach's alpha >0.90; some evidence underlining validity.
	Burden Interview (Zarit et al., 1980)	Frequently used; takes about 10 minutes to administer; Cronbach's alpha >0.70; some evidence underlining validity.
Physical environment	The Housing Enabler (Iwarsson, 1999)	Recently developed instrument; takes about 1.5 hours to administer; inter-rater reliability mean kappas for the different domains assessed 0.68–0.87; some evidence underlining validity.
	Multiphasic Environmental Assessment Procedure (Moos & Lemke, 1996)	Frequently used; data-collection time depends on the size of the institution to be assessed; can take up to about 1 week; Cronbach's alpha of subscales 0.44–0.96; some evidence underlining validity.

(*continued*)

Table 1.   Continued

Assessment domain	Prototypical instrument	Application issues and selected psychometric information[b]
Assessment of person×environment outcomes		
Subjective well-being and affect	Philadelphia Geriatric Center Morale Scale (PGCMS) (Lawton, 1975)	Very widely used; takes about 10 minutes to administer; Cronbach's alpha >0.80 (total score); broad evidence underlining validity.
	Scales of Psychological Well-Being (Ryff, 1989)	Frequently used; takes about 20 minutes to administer; Cronbach's alpha of all subscales >0.70; some evidence underlining validity.
	Positive and Negative Affect Schedule (PANAS) (Watson et al., 1988)	Frequently used; takes about 5 minutes to administer; Cronbach's alpha >0.70; some evidence underlining validity.
Mental health	Center of Epidemiological Studies of the Elderly Depression Scale (CES-D) (Radloff, 1977)	Very widely used; takes about 10 minutes to administer; Cronbach's alpha >0.80; broad evidence underlining validity.
	Mini-Mental State Examination (MMSE) (Folstein et al., 1975)	Very widely used; takes about 10 minutes to administer; inter-rater r >0.80; broad evidence underlining validity.

[a]See also additional description of these instruments in the text.
[b]The psychometric information given here is based on additional published evidence, which is not explicitly cited in this article due to space limitation.
[c]The estimation of duration always refers to the administration with old and very old persons.
[d]We recommend direct contact with the authors of this instrument for more information.

time: excellent, good, fair, or poor?') has proven to be a powerful predictor of subjective well-being in many studies. A multi-item assessment of this construct as well as other health-related aspects is provided by the now classic *SF-36* (Ware & Sherbourne, 1992). Frequently overlooked in its impact on everyday life and well-being, the assessment of pain and its psychosocial impact is recommended as a must for any comprehensive health evaluation of older adults (Parmelee, 1994).

Environment-Oriented Assessment

Social Environment

Aspects of the social environment include the objective size of the social network, the amount of real and perceived social support, interpersonal conflicts, and overall social network evaluations, such as loneliness. Caregivers are a significant part of elders' social environments. A classic instrument to measure social network size as well as some of its major qualitative characteristics is the *Social Networks in Adult Life Survey*

(Kahn & Antonucci, 1980). This instrument defines social network membership using concentric circles, an approach that has proven to be very helpful in differentiating members of the social network in terms of closeness and importance. Another well-established tool to assess the existing network is the *UCLA Loneliness Scale* (Russell, Peplau & Cutrona, 1980) addressing how often the respondent feels isolated and misunderstood and wishes to be involved in more social relationships. Caregiver persons deserve the attention of psychologists as well, given the extensive strain associated with this task and the increased risk of becoming physically and mentally ill. An instrument for assessing the stress of caregivers is the *Burden Interview* suggested by Zarit and colleagues in the early 1980s (Zarit, Reever & Bach-Peterson, 1980).

Physical Environment

Physical environments optimally adapted to the needs of frail elders can take on powerful supportive and stimulating functions in old age (for a review of the according empirical literature, see Wahl, 2001). Gitlin (1998) concluded in her review of checklists providing a comprehensive assessment of the home environment that the psychometric properties of most of these devices are at best unclear. Among the rare strictly tested instruments, we would recommend the 'Housing Enabler' as a promising tool that carefully considers the physical home environment as well as the functional profile of older persons acting within these environments (Iwarsson, 1999). Although many different suggestions have been tossed around, there is no single device with well-proven psychometric properties currently available. In contrast, the assessment of institutional environments serving the elderly has found much attention and more canalized research efforts. A comprehensive measurement device is the *Multiphasic Environmental Assessment Procedure* (MEAP), which is based on a wide-ranging research programme conducted by Moos and associates (Moos & Lemke, 1996) and has also been transferred to other countries (e.g. Fernandez-Ballesteros et al., 1991).

Assessment of Person × Environment Outcomes

Subjective Well-Being and Affect

Subjective well-being, or the cognitive and affective evaluation of the past and present life, has been regarded as a major indicator of successful ageing. The most highly renowned instrument probably is the *Philadelphia Geriatric Center Morale Scale* (PGCMS) (Lawton, 1975). This relatively easy-to-use 17-item scale covers three dimensions of subjective well-being, i.e. agitation, satisfaction with the ageing process, and general life-satisfaction. Due to the clinical nature of this instrument with many items addressing negative thoughts and emotions, it is particularly useful in the clinical, psychological evaluation of an older person, while other instruments more thoroughly address the positive facets of subjective well-being (e.g. Ryff, 1989).

Compared to subjective well-being, the measurement of affect has not yet found very much empirical attention (Labouvie-Vief, 1999). The term 'affect' includes emotions, moods, and feeling states, all of which can be assessed in terms of intensity, frequency, and duration.

A promising assessment tool for use with elders is the *Positive and Negative Affect Schedule* (PANAS) suggested by Watson, Clark, and Tellegen (1988).

Mental Health

Within the spectrum of mental health threats in later life, depression is, besides dementia, the major disease, whose optimal detection requires a combination of expertise from clinical psychology and psychiatry. The *Center of Epidemiological Studies of the Elderly Depression Scale* (CES-D) introduced by Radloff (1977) is widely used, has proven psychometric properties, and works well in elderly populations. Although a score of 17 is widely accepted as an indication of a depressive illness, it is wise to always include at least one other source of information (such as a clinical expert rating) before a final diagnostic decision is made. In addition, because severe cognitive impairments substantially increase as people age – with estimated dementia rates of about 25% beyond the age of 85 years – dementia assessment should be included as a routine part of every older person's clinical evaluation. A classic screening test in this regard is the *Mini-Mental State Examination* (MMSE), originally suggested by Folstein, Folstein, and McHugh (1975). A major advantage of this widely used device is its scoring system, which is well known among clinicians and thus significantly facilitates communication (a score of 23 is generally recommended as indicative of cognitive dysfunction).

SPECIFIC CHALLENGES OF ASSESSING OLDER ADULTS

A number of factors can threaten the internal and external validity of assessing older persons. In the following, only a selective overview of these issues can be provided.

Two messages are important in terms of practical test application: on the one hand, old age is associated with a slowing in fine motor functioning and reaction time, the loss of sensory functioning, and cognitive impairment. One consequence of this is that performance tests that require motor behaviour may not be adequate, at least in some elderly subpopulations (such as geriatric patients).

Furthermore, scales which are normally self-administered (e.g. personality tests) must frequently be administered by a third person, which means, as compared to other age groups, a substantial change in the social psychology of the test situation, for instance in terms of self-disclosure. The length of the instrument is particularly critical in case of very old persons. Furthermore, the response format should remain stable within testing sessions and should be as simple as possible (not more differentiated than a 5-point Likert-type scale). Also, motivational issues, including fatigue, must be considered when creating optimal test circumstances. On the other hand, test strategies found to be very effective and economic in younger persons, such as phone and computer-based assessment, can, in many cases, be transferred to older people as well. With respect to demented elders, the use of observational methods is frequently the only well-functioning assessment procedure for evaluating behaviour and inner states.

A major theoretical-methodological challenge of assessing older persons is the issue of construct invariance. For instance, constructs such as depression or pain might have a fundamentally different semantic at the age of twenty than at the age of ninety years. Moreover, measures might have age-related characteristics with respect to response bias, response format, or the production of missing data. These and other issues as well as tentative solutions have intensively been addressed by Teresi and Holmes (1994).

To conclude, we urge researchers and practitioners to adopt an attitude of 'constructive caution' in interpreting and using test results gathered in elderly populations.

FUTURE PERSPECTIVES AND CONCLUSIONS

The assessment of older persons is an important field of gerontology in terms of research and application. Due to the multitude of measurement instruments suggested in the gerontological literature, it is essential to carefully check the proven psychometric properties *and* practical usefulness of these devices for making adequate instrument selections. Standardized tests, semi-structured assessments, and observational methods should serve as complementary tools in any comprehensive clinical evaluation. An important

task of future research is, as is so often the case, replicative research including different subgroups of elders and the revision of existing devices in order to improve the critical mass of good instruments. The assessment procedures so developed should provide a broad, reliable, and valid description of both the positive and negative sides of the ageing individual.

Acknowledgement

Comments of David Burmedi and Mike Martin on an earlier draft of this entry are very much appreciated.

References

Costa, P.T. & McCrae, R.R. (1985). *The NEO-Personality Inventory. Manual Form S and Form R.* Odessa, FL: Psychological Assessment Resources.

Fernandez-Ballesteros, R. et al. (1991). Evaluation of residential programs for the elderly in Spain and United States. *Evaluation Practice, 12,* 159–164.

Folkman, S., Lazarus, R.S., Pimley, S. & Novacek, J. (1987). Age differences in stress and coping processes. *Psychology and Aging, 2,* 171–184.

Folstein, M.F., Folstein, S.E. & McHugh, P.R. (1975). Mini mental state: a practical method of grading the cognitive state of patients for the clinician. *Journal of Psychiatric Research, 12,* 189–198.

Gitlin, L.N. (1998). Testing home modification interventions: issues of theory, measurement, design, and implementation. In Schulz, R., Maddox, G. & Lawton, M.P. (Eds.), *Focus on Interventions Research with Older Adults,* Vol. 18 (pp. 190–246). New York: Springer.

Iwarsson, S. (1999). The housing enabler: an objective tool for assessing accessibility. *British Journal of Occupational Therapy, 62,* 491–97.

Kahn, R.L. & Antonucci, T.C. (1980). Convoys over the life course: attachment, roles, and social support. In Baltes, P.B. & Brim, O.G. (Eds.), *Life-Span Development and Behaviour* (pp. 253–286). New York: Academic Press.

Kane, R.L. & Kane, R.A. (Eds.) (2000). *Assessing Older People: Measures, Meaning and Practical Applications.* New York, NY: Oxford University Press.

Labouvie-Vief, G. (1999). Emotions in adulthood. In Bengtson, V.L. & Schaie, K.W. (Eds.), *Handbook of Theories of Aging* (pp. 253–267). New York: Springer Publishing.

Lawton, M.P. (1975). The Philadelphia Geriatric Center Morale Scale: a revision. *Journal of Gerontology, 30,* 85–89.

Lawton, M.P. & Brody, E.M. (1969). Assessment of older people: self-maintaining and instrumental activities of daily living. *The Gerontologist, 9,* 179–185.

Lawton, M.P. & Storandt, M. (1984). Assessment of older people. In Reynolds, P.M. & Chelune, G.J. (Eds.), *Advances in Psychological Assessment*, Vol. 6 (pp. 236–276). San Francisco: Jossey-Bass.

Lawton, M.P. & Teresi, J.A. (Eds.) (1994). *Focus on Assessment Techniques*, Vol. 14. New York: Springer.

Lehr, U.M. & Thomae, H. (2000). *Psychologie des Alterns* [Psychology of ageing] (9th ed.). Wiebelsheim: Quelle & Meyer.

Mannell, R.C. & Dupuis, S.L. (1994). Leisure and productive activity. In Lawton, M.P. & Teresi, J.A. (Eds.), *Focus on Assessment Techniques*, Vol. 14 (pp. 125–141). New York: Springer.

Moos, R.H. & Lemke, S. (1996). *Evaluating Residential Facilities: The Multiphasic Environmental Assessment Procedure*. Thousand Oaks, CA: Sage.

Parmelee, P.A. (1994). Assessment of pain in the elderly. In Lawton, M.P. & Teresi, J.A. (Eds.), *Focus on Assessment Techniques*, Vol. 14 (pp. 281–301). New York: Springer.

Radloff, L.S. (1977). The CES-D scale: a self-report depression scale for research in the general population. *Journal of Applied Psychological Measurement*, 1, 387–393.

Russell, D.W., Peplau, L.A. & Cutrona, C.E. (1980). The revised UCLA loneliness scale: concurrent and discriminant validity evidence. *Journal of Personality and Social Psychology*, 39, 472–480.

Ryff, C.D. (1989). Happiness in everything, or is it? Explorations on the meaning of psychological well-being. *Journal of Personality and Social Psychology, 57*, 1069–1081.

Smith, J. & Baltes, P.B. (1999). Trends and profiles of psychological functioning in very old age. In Baltes, P.B. & Mayer, K.U. (Eds.), *The Berlin Aging Study. Aging from 70 to 100* (pp. 197–226). Cambridge: Cambridge University Press.

Smith, J., Marsiske, M. & Maier, H. (1996). *Differences in Control Beliefs from Age 70 to 105.* Unpublished manuscript. Max Planck Institute for Human Development, Berlin.

Teresi, J.A. & Holmes, D. (1994). Overview of methodological issues in gerontological and geriatric measurement. In Lawton, M.P. & Teresi, J.A. (Eds.), *Focus on Assessment Techniques*, Vol. 14 (pp. 1–22). New York: Springer.

Wahl, H.-W. (2001). Environmental influences on ageing and behaviour. In Birren, J.E. & Schaie, K.W. (Eds.), *Handbook of the Psychology of Aging* (5th ed.). San Diego: Academic Press.

Ware, J.E. & Sherbourne, C.D. (1992). The MOS 36-item short-form healthy survey (SF-36). *Medical Care, 30*, 473–483.

Watson, D., Clark, L.A. & Tellegen, A. (1988). Development and validation of brief measures of positive and negative affect: the PANAS scales. *Journal of Personality and Social Psychology, 54*, 1063–1070.

Wechsler, D. (1981). *Wechsler Adult Intelligence Scale – Revised Manual*. New York: The Psychological Corporation.

Zarit, S.H., Reever, K.E. & Bach-Peterson, J. (1980). Relatives of the impaired elderly: correlates of feelings of burden. *The Gerontologist, 20*, 649–655.

Hans-Werner Wahl and Ursula Lehr

RELATED ENTRIES

DEMENTIA, QUALITY OF LIFE, HEALTH, DYNAMIC ASSESSMENT (LEARNING POTENTIAL THEORY, TESTING THE LIMITS), COGNITIVE PLASTICITY, COGNITIVE DECLINE/IMPAIRMENT, FLUID AND CRYSTALLIZED INTELLIGENCE, AUTOBIOGRAPHY, INTELLIGENCE ASSESSMENT THROUGH COHORT AND TIME, CAREGIVER BURDEN, BURNOUT ASSESSMENT

 APPLIED FIELDS: HEALTH

INTRODUCTION

Health psychology is a field within psychology that is devoted to understanding psychological influences on health-related processes, such as why people become ill, how they respond to illness, how they recover from a disease or adjust to chronic illness, and how they stay healthy in the first place (Schwarzer & Gutiérrez-Doña, 2000). Health psychologists conduct research on the origins and correlates of diseases. They identify personality or behavioural antecedents that influence the pathogenesis of certain illnesses. Health psychologists analyse the adoption and maintenance of health behaviours (e.g. physical exercise, nutrition, condom use, or dental hygiene) and explore the reasons why people adhere to risk behaviours (e.g. why they continue to smoke or drink alcohol). Health promotion and the prevention of illness are, therefore, agendas for research and practice, as is the improvement of the health care system in general.

In health psychology, a multitude of variables are assessed, such as physical conditions, health behaviours, quality of life, coping with stress or illness, coping resources, and premorbid personality. Since health behaviours dominate the discipline, the following contribution will focus on this particular subarea.

HEALTH BEHAVIOURS

Many health conditions are caused by such behaviours as problem drinking, substance use, smoking, reckless driving, overeating, or unprotected sexual intercourse. Health behaviours are often defined as behaviours that people engage in to maintain or improve their current health and to avoid illness. They include any behaviour a person performs in order to protect, promote, or maintain his or her health, whether or not such behaviours are objectively effective towards that end (Conner & Norman, 1996; Schwarzer & Renner, 2000).

People are inconsistent in the way they practise multiple health behaviours. For example, a person who exercises regularly does not necessarily adhere to a healthy diet. One reason people's current health habits are not more consistent is that they differ on a number of dimensions (see Table 1).

For a valid and reliable measurement of health behaviours, it is essential to distinguish between these dimensions and to define clearly the subject matter under investigation.

ASSESSMENT OF HEALTH BEHAVIOURS

There are various methods of assessing health behaviours (Renner, 2001). *Questionnaires* that

assess the frequency of past behaviour are the most commonly used methods. There are numerous questionnaires that ask for the average or typical quantity and frequency of alcohol consumption (for an overview, see Sobell & Sobell, 1995), dietary habits, or physical activity. However, the information provided by quantity and frequency measures (QF estimates) is limited because respondents must base their estimates on a large variety of experiences. QF estimates often reflect less drinking and tend to misclassify drinkers compared to daily diary or timeline reports. They also provide lower absolute food intake estimates than a longer, interviewer-administered diet history.

In rare occasions, *physiological methods* can be used, which are most accurate for measuring alcohol consumption (via blood or urine sampling), drug consumption (via immunoassay, hair or sweat bioassay procedures), habitual dietary intakes (via biochemical markers), or physical activity (via doubly labelled water). However, such bioassay methods are only required when a high level of accuracy about recent health behaviour is needed (e.g. for workplace drug testing). They can also be used in addition to self-report data in order to confirm or falsify self-report information (e.g. about recent drug use). However, in some circumstances it may only be necessary to lead respondents to believe that there is an objective way to identify their behaviours via physiological measures, which is done to reduce misreporting. Another direct method is *behavioural observation*, used to assess physical activity among children or a driver's speed, for example.

Unstructured or semistructured *interviews* are qualitative techniques for research on understanding individuals' cognitive and conceptual models of health behaviours and the frames of reference used to organize these behaviours. Therefore, qualitative methods are mainly concerned with exploration and analysis of health behaviour because they

Table 1. Dimensions of health behaviours

• Voluntary; consciously undertaken by the individual	• Involuntary; unconsciously undertaken by the individual
• Avoidance of harmful activities	• Engagement in protective activities
• Undertaken without medical assistance	• Needs professional medical assistance
• Vital	• Non-vital
• Occasional; unstable	• Habitual; stable
• Simple	• Complex, multifaceted

allow the interviewee to address the issues that are relevant to the topics raised by the investigator. One major disadvantage of qualitative methods is that generality is, by definition, not quantifiable. Furthermore, since anonymity is not given, self-reports may be affected by social desirability biases, which lead to overreporting of socially desirable behaviours as well as underreporting of socially undesirable behaviours.

Stone and Shiffman (1994) have labelled strategies for collecting self-reports of respondents' momentary or current state as *Ecological Momentary Assessment* (EMA). EMA studies usually consist of repeated assessment of participants' momentary state as they go about the tasks of daily living in their natural environment. Interval-contingent assessments require assessment at regular intervals. One example is the method of interactive voice response where alcoholics are asked to call in on a regular basis to report their drinking status to the interviewers. Another way is asking respondents to record every episode of smoking, eating, or another behaviour of interest. This event-contingent approach may not lead to a representative sample of the participant's general state, and it requires a clear definition of the triggering event. In contrast, signal-contingent sampling supplies participants with an external signal cue that is usually timed to be emitted at random to prompt them to complete a written assessment or an electronic diary. Signal device beepers, electronic watches, and palmtop computers can be used. EMA is a method that precisely assesses recent health behaviours. Its major advantage is that it minimizes deviations due to recall from memory by relying on respondents' reports of their experience at the very moment of inquiry.

A diary log is a data collection strategy that gathers information as time passes. The distinctive feature of this method is that it yields information that is temporally ordered. It shows the sequence of events and the profile of actions across time. Diary techniques can be particularly useful when data from the same person are required over a considerable period of time and/ or very frequently, such as assessing smoking behaviour, alcohol consumption, or dietary habits, in order to provide a general estimate of the amounts consumed. For example, alcohol consumption diaries often include questions about the frequency of drinking, the type of drink, and the typical quantity consumed on each occasion. In comparison to questionnaires, the diary log format minimizes recall biases associated with retrospective reporting, but daily reporting may be more reactive. In addition, diaries could be valuable for getting access to so-called 'intimate' information (e.g. sexual behaviour).

Timeline Followback Method Reports (TLFB), developed by Sobell and Sobell (1995), provide a detailed insight into health behaviours (smoking, taking drugs, or drinking, etc.) over a designated time period. Participants are asked to provide retrospective estimates of their daily behaviour by using a calendar over a certain time period, ranging up to 12 months prior to the interview. With this method, the pattern, variability, and level of drinking or smoking can be profiled, which is especially useful when precise estimates are needed or when researchers wish to evaluate specific changes in health behaviours before, during, and after interventions. However, this is a rather time-consuming method.

BIASES IN SELF-REPORTS

Some problems shared by all surveys relying on self-reports could seriously decrease internal and external validity (Schwarz & Strack, 1991). Short-term fluctuations, such as in substance use, produced by environmental (e.g. social settings) and psychological (e.g. mood or stress) variables, may affect the psychometric properties of usage measures. For example, there is a tendency for students to become increasingly exuberant as their high school graduation approaches. Increased party activity during the spring months contributes significantly to the actual level of drug use. Therefore, seasonal effects and short-term fluctuations may lead to superficial behavioural changes that could be misinterpreted by researchers as being genuine changes.

Questions about past behaviours assume accurate memory of events as well as willingness to report them to a researcher. However, respondents might not recall the actual events, employing instead various cognitive heuristics (rules of thumb) to estimate frequencies. This could result in certain biases. Individuals use different strategies to answer frequency questions over different time spans. Episodic enumeration (recalling and counting individual incidents) is more likely to be used with shorter time spans in frequency reports, whereas rate-based estimation (projecting the typical rate over the length of the recall period) is more likely to be used when longer time spans are involved. Reported behavioural frequencies for a year are generally lower than 12 times the equivalent frequencies for a month. People probably forget more behavioural instances over the time span of a year than over a month. Therefore, behavioural reports over a month are the more accurate of the two. The use of different time spans across or within studies may lead to inconsistent or even misleading results.

Accurate and reliable measurements of health behaviours, especially drug use and sexual activity, have proven to be difficult because of social desirability influences. People underreport smoking and underestimate alcohol consumption. Self-reports of alcohol consumption can account for as little as half the amount obtained from sales figures. Likewise, the total number of cigarettes sold or otherwise estimated to be consumed is substantially higher than the estimate calculated from smokers' self-reports. In addition, studies that focus on behavioural frequencies consistently yield illusory superiority: respondents report a lower frequency of unhealthy behaviours and higher frequency of healthy behaviours for themselves than for an average peer. Illicit problem behaviours, such as drug or alcohol use, may elicit stronger self-serving biases than more mundane health-threatening behaviours in adolescents (for details, see Renner, 2001).

REFERENCES

Conner, M. & Norman, P. (Eds.) (1996). *Predicting Health Behaviour: Research and Practice with Social Cognition Models*. Buckingham, England: Open University Press.

Renner, B. (2001). Assessment of health behaviours. In Smelser, N.J. & Baltes, P.B. (Eds.), *The International Encyclopedia of the Social and Behavioural Sciences*. Oxford, England: Elsevier.

Schwarz, N. & Strack, F. (1991). Context effects in attitude surveys: applying cognitive theory to social research. In Stroebe, W. & Hewstone, M. (Eds.), *European Review of Social Psychology*, Vol. 2, (pp. 31–50). Chichester, England: Wiley.

Schwarzer, R. & Gutiérrez-Doña, B. (2000). Health Psychology. In Pawlik, K. & Rosenzweig, M.R. (Eds.), *International Handbook of Psychology* (pp. 452–465). London: Sage.

Schwarzer, R. & Renner, B. (2000). Social-cognitive predictors of health behaviour: action self-efficacy and coping self-efficacy. *Health Psychology*, 19(5), 487–495.

Sobell, L.C. & Sobell, M.B. (1995). Alcohol consumption measures. In Allen, J.P. & Columbus, M. (Eds.), *Assessing Alcohol Problems* (pp. 55–73). NIAAA Treatment Handbook Series 4. Bethesda, MD: NIH.

Stone, A.A. & Shiffman, S. (1994). Ecological momentary assessment (EMA) in behavioural medicine. *Annals of Behavioural Medicine, 16*, 199–202.

Britta Renner and Ralf Schwarzer

RELATED ENTRIES

HEALTH, QUALITY OF LIFE, INTERVIEW IN BEHAVIOURAL AND HEALTH SETTINGS, BRAIN ACTIVITY MEASUREMENT, GOAL ATTAINMENT SCALING (GAS), PSYCHOPHYSIOLOGICAL EQUIPMENT AND MEASUREMENTS, OUTCOME ASSESSMENT/ TREATMENT ASSESSMENT, SELF-REPORTS (GENERAL), SELF-REPORT DISTORTIONS, SELF-PRESENTATION MEASUREMENT

APPLIED FIELDS: NEUROPSYCHOLOGY

INTRODUCTION

Neuropsychological assessment as a formal procedure is a relatively recent development. Its evolution has paralleled advances, in the past fifty years, in the areas of neuroscience in general, and cognitive neuroscience in particular. It has also been influenced by developments in applied clinical disciplines such as neurology, neuroradiology, rehabilitation medicine, special education, geriatrics, developmental psychology, etc. In this section, we review the historical trajectory of this aspect of clinical neuropsychology, and present the current state of the field.

HISTORICAL ANTECEDENTS

Neuropsychological assessment did not come of age until after the Second World War. In the second half of the 19th century, there had been a flurry of clinical studies that correlated brain structures and cognitive activity. The work of Broca, Déjerine, Jastrowitz, Korsakoff, Lichteim, Liepmann, Oppenheimer, Ribot, Wernicke, and many others in the latter part of the 19th century described the neurological substrates of disorders such as the aphasias, apraxias, amnesia, and frontal disinhibition (Walsh, 1978; Benton, 2000). However, these advances in localization of function lay dormant (except in the USSR) for over half a century. This approach regained its popularity in the 1950s and 1960s, in part as a result of the work of Brenda Milner and her colleagues in Montreal, who described the pivotal role of the hippocampus in memory (Scoville & Milner, 1957), and in part due to the work of Benton, Zangwill, Hécaen, Ajurriaguera, and Goodglass. Sperry's work and the seminal case study of a human deconnection syndrome (Geschwind & Kaplan, 1962) lent further impetus to the belief that higher cognitive functions could be componentialized and subjected to analysis via objective techniques. Interest in the pioneering 19th century studies and their potential contribution to the study of brain–behaviour relationships was revived by Norman Geschwind in Boston at approximately the same time (Geschwind, 1997).

PARADIGMS IN NEUROPSYCHOLOGICAL ASSESSMENT

Global Measures of Brain Damage

At the outset, the primary goal of the neuropsychological evaluation in the United States was to assist in differentiating behavioural disorders of 'organic' (i.e. structural) nature, from those of 'functional' (i.e. psychological) origin. This focus can be attributed to the influence of psychoanalytic thinking, which postulated that psychiatric disturbance could result from intra-psychic (moral and psychological) and disturbed inter-personal relationships (Hill, 1978: vii). Further, clinicians in the USA and Britain were formed in a positivist, psychometric culture, which has more readily trusted an actuarial, mechanistic approach to data gathering, and statistically driven decision-making algorithms (Meehl, 1954), while being less comfortable with the methodology of single-case studies. Thus Ward Halstead's purpose in designing tests was to determine whether a person had sustained brain damage or not, asking, 'more practically, can convenient indices be found which, like blood pressure, accurately reflect the normal and pathological range of variance for the individual? Is there a pathology of biological intelligence which is of significance to psychiatry and to our understanding of normal behaviour?' (Halstead, 1947: 7). He noted accurately that the tests developed by Binet and standardized by Terman (for the purpose of identifying 'subnormal' children who required remediation in school) were completely insensitive to the effects of brain damage. Citing the work of Hebb and Penfield (1940) he wrote, 'Evidence is now on record to the effect that surgical removal of one or both prefrontal lobes – that is, a mass of brain substance constituting about one-fourth of the total cerebrum – may not significantly alter the I.Q.' (Halstead, 1947: 7).

Fixed and Flexible Batteries

The Halstead–Reitan Battery (Reitan & Davison, 1974; Reitan & Wolfson, 1993) and extensions of it (e.g. Heaton, Grant & Mathews, 1991) gained widespread recognition in the USA from the 1950s as the best practice in neuropsychological assessment, since it provided a means of summarizing an array of observations into numerical values that can be compared across patients and situations, and which provide reliable predictions (Boll, 1981; Russell, 1986). This battery (the Halstead–Reitan Battery; Reitan & Davison, 1974) began as a selection of seven tests chosen for their ability to best discriminate patients with frontal versus non-frontal or non-injured controls. Currently, five of the original seven tests are typically administered to derive an Impairment Index (the proportion of scores in the impaired range), together with the Wechsler Intelligence scales, memory tests, and other tests of specific functions (Lezak, 1995: 709). The five tests include the Categories Test, the Tactile Perceptual Test, the Seashore Rhythm Test, the Finger Oscillation Test, and the Speech-Sounds Perception Test.

Halstead was fully aware of the view that prevailed in the 1930s (and well into the 1960s) that brain dysfunction is unitary (i.e. the notion of equipotentiality). Other tests sensitive to 'brain damage' were also available at that time. A well-known example is the Visual Motor Gestalt Test (Bender, 1938), now commonly referred to as the Bender–Gestalt test. Piotrowski might be credited with developing the first 'impairment index' when he stated (in reference to interpretation of responses to the Rorschach ink blot test) that, 'No single sign alone points to abnormality in the psychiatric sense, to say nothing of organic involvement of the brain. It is the accumulation of abnormal signs in the record that points to abnormality' (Piotrowski, 1937, cited in Lezak, 1995: 773). He considered five signs (out of the ten that he proposed) to be the minimal number needed to support an inference of brain damage, and noted that the number of signs increased with age. Halstead insisted on 'blind' administration of tests by trained technicians to ensure objectivity of results, although his qualitative observations were based on an impressive variety of sources. The use of cut-off scores (usually one and a half or two standard deviations from the mean, indicating impairment) and an Impairment Index (the number or proportion of tests on which the patient's score equals or exceeds the cut-off) as applied to the Halstead–Reitan battery (Reitan & Davison, 1974) attests to the influence of then prevalent theories of brain function on neuropsychological test interpretation. Nonetheless, both Halstead and later Reitan rejected the notion that brain function is unitary, based on the fact that patients with lesions in different areas produced different patterns of performance on the tests (Halstead, 1947; Reitan & Davison, 1974). Over time, there was recognition that identifiable neurological syndromes exist, and rather than apply a fixed battery of tests to everyone, regardless of the diagnosis, a flexible battery approach, espoused by Benton, in which standardized tests are selected to assess the functions most likely to be affected by the presenting conditions, has come to be preferred by the majority of clinicians in the United States.

Alternatives to the Psychometric Approach

The psychometric approach has not gone unchallenged. One of the pillars in the area of assessment in the USA, Anne Anastasi, expressed early concerns about the indiscriminate use of standardized assessment with diverse populations (Anastasi & Cordova, 1953). Further, the essential tenet of this approach is that 'the final solution to a problem, arrived at within a given time, is an objective measure of an underlying cognitive mechanism' (Kaplan, 1988: 129). A number of people have taken issue with such a premise, pointing to the multifactorial nature of the tasks used for assessment, and the various routes that an individual can take to reach a solution (e.g. Luria, 1966; Walsh, 1978; Kaplan, 1988). The score-based approach to assessment is quite different from an attempt to understand brain–behaviour relationships in terms of the way in which the organism or person interacts with the environment to attain a goal, regardless of the integrity of the nervous system. As early as the mid-1920s, Luria and his mentor Vygotsky in the USSR had decided that the best approach to understanding higher cognitive functions was two-pronged: to study their normal development on the one hand, and their 'decomposition' in brain-damaged individuals on the other. Vygotsky felt that the earlier work of the 19th century neurologists was limited by the absence of an adequate theory of psychology (Luria, 1979). Luria and his followers emphasized an analysis of performance based on the belief that behaviours are the result of functional brain systems that interact with each other. Thus, a function could be subserved by various subsystems, and difficulty in performing a task could be the result of a breakdown in any of those mechanisms. Conversely, compensatory routes engaging alternate subsystems can sometimes be utilized to achieve the same goal. This approach was particularly relevant to the rehabilitation of individuals who sustained brain damage during World War II. Analysis of the compensatory strategies that are or can be brought into play to reach a goal (that is, an analysis of the different circumstances that elicit or inhibit a given behaviour) provides a basis for intervention that can enhance the individual's success. Largely for this reason, Luria's approach to neuropsychological assessment has been widely adopted in rehabilitation centres throughout the world (e.g. Caetano & Christensen, 1997). His work has had a wide-ranging impact in neuropsychological practices and assessment in many countries.

Evolving Procedures and Roles for the Neuropsychologist

Christensen (1978) attempted to systematize Luria's approach to testing in order to make his procedures more accessible to a wider audience and to present stimuli in a format and sequence consistent with Luria's conceptualization of cortical functions. In the United States, this approach was assimilated within a quantitative scoring framework by Golden and his colleagues, and is now known as the Luria–Nebraska Neuropsychological Battery (Golden, Purisch & Hammeke, 1985). This battery is rarely in use today, as it has been widely criticized on a number of both conceptual and methodological grounds (Lezak, 1995). The publication in 1976 of Lezak's *Neuropsychological Assessment* (now in its 3rd edition), which describes and reviews many tests, as well as syndromes, provided an important resource to the field. One of the legacies of Luria's conceptualization of a hierarchy of cognitive abilities has been the need to separate the impact of primary on secondary functions (e.g. the need to assess activation and attention as they relate to memory and other higher mental processes). An important distinction must be made, especially in clinical practice, between psychometric testing (which in many clinics is performed by technicians) and neuropsychological assessment (which involves the interpretation and integration of information regarding the patient). A comprehensive neuropsychological evaluation will, at a minimum, address basic attentional, linguistic, visuoperceptual and visuoconstructional, motor, learning and memory, calculations, sequencing, executive and emotional functions, social interactions, and

problem-solving abilities. The importance of reviewing the records, obtaining a comprehensive history, family interviews, and an analysis of the person's goals and behaviour across different settings and over time, provide a more contextualized understanding of the individual as a whole, and better insights into how recommendations can be realistically formulated (Armengol, Kaplan & Moes, 2001). Attention to the role and possible impact on testing of medication, pain, physical limitations, and mental status (including neurovegetative functions such as sleep, appetite, sensorimotor changes, and mood) is essential.

Technological breakthroughs in the field of neuroimaging, specifically the advent of the CT scan in the early 1970s, and more recently with technologies that allow visualization of areas of brain activation (such as funtional Magnetic Resonance Imaging (fMRI) and PET/SPECT scanning), along with the availability of more sophisticated neuropsychological evaluation procedures in clinical settings, has gradually changed the focus and role of neuropsychological assessments. No longer is lesion localization the primary aim; rather, it has shifted in the direction of describing and understanding the functional consequences and rehabilitation implications of brain dysfunction. An important exception to this in the USA has been the area of forensic neuropsychology, where the focus continues to be on establishing the presence of structural brain damage following injury, with its functional and prognostic implications. This is particularly a concern in cases of minor head injury, where neuroimaging is likely to be unhelpful and where the potential for malingering is inevitably raised. This has led to interest in measures designed to detect deception (if only to be able to preemptively refute the assertion of malingering in the majority of cases), as well as an appreciation for the need to take into account the baseline incidence in the normal population of symptoms and patterns of test scores, in order to be able to establish the presence or absence of pathology.

In light of relatively new standards for presenting evidence in courtrooms (i.e. the Daubert rule of 1993), clinical neuropsychologists have had to rely on standardized instruments (rather than clinical experimental techniques) to document changes in functioning.

Over the years, within the experimental tradition of cognitive psychology, investigations of selective deficits in individuals with brain lesions led to the identification of discrete components of complex functions, as well as the development of ingenious and elegant laboratory procedures to demonstrate disconnections, levels of processing, and double dissociation of functions (e.g. Warrington, 1982; Shallice, 1988; McCarthy & Warrington, 1990; Gazzaniga, 1995). Experimental paradigms that have been used with lesioned non-human animals have also been applied in research and clinical settings to see if brain–behaviour relationships established for other species can be successfully applied to the study of humans. A good example is the use of delayed object alternation tasks with individuals who have sustained prefrontal damage (e.g. Oscar-Berman, McNamara & Freedman, 1991).

Current Trends

Edith Kaplan, who was trained by the developmental psychologist Heinz Werner, has formulated and championed a process approach to neuropsychological assessment. 'For Werner (1956) every cognitive act involves "microgenesis" (i.e. an "unfolding process over time"). Thus close observation and careful monitoring of behaviour en route to a solution (process) is more likely to provide more useful information than can be obtained from right or wrong scoring of final products (achievement)' (Kaplan, 1988). The Boston Process Approach, as it is known, attempts to bridge the case study method (grounded in an understanding of neuropsychological syndromes) developed by Luria on the one hand, and the focus on the need for replicable, empirical, and normatively standardized data on the other. This has been pursued in several ways. Following up on developments in cognitive neuroscience, new tests such as the California Verbal Learning Test (Delis et al., 1987) and the Delis–Kaplan Executive Function System (Delis, Kaplan & Kramer, 2001) were developed to better assess aspects of learning and executive function which are found to differ among patients with different neuropsychological disorders. This approach has also included (a) the addition of standardized procedures to existing tests to assist in clarifying the process underlying a patient's response (e.g. the Weschler Adult

Intelligence Scale as a Neuropsychological Instrument or WAIS-RNI, and the Wechsler Intelligence Scale for Children as a Process Instrument or WISC-III PI); (b) the addition of new indices to score existing data that allow for better capture of relevant process variables (e.g. new methods to score the Rey–Osterrieth Complex Figure drawings, as developed by Stern et al., 1995); and (c) a conceptual reanalysis of performance on existing tests based on alternative theoretical models (see Poreh, 2000 for examples of this last approach). Poreh (2000) refers to this new trend as the 'Quantified Process Approach'. One of the potential advantages of computerized approaches to assessment is the ability to capture sequential qualitative aspects of performance, although this potential remains largely unfulfilled at this time.

FUTURE PERSPECTIVES AND CONCLUSIONS

Neuropsychological assessment is central to attempts to understand the biological bases of behaviour. Even as our technology becomes more sophisticated and we unravel genetic codes, behavioural functions must be mapped, and behavioural and cognitive markers for particular syndromes and disorders become more relevant. Structural and functional in vivo neuroimaging techniques provide exciting opportunities to examine patterns of brain activation during the performance of tests and induced psychological states. Neuropsychological assessment must keep pace with the new demands imposed by technological advances and limitations. Tests adapted for presentation during fMRI are good examples of the latter (e.g. Whalen et al., 1998). In the immediate future, the greater use of computerized technologies will open possibilities for more naturalistic assessment, the evaluation of more complex behaviours, and the ability to collect a wide sample of measures, including the incorporation of physiological measures, concomitantly with performance of various activities. One area with particular promise for assessment and rehabilitation is the developing field of virtual reality (Riva, 1997). Neuroimaging has also permitted an analysis of brain functioning in individuals who differ in terms of the ecological demands placed upon them, such as illiterates and bilingual subjects (e.g. Castro-Caldas et al., 1998). The finding that structural and functional differences emerge under different environmental circumstances reinforces the need to take into account issues relating to ecological validity. That is, tests that have been developed for one population may have limited validity when administered to a different population (this certainly applies to populations in different stages or trajectories of development). Similarly, results that are obtained under one set of circumstances (e.g. the clinic or research laboratory) may not generalize to other, more typical daily tasks and situations. Clearly there is much work to be done in this area.

References

Anastasi, A. & Cordova, F.A. (1953). Some effects of bilingualism upon the intelligence test performance of Puerto Rican children in New York. *Journal of Educational Psychology, 44*, 1–19.

Armengol, C.G., Kaplan, E. & Moes, E.J. (2001). *The Consumer-Oriented Neuropsychological Report.* Odesssa, FL: Psychological Assessment Resources.

Bender, L. (1938). A visual motor gestalt test and its clinical use. American Orthopsychiatric Association, Research Monographs, No. 3.

Benton, A. (2000). Historical aspects of cerebral localization. In Riva, D. & Benton, A. (Eds.), *Localization of Brain Lesions and Developmental Functions* (pp. 1–14). London, England: John Libbey.

Boll, T. (1981). The Halstead–Reitan Neuropsychological Battery. In Filskov, S.B. & Boll, T.J. (Eds.), *Handbook of Clinical Neuropsychology.* New York: Wiley-Interscience.

Caetano, C. & Christensen, A.L. (1997). The design of neuropsychological rehabilitation: the role of neuropsychological assessment. In Leon-Carillon, J. (Ed.), *Neuropsychological Rehabilitation: Fundamentals, Innovations, and Directions.* Delray Beach, FL: St. Lucie Press.

Castro-Caldas, A., Petersson, K.M., Reis, A., Stone-Elander, S. & Ingvar, M. (1998). The illiterate brain. Learning to read and write during childhood influences the functional organization of the adult brain. *Brain, 121*, 1053–1063.

Christensen, A.-L. (1978). *Luria's Neuropsychological Investigation* (2nd ed.). Copenhagen: Munksgaard.

Delis, D.C., Kaplan, E. & Kramer, J.H. (2001). *Delis–Kaplan Executive Function System.* San Antonio, TX: The Psychological Corporation.

Delis, D.C., Kramer, J.H., Kaplan E. & Ober, B.A. (1987). *The California Verbal Learning Test Manual.* San Antonio: Psychological Corporation.

Gazzaniga, M.S. (1995). *The Cognitive Neurosciences.* Cambridge: Massachusetts Institute of Technology.

Geschwind, N. (1997). Selected writings. In Devinsky, D.O. & Schachter, S.C. (Eds.), *Norman Geschwind: Selected Publications on Language, Epilepsy, and Behaviour.* Boston: Butterworth-Heinemann.

Geschwind, N. & Kaplan, E. (1962). A human cerebral deconnection syndrome. *Neurology, 12*, 675–685.

Golden, C.J., Purisch, A.D. & Hammeke, T.A. (1985). *Luria–Nebraska Neuropsychological Battery: Forms I and II.* Los Angeles, CA: Western Psychological Services.

Halstead, W.C. (1947). *Brain and Intelligence: A Quantitative Study of the Frontal Lobes.* Chicago, IL: The University of Chicago Press.

Heaton, R.K., Grant, I. & Mathews, C.G. (1991). *Comprehensive Norms for an Expanded Halstead–Reitan Battery: Demographic Corrections, Research Findings, and Clinical Applications.* Odessa, FL: Psychological Assessment Resources.

Hill, D. (1978) Forward to the First Edition of Lishman, W.I., *Organic Psychiatry; The Psychological Consequences of Cerebral Disorder.* Oxford, England: Blackwell Scientific Publications.

Kaplan, E. (1988). A process approach to neuropsychological assessment. In Boll, T. & Bryant, B.K. (Eds.), *Clinical Neuropsychology and Brain Function: Research, Measurement, and Practice* (pp. 129–167). Washington, DC: American Psychological Association.

Lezak, M.D. (1995). *Neuropsychological Assessment* (3rd ed.). New York: Oxford University Press.

Luria, A.R. (1966). *Higher Cortical Functions in Man.* New York: Basic Books.

Luria, A.R. (1979). The making of mind. In Cole, M. & Cole, S. (Eds.), *The Making of Mind: A Personal Account of Soviet Psychology.* Cambridge: MIT Press.

McCarthy, R.A. & Warrington, E.K. (1990). *Cognitive Neuropsychology: A Clinical Introduction.* San Diego, CA: Academic Press.

Meehl, P.E. (1954). *Clinical versus Statistical Prediction.* Minneapolis: University of Minnesota Press.

Oscar-Berman, M., McNamara, P. & Freedman, M. (1991). Delayed response tasks: parallels between experimental ablation studies and findings in patients with frontal lesions. In Levin, H.S., Eisenberg, H.M. & Benton, A.L. (Eds.), *Frontal Lobe Function and Dysfunction.* New York: Oxford University Press.

Poreh, A. (2000). The quantified process approach: an emerging methodology to neuropsychological assessment. *The Clinical Neuropsychologist, 14*, 212–222.

Reitan, R.M. & Davison, L.A. (1974). *Clinical Neuropsychology: Current Status and Applications.* Washington, DC: V.H. Winston & Sons, Inc.

Reitan, R.M. & Wolfson, D. (1993). *The Halstead–Reitan Neuropsychological Test Battery: Theory and Clinical Interpretation.* Tucson, AZ: Neuropsychology Press.

Riva, G. (1997). Virtual reality in neuro-psycho-physiology: cognitive, clinical and methodological issues in assessment and treatment. *Studies in Health Technology and Informatics*, Vol. 44. Amsterdam: IOS Press.

Russell, E.W. (1986). The psychometric foundation of clinical neuropsychology. In Filskov, S.B. & Boll, T.J. (Eds.), *Handbook of Clinical Neuropsychology*. New York: John Wiley & Sons.

Scoville, W.B. & Milner, B. (1957). Loss of recent memory after bilateral hippocampal lesions. *Journal of Neurology, Neurosurgery, and Psychiatry*, 20, 11–21.

Shallice, T. (1988). *From Neuropsychology to Mental Structure*. New York: Cambridge University Press.

Stern, R.A., Singer, E.A., Duke, L.M., Singer, N.G., Morey, C.E., Daugherty, E.W. & Kaplan, E. (1995). The Boston qualitative scoring system for the Rey–Osterrieth complex figure: description and inter-rater reliability. *Clinical Neuropsychologist*, 3, 309–322.

Walsh, K. (1978). *Neuropsychological Assessment: A Clinical Approach*. New York: Churchill Livingstone.

Warrington, E. (1982). The fractionation of arithmetical skills: a single case study. *Quarterly Journal of Experimental Psychology*, *34A*, 31–51.

Whalen, P.J., Bush, G., McNally, R.J., Sabine, W., McInerney, S.C., Jenike, M.E. & Rauch, S.L. (1998). The emotional counting stroop paradigm: a functional magnetic resonance imaging probe of the anterior cingulated affective division. *Biological Psychiatry*, 44(12), 1219–1228.

Carmen Armengol de la Miyar,
Elisabeth J. Moes and Edith Kaplan

RELATED ENTRIES

MEMORY DISORDERS, VISUO-PERCEPTUAL IMPAIRMENTS, EXECUTIVE FUNCTIONS DISORDERS, VOLUNTARY MOVEMENT, EQUIPMENT FOR ASSESSING BASIC PROCESSES, NEUROPSYCHOLOGICAL TEST BATTERIES, OUTCOME EVALUATION IN NEUROPSYCHOLOGICAL REHABILITATION

A APPLIED FIELDS: ORGANIZATIONS

INTRODUCTION

Psychologists interested in describing, diagnosing or changing organizational behaviour are compelled to assess psychological properties of organizations at some stage of their work. It is for this reason that, as in other applied fields, multiple approaches and techniques concerning psychological assessment have been developed and used in organizations. This entry aims to describe a multilevel psychological assessment, adopting a social systems perspective. To this end, we define psychological assessment of organizations, analyse how it is implemented at different levels, and present future perspectives.

CONCEPT AND OBJECTIVES OF ORGANIZATIONAL ASSESSMENT

Psychological assessment of organizations refers to the measure of human behaviour in organizations using scientific instruments. The primary objective of this assessment is to describe the organization as an individual and collective behaviour system accurately. However, psychological measures should be also relevant in terms of practical implications, serving the purpose of helping managers and other members of the organizations to make decisions.

Traditionally, psychological assessment in organizations has been restricted to the measure of individual differences, implicitly assuming that organizational effectiveness is the result of the aggregation of the psychological characteristics of individuals. This individual level of analyses, however, is limited and the measurement of the work group and the organization as a whole offer a complementary and more comprehensive assessment. Psychological properties exist at different levels of analyses and all of them contribute to the effectiveness. Thus, a multilevel assessment is needed in obtaining a deeper description of the organizations.

MAIN TOPICS IN PSYCHOLOGICAL ASSESSMENT AT DIFFERENT LEVELS OF ANALYSES

The Individual Level

There is a persistent interest in the study of individual experiences in organizations and continuously there are emerging topics and controversies (Nord & Fox, 1996). Personality, cognitive, affective, and behavioural variables have been assessed during decades. With this in mind, the most relevant issues currently associated with the measurement of individuals in organizations are summarized in this section.

Personality

Individuals can be characterized by a number of enduring dispositional properties, which help to understand people's behaviours in organizations. One of the most popular methods of assessing personality is derived from the big five theory. Through self-report inventories, five dimensions of personality are measured: (1) extraversion; (2) emotional stability; (3) agreeableness; (4) conscientiousness; and (5) openness to experience. Several authors prefer the use of a composite of several big five constructs, labelled integrity test, because this broader measure can be more reliable in predicting overall job performance. However, narrower trait constructs can show better prediction of specific job performance criteria within specific occupations (Gatewood, Perloff & Perloff, 2000).

Knowledge, Abilities and Skills (KASs)

KASs are defined, respectively, as the amount of factual information known by an individual, his/her conduct of job specific activities, and his/her conduct of generalized job activities. With respect to the abilities, different goals are associated with the measure of general mental ability or 'g' versus specific abilities. Although there is some consensus about the predictive efficiency of the 'g' factor, measures of specific abilities tend to be more useful when the goals are understanding people's behaviours or their classification. Given that abilities, as they are measured by aptitude tests, refer to a wide and general range of human experiences, more circumscribed measures of skills and knowledge

have been developed in order to improve the validity of measures. This is the case of interpersonal skills, which are especially critical in customer service jobs, work groups, and leadership. Also, job knowledge and tacit-knowledge measures are closely related to specific job performance criteria. For instance, subjects can be exposed to a job-related situation, and their capabilities to solve problem situations can be measured through assessment centre procedures.

Individual Performance

Production (e.g. quantity) and other employee behaviour records (e.g. absenteeism) are used as objective direct or indirect measures of individual performance. Also, subjective evaluations from individuals familiar with the work of the focal person are considered (e.g. 360° feedback). These performance indicators are the result of task and contextual performance. The first is defined as the proficiency with which subjects perform core technical activities of well-defined jobs. Thus, cognitive abilities are relevant for predicting task performance. In contrast, contextual performance is defined as extra-task proficiency that contributes more to the organizational goals, including aspects such as enthusiasm and volunteering to make duties not formally part of one's job. It is assumed that personality variables are critical for predicting contextual performance criteria (Arvey & Murphy, 1998).

Work Attitudes

Work attitudes are defined as positive or negative evaluations about aspects of one's work environment (O'Reilly, 1991). The most common constructs measured by attitude instruments are job satisfaction, commitment, involvement, and stress. Satisfaction refers to a emotional state resulting from job experiences. The questionnaires used to measure job satisfaction can be classified in two groups: measures of overall satisfaction and measures of satisfaction with specific aspects of the job (Peiró & Prieto, 1996). The most frequently measured facets are satisfaction with pay, promotion, supervision, and job content (Gatewood et al., 2000). With regard to commitment, there is no generally accepted definition and measurement. While affective commitment measures include aspects such as loyalty towards the organization, the effort to achieve organizational goals, and the acceptance of organization's values, continuance commitment measures are related to the personal sacrifice associated with leaving the organization and the perceived employment alternatives. Finally, another measure of work attitudes refers to the degree to which the job experiences are perceived as stressful. However, caution is needed because self-report measures of stress may be easily inflated by the person's disposition toward negative affectivity (O'Reilly, 1991).

The Group Level

The work group consists of individuals who see themselves and who are seen by others as a social entity, who are interdependent because of the tasks they perform as members of a group, who are embedded in one or more larger social systems (e.g. organization), and who perform tasks that affect others (Guzzo & Dickson, 1996). Psychological assessment at group level is primarily focused on three aspects: design, processes, and performance.

Group Design

Although a good group design cannot guarantee a satisfactory group functioning, it is necessary to facilitate competent group behaviours. It is for this reason that group design should be measured and controlled. Of the different facets of group design (structure of task, group composition, and establishment of norms), composition of group has received increasing attention, especially heterogeneity (Guzzo & Dickson, 1996). Group heterogeneity refers to the mix of abilities, personalities, gender, attitudes, background, and demographic characteristics. In order to work effectively, a 'right mix' of group members is needed. Efforts have been devoted to assess the right mix of members in terms of abilities and personality (West & Allen, 1997). It is the case of 'skill mix', particularly popular within teams in health service settings, which refers to the efficient balance between trained and untrained, qualified and unqualified, and supervisory and operative staff. Also, personality compatibility can be measured. For instance, according to Schutz's theory of fundamental interpersonal relations orientations (FIRO) there are three basic needs expressed in group interaction: needs for inclusion, control, and affection. A compatible balance of initiators and receivers of control,

inclusion, and affection characterize effective groups.

Group Process

It is generally assumed that, in addition to group design, the process of interaction among group members affects the effectiveness of the group as a whole. As Hackman (1987) pointed out, assessing group process can pursue different goals. A trained observer can focus on the interpersonal transactions that reflect conscious and unconscious social and emotional forces (e.g. who is talking with whom). Group process assessment can also be focused on the issues of interaction directly related to work of group on its task (e.g. the degree to which knowledge and skill members are used). Group interaction can result in 'synergy'; that is, outcomes that are different from those that would be obtained by simply adding up the contributions of individuals (Hackman, 1987). Synergy can be positive (e.g. a very creative solution of a job-related problem) or negative (e.g. a severe failure of coordination). In general, different methods can be used to assess group process. It is the case of some assessment centre techniques (e.g. simulation), where real job tasks are represented and a group of individuals is assessed by a group of judges.

Group Performance

Three criteria are typically used to measure group performance: (1) group-produced outputs, (2) the influences of group for its members, and (3) the state of the group as a performing unit (see Guzzo & Dickson, 1996; Hackman, 1987). Although some objective indicators of group outputs can be measured (e.g. quantity), objective criteria are only available for a restricted number of work groups in organizations. In general, the assessment from others (e.g. a manager) is more critically associated with the consequences for a group and its members than objective measures. It is for this reason that there is a tendency to assess outputs in terms of satisfaction of the standards of the people ('clients') who receive and/or review the output. The second measure is related to the impact of group on individuals. It is assumed that the cost of generating group outputs is high if its members are dissatisfied. Accordingly, the degree to which the group experiences satisfy the needs of group members should be also assessed. The third measure reflects the probability that a group performs effectively in the future. Although the present outputs of a group can be satisfactory, it is possible that the social processes by which these outputs are obtained hamper the group as a performing unit, and its members are not willing anymore to work together on future tasks.

The Organization Level

Individuals and work groups are embedded in a more general organizational system that can be measured itself. Psychological properties of organizations as a whole, such as culture, climate, and performance, can also be assessed.

Culture and Climate

Although culture and climate have been sometimes used as synonyms, they refer to different concepts. As Schneider (1985) pointed out, culture is a deeper construct than climate has been. While organizational climate is defined as the shared perceptions of employees related to the practices, procedures, and behaviours that are rewarded and supported in an organization, culture refers to the beliefs, norms, and values underlying the policies and activities, as well as the manner in which the norms and values systems are communicated and transmitted. Consequently, the modes by which culture and climate are assessed are also different. Culture is usually measured by using qualitative and case study methodologies. In contrast, the survey approach is the dominant method in measuring climate (Schneider, 1985).

Organizational Performance

Financial performance and productivity are considered as the typical measures of organizational performance as a whole. In addition, other measures associated with customer responses of satisfaction and perceived quality have received increasing attention. While economic measures of performance reflect quantity of outputs, psychological measures of customer evaluations refer to quality of outputs as they are perceived by the customer (Fornell, 1992). Psychological measures offer information that is not included in current-term financial measures (Aaker & Jacobson, 1994). In the absence of alternatives, short-term financial gains are usually used as indicators of long-term prospects. However, the strategies devoted to increase long-term performance often diminish short-term earnings. The myopic management style, focused on short-term gains, can be corrected by considering non-financial measures. In fact, the measurement of customer perceptions of product quality is able to predict information concerning long-term competitiveness that is not captured by short-term financial measures (see Aaker & Jacobson, 1994).

FUTURE PERSPECTIVES

An Integrated Assessment of Organizations

In the preceding discussion, we have analysed how the psychological assessment is implemented at different levels of organizations. However, a more integrated perspective can be considered where the different levels of analyses are interrelated showing complex interactions. Herriot and Anderson (1997) proposed that the relationships between measures at individual, group, and organizational levels of analyses could show three kinds of patterns: complementary, neutral, and contradictory. The complementary interaction is observed when a high score at one level of analysis is desirable in combination with a high score at another level (e.g. when high interpersonal skills are required for both individual work and group working). The neutral interaction occurs when a high score on a construct is desired at one level and, simultaneously, it is not applicable at another level of analysis (e.g. when interpersonal skills are required for group working, but they are not related to individual performance). Finally, the contradictory interaction is observed when a high score at one level of analysis is desirable in combination with a low score at another level (e.g. when extraversion is desirable for team working, but introversion is positively related to individual performance). Because of its relevance to research and management, future efforts are needed in developing and testing these kinds of approaches. An integrated assessment is able to describe an organization more accurately, given that it serves to diagnose their complex and contradictory character.

Links between the Context of Organizations and Psychological Assessment

It is generally assumed by managerial orientations that organizations are free in order to design and implement practices and policies (see Morishima, 1995). However, the external context of organization impacts on the organizational choices, including the type of procedures and techniques used in the psychological assessment. For instance, Rousseau and Tinsley (1997) suggested that the culture of a country (e.g. in terms of individualism vs. collectivism) can be related to the appropriateness of individual versus group measures of performance, as well as to the emphasis on individual-job versus individual-organization or work-group fit measures. Also, Herriot and Anderson (1997) indicated that organizations are now subjected to an environment that changes with an increasing speed and unpredictability. In this context, organizations emphasize the psychological assessment related to employee flexibility, personality, and potential to innovate. Additionally, it is also likely to expect that, in some circumstances, organizations impact on their external context. For instance, organizations can demand an education system in which certifications are highly job-related, given that this type of education can facilitate the measurement and the managerial decisions (e.g. in a selection process). Thus, reciprocal influences between organizations and their contexts can be studied in the future. A contingency approach can be proposed where the psychological assessment depends on the characteristics of external contexts and the nature of the relations between these contexts and organizations.

The Political Face of Psychological Assessment in Organizations

Research and practice in organizations espouses a rational perspective in understanding psychological assessment. Organizations are often defined as rational and efficiency-seeking systems, and managers use psychological assessment in order to achieve valued organizational outcomes. However, their political 'face' should also be considered. Following this perspective, the organization is seen as a political system with competing groups and interests, each with its own perceptions of organizational realities. The political face is not everything, but it serves to understand some events related to psychological assessment. Additionally, the ignorance of power in organizations can result in managerial failures and incomplete assessment at different levels of analyses. For instance, there is not only a dominant culture in organizations but also 'countercultures' that reflect alternative values. Usually, individuals and work groups that have values and perceptions congruent with those of organizations, especially with the top-management group, also have more power and influence (Friedlander, 1987). Accordingly, it is reasonable to expect that divergent thinking will not be reflected in the measurement of culture. Also, psychological assessment is likely to be used to reinforce and justify the values and perceived tasks of the dominant coalition. Powerful coalitions act within their own reality, which is not necessarily better than other realities constructed within the organization as a whole. Alternative cultures can reflect adaptive values in terms of initiative and creativity. The ignorance of these cultures has contributed to long-term disasters in many companies (see Dachler, 1989). Thus, more effort is needed in order to include the diversity of organizational 'cultures' in psychological assessment, as well as in studying the impact of power forces and power games on measurement decisions at different levels of analyses.

CONCLUSIONS

A multilevel psychological assessment has important potential benefits. Using this perspective, the great complexity of organizations is diagnosed, given that the organization is considered as an open social system with different measurable subsystems. Psychologists can focus their psychological assessment at different levels of analyses. Thus, this perspective serves to consider both the micro domain's focus on individuals and groups and the macro domain's focus on the organization as a whole.

Additionally, the multilevel psychological assessment is enriched if three complementary perspectives are also incorporated in the future. First, a more integrated assessment can be considered, assuming that constructs measured at different levels of analyses can show complex, even contradictory, relationships. Secondly, there is a need to study the reciprocal influences, in terms of psychological assessment, between organizations and their external contexts. Finally, the political face of organizations should be measured and analysed in order to obtain a richer portrait of psychological assessment in organizations.

References

Aaker, D.A. & Jacobson, R. (1994). The financial information content of perceived quality. *Journal of Marketing Research, 31,* 191–201.

Arvey, R.D. & Murphy, K.R. (1998). Performance evaluation in work settings. *Annual Review of Psychology, 49,* 141–168.

Dachler, H.P. (1989). Selection and the organisational context. In Herriot, P. (Ed.), *Handbook of Assessment in Organisations* (pp. 45–69). Chichester: John Wiley & Sons.

Fornell, C. (1992). A national customer satisfaction barometer: the Swedish experience. *Journal of Marketing, 56,* 6–21.

Friedlander, F. (1987). The ecology of work groups. In Lorsch, J.W. (Ed.), *Handbook of Organisational Behaviour* (pp. 301–314). Englewood Cliffs: Prentice-Hall, Inc.

Gatewood, R.D., Perloff, R. & Perloff, E. (2000). Testing and industrial application. In Goldstein, G. & Hersen, M. (Eds.), *Handbook of Psychological Assessment* (pp. 505–525). Oxford: Elsevier Science Ltd.

Guzzo, R.A. & Dickson, M.W. (1996). Teams in organisations: recent research on performance and effectiveness. *Annual Review of Psychology, 47,* 307–338.

Hackman, J.R. (1987). The design of work teams. In Lorsch, J.W. (Ed.), *Handbook of Organisational Behaviour* (pp. 315–342). Englewood Cliffs: Prentice-Hall, Inc.

Herriot, P. & Anderson, N. (1997). Selecting for change: how will personnel and selection psychology survive? In Anderson, N. & Herriot, P. (Eds.), *International Handbook of Selection and Assessment* (pp. 1–34). Chichester: John Wiley & Sons.

Morishima, M. (1995). Embedding HRM in a social context. *British Journal of Industrial Relations, 33,* 617–640.

Nord, W.R. & Fox, S. (1996). The individual in organisational studies: the great disappearing act? In Clegg, S.R., Cynthia, C. & Nord, W.R. (Eds.), *Handbook of Organisation Studies* (pp. 148–174). London: Sage Publications.

O'Reilly, C.A. (1991). Organisational behaviour: where we've been, where we're going. *Annual Review of Psychology, 42,* 427–458.

Peiró, J.M. & Prieto, F. (Eds.) (1996). *Tratado de Psicología del Trabajo* (2 vols.). Madrid: Síntesis.

Rousseau, D.M. & Tinsley, C. (1997). Human resources are local: society and social contracts in a global economy. In Anderson, N. & Herriot, P. (Eds.), *International Handbook of Selection and Assessment* (pp. 39–61). Chichester: John Wiley & Sons.

Schneider, B. (1985). Organisational behaviour. *Annual Review of Psychology, 36,* 573–611.

West, M.A. & Allen, N.J. (1997). Selecting for teamwork. In Anderson, N. & Herriot, P. (Eds.), *International Handbook of Selection and Assessment* (pp. 492–506). Chichester: John Wiley & Sons.

José Maria Peiró and Vicente Martínez-Tur

RELATED ENTRIES

ORGANIZATIONAL CULTURE, LEADERSHIP IN ORGANIZATIONAL SETTINGS, OBSERVATIONAL TECHNIQUES IN WORK AND ORGANIZATIONAL SETTINGS, RISK AND PREVENTION IN WORK AND ORGANIZATIONAL SETTINGS, SELF-REPORTS IN WORK AND ORGANIZATIONAL SETTINGS, CENTRES (ASSESSMENT CENTRES), APPLIED FIELDS: WORK AND INDUSTRY

APPLIED FIELDS: PSYCHOPHYSIOLOGY

INTRODUCTION

The major focus of this entry will be to provide a clear rationale for the application of psychophysiological approaches and methods to areas of applied psychology. We will examine the reasons for their application, the psychological constructs and processes to be assessed, the methods employed, and specific issues concerning applied uses of these techniques. Specific guidance on psychophysiological recording has been dealt with elsewhere, together with entries on brain activity and ambulatory monitoring. For background reading and a general reference source, Cacioppo, Tassinary and Berntson's *Handbook of Psychophysiology*, 2nd Edition (2000) is recommended. Other useful introductory texts include Caccioppo and Tassinary (1990), Hugdahl (1995) and Stern, Ray and Davis (1980).

DEFINITIONS AND CONSTRUCTS

Psychophysiology can be loosely defined as the study of psychological constructs and processes using non-invasive physiological measures (see Cacioppo, Tassinary & Berntson, 2000; Turpin, 1989). Traditionally it is distinguished from physiological psychology by emphasizing the importance of studying the intact and conscious organism, usually in the absence of invasive techniques, which might disrupt and limit consciousness or behaviour. As such, the usual domain of psychophysiology has been the measurement of peripheral autonomic and central cortical measures within human participants studied whilst engaged in psychologically relevant tasks or natural situations. In contrast, physiological psychology has tended to use animal subjects and to measure invasively, usually directly from the nervous system, using implanted electrodes, and frequently employing invasive manipulations such as lesioning, infusion of pharmacological agents, direct stimulation etc. More recently, these boundaries have become less distinct since physiological psychology has been incorporated within the greater multidisciplinary arena of neuroscience, and psychophysiology has been extended by more direct but still non-invasive measures of brain activity and structure such as functional imaging, dense array electroencephalography and magnetography (see Cacioppo et al., 2000). Nevertheless the cardinal features of psychophysiology as being the study of psychological processes, largely from human participants and using non-invasive physiological measures, are central to the successful application of the discipline to more applied areas of study.

APPLIED PSYCHOPHYSIOLOGY

Psychophysiology has always been essentially an applied discipline since its identity has been very much to do with the measures employed and their various applications. Recently, Cacioppo et al. (2000) described this as systemic psychophysiology, which refers to the study of the various physiological systems (i.e. electrodermal, cardiovascular, cortical etc.) with respect to measurement, quantification and their relationships to psychological processes and paradigms. Much psychophysiological research has been methodologically focused in validating either specific physiological measures or their use as indices of psychological constructs. Subsequently, these measures have then been applied to theoretical questions derived from other branches of psychology including both fundamental and applied research. Traditional areas of application have included psychopathology research and the search for physiological markers of psychological disorder, as well as the development of clinical assessment and outcome measures (Keller, Hicks & Miller, 2000; Stoney & Lentino, 2000; Turpin, 1989). The measurement of stress and cognitive performance using psychophysiological parameters has also meant that these techniques have been used extensively within human factors and ergonomic research (Kramer & Weber, 2000). Other applied areas where psychophysiological approaches have been adopted have included attitude measurement, applied developmental psychology, environmental and specific polygraphy (i.e. lie detection) applications (Cacioppo et al., 2000).

What are the benefits of using psychophysiological approaches? The answer lies in the range of psychological constructs and paradigms for which psychophysiological indices or measures have been derived. Cacioppo et al. (2000), in addition to describing 'systemic psychophysiology', also identified 'thematic psychophysiology' which describes topical areas of psychophysiological research. They cited the following examples: cognitive psychophysiology (human information processing and physiological events); social psychophysiology (reciprocal relationships between social systems and physiology); developmental psychophysiology (developmental and ageing processes); clinical psychophysiology (study of disorders); environmental psychophysiology (person–space interactions); and applied psychophysiology (psychophysiological technologies such as biofeedback, lie detection, man–machine instruction etc.). These topics are exhaustively covered within their handbook. Similarly, we can identify at a more detailed level a myriad of psychological processes and constructs (e.g. attention, attitudes, emotion, memory consolidation) for which there are claimed to be psychophysiological indices or correlates (see Hugdahl, 1995). For example, a class of evoked potential measures of brain activity called the 'P300' is said to be associated with a variety of psychological processes surrounding stimulus evaluation, categorization and context updating (Donchin & Coles, 1988). Similarly, evoked potential Mis-Match-Negativity (Näätänen, 1992), cardiac deceleration (Graham, 1979) and the electrodermal response (Siddle, 1983) have all been associated with the detection of mismatches due to changes in stimulus novelty or significance.

It is apparent that psychophysiological correlates exist for a wide range of psychological constructs. The question, therefore, arises as to what advantages psychophysiological assessments present with respect to performance or self-report measures. It is claimed that psychophysiological measures have the following advantages: they are objective and free of either subjective or observer bias, they are continuous and unobtrusive measures, they can accurately indicate the timing of psychological events, and they may indicate the nature of mechanisms underlying the brain–behaviour relationships under study. Within an applied setting, many of these advantages become even more important. The ability to obtain objective and continuous measures which do not require either self-report or observation means that physiological measures indicating psychological changes in either state or processes may be studied in difficult or inaccessible environments. These could range from space flight to studying arousal processes in married couples during naturalistic social interaction (Gottman & Levenson, 1992). The emphasis on objective versus subjective report also means that data may be obtained from individuals with communication difficulties either due to cognitive impairment or age and temperament. Indeed, with respect to many psychological processes, it is argued that a comprehensive understanding is not possible without recourse to physiological measurement. Lang's classical work (Lang, 1968; Turpin, 1991) on the measurement of anxiety and the three systems approach which utilized

behavioural, cognitive and physiological approaches is a prime example of this argument. Moreover, there may be situations where systematic biases might be introduced with respect to self-report (i.e. forensic settings) where the assessment of 'truth and honesty' (i.e. lie detection) or the presentation of certain disorders (e.g. Post-Traumatic Stress Disorder) are claimed to be more accurately assessed using psychophysiological techniques. This raises the interesting question as to how objective psychophysiological indices truly are and whether they themselves can be subject to conscious manipulation and bias (Iocano, 2000).

Doubts concerning objectivity are not the only disadvantages to be considered when adopting psychophysiological techniques. Whether claimed psychophysiological indices of putative psychological constructs are either reliable or valid may also be subject to challenge. With respect to reliability, psychophysiological measures might be heavily influenced by the setting and situation in which they are obtained. This may give rise to problems of generalizability, if care is not taken to carefully standardize methods, settings, paradigms and materials. Reported test–retest reliabilities vary considerably across different psychophysiological indices (Strube, 2000). Similarly, due to the practical constraints of assessing large numbers of individuals, standardized norms for psychophysiological measures are few and far between. This provides very definite psychometric limits to the application of psychophysiology to the single case.

Specific psychophysiological theories are also limited and measures are usually interpreted within the context of other theoretical frameworks from cognitive psychology and elsewhere. Sometimes this results in psychophysiological measures having particular interpretations, which are assumed rather than empirically based. An example being whether cardiac deceleration, a common psychophysiological response, should be interpreted as an index of the orienting response, the detection of stimulus novelty or merely just stimulus registration (Ohman, Hamm & Hugdahl, 2000). Similarly, psychophysiological constructs can persist even though their empirical basis may be either insubstantial or even contradictory. Perhaps the best example, and one which is commonly used within applied settings, is the notion of arousal.

Arousal is still used as a major explanatory concept in many applied social and clinical settings despite much psychophysiological research, which has been deeply critical of the construct (Gardener, Gabriel & Diekman, 2000; Turpin & Heap, 1998). This can lead to major problems regarding interpretation and construct validity.

Finally there are issues to do with practical utility. Psychophysiological measures usually require complex electronic machinery for physiological measurement, sophisticated computer software for data acquisition and analysis, laboratory environments and trained technicians. These resources are expensive and may not be widely available. Furthermore, the reliance on laboratory settings may also preclude many applied settings. Consequently, many recent applications have relied on the development of ambulatory methods.

Applied Constructs and Uses

As discussed above, there are a wide range of potential applications for psychophysiological measures and approaches. Within the space limitations of this entry it is impossible to present even an overview of different types of applications. However, we will describe some recent examples. Before doing so, a distinction perhaps needs to be made between applied research and research in applied settings. Much psychophysiological research is geared to applied questions relating to psychological understanding of important issues such as health and disease. However, this tends to be laboratory-based experimental research and is directed at using psychophysiological measures to seek answers to fundamentally theoretically relevant questions but with consequences for applied areas. For example, there has been an impressive growth in studies employing the potentiated startle paradigm as a method of assessing emotional valence, and anxiety in particular (Lang, Bradley & Cuthbert, 1990). At a theoretical level, this research has increased understanding of how fear cues are processed at both conscious and pre-attentive levels, and the possible neural substrates underlying some of these mechanisms (Lang, Davis & Ohman, 2000). The question arises, therefore, whether these techniques can be transferred into an applied setting and used for more practical purposes. Could measures of potentiated startle be used to discriminate between different diagnostic groups of anxiety disorders, could they accurately track response to treatment and indicate therapeutic outcomes and gains? Unfortunately, there are in reality few areas of psychophysiology which are used routinely in professional psychology practice. Perhaps the only real examples are biofeedback treatments and polygraphy. Nevertheless, major areas of psychophysiological endeavour such as evoked potential research influence practical applications in other areas such as clinical neurology or audiometry.

Common clinical research applications of psychophysiological measures have been as measures of attention within schizophrenia: these have included electrodermal measures of orienting, P300 type event-related potentials (EP) and early sensory gating EPs (see Chapter by Miller et al., in Cacioppo et al., 2000). Recent applications of dense array EEG have looked at lateral distribution of brain activity, especially over prefrontal cortex and its relationship to affective processing and depression (Davidson, 1992). Anxiety disorders research has focused on the potentiated startle paradigm (Lang et al., 1990), as described above, together with studies of autonomic balance within Generalized Anxiety Disorders (Thayer & Lane, 2000). Therapeutic applications of psychophysiology continue in the form of studies of relaxation and meditation (Turpin & Heap, 1998) and biofeedback (Schwartz, 1995).

Psychophysiological studies within the discipline of health psychology continue to examine mechanisms underlying cardiovascular disease (Stoney & Lentino, 2000). Studies aimed at assessing cardiovascular reactivity to psychologically challenging events continue to be performed (e.g. Fredrickson & Matthews, 1990). A particular focus is the relationship between laboratory-based studies and ambulatory-monitoring based studies of reactivity. Psychophysiological measures have been particularly adopted to assess the role of stress in contributing to the aetiology and maintenance of common physical conditions. In addition to the usual autonomic measures such as heart rate and blood pressure reactivity, many studies examining 'stress' exploit techniques from psycho-immunology and endocrinology: using biochemical assays of immune or hormonal status (Uchino, Kiecolt-Glaser & Glaser, 2000).

Human factors psychophysiology has traditionally examined problems such as assessing alertness and sleep quality, mental workload and performance, and man–machine interactions. A full range of measures have been employed including endocrinological assays (Lovallo & Thomas, 2000) to evoked potential applications to man–machine interactions. Spectral analysis of physiological parameters over extended periods of time or different activities is a technique frequently employed in ergonomic applications. Mulder (1992), in particular, has exploited measures of heart rate variability to assess attentional and workload factors.

CONCLUSIONS

Psychophysiology has a long tradition as being used within applied settings. Advances in technology have broadened the range of settings in which psychophysiological measures can be obtained. Developments in neuro-imaging (e.g. Reiman, Lane, Van Petten & Bandettini, 2000) also mean that psychophysiological techniques can now address exciting questions of functional brain–behaviour relationships. Hopefully, these techniques will be extended so as to include more applied questions and applications.

References

Cacioppo, J.T. & Tassinary, L.G. (Eds.) (1990). *Principles of Psychophysiology: Physical, Social, and Inferential Elements*. Cambridge: Cambridge University Press.

Cacioppo, J.T., Tassinary, L.G. & Berntson, G.G. (Eds.) (2000). *Handbook of Psychophysiology*. Cambridge: Cambridge University Press.

Davidson, R.J. (1992). Anterior cerebral asymmetry and the nature of emotion. *Brain and Cognition, 20*, 125–151.

Donchin, E. & Coles, M.G.H. (1988). Is the P300 component a manifestation of context updating? *Behavioural and Brain Sciences, 11*, 354–356.

Fredrickson, M. & Matthews, K.A. (1990). Cardiovascular responses to behavioural stress and hypertension: a meta-analytic review. *Annals of Behavioural Medicine, 12*, 30–39.

Gardener, W.L., Gabriel, S. & Diekman, A.B. (2000). Interpersonal processes. In Cacioppo, J.T., Tassinary, L.S. & Berntson, G.G. (Eds.), *Handbook of Psychophysiology* (pp. 643–664). Cambridge: Cambridge University Press.

Gottman, J.M. & Levenson, R.W. (1992). Marital processes predictive of later dissolution: behaviour, physiology, and health. *Journal of Personality and Social Psychology, 63*, 221–233.

Graham, F.K. (1979). Distinguishing among orienting, defense and startle reflexes. In Kimmel, H.D., Van Olst, E.H. & Orlebeke, J.F. (Eds.), *The Orienting Reflex in Humans* (pp. 137–167). Hillsdale, NJ: Erlbaum.

Hugdahl, K. (1995). *Psychophysiology: The Mind-Body Perspective*. Cambridge: Harvard University Press.

Iocano, W.G. (2000). The detection of deception. In Cacioppo, J.T., Tassinary, L.S. & Berntson, G.G. (Eds.), *Handbook of Psychophysiology* (pp. 772–793). Cambridge: Cambridge University Press.

Keller, J., Hicks, B.D. & Miller, G.A. (2000). Psychophysiology in the study of psychopathology. In Cacioppo, J.T., Tassinary, L.S. & Berntson, G.G. (Eds.), *Handbook of Psychophysiology* (pp. 719–750). Cambridge: Cambridge University Press.

Kramer, A.F. & Weber, T. (2000). Applications of psychophysiology to human factors. In Cacioppo, J.T., Tassinary, L.S. & Berntson, G.G. (Eds.), *Handbook of Psychophysiology* (pp. 794–813). Cambridge: Cambridge University Press.

Lang, P.J. (1968). Fear reduction & fear behaviour: problems in treating a construct. In Shlien, J.M. (Ed.), *Research in Psychotherapy*. Washington, DC: American Psychological Association.

Lang, P.J., Bradley, M.M. & Cuthbert, B.N. (1990). Emotion, attention, and the startle reflex. *Psychological Review, 97*, 377–398.

Lang, P.J., Davis, M. & Ohman, A. (2000). Fear and anxiety: animal models and human cognitive psychophysiology. *Journal of Affective Disorders, 61*, 137–159.

Lovallo, W.R. & Thomas, T.L. (2000). Stress hormones in psychophysiological research. In Cacioppo, J.T., Tassinary, L.S. & Berntson, G.G. (Eds.), *Handbook of Psychophysiology* (pp. 342–367). Cambridge: Cambridge University Press.

Mulder, L.J.M. (1992). Measurement and analysis of heart rate and respiration for use in applied environments. *Biological Psychology, 34*, 205–236.

Näätänen, R. (1992). *Attention and Brain Function*. Hillsdale, NJ: Erlbaum.

Ohman, A., Hamm, A. & Hugdahl, K. (2000). Cognition and the autonomic nervous system. In Cacioppo, J.T., Tassinary, L.S. & Berntson, G.G. (Eds.), *Handbook of Psychophysiology* (pp. 533–575). Cambridge: Cambridge University Press.

Reiman, E.R., Lane, R.D., Van Petten, C. & Bandettini, P.A. (2000). Positron emission tomography and functional magnetic resonance imaging. In Cacioppo, J.T., Tassinary, L.S. & Berntson, G.G. (Eds.), *Handbook of Psychophysiology* (pp. 85–114). Cambridge: Cambridge University Press.

Schwartz, M.H. (1995). *Biofeedback – A Practitioner's Guide* (2nd ed.). New York: Guilford Press.

Siddle, D.A.T. (1983). *Orienting and Habituation: Perspectives in Human Research*. Chichester, UK: Wiley.

Stern, R.M., Ray, W.J. & Davis, C.M. (1980). *Psychophysiological Recording*. New York: Oxford University Press.

Stoney, C.M. & Lentino, L.M. (2000). Psychophysiological applications in clinical health psychology. In Cacioppo, J.T., Tassinary, L.S. & Berntson, G.G. (Eds.), *Handbook of Psychophysiology* (pp. 751–771). Cambridge: Cambridge University Press.

Strube, M.J. (2000). Psychometrics. In Cacioppo, J.T., Tassinary, L.S. & Berntson, G.G. (Eds.), *Handbook of Psychophysiology* (pp. 849–869). Cambridge: Cambridge University Press.

Thayer, J.F. & Lane, R.D. (2000). A model of neurovisceral integration in emotion regulation and dysregulation. *Journal of Affective Disorders, 61,* 201–216.

Turpin, G. (Ed.) (1989). *Handbook of Clinical Psychophysiology*. Chichester: Wiley.

Turpin, G. (1991). The psychophysiological assessment of anxiety disorders: three-systems measurement and beyond. *Psychological Assessment, 3,* 366–375.

Turpin, G. & Heap, M. (1998). Arousal reduction methods: relaxation, biofeedback, meditation and hypnosis. In Hersen, M. & Bellack, A. (Eds.), *Comprehensive Handbook of Clinical Psychology. Adults: Clinical Formulation and Treatment*, Vol. 6 (pp. 203–227), London: Elsevier.

Uchino, B.N., Kiecolt-Glaser, J.K. & Glaser, R. (2000). Psychophysiological modulation of cellular immunity. In Cacioppo, J.T., Tassinary, L.S. & Berntson, G.G. (Eds.), *Handbook of Psychophysiology* (pp. 397–424). Cambridge: Cambridge University Press.

Graham Turpin

RELATED ENTRIES

AMBULATORY ASSESSMENT, ANXIETY ASSESSMENT, ANXIETY DISORDERS ASSESSMENT, PSYCHOPHYSIOLOGICAL EQUIPMENT AND MEASUREMENTS, BRAIN ACTIVITY MEASUREMENT, EQUIPMENT FOR ASSESSING BASIC PROCESSES, APPLIED FIELDS: HEALTH, APPLIED FIELDS: CLINICAL

A APPLIED FIELDS: WORK AND INDUSTRY

INTRODUCTION

Very broadly, one might say that wherever people are busy there is a chance and a need for psychological assessment. However, it is impossible to name all fields in work and industry which are open for psychological assessment. The psychological assessor just has to look at the world of work and industry around him in order to find out what he might contribute. This may be done in terms of theories and constructs which allow evaluations of work and industriousness, by instruments which operationalize constructs and measures that are reliable and valid or in terms of methods, designs, and results to present to a customer or a team of experts.

One approach to systematize assessment in applied fields in general, and of work and organization in particular, is to take an Individual, Group, or Organizational perspective.

INDIVIDUAL PERSPECTIVE

Starting with assessing the individual within a company or an organization one might question 'what, when, what for': of course, psychological assessment is of interest in order to learn more about the individual's strengths and weaknesses, about his attitudes and beliefs, and about his competencies and potentials. Here, methods used in mental tests, reaction time studies, occupational personality scales (Ones & Viswesvaran, 2001), motivation scales, and opinion questionnaires are called for. The aim is to describe a person as fully as is needed to evaluate on how she or he will do (well) on a prospective job. Thus data at job entry are used to forecast the 'zone of proximal development' of an applicant. One has to recognize (see Furnham, 2001) that an individual:

- *chooses* a job based on pay, location, job security, and training based on his personality traits, attitudes, and values
- *adapts* to a job out of necessity, insight, motivation
- *changes* a job by altering the physical and social environments
- *evolves* with new technology, markets and global requirements according to what he understands are necessary requirements in the future.

All this is open for assessment. But assessment of an individual does not stop at job entry. Any job confronts incumbents with a variety of minor and major challenges. One of these is to learn to function well at a certain position. Thus learning gains or developing several competencies are of interest to assessors. Assessment results lead to improvement of the interaction with the individual and the work place by considering human factors for improved functioning, by motivating the individual, by designing up to date remuneration schedules, by considering aptitude treatment interactions in designing effective training programmes, by monitoring communication and coordination with others, by communication and coordination programmes, to name but a few.

A new aspect for assessment emphasizes licensing professionals as an aspect of overall quality assurance in production and service. Companies may want coworkers who have knowledge, skills, and competencies to deal with their products within the company itself but, even more important, they want this at all customer sites. The service person for a database product of a regional bank may create quite a loss if a new programme release is not handled with care. This is part of the liability movement in modern societies which assures that products and services do not do any harm to others. Here, with each new product and each new service, there has to be a model of proper use and a contingent assessment of its components. So assessment takes place in regard to accreditation and licensing.

During a person's professional life there are numerous occasions to assess what an incumbent's profile of competencies is like, or to find out about the set of strengths and weaknesses in order to assign someone to a proper position for the sake of himself and the benefit of the organization. Placement decisions should be based on sound assessment data.

Even at the end of a career, assessment may help to find a new position outside the organization by means of outplacement or early retirement plans. One might also have to look at the loss or weakening of competencies and skills over time and find means and measures to decide about rehabilitation programmes. Here, it is of interest what residual competencies are available, to which degree, and how they should be built upon in a rehabilitation training.

Seen as such, psychological assessment is a work-life-long companion activity which serves the individual and the organization in order to fruitfully monitor the interaction between both of them. The psychological well being of the individual is a target as is the reasonable use of his forces at work. Assessment emphasizes prerequisites to job demands, trainings, and personality developments (Roberts & Hogan, 2001). However, it also emphasizes effects of all the aforementioned after a new job was assigned, a training was accomplished, and a personal challenge was taken. Assessment data are vital to human resource management and thus have to be valid, reliable, and objective in the first place to sustain all personnel decisions that are taken.

GROUP PERSPECTIVE

Assessment at the group level is mainly oriented towards productivity, conflict resolution, good communication, and coordination. One may want to look at the social functioning of a team by means of a sociogram (Moreno, 1951; see entry on Sociometric Methods), by means of interaction analysis (Bales, 1950, SYMLOG), by means of a questionnaire about role ambiguity (Rizzo et al., 1970), or by observation studies in an obtrusive or non-obtrusive manner (Putnam and Jones, 1982).

Some assessments are status oriented and should allow judgement on what are the prevailing attitudes or obstacles in group life in order to go from there to improve it. Actions may involve changes in group memberships, group trainings, or re-groupings at large.

More of a process-oriented approach is called for if monitoring of actions is of interest. Longitudinal assessment data are needed to describe what changes take place in a group and explain why these changes occur. Cross-sectional data reveal how different groups develop independently from each other. Harrison and Shirom (1998: 161) present some key group factors: (1) Group Composition, Structure and Technology like nationality mix, divergence of professions, decision procedures, control procedures like evaluation, comprehensiveness of controls, and (2) Group Behaviour, Processes, and Culture like relations among members, reward types, direction of information flows, openness, decision making, supervisory behaviour (supportiveness, participation, goal setting, performance expectation, conflict management).

Topics may range from modern shift systems, remuneration schedules, new production techniques, new forms of cooperation and coordination, integrating minorities, client centredness of work, quality assurance at each production step, self-organization of the team, group cohesion, role conflicts/clarity, mobbing propensity, coworker–supervisor relationship, learning needs. This list is by far not complete but it displays minor and major topics which may be subject to an in-depth assessment. Practical problems are closely linked to some kind of sometimes political action on behalf of the management and the labour union representatives.

ORGANIZATIONAL PERSPECTIVE

Organizational assessment is by far more macroscopic than the foregoing two approaches (see Harrison & Shirom, 1998). First, it has to be defined: what is the organization under scrutiny? Some of them are small shops in a small region and others are global players operating on quite diverse markets. Second, the perspective may change if one considers an organization from within, its inner dynamics, its

members, in contrast to considering clients, suppliers, and organization members at the same time.

In order to assess, i.e. describe, an organization's climate, for example, quite different actions have to be taken. One has to look at what attracts people to an organization, what keeps them within, and what are the typical characteristics of those who are there for a given time (Schneider, 1987). So even for personnel marketing and in recruitment campaigns one may want to use self-assessment instruments. Pritchard and Karasick (1973) provide a scale with eleven dimensions like Autonomy, Conflict vs. Cooperation, Social Relations, and Structure, to name but a few. Based on this and other research, James and James (1989) provided a model which emphasizes (1) role stress and lack of harmony, (2) challenge at work and autonomy, (3) facilitation by leadership and support, (4) cooperation, friendliness, and warmth in a team. As Weinert (1998) points out these factors are related to roles, leadership, and teams.

Organizational culture (Schein, 1985; see entry on Organizational Culture), an adjacent construct, emphasizes common shared values, norms, goals, beliefs, and perspectives. Thus here the scope is on meaning, intentions, purpose of work and tasks, as well as on methods to achieve organizational essentials and underlying norms and values in all what members do. Artefacts and behaviour patterns are far more visible than beliefs, cognitions, and basic assumptions within a company. Sackman (1992) referred to cognitive orientations as part of organizational culture and identified four forms:

- dictionary knowledge – definitions of labels and definitions
- directory knowledge – assumptions of how common practices work and what are presumably causal relations
- recipe knowledge – prescriptions for improving remedy processes or urgencies
- axiomatic knowledge – about nature of things and why events occur.

The reasons for an assessment are manifold, too. There may be a constant interest in changes of the organization, a need to assess the organization prior or as a consequence of a re-organization, an in-depth view of what merging with another company had as an effect, to assure that new products and production techniques are adopted by the workforce, to find out how new markets would affect the members, and what challenges are perceived in the light of new clients. The scope is always to find out something about the organization as a whole. Most of this will be assessed by means of questionnaires, but some is discernible by interviews, observation, or unobtrusively browsing through documents, self-reports, marketing material, and guidelines. More qualitative than quantitative results are likely with the latter.

An investigation may be launched at the beginning of a change in organizational behaviour or the end of a campaign. In particular, many questionnaire-based actions are meant to shed light on aspects the management wants to emphasize. So the questions are one means to convey to the workforce what is considered essential to the organization. The questions altogether convey a message as such, and subsequent results tell everyone the degrees to which essentials are shared. If, for example, there are several questions about cooperation formats then the responders are geared to particularly perceive this construct and evaluate his momentary reflections on this. Thus the questionnaire is highlighting a concept which may be on the organization's agenda.

Scaffoldings of how to organize an assessment are given by the Open-Systems Analysis (Harrison & Shirom, 1998), Six Box Model (Weisbord, 1976), Stream Analysis (Porras, 1987), just to name a few.

ASSESSMENT INSTRUMENTS

There are published instruments which allow even standardized interpretation. But their drawback may be that they do not address the present problem and thus do not answer the question raised fully. In the case of assessment of an individual's behaviour there are numerous instruments from Differential Psychology. But if one addresses group and organizational problems one finds less and less formalized and standardized instruments. One help may be 'instruments' shared among psychological assessors who worked out a scale, evaluated it at one site or

within one company, but made it available to others. At least some kind of documentation about intended scope, design, and small scale results and evaluations are available (Drasgow & Schmitt, 2001).

So ad hoc instruments are created by internal staff or outside consultants. Often a sound explication and elaboration of constructs is missing. Some instruments lack a theory-based pre-evaluation of questions to be asked. This is sacrificed to immediate results because market forces drive the management to deciding. One may definitely wish that even a 'simple' questionnaire is considered and valued as a measuring instrument in itself. It provides sound data only if it has been designed and developed according to goals, established theory, constructs, and empirical results. In 'rapid practice' questions are ambiguous and so are results. Often the questionnaire falls short of a sound coverage of facets and so data are incomplete or highly one-sided.

There are, of course, good guidelines (Fleishman & Quaintance, 1984) as to how to construct a good measure. Many instruments ought be based on sound job descriptions to pre-define relevant target behaviours, task-related competencies, and job-related social skills (see entry on Job Characteristics). Also (item and/or person) sampling techniques (Shoemaker, 1973) allow cost saving at the expense of not asking everyone that should be invested in instrument design and evaluation.

As was mentioned above, apart from questionnaires, interviews, observations, survey-feedback approaches, simulations, grid-techniques (Jenkins, 1998), and scenario techniques may be used, for example. However, the less standardized they are, the more assessment errors that may be committed. In general, any instrument should be closely designed for the purpose it has to serve. Ad hoc instruments should be avoided, but instruments with some empirical underpinning should be preferred. The former only allow an assessment per fiat and the latter an assessment per fact.

ASSESSMENT DESIGNS

Designs of how to conduct an evaluation study (Cook & Campbell, 1979; Sanders, 1994) have been available for a long time. But in regard to sound assessment of effects of introduced changes at the person, group, or organizational level there ought to be more than one measure of an effect, and even a pre-measure should be available as a standard against which one may judge any changes. Restructuring of an organizational unit is quite an investment, and it is desirable to trace back to a prior measure what and how much has changed. Often enough an effect is ascertained but vanishes over time. So more than one post measure is advocated. Designs may be borrowed from Educational Psychology (Campbell & Stanley, 1963) to assure that assessed changes are true changes and not just valid for a short time.

Not only is it possible to sample individuals, but content areas can be sampled as well (Shoemaker, 1973; Hornke, 1978) in order to have a sound picture. It is not necessary to ask everyone the same questions, and have many duplicated answer patterns. Good design of individuals and content samples yield sufficient reliable and valid data and will help to save costs quite a bit. It just demands a bit of prior construct knowledge, some speculation about possible effects, and a kind of intelligent logistic in regard to data collection. An all-embracing survey is not always worth its efforts and investments. Sometimes, less is much more!

FUTURE PERSPECTIVES AND CONCLUSIONS

The initial and implicit question, of what the fields of psychological assessment are in regard to work and organization, can only be answered at a surface level. It is left to the ingenious assessor and his efforts, interests, and creativity to sense what the fields of assessment activities are. No one assigns them to him and even a contract allows for sound science-based assessments the contractor himself might not have had in mind. Applied fields in this sense are all those fields which help to improve an individual's, a group's, and an organization's life. The latter is for the benefit for all of them.

References

Bales, R.F. (1950). A set of categories for the analyses of small group interaction. *American Sociological Review, 15*, 146–159.

Campbell, D.T. & Stanley, J.C. (1963). Experimental and quasi-experimental designs for research on teaching. In Gage, N.L. (Ed.), *Handbook of Research on Teaching*. Chicago, IL: Rand McNally.

Cook, T.D. & Campbell, D.T. (1979). *Quasi-Experimentation-Design & Analysis Issues for Field Settings*. Chicago, IL: Rand McNally.

Drasgow, F. & Schmitt, N. (Eds.) (2001). *Measuring and Analyzing Behaviors in Organizations*. San Francisco: Jossey Bass Publishers.

Fleishman, E.A. & Quaintance, M.K. (1984). *Taxonomies of Human Performance: The Description of Human Tasks*. Orlando, FL: Academic.

Furnham, A. (2001). Personality and individual differences in the workplace–person–organization fit. In Roberts, B.W. & Hogan, R. (Eds.), *Personality in the Workplace* (pp. 223–252). Washington DC: American Psychological Association.

Harrison, M.I. & Shirom, A. (1998). *Organizational Diagnosis and Assessment: Bridging Theory and Practice*. Thousand Oaks, CA: Sage Publications.

Hornke, L.F. (1978). Personen-Aufgaben-Stichproben. In Klauer, K.J. (Ed.), *Handbuch der pädagogischen Diagnostik*, Band 1. Düsseldorf: Schwann.

James, L.A. & James, L.R. (1989). Integrating work environment perceptions. Explorations into the measurement of meaning. *Journal of Applied Psychology, 74*, 739–751.

Jenkins, M. (1998). *The Theory and Practice of Comparing Causal Maps*. London: Sage.

Moreno, J.L. (1951). *Sociometry, Experimental Method and the Science of Society*. New York: Beacon House.

Ones, D.S. & Viswesvaran, C. (2001). Personality at work: criterion-focused occupational personality scales used in personnel selection. In Roberts, B.W. & Hogan, R. (Eds.) *Personality in the Workplace* (pp. 63–92). Washington, DC: American Psychological Association.

Porras, J.I. (1987). *Stream Analysis*. Reading, MA: Addison-Wesley.

Pritchard, R.D. & Karasick, B. (1973). The effects of organizational climate on managerial job performance and job satisfaction. *Organizational Behaviour and Human Performance, 9*, 110–119.

Putnam, L.L. & Jones, T. (1982). Reciprocity in negotiations: an analysis of bargaining interaction. *Communication Monographs, 49*, 171–191.

Rizzo, J.R., House, R.J. & Lirtzman, S.I. (1970). Role conflict and ambiguity in complex organisations. *Administrative Science Quarterly, 15*, 150–153.

Roberts, B.W. & Hogan, R. (2001). *Personality in the Workplace*. Washington, DC: American Psychological Association.

Sackman, S. (1992). Cultures and subcultures: an analysis of organizational knowledge. *Administrative Science Quarterly, 37*, 140–161.

Sanders, J.R. (Ed.) (1994). *The Program Evaluation Standards* (2nd ed.). Thousand Oaks, NJ: Sage Publications.

Schein, E.H. (1985). *Organizational Culture and Leadership*. San Francisco, CA: Jossey-Bass.

Schneider, B. (1987). The people make the place. *Personnel Psychology*, 28, 447–479.

Shoemaker, D.M. (1973). *Principles and Procedures of Multiple Matrix Sampling*. Cambridge: Cambridge University Press.

Weinert, W. (1998). *Organisationspsychologie* (4th ed.). Weinheim: Psychologie Verlagsunion.

Weisbord, M.R. (1976). Diagnosing your organizations: six places to look for trouble with or without theory. *Group & Organizational Studies*, 1, 430–447.

Lutz F. Hornke

RELATED ENTRIES

<small>COGNITIVE/MENTAL ABILITIES IN WORK AND ORGANIZATIONAL SETTINGS, INTERVIEW IN WORK AND ORGANIZATIONAL SETTINGS, MOTOR SKILLS IN WORK SETTINGS, OBSERVATIONAL TECHNIQUES IN WORK AND ORGANIZATIONAL SETTINGS, WORK PERFORMANCE, PHYSICAL ABILITIES IN WORK SETTINGS, RISK AND PREVENTION IN WORK AND ORGANIZATIONAL SETTINGS, SELF-REPORTS IN WORK AND ORGANIZATIONAL SETTINGS, CENTRES (ASSESSMENT CENTRES), ACHIEVEMENT MOTIVATION, LEADERSHIP IN ORGANIZATIONAL SETTINGS</small>

A ASSESSMENT PROCESS

INTRODUCTION

In solving daily life problems, we automatically execute a lot of judgement and decision making. We also gather information or consult others in order to make well-informed decisions and judgements. The assessment process in the field of psychology is about the gathering and processing of information by a professional in order to get well-informed judgements and decisions concerning a specific request made by a person or an organization. The client is either a person or an organization that made the request; the subject is the person or organization who is the target of the assessment. Psychological assessment refers to the judgements and decisions made by the professional psychologist. Assessment process refers to how these judgements and decisions came about and how these judgements and decisions are communicated to the client.

Contrary to the layperson, the professional has the obligation to process his judgements and decisions according to three sets of standards: ethical standards, social standards, and methodological standards. Ethical and social standards apply to all fields of professional psychology. It is with respect to the methodological standards that the professional gets his or her identity as an academically educated expert in a particular field. Most methodological standards in the field of assessment published in the standards of the professional organizations are related to the methods and procedures the psychologist uses in collecting information. Standards or guidelines with respect to the assessment process are not so well articulated. Actually, it is only recently that the European Association of Psychological Assessment installed a Task Force to formulate Guidelines for the Assessment Process (GAP) (Fernández-Ballesteros, 1998).

This entry contains five sections. The first section highlights the distinction between assessment and testing. The second section analyses the assessment process. The third section mentions some of the biases that may disturb the intrinsic validity of the process and mentions some remedies proposed in the literature. The fourth section points to developments in the field that try to model the assessment process. The last section pays attention to the most recent contribution to the field, which is the production of professional guidelines for the assessment process.

ASSESSMENT AND TESTING

The relatively late attention to the quality of the assessment process might partly be explained by the dominant position of the psychometric approach in assessment. Psychometrics is the discipline that deals with formal statistical foundations of measuring and validating individual differences. In the field of applied psychometrics this tradition focuses on two issues: the development of psychometrically sound tests and the validation of these tests with respect to external criteria. A test is psychometrically sound when it proves to be an objective, quantitative, and reliable measure of individual differences. It is psychometrically valid when its scores predict the position of the examinee on some other criterion or characteristic. In order to be accepted as a test, the instrument must be constructed and validated according to the prescriptions of the existing psychometric theories (Allen & Yen, 1979, and Nunnally, 1978, for further documentation). The psychometric tradition has proven very valuable and both test theory and testing are integrated in the academic education of assessors. Moreover, the tradition has witnessed distinguished scholars who published fine books on testing and test use (Anastasi & Urbina, 1997; Cronbach, 1990).

Assessment is a summary term which refers to all the activities the assessor performs in producing an answer to the client's request. These activities may include testing among other activities, such as analysing the client's problem, generating hypotheses about its causes and searching for the appropriate intervention. It is the analytical and constructive quality of the assessment process that distinguishes assessment from mere testing.

THE PROCESS

The assessor has to analyse the request and to integrate his or her results in a case formulation, which takes into account the available knowledge in the field. In doing so he or she has to follow the same kind of logic any scientific researcher follows in deductively inferring hypotheses, in testing these hypotheses, and in formulating conclusions in the framework of the available knowledge. However, although the assessment process follows the same kind of logic as in any scientific search process the context differs basically from that of the scientific process (De Groot, 1969; Sloves et al., 1979).

For the scientific researcher in psychology the context of his or her work is the body of knowledge at a particular domain and the researcher is focused upon phenomena not yet explained within that particular domain. The goal of the scientific researcher is to find descriptions and explanations that generalize across persons and situations. It is not the concrete person who is the subject, but general phenomena such as perception, motivation, or personality dimensions. The assessor, however, focuses on the person with his or her particular problems in his or her past as well as present situation. The primary goal of the process is to contribute to the solution of a person's problems. The more the person's problems can be described and understood as representative for problems shared by other persons, the more the assessor can rely on a common body of knowledge and apply procedures and protocols developed for specific groups of clients. However, in many cases the assessor cannot just apply already established knowledge. Instead, he or she has to rely on his or her methodological and professional experience in using the state of the art in the field to design a client-tailored procedure and to make an educated interpretation of the outcome.

When talking about the client's problem, it is important to make a distinction between adjustment problems and clinical problems. By problem is meant a psychological state of uncertainty for which neither the client nor his or her social network sees a preferred course of action. Adjustment problems are problems all people encounter in their daily life, and for which they may want to seek professional advice. Examples of such problems are marital conflict, study choice, and career planning. Clinical problems are problems that have dysfunctional effects on the psychological and social well being of the client. In assessing adjustment problems, the assessor uses instruments and applies knowledge that belongs to the domain of general psychology. In assessing clinical problems, the assessor uses tools and knowledge that pertain to the domain of clinical psychology.

An important part of the assessment process is the explanation to the client of why and how the assessment tools are applied and how strong the evidence is, which may be the outcome of the process. The kind of assessment tools and knowledge involved are triggered by the requests the assessor has to answer. The simplest format to describe such requests is that of a question as if phrased by the client. Examples of such questions within the non-clinical domain are: 'Am I suited for this type of job?', 'Which qualities do I have to develop in order to be eligible for this particular education programme?', 'What conditions at the workplace are responsible for getting the high rate of job turnover?' Examples of questions in the clinical domain are: 'How serious are my anxieties?' 'Why does it happen to a person like me to have burn out', 'Do I need psychological treatment to master my feelings of self-worthlessness?'

Concrete requests and related questions automatically specify the kind of assessment activities the assessor should perform in order to answer the questions. For instance, in order to answer the question 'How serious are my anxieties?', the assessor first has to describe the anxieties and, secondly, he or she has to evaluate the anxieties against some standard or norm of severity. In answering the question 'What conditions are responsible for the labour turnover', the assessor first has to check whether the turnover is unusually high (again evaluation against a standard). Secondly – when the latter is the case – he or she has to hypothesize about conditions and, thirdly, to test these hypotheses by collecting data and evaluating the outcome.

Whatever the steps taken in the process, the process ends in an advice to the client. The oral and written report of the course and outcome of the assessment process must give the client a fair and evidence-based account of the given advice. The assessor should be careful in conveying the probabilistic and conditional nature of his or her statements.

FLAWS AND BIASES

The assessment process contains many instances in which the assessor, alone or in dialogue with the client, determines the course of action. The assessor should be aware of and protect him- or herself against the flaws and biases of clinical judgement. Clinical judgement refers to informal and subjective thinking and decision making. There is ample evidence that the professional psychologist who is not armed by proper decision

aids is as weak a decision maker as the less-trained professional or layperson.

The studies which demonstrate the fallibility of the clinical judgement and decision making belong to three different research streams which can be labelled as the psychometric, cognitive and social-psychological tradition. The *psychometric* tradition offers evidence for the fact that clinical prediction is nearly always less accurate than a prediction made by standardized formal predictions. Meehl already drew this conclusion in 1954, and ever since he was supported by many other reviews, the most recent one was presented by Grove et al. (2000). If one wants to predict a person's state of mind or behaviour in the future, the best thing to do is to base the prediction on the outcomes of empirical studies of the relationship between predictor (present state) and criterion (future state).

The *cognitive* research tradition presents evidence that cognitive heuristics which allow people to operate rather well in their daily lives nevertheless may have distorting effects in dealing with restricted and probabilistic information. Since the seminal work of Tversky and Kahneman (1974) the distorting effect of cognitive heuristics have been demonstrated in all kinds of choice and decision situations and with all kinds of people, professionals as well as laypersons (see Baron, 1994, and Goldstein & Hogarth, 1997, for a review). Of special critical interest for the assessment process are the heuristics people use in the generation and testing of hypotheses. One of the most famous heuristics in this respect has been called the confirmatory test strategy. People have the strong tendency to test hypotheses by searching the information that confirms the hypothesis and to neglect searching information that would disconfirm the hypothesis.

The *social-psychological* tradition presents evidence that in meeting the client the clinician is inclined to select and interpret information from the perspective of his causal attributions, stereotypes and characteristics. Of specific interest to the assessment process is the actor–observer bias hypothesized by Jones and Nisbett (1971) and empirically demonstrated in several studies (see Turk & Salovey, 1988, for a review). In explaining their behaviour actors tend to attribute it to situational factors while observers tend to attribute this behaviour to internal causes like traits and motives.

Studies of flaws and biases have automatically led to the question how these flaws and biases could be avoided or at least restricted. Several proposals have been made, ranging from further standardization of data-collection and empirical validation of prediction procedures involved up to debiasing reasoning techniques and computerized decision aids. Lists of such proposals are given in Garb (1998), Haynes and O'Brien (2000), and Turk and Salovey (1988).

MODELLING THE PROCESS

In many fields of professional psychology, one always has been well aware of the intricacies and fallacies of an assessment process that is not protected somehow against the flaws and biases of clinical judgement. Considerable progress has been made in standardizing the way in which information can be gathered by using reliable and valid tests by which a client's response can be compared with that of others. However, not only the data collection and statistical interpretation should proceed properly, the same should apply to the comprehensive assessment process, which starts with the client's requests and ends in the assessor's advice to the client.

In non-clinical domains, such as job and curriculum selection, the client's requests relate to the client's strengths and weaknesses with respect to a certain job or study curriculum. Here the relevant empirical body of knowledge is the relationship between the client's characteristics and the success or satisfaction in the job or curriculum at hand. What emanates from this empirical approach is – technically speaking – a multiple regression equation in which the scores on a standardized battery of tests are weighted according to their relationship with the criterion, and combined in such a way that the prediction of the criterion is as accurate as possible. The assessment process is modelled after a *statistical prediction model*. The assessment process reaches a level of standardization that equals the level of standardization of each of its components.

Uncertainty about which job or study to engage in most often presents a problem of choice. Not only the probability of success in each of the choice options is at stake, but also the value each of these options have for the client. The value of having success in a particular career is not restricted to

financial profits, but also depends upon more personal values such as social recognition, social identity, and emotional and intellectual satisfaction. The assessment process should result in advice in which probability of success is weighted by the value of that success. In the *utility model* the assessment process is formalized as the combination of probability and values that apply to each of the choice options (Baron, 1994; Von Winterfeld & Edwards, 1986).

Neither the statistical model nor the utility model are developed to model the full assessment process which starts with the client's request and results in an advice to the client. Nor do these models formalize the specific decision rules the diagnostician should follow in going through the main phases of the process. Westmeyer (1975) proposed an *algorithmic model*. In this formal model decision algorithms are supposed to work on an adequate empirical knowledge base which contains complete sets of conditional probabilities for a specified type of both problem and client.

All three models presented so far are *normative* in the sense that they process information according to statistical or decision rules. Strict normative models set formal conditions that usually cannot be met in psychological practice nor in the knowledge base this practice is supposed to work with (see Westmeyer & Hageböck, 1992, for a discussion). Therefore, many students of the assessment process have tried to model the process according to more heuristic principles that could guide the process. Most of these *heuristic models* have been restricted to a diagrammatic presentation of the assessment process (Maloney & Ward, 1976) while some others (De Bruyn, 1992; Haynes & O'Brien, 2000) have led to elaborations which show how the assessor can proceed if he or she wants to follow the logical decision flow depicted in the model.

FUTURE PERSPECTIVES AND CONCLUSIONS

Despite the growing interest in the quality of the assessment process, a comprehensive set of *heuristic guidelines* that could support the assessor in executing the process is still lacking. This is in contrast to the related fields of testing (American Psychological Association, 1999) and programme evaluation (Joint Committee on Standards for Educational Evaluation, 1994) which eventually have succeeded in the formulation of standards that monitor professional work. It is only recently (Fernández-Ballesteros, 1998) that a task force consisting of psychologists from different fields in psychology started to think of formulating guidelines to cover all phases of the assessment process. The task force formulated a set of guidelines to cover the phases of analysing the case, organizing and reporting results, planning the intervention, and evaluation and follow-up (Fernández-Ballesteros et al., 2001). Instead of being rigid rules, fixed forever, these guidelines represent recommendations for professional behaviour.

As already demonstrated in the fields of testing and evaluation, such guidelines highly contribute to the development of the profession. Therefore, as stated by Fernández-Ballesteros et al., 'We hope that the efforts made in developing and disseminating these Guidelines stimulate the discussion among interested scientific and professional audiences and, in the long run, will contribute to improve the practice of psychological assessment as well as the education and training of psychological assessors' (2001: 185).

References

Allen, Mary J. & Yen, Wendy M. (1979). *Introduction to Measurement Theory*. Monterey, CA: Brooks/Cole.

American Psychological Association (1999). *Standards for Educational and Psychological Tests*. Washington, DC: American Psychological Association.

Anastasi, Anne & Urbina, Susana (1997). *Psychological Testing*. Upper Saddle River, NJ: Prentice Hall.

Baron, Jonathan (1994). *Thinking and Decision* (2nd ed.). Cambridge: Cambridge University Press (1st ed., 1988).

Cronbach, Lee J. (1990). *Essentials of Psychological Testing* (5th ed.). New York: Harper & Row (1st ed., 1949).

De Bruyn, E.E.J. (1992). A normative-prescriptive view on clinical psychodiagnostic decision making. *European Journal of Psychological Assessment*, 8(3), 163–171.

De Groot, Adriaan D. (1969). *Methodology: Foundations of Inference and Research in the Behavioural Sciences*. The Hague: Mouton.

Fernández-Ballesteros, R. (1998). Task force for the development of guidelines for the assessment process (GAP). *Newsletter of the European Association of Psychological Assessment*, 1(1), 2–7.

Fernández-Ballesteros, R., De Bruyn, E.E.J., Godoy, A., Hornke, L.F., Ter Laak, J., Vizcarro, C., Westhoff, W., Westmeyer, H. & Zaccagnini, J.L. (2001). Guidelines for the assessment process (GAP): a proposal for discussion. *European Journal of Psychological Assessment*, 17(3), 178–191.

Garb, Howard J. (1998). *Studying the Clinician: Judgment Research and Psychological Assessment*. Washington, DC: American Psychological Association.

Goldstein, W.M. & Hogarth, R.M. (1997). *Research on Judgement and Decision Making: Currents, Connections and Controversies*. Cambridge: Cambridge University Press.

Grove, W.M., Zald, D.H., Lebow, B.S., Snitz, B.E. & Nelson, C. (2000). Clinical versus mechanical prediction: a meta-analysis. *Psychological Assessment*, 12(1), 19–30.

Haynes, Stephen N. & O'Brien, William (2000). *Principles and Practice of Behavioural Assessment*. New York: Kluwer Academic.

Hogarth, Robin M. (1987). *Judgement and Choice: The Psychology of Decision* (2nd ed.). Chichester: Wiley (1st ed., 1980).

Joint Committee on Standards for Educational Evaluation (1994). *The Program Evaluation Standards* (2nd ed.). Thousand Oaks, CA: Sage (1st ed., 1981).

Jones, Edward E. & Nisbett, Richard E. (1971). The actor and the observer: divergent perceptions of the causes of behaviour. In Jones, E.E., Kanouse, D.H., Kelley, H.H., Nisbett, R.E., Valins, S. & Weiner, B. (Eds.), *Attribution: Perceiving the Causes of Behaviour* (pp. 79–94). Morristown, NJ: General Learning Press.

Maloney, M.P. & Ward, M.P. (1976). *Psychological Assessment: A Conceptual Approach*. New York: Oxford University Press.

Meehl, Paul E. (1954). *Statistical versus Clinical Prediction*. Minneapolis, MN: University of Minnesota Press.

Nunnally, Jim C. (1978). *Psychometric Theory* (2nd ed.). New York: McGraw-Hill (1st ed., 1967).

Sloves, R.E., Doherty, E.M. & Schneider, K.C. (1979). A scientific problem-solving model of psychological assessment. *Professional Psychology*, 1(1), 28–35.

Turk, D. & Salovey, P. (Ed.) (1988). *Reasoning, Inference and Judgment in Clinical Psychology*. New York: Free Press.

Tversky, A. & Kahneman, D. (1974). Judgment under uncertainty: heuristics and biases. *Science*, 185(50), 1124–1131.

Von Winterfeld, Detlof & Edwards, Ward (1986). *Decision Analysis and Behavioural Research*. Cambridge: Cambridge University Press.

Westmeyer, H. (1975). The diagnostic process as a statistical-causal analysis. *Theory and Decision*, 6(1), 57–86.

Westmeyer, H. & Hageböck, J. (1992). Computer-assisted assessment: a normative approach. *European Journal of Psychological Assessment*, 8(1), 1–16.

Eric E.J. De Bruyn

RELATED ENTRIES

Assessor's Bias, Clinical Judgement, Case Formulation, Ethics, Prediction (General), Prediction: Clinical vs. Statistical, Report (General)

A | ASSESSOR'S BIAS

INTRODUCTION

Psychological assessment is subject to various errors of measurement. While some are random, as assumed in classical test theory, others are systematic and lead to consistent distortions of the true value of a characteristic. These latter errors may be partially due to assessor's biases. This term does not refer to elementary professional mistakes such as implementing test instructions incorrectly, but to systematic tendencies in case-related information processing that reduce the validity of data. Although these biases normally impair objectivity and reliability, they remain undetected when they are consistent across individuals and time. In addition, a low interrater agreement is not necessarily a sign of assessor's bias but may be due to valid differences between settings and informants (Lösel, 2002).

Not all types of assessment information are equally susceptible to assessor's biases. Whereas standardized tests or biographical inventories are less affected, their impact may be strong in unstructured interviews, behaviour observations, or trait ratings. For example, some studies on the judgement of job performance have shown that more than half of the variance is due to differences in the assessors (Scullen et al., 2000). In a meta-analysis, approximately 37% of the variance in ratings was attributed to them (Hyot & Kerns, 1999).

This entry concentrates on biases in assessments by other persons (e.g. psychologists, psychiatrists, teachers, or lay informants). Although these biases are similar to the numerous response sets and distortions in self-reports, some seem less important (e.g. lying, simulation, dissimulation, social desirability, or positive self-presentation) and others more relevant (e.g. halo, leniency, stringency, or contrast effects). In the following, we will first describe several of these errors and afterwards address factors that differentiate and moderate these distortions. Finally, we will take a brief look at approaches for detecting and reducing assessor's biases.

EXAMPLES OF ASSESSOR'S BIASES

Halo and Logical Error

In psychological assessment, a *halo effect* refers to an overgeneralization from one prominent characteristic of a person to other judgements on this individual. Most typically, it is an overestimation derived from a general impression. For example, if a person is judged to be good in general, he or she will be judged more positively on any specific dimension. Halo errors may arise particularly when there is insufficient information for a detailed assessment or when traits are not well defined. In these cases, the general impression is used to fill information gaps (Saal et al., 1980). A related bias is the *logical error*. Here, assessors are likely to give similar ratings to traits that seem logically related in their minds (Guilford, 1954). Whereas the halo effect derives from a perceived coherence of characteristics in an individual, the logical error refers to a more explicit and abstract coherence of variables or traits. The latter is often anchored in the assessor's subjective personality theory.

Both biases produce the same outcome, namely spurious and inflated correlations (Murphy et al., 1993). The underlying mechanisms are also related. Occasionally, a halo effect can have some advantage because it accentuates differences between individuals (Murphy et al., 1993). This is the case when a quick decision has to be made and the core determinants of the halo effect are empirically valid. Then, one can simply follow the useful decision rule 'take the best, ignore the rest' (Gigerenzer & Selten, 2001).

Position Effects

Whereas halo effects result from the psychological or logical closeness of the rated characteristics, their sequence or position may have a similar effect. One such distortion is the *proximity error*. Judgements that are close to each other in time or space contain a higher risk of mutual influence. A related error is the *primacy effect* in which the first impression of a person overshadows the assessment of their further behaviour. Its opposite is the *recency effect*: the last information on a person influences the evaluation of previous data. Early stereotyping (primacy) or easy remembering (recency) are among the mechanisms that underlie these modes of information processing. Although some experiments suggest that recency is more influential than primacy (e.g. Betz et al., 1992), it is questionable whether such findings can be generalized to real-life assessments.

Leniency and Stringency

These errors refer to the tendency to make relatively positive (leniency) or negative (stringency, severity) assessments. For example, somebody who is rather intelligent would be judged to be even more intelligent by a lenient rater but less intelligent by a stringent one. Leniency seems to be more frequent than stringency (Guilford, 1954). It may partially reflect tendencies toward social desirability, harmony, or other dispositions. Assessors who score high in self-monitoring tend to deliver more lenient ratings. Similarly, leniency correlates negatively with conscientiousness and positively with agreeableness (Bernardin et al., 2000). Nonetheless, other studies question the view that leniency is primarily due to personality dispositions. Situational and relational factors must also be taken into account.

Central Tendency

Leniency and stringency go along with polarizations between extreme judgements. In contrast, other assessors tend to produce scores in the middle range. Sometimes, this may express a lack of differentiated information on a person. In other cases, it involves indifferent perceptions or a general ambivalency or insecurity in the assessor.

Contrast and Projection Effects

Biases may also result from comparisons between a person's behaviour and the assessor's own dispositions. A *contrast error* is when the assessor attributes characteristics at the opposite pole to his self-perception; a *projection effect* when he evaluates a person as being similar to himself. Both tendencies relate to self-awareness and self-presentation processes in the assessor. For example, persons with behavioural problems may rate others higher on the same dimensions. Whereas projection errors can contribute to self-worth by reinforcing social comparability, contrast effects can serve a similar function by protecting the assessor's individuality.

Interactional Biases

Assessors' biases not only influence their own information processing but also how persons behave in the assessment situation. Although the assessor's age, gender, ethnicity, role, status, or institutional affiliation may have such effects (Hagenaars & Heinen, 1982), these should not be viewed as biases. Interactional biases refer to influences that derive from the assessor's information processing. One example is the self-fulfilling prophecy of positive expectations, although the typical Rosenthal effect has not been replicated sufficiently (Elashoff & Snow, 1971). In the practice of psychological assessment, even minor biases can have an effect (e.g. slightly nodding the head or providing other non-verbal reinforcements based on halo or leniency effects). Unstructured interviews are particularly vulnerable to biases derived from assessor's attitudes and expectations. Hyman et al. (1975) distinguish three forms: (a) *Attitude-structure expectations* refer to the belief that the attitudes of the respondent are unified. They resemble the halo effect and may reinforce uniform reactions. (b) *Role expectations* relate to the respondent's membership of a certain group. These stereotypes can result in assessor behaviour that triggers prototypical reactions in the respondent. (c) *Probability expectations* refer to the base rates of diagnostic characteristics in the respective population. They can lead to assessor behaviour that tries to confirm these specific assumptions. Other interactive biases contribute to *missing data*. For example, projection or contrast effects may lead an interviewer to evaluate a question as being

TOURO COLLEGE LIBRARY

extremely difficult or intimate. This can reduce emphasis and thus lead to more incomplete or 'don't know' answers. On the other hand, a very stringent assessor may elicit similar effects through behaviour that reduces the respondent's willingness to cooperate.

Overall, the impact of such interviewer biases seems to be small or not well-investigated (Hagenaars & Heinen, 1982). Probably, the more an assessor complies with professional standards and is not socially involved, the fewer biases will occur (Hyman et al., 1975).

DIFFERENTIAL ISSUES

Rater- versus Dyad-Specific Biases

Assessor's biases contain both rater-specific and dyad-specific components (Hyot & Kerns, 1999). In the former, the error variance is attributable to the assessor alone (e.g. a rater who generally tends to leniency when judging coworkers). In the latter, it is due to a specific relation between the assessor and the assessee (e.g. a teacher who judges a difficult student more negatively than he should). Rater-specific biases are a minor problem when only one assessor compares individuals on one dimension, because the error is the same across all judgements. It becomes more problematic when there are several assessors with different biases. The same holds for complex assessments by a single assessor who confounds specific information due to a halo effect.

Dyad-specific biases seem to be more powerful. Because they are less general, they are also more difficult to detect and correct. Neither rater-specific nor dyad-specific biases need to be stable. They may fluctuate over time and situations according to current influences such as emotional state, task involvement, or organizational factors.

Moderating Factors

The magnitude of biases also depends on what information is gathered. Their impact is relatively small (4% of variance) when ratings are based on explicit and objective criteria such as behaviour frequencies (Hyot & Kerns, 1999). However, it is much stronger (47% of variance) when assessors rate global trait characteristics. Training of assessors is another important moderator. When they are well-trained, less than 10% of variance is attributable to assessor's biases, but with minimal training, these sources may account for over 50% (Hyot & Kerns, 1999). Furthermore, rater agreement varies according to the observed behaviour samples. If assessors refer to different samples, they will agree less. However, as mentioned before, such interrater differences may indicate true variance rather than biases (reliability–validity trade-off; Scullen et al., 2000). For example, employees behave differently with their bosses than with their colleagues.

DETECTING AND REDUCING ASSESSOR'S BIASES

The valid assessment of an assessor's biases is a prerequisite for intervention. Unfortunately, there is little systematic and practice-oriented research on this issue.

One strategy is to reconstruct the errors from the assessor's judgements. If he rated specific dimensions in various persons and other assessors did the same, inter- and intrarater comparisons are possible. Different frequency distributions, means, variances, and correlations between variables may indicate halo, leniency, extremity, or other errors. However, as mentioned above, this is only possible when assessors work on the same samples of data. Another strategy is to compare the individual judgements with objective data structures. Brunswik's lense model can be used to compare regression weights between the respective data and both the assessor's judgement and an objective criterion. For example, a teacher may place too much weight on verbal intelligence in predicting student achievement. Similarly, configurational analyses can be used to detect biases in non-linear data structures.

Such reconstructions require a great deal of analogue data and judgements. If these are not available, one can try to assess directly what goes on in the assessor's mind (e.g. by the method of thinking aloud or analysing subjective theories by using structure-placing or repertory grid techniques). However, it is questionable how far these approaches can detect automatized and unconscious mental processes. Verbal ambiguities and social desirability effects must also be expected.

Assessor's biases may further be reduced through supervision by neutral experts or team feedback

TOURO COLLEGE LIBRARY

sessions. These approaches are most common in clinical contexts but can also be applied in other fields of psychological assessment.

Last, but not least, assessor's biases can be reduced by a systematic organization and quality management of the whole assessment process. This includes, for example, standardized procedures, detailed behavioural indicators of categories, intensive training of assessors, random-routine check of assessment quality, re-analysable data registration (e.g. video recordings), adequate time-spacing of judgements, techniques that enhance systematic comparisons (e.g. in pairs vs. ratings), the clear distinction between data description and interpretation, and explicit rules for data integration.

FUTURE PERSPECTIVES AND CONCLUSIONS

Assessor's biases are important sources of error variance. Although these biases cannot be eliminated completely in the human process of assessment, they can be reduced substantially. For example, this is possible by following the Guidelines for the Assessment Process recently proposed by a Task Force of the European Association of Psychological Assessment (Fernández-Ballesteros et al., 2001).

References

Betz, A.L., Gannon, K.M. & Skowronski, J.J. (1992). The moment of tenure and the moment of truth: when it pays to be aware of recency effects in social judgements. *Social Cognition*, 10(4), 397–413.

Bernardin, H.J., Cooke, D.K. & Villanova, P. (2000). Conscientiousness and agreeableness as predictors of rating leniency. *Journal of Applied Psychology*, 85(2), 232–236.

Elashoff, J.D. & Snow, E. (1971). *A Case Study in Statistical Inference: Reconsideration of the Rosenthal–Jacobson Data on Teacher Expectancy*. Stanford: Stanford University Press.

Fernández-Ballesteros, R., De Bruyn, E.E.J., Godoy, A., Hornke, L.F., Ter Laak, J., Vizcarro, C., Westhoff, K., Westmeyer, H. & Zaccagnini, J.L. (2001). Guidelines for the Assessment Process (GAP): a proposal for discussion. *European Journal of Psychological Assessment*, 17(3), 187–200.

Gigerenzer, G. & Selten, R. (Eds.) (2001). *Bounded Rationality: The Adaptive Toolbox*. Cambridge, MA: MIT Press.

Guilford, J.P. (1954). *Psychometric Methods* (2nd ed.). New York: McGraw-Hill.

Hagenaars, J.A. & Heinen, T.G. (1982). Effects of role-independent interviewer characteristics on responses. In Dijkstra, W. & van der Zouwen, J. (Eds.), *Response Behaviour in the Survey – Interview* (pp. 91–130). London: Academic Press.

Hyman, H.H., Cobb, W.J., Feldman, J.J., Hart, C.W. & Stember, C.H. (1975). *Interviewing in Social Research*. Chicago: University of Chicago Press.

Hyot, W.T. & Kerns, M.-D. (1999). Magnitude and moderators of bias in observer ratings: a meta-analysis. *Psychological Methods*, 4(4), 403–424.

Lösel, F. (2002) Risk/need assessment and prevention of antisocial development in young people. In Corrado, R., Roesch, R., Hart, S.D. & Gierowski, J.K. (Eds.), *Multiproblem Violent Youth*. Amsterdam: IOS Press.

Murphy, K.R., Jako, R.A. & Anhalt, R.L. (1993). Nature and consequences of halo error: a critical analysis. *Journal of Applied Psychology*, 78(2), 218–225.

Saal, F.E., Downey, R.G. & Lahey, M.A. (1980). Rating the ratings: assessing the psychometric quality of rating data. *Psychological Bulletin*, 88(2), 413–428.

Scullen, S.E., Mount, M.K. & Goff, M. (2000). Understanding the latent structure of job performance ratings. *Journal of Applied Psychology*, 85(6), 956–970.

Friedrich Lösel and Martin Schmucker

RELATED ENTRIES

ITEM BIAS, CLINICAL JUDGEMENT, ASSESSMENT PROCESS

ATTACHMENT

INTRODUCTION

Children are attached, if they tend to seek proximity to and contact with a specific caregiver in times of stress arising from factors such as distress, illness, or tiredness (Bowlby, 1984). Attachment is a major developmental milestone in the child's life, and it remains an important issue throughout the lifespan. In adulthood, attachment representations shape the way adults feel about the strains and stresses of intimate relationships, including parent–child relationships, and the way in which the self in relation to important others is evaluated. Attachment theory is a special branch of Darwinian evolution theory, and the need to become attached to a protective conspecific is considered one of the primary needs in the human species. Attachment theory is built upon the assumption that children come to this world with an inborn inclination to show attachment behaviour – and this inclination would have had survival value, or better: would increase 'inclusive fitness' – in the environment in which human evolution originally took place. Because of its ethological basis, assessment of attachment implies careful and systematic observations of verbal and non-verbal behaviour.

ASSESSMENT OF ATTACHMENT IN INFANTS

Attachment to a protective caregiver helps the infant to regulate his or her negative emotions in times of stress and distress, and to be able to explore the environment even if it is somewhat frightening. The idea that children seek a balance between the need for proximity to an attachment figure and the need to explore the wider environment is fundamental to the various attachment measures, such as the *Strange Situation* procedure (SSP; Ainsworth et al., 1978) and the *Attachment Q-Sort* (AQS; Vaughn & Waters, 1990) (see Table 1). Ainsworth and her colleagues observed one-year-old infants with their mothers in a standardized stressful separation procedure, and used the reactions of the infants to their reunion with the caregiver after a brief separation to assess the amount of trust the children had in the accessibility of their attachment figure.

The SSP consists of eight episodes, of which the last seven ideally take three minutes. Each

episode can however be curtailed when the infant starts crying. *Episode One* begins when the experimenter leads caregiver and child into an unfamiliar playroom. *Episode Two* is spent by the caregiver together with the child in the playroom. In *Episode Three* an unfamiliar adult (the 'stranger') enters the room and after a while starts to play with the infant. *Episode Four* starts when the caregiver departs, and the infant is left with the stranger. In *Episode Five* the caregiver returns, and the stranger unobtrusively leaves the room immediately after reunion. *Episode Six* starts when the caregiver leaves again: the infant is alone in the room. In *Episode Seven* the stranger returns. In *Episode Eight* the caregiver and the infant are reunited once again, and the stranger leaves unobtrusively immediately after reunion.

The Strange Situation procedure has been used with mothers, fathers, and other caregivers. Infants usually are between 12 and 24 months of age. For pre-schoolers, the same SSP is used, but the rating system for classifying the children is different and still is in the process of validation (Cassidy et al., 1992). On the basis of infants' reactions to the reunion with the caregiver, three patterns of attachment can be distinguished. Infants who actively seek proximity to their caregivers upon reunion, communicate their feelings of stress and distress openly, and then readily return to exploration are classified as secure (B) in their attachment to that caregiver. Infants who seem not distressed, and ignore or avoid the caregiver following reunion are classified as insecure-avoidant (A). Infants who combine strong proximity seeking and contact maintaining with contact resistance, or remain inconsolable, without being able to return to play and explore the environment, are classified insecure-ambivalent (C).

An overview of all American studies with non-clinical samples (21 samples with a total of 1584 infants, studies conducted in the years 1977–1990) shows that about 67% of the infants are classified secure, 21% are classified as insecure-avoidant, and 12% are classified insecure-ambivalent (Van Ijzendoorn, Goldberg, Kroonenberg & Frenkel, 1992). The Strange Situation classifications have been demonstrated to be valid. For example, secure infants have more sensitive parents than insecure infants (in 66 studies with more than 4000 infants,

Table 1.   Attachment measures

Attachment measure	12–24 months	24–48 months	12 years and older
Strange Situation	X		
Attachment Q Sort	X	X	
Adult Attachment Interview			X

DeWolff & Van Ijzendoorn, 1997). Furthermore, secure infants have more satisfactory peer relations, and they develop better language skills (Cassidy & Shaver, 1999). The SSP also shows discriminant validity in comparison with temperament. One of the most powerful demonstrations of the absence of a causal link between attachment and temperament is the lack of correspondence between a child's attachment relationship to his or her mother, and the same child's relationship to his or her father.

The concept of 'disorganized' attachment emerged from the systematic inspection of about 200 cases from various samples that were difficult to classify in one of the three organized attachment categories (Main & Solomon, 1986). In particular in studies on maltreated infants, the limits of the traditional Ainsworth et al. (1978) coding system became apparent because many children with an established background of abuse or neglect nevertheless had to be forced into the secure category. A common denominator of the anomalous cases appeared to be the (sometimes momentary) absence of an organized strategy to deal with the stress of the SSP. Disorganized attachment can be described as the breakdown of an otherwise consistent and organized strategy of emotion regulation. Whether secure or insecure, every child may show disorganization of attachment depending on the earlier child-rearing experiences. Maltreating parents are supposed to create disorganized attachment in their infants because they confront their infants with a pervasive paradox: they are potentially the only source of comfort for their children, whereas at the same time they frighten their children through their unpredictable abusive behaviour. Disorganization of attachment occurs in about 15% of non-clinical cases, where associations with parental unresolved loss have been found, and it is considered a major risk factor in the development of child psychopathology.

ATTACHMENT IN TODDLERS AND PRESCHOOLERS

Although the SSP has become remarkably popular and successful, it has been a drawback that attachment research was almost exclusively dependent on a single procedure for the measurement of attachment. Waters and his co-workers introduced another method for assessing attachment security in infants and toddlers, i.e. the *Attachment Q-Sort* (AQS). The AQS consists of 90 cards. On each card a specific behavioural characteristic of children between 12 and 48 months of age is described. The cards can be used as a standard vocabulary to describe the behaviour of a child in the natural home-setting, with special emphasis on secure-base behaviour (Vaughn & Waters, 1990). After several hours of observation the observer ranks the cards into nine piles from 'most descriptive of the subject' to 'least descriptive of the subject'. The number of cards that can be put in each pile is fixed, i.e. 10 cards in each pile. By comparing the resulting Q-sort with the behavioural profile of a 'prototypically secure' child as provided by several experts in the field of attachment theory, a score for attachment security can be derived.

The AQS has some advantages over the SSP. First, it can be used for a broader age range (12–48 months) than the SSP. Moreover, AQS scores for attachment security are based on observation of the child's secure-base behaviour in the home and may therefore have higher ecological validity. Furthermore, because the application of the AQS does not require the artificial induction of stress used in the SSP, the method can be applied in cultures and populations in which standard application of the SSP has proved to be somewhat complicated. Because the AQS is less intrusive than the SSP, it may be used more frequently with the same child, for example in repeated measures designs, in interventions studies, and in studies on children's attachment networks. Lastly, the application of the AQS in divergent cultures or populations may be attuned to the specific prototypical secure-base behaviour of the children from those backgrounds.

When the AQS is sorted by a trained observer it shows an impressive predictive validity. In particular, the observer AQS is strongly correlated with sensitive responsiveness. At the same time, it should be noted that the association between observer AQS security and SSP security is rather modest (Van Ijzendoorn, Vereijken & Risken-Walvaren, in press). The AQS and the SSP may therefore not measure the same construct, or they may be indexing different dimensions of the same construct. Support for the validity of the AQS as sorted by the mother is less convincing.

The association between the mother AQS and the SSP is disappointingly weak, and the instrument surprisingly shows a stronger association with temperament (Van Ijzendoorn et al., in press). Mothers of insecure children may lack the observational skills that are necessary for an unbiased registration of secure-base behaviours in their children.

In this contribution three assessment procedures are discussed that play a central role in attachment theory and research. The *Strange Situation Procedure* (SSP; Ainsworth et al., 1978) has been developed to assess attachment security of infants with their parents or other caregivers in a laboratory playroom. The *Attachment Q Sort* (AQS; Vaughn & Waters, 1990) is an instrument to observe secure-base behaviour and attachment security in children from 12–48 months at home. The *Adult Attachment Interview* (AAI; Main, Kaplan & Cassidy, 1985) is a semi-structured interview with a coding system (Main & Goldwyn, 1994) to assess adolescent and adult mental representations of attachment. We start with a brief discussion of the theoretical background of these assessment tools.

ASSESSMENT OF ATTACHMENT IN ADOLESCENCE AND ADULTHOOD

Attachment experiences are supposed to become crystallized into an internal working model or representation of attachment (Bowlby, 1984), which Main, Kaplan, and Cassidy defined as 'a set of rules for the organisation of information relevant to attachment and for obtaining or limiting access to that information' (1985, pp. 66–67). They developed an interview-based method of classifying a parent's mental representation of attachment, the *Adult Attachment Interview* (AAI). The AAI is a semi-structured interview that probes alternately for general descriptions of attachment relationships, specific supportive or contradicting memories, and descriptions of the current relationship with one's parents. The interview can be administered to parents, professional caregivers, and older adolescents, and stimulates respondents to both retrieve attachment-related autobiographical memories and evaluate these memories from their current perspective. For example, subjects are asked which five adjectives describe their childhood relationship with each parent, and what concrete memories or experiences led them to choose each adjective.

The AAI lasts about an hour and is transcribed verbatim. Interview transcripts are rated for security of attachment as derived from the subjects' present discussion of their attachment biographies (Hesse, 1999). The coding of the interviews is not based primarily on reported events in childhood, but rather on the coherency with which the adult is able to describe and evaluate these childhood experiences and their effects. The interview, therefore, does not assess the actual quality of childhood attachment relationships, and a secure representation of attachment is not incompatible with an insecure attachment history throughout childhood. This is a major difference with questionnaires that ask for descriptions of the relationship with parents or parents' parenting, in which descriptions of childhood experiences are decisive and taken for granted. Instead, the AAI takes into account that retrospection is not necessarily reliable, and that repression and idealization do take place. Hesse (1999) has suggested that the central task presented to the subject is that of producing and reflecting upon attachment-related memories while *simultaneously* maintaining coherent discourse with the interviewer.

The coding system of the AAI (Main & Goldwyn, 1994) includes scales for inferred childhood experiences with parents (e.g. loving, rejecting, role-reversing) and scales for state of mind with respect to attachment (e.g. anger, idealization, insistence on lack of recall, coherency). The scale scores for state of mind are of overriding importance when it comes to classification of an interview, in one out of three main categories. *Autonomous* or *secure* adults are able to describe their attachment-related experiences coherently, whether these experiences were negative (e.g. parental rejection or overinvolvement) or positive. They tend to value attachment relationships and to consider them important for their own personality. *Dismissing* adults tend to devalue the importance of attachment experiences for their own lives or to idealize their parents without being able to illustrate their positive evaluations with concrete events demonstrating secure interaction. They often appeal to lack of memory of childhood experiences. *Preoccupied* adults are still very much involved and preoccupied with their past attachment experiences and are therefore not able to describe them coherently. They may express anger or passivity when discussing current relationships with their parents. Dismissing and preoccupied adults are both considered insecure. Some adults indicate through their incoherent discussion of experiences of trauma (such as maltreatment, or the loss of an attachment figure) that they have not yet completed the process of mourning. They receive the additional classification *Unresolved,* which is superimposed on their main classification. In a meta-analysis on 33 studies, the distribution of non-clinical mothers was as follows: 24% dismissing, 58% autonomous, and 18% preoccupied mothers (Van Ijzendoorn & Bakermans-Kranenburg, 1996). About 19% of the mothers were additionally classified as unresolved. Fathers and adolescents showed about the same distribution of AAI classifications. Clinical respondents, however, showed highly deviating distributions, with a strong overrepresentation of insecure attachment representations. Systematic relations between clinical diagnosis and type of insecurity could not be established.

The test–retest reliability of the AAI has been established in several studies, and the same is true of the AAI's discriminant validity. AAI classifications turned out to be independent of respondents' IQ, social desirability, temperament, and general autobiographical memory abilities (for a review, see Hesse, 1999). The predictive validity of the AAI has been thoroughly tested in a large number of studies in different countries, and the results can best be described by meta-analytic findings. First, the AAI appears to be predictive of parents' sensitive responsiveness. Autonomous parents are more responsive to their child's attachment signals and needs than insecure parents (Van Ijzendoorn, 1995). Second, in several (cross-sectional as well as longitudinal) studies parents' representations of attachment were related to the security of the parent–child attachment relationship as measured through the Strange Situation procedure. Autonomous parents tended to have secure children, dismissing parents had insecure-avoidant children, preoccupied parents had insecure-ambivalent children, and parents with unresolved loss or other trauma more often had disorganized children (Van Ijzendoorn, 1995). In longitudinal studies covering the first 15 to 20 years of life, the infant SSP

classifications have been found to predict the later AAI classifications when major changes in life circumstances were absent (Waters, Hamilton & Weinfield, 2000).

FUTURE PERSPECTIVES AND CONCLUSIONS

We conclude that the Strange Situation Procedure, the Attachment Q Sort, and the Adult Attachment Interview have proven to be invaluable tools for testing empirical hypotheses. They have helped to advance attachment theory far beyond Bowlby's first draft some thirty years ago. During the past ten years or so, several other attachment measures have been developed, mostly based on the same construction principles that guided the development of the SSP, AQS, and AAI (Cassidy & Shaver, 1999). Some measures mirror the SSP and focus on attachment in preschoolers (the Preschool Assessment of Attachment), others involve projective techniques for preschoolers and older children, such as the SAT, drawings or photographs, or doll play. Other measures are adaptations of the AAI and cover younger (adolescent) age ranges or different representational dimensions (working model of the child; working model of caregiving). Self-report paper-and-pencil measures have been proposed for assessment of attachment in adolescence or adulthood, as well as interview measures for partner relationships. These alternative attachment measures are still in the process of validation, and do not yet present the psychometric qualities that SSP, AQS, and AAI have shown to possess (Cassidy & Shaver, 1999). In the near future, more data will become available on the reliability and validity of these promising measures. They may help to investigate attachment across the lifespan, in various contexts, populations, and cultures.

References

Ainsworth, M.D.S., Blehar, M.C., Waters, E. & Wall, S. (1978). *Patterns of Attachment.* Hillsdale, NJ: Lawrence Erlbaum.

Bowlby, J. (1984). *Attachment and Loss. Attachment,* Vol. 1 (2nd ed.). London: Penguin.

Cassidy, J., Marvin, R.S. & MacArthur Working Group on Attachment (1992). Attachment organization in pre-school procedures and coding manual. Unpublished Manuscript, University of Virginia.

Cassidy, J. & Shaver, P.R. (1999). *Handbook of Attachment. Theory, Research, and Clinical Applications.* New York: Guilford.

DeWolff, M.S. & Van Ijzendoorn, M.H. (1997). Sensitivity and attachment: a meta-analysis on parental antecedents of infant-attachment. *Child Development, 68*, 571–591.

Hesse, E. (1999). The Adult Attachment Interview: historical and current perspectives. In Cassidy, J. & Shaver, P.R. (Eds.), *Handbook of Attachment. Theory, Research, and Clinical Applications* (pp. 395–433). New York: Guilford.

Main, M. & Goldwyn, R. (1994). *Adult Attachment Classification System.* Department of Psychology, University of California at Berkeley. Unpublished manuscript.

Main, M., Kaplan, N. & Cassidy, J. (1985). Security in infancy, childhood, and adulthood: a move to the level of representation. In Bretherton, I. & Waters, E. (Eds.), *Growing Points of Attachment Theory and Research* (pp. 66–104). Chicago: Society for Research in Child Development.

Main, M. & Solomon, J. (1986). Discovery of an insecure-disorganized/disoriented attachment pattern. In Brazelton, T.B. & Yogman, M.W. (Eds.), *Affective Development in Infancy* (pp. 95–124). Norwood, NJ: Ablex.

Van Ijzendoorn, M.H. (1995). Adult attachment representations, parental responsiveness, and infant attachment. A meta-analysis on the predictive validity of the Adult Attachment Interview. *Psychological Bulletin, 117*, 387–403.

Van Ijzendoorn, M.H. & Bakermans-Kranenburg, M.J. (1996). Attachment representations in mothers, fathers, adolescents, and clinical groups: a meta-analytic search for normative data. *Journal of Consulting and Clinical Psychology, 64*, 8–21.

Van Ijzendoorn, M.H., Goldberg, S., Kroonenberg, P.M. & Frenkel, O.J. (1992). The relative effects of maternal and child problems on the quality of attachment: a meta-analysis of attachment in clinical-samples. *Child Development, 63*, 840–858.

Van Ijzendoorn, M.H., Vereijken, C.M.J.L. & Risken-Walvaren, J.M.A. (in press). Is the Attachment Q-Sort a valid measure of attachment security in young children? In Vaughn, B., Waters, E. & Posada, D. (Eds.), *Patterns of Secure Base Behaviour: Q-Sort Perspectives on Attachment and Caregiving in Infancy and Childhood.* Hillsdale, NJ: Erlbaum.

Vaughn, B.E. & Waters, E. (1990). Attachment behaviour at home and in the laboratory: Q-sort observations and Strange Situation classifications of one-year-olds. *Child Development, 61*, 1965–1973.

Waters, E., Hamilton, C.E. & Weinfield, N.S. (2000). The stability of attachment security from infancy to adolescence and early adulthood: general introduction. *Child Development, 71*, 678–683.

Marinus Van Ijzendoorn and
Marian J. Bakermans-Kranenburg

RELATED ENTRIES

Personality Assessment (General), Emotions, Motivation, Development (General), Development: Socio-Emotional, Pre-School Children

ATTENTION

INTRODUCTION

Attention involves being in a state of alertness, focusing on aspects of the environment that are deemed important for the task at hand, and shutting out irrelevant information. As the task demands change, attention involves the ability to flexibly shift focus to another target. Originally, attention was considered a unitary construct but currently it is conceptualized as a complex process involving (a) distributed neural systems, (b) perceptual, emotional, motivational and motor systems, as well as (c) links to multiple sources of environmental information.

Some commonly studied processes of attention include selecting, sustaining, and shifting. Selection refers to the ability to narrow the field of stimuli to which one attends for the purpose of enhanced processing. Sustained attention refers to the ability to maintain focus and alertness over time. Shifting refers to the ability to change focus of attention to suit one's goals and needs.

Research has focused on visual or auditory attention, although environmental stimuli are perceived through other modalities as well (i.e. touch, smell, taste). In addition, research has focused on attention to the external environment rather than to the internal environment (thoughts and emotions) since the internal environment is less amenable to objective and reliable methods of assessment (See Underwood, 1993).

WHY IS IT IMPORTANT TO ASSESS ATTENTION?

Attention is central to the ability to function perceptually, cognitively and socially. For that reason it is important to have basic scientific understanding of attention processes and the psychological and environmental conditions that govern the development of attention and its deployment under specific circumstances. With such knowledge in hand, one can design environments that promote optimal attention to important characteristics in those settings.

In addition, it is important to assess attention so as to map out individual differences in the development and use of attention. These differences are mostly in the normal range but may also include deficits that are quite marked as seen in children diagnosed with Attention Deficit Disorder or in adults diagnosed with schizophrenia, depression or substance abuse problems. The assessment of attention is important for parents and teachers who detect difficulties in a child's ability to focus attention and wish to have the child evaluated. Similarly, attention problems may be presented in adults who have suffered head injuries or stroke, and who would need to be evaluated to determine the seriousness of the deficits involved. Diagnosing such deficits is dependent on information about individual differences in attention and on the availability of appropriate assessment tools.

ASSESSMENT METHODS

Methods have been developed for the assessment of specific aspects of attention, including selective attention, sustained attention, and shifting attention. These methods include performance tests, mapping brain activity during performance of tasks and, finally, rating scales. Table 1 lists commonly used performance tasks, the aspects of attention they assess and the contexts in which they are used (clinical or research). Additional information can be found in Barkley (1994). Other tests include Trenerry, Crosson and

DeBoe's Visual Search and Attention Test (VSAT), Miller's California Computerized Assessment Package (CalCAP), Arthur, Barrett and Doverspike's Auditory Selective Attention Test (ASAT), and The Gordon Diagnostic System. Table 2 lists commonly used scales for rating attention.

FUTURE DIRECTIONS

Deal with Issues Pertaining to Assessment for the Purpose of Increasing Knowledge about Specific Processes

There is a need to understand to what extent the processes outlined above are really independent rather than different manifestations of the same core. This calls for a more integrated understanding of attention and for the development of a basic assessment battery that could be used when people are referred with problems in attention (see Ruff and Rothbart, 1996).

Checking Ecological Validity

To what extent are the assessments telling something about functioning under some specific environmental conditions but don't generalize to these processes as they operate in everyday, out of the lab environments? Questions remain about the extent to which it is possible to do well on all laboratory assessments but have problems in the everyday context. Similarly, is it possible to function well in the everyday environment and yet have problems on laboratory assessments.

Developing an Attention Battery

The battery would need to be based on normative data and would need to have specified cut off lines between the normal range and problem range. Children would benefit from a routine assessment using such a battery in the same way that they benefit from routine examination of their hearing and vision. Systematically evaluating how children perform in terms of their attention is important since children may have deficits that they mask through idiosyncratic cognitive strategies or by working harder than what would normally be required.

Table 1. Commonly used performance task

Process	Assessment Name	Short Description	Assessed Behaviour	Contexts of Use
I. Selective Attention	Children's Checking Task	Symbol cancellation	Number targets identified; Number targets missed; Incorrect identifications	Research
	Digit Symbol/Coding	Wechsler scales subtest	Timed task of correctly indicating which symbol corresponds to a number	Clinical Research
	Stroop Colour-World Interference Test	Naming the ink colour of words that spell a colour different from the ink colour	Time to complete each portion; Number of correct responses	Research Clinical
	The Trail Making Test	Connecting letters and numbers placed randomly on a page	Time to complete each part; Number of errors	Research Clinical
	Children's Embedded Figures Test	Identifying a target figure embedded among non-targets	Mean time to respond; Number of correct responses	Clinical Research
	Posner's Visual-Spatial Selective Attention Test	Responding to targets presented to the left/right visual fields	Difference in reaction time in the presence of valid and invalid cues	Research
II. Sustained Attention	Reaction Time Task(s)	Responding to simple target visual stimuli	Mean reaction time; Variability of response time	Research
	Continuous Performance Test (CPT)	Responding to target stimuli and inhibiting response to on-target stimuli	Response time; Number correct responses; Errors of omission; Errors of commission	Research Clinical
	KABC Hand Movements	Imitating progressively longer sequences of skilled hand movements	Standard score of successful number of sequences	Research Clinical

Category	Test	Description	Measure	Setting
III. Shifting Attention	Wisconsin Card Sorting Task	Sorting 128 cards containing sets of geometric designs – varying colour, form, number	% of correct; Number of categories achieved; Perseverative errors; Perseverative responses; Non-perseverative responses	Research Clinical
	Halstead–Reitan Neuropsych. Test Battery – Categories Test	Choosing from 1 of 4 choices from a projected stimuli based on a principle	Number of correct responses; Same behaviours as above	Clinical
IV. Numerical Mnemonic Attention	Digit Span	Wechsler scales subtest	Accurate memory for a specific string of numerical stimuli (forward & backward)	Research Clinical
	Arithmetic	Wechsler scales subtest	Correct solutions provided verbally	Research Clinical
V. Physiological	Heart Rate processes	Electrodes placed on chest record the electrocardiogram (EKG)	Decrements in heart rate reflect attention	Research
	Cortical Electrophysiology	Electrodes placed on scalp record the electroencephalograph (EEG)	Large, slow waves indicate lapses in attention during sustained attention task	Research
	Cerebral blood flow	Blood flow to brain regions is mapped by positron emission tomography (PET)	Denser distribution indicates more active metabolism	Research

Table 2.   Commonly used scales for rating attention

Rating scales
Title
ADD-H Comprehensive Teacher Rating Scale
ADHD Rating Scale
Attention Deficit Disorders Evaluation Scale
Behaviour Assessment System for Children
Child Attention Profile by Edelbrock
Child Behaviour Checklist
Conners' Parent and Teacher Rating Scale – Revised
Hyperactive Behaviour Code

CONCLUSIONS

Attention is central to cognitive and social functioning and has been the subject of scientific research for decades. It is regulated by neural, perceptual, emotional, motivational and motor systems and influenced by both internal and external stimuli. Because of its central and complex role in behaviour, there are many methods for assessing its various aspects. Despite the long history of interest in the topic, scientists are still working to achieve greater understanding of attention processes and on developing new assessment tools.

References

Barkley, R.A. (1994). The assessment of attention in children. In Lyon, G.R. (Ed.), *Frames of Reference for the Assessment of Learning Disabilities*. Baltimore: Paul H. Brookes Publishing.

Ruff, H.A. & Rothbart, M.K. (1996). *Attention in Early Development: Themes and Variations*. New York: Oxford University Press.

Underwood, G. (Ed.) (1993). *The Psychology of Attention*, Vols. I and II. New York: New York University Press.

Sarah Friedman and Anita Konachoff

RELATED ENTRIES

THEORETICAL PERSPECTIVE: COGNITIVE, INTELLIGENCE ASSESSMENT (GENERAL), AMBULATORY ASSESSMENT, BRAIN ACTIVITY MEASUREMENT, EQUIPMENT FOR ASSESSING BASIC PROCESSES

ATTITUDES

INTRODUCTION

Evaluation is a fundamental reaction to any object of psychological significance (Jarvis & Petty, 1996; Osgood, Suci & Tannenbaum, 1957). The present entry reviews some of the major techniques that have been developed to assess these evaluative reactions, or attitudes. A discussion of methods based on explicit evaluative responses – direct and inferred – is followed by a consideration of disguised and implicit assessment techniques. Emphasis is placed on questions of reliability, validity, and practicality.

EXPLICIT MEASURES OF ATTITUDE

Virtually any response can serve as an indicator of attitude toward an object so long as it is reliably associated with the respondent's tendency to evaluate the object in question. In contrast to implicit responses, which cannot be easily controlled, explicit evaluative responses are under the conscious control of the respondent. Most explicit attitude measures either rely on direct attitudinal inquiries or infer the respondents' evaluations from their expressions of beliefs about the attitude object.

Direct Evaluations

Single-item direct measures. Laboratory experiments and attitude surveys frequently use single items to obtain direct evaluations of the attitude object. Confronted with the item 'Do you approve of the way the President is doing his job?' respondents may be asked to express their degree of approval on a five-point scale that ranges from 'approve very much' to 'disapprove very much'. Such single items can be remarkably good indicators, especially for well-formed attitudes toward familiar objects. They are sometimes found to have quite high levels of reliability and to correlate well with external criteria. For example, the single item 'I have high self-esteem' (attitude toward the self), assessed on a five-point scale ranging from 'not very true of me' to 'very true of me', was found to have a test–retest reliability of 0.75 over a four-year period, compared to a reliability of 0.88 for the multi-item Rosenberg Self-Esteem Scale (Robins, Hendin & Trzesniewski, 2001, Study 1). Moreover, the single- and multi-item measures correlated highly with each other, and they had comparable correlations with various external criteria (e.g. self-evaluation of physical attractiveness, extraversion, optimism, life satisfaction).

However, single items do not always exhibit such favourable psychometric properties. They often have low reliabilities and can suffer from limited construct validity. Many attitude objects are multidimensional and a single item can be ambiguous with respect to the intended dimension (e.g. 'religion as an institution' vs. 'religious faith'). Furthermore, single items contain nuances of meaning that may inadvertently affect responses to attitudinal inquiries. An item inquiring whether the United States should *allow* public speech against democracy leads to different conclusions than one asking whether the United States should *forbid* such speech (see Schuman & Presser, 1981). In addition to such framing effects, research has revealed strong context effects in attitudinal surveys. Respondents tend to interpret a given item in light of the context created by previous questions. Thus, responses to questions about satisfaction with life in general and satisfaction with specific aspects of one's life, such as one's work or romantic relationship, are found to be influenced by the order in which these questions are asked (Schwarz, Strack & Mai, 1991).

Multi-item direct measures. It is possible to raise the reliability of a direct attitude measure by increasing the number of questions asked. The Rosenberg Self-Esteem Scale (Rosenberg, 1965), for example, contains 10 items, each a direct inquiry into self-esteem (e.g. 'I feel that I am a person of worth, at least on an equal basis with others'; 'All in all, I am inclined to feel that I am a failure'). Coefficients of internal consistency and test–retest reliability for this measure are typically quite high (see Robinson, Shaver & Wrightsman, 1991).

The most frequently employed multi-item direct measure of attitude, however, is the evaluative semantic differential (Osgood et al., 1957). Using large sets of seven-point bipolar adjective scales, Osgood and his associates discovered that evaluative reactions (i.e. attitudes) capture the most important dimension of any object's connotative meaning. Consequently, it is possible to obtain a measure of attitude by asking respondents to rate any construct on a set of bipolar evaluative adjective scales, such as *good–bad, harmful–beneficial, desirable–undesirable, pleasant–unpleasant*, and *useful–useless*. When a sufficient number of such scales is used, the evaluative semantic differential is found to have very high internal consistency and temporal stability. One caveat with respect to the semantic differential has to do with possible 'construct-scale interactions'. Although certain adjective pairs generally indicate evaluation, these adjectives can take on more specific denotative meaning in relation to particular attitude objects. Thus, the adjective pair *sick–healthy* usually reflects evaluation when rating people, but it may be a poor measure of evaluation when respondents are asked to judge the construct 'mental patients'.

Inferred Evaluations

Although multi-item direct attitude measures exhibit high degrees of reliability, they do not address the problems raised by the multi-dimensionality of attitude objects, or by framing and context effects, problems that jeopardize the validity of direct evaluations. Several standard attitude-scaling methods, such as Thurstone and Likert scaling, avoid these difficulties by sampling a broad range of responses relevant to the attitude object and then inferring the common underlying evaluation. Whereas responses to items on a Thurstone scale are required to have a curvilinear relation to the overall attitude, the more common Likert method requires that item operation characteristics have a linear or at least monotonic shape (Green, 1954). In practice, an investigator using Likert's method of summated ratings (Likert, 1932) begins by constructing a large set of items, usually statements of belief, that are intuitively relevant for the attitude object. To illustrate, the following items are part of a Likert scale that was designed to assess attitudes toward illegal immigrants (Ommundsen & Larsen, 1997).

- Illegal aliens should not benefit from my tax dollars.
- There is enough room in this country for everyone.
- Illegal aliens are a nuisance to society.
- Illegal aliens should be eligible for welfare.
- Illegal aliens provide the United States with a valuable human resource.
- We should protect our country from illegal aliens as we would our own homes.

The investigators initially constructed 80 items of this kind. Selection of items that had high correlations with the total score yielded a final 30-item scale. Most Likert scales ask respondents to indicate their degree of agreement with each statement on a five-point scale (*strongly agree, agree, undecided, disagree, strongly disagree*). Responses to negative items are reverse scored and the sum across all items constitutes the measure of attitude. The respondents' attitudes are thus *inferred* from their beliefs about the attitude object (see Fishbein & Ajzen, 1975).

By covering a broad range of issues relevant to the attitude object, multi-item belief-based scales can do justice to the multidimensional nature of the issue under consideration, avoiding the potential ambiguity of direct measures. Furthermore, by including many differently worded questions that appear in unsystematic order, they also avoid idiosyncratic framing and context effects. As a result, standard multi-item attitude scales tend to have high reliability and, in many applications, exhibit high degrees of predictive and construct validity (Ajzen, 1982). Collections of scales designed to assess social and political attitudes can be found in Robinson, Shaver, and Wrightsman (1991, 1999). The obvious disadvantage in comparison to direct attitude assessment lies in the increased time and effort required to develop multi-item inferred attitude scales and in the fact that such scales may not be suitable for large-scale telephone surveys.

DISGUISED ATTITUDE MEASURES

Notwithstanding the psychometric advantages of inferred attitude measures over direct assessment techniques, all explicit measures – direct and inferred – are subject to response biases that may jeopardize their validity. The most serious of these biases is the tendency to respond to attitudinal inquiries in a socially desirable manner (Paulhus, 1991). This tendency is a particularly severe threat to validity when dealing with such socially sensitive issues as racism and sexism, or with potentially embarrassing topics, such as sexual behaviour or tax evasion. Various methods have been developed in attempts to overcome or at least alleviate social desirability responding.

One approach assumes that individuals differ in their tendency to provide socially desirable responses. Scales are available to assess a person's general tendency to respond in a socially desirable manner (see Paulhus, 1991), and these scales can be used to select attitude items that are relatively free of general social desirability influences or to statistically remove variance due to individual differences in social desirability responding. Unfortunately, this approach fails to identify socially desirable responses that are not part of a general tendency but rather are unique to a given topic or assessment context.

The problem of social desirability responding arises because the purpose of explicit attitude measures is readily apparent. Other approaches to this problem therefore attempt to reduce the measure's transparency or completely disguise its purpose. In measures of whites' attitudes toward African Americans, for example, item wording has changed over the years to accommodate the changing social climate. The ethnocentrism scale (Adorno, Frenkel-Brunskwik, Levinson & Snaford, 1950), used in the 1950s, contained such blatantly racist statements as, 'Manual labor and unskilled jobs seem to fit the Negro mentality and ability better than more skilled or responsible work'. About 15 years later, the Multifactor Racial Attitude Inventory (Woodmansee & Cook, 1967) employed more mildly worded items, such as, 'I would not take a Negro to eat with me in a restaurant where I was well known'. The most popular explicit attitude scale used today, the Modern Racism Scale

(McConahay, Hardee & Batts, 1981), is an attempt at a relatively non-reactive measure that captures the ambivalence many people experience with respect to African Americans: negative feelings that contrast with a desire to live up to ideals of equality and fairness. Among the items on this scale are, 'It is easy to understand the anger of black people in America' and 'Blacks are getting too demanding in their push for equal rights'.

Although less blatant than earlier measures, the Modern Racism Scale is still quite transparent in its attempt to assess attitudes toward African Americans and is thus potentially subject to social desirability responding. The error-choice method (Hammond, 1948) was an early attempt to avoid social desirability responding by disguising the purpose of the measurement and exploiting the tendency of attitudes to bias responses without a person's awareness. Respondents are asked to choose which of two apparently factual items, equidistant from the known state of affairs, is true (e.g. '25% of African Americans attend college' versus '55% of African Americans attend college'). Choice of the low estimate may indicate a more negative attitude, but because the survey is presented as a fact quiz, participants will usually not be aware that their attitudes toward African Americans are being assessed and their responses may thus be uninfluenced by social desirability concerns.

IMPLICIT MEASURES OF ATTITUDE

Perhaps the most effective way to avoid response biases associated with explicit attitude measures is not to obscure the test's purpose but to observe evaluative responses over which respondents have little or no control.

Bodily Responses

A variety of physiological and other bodily responses have been considered as possible indicators of evaluation, including facial expressions, head movements, palmar sweat, heart rate, electrical skin conductance (GSR), and constriction and expansion of the pupil (see Petty & Cacioppo, 1983). By and large, measures of this kind have been found to have relatively low

reliability and to be of questionable validity as measures of attitude. The most promising bodily response measure to date is the facial electromyogram (EMG), an electrical potential accompanying the contraction of muscle fibres. Subtle contractions of facial muscles during exposure to attitude-relevant stimuli appear to reveal underlying positive or negative affective states (Petty & Cacioppo, 1983). Relatively few studies have been conducted to test the validity of this method, but even if its validity is confirmed, the facial EMG requires extensive training and complex technology. It is thus not a very practical method for conducting large-scale attitude surveys, although it may be quite useful in a laboratory context.

In a related method, electrodes are attached to various sites and an attempt is made to persuade respondents that physiological responses are being measured and that these responses provide a reliable indication of their true attitudes. Even though no physiological measures are actually taken, respondents believing that their true attitudes are being read by the machine are expected to provide truthful answers to attitudinal inquiries (Jones & Sigall, 1971). Empirical evidence suggests that the 'bogus pipeline' method can indeed help to reduce response biases due to social desirability concerns (Quigley-Fernandez & Tedeschi, 1978). This method, however, again requires a fairly complex laboratory setup.

Response Latency

Somewhat more practical are methods that rely on response latencies to assess implicit attitudes because the time it takes to respond to an attitudinal inquiry can be assessed with relative ease. The most popular response-latency method is the Implicit Association Test (IAT; Greenwald, McGhee & Schwartz, 1998) which is based on the assumption that evaluative responses or judgements can be activated automatically, outside the respondent's conscious awareness. Participants are asked to respond as quickly as possible to words that signify the attitude object and words with positive or negative valence. When measuring implicit attitudes toward African Americans, for example, the attitude object may be represented by first names recognized as belonging to white or black

Americans (e.g. 'Josh' vs. 'Jamel') and the valenced words by common positive or negative concepts (e.g. 'health' vs. 'grief'). Instructions that require highly associated categories to share a response key tend to produce faster reactions than instructions that require less associated categories to share a response key. Prejudiced individuals would therefore be expected to respond more quickly to combinations of black names with negative words than to combinations of black names with positive words, and they should show the reverse pattern for white names. The discrepancy between the response latencies for the two situations is taken as a measure of implicit acceptance of the association between an attitude object and valenced attributes, thus providing an implicit measure of attitude.

An alternative procedure relies on sequential evaluative priming (Fazio, Jackson, Dunton & Williams, 1995). Applied to the measurement of racial attitudes, photos of black and white faces may be presented as primes, followed by positive or negative target words. The participant is asked to judge the valence of each target word as quickly as possible. As in the IAT, a low response latency is taken as an indication of a strong association between the valenced word and the category ('black' or 'white') represented by the prime. Thus, if words with negative valence are judged more quickly when they follow a 'black' prime as compared to a 'white' prime, and when the opposite is true for positive words, it is taken as evidence for a negative attitude toward African Americans.

Response-latency measures have been used mainly in attempts to assess implicit racial and sexual stereotypes and prejudice. Test–retest reliabilities of implicit measures have been found to be of moderate magnitude (0.50 to 0.60) over a time span of one hour to three weeks (Kawakami & Dovidio, 2001); they tend to be virtually uncorrelated with corresponding explicit measures (Fazio et al., 1995; Greenwald et al., 1998; Kawakami & Dovidio, 2001), indicating that they indeed tap a different type of attitude; and they tend to reveal prejudice where explicit measures reveal little or none (e.g. Greenwald et al., 1998), suggesting that implicit measures may be subject to less social desirability bias than explicit measures. However, questions have been raised with respect to the

predictive validity of implicit attitude measures. It has been suggested that low response latencies reflect commonly shared and automatically activated stereotypes, but that privately held, explicit beliefs in conflict with the implicit stereotype can override the automatic response in determining actual behaviour (Devine, 1989).

FUTURE PERSPECTIVES AND CONCLUSIONS

The great effort that has been invested over the years in the development of attitude measurement procedures attests to the centrality of the attitude construct in the social and behavioural sciences. Table 1 summarizes the different types of measures commonly employed in attitude research. Single items are often used with considerable success to assess evaluative reactions to attitude objects, but multi-item instruments that infer attitudes from a broad range of responses to the attitude object tend to yield measures of greater reliability and validity. Implicit attitude measure hold out promise for overcoming people's tendencies to respond in socially desirable ways to explicit attitudinal inquiries, especially when dealing with sensitive issues or with domains in which attitudes are conflicted or ambivalent. However, more work is needed to establish the conditions under which implicit attitude measures are better indicators of response dispositions than are explicit measures. It appears that implicit attitudes may be predictive of actual behaviour in ambiguous contexts where the relevance of an explicit

Table 1.   Common attitude assessment techniques

Response type	Representative technique
Explicit – direct	
Single-item	Self-rating scale
Multi-item	Semantic differential
Explicit – infrared	Thurstone scaling, Likert scaling
Disguised	Error-choice method
Implicit	
Bodily responses	GSR, heart rate, papillary response, EMG
Response latency	Implicit association test, evaluative priming

attitude is unrecognized or can be denied, but explicit attitudes may override implicit response tendencies when the relevance of the explicit attitude is readily apparent (see Fiske, 1998 for a discussion of these issues).

References

Adorno, T.W., Frenkel-Brunskwik, E., Levinson, D.L. & Snaford, R.N. (1950). *The Authoritarian Personality*. New York: Harper.

Ajzen, I. (1982). On behaving in accordance with one's attitudes. In Zanna, M.P., Higgins, E.T. & Herman, C.P. (Eds.), *Attitude Structure and Function. The Third Ohio State University Volume on Attitudes and Persuasion*, Vol. 2 (pp. 3–15). Hillsdale, NJ: Erlbaum.

Devine, P.G. (1989). Stereotypes and prejudice: their automatic and controlled components. *Journal of Personality and Social Psychology, 56*, 5–18.

Fazio, R.H., Jackson, J.R., Dunton, B.C. & Williams, C.J. (1995). Variability in automatic activation as an unobstrusive measure of racial attitudes: a bona fide pipeline? *Journal of Personality and Social Psychology, 69*, 1013–1027.

Fishbein, M. & Ajzen, I. (1975). *Belief, Attitude, Intention, and Behaviour: An Introduction to Theory and Research*. Reading, MA: Addison-Wesley.

Fiske, S.T. (1998). Stereotyping, prejudice, and discrimination. In Gilbert, D.T., Fiske, S.T. & Gardner, L. (Eds.), *The Handbook of Social Psychology*, Vol. 2 (4th ed., pp. 357–411). Boston, MA: McGraw-Hill.

Green, B.F. (1954). Attitude measurement. In Lindzey, G. (Ed.), *Handbook of Social Psychology*, Vol. 1 (pp. 335–369). Reading, MA: Addison-Wesley.

Greenwald, A.G., McGhee, D.E. & Schwartz, J.L.K. (1998). Measuring individual differences in implicit cognition: the implicit association test. *Journal of Personality and Social Psychology, 74*, 1464–1480.

Hammond, K.R. (1948). Measuring attitudes by error choice: an indirect method. *Journal of Abnormal and Social Psychology, 43*, 38–48.

Jarvis, W.B.G. & Petty, R.E. (1996). The need to evaluate. *Journal of Personality and Social Psychology, 70*, 172–194.

Jones, E.E. & Sigall, H. (1971). The bogus pipeline: a new paradigm for measuring affect and attitude. *Psychological Bulletin, 76*, 349–364.

Kawakami, K. & Dovidio, J.F. (2001). The reliability of implicit stereotyping. *Personality and Social Psychology Bulletin, 27*, 212–225.

Likert, R. (1932). A technique for the measurement of attitudes. *Archives of Psychology, 140*, 5–53.

McConahay, J.B., Hardee, B.B. & Batts, V. (1981). Has racism declined in America? It depends on who is asking and what is asked. *Journal of Conflict Resolution, 25*, 563–579.

Ommundsen, R. & Larsen, K.S. (1997). Attitudes toward illegal aliens: the reliability and validity of a Likert-type scale. *The Journal of Social Psychology, 135*, 665–667.

Osgood, C.E., Suci, G.J. & Tannenbaum, P.H. (1957). *The Measurement of Meaning*. Urbana, IL: University of Illinois Press.

Paulhus, D.L. (1991). Measurement and control of response bias. In Robinson, J.P., Shaver, P.R. & Wrightsman, L.S. (Eds.), *Measures of Personality and Social Psychological Attitudes* (pp. 17–59). San Diego, CA: Academic Press.

Petty, R.E. & Cacioppo, J.T. (1983). The role of bodily responses in attitude measurement and change. In Cacioppo, J.T. & Petty, R.E. (Eds.), *Social Psychophysiology: A Sourcebook* (pp. 51–101). New York: Guilford Press.

Quigley-Fernandez, B. & Tedeschi, J.T. (1978). The bogus pipeline as lie detector: two validity studies. *Journal of Personality and Social Psychology, 36*, 247–256.

Robins, R.W., Hendin, H.M. & Trzesniewski, K.H. (2001). Measuring global self-esteem: construct validation of a single-item measure and the Rosenberg Self-Esteem Scale. *Personality and Social Psychology Bulletin, 27*, 151–161.

Robinson, J.P., Shaver, P.R. & Wrightsman, L.S. (Eds.) (1991). *Measures of Personality and Social Psychological Attitudes*. San Diego, CA: Academic Press.

Robinson, J.P., Shaver, P.R. & Wrightsman, L.S. (Eds.) (1999). *Measures of Political Attitudes. Measures of Social Psychological Attitudes*, Vol. 2. San Diego, CA: Academic Press.

Rosenberg, M. (1965). *Society and the Adolescent Self-Image*. Princeton, NJ: Princeton University Press.

Schuman, H. & Presser, S. (1981). *Questions and Answers in Attitude Surveys: Experiments on Question Form, Wording, and Context*. San Diego, CA: Academic Press.

Schwarz, N., Strack, F. & Mai, H.-P. (1991). Assimilation and contrast effects in part-whole question sequences: a conversational logic analysis. *Public Opinion Quarterly, 55*, 3–23.

Woodmansee, J. & Cook, S. (1967). Dimensions of racial attitudes: their identification and measurement. *Journal of Personality and Social Psychology, 7*, 240–250.

Icek Ajzen

RELATED ENTRIES

Personality Assessment (General), Interest, Emotions, Environmental Attitudes and Values, Values

ATTRIBUTIONAL STYLES

INTRODUCTION

Shortly after research on attribution theory blossomed, measures were developed to assess attributional style – the presence of cross-situational consistency in the types of attributions people make. Two approaches to measuring attributional style are reviewed here. The first involves global measures that assume attributional style and broadly applies across a variety of situations (see Table 1 for a list of the most widely used measures of attributional style). These measures were developed to test predictions from the reformulated theory of learned helplessness depression (Abramson, Seligman & Teasdale, 1978). The second approach involves more specific measures of attributional style. This approach emerged, in part, from critiques of the cross-situational consistency of the global measures. These measures assess attributional style in more limited contexts such as work, school, and relationships.

GLOBAL MEASURES OF ATTRIBUTIONAL STYLE

Dimensional Measures

Dimensional measures of attributional style require respondents to generate causes for hypothetical events and then to rate them along several attributional dimensions. The Attributional Style Questionnaire (ASQ; Peterson, Semmel, Von Baeyer, Abramson, Metalsky & Seligman, 1982) is the most widely known. It contains 12 hypothetical events, half describing positive events ('you meet a friend who compliments you on your appearance') and half describing negative events ('you go out on a date and it goes badly'). Events are further divided into an equal number of interpersonal and achievement contexts. The perceived cause of each event is rated along the dimensions of locus (due to the person or the situation), stability (likely or unlikely to occur again), and globality (limited in its influence or widespread) using seven-point scales. Scores can be computed for each dimension within positive and negative events. Factor analyses of the ASQ have supported the presence of distinct attributional styles for negative and positive events (Xenikou, Furnham & McCarrey, 1997), although results presented by Cutrona, Russell, and Jones (1985) indicate that each event on the ASQ represents its own factor. However, findings suggest that attributions for negative events are most strongly related to depression (Sweeney, Anderson & Bailey, 1986). Scores can be further analysed within interpersonal and achievement contexts, a distinction that appears to be more relevant to positive than negative events.

The ASQ has proven to be a valid predictor of depression. People who make internal, stable, and

Table 1.   Widely used measures of attributional style

Global measures
    Attributional Style Questionnaire (ASQ; Peterson et al., 1982)
    Attributional Style Assessment Test (ASAT; Anderson & Riger, 1991)
    Children's Attributional Style Questionnaire (CASQ; Seligman et al., 1984)
    Content Analysis of Verbatim Explanations (CAVE; Peterson, 1992)
Intermediate measures
    Academic Attributional Style Questionnaire (AASQ; Peterson & Barrett, 1987)
    Organizational Attributional Style Questionnaire (OASQ; Kent & Martinko, 1995)
    Relationship Attribution Measure (RAM; Bradbury & Fincham, 1990)

---

global attributions for negative events tend to be more depressed. However, there are at least four problems with the ASQ. First, internal consistency for the ASQ ranges from adequate to low, especially for the locus dimension. A frequent solution is to combine the three dimensions into a single index to increase reliability, as the dimensions tend to correlate highly with one another. However, this creates a second problem: one of interpretation. There are unique predictions for each attributional style dimension; using a composite score prevents valid tests of the model (Carver, 1989). Several authors advise researchers to analyse ASQ data in terms of both individual dimensions and composite scores. The third problem is also related; the ASQ does not assess the key attributional dimension of controllability. The few studies that included controllability consistently find that it is the most important attributional style dimension, whereas globality is the least important (e.g. Deuser & Anderson, 1995). The fourth problem concerns the affiliation versus achievement distinction; several of the 'achievement' items involve affiliative contexts. The *Expanded Attributional Style Questionnaire* (EASQ; Peterson & Villanova, 1988) uses an identical format to the ASQ and addresses the problem of low reliability by increasing the number of situations included in the measure. However, reliabilities remain modest and the other problems remain unresolved.

The third and fourth versions of the Attributional Style Assessment Test (ASAT-III and ASAT-IV) provide another dimensional assessment of attributional style (Anderson & Riger, 1991). These measures use a format similar to the ASQ but they incorporate a larger number of items (20 for the ASAT-III and 36 for the ASAT-IV), include the controllability dimension, and use success and failure items that mirror each other (e.g. 'succeeded' vs. 'failed' at coordinating an outing for a group of people...). The interpersonal versus non-interpersonal subsets of items are more clearly differentiated than the affiliation versus achievement items of the ASQ. Internal reliabilities at the subscale level tend to be weak to modest, in the 0.5–0.6 range; collapsing across situation types (e.g. ignoring the interpersonal vs. non-interpersonal distinction) yields somewhat larger alphas. These scales have successfully predicted depression, loneliness, and shyness as well as depressive-like motivational deficits in laboratory settings. Furthermore, this body of work has demonstrated the importance of assessing attributional styles separately for interpersonal and non-interpersonal situations. Finally, this work has shown substantial correlations between attributional styles for successful events and depression (and loneliness and shyness).

Several other dimensional measures of attributional style use the same basic approach as the ASQ and ASAT. The *Balanced Attributional Style Questionnaire* (BASQ; Feather & Tiggemann, 1984) uses a format similar to the ASQ but, like the ASAT, the positive and negative items mirror one another. The scales have moderate reliabilities and correlate with depression, self-esteem, and protestant work ethic. The *Real Events Attributional Style Questionnaire* (REASQ; Norman & Antaki, 1988) requires that respondents generate the positive and negative events for which they then make attributions. This may yield a better prediction of depression, but the loss of item standardization creates other problems.

Forced-Choice Measures

Forced-choice measures have respondents select a cause from a list of potential explanations. One benefit is that this method may more accurately mirror how people typically select a cause (i.e. without thinking about dimensions). Also, the types of causes in the list can be restricted to only those attributions of theoretical interest. Forced-choice measures also require less time to complete.

The ASAT-I and ASAT-II use this forced-choice format. Respondents are provided with a number of hypothetical situations (20 for the ASAT-I and 36 for the ASAT-II). On the ASAT-I, the listed types of causes are strategy, ability, effort, personality traits, mood, and circumstances. ASAT-II includes only strategy, effort, and ability causes. The number of times a particular cause is selected is summed to create a measure of attributional style for that dimension. Kuder–Richardson (K-R 20) reliabilities for the subscales tend to be in the low to moderate range. Correlations with loneliness and depression have established the validity of these scales in both US and Mainland China college student populations (Anderson, 1999).[1]

Measures for Children

The *Children's Attributional Style Questionnaire* (CASQ; Seligman et al., 1984) was developed to allow researchers to study attributional style in children aged 8–13. The CASQ includes 48 items divided equally between positive ('You get an "A" on a test') and negative events ('You break a glass'). The scale uses both a forced choice and a dimensional approach. Respondents select between two possible causes for the event, and each option represents the presence or absence of one attribution dimension (for example, an internal or external cause). Attributions for each dimension are computed by summing the number of internal, stable, or global responses. Scores similar to the ASQ can then be computed. Internal consistency of the CASQ is low to adequate and improves when the separate dimensions are combined into a single composite.

Content Analysis Measure

The *Content Analysis of Verbatim Explanations* (CAVE; Peterson, 1992) technique assesses attributional style through a content analysis of an individual's writing. This allows analysis of ecologically valid events without requiring the participant to complete a questionnaire. The CAVE can also be applied to historical data, and it has established the stability of attributional style over a 52-year period (Burns & Seligman, 1989). Coders first extract causal explanations from a text, then rate them along the dimensions of locus, stability, and globality. Inter-rater reliability for the CAVE technique is satisfactory, and internal consistency has been reported as low to adequate. More standard questionnaire measures of attributional style may be better predictors of depression, but the CAVE technique has proven useful when written content is all that is available.

INTERMEDIATE MEASURES OF ATTRIBUTIONAL STYLE

Global measures of attributional style assume a high degree of cross-situational consistency in the types of attributions people make. However, several studies have questioned this assumption. Cutrona et al. (1985) found that the ASQ was a poor predictor of attributions for actual events, suggesting that situational factors may play a more important role in predicting attributions. Factor analyses by Cutrona et al. (1985) suggest that there is little cross-situational consistency in global measures of attributional style. Intermediate measures of attributional style address this problem by limiting the situations about which an explanatory style is being assessed. Increased specificity should increase the ability of such measures to predict actual attributions. The ASAT's emphasis on four situation types (success/failure by interpersonal/non-interpersonal) is one approach to increasing specificity. Other research on this issue has been mixed, however (Henry & Campbell, 1995), suggesting that further work is needed to establish the appropriate level of specificity in attributional style measures.

Academic Settings

Two measures have been used to assess attributional style in academic settings. The *Academic Attributional Style Questionnaire* (AASQ; Peterson & Barrett, 1987) uses the same format as the ASQ and contains descriptions of 12 negative events that occur in academic settings. The measure has demonstrated high internal consistency, and findings suggest that students who make internal, stable, and global attributions for negative events tend to do more poorly in classes. Henry and Campbell (1995) also developed a measure of attributional style for academic events. Their measure contains 20 items, equally divided between positive and negative events. The measure displayed adequate to good reliability and also predicted academic performance.

Work Settings

The *Organizational Attributional Style Questionnaire* (OASQ; Kent & Martinko, 1995) was developed to assess attributional style for negative events in a work setting. The format is similar to that of the ASQ, and the measure contains descriptions of 16 negative events that can occur in a work setting. After writing down an explanation for the event, respondents rate the explanation along the dimensions of internal locus, external locus, stability, controllability, globality, and intentionality. The internal consistency for the scale is moderate to good.

Relationships

Several different types of intermediate attributional style measures have been developed for measuring attributions in the context of relationships. The *Relationship Attribution Measure* (RAM; Bradbury & Fincham, 1990) assesses the types of attributions people make for a spouse's negative behaviour. Respondents read a hypothetical negative action by their partner and rate the causes of that event along six dimensions: locus, stability, globality, and responsibility (intent, selfishness, and blame). Researchers can use either a four- or eight-item version. A composite of all attributional dimensions displays high internal consistency and predicts marital satisfaction. Partners who attribute negative partner behaviour to internal, stable, and global causes are more likely to be dissatisfied with the relationship. Fincham has also developed a version of the RAM for use with children to assess attributions for parent–child interactions. The *Children's Relationship Attribution Measure* (CRAM; Fincham, Beach, Arias & Brody, 1998) uses a format similar to the RAM, and contains descriptions of two negative events.

FUTURE PERSPECTIVES AND CONCLUSIONS

Measures of attributional style have generated several issues which require additional research. The first issue involves level of specificity. Many studies question the presence of a global attributional style, and it is not clear if intermediate measures provide a satisfying solution to this problem. Additional research is needed to resolve these issues. Furthermore, attributional style measures typically suffer from poor reliability. New measures need to be developed to address this shortcoming. Finally, more research is needed on the controllability dimension of attributional style and on the unique contributions of the various attributional dimensions.

There are numerous ways of measuring attributional style, each with particular strengths and weaknesses. In deciding which scale to use, the researcher needs to carefully consider the specific goals of the research project, and then pick the tool that best meets the needs of that project. The modest reliabilities of these scales suggests that considerable attention be paid to sample size and power.

Note

1 The various ASAT scales, as well as Chinese versions of that ASAT-I, the Beck Depression Inventory, and the Revised UCLA loneliness scales, can be downloaded from the following web site: psych-server.iastate.edu/faculty/caa/Scales/Scales.html

References

Abramson, L.Y., Seligman, M.E.P. & Teasdale, J. (1978). Learned helplessness in humans: critique and reformulation. *Journal of Abnormal Psychology, 87,* 49–74.

Anderson, C.A. (1999). Attributional style, depression, and loneliness: a cross-cultural comparison of American and Chinese students. *Personality and Social Psychology Bulletin, 25,* 482–499.

Anderson, C.A. & Riger, A.L. (1991). A controllability attributional model of problems in living: dimensional and situational interactions in the prediction of depression and loneliness. *Social Cognition, 9,* 149–181.

Bradbury, T.N. & Fincham, F.D. (1990). Attributions in marriage: review and critique. *Psychological Bulletin, 107,* 3–33.

Burns, M.O. & Seligman, M.E.P. (1989). Explanatory style across the life span: evidence for stability over 52 years. *Journal of Personality and Social Psychology, 56,* 471–477.

Carver, C.S. (1989). How should multifaceted personality constructs be tested? Issues illustrated by self-monitoring, attributional style, and hardiness. *Journal of Personality and Social Psychology, 56,* 577–585.

Cutrona, C.E., Russell, D. & Jones, R.D. (1985). Cross-situational consistency in causal attributions: does attributional style exist? *Journal of Personality and Social Psychology, 47,* 1043–1058.

Deuser, W.E. & Anderson, C.A. (1995). Controllability attributions and learned helplessness: some methodological and conceptual problems. *Basic and Applied Social Psychology, 16,* 297–318.

Feather, N.T. & Tiggemann, M. (1984). A balanced measure of attributional style. *Australian Journal of Psychology, 36*, 267–283.

Fincham, F.D., Beach, S.R.H., Arias, I. & Brody, G.H. (1998). Children's attributions in the family: the children's relationship attribution measure. *Journal of Family Psychology, 12*, 481–493.

Henry, J.W. & Campbell, C. (1995). A comparison of the validity, predictiveness, and consistency of a trait versus situational measure of attributions. In Marinko, M.J. (Ed.), *Attribution Theory: An Organizational Perspective* (pp. 35–52). Delray Beach, FL: St. Lucie Press.

Kent, R. & Martinko, M. (1995). The development and evaluation of a scale to measure organizational attributional style. In Martinko, M. (Ed.), *Attribution Theory: An Organizational Perspective* (pp. 53–75). Delray Beach, FL: St. Lucie Press.

Norman, P.D. & Antaki, C. (1988). Real events attributional style questionnaire. *Journal of Social and Clinical Psychology, 7*, 97–100.

Peterson, C. (1992). Explanatory style. In Smith, Charles P. & Atkinson, John W. (Eds.), *Motivation and Personality: Handbook of Thematic Content Analysis* (pp. 376–382). New York: Cambridge University Press.

Peterson, C. & Barrett, L. (1987). Explanatory style and academic performance among university freshmen. *Journal of Personality and Social Psychology, 53*, 603–607.

Peterson, C., Semmel, A., Von Baeyer, C., Abramson, L., Metalsky, G.I. & Seligman, M.E.P. (1982). The attributional style questionnaire. *Cognitive Therapy and Research, 3*, 287–300.

Peterson, C. & Villanova, P. (1988). An expanded attributional style questionnaire. *Journal of Abnormal Psychology, 97*, 87–89.

Seligman, M.P. et al. (1984). Attributional style and depressive symptoms among children. *Journal of Abnormal Psychology, 93*, 235–238.

Sweeney, P., Anderson, K. & Bailey, S. (1986). Attributional style in depression: a meta-analytic review. *Journal of Personality and Social Psychology, 50*, 974–991.

Xenikou, A., Furnham, A. & McCarrey, M. (1997). Attributional style for negative events: A proposition for a more reliable and valid measure of attributional style. *British Journal of Psychology, 88*, 53–69.

Robert M. Hessling, Craig A. Anderson and Daniel W. Russell

RELATED ENTRIES

PERSONALITY ASSESSMENT (GENERAL), COGNITIVE STYLES, MOTIVATION, IRRATIONAL BELIEFS

AUTOBIOGRAPHY

INTRODUCTION

Autobiography constitutes a critical resource for psychological assessment and yet a complex challenge to it. The essence of this challenge lies in the fact that autobiography can be seen as both a focus of assessment and a means of conducting it. Since autobiography does not lend itself to assessment by instruments or scales, the sections in this entry will focus on general issues associated with the defining, assessing, and researching of autobiography, as well as on future developments concerning it.

DEFINING AUTOBIOGRAPHY

Autobiography is a narrative accounting of a person's life as interpreted or articulated by the person him or herself. It is a self-report by which a person expresses, explains, or explores his or her subjective experience over time. It thus represents a route to what it means and feels like to *be* that person, on the inside. Such a definition distinguishes immediately between autobiography and biography (an account of a life, presumably with greater objectivity, by someone else). An equivalent term for autobiography would be life *story*. This can in turn be distinguished from life *history*, or indeed *case* history, which is an account of a life for specific purposes by, for example, a social worker or physician.

Starting from this basic definition, autobiography can be categorized according to whether it is formal or informal. Though the distinction can be a fine one, formal autobiography means a deliberate and comparatively structured recounting of one's life with the express intention of summing it up to date or making a public statement concerning it. While the expression may take many forms, including poetry and sculpture, obvious examples range from a published memoir to a curriculum vitae. Informal autobiography includes what one reveals about oneself in less intentional ways, through one's speech, as in conversation or therapy, one's words, as in letters or diaries, or one's gestures and deeds. Behind both formal and informal autobiography lies one's autobiographical memory, or the memory one has of one's life as a whole (Rubin, 1996). However, insofar as such memory is internal to a person, assessments of its structure and possible impairments are impossible except as it is mediated by that person's actions or words. In this entry, then, 'autobiography' means any autobiographical *activity* that has some mode of external expression.

Additional distinctions by which autobiography can be categorized – and assessed – are whether it is voluntary (spontaneous, self-directed) or involuntary (requested, assigned); intended for a public audience or for private reflection; partial (concerning a particular period or theme in one's life) or complete (concerning one's life as a whole); superficial or in-depth; and whether the cue prompting it is specific or general (for example, *What was it like growing up blind?* or simply *Tell me about your life*).

ASSESSING AUTOBIOGRAPHY

What is assessed from autobiographical activity, the method or instrument by which the assessment is carried out, and the theoretical perspective(s) in which the assessment is rooted, depends on the discipline or context that is involved.

Within the context of psychology, the most obvious example of this point is in relation to psychotherapy, and not least to the field of psychoanalysis. While the assessment and interpretation of autobiography constitute an integral source of information about an individual and about possible issues or themes on which the analysis can focus, the focus itself depends on the therapeutic perspective that is employed. Accordingly, it may be on, for example, a person's self-concept; degree of introversion–extroversion; obvious omissions from the person's self-report and their possible significance;

evidence of self-deception or of specific disorders; and/or locus of control.

Within developmental psychology, the focus may be on one's interpretation of life events; on one's life-course trajectory; on the evolution of personal identity (McAdams, 1988); on guiding personal metaphors; on the relationship between life story and values or emotions; and on changes over time in the content and form of one's self-report – or 'the development of autobiography' (Bruner, 1987). Within social psychology, sociology, and anthropology, the focus of assessment may be on the social constructedness of the self and on how 'narrative practice' (Holstein & Gubrium, 2000) concerning the self is portrayed and utilized. As conventions of self-talk and self-representation, or 'forms of self-telling' (Bruner, 1987), can vary profoundly by culture, language, gender, ethnicity, and class, they are necessarily of major concern in assessing differences in the accounts that individuals give of their lives.

Within cognitive science, the aim of assessment may be on the formation and function of one's autobiographical memory and on its completeness, reliability, and accuracy – that is, the interplay between fact and fiction within autobiographical memory (Rubin, 1996), or between 'historical truth' and 'narrative truth' (Spence, 1982).

Within a healthcare context, autobiographical activity can convey invaluable information concerning a patient's medical history, social networks and relationships, living conditions, and overall emotional and cognitive status. It can also provide a reference point for assessing differences between subjective and objective measures of physical health; and can assist in the detection and diagnosis of particular pyschopathologies, including dementia.

Within the humanities, and specifically literary criticism, assessment of autobiographical activity may draw upon psychological or psychoanalytic theory to focus on the various functions, personal and social, that autobiography serves for the person who engages in it (LeJeune, 1989). In addition, it can focus on the narrative structure and integrity of particular autobiographical texts in terms of, for instance, plot, genre, theme, metaphor, point of view, and voice; on the role of language, and thus culture, in the formation and development of self-awareness and subjectivity; on the complex inter-relationships between author, text, context, and audience (Olney, 1980); and on the philosophical and hermeneutical significance of being, at once, composer, narrator, editor, character, and reader in relation to one's own life story (Randall, 1995).

Finally, within gerontology, the study and assessment of autobiographical activity has perhaps a special significance insofar as gerontology is concerned with social and psychological development across the lifespan. Accordingly, the focus may overlap with that used in other disciplines and be on, for example, an individual's subjective experience of the ageing process, or *biographical* ageing; on the question of competence and of the relationship between person and environment (Svensson, 1996); and on the role played by autobiographical activity in relation to life review, generativity, spirituality, and preparing for death.

One particular method that uses autobiography in working with older adults – as a means not only of assessment but also of education, recreation, and (informal) therapy – is called 'guided autobiography' (Birren & Deutchman, 1991). In guided autobiography, persons write about their lives in relation to set themes – such as career, family, money, health, and love – and then share their writings with other individuals in a group setting. Such groups have been shown to be successful for those involved in increasing their sense of self-understanding and of personal integration.

In general, autobiographical activity in an advanced age can be assessed and utilized in terms of numerous functions that it can be said to serve:

- identifying and honouring key turning-points during one's life-course
- coming to grips with past resentments and negative feelings
- setting the record straight
- finding meaning amid life's struggles and challenges
- seeking answers to personal issues
- reviewing one's life to attain a sense of peace
- leaving a unique legacy of experience and wisdom.

It should be noted, though, that autobiographical activity can serve many of the above functions at any point throughout the lifespan, and not only in later life.

RESEARCHING AUTOBIOGRAPHY

From a research perspective, it would be valuable to examine the development of autobiography using qualitative methods within a longitudinal design. Of course, the very nature of autobiography leads us to treat it as 'longitudinal', since it provides a good characterization of how a person perceives his or her past in light of what life is like today and is expected to be like tomorrow, or in the future. However, such data represents not the past as it was at the time it occurred – not the 'true story' – but the past as perceived at the time it is recounted, and as portrayed to a particular audience. Of central interest in research on autobiography, then, would be how people's perception of their lives change, or remain stable, as they age, and what changes occur in both the selection of events that they recount and the angle or tone from which those events are interpreted and told.

One possible design is to ask people at age 60, for example, to tell about their lives at 60, at age 70 to tell about life at 70, and so on. This would enable an assessment of the degree of change or stability in the content of their autobiographies as they grow older. Similarly, asking people at 70 to tell about life at 60, and at 80 to tell about life at 70 (and 60), would permit an assessment of change and stability in people's perspectives on both their age and the ageing process. Finally, having people at 60 tell about their entire lifespan, at 70 the same, and so on, would provide a picture of the relative change and stability in their perspectives on the content and significance of their lives as a whole. Overall, such a design would permit a better understanding of how people perceive, represent, and interpret their lives at different stages.

FUTURE PERSPECTIVES AND CONCLUSIONS

In the future, due to rapid social change, there will probably be a more pronounced need and use of autobiography as a means for individuals to evaluate, understand, and integrate their lives, if not as a continuous process, then at different intervals over the lifespan. From a research perspective, there will most probably be a greater focus on using autobiographical data in longitudinal studies, especially of older persons, to gain a sense of change and stability in their inner experiences of the ageing process.

Though it presents many issues for consideration, autobiography constitutes a valuable tool in several disciplines for assessing people's perceptions of their lives. In many ways, however, it has not yet been fully exploited as a qualitative method, especially in longitudinal research. As a complement to various tests and measures, it merits greater use in order to provide a fuller description and a richer understanding of the process of human life.

References

Birren, J.E. & Deutchman, D. (1991). *Guiding Autobiography Groups for Older Adults: Exploring the Fabric of Life*. Baltimore, MD: The Johns Hopkins University Press.

Bruner, J. (1987). Life as narrative. *Social Research*, *54*(1), 11–32.

Holstein, J. & Gubrium, J. (2000). *The Self We Live By: Narrative Identity in a Postmodern World*. New York: Oxford University Press.

LeJeune, P. (1989). *On Autobiography* (trans. K. Leary). Minneapolis, MN: University of Minnesota Press.

McAdams, D. (1988). *Power, Intimacy, and the Life Story: Personological Inquiries into Identity*. New York: Guilford.

Olney, J. (Ed.) (1980). *Autobiography: Essays Theoretical and Critical*. Princeton, NJ: Princeton University Press.

Randall, W. (1995). *The Stories We Are: An Essay on Self-Creation*. Toronto: University of Toronto Press.

Rubin, D. (Ed.) (1996). *Remembering Our Past: Studies in Autobiographical Memory*. New York: Cambridge University Press.

Spence, D. (1982). *Narrative Truth and Historical Truth*. New York: W.W. Norton.

Svensson, T. (1996). Competence and quality of life: theoretical views of biography. In Birren, J.E., Kenyon, G.M., Ruth, J.-E., Schroots, J.J.F. & Svensson, T. (Eds.), *Aging and Biography: Explorations in Adult Development* (pp. 100–116). New York: Springer.

Torbjörn Svensson and William Randall

RELATED ENTRIES

Qualitative Methods, Theoretical Perspective: Constructivism, Self-Presentation Measurement, Subjective Methods, Self, The (General)

A AUTOMATED TEST ASSEMBLY SYSTEMS

INTRODUCTION

Historically, test construction in education and psychology has shown a development from: (1) the construction of standardized tests to the practice of assembling tests from item banks tailored to the test assembler's specifications; (2) the use of intuitive rules of test construction to the application of model-based algorithms; and (3) manual sorting of items on index cards to selection by a computerized system.

Test assembly can be characterized as the task of finding a combination of items from an item pool that satisfies a list of content specifications and is optimal in a statistical sense. Formally, the problem has the structure of a constrained combinatorial optimization problem in which an objective function is maximized subject to a set of constraints, both typically modelled using 0–1 decision variables for the inclusion of the items in the test. Currently, a large variety of test assembly problems have been modelled this way and powerful algorithms for solving them are available.

MODELLING TEST ASSEMBLY PROBLEMS

A common view underlying all attempts to automate test assembly is to see each item in the pool as a carrier of a set of *attributes* relevant to the psychological variable or the domain of knowledge or skills the pool is designed to measure. A formal distinction can be made between the following types of attributes:

1 Categorical attributes, such as item content, cognitive level, format, answer key, and item author. This type of attribute implies a discrete classification of the pool; that is, a partition with classes of items containing the same attribute.
2 Quantitative attributes, such as item parameter estimates, expected response time, previous exposure rate, and word counts. This type of attribute is a value on a variable or parameter that, for all practical purposes, is to be considered as continuous.
3 Logical attributes, which imply relations among subsets of items in the pool, mostly relations of inclusion or exclusion. A relation of inclusions exists if an item has to be presented with other items in the pool because they share a stem or the description of a case. A relation of exclusion exists if items cannot be in the same test form, for instance, because some of them clue the correct answer to the others.

In addition to item attributes, it is useful to introduce the notion of test attributes. A test attribute is defined as a (function on the) distribution of item attributes (van der Linden, 2000a). Examples of test attributes are: the distribution of item content or p-values in a test, its information function, the number of items with a gender orientation, and its (classical) reliability. A test can now be defined as a set of items from a pool that meets a list of specifications with respect to its attributes.

An important distinction is between test specifications formulated as constraints and as objective functions:

1 A specification is a *constraint* if it requires a test attribute to meet an upper limit, lower limit, or equality.
2 A specification is an *objective function* if it requires a test attribute to take a minimum or maximum value.

The standard format of a test assembly problem is illustrated by the following example of a classical test assembly problem:

Maximize test reliability

subject to

1 Number of items on knowledge of facts smaller than 15;

2 Number of items on application equal to 20;
3 All items having four response alternatives;
4 Number of items with graphics at least 10;
5 Total number of items equal to 50;
6 No items with more than 150 words;
7 All item difficulties larger than 0.40;
8 All item difficulties smaller than 0.60;
9 All item discrimination indices larger than 0.30;
10 Item 73 and 98 not together in the test.

When translating test specifications into constraints, each constraint is required to have a simple form. For example, though it seems convenient to combine Constraint 7 and 8 into a 'single' constraint ('All item difficulties between 0.40–0.60'), such a step would obscure the total number of constraints actually involved in the problem. Also, for each problem only one objective function can be optimized at a time. If we have more functions, optimizing one of them automatically gives a suboptimal solution for the others. Finally, exchanging objective functions and constraints does not sometimes have too much effect. For example, we can replace the objective function in the above example by one in which the test is constrained to have reliability close to an educated guess of its optimum value and replace Constraint 7 and 8 by an objective function that minimizes the distances between the item difficulties and a target value of 0.50. In large-scale testing programmes, test assembly problems in a standard format can easily have more than 200 constraints. For a more complete introduction to item and test attributes, test specifications, and rules for translating specifications into objective functions and constraints, see van der Linden (in preparation; Chapter 2).

A mathematical solution to test assembly problems becomes possible if the objective function and constraints are modelled using variables for the decision to select the items in the test. Let index $i = 1, \ldots, I$ denote the items in the pool. The most commonly used decision variables are binary variables x_i, where $x_i = 1$ denotes the selection of item i and $x_i = 0$ otherwise. (Other types of variables are sometimes necessary though; see section entitled 'Some Applications'.)

A few examples of constraints modelled in terms of decision variables are:

1 Constraint 2 in the above example is a constraint with respect to a categorical attribute. If V_a denotes the set of indices of the items with the attribute Application, the constraint can be modelled as:

$$\sum_{i \in V_a} x_i = 20. \qquad (1)$$

2 Constraint 7 is an example of a constraint with respect to a quantitative attribute. If p_i denotes the p-value of item i, it can be modelled as:

$$p_i x_i \leq 1, \quad i = 1, \ldots, I. \qquad (2)$$

3 Constraint 10 is a logical constraint. It can be modelled as:

$$x_{73} + x_{98} \leq 1. \qquad (3)$$

All these constraints are linear equalities or inequalities in the decision variables. The feature holds nearly universally for all test specifications used in practice. A simple recipe to check if constraints are modelled correctly is to substitute trial values for the decision variables and determine the truth-value of the constraint. Examples of objective functions modelled in terms of decision variables are given in the section on Applications, below.

SOLVING TEST ASSEMBLY PROBLEMS

Mathematical optimization problems with a linear objective function and linear constraints belong to the domain of Linear Programming (LP). The first to see the applicability of LP to test assembly were Feuerman and Weiss (1973) and Votaw (1952). If the decision variables are binary, the problem is known as a 0–1 LP problem. For a general introduction to these optimization techniques, see Nemhauser and Wolsey (1988) or Wagner (1972).

Once a test assembly problem has been modelled as a 0–1 LP problem, a solution can easily be found by solving the model for optimal values of the decision variables using one of the algorithms available from the literature. Although 0–1 LP problems are known to be NP-hard – that is, to have solutions that cannot generally be found in a time bounded by a polynomial in the size of the problem – current technology has reached a level of sophistication that allows us to find exact solutions to problems with 1000–2000 variables and hundreds of constraints within seconds. Sometimes, test assembly models have the special structure of a network-flow programming problem. For such structures solutions to problems of virtually unlimited size can be calculated within a second (for examples, see Armstrong, Jones & Wang, 1995). A very efficient general-purpose LP software package is CPLEX 6.5 (ILOG, 2000). A dedicated software package that helps test assemblers to define their problem and then translates the problem into an LP model is ConTEST (Timminga, van der Linden & Schweizer, 1997).

An alternative to model-based test assembly is test assembly based on a heuristic. Test assembly heuristics are computer algorithms that assemble a test in a sequential fashion, that is, by selecting one item at a time. They do so using an item-selection criterion designed to meet the test specifications. Because of their sequential nature, heuristics are generally fast. However, steps early in the sequential process cannot be undone later, and heuristics produce solutions that are not optimal. Another difference between the two approaches becomes manifest if a new class of test assembly problems has to be addressed. In an LP approach, the problem only has to be modelled and the model can be solved immediately by the algorithms and the software already available, whereas in a heuristic approach a new item-selection criterion and computer algorithm have to be developed and checked for the quality of their solutions. Examples of test assembly heuristics proven to be useful are given in Luecht (1998) and Swanson and Stocking (1993).

SOME APPLICATIONS

Target Information Function

The practice to assemble a test to meet a target for its information function was introduced in Birnbaum's (1968) pioneering work on

IRT-based test assembly. Theunissen (1985) was the first to realize that the problem can be solved using 0–1 LP, provided the information function is required to meet the target, $T(\theta)$, only in a series of discrete points, θ_k, $k = 1, \ldots, K$. Uniform approximation of the test information function to a series of target values is possible through a maximin approach (van der Linden & Boekkooi-Timminga, 1989). In this approach, test information is required to be in intervals about the target values, $(T(\theta_k) + y, T(\theta_k) - y)$, and the objective function minimizes the common size of the intervals. Formally, the model is

$$\text{minimize } y \qquad (4)$$

subject to

$$\sum_{i=1}^{I} I_i(\theta_k) x_i - T(\theta_k) \leq y, \quad k = 1, \ldots, K, \qquad (5)$$

$$\sum_{i=1}^{I} I_i(\theta_k) x_i - T(\theta_k) \geq -y, \quad k = 1, \ldots, K, \qquad (6)$$

where y is a real-valued decision variable with optimal value to be calculated by the algorithm. (LP problems with both integer and real-valued variables are known as mixed integer programming problems.) Of course, these equations should be extended with a set of constraints to meet the content specifications for the test.

An empirical example for a pool of 753 items from the Law School Admission Test (LSAT) is given in Figure 1. The test length was set at 75 items. (The actual LSAT is longer because it duplicates one of its sections.) In all, a 0–1 LP model with 804 variables and 276 constraints was needed to assemble the test to deal with all specifications (including an item-set structure of some of the sections; see subsection entitled 'Tests with Item Sets'). The test information function had to approximate the target at five values. Figure 1 shows both the information function of the test assembled and the full target.

Multiple Test Forms

If examinees are allowed to take tests at different sessions, tests are often assembled as sets of

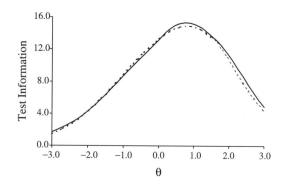

Figure 1. Information function for test form assembled from an LSAT pool (solid line represents target).

parallel forms. The best result is obtained if such sets are assembled simultaneously. If they are assembled sequentially, the value of the objective functions of each next form can be expected to be worse than those of its predecessors.

Multiple test forms can be assembled simultaneously if the following modifications are introduced:

1   The decision variables are replaced by variables x_{if}, with value 1 if item i is assigned to form $f = 1, \ldots, F$ and value 0 otherwise.
2   Constraints are added to the model to guarantee that each item is assigned to no more than one form:

$$\sum_{f=1}^{F} x_{if} \leq 1, \quad i = 1, \ldots, I \qquad (7)$$

For the same LSAT item pool, Figure 2 shows the information functions of three parallel forms assembled to meet the same target as in Figure 1. For more on this application as well as methods to deal with large multiple-form assembly problems, see van der Linden and Adema (1998).

Tests with Item Sets

Tests with item sets are popular because they allow for the testing of knowledge or skills using the same case for more than one item. Often, the item pool has more items per set than needed in the test. Let $s = 1, \ldots, S$ denote the item sets in the pool, $i_s = 1, \ldots, I_s$ the items in set s, and n_s the

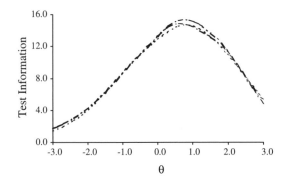

Figure 2.   Information functions for three parallel test forms assembled from an LSAT pool (same target as in Figure 1).

number of items required from set s if it is selected to be in the test.

Tests with item sets can be assembled if the following modifications are introduced:

1   In addition to decision variable for the items, 0–1 variables z_s for the selection of set s are introduced.
2   Constraints are added to the model that both coordinate the selection of item and sets and guarantee the correct number of items in each selected set:

$$\sum_{i_s}^{I_s} x_{i_s} - n_s Z_s = 0, \quad s = 1, \ldots, S. \quad (8)$$

The LSAT form assembled for Figure 1 had an item-set structure for some of its sections. For other empirical examples and approaches to assembling tests with item sets, see van der Linden (2000a).

Other Applications

The above applications illustrate only a few of the options made possible by 0–1 LP test assembly. Other options include: (1) classical test assembly, with Cronbach's alpha represented by a combination of an objective function and a constraint; (2) assembly of tests required to match a given test form item by item; (3) assembly of tests measuring a multidimensional ability; (4) assembly of multiple test forms that differ systematically – for example, a set of subtests for a multi-stage testing system or

testlets for testlet-based computerized adaptive testing (CAT); (5) assembly of tests with observed scores equated to those on a previous version of the test. A recent review of these and other applications is given in van der Linden (1998; in preparation).

FUTURE PERSPECTIVES

Though the development of computerized adaptive testing (CAT) was mainly motivated by statistical considerations, real-life CAT systems have to meet a host of non-statistical specifications as well. A recent development is the use of 0–1 LP test assembly to introduce non-statistical constraints in CAT (van der Linden, 2000b). The technique is applied through the assembly of a *shadow test* prior to the selection of the next item for an examinee. Shadow tests are tests that: (1) contain all items already assembled; (2) meet all constraints that have to be imposed on the adaptive test; and (3) have maximum information at the last update of the ability estimator. The item actually administered is the most informative item in the shadow test not administered to the examinee yet. Because after each update of the ability estimate the shadow test is re-assembled, the adaptive test is maximally informative. In addition, because each shadow test meets all necessary constraints, the adaptive test does.

Even though automated test assembly guarantees the best test from the pool, the result may be of low quality if the item pool is poor. In the parlance of 0–1 LP test assembly, the most important constraint imposed on the assembly of the test may be the poor composition of the item pool. It is therefore expected that an important future activity will be the development of methods to design item pools better targeted towards the tests to be assembled from them. A first attempt at optimal item pool design is given in van der Linden, Veldkamp and Reese (2000). A key notion in their approach is the one of a design space for the item pool. This space is defined as the Cartesian product of all statistical and non-statistical item attributes involved in the specifications for the tests from the pool. (This operation may require discretization of quantitative attributes.) A point in this space identifies a possible item in the pool. The technique of integer programming is then used to calculate an optimal blueprint of the item pool from the specifications for the tests the pool has to serve. The blueprint specifies the optimal number of items required for each point in the design space.

CONCLUSIONS

Over the last decade several models and algorithms for automated test assembly have been developed. Automated assembly is now possible for almost every type of test and every set of specifications. This development seems timely because automated test assembly is the key to any form of computer-based testing and the current expectations about the improvements in the practice of testing that have become possible by the introduction of computers in testing are high.

References

Armstrong, R.D., Jones, D.H. & Wang, Z. (1995). Network optimization in constrained standardized test construction. In Lawrence, K.D. (Ed.), *Applications of Management Science: Network Optimization Applications*, Vol. 8 (pp. 189–212). Greenwich, CT: JAI Press.

Birnbaum, A. (1968). Some latent trait models and their use in inferring an examinee's ability. In Lord, F.M. & Novick, M.R. (Eds.), *Statistical Theories of Mental Test Scores*. Reading, MA: Addison-Wesley.

Feuerman, F. & Weiss, H. (1973). A mathematical programming model for test construction and scoring. *Management Science*, 19, 961–966.

ILOG, Inc. (2000). *CPLEX 6.5* [Computer program and manual]. Incline Village, NV: Author.

Luecht, R.M. (1998). Computer-assisted test assembly using optimization heuristics. *Applied Psychological Measurement*, 22, 224–236.

Nemhauser, G. & Wolsey, L. (1988). *Integer and Combinatorial Optimization*. New York: Wiley.

Swanson, L. & Stocking, M.L. (1993). A model and heuristic for solving very large item selection problems. *Applied Psychological Measurement*, 17, 151–166.

Theunissen, T.J.J.M. (1985). Binary programming and test design. *Psychometrika*, 50, 411–420.

Timminga, E., van der Linden, W.J. & Schweizer, D.A. (1997). *ConTEST 2.0 Modules: A Decision Support System for Item Banking and Optimal Test Assembly* [Computer program and manual]. Groningen, The Netherlands: iec ProGAMMA.

van der Linden, W.J. (1998). Optimal assembly of educational and psychological tests, with a bibliography. *Applied Psychological Measurement*, 22, 195–211.

van der Linden, W.J. (2000a). Optimal assembling of tests with item sets. *Applied Psychological Measurement*, 24, 225–240.

van der Linden, W.J. (2000b). Constrained adaptive testing with shadow tests. In van der Linden, W.J. & Glas, C.A.W. (Eds.), *Computerized Adaptive Testing: Theory and Practice* (pp. 27–52). Norwell, MA: Kluwer Academic Publishers.

van der Linden, W.J. (in preparation). *Linear Models for Optimal Test Design*. New York: Springer-Verlag.

van der Linden, W.J. & Adema, J.J. (1998). Simultaneous assembly of multiple test forms. *Journal of Educational Measurement*, 35, 185–198.

van der Linden, W.J. & Boekkooi-Timminga, E. (1989). A maximin model for test design with practical constraints. *Psychometrika*, 54, 237–247.

van der Linden, W.J., Veldkamp, B.P. & Reese, L.M. (2000). An integer programming approach to item pool design. *Applied Psychological Measurement*, 24, 139–150.

Votaw, D.F. (1952). Methods of solving some personnel classification problems. *Psychometrika*, 17, 255–266.

Wagner, H.M. (1972). *Principles of Operations Research, with Applications to Managerial Decisions*. London: Prentice-Hall.

Wim van der Linden

RELATED ENTRIES

ITEM RESPONSE THEORY: MODELS AND FEATURES, ITEM BANKING, CLASSICAL AND MODERN ITEM ANALYSIS, ADAPTIVE AND TAILORED TESTING, THEORETICAL PERSPECTIVE: PSYCHOMETRICS

B BEHAVIOURAL ASSESSMENT TECHNIQUES

INTRODUCTION

A major impetus for behaviour therapy was disenchantment with the medical model of psychopathology that views problem behaviours as the result of an underlying illness or pathology. Behaviourists assert that both 'disordered' and 'non-disordered' behaviour can be explained using a common set of principles describing classical and operant conditioning.

Behaviourists believe that behaviours are best understood in terms of their function. Two 'symptoms' may differ in form, while being similar in function. For example, Jacobson (1992) describes topographically diverse behaviours such as walking away or keeping busy that all function to create distance between a client and his partner. Conversely, topographically similar behaviours may serve different functions. For example, tantrums may serve to elicit attention from adults or may be an indication that the present task is too demanding (Carr & Durand, 1985). Behaviour therapists try to understand not only the form but also the function of problem behaviours within the client's environment (Froyd et al., 1996).

The initial goals of assessment are to identify and construct a case formulation of the client's difficulties that will guide the clinician and patient towards potentially effective interventions. For the behaviour therapist, this involves identifying problem behaviours, stimuli that are present when the target behaviours occur, associated consequences, and organism variables including learning history and physiological variables (Goldfried & Sprafkin, 1976). The results of this functional analysis are used to design a behavioural intervention that is tailored to the individual client and conceptually linked to basic learning principles.

Assessing Target Behaviours

The process of defining and measuring target behaviours is essential to behavioural assessment. Vague complaints must be expressed as specific quantifiable behaviours. For instance, anger might include responses such as hitting walls, refusing to talk or other specific behaviours. The client's goals must be defined in terms of those specific behavioural changes that would occur if treatment were effective.

Target behaviour selection can be complicated by the complexity with which many responses are expressed. Behaviourists have long recognized that many clinical problems involve responses that cannot be readily observed. Some responses such as intrusive thoughts or aversive mood states are private by nature. Others, such as sexual responses, may be private and unobservable due to social convention. Many clinical complaints may include both observable and private responses. For example, depressed mood and suicidal ideation might be accompanied by crying, or other overt behaviours. Public and private responses may not always appear consistent. For example, an agoraphobic client may enter a shopping mall during an assessment but may do so only with extreme subjective distress.

Cone (1978) suggested that the bioinformational theory of emotion developed by Lang (1971) is useful for conceptualizing clinical problems. Lang (1971) asserted that emotional responses occur in three separate but loosely coupled response systems. These are the cognitive/linguistic, overt behavioural, and psychophysiological systems. A given response such as a panic attack may be divided into physiological responses such as increased heart rate and respiration, cognitive responses such as thoughts about dying or passing out, and overt behavioural responses such as escape from the situation, sitting down, or leaning against a wall for support. Ideally, each response mode should be assessed, there being no a priori reason to value one modality over another (Lang, 1971). Discrepancies are best considered with regard to the particular client, the goals of therapy, and ethical considerations. For example, it may be wise to take verbal reports of pain seriously even if they do not match evidence of tissue damage or physiological arousal.

The triple response conceptualization of clinical problems has encouraged the development and utilization of methods that more or less directly assess each response mode. Overt behaviours have been assessed by direct observation, with psychophysiological assessment used to assess bodily responses, and self-report measures developed to quantify subjective experiences. The apparent link between assessment methods and particular response modes is not absolute. For example, a client might verbally report sensations such as heart pounding, muscle tension, or other noticeable physical changes. However, in some cases, the method of assessment is more closely bound to a particular response mode. This is true of physiological processes such as blood pressure that are outside of the client's awareness, and in the case of thoughts or subjective states that can only be assessed by verbal report. In the following sections self-report measures, direct observation, and psychophysiological measurements are described in more detail.

SELF-REPORT METHODS

There are several formats for collecting self-report data. These include interviews, questionnaires and inventories, rating scales, think-aloud, and thought-sampling procedures. It is most often the case that an assessment would include several of these methods.

Interviews

The clinical interview is the most widely used method of clinical assessment (Watkins, Campbell, Nieberding & Hallmark, 1995), and is particularly advantageous in the early stages of assessment. The most salient of its advantages is flexibility. The typical interview begins with broad-based inquiry regarding the client's functioning. As the interview progresses, it becomes more focused on specific problems and potential controlling variables. Interviewing also provides an opportunity to directly observe the client's behaviour, and to begin developing a therapeutic relationship.

The clinical interview also has important disadvantages. Interviews elicit information from memory that can be subject to errors, omissions, or distortions. Additionally, the interview often relies heavily on the clinician to make subjective judgements in selecting those issues that warrant further assessment or inquiry. One could reasonably expect that different clinicians could emerge from a clinical interview with very different conceptualizations of the client (Hay, Hay, Angle & Nelson, 1979).

Structured and semi-structured interviews were developed in order to facilitate consistency across interviewers. Structured interviews are designed for administration by non-clinicians such as research assistants in large-scale studies. A structured interview follows a strict format that specifies the order and exact wording of questions. Semi-structured interviews are more frequently used by trained clinicians. They provide a more flexible framework for the course of the interview while providing enough structure to promote consistency across administrations. While specific questions may be provided, the interviewer is free to pursue additional information when this seems appropriate. In general, the goal of enhanced reliability has been attained with the use of structured and semi-structured interviews (Matarazzo, 1983). However, the majority of these interviews are designed for purposes of diagnosis rather than more particular target behaviours or functional assessment.

Just as the clinical interview proceeds from a general inquiry to more focused assessment of behavioural targets, other self-report measures vary in the degree to which they assess general areas of functioning versus particular problem behaviours. In general, those measures that assess general constructs such as depression or general domains of functioning are developed using group data and are meant to be applicable to a wide range of clients. Examples of these nomothetic measures include personality inventories and standardized questionnaires. Other self-report methods can be tailored more toward individual clients and particular problem responses. These include rating scales and think-aloud procedures. Each of these methods is described briefly in the following subsections.

Questionnaires

Questionnaires are probably the next most common assessment tool after interviews (Watkins, Campell, Nieberding & Hallmark, 1995). Questionnaires can be easily and economically administered. They are easily quantified and the scores can be compared across time to evaluate treatment effects. Finally, normative data is available for many questionnaires so that a given client's score can be referenced to a general population.

There has been a rapid proliferation of questionnaires over the last few decades (Froyd & Lambert, 1989). Some questionnaires focus on stimulus situations provoking the problem behaviour, such as anxiety provoking situations. Other questionnaires focus on particular responses or on positive or negative consequences. The process of choosing questionnaires from those that are available can be daunting. Fischer and Corcoran (1994) have compiled a collection of published questionnaires accompanied by summaries of their psychometric properties.

Many behaviourists have expressed concern with the apparent reliance on questionnaires both in clinical and in research settings. These criticisms stem in part from repeated observations that individuals evidence very limited ability to identify those variables that influence their behaviour. Additionally, behaviourists point out that we tend to reify the constructs that we measure. This may lead to a focus on underlying dispositions or traits in explaining behaviour rather than a thorough investigation of environmental factors and the individual's learning history. Behaviourists do make use of questionnaires but tend to regard them as measures of behavioural responses that tend to correlate rather than as underlying traits or dispositions.

Rating Scales and Self-Ratings

Rating scales can be constructed to measure a wide range of responses. They are often incorporated into questionnaires or interviews. For example, a client may be asked to rate feelings of hopelessness over the past week on a scale of 0–8. Clinicians might also make ratings of the client's noticeable behaviour during the interview or the client's apparent level of functioning.

The main advantage of rating scales is their flexibility. They can be used to assess problem behaviours for which questionnaires are not available. Additionally, rating scales can be administered repeatedly with greater ease than questionnaires. For example, rather than pausing to complete an anxiety questionnaire, a client might provide periodic self-ratings of discomfort during an anxiety-provoking situation. The main disadvantage of rating scales is the lack of normative data.

Thought Listing and Think-Aloud Procedures

Clinicians are sometimes interested in the particular thoughts that are experienced by a client in a situation such as a phobic exposure or role-play. The use of questionnaires may interfere with the situation and may not capture the more idiosyncratic thoughts of a particular client. Think-aloud and thought sampling procedures may be used under these circumstances.

These procedures require the client to verbalize thoughts as they occur in the assessment situation. Thoughts can be reported continually in a think-aloud format or the client may periodically be prompted to report the most recently occurring thoughts in a thought-sampling procedure. When the requirements of think-aloud procedures may interfere with the client's ability to remain engaged in the assessment situation, the client may be asked to list those thoughts that are recalled at the end of the task. These procedures carry the advantage of being highly flexible. Like other highly individualized methods, they also carry the disadvantage of lacking norms.

DIRECT OBSERVATION AND SELF-MONITORING

One of the most direct forms of assessment is observation by trained observers. Direct observation can be conducted by clinicians, professional staff, or by participant observers who already have contact with the client. Rather than reporting in retrospect, observers can record all instances of the target behaviour that they witness, thereby producing a frequency count. Depending on the type of target response, this task could be arduous. Recording all instances of highly frequent and repetitive behaviours can place undue demands on observers. There are several ways to decrease the demands on the observer and thereby facilitate more faithful data collection. One option is the use of brief observation periods. For example, a parent might be asked to record the frequency of the target behaviour at intervals during those specific situations when the behaviour is probable. When the target behaviour is an ongoing response, the observer might employ momentary sampling procedures and periodically check to see if the behaviour is occurring. For a more thorough discussion of alternative procedures of direct observation see Baird and Nelson-Gray (1999).

Direct observation carries some disadvantages. It can be costly and time-consuming. In the strictest sense it would be favourable to utilize multiple observers so that the concordance of their recording could be checked. It has been shown that the reliability of observations is enhanced when observers know that the data will

be checked (Weinrott & Jones, 1984). However, this may not be practical, particularly in clinical settings. The use of participant observers may be a less costly alternative in many cases.

Direct observation can also result in reactive effects. Reactivity refers to changes in behaviour that result from the assessment procedure. Making clients aware that they are being observed can alter the frequency or form of the target response (Kazdin, 1979). This can occur even with the use of participant observers (Hay, Nelson & Hay, 1980). The variables that influence observee reactivity are not well understood. For ethical reasons, it may be unwise to conduct observations without the client's awareness.

Self-Monitoring

In self-monitoring procedures, the client is asked to act as his or her own observer and to record information regarding target behaviours as they occur. Self-monitoring can be regarded as a self-report procedure with some benefits similar to direct observation. Because target behaviours are recorded as they occur, self-monitored data may be less susceptible to memory related errors. Like other self-report methods, self-monitoring can be used to assess private responses that are not amenable to observation. Self-monitored data also have the potential to be more complete than that obtained from observers, because the self-monitor can potentially observe all occurrences of target behaviours (Kazdin, 1974).

There are several formats for self-monitoring. Early in assessment, a diary format is common. This allows the client to record any potentially important behaviours and their environmental context in the form of a narrative. As particular target behaviours are identified, the client may utilize data collection sheets for recording more specific behavioural targets and situational variables. When behaviours are highly frequent or occur with prolonged duration, the client may be asked to estimate the number of occurrences at particular intervals or the amount of time engaged in the target response.

It is often desirable to check the integrity of self-monitored data. Making the client aware that their self-monitored data will be checked is known to enhance the accuracy of data collection (Lipinski & Nelson, 1974). Self-monitored data can be checked against data obtained from external observers or can be compared to measured by-products of the target response. For example, self-monitored alcohol consumption can be compared to randomly tested blood alcohol levels.

Among the disadvantages of self-monitoring are its demands on the client for data collection and the lack of available norms. Like direct observation, self-monitoring also produces reactive effects. However, this disadvantage in terms of measurement can be advantageous in terms of treatment. This is because reactive effects tend to occur in the therapeutic direction, with desirable behaviours becoming more frequent and undesired behaviours tending to decrease. This temporary effect of the procedure can produce some relief for the client and help to maintain an investment in treatment. More information on self-monitoring methods is provided in the self observation (Self-Monitoring) entry in this encyclopedia.

PSYCHOPHYSIOLOGICAL ASSESSMENT

Psychophysiological assessment is a highly direct form of measurement that involves assessing the byproducts of physiological processes that are associated with behavioural responses. For instance, a cardiotachometer can be used to measure electrical changes associated with activity of the heart. While clients can verbally report many physiological changes, a direct measurement via instrumentation carries several advantages. Physiological measures can be sensitive to subtle changes and to physiological processes that occur without the client's awareness. They can also provide both discrete and continuous data with regard to physiological processes while requiring only passive participation from the client (Iacono, 1991). Additionally, most clients lack familiarity with psychophysiological measurement, making deliberate distortion of responses improbable (Iacono, 1991). Korotitsch and Nelson-Gray (1999) provide a more detailed discussion of psychophysiological measures.

The main disadvantage of psychophysiological measurement is the cost of equipment and training. This problem is compounded by the observation that it is often desirable to include measures of multiple physiological channels. For example, there can be substantial variance across individuals in the degree of response exhibited on a given physiological index. Those measures that are most sensitive for a given individual may not be included in a limited psychophysiological assessment. With technological advances in this area, less costly instrumentation will likely become more available.

FUTURE PERSPECTIVES

Over the past two decades, research devoted to direct observation and self-monitoring procedures has declined dramatically. This trend has been mirrored by a rapid proliferation of questionnaires and research examining their psychometric properties. One likely reason for this shift is the current climate of managed healthcare. The goal of more efficient and less costly healthcare has created pressure for more rapid and inexpensive forms of assessment and treatment. Psychophysiological recording equipment is simply too expensive for most clinicians to afford and maintain. The task of training and paying trained observers can also be costly. Even when participant observers are used, the procedure can place inordinate demands on these individuals. While self-monitoring is less costly, it does place more demands on the client and more time is required to obtain useful information beyond an initial interview. In general, the more direct methods of behavioural assessment have the disadvantage of also being more costly and time consuming. The trend toward more rapid assessment seems to select for brief, easily administered, and relatively inexpensive questionnaires and rating scales. There have been calls for more research devoted to behavioural assessment methods (Korotitsch & Nelson-Gray, 1999; Taylor, 1999). This research might lead to more efficient methods for implementing these assessment procedures. There is also a need to determine if the data from these assessments facilitates more efficient and/or effective treatment (Korotitsch & Nelson-Gray, 1999). If empirical support for the utility of behavioural assessment techniques is generated, this may help to increase the receptiveness of third party payers to the use of these procedures.

CONCLUSIONS

The goals and conduct of behavioural assessment are directly linked to learning theory and to the goal of altering behaviour through the use of behavioural principles. The hallmark of behavioural assessment is an emphasis on the function rather than the form of problem behaviours, and on the specification of problem behaviours, as well as their environmental and organismic controlling variables in more detail than is typical of diagnostic classification. While diagnostic assessment tools might be included, behavioural assessment demands further molecular analysis of specific target behaviours and controlling variables.

Behaviour therapists have long recognized that clinical problems are often part of the client's private experience, and that many are a combination of verbal, physiological, and overt behavioural responses. A comprehensive assessment considers each of these modalities. While these ideas are still fundamental in behavioural assessment, the more costly and time-demanding methods of behavioural assessment are becoming more difficult to include in clinical assessment and are less apt to be the focus of research.

References

Baird, S. & Nelson-Gray, R.O. (1999). Direct observation and self-monitoring. In Hayes, S.C., Barlow, D.H. & Nelson-Gray, R.O. *The Scientist Practitioner* (2nd ed., pp. 353–386). New York: Allyn & Bacon.

Carr, E.G. & Durand, V.M. (1985). The social-communicative basis of severe behaviour problems in children. In Reiss, S. & Bootszin, R.R. (Eds.), *Theoretical Issues in Behaviour Therapy* (pp. 220–254). Orlando: Academic Press.

Cone, J.D. (1978). The behavioural assessment grid (BAG): a conceptual framework and a taxonomy. *Behaviour Therapy*, 9, 882–888.

Fischer, J. & Corcoran, K. (1994). *Measures for Clinical Practice: A Sourcebook* (2 vols., 2nd ed.). New York: Macmillan.

Froyd, J.E., Lambert, M.J. & Froyd, J.D. (1996). A review of practices of psychotherapy outcome measurement. *Journal of Mental Health*, 5, 11–15.

Goldfried, M.R. & Sprafkin, J.H. (1976). Behavioural personality assessment. In Spence, J.T., Carson, R.C. & Thibnut, J.W. (Eds.), *Behavioural Approaches to Therapy* (pp. 295–321). Morristown, NJ: General Learning Press.

Hay, W.M., Hay, L.R., Angle, H.V. & Nelson, R.O. (1979). The reliability of problem identification in the behavioural interview. *Behavioural Assessment*, 1, 107–118.

Hay, L.R., Nelson, R.O. & Hay, W.M. (1980). Methodological problems in the use of participant observers. *Journal of Applied Behaviour Analysis*, 13, 501–504.

Iacono, W.G. (1991). Psychophysiological assessment of psychopathology. *Psychological Assessment*, 3, 309–320.

Jacobson, N.S. (1992). Behavioural couple therapy: a new beginning. *Behaviour Therapy*, 23, 493–506.

Kazdin, A.E. (1974). Self-monitoring and behaviour change. In Mahoney, M.J. & Thorsen, C.E. (Eds.), *Self-Control: Power to the Person* (pp. 218–246). Monterey, California: Brooks-Cole.

Kazdin, A.E. (1979). Unobtrusive measures in behavioural assessment. *Journal of Applied Behaviour Analysis*, 12, 713–724.

Korotitsch, W.J. & Nelson-Gray, R.O. (1999). Self-report and physiological measures. In Hayes, S.C., Barlow, D.H. & Nelson-Gray, R.O. *The Scientist-Practitioner: Research and Accountability in the Age of Managed Care* (2nd ed., pp. 320–352). New York: Allyn & Bacon.

Lang, P.J. (1971). The application of psychophysiological methods to the study of psychotherapy and behaviour modification. In Bergin, A.E. & Garfield, S.L. (Eds.), *Handbook of Psychotherapy and Behaviour Change*. New York: Wiley.

Lipinski, D.P. & Nelson, R.O. (1974). The reactivity and unreliability of self-recording. *Journal of Consulting and Clinical Psychology*, 42, 118–123.

Matarazzo, J.D. (1983). The reliability of psychiatric and psychological diagnosis. *Clinical Psychology Review*, 3, 103–145.

Taylor, S. (1999). Behavioural assessment: review and prospect. *Behaviour Research and Therapy*, 42, 118–123.

Watkins, C.E., Campbell, V.L., Nieberding, R. & Hallmark, R. (1995). Contemporary practice of psychological assessment by clinical psychologists. *Professional Psychology: Research and Practice*, 26, 54–60.

Weinrott, M. & Jones, R.R. (1984). Overt versus covert assessment of observer reliability. *Child Development*, 55, 1125–1137.

William J. Korotitsch and
Rosemery O. Nelson-Gray

RELATED ENTRIES

THEORETICAL PERSPECTIVE: BEHAVIOURAL, THEORETICAL PERSPECTIVE: COGNITIVE-BEHAVIOURAL, OBSERVATIONAL METHODS (GENERAL), OBSERVATIONAL TECHNIQUES IN CLINICAL SETTINGS, SELF-REPORTS (GENERAL), SELF-REPORTS IN BEHAVIOURAL CLINICAL SETTINGS, PSYCHOPHYSIOLOGICAL EQUIPMENT AND MEASUREMENTS, APPLIED FIELDS: CLINICAL, ANALOGUE METHODS, SELF-OBSERVATION (SELF-MONITORING)

BEHAVIOURAL SETTINGS AND BEHAVIOUR MAPPING

INTRODUCTION

At first it might seem that behaviour settings and behavioural mapping are two separate and unrelated methods. Yet the true meaning of behaviour setting is that all behaviour is linked to a particular time and place; so any behavioural map is simply a record of behaviour that has always to be used within a behaviour setting. In a very literal sense behavioural mapping is really the footprint of a behaviour setting or settings.

For those unfamiliar with the term 'behaviour setting', it refers to a standing pattern of behaviour which is tied to a particular place and time, (these) are simply the easily observed events of everyday life like the grocery store, the lawyer's office, 3rd grade class. They can be observed to begin at a regular time and end at a regular time and contain a recognized pattern of behaviour which is constantly repeated. If it is unclear whether settings which are adjacent in time or place are really separate, the K-21 scale is used. This scale is available in Barker and Wright (1955), Schoggen (1989) or Bechtel (1997). The central idea is overlap of population and behaviour. If there is more than a fifty per cent overlap on the seven scales (population, space used, leadership, objects, action, time, mechanisms) the putative settings are really one. The score of 21 is arbitrarily chosen as the cut off point to separate two units but any score between 17 and 23 can indicate some boundary problems (Bechtel, 1977) of observed human behaviour. They are the units into which humans sort themselves to get the daily business of living done.

Behavioural mapping is the narrower recording of specific behaviours within settings. A behavioural map (Ittelson, Rivlin & Proshansky, 1976) is a recording of where behaviour takes place on a floor plan of the setting, providing a two-dimensional record of the behaviour. In special cases it is also possible to record the

behaviour automatically (Bechtel, 1967). Behavioural maps can include more than one behaviour setting.

BEHAVIOUR SETTINGS AS ASSESSMENT TOOLS

A behaviour setting census – that is, a complete count of behaviour settings in a community over a year – is used to assess either a community or an individual. Community assessment is done by counting the number of behaviour settings (with their population numbers) that occur in a defined community for one year. Assessment of an individual is done by collecting the *behavioural range*, the number of settings an individual enters in a year or a shorter time span, depending on the purpose of the assessment. A year is necessary in order to include the kinds of settings which only occur once a year like Christmas Eve, Easter, Fourth of July, etc. Merely counting the number of settings can provide a measure of health for both communities and persons.

A healthy community can be defined as one that provides an adequate, or, preferably, more than adequate, number of resources for its inhabitants. Healthy communities have about two settings available for each inhabitant. But there are other aspects which can be deduced from these numbers. For example, when two communities were compared (Barker & Schoggen, 1973), it was observed that one, a midwest town, had more behaviour settings available per child than a town in Great Britain. This was explained by the different philosophies on child rearing that existed in the two communities. In the midwest town it was assumed that the best way to rear children was to get them participating in adult life as soon as they could even though they might not be capable of performing at the adult level. In the British community children were withheld from participation until it was deemed they were capable of participating at a reasonably competent level. The result was the midwest town had twice as many settings where children were present. If one agreed that the midwest philosophy was more valid, then the greater participation would be a measure of a healthy environment for children (and could even quantify the number of settings available to children vs. number of children and be used to evaluate goals). Organizations can be assessed by use of behaviour settings. For example, in the study of school size (Barker & Gump, 1964), it was discovered that large schools had twenty times as many students as small schools but only five times as many settings. The consequence of this was that small schools can have twice the participation level of large schools in extra curricular activities, simply because there is more activity per student. The psychological consequences of this size discrepancy are also critical. Small schools report more satisfaction, competence, being challenged, engaging in important actions (leadership), being involved, achieving more cultural and more moral values. By contrast, large schools report more vicarious enjoyment (passive roles), large affiliation, and learning more about the school and persons in it.

Leadership is another important variable that can be measured when taking a behaviour-setting census. A simple scale is used for each behaviour setting: six is applied to a leader without whom the setting could not take place. A one-person radio station is an example. A teacher of an unfamiliar language like Urdu might be another. There are few truly six-rated settings because most are shared leadership. For example, any organization with a vice president has a shared leadership. Most settings have leaders rated at the five level. Fours are officials like secretaries, treasurers, board members, etc. Anyone who has a role above that of plain member is a four.

Even a janitor is a four. Threes are the bona fide members of the setting who are not officials in any way. Twos are visitors to the setting and ones are onlookers outside the setting looking in. Sidewalk superintendents are ones. This simple leadership breakdown for every setting can be used to calculate the leadership roles available per person in a town. To return to our midwest versus British towns, the midwesterners had control of four times as many settings as the British. This was because the British town had many outside persons entering

and controlling settings. It is obvious that this simple scale can also be used as a measure of opportunity. For example, in small versus large military bases in Alaska (Bechtel, 1977) it was shown that there was a much better chance at leadership roles in the smaller bases.

Using the Behavioural Range can be an effective way to measure the involvement of a patient outside of therapy (Bechtel, 1984). This method can be used to measure an average day, a month or a whole year in a person's life. The entire year is an accurate measure of lifestyle. For a quicker assessment, the therapist merely asks about the number of activities the patient engages in and assumes these are settings. Also critical is the role the patient takes in each setting, whether passive or some form of leadership. Two alcoholic women, aged 50, were assessed in this manner. The first patient had very few activities, and when she saw how sparse her day was remarked, 'Gee, I don't do very much.' Part of the therapy contract was to get her involved in more activities. The second patient made a rather impressive list of activities and was surprised by the breadth of engagement. Her contract was to use these settings as a better resource. The fact of participation was itself reassuring, however.

The Behavioural Range can also be used as a personal leadership measure by using the 1–6 scale for participation in each behaviour setting.

BEHAVIOUR MAPPING AS AN ASSESSMENT TOOL

Behavioural mapping was first used by Ittelson (1961) in a mental ward of a veteran's hospital (see Table 1). Patients in the ward were directly observed and their movements and behaviour coded on a floor plan of the ward. Cherulnik (1993) provides two examples of behavioural mapping used to evaluate changes in mental hospital wards. In both cases physical arrangements were modified to allow patients a closer proximity in order to encourage social interaction. And in both cases this was successful because pre–post behavioural mapping showed significant increases in social interaction.

A scale drawing of the place to be measured is first necessary with each physical feature labelled. The categories of behaviour should be observable and codable. One problem is the intrusiveness of

Table 1. Behavioural mapping categories from a mental ward (from Ittelson et al., 1976: 344)

Behaviour	Observational categories	Analytic categories
Patient reclines on bench, hand over face, but not asleep		
Patient lies in bed awake	Lie awake	
Patient sleeps on easy chair		
One patient sleeps while others are lined up for lunch	Sleeping	Isolated passive
Patient sits smiling to self	Sitting alone	
Patient sits, smoking and spitting		
Patient writes a letter on bench		
Patient takes notes from book	Write	
Patient sets own hair	Personal hygiene	
Patient sits, waiting to get into shower		
Patient reads newspaper and paces		
Patient reads a book	Read	Isolated active
Patient and nurse's aid stand next to alcove		
Patient stands in doorway smoking	Stand	
Patient paces between room and corridor		
Patient paces from room to room saying hello to other patients	Pacing	
Upon receiving lunch some patients take it to bedroom		
Patient sits at table and eats by self	Eating	
Patient cleans the table with sponge		
Patient makes bed	Housekeeping	
Two patients listen to record player	Phonograph-Radio	Mixed active
Patient turns down volume on radio		
Patient knits, sitting down	Arts	
Patient paints (oils), sitting down	and crafts	
Patient and registered nurses watch TV, together		
Patient watches TV, goes to get towel, returns	TV	
Patient stands and watches card games	Watching an activity	
Patient sits on cans in hall watching people go by		
Patient play soccer in corridor		
Patient and doctors play chess	Games	
One patient talks to another in reassurance tones		Social
Four patients sit facing corridor, talk sporadically		
Patient fails to respond to doctor's questions	Talk	
Patient introduces visitors to other patient		
Patient stands near room with visitors	Talk (visitor)	Visit
Patient comes in to flick cigarette ashes		
Patients go to solarium	Traffic	Traffic

observers. Usually observers are introduced as 'architecture students' who want to observe how the design elements are used. Another problem is the time sampling. If architectural features are to be evaluated, the time of maximum use must first be determined. Another aspect, however, may be the span of time where the features being studied are not used at all. Use and disuse are often problems with the same design feature. For example, in one study of a hospice done by Bill Ittelson and I, it was discovered that the chapel of the hospice was seldom used compared to other places. But when patients and staff were quizzed, it became apparent that the symbolic importance of the chapel made it more important than the actual use. An advantage of both the behaviour setting and behavioural mapping techniques is that they are essentially atheoretical and can be used to test any theory that proposes to influence behaviour or design.

FUTURE PERSPECTIVES AND CONCLUSIONS

The use of behaviour settings and behavioural mapping continue in many post-occupancy and other evaluation studies. It is often the practice to include them as part of several methods in post-occupany evaluation (POEs). However, many of the quantitative scales are often not used because researchers are not aware of their utility. For example, in several studies, the K-21 scale was used to measure boundary problems between two settings located adjacent to each other (see Barker, 1968 and Bechtel, 1984). Many times this scale can answer the question of whether a wall should be constructed between the settings.

The future of these measures is potentially greater than ever. The kind of data obtained is more readily understood by architects and engineers because it measures easily observed phenomenon (settings) which any layman can see and relate to. I can remember a conversation with Burgess Ledbetter, one of the architects I have worked extensively with in past years. He was designing a church of 10,000 members. I asked how he went about such an enormous task. He replied without hesitation, 'I just counted the potential behaviour settings.'

References

Baker, R. (1968). *Ecological Psychology*. Stanford, CA: Stanford University Press.

Barker, R. & Gump, P. (1964). *Big School, Small School*. Palo Alto, CA: Stanford University Press.

Barker, R. & Wright, H. (1955). *Midwest and its Children*. Evanston, IL: Row, Peterson.

Barker, R. & Schoggen, P. (1973). *Qualities of Community Life*. San Francisco: Jossey Bass.

Bechtel, R. (1967). Hodometer research in museums. *Museum News*, 45, 23–26.

Bechtel, R. (1977). *Enclosing Behaviour*. Stroudsburg, PA: Dowden, Hutchinson & Ross.

Bechtel, R. (1984). Patient and community, the ecological bond. In O'Connor, W. & Lubin, B. (Eds.), *Ecological Approaches to Clinical and Community Psychology* (pp. 216–231). New York: Wiley.

Bechtel, R. (1997). *Environment & Behaviour: An Introduction*. Thousand Oaks, CA: Sage Publications.

Cherulnik, P. (1993). *Applications of Environment–Behaviour Research*. Cambridge: Cambridge University Press.

Ittelson, W. (1961). *Some Factors Influencing the Design and Function of Psychiatric Facilities* (Progress Report). Brooklyn, NY: Brooklyn College.

Ittelson, W., Rivlin, L. & Proshansky, H. (1976). The use of behavioral maps in environmental psychology. In Proshansky, H., Ittelson, W. & Rivlin, L. (Eds.) *Environmental Psychology*, 2nd Ed. (pp. 340–351). New York: Holt, Rinehart & Winston.

Schoggen, P. (1989). *Behaviour Settings*. Stanford: Stanford University Press.

Robert B. Bechtel

RELATED ENTRIES

Behavioural Assessment Techniques, Observational Methods (General), Person/Situation (Environment) Assessment, Theoretical Perspective: Behavioural, Cognitive Maps, Post-Occupancy Evaluation for the Built Environment, Landscapes and Natural Environments

BIG FIVE MODEL ASSESSMENT

INTRODUCTION

The Big Five model of personality traits derives its strength from two lines of research, the psycholexical and the factoranalytic tradition, from which the interchangeably used names Big Five model and Five Factor model respectively originate. The two traditions have produced remarkably similar five-factor structures that mark a point of no return for personality psychology. An extensive review of history and theory with respect to the Big Five can be found in De Raad (2000).

The Big Five factors have been endorsed with a distinctive status, derived from the extensive, omnibus-character of the underlying *psycholexical* approach, and based on two characteristics, namely its *exhaustiveness* in capturing the semantics of personality and its recourse to *ordinary language*. Though both these characteristics may be improved upon, in comparison to other approaches to personality, the psycholexical approach outranks semantic coverage, and it has optimized the level of communication on personality traits by faring merely on readily intelligible units of description.

The model has served as a basis for the development of assessment instruments of various kinds. In the following paragraphs, different assessment forms based on the Big Five model, as well as some representative assessment systems, are briefly described, including Big Five trait-markers, Big Five inventories, and some instruments that have been moulded after the Big Five framework. To begin with, a brief content description of the Big Five constructs is given.

THE BIG FIVE CONSTRUCTS

The Big Five constructs, Extraversion, Agreeableness, Conscientiousness, Emotional Stability, and Intellect/Autonomy, made a long journey, covering about a whole century, towards a strong performance in the psychological arena during the last decade of the twentieth century. A straight count of the references made to each of the presently identified Big Five constructs in abstracts since 1887 tells that, of the total number of 17,262 references made, Extraversion (and Introversion) and Neuroticism (and Emotional Stability) are the absolute winners, with 8574 and 6189 references respectively. This picture sustains the historical 'Big Two' of temperament (Wiggins, 1968). The historical third, Intellect, with 1534 references, may refer to both traits and abilities.

Extraversion and Introversion

No single pair of traits of personality has been quite so widely discussed and studied as that of Extraversion and Introversion. Their main understanding at the onset of their appearance was Jungian. To Jung Extraversion is the outward turning of psychic energy toward the external world, while Introversion refers to the inward flow of psychic energy towards the depths of the psyche. Extraversion is denoted by habitual outgoingness, venturing forth with careless confidence into the unknown, and being particularly interested in

people and events in the external world. Introversion is reflected by a keen interest in one's own psyche, and often preferring to be alone.

Extraversion is a dimension in almost all personality inventories of a multidimensional nature, which in fact sustains its relevance and its substantive character. Moreover, many studies have provided behavioural correlates of this construct, such as the number of leadership roles assumed, and frequency of partying. Extraversion has also been found relevant in contexts of learning and education (De Raad & Schouwenburg, 1996) and of health (e.g. Scheier & Carver, 1987).

Agreeableness

Agreeableness is the personality dimension with the briefest history. Yet, while longtime constructs as Love and Hate, Solidarity, Conflict, Cooperation, Kindness, which are part and parcel of this dimension, may have been pivotal to the organization of social life throughout the history of mankind, as a personality dimension it essentially popped up with the rise of the Big Five. Agreeableness can be considered as being dominated by 'communion', the condition of being part of a spiritual or social community. Graziano and colleagues have described the details of the history of this construct (e.g. Graziano & Eisenberg, 1997).

Agreeableness is argued to play a role as a predictor of training proficiency (e.g. Salgado, 1997). In health psychological research, Agreeableness plays a documented role. Coronary heart disease is more likely to develop in competitive and hostile people than in those who are more easygoing and patient (*cf*. Graziano & Eisenberg, 1997).

Conscientiousness

Conscientiousness has been drawn upon as a resource in situations where achievement is of important value; that is, in contexts of work, learning and education. The construct represents the drive to accomplish something, and it contains the characteristics necessary in such a pursuit: being organized, systematic, efficient, practical, and steady.

Conscientiousness is found to be consistently related to school performance (e.g. Wolfe & Johnson, 1995), and job performance (e.g. Salgado, 1997).

Emotional Stability and Neuroticism

The first inventory measuring neurotic tendencies is Woodworth's (1917) Personal Data Sheet, developed to assess the ability of soldiers to cope with military stresses. Thurstone and Thurstone (1930) developed a neurotic inventory called 'A Personality Schedule' to assess the neurotic tendencies of university freshmen. As one of the 'Big Two', Neuroticism (or 'Anxiety') had been observed by Wiggins (1968) most notably in several of the works of Eysenck, Cattell, Guilford, and Gough.

Neuroticism has been found relevant as a predictor of school attainment (e.g. Entwistle & Cunningham, 1968). In the clinical situation, neuroticism is found relevant in the assessment of personality disorders (*cf*. Schroeder, Wormworth & Livesley, 1992). Neuroticism correlates significantly with measures of illness (e.g. Larsen, 1992).

Intellect and Openness to Experience

Feelings are usually running highest for the Fifth of the Big Five. This refers to its naming but also to its origin and its relevance as a personality trait factor. Discussions with respect to this factor incorporate the various points of criticism that are expressed over the Big Five as a model. Several candidates for factor five have been suggested, such as Culture, Intellectance, and Openness to Experience (see De Raad, 2000).

In assessment situations the Fifth of the Big Five may be relevant in psychiatry and clinical psychology. Aspects of Openness to Experience seem to be related to several disorders (Costa & Widiger, 1994). In contexts of learning and education, Openness to Experience has been related to learning strategies. Learning strategies possibly mediate a relationship between Openness to Experience and grade point average (*cf*. Blickle, 1996).

FACETS OF THE BIG FIVE

The Big Five factors represent an abstract level of personality description that may capture specificity at a lower level. Perugini (1999) distinguishes two ways to specify different levels of abstractness, a hierarchical and a circumplex approach. The *hierarchical* approach considers facets as first order factors and the Big Five as second order factors. The *circumplex* approach represents a fine-grained configuration in which facets are constituted as blends of two factors, based on the observation that many traits are most adequately described by two (out of five) substantial loadings. Because of its explicit coverage of the trait domain, the latter model provides an excellent starting point for the development of personality assessment instruments.

BIG FIVE TRAIT-MARKERS

Possibly the most direct way to arrive at an instrument assessing the Big Five is to select trait-variables as *markers* of the Big Five, on the basis of their loadings on those factors. Simply taking the first n highest loading trait-variables per factor might do the job. A frequently used marker list to measure the Big Five is the one described in Norman (1963). The list is based on earlier work by Cattell (1947). For the history of this and similar constructs from the same period, as well as for a comprehensive coverage of many psycholexical studies, see De Raad (2000). Goldberg (1992) developed an adequate list of 100 'unipolar' markers for the Big Five. In his 1992 article Goldberg concludes: 'It is to be hoped that the availability of this easily administered set of factor markers will now encourage investigators of diverse theoretical viewpoints to communicate in a common psychometric tongue.'

BIG FIVE INVENTORIES AND QUESTIONNAIRES

Several instruments have been developed to assess the Big Five factors. Besides those that are briefly described in the following sections, a few others should be mentioned such as the BFI (John, Donahue & Kentle, 1991), the HPI (Hogan & Hogan, 1992), the IPIP (Goldberg, 1999) and the HiPIC (Mervielde & De Fruyt, 1997). A few characteristics of some main Big Five instruments are summarized in Table 1.

Table 1. Summary of the some main Big Five inventories

Instrument	Authors	Factors					Variables
		I	II	III	IV	V	
100 Unipolar markers	Goldberg	Extraversion/ surgency	Agreeableness	Conscientiousness	Emotional stability	Intellect	100 adjectives
FFPI	Hendriks, Hofstee, De Raad	Extraversion	Agreeableness	Conscientiousness	Emotional stability	Autonomy	100 items
NEO-PI-R	Costa, McCrae	Extraversion	Agreeableness	Conscientiousness	Neuroticism	Openness to experience	240 items
BFQ	Caprara, Barbaranelli, Borgogni, Perugini	Energy	Friendliness	Conscientiousness	Neuroticism	Openness	120 + 12 Lie items
FF-NPQ	Paunonen, Ashton, Jackson	Extraversion	Agreeableness	Conscientiousness	Neuroticism	Openness to experience	60 non-verbal items

FFPI (Five Factor Personality Inventory)

This inventory (Hendriks, Hofstee & De Raad, 1999) is unique in several respects. It took its starting point in the circumplex approach with the so-called Abridged Big Five Circumplex (AB5C), distinguishing 90 facets that provide an optimal coverage of the semantics of the Big Five system. The pool of 914 items, that was agreed upon to represent the AB5C system, was made available with approximately identical phrasings in Dutch, German, and English. Items were only accepted for the final pool if clear, unambiguous translations in those languages could be found. The final instrument, comprising 100 items, 20 for each of the five scales, is trilingual in nature. The items have a simple and easy to understand behavioural format, put in third person singular, which makes them suitable for both other-ratings and self-ratings. Some examples of items are: Has a good word for everyone, Makes friends easily, Suspects hidden motives in others, Makes people feel uncomfortable, Feels at ease with people, Shows his/her feelings, Gives compliments, and Respects others. Besides scores for the Big Five dimensions, the FFPI enables the computation of an additional 40 bipolar facet scores, derived as blends of the Big Five.

NEO-PI-R (NEO Personality Inventory Revised)

Costa and McCrae's (1992) NEO-PI-R is the most frequently used personality questionnaire to assess the Big Five. The development of the N (Neuroticism), E (Extraversion), and O (Openness to Experience) scales started with cluster analyses of 16PF data, yielding two clusters called 'Adjustment-Anxiety' and 'Introversion–Extraversion', and a third cluster conceptualized as an Experiential Style dimension (openness versus closedness to experience). After taking knowledge of an early Big Five formulation, Costa and McCrae added Agreeableness and Conscientiousness to their three-dimensional system, assuming that their three dimensions, including Openness to Experience, captured the first three of the Big Five. Costa and McCrae's first Big Five version (the NEO-PI) included scales to assess six facets of Neuroticism, Extraversion, and Openness to Experience. Only the 240-item

NEO-PI-R (Costa & McCrae, 1992) also included six facets of Agreeableness and Conscientiousness.

BFQ (Big Five Questionnaire)

The Big Five Questionnaire (BFQ; Caprara, Barbaranelli, Borgogni & Perugini, 1993) has been developed using a top down approach, by first defining the five dimensions, and subsequently defining the most important facets for each dimension. The BFQ was developed alongside the first psycholexical study in Italian and some of its findings were taken into account, especially, to define the first factor. Accordingly, in the BFQ, the first factor is defined as Energy – rather than as Extraversion. The BFQ is easily administered and includes unique features such as a relatively small number of items (120) and scales to assess two facets per factor; in addition, it provides a Social Desirability response set scale of 12 items. Recently, a children version (BFQ-C, 65 items) has also been developed.

FF-NPQ (Five-Factor Nonverbal Personality Questionnaire)

A controversy with respect to verbal self- and other-ratings is that they may reflect consistencies in language rather than consistencies in observed behaviour. For this reason, Paunonen, Ashton, and Jackson (2001) developed an instrument that did not make use of verbal items, but included cartoon-like pictures, in which a person performs specific behaviours in specific situations. The investigators initially developed a non-verbal item pool for a person perception study and aiming to represent traits of Murray's system of needs. From this item pool a subset of 136 items was selected to form the Nonverbal Personality Questionnaire (NPQ) measuring 16 personality traits. With a few exceptions items were selected from the NPQ to form the 60-item FF-NPQ, with 12 items measuring each of the Big Five factors. This instrument takes about 10 minutes to finish.

QUESTIONNAIRES RELATED TO OR MOULDED AFTER THE BIG FIVE

The impact of the Big Five factors have been such that researchers often clarify the relations of their own alternative trait models with the Big Five. A few such alternative models have been proposed, such as a Big Three (Peabody & Goldberg, 1989), a Big Six (Jackson, Ashton & Tome, 1996), a Big Seven factor model (Almagor, Tellegen & Waller, 1995) and an alternative Five Factor model (Zuckerman, 1994). All these models share features with the Big Five but differ too.

In addition, some classic instruments to assess important personality dimensions have been moulded after the Big Five. Typically, this implied the development of a new coding format for existing items in those instruments so as to yield a measure of the Big Five factors. Examples of such instruments are the ACL (FormyDuval et al., 1995) and the 16PF (Hofer, Horn & Eber, 1997). A more specific situation is provided by the recoding of the MMPI-2 into the *Personality Psychopathology-Five Questionnaire* (PSY-5). The MMPI is one of the most used personality inventories for psychopathological assessment, originally developed in the 1940s and recently refurbished (MMPI-2). Harkness and McNulty (1994) developed the so-called PSY-5 constructs starting from a pool of symptoms and characteristics of both normal and dysfunctional personality functioning leading to the identification of 60 major topics in human personality. These topics were used to generate five higher order aggregates that have some resemblance with the Big Five, with especially the fifth factor remaining evidently uncovered.

FUTURE PERSPECTIVES

Because the Big Five model has acquired the status of a reference-model, its uses can be expanded to that of systems of classification and clarification for descriptive vocabularies that are not developed from a Big Five perspective, in order to evaluate the comprehensiveness of the trait-semantics of those vocabularies. Examples of such uses are given in De Raad (2000). Moreover, the model is expected to play an important role in modern theory building, because its five main constructs capture so much of the subject matter of personality psychology. An example is Digman (1997), who succeeded in relating the Big Five factors to

a higher order schema which brings together central concepts from various theories from the history of personality psychology.

Many more instruments along the main Big Five theme will be developed in the near future, as translations of existing instruments or as instruments that are completely developed within particular languages. Especially efforts may be expected to specify facets of the Big Five that can be cross-culturally validated.

CONCLUSIONS

Trait structures from different languages differ, and so do assessment instruments, imported or not. This conclusion is not dramatic; it is a challenge to cross-cultural research-programmes to isolate and identify what is valid across cultural borders, and to specify the particulars of the different cultures. A lot has yet to be done. The Big Five factor model has shown to be highly prolific in the construction of assessment instruments, notwithstanding the fact that its significance has only been recognized during the last decade of the twentieth century. Moreover, the Big Five factors are far from definitive, and the derived assessment instruments deserve constant atttention and an open eye for new facets and features to be included, in the model as well as in its assessment.

References

Almagor, M., Tellegen, A. & Waller, N.G. (1995). The Big Seven model: a cross-cultural replication and further exploration of the basic dimensions of natural language trait descriptors. *Journal of Personality and Social Psychology, 69*, 300–307.

Blickle, G. (1996). Personality traits, learning strategies, and performance. *European Journal of Personality, 10*, 337–352.

Caprara, G.V., Barbaranelli, C., Borgogni, L. & Perugini, M. (1993). The Big Five Questionnaire: a new questionnaire to assess the Five Factor Model. *Personality and Individual Differences, 15*, 281–288.

Cattell, R.B. (1947). Confirmation and clarification of primary personality factors. *Psychometrika, 12*, 197–220.

Costa, P.T., Jr. & McCrae, R.R. (1992). *Revised NEO Personality Inventory (NEO PI-RTM) and NEO Five-Factor Inventory (NEO-FFI) Professional Manual*. Odessa, FL: Psychological Assessment Resources.

Costa, P.T., Jr. & Widiger, T.A. (Eds.) (1994). *Personality Disorders and the Five-Factor Model of Personality*. Washington, DC: American Psychological Association.

De Raad, B. (2000). *The Big Five Personality Factors: The Psycholexical Approach to Personality*. Goettingen: Hogrefe & Huber Publishers.

De Raad, B. & Schouwenburg, H.C. (1996). Personality in learning and education: a review. *European Journal of Personality*, 10, 303–336.

Digman, J.M. (1997). Higher-order factors of the Big Five. *Journal of Personality and Social Psychology*, 73, 1246–1256.

Entwistle, N.J. & Cunningham, S. (1968). Neuroticism and school attainment – a linear relationship? *Journal of Educational Psychology*, 38, 123–132.

FormyDuval, D.L., Williams, J.E., Patterson, D.J. & Fogle, E.E. (1995). A 'big five' scoring system for the item pool of the Adjective Check List. *Journal of Personality Assessment*, 65, 59–76.

Goldberg, L.R. (1992). The development of markers of the Big-Five factor structure. *Psychological Assessment*, 4, 26–42.

Goldberg, L.R. (1999). A broad-bandwidth, public-domain, personality inventory measuring the lower-level facets of several five-factor models. In Mervielde, I., Deary, I., De Fruyt, F. & Ostendorf, F. (Eds.), *Personality Psychology in Europe*, Vol. 7 (pp. 7–28). Tilburg, The Netherlands: Tilburg University Press.

Graziano, W.G. & Eisenberg, N. (1997). Agreeableness: a dimension of personality. In Hogan, R., Johnson, J. & Briggs, S. (Eds.), *Handbook of Personality Psychology* (pp. 795–824). San Diego, CA: Academic Press.

Harkness, A.R. & McNulty, J.L. (1994). The Personality Psychopathology Five (PSY-5). In Strack, S. & Lorr, H. (Eds.), *Differentiation of Normal and Abnormal Personality*. New York: Springer.

Hendriks, A.A.J., Hofstee, W.K.B. & De Raad, B. (1999). The Five-Factor Personality Inventory (FFPI). *Personality and Individual Differences*, 27, 307–325.

Hofer, S.M., Horn, J.L. & Eber, H.W. (1997). A robust five-factor structure of the 16PF: strong evidence from independent rotation and confirmatory factorial invariance procedures. *Personality and Individual Differences*, 23, 247–269.

Hogan, R. & Hogan, J. (1992). *Hogan Personality Inventory Manual*. Tulsa, OK: Hogan Assessment Systems.

Jackson, D.N., Ashton, M.C. & Tome, J.L. (1996). The six-factor model of personality: facets from the Big Five. *Personality and Individual Differences*, 21, 391–402.

John, O.P., Donahue, E.M. & Kentle, R.L. (1991). *The Big Five Inventory – Version 4a and 54*. Berkeley, CA: University of California, Berkeley, Institute of Personality and Social Research.

Larsen, R.J. (1992). Neuroticism and selective encoding and recall of symptoms: evidence from a combined concurrent–retrospective study. *Journal of Personality and Social Psychology*, 62, 480–488.

Mervielde, I. & De Fruyt, F. (1997). *Hierarchical Personality Inventory for Children (HiPIC) aged 6 to 12*. Lisse: Swets and Zeitlinger.

Norman, W.T. (1963). Toward an adequate taxonomy of personality attributes: replicated factor structure in peer nomination personality ratings. *Journal of Abnormal and Social Psychology*, 66, 574–583.

Paunonen, S.V., Ashton, M.C. and Jackson, D.N. (2001). Nonverbal assessment of the Big Five personality factors. *European Journal of Personality*, 15, 3–18.

Peabody, D. & Goldberg, L.R. (1989). Some determinants of factor structures from personality trait-descriptors. *Journal of Personality and Social Psychology*, 57, 552–567.

Perugini, M. (1999). A proposal for integrating hierarchical and circumplex modelling in personality. In Mervielde, I., Deary, I., DeFruyt, F. & Ostendorf, F. (Eds.), *Personality Psychology in Europe*, Vol. 7 (pp. 85–99). Tilburg, The Netherlands: Tilburg University Press.

Salgado, J.F. (1997). The five factor model of personality and job performance in the European Community. *Journal of Applied Psychology*, 82, 30–43.

Scheier, M.F. & Carver, C.S. (1987). Dispositional optimism and physical well-being: the influence of generalized outcome expectancies on health. *Journal of Personality*, 55, 169–210.

Schroeder, M.L., Wormworth, J.A. & Livesley, W.J. (1992). Dimensions of personality disorder and their relationships to the Big Five dimensions of personality. *Psychological Assessment*, 4, 47–53.

Thurstone, L.L. & Thurstone, T.G. (1930). A neurotic inventory. *Journal of Social Psychology*, 1, 3–30.

Wiggins, J.S. (1968). Personality structure. *Annual Review of Psychology*, 19, 293–350.

Wolfe, R.N. & Johnson, S.D. (1995). Personality as a predictor of college performance. *Educational and Psychological Measurement*, 55, 177–185.

Woodworth, R.S. (1917). *Personal Data Sheet*. Chicago: Stoelting.

Zuckerman, M. (1994). An alternative five factor model of personality. In Halverson, C.F., Kohnstamm, G.A. & Martin, R.P. (Eds.), *The Developing Structure of Temperament and Personality from Infancy to Adulthood* (pp. 53–68). New York: Erlbaum.

Boele De Raad and Marco Perugini

RELATED ENTRIES

PERSONALITY ASSESSMENT (GENERAL), THEORETICAL PERSPECTIVE: PSYCHOMETRIC, TRAIT-STATE MODEL

B BRAIN ACTIVITY MEASUREMENT

INTRODUCTION

Electroencephalograms (EEGs) from the human scalp were first recorded in 1924 by Hans Berger. It is assumed that they are generated by brain activity related to information processing. EEG is mainly caused by nerve cell activity, whereas other brain imaging methods are more related to blood flow and metabolic parameters. Moreover, the direct coupling of EEG with biological flow of information allows a continuous and chronometric approach to the basis of cognitive processing. Variations of EEG require synchronous and massive parallel activity in wide-ranging populations of neurons and the measures are done in a great distance to the generators. Thus spatial resolution is less than in other brain imaging techniques.

Actually EEG potentials occur in several locations with alternating polarity. This finding is consistent with models of information processing assuming separate modules of cognitive functioning, which interact continuously in terms of uptake, processing and passing on of information.

The main fields of the psychological use of EEG are in *cognition*, in search of cognitive relevant modules in the brain and their temporal interaction. Distortion of common spatial or temporal regularity in potential dynamics (such as dimensional complexity) can be interpreted as a sign of uncommon or *emotional processing*. Brain activity is present when awake as well as during sleep, in which a number of *sleep stages* and sleep parameters can be differentiated by using certain criteria. Deviant patterns of EEG activity can be used to characterize *psychopathological states* or could be caused by *drug effects*.

PARAMETERS

Neurophysiological Basis

It is widely accepted that most of the time both excitatory and inhibitory postsynaptic potentials simultaneously are present in the pyramidal cells of the upper and middle cortical layers. Usually they are in balance without releasing considerable action potentials. It is assumed that this is particularly true when a module became charged without immediate output. A negative potential on the surface is measured because excitatory synapses are predominant in upper layers (negative interstitium in the upper layers). The release of action potentials (negative interstitium far below) will change the dipole causing a positive potential.

Basic Activity

Negative and positive potentials in EEG alternate with main fluctuations within about 0.1 s (equivalent to around 10 Hz). Dominant frequencies in the range of about 8–12 Hz are called *EEG alpha*. Alpha is observed in awake but resting subjects without demanding memory load. Alpha is generated by burst activity produced by loops between thalamic nuclei and the related cortical areas in case of attenuated stimulation. A lower portion of the alpha band (8–10 Hz) is discussed as reflecting attenuation of cortical activity during mental load while attending stimuli actively, for example in a time series resulting in partial loss of feature-related activation. The upper portion of alpha seems to be closer related to a more general attenuation of mental load mainly in processing stimuli, even by exogenous stimulation. Frequencies of 12–14 Hz (*EEG spindles*) seem to be indicative of active suppression of sensory stimuli during sleep.

Frequency 4–8 Hz (*EEG theta*) is discussed as indicative for extension of receptive fields, for example in coarse classification of stimuli. Theta is found to be increased during drowsiness and undirected memory search (flight of thought) as well as during top down or effortful processes causing directed memory search. The latter findings gave rise to the view that theta reflects involvement of hippocampal memory functions. Theta power can be found in posterior locations as well as above the premotor cortex indicating activated wide motor concepts. In learning response concepts, frontal theta is increased in good learners compared to poor learners.

Frequencies < 4 Hz (*EEG delta*) are found in slow wave sleep. Frequencies in the range of 40 Hz (*EEG gamma*) correspond to activities of neuronal ensembles, where some particular stimulus features are bound together building up a cognitive representation of an object or a gestalt. It is discussed that frequencies of 6 Hz may give rise to about seven oscillations of 40 Hz representing about seven distinct information chunks per second. There is a broad range of irregular frequencies between 14 and 40 Hz contributing to the shape of raw EEGs of awake subjects, which is called *EEG beta*.

Analysis of EEG basic activity needs data processing in the frequency domain and is useful for characterizing widespread cortical processes. It can be done for any time range as conceded by resolution and lower limit of the frequencies of interest, such as for mental states or for epochs chosen in relation to certain events.

Event-Related Potentials

Information processing can often be related to external events, such as the onset of a stimulus or a response. EEG potentials in the time domain corresponding to assumptions on expecting or processing of stimuli as well as preparing or evaluating of responses allow a kind of mental chronometry.

The most common potential observed before stimulus onset is a *contingent negative variation* (CNV) in the case of so-called imperative stimuli (which request fast responses) revealing increasing motor preparation. Consecutive to the onset of a stimulus, negative potentials reflect the load of certain brain areas stimulated by individually significant stimulus features. Physical features produce a load in modal specific areas in a time range of about 150 ms after onset, called *processing negativity* (N1). More abstract or related features lead to a load mainly depending on context information, for example in case of similar stimuli, in the context of a task, or in case of other kinds of involuntary or voluntary attention. Under these circumstances mental load mostly can be interpreted as a kind of mismatch and the related potential in the time range between 200–300 ms after onset is called *mismatch negativity* (N2).

Information load in individual brain areas is mostly followed by passing forward information to related or higher order areas, as revealed by a positive potential. An early positive deflection P1 (circa 100 ms) reflects forward processing of prepared (biological or overlearned) stimulation. A positive potential P2 (circa 200 ms) in the time range between N1 and N2 could be interpreted as forward processing from physical to psychological relevant features. Extraction of the psychological content ('semantics') means classification and relating to an abstract concept. Forward processing after this by a P3 or P300 (> 300 ms after onset) is discussed as cognition of the stimulus in terms of upgrading of the hitherto model of the environmental context. While most of the processes up to P3, even automatic respondings, are unconscious, forward processing after mismatch is assumed to be obligatory for being aware of the stimulus.

Longer-lasting processing increases P3 latency and widens the peak. Peak amplitude increases with task relevance and stimulus uncertainty. Important properties of stimulus processing can be studied by the odd ball paradigm. This paradigm consists of at least two classes of stimuli appearing randomly in time, where the instances of one stimulus are rare (20–30%) and a task should be done by using the rare stimuli (for example counting). Under these circumstances rare stimuli are responded by potentials with high P3s.

In case of mismatch of the extracted meaning of a stimulus compared to its semantic context, late negative and positive potentials can occur. *Semantic mismatch* occurs if a sentence ends with unexpected words or phrases (N400). Conducting information processing to a *reanalysis* is discussed in cases when a late positive potential follows (P600).

DATA ACQUISITION

The EEG Laboratory

EEG raw data have to be obtained in a laboratory protected against vibration and noise. Recording can be done without electric field protection, if external field generators are weak and well known (50/60 Hz). Usually a separate space for subjects (including display and response devices) and acquisition apparatus (amplifier and monitoring) should be provided. The electrical potentials recorded from the scalp are of low amplitude and have to be preamplified close behind the electrodes and amplified by high quality amplifiers. A/D converter is used to convert the analogue time-continuous voltage-time series into a digitalized time-discrete signal. Analogue–digital conversion rate (sampling rate) has to be at least twice as high as the highest frequency of interest in the signal to be measured to prevent the appearance of frequencies not present in the original signal. Preparation of derivation should be conducted by trained personnel. Otherwise all requirements, instruction, supervision and data acquisition by an examiner and/or computer has to be done as is usual in psychological experiments.

Electrode–Skin Interface

In the brain, a great variety of processes takes place, continuously generating time varying (bio)electric potential fields over the scalp. EEG signals are voltage time series reflecting the potential difference between two field points derived from the scalp by electrodes. Analyses of human EEG are usually based on frequencies of 0 to 100 Hz containing magnitudes approximately of 0 to 200 μV.

Employing high input impedance EEG amplifiers, a variety of different electrode materials (Ag/AgCl, tin, silver, gold) in combination with electrode jelly may be used. Caps with embedded electrodes permit simple handling and replication. Impedances up to 40 kΩ are permitted (Ferree et al., 2001), but less than 5000 Ω are usually preferred. This can be attained by abrading slightly the surface or even scratching the skin surface with a sterile needle. However, injuries have to be avoided.

Points of Derivation

Referential recording is based on the assumption that one electrode site is an inactive reference site and the active site of interest is recorded with respect to that reference. Reference sites with minor electrical activity such as the earlobes, mastoids, nose are preferred.

A reference-independent measure of the potential field is required for studying scalp topography and for source localization. One approach to overcome the reference-site problem is to use the so called average-reference using the mean of all recording channels at each time point to approximate an inactive reference. (Recording) problems arise because electrodes are not evenly distributed over the head surface. Another approach is to use reference-free transformations, such as current source density analysis (CSD), which is based on the second derivative of the interpolated potential distribution (Laplacian operator). The latter method accentuates local sources and masks interelectrode correlations. In order to get valid approximations, both approaches require a sufficient spatial electrode density.

Due to the prerequisites especially for successful topographic mapping and source localization a standardized system of electrode placement with up to 74 electrodes is usually used (10–10 system or '10% system'). Depending on certain research questions, a fewer number is used and/or interpolated sites are chosen. Advanced derivations use a 5% system with up to 345 electrodes (Oostenveld & Praamstra, 2001).

Common Steps in Artefact Rejection

The raw EEG signal may be contaminated by both technical (as power supply) and biological electric fields (electric activity of eyes, heart, muscle tension etc.). Parts of the EEG signal which are not generated by distinct brain processes are called 'artefacts'. Artefacts are not easy detectable and there are no common methods of artefact rejection. Thus contaminations of the brain signals have to be avoided by careful planning of the derivation setting (avoiding technical carelessness and unnecessary muscular activity as well as eyeblinks). After derivation the experimenter should do some 'eyeballing' on the signals. With DC-derivations it is useless to define an amplitude criterion for rejection (for example +80 μV). Noisy parts of the signal should be removed. Within one experiment the same criteria have to be applied for all subjects. Correction of ocular artefacts could be done in some cases (for uneasy children or patients) by use of special algorithms. Zero phase-shift low pass filters (about 20 Hz) are used for signal smoothing in ERP analyses.

DATA ANALYSIS

Signal Characteristics

Event-related potential (ERP) analysis is based on the assumption that part of the electrical brain activity is in a stable time relationship responding to a stimulus and the remaining brain activity is considered to be stationary noise. Hence segment-averaging is used to reduce variance depending on the ratio of time-locked to non-time-locked signal portion.

In general EEG signals are considered to be generated by stochastic processes with unknown probability density functions. Hence the processes are characterized by moments and moment functions. Usually EEG time series are studied up to second order of moments (mean, variance) and moment functions (covariance functions). *Higher-order statistics* (HOS) have to be used to analyse signal properties which deviate from Gaussian amplitude distribution (signal skewness, signal kurtosis). Given a signal of interest with non-zero HOS noised by Gaussian noise, then HOS is less affected by noise than second-order analyses.

Apart from the stochastic approach attempts have been made to describe EEG signals as the output of a complex *deterministic process* by use of non-linear difference equations. The corresponding mathematical base originates from the field of 'deterministic chaos'. One frequently used measure is called *EEG dimensional complexity* (DCx) and this yields information regarding the complexity of processes in the brain.

Methods of Spectral Estimation

One widely used method when analysing EEG time series is spectral analysis, which means analysing a given signal with respect to its properties within the frequency domain. (Problems arise in analysing rapid amplitude changes within low frequency bands.)

Spectra can be obtained by filtering the signal with a set of narrow bandpass filters. This procedure is common in determining *event-related desynchronization* (ERD) where activated cortical areas are assumed to be desynchronized compared to an idling state. After averaging over trials to discriminate between event-related and non-event-related power changes a standardized difference term between signal power in the analysed interval (A) and in a reference interval (R) is calculated:

$$\text{ERD} = ((R - A)/R) \times 100\%.$$

Fourier transform (FT) and wavelet transform (WT) are linear transformations of the signal from time to frequency domain. The most widely used approach for spectral estimation based on FT is the periodogram. Here the estimation is achieved by decomposing the signal recorded over time T in sines and cosines. To get reliable spectral estimates when analysing short epochs in the range of a few seconds (*short time Fourier transform* – STFT), a correction of the data segments is required. This could be done by tapering functions in the time domain (for example Hanning window). Additionally segment-averaging or smoothing is used to reduce variance. Note that frequency resolution (in hertz) is inverse proportional to the epoch length T (in seconds). With STFT, dynamics over time can be displayed in a time–frequency plane.

The idea behind *wavelets* is simply to have more appropriate functions than sines and cosines when dealing with non-stationary impulse-like events (spikes and transients, for example high-frequency bursts and K-complexes). The principal way of wavelet analysis is to define a wavelet prototype function $W(t)$ as an analysis template. The corresponding wavelet basis, $W_{s,l}(t)$, is obtained from the mother wavelet $W(t)$ by varying the scaling parameter s and the locating parameter l. Thus, the wavelets $W_{s,l}(t)$ are time shifted (l) and scaled (s) derivations of $W(t)$. Each analysis template $W_{s,l}(t)$ represents a band pass function with a central frequency f_0, localized in the time–frequency plane at $t = l$ and $f = f_0/s$. At any scale s the wavelet has not one frequency, but a band of frequencies, and the bandwidth is inverse proportional to s. The finer the resolution in time domain (small s) the less is the resolution in frequency domain and vice versa. The output can be displayed in the time–frequency plane analogous to STFT, reaching a maximum when the signal of interest most resembles the analysis template. Summing up, it may be said that the short-time Fourier transform is well adapted for analysing all kinds of longer lasting oscillatory like waveforms, whereas wavelets are more suited for the analysis of short duration pulsations and for signal detection, for instance in ERPs.

With *model based methods of spectral estimation* the raw EEG is interpreted as the output of a linear filter excited by white noise. EEG signal modelling and hence spectral estimation is based on derivates of the autoregressive moving average model (ARMA), which is described by a linear difference equation:

$$X_t = a_1 X_{t-1} + \cdots + a_p X_{t-p} + b_1 e_{t-1}$$
$$+ \cdots + b_q e_t - q + et \qquad (1)$$

where p denotes autoregressive lags and q denotes moving average lags. Terms containing e characterize white noise.

A multitude of models similar to Equation (1) is used. All of them are based on assumptions concerning the underlying stochastic processes rather than describing a certain biophysical model. Successful spectrum estimation depends critically on the selection of the appropriate model, the model order and the fitting method for estimating the coefficients (for example least-square-methods, maximum-likelihood-methods). Model-based spectral estimation compared to the Fourier transform approach is useful when dealing with very short segments.

Generally Used Spectral Estimations

The *power spectrum* (auto-spectral density function) displays the signals distribution of variance or power over frequency. The *cross-power spectrum* (cross-spectral density function) reflects the covariance between two EEG channels as a function of frequency.

A frequently used quantity is the cross-power spectrum normalized by the autospectra, the so called *coherence spectrum Coh*. EEG coherence analysis is regarded as a tool for studying interrelationships with respect to power and phase between different cortical areas during a certain psychological manipulation (such as sensory stimulation, voluntary movements). The values of the coherence function lie in the range from 0 to 1. It is assumed that a strong functional relationship between two brain regions is reflected by a high coherence value. To avoid trivial results (volume conduction) coherence should only be interpreted if the phase lag between the two channels is non-zero. Erroneous estimations may be caused for example by A/D converters producing artificial phase lag while sampling the data or by reference electrode effects.

The *bispectrum Bi* (the product of two spectra) and its normalized derivate *bicoherence* are third order measures in the frequency domain related to the signal skewness. They are tools for detecting the presence of non-linearity, particularly quadratic phase-coupling, i.e. two oscillatory processes generate a third component with a frequency equal to the sum (or difference) of two frequencies f1 and f2. As compared to the power spectrum, more data is usually needed to get reliable estimates.

Non-Invasive Localization of Neuronal Generators

The EEG can be used as a method for functional neural imaging. Its advantage is to display dynamic brain processes on a millisecond time scale. The problem of determination of intracerebral current sources from a given scalp surface potential is a so called inverse problem with no unique solution. It is necessary to make additional assumptions in order to choose a distinct three-dimensional source distribution among the infinite set of different possible solutions. Regularization methods are:

- *Equivalent dipole/dipole layer localization*: Scanning the head volume with the model source until an error function is minimized.
- *Weighted minimum norm*: Among all possible solutions, choosing the one containing the least energy.
- *Low resolution electromagnetic tomography* (Loreta): Assumes that neighbouring neurons are simultaneously and synchronously activated. Its aim is to find out the smoothest of all possible solutions.

High resistance of the skull is responsible for reduced spatial resolution. It has been shown

(Cuffin et al., 2001) that best average localization that can be achieved is approximately 10 mm using a spherical head model consisting of concentric spheres as brain, skull, and scalp.

FUTURE PERSPECTIVES AND CONCLUSIONS

Due to wavelet transform, there exists a great number of wavelet families. Selecting a certain wavelet depends on previous knowledge of the biophysics of brain processes. It would be desirable to build up a wavelet library for different EEG phenomena.

The reason for the use of a great number of EEG channels is to attain maximum spatial resolution of the scalp voltage distribution to improve topographic mapping considering the inverse estimate problem in neural imaging. A further goal might be to attain realistic head models, and to get individual parameters for the size of brain and skull.

References

Cuffin, B.N., Schomer, D.L., Ives, J.R. & Blume, H. (2001). Experimental tests of EEG source localization accuracy in spherical head models. *Clinical Neurophysiology, 112,* 46–51.

Ferree, T.C., Luu, P., Russel, G.S. & Tucker, D.M. (2001). Scalp electrode impedance, infection risk, and EEG data quality. *Clinical Neurophysiology, 112,* 536–544.

Oostenveld, R. & Praamstra, P. (2001). The five percent electrode system for high-resolution EEG and ERP measurements. *Clinical Neurophysiology, 112,* 713–719.

Rainer Bösel and Sascha Tamm

RELATED ENTRIES

PSYCHOPHYSIOLOGICAL EQUIPMENT AND MEASUREMENTS, EQUIPMENT FOR ASSESSING BASIC PROCESSES, THEORETICAL PERSPECTIVE: COGNITIVE, APPLIED FIELDS: PSYCHOPHYSIOLOGY, APPLIED FIELDS: NEUROPSYCHOLOGY

B URNOUT ASSESSMENT

INTRODUCTION

Job burnout is a prolonged response to chronic interpersonal stressors on the job. It has been recognized as an occupational hazard for various people-oriented professions, such as human services, education, and health care. Recently, as other occupations have become more oriented to customer service, and as global economic realities have changed organizations, the phenomenon of burnout has become relevant in these areas as well. Burnout is defined by the three dimensions of exhaustion, cynicism, and inefficacy. The standard measure that is used to assess these three dimensions is the Maslach Burnout Inventory (MBI).

As a reliably identifiable job stress syndrome, burnout places the individual stress experience within a larger organizational context of people's relation to their work. Interventions to alleviate burnout and to promote its opposite, engagement with work, can occur at both organizational and personal levels. The social focus of burnout, the solid research basis concerning the syndrome, and its specific ties to the work domain make a distinct and valuable contribution to people's health and well-being.

CONCEPTUALIZATION

Burnout is a psychological syndrome of exhaustion, cynicism, and inefficacy in the workplace. It is an individual stress experience embedded in a context of complex social relationships, and it involves the person's conception of both self and others on the job. Unlike unidimensional models of stress, this multidimensional model conceptualizes burnout in terms of its three core components.

Exhaustion refers to feelings of being over-extended and depleted of one's emotional and physical resources. Workers feel drained and used up, without any source of replenishment. They lack enough energy to face another day or another person in need. The exhaustion component represents the basic individual stress dimension of burnout.

Cynicism refers to a negative, hostile, or excessively detached response to the job, which often includes a loss of idealism. It usually develops in response to the overload of emotional exhaustion, and is self-protective at first – an emotional buffer of 'detached concern'. But the risk is that the detachment can turn into dehumanization. The cynicism component represents the interpersonal dimension of burnout.

Inefficacy refers to a decline in feelings of competence and productivity at work. People experience a growing sense of inadequacy about their ability to do the job well, and this may result in a self-imposed verdict of failure. The inefficacy component represents the self-evaluation dimension of burnout.

What has been distinctive about burnout is the interpersonal framework of the phenomenon. The centrality of relationships at work – whether it be relationships with clients, colleagues or supervisors – has always been at the heart of descriptions of burnout. These relationships are the source of both emotional strains and rewards, they can be a resource for coping with job stress, and they often bear the brunt of the negative effects of burnout. Thus, if one were to look at burnout out of context, and simply focus on the individual exhaustion component, one would lose sight of the phenomenon entirely.

In this regard, the multidimensional theory is a distinct improvement over prior unidimensional models of burnout because it both incorporates the single dimension (exhaustion), and extends it by adding two other dimensions: response toward others (cynicism) and response toward self (inefficacy). The inclusion of these two dimensions add something over and above the notion of an individual stress response and make burnout much broader than established ideas of occupational stress.

ASSESSMENT

The only measure that assesses all three of the core dimensions is the *Maslach Burnout Inventory* (MBI), so it is considered the standard tool for research in this field (see Maslach et al., 1996 for the most recent edition). There are now three versions of the MBI, designed for use with different occupations. The original version of the MBI was designed for people working in the human services and health care, given that the early research on burnout was conducted within these occupations and focused on the service relationship between provider and recipient. It is now known as the MBI–Human Services Survey (MBI-HSS). A second version of the MBI was developed for use by people working in educational settings (the MBI–Educators Survey, or MBI-ES). In both the HSS and ES forms, the labels for the three dimensions reflected the focus on occupations where workers interacted extensively with other people (clients, patients, students, etc.): emotional exhaustion, depersonalization, and reduced personal accomplishment.

Given the increasing interest in burnout within occupations that are not so clearly people-oriented, a third, general version of the MBI was developed (the MBI–General Survey, or MBI-GS). Here, the three components of the burnout construct are conceptualized in slightly broader terms, with respect to the general job, and not just to the personal relationships that may be a part of that job. Thus, the labels for the three components are: exhaustion, cynicism (a distant attitude toward the job), and reduced professional efficacy. The MBI-GS assesses the same three dimensions as the original measure, using slightly revised items, and maintains a consistent factor structure across a variety of occupations.

The items in the three MBI subscales are written in the form of statements about personal feelings or attitudes (e.g. 'I feel burned out from my work', 'Working all day is really a strain for me'). The items are answered in terms of the frequency with which the respondent experiences these feelings, on a seven-point, fully anchored scale (ranging from 0 = never to 6 = every day). Because such a response format is least similar to the typical format used in other self-report measures of attitudes and feelings, spurious correlations with other measures (due to similarities of response formats) should be minimized. Furthermore, the explicit anchoring of all seven points on the frequency dimension creates a more standardized response scale, so that the researcher can be fairly certain about the meanings assumed by respondents for each scale value. The MBI has been found to be reliable, valid, and easy to administer.

As a result of international interest in burnout research, the MBI has been translated into many languages. In most countries, the MBI has simply been translated and its psychometric properties taken for granted. However, some language versions, most notably the French, German, and Dutch versions, have been extensively studied psychometrically. Generally speaking, foreign language versions of the MBI have similar internal consistencies and show similar factorial and construct validity as the original American version. Moreover, the three-factor structure of the MBI appears to be invariant across different countries.

Despite these similarities in psychometric properties of the MBI measure, there are national differences in the average levels of burnout. For instance, several studies of various European workers have found lower average levels of exhaustion and cynicism, compared to similar North American samples.

CORRELATES OF BURNOUT

The current body of research evidence yields a fairly consistent picture of the burnout phenomenon (see Schaufeli & Enzmann, 1998). Because burnout is a prolonged response to chronic job stressors, it tends to be fairly stable over time. It is an important mediator of the causal link between various job stressors and individual stress outcomes. The exhaustion component of burnout tends to predict the rise of cynicism, while the inefficacy component tends to develop independently.

The primary antecedents of the exhaustion component are work overload and personal conflict at work. A lack of resources to manage job demands also contributes to burnout. The most critical of these resources has been social support among colleagues. Support underscores shared values and a sense of community within the organization, which enhances employees'

sense of efficacy. Another important resource is the opportunity for employees to participate in decisions that affect their work and to exercise control over their contributions.

Of the three burnout components, exhaustion is the closest to an orthodox stress variable, and therefore is more predictive of stress-related physiological health outcomes than the other two components. In terms of mental, as opposed to physical, health, the link with burnout is more complex. Is burnout itself a form of mental illness, or is it a cause of it? Much of this discussion has focused on depression and burnout, and research has demonstrated that the two constructs are indeed distinct: burnout is job-related and situation-specific, as opposed to depression which is general and context-free.

Burnout has been associated with various forms of job withdrawal – absenteeism, intention to leave the job, and actual turnover. However, for people who stay on the job, burnout leads to lower productivity and effectiveness at work. To the extent that burnout diminishes opportunities for satisfying experiences at work, it is associated with decreased job satisfaction and a reduced commitment to the job or the organization.

People who are experiencing burnout can have a negative impact on their colleagues, both by causing greater personal conflict and by disrupting job tasks. Thus, burnout can be 'contagious' and perpetuate itself through informal interactions on the job. There is also some evidence that burnout has a negative 'spillover' effect on people's home life.

Although the bulk of burnout research has focused on the organizational context in which people work, it has also considered a range of personal qualities. Burnout scores tend to be higher for people who have a less 'hardy' personality or a more external locus of control, or who score as 'neurotic' on the five-factor model of personality. People who exhibit Type-A behaviour tend to be more prone to exhaustion. There are few consistent relationships of burnout with demographic characteristics. Although higher age seems to be associated with lower burnout, it is confounded with both years of experience and with survival bias. The only consistent gender difference is a tendency for men to score slightly higher on cynicism.

FUTURE PERSPECTIVES

The extensive research on burnout has consistently found linear relationships of workplace conditions across the full range of the MBI subscales. Just as high levels of personal conflict are associated with high levels of exhaustion, low levels of conflict are strong predictors of low exhaustion. Conversely, high efficacy is associated with supportive personal relationships, the enhancement of sophisticated skills at work and active participation in shared decision making. These patterns indicate that the opposite of burnout is not a neutral state, but a positive one of job engagement. New research is defining engagement in terms of the positive ends of the three dimensions as burnout. Thus, engagement consists of a state of high energy (rather than exhaustion), strong involvement (rather than cynicism), and a sense of efficacy (rather than inefficacy).

One important implication of the burnout-engagement continuum is that strategies to promote engagement may be just as important for burnout prevention as strategies to reduce the risk of burnout. A workplace that is designed to support the positive development of the three core qualities of energy, involvement, and effectiveness should be successful in promoting the well-being and productivity of its employees, and thus the health of the entire organization.

FUTURE PERSPECTIVES AND CONCLUSIONS

The personal and organizational costs of burnout have led to the development of various intervention strategies. Some try to treat burnout after it has occurred, while others focus on how to prevent burnout by promoting engagement. Intervention may occur on the level of the individual, workgroup, or an entire organization. At each level, the number of people affected by an intervention and the potential for enduring change increases.

The primary emphasis has been on individual strategies to prevent burnout, rather than social or organizational ones, despite the fact that research has found that situational and organizational factors play a bigger role in burnout than individual ones. Also, individual strategies are relatively ineffective in the workplace, where the person has much less control of stressors than in other domains of his or her life. There are both philosophical and pragmatic reasons underlying the predominant focus on the individual, including notions of individual causality and responsibility, and the assumption that it is easier and cheaper to change people instead of organizations. However, any progress in dealing with burnout will depend on the development of strategies that focus on the job context and its impact on the people who work within it.

References

Maslach, C., Jackson, S.E. & Leiter, M.P. (1996). *Maslach Burnout Inventory Manual* (3rd ed.). Palo Alto, CA: Consulting Psychologists Press.

Schaufeli, W.B & Enzmann, D. (1998). *The Burnout Companion to Study & Practice: A Critical Analysis*. Philadelphia, PA: Taylor & Francis.

Christina Maslach

RELATED ENTRIES

APPLIED FIELDS: CLINICAL, APPLIED FIELDS: HEALTH, CAREGIVER BURDEN, APPLIED FIELDS: WORK AND INDUSTRY, PERSONALITY ASSESSMENT (GENERAL)

C CAREER AND PERSONNEL DEVELOPMENT

INTRODUCTION

The information revolution and globalization have affected the strategy and structures of larger organizations. They now engage in different forms of employment relationship with different groups of employees. For some employees, employers provide career assessment and manage their careers; for the majority, the onus is on them to assess themselves. Whilst employers use sophisticated tools such as assessment centres for the few, the majority use a variety of questionnaire and interactive methods. The exchange of career assessment information between organization and employee will aid subsequent necessary career dialogue.

CHANGES IN THE CONTEXT OF CAREERS

Traditionally, career assessment has been carried out by employers in order to enable them to manage the careers of employees more effectively. However, the nature of the employment relationship, and hence of career management, has been changing over the last three decades (Herriot, 2001a). Consequently, the purposes of career assessment, the responsibility for its conduct, and

the nature of what is being assessed have all changed too.

The changes in the nature of career have been profound. However, they have not been so radical as current managerial rhetoric alleges. The traditional organizational career is not at an end, as some argue (e.g. Bridges, 1995). Rather, in the USA and Europe at least, the length of time which an employee spends in each organizational employment has been gradually decreasing over a long period. Similarly, for the majority of employees, careers are not 'boundaryless' (Arthur & Rousseau, 1996). That is, employees are not free to move across or between organizations, or in and out of employment, as it suits them; the labour market power is more often with the employer than with the employee.

Nevertheless, fundamental changes have occurred. First, much *restructuring* of organizations has been undertaken. Downsizing, the removal of positions and their holders, has been a frequent managerial response to the perceived need to reduce costs to remain competitive; and delayering, the removal of levels of the organizational hierarchy, has also occurred. Delayering appears to be a consequence of information technology reducing the need for middle management; of work becoming more frequently organized into projects; and of responsibility being devolved further down the hierarchy. The second fundamental change to have occurred is that the variety of forms of employment contracts has increased. Management has sought to ensure *flexibility* in the supply of labour by offering temporary or part-time contracts; and it has aimed at increasing functional flexibility by designing work so as to break down craft and professional silos.

IMPLICATIONS FOR CAREERS

The consequences of these structural and contractual changes for careers have been considerable. Many employees have lost confidence in the possibility of progress in an upward direction within their organization, or indeed of retaining their present job. As a result, careers are more often subjectively than objectively defined (Ornstein & Isabella, 1993). That is, rather than concentrating upon a progressive sequence of positions held, employees construe their careers in a variety of ways. For example, they may view career as the acquisition over time of knowledge and skills and a consequent increase in employability; or as a narrative story, which makes some sort of sense of what may be chaotic past, present, and likely future experiences; or as a series of different forms of employment relationship.

As a consequence of these changes, the purposes of assessment in relation to career, the responsibility for and ownership of assessment data, and the nature of what is assessed, have all become more varied. First I will consider the increased variety of *purposes*.

There is now a major degree of *segmentation* in most larger organizations, such that different categories of employees have very different career deals (Hirsh & Jackson, 1996). For example, many organizations continue to separate out a cohort of high flyers, either on recruitment, or relatively early in their organizational career. A lot of development resource is put into these employees, in an effort to ensure that at least a good proportion of senior managers is internally recruited. In the case of these favoured employees, career assessment will be used initially to identify whether they have senior management potential; to discover their development needs; and to decide whether they are ready to be moved on to their next position.

Other employees, on the other hand, are perhaps less likely than before to have any attention paid to their future development. Rather, it is their present performance and its improvement which are of utmost concern to their managers. In terms of career assessment, they may have to make do with an annual appraisal which concentrates on performance, but which may make a gesture towards their career development (Drenth, 1998). Furthermore, their line manager, who is now likely to have complete responsibility for their appraisal, is unlikely to have the skills or knowledge to provide career advice. They are likely to have to rely on bulletin boards for internal job opportunities, and on advertisements for external ones. They will almost certainly have to find out for themselves what their interests and developmental capabilities are. The major purpose of this self-assessment is to help them to decide which career direction to seek to take. In order to aid them, their employer now, at best, gives them some help in formulating a personal development plan, and provides some sort of opportunity for self-assessment of interests, career aims, and development needs. However, such help is relatively rare.

Thus the *responsibility* for, and *ownership* of, career assessments has become varied also. For high flyers, the organization is likely to take most of the responsibility for assessment, and to own the data (although it will share much of it with the employee). For most others, the responsibility is now mostly their own to gain whatever assessment information they can. However, as a consequence, they are its owners, and can choose how much of it, if any, they share with their employer. If they enter into a psychological contract with their employer regarding their career development, they may use their assessment data as evidence of what they have to offer to the organization and what their development needs are.

Finally the *nature* of career assessment is becoming increasingly varied. High flyers are likely to undergo an expensive range of assessments, which are mostly conducted by others. Considerable effort is put into feeding back the results to the individual, and pointing them in the direction of ways to meet their development needs. Developmental placements in positions which will stretch the employee may be agreed as a consequence of the assessment (Kotter, 1982), often in negotiations at the highest level of the organization. The career assessment and management of this category of employee is normally integrated within a corporate resourcing strategy, aimed at ensuring that the appropriate levels of senior managerial capability will be available to the organization. Assessment and development centres are a favoured method of career assessment for this category of employees; and their development needs are likely to be described in terms of various managerial competencies (Sparrow, 1998).

Other employees, however, are more likely to assess themselves on the basis of their achievements, interests, and aspirations (Kidd, 1998), and to place their work career into the context of the rest of their lives when doing so. Moreover, the analysis hitherto has assumed that employees are located in large organizations with sophisticated Human Resource processes. Even in post-industrial and industrialized nations, up to half of the working population may be employed in small and medium sized enterprises. These are unlikely to have career management processes in place. Hence the majority of employees have to manage their own careers and conduct or purchase their own assessment methods.

ASSESSMENT TOOLS

First, I will review assessment tools used by organizations to assess potential and development needs. The assessment centre method has increased in popularity recently for both these purposes. It normally employs a variety of assessments, including individual and group exercises, structured interviews, and psychometric tests (Zaal, 1998). The exercises may assess performance at tasks required of employees at one or several levels ahead of the assessee's current position; or they may consist of off-the-shelf tasks designed to assess competencies, and not sampled from the organization's actual work. The results of these different modes of assessment are transformed into ratings of various competencies; that is, behavioural

repertoires which people input to a job, role, or organizational context. Typical examples of managerial competencies are oral communication, and planning and organizing. These competency ratings may then be reduced to a summary rating of potential, the overall assessment rating.

Assessment methods have traditionally been evaluated in terms of their reliability and validity. Assessment centres have demonstrated good levels of these psychometric properties, with particular success in predicting subsequent performance in training. Where applicants or employees have had little experience of the level of work for which they are being selected, the potential to be successfully developed for that level is what is being assessed. However, much predictive power is lost when assessments are reduced to an overall assessment rating. Moreover, it has been demonstrated repeatedly that even well-trained assessors assess on the basis of how well assessees perform overall on each exercise rather than on ratings of competencies. Thus the rationale for using assessment centres to assess competencies seems flawed, and a more realistic approach would regard the exercises as samples of the job.

There are two other types of criteria by which assessment centres should be evaluated. The first is their utility: the extent to which their benefits exceed their costs (Boudreau, 1991). Assessment centres are expensive, especially in terms of the time and training of the assessors, often senior managers. The method therefore needs to add validity above that obtained by cheaper methods if its expense is to be justified. On the other hand, it has other advantages, which are not normally included in utility estimates: it is acceptable to assessees (Iles & Mabey, 1993), and it gives assessors the belief that they are influencing important outcomes.

The second evaluative criterion relates to the time span for which the potential is being assessed. It is argued (Sparrow, 1998) that the competencies assessed are those which are required for the jobs of the present rather than those of the future. This is because of the method by which competencies are discovered. Typically, current good performers are compared to poor ones, with the consequence that the competencies inferred are those which are necessary to succeed at the time of the comparison. However, it is very difficult to predict what competencies will be required in the medium or longer term. One alternative is to assume that the key competencies will be meta-competencies of a more generic form; for example: the ability to learn new knowledge and skills rapidly; the capacity to manage one's own career and development; and the resilience and adaptability to make continuous career transitions. Many psychologists are convinced that psychometric tests of general intellectual aptitude are the best tools for the assessment of this more general potential (Schmidt & Hunter, 1998) but few organizations are willing to base decisions solely or mainly upon them, for a variety of good reasons.

The appraisal process is another method of assessing development needs. However, appraisers are usually line managers whose main purpose in appraisal is to assess employees' performance, set objectives, and allocate performance-related pay. Hence if appraisees admit to and identify their own development needs, they put their performance rating at risk. A recently popular alternative is 360 degree feedback, which requires appraisees to be assessed, usually anonymously, by superiors, peers, subordinates, and sometimes by clients or customers too. Of course, the advantage of this method is that different perspectives are obtained from different stakeholders, and hence a more rounded view of current development needs is obtained. However, the same difficulties arise as with the use of assessment centres if 360 degree feedback is used to assess potential: it is hard to decide what are the key competencies for the future.

Thus the assessment tools designed for the organizational purposes of assessing longer term potential or development needs have their problems. However, there exist a wide variety of instruments available to help individuals discover their interests and longer-term career aims (Kidd, 1998). For example, the Vocational Preference Inventory and Self-Directed Search (Holland, 1985a, 1985b) are valuable tools which can enable individuals to match their interests to occupations or organizations. These questionnaires are based upon Holland's theory of vocational preferences which could be more accurately described as a personality typology. Holland specifies six different orientations: Realistic,

Investigative, Artistic, Social, Enterprising, and Conventional. If one arranges these orientations into a hexagonal shape, in the above order, then those next to each other are considered to be more similar than those two or three places away. Similarity is construed in terms of whether or not the orientation is people-oriented, and whether it is more intellectual or practical in nature. The individual's top three interest orientations can then be matched to the coding given to each occupation, and an indication of individual/occupation fit obtained. The same exercise can be carried out to assess the individual's fit with an organization (provided, of course, that the questionnaire has been administered to existing employees). One of the issues which arises in the case of Holland's and other such methodologies is the degree to which interests change over time. In the course of organizational socialization, individuals' interests may change to the extent that what was originally a poor fit becomes a much better one.

The Career Anchors questionnaire (Schein, 1985) helps to identify those career values which are crucial to the individual. Again, the idea is that individuals have one particular career anchor (or set of talents, motives, and values) which they develop as adults and maintain over the course of their working lives. Although they may be successful in terms of upward career progression, it does not follow that their career has permitted them to express their favoured anchor. Schein identified five such anchors in his original version of the questionnaire, which were: technical/functional competence; managerial competence; security and stability; entrepreneurship; and autonomy and independence. He subsequently added three more: service/dedication; pure challenge; and lifestyle integration. For many people, the scores obtained on the questionnaire do not clearly indicate one anchor as much preferred to the others, and Schein argues that detailed career interviews are required to have a great deal of confidence in the identification of the anchor. One of the important outcomes of discovering one's anchor is that this enables the individual to identify which form of career relationship within an organization they will prefer. So, for example, an individual with a managerial anchor will welcome a position in a larger organization offering the opportunity

Table 1. Some career instruments, their authors, and assessment

Instrument	Author	Assessment
Adult Career Concerns Inventory	Super et al. (1988)	Career socialization
Adult Life Stage Questionnaire	Hopson & Scally (1989)	Stage norms
Career Anchors Questionnaire	Schein (1985)	Fundamental motive
Career Beliefs Inventory	Krumboltz (1991)	Attitudes to career
Career Concept Questionnaire	Driver & Brousseau (1981)	Job moves
Life Career Rainbow	Super (1980)	Work and life roles
Self-Directed Search	Holland (1985a)	Occupational interests
Vocational Preference Inventory	Holland (1985b)	Occupational interests
Work Locus of Control Scale	Spector (1988)	Self-development

of promotion and increasing power and responsibility; autonomous people will prefer small professional groupings or self-employment.

The Career Beliefs Inventory (Krumboltz, 1991) aims to reveal the individual's beliefs and attitudes regarding the nature of career itself. It offers five sets of questions: current career beliefs; what I need to be happy in my career; what influences my career decisions; what changes I am willing to make; and what effort I am willing to put in. While this instrument appears to offer the opportunity for some self-insight, its psychometric properties of validity and reliability are not good however.

These and other instruments are presented in Table 1, and they are some of the better known and more valid assessment tools. However, it should be noted that because of their age, some of them make normative assumptions about, e.g., the stages of adult life which are not now justified in the light of changed social norms.

Additionally, the Internet now permits access to a range of self-assessment techniques, including much more interactive procedures which provide some of the advantages of face-to-face career counselling.

FUTURE PERSPECTIVES AND CONCLUSIONS

One of the problems with assessment is that psychologists have concentrated so heavily on the theory and methods of assessment that they have paid too little attention to the uses to which it is put. This is true of career assessment, both in the case of assessment by the

organization for its own purposes, and of self-assessment by employees to help them discover their career direction.

As far as the organization is concerned, all too frequently career assessment has been introduced to meet a specific human resource need at a particular moment (for example, to retain a category of employees who were demonstrating a high rate of turnover). Instead, it should be integrated into an overall human resource strategy, which should itself be part of the overall business direction. It should, in other words, be a process which fits into a coordinated set of philosophies, policies, practices, and processes (Schuler, 1998).

In the case of individual self-assessment, practice has often been too narrowly confined. Work career cannot be seen in isolation from the individual's life career and identity. Hence the self-assessment of competencies or aptitudes is only part of the task. Rather, individuals need to reflect upon themselves: their identities, beliefs, and values, their past histories and their aspirations for the future.

Above all, career assessment has to be considered in the context of the employment relationship. The employment relationship is at present under great strain in many organizations in industrial and post-industrial economies; fundamental relational elements may be lost. Many organizations refer to employees as resources which they own, whilst many employees believe that they can rely only upon themselves (Herriot, 2001b). Hence the purposes of career assessment may, on the one hand, be considered solely those of maximizing the profitability of the firm's human capital; and on the other, those of securing one's personal survival during the turmoil of globalization and the information revolution. However, the sharing of the means and the products of career assessment between employers and employees is essential if a reciprocal employment relationship is to be maintained. For career assessment provides reliable and valid information about employees which meets the needs of both parties. It is therefore vital that such information is shared and forms the basis of informed career dialogue between them.

References

Arthur, M.B. & Rousseau, D.M. (1996). Introduction: the boundaryless career as a new employment principle. In Arthur, M.B. & Rousseau, D.M. (Eds.), *The Boundaryless Career*. New York: Oxford University Press.

Boudreau, J.W. (1991). Utility analysis for decisions in human resource management. In Dunnette, M.D. & Hough, L.M. (Eds.), *Handbook of Industrial and Organizational Psychology*, Vol. II (2nd ed.). Palo Alto, CA: Consulting Psychologists Press.

Bridges, W. (1995). *Jobshift: How to Prosper in a Workplace without Jobs*. London: Nicholas Brealey.

Drenth, P.J. (1998). Personnel appraisal. In Drenth, P.J.D., Thierry, H. & deWolff, C.J. (Eds.), *Handbook of Work and Organisational Psychology. Personnel Psychology*, Vol. III (2nd ed.). Hove: Psychology Press.

Driver, M. & Brousseau, K. (1981). *The Career Concept Questionnaire*. Los Angeles, CA: Decision Dynamics Corporation.

Herriot, P. (2001a). Careers. In Poole, M. & Warner, M. (Eds.), *The Handbook of Human Resource Management* (2nd ed.). London: International Thomson Business Press.

Herriot, P. (2001b). *The Employment Relationship: A Psychological Perspective*. London: Routledge.

Hirsh, W. & Jackson, C. (1996). *Strategies for Career Development: Promise, Practice, and Pretence*. Brighton: Institute for Employment Studies, Report 305.

Holland, J.L. (1985a). *The Self-Directed Search: Professional Manual*. Odessa, FL: Psychological Assessment Resources.

Holland, J.L. (1985b). *Manual for the Vocational Preference Inventory*. Odessa, FL: Psychological Assessment Resources.

Hopson, B. & Scally, M. (1989). *Build Your Own Rainbow: A Workbook for Career and Life Management*. Leeds: Lifeskills Associates.

Iles, P.A. & Mabey, C. (1993). Managerial career development techniques: effectiveness, acceptability, and availability. *British Journal of Management*, 4, 103–118.

Kidd, J.M. (1998). Assessment for self-managed career development. In Anderson, N. & Herriot, P. (Eds.), *International Handbook of Selection and Assessment*. Chichester: Wiley.

Kotter, J. (1982). *The General Managers*. New York: Free Press.

Krumboltz, J. (1991). *Career Beliefs Inventory*. Palo Alto, CA: Consulting Psychologists Press.

Ornstein, S. & Isabella, L.A. (1993). Making sense of career: a review 1989–1992. *Journal of Management*, 19, 243–267.

Schein, E.H. (1985). *Career Anchors: Discovering your Real Values*. San Diego, CA: University Associates.

Schmidt, F.L. & Hunter, J.E. (1998). The validity and utility of selection methods in personnel psychology: practical and theoretical implications of 85 years of research findings. *Psychological Bulletin*, 124, 262–274.

Schuler, R.S. (1998). Human resource management. In Poole, M. & Warner, M. (Eds.), *The Handbook of Human Resource Management*. London: International Thomson Business Press.

Sparrow, P.R. (1998). Organisational competencies: creating a strategic behavioural framework for selection and assessment. In Anderson, N. & Herriot, P. (Eds.), *International Handbook of Selection and Assessment*. Chichester: Wiley.

Spector, P.E. (1988). Development of the Work Locus of Control Scale. *Journal of Occupational Psychology*, 61, 335–340.

Super, D.E. (1980). A life-span, life-space approach to career development. *Journal of Vocational Behaviour*, 16, 282–298.

Super, D.E., Thompson, A.S., Lindeman, R.H., Myers, R.A. & Jordaan, J.P. (1988). *Adult Career Concerns Inventory*. Palo Alto, CA: Consulting Psychologists Press.

Zaal, J.N. (1998). Assessment centre methods. In Drenth, P.J.D., Thierry, H. & deWolff, C.J. (Eds.), *Personnel Psychology. Handbook of Work and Organisational Psychology*, Vol. 3 (2nd ed.). Hove: Psychology Press.

Peter Herriot

RELATED ENTRIES

PERSONNEL SELECTION, ASSESSMENT IN, ORGANIZATIONAL CULTURE, LEADERSHIP IN ORGANIZATIONAL SETTINGS, TOTAL QUALITY MANAGEMENT, APPLIED FIELDS: WORK AND INDUSTRY, APPLIED FIELDS: ORGANIZATIONS

C CAREGIVER BURDEN

INTRODUCTION

Caregiver burden refers to the physical, psychological and social consequences of taking care of a patient. Our aim is to raise the most important research issues on caregiver burden. After introducing the concept, we discuss the predictors, the impact of physical versus cognitive impairment and the gender differences, on burden. Most of the research has been made on demented individuals and elders but also on other chronic patients, as we will refer. Some widely used instruments are briefly presented and the future perspectives on this issue are pointed together with the concluding remarks.

The problem of caregiving has been studied extensively since the 1980s. This issue became of major importance namely because of the growing number of elders and the changing patterns of families and women, that traditionally assume the caregiver role (Biegel et al., 1991).

The conceptual framework to explain burden is the stress model. The physical overload of stress is derived from performing, or helping the patient perform, the activities of daily living (ADLs). The psychological and social costs of the caregiver role are much more difficult to measure but not less important in determining the stress of the caregiver.

According to Aneshensel et al. (1996) the stressors are the problematic conditions and difficult circumstances experienced by caregivers. The outcomes are the effects on individual health and emotional well being. There are also moderators that comprise social, personal and material resources that help modify or regulate the causal relationship between stressor and outcomes and the proliferation of stressors outside the boundaries of caregiving. The primary stressors are the objective conditions of caregiving (managing the patient's needs) and the subsequent sense of overload. The secondary stressors arise as a result of primary stressors and include strains in roles outside of caregiving (e.g. career) and intrapsychic strains.

Pearlin et al. (1990) view caregiver stress as a consequence of a process comprising a number of interrelated conditions, including the socio-economic characteristics and resources of caregivers and the primary and secondary stressors to which they are exposed. Primary stressors are hardships and problems anchored directly in caregiving. Secondary stressors are (1) the strains experienced in roles and activities outside of caregiving and (2) intrapsychic strains, involving the diminishment of self-concepts. Coping and social support can potentially intervene as buffers at multiple points along the stress process.

It is well established that caregiving is burdensome and is generally believed that caring for a demented individual present's the greatest challenge of all. We still know little about what is most distressing, the patient's decline, or providing daily care. The hypotheses that explain the evolution of caregiving are: (1) the wear-and-tear hypothesis suggesting that there will be a decrement in caregiver functioning as the illness progresses; (2) the adaptation hypothesis considering that caregivers will eventually adapt to the demands of the situation, stabilizing or even improving caregiving; (3) the trait hypothesis suggesting that caregivers maintain a constant level of functioning, depending on their resources of coping skills and social support; and (4) the glucocorticoid cascade hypothesis stating that the effect of chronic stressors could have persistent and severe consequences for immune function in elders (Schulz & Williamson, 1994).

Researchers frequently conceptualize caregiver behaviour in terms of specific tasks in relation to ADLs. The focus on tasks is very important but limits the understanding of caregiving to an objective burden and helps forget the subjective burden of the process that is embedded in personal relationships and extended to many other areas of the personal life of women caregivers (Abel, 1990).

According to Gottlieb (1989) the objective (primary demands of caregiving) and subjective burden (secondary demands involving dislocations) is determined by four sets of variables: (1) the past and present quality of the relationship between caregiver and care recipient; (2) the role's reverberations on other life spheres; (3) the support available from the caregiver's social ecology; and (4) psychosocial variables of the caregiver response to the demands of caregiving.

Risk factors for burden included the worsening of the relationship between caregiver and patient, being a spouse, shorter length of caregiving, poor caregiver self-rated health, greater physical disability, and behaviour and mood disturbances in the patient (Draper et al., 1995). Another model of caregiver burden (Vitalino et al., 1991) considers the distress as the relation of exposure to stress plus the vulnerability, over psychological and social resources; the caregivers with high vulnerability and low resources had higher burden.

The differential impact of physical versus cognitive impairment on caregiver burden is difficult to determine but a lot of studies show evidence that behavioural problems are the most difficult to manage for the caregivers and tend to produce more burden over time (e.g. Gaugler et al., 2000).

Next, we present a synthesis of objective and subjective variables appearing in literature on caregiving burden (Table 1).

Caregiving is gendered, defined and largely assumed by wives and daughters (Gottlieb, 1989), placing significant burden on women and generally considered their 'natural work' (Lee, 1999). It seems that caregiving burden affects females more than males in what concerns their mental and physical health (Pruchno et al., 1990).

Davis (1992) describes the profile of caregivers at risk as a middle aged or older woman, living with the care recipient, the sole care provider, with personal health problems, limited in personal, social or financial resources, has other family social or job-related obligations that compete with the demands of caregiving, previously has had problems in personal relationship with the care recipient and perceives the caregiver experience to be a major personal life disruption.

As the patient's disability and care demands increase over time the caregiver's capacity of coping with the demands of caregiving is eroded as the wear-and-tear hypothesis preview (Schulz et al., 1993). The pattern of coping of the caregiver is considered in several studies the most important factor of burden and most

Table 1.   Synthesis of variables of caregiving burden

Context of caregiving	Caregiver characteristics	Tasks performed (ADLs and IADLs): the level of work and effort the caregiver must expend with care	Caregiving outcomes
Household congruence between physical environment and patient capacities (architectonical barrier and aids)	Age, gender and SES	of work and effort	Physical burden
	Baseline physical and mental health	the caregiver must	Immunological functioning
	Development stage	expend with care	
	Beliefs and attitudes about caring	Time spent	Symptoms and complaints
Income	Conflicts between caregiving and job	Tasks performed	Medicine consumption
Available formal service	Conflicts between caregiving role and family life	Information	Psychological burden
		Competence	Depression, anxiety, irritability, cognitive distress
	Care recipient characteristics		Social burden
	Age, gender and SES		Isolation
	Type of impairment: physical, mental or both		Family disruption
	Level of disability		Career disruption
	The prognostic of illness (life expectancy, progressive or stable condition)		Satisfaction
	Relationship caregiver/ care recipient		
	Being a relative, friend, neighbour		
	Quality of the actual and past relationship		

researchers considered caregiver burden an individual problem of women who do not have the ability to cope with it (e.g. DeVries et al., 1997).

The competing role of working and giving care is of particular importance for employed women having to take care of a parent or parent-in-law. Contrary to employed men, the employed women provided similar care than the non-employed ones (Kramer & Kipnis, 1995).

One of the other areas of caregiver burden studies is the care for disabled children. The amount of children having chronic diseases is enormous, and so, the number of primary caregivers involved that suffer the impact of illness. Especially the mothers reported greater role strain, and less time spent in recreational activities (e.g. Quittner et al., 1998).

Recently, AIDS became a significant chronic illness. As in other progressive illnesses, the expanding demands of caregiving and the sense of captivity of caregiver role, invading social leisure and occupational life of the caregivers is responsible for the increased burden of caregiver (e.g. Pearlin et al., 1997).

Most of the studies exploring the burden of caregivers of patients with schizophrenia found a higher level of distress in primary caregivers and families (e.g. Brown & Wistle, 1998).

INSTRUMENTS TO ASSESS CAREGIVER BURDEN

Some of the most well-known measures of the impact of informal caregiving of elders are: *Burden Interview* (BI) (Zarit et al., 1980), with one factor that considered the impact as disruptions or changes in social activities, physical and financial strain, emotional upset and elder–carer relationship; *Caregiver Strain Index* (CSI) (Robinson, 1983), with one factor that measures physical tiredness, restriction of social life, loss of time to self, interference with life plans, emotional upset and financial loss; *Caregiver Burden Inventory* (CBI) (Novak & Guest, 1989) is a multidimensional instrument that measures the impact of burden on caregivers of cognitively impaired individuals with five factors: (1) Time dependence burden, (2) Developmental burden, (3) Physical burden, (4) Social burden and (5) Emotional burden;

Caregiving Appraisal (Lawton et al., 1989) represents the dimensions of subjective caregiving burden, caregiving satisfaction and caregiving impact factors. The major contribution of this instrument is the suggestion that caregiving may be appraised in positive or negative ways (see Orbell et al., 1993, for a review).

FUTURE PERSPECTIVES AND CONCLUSIONS

Longitudinal studies are needed to know the long-term impact of different illnesses on physical, psychological and social health burden of caregivers and on the well-being of care recipients.

Caregiver burden has consequences not only for the caregiver herself but also for all the family and the care recipient by disrupting the affective relationships between them, lowering patient well-being and fostering the risk of institutionalization resulting in a long term growth of health and social expenses with carer and care recipient.

Caregiver burden is not only an individual but also a society problem (e.g. Braithwaite, 1996) and our society should radically restructure care to meet the needs of different caregivers and care recipients. The study on caregiver burden should address the problem from a public policy perspective (Lee, 1999), fostering the buffering effect (e.g. Rapp et al., 1998) of social support on caregiver burden.

References

Abel, E. (1990). Informal care for the disabled elderly. *Research on Aging*, 12(2), 139–157.

Aneshensel, C., Pearlin, L., Mullan, J., Zarit, S. & Whitlatch, C. (1996). *Profiles in Caregiving: The Unexpected Carer*. Portland: Academic Press.

Biegel, D., Sales, E. & Shultz, R. (1991). *Family Caregiving in Chronic Illness*. Newbury Park, CA: Sage.

Braithwaite, V. (1996). Understanding stress in informal caregiving. *Research on Aging*, 18(2), 139–174.

Brown, S. & Wistle, J. (1998). People with schizophrenia and their families. *British Journal of Psychiatry*, 173, 139–144.

Davis, L. (1992). Building a science of caring for caregivers. *Family and Community Health*, 15(2), 1–9.

DeVries, H., Hamilton, D., Lovett, S. & Gallagher-Thompson, D. (1997). Patterns of coping preferences for male and female caregivers of frail older adults. *Psychology and Aging*, 12(2), 263–267.

Draper, B., Poulos, R., Poulos, C. & Ehrlich, F. (1995). Risk factors for stress in elderly caregivers. *International Journal of Geriatric Psychiatry*, 11, 227–231.

Gaugler, J., Davey, A., Pearlin, L. & Zarit, S. (2000). Modelling caregiver adaptation over time: the longitudinal impact of behaviour problem. *Psychology and Aging*, 15(3), 437–450.

Gottlieb, B. (1989). A contextual perspective in family care of the elderly care of the elderly. *Canadian Psychology*, 30(3), 596–607.

Kramer, B. & Kipnis, S. (1995). Eldercare and work-role conflict: toward an understanding of gender differences in caregiver burden. *The Gerontologist*, 15(3), 340–348.

Lawton, M., Kleban, M., Moss, M., Rovine, M. & Glicksman, A. (1989). Measuring caregiving appraisal. *Journal of Gerontology*, 44(3), 61–71.

Lee, C. (1999). Health, stress and coping among women caregivers. *Journal of Health Psychology*, 4(1), 27–40.

Novak, M. & Guest, C. (1989). Application of a multidimensional caregiver burden inventory. *The Gerontologist*, 29(6), 798–803.

Orbell, S., Hopkins, N. & Gillies, B. (1993). Measuring the impact of informal caring. *Journal of Community & Applied Social Psychology*, 3, 149–163.

Pearlin, L., Aneshensel, C. & Leblanc, A. (1997). The forms and mechanisms of stress proliferation: the case of AIDS caregivers. *Journal of Health and Social Behaviour*, 38, 223–236.

Pearlin, L., Mullan, J., Semple, S. & Skaff, M. (1990). Caregiving & the stress process: an overview of concepts and their measures. *The Gerontologist*, 30(5), 583–594.

Pruchno, R., Kleban, M., Michaels, E. & Dempsey, N. (1990). Mental and physical health of caregiving spouses: development of a causal model. *Journal of Gerontology*, 45(5), 192–199.

Quittner, A., Espelage, D., Opipare, L., Carter, B., Eid, N. & Eigen, H. (1998). Role strain in couples with and without a child with chronic illness: association with marital satisfaction, intimacy and daily mood. *Health Psychology*, 17(2), 112–124.

Rapp, S., Shumaker, S., Schmidt, S., Naughton, M. & Anderson, R. (1998). Social resourcefulness: its relationship to social support and well being among caregivers of dementia victims. *Aging and Mental Health*, 2(1), 40–48.

Robinson, B. (1983). Validation of a caregiver strain index. *Journal of Gerontology*, 38(3), 344–348.

Schulz, R. & Williamson, G. (1994). Health effects of caregiving: prevalence of mental and physical illness in Alzheimer's caregivers. In Light, E., Niederehe, G. & Lebowitz, B. (Eds.). *Stress Effects on Family Caregivers of Alzheimer's Patients* (pp. 38–63). New York: Springer Publishing Company.

Schulz, R., Williamson, G., Morycz, R. & Biegel, D. (1993). Changes in depression among men and women caring for Alzheimer's patients. In Zarit, S., Pearlin, L. & Shaie, K. (Eds.), *Caregiving Systems: Formal and Informal Helpers* (pp. 119–140). Hillsdale: Lawrence Erlbaum Associates Publishers.

Vitalino, P., Russo, J., Young, H., Teri, L. & Maiuro, R. (1991). Predictors of burden in spouse caregivers of individuals with Alzheimer disease. *Psychology and Aging*, 6(3), 392–402.

Zarit, S., Reever, K. & Bach-Peterson, J. (1980). Relatives of the impaired elderly correlates of feelings of individuals with dementia. *The Gerontologist*, 20(6), 649–655.

Constança Paúl and Ignacio Martin

RELATED ENTRIES

Applied Fields: Clinical, Applied Fields: Health, Burnout Assessment, Job Stress

C CASE FORMULATION

INTRODUCTION

One of the principal aims of a psychological assessment is to evaluate the form and function of target behaviours. The term case formulation can be defined as the process of operationalizing target behaviours[1] (determining the form) and evaluating relationships among target behaviours and potential controlling factors (determining the function) for an individual client.

The aforementioned definition has several important features. First, the identification of *causal functional relationships* is a central element of case formulation. Although functional relationships may be either correlational or causal, by itself, a functional relationship implies only covariation between two variables. Because a case formulation is primarily used in treatment planning, the identification and quantification of causal functional relationships among target behaviours and controlling factors are of primary interest.

Causal functional relationships are best thought of as elevated conditional probabilities (James, Mulaik & Brett, 1982), wherein the probability of observing a change in the form of a target behaviour (change in frequency, intensity, duration of response), given the occurrence of a hypothesized causal event (the conditional probability of the target behaviour), is greater than the probability of observing a change in the form of a target behaviour without the prior occurrence of the hypothesized causal event (the base rate or unconditional probability of the target behaviour). To illustrate, let A equal an increase in the frequency of worry experienced by a middle-aged client (the target behaviour), let B equal an increase in work stress (hypothesized causal event), and let P equal the probability. A tentative causal functional relationship between worry and work stress would be inferred if the probability of the frequency of worry after an increase in work stress [$P(A|B)$] was greater than the base rate probability of worry [$P(A)$].

Many internal and situational events may be causally associated with a target behaviour. For example, changes in central nervous system neurotransmitter levels, loss of response-contingent reinforcement, increased levels of family conflict, negative expectations, and seasonal changes may all exert causal influences on depressed mood for a particular client. Although several causal relationships may exist, in designing an intervention, we are most interested in the subset of causal relationships that exert significant causal effects on a target behaviour. Therefore, a second characteristic of case formulation is a focus on the identification of *important* causal functional relationships.

However, important causal functional relationships are often uncontrollable. For instance, two sets of potentially important causal factors that cannot be controlled or modified include significant historical events, such as exposure to trauma or economic changes, and biological attributes, such as genetic predisposition. Because interventions are designed to elicit change in target behaviours by modifying potential causes, a third characteristic of case formulation is an emphasis on *current* and *controllable* causal functional relationships.

In addition, a fourth characteristic of case formulation is its idiographic focus. Specifically, case formulations are typically designed to identify causal functional relationships applicable to a *specific* set of target behaviours for an *individual* client. This idiographic approach is consistent with the notion that important between-person differences exist in the causes of behaviour and that interventions should be individually tailored in order to maximize effectiveness.

Finally, because case formulation is not restricted to a specific type of target behaviour or causal factor, it is likely that a wide range of causal relationships may be examined during an assessment. As a result, assessors must consider incorporating complex variations of antecedent–response, response–response, response–consequence, and antecedent–response–consequence interactions into the case formulation.

IDENTIFYING CAUSAL FUNCTIONAL RELATIONSHIPS

The identification of causal relationships is a critical step in the development of a case formulation. To plausibly argue that two variables are causally related, one must rely on 'cues to causality' (Einhorn, 1988). The more important cues to causality identified in the research literature are: (a) elevated conditional probabilities, reliable co-variation, or concomitant variation, (b) temporal precedence – that is, the hypothesized causal variable precedes the observed effect on the target behaviour, (c) the exclusion of plausible alternative explanations for the observed relationship, and (d) a logical basis for inferring causality.

Several assessment methods can be used to evaluate the presence of these 'cues to causality'. Time series analysis and single subject designs can be used to evaluate covariation and temporal precedence (Barlow & Hersen, 1984). Self-monitoring of the target behaviour, its antecedents, and its consequences provides one source of data for such designs. These methodologies cannot, however, rule out third variable confounds or alternative accounts for the observed relationship. Furthermore, they can be problematic not only because they require multiple points of measurement and considerable effort from the client, but also because they typically evaluate the interactions among only a few variables.

Concurrent administration of different behavioural assessment devices, such as self-report inventories, psychophysiological measures, and behavioural interviews, can also provide information about causal functional relationships. For example, a client may report high levels of public speaking anxiety on a self-report inventory, demonstrate high levels of physiological reactivity during a simulated speech in a lab setting, and be observed to have poor social interaction skills during a behavioural interview. Given these data, a therapist may infer that the client's public speaking anxiety is caused by excessive physiological activation combined with deficiencies in social interaction skills. However, not only do these causal speculations fail to unambiguously demonstrate temporal precedence, they remain susceptible to alternative explanations for the observed relationships. For example, it may be equally plausible to hypothesize that public speaking anxiety and excessive physiological activation cause deficiencies in social interaction skills.

A third way to infer the presence of causal functional relationships focuses on the use of marker variables which are conveniently obtained indices of causal functional relationships (Haynes & O'Brien, 1988, 1990). For instance, the CO_2 inhalation challenge, which is sometimes used to assist the diagnosis of panic disorder, is an example of an empirically validated marker variable. Specifically, patients with panic disorder, relative to controls, have been shown to be significantly more likely to experience acute panic symptoms when they inhale air with high concentrations of CO_2 (Barlow, 1988; Clark, Salkovskis & Chalkley, 1985). Thus, the observation of panic symptoms in response to CO_2 inhalation can be used as a marker for the presence of the causal relationships between biological variables and behavioural responses that characterize panic disorder.

Although the marker variable strategy can provide information about causal functional relationships, few empirically validated marker variables have been identified in the assessment literature (Haynes & O'Brien, 2000). As a result, many assessors tend to rely on unvalidated marker variables, such as client reports of causal relationships. For example, clients frequently make causal attributions about their target behaviours and report them to the assessor during an interview. Such reliance on client report may be problematic because the reported causal relationships, although salient to the client, may not be accurate.

Although several assessment methods exist, their strengths vary in psychometric integrity, practicality, and relevance for assessing a particular set of target behaviours and controlling factors for an individual client. The selection and implementation of assessment tools throughout the case formulation process should take these factors into account and, when possible, should be guided by psychometric data and relevant empirical research. The use of multiple assessment methods can aid in the identification of functional causal relationships and provide corroborating evidence for, or disconfirming evidence against, the hypothesized relationships.

FUTURE PERSPECTIVES AND CONCLUSIONS

Case formulation emphasizes the identification and evaluation of important, controllable causal functional relationships for the purposes of intervention design. Identifying and evaluating causal functional relationships using rigorous empirical procedures, however, remains a challenging task for most assessors. Indeed, reviews of the assessment literature revealed that pretreatment causal analyses were conducted in only approximately 20 per cent of published case studies (Haynes & O'Brien, 1990; O'Brien & Haynes, 1995). Furthermore, many clinicians appear to be unfamiliar with the procedures needed to adequately evaluate causal relationships with an individual client (O'Brien, 1995). Finally, most clinicians do not appear to systematically construct case formulations in their clinical practices (Elliot et al., 1996).

A number of important questions about case formulation procedures need to be addressed in upcoming years. First, do interventions based on a comprehensive and systematic case formulation lead to significantly better outcomes? Second, can assessors be trained to consistently use valid case formulation procedures? Third, how generalizable are case formulations across persons, behaviours, and settings? And finally, what are the decisional processes that govern the generation of a case formulation among behavioural assessors?

Note

1   The term target behaviour refers to cognitive-verbal, affective-physiological, and overt-motor responses that are the focus of assessment. Target behaviours may be considered problematic (e.g. excessive anxiety in the presence of innocuous stimuli) or adaptive (e.g. using positive self-statements to reduce anxiety).

References

Barlow, D.H. (1988). *Anxiety and Its Disorders*. New York: Guilford.

Barlow, D.H. & Hersen, M. (1984). *Single Case Experimental Designs: Strategies for Studying Behaviour Change* (2nd ed.). New York: Pergamon (1st ed., 1976).

Clark, D.M., Salkovskis, P.M. & Chalkley, A.J. (1985). Respiratory control as a treatment for panic attacks. *Journal of Behaviour Therapy and Experimental Psychiatry*, 16(1), 23–30.

Einhorn, H.J. (1988). Diagnosis and causality in clinical and statistical prediction. In Turk, D.C. & Salovey, P. (Eds.), *Reasoning, Inference, and Judgment in Clinical Psychology* (pp. 51–70). New York: The Free Press.

Elliot, A.J., Miltenberger, R.G., Kaster-Bundgaard, J. & Lumley, V. (1996). A national survey of assessment and therapy techniques used by behaviour therapists. *Cognitive and Behaviour Practice*, 3, 107–125.

Haynes, S.N. & O'Brien, W.H. (1988). The Gordian knot of DSM-III-R use: integrating principles of behaviour classification and complex causal models, *Behavioural Assessment*, 10(1), 95–105.

Haynes, S.N. & O'Brien, W.H. (1990). Functional analysis in behaviour therapy. *Clinical Psychology Review*, 10(6), 649–668.

Haynes, S.N. & O'Brien, W.H. (2000). *Principles and Practice of Behavioural Assessment*. New York: Kluwer.

James, L.R., Mulaik, S.A. & Brett, J.M. (1982). *Causal Analysis: Assumptions, Models, and Data*. Beverly Hills: Sage.

O'Brien, W.H. (1995). Inaccuracies in the estimation of functional relationships using self-monitoring data. *Journal of Behaviour Therapy & Experimental Psychiatry*, 26(4), 351–357.

O'Brien, W.H. & Haynes, S.N. (1995). A functional analytic approach to the conceptualization, assessment, and treatment of a child with frequent migraine headaches. *In Session: Psychotherapy in Practice*, 1(2), 65–80.

Selected Bibliography

Dougher, M.J. (Ed.) (2000). *Clinical Behaviour Analysis*. Reno, NV: Context Press.

Elliot, A.J., Miltenberger, R.G., Kaster-Bundgaard, J. & Lumley, V. (1996). A national survey of assessment and therapy techniques used by behaviour therapists. *Cognitive and Behaviour Practice*, 3, 107–125.

Follette, W., Naugle, A.E. & Linnerooth, P.J. (2000). Functional alternatives to traditional assessment and diagnosis. In Dougher, M.J. (Ed.), *Clinical Behaviour Analysis* (pp. 99–125). Reno, NV: Context Press.

Haynes, S.N. & O'Brien, W.H. (2000). *Principles and Practice of Behavioural Assessment*. New York: Kluwer.

Iwata, B.A., Kahng, S.W., Wallace, M.D. & Lindberg, J.S. (2000). The functional analysis model of behavioural assessment. In Austin, J. & Carr, J. (Eds.), *Handbook of Applied Behaviour Analysis* (pp. 61–89). Reno, NV: Context Press.

Kazdin, A.E. (1998). *Research Design in Clinical Psychology* (3rd ed.). Boston: Allyn & Bacon (1st ed., 1980; 2nd ed., 1992).

William H. O'Brien, Allison Collins and Mary Kaplar

RELATED ENTRIES

CLASSIFICATION (GENERAL, INCLUDING DIAGNOSIS), DIAGNOSIS OF MENTAL AND BEHAVIOURAL DISORDERS, EXPLANATION, ASSESSMENT PROCESS

CENTRES (ASSESSMENT CENTRES)

INTRODUCTION

In general terms, 'assessment centres' are those processes used for marking, evaluating and predicting people's applied skills, know-how and knowledge based on situational tests.

The empirical base for this method is simple, and has been voiced on various occasions.

According to experiments carried out in the behavioural branch of psychology, the best indicator of a person's behaviour is his past behaviour, shown in a given situation. As a result, if we want to predict a person's efficiency in a given situation or before a set of tasks which could prove critical in carrying out his future professional responsibilities, we must observe, classify and evaluate his behaviour accurately in these types of situations in the present, or determine what type of conduct was shown in the past.

Origin of the Assessment Centre (AC) Methodology

Beginning in the second half of the past century (see McClelland et al., 1958), all evaluation technology which took this simple principle as a reference point – with variations and technical differences at various points and according to different specialists – was called *situational assessment method* and, in its application to the Psychology of Organizations, 'Assessment Centre Method'.

Professor D. McClelland's contributions are considered the most significant source in experimental and conceptual development for building current AC methods.

Current AC Concept

Though AC's basic concept can be applied in evaluating behaviour in any type of situation (e.g. in a clinical environment, to evaluate ability in stressful situations; in an educational environment, to evaluate students' learning behaviour regarding specific pedagogical contents; in a social environment to evaluate group behaviour in emergency situations; etc.), in practice, its current usage is basically related to organizational psychology.

Currently, AC is a process aimed at evaluating and predicting the behaviour of professionals whether in a job position which needs to be filled (*selection*), in a professional position which is being performed (*performance assessment*) or in a position the subject can perform in the future and in which he must show competence and extensive knowledge (*potential assessment*).

In all cases, the results of the individual and group assessment are used to plan *development and training programmes*, aimed at improving worker skills and eradicate deficiencies involving technical knowledge in handling personal and professional situations.

AC Determining Elements

AC is a logical and ordered process of observation, registration, classification and evaluation. It assesses the behaviour of one or various subjects who are faced with a series of situations in a standardized manner and where they must answer with a result or specific out-put.

In general terms, the elements which differentiate the assessment process centre from other evaluating techniques are the following:

- Evaluation is done through situational tests.
- The subject is asked to solve a specific problem or situation within standardized parameters.
- The situation has been designed so that specific characteristics can be observed in the subject's behaviour (called COMPETENCIES), either in general or technical knowledge.
- The criteria delimits whether the behaviour being observed draws near or far from the model of abilities being evaluated; the latter have been previously established and described in detail as 'observable behaviour'.
- The subjects perform the tests before a group of observers who carefully record the behaviour.
- *Potential* as well as current ability is evaluated.

TYPICAL AC PROCESS

How does a typical AC process develop?

Analysis Phase

First, a technical team defines the AC *parameters*. On the basis of detailed objectives (why is there an evaluation and who is to be evaluated), the factors or abilities to be evaluated are determined.

The set of abilities to be evaluated in an AC is called an assessment 'framework'. The analysis framework is achieved through various methods.

The objective is to know in detail the content and the dynamics of key situations which the subject must face in a given position or those tasks for which he is being evaluated.

As a result of the analysis, various aspects can be accurately determined:

- Content representative of the work done or which needs to be done, in particular *critical situations or incidents* which he must successfully solve to achieve results that are part of his responsibilities.
- Behaviour characteristics (basic knowledge and abilities put into practice) which the person must master to overcome critical situations, i.e. the *competencies* he must demonstrate.
- Specific behaviour which shows whether or not the subject possesses the essential *abilities* required in a given situation; these are defined as *criteria*.

Design Phase

The series of tests and exercises which those being evaluated will be subject to during the assessment process are drawn from the established framework. The selection has various well-defined objectives:

- That the set of tests and exercises reveals, without any doubt, the presence or absence of *competencies* in the framework.
- That they represent professional or personal working situations, and that they closely resemble real life.
- That 'test convergence' occurs. One of the elements which significantly increases the quality and reliability of the evaluation is the so-called test convergence, so that a specific *compentency* is identified through various tests done at different times.
- That these be revealed during an assessment session.
- That these combine individual working sessions, one-on-one situations and group integration, parallel to real life situations of those being evaluated.
- That the session be engaging, motivating and stimulating for the participants, so that the rhythm and intensity are maintained throughout the session.

The series of tests and exercises which can be applied during an AC are unlimited. At the same time, these are classified by common characteristics in the type of competencies they elicit. There follows a short description of each type:

- *Business games*: Simulation of complex and consecutive decisions, generally with the help of a computer, offering various management alternatives, so that each variable affects the others.
- *Group/s dynamics or discussion*: Consists of posing a 'problem-situation' to a group of participants so that they must discuss among themselves until they reach a common or individual solution.
- *Analysis exercises*: Analysis of situations or a set or group of complex information relating to a situation, where the participant is expected to identify relevant information, a given structure, and arrive at logical conclusions in order to take the proper action to best solve a situation.
- *Fact finding*: Correctly identify important facts missing from given information. Any additional information which the evaluators provide, on the request of the evaluees, is designed and structured by levels of depth in the analysis.
- *Presentation Exercises*: These are simulations where the participant must make a presentation before an audience, followed by a roundtable discussion of the subject's behaviour.
- *'In-baskets'*: The participant is shown a set of documents which he may find on any given work day in his in-basket. He must resolve the situation with the resources available. It is expected that he solve any technical, human, commercial, economic, financial and technical problems as best he can.
- *Role play*: The participant plays a brief role in a given situation (a difficult negotiation; a complaint; a sale; an unpleasant situation; etc.). Other roles are played by the evaluators or sometimes by professional actors trained for this purpose.
- *Mock interview*: Ask the participant to play the role of the evaluator in a given situation and with a specific goal which has been previously described. The nature of the

interview varies: sales interview, a counselling interview or an interview to discipline a co-worker.

Application Phase

When the AC is ready to be put into practice, several key factors, which have proved successful in past years, must be taken into account. Following are the most important:

- Number of participants: the ideal number is between 6 and 12.
- Number of observers/assessors: the ideal number of assessors or observers is one per three or four participants.
- Length of the evaluation process: there are some processes which are organized so that for each person being evaluated no more than half a work day is employed while there are some evaluations which can last up to 3 days per person being evaluated.
- Debate between assessors/participants: once the evaluation period is over, assessors and participants discuss individual results in a closing session until they reach a common ground.

FUTURE PERSPECTIVES AND CONCLUSIONS

In 2001, Professor Byham and his team developed a new perspective in the use of AC that has been labelled as *development centres*. The main aim of this version of AC processes is to enable the organizations not only to assess the actual capabilities and competencies shown by a given individual, but to predict the potential of development of such characteristics of behaviour – specially those related with the development of managerial potential – and to make reliable projections of the possible evolution of positive and necessary skills.

The concept of *potential derailers* as trends of behaviour which can miscarry the development of managerial capability is key to these *development centres*, and a lot of attention and focus is put in the early identification and reduction of them. A total of eleven possible *derailers* has been identified and described in terms of behavioural

criteria and is currently used in the development centres.

In sum, AC technology appears, in the beginning of the twenty first century, as the most powerful and reliable set of tools HR professionals can use to determine and develop human potential.

Bibliography

Bray, D.W. & Grant, D.L. (1966). The assessment centre in the measurement of potential for business management. *Psychological Monographs, 80* (17, whole no. 625).

Burrough, W.A., Rollins, J.B. & Hopkins, J.J. (1973). The effect of age, departmental experience, and prior rater experience on performance in assessment centre exercises. *Academy of Management Journal, 16*, 335–339.

Crawley, B., Pinder, R. & Herriot, P. (1990). Assessment centre dimensions, personality, and aptitudes. *Journal of Occupational Psychology, 63*, 211–216.

Dulewicz, V. & Fletcher, C. (1982). Experience, intelligence and background characteristics and their performance in an assessment centre. *Journal of Occupational Psychology, 55*, 197–207.

Flanagan, J.C. (1954). The critical incident technique. *Psychological Bulletin, 51*, 175–193.

Fletcher, C. (1991). Candidates' reactions to assessment centres and their outcomes: a longitudinal study. *Journal of Occupational Psychology, 64*(2), 117–128.

Frederiksen, N., Saunders, D.R. & Wand, B. (1957). The in-basket test. *Psychological Monographs, 71* (9, whole no. 438).

Gratton, L. (1989). Work of the manager. In Herriot, P. (Ed.), *Assessment and Selection in Organisations*. Chichester: John Wiley and Sons.

Howard, A. (1974). An assessment of assessment centres. *Academy of Management Journal, 17*, 115–134.

Huck, J.R. (1973). Assessment centres: a review of the external and internal validities. *Personnel Psychology, 26*, 191–212.

Klimoski, R. & Brickner, M. (1987). Why do assessment centres work? The puzzle of assessment centre validity. *Personnel Psychology, 40*, 234–260.

Klimoski, R. & Strickland, W.J. (1977). Assessment centre – valid or merely prescient? *Personnel Psychology, 30*, 353–361.

Lurie, J. & Watts, C. (1991). Using Assessment Centre in the Process of Organisational Change. Paper presented to British Psychological Society Occupational Psychology Conference, Cardiff, January 1991.

McClelland, D., Baldwin, A., Bronfenbrenner, U. & Strodbeck, F. (Eds.) (1958). *Talent and Society: New Perspectives in the Identification of Talent*. Princeton, NJ: Van Nostrand.

McEvoy, G.M. & Beatty, R.W. (1989). Assessment centre and subordinate appraisals of managers: a seven-year examination of predictive validity. *Personnel Psychology, 42*, 37–52.

Moses, J.L. (1973). The development of assessment centre for the early identification of supervisory potential. *Personnel Psychology, 26*, 569–580.

Moses, J.L. (1975). Task force on development of assessment centre standards, endorsed by Third International Congress on the assessment centre method, Quebec, May 1975.

Schmitt, N., Noe, R.A. & Fitzgerald, M.P. (1984). Validity of assessment centre ratings for the prediction of performance ratings and school climate of school administrators. *Journal of Applied Psychology, 69*, 207–213.

Thornton, G.C. III (1992). *Assessment Centres in Human Resource Management*. Reading, MA: Addison-Wesley.

Thornton, G.C. III & Byham, W.C. (1982). *Assessment Centre and Managerial Performance*. New York: Academic Press.

Walsh, J.P., Weinberg, R.M. & Fairfield, M.L. (1987). The effect of gender on assessment centre evaluations. *Journal of Occupational Psychology, 60*(4), 305–309.

Woodruffe, C. (1990). *Assessment Centres: Identifying and Developing Competencies*, London: Nelson.

Alvaro de Ansorena

RELATED ENTRIES

CHILD AND ADOLESCENT ASSESSMENT IN CLINICAL SETTINGS

INTRODUCTION

The assessment of behavioural and mental disorders in children and adolescents is one of the longest standing practices in the field of psychology. Amongst its pioneers are Itard, Preyer and Binet.

The American Academy of Child and Adolescent Psychiatry (1995) has outlined three main *purposes* in Child and Adolescent assessment: Determine whether psychopathology is present and, if so, establish a differential diagnosis. Determine whether treatment is suitable. Develop treatment programmes to encourage co-operative treatment between the family and patient.

Therefore certain *prerequisites* are essential:

- Assessment begins once the patient has had time to get used to the surroundings and the assessor.
- Multidisciplinary perspective. Paediatricians, neurologists, language specialists, psychologists, social workers, physiotherapists can contribute with additional points of view to the diagnosis of the problem and offer possible solutions.
- A variety of informants are consulted: parents, peers and teachers as well as the patient himself even if the various sources do not agree with each other. Assessment of very young children should be carried out in a variety of surroundings to see how these surroundings influence disturbed behaviour, especially when the probable cause is a reaction to the environment.
- Interaction and dynamics between different family members are assessed.
- Relationships with peers are assessed.
- The psychometric quality of instruments and possible variables during observation are controlled.
- Repetition of analyses as changes in behaviour in children and adolescents are typical.
- Evolutionary assessment since behaviour depends on the child's age.
- Children's behaviour is analysed within the cultural context in which it occurs to determine which behaviour is acceptable or not and whether its frequency or intensity is relevant.

Opportunity for child assessment depends on various factors:

Usually examination is requested by parents, advised by teachers or instructed by a law court or social services department. A child or adolescent should be examined when they show signs of slow development, difficulty in interpreting symbols, bad relationships with peers, inability to accept or follow rules or difficulty in controlling emotions.

During the assessment *initial contact* is very important. The first thing to consider is *information* about the patient and their consent. Then the professional must choose the best form of initial contact.

It is not necessary to give a preliminary explanation to children under 3 years old, but it may be worthwhile describing the kind of situations they are going to experience. Between 4 and 6 informing the child directly before the visit is recommended. Clear and concise information should be given. Explanations should be restricted to those which answer any questions the child raises, if at all. Children between 7 and 12 should be informed several days before to get used to the idea. Information should be clear and exact and should stimulate the child to question any doubts or fears they may have. Communication is more difficult with adolescents: only 5–10% request psychological help themselves. Parents usually make the decision for them and should inform the adolescent when doing so. If they are unable to persuade the adolescent to see the specialist they will need support from teachers or other adults. Any form of punishment at this age is inappropriate.

With very young children (0–3 years old) initial contact is usually with the parents alone. The parents are usually present when the child is interviewed for the first time except in potential cases of child abuse. Sometimes consultation is with the parents alone, particularly in cases of controlling behaviour. Between the ages of 4 and 6 consultation could begin together or just with the parents depending on the child and the type of problem. From 7 to 12 years there is greater flexibility. With adolescents the first meeting should be with the patient and begin with general questions about school, friends and hobbies before asking more personal questions. If the adolescent refuses to answer certain questions the professional should change topic and wait until a more comfortable relationship has been established before asking them again. When the professional is of the opposite sex care should be taken so as to offer the right amount of empathy and avoid the natural tendency to establish an excessively intense sentimental relationship.

The first session is used to focus on the problem and then additional, more specific information is obtained later. With younger children it is advisable to begin sessions with games. If the child is not talking the session is used to observe their behaviour. If they can talk then the child can be asked questions about their interests, which helps facilitate communication. By the end of the *first interview* the professional should have a clear idea of:

- Their opinion of the visit to the psychologist.
- Their view of the problem that has caused the patient (or parents) to seek help.
- The kind of relationship they have with their parents.
- Who their friends are and the relationship they have with them.
- Their school marks and the relationship they have with their teachers.
- The kind of interests they have.

Confidentiality should be respected except in cases of abuse, suicide, drug addiction, or if the patient is a danger to the lives of others. In cases of divorce where custody is in question, both parents are entitled to the information even though only one of them is the client. Confidentiality is extremely important with adolescent patients. Consent must be obtained from the patient before communicating anything to the parents.

Based on the first meeting the assessment is focussed in a certain direction.

The most important *areas of assessment* are:

- *Assessment of intellectual, social and psychomotor development.* This is investigated especially if the patient shows any signs of being immature or mentally retarded for his age.
- *Medical examination.* Carried out when the probable cause of the problem is physical and could involve a neurological or endocrine examination.
- *Assessment of the family environment.* Previous history of mental illness in the family, especially that being investigated, needs to be checked for. Family interaction is also evaluated.
- *Assessment of the social environment.* Social values and motivation in the child's environment need evaluating along with the resources and support the child receives.

The four basic assessment *procedures* are: norm-referenced test, interviews, observation and informal assessment. The choice of assessment type depends on the theoretical framework it belongs to, the child's age and the type of problem.

There are two main types of diagnostic orientation: *categorical* and *dimensional*. The former has been developed in the world of medicine and psychiatry and is based on a consensus of subjective criteria. The latter has been developed in the field of psychology and uses empirical categories and factorial analysis (Mash & Terdal, 1988).

The basic criteria for establishing different diagnostic categories are the causes and symptoms. Given that the causes of most syndromes cannot be identified but the risk factors that increase the probability of occurrence can be listed, a description of symptoms is often used. To avoid excessive diagnostic variability a general consensus of the basic characteristic symptoms of each syndrome is sought from experts. The well-known categorical diagnostic systems *International Classification of Disease* (ICD) and the *Diagnostic and Statistical Manual* (DSM) (Table 1) began as adult classification systems with few references to disorders in children except for mentally retarded children. The ICD is more common in Europe and DSM is more widely used in America, although the latter is gradually replacing the former system. The first classification of child mental disorders was done by Kanner (1953) and appears in the DSM II (1968). In Europe, Rutter (1965) wrote the first classification of child mental disorders which later appeared in the ICD-9 in 1978.

DSM-IV has some obvious advantages: (i) an increase in diagnostic complexity by including symptoms as well as duration and prediction; (ii) the use of ordinary vocabulary; (iii) the improvement in diagnostic reliability; and (iv) the possibility of cross-cultural use. Disadvantages include the need to improve categories of child diagnosis keeping developmental problems in mind.

Each diagnostic system has characteristic *assessment tools*. Categorical diagnosis opts for interviews to check for characteristic symptoms. Interviews can be open or more structured and therefore it is easier to control their reliability. One of the first structured *clinical interviews* with children was carried out by Graham and Rutter (1968) and served as a guide to subsequent interviews. The two that are most well known and commonly referred to are shown in Table 2.

Dimensional diagnosis is a continuum on which behavioural disorders vary in intensity. Alterations are grouped together empirically and defined as certain symptoms obtained through factorial analysis. The method is quantitative and empirical. To obtain information, which will give a reliable grouping of symptoms, 'clusters', extensive assessment is necessary using *questionnaires* or *checklists* to evaluate large numbers of people.

The dimensional system stipulates both *generic* and *specific* assessment. Disorders like depression, hyperactivity and autism need specific assessment and are useful in determining the effectiveness of treatment.

Multidimensional or generic evaluation covers a wider spectrum of disorders. Like 'screening', it is used in the early stages of diagnosis to confirm observations made during the first interview and

Table 1. Diagnostic systems: DSM and ICD

DSM-IV (1994), USA, APA	ICD-10, Europe, WHO
Mental Retardation	Mental Retardation
Learning Disorders	Developmental Disorders
Motor Skills Disorders	Developmental Disorders
Communication Disorders	Developmental Disorders
Pervasive Developmental Disorders	Developmental Disorders
(Touly in adults) Classification	Mixed Emotional and Asocial Disorders
(Touly in adults) Classification	Emotional Disorders
Attention Deficit and Disruptive Behaviour Disorders	Behavioural Disorders, Hyperactivity
Feeding and Eating Disorders of Infancy or Childhood	Other Disorders
Tic Disorders	Tic Disorders
Elimination Disorders	Other Disorders
Other Disorders of Infancy, Childhood, or Adolescence	Social Behaviour Disorders

Table 2.   Clinical interview types

Author	Name	Date	Age range	No of items	Applicant
Herjanic et al. (DICA)	Diagnostic Interview for Children and	1975	6–17	19 + 247	Parent Children
Reich Welner (DICA-R)	Adolescents	1978			Adolescent
Costello et al. (DISC)	Diagnostic Interview Schedule for Children	1984, 1986	6–17	246	Parent Children
Schaffer et al.		1997			

Table 3.   Multidimensional or generic evaluation

Author	Name	Date	Age range	No of items	Applicant
Peterson (BPCL)	Behaviour Problem Check-list	1961	5–16	55	Parent
Quay & Peterson (LBCL)	Louisville Behaviour Check-list	1967	4–12	164	Parent
Conners (CARS)	Conners Rating Scale	1969 1973	6–12	39 48	Teachers Parent
Wirt et al. (PIC)	Personality Inventory for Children	1977	3–16	600	Parent Children
Achenbach & Edelbrock (CBCL)	Child Behaviour Check-list	1978 1984	6–16	118 118	Parent Teachers
Achenbach & Edelbrock (YSR)	Youth Self Report	1987	11–18	103	Youth

check that no other problems have been over-looked. Some of the most significant are shown in Table 3.

The well-known *Child Behaviour Check-list* (CBCL, Achenbach & Edelbrock 1978) has two parts: the first compares the child's social skills to other children their age and the second rates behavioural problems. Factorial analysis creates subscales and two significant second order factors: internalizing and externalizing problems. Reliability is adequate as is validity.

The TRF checklist for teachers (Achenbach & Edelbrock, 1984, 1986) applies to children from ages 6 to 16. It is similar to the one given to parents but includes more detail about behaviour and achievement at school and has excellent psychometric qualities.

The more recent *Youth Self Report* (YSR, Achenbach & Edelbrock, 1987) is for adolescents and deals with social adaptation and behaviour disorders. Its psychometric qualities are adequate.

By referring to the frequently used taxonomy of child disorders we are going to use (i) *internalizing* and (ii) *externalizing* behavioural problems.

Anxiety is a basic cause of many internalizing disorders (e.g. phobias, post-trauma syndrome). Each has different characteristics but all reveal high levels of anxiety. Questionnaires are usually completed by parents, children or teachers (see Table 4).

The widely-used *State–Trait Anxiety Scale for Children* (STAIC, Spielberger et al., 1973) deals equally with state and trait anxiety. To avoid any bias there is a balance of positive and negative items and it refers to children from ages 9 to 15. The validity and reliability of the test is adequate.

Fear forms a part of child behaviour and cannot be considered pathological unless it affects the everyday life of the child considerably and requires treatment. One of the first epidemiological studies was made by Lapouse and Monk (1959). Scherer and Nakamura (1968) devised one of the first scales for children, *Fear Schedule for Children* – FSSC, answered by children and revised by Ollendick (FSSC-R, 1983). Its psychometric qualities are adequate. The well-known *Louisville Fear Survey Schedule* (LFSS, Miller, Barret, Hampe & Noble, 1972) refers to classic fears: fear of physical injury, fear of

Table 4. Anxiety questionnaires

Author	Name	Date	Age range	No of items	Applicant
Castañeda et al. (CMAS)	Children's Manifest Anxiety Scale	1956	6–15	42	Parent
Spielberger et al. (STAIC)	State–Trait Anxiety Scale for Children	1973	9–15	40	Children
Reynolds & Richmond (CMAS-R)	Revised Children's Manifest Anxiety Scale	1978	6–19	37	Children and Parent
Gillis (CAS)	Children Anxiety Scale	1980	6–8	20	Children

Table 5. Depression evaluation questionnaires

Author	Name	Date	Age range	No of items	Applicant
Kovacs & Beck	Children's Depression Inventory	1977	9–16	27	Children and Adolescent
Kovacs (CDI)		1992			
Birleson (DSRS)	Depression Self-Rating Scale	1981	9–17	18	Children and Adolescent
Lang & Tisher (CDS)	Children Depression Scale	1978	9–16	66	Children
Reynolds (RADS)	Reynolds Adolescent Depression Scale	1986	13–19	30	Adolescents
Reynolds (RCDS)	Reynolds Child Depression Scale	1989	9–12	30	Children

natural elements, social fears. Since then many lists of children's fears have appeared.

Another technique used with children is a test with visual support material such as the *Fear Thermometer* (FT, Walk, 1956), variations of which are still used today.

Due to the late acceptance of child depression by the scientific world, evaluation questionnaires are recent, and the best known are shown in Table 5.

The well-known *Children's Depression Inventory* (CDI, Kovacs & Beck, 1977; Kovacs, 1992) evaluates the presence of symptoms on a scale 0–2 and in the most recent version there are four factors. Designed for children, parents and teachers, the psychometric qualities are good and results are homogenous in different cultures.

There are structured interviews for emotional disorders such as the *Children's Depression Rating Scale* (CDRS, Poznanski, 1979) and tests for peer evaluation: *The Peer Nomination Inventory for Depression* (PNID, Lefkowitz & Tesing, 1980).

Obsessive-compulsive disorders usually occur during adulthood although there are a few cases during adolescence (0.3 or 0.7%). One of the most recent tools is the *Leyton Obsessional Inventory Child Version* (LOI-CV, Berg et al., 1986) with 44 yes/no questions and adequate psychometric qualities.

Anorexia Nervosa is among the internal behaviour disorders because of its comorbility with anxiety. This occurs when 25% of normal body weight is lost without illness or medical treatment and can be assessed with the *Eating Disorders Inventory* (EDI, Garner & Garfinkel, 1979).

Conduct disorders appear when children express their dissatisfaction and the society around them suffers as a consequence. Some forms are: opposition disorders, conduct disorder and delinquency. When social norms are not respected there is a problem of opposition or conduct, but when the law is broken it is delinquency. Most generic tests include points about conduct disorder. The best known specific tests are the *Behaviour Problem Checklist* (BPC, Peterson, 1961) revised by Quay (1983), the *New York Teacher Rating Scale for Disruptive and Antisocial Conduct* (NYTRS, Miller et al., 1995) and the *Child and Adolescent Disruptive Behaviour Inventory* (CADBI, Burns & Taylor, 1999).

Table 6.   Intelligence scales

Author	Name	Year	Age range
Binet & Simon-SB	Intelligence Scale	1905,	2–16
Terman & Merrrill	Stanford-Binet	1916	2–18
	Intelligence Scale	1937, 1960	
		1970, 1972	
Thordike et al.,	Revised L-M	1986	
Leiter (LIPS)	Leiter International	1929, 1948	2–20
	Performance Scale		
Roid & Miller (LIPS-R)	Leiter International	1997	
	Performance Scale – Revised		
Cattell (CIIS)	Cattell Infant	1940	
	Intelligence Scale		
Wechsler (WISC)	Weschler Intelligence Scale	1949	6–12
	for Children		
Weschler (WISC-R)	Revised	1974	6–15
Weschler (WISC-III)		1991	6–12
Weschler (WPPSI)	Wechsler Preschool and	1963	4–6 1/2
	Primary Scale of Intelligence		
Bayley (BSID)	Bayley Scales for	1969	0–2 1/2
	Infant Development		
Raven (PM)	Raven's Progressive Matrices		5–11
Raven (PM-R)	Raven's Progressive	1986	
	Matrices – Revised		
McCarthy (MSCA)	McCarthy Scales of	1972	2–8 1/2
	Children Abilities		
Kaufman & Kaufman (K-ABC)	Kaufman Assessing Battery	1983	2–12
	for Children		
Bracken & McCallum	Universal Test of Nonverbal	1997	3–17
	Intelligence		
Naglieri & Das (CAS)	Cognitive Assessment System	1997	5–17

Among the most common causes of disruptive behaviour are hyperactivity and aggression. The well-known *Werry–Weiss–Peters Activity Rating Scale* (WWPARS, Werry, 1968) evaluates hyperactivity. It has been updated and is completed by parents. The *Home Situations Questionnaire* (HSQ, Barkley, 1981) evaluates the home environment. Physical and verbal aggression is evaluated in the *Aggression Fisical y Verbal* checklist (AFV, Caprara & Pastorelli, 1993). The evaluation covers two main areas: psychotic disorders and autism.

Psychotic Disorders assessment is complex and neurological and physiological alterations as well as mental retardation need to be investigated. In the field of psychology the well-known *Kiddie-Schedule for Affective Disorders in Present Episode* (K-SADS-P, Chambers et al., 1985) is a semi-structured interview for children and parents and detects affective, anxiety, conduct and psychotic disorders. It discriminates between illusions and delusions. The reliability and validity are good for *psychotic disorders*. The *Brief Mental Status Interview* is suitable for adolescent patients. In adolescents it is possible to use MMPI-A (Archer, 1992).

More specific evaluation is needed when dealing with autism. The well-known *Childhood Autism Rating Scale* (CARS, Schopler et al., 1980) explores, through 15 subscales, relationships, adaptation to change, verbal communication etc. Another big syndrome is *Mental Retardation*. A child is considered mentally retarded when his performance is two or more standard deviations below the population mean. The patient's mental age initially determined general cognitive functioning. The first scale, created by Binet (1905), was to locate children in schools according to their learning abilities following the compulsory schooling law in France (see Table 6). The scale was introduced in the USA by Goddard and revised by Terman (1916) and Terman–Merrill (1937, 1960, and

1972) who adopted Stern's concept of IQ. In 1949 the *Wechsler Intelligence Scale for Children* (WISC) was published and revised in 1974 (WISC-R). This scale contains items taken from Binet, Yerkes and Kohs and is probably the most used scale in the world with children. It has two factors, Verbal and Performance, and validity and reliability of this scale are good.

Since Cattell and Horn proposed their innovative theory about fluid (capacity) and crystallized (learning) intelligence, the effort to assess the other side of intelligent behaviour has been challenged. With the Russian prohibition of intelligence tests and the American idea that tests were culturally biased there were strong reasons to develop other forms of assessing children's intelligent behaviour. Stenberg distinguished three different types of intelligence: componential (internal mental mechanism), experiential (internal and external world interaction) and contextual (adaptation). Finally, today's concept of intelligence has become more Piagetian. Social and emotional adaptive behaviour is today the most important subject when assessing children's capacities which are considered holistic rather than purely mental. In fact the idea of intelligence being the capacity of adaptation has been present from Binet to Sternberg. There are special tools to assess this field: *Adaptative Behaviour Scales* (ABS, Nihira et al., 1974); *Balthazar Scales Adaptative Behaviour* (BSAB, I, II, Balthazar, 1971).

The Baby Tests and Development assessment are the best way to detect early problems in children. The *Minnesota Child Development Inventory* (MCDI, Ireton & Thwing, 1977), the *Neonatal Behavioural Assessment Scale* (NBAS, Brazelton, 1973), *Development Scales* (DS, Gessell & Amatruda, 1940), *Bayley Scales for Infant Development* (BISID, Bayley, 1969) are some of them.

In recent years, neuropsychological assessment of cognition is growing dramatically and it permits to have an independent evaluation of attention; auditory, visual, tactile, verbal, spatial perceptual functions; memory, reading, reasoning, problem solving, cognitive planning and learning. This technique also permits application on infants and handicapped children early and objectively.

Adaptive behaviour is assessed especially in handicapped children. The well-known *Adaptive Behaviour Scale* (ABS, Nihira et al., 1974) covers the 3–69 age group and assesses behavioural and affective problems in mentally retarded people. Today the learning potential and problem solving abilities are included in intelligence assessment tests.

Intelligence assessment has defenders and critics. The former think that knowing the child's capacity will promote the best education for him, the latter consider that testing places the minority in an unfavourable position.

FUTURE PERSPECTIVES AND CONCLUSIONS

To conclude, it is clear that child assessment is a special task. Although its goals and methods are similar to adult assessment, its subject is absolutely different. It needs to take into account development, and tools, techniques and perspectives must conform themselves to such a dimension.

If children are subordinated to their parents and teachers, this does not mean that the psychologist may neglect their privacy and rights.

Finally, it is necessary to emphasize that all clinical assessments must not only diagnose the problem, but also consider its seriousness, its possible solution, design a treatment plan and follow up the subsequent intervention.

Among the questions that remain open to future research we may point to the following ones:

1 The need to reconcile data coming from multiple informants by the OR rule, and to secure the reliability of these different sources (parents, child, teachers, peers, nurses), specially in what relates to emotions and behaviours.

2 To strengthen multicultural assessment, as children need to be assessed in their own cultural contexts, language and social values.

3 To isolate new risk factors for the main disorders, in order to facilitate preventive intervention in those cases.

4 Full prevention is the new goal for the coming future, a task that must be related not only to pathological events, but also to positive dimensions of behaviour, such as autoefficacy, happiness, success, well being, and achievement.

Basic References

Achenbach, T.M. & McConaghy, S.H. (1996). *Empirically Based Assessment of Child and Adolescent Psychopathology: Practical Applications* (2nd ed.). Newbury Park, CA: Sage.

del Barrio M.V. (1995). Evaluación clínica infantil y adolescente. In Silva, F. (Ed.). *Evaluación psicológica en niños y adolescents*. Madrid: Síntesis.

Harrison, S.I. (1998). *Handbook of Child and Adolescent Psychiatry: Clinical Assessment and Intervention Planing*, Vol. 5. New York: Wiley.

Hopper, S.R., Hynd, J.W. & Mattison, R.E. (1992). *Child Psychopathology: Diagnostic Criteria and Clinical Assessment*. Hillsdale, NY: Lawrence Erlbaum.

Hughes, J. & Baker, D.B. (1990). *The Clinical Child Interview*. New York: Guilford Press.

Johnson, J.H. & Goldman, J. (1990). *Developmental Assessment in Clinical Child Psychology*. New York: Pergamon Press.

Kazdin, A. (1996). Evaluation in clinical practice (Special Series). *Clinical Psychology: Science and Practice*, *3*, 144–181.

Mash, E.J & Terdal, L.G. (Ed.) (1988). *Behavioural Assessment of Childhood Disorders* (2nd ed.). New York: Guilford Press.

Morrison, J. & Anders, T.I. (1999). *Interviewing Children and Adolescents*. New York: Guilford Press.

Ollendick, T.H. & Hersen, M. (1986). *Handbook of Child Psychopathology*. New York: Plenum Press.

Quittner, A.L. (2000). Improving assessment in child clinical and paediatric psychology: establishing links to process and functional outcomes. In Drotar, D. (Ed.), *Handbook of Research in Paediatric and Clinical Child Psychology*. New York: Plenum Publishers.

Rutter, M. & Hussain, T.A. (1988). *Assessment and Diagnosis in Child Psychopathology*. London: David Fulton Publishers.

Sattler, M. (1988). *Assessment of Children* (3rd ed.). San Diego, CA: J. Sattler Publishers.

Schaffer, D. & Lucas, C.P. (1999). *Diagnostic Assessment in Child and Adolescent Psychopathology*. New York: Guilford Press.

María Victoria del Barrio

RELATED ENTRIES

APPLIED FIELDS: CLINICAL, CHILDREN WITH DISABILITIES, CHILD CUSTODY, PRE-SCHOOL CHILDREN, MENTAL RETARDATION, LEARNING DISABILITIES

C CHILD CUSTODY

INTRODUCTION

More families go through divorce and break-up than ever before. Parents are faced with critical decisions, and children are influenced by the dramatic changes in their families. In such a crisis, the child's natural support system may not always address his/her best interests. One outcome of this situation is an increasing need for diagnostic and therapeutic involvement, best executed by a multidisciplinary team.

Relevant Facts

The marked increase in the recent rate of divorce has brought about an increase in the number of children being raised in non-traditional families: blended families (Arda, 1994), father-headed households (Cohen, 1995), and families in which unmarried parents raise their children on their own, accompanied by steady or changing partners.

Children are being raised within or outside the nucleus family and are impacted by social mobility and immigration. Concomitantly we see a significant decrease in the influence of religion, family values, and social values, resulting in a lack of traditional regulations and guidelines.

General Guidelines for Custody Assessment

The purpose of assessment is to reach a recommendation that will stand in court and serve as a basis for a long-lasting arrangement, taking into account the changing needs of each family member and those of the family as a system. This resulting recommendation may have a deep, sometimes irreversible, effect on the lives of all concerned, especially children. The experts who make these recommendations carry a heavy responsibility.

Despite the variety of opinions, most Western professionals and courts have agreed upon several criteria regarding child custody (APA, 1994; Miller, 1993; Wall & Amadio, 1994; Goldstein, Freud & Solnit, 1979; Kaslow & Schwartz, 1987). The guiding principle is the best interest of the child, a difficult endeavour when the authentic details are overshadowed by crisis. The following general guidelines should be followed.

Security and Consistency

Preference for an environment that will ensure consistent living conditions, security, and protection.

The Least Harmful Choice

Where there is no optimal solution, select the option least damaging to the child.

The Child's Relationship with the Non-Custodial Parent and his Family

The parent willing to allow this contact is usually considered the preferable choice, as this willingness is regarded as a manifestation of sensitivity and respect to the needs of the child.

These guidelines concur with distinct legal criteria defining relevant legal aspects such as natural guardianship, requisition of the rights of natural guardians (sending the child to a foster home and adoption), economic and physical responsibility, and definition of children at risk.

The court, as the 'client' of the custody assessment, expects recommendations based on accepted and admissible legal tools and data-backed findings. Data gathering must be responsible, professional, and authorized. The recommendations must be adaptable to the changing developmental needs of each individual separately and those of the family as a whole. These recommendations should be long enduring and applicable until the family is able to change the circumstances on its own or with their consent. The recommendations refer to the flexibility and the maturity of each family member and the family as a whole, their ability to change, develop, and be sensitive as well as respect the individual's needs. These widely accepted guidelines serve as a very general framework. Adhering to them enables the experts to work with a certain degree of unity.

BEST INTERESTS OF THE CHILD

This basic principle generally means that where a conflict exists between the needs of the child and the needs of the adult, first priority is given to those of the child.

Legal Aspects

This principle is the foundation of laws legislated to ensure the safety of the child during various crises by enabling, among other things, separate legal representation for children. It also takes precedence over other commonly applied legal principles (e.g. non-disclosure vs. public trial). Decisions have time limits and may be reevaluated – not following the principle of finality of judgement after appeals have been heard. *The Hague Child Abduction Convention* differs on this, and holds legal considerations above the concept of child's best interest (Silberman, 1994).

It is important to note that the child's best interest is not always the sole and foremost issue for the disputing parents, thus raising the need for separate *children's legal representation*.

Developmental Aspects

Children's needs vary according to their developmental stages, a fact that must come to bear on the evaluation (e.g. considerations regarding the separation of a very young child from his/her mother are different than those regarding an adolescent). Religious, cultural and intercultural issues must be taken into account, as should the needs of special populations (e.g. single-parent family, single-gender family, HIV/AIDS and addicted families).

CHILD CUSTODY ASSESSMENT

Diagnostic Process

The main elements of the diagnostic process are:

The Events

The events, individual tests and examinations of the child and relevant family members, as well as interactive meetings, home visits, contact with appropriate services, and professional discussions among team members.

Intentionally Premeditated Continuous Process

The process is deliberately slow and drawn-out, to enable the team to assess the ability to change and the ability of the child and other significant figures to accept and utilize help and support from the team. The team also provides support and advice.

1   The diagnosis is based on a holistic concept taking into account a wide variety of aspects of the child's life. Material must be collected from various sources (e.g. teachers and doctors). Social relations, extra-curricular activities, hobbies, etc. should also be examined directly.
2   Most Discreet Objectivity. Objectivity is a critical factor, as is discretion, especially in cases where a choice must be made. Each party must feel that it has the impartial opportunity to present itself and its position, and be examined by the team respectfully, objectively and be openly heard without prejudice. The team must transmit reliability, strict confidentiality and privacy of all the information collected.

Observational Techniques

Observational techniques are tools for providing information about details of daily life, emotional climate, and behaviour patterns. The integration of this information with the results of the psychological testing is crucial for obtaining an overall understanding of the family's situation.

Interactions

Interactions are in vivo meetings with all relevant, significant figures in the child's life. The meetings provide an opportunity to observe the relationships in the 'here and now', and reflect the family's behavioural and emotional climate. Although family resistance may prevent these meetings, they should be considered an important asset to any recommendation.

Home Visits

Home visits should provide a first-hand impression of the child's situation: how he lives and with whom, and even what clothes he wears, what toys he has, the physical conditions of his surroundings and other daily, practical information. The alternative living place should also be visited and assessed to reach a fact-based choice.

Psychological Tests

Psychological tests are commonly used and have defined scientifically based norms, validity, and reliability. Tests complete and balance the information gathered from the observational techniques.

The following tests are widely used and accepted evaluation of personality and capability, and therefore are best suited for custody assessment.

The Bender Gestalt Test (BGT)

The Bender Gestalt Test (BGT), originally known as the Bender Visual Motor Gestalt Test (Bender, 1938), using the Hutt (1985) adaptation can be used. The test is a screening instrument for neurological and personality abnormalities, and assesses one type of constructional and memory ability.

The Wechsler Intelligence Scale for Children (WISC-R) and WAIS

The Wechsler Intelligence Scale for Children (WISC-R) and WAIS, for adults, are commonly used for the evaluation of intelligence: Verbal-, Performance- and Total IQ. The results help determine psychological and educational interventions (Wechsler, 1991).

The Rorschach Inkblot Test

The Rorschach Inkblot Test – Exner (1993) and Weiner (1998), the CAT and TAT (Bellak, 1986), MMPI-2 (Greene, 1991) and 'drawing Person', 'House', 'Tree', and 'Family' as projective tests, as well as various Questionnaires (Mullett & Stolberg, 1999; Heflinger et al., 2000).

Recording Special Circumstances

Custody assessment is based on the diagnostic process, on observational techniques, and on psychological tests. In addition, consideration must be given to issues and circumstances that are not quantifiable, but are nonetheless crucial to the assessment. Examples of such issues are new circumstances caused by the remarriage of one parent; choosing between a parent and a member of the extended family as legal guardian; separating siblings; and false allegations by one parent that the other is abusing the child.

MULTIDISCIPLINARY TEAM

In the arena of family disputes courtesy and rules are discarded; a barehanded, cutthroat, war is fought between parties who once shared a life and perhaps love. It is a most demanding, confusing, and absorbing field in which one may easily lose perspective. In this complex atmosphere the family may try to seduce and bribe or threaten and blackmail. The team can help keep clear perspective and focus, help identify and acknowledge the possible bias and neutralize any interference that may undermine the process.

The multidisciplinary team engages with the family, studying every relevant aspect and collecting information from various sources. At the same time it acts as an anchor to the family in crisis. All initiatives of independent expression are encouraged, especially those of children. Members of the team share the burden and the responsibility.

A typical multidisciplinary team for child custody cases consists of the school psychologist, a clinical psychologist, family therapists, and a social worker. For specific cases the team may include an expert in learning disabilities and a psychiatrist. At times legal or religious experts may be called in, as well as dieticians, occupational therapists, or speech therapists. The team usually consists of three people of different disciplines, one of whom is the case-manager (Levi & Romi, 2000).

The usual decision-making process has five stages:

1 Data collection and initial impression
2 Analysis and integration of the diagnostic material
3 Consolidation of findings and defining recommendations for intervention
4 Intervention
5 Follow-up and evaluation of the results of the intervention

Possible criticism of multidisciplinary teams may refer to the cost in terms of time, energy, and funds, and to the difficulty of involving the family with several professionals.

FUTURE PERSPECTIVES AND CONCLUSIONS

Many children are in crisis and lead a complex life as a result of not having a 'natural stable home'. These transitional periods may constitute risk to the child and require active intervention by social services and courts to ensure the safety and best interest of the child.

Despite vast accumulated knowledge, it still seems impossible to reach a common ground for dealing with the variety of situations needing intervention and requiring multidomain thought. Each aspect of the situation must be considered, and using a multidisciplinary team, as detailed here, seems to provide an optimal approach to a complex human issue.

References

American Psychological Association (1994). Guidelines for Child Custody Evaluations in Divorce Proceedings. *American Psychologist*, Vol. 49, No. 7, 677–680.

Arda, I. (1994). Tension factors in remarriage families – a qualitative pioneer study. *Society and Welfare*, 14(3–4), 311–291 (in Hebrew).

Bellak, L. (1986). *The TAT, CAT, and SAT in Clinical Use* (4th ed.). Larchmont, New York: C.P.S., Inc.

Bender, L. (1938). A visual motor Gestalt test and its clinical use. *Research Monographs of the American Orthopsychiatric Association*, No. 3.

Cohen, O. (1995). Feeling of relief – divorced mothers and fathers raising the children by themselves. *Society and Welfare*, 15, 4 (in Hebrew).

Exner, J.E., Jr. (1993). *The Rorschach: A Comprehensive System, Basic Foundations*, Vol. 1 (3rd ed.). New York: John Wiley & Sons, Inc.

Goldstein, J., Freud, A. & Solnit, A.Z. (1979). *Before the Best Interests of the Child*. New York: Free Press.

Greene, R.L. (1991). *The MMPI-1/MMPI: An Interpretive Manual*. New York: Allyn and Bacon.

Heflinger, C.A., Simpkins, C.G. & Combs, O.T. (2000). Using the CBCL to determine the clinical status of children in state custody. *Children and Youth Services Review*, 22(1), 55–73.

Hutt, M.L. (1985). *Hutt Adaptation of the Bender Gestalt Test* (4th ed.). New York: Grune & Stratton.

Kaslow, F.W. & Schwartz, L.L. (1987). *The Dynamics of Divorce: A Life Cycle Perspective*. New York: Brunner/Mazel.

Levi, N. & Romi, S. (2000). A multi-disciplinary professional team to clarify the dilemmas in children's custody. In Singh, N.N., Leung, J.P. & Singh, A.N. (Eds.), *International Research and Practice in Child and Adolescent Mental Health* (Chapter 21, 357–379). Oxford: Elsevier Science Ltd.

Miller, G. (1993). The psychological best interests of the child. *Journal of Divorce and Remarriage*, 19(1–2), 21–36.

Mullett, E.K. & Stolberg, A. (1999). The development of the co-parenting behaviours questionnaire: an instrument for children of divorce. *Journal of Divorce and Remarriage*, 31(3–4), 115–137.

Silberman, L. (1994). Hague convention on international child abduction: a brief overview and case law analysis. *Family Law Quarterly*, 28(1), 9–34.

Wall, J.C. & Amadio, C. (1994). An integrated approach to child custody evaluation: utilizing the 'best interest' of the child and family systems frameworks. *Journal of Divorce and Remarriage*, 21(3–4), 39–57.

Wechsler, D. (1991). *Manual for the Wechsler Intelligence Scale for Children – 111*. New York: Psychological Corporation.

Weiner, B.I. (1998). *Principles of Rorschach Interpretation*. Mahwah, NJ: Lawrence Erlbaum Associates, Publishers.

Selected Bibliography

Exner, J.E. & Weiner, I.B. (1982). *The Rorschach: A Comprehensive System, Assessment of Children and Adolescents*, Vol. 3. New York: Wiley.

Gardner, R.A. (1986). *Child Custody Litigation: A Guide for Parents and Health Care Professionals*. Cresskill, NJ: Creative Therapeutics.

Gardner, R.A. (1989). *Family Evaluation in Child Custody Mediation, Arbitration, and Litigation*. Cresskill, NJ: Creative Therapeutics.

Gardner, R.A. (1999). Assessment for the stronger, healthier psychological bond in child-custody evaluations. *Journal of Divorce and Remarriage*, 31(1–2), 1–14.

Schutz, B.M., Dixon, E.B., Lindergerger, J.C. & Ruthner, N.J. (1989). *Solomon's Sword: A Practical Guide to Conducting Child Custody Evaluations*. San Francisco: Jossey-Bass.

Stahl, P.M. (1994). *Conducting Custody Evaluation: A Comprehensive Guide*. Thousand Oaks, CA: Sage Publishers.

Woody, R.H. (2000). *Child Custody: Practice Standards, Ethical Issues, and Legal Safeguards for Mental Health Professionals*. Professional Resource Press.

Shlomo Romi and Nurit Levi

RELATED ENTRIES

Applied Fields: Forensic, Family, Couple Assessment in Clinical Settings

C CHILDREN WITH DISABILITIES

INTRODUCTION

There are many types of disabilities that affect children in very different ways. Development, learning processes and individual needs vary according to the nature of the disability. Children are differently affected by the extent, severity and multiplicity of the deficiencies. Assessing children with disabilities requires that aspects which differentiate each case be known and taken account of. It also requires that both resources and support from the surrounding environment be evaluated, since the child's chances of playing

a full part in the community often depend on these factors.

In this entry we will refer to key aspects that should be taken into account when assessing children with disabilities. When we talk of children with disabilities we are referring to children with intellectual disabilities (mental retardation), hearing impairments including deafness, speech or language impairments, visual impairments including blindness, serious emotional disturbance, orthopaedic impairments, autism, traumatic brain injury, other health impairments or specific learning disabilities.

Under the category of children with disabilities we currently include groups which were not previously included within this category, this being the case of autistic children and children with traumatic brain injury. In the past, children with these types of disabilities received isolated, specific, and different attention to other children. Without underestimating the need for such attention at certain stages of these children's development, today many of the problems that they have in common with other children of their own age are the ones to be assessed.

Many of the tests and assessment tools used to assess children with disabilities are frequently the same used with other children who have no disability. For this reason, this entry focuses on those aspects which are essential for the assessment of children with disabilities, without embracing other areas specifically related to the subject of assessment, dealt with in other entries of this encyclopedia.

THE EVOLUTION OF ASSESSMENT CRITERIA

Assessment used in schools in the first half of the last century started out with and was characterized by the use of standardized tests which focused on general processes of intelligence, personality and achievement when faced with general tasks. Subsequently, in the 1970s, many specific standardized tests were developed, with great attention paid to students with learning disabilities. At the time, tests such as the Illinois Tests of Psycholinguistic Abilities (Kirk, McCarthy & Kirk, 1968) and the Developmental Test of Visual Perception (Frostig, Lefever & Whittlesey, 1966; Hammill, Pearson & Voress, 1993) acquired great importance. However, in the 1970s, standardized tests suffered from significant limitations with respect to generating useful information about the difficulties that students with deficiencies suffered from.

In the 1980s, schools started to propose alternative strategies to the standardized tests. Informal measures, mainly in curriculum-based measurement, acquired great relevance (Taylor, 1997). And the need to use both types of measurement was raised. While standardized tests are of greater use in diagnosis and the obtaining

of general and preliminary information about an individual, informal measurement is of greater relevance when we require useful data for the education process because it concentrates on measuring the progress of the student in the curriculum.

At present, the assessment process in schools – principal setting in which the assessment of children with disabilities is described – varies according to the different purposes it pursues. Education decisions refer not only to the initial screening stage but also to the type of programme that should be employed, as well as the progress of the student in the programmes. The main goals of assessment in schools are (Taylor, 1997): (1) initial identification or screening; (2) determination and evaluation of teaching programmes and strategies; (3) determination of current performance level and educational level; (4) decisions about classification and programme placement; and (5) development of Individualized Educational Programmes (including goals, objectives and evaluation procedures). The nature of the different procedures used in the different situations described is always a result of combining formal and informal assessment procedures. And the responsibility for the assessment process falls on different professionals.

ASSESSMENT OF THE PROGRESS OF STUDENTS IN INCLUSIVE SCHOOLS

Norm-Referenced and Criterion Referenced Testing

Norm-referenced tests provide performance measures, which allow comparisons of scores obtained from students from different grades, regions, ages and settings. Norm-referenced tests are usually used to make a preliminary analysis, like screening tests of student performance, and compare it to that of other students of similar characteristics. Subsequently, a decision is made over whether a more profound analysis of the student's academic performance is needed.

The results of norm-referenced tests are also used to determine whether a student needs to receive special education services, or to determine curricular areas in which the student will need special help, as well as to assess the progress of the student in education contexts (Salend, 1998). Additionally, these tests usually give adequate information about the reliability and validity they offer.

The main problem with norm-referenced tests is that they do not offer data useful for planning the education process. The data is normally very general, and from an inclusive education point of view they are criticized because the test format can be difficult for many students, biased with respect to curriculum content, and test items and standardization do not reflect a multicultural perspective (Salend, 1998).

Criterion-referenced tests 'relate a student's score on an achievement test to a domain of knowledge rather than to another student's score' (Sax, 1997). The essential aim of criterion-referenced testing is to help to define what to teach, and the determination and evaluation of objectives and teaching strategies. Similarly, they are used to plan and evaluate the progress of the student in the individual's education plan. Although there are many criterion-referenced tests published commercially, it is recommended that the professionals who take part in the diagnosis (especially the teachers) devise their own tests. In this way the choice of content and items is more likely to be relevant to the goals defined.

Curriculum-Based Measurement

Curriculum-based measurement implies assessing classroom learning and content and is centred on practical education applications. Normal curricular material is used to assess the degree of learning, the difficulties and the instruction needs of the students (Tucker, 1985). As an assessment method, importance is placed on direct observation and frequent registry of student curricular performance, information used to take decisions related to the instruction (Deno, 1987). Curriculum-based measurement emphasizes the integration of concepts and applied tools coming from a variety of sources and psycho-pedagogical approaches: applied behavioural analysis, test construction theory, curricular development and assessment and precision teaching (Salvia & Hughes, 1990). Environmental models and education efficiency, along with evidence from instructional and cognitive psychology and the social psychology of education, have also allowed

us to understand the progressive movement away from student results and towards the area of teaching–learning (Meyers, Pfeiffer & Erlbaum, 1985).

It is evident that currently both types of assessment, standardized and curriculum-based, have a place, depending on the objectives set. It is also clear that both school psychologists as well as education professionals involved directly in the teaching of students with difficulties (general education teachers, special education teachers, therapists, and others) need to be included in the assessment process, as on many occasions do the parents.

Assessment Alternatives in Education

In recent years, movements of education reform have been proposing substantial changes in school assessment practice. The prejudicial effects of using standardized test in schools, particularly in relation to children from marginal and minority groups and including those families with financial problems, have led to a variety of alternative procedures aimed at fairer assessment. The tests are highly limited when giving information on the school instruction needs of children with disabilities. As a result, different types of procedures have been proposed. The aim is to develop a more flexible and multi-methodological system of school assessment than has previously been used, opening the door to qualitative procedures and making teachers and other education professionals directly responsible for such tasks.

In recent years several models have been proposed to take the place of 'traditional objective assessment procedures', the so-called post-modernist models being especially notable, models which aim to underline the multiplicity of assessment methods as well as emphasizing a different type of relation between the assessor and the assessed (Goodwin, 1997). In this sense, one of the most recent assessment trends in school learning processes, especially appropriate for children with disabilities and other limitations, is the so-called authentic assessment, also called performance or alternative assessment. This kind of procedure, centred on education and improving the professional practice of teachers, is particularly recommendable when favouring equity and inclusion in schools of students with special needs.

Some of the most important principles or characteristics proposed in order to achieve these changes in school learning assessment practice include (Darling-Hammond & Falk, 1997): (1) basing assessments on standards for learning; (2) representing performances of understanding in authentic ways; (3) embedding assessment in curriculum and instruction; (4) providing multiple forms of evidence about student learning; (5) evaluating standards without unnecessary standardization; and (6) involving local educators in designing and scoring assessments.

Extending responsibility for assessment to teachers and other persons who have direct contact with the student at school is a key factor for improving teaching.

Only by obtaining specific and concrete assessment of classroom learning difficulties can accurate conclusions be reached, in order to adapt and improve the efficacy of learning in students with limitations. However, the aims of assessment in children with disabilities are much wider than the learning assessment in the classroom. As in other contexts, there exist other notable aims of the psychological assessment and the use of tests such as (Meyer et al., 2001): (a) describing current functioning, including cognitive abilities, severity of disturbance, and capacity for independent living; (b) confirming, refuting, or modifying the impressions formed by clinicians through their less structured interactions with patients; (c) identifying therapeutic needs, highlighting issues likely to emerge in treatment, recommending forms of intervention, and offering guidance about likely outcomes; (d) aiding in differential diagnosis of emotional, behavioural and cognitive disorders; or (e) monitoring treatment over time to evaluate the success of interventions or to identify new issues that may require attention as original concerns are resolved.

LABELLING AND CLASSIFICATION

Contrary to previous practice, we no longer only identify children with disabilities in relation to their diagnostic label; neither do we identify them with separate special services in normal schooling. We are currently more interested in identifying education and other special needs of children with limitations or disabilities, prioritizing schools with full inclusion. The label is less important than before. Assessment focuses on observing the child and its surroundings.

The detrimental effects of labelling have been thoroughly described in educational contexts (Verdugo, 1994). Those authors who oppose the use of classifications remark that they (Langone, 1990): (a) exaggerate weaker areas of the subject; (b) are the cause of the so-called self-fulfilling prophecy which explains why students do not improve; (c) give rise to a negative self-concept in the students; and (d) allow teachers to have students outside normal educational programmes. Gallagher (1976) pointed out three negative characteristics of labelling in education, which are especially important and have been barely commented on by other authors: (a) categorizing may lead to a social hierarchy; (b) categorizing or classifying may be regarded by professionals as the end product of the process and would not produce a change; and (c) the classification is a particular treatment which may lead us to ignore complex social and environmental problems that have to be regenerated.

Those authors who propose the use of classifications in education base themselves on the following facts (Langone, 1990; Meyen, 1988): (a) labels allow better funding to be obtained for those categories in which there is a stronger need, given that the lack of a label would mix up data-gathering procedures; (b) non-disabled classmates may accept more easily the behaviour of students labelled as disabled; and (c) professionals may communicate more easily research results when individuals are divided into specific categories. Other reasons determine that categories and labels allow us to establish realistic aims for students or that labelling is required in order to ensure appropriate service delivery (Verdugo, 1994).

The use of labelling and classification has been heavily criticized in recent decades, but it has continued to be used in different ways, mainly in order to establish priorities and obtain special resources for specific students. Even so, labelling should disappear from daily education practice and direct contact with children with disabilities. Labelling should only remain when restricted to those professional and administrative situations which favour support and resources dedicated to promoting the equal opportunities of children with disabilities.

ACCOMMODATIONS AND MODIFICATIONS WHEN TESTING CHILDREN WITH DISABILITIES

Tests are applied to children with disabilities with different aims in mind, mainly in relation to their education. For example, they are used in decision-making processes to make placements, selection, identify needs, adapt educational programmes, or as a tool for educational accountability. However, standardized tests are frequently designed without taking into account procedures for their application in relation to children with language, sensorial, motor or psychological problems, when such problems do not affect the construct to be measured. In the case of children with disabilities, modifications and accommodations of assessment practices should be made to avoid prejudicing the results of the process as a consequence of characteristics that have nothing to do with what is to be measured (Salvia & Ysseldyke, 1998).

When tests are used with children who show some sort of disability, a series of specific considerations should be kept in mind, which facilitates the application process of the same with the aim of obtaining the most representative score of the individual. The goal is to reduce the influence of certain characteristics of the individual which have nothing to do with the main objective of the assessment, thus allowing valid inferences to be obtained of the construct analysed in the individual. This means that different types of accommodations and modifications need to be taken into account, types clearly synthesized and defined in the *Standards for Educational and Psychological Testing* written by the American Educational Research Association, American Psychological Association, and National Council on Measurement in Education (1999), the essence of which we describe in the following paragraphs.

Accommodation is a general term used to describe any action (contents or administration) which modifies the protocol established in a test in order to apply it to a person with disability, without affecting the construct to be measured. This means that situations exist where it is unnecessary to make accommodations because, precisely, the objective of the assessment is related to discovering the impact of the disability on the individual. Any accommodation should be directly related to the specific needs of the child who takes the test. The very same disability may require accommodation in one case but not in others, or require a different degree or extension in each case. Professional judgement plays a key role in decisions over accommodation.

Test modification can be carried out with respect to presentation format, response format, altering the timing, modifying the setting, using only a portion of the test or using alternative assessments. The professional in charge of the assessment process is the person who should decide in each case or cases what modifications should be made.

A great deal of caution should be taken when interpreting scores obtained after taking decisions related to accommodation of content or test administration procedures. The psychometric qualities of the test may become altered, in which case it may be difficult to compare student scores with scores from the original test. Similarly, decisions taken on modification may have affected the construct measured. For these reasons, the assessment report should always include the modifications which have been carried out in the tests, and should analyse whether these modifications affect the validity of the inferences carried out.

FUTURE PERSPECTIVES AND CONCLUSIONS

There are many different disabilities and each person presents a different situation depending not only on the type of disability, but also its extent, severity and intensity. Furthermore, environmental considerations also determine disability. Assessment should be centred on identifying multidimensional individual needs, but the use of severity labels to designate educational placement will be eliminated. Assessment and diagnosis of disability should lead 'to a profile of individually defined supports, not to a specific school or educational program placement' (Luckasson et al., 1992: 113).

In this entry we reviewed some of the central issues in assessing children with disabilities: (a) the evolution of assessment criteria, from standardized tests which focused on general processes to a more interdisciplinary approach using formal and informal procedures according to assessment goals; (b) assessment in inclusive schools, based on both standardized tests and curriculum-based measurement; (c) labelling and classification, that must be restricted only to specific professional and administrative situations; and (d) accommodations and modifications when testing any child with disabilities, in order to avoid influences of the individual which are not related to the assessment objective.

In the future, today's perspective of a more flexible and multimethodological system of school assessment will remain and active participation of teachers and other school personnel will increase. Simultaneously, psychologists will develop new methods and techniques to assess specific disabilities, although most of the assessment tools used to assess children with disabilities are the same as those used with other children who have no disability. Specific methods should take into account specific skills (and the lack of these) in each person, and accommodate and modify procedures according to those skills.

There will be psychologists and professionals trained in assessing specific problems or situations related to disabled people; for example, mental health problems in intellectually or sensory disabled people, or ageing in Down syndrome and other intellectually disabled people. Comprehensive bio-psycho-social assessment approaches should be implemented with interdisciplinary teams specialized in specific situations.

The new International Classification of Functioning, Disability and Health (World Health Organization, 2001) will be used to develop new tools and techniques to assess persons in different situations related to a bio-psycho-social rehabilitation. The emphasis on environment of this classification must be followed by new assessment approaches to assess activities (limitations) and participation (restrictions) in each disabled person.

References

American Educational Research Association/American Psychological Association/National Council on Measurement in Education (1999). *Standards for Educational and Psychological Testing.* Washington, DC: American Educational Research Association.

Darling-Hammond, L. & Falk, B. (1997). Supporting teaching and learning for all students: policies for authentic assessment systems. In Goodwin, A.L. (Ed.), *Assessment for Equity and Inclusion* (pp. 51–75). New York: Routledge.

Deno, S. (1987). Curriculum-based measurement. *Teaching Exceptional Children, 20,* 1–4.

Frostig, M., Lefever, W. & Whittlesey, J. (1966). *Administration and Scoring Manual: Marianne Frostig Developmental Test of Visual Perception.* Palo Alto, CA: Consulting Psychologists Press.

Gallagher, J.J. (1976). The acred and profane use of labeling. *Mental Retardation, 14,* 2–3.

Goodwin, A.L. (1997). *Assessment for Equity and Inclusion.* New York: Routledge.

Hammill, D., Pearson, N. & Voress, J. (1993). *Developmental Test of Visual Perception – 2.* Austin, TX: Pro-Ed.

Kirk, S., McCarthy, J. & Kirk, W. (1968). *Illinois Tests of Psycholinguistic Abilities.* Urbana, IL: University of Illinois Press.

Langone, J. (1990). *Teaching Students with Mild and Moderate Learning Problems.* Boston: Allyn & Bacon.

Luckasson, R., Coulte, D.L., Polloway, E.A., Reiss, S., Schalock, R.L., Snell, M.E., Spitalnik, D.M. & Stark, S.A. (1992). *Mental Retardation: Definition, Classification and Systems of Support.* Washington, DC: American Assiciation of Retardation.

Meyen, E. (1988). A commentary on special education. In: Meyen, E. & Skrtic, T. (Eds.), *Exceptional Children and Youth* (3rd ed., pp. 3–48). Denver: Love.

Meyer, G.J., Finn, S.E., Eyde, L.D., Kay, G.G., Moreland, K.L., Dies, R.R., Eisman, E.J., Kubiszyn, T.W. & Reed, G.M. (2001). Psychological testing and psychological assessment. A review of evidence and issues. *American Psychologist, 56,* 128–165.

Meyers, K., Pfeiffer, J. & Erlbaum, V. (1985). Process assessment: a model for broadening assessment. *The Journal of Special Education, 19,* 73–89.

Salend, S.J. (1998). *Effective Mainstreaming. Creating Inclusive Classrooms* (3rd ed.). Upper Saddle River, NJ: Prentice Hall.

Salvia, J. & Hughes, C. (1990). *Curriculum-Based Assessment: Testing What is Taught.* New York: Macmillan.

Salvia, J. & Ysseldyke, J.E. (1998). *Assessment* (7th ed.). Boston: Houghton Mifflin.

Sax, G. (1997). *Principles of Educational and Psychological Measurement* (4th ed.). Belmont, CA: Wadsworth.

Taylor, R.L. (1997). *Assessment of Exceptional Students. Educational and Psychological Procedures* (4th ed.). Boston: Allyn & Bacon.

Tucker, J.A. (1985). Curriculum-based assessment: an introduction. *Exceptional Children, 52,* 199–204.

Verdugo, M.A. (1994). *Evaluación curricular*. Madrid: Siglo Veintiuno.

World Health Organization (2001). *International Classification of Functioning, Disability and Health. ICIDH-2*. Geneva, Switzerland: Author.

Miguel Angel Verdugo

RELATED ENTRIES

CLASSICAL AND MODERN ITEM ANALYSIS

INTRODUCTION

Up until 25 years or so ago, item analysis was straightforward: multiple-choice test items were field-tested on reasonably sized samples of examinees to determine their level of difficulty and discrimination, and distractors were evaluated to determine their effectiveness in attracting examinees who were without the appropriate knowledge required for successfully answering the test items (see Crocker & Algina, 1986; Gulliksen, 1950; Lord & Novick, 1968). Items that were too easy or too hard, or less discriminating than other test items available to the test developer, were less likely to be selected for the final version of a test. In the 1970s, criterion-referenced tests were introduced into the testing field, and item analysis for these tests became less focused on determining levels of item difficulty and discrimination because these item statistics were relatively unimportant in the criterion-referenced test development process. Item congruence with the objectives they were designed to measure became one of the determining factors for item selection. Item difficulties of items measuring the same objective were used to identify potentially flawed items rather than to assess item difficulty per se. Outliers among the item difficulties were helpful in flagging potentially flawed test items. Identifying items with negative or very low item discrimination indices became important but that was about all that was important about item discrimination indices for constructing criterion-referenced tests. Clearly the use of item statistics with criterion-referenced test development was different from norm-referenced test development.

In the 1970s, modern test theory, perhaps better known as 'item response theory (IRT)', was introduced into the testing field and the item statistics of interest were different from the classical item statistics and also depended upon the choice of test model (Hambleton, Swaminathan & Rogers, 1991; Lord, 1980; Wright & Stone, 1979). Even the number of item statistics available to the test developer was dependent on the choice of IRT model. Modern test theory was very much focused at the item level as a strategy for gaining more flexibility in the test development process. At the same time, modern test theory is associated with stronger modelling of the item response data. Advantages, in principle, accrue from such an approach, but these advantages only come when the models being applied fit the data (e.g. the one-, two-, and three-parameter logistic test models). Model-data fit then is a critical element of modern test theory. IRT item statistics have the attractive feature that they are invariant across samples of examinees from the population of examinees for whom the test under construction is intended and this item invariance property is a major advantage to test developers. After statistically adjusting item statistics for differences in examinee samples, item statistics can be compared and contrasted, though the examinee samples on which they were based can be quite different.

One other major change in assessment has taken place that impacts strongly on item analysis practices today. Today, it is common to use performance test items that are scored polytomously. There are no multiple-choice item distractors needing to be evaluated. But, item statistics for assessing difficulty and discrimination that can be applied to polytomous response data have become important.

The remainder of this entry is divided into three sections: classical item analysis and modern item analysis will be described in the first two sections. References will be used to point to the actual item statistics formulas. Conclusions and future directions will be presented in a final section.

CLASSICAL ITEM ANALYSIS

Perhaps it is useful to restate the purposes of item analysis in norm-referenced test development: to determine flaws in test items, to evaluate the effectiveness of distractors (if the items are in a multiple-choice format), and to determine item statistics for use in subsequent test development work.

Item Difficulty

With dichotomously scored items, item difficulty is defined as the proportion of examinees answering an item correctly. The symbol 'p' is often used to designate item difficulty. As has been noted often, it was unfortunate that this statistic was not called 'item easiness' as this term would have been more descriptive.

Item difficulty statistics answer the question about the proportion of examinees in a sample of examinees who are tested who can answer each test item correctly. This is different from the proportion of examinees who know the correct answer because at least some proportion of examinees answer the item correctly by guessing the correct answer. Thus, the proportion of examinees answering an item correctly is an overestimate of the proportion of examinees who actually know the correct answer. By using the same assumption that is made to derive the correction for guessing formula (see Crocker & Algina, 1986), revised item statistics can be reported reflecting estimates of the proportion of examinees who actually know the correct answer to each test item. This information may be especially important with criterion-referenced test items.

Item difficulty statistics as typically defined in classical test theory have ordinal scale properties. Therefore, they cannot be statistically manipulated. For example, the test developer may want to study the linear relationship between item difficulty statistics and item discrimination indices. This should not be done. One solution is to place item difficulty statistics onto a scale that is considered to have equal intervals. ETS introduced the delta scale (a scale on which ability scores are assumed to be normally distributed with a mean = 13, and a standard deviation = 4). The item difficulty on this new scale (referred to as the 'item delta value') is the point on the delta scale beyond which p% of the examinees would fall in a normal distribution of ability. Thus, for example, an item with a p-value equal to 0.16 would have a corresponding delta value of 17. An item with a p-value of 0.50 would have a delta value of 13. On the delta scale, the transformed p-values are considered to be equal interval measurements and can be averaged, used in correlational analyses, etc.

Item Discrimination

The most obvious statistic to reflect item discrimination with 0–1 item level data is the Pearson product-moment correlation between item score and total test score being used as the criterion. Variations include correlating item level performance with total test scores (excluding the item itself, and the corresponding bias in the correlation) or correlating item scores with a criterion external to the test (a good idea, but rarely convenient). In this special case of the Pearson correlation because one of the variables is dichotomously scored, the correlation is called the 'point biserial correlation'. In many practical test development studies, the goal is to find items with point biserial correlations in excess of 0.20. When content specifications cannot be met, it is common to lower the threshold for acceptable discriminating powers of test items.

The point biserial correlation is very popular in norm-referenced test development because it is helpful in distinguishing the more discriminating from the less discriminating and negatively discriminating items, and it has a simple relationship to the standard deviation of test scores (see, for example, Lord & Novick, 1968). It does tend to be a bit higher for middle difficulty items than easier and harder items because item variability is higher and so to remove the bias that tends to favour middle difficulty items, an assumption can be made that despite the 0–1 scoring, underlying performance on the item is a normal distribution of ability. With this special assumption, the 'item biserial correlation' can be estimated, and this correlation tends to be more invariant over various samples of examinees that may take the item. This is a good property for an item statistic to have (because the choice of examinee sample in field-testing is less influential). It is easy to show that item biserial correlations tend to be a bit higher than item point biserial correlations (about 0.10 higher), though the calculations are more complicated and the statistic itself is harder to explain to users. Major testing agencies tend to prefer biserial correlations; smaller testing agencies and individual test developers seem more inclined to use point biserial correlations. The impact of this choice though seems minor in practice.

When both the criterion and the item are scored dichotomously, the Pearson product-moment correlation simplifies and is often called a 'phi correlation'. If both the item level and the criterion level variables are dichotomous, and if normality assumptions are made about ability underlying performance on the item and the criterion, the correlation used is called the 'tetrachoric correlation'.

Other item discrimination statistics can be found in Crocker and Algina (1986) including some that are principally used with criterion-referenced tests to describe the power of items to distinguish masters and non-masters. Extensions of these item level statistics to handle polytomously scored items are also emerging. As a starter, the Pearson correlation can easily handle the extension, but there are newer statistics being introduced also that assume a normal distribution of ability underlying item performance when items are scored polytomously.

Effectiveness of Distractors

With multiple-choice items, it is common to determine if the distractors are enhancing the measurement properties of the item, and if not, what changes can be made. First, an analysis is made to see if the distractors are being chosen. When the per cent of examinees choosing a distractor is low (say, less than 5%), and especially when the discriminating power of the test item is not as high as is desired, that distractor is studied to see if a more attractive answer for low-performing examinees can be substituted. Second, an analysis is made of the choice patterns of relatively high and relatively low performing examinees. Relatively popular distractors among the more capable examinees may suggest that there are two correct answers or even that the intended correct answer is not correct.

Role in Test Development

With norm-referenced tests, items are typically selected that maximize test score variability and contribute to content validity. This means that items with middle levels of difficulty and high item discrimination tend to be selected. With criterion-referenced tests, item statistics tend to be less important in test development. Maximizing test score variance would rarely be a criterion in item selection. Still, items with very low or negative discrimination levels would be of minimal value in a criterion-referenced test. On the other hand, items that have difficulty levels that decrease measurement errors for examinees near the performance standards may be of special value in a criterion-referenced test.

MODERN ITEM ANALYSIS

Until recently, among users of modern test theory, it has been common to carry out item analyses with both classical and modern procedures (Hambleton, Swaminathan & Rogers, 1991). In the introduction, a brief discussion of the advantages of IRT item statistics was provided. But classical item analysis remains popular for obtaining some initial views about item quality, even by test developers working in an IRT framework.

The key concept in IRT is that of the 'item characteristic curve' (ICC). This looks like a non-linear regression line (item performance regressed on ability) and provides an estimate of the probability of success on a test item for examinees at different ability levels. More capable examinees always have higher probabilities of success than less capable examinees. The interested reader is referred to the entry on item response theory in this encyclopedia to learn more about item characteristic curves. Estimating these ICCs can be complicated, require complex IRT software, and usually requires larger sample sizes than are needed to do a proper classical item analysis.

Item Difficulty

For harder items the ICCs are shifted to the higher end of the ability scale. Thus, examinees always have lower probabilities of success on harder items than easier items (as it should be). For easier items the ICCs are shifted to the lower end of the ability scale. The special property of ICCs is that they are defined over the ability scale on which items and scores are reported, and are independent of the examinee samples to which they are applied. For a given item and at a particular ability level, the probability of a successful response might be 0.75. All examinees at THAT ability level, regardless of the sample from which they came, have exactly the same probability.

Item Discrimination

The discriminating power of a test item influences the slope of the ICC. More discriminating items have steeper slopes, less discriminating items have lower slopes. The slope of the ICC has a substantial influence on the usefulness of a test item for estimating ability.

Effectiveness of Distractors/ Polytomously Scored Items

With 0–1 scored data, there are IRT models that allow for a full analysis of the distractors (see, for example, the nominal response model). Wainer (1989) provides an excellent discussion of an IRT distractor analysis. With polytomously scored items, there are additional IRT models that permit a full investigation of the effectiveness of each score point for assessing examinee ability. For example, it is possible to determine over what intervals on the ability scale a particular score point is useful for estimating ability.

Role in Test Development

There is one special feature of IRT item statistics, in addition to the property of item parameter invariance. Item statistics and ability scores are reported on the same scale. This feature makes it possible to choose test items that provide maximum information about examinee ability. For example, within a computer adaptive test administration, using the available ability estimate at any point in the test administration process, the best item can be selected to maximize what can be learned about examinee ability. The basic rule is that the items that are discriminating, and where the expected probability of the examinee's correct response is 50%, are the most useful for test administration. Items that are too easy or too hard, or provide modest discriminating power, are less useful in test administration. Of course, item selection is normally constrained by the need to ensure content validity of the total set of administered items, and by the need to limit the exposure of test items.

The amount of information an item provides for estimating ability at each ability level is given by the item information function (see Hambleton, Swaminathan & Rogers, 1991). Largely, the amount of information provided by an item tends to be maximum in the region on the ability continuum where examinees have about a 50% probability of a correct answer, and tends to zero for ability levels far from this point. The information function tends to be higher with more discriminating items. For a full discussion, see Hambleton, Swaminathan and Rogers (1991).

When performance levels are set on the ability continuum for assigning examinees to performance categories (e.g. below basic, basic, proficient, and advanced) it is common to try and minimize errors of measurement for ability scores near these performance levels to maximize both decision consistency and decision accuracy. This is accomplished quite easily within an IRT framework by selecting relatively more items and/ or more discriminating items functioning near the performance levels on the ability continuum.

FUTURE PERSPECTIVES AND CONCLUSIONS

The topic of item analysis has developed nicely as changes in test development have taken place. As the testing field has moved from normed-referenced testing to criterion-referenced testing, from dichotomously scored data to polytomously scored data, and from classical to modern test theory models, item analysis procedures have been introduced and/or modified to keep up with the needs of test developers. Wainer (1989) offered some clever suggestions for improving item analysis – these suggestions involve increased use of graphical procedures, and increased use of complex IRT models for reporting the effectiveness of multiple-choice test item distractors. He also envisioned a dynamic system where test developers have immediate access to item statistical information (literally by pushing a button or touching a screen) and in the course of building a test developer can monitor such statistics as test mean, standard deviation, test information, conditional standard errors, content specifications, etc. Wainer's ideas were sound in 1989, and remain sound today – he has offered some excellent ideas for making item analysis more useful to test developers. Interested readers are referred to Crocker and Algina (1986), Hambleton, Swaminathan, and Rogers (1991), Henrysson (1971), McDonald (1999), Wainer (1989), and Wright and Stone (1979) for follow-up reading on this topic.

References

Crocker, L. & Algina, J. (1986). *Introduction to Classical and Modern Test Theory*. Orlando, FL: Holt, Rinehart, & Winston, Inc.

Gulliksen, H. (1950). *Theory of Mental Tests*. New York: Wiley. (Republished by Lawrence Erlbaum Associates, Publishers, 1987.)

Hambleton, R.K., Swaminathan, H. & Rogers, H.J. (1991). *Fundamentals of Item Response Theory*. Newbury Park, CA: Sage Publications.

Henrysson, S. (1971). Gathering, analysing, and using data on test items. In Thorndike, R. (Ed.), *Educational Measurement* (2nd ed., pp. 130–159). Washington, DC: American Council on Education.

Lord, F.M. (1980). *Applications of Item Response Theory to Practical Testing Problems*. Mahwah, NJ: Erlbaum.

Lord, F.M. & Novick, M.R. (1968). *Statistical Theories of Mental Test Scores*. Reading, MA: Addison-Wesley.

McDonald, R.P. (1999). *Test Theory: A Unified Treatment*. Mahwah, NJ: Lawrence Erlbaum.

Wainer, H. (1989). The future of item analysis. *Journal of Educational Measurement*, 26, 191–208.

Wright, B.D. & Stone, M.H. (1979). *Best Test Design*. Chicago: MESA Press.

Ronald K. Hambleton and Mohamed Dirir

RELATED ENTRIES

ACHIEVEMENT TESTING, ITEM RESPONSE THEORY: MODELS AND FEATURES

CLASSICAL TEST THEORY

INTRODUCTION

Classical test theory (CTT) embraces a whole set of models and technical procedures designed to provide solutions to the problems involved in measuring psychological variables. When psychologists measure a variable, thus obtaining an empirical score, their interest lies not in the score itself, but in the inferences and interpretations that can be made from it and that can provide information on some aspect of the assessed person's behaviour. Of course, for these interpretations and inferences to be well founded it is necessary to have precise knowledge of the different psychometric properties of the instrument employed. CTT offers such coverage, allowing detailed description of the metric characteristics of the measurement instruments normally used by social scientists and professionals. On labelling this set of knowledge as 'classical' the intention is, on the one hand, to indicate that it is well established, having resisted the erosion of time, and, on the other, to differentiate it from new psychometric models; that is, the so-called item response theory (IRT) models that have emerged since the 1960s, and which reached their most successful period to date in the 1980s and 1990s. For a description of these models see the corresponding IRT entry.

Origins and Development of Classical Test Theory

The initial proposals of what we now refer to under the generic term classical test theory (CTT)

date from the beginning of the twentieth century. The beginnings of this approach were not particularly easy, as the quantitative orientation of psychology was at that time not the dominant paradigm. Nevertheless, it established itself little by little, and soon the majority of universities were including courses on test theory. As Joncich (1968) recounts in his biography of E.L. Thorndike, when the latter sent a copy of his pioneering work on measurement (Thorndike, 1904) to his *maestro* William James, he included a note advising him to oblige his students to read the book, but adding that under no circumstances should James himself even open it, as the figures, curves and formulas it contained would drive him mad. This anecdote serves to indicate the, at best, lukewarm reception to be expected from the psychological establishment for these psychometric issues that were taking their first steps. However, the period that followed was one of great activity and progress for psychometrics. New tests were constructed, psychometric technology was developed, and important advances were made in psychological and psychophysical scaling (Thurstone, 1927, 1928; Thurstone & Chave, 1929).

In 1936, Guilford would attempt to synthesize in his classic work *Psychometric Methods* all the basic developments up to that time in the fields of test theory, psychological scaling, and psychophysical scaling. These three fields share many concepts and models, and at that time it was still possible to treat them jointly, but the development and specialization of each of them has since made it necessary to deal with them separately, the latest edition of Guilford's 1954 book constituting an understandable exception.

At the same time as the test theory corpus of knowledge was becoming consolidated, the first steps were taken toward its institutionalization. The year 1936 saw the formation of the American Psychometric Society, with Thurstone as its president, and whose organ of expression would be the journal *Psychometrika*. Little by little, more and more journals specializing in psychological and educational measurement would appear, and today they are many. In 1947, Thurstone published his classic work *Multiple Factor Analysis*, presenting a multivariate technique with its origins in the psychometric field, and which has made an enormous

contribution to the construction, analysis and validation of tests. From the publication of Thurstone's book until today, factor analysis has made gigantic strides, thanks to new methods of extraction and rotation of factors, and thanks above all to the power and speed of calculation afforded by modern computers; nevertheless, it is still gratifying today to re-read Thurstone's book and wonder at the wisdom and psychological substance with which it is imbued. Thurstone was without doubt one of the great pioneers and personalities of classical psychometrics. As my own *maestro*, Mariano Yela, who studied under him in Chicago in the mid-1940s, relates, Thurstone 'was, above all, a creator. ... He always remained the engineer-inventor that as a young man had worked with Edison. He was as clear and incisive as crystal, shy, hard, sarcastic, implacable. With me, he was understanding, tolerant and cordial. He was totally devoted to his specialty, psychology as a rational experimental and quantitative science, and to his photographic interests. Nothing else existed for him' (Yela, 1996).

In parallel to the psychometric proposals of these early years, there was also an intense debate on the theory of measurement, led mainly by physicists somewhat wary of psychological measurement (Campbell, 1928) innovative proposals with regard to measurement scales would give a new direction and renewed momentum to the field, which would oblige psychometrists to review the metric status of the scores obtained in tests. Stevens' proposals for measurement scales (nominal, ordinal, interval and ratio) gave rise to an interesting debate – which is still going on today – on the connections between scales and statistical techniques, with postures ranging between two extremes: those claiming that scales determine the type of statistical techniques to use, and those that consider scales and statistics to be worlds apart, and totally unrelated (Gaito, 1980; Lord, 1953; Michell, 1986; Stine, 1989; Townsend & Ashby, 1984). Although the debate is an interesting one, and from a theoretical point of view there are arguments for defending either position, our humble advice to professionals is that they take a careful account of the scale used for measuring their data on processing them statistically and making inferences, since, while numbers do not know where they come from, researchers and professionals do indeed know how they were obtained and for what purpose they will be used. From the 1960s, a new perspective within measurement theory appeared on the scene, the axiomatic approach (Coombs, 1964; Krantz et al., 1971; Luce & Narens, 1986; Michell, 1990, 1997; Narens, 1985; Narens & Luce, 1986; Pfanzagl, 1968; Roberts, 1979; Savage & Ehrlich, 1990; Schwager, 1991; Suppes & Zinnes, 1963). This approach, highly formalized and attractive from a theoretical point of view, has had little impact on psychological assessment practice.

Returning to psychometrics, it could be said that the canonical work setting out the essentials of classical test theory developed up to that time was Gulliksen's book (1950) *Theory of Mental Tests*. Gulliksen had been a student of Thurstone, and later his assistant and colleague, and recognized the influence of his mentor, especially that of his book *The Reliability and Validity of Tests* (Thurstone, 1931). But Thurstone's book was already out of print by the time Gulliksen wrote his in 1950. The year 1954 saw the appearance of the first technical recommendations for the use of tests (*Technical Recommendations for Psychological Tests and Diagnostic Techniques*), and since then these recommendations, drawn up jointly by the American Educational Research Association, the American Psychological Association and the National Council on Measurement in Education, have undergone several revisions, the last of them as recently as 1999.

A fundamental text, which establishes a bridge between the classical approach and the new psychometric models, is that of Lord and Novick (1968). This important work, which benefits from the collaboration of Birnbaum, reanalysed the classical perspective and promoted the new item response theory models, which provided solutions to some problems that could not be adequately solved within a classical framework. Apart from the texts cited by Gulliksen and Lord and Novick, there is an abundance of works that offer clear and well-documented expositions of classical test theory, among them Magnuson (1967), Allen and Yen (1979), Thorndike (1982), Crocker and Algina (1986) and Muñiz (1996, 2000).

Below is a chronology detailing some of the milestones of classical test theory, adapted from Muñiz (2000):

Psychometric Chronology

1883	Galton publishes the book *Inquiries into Human Faculty and its Development*
1884	Galton opens the Anthropometric Laboratory in London
1891	J. McKeen Cattell found the Laboratory of Psychology at Columbia University, United States
1894	Kraepelin proposes the use of tests in psychopathology
1896	Ebbinghaus proposes the phrase-completion test
1904	Spearman publishes his two-factor theory of intelligence and the attenuation formulas; E.L. Thorndike publishes the book *An Introduction to the Theory of Mental and Social Measurements*
1905	Binet and Simon publish the first intelligence scale
1907	Krueger and Spearman coin the term *reliability coefficient*
1908	Introduction of the concept of *mental age* in the second edition of the Binet scale
1910	Spearman–Brown formula that relates reliability to the length of tests is published
1912	Stern proposes the concept of intelligence quotient
1916	Terman publishes Stanford's revision of the Binet–Simon scale
1918	Creation of the Army Alpha tests
1921	Publication of the Rorschach test
1931	Thurstone publishes *The Reliability and Validity of Tests*
1935	The Psychometric Society is founded; Buros publishes his first review of tests (*Mental Measurements Yearbook*)
1936	Guilford publishes *Psychometric Methods*; First issue of the journal *Psychometrika*
1937	Kuder and Richardson publish in *Psychometrika* their formulas KR_{20} and KR_{21}

1938	Bender, Raven and PMA tests are published
1939	Wechsler proposes his scale for measuring intelligence
1940	Appearance of the personality questionnaire *Minnesota Multiphasic Personality Inventory* (MMPI)
1946	Stevens proposes his four measurement scales: nominal, ordinal, interval and ratio
1948	Educational Testing Service (ETS) in the United States is established
1950	Gulliksen publishes *Theory of Mental Tests*
1951	Cronbach introduces the coefficient alpha; First edition of *Educational Measurement* is edited by Lindquist
1954	First edition of *Technical Recommendations for Psychological Tests and Diagnostic Techniques* is published
1955	Construct validity is introduced by Cronbach and Meehl
1958	Torgerson publishes *Theory and Methods of Scaling*
1959	Discriminant convergent validity is introduced by Campbell and Fiske
1960	Rasch proposes the one-parameter logistical model
1963	Criterion-referenced testing is introduced by Robert Glaser
1966	Second edition of *Standards for Educational and Psychological Tests* is published
1968	Lord and Novick publish *Statistical Theories of Mental Tests Scores*
1971	Second edition of *Educational Measurement* is published, edited by Thorndike
1974	Third edition of *Standards for Educational and Psychological Tests* is published
1979	BICAL computer program for estimating Rasch model parameters is introduced
1980	Lord publishes *Applications of Item Response Theory to Practical Testing Problems*
1982	The computer program LOGIST, for estimating IRT model parameters, is introduced
1984	The computer program BILOG, for estimating IRT model parameters, is introduced
1985	Fourth edition of *Standards for Educational and Psychological Tests* is published; Hambleton and Swaminathan's book on *Item Response Theory* is published
1989	The third edition of *Educational Measurement*, edited by Linn, is published
1997	Seventh edition of Anastasi's *Psychological Testing* is published; *Handbook of IRT models*, by Van der Linden and Hambleton (1997), is published
1999	Fifth edition of *Standards for Educational and Psychological Tests* is published

Classical Linear Model

The basic body of knowledge covered by the general term *classical test theory* (CTT) derives from the developments of the linear model, which has its origins in the pioneering works of Spearman (1904, 1907, 1913). In this model a person's empirical score from a test (*X*) is assumed to be made up of two additive components, the true score that actually corresponds to the person assessed in the test (*T*), and a certain error of measurement (*e*). Formally, the model can be expressed as:

$$X = T + e$$

where *X* is the empirical score obtained, *T* the true score and *e* the measurement error.

In order to derive the formulas necessary for calculating reliability, the model requires three assumptions and a definition. It is assumed that: (a) a person's true score in a test is that which s/he would obtain on average if the test were administered an infinite number of times ($E(X) = T$), (b) person true score and measurement error are uncorrelated ($\rho_{te} = 0$), and (c) measurement errors across parallel-forms of a test are uncorrelated. In addition, parallel tests are defined as tests that measure the same construct, where an examinee has the same true score on each, and where the sizes of errors in the tests (standard error of measurement) are identical.

From this model, through the corresponding developments, it is possible to arrive at operative formulas for the estimation of errors (*e*), and person true scores (*T*). All of these necessary deductions make up the psychometric corpus of classical test theory, whose formulation can be found in the classic texts already mentioned.

Through the corresponding developments the reliability coefficient $(\rho_{xx'})$ is obtained, a coefficient that permits the estimation of the size of the errors committed in the measurement process (see the corresponding entry in this encyclopaedia). Its formula expresses the amount of variance of true measurement (σ^2_T) in the empirical variance (σ^2_x).

The ideal situation is that all the empirical variance is due to true variance, which is what would occur when $\sigma^2_T = \sigma^2_x$, in which case the reliability is perfect, and the test measures with no error. The empirical calculation of the reliability coefficient value cannot be carried out by means of this formula, which is merely conceptual; empirical estimation can be obtained using various designs, among which are: (a) the correlation between two parallel forms of the test, (b) the correlation between scores on two random halves of the test corrected with the Spearman–Brown formula, and (c) the correlation between two applications of the same test to a sample of examinees. Each one of these procedures has its advantages and disadvantages, and is more appropriate for some situations than for others. In all cases the value obtained is a numerical value between 0 and 1, and the test's precision is greater the closer this value is to 1. Given that this formula is conceptual rather than operative, the psychometric literature offers an abundance of classical formulas for obtaining the empirical value of the reliability coefficient, important among them are those of Rulon (1939), Guttman (1945), Flanagan (1937), the KR_{20} and KR_{21} (Kuder & Richardson, 1937) and the popular alpha coefficient (Cronbach, 1951) that expresses the reliability of the test as a function of its internal consistency. An alternative, though equivalent form of expressing the reliability of tests is through the *standard error of measurement*.

Whichever index is used, and in each case there are technical reasons for using one or another, the important point is that all measurements have an associated degree of precision that is empirically calculable. The most common sources of error in psychological measurement have been widely researched by specialists, who have arrived at a highly detailed classification of all possible error sources (Cronbach, 1947; Schmidt & Hunter, 1996; Stanley, 1971; Thorndike, 1951). In quite simplified terms, we can identify three principal avenues through which random errors infiltrate psychological measurement: (a) the *actual person* assessed, who will arrive at the test situation in a certain mood and with particular attitudes, fears, and anxieties in relation to the test, and who is affected by any type of previous event, all of which may introduce error, (b) the *measurement instrument* used, whose specific characteristics may have a differential influence on those persons assessed (e.g. the questions in the test may be unclear to persons), and (c) the *application, correction and interpretation* made by professionals (Muñiz, 1998).

Variations on the Classical Test Model

The classical linear model permits the estimation of measurement error, but not its particular sources which are assumed to be unknown, and the errors random. Some models, also within the classical framework, have attempted to provide a breakdown of errors, thus offering not only overall reliability, but also reliability as a function of error sources (Bock & Wood, 1971; Novick, 1966; Sutcliffe, 1965). The technical–formal complexity and operative complications introduced by these models, offset against the advantages they offer, has meant that none of them has become popular in practice. Worthy of special mention in this respect is *generalizability theory*, proposed by Cronbach and his colleagues (Cronbach, Rajaratnam & Gleser, 1963; Gleser, Cronbach & Rajaratnam, 1965). Through the use of complex analysis of variance designs, this theory permits estimation of the size of different error sources, considered in the measurement process. In 1972, these authors published an exhaustive treatise (Cronbach, Gleser, Nanda & Rajaratnam, 1972), a veritable bible for the theory; systematic and more accessible accounts can be found in Brennan (1983), Crocker and Algina (1986),

Shavelson and Webb (1991), and Shavelson, Webb, and Rowley (1989).

FUTURE PERSPECTIVES

The simplicity and versatility, it can be used in many different situations, of the Classical Test Theory (CTT) approach will guarantee this psychometric model to be abundantly used in the future, in conjunction with the powerful and psychometrically sophisticated models developed under the framework of the Item Response Theory (IRT). These new models have to be seen as complementary to the Classical approach, never as substitutes of the CTT. Needless to say, most of the psychological tests currently used by professionals have been developed within the framework of the Classical Test Theory.

CONCLUSIONS

Classical Test Theory embraces a set of models and technical procedures designed to provide solutions to the problems involved in measuring psychological variables. After a century of developments, especially during the first half of this century, the Classical Test Theory approach appears as a solid corpus of knowledge giving reasonable solutions to most of the practical problems psychologists face when measuring their variables of interest. New psychometric models, such as Item Response models, have been proposed to overcome some of the problems faced by the classical approach; these models constitute a complementary tool that psychologists can use combined with the classical approach.

References

Allen, M.J. & Yen, W.M. (1979). *Introduction to Measurement Theory*. Monterrey, CA: Brooks/Cole Publishing Company.

American Educational Research Association, American Psychological Association, National Council on Measurement in Education (1999). *Standards for Educational and Psychological Testing*. Washington, DC: Author.

Anastasi, A. & Urbina, S. (1997). *Psychological Testing* (7th ed.). Upper Saddle River, NJ: Prentice Hall.

Bock, R.D. & Wood, R. (1971). Test theory. *Annual Review of Psychology*, 22, 193–224.

Brennan, R.L. (1983). *Elements of Generalizability Theory*. Iowa City, IA: American College Testing.

Campbell, N.R. (1928). *An Account of the Principles of Measurement and Calculation*. London: Longmans Green.

Coombs, C.H. (1964). *A Theory of Data*. New York: Wiley.

Crocker, L. & Algina, J. (1986). *Introduction to Classical and Modern Test Theory*. New York: Holt, Rinehart & Winston.

Cronbach, L.J. (1947). Test reliability: its meaning and determination. *Psychometrika*, 12, 1–16.

Cronbach, L.J. (1951). Coefficient alpha and the internal structure of tests. *Psychometrika*, 16, 297–334.

Cronbach, L.J., Gleser, G.C., Nanda, H. & Rajaratnam, N. (1972). *The Dependability of Behavioural Measurement: Theory of Generalizability for Scores and Profiles*. New York: Wiley.

Cronbach, L.J., Rajaratnam, N. & Gleser, G.C. (1963). Theory of generalizability: a liberalization of reliability theory. *The British Journal of Statistical Psychology*, 16(2), 137–163.

Flanagan, J.L. (1937). A note on calculating the standard error of measurement and reliability coefficients with the test score machine. *Journal of Applied Psychology*, 23, 529.

Gaito, J. (1980). Measurement scales and statistics: resurgence of an old misconception. *Psychological Bulletin*, 87, 564–567.

Galton, F. (1883). *Inquiries into Human Faculty and its Development*. London: Macmillan.

Gleser, G.C., Cronbach, L.J. & Rajaratnam, N. (1965). Generality of scores influenced by multiple sources of variance. *Psychometrika*, 30, 395–418.

Guilford, J.P. (1936, 1954). *Psychometric Methods*. New York: McGraw-Hill.

Gulliksen, H. (1950). *Theory of Mental Tests*. New York: Wiley.

Guttman, L. (1945). A basis for analyzing test–retest reliability. *Psychometrika*, 10, 255–282.

Hambleton, R.K. & Swaminathan, H. (1985). *Item Response Theory: Principles and Applications*. Boston: Kluwer.

Joncich, G. (1968). *The Sane Positivist: A Biography of Edward L. Thorndike*. Middletown: Wesleyan University Press.

Krantz, D.H., Luce, R.D., Suppes, P. & Twersky, A. (1971). *Foundations of Measurement. Additive and Polynomial Representations*, Vol. 1. New York: Academic Press.

Kuder, G.F. & Richardson, M.W. (1937). The theory of estimation of test reliability. *Psychometrika*, 2, 151–160.

Lord, F.M. (1953). On the statistical treatment of football numbers. *The American Psychologist*, 8, 750–751.

Lord, F.M. (1980). *Applications of Item Response Theory to Practice Testing Problems*. Hillsdale, NJ: Erlbaum Associates.

Lord, F.M. & Novick, M.R. (1968). *Statistical Theories of Mental Tests Scores*. Reading, MA: Addison-Wesley.

Luce, R.D. & Narens, L. (1986). The mathematics underlying measurement on the continuum. *Science, 236*, 1527–1532.

Magnuson, D. (1967). *Test Theory*. Reading, MA: Addison-Wesley.

Michell, J. (1986). Measurement scales and statistics: a clash of paradigms. *Psychological Bulletin, 100*, 398–407.

Michell, J. (1990). *An Introduction to the Logic of Psychological Measurement*. Hillsdale, NJ: Lawrence Erlbaum Associates.

Michell, J. (1997). Quantitative science and the definition of measurement in psychology. *British Journal of Psychology, 88*, 355–383.

Muñiz, J. (Ed.) (1996). *Psicometría*. Madrid: Universitas.

Muñiz, J. (1998). La medición de lo psicológico. *Psicothema, 10*, 1–21.

Muñiz, J. (2000). *Teoría clásica de los tests*. Madrid: Pirámide.

Narens, L. (1985). Abstract measurement: the theory of numerical assignment. *Psychological Bulletin, 99*, 166–180.

Narens, L. & Luce, R.D. (1986). Measurement: the theory of numerical assignment. *Psychological Bulletin, 99*, 166–180.

Novick, M.R. (1966). The axioms and principal results of classical test theory. *Journal of Mathematical Psychology, 3*, 1–18.

Pfanzagl, J. (1968). *Theory of Measurement*. New York: Wiley.

Roberts, F.S. (1979). *Measurement Theory*. Reading, MA: Addison Wesley.

Rulon, P.J. (1939). A simplified procedure for determining the reliability of a test by splithalves. *Harvard Educational Review, 9*, 99–103.

Savage, L.W. & Ehrlich, R. (Eds.) (1990). *Philosophical and Foundational Issues in Measurement Theory*. Hillsdale, NJ: Lawrence Erlbaum Associates.

Schmidt, F.L. & Hunter, J.E. (1996). Measurement error in psychological research: lessons from 26 research scenarios. *Psychological Methods, 1*, 199–223.

Schwager, K.W. (1991). The representational theory of measurement: an assessment. *Psychological Bulletin, 110*, 618–626.

Shavelson, R. & Webb, N. (1991). *Generalizability Theory*. Beverly Hills, CA: Sage.

Shavelson, R., Webb, N. & Rowley, G.L. (1989). Generalizability theory. *American Psychologist, 44*, 922–932.

Spearman, C. (1904). The proof and measurement of association between two things. *American Journal of Psychology, 15*, 72–101.

Spearman, C. (1907). Demonstration of formulae for true measurement of correlation. *American Journal of Psychology, 18*, 161–169.

Spearman, C. (1913). Correlations of sums and differences. *British Journal of Psychology, 5*, 417–426.

Stanley, J.C. (1971). Reliability. In Thorndike, R.L. (Ed.), *Educational Measurement*. Washington, DC: American Council on Education.

Stevens, S.S. (1946). On the theory of scales of measurement. *Science, 103*, 677–680.

Stine, W.W. (1989). Meaningful inference: the role of measurement in statistics. *Psychological Bulletin, 105*, 1, 147–155.

Suppes, P. & Zinnes, J.L. (1963). Basic measurement theory. In Luce, R.D., Bush, R.R. & Galanter, E. (Eds.), *Handbook of Mathematical Psychology*, Vol. I (pp. 1–76). New York: Wiley.

Sutcliffe, J.P. (1965). A probability model for error of classification, I: General considerations. *Psychometrika, 30*, 73–96.

Thorndike, E.L. (1904). *An Introduction to the Theory of Mental and Social Measurements*. New York: Science Press.

Thorndike, R.L. (1951). Reliability. In Lindquist, E.L. (Ed.), *Educational Measurement* (pp. 560–620). Washington, DC: American Council on Education.

Thorndike, R.L. (1982). *Applied Psychometrics*. Boston: Houghton Mifflin.

Thurstone, L.L. (1927). A law of comparative judgment. *Psychological Review, 34*, 273–286.

Thurstone, L.L. (1928). Attitudes can be measured. *American Journal of Sociology, 33*, 529–554.

Thurstone, L.L. (1931). *The Reliability and Validity of Tests*. Ann Arbor, MI: Edward Brothers.

Thurstone, L.L. (1947). *Multiple Factor Analysis*. Chicago: University of Chicago Press.

Thurstone, L.L. & Chave, E.G. (1929). *The Measurement of Attitudes*. Chicago: University of Chicago Press.

Torgerson, W.S. (1958). *Theory and Methods of Scaling*. New York: Wiley.

Townsend, J.T. & Ashby, F.G. (1984). Measurement scales and statistics: the misconception misconceived. *Psychological Bulletin, 96*, 394–401.

Van der Linden, W.J. & Hambleton, R.K. (Eds.) (1997). *Handbook of Modern Item Response Theory*. New York: Springer-Verlag.

Yela, M. (1996). La forja de una vocación. *Psicothema, 8*(Supplement), 43–51.

José Muñiz

RELATED ENTRIES

Theoretical Perspective: Psychometrics, Item Response Theory: Models and Features, Classical and Modern Item Analysis, Reliability, Validity (General)

CLASSIFICATION (GENERAL, INCLUDING DIAGNOSIS)

INTRODUCTION

This entry treats formal classification procedures, not psychological models of classification behaviour. After specifying the terminology, fundamental concepts of classification are briefly introduced, followed by a short review of the empirical basis of classification. Finally, assignment procedures and the evaluation of a classification system are emphasized.

According to Gordon (1996: 65) classification 'is concerned with the investigation of a set of objects in order to establish whether or not they fall naturally into groups (or classes, or clusters) of objects with the property that objects in the same group are similar to one another and different from objects in other groups'.

Differential and clinical psychology frequently solve problems of classification in several different areas: persons are characterized by typologies, one finds classifications of tasks and situations, intervention procedures are analysed and ordered in this way, and above all diagnosis as the assignment of persons to (nosological) categories is based on classification. Many examples from psychology and the social sciences are provided by and referred to in Reinecke and Tarnai (2000). Several classificatory systems for clinical assessment are found in Baumann and Perrez (1990). These systems are classified as distortion of psychological functions (like learning, memory, sensory-motor skills, sleep, emotion and motivation), distortion of patterns of functions (neuroses, depression, psychosomatic, schizophrenic, distortions specific to children, adolescents and old people), and distortions to interpersonal systems (in school, work organizations or community).

TERMINOLOGY

The *objects* mentioned in Gordon's definition are also called cases, persons, patients, clients, elements, units, exemplars, specimens or items.

This reflects the interdisciplinary research tradition of the field. Physics provides in the table of elements a well known example, and biology can be seen as an ongoing struggle to give a systematic, i.e. taxonomic, overview of all living beings. In clinical psychology and psychiatry, DSM (Diagnostic and Statistical Manual of Mental Disorders) as well as ICD (International Classification of Diseases) are used extensively.

What Gordon calls 'groups' is usually called *classes* or, more formally, sets and partitions, or a taxon in biology. In the behavioural and social sciences, quite often neither the kind nor the number of classes are known in advance and have to be determined in the process of establishing a classificatory system. They are the target of permanent revision to incorporate the increasing knowledge in a subject area.

Searching for classes means analysing the relationships between objects. Two fundamentally different though not mutually exclusive bases exist for this analysis: either judgements of similarity are studied, or patterns of features describing the objects are compared.

Similarity may be either based directly on judgements, expert opinions etc. on likeness or of belonging together, or on confusion frequency or other behavioural observations. Or the similarities may be derived from co-occurrence patterns or correlations between properties. A large variety of coefficients exists to derive similarity measures on which procedures like cluster analysis or multi-dimensional scaling might be based.

The objects may be characterized by *properties*, traits, characteristics, symptoms, features or variables. They describe the variability between the objects by categories. These categories exist in at least two values (states, labels). The variables may be qualitative or quantitative, discrete or continuous, and of any scale level. Within the context of classification, it is useful to consider *sets* of variables, also called profiles, vectors, syndromes, or feature patterns.

THE CONCEPTUAL BASIS OF CLASSIFICATION

To solve all major parts of a classification task, we have to find predictors, delimit the classes, and specify the relationship between predictors and classes. Here, we briefly discuss some class concepts, mention approaches to prediction and comment on a specific way to identify class membership, the diagnostic key.

What defines a class? Several quite different conceptions exist:

1 Each object with a specific, 'essential' property belongs to a class. e.g., when a certain genetic anomaly exists, the child is diagnosed as showing the 'Down Syndrome'. The assumption that (a few) necessary properties decide about class membership characterizes the *monothetic position* (Sutcliffe, 1993).

2 There exist some properties to be used for classification, and the observation of some of these properties in an object (but not necessarily the same for every object) is necessary and sufficient to be a member of a specified class. This is the *polythetic* contraposition to definition (1) (Gyllenberg & Koski, 1996).

3 A variant of position (1) refers to a 'nosological unit', a syndrome, as genetically determined dyslexia. The identification of a few symptoms are essential.

4 A variant of position (2) refers to *prototypes*, relatively well known members conceived as the 'centre' of a class. A member of the same class must be similar to the prototype.

5 Classes are more or less identical with *clusters*. A cluster is a formal representation of several objects and of the relations between these objects. The relations may be similarities represented usually by distances, or may be vectors of properties. Data reveal clustering if – to a significant extent – the objects can be sorted into sets so that they are (a) more similar to each other if they are members of the same set (compactness), and (b) more dissimilar to objects in other sets (isolation), or both.

With more than 200 procedures designed to find clusters, the various cluster concepts have to be classified themselves. The procedures vary with the emphasis they give to compactness or isolation. Some fundamental distinctions between cluster concepts are: all clusters are on the same level vs. there exists a hierarchical structure among the clusters, and an element may be a member in only one vs. in more than one cluster (*disjunct or overlapping membership*).

6 Most cluster concepts refer only to contingencies of the first order, i.e. to relationships between two variables, but not three or more. Several notable exceptions exist, such as Configural Frequency Analysis (Krauth & Lienert, 1973), Pattern-Analytic Clustering (McQuitty, 1987) and Hierarchical Classes (HICLAS; Rosenberg, Van Mechelen & De Boeck, 1996); for a theoretical overview, see Feger and Brehm (2001).

Classification is that special case of *prediction* (see 'Prediction (General)' entry) in which at the start of the analytical process it may be unknown, as also how many and which categories of the dependent variable exist. The dependent variable here is equivalent with the set of classes called the 'criterion'. All ideas available to perform prediction in general can in principle be applied in classification to bridge the gap between predictors and this criterion. The most common formal prediction models – prediction rules, correlational approaches, regression, discriminant analysis – are briefly discussed in the entry 'prediction'. Here comments are given only on the old procedure of building and using a diagnostic key which is becoming more popular recently.

Dunn and Everitt (1982: 106) distinguish between two main approaches to formal classification. 'In the first one employs characters in a *sequence* (as in a *diagnostic key*). Here possible alternatives are successively eliminated by considering more and more characters until only one possibility remains.' In the second approach all features are considered simultaneously in a kind of 'matching'. In this process, all information about the new case is compared to the template provided by every class. A diagnostic key is like performing a series of tests in a fixed order. The results of a test may determine which test or other procedure should be applied next. If errors cannot be corrected, the first tests should be very reliable. The earlier in the diagnostic process a test is given, the more serious a mistake in the identification procedure may turn out.

A diagnostic key is often graphically represented as a (rooted) tree and then called a 'dendrogram'. Every test is a node in this graph. Two tests are connected by an edge if they constitute a part of a possible sequence of tests to be applied. Depending on the result of the test, a different path – a different branch of the tree – may be followed. An end node or 'leaf' represents the class of the assignment technique.

Working with a diagnostic key vs. using all predictors simultaneously also reflects the dispute between the monothetic and polythetic position and the question whether to use only contingencies of the first or of higher orders. If essential variables are found – perhaps the causes of a syndrome or unique properties of members of a certain class – the essential variables will be used unless they are ethically dubious, or it is dangerous to obtain this information, or very expensive. Working with more variables one might be able to exploit different relationships between predictors and criterion. In some predictors, a direct association exists between predictor and criterion, perhaps of different aspects in different predictors. Some predictors serve to suppress the error in other predictors (suppressor variables) or function as moderator variables (see 'Prediction (General)'). In a diagnostic key, the first item is related to the criterion by a contingency of the first order. Later items in the key imply all previous items. Thus the feature pattern on which the decision is based becomes longer and longer, and the order of the contingency increases. Furthermore, the number of cases on which the construction of the later parts of the tree is based becomes increasingly smaller. Also considering cost of obtaining information and of possible misclassifications may lead to the strategy to use many but relatively short rules (see Breiman, Friedman, Olshen & Stone, 1993).

ESTABLISHING A CLASSIFICATORY SYSTEM

When developing a classificatory system, some decisions have to be made; only a few are

mentioned here. How should the field be defined from which to select, perhaps even to *sample*, cases? Preferably, this *extension* of a classification is defined explicitly. The same is true for the *intension* of a system, i.e. the list of the properties to characterize the cases as strictly as possible. The two lists implicitly take a basic tenet of classification for granted: variables or relations like similarity have the same meaning even when applied to different objects. If properties are to be used, the question of their 'usefulness' arises, including considerations of differential weighting, transformations, and costs (see Pankhurst, 1991).

If the decision is to investigate similarities between objects to find classes, one faces the next decision: should experts or clients define the 'similarity in the eye of the subjects' or should the researcher calculate similarity coefficients from properties and thus determine the 'similarity in the mind of the researcher'? For both procedures inherent problems exist which can not be treated here.

EVALUATION OF A CLASSIFICATION PROCEDURE

The prototypes of classificatory systems in physics and biology are successful because they satisfy some criteria:

1 They are founded by and contribute to substantial theories.
2 The assignment of elements to classes uses only a small part of the available, usually quite reliable information and can be performed objectively.
3 The system allocates all elements, each in just one class, and does not use a class with many unidentifiable objects.
4 There exists order between the classes and among the properties allowing prediction of 'missing elements' and their properties.
5 The system is open for permanent extension and revision.

All steps bringing a classificatory system closer to satisfying these criteria will increase its theoretical and practical importance. DSM and ICD, to mention the most popular approaches to clinical assessment, do not satisfy all of these criteria. They are the result of professional experience, convention and sometimes even political compromise.

All parts of the classification system should be evaluated, (1) the conceptualization of the classes, especially if the classes are derived from clustering, (2) the predictive success, and (3) the selection of predictors.

First, all popular clustering algorithms lead always to a result, a set of clusters. To find clusters is not an *empirical* result but an exercise in calculation. Therefore, inferential statistics has to secure that the degree of compactness or isolation in the data is significant (Bock, 1996; Milligan, 1996). Second, predictive success in one study may capitalize on chance. Replication with different samples and methods and at various circumstances is essential, especially in the form of *cross validation*. The principle of cross validation is to use two comparable samples, either the old and a new one, or a random split of the one and only sample available if its number of cases is large enough. Then the prediction rules derived from one sample are applied in the other sample. Ideally, the predictive success in the replication is not lower than before. Even the previous determination of the classes may be tested in this way (Everitt, 1993). Third, the selection of predictors might be a topic of continuous evaluation. Their reliability and validity is not necessarily constant. It is quite likely that a revision of a test or questionnaire changes the properties of these instruments as predictors. The *a priori* frequencies (base rates) of how the cases are distributed over the categories of the variables may also change with time and from institution to institution. Therefore, it is not surprising to find dozens of publications every year concerned with the development of new and the modification of already existing classifications.

References

Baumann, U. & Perrez, M. (Eds.) (1990). *Lehrbuch Klinische Psychologie. Grundlagen, Diagnostik, Ätiologie*. Band 1. Bern: Huber.

Bock, H.-H. (1996). Probability models and hypothesis testing in partitioning cluster analysis. In Arabie, P., Hubert, L.J. & De Soete, G. (Eds.), *Clustering and Classification* (pp. 377–453). Singapore: World Scientific.

Breiman, L., Friedman, J.H., Olshen, R.A. & Stone, C.J. (1993). *Classification and Regression Trees* (2nd ed.). Boca Raton: Chapman and Hall.

Dunn, G. & Everitt, B.S. (1982). *An Introduction to Mathematical Taxonomy*. Cambridge: Cambridge University Press.

Everitt, B.S. (1993). *Cluster Analysis* (3rd ed.). London: Edward Arnold.

Feger, H. & Brehm, M. (Eds.) (2001). *New Developments in Feature Pattern Analysis*. Lengerich: Pabst.

Gordon, A.D. (1996). Hierarchical classification. In Arabie, P., Hubert, L.J. & De Soete, G. (Eds.), *Clustering and Classification* (pp. 65–121). Singapore: World Scientific.

Gyllenberg, M. & Koski, T. (1996). Numerical taxonomy and the principle of maximum entropy. *Journal of Classification*, 13, 213–229.

Krauth, J. & Lienert, G.A. (1973). *KFA-Die Konfigurationsfrequenzanalyse*. Freiburg: Alber.

McQuitty, L.L. (1987). *Pattern-Analytic Clustering: Theory, Method, Research and Configural Findings*. New York: University Press of America.

Milligan, G.W. (1996). Clustering validation: results and implication for applied analyses. In Arabie, P., Hubert, L.J. & De Soete, G. (Eds.), *Clustering and Classification* (pp. 341–375). Singapore: World Scientific.

Pankhurst, R.J. (1991). *Practical Taxonomic Computing*. Cambridge: Cambridge University Press.

Reinecke, J. & Tarnai, C. (Eds.) (2000). *Angewandte Klassifikationsanalyse in den Sozialwissenschaften*. Münster: Waxmann.

Rosenberg, S., Van Mechelen, I. & De Boeck, P. (1996). A hierarchical classes model. Theory and method with applications in psychology and psychopathology. In Arabie, P., Hubert, L.J. & De Soete, G. (Eds.), *Clustering and Classification*. Singapore: World Scientific.

Sutcliffe, J.P. (1993). Concept, class, and category in the tradition of Aristotle. In Van Mechelen, I., Hampton, J., Michalski, R.S. & Theuns, P. (Eds.), *Categories and Concepts* (pp. 35–65). London: Academic Press.

Hubert Feger

RELATED ENTRIES

DIAGNOSIS OF MENTAL AND BEHAVIOURAL DISORDERS, EXPLANATION, PREDICTION (GENERAL)

CLINICAL JUDGEMENT

INTRODUCTION

'Clinical judgement' refers generally to the result of a set of cognitive activities that aim to: (a) classify an observed behavioural pattern into a nosological system category (*diagnostic judgement*); (b) predict the development of an observed behavioural pattern under a given treatment, or under particular environmental conditions (*predictive judgement*, or *prognosis*); (c) estimate the degree of severity of a disorder (*severity judgement*); and (d) make an informed decision about the best treatment (*treatment judgement*).

Many published works describe how diagnostic and prognostic judgements are made. Some propose theoretical models to represent diagnostic and prognostic judgements, but little has been published about severity- and treatment-judgements.

A clinical judgement is the result of three main complex activities: data collection, data evaluation, and information integration. Because these activities are sequential, clinical-judgement making is often considered a process and, in this case, each activity might be considered a process stage. Usually, at the conclusion of the last stage, the judgement is communicated externally as a formal 'clinical report' or 'diagnostic report'.

Many psychological models of judgement-making only focus on one or two stages of the internal cognitive process, not all three, and none includes the clinical report stage.

PSYCHOLOGICAL STUDY OF CLINICAL JUDGEMENT

The empirical study of clinical judgement was stimulated by the so called clinical–statistical controversy (see entry *Prediction: Clinical vs. Statistical*). From the beginning these studies revealed that statistical predictions are more accurate than the intuitive predictions of clinicians, and two research strategies evolved. One describes professional judgements empirically and develops theoretical models to improve clinical training and judgement performance. The other aims to develop expert systems and computerized support systems to help clinicians to solve clinical problems. Computerized strategies helped develop artificial intelligence that, although closely associated with cognitive psychology, lies beyond the scope of this entry.

Lineal Models

Early and important methods for the study of clinical judgement were the lens and the policy-capturing models.

Hoffman's *policy-capturing* research strategy (1960) uses regression equations to simulate clinical-judgement making. It aims to discover the subjective relative importance the clinician gives to the several data elements used to make the final judgement. In regression equations the relative importance of the same data elements is expressed objectively by 'regression weights'. In addition, the researchers in this type of study take into account the different strategies the clinicians use when they integrate this information to make their judgement. Several important conclusions have emerged from policy-capturing research:

(a) clinicians generally use only a few cues to make a clinical judgement;

(b) the subjective importance that clinicians give to their data often does not agree with the regression weights of the same data;

(c) the disparities between objective and subjective 'weights' suggests that most clinicians are unaware of the subjective importance they attribute to their data;

(d) although lineal regression equations often represent and predict very well how clinicians make clinical judgements, most clinicians believe that they use configurational and non-lineal reasoning;

(e) configurational modelling of clinical judgement (by using: analysis of variance;

interaction-effects in the regression equations; or one of several other analytical procedures) does not depict or predict clinicians' judgements better than lineal modelling;

(f) configurational modelling does not improve judgement accuracy. Nevertheless, the configurational-reasoning idea strongly influenced clinical judgement studies and contributed to the development of Anderson's information-integration theory (Anderson, 1981).

The *lens model* is based on original work by Brunswik. Hammond (1955) adapted it for use in the field of clinical judgement. This theoretical approach proved highly effective to depict the relationships between intuitive judgement and an objective criterion. The lens model also depicts:

(a) the interrelationship between available data (information redundancy);
(b) the relationships between data and criterion (ecological validity of available data);
(c) between data and clinician's judgement (validity of clinician's inferences);
(d) between clinical judgement and criterion (judgement validity);
(e) between objective judgement and predicted judgement (judgement predictability, or cognitive control);
(f) between the objective- and predicted-criterion values (environment predictability, or task predictability); and
(g) between the predicted judgement and the predicted criterion value (knowledge of the nature of the clinical task).

Some important results from research carried out with lineal models of clinical judgement are:

(a) judgements formed by intuition can be precisely represented by mathematical expressions like regression equations, analysis of variance, or conjoint measures;
(b) clinicians' judgements can be accurately predicted;
(c) several task-related factors strongly influence judgements: the amount of data collected, the order in which data items are collected or dealt with, the coherence of data elements, the different types of data-presentation to subject, the

subject-response formats, and the constraints imposed by limited time;

(d) an important result that contradicted widely accepted ideas in psychological assessment is that when low-validity data elements are added to high-validity data, judgement validity decreases. Consequently, and surprisingly, the more data of the same type the clinician has (information redundancy), the lower is judgement validity and predictability, and the clinician not only tends to show overconfidence but, paradoxically, abundant data often induces the clinician to overlook inconsistent data.

Decision-Making Theories

Decision-making theories represent a great advance in the study of clinical judgement, especially in medicine. The main subjects of this theoretical approach in psychological assessment are described in the entry about decisions. It is sufficient to say that clinical-judgement research uses several established decision-making theories to study the ways clinicians select a final decision from an array of potential decisions (options) by taking into account their objective probabilities and subjective 'attractiveness' for the decision-maker. The accumulated conclusions of decision-making research suggest that clinicians' judgements are often subjectively biased (Dowie & Elstein, 1988).

Problem-Solving Theories

Elstein, Shulman and Sprafka (1978) propose a model of clinical judgement based on problem-solving theories that has stimulated much new research and is now widely accepted by other authors in the field of clinical judgement. Their research model employs *process-tracing* methods and the concepts used are very different to those of the statistical theories like 'policy-capturing' and 'lens' models. Elstein, Shulman and Sprafka consider clinical-judgement making as a four-step process, namely: limited data collection; formation of orientative hypotheses; data evaluation; and finally, testing to select one hypothesis. In the first step, data collection, the clinicians assemble a number of data items concerning the motive for consulting: this step usually lasts a few minutes and then the clinicians pass quickly to the activity of generating several hypotheses that might explain some of the accumulated data. When these hypotheses have been made, the significance of each element of the remaining data is evaluated again in the light of each hypothesis being considered and only those data elements that fit that hypothesis are considered relevant. When required, clinicians assemble new data elements to test hypotheses. In the fourth and final step, the hypothesis that best fits the available data is accepted as the final clinical judgement.

The book by Elstein, Shulman and Sprafka (1978) presents several important findings about the four steps of clinical-judgement process and their research helps enormously trainer clinicians to show their trainees how to make clinical assessments. Although this research refers mainly to diagnostic judgements, it applies equally to treatment judgements.

TRAINING FOR CLINICAL JUDGEMENT-MAKING

The policy capturing, lens, or decision-making models do not take into account data gathering, the first phase of the judgement process. They assume that data are available at the beginning of the process. Consequently, these models merely exploit data available at a given time, but they do not represent or prescribe what types of data are desirable. The problem-solving model does represent the phase of data collection. Interestingly, no published psychological model of clinical judgement takes into account judgement expression, the last step of the process. Consequently, they limit prescriptions and suggestions about how to form clinical judgements to the previous steps: data gathering, data appraisal, data integration, hypothesis generation, and hypothesis evaluation.

One proven policy-capturing strategy to enhance judgement accuracy (the so-called 'bootstrapping') is for a clinician to make his judgements conform strictly to the regression equation that represents his or her previous reliable performances (nevertheless, in theory, we could simply substitute the clinician by using this regression equation).

The lens model is useful to enhance the validity of clinical judgement. Hammond and associates suggested three general ways to enhance judgement quality:

(a) gather more data relevant to the task, use more valid data, or increase the independence between data, and so increase criterion predictability;

(b) increase the clinician's knowledge of the task structure by helping the clinician to learn to adjust his or her usual judgement-forming strategy to the objective weights of each data element and to the curve of the mathematical function that best associates the data elements with the criterion; and

(c) increase the clinician's cognitive control to consistently fine-tune actual judgements to conform to his or her usual judgement-making strategy. Other theoretical models include (a) above (increase criterion predictability) and (b) (to fit the clinician's strategy to the regression equation). However, only the lens model suggests that clinical judgement may be improved by increasing cognitive control.

Elstein, Shulman and Sprafka (1978) offer also important insights and conclusions with great value in clinical training:

(a) Quality of clinical judgement depends on the amount, nature, and structure of the clinician's expert knowledge. Consequently, the training of clinicians must include knowledge of basic disciplines. Furthermore, isolated knowledge of heuristics and procedural rules of information integration (e.g. regression equations or the Bayes' Theorem) do not ensure that clinicians will always make accurate judgements. The rules of information-integration are invaluable for clinical judgement making, but equally important is basic knowledge of the nature and the appropriateness of the data to be integrated.

(b) Because specialized knowledge is fundamentally important to solve clinical problems, the types of clinical cases used to train novice clinicians must be carefully selected for the particular clinical speciality. The range of cases chosen for training must include all the professional tasks undertaken by the specialists because the information-gathering and data-integration strategies are highly task dependent.

(c) Most clinicians appear to use the hypothetical-deductive method.

(d) Interpretation of information is not a simple process in which knowledge recovered from memory is applied mechanically to any available data: the skills needed to propound hypotheses that might guide the subsequent steps (activities) of the assessment process must be learned.

(e) Judgement quality suffers more from misinterpretations made while data elements are appraised and from the errors and mistakes made while they are integrated into the final judgement than from an insufficient collection of data.

(f) Many errors and omissions that might lead to erroneous or distorted final clinical judgements disappear or are reduced when the clinician generates as many hypotheses as available data permit.

FUTURE PERSPECTIVES

Judgement formation, decision making and problem solving are the three classical approaches to the study of clinical judgement. However, in the future, clinical judgement research will take into account some new theories of cognitive psychology such as 'categorization by prototypes' (Cantor, Smith, French & Mezzich, 1980), pattern matching (Kassirer, Kuipers & Gorry, 1982), 'mental scripts' (Feltovich & Barrows, 1984; Boshuizen & Schmidt, 1992), situational models (Patel, Evans & Groen, 1989), semantic structures (Lemieux & Bordage, 1992), a diagnostic cycle derived from De Groot's scientific cycle (De Bruyn, 1992), a special case of the application of scientific explanations (Westmeyer & Hageböck, 1992), and parallel processing of information (Berrios & Chen, 1993). The researchers who use some of these approaches are highly productive and their works have great potential to influence many other workers in this field.

CONCLUSIONS

Some important conclusions from the research about clinical judgement are:

(a) Clinical intuitive judgement-making can be theoretically and mathematically represented, and the clinician's judgements accurately predicted.

(b) The research of clinical judgement has produced promising computerized support systems for clinical judgement, as well as a great amount of knowledge and procedural guidelines for clinical training and clinical judgement-making.

(c) Emerging trends in clinical-judgement research are contributing not only to our understanding of clinical judgement, but also to the development of the psychology of judgement, decision making, problem solving, and categorization.

References

Anderson, N.H. (1981). *Foundations of Information Integration Theory*. New York: Academic Press.

Berrios, G.E. & Chen, E.Y.H. (1993). Recognising psychiatric symptoms. Relevance to the diagnostic process. *British Journal of Psychiatry*, 163, 308–314.

Boshuizen, H.P. & Schmidt, H.G. (1992). On the role of biomedical knowledge in clinical reasoning by experts, intermediates and novices. *Cognitive Science*, 16, 153–184.

Cantor, N., Smith, E.E., French, R.D. & Mezzich, J. (1980). Psychiatric diagnosis as prototype categorization. *Journal of Abnormal Psychology*, 89, 181–193.

De Bruyn, E.E.J. (1992). A normative-prescriptive view on clinical psychodiagnostic decision making. *European Journal of Psychological Assessment*, 8, 163–171.

Dowie, J. & Elstein, A. (1988). *Professional Judgement. A Reader in Clinical Decision Making*. Cambridge: Cambridge University Press.

Elstein, A.S., Shulman, L.E. & Sprafka, S.A. (1978). *Medical Problem Solving: An Analysis of Clinical Reasoning*. Cambridge, MA: Harvard University Press.

Feltovich, P.J. & Barrows, H.S. (1984). Issues of generality in medical problem solving. In Schmidt, H.G. & De Volder, M.L. (Eds.), *Tutorials in Problem-Based Learning: A New Direction in Teaching the Health Professions* (pp. 128–142). Assen, Holland: Van Gorcum.

Hammond, K.R. (1955). Probabilistic functioning and the clinical method. *Psychological Review*, 62, 255–262.

Hoffman, P.J. (1960). The paramorphic representation of clinical judgement. *Psychological Bulletin, 47,* 116–131.

Kassirer, J.P., Kuipers, B.J. & Gorry, G.A. (1982). Toward a theory of clinical expertise. *American Journal of Medicine, 73,* 251–259.

Lemieux, M. & Bordage, G. (1992). Propositional versus structural semantic analysis of medical diagnostic thinking. *Cognitive Science, 16,* 185–204.

Patel, V.L., Evans, D.A. & Groen, G.J. (1989). Reconciling basic science and clinical reasoning. *Teaching and Learning in Medicine, 1,* 116–121.

Westmeyer, H. & Hageböck, J. (1992). Computer-assisted assessment: a normative perspective. *European Journal of Psychological Assessment, 8,* 1–16.

Antonio Godoy

RELATED ENTRIES

COACHING CANDIDATES TO SCORE HIGHER ON TESTS

INTRODUCTION

Applicants for higher education, jobs, etc. are usually required to take aptitude tests for selection and sometimes for placement. Applicants strive for high scores to increase their chances in the selection or placement process. To achieve such scores, examinees may utilize various forms of coaching. Coaching was defined by Cole (1982) as a 'wide variety of test preparation activities undertaken by individuals in an attempt to improve test scores'. These may range from solving some items to extensive courses.

Today most testing institutions offer free (or inexpensive) explanations of test instructions, a multitude of practice items and tests, and test-taking strategies. These provide fundamental coaching to examinees and facilitate practice with 'official material'.

After a brief historical review, we shall describe coaching – its components, the various forms it can take, and its prevalence. This will be followed by a review of studies that have attempted to evaluate the coaching effect – the size of the score gain. A separate section will deal with social and test validity issues associated with coaching.

HISTORICAL BACKGROUND

Coaching is as old as testing. The earliest example can be found in China, where coaching for civil service examinations has been in existence for some 3000 years. In the modern testing era, coaching research began with the Binet intelligence tests in France. Binet and Simon (1916) discovered that test scores improved in the second administration of intelligence tests to 9-year-old pupils. The gain was attributed to several factors, including familiarity with the test content. In England, studies were conducted on coaching for the eleven-plus examinations, which were used extensively for pupil selection after primary school. Yates (1953) and others showed that coaching for these examinations can improve scores. However, their studies were not methodologically sound, therefore limiting generalization from these findings.

The question of whether aptitude test scores are affected by coaching has been extensively discussed (e.g. Bond, 1989). Until about 1970, the commonly held view was that improvement due to coaching was very small, if not negligible. This view is clearly demonstrated by the following typical quote from the publication of ETS (Educational Testing Service, which is responsible for several of the largest testing programmes in the world): 'The magnitude of the gains resulting from coaching vary slightly but they are always small regardless of the coaching method used or the differences in the students coached' (ETS, 1965: 4).

Later, as data accumulated, views of coaching effectiveness changed. Today, educational researchers agree that coaching usually results in small score gains, and the question to be addressed is no longer 'Does coaching help?' but 'How much does coaching help?'

COACHING COMPONENTS, FORMS AND PREVALENCE

Components

Coaching for a test involves three interrelated components (Allalouf & Ben-Shakhar, 1998): acquiring familiarity with the test, reviewing relevant material and acquiring testwiseness:

1 Acquiring familiarity with the test – becoming acquainted with the test instructions, item types, time limits, and the answer sheet format. This can be achieved by answering questions similar to the test questions under conditions as similar as possible to those encountered during the actual test administration.
2 Reviewing relevant material – reviewing the academic material included in the test, such as reviewing mathematics when the test contains mathematical reasoning.
3 Acquiring testwiseness (TW) – improving the 'subject capacity to utilize the characteristics and formats of the test and/or the test-taking situation to receive a high score' (Millman, Bishop & Ebel, 1965: 707). The following TW strategies, independent of test content or purpose, were identified by Millman et al. (1965): efficient use of available time, error avoidance and intelligent guessing. In addition, they found test-specific testwiseness – elements dependent upon specific flaws and clues in a particular test.

Those who construct aptitude tests should be aware of these coaching components. This awareness will enable them to: (1) formulate clear test instructions, (2) make the test less dependent upon scholastic knowledge, and (3) avoid including clues which might help the sophisticated examinee.

It should be noted that in some studies (e.g. Cole, 1982), coaching includes a cheating component, where examinees have access to test items, and even to the correct answers, before the

test. In this entry, cheating is not regarded as a component of coaching. It also should be noted that one of the purposes of coaching is to decrease anxiety resulting from an unfamiliar test.

Forms

Different forms of coaching can be characterized by five variables: (1) amount of material: from a small number of items to very detailed guides, (2) institution/company responsible: commercial or non-commercial, (3) method of learning: self-study or instructed, (4) medium: books or computerized, and (5) amount of time devoted: from several hours to over a hundred hours. Examinees choose the form of coaching most suitable to them, based on availability, financial considerations and even fashion.

Prevalence

Special preparation for scholastic aptitude entrance exams to institutions of higher learning and for other high-stakes tests is very common. The following two examples deal with scholastic aptitude tests for admission to higher education. In the United States, according to a survey conducted by Powers and Rock (1999) on the Scholastic Assessment Tests (SAT), 97% of students engaged in some form of preparation before taking the test, with a median of 11 hours of preparation. 12% of the SAT examinees participated in out-of-school coaching programmes, 18% participated in in-school coaching programmes, 58% used the official booklet, and 81% took the Preliminary SAT beforehand. In Israel, 83% (!) of examinees participated in coaching courses for the Inter-University Psychometric Entrance Test (PET) in the year 2000 and 63% used the official booklet.

STUDIES ON COACHING EFFECT

A major coaching issue is its effect. Many studies have dealt with the effect of coaching on the performance on test scores. Some studies were done on the differential effect of coaching on specific item types.

Score Gains Due to Coaching

Examinees and the public are often exposed to rumours and extreme individual examples of large score gains following coaching. This information sometimes is disseminated by the large commercial coaching companies which have financial interest in advertising themselves. A different picture is obtained from objective information based on scientifically controlled studies: score gains do occur, but they are generally small, especially when compared to the claims made by the commercial companies.

Since the early 1970s, many studies focusing on the effects of preparation on scholastic aptitude tests have been conducted. These studies estimated the coaching effect beyond the gain achieved due to retesting. Recent meta-analyses of many studies (Messick, 1981; Powers, 1993) have demonstrated that scores on scholastic aptitude tests can be improved by focused preparation. The expected gain in an examinee's score following several weeks of coaching is generally small, and the mean gain on the SAT, according to these meta-analyses, is approximately one fifth of a standard deviation (beyond the gain that would be expected as a result of retesting only, which, according to Donlon, 1984, is about one seventh of a standard deviation). Similar results were obtained for the American College Testing (ACT) Assessment (McCoy, 1999) and the Israeli PET (Oren, 1993).

Differential Effect

Studies show that coaching is more effective for mathematical items than for verbal items. The effect depends on the time devoted to coaching. According to Messick (1981), the improvement resulting from the first 20 hours of coaching for the SAT is about 20% of a standard deviation in the mathematical subtest, and about 12.5% of a standard deviation in the verbal subtest. They estimate that 120 hours are needed to double these gains in the mathematical subtest and 250 hours in the verbal subtest. Figure 1 (based on Messick, 1981), who performed a logarithmic interpolation on the basis of the studies included in his meta-analysis) presents the marginal gains in the mathematical and verbal aptitudes.

Coaching has a differential effect on different item types. For example, Swinton and Powers (1983) found that in the analytic part of the Graduate Record Examinations (GRE), the performance on two item types (analysis of explanations and logical diagrams) was greatly affected by coaching. As a result, these item types were removed from the test.

SOCIAL AND VALIDITY CONSIDERATIONS

Tests are administered in order to offer all candidates the same fair chance to succeed.

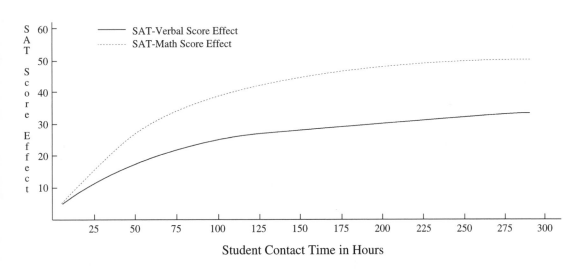

Figure 1.   Expected score effects associated with the amount of examinees' contact time for verbal and math subtests (based on Messick, 1981).

However, it can be argued that coaching works against equity: since not everyone prepares for a test, fairness may be impaired.

Social Considerations

Not every applicant can afford expensive commercial courses. Moreover, the 'prestigious coaching courses' are usually given in wealthy neighbourhoods. As Cole (1982) noted, if those who can afford expensive courses gain an advantage, then testing becomes linked to economic status – which is completely counter to the testing goal of offering equal opportunity for all. The solution to this threat to fairness is, of course, to expose every candidate to coaching at a reasonable price.

Validity Considerations

Some critics believe that if you can coach for an aptitude test, something is wrong with the test, and it cannot be valid. These critics believe (actually, they have the illusion) that somewhere an 'ideal test' exists that cannot be coached for. Reality proves otherwise. The disclosure policy characterizing today's testing, whereby examinees are provided with coaching material, makes this 'ideal' even less realizable.

Other critics of scholastic aptitude tests typically claim that preparation improves scores on these tests by teaching examinees special techniques for solving multiple choice items, thus lowering test validity. Many researchers, among them Anastasi (1981) and Bond (1989), have raised the question of the possible detrimental effects of coaching on test validity. Bond (1989: 440) wrote: 'A continuing concern on the part of testing specialists, admissions officers, and others is that coaching, if highly effective, could adversely affect predictive validity and could, in fact, call into question the very concept of aptitude.' However, in contrast to the concern raised by Bond, most studies indicate that coaching in fact leads to slight improvement in the predictive validity of aptitude tests (see Allalouf & Ben-Shakhar, 1998). This may be explained by the improvement, resulting from coaching, in inaccurately low scores that are due to poor test-taking skills. Coaching may also have a small influence on the cognitive skills necessary for success in meeting specific criteria (e.g. achievement in higher education).

FUTURE PERSPECTIVES AND CONCLUSIONS

As long as tests are used, coaching issues will remain a matter of public concern. The public and the examinees should realize that score gains due to coaching are usually small, and large gains are very rare. Institutions that require or administer aptitude tests should provide examinees with inexpensive coaching material. It should be remembered that coaching tends to improve general skills, such as verbal and mathematical skills, and this improvement is beneficial for every applicant. Of course, if coaching does not impair predictive validity and fairness, and even increases the predictive validity of the test (especially when everyone is coached to a similar extent), coaching is desirable.

References

Allalouf, A. & Ben-Shakhar, G. (1998). The effect of coaching on the predictive validity of scholastic aptitude tests. *Journal of Educational Measurement, 35,* 31–47.

Anastasi, A. (1981). Coaching, test sophistication, and developed abilities. *American Psychologist, 36,* 1086–1093.

Binet, A. & Simon, T. (1916). *The Development of Intelligence in Children.* Reprinted, 1983. Salem, New Hampshire: Clyer.

Bond, L. (1989). The effects of special preparation on measures of scholastic ability. In Linn, R.L. (Ed.), *Educational Measurement* (3rd ed.). New York: Macmillan.

Cole, N. (1982). The implication of coaching for ability testing. In Wigdor, A.K. & Garner, W.R. (Eds.), *Ability Testing: Uses, Consequences, and Controversies (Part II).* Washington DC: National Academy Press.

Donlon, T.E. (1984). *The College Board Technical Handbook for the Scholastic Aptitude Test and Achievement Tests.* New York: College Entrance Examination Board.

ETS (1965). *Effects of Coaching on Scholastic Aptitude Tests Scores.* New York: College Entrance Examination Board.

McCoy, T.R. (1999, April). *Differential Effects of Test Preparation Activities and Subject Content on ACT Assessment Scores.* Paper presented at the annual meeting of the National Council on Measurement in Education, Montreal, Quebec, Canada.

Messick, S. (1981). The controversy over coaching: issues of effectiveness and equity. In Green, B.F. (Ed.), *Issues in Testing: Coaching, Disclosure and Ethnic Bias.* San Francisco: Jossey Bass.

Millman, J., Bishop, C.H. & Ebel, R. (1965). An analysis of test-wiseness. *Educational and Psychological Measurement*, 25, 707–726.

Oren, C. (1993). *On the Effect of Various Preparation Modes on PET Scores* (Report No. 170). National Institute for Testing and Evaluation, Jerusalem.

Powers, D.E. (1993). Coaching for the SAT: summary of the summaries and an update. *Educational Measurement: Issues and Practice*, 12, 24–30.

Powers, D.E. & Rock, D.A. (1999). Effects of coaching on SAT I: reasoning test scores. *Journal of Educational Measurement*, 36, 93–118.

Swinton, S.S. & Powers, D.E. (1983). A study on the effect of special preparation on GRE analytical scores and item types. *Journal of Educational Psychology*, 75, 104–115.

Yates, A.J. (1953). Symposium on the effects of coaching and practice in intelligence tests. *British Journal of Educational Psychology*, 23, 147–162.

Avi Allalouf

RELATED ENTRIES

Applied Fields: Education, Achievement Testing

C COGNITIVE ABILITY: *g* FACTOR

INTRODUCTION

There is an unlimited variety of human mental abilities, defined as any form of information processing capability that can be assessed objectively and quantitatively by means of psychometric tests or various laboratory apparatuses. Information processing includes diverse cognitive functions such as stimulus apprehension, attention, perception, sensory discrimination, generalization, conditioning, learning, short-term and long-term memory, recall, learning-set acquisition, concept formation, thinking, reasoning, inference, problem solving, planning, invention, and use of language. Quantitative assessments of such information processing functions by objective means typically show a wide distribution of individual differences. It is well established in psychometrics that individual differences in a wide variety of cognitive tasks, however diverse in specific knowledge content and required skills, are all positively correlated in the general population. This phenomenon of all-positive correlations among measures of individual differences in cognitive abilities is the basis of the theoretical construct of general *ability*, or *g*.

FACTOR ANALYSIS OF MENTAL TESTS

The *g* factor is conceived technically as a *latent variable* that accounts for the empirical fact of all-positive correlations among diverse cognitive tests. By means of *factor analysis* one can determine the *g factor loadings* of various tests, i.e. their degree of correlation with the one factor that is common to a number of different cognitive tests, and from which *g factor scores* of individuals can be estimated.

'General Ability' and 'Ability in General'

It is important to distinguish between *general ability* (or the *g* factor), on the one hand, and what can be called *ability in general*, on the other. The latter refers to the sum (or average) of the scores on a collection of different subtests, such as the Stanford–Binet and the Wechsler batteries, and many other heterogeneous tests of 'intelligence'. The total score or Full Scale IQ on such tests is based on an arbitrary selection of a number of diverse tests. The *g* factor, however, in a linear decomposition of the total variance into uncorrelated components or factors, reflects only the source of variance that is common to all of the different ability measures represented by the various subtests of a cognitive test battery. Hence the *simple sum* of the subtest standardized scores on a test battery and the factor scores obtained from the *g loadings* of various subtests are not necessarily the same and may even be quite different. Typically, however, in the most widely used and broadly valid standardized test batteries the sum of the subtest scores (e.g. the full scale IQ) and the *g* factor scores are very highly correlated. Therefore the labour of calculating factor scores has little justification for the practical use of tests; the total standardized score, or IQ, is a fair substitute for the estimated *g* factor score.

Test Construction for the Measurement of *g*

The psychometric procedures for constructing an IQ test are intended to yield high practical validity for predicting many different outcomes involving cognitive abilities, such as scholastic achievement, college grade-point average, job performance, occupational level, and success in various armed services training programmes. This aim of IQ test construction and the psychometric means for achieving it inevitably results in the production of highly *g* loaded IQ scores, even when factor analysis is not used and the test designers have no interest in maximizing the test's overall *g* saturation per se.

Psychometrics of *g*

It has proved absolutely impossible to devise various tests involving information processing of any kind that, within a broad range of talent, are not positively correlated with each other. The more such diverse tests that are included in a battery, the greater is the proportion of the common factor variance (CFV) and, generally, the larger is the proportion of CFV consisting of *g*. The total variance, V_T, of any test composed of a number, n, of parts (i.e. items or subtests), i and j, consists of the sum of the item variances plus twice the sum of the item covariances: $V_T = \sum V_i + 2\sum \text{Cov}_{ij}$. The first term in this equation ($\sum V_i$) increases linearly as a function of n, while the second term ($2\sum \text{Cov}_{ij}$) increases exponentially, such that in most ability tests consisting of many parts (items or subtests), the second term typically constitutes some eight to ten times more of the total variance than does the first term. Hence most of a test's total variance is contributed by the item covariances, rather than by the item variances. In a factor analysis, the total variance is partitioned into two parts: (1) the *common factor* variance (i.e. the total *communality*, composed of the sum of all the

items' loadings on *g* and on one or more *group factors*, if any) and (2) the items' unshared or *specific* variance (i.e. item *specificity*) and *measurement error*. In a test composed of sufficiently diverse subtests or very heterogeneous items, *g* is typically larger than any group factor independent of *g* and can even be larger (in terms of the proportion of variance accounted for) than all of the group factors (independent of *g*) combined. This is true even for test batteries that were not expressly designed to maximize *g*.

Practical Validity of *g*

The *g* factor itself contributes more to a test's practical validity than any of the group factors used alone or in combination independently of *g* (Jensen, 1998, Chapter 9; Schmidt & Hunter, 1998). The most highly *g* loaded tests are the highest in *validity generalization* (i.e. a test's validity across many different predictive criteria), although certain group factors in addition to *g* (e.g. verbal, numerical, spatial, mechanical, and clerical speed/accuracy) may increase a test's validity for predicting a specific criterion.

Research on the Nature of Intelligence

The *g* factor per se is mainly of importance in research on the biological basis of intelligence, rather than in clinical assessment of individuals. Research on the properties of *g* itself has shown it to be more highly correlated with various genetic, anatomic, and physiological brain variables than are the major group factors or other psychometric variables after *g* is statistically removed. The chief focus in such research is on the correlation of *g* with various non-psychometric variables, such as brain size, brain evoked potentials, brain glucose metabolic rate, nerve conduction velocity, tests' heritability coefficients, and the like (Jensen, 1998). For such purposes, it is unnecessary to obtain *g* factor scores for individuals, as the factor loadings of the biological variables of interest can be obtained directly by factor analysing them within a suitable correlation matrix of psychometric tests that strongly identify *g*.

Clinical Assessment of *g*

Factor scores on *g* (or other factors) are seldom called for in clinical assessment. The global IQ derived from one of the standard IQ tests, such as the Wechsler Intelligence Scales, the Kaufman Assessment Battery for Children, the Woodcock–Johnson Tests of Cognitive Ability, and the British Ability Scales (which provides conversion tables for *g* factor scores), is generally an adequate indicator of mental level, and extreme deviations in the profile of subtest scores may occasionally cue the examiner of the need for other, more specialized tests. If, however, it is important to assess individuals' relative level of *g* as uncontaminated as possible by other ability factors, *g* factor scores can be obtained, given a proper factor analysis or components analysis of the battery on a large enough group of individuals to ensure high reliability of the tests' *g* factor loadings.

Assessment of *g* in Individuals

It is axiomatic that no single test can yield a pure measure of *g*. Although every cognitive test contains *g* variance, every test also has its own specificity variance and often reflects one or more group factors as well. Therefore, *g* factor scores of individuals can be estimated only by a special mathematical treatment of the data. There are several methods for calculating factor scores, the detailed methodology for which is beyond the scope of this entry (see Harman, 1976, Chapter 16). The method of factor analysis or principal components analysis used for extracting the *g* factor from a suitable test battery usually makes little difference in the end result (Jensen & Weng, 1994). The three main choices are between (1) the first factor in a principal factor analysis, (2) the first principal component in a components analysis, and (3) the highest-order factor in an orthogonalized hierarchical factor analysis. Although it makes little practical difference, the choice here depends on quite technical psychometric considerations discussed in the above references. The presently preferred method for statistically estimating factor scores is by multiple regression, in which all of the subtests' intercorrelations and the tests' *g* factor loadings, in addition to the individuals' standardized scores on each subtest, are used to calculate each individual's *g* factor score. This procedure is described in most modern textbooks on factor analysis and, fortunately, is now available in statistical computer programs.

Spearman's 'Law of Diminishing Returns'

A seldom recognized problem in the estimation of *g* factor scores arises from a phenomenon first discovered by Spearman, which he termed the *law of diminishing returns* (Jensen, 1998, Appendix A). This seemingly paradoxical effect, which has been well established in several recent studies, consists of the fact that tests' *g* loadings are smaller, on average, for individuals of higher general ability. If we divide the bell-curve distribution of IQ at the median (IQ 100) and extract the *g* factor separately from the upper-half and the lower-half of the distribution, we find that *g* accounts for significantly less of the total variance in the upper-half than in the lower-half. For instance, in the Wechsler scales (both for adults and for children) the *g* variance is about one and a half times greater for the distribution of IQ below 100 than for that of IQ above 100. In general, the higher the Full Scale IQ score, the less it reflects *g*. A corollary is that the various subtests are less highly correlated with each other at the higher levels of IQ. The cognitively more able subjects have more highly differentiated abilities. Relatively more of their individual difference variance exists in the group factors and test specificity. But it is also a fact that the subtests with the larger *g* loadings manifest this effect by far the least; it is almost entirely attributable to those tests with the smaller *g* loadings. This implies that in constructing a test battery that comes as close as possible to measuring *g* equally well across the full range of ability, all of the subtests in the battery should have as large and as nearly equal *g* loadings as possible. Also every subtest's *g* loading should greatly exceed its loadings on any group factors. Then the total standardized scores on such a test, assuming it also meets all the usual psychometric desiderata, should provide a defensible estimate of *g*. The total scores would scarcely differ from the optimal *g* factor scores.

FUTURE PERSPECTIVES

Both in research and in applied assessment, the most promising future trends in the measurement of *g*, as well as of other ability factors, will take advantage of recent advances in the methods of *computerized adaptive testing* (CAT), *item response theory* (IRT), and *mental chronometry* (MC), which, used in combination, would optimize mental testing. CAT greatly increases the efficiency of test-taking by quickly zeroing-in on the level of item difficulty that is most reliably discriminating of an individual's level of ability. Scaling item difficulty by IRT and the use of the item characteristic curve permits more unidimensional item selection for CAT-administered subscales. A composite score based on chronometric measures of the time required to perform various elementary cognitive tasks (ECT) are *g*-loaded and yet performance on ECTs has minimal dependence on prior acquired knowledge and skills, thereby minimizing the cultural loading of the cognitive ability measures.

CONCLUSIONS

It should not be forgotten that any psychometric estimate of *g* is just an approximation of a latent variable or hypothetical construct. The best derived *g* factor scores are an ordinal scale, which, without additional theoretical assumptions, can only rank individuals with respect to the estimate of *g* derived from a particular battery of tests.

It should also be recognized that every psychometric test, however well designed it is to measure a particular factor (especially *g*), always has some 'excess baggage', or test specificity. The specific knowledge and cognitive skills sampled

by a test battery do not themselves represent *g*, but are merely vehicles for estimating the latent variable *g*, which can be achieved with diverse test batteries calling for different knowledge and skills. In testing individuals or groups, one must always question whether a test score is reflecting mainly the latent variable *g* or mainly the specificities of the vehicles used to estimate *g*. Despite its metrical limitations, the *g* factor is related both to more individually and socially important variables and to more possibly causal biological variables than is any other construct in psychology (Gottfredson, 1997; Jensen, 1998).

References

Gottfredson, L.S. (Ed.) (1997). Intelligence and social policy (special issue). *Intelligence*, *24*(1), 1–320.

Harman, H.H. (1976). *Modern Factor Analysis* (3rd ed.). Chicago: University of Chicago Press.

Jensen, A.R. (1998). *The g Factor*. Westport, CT: Praeger.

Jensen, A.R. & Weng, L.-J. (1994). What is a good *g*? *Intelligence*, *18*(3), 231–258.

Schmidt, F.L. & Hunter, J.E. (1998). The validity and utility of selection methods in personnel psychology: practical and theoretical implications of 85 years of research findings. *Psychological Bulletin*, *124*, 262–274.

Arthur R. Jensen

RELATED ENTRIES

INTELLIGENCE ASSESSMENT (GENERAL), COGNITIVE ABILITY: MULTIPLE COGNITIVE ABILITIES, COGNITIVE/MENTAL ABILITIES IN WORK AND ORGANIZATIONAL SETTINGS

COGNITIVE ABILITY: MULTIPLE COGNITIVE ABILITIES

INTRODUCTION

There are some theories supporting the view of intelligence as a collection of separate cognitive abilities (Gardner, 1993; Guilford and Hoepfner, 1971). Those theories follow the often-called 'Thurstone tradition' (Gustafsson, 1984).

Guilford's Structure-of-Intellect (SOI) model postulates 180 separate abilities resulting from the combination of three cognitive facets: operations, contents, and products. Cattell's Gf-Gc theory distinguishes culture-reduced (Gf) and culture-specific (Gc) abilities (Cattell, 1987). Horn expanded Gf-Gc theory to include other abilities like Gv (visualization capacity), Gps (general perceptual speed), Gm (general memory capacity), and Gr (general retrieval capacity) (Horn, 1994). Although the Gf-Gc theory can be considered as a hierarchical model covering many domains of intelligence, it does not provide a higher order factor (g) to account for correlations among the identified (second-order) general cognitive abilities. Gardner's theory postulates several independent intelligences (spatial, musical, verbal, and so forth) (Gardner, 1993). Sternberg's triarchic theory distinguishes analytic, practical, and creative intelligence (Sternberg, 1985). What all these theories have in common is that group abilities are thought to be more prominent than the g factor.

However, it must be said at the outset that there is no conflict between group or specific cognitive abilities and g (Brody, 1992; Carroll, 1993; Jensen, 1998). Thurstone recognized that his primary cognitive abilities were correlated, admitting the possible existence of Spearman's general factor (g) at the second order of analysis. The Thurstone model is not really different from the Spearman model: there are group factors and a general cognitive ability (g). Guilford SOI abilities are in fact correlated: the near-zero correlations he found in his data were the result of sampling error, restriction of range, measurement error, and the inclusion of tests of divergent production (Carroll, 1993). When proper corrections are made for restriction of range and attenuation, all the correlations are above zero, with a mean of $+0.45$. Therefore, there is no empirical evidence in the SOI model that contradicts a hierarchical picture of intelligence with g at the apex: all cognitive tests are positively correlated (Colom & Andrés-Pueyo, 2000; Jensen, 1998). Gustafsson suggested an expansion of Gf-Gc theory: the HILI model (Hierarchical Lisrel). The HILI model proposes that the g factor subsumes Gf, Gc and Gv. Moreover, g is supposed to be identical to Gf. Therefore, there is no contradiction between the Gf-Gc view of intelligence and g (Gustafsson, 1984).

Sternberg and Gardner cannot be included within this framework so easily, because they both go far beyond. This is what they usually claim, although one can have some reasonable reservations. First, the specific measurements of analytical, practical and creative abilities taken through the Sternberg Triarchic Abilities Test (STAT) correlate higher than $+0.6$. Correlations of this magnitude

are telling a familiar story within the abilities domain: the positive manifold of the currently known measures. Second, there are some sample problems: university undergraduates or creative people are not the best samples to test the likelihood of the g factor (in addition to the non-questioned specific cognitive abilities). These samples represent the top 10% of the intelligence distribution in the entire population, and, therefore, there is a considerable restriction of range. Third, practical and creative intelligences in Sternberg's theory can be viewed as achievement variables reflecting how g is invested in activities as affected by opportunities, motivation, personality, and interests. The triarchic theory 'itself' is not the opposite of g, although separate abilities are considered more prominent in Sternberg's view of intelligence. Finally, Gardner's taxonomy is arbitrary and without empirical foundation. His view can have some interest in contexts like education, but there is nothing in the literature that gives an empirical foundation for Gardner's theory contradicting a hierarchical picture of intelligence with g at the apex.

Carroll supports that intelligence has a hierarchical structure in his famous survey of factor analytic studies (Carroll, 1993; Mackintosh, 1998). There is strong evidence for a factor representing *general* intelligence (g) located at the apex of the hierarchy (stratum III) and representing the level of difficulty that can be handled in performing induction, reasoning, visualization, and language comprehension tests. At a lower order in the hierarchy (stratum II) several broad ability factors are distinguished: fluid intelligence, crystallized intelligence, general memory, visual perception, auditory perception, retrieval, and cognitive speediness. Finally, the stratum I abilities are dominated by stratum II abilities. Stratum I includes narrow abilities, stratum II broad abilities, and stratum III the general ability (g) (Figure 1).

Any cognitive ability refers to variations in performance on some defined class of tasks (Jensen, 1980; Neisser et al., 1996). Abilities reflect observable differences in individuals' performance of certain tests. However, a given task involves a variety of abilities: 'verbal ability', for instance, can be regarded as an inexact concept that has no scientific meaning unless it is referred to the structure of abilities that compose it. The problem of defining intelligence is the problem of defining the factorial constructs that underlie it and specifying their structure.

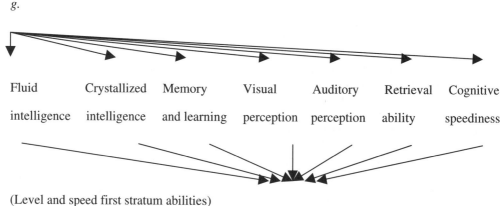

(Level and speed first stratum abilities)

Figure 1. A simplified picture of the three-stratum theory. The general three-stratum factor (*g*), broad second stratum abilities, and narrow first stratum abilities are located within the hierarchical structure representing the concept of intelligence.

Carroll reanalysed various datasets from several countries through a method of hierarchical factor analysis known as the Schmid–Leiman transformation (Loehlin, 1992): the higher order factors are allowed to account for as much of the correlation among the observed variables as they can, while the lower order factors are reduced to residual factors uncorrelated with each other and with the higher order factors. Therefore, each factor represents the independent contribution of the factor in question. Two main findings emerge from the analyses: (a) the *g* factor constitutes more than half of the total common factor variance in a cognitive test, and (b) various specific cognitive abilities can be identified in the domains of language, memory and learning, visual perception, information processing, knowledge and so forth, indicating certain generalizations of abilities; there are more than sixty specific abilities, although not all of them are equal in importance. Cognitive abilities are analogous to the elements in the periodic table: some, like fluid intelligence, are as important as carbon or oxygen, while others are more like the rare earth elements whose importance has not become apparent (Carroll, 1993).

'VEHICLES' OF COGNITIVE ABILITIES

Cognitive abilities can be elicited in many different ways. They are sources of variance evidenced by the correlations among several diverse tests, each of which reflects *g*, specific abilities, and test specificity. Tests are 'vehicles' used to elicit the cognitive abilities. The vehicle is not the ability and the ability is not the vehicle: two tests with quite different item contents can each be a good vehicle of a given cognitive ability.

There are several batteries that yield a profile of test scores in a set of separate cognitive abilities identified through factor-analytic research. Some examples follow: the Chicago Tests of Primary Mental Abilities (PMA), the Differential Aptitude Test (DAT), the Guilford–Zimmerman Aptitude Survey (GZAS), the Comprehensive Ability Battery (CAB), the British Ability Scales (BAS), the Woodcock–Johnson Psycho-Educational Battery (WJ-R), the Armed Services Vocational Aptitude Battery (ASVAB) and the General Aptitude Test Battery (GATB). Only the PMA, the DAT, and the WJ-R are briefly described.

The Chicago Tests of Primary Mental Abilities (PMA)

They represent the first effort to construct a multiple aptitude battery. The PMA can be administered from 10 years of age to late adulthood.

The PMA include five timed subtests:

- Verbal (V): composed by vocabulary items.
- Number (N): speed and accuracy of simple arithmetic computations.
- Spatial (S): changed positions or transformations must be visualized.

- Reasoning (R): a rule must be found (letter series completion).
- Fluency (F): produce words beginning with a given letter.

The split-half reliabilities are in the 0.90s. A global score can also be obtained through the next formula: $1.5 \times V + S + 2 \times R + N + F$. The PMA provide gross measures of their intended abilities.

The Differential Aptitude Test (DAT)

It is one of the most widely used multiple aptitude batteries. The DAT was originally designed for use in the educational and career counselling of students in Grades 8 and 12. The administration is timed, but most of the subtests are measures of the level the person can reach.

The DAT measures follow:

- Verbal reasoning (VR): based on the relationships among word meanings, it is a typical analogies test.
- Numerical ability (NA): a numerical reasoning test, not based in the ability to make computations.
- Abstract reasoning (AR): ability to reason with figures and geometric shapes. A rule underlies an array of figures.
- Clerical speed and accuracy (PSA): ability to quickly compare printed documents.
- Mechanical reasoning (MR): based on basic mechanical principles.
- Space relations (SR): ability to visualize an object in three dimensions. The object must be folded and then rotated to compare it with several alternatives.
- Spelling (SP): ability to spell common words.
- Language usage (LU): assesses typical syntactic mistakes.

The split-half reliabilities are in the 0.90s. There is evidence of a large general factor underlying performance in the DAT (correlations range from +0.2 to +0.8). VR + NA index was introduced as an estimation of scholastic aptitude. This index correlates in the 0.70s and 0.80s with composite criteria of academic achievement.

The last version (DAT-5) includes level 1 and level 2 batteries. The DAT-5 level 1 is adapted for grades 7–9, while the DAT-5 level 2 is adapted for 10–12 grades.

The Woodcock–Johnson Psycho-Educational Battery (WJ-R)

The WJ-R battery can test individuals from ages 2 to 90 years and includes a cognitive and an achievement section.

The WJ-R cognitive section assesses:

- Fluid reasoning (Gf): solving of new problems not facilitated by one's acculturation.
- Comprehension-knowledge (Gc): breadth and depth of one's education-related knowledge of a culture.
- Long-term retrieval (Glr): retrieval of information stored minutes or a couple of days earlier measured with paired-associate learning tasks.
- Short-term memory (Gsm): storage and retrieval of auditory information, measured by tasks requiring the recall of sentences, words, and numbers in their reversed sequence.
- Visual processing (Gv): ability in perceiving patterns, rotating objects in space, and retaining visual images.
- Auditory processing (Ga): ability to perceive patterns fluently among auditory stimuli.
- Processing speed (Gs): working quickly on clerical, visual-motor tasks.

Quantitative ability is assessed by several subtests of the achievement section.

Each ability score yields standard scores with a mean of 100 and a standard deviation of 15. A global score (g) is also provided. One psychometric grouping of selected subtests permits the detection of possible disabilities in specific areas.

The internal consistency values for ages 2 to 79 ranged from 0.69 to 0.93. The g composite score yields a median internal consistency coefficient of 0.94. Factor analytic support for the measured cognitive abilities is robust. The measured abilities closely resemble the broad abilities identified in Carroll's survey.

Comment

There are specific measures in different countries. That is why a theoretical background to group cognitive tests is heavily recommended: try to refer the specific measure to any given cognitive ability within the hierarchical structure of intelligence. Remember that you must go from the gross anatomy (broad) to the microscope (narrow) within the rich world of multiple cognitive abilities (Carroll, 1993).

FUTURE PERSPECTIVES AND CONCLUSIONS

Cognitive tests need to be redesigned with two main purposes in mind: (a) to improve the construct validity of the testing materials and the procedures of administration, by considering what aspects of cognitive performance are tapped by the tests, and (b) to better appraise and differentiate the speed and the level aspects of cognitive abilities.

There are some questions related with the problem of raising intelligence and cognitive abilities. To what extent are cognitive abilities malleable? It is important to know how to measure the cognitive abilities that we are trying to improve. Remember that the measure is not the ability; the measure is only a 'vehicle' of the ability. A related question is, what are the effects of schooling? There are many gaps in what we know about this topic. Changes in the contrast between spatial and verbal abilities are related to the type of education and occupational experiences of the people. Therefore, there can be some important questions that the measurement of specific cognitive abilities could help to answer.

There is an important topic yet addressed in the literature, but that will probably be revisited in the future: the configuration of abilities in human groups (sex, ethnicity, and so forth) (Colom et al., 2000, 2001; Loehlin, 2000; Deary et al., 1996). Some recent handbooks of intelligence note the problem of the configuration of cognitive abilities in several social groups, because of its relevance for many psychological assessment purposes.

Although there are some multiscore cognitive batteries not explicitly guided by factor analytic research, most of them are inspired by it. However, more confidence should rely on batteries derived from the factor analytic approach. Statistical techniques are especially fitted to answer questions related to the ability that is tapped by any specific cognitive test. Most of the available tests measure general intelligence (g) in addition to several cognitive abilities and specific skills. We know now how to separate these influences on performance. There are some measures highly

g-loaded, while others are less g-loaded. Moreover, the same measure loads differently in general and specific cognitive factors depending on the sample analysed. Thus, for instance, the letter–number series test of the WAIS-III has a g-loading of +0.84 in people with basic studies, but a g-loading of +0.59 in people with university studies (Colom et al., 2002).

The measurement of specific cognitive abilities is important for some psychological assessment purposes. Most of them are in the domain of individual clinical counselling as well as educational and vocational guidance. The profiles that derive from the administration of a multi-score cognitive battery are informative of the strengths and weaknesses of a given person. And this information is vital for the counsellor. However, specific abilities are usually seen as less germane for personnel selection, because g is the ability mostly responsible for the validity indices associated with cognitive measures. Make your choice, but do it with wisdom.

References

Brody, N. (1992). *Intelligence* (2nd ed.). San Diego: Academic Press.

Carroll, J.B. (1993). *Human Cognitive Abilities. A Survey of Factor-Analytic Studies.* Cambridge: Cambridge University Press.

Cattell, R.B. (1987). *Intelligence: Its Structure, Growth and Action.* Amsterdam: North-Holland.

Colom, R. & Andrés-Pueyo, A. (2000). The study of human intelligence: a review at the turn of the millennium. *Psychology in Spain,* 4(1), 167–182.

Colom, R., Juan-Espinosa, M., Abad, F.J. & García, L.F. (2000). Negligible sex differences in general intelligence. *Intelligence,* 28(1), 57–68.

Colom, R., Juan-Espinosa, M. & García, L.F. (2001): The secular increase in test scores is a 'Jensen effect'. *Personality and Individual Differences,* 30, 553–559.

Colom, R., Abad, F.J., García, L.F., Juan-Espinosa, M. (2002). Education: Wechsler's Full Scale 1a. Intelligence, 30, 449–462.

Deary, I.J., Egan, V., Gibson, G.J., Austin, E.J., Brand, C.R. & Kellaghan, T. (1996). Intelligence and the differentiation hypothesis. *Intelligence,* 23, 105–132.

Gardner, H. (1993). *Multiple Intelligences: The Theory in Practice.* New York: Basic.

Guilford, J.P. & Hoepfner, R. (1971). *The Analysis of Intelligence.* New York: McGraw-Hill.

Gustafsson, J.E. (1984). A unifying model for the structure of intellectual abilities. *Intelligence,* 8, 179–203.

Horn, J. (1994). Theory of fluid and crystallized intelligence. In Sternberg, R.J. (Ed.), *Encyclopedia of Human Intelligence.* New York: Macmillan.

Jensen, A. (1980). *Bias in Mental Testing.* New York: Free Press.

Jensen, A.R. (1998). *The g Factor*. New York: Praeger.

Loehlin, J.C. (1992). *Latent Variables Models: An Introduction to Factor, Path, and Structural Analysis* (2nd ed.). Hillsdale, NJ: Erlbaum.

Loehlin, J.C. (2000). Group differences in intelligence. In Sternberg, R.J. (Ed.), *Handbook of Intelligence*. Cambridge: Cambridge University Press.

Mackintosh, N.J. (1998). *IQ and Human Intelligence*. Oxford: Oxford University Press.

Neisser, U., Boodoo, G., Bouchard, T., Boykin, A., Brody, N., Ceci, S., Halpern, D., Loehlin, J., Perloff, R., Sternberg, R. & Urbina, S. (1996). Intelligence: knowns and unknowns. *American Psychologist*, *51*(2), 77–101.

Sternberg, R.J. (1985). *Beyond IQ: A Triarchic Theory of Human Intelligence*. New York: Cambridge University Press.

Roberto Colom

RELATED ENTRIES

INTELLIGENCE ASSESSMENT (GENERAL), COGNITIVE/MENTAL ABILITIES IN WORK AND ORGANIZATIONAL SETTINGS, FLUID AND CRYSTALLIZED INTELLIGENCE, THEORETICAL PERSPECTIVE: COGNITIVE, THEORETICAL PERSPECTIVE: PSYCHOMETRICS, COGNITIVE ABILITIES: *g* FACTOR.

COGNITIVE DECLINE/ IMPAIRMENT

Cognitive decline is defined as a negative change in cognitive status over time that can be a function of normal ageing, brain injury, dementing brain pathology (e.g. Alzheimer's disease), or other mechanisms. There are two major areas in which assessment of cognitive decline is important: (1) research on the nature of ageing and how it affects cognitive processes and mechanisms, and (2) individual assessment, in which cognitive testing is used to determine whether a specific individual has undergone cognitive decline, possibly due to age-related disease processes, such as Alzheimer's disease or stroke. Assessment of normative age-related change often involves use of panel designs, in which a large sample of individuals are given a set of cognitive tests and tasks. Prototypic examples of this kind of research are the Seattle Longitudinal Study (Schaie, 1996), the Berlin Aging Study (Baltes & Mayer, 1999), and the Victoria Longitudinal Study (Hultsch, Hertzog, Dixon & Small, 1998). These kinds of studies focus on characterizing the normative patterns of cognitive decline, and also on assessing individual differences in rates of cognitive decline. In order to address the latter question, it is important that the same persons are followed over time in a longitudinal design, so that individual differences in rates of cognitive change can be estimated (Baltes, Reese & Nesselroade, 1988). When the goal is assessment of individuals with respect to cognitive decline,

change is often assessed indirectly. That is, the typical neuropsychological assessment of decline is made through norm-referenced evaluation – low performance relative to same-aged peers. However, it is also possible to follow individuals over time for purposes of assessment, as we discuss further.

One of the challenges with assessing cognitive decline in adulthood is that there are a large number of different types of cognitive abilities (Carroll, 1993). Research on cognitive decline must allow for the possibility that different abilities may be affected in different ways by the ageing process (Dixon & Hertzog, 1996). It is well known, for example, that tests of recognition vocabulary (knowledge of word meanings) show relatively little decline until late in the lifespan, whereas tests of inductive reasoning (the ability to observe patterns or regularities in phenomena) or deductive reasoning show earlier decline (Salthouse, 1991). Another challenge to assessing cognitive decline is that changes are often slow and gradual (occurring over years or decades, in the absence of significant pathology in the central nervous system). Hence researchers often use cross-sectional designs, in which persons of different ages are tested at a single point in time, and age differences within the sample are used to estimate magnitudes of average age-related declines. Although this approach probably provides accurate general information about abilities that are influenced by age, generational (or cohort) differences can lead to overestimation of the magnitude of decline. Moreover, cross-sectional data cannot be used to evaluate individual differences in rates of cognitive change. Cross-sectional studies allow quick assessment of possible cognitive decline, but the inferences in such cases should be validated with longitudinal data as rapidly as possible (Hertzog, 1996).

A critical issue for research on cognitive decline is whether tests are prone to measurement bias in the evaluation of older adults. This issue can be understood as one of assuming measurement equivalence (Baltes et al., 1988) at different points in the adult lifespan. Does a test measure the same construct with the same measurement properties (e.g. reliability, validity) for persons of different ages? Psychometric techniques, such as item-response theory (Embretson & Reise, 2000), can be used to evaluate measurement equivalence of tests for persons of different ages, although they have rarely been used in age-comparative studies. Factor analysis of test batteries and items has been more widely used to assess measurement equivalence of cognitive tests, and the evidence is mixed. In some cases, test batteries show invariant factor structures (Brickley, Keith & Wolfle, 1995); in other cases, it appears that tests show at least some change in measurement properties in assessing older adults (Schaie, Maitland, Willis & Intrieri, 1998). Moreover, there is at least some evidence that tests can be constructed in ways that unintentionally penalize the performance of older adults. It is well known that ageing causes slowing in the speed of cognitive processes (Salthouse, 1996). Hence, tests that are highly speeded (where the total score depends more on the number of items answered correctly, rather than the difficulty of items answered correctly; see Anastasi, 1988) can become poor measures of a target construct in older populations because older adults are unduly penalized by slow response latencies. For example, Hertzog (1989) showed that the test of vocabulary used in the Seattle Longitudinal Study showed early decline that could be attributed to the processing speed requirements of the test, not to the decline of verbal ability (see also Hertzog & Bleckley, 2001). Recent results indicate that tests explicitly designed to cover a wide range of item difficulty, such as the Woodcock–Johnson, may provide better assessment of adult cognitive performance. Table 1 lists several widely used intelligence tests that are appropriate for research with older adults (for an excellent set of test reviews, see Flanagan, Genshaft & Harrison, 1997). Despite recent progress in our understanding of tests appropriate for assessment of adults, continuing work is needed that focuses on the issue of construct validity of tests in older populations.

Another important measurement issue is that standardized tests, even when well-designed, may not cover important aspects of cognitive function. For example, working memory, defined as the ability to hold information in an active state while analysing it (e.g. mentally summing four two-digit numbers), is a critical construct in contemporary cognitive psychology. Indeed, some scientists argue that age changes in working memory capacity account for age changes in a variety of complex psychological tasks, including tests of reasoning (Salthouse, 1991; Hultsch et al., 1998). Often, however, standardized psychometric test batteries do not measure new constructs deriving from contemporary cognitive psychology. If the goal is characterizing age-related changes in cognition, then individuals may wish to use newly developed tests or experimental tasks that are not commonly used for norm-referenced psychological assessment, rather than the standardized tests cited in Table 1.

Assessment of cognitive change in an individual is often done using standardized tests, evaluating an individual's test performance against age-graded population norms. Poor performance, relative to the norm, is taken as presumptive evidence of decline. However, this approach cannot rule out stable, low levels of performance, and it presumes the reliability and validity of an assessment of cognitive function at a single point in time. As such it does not address the possibility of transient fluctuations in test performance. Pathological change may also be associated with increased variability in performance – a person could be relatively intact on one day and relatively impaired on the next day. An alternative approach to norm-referenced assessment is to directly measure change by assessing individuals repeatedly over time, as in a longitudinal research design. Despite potential problems such as positive bias due to practice

Table 1. Cognitive tests measuring multiple abilities appropriate for use with older adults

Test name[a]	Publisher	Group/Individual testing	Comments
Das–Naglieri (CAS)	The Riverside Publishing Co.	Individual	Based on little-known information-processing theory; unique ability structure
ETS Factor Reference Kit	Educational Testing Service	Group	Excellent coverage of different ability; poor graphics; many speeded tests;
STAMAT	Consulting Psychologists Press, Inc.	Group	Revision of Thurstone tests; low item difficulty level; highly speeded
WAIS III		Individual	Widely used in clinical ability assessment; factorially complex, limited ability sampling;
WMS III	The Psychological Corp.	Individual	Widely used in clinical ability assessment; norms available
Woodcock–Johnson III	The Riverside Publishing Co.	Individual	Based on fluid/crystallized theory of intelligence; excellent ability/item sampling

[a]Tests are listed in alphabetical order.

221

effects, direct estimates of change through repeated assessments may produce more valid inferences about whether an individual is declining. Longitudinal studies of persons initially diagnosed with possible Alzheimer's disease have proved valuable in charting the progression of the cognitive consequences of the disease (e.g. Rubin et al., 1998).

Recent statistical advances in the techniques for estimating individual change functions have had an important impact on scientific studies of age-related changes in cognition and other variables. Longitudinal data on memory decline suggest that there are reliable individual differences in cognitive change late in life (Hultsch et al., 1998). Some individuals decline more than others. In at least some cases, these individual differences have been shown to be associated with risk factors for Alzheimer's disease, even prior to the diagnosis of the disease itself. Other factors, such as cardiovascular disease or life styles that do not provide adequate intellectual stimulation (Schooler, Mulatu, & Oates, 1999), may also affect cognitive change in adulthood. Thus, repeated testing may be an important way of identifying individuals who are showing greater cognitive decline than would be expected.

The approach of repeated testing of individuals can be applied to individual assessment. What is needed is a set of cognitive tests that are resistant to distortion due to repeated testing and that can be administered frequently. In one example of this approach, Hertzog, Dixon, and Hultsch (1992) used a set of 25 stories to assess long-term memory for text information. The stories were constructed to be highly similar in their narrative structure, even though the specific content of the stories was different. A small group of older adults were assessed on text recall once a week for about two years. The older individuals all showed variability in test performance from week to week, suggesting that transient variability in performance might have a greater impact on the reliability of norm-referenced assessment than has been generally believed. More importantly, the older adults showed different patterns of average changes across the two-year period. A few individuals declined in text recall, a few individuals remained stable, and a few individuals improved their performance. The declining individuals may have been experiencing pathological late-life decline

prior to death, or what is referred to as terminal decline (Berg, 1996). The advantage of the repeated assessment of change was that enough data points were collected on each person so that one could compute a standard deviation of scores for each individual. This statistic could then be used to estimate a standard error of estimate for the observed change over the two-year period, eliminating the need for a comparison to norms as a way of inferring reliable change.

To date, repeated testing of individuals has had little impact on neuropsychological assessment practices. A number of practical problems need to be solved. For example, to be practically meaningful, individuals would need to have regular test assessments prior to the development of any pathology, so that a baseline pattern of change could be established, as with attempts to estimate premorbid intelligence for norm-referenced assessment. This approach is analogous to routine medical testing (e.g. blood tests for cholesterol or blood pressure assessment) to establish a measured patient history on critical physiological functions. Routine and regular cognitive testing of individuals could provide a more valid baseline against which to assess the possibility of cognitive change.

References

Anastasi, A. (1988). *Psychological Testing* (6th ed.). New York: Prentice-Hall.

Baltes, P.B. & Mayer, K.U. (Eds.) (1999). *The Berlin Aging Study: Aging from 70 to 100*. New York: Cambridge University Press.

Baltes, P.B., Reese, H.W. & Nesselroade, J.R. (1988). *Life-Span Developmental Psychology: Introduction to Research Methods*. Hillsdale, NJ: Lawrence Erlbaum Associates.

Berg, S. (1996). Aging, behaviour, and terminal decline. In Birren, J.E. & Schaie, K.W. (Eds.), *Handbook of the Psychology of Aging* (4th ed.). San Diego, CA: Academic Press.

Brickley, P.G., Keith, T.Z. & Wolfle, L.M. (1995). The three-stratum theory of cognitive abilities: test of the structure of intellect across the adult life span. *Intelligence*, 20, 229–248.

Carroll, J.B. (1993). *Human Cognitive Abilities: A Survey of Factor-Analytic Studies*. New York: Cambridge University Press.

Dixon, R.A. & Hertzog, C. (1996). Theoretical issues in cognition and ageing. In Blanchard-Fields, F. & Hess, T.M. (Eds.), *Perspectives on Cognitive Change in Adulthood and Aging* (pp. 25–65). New York: McGraw-Hill.

Embretson, S.E. & Reise, S.P. (2000). *Item Response Theory for Psychologists*. Mahwah, NJ: Lawrence Erlbaum Associates.

Flanagan, D.P., Genshaft, J.L. & Harrison, P.L. (Eds.) (1997). *Contemporary Intellectual Assessment: Theories, Tests, and Issues*. New York: Guilford Press.

Hertzog, C. (1996). Research design in studies of aging and cognition. In J.E. Bitten & K.W. Schaie (Eds.), *Handbook of the Psychology of Aging* (5th Ed.). San Diego, CA: Academic Press.

Hertzog, C. (1989). Influences of cognitive slowing on age differences in intelligence. *Developmental Psychology*, 25, 636–651.

Hertzog, C. & Bleckley, M.K. (2001). Age differences in the structure of intelligence: influences of information processing speed. *Intelligence*, 29, 191–217.

Hertzog, C., Dixon, R.A. & Hultsch, D.F. (1992). Intraindividual change in text recall of the elderly. *Brain and Language*, 42, 248–269.

Hultsch, D.F., Hertzog, C., Dixon, R.A. & Small, B.J. (1998). *Memory Change in the Aged*. New York: Cambridge University Press.

Rubin, E.H., Storandt, M., Miller, P., Kinscherf, D.A., Grant, E.A., Morris, J.C. & Berg, L. (1998). A prospective study of cognitive function and onset of dementia in cognitively healthy elders. *Archives of Neurology*, 55, 395–401.

Salthouse, T.A. (1991). *Theoretical Perspectives on Cognitive Aging*. Hillsdale, NJ: Lawrence Erlbaum Associates.

Salthouse, T.A. (1996). The processing-speed theory of adult age differences in cognition. *Psychological Review*, 103, 403–428.

Schaie, K.W. (1996). *Intellectual Development in Adulthood*. New York: Cambridge University Press.

Schaie, K.W., Maitland, S.B., Willis, S.L. & Intrieri, R.C. (1998). Longitudinal invariance of adult psychometric ability factor structures across 7 years. *Psychology and Aging*, 13, 8–20.

Schooler, C., Mulatu, M.S. & Oates, G. (1999). The continuing effects of substantively complex work on the intellectual function of older workers. *Psychology and Aging*, 14, 483–506.

Christopher Hertzog and Simeon Feldstein

RELATED ENTRIES

Applied Fields: Gerontology, Fluid and Crystallized Intelligence, Cognitive Plasticity, Intelligence Assessment through Cohort and Time

COGNITIVE MAPS

INTRODUCTION

This entry discusses cognitive maps and the methodologies used to define them. The concept is traced from its emergence in psychology through attempts to operationalize it and use it in disciplines such as planning, behavioural geography, artificial intelligence, and computer science. Assessment tasks include sketch mapping, written and verbal descriptions, orientation and direction estimation, interpoint distance estimation, establishing frames of reference, establishing configurational or layout knowledge using trilateration or non-metric multidimensional scaling, and completion of navigation or wayfinding tasks. Future research directions involve more work on spatial cognition and spatial abilities, research at macrospatial scales, evaluation of potential contribution of virtual environments, and investigation of the neurobiology of place cells.

DEFINITION OF TERMS AND BACKGROUND

Although cognitive maps have been used for environmental knowing and wayfinding throughout the entirety of human history, they have only become a matter of scientific experimentation and analysis since the advent of Tolman's place learning theory (Tolman, 1948). This theory suggests that a *cognitive map* develops in the long-term memory of humans and other animals. Continuing multidisciplinary efforts have been made to examine the content, validity, and reliability of these internal representations.

Defined as *one's internal representation of the experienced world*, the concept of a cognitive map has spread among many disciplines. Beyond the original work in psychology, the first application of a 'cognitive map' was made by planner Kevin Lynch (1960). He examined what people knew about environments, suggesting that knowledge depended on environmental legibility. Legibility was defined as the ease with which an environment could be perceived, comprehended, and used. To determine what people knew about environments, Lynch asked them to externalize their knowledge (of selected cities) by producing 'sketch maps'. These were examined to find which features (landmarks and other reference points, paths and boundaries, and neighbourhoods or districts) were included. Using the sketches made by many individuals, he produced (for specific cities) a composite sketch (or 'city image') of those locational, path, and district features that were represented by the majority of the participants.

Following Lynch's efforts, geographers became interested in the cognitive map concept. Initially termed 'mental maps' (Gould, 1966), these were cartographic representations of the rank orders of stated preferences for living in places. The rank orders were aggregated, and a cartographic isoline map of the places – or a map represented as a continuous surface using lines of uniform preference value – was constructed. Remarkable regional differences in preferences were found, and the results were often interpreted as a regionalized 'view of the world' – such as 'a Californian view of the US'.

Piaget and Inhelder (1967) provided both a theoretical structure and empirical evidence that cognitive maps develop over time as age and intellectual maturity advanced. Their developmental theory of knowledge acquisition was made explicitly spatial by Hart and Moore (1973) and Siegel and White (1975), who argued that there was a continuous transformation of spatial knowledge from an egocentric structure that dominated the first two years of infancy and was epitomized by a projective form of representation, to a topological knowledge structure as children advanced to pre-operational learning stages, to a semi-metric and metric understanding as children passed through concrete operational and abstract stages of thinking and reasoning. In recent years, Montello (1998) vigorously challenged these ideas, not for their relevance to the spatial knowledge acquisition of children as they age, but in terms of adult learning about new environments. His argument suggests that adult humans have the ability to reason abstractly about space and to represent it metrically, and, thus, would not need to go through the earlier stages outlined in developmental theories.

Moore and Golledge (1976) had distinguished between the cognitive map as an *internal representation* of sensed environmental phenomena and the *externalization* of that knowledge in the form of sketches, verbal descriptions, artistic renderings, or other spatial products. Research interest in the construction, organization, and use of cognitive mapping information stimulated multidisciplinary research in spatial cognition. In psychology, attention was focused on how environments are perceived, and theories of imagery speculated about how spatial information was stored in the brain and recalled into working memory. Focusing on the use of cognitive maps in wayfinding and navigation, mathematicians and computer scientists interested in artificial intelligence, and, in particular, robotic modelling, have also developed a research agenda focusing on cognitive maps and cognitive mapping. Kuipers (1978) produced a specific artificial intelligence-based model (TOUR) of wayfinding that emphasized the process of route-based learning and cognitive map development. During the 1970s and 1980s, efforts were made to produce various computational models that embedded the idea of cognitive maps and their use in navigational processes. All these models were based on cognitive mapping and environmental learning. Knowledge accumulation was modelled as a production process using ⟨ 'if ____, then ____' ⟩ rules that could anchor a software package designed to guide a mechanical or human traveller through an unfamiliar environment.

RELEVANT METHODOLOGIES

Currently, to know the contents of a cognitive map requires an external representation. The most common methodologies include: (i) sketch mapping; (ii) verbal or written descriptions; (iii) completion of orientation and direction tasks; (iv) interpoint distance estimation; (v) recovering latent structure using non-metric multidimensional scaling; and (vi) conducting wayfinding and navigation tasks.

Sketch Mapping. Originally, subjects were simply given a standard sheet of paper and asked to draw (to the best of their ability in a given time) a sketch 'map' of a given environment. The results were interpreted in terms of five dominant features: landmarks, nodes, paths, boundaries, and districts. All these are obvious except for 'node'; this represented minor features, less important cues, or unnamed road intersections or other point features. Later attempts to produce sketch maps provided a standard reference location (usually centred on the page) and, sometimes, a north line and a scale on the drawing surface. A scale was used to provide metric information from the sketch, while the north line was to give common orientation and direction that would help interpret angularity between sketch features. Sometimes, information was simply aggregated and the results transferred to a cartographic map on which was plotted the relative importance of map features (Milgram & Jodelet, 1976). Research by psychologist Blades (1990) showed that similar sketch maps would be repeatedly produced by the same individual at different time periods, thus giving a semblance of reliability and validity to this methodology. *But* there was consistent criticism that, because of the absence of scales and north lines, spatial concepts such as distance, angular direction, configural layout, and orientation could not be reliably extracted from these products. While the sketches provided a useful inventory of environmental knowledge, they did not necessarily contain the spatial relations that would make them map-like. Sketch mapping is now used as part of a bundle of tasks for defining a person's environmental knowledge structure.

Verbal or Written Description. Verbal or written products offset graphicacy skills required for sketch mapping. Content analysis of the material so produced is used to compile lists of features (usually classified according to Lynch's five categories of phenomena). Both verbal and written descriptions are often heavily laced with fuzzy spatial prepositions such as 'close to', 'near', 'behind', or 'to the left of' which are spatially inexact (Landau & Jackendoff, 1993). This linguistic problem inhibited the creation of reasonably accurate map-like representations of the spatial content of such expositions. While this problem has spawned multidisciplinary interest in spatial linguistics, naïve geography, and natural language software programming in computer science, the task of extracting accurate spatial information from verbal and written descriptions is still a taxing one. When used in conjunction with other tasks, however, they do provide useful insights into a person's spatial knowledge structure.

Orientation and Direction. Establishing the orientation and directional features of a person's cognitive map relies on finding the frame of reference being used. In the cognitive domain, relative location (e.g. tied to a street system rather than a global frame) and idiosyncratic frames of reference are common. Cardinal directions (north, south, east, and west) are infrequently used in comparison to frames tied to local knowledge. The frame of reference used to encode, locate, and recall spatialized information stored in long-term memory can be projective (related to a dominant landmark such as a home or workplace), locally metric (related to a street network or numbering system), or egocentrically arbitrary (with respect to the relative positions of self or dominant natural or built environmental features). Orientation is of critical importance in aligning cognitive maps with the real world (Tversky, 1981).

One traditional way of determining knowledge of angularity between environmental features is *to point* in the direction of the particular feature, either from current location or from some imaginary location. A compass can be used to measure the pointing angle and, if the frame of reference is known, a matching of pointing with the idiosyncratic reference-base can be obtained. Pointing has been a common form of indicating directional knowledge throughout human history. It is a simple task that is often used in experiments when attempting to discover layout knowledge in real, imaginary, or virtual environments.

Interpoint Distance Estimation. Distance measurements are usually obtained between specific pairs of points alone or in sequence (as along a route). Multidisciplinary work on psychological distance (or *subjective distance*) estimation has shown: (i) distances are often perceived asymmetrically (A → B ≠ B → A); (ii) shorter distances are usually overestimated while longer distances are usually underestimated (regression toward the mean); (iii) distances uphill are perceived to be different to distances downhill; and (iv) distances along curved lines or along traces with multiple turn angles are perceived to be longer than equivalent straight line distances. Layouts of points (spatial configurations) can be constructed using a matrix of interpoint distance estimates. The methodology is known as *trilateration* and manipulates the interpoint distances in a multidimensional space until a feasible layout is constructed. If actual distances were used (such as an interpoint distance matrix from a road atlas), trilateration would closely reproduce the actual layout of towns in an environment. When perceived distances are used, trilateration produces a configuration that represents the interpoint distance knowledge stored in a person's long term memory after sensory bias and error have been taken into consideration. Since many individuals have different concepts of components of distance (yards, miles, etc.), Golledge and Rushton (1972) suggested that a less formal measure (proximity) could be used to construct the interpoint distance matrix. Using a nine-point scale anchored at each end by the perceived shortest and longest distance, the scaled proximities are input to a non-metric multi-dimensional scaling procedure (KYST or other procedures found in many standard statistical software packages) to produce a minimum dimensional configuration of the proximity information. These can be matched against a real world configuration using indexes of Stress (Badness of Fit) or using cross-correlation matrices. Thus, with either direct or indirect interpoint measurements among known places, a layout representation or configurational structure of latent spatial knowledge contained in long term memory can be obtained. Once obtained, the different distortions and errors in one's cognitive map can be highlighted.

Wayfinding and Navigation. Wayfinding or navigation tasks include: (i) walking a specified distance (to examine distance estimation and veering tendencies); (ii) following simple paths with a minimal number of turns; (iii) undertaking triangle completion (shortcutting, homing, or path integration tasks); (iv) examining different route following strategies including route chunking and rote memorization of paths; and (v) conducting post-hoc tasks to examine the effects of different reinforcing techniques such as: during travel, estimating interpoint distances or directions; after route completion, giving verbal or written descriptions of the course just completed such that another person could follow the same path; and construction of maps or models of the route just followed. Research tasks have varied in scale from triangle completion in small laboratory settings (using path legs of three, six, and nine metres), to wayfinding in institutional settings (universities, hospitals, and airports), to larger scale wayfinding in suburban neighbourhoods.

FUTURE PERSPECTIVES

Further research on cognitive maps is dependent on further research on the nature of spatial cognition. Future research will need to concentrate on (i) problems of mental rotation, (ii) cognitive alignment problems, (iii) frame of reference concerns, and (iv) distance and directional estimations. This research can take place in (i) real geographic environments, (ii) imaginary environments, and (iii) virtual environments. Although the bulk of the latter are visual virtual spaces, some work has been undertaken in virtual auditory environments (Loomis, Golledge & Klatzky, 1999). As a complement to this virtual domain research, there is an increasing interest in assessing human spatial abilities. Over time, a significant number of spatial tests have been developed and evaluated (see Eliot & Smith, 1983). Specific test scores derived from tests designed to measure the three dominant psychometric factors (visualization, speeded rotation, and orientation) do not predict real world behaviours at various scales.

Other areas for future research include:

- Simple tests to assess the variety of spatial skills ranging from distance and direction estimation to spatial rotation, spatial alignment, spatial orientation, defining appropriate reference frames, wayfinding, producing different spatial products, and comprehending spatial relations such as geographic association, spatial autocorrelation, spatial sequence, scale transformation, transforming among different dimensionalities and reversing those transformations, overlaying or dissolving different information layers, and many others.
- Defining tests to evaluate if people have the skills needed for using spatial databases, georeferenced systems, and spatialization metaphors in Internet search engines.
- Systematic examination of the process of spatial knowledge acquisition.
- Determination of the relevance of developmental theory and its competitors in the area of spatial knowledge acquisition over time and with increasing age.
- Investigation of how spatial information is encoded in 'place cells' (Nadel, 1999). The use of MRIs, CT scans, and PET scans has

indicated that spatial information is more generally distributed than just in the hippocampus, but the exact pattern of concentration or dispersion of place cells is as yet poorly known. It is likely that assessment tasks will focus in the near future on brain damaged individuals to help determine if specific spatial knowledge is highly localized in the brain.

FUTURE PERSPECTIVES AND CONCLUSIONS

Overall, a cognitive map is a useful tool for educating about spatial knowledge acquisition, for examining wayfinding and navigation behaviours, for assessing individual differences in spatial abilities and spatial skills, for investigating the possibility of sex-based differences in spatial cognition and the use of cognized spatial information, and for providing a schemata for investigating environmental knowledge acquisition at scales ranging from micro to macro. Societal needs for well-trained participants for a future workforce have emphasized the need to understand and use cognitive maps and spatial knowledge acquisition principles. Cognitive map construction and development depends on spatial abilities and, in particular, the abilities to think and reason in a spatial manner. Cognitive mapping research is still in its relative infancy, and determination of ways to assess and use cognitive mapping ability in different task domains still remains as a primary focus of future research.

Acknowledgement

Partial support was provided by NSF Grant No BCS-0083110.

References

Blades, M. (1990). The reliability of data collected from sketch maps. *Journal of Environmental Psychology*, 10(4), 209–231.

Eliot, J. & Smith, I.M. (1983). *An International Directory of Spatial Tests*. Windsor, UK: NFER-NELSON.

Golledge, R.G. & Rushton, G. (1972). *Multidimensional Scaling: Review and Geographical Applications* (Technical Paper 10). Washington, DC: AAG Commission on College Geography.

Gould, P. (1966). *On Mental Maps*. Discussion Paper No. 9 presented at the Community of Mathematical Geographers, Michigan University, Ann Arbor, MI.

Hart, R.A. & Moore, G.T. (1973). The development of spatial cognition: a review. In Downs, R.M. & Stea, D. (Eds.), *Image and Environment: Cognitive Mapping and Spatial Behaviour* (pp. 246–288). Chicago: Aldine.

Kuipers, B.J. (1978). Modelling spatial knowledge. *Cognitive Science*, 2, 129–153.

Landau, B. & Jackendoff, R. (1993). 'What' and 'where' in spatial language and spatial cognition. *Behavioural and Brain Sciences*, 16, 217–238.

Loomis, J.M., Golledge, R.G. & Klatzky, R.L. (1999). Auditory distance perception in real, virtual, and mixed environments. In Ohta, Y. & Tamura, H. (Eds.), *Mixed Reality: Merging Real and Virtual Worlds* (pp. 201–214). Tokyo: Ohmsha, Ltd.

Lynch, K. (1960). *The Image of the City*. Cambridge, MA: The MIT Press.

Milgram, S. & Jodelet, D. (1976). Psychological maps of Paris. In Proshansky, H.M., Ittelson, W.H. & Rivlin, L.G. (Eds.), *Environmental Psychology People and Their Physical Settings* (2nd ed., pp. 103–124). New York: Rinehart and Winston.

Montello, D.R. (1998). A new framework for understanding the acquisition of spatial knowledge in large-scale environments. In Egenhofer, M.J. & Golledge, R.G. (Eds.), *Spatial and Temporal Reasoning in Geographic Information Systems* (pp. 143–154). New York: Oxford University Press.

Moore, G.T. & Golledge, R.G. (Eds.) (1976). *Environmental Knowing: Theories, Research and Methods*. Stroudsburg, PA: Dowden, Hutchinson & Ross.

Nadel, L. (1999). Neural mechanisms of spatial orientation and wayfinding: an overview. In Golledge, R.G. (Ed.), *Wayfinding Behaviour: Cognitive Mapping and Other Spatial Processes* (pp. 313–327). Baltimore, MD: The Johns Hopkins University Press.

Piaget, J. & Inhelder, B. (1967). *The Child's Conception of Space*. New York: Norton.

Siegel, A.W. & White, S.H. (1975). The development of spatial representation of large scale environments. In Reese, H.W. (Ed.), *Advances in Child Development and Behaviour*, Vol. 10 (pp. 9–55). New York: Academic Press.

Tolman, E.C. (1948). Cognitive maps in rats and men. *Psychological Review*, 55, 189–209.

Tversky, B. (1981). Distortions in memory for maps. *Cognitive Psychology*, 13, 407–433.

Reginald G. Golledge

RELATED ENTRIES

COGNITIVE PROCESSES: CURRENT STATUS, COGNITIVE STYLES, THEORETICAL PERSPECTIVE: COGNITIVE

COGNITIVE/MENTAL ABILITIES IN WORK AND ORGANIZATIONAL SETTINGS

INTRODUCTION

Cognitive processing of information is a critical requirement of many jobs in the workplace. There have been many changes in the nature of work and organizations with regard to the amount and nature of information, which must be dealt with by those working in organizations, as well as in the speed with which this information must be processed and applied. Thus the assessment of individual differences in those cognitive abilities relevant to effective performance in the workplace has become especially critical. This entry deals with the definition and organization of cognitive abilities, presents examples of standardized, diagnostic, and reliable measures for assessing these cognitive abilities, and provides examples of jobs and tasks requiring each of these abilities.

Some Definitions

Both Carroll (1993) and Fleishman (1972) define abilities as relatively enduring attributes of an individual's capability for performing a particular range of different tasks; however, these abilities may develop over time and with exposure to multiple situations (Snow & Lohman, 1984).

Recently, the term 'competencies' has come into use to describe individual attributes related to quality of work performance (see e.g. McClelland, 1973). A competency has been defined as an 'underlying characteristic of an individual which is causally related to effective or superior performance in a job' (Boyatzis, 1982). This definition is, of course, consistent with our definition of ability. However, lists of competencies often contain a mixture of knowledges, skills, abilities, motivation, beliefs, values, and interests.

The distinction between 'abilities' and 'skills' is often made (see e.g. Fleishman, 1966, 1972); where an ability is a general trait of an individual that is inferred from the relationships among performances of individuals observed across a range of different tasks, skills are more dependent on learning and represent the product of training in particular tasks. The development of a given skill (e.g. airplane piloting) is predicated, in part, on the individual's possession of relevant underlying abilities (e.g. spatial orientation, multi-limb coordination). These underlying abilities are related to the rate of acquisition and final levels of performance that a person can achieve in particular skills (see Ackerman, 1988; Fleishman, 1972).

Fleishman (1982) and Fleishman and Quaintance (1984) have described the different conceptual bases for defining 'tasks'. Wheaton (1973) proposed that a task reflects an organized set of responses to a specified stimulus situation intended to bring about the attainment of a goal state. This definition of a task is similar to one proposed by Hackman (1968) and McCormick (1976) and, more recently, by Carroll (1993), who defines a task as 'an activity in which a person engages in order to achieve a specified objective or result'.

Tasks can be described in terms of the abilities required to perform them (Fleishman, 1972). Tasks requiring the same ability or a similar group of abilities would be placed in the same category. The use of empirical information on the relationships among performances of individuals performing different tasks allows us to identify the basic underlying abilities (Fleishman, 1972; Carroll, 1993).

STRUCTURE OF HUMAN ABILITIES

Critical questions have concerned the generality of the constructs used to describe individual differences in human abilities. Elsewhere, constructs such as 'mental abilities', 'motor abilities', 'problem solving ability', 'decision making ability', and 'agility' have turned out to be too broad; the tasks required by such broad categories are too diverse to yield high correlations between performances of these tasks. Factor analyses of the correlations among performances within these domains typically yield somewhat more narrowly defined abilities. Similarly, expressions like 'athletic ability' and 'musical ability' are often used, but it is known that there are a number of separate constructs that better define several different abilities involved in the tasks comprising these broad activities. However, characterizing an individual as having the ability to 'lift barbells of a given weight' or to 'solve quadratic equations of a given complexity' yields information that is too specific and not very descriptive of an ability that extends to performance in a variety of tasks requiring the same underlying ability.

It is recognized that the study of human abilities has a long history and that a number of alternative factor analytic models and theories regarding the structure of human cognitive abilities have been proposed (Sternberg & Detterman, 1986). Carroll (1993) has recently reviewed these models and other historical developments in the factor analysis of human cognitive abilities. Structural issues often involve the presence and nature of 'general cognitive ability', the importance of ability factors found among sub-groups of performances relative to such a general ability, and the existence and nature of hierarchical structures that relate general and more narrow ability categories. Thus, Spearman's (1923) hierarchy emphasized a general factor ('g'); Cattell and Horn's (1978) work stressed broader group factors (e.g. fluid and crystallized intelligence); and the work of Thurstone (1947) and Guilford (1985) emphasized a larger number of more narrowly defined abilities spanning a more limited range of performances (e.g. numerical and verbal abilities, inductive reasoning).

Hierarchical models investigated in previous work have been largely confined to performance in the cognitive areas of human performance. Carroll's (1993) review has proposed a hierarchical theory of cognitive abilities recognizing abilities classified at three strata: (a) numerous, narrow first-stratum factors; (b) a smaller number of broader, second-order factors; and (c) a single general factor at stratum three. He has also shown the difficulties and limitations in designing and carrying out hierarchical factor analysis studies to adequately name and define general and second-order factors and in matching these factors across studies.

COGNITIVE ABILITIES TAXONOMY

The ability taxonomy developed by Fleishman and his associates (e.g. Fleishman, 1975; Fleishman & Quaintance, 1984) falls into the first stratum of Carroll's system. The abilities in the taxonomy cover a broad spectrum of performances likely to be found in the world of work and include cognitive, psychomotor, physical, and sensory-perceptual abilities. Most of the abilities at this level have been identified in programmatic research and replicated across many studies. Furthermore, operational definitions of each of these abilities have been developed, linkages of job tasks with each ability have been established, and a methodology has been developed for evaluating jobs in terms of their requirements for these abilities (Fleishman, 1992; Fleishman & Reilly, 1992).

Table 1 presents the 21 cognitive abilities in the taxonomy with brief definitions of each ability. These abilities are organized into a hierarchy of seven broader categories. More detailed definitions can be found elsewhere in Fleishman and Reilly (1992).

MEASURES FOR ASSESSING COGNITIVE ABILITIES

Table 2 provides examples of tests available to measure each of the abilities described in Table 1. Tests have been chosen, based on an extensive review (Fleishman & Reilly, 1992). For most of these abilities, there are many more tests available. For the most part, tests listed have been shown to have relatively high reliabilities, normative data, and manuals describing conditions of administration, validity and normative information. Fleishman and Reilly (1992) include many more tests for each ability, including publishers' addresses. The tests they include are classified by ability measured.

Table 1.   Cognitive abilities and their definitions: Fleishman's Taxonomy of Human Abilities

Verbal Abilities

Oral Comprehension	The ability to listen and to understand information and ideas presented through spoken words and sentences.
Written Comprehension	The ability to read and understand information and ideas presented in writing.
Oral Expression	The ability to communicate information and ideas in speaking so others will understand.
Written Expression	The ability to communicate information and ideas in writing so others will understand.

Idea Generation and Reasoning Abilities

Fluency of Ideas	The ability to generate a number of ideas about a given topic. It concerns the number of ideas produced and not the quality of the ideas.
Originality	The ability to come up with unusual or clever ideas about a given topic or situation, or to develop creative ways to solve a problem.
Problem Sensitivity	The ability to tell when something is wrong or likely to go wrong. It does not involve solving the problem, only recognizing there is a problem.
Deductive Reasoning	The ability to apply general rules to specific problems to come up with logical answers. It involves deciding if an answer makes sense.
Inductive Reasoning	The ability to combine separate pieces of information, or specific answers to problems, to form general rules or conclusions. It includes coming up with a logical explanation for why a series of seemingly unrelated events occur together.
Information Ordering	The ability to correctly follow a given rule or set of rules in order to arrange things or actions in a certain order. The things or actions can include numbers, letters, words, pictures, procedures, sentences, and mathematical or logical operations.
Category Flexibility	The ability to produce many rules so that each rule tells how to group (or combine) a set of things in a different way.

Quantitative Abilities

Mathematical Reasoning	The ability to understand and organize a problem and then to select a mathematical method or formula to solve the problem.
Number Facility	The ability to add, subtract, multiply, or divide quickly and correctly.

Memory

Memorization	The ability to remember information such as words, numbers, pictures, and procedures.

Perceptual Abilities

Speed of Closure	The ability to quickly make sense of information that seems to be without meaning or organization. It involves quickly combining and organizing different pieces of information into a meaningful pattern.
Flexibility of Closure	The ability to identify or detect a known pattern (a figure, object, word, or sound) that is hidden in other distracting material.
Perceptual Speed	The ability to quickly and accurately compare letters, numbers, objects, pictures, or patterns. The things to be compared may be presented at the same time or one after the other. This ability also includes comparing a presented object with a remembered object.

Spatial Abilities

Spatial Organization	The ability to know one's location in relation to the environment, or to know where other objects are in relation to one's self.
Visualization	The ability to imagine how something will look after it is moved around or when its parts are moved or rearranged.

Attentiveness

Selective Attention	The ability to concentrate and not be distracted while performing a task over a period of time.
Time Sharing	The ability to efficiently shift back and forth between two or more activities or sources of information (such as speech, sounds, touch, or other sources).

Source: Adapted from Fleishman (1992), Fleishman and Quaintance (1984), Fleishman and Reilly (1992), Fleishman, Costanza, and Marshall-Mies (1999). The complete taxonomy also covers psychomotor, physical and sensory-perceptual abilities.

Table 2.   Example of tests available to measure each cognitive ability

Ability	Tests
Oral Comprehension	The PSI Basic Skills Tests: Following Oral Directions, Psychological Services, Inc. Watson–Barker Listening Test, SPECTRA Communication Associates
Written Comprehension	Guilford–Zimmerman Aptitude Survey: Verbal Comprehension, Consulting Psychologists Press Nelson–Denny Reading Test: Forms E & F-1, The Riverside Publishing Co.
Oral Expression	No standard tests of oral expression were identified.
Written Expression	Expressional Fluency, Consulting Psychologists Press Ideational Fluency, Consulting Psychologists Press Employee Aptitude Survey Test # 8 – Word Fluency (EAS #8), Psychological Services, Inc.
Fluency of Ideas	Ideational Fluency, Consulting Psychologists Press Topic Tests – F-1, Educational Testing Services
Originality	Consequences, Consulting Psychologists Press Flanagan Aptitude Classification Tests (FACT): Ingenuity, Science Research Associates
Memorization	The PSI Basic Skills Tests: Memory, Science Research Associates Flanagan Aptitude Classification Tests: Memory, Science Research Associates
Problem Sensitivity	No standard tests of problem sensitivity were identified.
Mathematical Reasoning	Guilford–Zimmerman Aptitude Survey: General Reasoning, Consulting Psychologists Press Flanagan Industrial Tests (FIT): Mathematics and Reasoning, Science Research Associates
Number Facility	Comprehensive Ability Battery: Numerical Ability, Institute for Personality & Ability Testing, Inc. Differential Aptitude Test: Numeric Ability, The Psychological Corporation
Deductive Reasoning	Nonsense Syllogisms – RL-1, Educational Testing Service The PSI Basic Skills Tests for Business: Decision Making, Psychological Services, Inc.
Inductive Reasoning	Letter Sets – 1, Educational Testing Services Critical Reasoning Test Battery, Saville & Holdsworth, Ltd.
Information Ordering	Calendar Test, Educational Testing Services Following Directions, Educational Testing Services
Category Flexibility	Making Groups – (XU-3), Educational Testing Services Halstead Category Test, Precision People, Inc.
Speed of Closure	Gestalt Completion Test – (CS-1), Educational Testing Services Closure Speed (Gestalt Completion), London House Press
Flexibility of Closure	Comprehensive Ability Battery: Hidden Shapes, Institute for Personality & Ability Testing, Inc. Closure Flexibility (Concealed Figures), London House Press
Spatial Orientation	Guilford–Zimmerman Aptitude Survey: Spatial Orientation, Consulting Psychologists Press Right–Left Orientation, Oxford Press University
Visualization	Minnesota Spatial Relations Test, American Guidance Service Guilford–Zimmerman Aptitude Survey: Spatial Visualization, Consulting Psychologists Press
Perceptual Speed	Guilford–Zimmerman Aptitude Survey: Perceptual Speed, Consulting Psychologists Press Minnesota Clerical, The Psychological Corporation
Selective Attention	No standard tests of selective attention were identified.
Time Sharing	No standard tests of time sharing were identified.

Source: Extracted from the more comprehensive definitions, test specifications and publisher listings in Fleishman & Reilly (1992). Reprinted with permission.

RELATING THE COGNITIVE ABILITIES TO JOB REQUIREMENTS

The cognitive ability constructs described, and their definitions, provide a framework for thinking about the abilities required for the performance of many different job tasks. These 21 cognitive ability factors have been included as part of a more comprehensive taxonomy of human abilities, which also include cognitive, psychomotor, and sensory-perceptual abilities (Fleishman, 1975; Fleishman & Quaintance, 1984; Fleishman & Reilly, 1992). A methodology has been developed for describing the ability requirements of jobs and job tasks in terms of the complete taxonomy of 52 abilities (Fleishman, 1975, 1992; Fleishman & Mumford, 1991). The Fleishman–Job Analysis Survey (F-JAS) (Fleishman, 1992) provides the job analysis method for linking the cognitive ability constructs described here to the requirements of occupational tasks.

In this job analysis methodology, each of the carefully defined ability definitions are presented, each with a corresponding seven-point rating scale containing empirically derived task anchors at high, middle, and low points on each scale (see Fleishman, 1992). Respondents (job incumbents, supervisors, or job analysts) rate the level of each ability required for particular jobs or job tasks on ability rating scales, providing a profile of the job's ability requirements.

Using these and related methods, the cognitive ability requirements of thousands of jobs have been determined, including computer programmers, high level executives, accountants, building inspectors, fire fighters, medical personnel, telephone repair workers, police, administrators, attorneys, automotive mechanics, sales personnel, refinery workers, and many military specialities. Table 3 provides examples of jobs likely to require each of these cognitive abilities.

Interrater reliabilities obtained from use of the F-JAS to describe the ability requirements of jobs are high and there is very high agreement between profiles of ability requirements obtained from incumbents, supervisors, and job analysts. It is important to note that the methodology recognizes the centrality of the notion of 'level' of ability requirements. Thus jobs requiring a particular ability may require different levels of that ability. For example, oral comprehension is important for secretaries and lawyers, but a higher level of oral comprehension is required for most lawyers than for most secretaries in terms of task requirements.

FUTURE PERSPECTIVES AND CONCLUSIONS

A taxonomy of cognitive abilities was presented to provide a framework for describing the

Table 3.   Examples of jobs requiring each ability

Oral Comprehension:	executive, interpreter, counsellor
Written Comprehension:	lawyer, book editor, translator
Oral Expression:	politician, actor, college professor
Written Expression:	judge, reporter, author
Fluency of Ideas:	advertising executive, song writer, interior designer
Originality:	artist, choreographer, inventor
Memorization:	actor, concert pianist, scientist
Problem Sensitivity:	medical doctor, air traffic controller, mathematician
Mathematical Reasoning:	engineer, statistician, physicist
Number Facility:	accountant, cashier, mortgage banker
Deductive Reasoning:	auto mechanic, pathologist, computer programmer
Inductive Reasoning:	statistician, meteorologist, psychologist
Information Ordering:	librarian, astronaut, file clerk
Category Flexibility:	archivist, biology taxonomist, museum contractor
Speed of Closure:	meteorologist, cryptographer, navigator
Flexibility of Closure:	microbiologist, radar operator, radiologist
Spatial Orientation:	cartographer, surveyor, pilot
Visualization:	architect, engineer, dentist
Perceptual Speed:	maintenance troubleshooter, inspector, proofreader
Selective Attention:	radar monitor, lifeguard, early warning system monitor
Time Sharing:	air traffic controller, athletics coach, helicopter pilot

Source: From Fleishman & Reilly (1992). Reprinted with permission.

requirements of jobs on the workplace. The 21 ability definitions, arranged in an hierarchy of seven broader categories of cognitive functioning, provide distinctions between the abilities and indicate their limits and generality across different kinds of human tasks. Tests were identified that reliably assess each cognitive ability. A job analysis methodology was described to identify the extent to which the tasks in particular jobs require the different cognitive abilities. These methods have resulted in the selection of tests to assist in matching individuals with jobs requiring different abilities.

Recent research has examined newer methods of assessing cognitive abilities, especially those involved in highly demanding complex organizational environments. Leadership, at high levels of management, for example, can be seen as involving complex problem solving, and decision-making, in ill defined, changing, and other novel organizational domains (Fleishman et al., 1999). A number of investigations have emphasized the importance of metacognitive skills in this context, to guide the problem solving process. Recently, Marshall-Mies, Fleishman, Martin, Zaccaro, Baughman, and McGee (2000) have shown how novel computer interactive assessments can be developed to identify these skills and have demonstrated the validity of such measures in predictor performance of high level organizational leaders. Future research should be directed at delineating the relations between such cognitive abilities and performance, using more flexible and adaptive assessment methods.

References

Ackerman, P.L. (1988). Determinants of individual differences during skill acquisition: cognitive abilities and information processing. *Journal of Experimental Psychology: General*, 117, 288–318.

Boyatzis, R.E. (1982). *The Competent Manager: A Model for Effective Performance*. New York: Wiley-Interscience.

Carroll, J.B. (1993). *Human Cognitive Abilities*. New York: Cambridge University Press.

Cattell, R.B. & Horn, J.L. (1978). A check on the theory of fluid and crystallized intelligence with description of new subtest designs. *Journal of Educational Measurement*, 15, 139–164.

Fleishman, E.A. (1966). Human abilities and the acquisition of skill. In Bilodeau, E.A. (Ed.), *Acquisition of Skill*. New York: Academic Press.

Fleishman, E.A. (1972). On the relation between abilities, learning, and human performance. *American Psychologist*, 27, 1017–1032.

Fleishman, E.A. (1975). Toward a taxonomy of human performance. *American Psychologist*, 30, 1127–1149.

Fleishman, E.A. (1982). Systems for describing human tasks. *American Psychologist*, 37, 821–834.

Fleishman, E.A. (1992). *Fleishman–Job Analysis Survey (F-JAS)*. Potomac, MD: Management Research Institute, Inc.

Fleishman, E.A., Costanza, D.P. & Marshall-Mies, J.C. (1999). Abilities. In Peterson, N., Mumford, M., Borman, W., Jeanneret, P. & Fleishman, E. (Eds.), *An Occupational Information System for the 21st Century: The Development of O*Net*. Washington, DC: American Psychological Association.

Fleishman, E.A. & Mumford, M.D. (1991). Evaluating classifications of job behaviour: a construct validation of the ability requirement scales. *Personnel Psychology*, 44(3), 523–575.

Fleishman, E.A. & Quaintance, M. (1984). *Taxonomies of Human Performance: The Description of Human Tasks*. Potomac, MD: Management Research Institute, Inc.

Fleishman, E.A. & Reilly, M.E. (1992). *Handbook of Human Abilities: Definitions, Measurements, and Job Task Requirements*. Potomac, MD: Management Research Institute, Inc.

Guilford, J.P. (1985). The structure-of-intellect model. In Wolman, B.B. (Ed.), *Handbook of Intelligence: Theories, Measurements, and Applications* (pp. 225–266). New York: Wiley.

Hackman, J.R. (1968). Tasks and task performance in research on stress. In McGrath, J.E. (Eds.), *Social and Psychological Factors in Stress*. New York: Holt, Rinehart & Winston.

Marshall-Mies, J.C., Fleishman, E.A., Martin, J.A., Zaccaro, S.J., Baughman, W.A. & McGee, M.L. (2000). Development and evaluation of cognitive and metacognitive measures for predicting leadership potential. *Leadership Quarterly*, 11(1) 135–153.

McClelland, D.C. (1973). Testing for competence rather than intelligence. *American Psychologist*, 28, 1–14.

McCormick, E.J. (1976). Job and task analysis. In Dunnette, M.D. (Ed.), *Handbook of Industrial and Organizational Psychology* (pp. 651–696). Chicago, IL: Rand-McNally.

Snow, R.E. & Lohman, D.F. (1984). Toward a theory of cognitive aptitude for learning from instructions. *Journal of Educational Psychology*, 16, 349–376.

Spearman, C. (1923). *The Abilities of Man: Their Nature and Measurement*. New York: Macmillan. [Reprinted: New York: AMS Publishers, 1981.]

Sternberg, R.J. & Detterman, D.K. (1986). *What is Intelligence?* Norwood, NJ: Alex Publishing Company.

Thurstone, L.L. (1947). *Multiple Factor Analysis: A Development and Expansion of the Vectors of Mind*. Chicago, IL: University of Chicago Press.

Wheaton, G.R. (1973). Development of a taxonomy of human performance: a review of classificatory systems related to tasks and performance. *JSAS Catalog of Selected Documents*, 3, 22–23 (Ms. No. 317).

Edwin A. Fleishman

RELATED ENTRIES

APPLIED FIELDS: WORK AND INDUSTRY, INTELLIGENCE ASSESSMENT (GENERAL), COGNITIVE ABILITY: G FACTOR, COGNITIVE ABILITY: MULTIPLE COGNITIVE ABILITIES, PERSONNEL SELECTION, ASSESSMENT IN, COGNITIVE/MENTAL ABILITIES IN WORK AND ORGANIZATIONAL SETTINGS

COGNITIVE PLASTICITY

INTRODUCTION

Cognitive functions are typically assessed with psychometric tests in a single test session. Usually this type of assessment does not provide direct information about an individual's learning potential given suitable instructional and social settings; it may provide this information only indirectly via predictive correlations with external criteria. Such predictability, however, is difficult to obtain because static measurements are influenced by numerous other factors such as specific school education, experience with test taking, or disruptive and supportive conditions in the individual's social setting. 'Cognitive plasticity assessment' represents alternative concepts to such state-oriented measurement. They directly assess the change in performance in response to educational practices or theory-guided cognitive interventions. We describe three approaches to cognitive plasticity assessment (Learning Potential Assessment, Learning Tests, and Cognitive Engineering) to exemplify the broad range of

perspectives on this topic. Our conceptualization of 'cognitive plasticity assessment' corresponds roughly to 'dynamic assessment' in the sense of Grigorenko and Sternberg (1998); Lidz and Elliot (2000) summarize learning potential assessment and learning tests under 'dynamic assessment'. Table 1 highlights differences between the approaches in disciplinary origin as well as their primary thematic, theoretical and methodological orientations. In general, however, the commonalities between them probably outweigh their differences.

LEARNING POTENTIAL ASSESSMENT

Probably the best known assessment of cognitive plasticity derives from Vygotsky's (1962) determination of the zone of proximal development. According to Vygotsky, learning is to be structured so that a higher state of intellectual

Table 1. Three approaches to cognitive plasticity assessment

Approach	Learning potential assessment	Learning tests	Cognitive engineering
Origin	Educational psychology	Differential psychology	Cognitive psychology
Focus	Remediation of specific learning deficits	Dynamic assessment of psychometric intelligence	Acquisition of expertise in narrowly defined skill
Theory	Zone of proximal development, direct and mediated learning	Zone of proximal development, complexity of information	Skill assembly, deliberate practice, tailored learning
Method	Psychometric tests	(Psychometric) Learning tests	Laboratory experiments
References	Feuerstein (1979)	Budoff (1987)	Kliegl & Baltes (1987)
	F.-Ballesteros & Calero (2000)	Guthke & Wiedl (1996)	Kliegl et al. (2000)

potential is reached, a further development of the child is initiated from the point of current ability (i.e. zone of actual development) to a state that encompasses skills not in the current cognitive repertoire but within reach, given an appropriate instructional and social setting (i.e. zone of proximal development). Such a change in cognitive structures causes not only a performance increase at the time when the programme is administered but facilitates also future cognitive development. In the end, children and adolescents should be enabled to initiate and control their own learning activities; they should learn to learn. This thought set up a line of research exemplified by Feuerstein's (1979) learning potential assessment device (LPAD) and, in a methodologically refined way, Fernández-Ballesteros and Calero's (2000) 'Evaluación del Potencial de Aprendizaje' (EPA). Development and modification of cognitive structures are determined by two types of learning (aside from physiological preconditions): direct and mediated learning experience (MLE). MLE is critical for the modification of cognitive structures. Mediators (e.g. parents and/or especially teachers) orient and organize the child's phenomenological world by selecting, structuring and focusing learning experiences and by providing feedback.

The LPAD was applied primarily to identify and overcome specific learning disabilities in children and adolescents; the EPA has been applied to persons ranging in age from 12 to 90 years and varying widely in psychometric intelligence. Starting point of an intervention is the determination of the objective state and of the causes of learning deficits with the help of psychometric tests such as WISC-R or Raven. Subsequently, a set of tasks is assembled in a standardized training programme that is adjusted to the individual child's strengths and weaknesses. The intervention starts with simple tasks derived from psychometric tests and in the course of practice tasks of increasing complexity and novelty are introduced. Feuerstein assumed that practice with verbal, numerical, figural, and spatial tasks leads to an improvement in basic cognitive processes (e.g. analogical reasoning, categorization, deductive thinking). The effectiveness of LPAD has been claimed repeatedly for children with learning disabilities and deaf children but various authors have criticized the

eclectic, non-theoretic construction of tasks. EPA training significantly improves Raven scores and appears to be stable over time.

LEARNING TESTS

Proponents of learning tests (Budoff, 1987; Guthke & Wiedl, 1996) focus the psychometric quality of learning-test indicators to establish the added value of direct observation in learning tests over the indirectly inferred contribution of state measures. Furthermore, they are trying to link individual learning potential to the effects of standardized learning cues. Theoretically, the learning-test concept can also be traced to Vygotsky's (1962) theory about a zone of proximal development.

Learning tests are implemented in a pretest–instruction/practice–post-test design. During the first phase of a long-term learning test (e.g. Raven Learning Potential Test, RLPT, Budoff, 1987) baseline performance is determined with an intelligence test. During post-test either the pretest tasks are repeated or a parallel form is administered. Variations of test items are used to check transfer gradients. Post-test results are interpreted as the outcome of learning potential testing. Learning tests differ in the extent of the instruction/practice phase which can be quite extensive, including coaching to higher levels of performance with examples, explanations, demonstration of solution strategies or metacognitive cues. Obviously, such long-term learning tests may not be economical enough for practical settings. Consequently, much effort has been invested in the development of short-term learning tests in which the instruction and practice phase is embedded in the test procedure with the aim to extract indicators of learning potential within a single session. Accordingly, the tester still povides simple feedback and solution cues and varies item difficulty as required by the subject's performance.

There have been some encouraging results from the learning test approach compared to standard IQ tests. Construct validity is indicated by a reduction of individual differences in children that are linked to their social and ethnic backgrounds and of the influence of qualitative differences in school settings. Also emotional–motivational stress is lower in learning tests. With an adaptive computer-based intelligence learning test battery

(Guthke et al., 1995) it is possible to monitor and document not only progress by learning but also the learning process itself (i.e. individual learning trajectories, individual strengths and weaknesses). Moreover, this approach goes beyond earlier diagnostic procedures because (1) test construction was guided by a theory of information complexity, (2) a description of the inherent processing demands is available for the complete battery, and (3) item selection is graded by difficulty leading from simple to complex items. Finally, a systematic process of the learner is promoted by continuous feedback and error-related cues.

COGNITIVE ENGINEERING

The third approach to cognitive plasticity assessment, cognitive engineering, originates in developmental and cognitive learning theory (Baltes & Kliegl, 1992; Kliegl & Baltes, 1987; Kliegl et al., 2000). The guiding idea of this approach has been that the best estimate of learning potential in a narrowly defined cognitive skill (e.g. memory for digits) is reflected in the performance of experts (i.e. mnemonists). Such expert performances are well understood in the context of cognitive learning theory; the required declarative and procedural knowledge can be developed and practised under laboratory conditions. Using these performance levels as benchmarks one can check to what degree 'normal' individuals can approximate such expert levels of performance. Moreover, acquisition of cognitive skills follows the power law of practice. Therefore individual differences in asymptotic performance of a skill can be used as indicators of limits of learning potential relative to a given theory-based implementation of the cognitive skill in question. Unfortunately, there have been only a few cognitive engineering studies. These studies compared young and old adults with respect to various mnemonic skills for digits, words, or face–name associations. They have led to very clear evidence documenting the learning potential of healthy and mentally fit older adults (e.g. a 70-year-old woman remembering well over 100 random digits; Kliegl & Baltes, 1987) as well as a remarkable inability of the same type of older adults to improve on learning new face–name associations (Kliegl et al., 2000).

Laboratory-based acquisition of cognitive skill is referred to as cognitive engineering and comprises three major components: skill assembly, deliberate practice, and tailored learning.

Skill assembly. Skill assembly refers to the programme part where a qualitatively different organization of behaviour is implemented, that is one that allows to circumvent general constraints of cognition or intelligence (e.g. using mental imagery rather than rehearsal to memorize verbal information). Consequently, according to this perspective, expertise is not primarily a function of normal intelligence and cannot be achieved by practising and automatizing the normal routines already available in the behavioural repertoire. This perspective is also compatible with limited transfer to tasks outside the domain of expertise.

Deliberate practice. The need for deliberate practice as an essential component of a skill acquisition programme recognizes that high levels of performance are tied to specific training schedules with attention to effort, intensity, and motivation (Ericsson et al., 1993). Effort can be quantified as the number of hours devoted to skill acquisition. Intensity aspects (i.e. focus and concentration) are operationalized in detailed feedback, ideally provided by a master coach in individualized training regimes. Finally, a high level of motivation is a precondition to subject oneself to strenuous training regimes required for achieving expert-like performance levels.

Tailored learning. The question as to how one can sustain the high level of motivation is critically tied up with the implementation and features of practice programmes. In general, the goal must be to avoid both boredom, due to lack of challenge, and frustration, due to task conditions that are simply too difficult for a given level of the skill to be acquired. Most of these problems can be handled with computerized training programs that keep track of the learning progress and adapt to the individual's level of performance. Interestingly, once established, testing a skill *beyond* its functional limits tends to induce compensatory strategies that allow the expert to maintain his or her high level of performance (Kliegl & Baltes, 1987). Such extension of an expertise is quite reminiscent of real-life examples where experts often exhibit a tendency to test the limits of their skill by extending it to new domains.

FUTURE PERSPECTIVES AND CONCLUSIONS

Dynamic testing and cognitive plasticity assessment have much appeal because they focus the highly attractive concept of learning potential. Unfortunately, neither have learning potential and learning test research so far convincingly demonstrated that they account for unique variance relative to static assessments (Grigorenko & Sternberg, 1998), nor has cognitive engineering been applied to a sufficiently large number of content domains to warrant an unqualified endorsement. Moreover, these approaches originate at very different conceptual starting points (i.e. the concept of psychometric intelligence and cognitive skill acquisition theory) and so far concern themselves with very different persons: children with learning disorders on the one hand and highly motivated, mentally very fit older adults on the other. Nevertheless, a future convergence of these approaches might be useful, if only because thinking about learning disorders from the perspective of cognitive expertise could open a new window on some old remediational problems.

References

Baltes, P.B. & Kliegl, R. (1992). Further testing of limits of cognitive plasticity: negative age differences in a mnemonic skill are robust. *Developmental Psychology, 28,* 121–125.

Budoff, M. (1987). Measures for assessing learning potential. In Lidz, C. (Ed.), *Dynamic Assessment* (pp. 173–195). New York: Guilford Press.

Ericsson, K.A., Krampe, R. Th. & Tesch-Roemer, C. (1993). The role of deliberate practice in the acquisition of expert performance. *Psychological Review, 100*(3), 363–406.

Fernández-Ballesteros, R. & Calero, M.D. (2000). The assessment of learning potential: the EPA instrument. In Lidz, C. & Elliot, J.G. (Eds.), *Dynamic Assessment: Prevailing Models and Applications in Advances in Cognition and Educational Practice,* Vol. 6 (pp. 293–323). Oxford: Elsevier Science.

Feuerstein, R. (1979). *The Dynamic Assessment of Retarded Performers.* Baltimore: University Park Press.

Grigorenko, E.L. & Sternberg, R.J. (1998). Dynamic Testing. *Psychological Bulletin, 124*(1), 75–111.

Guthke, J., Beckmann, J.F., Stein, H., Pillner, S. & Vahle, H. (1995). *Adaptive Computergestützte Intelligenzlerntestbatterie (ACIL).* Mödling: Dr. Schuhfried.

Guthke, J. & Wiedl, K.H. (1996). *Dynamisches Testen.* Göttingen: Hogrefe.

Kliegl, R. & Baltes, P.B. (1987). Theory-guided analysis of mechanisms of development and ageing through testing-the-limits and research on expertise. In Schooler, C. & Schaie, K.W. (Eds.), *Cognitive Functioning and Social Structure Over the Life Course* (pp. 95–119). Norwood, NJ: Ablex.

Kliegl, R., Philipp, D., Luckner, M. & Krampe, R. Th. (2000). Face memory skill acquisition. In Charness, N., Park, D.C. & Sabel, B.A. (Eds.), *Communication, Technology, and Aging* (pp.169–186). New York: Springer.

Lidz, C. & Elliot, J.G. (Eds.), *Dynamic Assessment: Prevailing Models and Applications in Advances in Cognition and Educational Practice,* Vol. 6. Oxford: Elsevier Science.

Vygotsky, L.S. (1962). *Thought and Language.* Cambridge, MA: MIT Press. (Original Russian work published in 1934.)

Reinhold Kliegl and Doris Philipp

RELATED ENTRIES

Dynamic Assessment (Learning Potential Testing, Testing the Limits), Cognitive Plasticity, Cognitive Decline/Impairment

COGNITIVE PROCESSES: CURRENT STATUS

INTRODUCTION

Cognitive process assessment is not a specific, universally agreed upon approach to assessment, but rather refers to a general orientation concerning mostly what kinds of knowledge, skills, and abilities ought to be assessed, and to a lesser extent perhaps, to how they ought to be assessed. Cognitive process assessment is often defined at least partly by what it is not – it is not 'behaviourism' and it is not 'psychometrics'. It is not behaviourism, because behaviourist approaches focus on observable behaviour, which can be recorded on checklists. In contrast, cognitive process approaches focus on internal thoughts, feelings, strategies, orientations, predispositions, and other attributes that can only be inferred, based on patterns of behaviour. It is not psychometrics, because psychometric approaches are typically driven by correlational findings rather than by theory. Psychometric approaches are characterized as primarily empirical, involving the administration of a variety of tests, followed by an exploratory factor analysis to identify test clusters, the analysis of which might reveal common processes underlying test performance. In comparison, cognitive processes assessment is said to be more theoretical based on our understanding from cognitive and brain science of how the mind works. These characterizations are, of course, often overstated and, in practice, the distinction between the approaches is frequently blurred, but there are differences in emphases.

COGNITIVE PROCESSING FRAMEWORKS

There are many models and theories of cognitive processes, but one useful distinction might be made between macro- and micro-theories, or between cognitive architectures (a macro-theory) and models of cognitive tasks (micro-theories). Much of the cognitive process work originated as micro-theories of particular tasks, such as the kinds of tasks that routinely appear in intelligence tests. For example, analyses have been conducted on inductive and deductive reasoning tasks, spatial relations tests, vocabulary tests, and so on. From this work, important concepts and distinctions emerged. Some examples are the differentiation between short-term, or working, memory and long-term memory, the distinction between declarative and procedural memory, the concept of automaticity, the distinction between imaginal and verbal processing, the delineation of stages of processing (e.g. apprehension, encoding, retrieval, decision, etc.). Other examples are the identification of task-specific strategies, the positing of metacognitive skills, such as planning, self-monitoring, and self-regulation, and many more. Also, from this work, we now know how to manipulate item difficulty levels on some tasks,

particularly the more arid ones found on intelligence tests. Such a capability has implications for item design and automatic item generation (see Irvine & Kyllonen, 2002; Kyllonen, 2002).

However, it was recognized, early on, that the micro-theory approach was severely limited, and that real progress would only be made when grander theories were attempted that incorporated what we know about cognition. Consequently, there have been several macro-theories of cognitive processes, formulated along these lines, including ACT-R (Anderson, 1993), SOAR (Newell, 1990), and EPIC (Kieras & Meyer, 1994). It is useful to note that these all contain some common elements. An important distinction, for example, in all is the one between the current focus of thought, and long-term memory, the current focus of thought usually being called 'working memory'. Another characteristic is the simultaneous-sequential distinction, in which some processes, such as vision, and memory retrieval, are assumed to be simultaneous, while others, such as problem solving, are assumed to be more deliberative, and sequential.

There have been some attempts to incorporate these grand cognitive architectures into theories of individual differences in cognition. For example, in the Cognitive Abilities Measurement (CAM) framework (e.g. Chaiken, Kyllonen & Tirre, 2000; Kyllonen, 1994), cognitive processing factors, such as working memory, processing speed, temporal processing, and declarative and procedural knowledge, and declarative and procedural learning, are crossed with verbal, spatial, and quantitative content to create a wide variety of cognitive processing tests. However, no operational intelligence test is actually based on the cognitive architectures. Instead, it seems that distinctions made in these theoretical frameworks, and in the micro-theories that have been developed, are reflected in particular item types appearing either in the research literature, or even in intelligence tests. For example, Sternberg et al. (2000) take advantage of the distinction made in the cognitive processing literature between explicit or declarative knowledge, and tacit or procedural knowledge, in their discussion of 'Practical intelligence' from which they have developed several experimental assessments.

There has been some merging of traditional conceptions of intelligence, based on factor-analytic studies, with the cognitive processes framework. The prototypical example is Carroll's (1993) taxonomy, which summarizes much of what is known about the structure of intelligence, from the correlational literature, based on a reanalysis of all known published studies of both conventional and cognitive process measures. Based on his findings, Carroll posited a three-stratum hierarchy, with a general factor at the top. Below this, at the second-stratum, are eight intermediate factors – fluid and crystallized ability, memory and learning, visual perception, auditory reception, retrieval ability, cognitive speediness, and decision speed. In turn, these second-stratum concepts are defined by more specific primary abilities, such as simple and choice reaction time, mental comparison time, and semantic processing speed. Importantly, several of the intermediate factors, and many of the specific abilities, such as the reaction time ones just listed, are essentially cognitive processing abilities.

COGNITIVE PROCESSING FRAMEWORKS AND PSYCHOLOGICAL ASSESSMENT

Perhaps the first intelligence test battery, suggested by Sir Francis Galton and later realized by the pioneer of the mental testing movement, James McKeen Cattell, might today be called a 'cognitive processing' battery. It was based on an idea of basic information-processing elements, and consisted of tests of discrimination, sensory judgement, memory, and reaction time. Interestingly, this approach was abandoned, in favour of Binet's alternative framework of sampling more complex tasks from the school curriculum, such as reading and problem solving. It is commonly thought that Galton's basic processes approach was a failure, yielding uncorrelated measures with poor reliabilities, in contrast with Binet's approach, which yielded tests with high validity against school outcomes. Recent re-analyses suggest that this may not have been a fair characterization of findings obtained under the Galtonian framework (Jensen, 1998). Nevertheless, Binet's approach was considered more fruitful, and traditional intelligence test batteries, such as the Wechsler, Kaufman, and Stanford–Binet scales, have worked primarily

within the Binet tradition, inserting some modifications, such as the distinction between verbal and performance IQ, to provide additional practical and clinical utility.

However, several contemporary intelligence tests have embraced cognitive processing notions. One example is Das, Naglieri, and Kirby's (1994) Cognitive Assessment System (CAS), based on their Planning, Attention, Simultaneous, Successive (PASS) theory. The CAS battery consists of tests of each of the PASS factors, planning (e.g. find two numbers that are the same), attention (e.g. underline pairs that match), simultaneous processing (e.g. figure memory), and successive processing (e.g. repeat strings of words in order). The theoretical underpinning of the battery may be superfluous, or even wrong (Kranzler & Keith, 1999), but at least the intention behind the battery is to use tasks to identify cognitive processes.

Another contemporary intelligence test that has done so is the Woodcock–Johnson III (WJIII; Woodcock, McGrew & Mather, 2001). This test battery has the additional virtue of being neatly aligned with the contemporary consensus view of the hierarchical structure of the intellect, as exemplified by the Carroll (1993) taxonomy, noted above. The WJIII consists of numerous tests of cognitive processes, including attention, working memory, and executive processes. In addition, it measures fluid and crystallized intelligence, and many of the higher-order (or second-stratum) factors of the Carroll (and closely related Horn–Cattell) framework, such as processing speed, short-term memory, long-term retrieval, and auditory processing, use tests such as visual matching, decision speed, auditory working memory, retrieval fluency, and so forth.

FUTURE PERSPECTIVES

Current intelligence tests are paper-and-pencil measures. The precise measurement of many cognitive processes, enacted within fractions of a second, is virtually impossible. For this reason, perhaps, the range of commercially available, standardized intelligence tests attempting to assess disparate cognitive processing constructs has been restricted. Intelligence testing is likely to move toward assessment of cognitive processing constructs both for improved construct validity, and for more potentially meaningful diagnosis and re-mediation of cognitive impairments. Measuring an increased range of cognitive processes is possible through the implementation of computer and web technologies, more automated, real-time data capture and analyses, item-generative procedures, and advances in statistical techniques such as item-response theory and structural equation modelling.

Attempts to measure some cognitive processing constructs using paper-and-pencil methodologies are likely to be not very accurate. The correlation between paper-and-pencil measures of processing speed and speed of response in a computerized test has often been found to be low (Van de Vijver & Harsveld, 1994). And parameters other than total response time, such variability, slope, and intercept – which are impossible to measure with paper-and-pencil – may be important (Jensen, 1998). Paper-and-pencil attempts to measure processing speed may include a host of extraneous variables (e.g. handwriting speed, memory for stimuli, reading speed), which may be reduced, measured, or otherwise eliminated under the controlled conditions afforded through computerized testing.

A cognitive processes approach also promises to identify new forms of intelligence that have proven difficult to assess using traditional psychometric procedures. For example, the concept of emotional intelligence (EI), which reflects the individual's propensity for perceiving, assimilating, understanding, and managing one's own (and others') emotions, to date, has been assessed using either self-report or consensual techniques. Both procedures are problematic (see Matthews, Zeidner & Roberts, 2003). However, a number of experimental paradigms assess the basic cognitive processing routines associated with stimuli that provoke emotions. For example, the Emotional Stroop task measures diversion of attention from naming the ink-colour of words onto the emotional meanings of the words. No systematic attempts have yet been made to use these particularly sensitive instruments in the research on EI. Cognitive processing tasks of this nature provide an opportunity for the development of objective indices of various factors of emotional intelligence and a robust construct validation methodology. Moreover, these types of task may provide precisely controlled conditions whereby explanatory models of EI may be tested, refined, or otherwise developed.

CONCLUSIONS

Cognitive processes assessment has its roots in Galton's basic process ideas, but its more recent revival in the last decades of the twentieth century might be seen as a reaction to the predominant behavioural and psychometric approaches to assessment in education, industry, and clinical practice. Initially, cognitive processes assessment was seen as a stark alternative to the dominance of psychometric frameworks. But with the publication of Carroll's (1993) taxonomy, which placed cognitive processes within a hierarchical model of abilities, a synthesis between the schools of thought has emerged. The widespread acceptance of Carroll's framework, at least in a general sense, within the field of intelligence research, suggests that cognitive processes assessment is now part of the mainstream. Attempts to follow this model in the development of commercially available intelligence test batteries, as seen currently in the Woodcock–Johnson III battery, are likely to continue. In addition, advances in technology, such as computerized and web testing, and the extension of cognitive processing notions into the realm of social and emotional behaviour, promise significant expansion and development in cognitive processes assessment.

References

Anderson, J.R. (1993). *Rules of the Mind*. Hillsdale, NJ: Lawrence Erlbaum Associates.

Carroll, J.B. (1993). *Human Cognitive Abilities: A Survey of Factor-Analytic Studies*. Cambridge, UK: Cambridge University Press.

Chaiken, S.R., Kyllonen, P.C. & Tirre, W.C. (2000). Organization and components of psychomotor ability. *Cognitive Psychology*, 40, 198–226.

Das, J.P., Naglieri, J.A. & Kirby, J.R. (1994). *Assessment of Cognitive Processes: The PASS Theory of Intelligence*. New York: Allyn & Bacon.

Irvine, S. & Kyllonen, P.C. (Eds.), (2002). *Generating Items for Cognitive Tests: Theory and Practice*. Mahwah, NJ: Lawrence Erlbaum Associates.

Jensen, A.R. (1998). *The g factor: The Science of Mental Ability*. Westport, CT: Praeger Publishers.

Kieras, D.E. & Meyer, D.E. (1994). *The EPIC Architecture for Modelling Human Information-Processing and Performance: A Brief Introduction* (EPIC Technical Report No. 1, TR-94/ONR-EPIC-1). Ann Arbor: University of Michigan, Department of Electrical Engineering and Computer Science.

Kranzler, J.H. & Keith, T.Z. (1999). Independent confirmatory factor analysis of the Cognitive

Assessment System (CAS): What does the CAS measure? *School Psychology Review*, 28, 117–144.

Kyllonen, P.C. (1994). CAM: a theoretical framework for cognitive abilities measurement. In Detterman, D.K. (Ed.), *Current Topics in Human Intelligence*. Vol. 4, *Theories of Intelligence* (pp. 307–359). Norwood, NJ: Ablex.

Kyllonen, P.C. (2002). Developments in test design. In Fernández-Ballesteros, R. et al., *Encyclopedia of Psychological Assessment* pp. 237–241. London: Sage.

Matthews, G., Zeidner, M. & Roberts, R.D. (2003). *Emotional Intelligence: Science and Myth*. Cambridge, MA: MIT Press.

Newell, A. (1990). *Unified Theories of Cognition*. Cambridge, MA: Harvard University Press.

Sternberg, R.J., Forsythe, G.B., Hedlund, J., Horvath, J., Snook, S., Williams, W.M., Wagner, R.K. & Grigorenko, E.L. (2000). *Practical Intelligence*. New York: Cambridge University Press.

Van de Vijver, F.J.R. & Harsveld, M. (1994). The incomplete equivalence of the paper-and-pencil and computerized versions of the General Aptitude Test Battery. *Journal of Applied Psychology*, 79, 852–859.

Woodcock, R., McGrew, K. & Mather, N. (2001). *Woodcock–Johnson III Complete Battery*. Chicago, IL: Riverside.

Patrick C. Kyllonen and Richard D. Roberts

RELATED ENTRIES

Cognitive Processes: Historical Perspective, Cognitive Styles, Theoretical Perspective: Cognitive

C COGNITIVE PROCESSES: HISTORICAL PERSPECTIVE

INTRODUCTION

Cognitive processes range from the most basic (such as simple reaction time, choice reaction time, letter comparisons, and so on) to the most complex forms of human cognition (such as planning, attention, reasoning, and memory). Numerous attempts have been made to operationalize measurement of cognitive processes – indeed, process measures are prominent among the individual scales of most omnibus intellectual ability tests. However, the identification of individual differences in specific cognitive processes has been fraught with difficulties, due to two major factors. The first factor is that tests of cognitive processes tend to be correlated with one another. The second factor is that the content of the test items also determines individual differences in test performance, sometimes to a much greater degree than the underlying processes. The history of cognitive process assessment is described, and a brief review of contemporary issues and problems is presented.

In the hundred or so years of modern psychological assessment, there has been substantial interest in the efficient, reliable, and valid assessment of cognitive processes. The list of cognitive processes considered for assessment range from the most basic sensory and perceptual activities (such as brightness discrimination, and differential weight judgements) through to the most complex activities (such as analogical reasoning and creativity). A comprehensive list of cognitive processes studied through individual-differences assessments would include nearly all of the tasks studied by experimental psychologists concerned with discovering fundamental building blocks for mental life, and additional processes that are mostly of interest to differential psychologists.

EARLY ASSESSMENTS OF COGNITIVE PROCESSES

In a classic *Manual of Mental and Physical Tests*, Whipple (1910/1914) divided the range of mental assessments into two broad categories, simpler processes and complex processes. For the simpler tests, Whipple listed sensory tests (e.g. colour blindness, discrimination of pitch, discrimination of lifted weights), and tests of attention and perception. Some of these tests were apparatus tests, while others were the kinds of paper and pencil tests familiar to modern psychologists. Measurement of 'visual apprehension' – that is, how many objects can be perceived in a brief presentation – was administered with a tachistoscope, an instrument that could be adjusted to provide only the briefest exposure of the stimuli to the examinee. Tests of attention included cancellation tests (of which the modern Symbol–Digit test is an exemplar), simultaneous adding, and counting dots. Complex tests described by Whipple included tests of description, association, suggestibility, imagination, and intellectual ability. While one might argue that intellectual ability is not a cognitive 'process' per se, Binet's method for assessment of intellect was specifically predicated on an amalgamation of several different cognitive processes, such as recognition and recall forms of memory, visual and tactile judgements, and spatial visualization, among other processes (e.g. see Binet–Simon, 1905/1973). Even though the Binet–Simon scales are themselves measures of cognitive processes, people traditionally think of the Binet–Simon and more recent tests as intelligence tests, mainly because the Binet–Simon test yields a single amalgamated score (Mental Age), even though it is possible to examine the individual cognitive processes scale scores.

The Binet–Simon scales illustrate one of the most important characteristics of cognitive processes assessments. This characteristic is called 'positive manifold' – and it refers to the nearly universal property of mental assessments that they are positively intercorrelated. That is, in any large sample of examinees and cognitive process measures, an intercorrelation matrix of the measures will show positive correlations throughout the matrix. In simple terms, this means that all cognitive assessments tend to share some variance – individuals who perform well on one cognitive process assessment will also tend to perform better than average on another cognitive process assessment, *even though the measures may seem to assess theoretically and practically different cognitive processes*. This property of cognitive process assessments made it possible for Binet and Simon to develop a coherent and comprehensive assessment of intelligence. Because the individual cognitive process scales were themselves positively and often substantially correlated, aggregation of the separate measures resulted in a diminution of scale-specific variance contributions, and an accentuation of the general intellectual ability, common to the specific process measures. The result was a robust measure that could be well-replicated with a wide variety of instruments, as long as there was a broad sampling of the underlying cognitive processes assessed.

This positive manifold characteristic of cognitive process assessments was also one of the major justifications for Spearman's (1904) theory of general intelligence. In Spearman's formulation, the positive correlations among cognitive assessments were said to be a result of their shared loading on a general factor of intelligence, called g. This g factor was proposed to be involved in determining individual differences in all cognitive assessments, though to a greater or lesser degree in each assessment, depending on the specific cognitive processes tapped by the assessment instrument. Later developments in theory and in statistical procedures from the 1910s to the 1950s resulted in suggestions that something more than a single general (g) factor was responsible for the common variance among cognitive process measures. In addition to a general factor, several investigators found broad content factors, which represent the type of material used in the assessments – such as spatial (or figural), verbal, and numerical contents. Assessment instruments that share the same item content tend to have higher correlations with one another than instruments with different item content. This finding holds sometimes even when instruments are believed to assess the same underlying cognitive processes. Thus, a test of verbal reasoning may have a higher correlation with a test of vocabulary than it does with a test of spatial reasoning. Such a result substantially complicates the identification of a test as assessing a single kind of cognitive processing, because the content may make a larger contribution than the process to the rank ordering of individuals in their test performance.

COGNITIVE PROCESSES AND DIFFERENTIAL APTITUDE ASSESSMENTS

From the late 1930s to the early 1970s, substantial effort was devoted toward the development of cognitive assessments that were diagnostic of particular cognitive processes. For example, Thurstone's (1938) theory of Primary Mental Abilities included assessments of the cognitive processes of Memory, Inductive Reasoning, Perception, Space, Verbal Meaning, Word Fluency, and Perceptual Speed. The hope for measures based on this theory was that a battery of such scales could reveal the relative strengths and weaknesses of an individual's cognitive processes. By extending Thurstone's framework, Guilford's (1967) taxonomy of 120 different abilities was perhaps the first explicit representation of a wide array of cognitive processes that were believed to constitute intelligence. Guilford identified operations of: cognition, memory, divergent production (prominent in creative activity), convergent production, and evaluation, along with describing a variety of different contents and products. Exploration of cognitive process assessments by Guilford and his colleagues found mixed success. In the area of creativity, many specific instruments were created that assessed divergent production processes with particular combinations of item contents and item products. However, many of these and other cognitive process tests developed by these investigators remain useful mostly for research purposes, and have generally failed to demonstrate substantial validity for application purposes, such as selection, training, and counselling (that is, over and above general cognitive/intellectual ability batteries).

INFORMATION PROCESSING AND INDIVIDUAL DIFFERENCES ASSESSMENTS

Until the 1970s most attempts to develop assessment instruments for cognitive processes were undertaken by a rational approach (such as Guilford's). Starting in the mid-1970s with work by Hunt, Frost and Lunneborg (1973), several investigators attempted to assess individual differences in tasks designed by experimental psychologists of basic information processing. From an experimental psychology perspective, such tasks were viewed as powerful paradigms for identification of the building blocks of cognitive processes. Tasks such as memory scanning, letter matching, colour naming, and others were used for testing competing models of memory, inhibition, lexical access, and other cognitive processes. Similarly, tests inspired by the Donders' subtraction technique (simple reaction time and choice reaction time) were examined to determine whether efficient, reliable and valid assessments of individual differences could be obtained. Carroll (1980; see also Carroll, 1993), for example, prepared a taxonomic representation of basic information processing tasks. Throughout the late 1970s and 1980s, many studies were conducted in this

framework, yielding a variety of claims that the fundamental cognitive processes underlying intelligence could be identified and measured. Some investigators, such as Jensen (1998), claimed that assessments of individual differences in the rate of information acquisition (measured as the slope of an equation relating reaction time to the number of bits of information in a display) were substantially related to general intelligence. Other investigators focused on tasks like the inspection time paradigm (which involves line-length judgements with very brief stimulus presentations).

A few of these basic information processing tasks, however, have made it into the realm of operational assessments. One notable exception is the framework by Das, Naglieri, and their colleagues and his colleagues, called PASS for planning, attention, simultaneous, and successive processing. Their framework has been incorporated into a testing instrument, called the Das–Naglieri Cognitive Assessment Systems (for a description, see Naglieri, 1997). Although the test is a recently developed product, there are several sources of empirical data on the validity of the individual scales and the omnibus intelligence scale from the test. There is considerable disagreement in the academic and practice community, however, as to whether these scales provide sufficiently differential diagnostic information (i.e. that requires low intercorrelations among the scales), or that the information obtained from the scales is demonstrably different from that obtained from the traditional Binet and Wechsler scales. Substantial correlations appear to be obtained from the aggregated scales and the traditional IQ measures, a finding that is consistent with the discussion above regarding the positive manifold found in cognitive process assessments.

FUTURE PERSPECTIVES AND CONCLUSIONS

Assessment of cognitive processes is a tradition that stretches back to the early days of modern assessment. The intelligence scales developed by Binet and his colleagues were themselves predicated on both theoretical and empirical foundations. Research conducted in the subsequent decades has demonstrated that such process measures are an integral part of any broad intellectual ability assessment system. Nonetheless, attempts at developing assessments of cognitive processes, in isolation, have largely failed to be useful for applications purposes, partly because of substantial common variance with assessments of other cognitive processes (i.e. positive manifold), and partly because the content of the assessment instruments (such as verbal, spatial, or numerical content) play a much larger role in determining the rank ordering of individuals than do the underlying theoretical cognitive processes. For most intents and purposes, psychometric instruments that sample widely among numerous processes and contents have been found to have greater validity for real-world applications. Cognitive process assessments have found utility mostly in the domain of laboratory research, and only limited success in those environments. Future investigations might usefully focus on those abilities that show reliable and valid assessments, but that are generally distant from general intelligence. Most prominent among such cognitive process assessments are perceptual speed abilities, such as scanning, memory, and pattern recognition (Ackerman & Cianciolo, 2000). Such process assessments tend to correlate much less with the general and content abilities, partly because they use simple or uniform stimuli, rather than complex stimuli. In addition, such measures have been found to be useful predictors of skilled performance, especially for tasks that have substantial demands on speed of processing for high levels of performance.

References

Ackerman, P.L. & Cianciolo, A.T. (2000). Cognitive, perceptual speed, and psychomotor determinants of individual differences during skill acquisition. *Journal of Experimental Psychology: Applied*, 6, 259–290.

Binet, A. & Simon, T. (1905/1973). New methods for the diagnosis of the intellectual level of subnormals. *L'Année Psychologique*, *13*, 191–244. Translated by Kite, E. and reprinted in: *The Development of Intelligence in Children*. New York: Arno Press.

Carroll, J.B. (1980). *Individual Difference Relations in Psychometric and Experimental Cognitive Tasks*, (Tech. Rep. No. 163). Chapel Hill: University of North Carolina, The L.L. Thurstone Psychometric Laboratory.

Carroll, J.B. (1993). *Human Cognitive Abilities* (Chapter 16, pp. 631–655). New York: Cambridge University Press.

Guilford, J.P. (1967). *The Nature of Human Intelligence*. New York: McGraw-Hill.

Hunt, E., Frost, N. & Lunneborg, C. (1973). Individual differences in cognition: a new approach to intelligence. In Bower, G. (Ed.), *Advances in Learning and Motivation*, Vol. 7 (pp. 87–122). New York: Academic Press.

Jensen, A.R. (1998). *The g Factor: The Science of Mental Ability*. Westport, CT: Praeger.

Naglieri, J.A. (1997). Planning, attention, simultaneous and successive theory and the cognitive assessment system: a new theory-based measure of intelligence. In Flanagan, D.P., Genshaft, J.L. & Harrison, P.L. (Eds.), *Contemporary Intellectual Assessment: Theories, Tests, and Issues* (pp. 247–267). New York: Guilford Press.

Spearman, C. (1904). 'General intelligence,' objectively determined and measured. *American Journal of Psychology*, *15*, 201–293.

Thurstone, L.L. (1938). Primary mental abilities. *Psychometric Monographs*, *1*, 1–121.

Whipple, G.M. (1910/1914). *Manual of Mental and Physical Tests. Part 1: Simpler Processes; Part 2: Complex Processes* (2nd ed.). Baltimore: Warwick & York.

Phillip L. Ackerman

RELATED ENTRIES

COGNITIVE PSYCHOLOGY AND ASSESSMENT PRACTICES

INTRODUCTION

An assessment is a tool designed to observe a person's behaviour and produce data that can be used to draw inferences concerning some characteristic of that person, such as what the person knows, or feels, or believes (the 'construct'). This process of reasoning from evidence

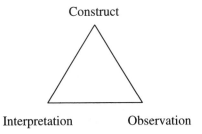

Figure 1.   The assessment triangle.

(i.e. the data) can be portrayed as an *assessment triangle*. As shown in Figure 1, the vertices of the triangle represent the three key elements underlying any assessment: (a) a model of the *person construct*; (b) a set of beliefs about the kinds of *observations* that will provide evidence about the construct; and (c) an *interpretation* process for making sense of the evidence (NRC, 2001). An assessment cannot be designed and implemented without some consideration of each of these three elements. The three are represented as vertices of a triangle because each is connected to and dependent on the other two. Thus, for an assessment to be effective, the three elements must be in synchrony. The assessment triangle provides a useful framework for analysing current assessments or designing future assessments.

Given this framework then, the essential relationship between cognitive psychology and assessment is that, for many of the constructs that we wish to assess, the source of that construct will be a theory from the area of cognitive psychology. Moreover, the research that was the basis for that theory will oftentimes include instrument development that will also be the basis for the design of the assessment items. Unfortunately, there are constructs of a cognitive nature that one might like to assess that have not been thoroughly investigated within cognitive psychology. In that case, the assessment instrument developer must take on the role of cognitive psychologist as part of instrument development.

The following paragraphs are structured as: (a) a survey of recent advances in cognitive psychology, (b) commentary on their relevance to assessment, (c) a discussion of the situative perspective on cognitive psychology and its implications for assessment, and finally (d), as a conclusion, a discussion of future perspectives.

THE COGNITIVE PERSPECTIVE

The theories of cognitive psychology are built up to explain how people develop knowledge structures, such as the ideas associated with a certain domain of knowledge or a subject matter discipline, and ways of reasoning and problem-solving. The discipline of cognitive psychology seeks to understand how knowledge is encoded, stored, organized, and retrieved, and how different types of internal representations are created as people learn about a concept (NRC, 1999). One major principle of cognitive theory is that learners actively construct their understanding by trying to connect new data with their existing knowledge.

To cognitive psychologists, *knowing* is not merely the accumulation of factual information and routine procedures. Knowing means being able to combine knowledge, skills, and procedures in ways that are useful for interpreting new situations and solving problems. Thus, assessment of cognitive constructs should not overemphasize basic information and skills – these should be seen as resources for more meaningful activities. As Wiggins (1989) points out, children learn a sport not just by practising the component skills (e.g. in soccer, dribbling, passing, and shooting), but also by actually playing the sport.

While the earlier differential (Carroll, 1993) and behaviourist (Skinner, 1938) approaches focused on the extent of knowledge possessed by a person, cognitive theory has emphasized what sort of knowledge a person has. Thus, from a cognitive perspective, one must not only assess *how much* people know, but also assess how, when, and whether they *use* what they know. From this perspective, traditional tests, which usually record how many items examinees answer correctly or incorrectly, fall short. What is needed is data about how they reach those answers and/or how well they understand the underlying concepts. For this, more complex tasks are required that reveal information about thinking strategies, and growth in understanding over time.

IMPLICATIONS FOR ASSESSMENT

Cognitive psychology theories focus on the way knowledge is represented, organized, and processed in the mind (NRC, 1999). Consideration is also given to social dimensions of learning, including social and participatory practices that support knowing and understanding (Anderson et al., 2000). The implication is that assessment practices need to include the more complex aspects of cognition as well as component skills and discrete bits of knowledge.

The mind's cognitive structure includes short-term (or working) memory, a very limited system, and long-term memory, an almost limitless store of knowledge (Baddeley, 1986). In many contexts, what is most important is how well the person can utilize the knowledge stored in long-term memory and use it to reason efficiently about current information and problems. The contents of long-term memory include both general and specific knowledge, but much of what a person knows is domain- and task-specific and is organized into structures known as schemas (e.g. Cheng & Holyoak, 1985). Thus, assessments should evaluate what schemas an individual has and under what circumstances the person regards the information as important. This evaluation should include how a person organizes acquired information, encompassing both strategies for problem-solving and ways of chunking relevant information into workable units.

Studies of expert–novice differences in subject domains illuminate critical features of knowledge structures that should be the targets for assessment. Experts in a subject domain typically organize factual and procedural knowledge into schemas that support pattern recognition and the rapid retrieval and application of knowledge (Chi et al., 1982).

Metacognition – the process of reflecting on and directing one's own thinking – is one of the most important aspects of cognition (Newell, 1990). It is crucial to effective thinking and problem solving and is one of the principal features of expertise in specific areas of knowledge and skill. Experts use metacognitive strategies for monitoring understanding during problem-solving and for performing self-correction (Hatano, 1990). The implication here is that assessments should seek to determine whether an individual has good metacognitive skills.

People learn in different ways and follow different paths to mastery. The growth process is not a uniform progression, nor is there invariant change from erroneous to optimal solution strategies – but, a person's problem-solving strategies do become more effective over time and with practice (Siegler, 1998). The implication of this is that assessments should focus on identifying the range of strategies that are being used for problem solving, giving particular consideration to where those strategies fall on a developmental continuum of efficiency and suitability for a particular domain of knowledge and skill.

People have rich intuitive knowledge of their world that undergoes significant alteration as they mature and change. Learning entails the transformation of naïve understanding into more complete and accurate comprehension, and assessment can be used as a tool to facilitate this process (Case, 1992). Thus, assessments should focus on making people's thinking visible to both the assessor and, where appropriate, to the person under assessment. This way useful strategies can be selected to support an appropriate course for future growth.

Practice and feedback are crucial aspects of the development of skills and expertise (Rosenbloom & Newell, 1987). Thus, timely and informative feedback to a person during instruction and learning is one of the most important roles for assessment, ensuring that their practice of a skill and its subsequent acquisition will be effective and efficient.

Knowledge often develops in a highly contextualized and inflexible form, and hence does not transfer very effectively. The possibility of transfer is dependent on the development of an explicit understanding of when to apply what has been learned (Bassok & Holyoak, 1989). When assessing achievement, then, the assessor needs to consider the pre-requisite knowledge and skills needed to answer a question or solve a problem, including the context in which it is presented, and whether an assessment task or situation is functioning as a test of near, far, or zero transfer.

THE SITUATIVE PERSPECTIVE AND ITS IMPLICATIONS FOR ASSESSMENT

The situative, or sociocultural, perspective was, in part, prompted by concerns with the cognitive perspective's almost exclusive focus on the thinking of the individual. Instead, the situative perspective describes behaviour at a different level of analysis, one oriented toward practical activity and context. Here, 'context' refers to engagement in particular forms of practice within particular communities. (A community can be any purposeful group, large or small, from the global society of professional archaeologists to a local swimming club or classroom.) In these accounts, the fundamental unit of analysis is *mediated activity*, a person or group's activity mediated by cultural artefacts, like tools and language (Wertsch, 1998). In this view, one learns to participate in the practices, goals, and habits of mind of a particular community.

One of the prime features of this approach is attention to the artefacts generated and used by people to shape the nature of cognitive activity. From a traditional cognitive perspective, physics is a particular knowledge structure – from the situative perspective of mediated activity, working in a physics laboratory is also strongly dependent on the participants' abilities to collaborate in such activities as formulating and understanding questions and problems (Ochs et al., 1994).

The situated perspective proposes that every assessment is, at least in part, a measure of the degree to which one can participate in a form of practice. From this perspective, filling in a Likert scale is a form of practice. There will be some students who, by virtue of their histories, inclinations, or simple interests, will be better prepared than others to participate effectively in this practice. Hence, simple assumptions about these or any other forms of assessment as indicators of knowledge must be examined.

Discourse and interaction with others is the basis of much of what humans learn. Thus, knowledge is often embedded in particular social and cultural contexts, including the context of the assessments themselves, and it encompasses understandings about the meaning of specific practices such as question asking and answering. The implication is that assessments need to examine how well students engage in communicative practices appropriate to a domain of knowledge and skill, what they understand about those practices, and how well they use the tools appropriate to that domain.

FUTURE PERSPECTIVES AND CONCLUSIONS

From the perspective outlined above, one can see that models of cognition and learning provide a basis for the design and implementation of theory-driven assessment practices. Such programmes and practices already exist and have been used productively in certain areas (e.g. Hunt & Minstrell, 1996; Marshall, 1995; White & Frederiksen, 1998; Wilson & Sloane, 2000). However, the vast majority of what is known has yet to be applied to the design of assessments for classroom or external evaluation purposes, and there are many subject areas where the cognitive foundations are not yet established. Therefore, further work is needed to utilize what is already known within cognitive science in assessment practice, as well as to develop additional cognitive analyses of domain-specific knowledge and expertise.

Many highly effective tools exist for probing and modelling a person's knowledge and for examining the contents and contexts of learning (such as reaction-time studies, computational modelling, analysis of protocols, microgenetic analysis, and ethnographic analysis – see NRC, 2001). The methods used in cognitive science to design tasks, observe and analyse cognition, and draw inferences about what a person knows are applicable to many of the challenges of designing effective assessments.

Contemporary assessment practices are, in general, not in concert with the situative perspective. There is good evidence to expect that someone's performance in an abstract assessment situation will not accurately reflect how well they would participate in organized, cumulative activities that may hold greater meaning for them. From the situative standpoint, assessment means observing and analysing how students use knowledge, skills, and processes to participate in the real work of a community. For example, to assess performance in science, one might look at how productively students find and use information resources; how clearly they formulate and support arguments and hypotheses; how well they initiate, explain, and discuss in a group; and whether they apply their conceptual knowledge and skills according to the standards of the discipline.

Acknowledgement

Much of the material in this entry is based on the report of the US National Research Council's Committee on the Foundations of Assessment (NRC, 2001), of which the author was honoured to be a member.

References

Anderson, J.R., Greeno, J.G., Reder, L.M. & Simon, H.A. (2000). Perspectives on learning, thinking, and activity. *Educational Researcher*, 29(4), 11–13.

Baddeley, A. (1986). *Working Memory*. Oxford: Clarendon Press/Oxford University Press.

Bassok, M. & Holyoak, K.J. (1989). Interdomain transfer between isomorphic topics in algebra and physics. *Journal of Experimental Psychology: Memory, Learning, and Cognition*, 15(1), 153–166.

Carroll, J.B. (1993). *Human Cognitive Abilities*. Cambridge: Cambridge University Press.

Case, R. (1992). *The Mind's Staircase: Exploring the Conceptual Underpinnings of Children's Thought and Knowledge*. Hillsdale, NJ: Lawrence Erlbaum Associates.

Cheng, P.W. & Holyoak, K.J. (1985). Pragmatic reasoning schemas. *Cognitive-Psychology*, 17(4), 391–416.

Chi, M.T.H., Glaser, R. & Rees, E. (1982). Expertise in problem-solving. In Sternberg, R.J. (Ed.), *Advances in the Psychology of Human Intelligence*, Vol. 1. Hillsdale, NJ: Lawrence Erlbaum Associates.

Hatano, G. (1990). The nature of everyday science: a brief introduction. *British Journal of Developmental Psychology*, 8, 245–250.

Hunt, E. & Minstrell, J. (1996). Effective instruction in science and mathematics: psychological principles and social constraints. *Issues in Education: Contributions from Educational Psychology*, 2(2), 123–162.

Marshall, S.P. (1995). *Schemas in Problem-Solving*. New York: Cambridge University Press.

National Research Council (NRC) (1999). In Bransford, J.D., Brown, A.L. & Cocking, R.R. (Eds.), *How People Learn: Brain, Mind, Experience, and School*. Committee on Developments in the Science of Learning. Commission on Behavioural and Social Sciences and Education. Washington, DC: National Academy Press.

National Research Council (NRC) (2001). In Pellegrino, J., Chudowsky, N. & Glaser, R. (Eds.), *Knowing What Students Know: The Science and Design of Educational Assessment*. Committee on the Foundations of Assessment. Division on Behavioural and Social Sciences and Education. Washington, DC: National Academy Press.

Newell, A. (1990). *Unified Theories of Cognition*. Cambridge, MA: Harvard University Press.

Ochs, E., Jacoby, S. & Gonzalez, P. (1994). Interpretive journeys: how physicists talk and travel through graphic space. *Configurations*, 2, 151–172.

Rosenbloom, P. & Newell, A. (1987). Learning by chunking: a production system model of practice. In Klahr, D. & Langley, P. (Eds.), *Production System Models of Learning and Development* (pp. 221–286). Cambridge, MA: MIT Press.

Siegler, R.S. (1998). *Children's Thinking* (3rd ed.). Upper Saddle River, NJ: Prentice Hall.

Skinner, B.F. (1938). *The Behaviour of Organisms: An Experimental Analysis*. New York: Appleton-Century-Crofts.

Wertsch, J.V. (1998). *Mind as Action*. New York: Oxford University Press.

White, B.Y. & Frederiksen, J.R. (1998). Inquiry, modelling, and metacognition: making science accessible to all students. *Cognition and Instruction*, 16(1), 3–118.

Wiggins, G. (1989). Teaching to the (authentic) test. *Educational Leadership*, 46(7), 41–47.

Wilson, M. & Sloane, K. (2000). From principles to practice: an embedded assessment system. *Applied Measurement in Education*, 13(2), 181–208.

Mark Wilson

RELATED ENTRIES

Applied Fields: Education, Theoretical Perspective: Cognitive, Achievement Testing

COGNITIVE STYLES

INTRODUCTION

This entry is structured in five sections. In the first section the concept of 'cognitive styles' (CS) is defined and the evolution of how CS have been theorized and assessed is briefly outlined. In the second section an overall picture of the kinds of instruments and procedures employed to measure CS is given. In the third section some main CS are reported together with the description of the corresponding testing tools. In the fourth section future directions concerning CS assessment are discussed. Finally, a perspective about the integration of different CS is proposed.

WHAT ARE COGNITIVE STYLES?

A Definition

CS refer to a person's habitual, prevalent, or preferred mode of perceiving, memorizing, learning, judging, decision-making, problem-solving. Individual differences about how people carry out tasks involving these functions may constitute a style if they appear to be:

- pervasive; that is, they emerge consistently in different contexts, independently of the particular features of situation;
- stable; that is, they are always the same at different times.

CS induce persons to adopt similar attitudes and behaviours in a variety of domains; they concern in fact general approaches in mental functioning, irrespective of the incidental demands of specific cases.

CS differ from abilities because the latter are measured in terms of *level* of performance whereas the former in terms of *manner* of performance. Abilities are uni-polar dimensions while styles are bi- or multi-polar. Finally most styles, but not abilities, are neutral in terms of value and desirability (a style cannot be absolutely 'good'; its relevance depends on the features of the situation and on the individual's goals).

CS can be conceptualized as a cross-road of thinking, personality, and motivation. In fact they concern the kind of strategies which an individual tends to apply when he/she faces a situation or the preferred way of processing information. CS are also grounded in the deep psychological structure of a person and in his/her basic orientation and affective disposition toward reality. Furthermore, CS are linked to the kind of purposes and expectations which people develop in their life.

Historical Trends

Research on CS began in the 1950s at the Menninger Foundation and concerned the topic of 'cognitive control', a construct which deals with mediation between the ego and the demands of inner needs. Seven profiles were identified: tolerance for unrealistic experience, conceptual differentiation, constricted–flexible control, levelling–sharpening, scanning, contrast reactivity, field articulation. These early styles – as well as field dependence–independence (see below) which was proposed at about the same period – were measured prevalently by means of perceptual probes and by considering the outcomes of the cognitive process. Observation of behaviour during tasks and analysis of how subjects performed tasks were introduced in the 1960s; styles – such as tolerant–intolerant, complexity–simplicity, risk taking–caution – went beyond cognition and were related to personality. In the 1970s and 1980s a variety of bi-polar styles emerged; the tendency was to identify styles integrating differences in thinking processes and in attitudes, emotions, and interpersonal relationships and to use quick measures such as those provided by self-administered questionnaires. Finally, in the 1990s doubts were raised about the bi-polarity of styles and complex, multi-dimensional constructs were proposed. For instance, Sternberg (1997) analysed styles in terms of function (legislative, executive, or judicial), form (monarchic, hierarchic, oligarchic, or anarchic), level (global or local), scope (internal or external), use (producing or consuming), and leaning (conservative or progressive). The combination of these dimensions produces fifteen different styles.

HOW ARE COGNITIVE STYLES ASSESSED?

A Taxonomy

Three main kinds of data can be employed to measure CS: behavioural, self-report, and physiological (see Table 1).

Behavioural data can be obtained by recording the final result of a given task or the procedure followed in performing the task. The task may consist in filling out a paper-and-pencil test or a sorting test, in carrying out trials by means of an experimental apparatus, or in interacting with the computer within an ad-hoc designed virtual environment.

Table 1. A taxonomy of methods to assess cognitive styles with examples of procedures and/or instruments

Method	Cognitive style	Examples of procedures and/or instruments
Behavioural		
Paper-and-pencil tests	Field Dependence–Independence	Embedded Figure Test
Sorting tasks	Categorization style	Classification tasks
Experimental apparatus	Impulsivity–Reflectivity	Speed–accuracy trials
Computer interaction	Analytic–Global	Conversational analysis
Self-report		
Introspection	Verbalizer–Visualizer	Strategies of Thinking Retrospective Report
Checking personal features	Adaptation–Innovation	Kirton Adaptation–Innovation Inventory
Statement endorsement	Left–Right	Your Style of Learning and Thinking
Physiological	Verbalizer–Visualizer	LEMs
		Breathing patterns

Self-reports require that people evaluate themselves by describing introspectively the way in which they performed tasks, by checking personal habits or preferences, or by endorsing statements about what they think of themselves. This may be done by asking subjects to keep a diary of what occurred to them during a period of their life, by interviewing them, or by administering questionnaires.

Finally, some physiological measures can be interpreted as indices of particular cognitive preferences in processing stimuli.

An Example

In order to exemplify the procedures described above, we can consider the case of the visualizer–verbalizer style (for references of this section see Antonietti & Giorgetti, 1998). Various cognitive tasks may be performed by means of operations which require either the use of visual or of abstract and verbal representations and processes. Though it is likely that most people can switch strategies according to the nature of the task, there are some persons who appear to be heavily dependent upon one or other of the two strategies because of their different promptness to employ visual or verbal mental operations. The tendency to privilege visual or verbal functioning has been conceptualized as a cognitive style.

Behavioural Data

To assess whether a person is a visualizer or a verbalizer, it is possible to present him/her with tasks which can be performed through both visual and verbal–abstract strategies and to record the extent to which each of the two kinds of procedures has been followed. For instance, subjects can be asked to solve categorical syllogistic problems and then can be classified according to the representational strategy they used: 'elemental' if they used several concrete figures, 'diagrammatic' if they used diagrams (for example Venn's diagrams) representing the logical relations, and 'verbal' if they thought intuitively on the basis of verbal expressions of premises.

Self-Reports

In order to understand how much an individual tends to visualize, he/she can be requested to keep a record of the times in which he/she has experienced imagery during the day. Information of this kind may be derived also through questionnaires in which people are asked to rate how frequently they create and process various kinds of mental images. These instruments incite subjects to consider their habitual modes of thinking as they emerge in the complete range of mental activities and to assess the occurrence of visual images in different tasks, domains, contexts, and so on. Finally, introspective judgements are involved in instruments where subjects are asked to describe the cognitive strategy (visual vs. verbal/abstract) previously employed in answering questions (for example 'Albert is taller than Bob; Charles is taller than Albert; who is the tallest?', 'List five parts of the human body') that can be answered by means of either a visual or a verbal–abstract strategy.

Physiological Measures

Observations have indicated that when someone is asked a question requiring a little thought the eyes make an initial movement to the left or right. Since it was argued that the right cerebral hemisphere is associated with the processing of visual information and that the spontaneous lateral eye movements (LEMs) are under the control of the counter-lateral hemisphere, it was claimed that the presentation of a visual-spatial question produces the activation of the right hemisphere and, consequently, left LEMs. However, verbalizers should turn their eyes consistently to the right and visualizers to the left, whatever the kind of question. Thus, it has been suggested to use LEMs as a criterion to assess the preference for either a visual or a verbal processing. Furthermore, it was hypothesized that implicit laryngeal and tongue movements accompany or precede verbal thinking, so that the individual's regular breathing rhythm is disrupted. Under this assumption, it is possible to detect whether the silent reasoning that a person accomplishes while he/she is answering a question is visual or verbal by recording his/her breathing pattern. According to these conjectures, it was found that verbalizers had significantly more disruptions of their regular breathing rhythm, both in rest and in work conditions, than visualizers.

WHAT ARE THE MAIN COGNITIVE STYLES?

Field Dependence–Independence

This style refers to the tendency to overcome embedding contexts; that is, to identify and to isolate elements included in complex patterns. Such a tendency is associated to personality traits linked to psychological differentiation. Field independent people tend to analyse rather then leave items of information global and confused. Field dependent–independent individuals were originally recognized by asking them to adjust a rod in a tilted rectangular frame so that it might appear vertical (Rod-and-Frame Test): field-independent subjects arrange the rod perfectly vertical since, unlike field-dependent persons, they are not influenced by the tilted nature of the frame. However, the most widely used instrument to test field dependence–independence is the Embedded Figure Test (Witkin et al., 1973), devised both for individual and for group administration. The test consists of a series of perceptual restructuring items requiring subjects to pick out a simple figure hidden in a larger, entangled design.

Impulsivity–Reflectivity

The impulsive person tends to put forward the first idea that comes to him/her, whereas the reflective person considers alternatives (Messer, 1976). This style is generally assessed by measuring differences in decision-making under conditions of uncertainty. Tasks used present several plausible choices, only one of which is correct: who responds quickly often errs; who pauses to reflect is more often correct. Different stylistic combinations of speed and accuracy can be found. For instance, the Matching Familiar Figures Test identifies four categories of respondents: fast-responding/high-error, fast-responding/low-error, slow-responding/high-error, slow-responding/low-error.

Categorization Styles

Consistent individual differences have been detected by giving a number of objects and by requiring subjects to sort them into categories (Guilford, 1980). Some persons (narrow categorization style) place objects into a wide number of small, well-defined, categories, so that each category contains only objects sharing a high number of similar features; other persons (broad categorization style) place objects into a small number of wide categories which include items with few common features.

Stylistic differences were highlighted with reference not only to the width of categorization but also to the kind of criteria employed to construct categories: analytic-descriptive style induces to include in the same category items showing surface physical–perceptual similarities; conceptual-inferential style induces to define categories on the basis of similarities in objects' functions; thematic-relational style induces to include in the same category disparate objects which have in common only the fact that they occur in the same action or situation.

Analytic–Global

Different authors converged in maintaining that a consistent dimension which differentiates people is the tendency to consider either details of a situation or the whole picture (Schmeck, 1988). Analytic individuals have a focused attention, have an interest in operations and procedures or the 'proper' ways of doing things and prefer step-by-step schemes; their thinking is controlled and consciously directed. Global persons tend toward scanning, leading to form overall impressions, including entry of feelings into decisions; their organizational schemes involve random or multiple accessibility of components and varied associations between them.

Tests of the Cognitive Styles Analysis (Riding & Rayner, 1998) allow measurement of the analytic dimension by presenting items each comprising a simple geometrical shape and a complex figure and by asking to indicate whether or not the simple shape is contained in the complex figure; the holistic dimension is measured by presenting pairs of complex geometrical figures and by requiring to judge the overall similarity between them. The ratio between response times in the two tasks reveals preference for one of the two extremes of the style.

By means of conversational analysis – carried out involving subjects in a dialogue either with a human interlocutor or with a virtual, computer implemented partner – it is possible to recognize peculiar mental operations related to the analytic–global distinction (Pask, 1976): holistic persons have many goals, assimilate information from many topics, ask questions about broad relations and form generalized hypotheses; the opposite individuals have one goal at a time, move to another topic only when they are completely certain about the one they are currently working on, ask questions about narrow relations and their conjectures are specific.

Styles Related to Hemispheric Asymmetry

Hypotheses derived from research into brain lateralization induced Torrance (1988) to propose the distinction between a left and a right style of thinking. Left style is concerned with verbal, logical, analytical, and abstract tasks; right style refers to non-verbal, holistic, spatial, and concrete thinking. The left style implies preference for sequential processing of information and systematicity in solving problems; the right style implies preference for parallel processing, perceptual representation in the form of synthesized patterns,

intuitive and creative problem-solving. The Your Style of Learning and Thinking is a self-report inventory designed to estimate the relative psychological dependence of an individual on the left or on the right mode of thinking. The instrument consists of items each reporting a pair of statements (one referred to the left and the other to the right style of thinking). Subjects have to place a check mark whether the statement is true of them; they may check one or both of the statements in a pair or neither. Three scores are computed: the number of items in which subjects check only the statement concerning the left style (left scale), the number of items in which subjects check only the right statement (right scale), and the number of items in which both or neither of the statements are checked (integrative scale).

Adaptation–Innovation

Adaptors are inclined to employ well-known information and strategies and to improve what is already available. On the one hand, innovators are more likely to neglect past experience and to look for possible novel solutions. The adaptation–innovation style is conceptualized as a continuum ranging from the habit 'to do things better' to the habit 'to do things differently'. In problem-solving settings, adaptors tend to reduce problems by improvement with a maximum of continuity and stability and by seeking solutions in understood ways; on the other, innovators try to discover problems, query problem assumptions, and manipulate them (Kirton, 1989).

Such a style can be measured through the Kirton Adaption–Innovation Inventory, a self-report questionnaire constituted by statements each describing a certain personal attribute. Respondents must imagine that they have been asked to present, consistently and for a long time, a certain image of themselves to others. They have to state the degree of difficulty that such a task would entail for them on a five-point scale from very easy to very hard. The scoring system used leads to innovators scoring higher and adaptors scoring lower.

FUTURE PERSPECTIVES

CS assessment involves a series of testing and psychometric issues which have been largely discussed (Tiedemann, 1987). These issues are closely related to methodological and theoretical topics which future research should highlight. For instance, it is not still clear whether CS are homogeneous, unitary psychological dimensions or are multi-componential products of more specific sub-tendencies. Furthermore, the question whether CS are unique, dichotomous dimensions or are the result of two or more parallel (or orthogonal) dimensions should be answered. Finally, empirical investigations should allow assessment of whether CS are 'all-or-nothing' attributes or are continuous dimensions, so that individuals may share a style in various degrees of intensity.

Answers given to these questions have relevant implications for the ways in which CS can be assessed. For instance, the structure of most CS tests is designed to include pairs of opposite items, each concerning a pole of the style at hand. Thus, the rejection of the bi-polarity of CS undermines one of the basic assumptions of a large number of instruments.

Currently CS are measured prevalently by means of self-reports. This kind of assessment implies that individuals consider themselves introspectively in order to judge some personal features. However, the assumption that people can have direct access to the stylistic dimensions to be evaluated is under discussion. Can a person estimate adequately his or her cognitive tendencies? Doubts can be cast. For example, if a subject is requested – as questionnaires ask – to give a global judgement about the generality of his or her own experience, he or she risks reporting what he or she thinks about his or herself rather than what actually occurs to him/her; by contrast, if attention is focused – as diaries or retrospective interviews ask – on short time intervals, reports reflect only the specific experience of those periods or tasks but do not give an overall picture.

A promising direction seems to be the integration of different kinds of data, as computer-supported assessment procedures allow: recording effective behaviour in strategic tasks can show stylistic differences which might be supported both by ecological observation of everyday-life situations and by investigating how the subject perceives his or her own mental functioning.

CONCLUSIONS

Research has yielded a long list of putative CS which show a variety of shared features and overlapping distinctions, so that the need for integrative models emerges (Miller, 1987). In this perspective a promising direction does not seem to be the attempt to concentrate CS into a reduced number of same-level dimensions but to consider CS within a hierarchic model, with some styles (for instance the analytic–global dichotomy: Riding & Rayner, 1998) playing the role of super-ordinate constructs which include other styles. This should lead to drawing a structural picture of individual differences concerning the manners in which cognitive tasks can be performed.

References

Antonietti, A. & Giorgetti, M. (1998). The verbalizer-visualizer questionnaire: a review. *Perceptual and Motor Skills*, 86, 227–239.

Guilford, J.P. (1980). Cognitive styles: what are they? *Educational and Psychological Measurement*, 40, 715–735.

Kirton, M. (Ed.) (1989). *Adaptors and Innovators*. London: Routledge.

Messer, S.B. (1976). Reflection-impulsivity: a review. *Psychological Bulletin*, 83, 1026–1052.

Miller, A. (1987). Cognitive styles: an integrated model. *Educational Psychologist*, 7, 251–268.

Pask, G. (1976). Conversational techniques on the study and practice of education. *British Journal of Educational Psychology*, 46, 12–25.

Riding, R. & Rayner, S. (1998). *Cognitive Styles and Learning Strategies*. London: Fulton.

Schmeck, R.R. (Ed.) (1988). *Learning Strategies and Learning Styles*. New York: Plenum.

Sternberg, R.J. (1997). *Thinking Styles*. Cambridge: Cambridge University Press.

Tiedemann, J. (1987). Measures of cognitive styles: a critical review. *Educational Psychologist*, 24, 261–275.

Torrance, E.P. (1988). *Your Style of Learning and Thinking*. Bensenville, IL: Scholastic Testing Service.

Witkin, H.A. Goodenough D.R. & Oltnson, P.K. (1973). *Field-Dependence–Independence and Psychological Differentiation*. Princeton: Educational Testing Service.

Alessandro Antonietti

RELATED ENTRIES

PERSONALITY ASSESSMENT (GENERAL), THEORETICAL PERSPECTIVE: COGNITIVE, THEORETICAL PERSPECTIVE: COGNITIVE-BEHAVIOURAL, ATTRIBUTIONAL STYLES, COPING STYLES

COMMUNICATIVE LANGUAGE ABILITIES

INTRODUCTION

As is often the case with other psychological functions, most people think they know the meaning of communication. Problems arise, however, when experts try to define communication, specify what it consists of, and determine its limits. Definitions can range from very broad concepts, where the simple transmission of information is considered to constitute valid communication, to more restrictive ones that imply both intent and awareness of the communicative act. Below we briefly describe the basic skills needed to communicate, as well as ways of assessing them.

BASIC COMMUNICATION SKILLS

Although linguistic abilities used to be considered sufficient for good communication, language and communication are now seen as two different functional systems. However, the relationship between them is not clear.

Among the communicative skills attributed to the speaker, the message has always had a privileged position and has been seen as responsible for the success or failure of the communicative exchange. To formulate good messages, speakers have to know what they want to communicate, identify and select the information to be transmitted, and produce unambiguous messages. However, it is not easy, even for adults, to provide unambiguous messages, nor to detect ambiguous or incomplete ones.

In order to produce and above all to restructure messages, speakers or listeners have to articulate knowledge about the message itself (meaning), about the partner (status, age, linguistic and cognitive skills, etc.) and about the context (its characteristics and the extent to which context is shared by interlocutors).

Knowledge of the roles and rules governing the communicative exchange should also be taken into account (turn-taking, topic maintenance or change, etc). Furthermore, the distinction between what is meant (communicative intention and message representation) and what is said has to be made (Bonitatibus, 1988; Robinson & Mitchell, 1992).

Messages are directed to others (social language), but sometimes they can be directed inward (private speech) (see Table 1). To formulate social messages the speaker has to be skilled in role taking, taking into account the partner's characteristics and adapting the message accordingly. Likewise, the listener also has to understand messages from the speaker's perspective. Any lack of ability in role taking has a negative effect on the negotiation process.

Even though communicative responsibility is shared, a skilled listener can change the course of communication (Patterson & Kister, 1981). The listener's most powerful skill for disambiguating messages is asking questions, and then contributing any relevant information held. A well-formed query exercises two functions: a selective one with respect to the previous message (indicating the confusing terms, pointing out potential new information, etc.), and a determining function regarding the requested response (repetition, confirmation, specification, etc.) (Garvey, 1979).

Communicative exchange is not limited solely to the sharing of information. Partners, throughout communicative exchange, actively and deliberately attempt to control their own behaviour (self-regulation) and that of their partner (interlocutor regulation) through verbal utterances of different regulatory force (strong or weak). Regulation can also be carried out by a more capable outside agent such as a tutorial support system.

Private speech or internal regulation is a dialogic form of internal language linked to the egocentric developmental stage. It reappears

Table 1. Basic communication skills

	Speaker	Listener	Adult
Verbal information related to the referent	Message Restructuring and repairing of the message Ask questions Interlocutor regulation Self-regulation	Contribute relevant information	Guiding interventions
Private language	Internal regulation		
Verbal information unrelated to referent	Weak regulation		
Manipulative abilities		Adapting performance to the message	
Verbal, non-verbal, social and cognitive abilities related to the communicative process	Maintaining principle of co-operation Understanding exchange context Understanding partner's role Using and understanding communicative rules Expressing communicative intention Analysing the referent and non-referents Assessing messages		

(through lip movement, muttering, murmuring, etc.) when the subject has to deal with a difficult task.

The communicative exchange is only successful when the ensemble of skills is harmonized in a coherent and flexible way. When communication is approached from the perspective of regulation, an interface is produced between communicative, cognitive, linguistic and/or social processes.

ASSESSMENT OF VERBAL COMMUNICATION SKILLS

The assessment of communicative skills involves the identification of the functions, rules and patterns that operate in a communicative exchange. The assessment of communicative skills has been developed basically within the domains of (a) language development and pragmatics, and (b) psychopathology (studies about communicative difficulties in childhood, learning disabilities and adult aphasia). Different instruments for analysing communicative functions have been designed in both domains. These can be organized as follows: (1) observational

checklist, profiles and interview, (2) standardized tests and (3) referential tasks. McTear and Conti-Ramsden (1989) and Smith and Leinonen (1992) provide good descriptions of pragmatic and communicational assessment.

Observational Checklist, Profiles and Interview

These are instruments designed to identify the strengths and weaknesses of communicative skills, and elaborated under a qualitative approach. They have proved very useful in research and in educational and clinical contexts. The interpretation of results from such techniques is usually based on the theory of speech acts.

Tough (1977) produced one of the first and most widely used instruments which aimed to classify the functions of language. It analyses four functions (directive, interpretative, projective and relational), each one being sub-divided into several more specific functions (referring to needs, planning, expressing feelings, etc.) and communicative strategies.

The Pragmatic Protocol (Prutting & Kirchner, 1987) is a checklist suitable for children older than five years of age. It analyses pragmatic skills using the conceptual framework of speech acts and thus examines three main aspects: utterance acts (or expressed intentions), propositional acts (lexical, grammar, style) and illocutionary and perlocutionary acts (speech acts, topic management, turn-taking).

The Pragmatic Profile of Early Communication Skills (Dewart & Summers, 1988) analyses speech acts, responses to communication, interactive aspects of communication, and the effect of contextual conditions on communicative success. Information is obtained through a semi-structured interview given to parents or caregivers. The profile is useful for assessing communication in very young children or children without language. It can also be useful for analysing children from different cultural backgrounds who are not very able in the language of the community.

The MacArthur Communicative Development Inventory (CDI) (Fenson, Dale, Reznick, Thal, Bates, Hartung, Pethick & Reilly, 1993) is suitable for children from 8 to 30 months. It analyses, on the basis of parental report, early language development and symbolic and communicative gestures. Also, the Sequenced Inventory of Communication Development (Hendrick, Prather & Tobin, 1975), for young children between four months and four years of age, deals with the child's prelinguistic behaviours (reaction to environmental sounds and speech, imitation, play routines, etc.) and first language.

The McTear Conversation Checklist (1985) analyses the communication skills of school-age children, with respect to turn-taking, initiation of conversational exchanges, response, cohesion and repairing the conversational breakdown. The aim of this checklist is not only to provide an instrument capable of grasping the development of pragmatics, but also to detect disordered conversation.

As can be seen, the tools used within the pragmatic perspective simultaneously embrace both verbal and non-verbal communication, whilst those for very young children particularly emphasize pre-conversational abilities. The main weakness of these tools is that the guidelines for coding and interpretation are often not very well defined.

Standardized Tests

The Test of Pragmatic Skills (Shulman, 1985) was designed to assess a child's difficulties with conversational intentions. The test focuses on the use of illocutionary acts including requesting information or action, rejection/denial, naming/labelling, answering/responding, summoning/calling, greeting and closing conversation. It is suitable for children between 3 and 9 years of age. Speech acts are elicited in four situations while children are playing with familiar objects (puppets, pencils, telephones and blocks). The responses are evaluated according to their context appropriateness, the use of verbal or non-verbal language, and the verbal range and elaboration of expressed intention.

The *Bateria de Lenguaje Objetiva y Criterial* (BLOC) (Puyuelo, Wiig, Renom & Solanas, 1998), for children from 5 to 14 years old, analyses child development according to semantic, morphological, syntactic and pragmatic language parameters. The pragmatic part analyses communicative functions such as: greetings, saying goodbye, thanking, asking for attention, asking/giving/preventing, querying, etc. The test allows the child's performance to be compared with both educational and developmental age norms. Also, a cut-off point differentiates between risk and normal pragmatic competence.

Other tests are based upon the need to assess the functional communicative skills of aphasic adults. The Assessment Protocol of Pragmatic-Linguistic Skills (APPLS) (Gurland, Chwat & Gerber Wollner, 1982) aims to identify the linguistic abilities used in a pragmatic context, the pragmatic abilities themselves, and the specific ability to repair discourse. And the Amsterdam–Nijmegen Everyday Language Test (ANELT) (Blomert, Kean, Koster & Schokker, 1994) aims to analyse the verbal communicative abilities and changes in them over time, focusing on everyday situations involving verbal social interaction.

The main criticism of these instruments, apart from the ANELT, is that they analyse speaker competence rather than the interactional conversation.

Referential Tasks

The referential communication paradigm focuses specifically on the analysis of verbal communication skills and explicitly avoids the analysis of non-verbal communication. There are not standardized tests developed from this perspective which uses specific tasks to elicit verbal behaviour. The most widely used tasks are:

(a) Identification, naming and describing physical objects, drawings, photographs, etc. The 'Abstract Shapes' task of Glucksberg and Krauss (1967) is one of the best-known.

(b) Giving instructions and directions: how to draw or assemble parts of an object or building blocks, communicating routes, etc. 'Route finding task' and 'Room construction task' (Lloyd, Boada & Forns, 1992), 'Tangram figures' or 'Island Map task' (see Yule, 1997) are also well known.

(c) Giving accounts of incidents, telling stories (constructing a narrative from visual or videotaped material) or expressing opinions. The 'supermarket' and 'disco' tasks are good examples (see Yule, 1997).

The main criticism of this area is the lack of a unified model able to integrate the research carried out from this perspective.

FUTURE PERSPECTIVES

Communication is an area of growing interest, both from a research and applied point of view. How meaning is negotiated, unambiguous messages are produced, and instructions understood and accurately responded to are all-important areas of study for developmental and educational psychologists, as 'learning' is, in part, a verbal communicative process.

Effective communication is also necessary for proper social development and social life (from personal to international relationships).

The study of communication skills also has special relevance from a psychopathological perspective because the correct use of these skills appears to be affected in various disorders. Communicative dysfunction and errors (absence of message reparation, poor topic maintenance, use of deviant words, excessive verbal distractions, flaws in interactive skills, etc.) seem to be particularly frequent in psychotic pathologies, in several linguistic disorders (semantic–pragmatic deficit), in cognitive deficit pathologies and in aphasic disorders. Internal regulation difficulties could lie behind hyperactive pathologies and recent studies have suggested that a lack of communication skills could explain some anti-social disorders in children.

A new and increasing area of interest, focusing on communicative verbal exchange, is the study of elderspeak language and secondary baby talk.

CONCLUSIONS

In order to develop better tools for the accurate assessment of communication skills, some aspects must be studied in greater detail.

Firstly, further studies are needed to clarify the relationship between communicative, cognitive, socio-emotional and linguistic skills. Despite the considerable amount of research carried out in this area, it is still not clear whether communicative competence is a result – the outcome of a combination of these skills – or one of the cognitive processes underpinning the development of other skills. Therefore, some tests labelled as 'communication tests' may actually be exploring cognitive or linguistic skills, or even social development or personality styles.

Secondly, a more precise knowledge of communicative developmental skills is needed. To date, there have been some developmental studies covering a wide range of ages (Camaioni, Ercolani & Lloyd, 1998) and very few provide a longitudinal perspective (Bivens & Berk, 1990; Forns & Boada, 1997; Martínez, Forns & Boada, 1997).

Thirdly, in order to grasp the nature of communicative exchange and evaluate communicative abilities, any new test has to address two main aspects: one concerns the interlocutor, and the other, the test situation. In the future, the usual interlocutor in communicative testing will be a relative, colleague or friend, not only the psychologist. And the testing will be conducted in a familiar context, besides the standardized one. Without these two conditions the conversational sample obtained by psychologists may be very different to real conversation.

Finally, although there are more tools than those described here, it is clear that the area of verbal communicative assessment is lacking a test of high technical quality. It should be acknowledged that this reflects the absence of reliable outcomes in our understanding of human communication.

References

Bivens, J.A. & Berk, L.E. (1990). A longitudinal study of the development of elementary school children's private speech. *Merrill-Palmer Quarterly, 36*(4), 443–463.

Blomert, L., Kean, M.L., Koster, Ch. & Schokker, J. (1994). Amsterdam–Nijmegen Everyday Language Test, ANELT: construction, reliability and validity. *Aphasiology, 8*(4), 381–407.

Bonitatibus, G. (1988). What is said and what is meant in referential communication. In Astington, J.W., Harris, P.L. & Olson, D.R. (Eds.), *Developing Theories of Mind* (pp. 326–338). Cambridge: Cambridge University Press.

Camaioni, L., Ercolani, A.P. & Lloyd, P. (1998). The development of referential communication: learning to speak and learning to process verbal information are not the same thing. *Cahiers de Psychologie Cognitive. Current Psychology of Cognition, 17*(1), 3–30.

Dewart, H. & Summers, S. (1988). *The Pragmatics Profile of Early Communication Skills.* Windsor: NFER-Nelson.

Fenson, L., Dale, P., Reznick, J.S., Thal, D., Bates, E., Hartung, J., Pethick, S. & Reilly, J. (1993). *The MacArthur Communicative Development Inventories User's Guide and Technical Manual.* San Diego: Singular Publishing Group.

Forns, M. & Boada, H. (1997). Estudi longitudinal de la reestructuració del missatge en nens bilingües i monolingües dins d'un programa escolar d'immersió lingüística. *Anuario de Psicología, 75,* 77–93.

Garvey, C. (1979). Contingent queries and their relationship in discourse. In Ochs, E. & Schieffelin, B. (Eds.), *Developmental Pragmatics* (pp. 363–372). New York: Academic Press.

Glucksberg, S. & Krauss, R.M. (1967). What do people say after they have learned to talk? Studies in the development of referential communication. *Merrill-Palmer Quarterly, 13,* 310–316.

Gurland, G.B., Chwat, S.E. & Gerber Wollner, S. (1982). Establishing a communication profile in adult aphasia: analysis of communicative acts and conversational sequences. In Brookshire, R. (Ed.), *Clinical Aphasiology Conference Proceedings.* Minneapolis: BRK Publishers.

Hendrick, D.L., Prather, E.M. & Tobin, A.R. (1975). *Sequenced Inventory of Communication Development.* Seattle: University of Washington.

Lloyd, P., Boada, H. & Forns, M. (1992). New directions in referential communication research. *British Journal of Developmental Psychology, 10,* 385–403.

Martínez, M., Forns, M. & Boada, H. (1997). Estudio longitudinal de la comunicación referencial en niños de 4 a 8 años. *Anuario de Psicología, 75,* 37–58.

McTear, M. (1985). *Children's Conversations.* Oxford: Blackwell.

McTear, M. & Conti-Ramsden, G. (1989). Assessment of pragmatics. In Grundy, K. (Ed.), *Linguistics in Clinical Practice.* London: Taylor and Francis.

Patterson, C. & Kister, M. (1981). The development of listener skills for referential communication. In Dickson, W.P. (Ed.), *Children's Oral Communication Skills* (pp. 143–166). New York: Academic Press.

Prutting, C.A. & Kirchner, D.M. (1987). A clinical appraisal of the pragmatic aspects of language. *Journal of Speech and Hearing Disorders, 52*(2), 105–119.

Puyuelo, M., Wiig, E.H., Renom, J. & Solanas, A. (1998). *Batería de Lenguaje Objetiva y Criterial (BLOC).* Barcelona: Masson.

Robinson, E.J. & Mitchell, P. (1992). Children's interpretation of messages from a speaker with a false belief. *Child Development, 63*(3), 639–652.

Shulman, B.B. (1985) *Test of Pragmatic Skills.* Arizona: Communication Skills Builders.

Smith, B.R. & Leinonen, E. (1992). *Clinical Pragmatics.* London: Chapman and Hall.

Tough, J. (1977). *The Development of Meaning: A Study of Children's Use of Language.* London: Allen and Unwin.

Yule, G. (1997). *Referential Communication Tasks.* New Jersey: LEA.

María Forns

RELATED ENTRIES

Language (General), Development: Language, Testing in the Second Language in Minorities

C|OMPUTER-BASED TESTING[1]

INTRODUCTION

Computer-based testing (CBT) has become a viable and well-developed method for administering a variety of tests in many different contexts. Various achievement, psychological, licensure, and certification tests have all benefited from computerization. The emergence of sophisticated computer technology has enabled the implementation of measurement models that were proposed theoretically years ago.

The underpinnings of CBT are grounded in item response theory (IRT), which began to develop in the 1960s (Birnbaum, 1968; Rasch, 1960) and reached a relatively mature state by the 1980s (Lord, 1980). However, the recent expansion of operational CBT programs has introduced challenges that have considerably expanded the psychometrics supporting CBT. The purpose of this entry is to provide an overview of CBT, including its advantages, the psychometric models that support it, and some of the issues and challenges that are currently being addressed by researchers and practitioners. In addition, we offer some thoughts about how CBT may evolve to support future assessment needs.

ADVANTAGES OF CBT

The advantages of CBT include psychometric benefits, benefits to test-takers, and benefits to test-users. CBT permits automated processes that are not possible with paper-and-pencil testing, such as automatic item and form selection, immediate scoring and reporting of results, and immediate transmission of examinee data to the sponsoring organization. CBT systems also offer generally better data capturing functionality than the traditional scannable answer sheets used with paper-and-pencil testing programmes. Advantages to test-takers include convenient exam scheduling, a wide variety of appointment times, a comfortable test-taking environment, intuitive examinee interfaces, and faster score results processing.

Some advantages to test-users include excellent display and graphics options and a wide choice of item formats that may be administered, allowing sponsoring organizations to pretest many new item types with innovative graphics and user response options. Other advantages to test-users include the frequent transmission of data back to the processing centre and the ability to detect trends or problematic issues more quickly than with single batch-type test administration. Irregularities that may occur during a traditional test administration will often affect entire groups of examinees, but irregularities with software or hardware are usually more isolated

and limited in scope to individual test sessions. Multiple-choice items that might be mis-keyed or problematic in a computer-based testing environment can usually be deactivated quickly with far fewer complications than in traditional paper-and-pencil test settings.

PSYCHOMETRIC MODELS FOR CBT

A number of psychometric models are available for use in CBT. The computerized linear test (CLT) is most similar to the traditional paper-and-pencil test. CLTs consist of fixed forms with a fixed number of items per form. Usually, a number of forms are assembled, pre-equated to one another and deployed simultaneously to ensure that items are not exposed too quickly to examinees. These forms sometimes include a process that randomizes the presentation of items to each examinee within a test or within a well-defined section of the test, to guard against memorization of keys or further exposure of items. In some applications, CLTs are administered by dynamically choosing the fixed number of items to be administered to each examinee from a larger pool of questions.

Computerized-adaptive testing (CAT) utilizes item response theory (IRT) to select subsets of items from a large item pool so that the statistical characteristics of the selected items are optimally targeted to each test-taker. With CAT, performance on the first few items provides initial estimates of examinee ability. Each estimate of ability is used to select items that will provide the most information about the examinee's new ability at every point in the test. As more items are administered, the examinee ability estimate becomes increasingly precise because the computer adjusts the characteristics of each question to match the performance of the test-taker.

One principal advantage of CAT is efficiency. Since the items on the test are targeted to examinee ability, more information is gained about the examinee with fewer items than in a traditional paper-and-pencil test or a CLT. Because of this efficiency, a shorter test length can be established with CAT that will yield scores or pass/fail decisions that are equally precise or more precise than those based on traditional testing methodologies. With an appropriate decision rule, a variable-length testing process can be established that is based on giving each test-taker only as many questions as are needed for the computer to make a reliable estimate of examinee ability or to accurately classify an examinee as passing or failing compared to a minimum performance standard.

Much work on CAT in recent years has concentrated on adaptive testing algorithms. The most commonly accepted statistical criterion for CAT item selection is maximum information. However, use of this criterion alone leads to unrealistic results in most applications because test content is not accounted for. Several researchers have proposed algorithms to control content in CAT item selection. Kingsbury and Zara (1989) proposed a simple method of balancing item selection with respect to test content that involved partitioning the item pool according to content categories and choosing specified numbers of items from each content strata. Stocking and Swanson (1993) developed a weighted deviations model to account for content in CAT item selection. In their approach, content specifications are articulated as a series of upper and lower boundaries on the numbers to be selected. In addition, the maximum information objective is also reformulated as a boundary (although in this case the lower and upper boundaries are set equal at an artificially high level). A weighted sum of the deviations from all bounds is taken as the objective function, with weights reflecting the importance of both the content specifications and information. CAT item selection proceeds sequentially with the goal of minimizing the objective function.

An adaptive testing approach that constrains item selection as the test proceeds was introduced by van der Linden and Reese (1998) and van der Linden (2000). The idea behind this method is to satisfy all CAT content constraints through a series of shadow tests assembled to be optimal at the point of each interim estimate of examinee ability. The shadow test is a full-length test that includes all items previously administered and that satisfies all of the test constraints. From the full shadow test, only the most informative item at the interim ability level is selected. The remaining items are returned to the pool and the process is repeated for the next item, and subsequently until the adaptive test is completed.

Chang and Ying (1999) proposed an adaptive item selection approach based on classifying item discrimination parameter estimates into strata. In their approach, items are chosen from the lower discriminating strata early in the test when little is known about the ability of the test-taker, and strata with higher discriminating items are utilized late in the test when a more reliable estimate of ability is available. The goal of this approach is to avoid choosing highly discriminating items early in the test that may be poorly targeted due to an unreliable estimate of the test-taker's ability.

ISSUES WITH CBT

Despite the explosion of research and operational applications of CBT, there remain a number of issues with its use. Although discussion of all these issues is beyond the scope of this entry, we briefly discuss four potentially challenging areas for CBT testing programs: (1) establishing comparability between CBT and paper-and-pencil versions of an exam, (2) ensuring the security of computerized testing item pools, (3) monitoring CBT results, and (4) pretesting, calibrating and linking new items for an ongoing CBT program.

CBT Comparability

Many applications of CBT involve transitioning an existing testing programme to computer administration. In making such a transition, there is concern with maintaining the score scale established for the paper-and-pencil testing programme and ensuring that test scores or pass/fail decisions based on CBT are comparable to those based on paper-and-pencil testing. Kolen and Brennan (1995) list several significant comparability issues that arise when paper-and-pencil forms are transitioned to computer, including ease of reading passages, ease of reviewing or changing answers to previous questions, effects of time limits, and responding by keyboard or mouse versus using an answer sheet. In recent years, improvements in computerized testing interfaces and increasingly computer literate test-takers have lessened comparability concerns. Furthermore, a number of studies in a variety of contexts have supported the comparability of paper-and-pencil and computerized tests (e.g. Spray, Ackerman, Reckase & Carlson, 1989). Despite these encouraging results, comparability remains an important issue that must be addressed whenever CBT and paper-and-pencil test scores are to be used interchangeably or an existing score scale for a paper-and-pencil test is to be retained with the introduction of a CBT version.

Ensuring the Security of Computerized Testing Item Pools

A primary advantage of computerized testing is continuous administration, which allows test-takers flexibility in deciding when they will take a test. However, continuous testing requires exposing test items repeatedly over time, which introduces the possibility that the security of test questions can become compromised. This practical problem is an extremely important one, as a threat to the security of test questions is a threat to the validity of the test. Protecting the integrity of CBT item pools involves secure administrative procedures, statistical algorithms to limit the over-use of individual test questions in a particular item pool, and approaches for constructing and rotating item pools or test forms to further control item exposure. Stocking and Lewis (2000) describe one method of controlling the exposure of items in CAT. Way (1998) reviews the literature on protecting item pool security in CBT.

Monitoring CBT Results

Most CBT applications utilize IRT in ways that rely heavily upon the strong assumptions of the underlying models. As a result, model–data fit becomes an especially critical issue with CBT programs. A number of well-known methods exist for assessing model–data fit in traditional IRT applications (Hambleton & Swaminathan, 1985). However, with CBT applications utilizing CAT or other tailored item selection procedures, the features of continuous testing and adaptive item selection create challenges in monitoring CBT results. Glas (2000) addresses the issue of monitoring CAT data to assess changes in item performance. Another side of monitoring CBT is assessing aberrant responses by individual test-takers, or person fit, based on CBT results. Many factors can contribute to person misfit, including multidimensionality of test content, pre-knowledge of a subset of questions on the test,

and random guessing on multiple-choice items due to time pressures.

Pretesting, Calibrating and Linking New Items for an Ongoing CBT Program

CBT provides a flexible mechanism for trying out (or pretesting) new items because tests are administered electronically and many forms with different sets of pretest items can be published with little added expense. Most CBT programs pretest items by randomly selecting a subset of items from a larger pretest pool and interspersing them in with the operational items given to each test-taker. This on-line pretesting is easy to do if the test is composed of discrete items. However, if the pretest items are associated with passages and the number of items associated with each passage differs, sophisticated algorithms may be necessary to ensure that the pretest and operational items are administered seamlessly. For tests based on CAT, on-line pretesting places special demands on traditional IRT estimation methods. Recent studies (see, for example, Ban, Hanson, Wang, Yi & Harris, 2000) suggest that operational on-line calibration is feasible with CAT if appropriate data collection designs and estimation procedures are utilized.

FUTURE PERSECTIVES AND CONCLUSIONS

Both researchers in the area of CBT and practitioners that have interest in CBT applications have a strong sense that CBT will continue to evolve and expand rapidly in the future, primarily because of the way the technology and the Internet are transforming our society. Bennett (2001) provides a compelling vision of how the Internet will change the landscape of large-scale assessment for both purveyors and the consumers of CBT. He synthesizes a number of trends in the global economy and distance learning, and argues that assessment will have to be reinvented if it is to remain relevant to what and how students learn.

Several innovative aspects of CBT are likely to evolve most quickly. Among them is the continued development of features that can be used with computer-administered items, including sound, graphics, animation, and video. Bennett, Morley, and Quardt (1998) provide one example of a graphical modelling item type, which test-takers respond to by plotting points on a set of axes and using curve or line tools to connect the points.

Another potential CBT development is the use of the computer to generate test questions in real time. Bejar (1993) presents a rationale for and examples of what he refers to as a 'generative approach' to measurement. According to Bejar, the two major requirements for item generation are having a reliable mechanism for generating instances of items, and having sufficient knowledge about the response process to estimate the psychometric parameters (e.g. difficulty and discriminating power) of the generated items.

One major issue with item generation is developing psychometric models that can deal with the uncertainty inherent in item modelling, in which statistical characteristics of the computer-generated items are based on predictions rather than pretest data collections. Mislevy, Sheehan, and Wingersky (1993), Mislevy, Wingersky, and Sheehan (1994), Embretson (1999), and Glas and van der Linden (2001) present and discuss IRT models that hold potential for use in an item modelling context. A second issue is the investment in time and resources that is necessary to develop credible item models for each content domain of interest. This is further complicated by the fact that the linguistic and technological tools that are successful for one construct (e.g. quantitative reasoning) may be completely inadequate for developing item models in another construct (e.g. reading comprehension).

Still another aspect of CBT that will continue to rapidly evolve is the computer's ability to interact with test-takers and to simulate realistic assessment scenarios. Recent applications of interactive simulations to high-stakes assessment have included design problems used in an architect licensure exam (Kenney, 1997) and a computerized performance test to measure the patient management skills of physicians (Clauser, Margolis, Clyman & Ross, 1997). These efforts underscore one of the greatest challenges in developing realistic CBT simulations, which is developing valid and reliable measures while at the same time presenting tasks in as authentic a

manner as possible. Assessing complex behaviours through simulation requires approaches that can reveal how experts organize and apply their knowledge in a particular domain, a practice that has been referred to as cognitive task analysis (Means & Gott, 1988; Mislevy et al., 1999). Such methodological approaches are closely linked to efforts in cognitive psychology and intelligent tutoring (cf. Nichols, Chipman & Brennan, 1995). In many ways, these disciplines hold the key to integrating the explosion of technology tools that can be applied in a CBT with the traditional values of valid and reliable assessment.

Note

1 The positions expressed are those of the authors and not necessarily of Educational Testing Service or CTB McGraw-Hill.

References

Ban, J., Hanson, B.A., Wang, T., Yi, Q. & Harris, D.J. (2000). *A Comparative Study of Online Pretest Item Calibration/Scaling Methods in Computerized Adaptive Testing* (ACT Research Report 00-11). Iowa City, IA: ACT, Inc. [Available at *http://www.b-a-h.com/papers/paper0003.html*]

Bejar, I.I. (1993). A generative approach to psychological and educational measurement. In Frederikson, N., Mislevy, R.J. & Bejar, I.I. (Eds.), *Test Theory for a New Generation of Tests*. Hillsdale, NJ: Erlbaum.

Bennett, R.E. (2001). How the internet will help large-scale assessment reinvent itself. *Education Policy Analysis Archives* [On-line], 9(5). [Available at *http://epaa.asu.edu/epaa/v9n5.html*]

Bennett, R.E., Morley, M. & Quardt, D. (1998). Three response types for broadening the conception of mathematical problem solving in mathematics. *Applied Psychological Measurement*, 24, 294–309.

Birnbaum, A. (1968). Some latent trait models and their use in inferring an examinee's ability. In Lord, F.M. & Novick, M.R. (Eds.), *Statistical Theories of Mental Test Scores*. Reading, MA: Addison-Wesley.

Chang, H.H. & Ying, Z. (1999). Alpha stratified multistage computerized adaptive testing. *Applied Psychological Measurement*, 23, 211–222.

Clauser, B.E., Margolis, M.J., Clyman, S.G. & Ross, L.P. (1997). Development of automated scoring algorithms for complex performance assessments: a comparison of two approaches. *Journal of Educational Measurement*, 34, 141–161.

Embretson, S.E. (1999). Generating items during testing: psychometric issues and models. *Psychometrika*, 64, 407–433.

Glas, C.A.W. (2000). Item calibration and parameter drift. In van der Linden, W.J. & Glas, C.A.W. (Eds.), *Computerized Adaptive Testing: Theory and Practice*. Boston: Kluwer Academic Publishers.

Glas, C.A.W. & van der Linden, W.J. (2001, July). *Modelling Variability in Item Parameters in CAT*. Paper presented at the international meeting of the Psychometric Society, Osaka, Japan.

Hambleton, R.K. & Swaminathan, H. (1985). *Item Response Theory: Principles and Applications*. Boston: Kluwer-Nijhoff.

Kenney, J.F. (1997). New testing methodologies for the Architect Registration Exam. *CLEAR Exam Review*, 8(20), 23–28.

Kingsbury, G.C. & Zara, A.R. (1989). Procedures for selecting items for computerized adaptive tests. *Applied Measurement in Education*, 2, 359–375.

Kolen, M.J. & Brennan, R.L. (1995). *Test Equating: Methods and Practices*. New York: Springer-Verlag.

Lord, F.M. (1980). *Applications of Item Response Theory to Practical Testing Problems*. Hillsdale, NJ: Erlbaum.

Means, B. & Gott, S.P. (1988). Cognitive task analysis as a basis for tutor development: articulating abstract knowledge representations. In Postka, M.J., Massey, L.D. & Mutter, S.A. (Eds.), *Intelligent Tutoring Systems: Lessons Learned*. Hillsdale, NJ: Erlbaum.

Mislevy, R.J., Sheehan, K.M. & Wingersky, M.S. (1993). How to equate tests with little or no data. *Journal of Educational Measurement*, 30, 55–78.

Mislevy, R.J., Steinberg, L.S., Breyer, F.J., Almond, R.G. & Johnson, L. (1999). A cognitive task analysis, with implications for designing a simulation-based performance assessment. *Human Computers in Human Behaviour*, 15, 335–374.

Mislevy, R.J., Wingersky, M.S. & Sheehan, K.M. (1994). *Dealing with Uncertainty About Item Parameters: Expected Response Functions* (ETS Research Report 94-28-ONR). Princeton, NJ: Educational Testing Service.

Nichols, P.D., Chipman, S.F. & Brennan, R.L. (1995). *Cognitively Diagnostic Assessment*. Hillsdale, NJ: Erlbaum.

Rasch, G. (1960). *Probabilistic Model for Some Intelligence and Attainment Tests*. Copenhagen, Denmark: Danish Institute for Educational Research.

Spray, J.A., Ackerman, T.A., Reckase, M.D. & Carlson, J.E. (1989). Effect of medium of item presentation on examinee performance and item characteristics. *Journal of Educational Measurement*, 26, 261–271.

Stocking, M.L. & Lewis, C. (2000). Methods of controlling the exposure of items in CAT. In van der Linden, W.J. & Glas, C.A.W. (Eds.), *Computerized Adaptive Testing: Theory and Practice*. Boston: Kluwer Academic Publishers.

Stocking, M.L. & Swanson, L. (1993). A method for severely constrained item selection in adaptive testing. *Applied Psychological Measurement*, 17, 277–292.

van der Linden, W.J. (2000). Constrained adaptive testing with shadow tests. In van der Linden, W.J. & Glas, C.A.W. (Eds.), *Computerized Adaptive Testing: Theory and Practice*. Boston: Kluwer Academic Publishers.

van der Linden, W.J. & Reese, L.M. (1998). A model for optimal constrained adaptive testing. *Applied Psychological Measurement*, 22, 259–270.

Way, W.D. (1998). Protecting the integrity of computerized testing item pools. *Educational Measurement: Issues and Practice*, 17, 17–26.

Walter D. Way and Jerry Gorham

RELATED ENTRIES

ADAPTIVE AND TAILORED TESTING, AUTOMATED TEST ASSEMBLY SYSTEMS, ITEM RESPONSE THEORY: MODELS AND FEATURES

C COPING STYLES

INTRODUCTION

The term coping is generally used in association with the concepts of adaptation and stress, but it bears links to many other concepts as well. Adaptation is a very broad concept which covers many aspects of human behaviour, and coping, in turn, refers to a person's means to achieve or maintain adaptation. Situations which call for readaptation are usually stressful, and coping refers generally to managing stress, or emotional states connected to stress, but also to managing the stressful situations. Coping is the way to avoid the harmful effects of stress. The best known, and in psychological literature the most often quoted, definition of coping comes from Lazarus and Folkman (1984: 141), who define coping as 'constantly changing cognitive and behavioural efforts to manage specific external and/or internal demands that are appraised as taxing or exceeding the resources of the person'.

There are many other concepts closely related, or sometimes even comparable, to coping. This group consists of concepts such as sense of coherence, hardiness, self-efficacy, locus of control, perceived control, and many others which refer to persons' goals, perceptions or possibilities to control their own life and environment or, at least, to manage them. Also defences may be mentioned here, although many writers and researchers want to separate defences from coping, specifically because defences are considered less conscious than coping. Haan (1977), for example, has made a clear distinction between coping and defences, whereas Kahana et al. (1982) have used the concepts of coping, defence and even adaptation interchangeably.

The above mentioned concepts close to coping refer to dispositional attitudes and behaviours and are thus quite similar to the concept of coping styles. That, in turn, is associated with personality traits, which may be seen quite stable and changing, perhaps, only with life-time individual development. In other words, coping styles refer to rather stable, personality traits like dispositions to handle problematic situations and stress by various ways or strategies. Traditionally, this perspective was predominant in coping research, and it still has its proponents. In recent literature, however, the concept of coping styles has often been used quite loosely, referring also to any broader coping dimensions or even to specific strategies or ways of coping irrespective of whether they are situation specific or dispositional.

Contrary to the style or trait model, the process model emphasizes situation specific ways and strategies of coping. The process model also regards coping as highly conscious behaviour, whereas the trait model includes an idea of coping as a less conscious phenomenon, specifically when defences are accepted as ways of coping. At present, the process model seems to be more generally appreciated than the trait model. In this development the writings of Lazarus and his colleagues have played a major role (e.g. Lazarus & Folkman, 1984). This perspective depicts coping behaviour as very contextual. The process-oriented approach to coping concentrates on the actual thoughts and actions of people in specific events or situations as well as on changes in these thoughts and actions. It differs from the trait or disposition approaches, because it is not trying to identify what a person usually does. Coping is not static, unchanged from a situation or moment to another, but characterized by flexibility: specific ways to handle stress and stressful situations change according to the demands of the situations.

The choice and use of coping strategies may, however, at least partly depend on the personality characteristics of an individual. Thus, the trait and process perspectives might also be united. Unfortunately, in the recent literature and research they appear more mixed than united. This is seen, for example, in many publications describing studies where the coping styles of various groups of people are investigated using methods developed for assessing coping processes.

In all, coping research has been, and still is, characterized by conceptual vagueness and even controversy, as shown by De Ridder (1997), for example. Therefore coping assessment methods cannot be effectively developed by trying to improve their psychometric properties only (*cf.* Parker & Endler, 1992).

ASSESSMENT

When looking at publications mentioned in the PsycINFO database 1996 to 2000, only, I found over 70 differently named coping questionnaires, of which about 30 were intended for general measures of coping styles or processes, while the rest were targeted at certain age groups or problem areas. These figures do not include direct translations of original methods into other languages. Most of the methods have a North-American origin, but a few were developed in Germany, Holland or Britain and very few in other European or Asian countries. The North-American questionnaires, especially, have often been used as (almost) direct translations in other cultures on all continents. Sometimes, at least, these translations have tried to pay more attention on specific cultural features, but basically own ('domestic') methods are rare even in Europe, or at least they have not been introduced in international publications.

The methods that are used in the studies of coping reflect certain underlying theoretical or conceptual views. For example, clinical evaluation is closely related to views on egopsychological processes, and when personality tests are used the idea of coping focuses on personality traits. If it is assumed that coping is manifested especially in behavioural reactions and activities, observation of behaviour in natural, real-life situations is needed, or at least people should be asked to tell about their behaviour in stressful situations. However, observational studies on coping seem rare, and it is also hard to find studies where subjects have freely described their coping behaviour.

In most cases coping has been studied using questionnaires based on self-evaluations. These questionnaires include either hypothetical events and situations, or situations which the subjects have really experienced. The hypothetical situations have been specified with varying accuracy. In the case of authentic, really experienced events, the subjects have usually been asked to think about the most difficult or stressful situation in their life during the preceding week, month, year or some other time span. Hence, studies of this kind have been characterized by a wide range of events to be coped with. Often it has been a question of major life events and changes, but coping behaviour in habitual everyday situations has also been examined (e.g. Stone & Neale, 1984).

The questionnaires have usually listed numerous, even dozens of, ways of coping. The subjects have had to indicate, whether, or to what extent they have used each of the ways in the situations they are thinking about. These different ways are meant to represent various coping dimensions. The styles or strategies which the more or less numerous items (ways of coping) represent may be numerous, as well. However, most often three different dimensions are proposed: task- or problem-oriented, emotion-oriented and avoidance-oriented coping.

The two most often used methods in recent research are the Ways of Coping Questionnaire (Folkman & Lazarus, 1988) and the Coping Inventory for Stressful Situations (Endler & Parker, 1990). These two methods are also those that are most often translated into various European and Asian languages. They both use factor-analytically derived scales or dimensions of coping and are much alike otherwise, as well, like most coping questionnaires in general.

The Ways of Coping Questionnaire (WCQ) is the best known coping questionnaire, originally developed by Lazarus and his colleagues over twenty years ago. It is based on earlier methods, empirical findings and Lazarus' own theory about stress and coping. Several versions of the questionnaire have been presented, but the recently most often used version comes from Folkman and Lazarus (1988). The respondent is asked to think about the most stressful event or situation in his/her life recently and to indicate, using a four-point scale (from not used to used a great deal), which of the 66 given ways of coping he/she has used in the situation. Fifty of these ways contribute to eight scales representing problem and emotion-focused coping (the others remaining as buffer items). The WCQ is meant to measure coping processes, and dynamic and changing strategies in specific situations, not coping dispositions or styles.

The Coping Inventory for Stressful Situations (CISS) includes 48 items representing three different factors (16 items for each): task-oriented coping, emotion-oriented coping and avoidance-oriented coping. The last factor may also be divided into two different factors (distraction and social diversion). The items are answered using a five-point frequency scale (from not at all to very much). Although the developers of the method acknowledge situational effects on the chosen coping strategies, the CISS is meant to assess trait-like coping styles rather than situation-specific coping processes.

The *COPE questionnaire* (Carver et al., 1989) represents a theoretically based approach to assessment of coping styles, but its developers used it also to assess situational coping strategies. Being otherwise quite similar to the factor-analytical methods, it includes 13 scales of coping, each assessed by four items (plus one one-item dimension) on a four-point scale. In later studies those scales have not received psychometric support, but that is often the case with factor-analytical methods, as well.

Table 1 summarizes the main characteristics of the above mentioned three questionnaires, while Table 2 shows a selected list of coping questionnaires including these three and a few other instruments. For other listings on varying grounds and critical evaluations of coping questionnaires,

Table 1.   Characteristics of three notable questionnaires of coping styles and/or processes

	Coping Inventory for Stressful Situations	COPE Questionnaire	Ways of Coping Questionnaire
Style or Process	Style	Style (Process)	Process
Basis for dimensions and/or scales	Factor-analytical	Theoretical	Factor-analytical
Dimensions	Task-oriented Emotion-oriented Avoidance-oriented	Problem-focused Emotion-focused Avoidance	Problem-focused Emotion-focused
Scales	As dimensions + avoidance divided Planning	Active coping	Confrontive coping
			Distancing
		Suppression of competing activities	Self-controlling
	Distraction Social diversion		Seeking social support
		Restraint coping	Accepting responsibility
		Seeking social support – instrumental	Escape-avoidance
		Seeking social support – emotional	Planful problem-solving
		Positive reinterpretation and growth	Positive reappraisal
		Acceptance Turning to religion Focus on and venting of emotions Denial Behavioural disengagement Mental disengagement Alcohol–drug disengagement*	
Number of items	48	53	50 (66)
Item scale	5-point (not at all–very much)	4-point	4-point (not at all–a lot) (not used–used a great deal)

*Includes only one item.

see e.g. De Ridder (1997), Moos and Schaefer (1993), and Parker and Endler (1992). (See also Kahana et al., 1982, for some older methods.)

Many of the most often used coping questionnaires are general measures of coping behaviour. The WCQ and CISS, for example, have been used across all age groups from school children to old persons, and also in a great variety of contexts, as a general measure of coping, as well as with problem groups of various kinds. Some instruments, on the other hand, have been developed for specific purposes, e.g. for evaluating coping in case of depression, pain, epilepsy, heart disease, hearing problems, and family problems, to name just a few. Some questionnaires, in turn, have been designed to assess coping styles or processes among children,

adolescents, students, older people or other defined populations. Some of these more specific measures have been developed from the general questionnaires by modifying the items and, perhaps, adding new ones.

A number of interview methods have also been developed to study coping. However, in most cases this has involved a few open-ended interview questions (or perhaps an oral presentation of a questionnaire with some extra questions) rather than specific interview methods. The Stress in Life Coping Scale developed by Pearlin and Schooler (1978) is one of the few exceptions. It includes numerous questions for evaluating general coping responses across different areas of life, but unattached to specific life events. These questions

Table 2. Selected list of general coping questionnaires

Name and reference
COPE; Carver et al. (1989)
Coping Inventory for Stressful Situations; Endler and Parker (1990)
Coping Responses Inventory; Moos (1992)
Coping Strategy Indicator; Amirkham (1990)
Coping Styles Questionnaire; Rogers et al. (1993)
General Coping Questionnaire; Joseph et al. (1992)
Life Situations Inventory; Feifel and Strack (1989)
Mainz Coping Inventory (original German name Angstbewaeltigungs Inventar); Egloff and Krohne (1998)
Stress in Life Coping Scale; Pearlin and Schooler (1978)
Ways of Coping Questionnaire; Folkman and Lazarus (1988)

form a part of a wider structured interview concerning psychological resources, strain and coping in stressful situations. The whole method has not been used much, because it is rather laborious, and recent studies with partial use of the method are not easy to find, either.

In-depth or theme interviews to study coping have been used quite seldom, but there are some exceptions, such as the Duke Longitudinal Studies of Aging, the Bonn Longitudinal Study on Aging and the Jerusalem Longitudinal Study of Midadulthood and Aging, as well as few studies concentrating on certain specific problems. However, in most such cases the method has not been described in detail, and so it is quite difficult to evaluate the variety of interview methods used in coping studies to date.

In addition to the methods mentioned above, coping has sometimes been studied more or less indirectly by methods originally developed to examine concepts close to coping. This category includes questionnaires and other methods to evaluate, for example, activity, mood, competence, recent life events and internal vs. external locus of control. There have also been attempts to examine coping and adaptation holistically, using long and demanding interviews and a variety of different tests. Usually these techniques have been originally developed for other purposes, and are often non-repeatable in their original form to confirm the results.

The validity of the coping methods has usually not been adequately examined. The construct validity of the methods is questionable, partly because of the incoherent use of the concept of coping as well as other concepts close to it, as described above. There are problems in the external validity of the methods, as well. Many of the methods were originally used with certain age and cultural groups, and would need revalidation when used with other populations. Information on the internal consistency and test–test reliability of the method is too often missing, or indicates unsatisfactory levels. For critical evaluation of the validity and reliability issues, see De Ridder (1997), Parker and Endler (1992), and Schwarzer and Schwarzer (1996). In addition, Aldwin (1994) as well as Zeidner and Endler (1996) provide informative reading also on other important aspects of coping research.

FUTURE PERSPECTIVES AND CONCLUSIONS

In this entry, some conceptual and theoretical views on coping behaviour and various methods to study coping have been examined. These two sides of the issue include some vagueness and interrelated problems. Especially, the validity problems of the assessment methods are related to the vagueness of the concepts of coping. Both theoretical and methodological aspects need further development to guarantee sufficient consistency for valid and reliable comparisons.

During the last twenty years numerous coping-behaviour questionnaires have been used, and many of these questionnaires have sprouted various versions and modifications. The use of these self-report questionnaires is connected to an emphasis on coping processes on the theoretical side. However, if coping is seen as a process or a behavioural progress of even long duration rather than a momentary reaction, completing a coping questionnaire at one point of time cannot describe this process, but the questionnaire should be repeated a number of times during the person's possible progress toward eventual adaptation. There are very few studies which have even tried this kind of design.

Questionnaires on coping styles or processes often have notable psychometric and conceptual shortcomings. In spite of that, other methods have not been used much during the last decades. For example, projective coping methods have been used in few studies only. On the other hand, their use is closely connected to personality assessment and the conception of coping style, which has lately been less popular in coping research than a few decades ago. Processes and styles of coping are not, however, opposite or mutually exclusive concepts but coping behaviour is probably affected both by situational factors and dispositional ways of acting and reacting. Acknowledgment of this relationship gives but more reason to try and develop more versatile assessment methods.

When designing individual or group-level coping assessments one should always carefully consider what methods to use. For example, is it wise to use a method developed in different cultural surroundings as such, or should some modifications be made, which, then again, tends to weaken comparability? Consideration is needed, and perhaps even more so, also when one decides to develop or formulate a new method, because of the huge amount of different assessment tools available already. Some of the most often used (North-American) questionnaires have been translated into many languages and used in varying cultures, but the validity of these translated versions remains often questionable and they often lack any other psychometric evaluation than internal consistency.

The criticism towards the coping assessment methods proposed above does not mean that they should not be used at all in population studies or in clinical work. It means that one should be careful when choosing assessment methods and interpreting their results, and take into account the shortcomings and problems which these methods often have. The user should be aware of the origins and intended purposes of different methods when trying to find the best one for the particular setting.

What are then the most important questions to be answered when developing coping behaviour assessment? The primary challenge and necessity may be to clarify the concept of coping, reconciling various theoretical views, not least because the differing conceptions and views affect the assessments and weaken the comparability of different studies. The psychometric properties of the assessment tools already in use and those to be developed in the future should be improved in order to gather valid and reliable information on coping behaviour. For the comparability of the coping studies it would be better if there were fewer and less diversifying methods in use. On the other hand, if coping behaviour is indeed quite contextual and affected by cultural factors, we also need methods that are sensitive to these differences in order to increase our knowledge on coping in different settings.

Does the rise of self-report questionnaires represent a desirable trend or should other kinds of methods be encouraged instead? Possible alternative methods include, at least, various interview techniques and perhaps even reintroduction of projective and semiprojective assessment tools after their relative decline since the 1970s. In clinical settings or in other individual assessment, at least, many-sided up-to-date methods are needed beside the coping questionnaires.

Furthermore, it may be asked if the assessment methods should be grounded more heavily on the specific features of varying cultural (economic, social) surroundings. At the moment, most of the coping assessment methods used all over the world are originally English and developed in North America, and they have been more or less directly translated into other languages without paying much attention to the variability of attitudes and behaviours in different cultures.

What would be the most important targets of coping research in the future? More information is needed concerning various specific situations and groups of people. Even here the list of targets could become almost endless including, for example, coping behaviour with different illnesses, varying problems in social life and interpersonal communication, challenges caused by new technologies and flood of information as well as the rapid changes of various life domains in modern times. Most coping studies so far have concentrated on young and middle-aged adults. Other age groups have been studied as well, but very little information has been obtained from the youngest as well as the oldest age groups.

One point in order to improve coping research is to reconsider whether there is any sense to label certain ways of coping as inefficient or unuseful, as such. The individual processes of coping have various phases, and sometimes even those seemingly 'bad' ways or strategies may serve as an important link in the chain towards eventual adaptation. This notion is connected with another issue, i.e. the need to describe the coping process in detail. In one of his recent writings Lazarus (1998), being critical also toward his own coping studies and methods, has proposed that the ultimate goal of methodological development should be the ability to reveal and describe individual coping behaviour, reactions and ways to handle stressful situations, as well as inter-individual differences and intra-individual changes in these ways and reactions. Better understanding of human behaviour in stressful situations would also lend possibilities to enhance individuals' coping capacity and thus improve the quality of their life.

References

Aldwin, C.M. (1994). *Stress, Coping, and Development: An Intergrative Perspective.* New York: Guilford Press.

Amirkham, J.H. (1990). A factor analytically derived measure of coping: the Coping Strategy Indicator. *Journal of Personality and Social Psychology, 59,* 1066–1074.

Carver, S.C., Scheier, M.F. & Weintraub, J.K. (1989). Assessing coping strategies: a theoretically based approach. *Journal of Personality and Social Psychology, 56,* 267–283.

De Ridder, D. (1997). What is wrong with coping assessment? A review of conceptual and methodological issues. *Psychology and Health, 12,* 417–431.

Egloff, B. & Krohne, H.W. (1998). Die Messung von Vigilanz und kognitiver Vermeidung: Untersuchungen mit dem Angstbewaeltigungs-Inventar (ABI). *Diagnostica, 44,* 189–200.

Endler, N.S. & Parker, J.D.A. (1990). *Coping Inventory for Stressful Situations (CISS): Manual.* Toronto: Multi-Health Systems.

Feifel, H. & Strack, S. (1989). Coping with conflict situations: middle-aged and elderly men. *Psychology and Aging, 4,* 26–33.

Folkman, S. & Lazarus, R.S. (1988). *Manual for the Ways of Coping Questionnaire* (Research ed.). Palo Alto, CA: Consulting Psychologists Press.

Haan, N. (1977). *Coping and Defending. Processes of Self-Environment Organization.* New York: Academic Press.

Joseph, S., Williams, R. & Yule, W. (1992). Crisis support, attributional style, coping style and post-traumatic symptoms. *Personality and Individual Differences, 13,* 1249–1251.

Kahana, E., Fairchild, T. & Kahana, B. (1982). Adaptation. In Mangen, D.J. & Peterson, W.A. (Eds.), *Research Instruments in Social Gerontology.* Vol. I, Clinical and Social Psychology (pp. 145–193). Minneapolis: University of Minnesota Press.

Lazarus, R.S. (1998). Coping with ageing: individuality as a key to understanding. In Nordhus, I.H., VandenBos, G.R., Berg, S. & Fromholt, P. (Eds.), *Clinical Geropsychology* (pp. 109–127). Washington, DC: American Psychological Association.

Lazarus, R.S. & Folkman, S. (1984). *Stress, Appraisal, and Coping.* New York: Springer.

Moos, R.H. (1992). *Coping Responses Inventory Manual.* Palo Alto, CA: Center for Health Care Evaluation, Department of Veterans Affairs and Stanford University Medical Centers.

Moos, R.H. & Schaefer, J.A. (1993). Coping resources and processes: current concepts and measures. In Goldberger, L. & Breznitz, S. (Eds.), *Handbook of Stress. Theoretical and Clinical Aspects* (2nd ed., pp. 234–257). New York: Free Press.

Parker, J.D. & Endler, N.S. (1992). Coping with coping assessment: a critical review. *European Journal of Personality, 6,* 321–344.

Pearlin, L.I. & Schooler, C. (1978). The structure of coping. *Journal of Health and Social Behaviour, 19,* 2–21.

Rogers, D., Javis, G. & Najarian, B. (1993). Detachment and coping: the construction and validation of a new scale for measuring coping strategies. *Personality and Individual Differences, 15,* 619–626.

Schwarzer, R. & Schwarzer, C. (1996). A critical survey of coping instruments. In Zeidner, M. & Endler, N.S. (Eds.), *Handbook of Coping: Theory, Research, Applications* (pp. 107–132). New York: John Wiley & Sons.

Stone, A.A. & Neale, J.M. (1984). New measure of daily coping: development and preliminary results. *Journal of Personality and Social Psychology, 46,* 892–906.

Zeidner, M. & Endler, N.S. (Eds.) (1996). *Handbook of Coping: Theory, Research, Applications.* New York: John Wiley & Sons.

Timo Suutama

RELATED ENTRIES

Personality Assessment (General), Type A: A Proposed Psychosocial Risk Factor for Cardiovascular Diseases, Type C: A Proposed Psychosocial Risk Factor for Cancer, Cognitive Styles, Emotions

C
COUNSELLING, ASSESSMENTS IN

INTRODUCTION

The allied fields of counselling and counselling psychology have long shared a core set of values that have sustained their scholarly and professional contributions. Recent research has identified three central commitments that distinguish the field (Neimeyer & Diamond, 2001). These include a commitment to a lifespan developmental model of adjustment (as opposed to pathology), a commitment to vocational and career issues, and a commitment to issues of diversity and multiculturalism. Each of these commitments, in turn, have clear expressions within the field's contributions to the domain of assessment.

THE ASSESSMENT OF DEVELOPMENT AND ADJUSTMENT

Conceptualizing clients' problems through a lifespan developmental model of adjustment is a central feature of the field of counselling. This commitment is reflected in the interpretation and selection of various assessment instruments. For example, Blocher (2000a, 2000b) highlights the importance of interpreting assessments within the full context of an individual's life situations. This contextual awareness encourages counsellors to conceptualize client problems in terms of adjusting to a life stage or novel environment rather than pathologizing the problem as a deficiency. Danish (1981) states that issues of adjustment occur throughout the lifespan and can be categorized in the following ways: (a) normative influences that are usually either biologically or socially determined, e.g. menopause or compulsory retirement, (b) historical influences that tend to affect all individuals within a particular generation, e.g. Vietnam War or the Civil Rights Movement, and (c) non-normative life events, e.g. loss of a job or divorce. Although

there has been much theorizing about lifespan developmental models of adjustment, these considerations have not yet produced an array of assessment instruments designed for use in individual counselling (Hood & Johnson, 1997). Instead, the lifespan development framework represents a context within which various assessment tools can be understood and utilized.

While counselling psychologists strive to understand assessments within the context of the individual, there are particular assessment tools that specifically embrace the field's commitment to more normative and positive adjustment. These assessment tools provide the counsellor with information regarding individual adjustment to a particular problem or situation. Personality inventories such as the California Personality Inventory (CPI) and the Myers–Briggs Type Indicator (MBTI) accomplish this by investigating enduring interpersonal personality characteristics. These inventories contrast sharply with more pathology-based personality assessments, such as the MMPI-II, that focus assessment on aspects of pathology, dysfunction, and deficiency, rather than strengths, competencies, and capacities. Additionally, the concentration on this person–environment fit, on personal capacities and strengths, and on effective adjustment and growth are clearly reflected in the field's long-standing dedication to vocational and career assessment.

VOCATIONAL AND CAREER ASSESSMENT

Early career counselling was conceptualized as a process of helping the individual to select an appropriate career. Consequently, most assessment tools focused on aspects of trait–factor matching (e.g. matching skills or abilities to occupations). The redefining of vocational counselling as a developmental process (Super, 1957), however, turns the attention in the field away from a focus on the choice itself, and instead towards developmental features of the person making the choices. Attention to career preparedness, uncertainty, maturity, self-efficacy, and commitment all reflect this shift towards a developmental framework.

These and many other features of career development and decision making have been operationalized in assessment instruments in the field. Kapes, Mastie, and Whitfield (1994), for example, provide a review of 52 such instruments, and Kapes and Vacha-Haase (1994) provide synoptic coverage of an additional 245 assessment measures. Despite their remarkable variation, most career assessment measures are designed to fulfil one or more of four distinct functions (Herr & Cramer, 1992): *prediction* (e.g. forecast success or satisfaction); *discrimination* (e.g. determine matching of skills and demands); *monitoring* (e.g. assess ongoing identity development); and *evaluation* (e.g. assess change or effectiveness of outcome).

Selecting the most suitable assessment tool for use can be a challenging task for the counsellor and/or his or her client. Womer (1988) has provided a practical step-by-step procedure for evaluating and choosing appropriate career counselling assessments. Prediger and Garfield (1988) provide a useful complement to this by furnishing a checklist of counsellor competencies to assist the practitioner in determining his or her own suitability to administer, score, and interpret various career assessment measures.

DIVERSITY, MULTICULTURALISM AND ASSESSMENT

Attention to issues of diversity in counselling has found a number of expressions within the fields of assessment. These include (1) attention to the evaluation and development of culturally fair instruments and (2) explicit focus on the assessment of multicultural counselling competence.

Culturally Fair Assessment

Regarding cultural fairness, the field of counselling has directed its attention to the critique and development of cultural sensitivity in relation to the assessment instruments utilized within the discipline. The *Handbook of Multicultural Counselling* (Ponterotto, Casas, Suzuki & Alexander, 1995) reflects one representative resource in this regard. This handbook articulates two primary components of diversity in assessment: culturally sensitive or adapted assessment and the assessment of multicultural counselling competencies.

A framework for assessment in multicultural counselling has been advanced by Grieger and Ponterotto (1995). This framework takes into account cultural worldviews and levels of acculturation, within both clients and their families. Levels of 'psychological mindedness', and attitudes towards helping, are critical at the individual and familial levels. Additionally, recent work by Rodriguez (2000) identifies a range of culturally sensitive assessment instruments that are currently available in the field. These include intelligence tests (e.g. Wechsler Intelligence Scale for Children – Third Edition, and Woodcock–Johnson Psycho-Educational Battery – Revised) and non-verbal instruments (e.g. the Test of Nonverbal Intelligence – Third Edition, and The Leiter International Performance scale). In addition, alternate assessment strategies are utilized to accommodate cultural differences. These strategies include suspending time limits, contextualizing vocabulary, encouraging use of paper and pencil on arithmetic tests, clients target performances on tasks more familiar to the mainstream culture. The collective goals of efforts in this field are to examine and establish 'culturally fairness' in assessment in order to support the counsellor's overall dedication to cultural competence in the process of counselling.

The Assessment of Cultural Competence

The need for culturally sensitive assessment has also extended to the assessment of the counsellor's own multicultural competencies, as well. Rodriguez (2000) notes specific standards of culturally competent counsellors. These standards include (1) continued awareness and development of culturally sensitive assessment theories and (2) a thorough understanding of the instruments accessible for diverse populations. Ponterotto, Rieger, Barrett, and Sparks (1994) provide a review of four different assessment instruments created to assess the cultural competence of counsellors. The first assessment measure, the Cross-Cultural Counselling Inventory – Revised, is based on 11 discrete cross-cultural counselling competencies. The second measure is the Multicultural Counselling Awareness Scale-Form B: Revised Self Assessment, which measures multicultural knowledge/skills and awareness. Third, the Multicultural Counselling Inventory is an instrument that measures multicultural counselling competence according to four categories: skills, awareness, knowledge, and the counselling relationship. And fourth, the Multicultural Awareness–Knowledge-and-Skills Survey is used in counsellor training programmes to assess the effect of instructional strategies on students' multicultural counselling development.

This work is complemented by related efforts in the field to develop models of racial and cultural identity development (Helms, 1990) and associated assessment instruments. Importantly, this work has been extended towards identifying the ways in which a counsellor's own identity development relates to the development of professional competencies in multicultural counselling contexts (Vinson & Neimeyer, 2000).

In sum, issues of diversity constitute an important expression of the counselling field's commitment to multiculturalism. This commitment finds expression both in the ongoing need for the development of culturally relevant assessment tools, and in sustained self-reflection regarding the counsellor's own cultural awareness and multicultural skills (Gill & Bob, 1999).

FUTURE PERSPECTIVES AND CONCLUSIONS

Explicit attention to issues concerning the field's future has been the subject of recent empirical research. Neimeyer and Norcross (1997), for example, have identified specific predictions associated with future directions in the area of counselling and counselling assessment. Together with the results of systematic Delphi Polling (Neimeyer & Diamond, 2001), this work suggests continued attention to the three themes identified in this entry. This likelihood is further enhanced by related developments in allied fields, such as the renewed interest in 'positive psychology' and models of growth and development, technological advances in computer-assisted career assessment, and the inclusion of diversity as a core domain in the accreditation of counselling training programmes.

The field of counselling supports a broad array of interests and instruments in relation to the area of assessment. Distinctive contributions are marked by the field's ongoing commitment to models of growth and development, to a sustained focus on career and vocational issues, and on an enduring commitment to issues of diversity. Each of these areas, in turn, has spawned a wide assortment of assessment instruments designed to maximize the effectiveness of the work that is done between counsellors and their clients across a broad domain of professional practice.

References

Blocher, D.H. (2000a). *Counseling: A Developmental Approach* (4th ed.). New York: John Wiley & Sons.

Blocher, D.H. (2000b). *The Evolution of Counseling Psychology*. New York: Springer Publishing Company.

Danish, S.J. (1981). Life span development and intervention: a necessary link. *Counseling Psychologist*, 24, 144–160.

Gill, E.F. & Bob, S. (1999). Culturally competent research: an ethical perspective. *Clinical Psychology Review*, 19(1), 45–55.

Grieger, I. & Ponterotto, J.G. (1995). A framework for assessment in multicultural counseling. In Ponterotto, J.G., Reiger, B.P., Barrett, A. & Sparks R. (Eds.), *Handbook of Multicultural Counseling*. London: Sage.

Helms, J.E. (1990). *Black and White Racial Identity: Theory, Research, and Practice*. Westport, CT: Greenwood.

Herr, E.L. & Cramer, S.H. (1992). *Career Guidance and Counseling Through the Life Span: Systemic Approaches* (4th ed.). Boston: Little, Brown.

Hood, A.B. & Johnson, R.W. (1997). *Assessment in Counseling: A Guide to the Use of Psychological Assessment Procedures* (2nd ed.). Virginia: American Counseling Association.

Kapes, J.T., Mastie, M.M. & Whitfield, E.A. (Eds.) (1994). *A Counselor's Guide to Career Assessment Instruments*. Alexandria, VA: National Career Development Association.

Kapes, J.T. & Vacha-Haase, T. (1994). A counselor's guide user's matrix: an alphabetical listing of career assessment instruments by category and type of use. In Kapes, J.T., Mastie, M.M. & Whitfield, E.A. (Eds.), *Counselor's Guide to Career Assessment Instruments* (pp. 473–489). Alexandria, VA: National Career Development Association.

Neimeyer, G.J. & Diamond, A.K. (2001). The anticipated future of counselling psychology in the United States: a Delphi Poll. *Counseling Psychology Quarterly, 14*, 49–65.

Neimeyer, G.J. & Norcross, J.C. (1997). The future of psychotherapy and counseling psychology in the USA: Delphi data and beyond. In Palmer, S. & Varma, V. (Eds.), *The Future of Counseling and Psychotherapy* (pp. 65–81). London: Sage Publications.

Ponterotto, J.G., Casas, J.M., Suzuki, L.A. & Alexander, C.M. (Eds.) (1995). *Handbook of Multicultural Counselling*. London: Sage.

Ponterotto, J.G., Reiger, B.P., Barrett, A. & Sparks, R. (1994). Assessing multicultural counseling competence: a review of instrumentation. *Journal of Counseling and Development, 72*, 316–322.

Prediger, D.J. & Garfield, N.J. (1988). Testing competencies and responsibilities: a checklist for counselors. In Kapes, J.T. & Mastie, M.M. (Eds.), *Counselor's Guide to Career Assessment Instruments* (pp. 49–54). Alexandria, VA: National Career Development Association.

Rodriguez, C. (2000). Culturally sensitive psychological assessment. In Canino I. & Spurlock J. (Eds.), *Culturally Diverse Children and Adolescents: Assessment, Diagnosis, and Treatment* (2nd ed.). New York: Guilford Press.

Super, D.E. (1957). Vocational adjustment: implementing a self-concept. *Occupations, 30*, 88–92.

Vinson, T. & Neimeyer, G.J. (2000). The relationship between racial identity development and multicultural counseling competency. *Journal of Multicultural Counseling and Development, 28*, 177–192.

Womer, F.B. (1988). Selecting an instrument: chore or challenge? In Kapes, J.T. & Mastie, M.M. (Eds.), *Counselor's Guide to Career Assessment Instruments* (pp. 27–35). Alexandria, VA: National Career Development Association.

Greg J. Neimeyer, Jocelyn Saferstein and Jason Z. Bowman

RELATED ENTRIES

APPLIED FIELDS: CLINICAL, APPLIED FIELDS: EDUCATION

COUPLE ASSESSMENT IN CLINICAL SETTINGS

INTRODUCTION

The process for assessing couples is both quantitatively and qualitatively distinct from that for assessing individuals. With couples one has not only both partners to evaluate, but also the patterns of interaction that define their relationship. Whereas persons pursuing individual therapy typically acknowledge some culpability for their distress and assume at least token responsibility for change, partners entering couple therapy often attribute greater responsibility for relationship difficulties and burden for change to each other. A unique advantage to assessing couples is the opportunity to observe directly many of the patterns of communication and interaction that partners describe as problematic.

A CONCEPTUAL MODEL FOR ASSESSING COUPLES

Snyder and colleagues (Snyder, Cavell, Heffer & Mangrum, 1995) advocated a comprehensive model for directing and organizing assessment strategies for couples and families. They proposed five construct domains: (a) cognitive, (b) affective, (c) behavioural and control, (d) structural/developmental, and (e) communication and interpersonal. Constructs relevant to each of these domains can be assessed at each of the multiple levels comprising the psychosocial system in which the couple or family functions: (a) individuals, (b) dyads, (c) the nuclear family, (d) the extended family and related social systems, and (e) the community and cultural systems. Each of the five target domains may be assessed with varying degrees of relevance and specificity across each of the five system levels using both formal and informal assessment approaches to self-report and observational techniques.

SPECIFIC ASSESSMENT STRATEGIES

The Clinical Interview

The initial clinical interview serves as a means for obtaining important information, informally observing partners' communication patterns, and establishing a collaborative alliance for subsequent interventions. Snyder and Abbott (2002) advocated an extended initial assessment interview lasting about two hours in which the following goals are stated at the outset: (a) first getting to know each partner as an individual separate from the marriage; (b) understanding the structure and organization of the marriage; (c) learning about current relationship difficulties, their development, and previous efforts to address these; and (d) reaching an informed decision together about whether to proceed with couple therapy and, if so, discussing respective expectations.

L'Abate (1994) recommended attending to the following questions when conducting the initial interview: What types of communication and relational patterns exist between partners? To what degree have partners been able to develop a coalition enabling them to set goals, solve problems, negotiate conflicts, handle crises, and complete individual and family developmental tasks? To what extent have the partners and extended family members been able to negotiate mutually acceptable patterns of separateness and connectedness? To what extent are members emotionally supportive of each other? What are the recurrent themes in the marriage and the extended family? Information regarding transgenerational family structures, dynamics, and critical family events potentially influencing family members' interactions with one another can be graphically depicted using the family genogram method (McGoldrick, Gerson & Shellenberger, 1999).

Observational Approaches

More than 30 years of observational research indicate that distressed couples: (a) are more hostile; (b) start their conversations with greater hostility and maintain more hostility during the course of conversation; (c) are more likely to reciprocate and escalate their partner's hostility; (d) are less likely to edit their behaviour during conflict, resulting in longer negative reciprocity loops; (e) emit less positive behaviour; and (f) are more likely to show 'demand → withdraw' patterns (Heyman, 2001). These findings affirm the importance of integrating 5–10 minute observations of non-structured problem-solving discussions without therapist intervention into the initial assessment process. How does the conversation start? Does the level of anger escalate, and what happens when it does? Do the partners enter repetitive negative loops? Are the couple's communication patterns consistent across different domains of conflict?

Partners' communication exchanges can be subjected to various systems for coding verbal and non-verbal behaviour (for reviews see Sayers & Sarwer, 1998; Snyder & Abbott, 2002). The most widely used of these is the Marital Interaction Scoring System (MICS) that includes 37 codes of both verbal and non-verbal behaviours such as criticism, disagreement, negative affect, problem description, acceptance of responsibility, agreement, and humour. An abbreviated adaptation of the MICS designated as the 'rapid-MICS' (RMICS) reduces these codes to 9 and has demonstrated both reliability and discriminant validity.

Self-Report Techniques

The use of self-report measures in couples assessment is based on the rationale that such techniques: (a) are convenient and relatively easy to administer, obtaining a wealth of information across a broad range of issues germane to clinical assessment or research objectives; (b) allow disclosure about events and subjective experiences respondents may be reluctant to discuss; and (c) provide important data concerning internal phenomena opaque to observational approaches including values and attitudes, expectations and attributions, and satisfaction and commitment. However, self-report measures also exhibit susceptibility to efforts to bias self- and other-presentation in either a favourable or unfavourable manner, and typically provide few finegrained details concerning moment-to-moment interactions.

Published measures for assessing couples and families number well over 1000, although few have achieved widespread adoption. Several comprehensive sourcebooks regarding self-report marital and family measures are available (e.g. Touliatos, Perlmutter & Straus, 1990), as are pragmatic reviews and recommendations regarding selected measures for clinical use (e.g. Sayers & Sarwer, 1998; Snyder & Abbott, 2002).

Self-report measures of couples' *behaviour* emphasize specific behaviour exchanges, communication, verbal and non-verbal aggression, and the sexual relationship. Exemplars in this domain include the Spouse Observation Checklist (SOC) and Areas of Change Questionnaire (ACQ). Such measures of behaviour exchange typically ask each partner to indicate which behaviours their partner had emitted or the couple had participated in over some specified time period and to rate these as either pleasing or displeasing. Measures vary in their length and the extent to which they group behaviours into discrete categories (e.g. affection, companionship, communication, parenting, household tasks). Partners' responses serve to delineate relative strengths and weaknesses in the relationship and can be used as a basis for articulating specific requests and for generating behaviour exchange agreements.

Measures of partners' *cognitions* emphasize couples' assumptions, standards, expectancies, and attributions for relationship events. For example, the Dyadic Attributional Inventory (DAI) asks respondents to imagine hypothetical marital events and then, for each event, generate explanations for their partner's behaviour in that situation. The intent of such measures is to assist in identifying and modifying dysfunctional attributional sets contributing to subjective negativity. Related cognitive measures such as the Relationship Beliefs Inventory (RBI) examine unrealistic relationship assumptions or beliefs about marriage – for example, that disagreements are necessarily destructive or that spouses should know each other's feelings and thoughts without asking.

Measures of relationship *affect* or satisfaction abound. Some (e.g. the Kansas Marital Satisfaction Scale; KMSS) are as brief as 3–4 items that ask partners to rate their overall satisfaction with their relationship. A more widely used global measure in marital research is the 32-item Dyadic Adjustment Scale (DAS) assessing relationship cohesion, satisfaction, consensus, and affectional expression. Other multidimensional measures are far more extensive and are designed to identify both the nature and intensity of relationship distress in distinct areas of interaction. One such measure widely used in both research and clinical settings is the Marital Satisfaction Inventory – Revised (MSIR; Snyder, 1997), a 150-item inventory that includes two validity scales, one global scale, and ten specific scales assessing relationship satisfaction in such areas as affective and problem-solving communication, aggression, leisure time together, finances, the sexual relationship, role orientation, family of origin, and interactions regarding children.

FUTURE PERSPECTIVES

Future developments in couple assessment are likely to focus on three objectives. First, increasing attention needs to be placed on the psychometric adequacy of both self-report and observational techniques, something that to date has been sorely lacking (Snyder & Rice, 1996). Second, both clinical and empirical evaluation of optimal assessment strategies needs to be conducted. The current preferred strategy is to adopt a semi-structured clinical interview with informal observation of couples' communication, followed by a self-report strategy adopting a multidimensional measure or set of measures that differentiate among levels and sources of relationship distress. Areas of individual or relational distress revealed by these approaches can then be assessed further using structured observations or narrow-band self-report techniques with clear evidence of reliability and validity. Third, the clinical utility of specific assessment strategies needs to be evaluated by examining guidelines for linking findings to treatment and observing their differential impact on outcome.

CONCLUSIONS

Couple therapists and researchers face a vast array of measurement techniques intended to assess relevant behaviours, cognitions, affect, and patterns of interaction relevant to couples' concerns. A constructive assessment strategy is one guided by well-formulated conceptual models of assessment and treatment, use of assessment techniques with demonstrated psychometric adequacy as well as clinical utility, and an explicit case formulation that links assessment findings to clinical intervention. Specific assessment strategies – whether they emphasize informal or structured self-report or observational methods – should complement one another in serving dual purposes of generating information and helping the couple to construct a more optimistic formulation of their current difficulties, how they came about, and how they can be remedied.

References

Heyman, R.E. (2001). Observation of couple conflicts: clinical assessment applications, stubborn truths, a shaky foundations. *Psychological Assessment, 13*, 5–35.

L'Abate, L. (1994). *Family Evaluation: A Psychological Approach*. Thousand Oaks, CA: Sage.

McGoldrick, M., Gerson, R. & Shellenberger, S. (1999). *Genograms: Assessment and Intervention* (2nd ed.). New York: Norton.

Sayers, S.L. & Sarwer, D.B. (1998). Assessment of marital dysfunction. In Bellack, A.S. & Hersen, M. (Eds.), *Behavioural Assessment: A Practical Handbook* (4th ed., pp. 293–314). Boston: Allyn and Bacon.

Snyder, D.K. (1997). *Manual for the Marital Satisfaction Inventory – Revised*. Los Angeles, CA: Western Psychological Services.

Snyder, D.K. & Abbott, B.V. (2002) Assessing couples: a practical approach to planning and evaluating relationship interventions. In Antony, M.M. & Barlow, D.H. (Eds.), *Handbook of Assessment and Treatment Planning*. New York: Guilford.

Snyder, D.K., Cavell, T.A., Heffer, R.W. & Mangrum, L.F. (1995). Marital and family assessment: a multifaceted, multilevel approach. In Mikesell, R.H., Lusterman, D.D. & McDaniel, S.H. (Eds.), *Integrating Family Therapy: Handbook of Family Psychology and Systems Theory* (pp. 163–182). Washington, DC: American Psychological Association.

Snyder, D.K. & Rice, J.L. (1996). Methodological issues and strategies in scale development. In Sprenkle, D.H. & Moon, S.M. (Eds.), *Research Methods in Family Therapy* (pp. 216–237). New York: Guilford Press.

Touliatos, J., Perlmutter, B.F. & Straus, M.A. (Eds.) (1990). *Handbook of Family Measurement Techniques*. Newbury Park, CA: Sage.

Douglas K. Snyder

RELATED FIELDS

APPLIED FIELDS: CLINICAL, CHILD CUSTODY

CREATIVITY

INTRODUCTION

Creativity is usually defined as the capacity to generate ideas that are jointly original and adaptive. Original ideas are those that have a low statistical likelihood of occurring in the population, whereas adaptive ideas are those that satisfy certain scientific, aesthetic, or practical criteria. An idea that is original but maladaptive is more likely to be considered a sign of mental disturbance than creativity, while an idea that is adaptive but unoriginal will be dismissed as mundane or perfunctory rather than creative. Although almost universal consensus exists on this abstract definition of the phenomenon, much less agreement is apparent regarding how best to translate this definition into concrete instruments or tests.

TESTS

Psychologists wishing to assess individual differences in creativity have a tremendous range of instruments to choose from. Therefore, before investigators can settle on any single test or battery of tests, it is first necessary that they address four major questions:

1 What is the age of the target population? Some measures are specifically designed for

school-age populations, whether children or adolescents, whereas other measures are targeted at adult populations.

2 Which domain of creativity is to be assessed? Not only may creativity in the arts differ substantially from creativity in the sciences, but also there may appear significant contrasts within specific arts (e.g. music vs. literature) or sciences (e.g. mathematics vs. invention).

3 What is the magnitude of creativity to be evaluated? At one extreme is everyday problem-solving ability ('little c' creativity) where at the other extreme is eminent creativity that earns awards and honours appropriate to the domain ('Big C' Creativity, or genius).

4 Which manifestation of creativity is to be targeted? That is, the investigator must decide whether creativity manifests itself primarily as a product, a process, or a person. Some instruments postulate that creativity takes the form of a concrete product, others assume that creativity involves a particular type of cognitive process, while still others posit that creativity entails a personal disposition of some kind.

Of these four questions, it is the last that is perhaps the most crucial. Assessment strategies differ dramatically depending on whether creativity is best manifested as a product, process, or person. As a consequence, the description of creativity measures that follows will be divided into three subsections.

Product Measures

Ultimately, a creative idea should take some concrete form, such as a poem, story, painting, or design. Hence, one obvious approach to creativity assessment is to measure the quantity or quality of productive output. A case in point is the Consensual Assessment Technique devised by Amabile (1982). Here a research participant is asked to make some product, such as a collage or a poem, which is then assessed by an independent set of experts. This technique has proven especially useful in laboratory experiments on the social circumstances that are most likely to favour creative behaviour. However, this approach has at least two disadvantages. First,

the creativity of an individual is decided according to performance on a single task. Second, the assessment is based on a task that may not be representative of the domain in which the individual is most creative. For instance, a creative writer will not necessarily do well on a task in the visual arts, such as making collages.

An alternative is to assess individual differences in creativity according to products that the person has spontaneously generated. For example, the Lifetime Creativity Scales assess creative behaviour by asking participants to self-identify examples of their own creative achievements (Richards et al., 1988). According to this approach, creativity assessment is based on multiple products in the domain that the individual finds most germane to personal creative expression. Although this instrument has proven validity and utility, it can be objected that a product's creativity requires an external assessment, such as that provided in the Consensual Assessment Technique. Furthermore, this instrument is clearly aimed at everyday creativity rather than creative output that is highly valued professionally or socially.

One way to assess such Big-C Creativity is to use some variety of productivity measure. Thus, the creativity of scientists may be gauged by journal articles, that of inventors by patents. Often such measures of pure quantity of output are supplemented by evaluations of quality. For example, the quality of a scientist's productivity may be assessed by the number of citations to his or her work. Another approach is to assess creative impact in terms of awards and honours received or the evaluations of experts in the field – a tactic that dates back to Francis Galton (1869). One especially innovative strategy is Ludwig's (1992) Creative Achievement Scale, which provides an objective approach to evaluating a creator's life work. This scale has proven useful in addressing the classic question of whether exceptional creativity is associated with some degree of psychopathology (the 'mad-genius' debate).

Process Measures

One major drawback of all product measures of creativity is that they appear barren of truly psychological content. These measures stress outward behaviour and its impact rather than internal mental states. Yet presumably there exists some special thought processes that underly these creative products. Accordingly, psychologists can instead devise instruments that tap into these crucial processes. For example, Mednick (1962) theorized that creativity requires the capacity to generate remote associations that can connect hitherto disparate ideas. He implemented this theory by devising the Remote Association Test, or RAT, that has seen considerable use in subsequent research. A person taking the RAT must identify a word that has an associative linkage with three separate stimulus words (e.g. associating the word 'chair' with the given words 'wheel, electric, high').

An even more popular set of measures was devised by Guilford (1967) in the context of his multidimensional theory of intelligence. These measures assess various kinds of *divergent thinking*, which is supposed to provide the basis for creativity. Divergent thinking is the capacity to generate a great variety of responses to a given set of stimuli. Unlike *convergent thinking*, which aims at the single most correct response, ideational productivity is emphasized. A specific instance is the Unusual Uses test, which asks research participants to come up with as many uses as possible for ordinary objects, such as a toothpick or paperclip. The participants' responses can then be scored for fluency (number of responses), flexibility (number of distinct categories to which the responses belong), and originality (how rare the response is relative to others taking the test).

Although the foregoing measures were initially conceived for assessing creativity in adults, comparable measures have been devised for use with children and adolescents. Indeed, such measures have become especially commonplace in educational settings. Probably the most well-known instruments for this purpose are the Torrance Tests of Creative Thinking (Torrance, 1966; see also Crammond, 1994). Although designed to assess creativity in the early developmental years, these tests have been shown to have long-term predictive validity well into adulthood.

Person Measures

Process measures of creativity operate under the assumption that creativity requires the capacity to engage in somewhat distinctive cognitive processes. Not all psychologists agree with this position. In the first place, often performance on process instruments can be enhanced by relatively straightforward training procedures, and sometimes performance enhancements can occur by changing the instructional set when administering the test (i.e. the command to 'be creative!'). In addition, creative individuals appear to have distinctive non-cognitive characteristics that set them apart from persons who fail to display creativity. This has led some psychologists to propose that creativity be assessed by person-based measures.

The most frequently used instruments assess creativity via the personality characteristics that are strongly correlated with creative behaviour. These personality assessments are of three kinds. First, the assessment may simply depend on already established scales of standard tests, such as the Minnesota Multiphasic Personality Inventory or Eysenck's Personality Questionnaire. These measures will tend to yield the lowest validity coefficients. Second, the assessment may be based on the construction of a specialized subscale of an already established personality test. For instance, Gough (1979) devised a Creative Personality Scale from his more general Adjective Check List. Third, the assessment may rely on a measure that is specially constructed to gauge individual differences in creative personality. An example is the How Do You Think questionnaire that gauges whether a person has the interests, values, energy, self-confidence, humour, flexibility, playfulness, unconventionality, and openness associated with creativity (Davis, 1975).

An alternative person-based approach is predicated on the assumption that creative potential emerges by means of a particular set of developmental experiences. These experiences may reflect either genetic predilections (nature) or acquired inclinations (nurture). For example, Schaefer and Anastasi (1968) designed a biographical inventory that identifies creativity in adolescent boys (see also Schaefer, 1970). The items tap such factors as family background, school activities, and extracurricular interests. Moreover, the inventory discriminates not only creative from non-creative adolescents but also between scientific and artistic creativity. Similar biographical inventories have been devised for both children and adults.

Table 1.   Summary table of representative creativity measures

Product Measures	Consensual Assessment Technique (Amabile, 1982)
	Lifetime Creativity Scales (Richards et al., 1988)
	Creative Achievement Scale (Ludwig, 1992)
Process Measures	Remote Associates Test (Mednick, 1962)
	Unusual Uses Test (Guilford, 1967)
	Torrance Tests of Creative Thinking (Torrance, 1966; Crammond, 1994)
Person Measures	Creative Personality Scale of the Adjective Check List (Gough, 1979)
	How Do You Think Inventories (Davis, 1975)
	Biographical Inventory – Creativity (Schaefer, 1970; Schaefer & Anastasi, 1968)

The above list by no means exhausts the inventory of tests that purport to measure creativity. The instruments listed were merely chosen as representative of the various types of tests that have been developed since the 1960s. For a more detailed inventory, see Hocevar and Bachelor (1989).

FUTURE PERSPECTIVES

Ideally, scores on the diverse creativity measures should intercorrelate so highly that all alternative instruments could be said to assess the same underlying latent factor. The various measures can then be said to display convergent validity. Yet many empirical studies have found that alternative instruments often fail to converge on a single, psychometrically cohesive dimension. Even worse, many measures seem to lack divergent validity as well. For instance, some of the process-type instruments exhibit unacceptably high correlations with scores on intelligence tests. These correlations have driven some researchers to question whether creativity can be reliably separated from the problem-solving ability associated with general intelligence (i.e. 'Spearman's G'). In contrast, other creativity researchers have advocated more positive conclusions, believing that there indeed exists a subset of instruments that have the desired convergent and divergent validity – as well as the requisite predictive validity. Whether this optimistic position will receive empirical justification in future research remains to be seen.

CONCLUSIONS

Clearly, psychologists who want to assess creativity must confront a tremendous number of alternative creativity measures. Not only do the various instruments differ in their respective reliabilities and validities, but also the alternative measures are often based on rather contrary conceptions about what has to be measured. Even within a single approach there is available several rival measurement tools. Thus, the person-type measures include both biographical inventories and personality questionnaires, and the latter may be subdivided into more than one kind. Complicating matters even more, the choice of instrument is contingent on such criteria as the age of the target population, the domain of creativity involved, and the magnitude of creativity to be assessed. Creativity assessment is no easy task, and may even require some creativity.

References

Amabile, T.M. (1982). Social psychology of creativity: a consensual assessment technique. *Journal of Personality and Social Psychology, 43*(5), 997–1013.

Crammond, Bonnie (1994). The Torrance tests of creative thinking: from design through establishment of predictive validity. In Subotnik, R.F. & Arnold, K.D. (Eds.), *Beyond Terman: Contemporary Longitudinal Studies of Giftedness and Talent* (pp. 229–254). Norwood, NJ: Ablex.

Davis, G.A. (1975). In frumious pursuit of the creative person. *Journal of Creative Behaviour, 9*(2), 75–87.

Galton, Francis (1869). *Hereditary Genius: An Inquiry into its Laws and Consequences.* London: Macmillan.

Gough, H.G. (1979). A creative Personality Scale for the Adjective Check List. *Journal of Personality and Social Psychology, 37*(8), 1398–1405.

Guilford, J.P. (1967). *The Nature of Human Intelligence.* New York: McGraw-Hill.

Hocevar, Dennis & Bachelor, Patricia (1989). A taxonomy and critique of measurements used in the study of creativity. In Glover, J.A., Ronning, R.R. & Reynolds, C.R. (Eds.), *Handbook of Creativity* (pp. 53–75). New York: Plenum Press.

Ludwig, A.M. (1992). The Creative Achievement Scale. *Creativity Research Journal, 5*(2), 109–124.

Mednick, S.A. (1962). The associative basis of the creative process. *Psychological Review, 69*(3), 220–232.

Richards, R., Kinney, D.K., Lunde, I., Benet, M. & Merzel, A.P.C. (1988). Assessing everyday creativity: characteristics of the Lifetime Creativity Scales and validation with three large samples. *Journal of Personality and Social Psychology, 54*(3), 476–485.

Schaefer, C.E. (1970). *Biographical Inventory – Creativity*. San Diego, CA: Educational and Industrial Testing Service.

Schaefer, C.E. & Anastasi, A. (1968). A biographical inventory for identifying creativity in adolescent boys. *Journal of Applied Psychology, 58*, 42–48.

Torrance, E.P. (1966). *Torrance Tests of Creative Thinking*. Princeton, NJ: Personnel Press.

Dean Keith Simonton

RELATED ENTRIES

Intelligence Assessment (General), Personality Assessment (General), Applied Fields: Education

CRITERION-REFERENCED TESTING: METHODS AND PROCEDURES

INTRODUCTION

Criterion-referenced tests are constructed to allow users to interpret examinee test performance in relation to well-defined domains of content and/or behaviours. Normally, performance standards are set on the test score reporting scale to permit examinee test performance to be classified into performance categories such as below basic, basic, proficient, and advanced. Criterion-referenced tests are well suited for many of the assessment needs that exist in education, the professions, the military, and industry. Today, criterion-referenced tests are called by many names – domain-referenced tests, competency tests, basic skills tests, mastery tests, performance tests, authentic assessments, objectives-referenced tests, and more. In different contexts, test developers and users have adopted these different names. For example, in school contexts, the term 'mastery testing' is common. When criterion-referenced tests are developed to model classroom activities or exercises, the term 'authentic test' is sometimes used. When criterion-referenced tests consist of many performance tasks, the terms 'performance test' or 'performance assessment' are used. Regardless, all of these terms refer to a type of assessment where what examinees know and can do is estimated, and often performance standards are used for interpreting examinee performance.

This entry has been divided into three sections. First, the most important criterion-referenced testing concepts will be presented. Second, criterion-referenced tests will be compared to norm-referenced tests. Finally, some conclusions and predictions about the future for criterion-referenced tests will be offered.

KEY CRITERION-REFERENCED TESTING CONCEPTS

Defining Content Domains

When this approach to assessment was introduced by Glaser (1963) and Popham and Husek (1969), criterion-referenced tests were constructed to assess a set of behavioural objectives. Over the years, it became clear that behavioural objectives did not have the specificity needed to guide instruction or to serve as targets for test development and test score interpretation (Popham, 1978). Numerous attempts were made to increase the clarity of behavioural objectives including the development of detailed domain specifications that included a clearly written objective, a sample test item or two, detailed specifications for appropriate content, and details on the construction of relevant assessment materials (see Hambleton, 1998). Domain specifications seemed to meet the demand for clearer statements of the intended targets for assessment but they were very time-consuming to write and often the level of detail needed for good assessment was impossible to achieve for higher order cognitive skills, and so test developers found domain specifications to be limiting.

Recently the trend in criterion-referenced testing practices has been to write objectives focused on the more important educational outcomes (fewer instructional and assessment targets seem to be preferable) and then offer a couple of sample assessments, preferably samples that show the diversity of approaches that might be used for assessment (Popham, 2000). Coupled with these looser specifications of the objectives is an intensive effort to demonstrate the validity of any assessments that are constructed.

Writing Valid Test Items

The production of valid test items, that is test items that provide a psychometrically sound basis for assessing examinee level of proficiency or performance, require (1) well-trained item writers, (2) item review, (3) field testing, and (4) the use of multiple item formats. Well-trained item writers are persons who have had experience with the intended population of examinees, know the intended curricula, and have experience writing test items using a variety of item formats. Item review often involves checking test items for their validity in measuring the intended objectives, their technical adequacy (that is, being consistent with the best item writing practices), and ensuring items are free of bias and stereotyping. Field-testing must be carried out on samples large enough to provide stable statistical information and representative of the intended population of examinees. Unstable and/or biased item statistical information only complicates and threatens the validity of the test development process. And, finally, one of the most important changes today in testing is the introduction of new item formats, formats that permit the assessment of higher level cognitive skills (see Zenisky & Sireci, in press).

Setting Performance Standards

Perhaps the most difficult step in the criterion-referenced testing process is the setting of performance standards. Ultimately, this process is judgemental, and the goal is to create a framework in which judgements provided by panellists lead to reliable and valid ratings and ultimately reliable and valid performance standards. Many factors about the standard-setting process have changed over the years (for an excellent up-to-date review, see Cizek, 2001). For one, more emphasis today is given to the selection and training of panellists to set the performance standards. Panellists need to be representative of the appropriate stake-holder groups, and be thoroughly trained in the method being implemented. Second, detailed descriptions of the performance categories are being set. These are needed to provide the framework for panellists to make meaning judgements about the performance standards. Third, new methods for standard-setting have emerged for use with criterion-referenced tests, but research remains to be done to determine the most valid ways in which these methods can be implemented. Cizek (2001) describes a number of these new methods including the book-mark method, the body-of-work method, the analytic judgement method, and more. Fourth, the topic of feedback to panellists has become very important. How much and what kind of information do panellists need to set valid standards: information about their own consistency over items and over rounds of ratings; their agreement with other panellists; their consistency with empirical evidence about the test items and the examinees?

Assessing Reliability and Validity

Criterion-referenced test scores are used to assign examinees to performance categories. It is obvious then that reliability of test scores is less important than the reliability of the classifications of examinees to performance categories. This point is well-accepted in the criterion-referenced testing field (see Hambleton, 1998). But it is difficult, if not impossible, in practice to administer parallel forms (or even a retest) of a criterion-referenced test to assess the consistency with which examinees are assigned to performance categories. What have evolved then are single-administration estimates of decision consistency for criterion-referenced tests when items are scored 0–1, and there are two performance categories (Hambleton, 1998) and single-administration estimates of decision consistency when items are polytomously scored (i.e. more than two score categories are used per test item) and when more than two performance categories are used (see, for example, Livingston & Lewis, 1995). Both statistical procedures for obtaining single administration estimates of decision consistency involve strong true score modelling of the available data to obtain the estimates.

Validity assessment might focus on the relationship between classifications made on the basis of the test scores and classifications or performance ratings provided external to the test (e.g. teacher ratings, or job performance ratings). Other evidence to support the score inferences from a criterion-referenced test can come from the compilation of content, criterion-related, and construct validity evidence. See the AERA, APA, and NCME (1999) Test Standards for guidance.

Documenting the Technical Adequacy of a Test

The American Educational Research Association (AERA), American Psychological Association (APA), and the National Council for Measurement in Education (NCME) *Test Standards* (AERA, APA & NCME, 1999) make very clear that a test developer's job is not completed with the administration of his/her test. A major initiative is needed to compile the relevant procedural and technical information to document the usefulness of the test for achieving particular purposes. To quote the *Test Standards*, 'Test documents need to include enough information to allow test users and reviewers to determine the appropriateness of the test for its intended purposes' (AERA, APA & NCME, 1999: 67).

DIFFERENCES BETWEEN CRITERION-REFERENCED AND NORM-REFERENCED TESTS

Criterion-referenced tests are sometimes incorrectly assumed to be very similar to norm-referenced tests. It has been said, incorrectly, that these two types of tests are really no different,

and both criterion-referenced tests and norm-referenced tests are constructed in the same way. The only difference is the way in which the test scores are used. It is certainly true that scores from criterion-referenced tests and norm-referenced tests are used differently – criterion-referenced test scores are used to interpret examinee performance in relation to well-defined content areas and to make performance classifications. Norm-referenced test scores are used in comparing examinees on the construct that is measured by the test. Percentile norms, grade norms, age norms, and standard-score norms are all very popular and in common use. But these fundamental differences in test score interpretations have serious implications for the development and evaluation of criterion-referenced and norm-referenced tests. Criterion-referenced tests and norm-referenced tests differ in three important ways.

First, criterion-referenced tests require very precise definitions of the content to be measured. How else can content-referenced interpretations of scores be possible? With norm-referenced tests, content specifications are important because they impact on their construct validity. At the same time, the level of detail need not be as great because content-referencing of norm-referenced test scores is not done, and if it is done, this type of interpretation is only of secondary importance.

Second, with criterion-referenced tests, precise matching of test items to the content being measured is very important, and test items are chosen because of their content validity. Item statistics are important in identifying flaws in test items such as two correct answers or non-functioning distractors but items are selected because of judgemental and statistical evidence that they provide a basis for assessing the objectives of interest. When item statistics are used, it may be to assist in building tests that can maximize the precision of scores in and around the performance standards. In this way, decision consistency and decision accuracy can be increased by reducing measurement errors for examinees near the performance standards. In contrast, with norm-referenced tests, item match to the content specifications for the test is important, though not to the same degree, and most importantly, item statistics often play a critical role in item selection. In general, items with moderate difficulty levels and high levels of discriminating power, along with the appropriate content characteristics, are chosen to produce a test with a desired mean, and to maximize test score variance and test score reliability.

Finally, criterion-referenced tests and norm-referenced tests are judged against different criteria. For criterion-referenced tests, the consistency with which examinees are assigned to performance categories (e.g. below basic, basic, proficient, and advanced) and the accuracy of these classifications (that is, the consistency between performance classifications made based on test scores, and classifications based on an independent criterion) are important. Norm-referenced tests are judged based on a consideration of classical reliability estimation (e.g. test–retest, parallel-form, and internal consistency estimates of reliability) and criterion-related validation. Content and construct validation evidence is normally important for both criterion-referenced and norm-referenced tests.

In summary, it might be said that criterion-referenced and norm-referenced tests share many common features; for example, they often use similar test directions and similar item formats. On the other hand, since the purposes are fundamentally different, there are important differences in the ways the test content is specified for each, and the ways these two types of tests are constructed and evaluated.

FUTURE PERSPECTIVES AND CONCLUSIONS

The number of criterion-referenced tests being constructed today is substantial. These tests are being used in (1) the diagnosis of individual skills, (2) the evaluation of learning and achievement, (3) programme evaluation, and (4) credentialling. There is simply no shortage of situations where there is interest in assessing what examinees know and can do, and interpreting criterion-referenced test scores in relation to levels of expected or desired performance. But criterion-referenced testing continues to change – more focus is being placed on the definition and clarification of constructs to be measured (without clarity of content domains, neither instruction nor test development can be done well), more

item formats are being used in the tests (whereas 20 years ago multiple-choice items were common, today item formats extend to many variations of performance assessments), and more technical sophistication is being applied in the setting of performance standards and the assessment of reliability and validity (Hambleton, 1994).

References

AERA, APA & NCME (1999). *Standards for Educational and Psychological Testing*. Washington, DC: AERA.

Cizek, G. (Ed.) (2001). *Setting Performance Standards: Concepts, Methods, and Perspectives*. Mahwah, NJ: Erlbaum Publishers.

Glaser, R. (1963). Instructional technology and the measurement of learning outcomes. *American Psychologist*, 18, 519–521.

Hambleton, R.K. (1994). The rise and fall of criterion-referenced measurement? *Educational Measurement: Issues and Practice*, 13, 21–26.

Hambleton, R.K. (1998). Criterion-referenced testing principles, technical advances, and evaluation guidelines. In Reynolds, C. & Gutkin, T. (Eds.), *Handbook of School Psychology* (3rd ed., pp. 409–434). New York: Wiley.

Livingston, S. & Lewis, C. (1995). Estimating the consistency and accuracy of classifications based on test scores. *Journal of Educational Measurement*, 32, 179–197.

Popham, W.J. (1978). *Criterion-Referenced Measurement*. Englewood Cliffs, NJ: Prentice-Hall.

Popham, W.J. (2000, June). Assessments that illuminate instructional decisions. Presentation at the 30th Annual Conference on Large-Scale Assessment, Council of Chief State School Officers, Snowbird, Utah.

Popham, W.J. & Husek, T.R. (1969). Implications of criterion-referenced measurement. *Journal of Educational Measurement*, 6, 1–9.

Zenisky, A. & Sireci, S.G. Feasibility review of selected performance assessment item types for computerized examinations. *Applied Measurement in Education* (in press).

Ronald K. Hambleton

RELATED ENTRIES

ACHIEVEMENT TESTING, CLASSICAL AND MODERN ITEM ANALYSIS, PERFORMANCE STANDARDS: SELECTED RESPONSE ITEM FORMATS, PERFORMANCE STANDARDS: CONSTRUCTED RESPONSE ITEM FORMATS, VALIDITY: CRITERION-RELATED, THEORETICAL PERSPECTIVE: PSYCHOMETRICS

CROSS-CULTURAL ASSESSMENT

INTRODUCTION

Cross-cultural assessment refers to the use of assessment procedures with testees from different cultural backgrounds. Various instances can be distinguished: (i) an existing procedure is used in another country than the one in which it was originally designed, (ii) individuals within a single country differ from each other in ethnic or cultural background, or (iii) testees currently living in different countries take part in the same assessment procedure. Underlying all these forms of cross-cultural assessment are certain issues about the cross-cultural comparability or equivalence of test scores. These are briefly discussed in the first section. In the second section some traditions of cross-cultural test use are mentioned with a view to evaluate how serious the threats are to meaningful and valid cross-cultural assessment.

EQUIVALENCE ISSUES

Suppose a second generation migrant takes a test of word knowledge in a language that is not the home language of the parents. Then the question arises whether the obtained score is affected by the home language of this testee, and whether this is relevant for the interpretation of the score. Common sense tells us that the score can be a valid indicator of the current level of skill or achievement, but that it is likely to give a biased impression of the testee's language abilities, and about the testee's intellectual capacities in case the word knowledge test is part of an intelligence battery. This example shows that scores on one and the same instrument can be used to make inferences or generalizations about more than a single trait.[1]

If persons from different cultural backgrounds, who have the same test score, do not have the same standing on the trait to be assessed, the instrument concerned is called biased or

inequivalent. Thus, it often depends on the generalization whether or not scores are biased for testees belonging to a certain cultural population. A definition in which this is taken into consideration is the following: cultural biasedness or inequivalence implies that an observed difference between two cultural groups on a score variable is not matched by a corresponding difference in respect of the trait in terms of which the scores are interpreted.

From the 1960s cultural bias or inequivalence began to be addressed as a psychometric issue. Initially the focus was very much on item bias; items that were unexpectedly difficult for a new cultural group, to which a test was applied, were identified as biased and removed from the instrument. Gradually awareness increased that inequivalence is a more comprehensive issue (e.g. Malpass & Poortinga, 1986; Poortinga & Malpass, 1986). A framework for the analysis of cultural equivalence (or absence of bias) has been described by Van de Vijver and Leung (1997; Van de Vijver & Poortinga, 1997). They distinguish three levels of equivalence that are hierarchically ordered:

(i) structural or functional equivalence; viz., a test measures the same trait (or set of traits) cross-culturally.
(ii) metric or measurement unit equivalence; viz., differences between scores have the same meaning across cultures; the metric of the score variable is the same.
(iii) scale equivalence or full score equivalence; viz., scores have the same meaning cross-culturally and allow identical (quantitative) interpretations in terms of norms or criteria.

The general consequence of all forms of bias is that they make the scores of a test in some way incomparable across the cultural populations concerned. The test user or test author has to show that scores are not affected by bias

(Poortinga & Malpass, 1986). This is done by demonstrating that scores meet certain conditions of invariance of relationships cross-culturally. The remainder of this section gives examples of various levels of bias and how these can be identified.

Before the translation of a test, a panel of judges can examine the content validity of the items for the new cultural context. It is considered part of the translation of a test that the identity of linguistic meaning is being checked. However, most analyses of equivalence are carried out after data sets from different cultures have been obtained.

A first set of controls pertains to the question whether the same trait is measured in the various cultural groups. Bias occurs, if important aspects of the relevant trait are not included in the test, or somehow misrepresented. An example is the notion of being smart or clever, which in African societies much more than in Western countries appears to be associated with positive social behaviour. Another example is found in an analysis of Kagitcibasi (1970) who found that components of authoritarianism on an American scale showed lower intercorrelations in Turkey than in the USA, suggesting that the scale had a different meaning in Turkey. Needless to say, if a test or scale does not measure the same trait, cross-culturally, any comparison of scores is meaningless; it amounts to comparing apples with pears.

Relevant information can be obtained by examining structural relationships between item variables or (if there is a set of tests referring to a nomological network) between test score variables. This is called analysis of structural equivalence (Van de Vijver & Leung, 1997). For equivalent tests such structural relationships should be invariant. Usually this is taken to imply that correlations between variables should be equal across cultures. In practice it is usually not the similarity between correlation matrices that is determined, but the similarity of factor structures. The most common statistic to assess this similarity is Tucker's [phi]; values larger than 0.90 are seen as evidence that the same traits are being assessed cross-culturally.

A second level of inequivalence distinguished by Van de Vijver and Leung (1997) is called metric equivalence. This form of equivalence implies that quantitative differences between individual scores have the same meaning in different countries. An example of metrically equivalent scales is the Kelvin and Celsius scales. Both are measures of temperature and a difference of a certain numerical value has the same meaning everywhere, but an identical value on these two scales has quite a different meaning. In a similar sense the same word knowledge score of migrant and non-migrant testees may reflect different levels of underlying verbal ability. And cultural differences in the emphasis on speed versus accuracy may lead to differences on speeded tests that are not found on power tests. Still another example concerns unequal effects across groups of response styles. Van Herk (2000) found evidence for a systematic tendency towards higher scoring on item response scales in representative samples from Greece, and to a lesser extent Italy, than in Western European countries.

There are no clear traditions for the analysis of the numerous sources of metric inequivalence (Van de Vijver & Tanzer, 1997). Since most of them tend to affect all the items of an assessment procedure to a similar extent, psychometric conditions to rule out metric equivalence depend on some external standard, or repeated administration of the instrument under different conditions or with different samples. For example, suspected effects of social desirability can be evaluated by the use of a separate scale for social desirability, and effects of speededness can be identified by allowing extra time to an experimental group. All in all, test users and test authors should realize that it is virtually impossible to rule out all of the many possible, and even plausible, sources of bias leading to metric inequivalence.

Most controls concern scale equivalence or full score comparability, i.e. the state of affairs where a test score has the same meaning in terms of the intended trait independent of the cultural background of the testee. Sometimes these controls are in the form of an extension of analyses for structural equivalence. Structural equation models like LISREL allow an ordered sequence of tests examining increasingly strict conditions, including aspects of scale equivalence as well as structural equivalence (Marsh & Byrne, 1993).

An important set of control procedures for scale equivalence are directed at finding evidence of item bias, also called *differential item functioning* (DIF). In these analyses the other items on a test are taken as a standard against which the target item is evaluated. The general condition for equivalence is, then, that testees with the same test score, independent of culture, should have the same expected item score. An item can be biased because of problems with translation, or because its contents refer to cultural specific knowledge or practices. Item difficulty, or the rate of endorsement in typical performance tests, can be influenced in various subtle ways. For example, in a study with French and German respondents, Ellis (1989) could make plausible that some items were biased because of slight shifts in linguistic meaning. For bias in other items no reason could be given and on replication of the study not all the same items came out as biased. This is to be expected as a statistical decision rule invariably leads to some false positive and false negative outcomes.

Various statistical procedures have been developed to test for item bias (e.g. Berk, 1982; Holland & Wainer, 1993; Van de Vijver & Leung, 1997). Initially these were based on classical test theory, with the difficulty index (p_i) as the most important item parameter. An item with a larger, or smaller, difference between cultural groups in p_i than expected would be identified as biased. One common technique, which continues to be handy to gain a first impression, is the preparation of a plot of the p_i values in two groups and to visually inspect these for outliers. Another common technique is analysis of variance, with the item by culture interaction term as the main index for bias.

For dichotomous (yes–no, correct–incorrect) items the p_i index has several disadvantages (Lord, 1980). Therefore, analyses based on item response theory (IRT) models and contingency tables (so-called χ^2 procedures) were developed. Such models not only lead to better estimates, they also allow the researcher to distinguish between different forms of item bias, although the numbers of respondents required for stable estimates may be large, especially with IRT models. Moreover, these more recent procedures are so-called 'conditional' methods, in which item bias is investigated per ability level. In 'unconditional' methods, like those based on correlations between p_i values, the implicit assumption is that item bias is invariant across the entire range of scores.

Currently the most popular technique with dichotomous items is the Mantel–Haenszel statistic (e.g. Holland & Wainer, 1993). In a first step, each of two groups of testees are split up in subgroups with equal test scores. The procedure then compares the means of the items across these subgroups. An unbiased item will show means that are the same for all pairs of subgroups; an item is biased when it shows differences in difficulty between at least some of the pairs of subgroups.

USING THE SAME TESTS ACROSS CULTURAL GROUPS

The evidence on the feasibility of using the same tests across cultural populations comes mainly from three (overlapping) sources, viz., (i) adaptation and transfer of tests, (ii) analysis of bias in cross-cultural studies, and (iii) analysis of fairness of tests in multicultural societies.

Most well-known psychometric tests, especially from the USA and the UK, have been translated into many languages. Sometimes translated tests are used without even determining new norms. Although no cross-cultural comparison of scores may be intended, it should be clear that full score equivalence is assumed if scores in one country are interpreted on the basis of norms from another country. At other times elaborate adaptation procedures are followed, especially with intelligence batteries like the Wechsler intelligence scales. In projects of this kind new norms are established on the basis of a local sample. The scores are not used for cross-cultural comparison, but usually it is assumed that the research conducted in the country of origin is also valid for the adapted version. Thus, structural equivalence is assumed, but other levels of equivalence are of limited concern. Available evidence tends to be in support of construct equivalence. For example, Vander Steene et al. (1986) found for a Dutch version of the WISC that the factor structure was similar to that reported by Kaufman (1975) for the USA. However, it should be noted that 'similarity' is often decided on an impressionistic basis rather than on the basis of formal statistical procedures of the kind mentioned earlier on.

In the area of personality there is at present much interest in the so-called Five-Factor Model

(FFM) or 'Big Five' personality dimensions. Research on structural equivalence indicates that more often than not these dimensions travel well from culture to culture (e.g. McCrae, Costa, Del Pilar, Rolland & Parker, 1998). These findings are moderated by studies in which locally constructed scales have led to the identification of additional factors beyond those found with the FFM (cf. Cheung & Leung, 1998). But this may mean that the FFM model does not represent the entire domain of personality traits, rather than questioning the structural equivalence of dimensions that are represented.

Another example of a much used instrument is the MMPI, including the MMPI/2. In a number of countries the validity of diagnostic profiles originally established for the USA has been investigated. By and large these were found to be rather similar, although it would be a step too far to assume strict metric equivalence even across the industrialized countries (cf. Butcher, 1996). Other findings have been reported for the *Eysenck Personality Questionnaire* (EPQ). Similarity in factor structures was found by Barrett, Petrides, Eysenck, and Eysenck (1998) in comparisons of numerous countries with the original factor structure in the UK.

The second source of empirical evidence derives from cross-cultural research in which equivalence is an explicit target of investigation. In the previous section various examples have been discussed. The largest volume of research has been directed at item bias. No studies were found that were based on samples from cultures with substantial differences in behaviour repertoires that did not show statistical evidence of item bias. A conservative conclusion from such findings is that the trait domain from which items were sampled is not identical across cultures and that this preempts any comparison. On the other hand, in such studies the majority of items tend to behave fairly similar; an item that is difficult, or has a high rate of endorsement in one population, also does so in another population. This kind of evidence justifies the practice of removing biased items to improve the equivalence of tests.

The empirical evidence derived from analyses of bias in multicultural societies is difficult to interpret. One reason is that recent minority groups as a rule are culturally heterogeneous, not only in terms of background, but also in terms of the extent of their acculturation to the new society. Most research has been conducted in the USA, where some minorities have been part of the society for a number of generations. Here limited, though non-negligible, effects of item bias have often been found (e.g. Berk, 1982; Holland & Wainer, 1993). In countries in Europe that in recent decades have become more multicultural systematic attention for test use is now emerging (e.g. Bleichrodt & Van de Vijver, 2001).

With test use in multicultural settings score distributions from different ethnic groups can be evaluated in terms of common criteria (e.g. job performance). In this way, the 'fairness' of the tests can be assessed. One problem is that analyses of fairness are rather underdeveloped. Criterion ratings and test scores may suffer from common sources of bias (e.g. poor quality of schooling for minorities) when interpretations are made to more encompassing traits, like intellectual capacities. In studies of differences in intelligence between African-Americans and European-Americans this difficulty has been seriously underestimated (cf. Herrnstein & Murray, 1994). On the other hand, there is a growing emphasis on broader views of assessment for higher education, including the potential of the student for growth and development, and for fairness in employment testing (Sireci & Geisinger, 1998).

FUTURE PERSPECTIVES AND CONCLUSIONS

Across the educated groups in the world to whom psychometric tests are administered there is limited evidence of structural inequivalence. Therefore, transfer and adaptation of existing tests appears to make sense. An important advantage is that the knowledge and expertise can be used which has gone into the original development. Moreover, the information on validity can be employed that has been accumulated, sometimes over many years. About metric equivalence there remains uncertainty. To what extent profiles of personality scales, as used in clinical diagnosis, and profiles of cognitive abilities allow the same interpretation remains unclear and will have to be judged from instance to instance on the basis of concrete evidence. The extensive record of item bias makes clear that full score equivalence can hardly ever be assumed and this imposes strong limitations on the interpretation of scores of testees with different cultural backgrounds, in terms of the same norms or standards. This is especially the case if scores are interpreted in terms of comprehensive psychological traits like cognitive abilities and personality dimensions.

Note

1 'Trait' is used for the behaviour domain, personality trait, cognitive ability, etc., in terms of which a test score variable is interpreted. The notion is similar to that of 'universe of generalization' (Cronbach, Gleser, Nanda & Rajaratnam, 1972).

References

Barrett, P.T., Petrides, K.V., Eysenck, S.B.G. & Eysenck, H.J. (1998). The Eysenck Personality Questionnaire: an examination of the factorial similarity of P, E, N, and L across 34 countries. *Personality and Individual Differences*, 25, 805–819.

Berk, R.A. (Ed.) (1982). *Handbook of Methods for Detecting Test Bias.* Baltimore, MD: Johns Hopkins University Press.

Bleichrodt, N. & Van de Vijver, F.J.R. (Eds.) (2001). *Het Gebruik Van Psychologische Tests Bij Allochtonen.* Amsterdam: Swets.

Butcher, J.N. (Ed.) (1996). *International Adaptations of the MMPI-2: Research and Clinical Applications.* Minneapolis: University of Minnesota Press.

Cheung, F.M. & Leung, K. (1998). Indigenous personality measures: Chinese examples. *Journal of Cross-Cultural Psychology*, 29, 233–248.

Cronbach, L.J., Gleser, G.C., Nanda, H. & Rajaratnam, N. (1972). *The Dependability of Behavioural Measurements.* New York: Wiley.

Ellis, B.B. (1989). Differential item functioning: implications for test translations. *Journal of Applied Psychology*, 74, 912–921.

Herrnstein, R.J. & Murray, C. (1994). *The Bell Curve: Intelligence and Class Structure in American Life.* New York: Free Press.

Holland, P.W. & Wainer, H. (Eds.) (1993). *Differential Item Functioning.* Hillsdale, NJ: Erlbaum.

Kagitcibasi, C. (1970). Social norms and authoritarianism: a Turkish–American comparison. *Journal of Personality and Social Psychology*, 16, 444–451.

Kaufman, A.S. (1975). Factor analysis of the WISC-R at 11 age levels between 6 1/2 and 16 1/2 years. *Journal of Consulting and Clinical Psychology*, 43, 135–147.

Lord, F.M. (1980). *Applications of Item Response Theory to Practical Testing Problems.* Hillsdale, NJ: Erlbaum.

Malpass, R.S. & Poortinga, Y.H. (1986). Designs for equivalence. In Lonner, W.J. & Berry, J.W. (Eds.), *Field Methods in Cross-Cultural Psychology* (pp. 47–83). Beverly Hills, CA: Sage.

Marsh, H.W. & Byrne, B.M. (1993). Confirmatory factor analysis of multigroup–multimethod self-concept data: between-group and within-group invariance constraints. *Multivariate Behavioural Research*, 28, 313–349.

McCrae, R.R., Costa, P.T., Jr., Del Pilar, G.H., Rolland, J.-P. & Parker, W.D. (1998). Cross-cultural assessment of the five-factor model: the revised NEO personality inventory. *Journal of Cross-Cultural Psychology*, 29, 171–188.

Poortinga, Y.H. & Malpass, R.S. (1986). Making inferences from cross-cultural data. In Lonner, W.J. & Berry, J.W. (Eds.), *Field Methods in Cross-Cultural Psychology* (pp. 17–46). Beverly Hills, CA: Sage.

Sireci, S.G. & Geisinger, K.F. (1998). Fairness in employment testing. In Sandval, J., Frisby, C.L., Geisinger, K.F., Scheunneman, J.D. & Grenies, J.R. (Eds.), *Test Interpretation and Diversity: Achieving Equity in Assessment* (pp. 105–140). Washington, DC: American Psychological Association.

Van de Vijver, F.J.R. & Leung, K. (1997). *Methods and Data Analysis for Cross-Cultural Research.* Thousand Oaks, CA: Sage.

Van de Vijver, F.J.R. & Poortinga, Y.H. (1997). Towards an integrated analysis of bias in cross-cultural assessment. *European Journal of Psychological Assessment*, 13, 21–29.

Van de Vijver, F.J.R. & Tanzer, N.K. (1997). Bias and equivalence in cross-cultural assessment. *European Review of Applied Psychology*, 47, 263–279.

Vander Steene, G., Van Haassen, P.P., De Bruyn, E.E.J., Coetsier, P., Pijl, Y.J., Poortinga, Y.H., Spelberg, H.C. & Stinissen, J. (1986). *WISC-R: Wechsler Intelligence Scale for Children – Revised. Nederlandstalige Uitgave.* Lisse: Swets & Zeitlinger.

Van Herk, H. (2000). *Equivalence in Cross-National Context: Methodological and Empirical Issues in Marketing Research.* Unpublished Ph.D. Thesis. Tilburg: Tilburg University.

Ype H. Poortinga

RELATED ENTRIES

Test Adaptation/Translation Methods, Testing in the Second Language in Minorities, Theoretical Perspective: Psychometrics

D DANGEROUS/VIOLENCE POTENTIAL BEHAVIOUR

INTRODUCTION

The past decade has witnessed a growing interest in the clinical assessment of dangerousness and violence risk (Monahan & Steadman, 1994; Quinsey, Harris, Rice & Cormier, 1998). Successful prediction of often covert, low-frequency events can be particularly difficult to demonstrate. Within groups of mentally ill, criminal offenders, and/or mentally ill criminal offenders, major predictors of violent recidivism are largely the same, with criminal history variables most predictive of future violence relative to clinical variables associated with diagnosis of mental illness (Bonta, Law & Hanson, 1998).

Several assessment protocols have been advanced, including those adapted for specialized types of violence, such as sexual offending. Reliable and valid procedures such as the Psychopathy Checklist – Revised (PCL-R, Hare, 1991), Violence Risk Appraisal Guide (VRAG, Quinsey et al., 1998), Sex Offender Risk Appraisal Guide (SORAG, Quinsey et al., 1998), HCR-20 (Webster, Douglas, Eaves & Hart, 1997), and Rapid Risk Assessment for Sexual Offense Recidivism (RRASOR, Hanson, 1997) allow forensic practitioners to anchor their clinical opinions in empirically based nomothetic data while providing an estimate of violence potential over a given period of time.

While historical information forms a starting point for assessing potentially dangerous and violent individuals, idiographic data obtained from *individualized personality assessment* fills in the 'missing middle' (adding clinical and dispositional information to substantiated historical and contextual data) to inform and guide the tasks of understanding and treating dangerous and violent patients (Gacono, 2000; Gacono & Meloy, 1994, 2002).

VIOLENCE PREDICTION

Debate over the superiority of actuarial versus clinical approaches in the prediction of behaviour may hazard the creation of an artificial dichotomy. For example, a patient possessed by the delusion that he must hurt or kill another (to save himself, humankind, the earth) should be considered potentially quite dangerous, regardless of actuarially determined risk. In assessing individuals, actuarial tools are used as guides to inform clinical judgement.[1] With this caveat in mind, we turn to the most intensive actuarially oriented project assessing violence risk.

The MacArthur Violence Risk Assessment Study

Monahan and Steadman's (1994) work outlining the beginnings of the MacArthur Violence Risk Assessment Study is sometimes credited with reinvigorating a more collaborative, second generation effort to standardize an actuarial approach in the prediction of violence. Drawing upon a panoply of previously identified but variously operationalized risk variables, Monahan and Steadman adapted a number of standardized tests and variables to operationalize prospective violence risk factors found in four general groupings:[2]

1 Dispositional factors, including anger, impulsiveness, psychopathy, and personality disorders.
2 Clinical or psychopathological factors, including diagnosis of mental disorder, alcohol or substance abuse, and the presence of delusions, hallucinations, or violent fantasies.
3 Historical or case history variables, including previous violence, arrest history, treatment history, history of self-harm, as well as social, work, and family history.
4 Contextual factors, including perceived stress, social support, and means for violence.

Dependent on the referral context and setting, an assessment of potentially violent individuals requires gathering data from each of these four domains.

Assessing Historical, Dispositional, Clinical, and Contextual Factors

Assessing potentially violent individuals begins with a thorough review of documented historical information, whether performed in institutional or community setting. Documentation, often obtained from legal authorities, must be reviewed relating to history of violence (including sexual assault), previous offences, weapon use, and so forth. Contemporary data including mental status markers (acute paranoid ideation, delusions, etc.) can be substantiated from a review of treatment records, staff interviews, and other corroborative sources. Antecedents and consequents surrounding previous violent acts should be noted along with the mode of violence (affective versus predatory). While a history of *affective violence* in an unmedicated psychotic patient (without concurrent psychopathy or character pathology) will likely respond, first, to neuroleptic intervention and, second, to anger management instruction, the same interventions will not likely impact

the psychotic psychopath with a documented history of *predatory violence*.[3] Evaluation of a patient's past violence includes assessment of the cognitive, affective, and behavioural patterns prior to, during, and consequent to violent episodes, as well as any current situational or dynamic factors that could be impacted by immediate intervention.[4] In addition to relevant historical, dispositional, clinical, and contextual factors, victim characteristics (age, gender, circumstances) should also be noted.

Subsequent to assessing the above history and mental status, clinical opinions are anchored by completing an established actuarial risk assessment instrument. Historical information and semi-structured interview data are used to complete these procedures. The Violence Risk Appraisal Guide (VRAG) and the Sex Offender Risk Appraisal Guide (SORAG; Quinsey et al., 1998) are two protocols that produce a violence prediction probability estimate based on the summation of demographic, historical and clinical findings, with a significant contribution made by the patient's score on the PCL-R (requiring record review and semi-structured interview; Hare, 1991).

The PCL-R (Hare, 1991) assesses psychopathy level and is an integral part of the VRAG and SORAG. The PCL-R is a 20 item protocol based on interview findings anchored in a thorough record review and substantiation through related corroborative sources. High psychopathy scores have consistently been related to findings of criminal recidivism, including violent recidivism, and are viewed as a particularly intractable dispositional factor that should never be ignored (Bodholdt et al., 2000; Gacono, 2000).

Provided the data from the evaluation protocol described above, personality testing, like the Rorschach, refines our understanding of dispositional or clinical factors such as impulsivity, levels of anger and hostility, presence of thought disorder, problems with affect regulation, methods of coping with emotions, and so forth. Standardized psychological testing aids in teasing out the similarities and differences among individuals to an extent not possible with risk assessment guides and instruments such as the PCL-R alone (Gacono, 1998, 2000). Combined historical information, risk assessment guide scores, PCL-R scores, and testing data allow the clinician to provide opinions highlighting *individualized context–person dynamics*; that is, under what set of circumstances is a given patient more likely to perpetrate a particular type of violence directed at a particular type of victim.

Conducting the Evaluation

The choice of actuarial tools and evaluation format is dictated by setting, referral question, clinical presentation, resource availability such as treatment, and the purposes served by the evaluation. Probabilities and other correlations determined from actuarially derived methods require a consideration of their clinical application.[5] The following case example illustrates the use of historical, dispositional, clinical, and contextual factors in evaluation of a previously violent, and prospectively, potentially dangerous individual.

Case Example. Mr. Jones is a married, Caucasian male, in his mid-twenties, referred for a psychological evaluation to determine risk of future offending, amenability to parole supervision, and to better understand offence and substance abuse history. Mr. Jones is currently serving a 3-year sentence for assault with a deadly weapon.

Mr. Jones' history reveals a sporadic work history, a lengthy history of substance and alcohol abuse, and the absence of a major mental disorder. He meets criteria for multiple substance dependencies, dysthymia, and Antisocial Personality Disorder (historical, clinical, dispositional). His violence has never been predatory, rather, it has always been impulsive, unplanned, driven by intense affect, and associated with intoxication (dispositional, contextual factors).

PCL-R (28) and VRAG (+23, category 8) scores, both static variables based primarily on historical data, place him at a high risk for violent re-offence within the next 7 to 10 years. Rorschach and MMPI-2 findings highlight dispositional and clinical factors suggesting problems managing emotions, high levels of hostility, difficulties handling complexity, and associated problems with perception and judgement. Legal factors are also of consequence. The state has two remaining years of hold over an individual, who discharging 'as is' presents a fairly substantial risk of re-offence. There are no institutionally based resources (no substance abuse, anger management, or similar treatment) to target the somewhat more malleable (dynamic) but difficult dispositional and clinical risk factors. Thus, any treatment impact on those risk factors highlighted through psychological assessment would need to come from a community setting, preferably offered under parole supervision and paid for by Mr. Jones' family.

The parole board decision to release or retain becomes more straightforward when presented with evaluation findings. They can: (1) incarcerate Mr. Jones until his time is completed and subsequently release him unsupervised to the community with all the 'static' actuarial risk unmitigated; or (2) use his supervision period in an attempt to impact any dynamic (changeable) factors relevant to re-offence rates. The senior author (CBG) recommended the latter, including recommendations that the parole board consider a nine to twelve month residential substance abuse treatment programme followed by transition to a halfway house.

FUTURE PERSPECTIVES

The immediate future involves the task of assimilating into clinical practice the vast amount of data and findings on violence and violence prediction from the ongoing MacArthur Violence Risk Assessment Project and other programmatic research (see also Gacono, 2000). To be of practical use, we expect further refinement of assessment protocols, followed by necessary cross-validation and normative studies. Item Response Theory item analysis may be particularly well suited to cross-cultural studies as well as test or protocol refinement (Bodholdt et al., 2000). Further, as computational algorithms continue to be developed, and computer memory and processing speed become less of an obstacle, we expect neural network modelling to assist prediction accuracy by extracting more relevant and less redundant predictors and also quantifying non-linear relationships among variables found to be highly interactive (Marshall & English, 2000). In this light, we are hopeful that data obtained regarding factors tending to mitigate or worsen potential for violence will be applied in efforts involving early intervention, with special attention to social and societal forces impacting violence and aggression.

CONCLUSIONS

In any setting, assessing potentially dangerous and violent patients quite frequently becomes an exercise in harm reduction. Had our case example involved a highly predatory psychopathic individual, with or without substance abuse problems or a supportive family, available data concerning amenability to treatment would very likely have resulted in a harm reduction strategy involving no parole, thus minimizing exposure to the public for a year or two, but not impacting subsequent risk (Gacono, Nieberding, Owen, Rubel & Bodholdt, 2001).

Advances in the actuarial prediction of violence have been impressive, and continue to be more fully elaborated and refined. In assessing individuals, actuarial protocols can inform clinical judgement, but not replace clinical judgement. The evaluation begins with historical and actuarial formulations, but it also assesses dynamic factors addressing risk reduction, setting, available resources, as well as ethical and legal constraints. Not only should the assessment consider the probability of violence within a given setting, it must also consider the capacity of the setting to control or contain the potential violence to staff or other patients. A harm reduction approach allows the evaluator to organize his or her data into a cogent conceptual model.

Notes

1   We note that more recent studies have found clinical judgement, in the absence of formalized actuarial tables, to be less lacking than initially suspected (Gardner, Lidz, Mulvey & Shaw, 1996; Mossman, 1994).

2   A complete listing of well over 100 variables and tests would exhaust the space allotted for this entry.

3   Contrasted to *affective violence* which has been characterized as 'flight or fight', increased autonomic arousal, reactivity, and possible loss of reality testing, *predatory violence* has been linked to psychopathy and is associated with minimal or absent autonomic arousal, minimal perceived threat, planned and purposeful behaviour, and unimpaired reality testing (Meloy, 1988).

4   This includes identification of specific person–context factors (e.g. medication non-compliance, alcohol or drug use, level of supervision or

custody) expected to mitigate or amplify more immediate risk of re-offence, including violent re-offence.

5   For example, empirical data indicating the rare use of the insanity defence (NGRI) and even rarer occurrence of those who malinger, when used to dismiss the need for considering psychopathy level in these evaluations, the relevance of questioning NGRI statutes, or ignoring the undue burden of attempting to treat the NGRI psychopath, are of little consolation to forensic hospital staff who are forced by legal statute into the untenable position of managing the serious behaviours of a malingering psychopath (Gacono, 2000).

References

Bodholdt, R.H., Richards, H.R. & Gacono, C.B. (2000). Assessing psychopathy in adults: the psychopathy checklist – revised and screening version. In Gacono, C.B. (Ed.), *The Clinical and Forensic Assessment of Psychopathy: A Practitioner's Guide* (pp. 55–86). Mahwah, NJ: Erlbaum.

Bonta, J., Law, M. & Hanson, K. (1998). The prediction of criminal and violent recidivism among mentally disordered offenders: a meta-analysis. *Psychological Bulletin, 123*, 123–142.

Gacono, C. (1998). The use of the psychopathy checklist – revised (PCL-R) and Rorschach in treatment planning with antisocial patients. *International Journal of Offender Therapy and Comparative Criminology, 42*(1), 49–64.

Gacono, C. (2000). Suggestions for implementation and use of the psychopathy checklists in forensic and clinical practice. In Gacono, C.B. (Ed.), *The Clinical and Forensic Assessment of Psychopathy: A Practitioner's Guide* (pp. 175–202). Mahwah, NJ: Erlbaum.

Gacono, C. & Meloy, R. (1994). Rorschach assessment of aggressive and psychopathic personalities. Mahwah, NJ: Erlbaum Publishers.

Gacono, C. & Meloy, R. (2002). Assessing antisocial and psychopathic personalities. In Butcher, J. (Ed.), *Clinical Personality Assessment: Practical Approaches* (2nd ed.; pp. 361–375). New York: Oxford.

Gacono, C., Nieberding, R., Owen, A., Rubel, J. & Bodholdt, R. (2001). Treating conduct disorder, antisocial, and psychopathic personalities. In Ashford, J., Sales, B. & Reid, W. (Eds.), *Treating Adult and Juvenile Offenders with Special Needs* (pp. 99–129). Washington, DC: American Psychological Association.

Gardner, W., Lidz, C.W., Mulvey, E.P. & Shaw, E.C. (1996). Clinical versus actuarial predictions of violence in patients with mental illness. *Journal of Consulting and Clinical Psychology, 64*, 602–609.

Hanson, K. (1997). The development of a brief actuarial risk scale for sexual offender recidivism (User Report No. 97-04). Ottawa, Canada: Department of the Solicitor General of Canada.

Hare, R.D. (1991). *The Hare Psychopathy Checklist – Revised*. Toronto: Multi-Health Systems.

Marshall, D.B. & English, D.J. (2000). Neural network modelling of risk assessment in child protective services. *Psychological Methods*, 5, 102–124.

Meloy, R. (1988). *The Psychopathic Mind: Origins, Dynamics, and Treatment*. Northvale: Jason Aronson.

Monahan, J. & Steadman, H.J. (1994). Toward a rejuvenation of risk assessment research. In Monahan, J. and Steadman, H.J. (Eds.), *Violence and Mental Disorder: Developments in Risk Assessment* (pp. 1–17). Chicago: The University of Chicago Press.

Mossman, D. (1994). Assessing predictions of violence: being accurate about accuracy. *Journal of Consulting and Clinical Psychology*, 62, 783–792.

Quinsey, V.L., Harris, G.T., Rice, M.E. & Cormier, C.A. (1998). *Violent Offenders: Appraising and Managing Risk*. Washington, DC: American Psychological Association.

Webster, C.D., Douglas, K.S., Eaves, D. & Hart, S.D. (1997). *HCR:20 Assessing Risk for Violence, Version 2*. Burnaby, British Columbia: Simon Fraser University Press.

Carl B. Gacono and Robert H. Bodholdt

RELATED ENTRIES

APPLIED FIELDS: CLINICAL, ANGER, HOSTILITY AND AGGRESSION ASSESSMENT, ANTISOCIAL DISORDERS ASSESSMENT

DECISION (INCLUDING DECISION THEORY)

INTRODUCTION

Most problems dealt with in the practice of psychology can be solved only by the application of a treatment, e.g. an intervention. In most cases, more than one treatment is available. The psychologist has to choose between several options. His or her choice of or decision for a certain treatment cannot be made in an arbitrary way but has to follow certain rules which are the subject of a field of study called decision theory (*cf.* Klein et al., 1993). In the practice of psychology, an important component of the decision rules are case-related assessment data, which are collected in the course of an assessment process. The role of assessment data in the decision-making process is the topic of this entry.

A CLASSIFICATION OF DECISIONS

For every decision it is necessary that a minimum of two alternative treatments is given, e.g. acceptance versus rejection of an applicant. Decisions which occur during the assessment process can be classified within a system proposed by Cronbach and Gleser (1965), who distinguished between six kinds of assessment-related decisions.

The first feature of decisions refers to whether the gain of a decision is in favour of an institution or an individual. A decision is *institutional*, for example, when an organization tests all individuals using the same standardized procedure. In such a case, a decision rule is required that yields as much benefit to the institution as possible from multiple (homogeneous) decisions over all individuals. Individual interests may be taken into account, but only insofar as they affect the realization of the goals of the institution. A decision is *individual*, for example, when an individual asks an institution for help in a decision making process. In order to get information that can support the individual in the decision, the institution arranges a specific test programme. Individual decisions are often unique. The choice confronting the decision maker may rarely or never recur. In this case only the individual benefit is important.

The second feature of decisions distinguishes between fixed and variable rates of acceptance. A *fixed rate of acceptance* exists, for example, when job openings in a company are limited to a certain number. In such a case the decisions depend on each other. A *non-fixed* or *variable acceptance rate* exists, when independence of the decisions is given. This is the case, for example, when there is a job for every applicant who fulfils the respective requirements.

Cronbach and Gleser (1965) also differentiate between *single-stage* and *multi-stage (sequential) tests*. In the first case, the decision is made in only one step, in the second case in multiple steps on the basis of a sequential procedure.

The fourth feature of decisions refers to whether persons are *selected* (e.g. for a job, training, therapy) or *placed* to different treatments. When people are selected, only a certain number is accepted. However, when they are placed, nobody is excluded from the institution, but each person is assigned to the treatment with the best fit to his or her individual characteristics.

Assessment data are either restricted to only one dimension (*univariate* information) or composed of more dimensions (*multivariate* information). The use of multiple predictors increases the validity of a decision, because multiple facets of the criterion can be considered.

The last feature of decisions distinguishes between terminal and investigative decisions. If the individual is assigned to a treatment in which the person will stay in for a relatively long period of time, the decision is considered to be *terminal* and the assessment process to be complete. If the person is assigned to a temporary treatment, the decision is considered to be *investigative* and the treatment will lead to further questions.

The combination of the six features of classification results in $2^6 = 64$ different types of decisions in an assessment process. Tack (1976) combines these different components in his circular model and emphasizes especially the objective of the decision, which is important for the decision-making strategy. He defines a strategy as a normative system of rules that are applied to given data considering the prevailing objectives. The fundamental types of these strategies are referred to in the following sections.

COMPENSATORY AND CONJUNCTIVE DECISION STRATEGIES

In a *compensatory* model, a certain decision can be made on the basis of various combinations of predictor scores (i.e. low scores in some of the predictors can be compensated by high scores in other predictors). In compensatory models the combination of the predictor scores is linear. In addition to these combinatory-compensatory strategies, *disjunctive strategies* (Or-strategies) exist as another class of compensatory strategies. Using the Or-strategies, an applicant needs to obtain a certain score in only one predictor to be accepted, not a sum of many competencies. Compensatory strategies are always dysfunctional when certain minimum requirements in all tests are necessary to obtain a result, e.g. success in a particular job. In those cases *conjunctive* strategies (And-strategies) need to be applied.

SINGLE-STAGE VS. MULTI-STAGE DECISION STRATEGIES

Decision strategies can be single-stage and multi-stage. A single-stage strategy is called 'non-sequential battery', in which persons are selected who achieve the highest sum score in the whole battery of tests. Another one is called 'single screen', which means that only one test is administered and all further decisions are based on that test.

Multi-stage decision strategies can be divided into three different procedures: the first one is called the *pre-reject strategy*, in which all persons who do not achieve a certain score are excluded from further testing and are rejected.

Using the *pre-accept strategy* all persons are accepted who achieve a particular score. The rest of the persons are further tested.

The *complete sequential strategy* is a combination of the former two procedures: those individuals who score higher than a certain score are accepted, and those who are below another score are rejected. Persons in the medium range are further tested for acceptance or rejection.

Sequential strategies (multi-stage) are in general superior to non-sequential strategies (single-stage), but this superiority disappears when extreme selection rates are given (see Cronbach & Gleser, 1965: 77ff). Sequential decisions can be reduced to a series of single-stage procedures.

DECISION-ERRORS

The central task of assigning-strategies is to avoid classification errors. Such errors occur when the assignment on the basis of predictor variables does not overlap with the real class affiliation. Two types of assigning errors can be distinguished: the type-one-error consists of false positive decisions (for example, people are diagnosed as being sick although they are healthy); the type-two-error consists of false negatives (for example, people are diagnosed as being healthy although they are sick). Four evaluation criteria can be distinguished: (1) *Sensitivity* is the probability with which a given positive state is recognized as such. (2) *Specificity* is the probability with which a given negative state is recognized as such. (3) *Positive prediction value* is the probability with which a positive decision or diagnosis is correct. (4) *Negative prediction value* is the probability with which a negative decision or diagnosis is correct.

The ratio of the number of persons that are successful in the criterion and the number of all persons considered defines the *base rate*, which is also called the *success rate without use of test*. The efficiency of the selection can be calculated as the ratio of the number of selected and qualified persons and the number of all selected persons, which is also called the *selective qualification quotient*. This quotient is identical with the positive prediction value.

FIXING CUT-OFF SCORES

Increasing or decreasing the cut-off score of a predictor or predictor combination, which separates negative from positive decisions, can alter the size of the positive prediction value (and the selective qualification quotient). The more the critical cut-off score is moved towards the characteristic or attribute that has to be identified (e.g. illness or qualification), the larger will be the size of the quotient. But then, only the error of a false positive decision is considered, whereas the risk of a false negative decision is neglected. For setting the cut-off score, the base rate and the success rate without use of test are important. With the help of the

ROC-curve (Receiver Operating Characteristic), specificity and sensitivity can be determined simultaneously and independently of the base rate for various cut-off scores, if the test score distribution of the different groups could be determined on the basis of empirical studies.

To reconcile the particular aspects, an additional evaluation of the certain outcomes and possible errors, which is completely independent of methodological approaches, is necessary. Wieczerkowski and Oeveste (1982: 929) point out that there is no unequivocal solution for setting critical cut-off scores but that personal, social, and economic factors must be considered.

UTILITY CONSIDERATIONS

Institutional and individual decisions are made because the respective organizations or persons want to achieve positive economic results, i.e. gains, whereas losses are a result of wrong decisions. Cronbach and Gleser (1965) formalized this economic dimension of institutional decisions and developed a utility function with which the total utility of a certain decision strategy can be estimated. To do that, a *strategy matrix* is an important requirement. A strategy matrix includes rules according to which decisions can be made on the basis of assessment data. The entries of such a matrix are the probabilities with which the alternative treatments are assigned to groups of persons which are characterized by certain classes of assessment data. For a treatment t and a group of persons characterized by assessment information x_r the entry would be the conditional probability $p(t \mid x_r)$.

In addition to the frequently used 0/1-rule, which confines the range of the conditional probabilities $p(t \mid x_r)$ to the values 0 (i.e. no assignment to treatment t in case of assessment data x_r) and 1 (i.e. assignment to t given x_r), probabilistic links are also possible. Despite this, it is also important to link the considered treatments to their results as well as to the success in the criterion. This link is included in the so-called *validity matrix*. Its entries stand for the probability that persons characterized by assessment information x_r and assigned to treatment t achieve a criterion score c_r: $p(c \mid x_{r,t})$. In the simplest case, the criterion scores can be dichotomous categories (successful versus not successful, healthy versus ill). Continuous categories are possible as well.

Finally, it is necessary to assign to every criterion class a utility-vector e_c and to every class of assessment data a cost vector c_c. The utility is the value, which can be calculated for every stage of the criterion in the respective institution. Costs come into existence through the efforts of getting certain information. It is important that utilities and costs are put on the same scale and that the scale consists of equal intervals (interval level). For monetary units, those restrictions are fulfilled.

Based on the strategy matrix and the validity matrix as well as on the values of the utility and cost vectors, the following non-parametric gain function can be established (after Cronbach & Gleser, 1965: 24):

$$U = N \underbrace{\sum_r p(x_r) \underbrace{\sum_t p(t|x_r) \overbrace{\sum_c p(c|x_{r,t}) e_c}^{III}}_{I}}_{II}$$

$$- N \underbrace{\sum_r p(x_r) \cdot c_r}_{IV}$$

$U =$ Utility

$e_c =$ Gain of the achievement of the criterion c

$p(c \mid x_{r,t}) =$ Value from the validity-matrix for the treatment t

$p(t \mid x_r) =$ Value from the strategy-matrix

$p(x_r) =$ Probability of the class of assessment data x_r

$c_r =$ Costs for getting assessment data x_r

$N =$ Number of persons the strategy is applied to

$I =$ Expected gain of an individual in the criterion, if the individual is characterized by a class of assessment data x_r and treatment t is applied

$II =$ Expected gain of an individual who is characterized by the class of assessment data x_r

$III =$ Expected gain of an individual (mean over criterion classes, treatments, and classes of assessment data)

$IV =$ Expected cost for getting the information from a person

The multiplication of utility and cost by the number of tested persons results in the expected net-utility of a strategy when it is applied to a group of N individuals. This model merges with the model of Brogden (1949), when assumptions of continuity are made for the information and criterion categories. Constant costs for all persons are presumed and the test scores are linearly related with the achievement in the criterion. The central formula of this model is:

$$U = N \cdot s_e \cdot r_{xe} \cdot V_{(xiT)} + N\varphi_{(xiT)}e_{t(A)} - NC_x$$

$e_t(A) =$ Average gain of a person after treatment A (accept) for the institution

$s_e =$ Deviation of the expected gain values

$r_{xe} =$ Correlation between the predictor and (gain differences in) the criterion; $e_{t(A)}$, s_e, r_{xe} have to be specified in the population before the test is applied

$V_{(xiT)} =$ Ordinate of the standard normal distribution in the (standardized) cut-off score x_{iT}

$\phi_{(xiT)} =$ Selection rate for the cut-off score x_{iT}

$C =$ Costs

The a priori utility results, when $N^*\varphi_{(xiT)}$ persons out of a population are selected randomly:

$$U_o = N\varphi_{(xiT)}e_{t(A)}$$

The utility of applying the test (net utility) on N persons is therefore:

$$U - U_0 = N \cdot s_e \cdot r_{xe} \cdot V_{(xiT)} - NC_x$$

Divided by the number of tested persons, the net utility 'per man tested' (Cronbach & Gleser, 1965: 308) evolves. As seen in the equations, the validity of the tests, the variability of the utilities and the selection ratio are important for the utility.

FUTURE PERSPECTIVES AND CONCLUSIONS

The requirement of a linear relation between the predictor and the utility is often not fulfilled. It is also very difficult to get the entries for the validity matrices because, for their specification, no earlier selection should have taken place. The respective persons should have been (randomly) assigned to the treatments and then observed longitudinally to demonstrate adequate success rates.

Next to this basic problem, the determination of the monetary equivalence is comparatively simple because it is easy to determine what has to be paid for a test, its administration, and its evaluation. On the other hand, the efforts of developing a test and the training of assessors should also be included as well as the loss of a (right or wrong) rejection.

Although the requirements of the model are sometimes empirically not fulfilled and the difficulties of collecting the necessary information are notorious, there are some publications which demonstrate the usefulness of the model for practical purposes (Brandstätter, 1970; Weinstein and Fineberg, 1980) and underline that psychological testing may yield enormous benefits to institutions and the society in total (Amelang, 1999).

Acknowledgement

I am grateful to Birgit Koopmann for the application of her English skills to this entry.

References

Amelang, M. (1999). Zur Lage der Psychologie: Einzelaspekte von Ausbildung und Beruf unter besonderer Berücksichtigung der ökonomischen Implikationen psychologischen Handelns [On the state of psychology: educational and professional aspects with special regard to the economic implications of psychological action]. In *Psychologische Rundschau*, 50, 2–13.

Brandstätter, H. (1970). *Leistungsprognose und Erfolgskontrolle [The Prediction of Achievement and the Evaluation of Success]*. Bern: Huber.

Brogden, H.E. (1949). When testing pays off. *Personnel Psychology*, 2, 171–185.

Cronbach, L.J. & Gleser, G.C. (1965). *Psychological Tests and Personnel Decisions* (2nd ed.). Urbana, IL: University of Illinois Press.

Klein, G.A., Orasanu, J., Calderwood, R. & Zsambok, C.E. (Eds.) (1993). *Decision Making in Action: Models and Methods*. Norwood, NJ: Ablex.

Tack, W.H. (1976). Diagnostik als Entscheidungshilfe [Assessment as decision aid]. In Pawlik, K. (Ed.), *Diagnose der Diagnostik [Assessment of Psychological Assessment]* (pp. 103–130). Stuttgart: Klett.

Weinstein, M.C. & Fineberg, H.V. (1980). *Clinical Decision Analysis*. Philadelphia: Saunders.

Wieczerkowski, W. & Oeveste, H.Z. (1982). Zuordnungs- und Entscheidungsstrategien [Assigning and decision strategies]. In Klauer, K.J. (Ed.), *Handbuch der Pädagogischen Diagnostik [Handbook of Educational Assessment]*, Band. 2, Vol. 2 (pp. 919–951). Düsseldorf: Schwann.

Manfred Amelang

RELATED ENTRIES

CLASSIFICATION (GENERAL, INCLUDING DIAGNOSIS), EXPLANATION, OUTCOME ASSESSMENT/TREATMENT ASSESSMENT, PREDICTION (GENERAL), UTILITY

D EMENTIA

INTRODUCTION

Dementia is currently defined as 'a syndrome consisting of progressive impairment in both memory and at least one of the following cognitive deficits: aphasia, apraxia, agnosia or disturbance in executive abilities, sufficient to interfere with social or occupational functioning, in the absence of delirium or major non-organic psychiatric disorders' (American Psychiatric Association, 1994). This narrow definition is a remnant of the 'cognitive paradigm' of dementia (Berrios, 1989). According to the latter view (developed during the late 19th century), cognitive deficits are the only pathognomonic features of dementia and psychiatric and behavioural symptoms are just coincidental encumbrances. Due to the work of Ebbinghaus, memory became the first measurable cognitive deficit and this introduced a lasting bias in that ever since memory impairment has tended to be considered as the main cognitive deficit of the dementias.

Up to the 1970s, the cognitive paradigm seriously emasculated clinical research, particularly into the diagnosis of 'early dementia' and the identification of varieties and subtypes of dementia. The realization that neuropsychological assessment alone was not going to resolve these problems led during the 1980s to the acceptance that psychiatric symptoms were, after all, central to dementia (Berrios, 1992). In due course, this allowed for a better understanding of the disease and the identification of subtypes such as, for example, Lewy body Dementia.

The problem of what is 'early dementia' and how it can be identified has not yet been resolved in spite of the desperation of the pharmaceutical industry which would like to have a reason to start pro-cholinergic 'treatment' early. Likewise, little is known about 'symptom-sequencing', namely the finding that psychiatric and personality changes may precede or follow the cognitive deficits. The central questions in this regard are whether the sequencing is random or reflects the influence of clinical and genetic factors. The development of neuroimaging and genetics (*inter alia*) has of late led to important advances in the classification of the dementias.

The dementias are complex neuropsychiatric disorders with a clinical profile that includes disorders of personality, emotions, mood, and will; conventional mental symptoms (hallucinations, delusions, agitation, sadness, anxiety, etc.); disorders of awareness and consciousness; psychosocial incompetence; and the full gamut of neuropsychological deficits. It follows from this that subjects suffering from dementia should be clinically looked after by *multidisciplinary teams* and that it should be considered unethical for neurologists, psychiatrists or psychologists *alone* to monopolize their diagnosis and/or care (Berrios & Hodges, 2000).

It also follows from the symptomatic complexity of the dementias that their assessment must be exhaustive and longitudinal. Together with the finding of specific markers such as volumetric changes in the medial temporal lobes, analysis of these clinical data should contribute to resolve the problems of symptom-sequencing and 'early dementia'. In this latter case, it is expected that the old concept of early dementia as a 'mini-dementia' (i.e. one dependent upon instrument sensitivity) will change to one with a broader symptom profile which may include personality and behavioural changes as markers of early dementia.

It has been said that the assessment of dementia should be carried out by a multi-disciplinary process involving the neurologist, neuropsychiatrist, neuropsychologist and occupational therapist. In terms of the objectives of assessment, as important as determining a 'diagnosis' is the profiling of deficits and assets. Outcome measures, developed on the basis of this knowledge, will have the adequate sensitivity and specificity to help select the right treatments for the right patients and also to take other hard therapeutic decisions (e.g. rationing of expensive treatments such as pro-cholinergic medication).

The concept of assessment is a dynamic one. It should start by reconstructing a premorbid profile, for it is only against this information that the progressive effect of the disease can be evaluated. When seen, most subjects are already affected by the disease so that the assessment must look both backwards and forwards. This model is followed at the Cambridge Memory Clinic (CMC) (Berrios & Hodges, 2000).

ASSESSMENT BY THE NEUROLOGIST

The neurological assessment includes an interview with the patient and carer, a bedside cognitive examination and physical examination. The interview should be aimed at getting the details of cognitive functions which includes memory, language, numerical skills, visuospatial skills, neglect phenomenon, visual perception, personality changes, self-care, thinking and problem solving abilities. Many patients lack insight into the nature and extent of their cognitive deficits. The interview with the carer is essential to get objective data and to plot the progression of the illness. The Addenbrooke's Cognitive Examination (ACE) (Mathuranath et al., 2000) constitutes the core instrument. All patients have a full general, physical and neurological examination, blood pressure, cardiac auscultation, frontal release signs, eye movements and fundal examination, gait, tone, abnormal movements and blood screen to rule out reversible dementias. Neuroimaging (CT Scan, MRI, PET scan, SPECT scan) provides structural and functional aspects of the brain, which can be crucial for the differential diagnosis.

ASSESSMENT BY THE NEUROPSYCHIATRIST

The neuropsychiatric assessment of the dementias entails *more than* the search for 'associated' psychiatric disorders such as depression, anxiety or delusional disorder. Since the dementias are first and foremost *neuropsychiatric* disorders, the main objective of the assessment is psychiatrically to diagnose the condition and to profile deficits and assets. The mapping of the symptoms is made by means of the 'Cambridge Behavioural Inventory' (CBI) (completed by a relative) and the 'Insight into Memory Questionnaires' (self and relative) (IMQ) (Marková & Berrios, 2000).

Like with other neuropsychiatric disorders, the psychopathology of the patient with dementia is better captured at the symptomatic level (Berrios et al., 2001). Trying to reach formal categorical diagnoses is ending up with the empty claim that the patient 'does not meet diagnostic DSM IV criteria for disease XX'. This is misleading because a great deal of the rich psychiatric and behavioural symptomatology of dementia is expressed in isolated mental symptoms which are never sufficient to 'meet criteria' for anything; and also because it may delay treatment. Being told that a morose, sad and distractible patient does not meet DSM IV criteria for major depression means little and can be positively misleading given that some clinicians may want to go ahead with antidepressants in some cases.

In view of the above, it is essential that instruments be used in the neuropsychiatric assessment that generate information analysable at both levels (symptomatic and nosological). It is the combination of all this information, usually carried out in special meetings of the multi-disciplinary team at the end of the assessments, that differential diagnosis and behavioural

phenocopies of dementia are ruled out (Berrios & Marková, 2001).

The Cambridge Computerized Neuropsychiatry Battery includes 9 core instruments and another 11 (to measure hypochondria, mania, attention, metamemory, etc.) which are chosen according to clinical findings (see Table 1).

ASSESSMENT BY THE NEUROPSYCHOLOGIST

Clinical neuropsychology (whether cognitive or not) is concerned with the evaluation of mental function and plays a crucial role in the differential diagnosis and the profiling of deficits and assets. The experienced neuropsychologist will interpret the data against his assessment of the patient and this usually leads to greater discrimination. The assessment should be comprehensive enough to generate information about attention, general intellectual skills, executive functions and to identify impairment in specific areas such as memory, language, calculation, praxis and visuospatial skills. Practical aspects of the assessment procedure are of particular importance in the case of patients with dementia given that they tend to become fatigued, distracted and bored easily. In the CMC, a standard set of core tests is administered. They include tests of general intelligence such as Wechsler Adult Intelligence Scale – Revised, assessment of premorbid IQ, assessment of frontal lobe functions, tests of verbal and visual memory, visuospatial and perceptual tasks (a full description in Hodges, 1994).

FUTURE PERSPECTIVES AND CONCLUSIONS

So far in the history of mankind, it is an observed fact that upon reaching certain age, mind and body deteriorate; and to explain this fact a number of narratives have been put together (Berrios, 1994). Straddling the legal and medical narratives, the concept of 'dementia' developed early in the cultural history of Europe; by the end of the 18th century it had become enthroned as a 'disease' (Berrios & Freeman, 1991).

Neither the deterioration in question nor the concept of dementia are, however, ineluctable. Whether by dint of genetic engineering or by social

Table 1.   Cambridge Computerized Neuropsychiatry Battery

Core instruments	Reference	Commentary
28-General Health Questionnaire	Goldberg & Hillier, 1979	Self-administered; yields 4 factors: somatic symptoms, anxiety and insomnia, social dysfunction and depression.
Personality Deviance Scale	Bedford & Foulds, 1978	Measures 'Extrapunitiveness', 'Intropunitiveness' and 'Dominance'. Normative data available; good reliability and validity.
Beck Depression Inventory	Beck et al., 1979	Self-administered measure of depression. Emphasizes subjective states.
Snaith's Irritability Scale	Snaith et al., 1978	Yields 4 factors: anxiety, depression, outward irritability and inward irritability. Good measure of irritability. Normative data available.
Cognitive Failures Questionnaire	Wagle et al., 1999	Measures lapses of perception, memory and motor behaviour in daily life.
Signal Detection Memory Test	Miller & Lewis, 1977	Recognition memory test based on signal detection theory; developed at Addenbrooke's hospital, Cambridge, UK. Standardized in 3000 normal subjects. A d = 1.50 cut off discriminates with a sensitivity of 85% and a specificity of 82% ($N = 350$).
Maudsley Obsessive-Compulsive Questionnaire	Rachman & Hodgson, 1980	Self-administered scale; yields 4 factors: checking, washing, slowness-repetition and doubting-conscientious.
Dissociation Questionnaire	Riley, 1988	Assesses degree of dissociation construed as a failure to integrate thoughts, feelings and actions into consciousness. Tested in the general population, it has good reliability and validity.
Zung Anxiety Scale	Zung, 1971	Self-administered measure of *state* anxiety.

whim, mankind may decide to prolong life and/or create a new terminus for it. The assessors of the future will soon create a new 'science' to accommodate the consequences of such momentous decisions. In the meantime, dementia remains a fashionable area of research and much has been invested in finding a cure. The implications of a successful outcome, in terms of *Lebensraum* and economy, have not yet been contemplated.

In terms of conventional nosology, the 'syndrome' dementia is considered as a final common pathway to a gamut of aetiologies which in turn create their own clinical profiles. The classifications issued out of the latter have of late been challenged by categories based on the new neuropsychology and genetics. For example, 'Alzheimer's disease', a notion constructed during the early part of the 20th century, has

now all but been broken up into a growing number of overlapping disorders (Berrios, 1990).

In conclusion, dementia is a neuropsychiatric disorder warranting a multidisciplinary approach which should include neurologists, neuropsychiatrists, neuropsychologists, occupational and nurse therapists. Combined they should generate a patient-centred narrative describing his/her current state and including educated guesses about his/her past and future.

If the cross-sectional examination does not provide a clear diagnosis, the patient should be followed up. Initial assessments are never definitive but only provide a baseline. From the start, dementia sets up 'self-damaging loops' (e.g. patients realize that they cannot do something well and voluntarily abstain and this leads to forgetting and functional loss). These loops complicate the assessment as voluntary abstentions may be taken to be real deficits. It is understood that often enough behavioural analysis is more important to the patient's understanding and management than measuring his apolipoproteins.

References

American Psychiatric Association (1994). *Diagnostic and Statistical Manual of Mental Disorders* (4th ed.). Washington DC: American Psychiatric Association.

Beck, A.T., Rush, A.J., Shaw, B.F. & Emery, E. (1979). *A Cognitive Theory of Depression*. New York: Guilford Press.

Bedford, A. & Foulds, G. (1978). *Personality Deviance Scale*. UK: NFER Publishing Company.

Berrios, G.E. (1989). Non-cognitive symptoms and the diagnosis of dementia. Historical and clinical aspects. *British Journal of Psychiatry*, *154*, 11–16.

Berrios, G.E. (1990). Alzheimer's disease: a conceptual history. *International Journal of Geriatric Psychiatry*, *5*, 355–365.

Berrios, G.E. (1992). Psychotic symptoms in the elderly: concepts and models. In Katona, C. & Levy, R. (Eds.), *Delusions and Hallucinations in Old Age*. London: Gaskell.

Berrios, G.E. (1994). Pathological ageing: a conceptual history in the nineteenth century. In Copeland, J.M.R., Abou-Saleh, M.T. and Blazer, D.G. (Eds.), *Principles and Practice of Geriatric Psychiatry* (pp. 11–16). Chichester: Wiley.

Berrios, G.E. & Freeman, H. (1991). *Alzheimer and the Dementias*. London: Royal Society of Medicine.

Berrios, G.E. & Hodges, J.R. (2000) *Memory Disorders in Psychiatric Practice*. Cambridge: Cambridge University Press.

Berrios, G.E. & Marková, I.S. (2001). Psychiatric disorders mimicking dementia. In Hodges, J.R. (Ed.), *Early Onset Dementia. A Multidisciplinary Approach*. Oxford: Oxford University Press.

Berrios, G.E., Paykel, E.S. & Wagle, A. (2001). Psychiatric assessment. In Fawcett, J.W., Rosser, A. &

Dunnett, S.B. (Eds.), *Brain Damage, Brain Repair*. Oxford: Oxford University Press.

Goldberg, D.P. & Hillier, V.F. (1979). A scaled version of general health questionnaire. *Psychological Medicine*, *9*, 139–145.

Hodges, J.R. (1994). *Cognitive Assessment for Clinicians*. Oxford: Oxford University Press.

Marková, I.S. & Berrios, G.E. (2000). Insight into memory deficits. In Berrios, G.E. & Hodges, J.R. (Eds.), *Memory Disorders in Psychiatric Practice*. Cambridge: Cambridge University Press.

Mathuranath, P.S., Nestor, P.J., Berrios, G.E., Rakowicz, W. & Hodges, J.R. (2000). A brief cognitive battery to differentiate Alzheimer's disease and frontotemporal dementia. *Neurology*, *55*, 1613–1620.

Miller, E. & Lewis, P. (1977). Recognition memory in elderly patients with depression and dementia: a signal detection analysis. *Journal of Abnormal Psychology*, *86*, 84–86.

Rachman, S.J. & Hodgson, R.J. (1980). *Obsessions and Compulsions*. New Jersey: Prentice Hall.

Riley, K.C. (1988). Measurement of dissociation. *The Journal of Nervous & Mental Disease*, *176*, 449–450.

Snaith, R.P., Constantopoulos, A.A., Jardine, M.Y. & McGuffin, P. (1978). A clinical scale for the self-assessment of irritability. *British Journal of Psychiatry*, *132*, 164–171.

Wagle, A.C., Berrios, G.E. & Ho, L.W. (1999). Cognitive failures questionnaire in psychiatry. *Comprehensive Psychiatry*, *40*, 478–484.

Zung, W.W.K. (1971). A rating instrument for anxiety disorders. *Psychosomatics*, *12*, 371–379.

Suvarna Wagle, Ajay Wagle and
German E. Berrios

RELATED ENTRIES

APPLIED FIELDS: CLINICAL, APPLIED FIELDS: NEUROPSYCHOLOGY, APPLIED FIELDS: GERONTOLOGY, MEMORY DISORDERS, BRAIN ACTIVITY MEASUREMENT, COGNITIVE DECLINE/IMPAIRMENT

DEVELOPMENT (GENERAL)

INTRODUCTION

Human behaviour takes place in both a temporal and social context. Psychological development refers to the temporal context, and deals with (dis)continuous progression, increasing complexity and non-entropy of behaviours, cognitions and emotions. Development dominates the first half of life, and is latent in the second half. It refers to behavioural changes that cannot be instantly turned back. Firstly, in this contribution, characteristics and purposes of assessment and of development are described. Secondly, the role of developmental constructs and test theory for assessment of behavioural development are both discussed. Thirdly, instruments for assessing behavioural development, specifically in children, are described. Finally, some thoughts are presented on the future of assessment of development.

GENERAL AND DEVELOPMENTAL ASSESSMENT: PURPOSES

Assessment in general is characterized as solving a client's problem by following specific decision rules, by measuring individual differences, by gathering and integrating information about a client's behaviour and environment in order to help, and by deciding for interventions using information about the client's behaviour and his or her social environment (Fernández-Ballesteros et al., 2001). Assessment of development usually refers to children and is defined as assessing the levels of behavioural, cognitive, and socio-emotional functioning in order to show the strong and weak sides of a client (Johnson & Sheeber, 1999).

Both general and developmental assessments have three main objectives. The first is to diagnose the presence or absence of disorders. This refers to the activity of ascribing a person to a category by means of explicit rules; for example, those presented in the *Diagnostic and Statistical Manual of Mental Disorders* (DSM-IV, 1994). A child can be fitted into a ADHD or Conduct Disorder category (see 'Classification' entry). The second purpose is prediction (see 'Prediction (General)' entry). If one knows, for example, the level of intelligence, extroversion or conscientiousness of a child, one can predict the probability of school success or future behavioural adaptation. The third main objective is the explanation as expressed in the Hypotheses-Testing-Model (HTM) of assessment (see 'Explanation' entry). Explanation is pre-eminently relevant in developmental assessment, because it looks for the cause of problematic and deviant behaviours and helps to design effective interventions.

While development implies progression, change, increasing complexity, and seemingly even erratic change, it is easily presupposed (partly because of the frequent use of trait-like concepts and instruments) that the categories, the individual differences, and the effects of intervention are stable (Lewis, 1999). In addition, hypotheses testing in the HTM does not refer to testing a population parameter, but to comparing an assessment result with a pre-established criterion. An example is the hypothesis that this child is not able to profit from normal education, because its IQ is lower than 80. To conclude, developmental assessment is aimed at classifying, predicting, and explaining. This last goal is important because of the explaining and changing of children's problematic behaviours.

ASSESSMENT AND DEVELOPMENTAL PSYCHOLOGY: METHOD AND CONTENT

Assessment is not a separate and independent psychological discipline. It borrows from methods and theories of all psychological (sub)-disciplines. Developmental assessment uses developmental theories, models, and constructs but also test theory in order to design appropriate instruments. Moreover, it is based on the methodological rules that come from the empirical-analytical tradition. This disciplines the assessment process scientifically (ter Laak, 1997). The quality of developmental assessment depends on how well the structure of developmental constructs, test theory, instruments, and the rules followed during the assessment process '*fits*'. The first three, and how they fit, are discussed below.

As a scientific discipline developmental psychology has to offer *theories, models and constructs, and methods* to describe and explain behavioural development. Theories primarily determine the 'what' of assessment, and in principle they have to guide decisions about appropriate methods and data analyses. The latter refer to the 'how' of assessment.

With respect to the 'how', in psychology two research approaches dominate (Cronbach, 1957) that are appropriate in experimental, social, personality, and educational psychology. They are the correlational or observational (e.g. Spearman's analysis of intelligence), and the experimental disciplines (e.g. Fisher's analysis of variance for the crops in the fields). The correlational discipline elicited developmental studies that investigate stability and (linear) predictability of test scores over time, and individual differences between age groups. The experimental approach elicited studies designed to accelerate cognitive achievements and behavioural adaptations particularly in youngsters. To conclude, the fit between the experimental and correlational methodology and developmental questions is limited. Cronbach did not distinguish a 'third developmental discipline' of scientific psychology besides his 'two disciplines of scientific psychology'.

The 'what' of developmental assessment is traditionally determined by organismic and mechanistic developmental theories, models or constructs. These connect the behavioural past to the present as qualitatively different steps or stages (organismic), or as gradual growth taking the immediate context into account (mechanistic). In organismic theory strong (Piaget, Kohlberg) and weak (Erikson, Loevinger) constructs dominate. Recently, non-linear dynamic models have been applied to developmental phenomena (Van Geert, 1994).

According to strong organismic theories qualitatively different stages exist. These are strictly ordered in time, with an unavoidable final equilibrated stage, and sudden stage transitions are expected to occur. Conceptual analysis and research are conducted to prove the existence of stages, e.g. criteria are used to determine if children are in the pre-operational or concrete operational stage. Kerssies, Rensen, Oppenheimer and Molenaar (1989) offer empirical support for the ordering of the six Piagetian sub-stages in the sensorimotor period. Boom, Brugman and van der Heijden (2001) have analysed the arguments in moral dilemmas and found support for the expected ordering of Kohlberg's stages of moral development in Dutch and Russian adolescents. These two studies owe the descriptions of developmental levels or stages to the work of Piaget and the Brunet–Lezine. The claim that there is an unavoidable last and equilibrated stage for every person was doubted from the beginning, because of lack of empirical support. People usually only reach the formal operational level in their own profession. Van der Maas (1993) has used eight transition criteria from chaos theory and non-linear dynamics to test

the sudden change from the Piagetian pre-operational stage to the concrete operational stage. He reports support for a few of these criteria, e.g. much variation, and a bimodal distribution of responses in the transitional period.

'Weak' organismic theories resemble 'strong' ones, but do not require a strict progression and an equilibrated last stage. Erikson simply presupposed the existence and the ordering of the seven stages, and connected the sequence to increasing age, and to different social and cultural tasks. Loevinger supported the claim of existence by results from a sentence completion questionnaire that classified a person in or between two adjacent stages of Ego development. The ordering from impulsive, symbiotic, pre-social (level 1) to autonomous and integrated (level 7) during life has, however, not been empirically tested.

Mechanistic models can be used to describe and explain development, but they are not popular. Lewis (1999) recently argues for a mechanistic, context-bound interpretation of development, and he also makes it plausible that in order to explain the development of attachment and depression organismic models are not sufficient. To conclude, there is limited empirical research and support for the claims of the strong and weak organismic constructs. They elicited, however, the construction of some theoretically based developmental scales. In explaining behavioural development mechanistic models are probably underestimated.

Classical (CTT) and Modern Test Theory or Item Response Theory (IRT) comprise models for subjects' answers on items. CTT is a true score model for estimating errors in answers on items and tests, and not for describing the development of behaviours. Nevertheless, reliable tests can show average differences in test scores for different age groups as well as changes in test scores for the same group or individual over time. These differences can, under certain conditions, be interpreted as development. Most intelligence, aptitude and achievement tests, and personality questionnaires, use a true score model of CTT. This implies that the cause of age-groups, and inter-individual differences, is not interpreted developmentally, and that test items are not designed to depict development. To conclude, Classical Test Theory helps to measure reliably age- and inter-individual differences, but it is not related to developmental theory. IRT meets some technical shortcomings of CTT by using specific estimation procedures to assess the probability that a subject answers an item correctly or agrees upon an item. Items measure latent traits, such as spatial ability, reading skill, openness to experience or short-term memory. IRT models can be helpful in designing and testing developmental scales. For example, a developmental stage-like scale requires that items represent each stage by steep, similarly shaped, non-overlapping item characteristic curves. Some developmental constructs imply stages or developmental levels, but, as stated above, there is seldom interest in testing characteristics of these stages. To conclude, IRT offers possibilities to design developmental scales, but they are not regularly used until now.

Developmental constructs must be operationalized, i.e. their meaning and structure have to be reflected in measurement procedures and results, such as *developmental quotients, developmental scales, tests, questionnaires, observation* and *judgement procedures*. Several instruments have been reported that are designed from a developmental perspective. Most instruments that are called 'developmental' are, however, instruments for children, and are constructed from a non-developmental individual differences or correlational perspective.

INSTRUMENTS: CHILDREN DEVELOPMENT

The instruments described below have been adapted from American instruments and are widely used. The reliability and validity of these adaptations must be researched empirically for each country. The judgements about their psychometric qualities have been taken from the third and fourth review of Dutch test research (Evers, Van Vliet-Mulder & ter Laak, 1992; Evers, Van Vliet-Mulder & Groot, 2000). It is likely that these judgements apply, at least partly, to other language communities.

Firstly, a series of instruments to measure cognitive and motor development is available.

An old concept is the developmental quotient (*Gessell Scales for Motor Development*), in which a developmental scale is supposed that is

empirically reflected in the age of the children. So (the lack of) age-adequate behaviour can be determined, i.e. the amount a child is behind or in front of the developmental level of same aged peers. The test can be administered from 4 weeks up to 6 years. The observed behaviour is, however, not limited to motor behaviour, it also includes adaptation, speaking and social behaviour (Gesseff, 1947).

The *Denver Developmental Screening Test* can be used for children between 6 days and 6;6 years. It estimates the presence of motor and cognitive developmental disorders and of retardation. It consists of 105 items, 25 of which have to be scored by observation, the remaining items are scored by asking the parents. The reliability and predictive validity are sufficient. The items are not chosen with a developmental construct in mind. A child's result is compared with norms established for the age group. If a child deviates substantially then further investigation is recommended.

The *McCarthy Scales of Children's Abilities* aim to assess the cognitive and motor developmental level of children between 2;6 and 8;6 years. There are six scales (verbal, perceptual, quantitative, cognitive, memory, and motor behaviour) that use 18 subtests. Because empirical research is scarce, reliability and validity are insufficient. The scales presuppose a developmental pattern that is plausible, but has not been empirically tested.

The *Bayley Scales of Infant Development* (BSID) are the most used scales for measuring mental and motor behaviour in children between 2 and 30 months. The mental scale consists of 163 dichotomous items of increasing difficulty level. The bases for this increase in difficulty levels are empirical findings, but not a developmental construct. The scale for motor behaviour consists of 81 dichotomous items. Finally, 25 items are scored on a 9-point scale, that contains evaluations of (social) behaviours using observations of the child during the testing. Norms for 14 age groups are developed, and by interpolation 33 norm groups are available. This test is well constructed. Sufficient norms are available, reliability (both internal consistency and test–retest) is between 0.80 and 0.96, and validity is good, respectively sufficient. Although the scales correlated very highly with another test measuring the developmental level (i.e. the

Bühler–Hetzer Test, 1953: correlation from 0.83 to 0.89), it is frequently reported that the scales do not predict IQ at school age well. An extensive training is necessary before taking the test with these young children. There is a substantial relationship between the scores on the two scales and age in normal healthy children. Correlation between 0.25 and 0.30 are found between the BSID and the educational levels of fathers and mothers.

The *Stanford–Binet Scale* was aimed at measuring the cognitive level of children. The scale has been translated the world over and became popular in the US due to Goddard and Terman. The scale is used from age 2 years on and contains different sets of items for different age groups.

Nevertheless, for the estimation of children's IQ the *Wechsler Scales* (WIPPSI and WISC-R) and the deviation IQ became more popular. There is no developmental construct and the age differences are not interpreted developmentally in the Wechsler scales. The psychometric properties show a test that works well.

Secondly, instruments measuring school achievement are available in many language communities. The CITO, the Dutch Institute of Educational Testing, develops all achievement tests in the Netherlands. These achievement tests are all IRT modelled and of high psychometric quality. Well known is the 11+ achievement test taken before entering secondary school. Almost all 11–13 year olds are investigated using this battery. The achievement tests are not based on an explicit idea of language, arithmetic, and cognitive development. They do, however, predict later school achievement very well.

Thirdly, social and emotional development in children can be assessed. The *School* uses 52 items measuring social and emotional functioning in the classroom. They parallel four of the Big Five factors and add the attitude towards school tasks. The questionnaire is not based on an developmental construct. It can be used for pupils between 4 and 11. The reliability and validity are sufficient (see Evers et al., 2000).

The *Self-Perception Profile for Children* was originally constructed by Harter and adapted for Dutch children from 8–12 years. It measures, using 36 items, six scales, e.g. social acceptation, physical appearance, ability in sports, and feelings of self-worth. Reliability and construct validity are sufficient; data for predictive validity

is too scarce, and is consequently judged as insufficient. A developmental construct was absent in the constructing of the test.

Fourthly, several instruments help in the assessment of pathology and adaptation in children. Most frequently an adaptation of the *Child Behaviour Check List* (CBCL) is used. This list can be used for children between 4 and 18 years old and the questions can be answered by parents and teachers. The norms are good, and both reliability and predictive and construct validity are good, respectively sufficient. It yields a profile of the child that informs about the level of problematic internalizing and externalizing behaviours. Although the empirical data show age and gender differences there is not a developmental construct to explain these differences.

There is a 102-item *Children Depression Scale* available, yielding 10 different facets of depression for children from 9–12 years old. The Kovacs questionnaire is usually the basis of these scales. Reliability is sufficient as is construct validity. Predictive validity is insufficient (see Evers et al., 2000).

The *DSM IV R* is appropriate for persons of 18 years and older. Nevertheless, some specific disorders can be measured in children. The *ADHD Questionnaire for Children* can be used to assess Hyperactivity, Impulsivity, and Attention Deficit in 4 to 18 year olds, using 18 items. The psychometric properties allow to judge it as a good and sufficient instrument for measuring ADHD. There is no developmental interpretation of the age differences in amount and type of expression of this syndrome.

Lastly, personality in children is assessed from 8 years on using adaptations of scales for adults. Eysenck's three factors, extroversion, neuroticism and psychoticism, are adapted for children (see *ABV-J Questionnaire* in Evers et al., 2000). They are used for children from 8–15 years old and are sufficiently reliable and valid to measure Extraversion. Slotboom and Elphick (1997) adapted the questionnaire for youngsters: *Big Five for Children* from 2;6 to 18 years old. They used three partly different sets of items for the very young and the adolescent subjects. For the younger children the parents fill the questionnaire in. The authors found sufficient support for the existence of the Big Five in these age groups. Judgements of reliability and validity are not yet available. The preliminary results are promising. There is no developmental construct that explains age differences in either instrument, and there is no developmental theoretical explanation for the necessity to use different items for the age groups.

Loevinger's Ego development model uses a sentence completion test (*Ego Development Scale*) to assess the level of ego development. The children can be assigned to a level or between two levels. Scoring is reliable and there is some validity data. There is a developmental construct and scoring is rather time consuming. The scale is not very sensitive for differences within the period of 0 to 12 years, because it is based on a life-span model.

To conclude, there are many sufficiently reliable and valid instruments and procedures available to assess motor and mental status, school achievement, social emotional development, pathology, and personality in the formative years of life (see Table 1). Very few, however, are inspired by developmental constructs. This implies, that in addition to the moderate fit between test theory and developmental constructs, the fit between developmental constructs and instruments measuring changing and developing behaviours is partly lacking.

Table 1. Summary of the instruments

Instrument	What is measured?	Methodological discipline	Developmental construct?	Age
Gessell Motor Scales	Motor speech, social behaviour	Developmental	Yes	4 weeks–6 years
Denver Developmental Screening Test	Presence of cognitive and motor delay	Correlational/ Observational	No	6 days–6;6 years
McCarthy Scales	Verbal, perceptual, motor, etc. behaviour	Developmental: conceptual not empirical	Yes and No	2;6–8;6 years
Bayley Scales of Infant Development	Mental, motor behaviour; adaptation	Correlational/ Observational	No	2–30 months
Stanford–Binet Scale	Intelligence	Developmental: conceptual not empirical	Yes and No	Lifespan
School Achievement Tests	School achievement	Correlational/ Observational	No	6–30 years
Social-Emotional Development	Socio-emotional functioning at school	Correlational/ Observational	No	4–11 years
Self-Perception	Social acceptation, physical appearance, self-worth	Correlational/ Observational	No	8–12 years
Child Behaviour Check List	Childhood pathology: internalizing, externalizing behaviour	Correlational/ Observational	No	4–18 years
Childhood Depression Scale	Clinical depression	Correlational/ Observational	No	9–12 years
Attention Deficit Hyperactive Disorder	See above	Diagnosis; based on expert agreement	No	4–18 years
Personality	Extroversion, neuroticism, test attitude	Correlational/ Observational	No	8–14 years
Personality	The Big Five	Correlational/ Observational	No	2;6–18 years
Personality	Stages of ego development	Conceptual developmental, and empirical	Yes and No	Almost whole lifespan

FUTURE PERSPECTIVES AND CONCLUSIONS

The quality of assessment of behavioural development depends on the fit between test theoretical models, substantive developmental constructs, and instruments. Classical test theory is not designed to assess development. Nevertheless, it shows test score differences between age groups and within individuals. Combined with a substantial developmental theory these differences can be interpreted developmentally. In the future, age differences between and within individuals can be interpreted from a developmental perspective (Willett, Singer & Martin, 1998). Item response theory and non-linear dynamic theory offer explicit models to test developmental hypotheses. In the future, these models and theory will be used more, and also enhance insight in behavioural development. Developmental models and theories contain mainly strong and weak organismic constructs. In the future these constructs' claims will be tested empirically, and different constructs will be added to allow for other than stage-like developmental patterns. Most instruments for assessing children's behaviours are based on the correlational/observational individual differences approach. Many of these instruments meet their goals. They will remain important in the future, but they will be enriched with developmental insights and constructs to interpret inter-individual and intra-individual age differences of cognitions, behaviours, and emotions.

References

Boom, J., Brugman, D. & van der Heijden, P.G.M. (2001). Hierarchical structure of moral stages by a sorting task. *Child Development*, 72(2), 535–548.

Bühler, Ch. & Hetzer, H. (1953). *Kleinkindertests 2e Auflage* [Small Chidren's Test]. München: Verlags Union.

Cronbach, L.J. (1957). The two disciplines of scientific psychology. *American Psychologist*, 12, 671–684.

Diagnostic and Statistical Manual of Mental Disorders IV (1994). Washington DC: American Psychiatric Association.

Evers, A., Van Vliet-Mulder, J. & Laak, J. ter (1992). *Documentatie van Tests en Testresearch in the Netherlands* [Documentation of Tests and Test Research in the Netherlands]. Assen/Maastricht: Van Gorcum.

Evers, A., Van Vliet-Mulder & Groot, C.J. (2000). *Documentatie van Test en Testresearch in Nederland, Deel I en Deel II* [Documentation of Test and Test Research in the Netherlands, Part I and Part II]. Assen/Maastricht: Van Gorcum.

Fernández-Ballesteros, R., De Bruyn, E., Godoy, A., Hornke, L., Laak, J. ter, Vizcarro, C., Westhoff, K., Westmeyer, H. & Zaccagnini, J. (2001). Guidelines for the assessment process (GAP): a proposal for discussion. *European Journal of Psychological Assessment*, 17(3), 178–191.

Gessell, A. (1947). *Developmental Diagnosis*. New York: Wiley.

Johnson, J.H. & Sheeber, L.B. (1999). Developmental assessment. In Silverman, W.K. & Ollendick, T.H. (Eds.), *Developmental Issues in the Clinical Treatment of Children* (pp. 44–59). Needham Heights, Ma: Allyn & Bacon.

Kerssies, I.J., Rensen, F.S.X., Oppenheimer, L. & Molenaar, P.C.M. (1989). *De ordinale schalen voor het bepalen van de Psychologische Ontwikkeling in de Sensorimotorische Periode* [Ordinal scales for the determination of psychological development in the sensorimotor period]. Lisse: Swets & Zeitlinger.

Laak. J. ter (1997). *Assessment: Content and Method*. Utrecht: Reproduction General Services: Faculty of Social Sciences [In Dutch: *Psychologische Diagnostiek, Inhoud en Methode* (3rd ed.). 1999. Lisse: Swets & Zeitlinger].

Lewis, M. (1999). On the development of personality. In Pervin, L.A. and John, O.P. (Eds.), *Handbook of Personality: Theory and Research* (pp. 327–346). New York: Guilford Press.

Slotboom, A. & Elphick, E. (1997). Parent's perception of child personality. Doctoral Dissertation. University of Leiden, The Netherlands. Alblasserdam: Haveka B.V.

Van der Maas, H. (1993). *Catastrophe Analysis of Stage Wise Cognitive Development: Model, Method and Applications*. Amsterdam: Academisch proefschrift Universiteit van Amsterdam.

Van Geert, P. (1994). *Dynamic Systems of Development, Change Between Complexity and Chaos*. New York: Harvester Wheatsheaf.

Willett, J.B., Singer, J.D. & Martin, N.C. (1998). The design and analysis of longitudinal studies of development and psychopathology in context: statistical models and methodological recommendations. *Development and Psychopathology*, 10, 395–426.

J. ter Laak, G. Brugman and M. de Goede

RELATED ENTRIES

DEVELOPMENT: PSYCHOMOTOR, DEVELOPMENT: SOCIO-EMOTIONAL, DEVELOPMENT: LANGUAGE, DEVELOPMENT: INTELLIGENCE/COGNITIVE

DEVELOPMENT: INTELLIGENCE/COGNITIVE

INTRODUCTION

Cognitive development is the study of how fundamental processes of acquiring knowledge and information about the self and environment develop. The evaluation of cognitive development, known as cognitive assessment, is an important part of monitoring normal child development. The study of cognitive development, indeed the roots of cognitive assessment, can be traced to the French psychologist Jean Piaget (1896–1980). In many respects, Piaget's theories formed the basis for the modern study of cognitive development. Although not all of Piaget's tenets have withstood the test of time, they continue to influence modern cognitive assessment, if only conceptually (Wadsworth, 1996). Here we will briefly describe Piaget's theory of cognitive development as well his observations of the A-not-B tasks. Finally, we will illustrate the modern tools of cognitive assessment with the Bayley Scale of Infant Development, two Slosson tests, and the Kaufman Adolescent and Adult Intelligence Test (KAIT).

FOUR STAGES OF PIAGET'S THEORY

In 1920, Piaget began testing infants and children to see at what age they could solve certain problems correctly and how they did so. Based on his observations, Piaget became more interested in the children's errors on specific tasks which he noticed occurred at distinct ages of development for the majority of children tested. Piaget's first developmental stage, the sensorimotor stage, encompasses the first two years of life. During this stage, the infant uses the motor movements and sensory stimulation of touching, mouthing, looking, and other actions to organize the properties of its environment. It is through these interactions with the environment that the infant begins to develop schemas. Piaget believed

that sensorimotor stage infants lacked cognition; in other words, infants did not think about the environment, they merely organized it. Most patterns of infant behaviour are dominated by reflex. After eight months, the infant begins to develop the concept of object permanence, or the awareness that an object still exists despite its being taken from view. By the end of the second year, the infant begins to have internal representations of objects and events and understand that objects may affect the environment as the infant can (Halford, 1978).

Piaget's second stage, the pre-operational stage, encompasses ages 2 through 6 or 7 years. In this stage, the child begins to represent objects and events symbolically through, for example, representational behaviours such as symbolic play, drawing, and mental image memory. Language develops rapidly during this period. As the child progresses through this stage, language is increasingly used as a social tool and moral feelings and reasoning start to develop. However, thoughts and language are largely egocentric with the child having difficulty distinguishing perception and logical reasoning. As a result, the capacity for structured conversation is not yet apparent. Affective and social schemata are continuously assimilated and accommodated throughout this stage (Inhelder & Piaget, 1958; Piaget, 1972).

Piaget believed that a third process, equilibrium, prevented an extreme use of either assimilation or accommodation to classify stimuli. Equilibrium is a self-regulatory mechanism that created a balance between accommodation and assimilation. When schemata cannot assimilate to a new stimulus or situation, the child is said to be in a state of disequilibrium. As the schemata adapt to the new stimulus, a cognitive balance is achieved, or equilibrium. This process is referred to as equilibration (Piaget, 1977). In combination, these three processes facilitate cognitive development throughout an individual's life.

From the age of 7 to 11, Piaget noted a third stage, the concrete operational stage, in which the child's logical reasoning abilities increase. The child is successful at seriation (the ability to accurately categorize or mentally arrange a set of stimuli according to a dimension such as size, weight, or volume), and classification of concrete objects, and is capable of understanding conversation tasks, such as conversation of number. Even though some logical reasoning skills have started to develop, the child is unable to apply these skills to abstract problems and hypotheses. Perception plays a greatly reduced role in judgements (Kaufman & Flaitz, 1987).

Piaget's last stage of development, the formal operations stage, encompasses ages 11 to 15+ years. During this period, the child is able to apply logical reasoning to abstract verbal and hypothetical problems. By the end of the formal operations stage, the child's cognitive behaviour is qualitatively similar to that of an adult. Indeed, Piaget (1972) wrote, in these years 'a whole series of novelties highlights the arrival of a more complete logic' (p. 3). This stage is focused on a development of a capacity for dealing with possibilities; thinking becomes increasingly flexible (Kaufman & Flaitz, 1987).

HOW EACH STAGE IS QUALITATIVELY DIFFERENT

Piaget's theory included four main stages with each stage reflecting a qualitative change in a child's reasoning abilities. Common changes to each stage are: (a) cognitive reasoning becomes superior with the advancement of each step; (b) each improvement in a reasoning ability is generalized across all things associated with the reasoning ability; (c) each progressive step incorporates past learning and skills with the new knowledge; and (d) cognitive and intellectual development depend on four variables which include maturation, experience, social interaction, and equilibration (Piaget & Inhelder, 1969).

COGNITIVE DEVELOPMENT ASSESSMENT DERIVED FROM PIAGET'S THEORY

Throughout Piaget's observations of child behaviour, he derived several tasks to assess a child's current level of cognitive functioning, according to his theory. A familiar task demonstrating object permanence for the sensorimotor stage (infancy) is the 'A-not-B' task. In this task, the experimenter shows an infant a toy and then places the toy underneath a nearby cloth, designated as location 'A'. At around 12 months of age, the infant will find the toy in the 'A' cloth. Once this is accomplished, the experimenter then places the toy under a second cloth at location 'B'. Despite having seen the toy being placed under cloth 'B' and despite showing success previously at retrieving the toy from cloth 'A', many infants continue to search for the toy under cloth A. This is the A-not-B error. The average age for infants to accomplish this task (i.e. searching for the toy under the 'B' cloth) is from 12–18 months of age.

BEYOND PIAGET: CONTEMPORARY COGNITIVE ASSESSMENT

While influenced by Piaget's theories of cognitive development, most contemporary tools of cognitive assessment use more general theories of intelligence, not theories that are specific to child development. Many of these tests, such as the Wechsler Primary Preschool Scales of Intelligence – Revised (WPPSI-R), Kaufman Assessment Battery for Children (K-ABC), and Cognitive Assessment System (CAS) are explored in greater details elsewhere in this encyclopedia (see 'Intelligence Assessment (General))'. Three other instruments for the assessment of cognitive development will be addressed below.

BAYLEY SCALES OF INFANT DEVELOPMENT – SECOND EDITION (BSID-II; BAYLEY, 1993)

The Bayley Scales of Infant Development – Second Edition (BSID-II; Bayley, 1993) are a revision of the original BSID that was developed by Bayley (1969) to assess the development of infants and very young children. The BSID-II may be administered to infants between the ages of one month and 42 months. Comprised of three scales (Mental, Motor, and Behaviour Rating), the BSID-II is one of the most commonly used tests in the psychological testing of an infant's current level of development and achievement of specific developmental milestones. The Mental scale contains items for the assessment of precursors of intelligence, including memory, habituation, problem solving, early number concepts, language, and logical thinking. The mental scale contains no subtests and yields a single global index or Mental Development Index (MDI), ($M = 100$, $SD = 15$), which is interpreted as a measure of overall cognitive development, not as a measure of intelligence, language or visual perception. The BSID-II has high psychometric quality, more specifically high internal consistency coefficients, and good test–retest reliability. Overall, the average reliability for the BSID-II is 0.88 across all age levels and the coefficients for internal consistency are 0.89 and 0.90 for ages of 36 months and 42 months, respectively (Alfonso & Flanagan, 1999; Bracken & Walker, 1997).

SLOSSON TESTS

The Slosson Intelligence Test Primary – (SIT-R; Erford, Vitali & Slosson, 1999) and the Slosson Full-Range Intelligence Test (S-FRIT; Algozzine, Eaves, Mann & Vance, 1993) are assessment tools that are useful for a variety of practical purposes such as evaluating the cognitive ability of individuals with learning disabilities, mental retardation, visual impairments, orthopaedic disabilities, or children who are considered potentially gifted. The SIT-R is appropriate for individuals from the age of 4 years old and up, while the S-FRIT is appropriate for individuals from 5 years old to 21 years old. The SIT-R measures General Information, Similarities and Differences, Vocabulary, Comprehension, Arithmetic, and Auditory Memory, while the S-FRIT has a Verbal Index, Performance Index, and Memory Index, that combine to produce a Full-Range Intelligence Quotient (Algozzine et al., 1993).

CONCLUSIONS

The assessment of cognitive development emphasizes the examination of variables relevant to the current developmental functioning of a child. Cognitive development assessments, historically, have been an important part of Western society's emphasis on education and have enabled the identification of children who may need early intervention services due to developmental delay. Piaget was one of the first theorists to identify the importance of the assessment of cognitive development. Over time, not all of Piaget's theory has been supported by modern research. It nonetheless continues to remain one of the most important preliminary theories of cognitive development today, and its influence remains in the assessment of cognitive development, and, occasionally, in clinical assessment.

References

Alfonso, V.C. & Flanagan, D.P. (1999). Assessment of Cognitive Functioning in Preschoolers. In Nuttall, E.V., Romero, I. & Kalesnik, J. (Eds.), *Assessing and Screening Preschoolers: Psychological and Educational Dimensions* (pp. 186–218). Boston: Allyn and Bacon.

Algozzine, B., Eaves, R.C., Mann, L. & Vance, H.R. (1993). *Slosson Full-Range Intelligence Test (S-FRIT)*. East Aurora, NY: Slosson Educational Publications.

Bayley, N. (1969). *Manual for the Bayley Scales of Infant Development*. San Antonio, TX: Psychological Corporation.

Bayley, N. (1993). *Bayley Scales of Infant Development* (2nd ed.). San Antonio: Psychological Corporation.

Bracken, B.A. & Walker, K.C. (1997). The utility of intelligence tests for preschool children. In Flanagan, D.P., Genshaft, J.L. & Harrison, P.L. (Eds.), *Contemporary Intellectual Assessment: Theories, Tests and Issues* (pp. 484–503). New York: Guilford Press.

Erford, B.T., Vitali, G.J. & Slosson, S. (1999). *Slosson Intelligence Test – Primary (SITP)*. East Aurora, NY: Slosson Educational Publications.

Halford, G.S. (1978). Introduction: the structural approach to cognitive development. In Keats, J.A., Collis, K.F. & Halford, G.S. (Eds.), *Cognitive Development* (pp. 1–27). New York: John Wiley & Sons.

Inhelder, B. & Piaget, J. (1958). *The Growth of Logical Thinking from Childhood to Adolescence*. New York: Basic Books.

Kaufman, A.S. & Flaitz, J. (1987). Intellectual growth. In Van Hasselt, V.B. & Hersen, M. (Eds.), *Handbook of Adolescent Psychology* (pp. 205–226). New York: Pergamon Press.

Piaget, J. (1972). Intellectual evolution from adolescence to adulthood. *Human Development, 15*, 1–12.

Piaget, J. (1977). *The Development of Thought*. New York: Viking Press.

Piaget, J. & Inhelder, B. (1969). *The Psychology of the Child*. New York: Basic Books.

Wadsworth, J.B. (1996). *Piaget's Theory of Cognitive and Affective Development: Foundations of Constructivism* (5th ed.). White Plains, NY: Longman Publishers.

Jennifer M. Gillis, James C. Kaufman and
Alan S. Kaufman

RELATED ENTRIES

Development (General), Development: Psychomotor, Development: Socio-Emotional, Development: Language, Applied Fields: Clinical, Applied Fields: Education, Applied Fields: Neuropsychology

D DEVELOPMENT: LANGUAGE

INTRODUCTION

The assessment of language development is aimed at establishing the level of competence or proficiency attained by children and second-language learners in the linguistic knowledge and abilities involved in speaking, listening, reading and writing activities.

From a theoretical point of view, language development assessment rests on similar assumptions and biases as adult language assessment. See Language (General) in this volume. Unlike language adult testing, however, language development assessment presupposes that the linguistic subject's competencies and abilities are not yet fully developed, and thus should be assessed at some intermediate point between an *initial non-linguistic state* (typical of newborns and people beginning to learn a second language), and the *final state* typical of people possessing a basic linguistic competence (e.g. normally developed children above 6–7 years old with a good command of their native/mother tongue, and highly proficient second-language learners).[1]

Individual language tests are used for a number of different practical purposes. According to Stark et al. (1982: 150–151), these include: (1) screening large groups of children in preschool or early school years for language disorders; (2) determining level of language functioning or degree of deficit in language in children considered to be at risk for a language disorder (these measures being often employed in making decisions as to whether a child should be admitted to a treatment programme, assigned to a given level of educational placement, or included in a research study); (3) in-depth evaluation of language and language-related skills in a child who has been admitted to a clinical, educational or research programme; and (4) determining to what extent an intervention programme has benefited individual language-impaired children.

As in adult language assessment, two general perspectives underlie the tools created to assess developing language: a psychometric approach and a cognitive approach.

Classical psychometric assessment – which largely rests on the behaviourist assumptions on language prevailing in the 1950s and 1960s – implicitly views the linguistic progress of children as a relatively linear process that can be adequately outlined through the quantitative scores that subjects obtain in a number of standardized linguistic tasks. Test items (which are not contextually relevant) are selected on the basis of their ability to discriminate between typically developing children at different ages, but not necessarily on developmental considerations. The examiner can derive conclusions about the developmental 'normality/non-normality' of a child by merely comparing the language ages and quotients that the child obtains with those expected by age.

The *cognitive approach* – which is the prevailing one since the early 1970s – views linguistic behaviours as reflecting both the abstract knowledge that a speaker–listener possesses about language (the so-called 'linguistic competence'), and the ongoing mental processes that operate on linguistic representations in real-time language production and comprehension ('linguistic performance'). Therefore, language development assessment is primarily focused on the description of the underlying competence of subjects over time, as well as on characteristics and changes in utterances during actual verbal performance.

The cognitive approach implicitly assumes the representational complexity of linguistic competence (which is viewed as consisting of phonological, morphological, syntactic, lexical, semantic and pragmatic principles), as well as the differential constraints that speaking and comprehension activities impose on the cognitive system.

Therefore, from this perspective, it is virtually impossible to make a good developmental diagnosis of language if the examiner (a) does not possess an extensive knowledge of the *stages* at which the different subsets of linguistic principles are acquired, or (b) ignores the specific mechanisms involved, or (c) lacks a theoretically grounded *model* about human cognitive growth and organization (that appears to be not as modularized in children as it seems to be in adults – see Karmiloff-Smith, 1992). Diagnostic conclusions about the linguistic *competence* of subjects must also take into account that verbal comprehension abilities develop faster than speaking, which is particularly true for the youngest children.

THE CONTENTS OF LANGUAGE DEVELOPMENT ASSESSMENT

During the last decades, the contents of language development assessment have undergone several critical changes. These changes mirror the different theoretical models on language yielded by both psychologists and linguists, but also run in parallel to the ongoing diversification of professional settings in which language development assessment has been required (these settings being, at first, highly restricted to speech *therapists* and second-foreign language *teachers*, and now also involving *psychologists*).

In the 1960s and 1970s, the emphasis of language examiners was primarily focused on deficits and disorders in phonology and grammar. The use of the *mean length of utterance in morphemes* (MLU) to assign the child to a developmental level is a good example of strategies focused on the structural aspects of language, which were developed in these years and have been extensively used around the world since then (although MLU cannot be applied without adaptations to languages other than English – e.g. languages with more complex morphologies such as Spanish, German or Hebrew). The

batteries included in Table 1 are also classical and well-known examples of psychometric tests based on models of linguistic competence.

In the late 1970s and mid-1980s, a number of strands emerged that resulted in both an enlargement of the contents to be assessed, and a double shift away from the deficit-centred focus on the formal aspects of language towards client-centred approaches focused on the subject's linguistic abilities in natural settings (Howard & Müller, 1995).

In the theoretical domain, an increasing interest in *discourse* and *pragmatic* abilities grew in these years which has been frequently referred to as the 'pragmatics revolution'. This pragmatic revolution was brought about by the innovative proposals of authors such as Austin (1962), Searle (1969), and Bates (1976). Generally speaking, it allowed researchers to criticize the grammatical bias of previous language models and to become more and more interested in analysing how *real people* use language in social contexts (as opposite to the *ideal speakers* referred to in the previous psychometric and linguistic traditions). In the clinical domain, a huge body of observations had also been accumulated at that time concerning children who did not show difficulties to construct phonologically and grammatically well-formed utterances, but used language in an odd and inappropriate fashion (the so-called 'semantic pragmatic disorder').

Taken together, these new clinical and theoretical interests paved the way to the construction of assessment tools and measures now focused in communicative and pragmatic abilities. See Communicative Language Abilities in this volume. Besides, methods originally devised for adult language assessment, such as the analysis of spoken discourse and conversations, began to be used for children assessment purposes, largely exceeding the limits of previous psychometric and grammatical testing (see, for example, Brinton & Fujiki, 1989; McTear, 1985).

METHODS FOR LANGUAGE DEVELOPMENT ASSESSMENT

Four main categories of techniques of language development assessment will be presented here that try to simultaneously collect informative data about a broad range of language functions,

Table 1.   Commonly used standardized tests for the assessment of language development

Illinois Test of Psycholinguistic Abilities (ITPA) (Kirk & McCarthy, 1961). Based on Osgood's neobehaviouristic model on language, this test includes 12 different tasks which explore a wide repertoire of abilities (phonological, syntactic, semantic and visual abilities, gestural expression, fluency and memory) that, according to its underlying theoretical model, are involved in the communicative process. Although the use of this battery is very usual in ordinary and special schools, some authors have questioned its usefulness for language development assessment due to its lack of developmental foundations.

Peabody Picture Test of Vocabulary (PPVT) (Dunn, 1965; revised in Dunn & Dunn, 1981). This test (also very commonly used) assesses the recognition of a set of 100 words presented by the examiner and ordered by difficulty. Its materials are plates with four pictures each, and the child is asked to identify the one that matches the target word. It can be applied to children above 2.6 years.

Reynell Expressive Developmental Language Scale (Reynell, 1969). This scale allows assessment of the verbal comprehension and expression abilities of children between 18-months and 6 years of age. The complete battery includes two different scales. In the comprehension scale, the child is asked to carry out a set of verbal instructions that the examiner proposes in a semi-structured play situation. The expressive scale allows estimations of the vocabulary, structure and creative use of language of children without visual aids of pictures or objects.

The Edinburgh Articulation Test (Anthony et al., 1971) and *The Goldman–Fristoe Test of Articulation* (Goldman & Fristoe, 1972). Probably the most commonly used phonological tests, these two tests involve the production by the child of a small set of lexical items from pictures presented by the examiner. The lexical items are designed to contain a representative sample of the phonemes of the English language in various positions within the word (word-initial, word-medial, word-final). The responses are tape-recorded, transcribed and categorized by the examiner, and then compared with the targets.

The Northwestern Syntax Screening Test (NSST) (Lee, 1971). This test evaluates the morphosyntactic proficiency of children between 3–8 years by means of expressive (imitation) and receptive tasks (pointing to the correct choice among four different pictures). The morphosyntactic contrasts evaluated include, among others, the affirmative/negative contrast, inflectional marking of tense and number, prepositions, and different kinds of pronouns and interrogative adverbs (such as 'who', 'what', 'where').

The Carrow Auditory Test of Language Comprehension (CATLC) (Carrow, 1974). This test assesses the morphosyntactic proficiency of children between 3–6 years. Children are asked to choose among three pictures the one that best matches the input provided by the examiner. The pictures depict contrasts about different kinds of function words (e.g. prepositions, determiners, etc.), inflectional morphemes, various sorts of syntactic structures, etc.

and meet the constraints of limited time and resources typical of clinical explorations: (1) *structured tests*, (2) *language sampling*, (3) *parental reports*, and (4) *non-standarized elicitations* McDaniel et al. (1996).

Structured tests are the best exponents of the psychometric tradition in language development assessment, and the most common method still used in educational and clinical settings. Structured tests have steadily been developed from the 1960s, and currently they could be counted in tens.

Individual language testing typically involves asking children to solve linguistic tasks such as discrimination of individual phonemes, naming or pointing to objects and pictures, carrying out actions asked by the examiner, etc. in isolated, fixed and non-natural communicative situations where contextual and particular variations must be avoided. Although some differences exist

between batteries of tests developed for the assessment of language level or of the degree of language deficit, they are usually treated as a scale, their results being expressed in the form of language ages or language quotients.

The assessment of language of children by using standardized tests is usually expensive, requires the cooperation of children, and shows a limited validity for children under 3 years. Besides, most of the available tests do not fit well under current cognitive theories and data on normal language development, and lack updated theoretical foundations. A remarkable and worthy exception is the *Test for the Reception of Grammar* – TROG – developed by Bishop (1983), where the targets were carefully selected on the basis of psycholinguistic criteria, and errors are informative about the linguistic *strategies* the children use when listening to messages.

The *language sampling* methodology consists of recording samples of spontaneous language in natural and meaningful settings. These samples (recorded in audio- or videotape) are supposedly representative of language children use in day-to-day conversations.

Language sampling became the true 'method of choice' for early language assessment, given its great ecological validity and versatility (it made it possible to gather information about grammatical and pragmatic components of language from a single sample, as well as to compare samples from a same subject in different conversational conditions: familiar and unfamiliar settings, peers, adults, and younger people as partners, etc.).

Until now, a wide variety of indices (phonological, morphological, lexical, syntactic, semantic, and pragmatic) have been thought to be derived from linguistic sampling (see Miller, 1981 for a review). However, normative data are lacking for most of these indices, and a great variability could be induced in them when minimal changes in conversational or environmental conditions occur.

The use of a sample-based methodology for assessing language development requires highly trained personnel, and consumes a substantial amount of time for analysis. In the last few years software has been designed to derive linguistic profiles and measures by computer (e.g. the *Systematic Analysis of Language Transcripts* – SALT – developed by Miller & Chapman, 1983, and the *Child Language Analysis Program* – CLAN – see MacWhinney, 1991). However, although the computerized analysis of speech samples has become a formidable tool for researchers, their clinical use for diagnostic purposes is still limited.

Even under ideal circumstances, the representativeness of measures gathered from language samples analyses is not always guaranteed, which poses the problem of their reliability. Another methodological problem is that a child might simply choose not to produce a particular linguistic construction (or pragmatic function) even though she has acquired it, and that examiners interpret the *non-observed* targets as a sign of a *non-acquired* ability.

The *parental reports*, as Dale has stated (1996: 162), involve 'the systematic utilization of the extensive experience of parents (and potentially other caregivers) with their children'. This method usually adopts the form of diary studies, retrospective reports, and/or free-form reports elicited by the examiner through questionnaires or interviews.

Parental reports about children's language are basically used for young children, and have significant advantages because, among other things, they are 'likely to reflect what a child knows, whereas [a sample of] free speech reflects those forms that she is more likely to use' (Bates, Bretherton & Snyder, 1988).

Although the parental report's validity could be negatively affected by numerous different variables (e.g. social class, interests and skills of parents, age and disability of the child, etc.), this old and 'low-tech' procedure is still commonly used by researchers and clinicians, especially for purposes of initial screening. Excellent examples of language development measures based in parent reports are the *MacArthur Communicative Development Inventories* (CDI) (Fenson et al., 1993), and the *Receptive-Expressive Emergent Language Scale* (REEL) (Bzoch & League, 1994).

The *elicited non-standardized production* is an experimental technique in which the adult suggests certain tasks and probes to the child (usually in the broader context of a game with puppets) in order to elicit particular linguistic responses. Elicited non-standardized production has been successfully used both in clinical and psycholinguistic research contexts to evoke morphological and syntactic structures (as well as pragmatic and communicative functions) that occur only rarely, if at all, in children's spontaneous speech. It allows the diagnostic impressions derived from language testing and spontaneous speech analyses to be contrasted, and enables examiners to obtain robust samples of data of the targeted structures within a single experimental session.

LANGUAGE VARIABILITY AND LANGUAGE DIFFERENCE IN CHILDREN DEVELOPMENT

Individual variations in patterns of linguistic development of clinically normal children have been repeatedly noted by researchers and clinicians since the 1980s (e.g. Bates & MacWhinney, 1987), which points out the need to bear in mind the non-linear character of language learning, and the intrinsic variability of language performance (moment to moment, across contexts and subjects, and developmentally over time). On the other hand, there is an issue of deep concern regarding the data that have been recently published, showing an increasing number of children from 'minority' ethnic groups who are misdiagnosed as having language disabilities (and are included in special education classes) because of their low scores in standardized language tests.

In order to neutralize the cultural bias in language assessment, practical suggestions could be recommended when testing these 'minority' children, such as 'rewording instructions, providing additional time or practice, asking the child to provide an explanation for incorrect responses, having a parent or another trusted adult administer the test, and using repeated presentations of test stimuli' (Gutiérrez-Clelles, 1996: 49). However, children speaking languages or dialects other than the official ones could constitute more than 50% of the school population in some states, and the practical problem arises of how to adequately differentiate language disorder from language difference. Because of the great variability within the clinically normal population itself, rigid norm-based criteria cannot be established to distinguish specific language disorders and delays from normal individual variations.

Standardized tests and competence-based measures in language development assessment used so far seem unable to adequately capture both variability and stability in a child's verbal performance. Consequently, an increasing number of specialists have recently proposed to complement (if not to substitute) the classical strategies in language development assessment with *dynamic methods* that allow comparisons of the child's performance as it changes during ongoing language processing, and to obtain language-learning measures (e.g. Evans, 1996; Peña, 1996).

Undoubtedly, these new proposals will imply wide and profound changes both in theoretical assumptions and assessing practices. Perhaps they must be considered as the first signs of an imminent and largely necessary new 'revolution' in language development assessment.

FUTURE PERSPECTIVES AND CONCLUSIONS

In our review of the current state of language development assessment, we have pointed out three relevant issues.

First, we have referred to the great enlargement of the contents of the assessment in the last two decades, showing that the assessment was initially limited to structural aspects of language, whereas now it is also focused on pragmatic and communicative abilities.

Secondly, we have briefly described the methods and strategies commonly used in language development assessment, and identified both their advantages and limitations. Because the individual language tests only provide limited information about a narrow range of linguistic abilities, and since they must be applied outside the natural context in which language is used, we strongly claim against using standardized tests as the only basis for the assessment of linguistic competence in children, and recommend usage of complementary methodologies such as speech-sample analyses, parental reports, and elicited productions.

Finally, and on the basis of recent data revealing the great variability of language development in normal children (and the cultural differences that negatively affect the performance of children from minority ethnic groups in standard language testing), we have pointed out the need of distinguishing between language variation and language difference. We have also warned about the current lack of operative criteria for such a distinction, and feel confident that a dramatic change will soon ensue (which already seems to emerge) in the theoretical and practical assumptions of current language development assessment.

In future, language development assessment must still go towards a more theoretically grounded case-study approach, and an acknowledgement of the individual nature of the linguistic profiles of children. Strategies which allow the examiners to simultaneously exploit normative references and obtain individual language samples, in a range of different communicative contexts, could be the most useful strategy in order to conjure up a complete and representative picture of the language abilities of children.

Note

1 In a recent charming book, the cognitive psychologist Steven Pinker (1994: 15) referred to human language as 'an instinct to acquire an art' to emphasize the idea that it is not possible for human beings to develop the *natural* faculty of language (which is part of our biological – phylogenetically inherited – endowment) without *learning* any particular language.

References

Anthony, A., Bogle, D., Ingram, T. & McIsaac, M. (1971). *The Edinburgh Articulation Test*. Edinburgh: Livingstone.

Austin, J.L. (1962). *How to do Things with Words*. Oxford: Clarendon Press.

Bates, E. (1976). *Language and Context: The Acquisition of Pragmatics*. New York: Academic Press.

Bates, E. & MacWhinney, B. (1987). Competition, variation, and language learning. In MacWhinney, B. (Ed.), *The Crosslinguistic Study of Sentence Processing*. New York: Cambridge University Press.

Bates, E., Bretherton, I. & Shyder, L. (1988). *From First Words to Grammar Individual Differences and Dissociable Mechanisms*. New York: Cambridge University Press.

Bishop, D. (1983). *Test for Reception of Grammar (TROG)*. Manchester: University of Manchester Press.

Brinton, B. & Fujiki, M. (1989). *Conversational Management with Language-Impaired Children. Pragmatic Assessment and Intervention*. Rockville, MA: Aspen Publ.

Bzoch, K.R. & League, R. (1994). *Receptive-Expressive Emergent Language Scale (REEL)* (2nd ed.). Austin, TX: PRO-ED.

Carrow, E. (1974). *Test for Auditory Comprehension of Language*. Austin, TX: Learning Concepts.

Dale, Ph.S. (1996). Parent report assessment of language and communication. In Cole, K.N., Dale, Ph.S. & Thal, D.J. (Eds.), *Assessment of Communication and Language*. Baltimore: Paul H. Brookes Publ. Co.

Dunn, L. (1965). *Peabody Picture Vocabulary Test*. Circle Pines, MN: American Guidance Service.

Dunn, L.M. & Dunn, L.M. (1981). *Peabody Picture Vocabulary Test – Revised*. Circle Pines, MN: American Guidance Service.

Evans, J.L. (1996). Plotting the complexities of language sample analysis: linear and non-linear dynamical models of assessment. In Cole, K.N., Dale, Ph.S. & Thal, D.J. (Eds.), *Assessment of Communication and Language*. Baltimore: Paul H. Brookes Publ. Co.

Fenson, I., Dale, Ph.S., Reznick, J.S., Bates, E., Hartung, J.P., Pethick, S. & Reilly, J.S. (1993). *MacArthur Communicative Development Inventories (CDI)*. San Diego: Singular.

Goldman, R. & Fristoe, M. (1972). *Test of Articulation*. Circle Pines, MN: American Guidance Service.

Gutiérrez-Clellen, V.F. (1996). Language diversity: implications for assessment. In Cole, K.N., Dale, Ph.S. & Thal, D.J. (Eds.), *Assessment of Communication and Language*. Baltimore: Paul H. Brookes Publ. Co.

Howard, S. & Müller, D. (1995). The changing face of child language assessment: 1985–1995. *Child Language Teaching and Therapy*, 11, 7–22.

Karmiloff-Smith, A. (1992). *Beyond Modularity*. Cambridge, MA: The MIT Press.

Kirk, S. & McCarthy, J. (1961). *Illinois Test of Psycholinguistic Abilities*. Urbana, IL: University of Illinois Press.

Lee, L. (1971). *Northwestern Syntax Screening Test (NSST)*. Evanston, IL: Northwestern University Press.

MacWhinney, B. (1991). *The CHILDES project: Tools for Analyzing Talk*. Hillsdale, NJ: Lawrence Erlbaum Associates.

McDaniel, D., McKee, C. & Smith, H. (1996). *Methods for Assessing Children's Syntax*. Cambridge, MA: The MIT Press.

McTear, M. (1985). *Children's Conversations*. Oxford: Basil Blackwell.

Miller, J. (1981). *Assessing Language Production in Children: Experimental Procedures*. Austin, TX: PRO-ED.

Miller, J. & Chapman, R. (1983). *SALT: Systematic Analysis of Language Transcripts: User's Manual*. Madison: University of Wisconsin Press.

Peña, E.D. (1996). Dynamic assessment: the model and its language application. In Cole, K.N., Dale, Ph.S. & Thal, D.J. (Eds.), *Assessment of Communication and Language*. Baltimore: Paul H. Brookes Publ. Co.

Pinker, S. (1994). *The Language Instinct: How the Mind Creates Language*. New York: William Morrow and Company.

Reynell, J. (1969). *Reynell Expressive Developmental Language Scale*. Slough, England: National Foundation for Educational Research.

Searle, J. (1969). *Speech Acts*. Cambridge: Cambridge University Press.

Stark, R.E., Tallal, P. & Mellit, E.D. (1982). Quantification of language abilities in children. *Speech and Language*, 7, 149–184.

Mercedes Belinchón

RELATED ENTRIES

DEVELOPMENT (GENERAL), DEVELOPMENT: PSYCHOMOTOR, DEVELOPMENT: SOCIO-EMOTIONAL, DEVELOPMENT: INTELLIGENCE/COGNITIVE, LANGUAGE (GENERAL), COMMUNICATIVE LANGUAGE ABILITIES, APPLIED FIELDS: EDUCATION, APPLIED FIELDS: CLINICAL, THEORETICAL PERSPECTIVE: COGNITIVE

D EVELOPMENT: PSYCHOMOTOR

INTRODUCTION

Assessing psychomotor development is an important component in the interdisciplinary process of evaluating young children. Movement is an avenue through which infants and children interact with their environment, and is closely tied to and interrelated with both perceptual and emotional development. Hence, it may appear in the literature under the name of psychomotor. Nonetheless, this entry will refer to motor development, defined here as changes in the level of movement performance based on neurological and environmental influences.

This entry will address the assessment of motor development in children from birth to 6 years of age, relating only to observable, quantifiable development.

HISTORICAL TRENDS

In the early 1900s the trend was for psychological examination of relationships between cognitive abilities and motor abilities, represented, for the most part, by fine motor manual dexterity skills.

From Motor Abilities Assessment to Motor Skills Assessment

In the 1920s, assessments focused mainly on motor abilities and capacities were expressed in a single composite score.

From the 1940s, assessments began focusing more on direct measures of motor skills. Gesell and Bayley laid the foundations for the assessment of motor skills in infants and young children from the early 1900s and into the 1950s.

From Product-Oriented Assessment to Process-Oriented Assessment

In the field of assessing fundamental motor skills, the era between the 1930s to the 1960s was dominated by product-oriented assessments. The 1970s saw a shift to more process-oriented assessments, pioneered by the work of Seefeldt and Hubenstricker (1982), and on fundamental motor patterns development.

From Neuromaturational Hierarchical Frameworks to Functional Activities

Since the 1930s and 1940s, functional movement skills have been the main focus in assessment of daily living activities. This shift from the use of neuromaturational and reflex hierarchical frameworks for evaluation of children to the measurement of disablement related to functional activities was driven by contemporary theories of motor development and motor control, which supported motor learning and systems approaches to evaluation and intervention.

The focus on functional movement skills can also be seen today in the area of adapted physical education and special education (Davis & Burton, 1991), as in the development of the Movement Assessment Battery for Children Checklist (Henderson & Sugden, 1992).

TERMINOLOGY

Motor Development

Adaptive or functional changes in movement behaviour throughout life, and the processes underlying this behaviour. Changes occur in observable movement behaviours, usually categorized as non-locomotor (stabilizing), locomotor, or manipulative, or any combination of the three. Maturation, growth, and experience are variables that may lead to change in movement behaviour.

Psychomotor Development

Changes in behaviour throughout life, emphasizing the interaction between psychological and motor process.

Motor Abilities

General traits or capacities which underlie movement skills and are not easily modified by practice or experience.

Movement Skill

Specific and goal-directed movement patterns (e.g. running, writing). Also used as a qualitative expression of movement performance.

Psychomotor Development Assessment

Any activity, either formal (standardized, norm-referenced, criterion-referenced) or informal (using developmental, observational checklists or profiles), designed to elicit accurate and reliable samples of movement behaviour, that represent the developmental status of an individual.

A THEORETICAL MODEL OF MOTOR DEVELOPMENT

Gallahue (1982) suggested a four-phase model of motor development: (1) reflexive movement, (2) rudimentary movement, (3) fundamental movement, and (4) sport-related movement. This model can serve as a framework and used as a tool for assessment. In this discussion, we refer to motor development only in regard to the sequential progression of movement in the first three phases, representing motor development of preschool children. These phases parallel the *motor abilities*, *early movement milestones*, and *fundamental movement skill* levels of movement skill described in the six-level movement skill taxonomy developed by Burton and Miller (1998).

Phase 1. Reflexive Movement (in utero–1 year)

Neonatal movements are reflexive. Rooting and sucking are primitive survival mechanisms, controlled by lower levels of the central nervous system. Postural reflexes (e.g. stepping and crawling) are another form of involuntary movement. As the child grows, the developing cerebral cortex inhibits lower-level reflexes, and movement milestones follow a predictable sequence.

Phase 2. Rudimentary Movement (birth–2 years)

Rudimentary movement abilities involve stability movements (e.g. control of head, neck, and trunk muscles), manipulative tasks (reaching, grasping, and releasing), and locomotor movements (creeping, crawling, and walking). In the first year, motor development is mostly a matter of biological maturation, and rudimentary movements appear in a highly predictable sequence whose rate varies from child to child, depending on biological and environmental factors (Gallahue, 1982; Burton & Miller, 1998).

Phase 3. Fundamental Movement (2–7 years)

The fundamental movement abilities of early childhood grow from the rudimentary movement phase of infancy. It is then that children acquire and refine fundamental motor patterns and begin to develop more complex locomotor, stability, and manipulative movements, first in isolation and then in combination with other motor skills. Fundamental locomotor skills include walking, running, jumping, sliding, galloping, hopping, and leaping, while fundamental object-control skills include throwing, catching, striking, bouncing, kicking, pulling, and pushing (Gallahue, 1982; Burton & Miller, 1998). Maturation and factors such as opportunity, motivation, and instruction have a significant influence on the degree of skill development. Fundamental motor patterns provide the infrastructure for learning more complex games, sports, and dance skills in later life. Without these prerequisite skills, children may experience a high failure rate both in school and in the playground.

AIMS OF MOTOR-DEVELOPMENT ASSESSMENT

Categorization or Identification

Assessing eligibility for special educational services or appropriate placement as provided by law. Screening to determine whether a child is lagging, and his/her level of development/ performance in relation to peers. Planning intervention or instruction: providing a baseline measurement of the child's skills and of desired family outcomes, to determine appropriate goals and objectives for intervention (Bricker, 1993).

Evaluating Change over Time

Assessing the child's age-related progress with no special intervention. Evaluating progress or intervention effectiveness. Predicting a child's future performance (e.g. using the APGAR score).

Research

For data collection as a research tool. Note that assessment is highly recommended for screening and evaluating individuals with noticeable delays, but it does not generate labels or identify causes of deficiency (Burton & Miller, 1998).

For purposes of assessment various tests have been constructed. Table 1 presents one selection of such tests. This is by no means an exhaustive list, and tests should be carefully chosen for each case.

MOTOR DEVELOPMENT TESTS: CLASSIFICATION AND SELECTION

Some of the myriad tests for motor development use Gallahue's (1982) four phases as a framework for description and selection. These are:

Assessment of Motor Abilities

Motor abilities are general traits or capacities of an individual that underlie the performance of a variety of movement skills. The Bruininks–Oseretsky Test of Motor Proficiency (Bruininks, 1978), the Basic Gross Motor Assessment, and the Movement Assessment Battery for Children Test (Henderson & Sugden, 1992) are examples of motor ability assessments.

Assessment of Early Movement Milestones

Most of the early movement assessment instruments, such as the Movement Assessment of Infants, focused on neuromotor aspects (evaluation of posture, tone, and various reflexes or 'reactions'). Other tools measure acquisition of early milestones, e.g. the Bayley Scales of Infant Development, the Peabody Developmental Motor Scales, and the Gesell Developmental Scales. Though these instruments differ considerably in their stated aims, in practice the differences are sometimes ignored. Some were designed as screening tests (e.g. the Denver Developmental Screening Test), others for designing intervention programmes such as the Bayley-II (Bayley, 1993), but all may be used for assessment too.

Few of the early movement milestone assessment tools were constructed specifically to document change, such as the Gross Motor Function Measure. Some tests provide normative data on the whole range of abilities (e.g. Bruininks, 1978).

Assessment of Fundamental Movement Skills

Most contemporary movement skill assessments are designed for males and females. Gender differences may be apparent in tests of fundamental movement skills, when norms are established for individual skills. The main two approaches to assessing fundamental movement skills are product-oriented assessments and process-oriented assessments.

Product-Oriented Assessment

Product-oriented assessment focuses quantitatively on movement performance, i.e. how fast children can run (regardless of their stage or maturity of running style), how high they can jump, and the number of repetitions they can perform for a given motor skill. Before 1975, specific fundamental movement skill assessment instruments were product-oriented; for example, the Bruininks–Oseretsky Test of Motor Proficiency (Bruininks, 1978) and Test of Motor Impairment – Henderson Revision.

Table 1. Assessment tools

Assessment Instrument	Movement Category	Purpose	Description	Ages	Time Required
Bayley II – Bayley Scales of Infant Development (Bayley, 1993)	Motor abilities; Early movement milestones; Fundamental movement skills	Identify developmental delays; Design intervention programmes; Monitor programmes' effectiveness	Criterion- and norm-referenced test. Three scales: Mental, Motor, Behaviour Rating	1–42 months	Under 15 months 25–35 minutes Over 15 months up to 60 minutes
BOT – Bruininks-Oseretsky Test of Motor Proficiency (Bruininks, 1978)	Motor abilities; Fundamental movement skills; Specialized movement skills	Determine educational placement; Assess gross and fine motor skills; Develop and evaluate motor training programmes; Special screening; Assist clinicians and researchers	Long- and Short Form, norm-referenced, product-oriented test. LF: 46 items in 8 subtests; SF: 14 items	4.5–14.5 years	LF: 45–60 minutes SF: 15–20 minutes
Denver II (Frankenburg et al, 1990)	Early movement milestones; Fundamental movement skills	Screen asymptomatic children; Confirm intuitive suspicions; Monitor children at risk for developmental problems	Norm referenced; 125 tasks. Categories: Personal-Social, Fine Motor – Adaptive, Language, Gross Motor	Birth–6 years	15–30 minutes
I CAN Instructional Management System (Wessel, 1976)	Early movement milestones; Fundamental movement skills; Specialized movement skills	Prescribe appropriate movement activities for students; Evaluate skill-specific progress	Criterion-referenced checklists; process and product items. Categories: Preprimary, Primary, Sport/Leisure/ Recreation	Not specified	Specific to individual checklist
MABC Checklist – Movement Assessment Battery for Children Checklist (Henderson & Sugden, 1992)	Motor abilities; Fundamental movement skills; Specialized movement skills; Functional movement skills	Checklist: Screening; Identifying special problems; Research. Test: Clinical exploration; Intervention planning; Programme evaluation	Criterion-referenced test; 5 12-item categories: C (child) stationary/ E (environment) stable; C moving/ E stable; C stationary/ E changing; C moving/ E changing; Behaviours which may interfere with performance	5–11 years	Recommendation: Complete over 1–2 week period of observation

320

Test	Focus	Purpose	Description	Age range	Time
PDMS – Peabody Development Motor Scales (Folio & Fewell, 1983)	Motor abilities; Early movement milestones; Fundamental movement skills	Identify children with delayed or aberrant skills; Determine need and/or eligibility for intervention; Plan programme; Evaluate changes over time	Two-scaled criterion- and norm-referenced instrument; Gross Motor and Fine Motor	Birth–6 years, 11 months	20–30 minutes per scale, total of 45–60 minutes
SIGMA – Ohio State U. Scale of Intra-Gross Motor Assessment (Loovis & Ersing, 1979)	Fundamental movement skills	Determine most logical starting point for planning intervention	Criterion-referenced instrument for assessing qualitative aspects of 11 fundamental movement skills	2.5–14 years	Not reported
TGMD – Test of Gross Motor Development (Ulrich, 1985)	Motor abilities; Fundamental movement skills	Identify children significantly below age norms in GMS; Plan programme to improve skills; Assess improvement as function of age or experience/of instruction and intervention	Criterion-referenced test on the movement patterns used to perform 12 fundamental movement skills; Subtests: locomotor and object-control	3–10 years	About 15–20 minutes
TPBA – Trans-disciplinary Play-Based Assessment (Linder, 1993)	Early movement milestones; Fundamental movement skills	Identify service needs; Develop intervention programmes based on individual treatment objectives; Evaluate progress	6-phase criterion-referenced tool: 1. Unstructured facilitation; 2. Structured facilitation; 3. Child–adult interaction; 4. Parent–child interaction; 5. Motor play; 6. Snack	Birth–72 months	Varies: up to 25 minutes per test

321

Process-Oriented Assessment

Process-oriented assessment looks at the quality or form of motor performance and provides a detailed description of the nature of the child's movement, based on observation of components and sequential elements. Among process-oriented tools we find the test of Gross Motor Development, the Ohio State University Scale of Intra-Gross Motor Assessment, and the I CAN Fundamental Skills assessment instrument.

FUTURE PERSPECTIVES

This section will address the challenges inherent in assessing young children.

From a 'Single Assessor' Model to an Environmental Model

Using a team approach, children are evaluated in the presence of family members, also considering home and social environment. Parents/guardians, who see their child in natural settings, are taught to observe motor development. Often they are motivated to take an active role in their child's assessment and intervention, working with educators.

From Isolated/Formal Settings to Natural/Informal Environments

Children's motor behaviours in an isolated therapy setting are not taken as a prediction of their behaviours in real-life environments, nor is performance in a therapeutic setting transferred to tasks that children must accomplish in real-life situations. An 'authentic' assessment (e.g. Play-Based Assessment) is recommended, since young children tend to produce their true behaviour in their natural environment, be it home, preschool, or childcare facilities. Each child's interaction with toys and playmates can be systematically observed and reliably recorded as in the Trans-disciplinary Play-Based Assessment (Linder, 1993). The assessment is constructed so that the team can communicate with the play facilitator concerning unobserved skills (e.g. can the child stack three blocks?).

From Standardized Assessments to Assessments Accommodating Special Needs

The importance of interaction between individuals and all aspects of their environment is best supported through the ecological assessment approach. The ecological theory forms the framework for families and professionals working with an interdisciplinary approach. According to the Ecological Task Analysis (ETA) model, a goal is selected and the environment is structured in such a way that it elicits various movement patterns from the child interacting within it. The assessor can challenge, direct, and manipulate the environment, and at the same time observe and record the change(s) in motor behaviour.

From Neuromuscular Explanations to an All-Inclusive Outlook

Rather than looking only at the neuromuscular factor, the systems approach looks at the physiological and mechanical systems underlying motor control. This approach addresses motor control in terms of a group of physically based interactive systems (sensory, motor, musculoskeletal, higher level adaptational, etc.), which in combination produce movement. This approach is aimed at identifying the contributions of the different systems to a given task. In people who are observed to have motor problems, this approach aims at identifying the deficits in terms of the dysfunctional systems. The systems approach assumes a high degree of interdependence between the individual systems that contribute to a movement.

In children identified as having a motor deficiency of unknown aetiology, systems and modular approaches can be used to try and identify the underlying dysfunction and to design appropriate remedial programmes. Identifying the dysfunctional system rather than the problematic skill facilitates the development of a remedial programme for training the underlying deficit instead of training the specific behavioural task (Case-Smith, 1996).

Employing Technology

Videotapes and computers may be employed. Videotaping produces a permanent record of the child's motor behaviour. Tapes can be categorized, analysed, and recorded for use in the child's file, though the process is time-consuming and expensive. To ensure valid results, recorders ensure that children are unaware of the crew and the equipment.

Movement and motor development can also be recorded on a camera connected to a computer, and compared with previously stored data. The computer can provide a printout with the child's profile, indicating the skill observed, level of development, and age comparison, as well as suggestions for professionals to enhance skill development.

CONCLUSIONS

Despite the well-established use of development instruments, it is only in the last decade that have we become more sensitive to their use, misuse, and limitations, especially when very young children are being assessed (National Association for the Education of Young Children [NAEYC], 1988; Bredekamp & Rosegrant, 1993). During the early formative years, young children display wide variations in their motor development making it difficult to compare motor behaviour based on standardized scores. Young children are environmentally influenced, constantly changing, and unpredictable in their behaviour. Careful, day-to-day, repeated observations are needed to document behaviour reliably. Many published tests are both extremely complex to administer and time-consuming, decreasing valuable time for direct intervention and contact with the child. Some assessments may also stigmatize individuals.

The dynamic nature of growing children requires a thorough understanding of their cognitive, social, emotional, and physical development, and how these aspects affect their responses to testing. The use of a valid and reliable test instrument, in itself, is insufficient. The test must come in conjunction with knowledge of each child's unique developmental needs, incorporating new approaches and alternative assessment instruments while adhering to specific evaluation guidelines.

References

Bayley, N. (1993). *Bayley Scales of Infant Development* (2nd ed.). San Antonio: Therapy Skill Builders.

Bredekamp, S. & Rosegrant, T. (Eds.) (1993). *Reaching Potentials: Appropriate Curriculum and Assessment for Young Children*, Vol. 1. Washington, DC: National Association for the Education of Young Children.

Bricker, D. (1993). *AEPS Measurement for Birth to Three Years*. Baltimore, MD: Brookes.

Bruininks, R.H. (1978). *Bruininks–Oseretsky Test of Motor Proficiency Examiner's Manual*. Circle Pines, NM: American Guidance Service.

Burton, A.W. & Miller, D.E. (1998). *Movement Skill Assessment*. Champain, IL: Human Kinetics.

Case-Smith, J. (1996). Analysis of current motor development theory and recently published infant motor assessments. *Infants and Young Children*, 9(1), 29–41.

Davis, W.E. & Burton, A.W. (1991). Ecological task analysis: translating movement behaviour theory into practice. *Adapted Physical Activity Quarterly*, 8, 145–177.

Folio, M.R. & Fewell, R.R. (1983). *Peabody Developmental Motor Scales and Activity*. Austin, TX: Pro-Ed.

Frankenburg, W.K., Dodds, J.B. & Archer, P. (1990). *Denver II Technical Manual*. Denver: Denver Developmental Materials.

Gallahue, D.L. (1982). *Understanding Motor Development Infants and Children*. New York: John Wiley & Sons, Inc.

Henderson, S.E. & Sugden, D.A. (1992). *Movement Assessment Battery for Children*. Sidcup, Kent, England: Therapy Skill Builders.

Linder, T.W. (1993). *Transdisciplinary Play-Based Assessment: A Functional Approach to Working with Young Children* (2nd ed.). Baltimore: Brookes.

Loovis, M. & Ersing, W.F. (1979). *Assessing and Programming Gross Motor Development for Children*. Bloomington, IN: Tichenor.

National Association for the Education of Young Children (NAEYC) (1988, March). NAEYC positions statement on standardized test of young children 3 through 8 years of age. Adopted November 1987. *Young Children*, 43(3), 42–47.

Seefeldt, V. & Hubenstricker, J. (1982). Patterns, phases, or stages: an analytical model for the study of developmental movement. In Keslo, J.A.S. & Clark, J.E. (Eds.), *The Development of Movement Control and Co-ordination* (pp. 309–318). Austin, TX: Pro-Ed.

Ulrich, D.A. (1985). *Test of Gross Motor Development*. Austin, TX: Pro-Ed.

Wessel, J.A. (1976). *I CAN Fundamental Skills*. Austin, TX: Pro-Ed.

Orli Yazdi-Ugav and Shlomo Romi

RELATED ENTRIES

D DEVELOPMENT: SOCIO-EMOTIONAL

Emotional life, which develops earlier than rational life, is the key to understanding the world in early childhood. However, up to now, less research has been carried out on this important aspect than on others, such as intellectual, linguistic, motor or moral aspects, and this has had a corresponding effect on assessment.

The mechanism of emotional development still remains obscure. Thus, there are very few scales for assessing emotional development, compared to the number of instruments for assessing, for example, cognitive or motor development. Of the emotional assessment scales that do exist, the most notable are those of: Erikson (1963), who described the psychosocial development of children, and whose theory involves a polar evolution of emotions with five different stages: Trust–Mistrust (0–18 months), Autonomy–Shame (18 months–3 years), Inactive–Guilt (3–5 years), Industry–Inferiority (6–11 months) and Identity–Confusion (12–17 months); Jersild, who proposed five psycho-affective stages based on different fear elicitors, the most important of which were: strange, being different, ridicule, separation and imagination; and Sroufe (1979), who identified the following stages: smile (1–3 months), positive affect (3–6 months), active participation (7–9 months), attachment (9–12 months), practising (12–18 months) and self-concept (18–36 months).

Experts in this field are concerned with clarifying certain issues such as the age at which children show emotions and how we can notice them, the age at which they detect other people's emotions, or when they begin to recognize their own emotions. Serious assessment is necessary if we are to answer such questions (Campus & Barret, 1984).

There are three main strategies for measuring infants' emotions: laboratory procedures, parental reports and observation in natural contexts. When children grow up – and depending on their age at the time of assessment – it is possible to add other methods, including pictorial tests, questionnaires to be answered by the child, matching pictures, drawing and playing.

While assessing emotions in children, it is often necessary to focus on some of their components, such as elicitors, receptors, states, expressions or experiences (Lewis, 1998). Therefore, the psychological assessment of emotions should take into account physiological factors, facial expressions and body postures, as well as vocalizations and language.

We can also analyse the physical basis of emotion by means of skin conductance, cortisone rates, electromyography, and so on. These methods are normally used in clinical settings, and rarely in developmental research.

The commonest method for assessing emotions in children is observation of the relationship between elicitors and expressions. The emotional behaviour is usually studied by means of video recording while the child is performing a specific task in the laboratory. Observation in natural environments is also possible, but is much more rarely used.

All experts accept the fact that basic emotions are present in children from birth, and that the more complex ones become established successively according to a schedule. The basic emotions of joy, sadness, anger, fear and interest appear before the more complex ones, such as guilt, empathy, pride or shame.

Observing the child's reactions to elicitors such as sweet and bitter drinks, restraints or sudden noises has constituted the basis of many experiments on children's emotions (Watson & Morgan, 1917). Another procedure has consisted in taking photos of children in the presence of elicitors in a natural context and showing the pictures to judges who are requested to identify the emotions in them. The emotions identified most accurately through this method in children 1 to 9 months old are: happiness (81%), sadness (78%), surprise (69%), anger (41%) and disgust (37%) (Izard, 1980). Concordance among judges improves when they are able to see the sequence elicitor-expressive facial response. Another assessment strategy has been to observe child–mother, child–stranger or child–peers interaction during a playing task. The facial emotional response has been found to be similar in many cross-cultural studies (Mesquita & Frijda, 1992), with judges clearly identifying emotions on looking at photographs of people from other cultures (Ekman, 1973).

Another strategy has been to observe emotional reactions in mother–infant play. The situations most often used are the following: 'tell me a story', 'gonna-get-you', 'walking fingers so big', 'pat-a-cake' and 'peek-a-boo', with children aged 1–6 months; and 'tactile games', 'body movement', 'visual games', 'horsie' and 'ball', with those aged 3 to 8 months; and 'independent toy play', 'co-ordinated toy play', 'give and take', 'tower', 'role games', 'reading' and 'pretending', with children aged 7 to 17 months.

The first assessment of children's emotional development was carried out through laboratory observation. Based on data from different authors, whose laboratory experiments consisted of adults identifying children's emotions, we can develop a schedule of emotion appearance (see Table 1).

The basic emotions are present from birth, but as the child grows up, they mature and become more differentiated, complex and focused. Social learning plays an important role in this process. Children's social adaptation depends on their ability to express and detect emotions.

A different question is that of locating and assessing the age at which a child is able to recognize and identify other people's emotions. Empathy is the emotion that allows us to identify this ability. Haviland and Lelwica (1987) detected this capability in children aged 2 months, while Yarrow and Waxler (1975) identified complex responses to help adults cope with their distress in children aged 10 to 20 months. Sorce et al. (1985) showed that children 9 to 12 months old change their behaviour with regard to a visual cliff by understanding facial emotions (joy or fear) in their mother's face. Also, a child's acceptation or avoidance of a new toy is mediated by his/her mother's behaviour at the age of 1 (Hornick et al., 1987): Feiring (Feiring et al., 1984) found that the child looks at the caregiver's face before reacting to a new stimulus, which shows that 1-year-old children

are able to comprehend other people's emotions. By the age of 3, children can correctly point out the mentioned picture among others (Müller, 1954).

It is difficult to establish when self-awareness of emotions appears in a child; Lewis and Brooks claim that self-emotion awareness begins at the age of 18 months, and also that 2-year-old children are able to use emotional terms (Breterton et al., 1986). However, Dunn (1988) showed that children could rarely talk about inner states at the age of two, and that it was not until the age of 3 that 30% of children could do so without any trouble. Trotter (1982) agrees with Dunn, and locates the capability of self-emotion awareness at about the age of 2. At two and a half years of age, the child understands the relationship between desire and emotion. At about 3, children are able to match pictures of emotions with the words that name them, and can also use proper words to describe situations related to different emotions (Wellman et al., 2000), as well as identifying individual emotions and situations that elicit them (Borke, 1971). Finally, it can be stated that children from 2 to 4 years old have some knowledge of their own emotions, which experts affirm that they can perceive from around age two.

At the age of 4, children can draw basic emotions by means of selecting the discriminative emotion factors, especially those related to mouth shape. (del Barrio, 2000).

Also by the age of 4, the child can match photos that represent similar feelings, name different emotions represented in pictures and answer questions about them. It is widely accepted, then, that a child of 4 years old is capable of perceiving his or her emotions and the situations that elicit them.

Language is used to assess emotions in two ways: through the *Mean Length Utterance*, in that greater length implies a more positive feeling, and through the *Feeling State Talk*, which consists of analysing the content of the child's utterances; this procedure can only be used after language capabilities have developed. Dunn et al. (1991) analysed children's talk through a categorization system of conversational patterns, referents, themes, disputes and causal references. They found out a strong relationship between the language of mother and child about feelings when children are 3 years old; these data also revealed that children improve their ability to

Table 1. Schedule of appearance of the expression of emotions

Emotion	Author	Expression	Age
Interest Smile Dislike Startle	Trotter, 1982	Facial, body	From birth
Smile Dislike	Sroufe, 1979	Facial, body	From birth
Excitement	Bridges, 1932	Body	From birth
Anger	Stenberg & Campos, 1990	Facial	First month
Interest Distress	Sroufe, 1979	Facial	First month
Anguish	Bridges, 1932	Facial	First month
Enjoyment Dislike	Ganchrow et al., 1983	Facial	First month
Anger Surprise Sadness	Trotter, 1982	Facial	3–4 months
Distress Delight	Bridges, 1932	Facial	3–4 months
Pleasure Rage Anger	Sroufe, 1979	Facial	3 months
Enjoyment	Sroufe, 1979	Facial	4 months
Anger	Lewis, 1998	Facial, motor	2 months
Love Anger Fear	Watson, 1917	Facial, body	2 months
Sadness	Gaensbauer, 1980	Facial	3.5 months
Enjoyment Anger Sadness Interest Fear Surprise Dislike	Izard et al., 1980	Facial	5–9 months
Fear	Trotter, 1982	Facial, body	5–6 months
Joy Sadness Interest Fear	Izard et al., 1980	Facial	5–9 months
Shame Timidity	Izard et al., 1980	Facial	6–9 months
Fear Disgust Anger	Bridges, 1932	Facial	6 months
Anger	Sroufe, 1979	Facial, body	7 months
Attachment	Sroufe, 1979	Facial, body	9 months
Anxiety Elation Petulance	Sroufe, 1979	Facial, body	12 months

(continued)

Table 1.   Continued

Emotion	Author	Expression	Age
Guilt	Case, 1991 Trotter, 1982 Bridges, 1932	Facial, body	18–24 months
Pride	Heckhausen, 1987	Facial, body	14–20 months
Shame	Heckhausen, 1987 Sroufe, 1979	Facial, withdrawal	9–14 months
Elation Affection Jealousy	Bridges, 1932	Facial	12 months
Joy	Bridges, 1932	Facial, body	2 years
Pride	Sroufe, 1979	Facial, body	2 years

Source: From del Barrio (2002).

judge other people's emotions when they reach the age of six.

An interesting study by Harris et al. (1987) showed differences in emotional self-awareness in children aged 5 to 14. The task consisted of giving examples of words related to emotions such as 'happy', 'sad', 'angry', 'proud', 'jealous' or 'guilty'. At the age of 5, children can explain basic emotions verbally, at 7 they explain complex emotions, and at 14 a child's verbal explanations are similar to those of an adult.

The observation of facial expressions and body movements in different situations, such as mother–child interaction, is the principal method of assessing emotion in young children.

Strange Situation Technique (STT, Ainsworth & Wittig, 1969). This is a standard procedure for assessing the quality of infants' attachment to parents. A secure attachment is considered the basis for good emotional development, this concept being quite similar to that of 'ethological imprinting'. The suitable age range for the application of this tool is 9 to 34 months. Observed situations are: (1) Mother–child interaction in a playroom. (2) An unknown woman goes into the room and talks to both mother and child. (3) While the stranger is talking to the child, the mother leaves the room. (4) The stranger tries to interact with the child. (5) The mother returns and the stranger leaves the room. (6) The mother goes out and the child remains alone. (7) The stranger returns and tries to make contact with the child. (8) The mother comes back.

Each situation described above takes three minutes, or even less in the case of the child becoming distressed. The child's behaviour is recorded and evaluated by three different judges. The behaviour units to be observed are: seeking contact, maintaining contact, avoiding contact and resistance to contact. The child's behaviour is classified into four different types: 'A' Anxious/avoiding attachment, 'B' Secure attachment, 'C' Ambivalent attachment and 'D' Disorganized attachment.

Maximally Discriminative Facial Movement Coding System (MAX, Izard, 1979). This system was developed as an objective system for identifying the discrete facial changes of fundamental emotions. It identifies the following affects: fear, joy, anger, shame, sadness, interest, disgust and surprise. The AFFEX (Izard, 1980) is used with children, and is a system in which the basic emotions are identified through observing the whole face. These two instruments are complementary, but have been criticized on the grounds of the low reliability of their subjective judgements. Another tool designed by Izard is the Mother's Perception of Baby's Emotion Expressions (MPBEE, Izard et al., 1979), which assesses the frequency with which children aged 2 to 9 months express emotions.

Facial Action Coding System (FACS, Ekman & Friesen, 1978). This system is an anatomically comprehensive system that codes all observable facial expressions and identifies the following affects: joy, surprise, disgust, anger and fear. It assesses action units (AUs), and has been adapted for use with infants from 0 to 3 months old (Oster, 1978). There are 24 different AUs, which represent different positions of the child's brows, mouth, eyes and cheeks. There are also three different movement intensity levels. The child's face is recorded and different judges subsequently assess the tape. Agreement between judges increases as child's age increases from 3 (58%) to 8 weeks (92%); these data are interpreted as reflecting an evolution of the child's facial expressions, which shift from ambiguity to clarification. The child's facial movements can be observed in combination, so that it is possible to obtain patterns of the basic emotions.

The most structured laboratory observation system for assessing a child's emotional behaviour is the *Attachment Q-Set* (AQS, Walters & Deane, 1985). This is an instrument designed to describe the basic security behaviour of 1 to 5-year-old children. It is made up of 100 items using the Q methodology, and has a three-point scale: (1) non-confident, (2) somewhat confident and (3) very confident. This scale can be used to assess the observer's confidence of the adequacy of the Q-descriptions. There is also a *Q-Short* (Q-S, Walters & Deane, 1985). This is a short scale consisting of two lists with 90 items related to traits and behaviours; both can be filled out by parents and trained observers.

Kiddie-Infant Descriptive Instrument for Emotional States (KIDIES, Stern et al., 1989). This is a clinical instrument designed to assess emotional and behavioural state levels as well as disorders of infants and young children. It measures 16 affective and behavioural dimensions, and quantifies frequency (0–4) and intensity (presence or absence of observable behaviours). The affective dimensions assessed are happiness, sadness, anger, fear, disgust, surprise, distress and soberness. All channels of expression of emotional states can be assessed, especially the face (smile), the posture (jumping up), the voice (pleasant vocalizations) and the gesture (arms flapping).

AIMS: Developmental Indicators of Emotional Health (AIMS: DIEH, Partridge, 1990). This consists of a structured dialogue between parents and practitioners about the emotional health of children aged 2 weeks to 5 years. It explores four areas: Attachment, Interaction, Mastery and Social Support. Each dimension is assessed through 10 items and rated using a Likert scale (1–5).

When the child is over 3 years old, the emotional assessment may include children's actions such as labelling, pointing, matching or telling stories.

Test of Social Sensitivity (TSS, Rothenberg, 1970). Children listen to four tape-recorded scenarios in which a man and a woman interact. The emotions presented in this task are 'Happiness', 'Anger', 'Anxiety' and 'Sadness'. Photos of a man and a woman depicting the four emotions are used, as well as the tapes. The child must identify how the actor feels. Responses are scored according to their accuracy: (2) the child mentions emotion changes, (1) the child mentions only one emotion, (0) the child does not mention any feeling, and (−1) the child chooses a wrong emotion.

Affect in Play Scale (APS, Howe & Silvern, 1981). This is a standardized measure of the affective expression in children's pretend play. The first form was elaborated for children 6 to 10 years old. There is also an adaptation for pre-school children aged 4 to 5, called *PAPS*. The play task uses human puppets, a boy and a girl with neutral expressions, and three coloured blocks. Animal puppets can also be used instead of the human ones. The child is encouraged to play with the puppets for five minutes, in a situation of free play without any instruction. The play is videotaped. Emotion-loaded content and expressions of emotion during the play are coded. There are three major affect-related scores: Frequency of affective expression units (verbal or moving/motor), Categorization of the units (Happiness, Anxiety, Sadness, Frustration, Affection, Aggression, Oral aggression, Sexual aggression and Competition) and Intensity of the units. These dimensions are rated 1 to 5.

Fantasy and Imagination are also scored according to the following elements: Organization, Elaboration and Imagination (rated 1 to 5), and Quality of Fantasy (mean of previous scores). Comfort while playing is also scored (rated 1 to 5). Total score is obtained by means of multiplying quality of fantasy by frequency of the affect score.

Affective Labelling Task (ALT, Denham, 1986). Children over 4 years old are asked to identify verbally and point out the appropriate expressions of 'Happiness', 'Sadness', 'Anger' and 'Fear' in four drawings of faces. First, they have to identify emotions, answering questions such as: 'Who is sad in these four drawings?'

They are then required to name the emotion represented in the picture, answering the following question: 'What is he feeling?' As an answer, children have to point to the corresponding drawing. Responses are scored 1 if the child identifies the emotion as positive or negative, or 2 if the child has a specific label for the emotion.

The same task can also be presented as a story performance, using puppets as actors that express the four emotions.

Conflicting emotions (CE, Gordis et al., 1989). This is composed of two set stories that each describe three different events. In the first one (Explain), a character experiences two opposite emotions mentioned in the story, saying, for example, 'You know I feel both happy and sad, about the last day of school.' The task consists in explaining the reasons why the actor feels that way. Possible scores are: (0) no explanation, (1) explanation of one of the emotions, and (2) explanation of both emotions. In the second set story (Explain/Detect), the child is told the story alone and asked what the character is feeling. It is scored in the same way as the first one, though in this second task the child can be prompted.

At the end, the child is asked to recount a similar event that he or she has experienced (Own Story). This third part is scored as follows: (2) the story contains two opposite emotions, and (1) it contains only one emotion.

Total possible score is 14.

Teddy Bears' Picnic (TBP, Mueller, 1996). This is an adaptation of the 'MUG and TAT' instrument for assessing emotional and behavioural problems in younger children. It was developed to be used with 4- to 6-year-old children. It utilizes a bear family: a mother, a father and two children, a boy and a girl. The young bear with the same sex as the child's is introduced to him/her. The child then has to answer some questions about each of the ten different stories presented, such as: 'What happens next?', or 'What does this bear do?' The TBP provides quantitative information about several problems, such as disorientation, drive expressions, aggression, helplessness or vulnerability.

There are also instruments for assessing children's development that include the assessment of emotional development. Some examples are shown in Table 2.

Children usually learn to regulate their emotions in their relationships with other people; this is called 'emotional competence'. The most important instruments for assessing emotional competence are shown in Table 3.

Greenspan described the following developmental sequence by means of the *FEASIE* instrument:

18 months: the child has a representational/affective communication system.
24 months: the child can create mental representations of intentions, wishes, needs or feelings.
30 months: the child has a representational elaboration system.
36 months: the child has a representational differentiation, so that he can distinguish real versus unreal events.
42 months: the child has a matured representational differentiation.

Finally, we can identify two main conceptions of children's emotions: it can be argued that children cannot experience emotions until they develop the capacity for reflective, self-conscious awareness, which they attain around the end of their first year of life (Lewis & Brooks, 1978). On the other hand, there is a claim for the existence of basic emotions more or less from birth (3 to 4 weeks old), which undergo developmental changes according to the child's mental growth (Oster, 1978).

The assessment of emotions also changes with the child's age. The best way to assess infants is through the observation of facial expressions and body movements, but once the child attains mastery of language, more complex tasks can be used, such as matching, answering questions or playing. With children over 7 years old, questionnaires offer a wider range of possibilities, and from this age onwards there are also specific tools for assessing each different emotion.

FUTURE PERSPECTIVE AND CONCLUSIONS

As it is well known, emotional life is the key to understanding the world in early childhood. Although emotions are an important subject in

Table 2.   Instruments for assessing children's development

Name	Author	Age (Years)	Applicant
Early Learning Accomplishment Profile* (LAP)	Glover et al., 1978	0–3	Psychologist
Minnesota Infant Development Inventory	Ireton & Thwing, 1980	1–16	Psychologist
Battelle Developmental Inventory* (BDI)	Newborg et al., 1988	0–8	
Early Screening Profiles	Harrison et al., 1990	2–6	Parents, teachers, caregivers
Carolina Curriculum for Infants (AGS)	Johnson-Martin et al., 1991	0–2	Psychologist
Assessment Evaluation and Programming System (AEPS)	Bricker, 1992	0–6	Parents, psychologist
Denver-II	Frankenbrg, 1992	0–6	Psychologist
Bayley Scales of Infant Development-II (BSID-II)	Bayley, 1993	0–3	Psychologist

Source: From del Barrio (2002).
*The most useful instruments for assessing emotions.

Table 3.   Emotional competence screening tools

Name	Author	Tasks	Age
Denver Developmental Screening Test (DDST)	Frankeburg et al., 1971	Interactive play and Mother separation	18–54 months
Tool Use Task (TUT)	Matas et al., 1978	Free-play, cleanup, reunion, separation	18–54 months
Minnesota Pre-school Affect Check-list (MPAC)	Sroufe et al., 1984	Peer interaction	3–6 years
Hawaii Early Learning Profile (HELP)	Parks, 1992	Play, living activities	0–3 years
Functional Emotional Assessment Scale for Infancy and Early Childhood (FEASIE)	Greenspan, 1992	Family, clinician and caregivers interaction	18–42 months
Pre-school Socio-affective Profile (PSP)	La Freniere & Dumas, 1996	Social interaction with family and peers	3–6 years

Source: From del Barrio (2002).

psychology, up to now less research has been carried out on this important aspect, having a corresponding negative effect on assessment. Much more research is required in order to improve the assessment of emotional development.

References

Ainsworth, M. & Wittig, B.A. (1969). Attachment and exploratory behaviour of one-year-olds in a strange situation. In Fox, B.M. (Ed.), *Determinants of Infant Behaviour*. Vol. 4. London: Methuen.

Borke, H. (1971). Interpersonal perception of young children: egocentrism or empathy? *Developmental Psychology*, 5, 263–269.

Breterton, I., Fritz, J., Zahn-Waxler, C. & Ridgeway, D. (1986). Learning to talk about emotions: a functionalist perspective. *Child Development*, 57, 529–548.

Campos, J. & Barret, K. (1984). Towards a new understanding of emotions and their development. In Izard, C., Kagan, J. & Zajonc, R. (Eds.), *Emotions, Cognition and Behaviour* (pp. 229–263). New York: Cambridge University Press.

del Barrio, V. (2000). Emotional knowledge children from 4 to 8 years of age. *Ausiedad y Estrés*, 6, 143–202.

del Barrio, V. (2002). *Emociones Infantiles [Children's Emotions]*, Madrid: Piramide.

Denham, S. (1986). Social cognition, pro-social behaviour and emotion in preschoolers. *Child Development*, 57, 194–201.

Dunn, J. (1988). *The Beginning of Social Understanding*. Cambridge, MA: Harvard University Press.

Dunn, J., Brown, J. & Beardsall, L. (1991). Family talk about feeling states and children's later understanding of others' emotions. *Developmental Psychology, 27*, 448–455.

Ekman, P. (1973). Cross-cultural studies of facial expression. In Ekman, P. (Ed.), *Darwin and Facial Expression*. New York: Academic Press.

Ekman, P. & Friesen, W.V. (1978). *Manual for the Facial Action Coding System*. Palo Alto, CA.: Consulting Psychologist Press.

Erinson, E.H. (1963). *Childhood and Society*. New York, Norton.

Feiring, C., Lewis, M. & Starr, M.D. (1984). Indirect effects and infants' reactions to strangers. *Developmental Psychology, 20*, 485–491.

Gordis, F.W., Rosen, A.B. & Grand, S. (1989). Young children's understanding of simultaneous conflicting emotions. Paper presented at the biennial meeting of the Society for Research in Child Development. Kansas City, MO.

Harris, P.L., Olthof, T., Meerum Terwogt, M. & Hardman, C.E. (1987). Children knowledge of situations that provoke emotions. *International Journal of Behavioural Development, 10*, 319–344.

Haviland, J.M. & Lelwica, M. (1987). The induced affect response: 10-week-old infants' responses to three emotional expressions. *Developmental Psychology, 16*, 132–104.

Hornick, R., Riesenhoover, N. & Gunnar, M. (1987). The effects of maternal positive neutral and negative affective communications on infant response to new toys. *Child Development, 58*, 937–944.

Howe & Silvern (1981). Behavioural observation during play therapy: preliminary development of a research instrument. *Journal of Personality Assessment, 45*, 168–182.

Izard, C.E. (1980). *AFFEX: A System for Identifying Affect Expressions by Holistic Judgements*. Newark: Instructional Resources Center. University of Delaware.

Izard, C.E., Buechler, S. & Huebner, R.R. (1979). Mother's perception of infants' emotion expression. Unpublished Work. University of Delaware.

Izard, C.E., Hebner, R.R., Risser, D., McGuinness, G.C. & Dougherty, L.M. (1980). *Developmental Psychology, 23*, 97–140.

Lewis, M. (1998). The development and structure of emotions. In Mascolo, M.F. & Griffin, S. (Eds.), *What Develops in Emotional Development?* (pp. 29–50). New York: Plenum Press.

Mesquita, B. & Frijda, N.H. (1992). Cultural variations in emotions: a review. *Psychological Bulletin, 112*, 179–204.

Mueller, N. (1996). The Teddy Bears' Picnic. Four-year-old children's personal construct in relation to behavioural problems and to teacher global concern. *Journal of Child Psychology and Psychiatry, 37*, 381–389.

Müller, J. (1954). Physiognomic Aussagen über Menschen bei Kleinkinder. Unpublished manuscript.

Oster, H. (1978). Facial expression and affect development. In Lewis, M. & Rosenblum, L.A., (Eds.); *The Development of Affect* (pp. 43–79). New York: Plenum Press.

Partridge, S. (1990). AIMS: *Developmental Indicators of Emotional Health*. Portland: University of Maine, Department of Human Services Development Institute.

Rothenberg, B. (1970). Children's social sensitivity and the relationship to interpersonal competence, interpersonal comfort and intellectual level. *Developmental Psychology, 2*, 335–350.

Sorce, J.F., Emde, R.N., Campos, J.L. & Klinnert, M.D. (1985). Maternal emotion signalling: its effects on visual cliff behavior of 1 year old. *Developmental Psychology, 21*, 195–200.

Sroufe, L.-A. (1979). Socioemotional development. In Osofsky, J.D. (Ed.), *Handbook of Infant Development*. New York: Wiley.

Stern, D.N., Robert-Tisson, C., de Mulralt, M. & Cramer, B. (1989). The KIA profile: Un instrument de recherche clinique pour l'évaluation des états affectives du jeune enfant. In Lebovici, S., Mazet, P. & Visier, J.P. (Eds.), *L'évaluations précoces entre le bébé et ses partenaires* (pp. 131–149). Paris: Eshel.

Trotter, V.T. (1982). The consistence with which teachers at various grade levels convey affect via different channels of communication. *Dissertation Abstracts International, 43*, 371–373.

Walters, E. & Deane, K.E. (1985). Defining and assessing individual differences in attachment relationship: Q-methodology and the organization of behaviour in infancy and early childhood. In Breterton, I. & Waters, E. (Eds.), *Growing Points of Attachment Theory Research* (pp. 41–65). Monographs of the Society for Research in Child Development, 50 (1-2, Serial. No. 209).

Watson, J.B. & Morgan, J.J.B. (1917). Emotional and psychological reactions. *American Journal of Psychology, 28*, 514–527.

Wellman, H.M., Phillips, A.T. & Rodriguez, T. (2000). Young children's, understanding of perception, desire, and emotions. *Child Development, 71*, 895–912.

Yarrow, M.R. & Waxler, C.Z. (1975). The emergence and functions of prosocial behaviour in young children. Paper presented at the Society for Research in Child Development meeting, Denver.

Maria Victoria del Barrio

RELATED ENTRIES

DIAGNOSIS OF MENTAL AND BEHAVIOURAL DISORDERS

INTRODUCTION

Mental and behavioural disorders have been the object of many classifications, from the Greek Antiquity during which they were divided into mania, melancholia, phrenitis and lethargia, to the most recent diagnostic manual, the DSM-IV, published in 1994.

The purpose of medical classifications is to divide the population of patients into distinct and homogeneous sub-groups, by using as criteria the observed symptoms and, if it is known, their cause, in order to choose the most adequate therapy. The process leading to the attribution of a given patient to one of the sub-groups constitutes the diagnosis. Sub-groups defined by a specific pattern of symptoms are called syndromes. The term disease is theoretically reserved to those defined by a common aetiology, although it has often been applied to purely syndromic entities. Today, psychiatry uses the more vague term Disorder for both. Several Syndromes may originate from the same cause and, conversely, a single syndrome may have diverse aetiologies.

HISTORICAL PERSPECTIVE

The first general classification of mental disorders appeared in the second half of the 18th century. Its author, Boissier de Sauvages, had compiled all the descriptions proposed since Antiquity and presented them according to the formal structure introduced in the botanical classification by his friend Linnaeus. It had little influence on modern psychiatry which began around 1800 with Pinel. During the greatest part of the 19th century, the main contribution of the psychiatrist consisted in the accurate description of syndromes. They belonged mainly to those aspects of mental disorders later known as psychoses, which led to the commitment to asylums. Among the less severe psychological manifestations, the neuroses,

a term coined by Cullen to emphasize what he considered to be their hypothetical aetiology: a dysfunction of the nervous system, and whose main forms were hysteria, hypochondriasis, and later neurasthenia, were studied by neurologists like Charcot and the character peculiarities, formerly the object of descriptions by writers and moralists, constituting today the personality disorders were incorporated into psychiatry only at the end of the century.

Between 1883 and 1917, in the eight successive editions of his Textbook, Kraepelin elaborated progressively the classification whose main outlines are the basis of the future ones. His aim was to describe separate diseases, each defined by its cause, its psychopathological mechanisms, and by its clinical manifestations. He postulated in each one a strict correspondence between the three levels. In most cases he had to evoke only hypothetical causes, but affirmed that, because of its postulates, the classification based on the clinical manifestations would not be modified when the aetiology would be later proved, provided that one would not only take into account the transversally observed symptoms, as in the syndromic perspective, but also 'the developmental conditions, the course and the outcome of the individual disorder'. Kraepelin's classification distinguished four main groups of disorders:

1   those whose origin was a proven anomaly of the brain structure, either acquired as in the dementias, or congenital as in mental retardation;
2   the psychoses, for which the postulated and endogenous origin, possibly metabolic or hereditary, the isolation of their two main forms, Dementia pracox – later renamed by Bleuler Schizophrenia. And manic-depressive psychosis being the most often evoked contribution of Kraepelin;
3   the neuroses of psychogenic nature; and
4   the personality disorders, relatively permanent anomalies related to constitutional

factors. In the following decades, many modifications were introduced in this general scheme, such as the expansion of the concept of neurosis under the growing influence of psychoanalysis.

MODERN CLASSIFICATION SYSTEMS

Many of those modifications were restricted to a national or ideological school and this led to many difficulties to communication between specialists, even if they used the same terminology: the low-inter-raters reliability of the psychiatric diagnosis was demonstrated by many experimental studies. Efforts towards a consensus came mainly from two organizations. The World Health Organization (WHO) published periodically an International Classification of Diseases (ICD) which included a chapter on mental disorders. Initially, only an enumeration of the names of the disorders, it included only with its ninth revision (1975) a glossary giving a short description of the characteristics of each one. The American Psychiatric Association began in 1952 for the benefit of its members to publish a Diagnostic and Statistical Manual (DSM) which contained a glossary added to the terms recommended.

The third edition of this Manual (DSM-III) published in 1980 constitutes a fundamental step in the history of psychiatric classifications. Although initially intended to be used only by the American psychiatrists, it acquired rapidly such a world wide influence that the ICD-10 (1992) has practically adopted its positions. It was succeeded by a revised edition (DSM-III-R) in 1987 and by the DSM-IV in 1994 which have retained its main features. The classification is strictly categorical, this being a reaction against the antinosologism which had prevailed in the preceding decades, especially in the United States, under the influence of psychodynamism and, according to its authors, in this respect a return to the Kraepelinian medical tradition. Each disorder is characterized by a pattern of diagnostic criteria, generally constituted by the presence of a definite number of precisely defined symptoms, obviously influenced in their presentation and mode of utilization by statistical psychology and by the computer

assisted diagnostic procedures. The criteria are usually of a purely descriptive nature. The DSMs exclude from nosology any not objectively demonstrated aetiological concepts: in practice their categories are for the most part only syndromic, a situation specific to psychiatry. Among the many consequences, one of the most notable is the disappearance of the concept (and term) of neurosis, the justification being that it implied for many an aetiology based on purely hypothetical psychological conflicts. Most of the former neurotic disorders belong now to the group of the Anxiety Disorders, defined by the existence of anxiety as the prominent symptom. But for that reason, Hysteria has been excluded from the group, the manifestations formerly reattached to it being attributed, according to their objective characteristics, to the newly constituted groups of the somatoform and of the dissociative disorders.

Another originality of the DSMs has been the introduction of the multi-axial system. Possibly useful information about a given patient are coded of five axes. The diagnostic category to which he belongs is reported on Axes 1 and 2, the last one being reserved to the personality disorders and to mental retardation. This disposition facilitates the description of the frequently occurring situation in which an Axis 1 disorder develops in a patient affected by one of the permanent mental abnormalities of Axis 2. Axis 3 records the general physical conditions potentially relevant to the understanding and management of the mental disorder. Axis 4 in the same perspective the psychological and social problems, and Axis 5 the general assessment to the level of global functioning, of the patient. Despite its striking originalities, despite the introduction of many new categories and sub-categories in order to increase the homogeneity of each one, the basic structure of the Kraepelinian nosology can still be recognized in the DSM-IV. It is true that the ICD-10 is slightly more conservative in its technical aspects – its multi-axial system is simpler – and in its vocabulary – the term neurosis has been retained – but the categories and their criteria are very similar.

Finally, it can be stated that the DSM-IV and ICD-10 are presently by far the most commonly used diagnostic manuals, one is now nearing a general consensus in the classification of mental and behavioural disorders.

FUTURE PERSPECTIVES AND CONCLUSIONS

However, this classification is the object of criticisms. If its interraters reliability is recognized, the purely descriptive nature of most of the diagnostic criteria is considered by many as a too superficial approach, and its growing complexity does not result in an evident increase of its validity. A classification is basically a technique of condensation of information. But such a condensation can be obtained in a completely different way by using a dimensional model of the type developed by psychologists in the description of personality. Whereas a classification regroups the individuals according to their characteristics, the dimensional model regroups empirically, using habitually the statistical method of factor analysis, those characteristics into a small number of linear dimensions. Each subject can be described in a simplified way by his position on each of them, by his dimensional profile. This model is commonly used in the description of the normal and pathological personality, has been introduced in psychiatry in the construction of the rating scales and is even proposed by the DSM-IV for the specification of the patients receiving the diagnosis for schizophrenia by their attribution to one of the sub-categories of the disorder. The substitution of the dimensional model to the categorical one seems particularly advisable in the group of Personality Disorders in which the present categorical approach is obviously inadequate, and the whole of mental pathology had even been considered by the authors of the DSM-IV. Such a fundamental change has been provisorily rejected for reasons of tradition – the various branches of medicine use the categorical model – and for practical ones: the researchers have not yet reached an agreement of the best system on dimensions to be used. Future developments will improve those flaws.

References

American Psychiatric Association (1994). *Diagnostic and Statistical Manual of Mental Disorders. DSM-IV* (4th ed.). Washington: American Psychiatric Association.

World Health Organization (1992). *The ICD-10 Classification of Mental and Behavioural Disorders. Clinical Descriptions and Diagnostic Guidelines.* Geneva: World Health Organization.

World Health Organization (1992). *The ICD-10 Classification on Mental and Behavioural Disorders. Diagnostic Criteria for Research.* Geneva: World Health Organization.

Pierre Pichot

RELATED ENTRIES

APPLIED FIELDS: CLINICAL, CLASSIFICATION (GENERAL, INCLUDING DIAGNOSIS), CLINICAL JUDGEMENT

DIAGNOSTIC TESTING IN EDUCATIONAL SETTINGS

INTRODUCTION

Diagnostic testing in education refers to an in-depth assessment of pupils' learning difficulties, whatever their causes. The way to conduct such an assessment is not obvious. An essential distinction should be made between an assessment that focuses on performance and an assessment that focuses on competence. The first section clarifies this distinction. The second and the third sections analyse the usefulness and the limits of each of these two levels of assessment.

TWO LEVELS OF DIAGNOSTIC TESTING: PERFORMANCE AND COMPETENCE

In the field of linguistics, Chomsky (1965) made a fundamental distinction between performance and competence. Performance refers to the use of language in functional situations. Competence refers the underlying system of rules mastered by the speaker. The speaker's competence cannot be observed directly. This is only inferred from the speaker's performance, which imperfectly reflects his competence. This distinction between performance and competence is essential for the diagnosis of learning difficulties. The diagnostic testing can focus on the quality of the behaviours produced by a subject – the performance – (e.g. the correctness of a text reading) or on the cognitive abilities underlying these behaviours – the competence – (e.g. the mental processes used when reading a word). Diagnostic tests are very different if they target the assessment of performance or competence.

Performance tests are basically a-theoretical, in the sense they do not refer to any model of the mental activity being at work in the items. The test items are usually selected on the basis of an accurate definition of the knowledge domain to be assessed and on a specific description of the behaviours corresponding to the mastery of a particular knowledge. The validation of the performance test items relies on experts of the domain who judge the pertinence of the selected items with regard to the learning goals.

On the other hand, competence tests rely on models of cognitive processes involved in the items. To validate these tests, the pertinence of the items chosen as indicators of the mental processes to be measured should be proved. Are the selected tasks involving the intended processes, and only these? Validation of the competence tests is often difficult because the cognitive activities involved in the items are never straightforward. Even apparently very simple tasks involve rather complex cognitive processes (e.g. Longstreth, 1984). Since a pure measure of the intended processes does not exist, the interpretation of the scores in competence tests is often difficult. Moreover, the models underlying the competence tests are only partial and temporary representations of the mental reality. Therefore, the difficulty of building and interpreting such tests could stem from model shortcomings.

DIAGNOSTIC TESTING THAT FOCUSES ON PERFORMANCE

There are two main arguments for using performance tests to diagnose learning difficulties. The first is that the performance measurement guarantees the ecological validity of the diagnostic testing. Performances are useful behaviours allowing subjects to cope with everyday problems. When the diagnostic assessment only focuses on mental processes, there is a risk of unduly emphasizing disabilities without any real consequences for the subject's environmental adaptation. The second argument for using performance tests is that their items match the teaching goals. Performances are essential information for appraising the child's adjustment to the school demands. Referring to school demands avoids describing an imperfect performance, but corresponding to a sufficient performance at a given school level, as an indication of learning disability. Learning is a step-by-step process. It is essential to distinguish between what is related to the normal learning process and what is related to disability.

Unfortunately, as performance tests are built without any reference to a model of the cognitive functioning, they do not open to an in-depth understanding of the observed phenomena. As Snow and Lohman emphasized (1988: 268), 'item writers are more likely to be content specialists working from test specifications that bear no relation to the specifications of relevant psychological theory'. The items of the performance tests are more often a sample of relevant content domain knowledge, but not of learning. Consequently, the scores are not keys for really understanding success or failure. They do not provide a sound foundation for identifying learning disabilities and how they might be corrected.

Another problem with performance tests is the interpretation of the discrepancy between the observed score and the expected score. For example, according to the DSM-IV (American Psychiatric Association, 1994), one of the criteria for 'reading disorder' is a reading achievement, measured by a performance test, below expectation. This criterion is inaccurate. When does a discrepancy between an observed score and an expected score allow one to talk about learning disabilities? Usually, a 2-year delay with regard to the expected score (expressed on the grade-equivalent score scale) is considered as a criterion of learning disabilities (Kavale & Forness, 1995). Such a criterion is arbitrary, but there is no way to determine a more appropriate criterion using a performance test. The best answer to this problem is to refer to an identified disorder of the cognitive processes relating to the low observed score. For that purpose, a competence test is required.

DIAGNOSTIC TESTING THAT FOCUSES ON COMPETENCE

Historically, the Piagetian theory is the first reference to an assessment that focuses on competence (Inhelder, 1943). The Piagetian model was very appealing to practitioners during the 1960s and the 1970s. Today, it is less popular, but it is still used for the diagnosis of mathematical learning disorders. The Piagetian theory provides a particularly strong conceptual framework for understanding the construction of the logical structure of thought. It is especially helpful for understanding the development of certain concepts, like the concept of number. In this case, it focuses the diagnostic assessment on logical operations that constitute the roots of the concept of number. Diagnostic tests developed in reference to the Piagetian theory allow one to go further than the sole report of success or failure, and enable one to catch the person's way of thinking. Unfortunately, the tests based on the Piagetian theory are not without shortcomings. Although these tests are strong from a theoretical viewpoint, they are often weak from a psychometric viewpoint. Standardization and norms of the tasks used for diagnostic testing are generally inadequate. But, the main methodological problem refers to the validity of the tasks used for assessment. Are Piagetian tasks measuring what they are intended to measure, and only that? When a test is focused on competence, empirical evidence is required to prove that the selected tasks have correctly measured the targeted competence. Numerous studies on Piagetian tasks have shown that this requirement is often imperfectly met.

For more than twenty years, cognitive psychology has provided another framework for diagnostic testing that focuses on competence. In comparison with the Piagetian theory, cognitivist models try to describe the complexity of information processing without limitation to the logical components alone. They pay more attention to the representations and to the kind of knowledge used by the subject. Particularly, the concepts of declarative and procedural knowledge, and the relationship between the

two, have been widely applied to understand school learning. This goes together with great attention paid to the level of automatism of procedures, which is appraised via the speed of process and/or the resistance to interference from other tasks performed simultaneously.

Some of the competence tests developed within the cognitive psychology framework try to assess general procedures, applying to a wide range of tasks. For example, the *Kaufman Assessment Battery for Children* (K-ABC; Kaufman & Kaufman, 1983) was designed to assess the simultaneous and sequential processing. Defects in these processes seem to be the root of some learning disabilities. Unfortunately, the K-ABC, as other tests assessing general procedures, raises some questions about its validity and its usefulness. Diagnostic tests, which focus on more specific procedures, seem to be the more promising. This is the case of tests measuring the procedures involved in the reading of words. These tests are built on componential models, which organize the processes involved in oral reading. The effectiveness of each component is appraised using very specific tasks. The score for each task needs to be interpreted in relation to the scores for the other tasks. These tests provide specific information, but they are generally more valid than tests assessing general procedures and, consequently, are more useful for practitioners.

FUTURE PERSPECTIVES

Research in cognitive and neuropsychology has improved sharply our knowledge of the mental processes involved in school learning. We have now powerful models to explain how children read words or memorize multiplication tables. These models can also be used to understand learning disabilities. Diagnostic tests built on these models are progressively available (e.g. *Test of Phonological Awareness*, Torgesen & Bryant, 1994). In the near future, the development and publication of such tests will accelerate.

However, all learning disabilities cannot be understood through very specific models of mental processes. Some problems are related to more general cognitive processes involved in a wide range of learning tasks. Using only tests focusing on very specific processes, there is a risk to miss some important cognitive problems. Consequently, in the future, practitioners will also need tests assessing broad cognitive processes, but these tests will be built on stronger models than in the past. The *Revision of the Leiter International Performance Scale* (Roid & Miller, 1997) and the *Cognitive Assessment System* (Naglieri & Das, 1987) illustrate of this trend.

CONCLUSIONS

The assessments that focus on competence give more interesting information for special education than the assessments that focus on performance. The purpose of diagnosis is not only to quantify success and failures but it is also, and above all, to understand the meaning of the observed performance. For such an understanding, we need to refer to models of learning and cognitive functioning. These models allow us to really interpret the observed scores and to provide useful information to effectively help children with learning disabilities.

References

American Psychiatric Association (1994). *Diagnostic and Statistical Manual of Mental Disorders.* *DSM-IV*. Washington, DC: American Psychiatric Association.

Chomsky, N. (1965). *Aspects of the Theory of Syntax*. Cambridge, MA: MIT Press.

Inhelder, B. (1943). *Le diagnostic du raisonnement chez les débiles mentaux*. Neuchâtel: Delachaux et Niestlé.

Kaufman, A.S. & Kaufman, N. (1983). *Kaufman Assessment Battery for Children*. Circle Pine, MN: American Guidance Service.

Kavale, K.A. & Forness, S.R. (1995). *The Nature of Learning Disabilities*. Mahwah, NJ: Lawrence Erlbaum.

Longstreth, L.E. (1984). Jensen's reaction time investigations of intelligence: a critique. *Intelligence, 8*, 139–160.

Naglieri, J.A. & Das, J.P. (1987). *Cognitive Assessment System*. Itasca, IL: Riverside.

Roid, G.H. & Miller, L.J. (1997). *Leiter International Performance Scale – Revised*. Wood Dale, IL: Stoelting.

Snow, R.E. & Lohman, D. (1988). Implications of cognitive psychology for educational measurement. In Linn, R.L. (Ed.), *Educational Measurement* (3rd ed., pp. 263–331). New York: Macmillan.

Torgesen, J.K. & Bryant, B.R. (1994). *Test of Phonological Awareness*. Austin, TX: Pro-Ed.

Jacques Gregoire

RELATED ENTRIES

APPLIED FIELDS: EDUCATION, CLASSIFICATION (GENERAL, INCLUDING DIAGNOSIS), CLINICAL JUDGEMENT, PSYCHOEDUCATIONAL TEST BATTERIES

DYNAMIC ASSESSMENT (LEARNING POTENTIAL TESTING, TESTING THE LIMITS)

INTRODUCTION

This entry discusses the characteristics and procedures of dynamic assessment and learning potential testing, differentiating these approaches from testing-the-limits. The entry will briefly discuss examples of dynamic assessment procedures that have been developed by researchers in a number of countries, as well as developing applications and evidence for validity of these approaches.

Dynamic assessment is a generic term for approaches to assessment that are characterized by inclusion of interactions between the assessor and learner during the course of the assessment. These are sometimes referred to as learning potential or interactive assessment procedures because the information derived from the interaction relates to what the learner is able to accomplish with the help of a more experienced collaborator, going beyond independent functioning. This extension beyond the current level of functioning operationalizes the concept of potential. The focus of the assessment is on the learner's responsiveness to the interaction-as-intervention, and the level of functioning of the learner following, rather than preceding, this interaction. Dynamic assessment assesses the learner in the process of learning, as well as the learning processes per se.

Dynamic assessment goes far beyond testing-the-limits. In testing-the-limits, assessors typically make minor changes in the administration of tests that typically have standardized scripted instructions. The intent is to explore what the learner can do if, for example, given more time, or if the vocabulary were more accessible. Testing-the-limits does not look at the process of learning or explore how problems were solved or errors made and then overcome, or redefine level of performance in terms of abilities demonstrated following the provision of scaffolded interventions. An exception to this is the work by Carlson (1995), who refer to their dynamic assessment approach as testing-the-limits. The work of these researchers documented the impact of assessor's elaborated feedback and learner's verbalization during the course of problem solving as potent factors in facilitating problem solution. Their approach to dynamic assessment emphasizes these types of interactions during the course of assessment interactions.

The theoretical bases for dynamic assessment derive primarily from the works of Vygotsky (1978) in Russia, and Feuerstein and his colleagues (Feuerstein, Rand & Hoffman, 1979) in Israel. Vygotsky's description of the 'zone of proximal development' and his advocacy for determining both the zones of actual and proximal development have served to describe the nature of dynamic assessment as providing information not only about what the learner can accomplish independently, but, also, what the learner can demonstrate with the help of a more experienced collaborator. Feuerstein et al.'s work has provided both detailed elaboration of the nature of the interactions that need to take place in order to facilitate learning, as well as the design of a specific dynamic assessment procedure to operationalize these ideas.

MEASUREMENT DEVICES

Since Feuerstein's work, along with significant parallel developments in Germany (Guthke, 1992), there has been considerable research and development of dynamic assessment procedures. Five approaches to dynamic assessment have served as models for most of the work that has developed during the late twentieth century. These include the work of Feuerstein et al. (1979), Budoff (1987), Campione and Brown (1987), Carlson (1995), and Lidz (1991).

Feuerstein's remains the most clinical and intuitive. Using a battery of tests, many of them designed by André Rey, though also including the Raven's Progressive Matrices and a modification of the Arthur Stencil Designs Test, Feuerstein's Learning Potential (now Propensity) Assessment Device adds an interaction component to each of the tests. Learner performance is analysed in terms of an array of cognitive deficiencies and responsiveness to the interactions of the assessor that follow the expressed needs of the learner during the course of the assessment.

Budoff's learning potential assessment uses some of the same and similar tests as Feuerstein, but differs in both procedure and purpose. While Feuerstein's approach provides detailed descriptive information about the problem-solving nature of the learner, Budoff designed his procedure to address issues of classification, specifically misclassification of children as mentally retarded. This approach provides standardized, scripted instructions for all learners. The content of the script addresses principles and strategies of problem solution, and learner response is analysed in terms of ability to profit from this experience.

Campione and Brown initially designed their approach to dynamic assessment as an attempt to operationalize Vygotsky's notion of zone of proximal development. Therefore, their approach was specifically an attempt to represent a theory of assessment. These researchers designed a graduated prompting approach, during which learners who did not succeed in solving a problem received a standard set of predetermined hierarchically ordered series of hints that increasingly approached total task solution by the assessor.

Carlson (1995), as described above, offer a testing-the-limits approach, where learners are asked to verbalize their problem solutions, and where they are provided with ongoing elaborated feedback regarding their performance.

Finally, Lidz (1991) combined dynamic with curriculum-based assessment to link the assessment with the learner's actual curriculum. This can be done either clinically, offering embedded interventions responsive to the behaviours of the learner during the course of the assessment, following a neuropsychological processing model, or by use of structured scripts that provide principles of problem solution and relevant strategies to all learners regardless of their specific functioning.

The procedures available at the time of writing this entry were many, and included (see chapters in Lidz & Elliott, 2000 for detailed descriptions, research, and case examples of each): The Leipzig Learning Test and Adaptive Computer Assisted Intelligence Learning Test Battery, both described by Guthke and Beckmann, Swanson's Cognitive Processing Test, Hessels' Learning Potential Test for Ethnic Minorities, Karpov's dynamic assessment of the level of internalization of children's problem-solving activity, Buchel and Schlatter's Analogical Reasoning Learning Test, Jensen's Mindladder Model, Resing's Learning Potential for Inductive. Reasoning in Young Children, Gerber's Dynomath, the Evaluacion del Potencial de Aprendizaje by Fernandez-Ballesteros and Calero, Kahn's Dynamic Assessment of Infants and Toddlers' Abilities, Tzuriel's Cognitive Modifiability Battery (plus three other instruments developed by the same author), and The Application of Cognitive Functions Scale by Lidz and Jepsen. These procedures, with summary information, appear in Table 1.

There have been criticisms of dynamic assessment approaches as lacking evidence of reliability and validity. The emphasis of some approaches to dynamic assessment on change and the plasticity of the learner presents challenges to traditional evidence of both reliability and validity; however, the research literature addressing these issues has increased, and the evidence, for example, of increased validity of post test compared to pretest scores is available (e.g. Guthke, Beckman & Stein, 1995).

FUTURE PERSPECTIVES

Development of dynamic assessment approaches and research concerning issues of dynamic assessment have become an international enterprise. It is a relatively recent phenomenon that the researchers and procedure designers are aware of each other's work and are in communication with each other. Dynamic assessment has many faces and many diverse applications. It seems that there will never be just one thing called dynamic assessment, yet there are shared characteristics of these approaches. The future is likely to see increasing development of new procedures to meet various needs and applications, as well as increasingly sophisticated research on existing approaches. The future will also likely include increased dissemination of these approaches to practitioners, who will need exposure to these practices during their preservice training, and not just during brief workshops or inservice experiences. The influence of the thinking and attitudes generated by dynamic assessment are already apparent in the narratives, and occasionally the practices, of new, more traditionally psychometric procedures released by major publishers. Practitioners from different domains, such as psychology, education, and speech/language, are becoming increasingly aware of dynamic assessment, and are developing a common vocabulary and point of view regarding approaches to assessment, while still remaining within their area of expertise. The more emphasis there is on linking assessment with intervention and on proportionate representation of learners from diverse backgrounds in specialized services, the more need there will be for dynamic assessment approaches. Yet assessors need to continue to be aware of the information yielded by these procedures, just as they are of any other approach to assessment, and apply them when appropriate.

CONCLUSIONS

Dynamic assessment is a relatively recent addition to the assessment repertory. It represents not just approaches to conducting an assessment, but an attitude toward the learner and toward the learning experience as well. The value of observing learners during the course of learning, and viewing learning outcomes as open-ended and malleable, is an important contribution of these approaches, and consonant with evidence regarding neurological processing of the human

Table 1. Dynamic assessment models (See, Lidz & Elliott, 2000)

Test	Author(s)	Population	Content	Intervention	Properties
Adaptive Computer Assisted Learning Test Battery (ACIL) (German)	Guthke & Beckmann (Germany)	Grades 5 through 9	Three independent short term learning tests: sequential figures, number sequences, and analogies	Computerized adaptive assistance with feedback, prompts, and additional tasks; assesses need for assistance	Norms for regular and high achieving students. Satisfactory prediction of school grades. Factor analysis yielded a learning ability factor
Analogical Reasoning Learning Test (ARLT) (French)	Schlatter & Buchel (Switzerland)	Children and adults with mental retardation with mental age between 3 and 7 years	2×2 analogical matrices in figurative and geometrical modalities, constructed in wooden box	Standardized hierarchical hints based on research relevant to nature of error	Maintenance and transfer scores. Distinguishes between gainers and non-gainers. Evidence of discriminant and predictive validity, internal consistency, test–retest stability
Application of Cognitive Functions Scale (ACFS) (English)	Lidz & Jepsen (USA)	Children functioning between ages three through five years	Six process-oriented subtests tapping preschool curriculum demands and a behaviour rating scale	Semi-scripted teaching related to process demands of subtests	Documented pre to posttest gains, predictive validity, discriminant validity and reliability
Cognitive Modifiability Battery (CMB) (English)	Tzuriel (Israel)	Children in kindergarten through fourth grade	Manipulable materials with tasks tapping six areas of seriation, pattern reproduction, analogies, sequences (levels 1 and 2), and memory	Mediation-based teaching involves focusing attention on important dimensions, explanation of rules for problem solution, applying relevant strategies, and practice with sample items	Can be used clinically, or formally scored. Yields all/none or partial scores. Evidence provided internal consistency, construct and predictive validity
Dynamic Assessment of Infants' and Toddlers' Abilities (DAITA) (English)	Kahn (USA)	Infants and toddlers	Follows administration of standardized approaches. Uses items refused or failed on these procedures. The Hawaii Early Learning Profile Activity Book is recommended	Mediation-based clinical intervention	Clinical, qualitative information regarding children's level of functioning and responsiveness to intervention. Guidelines provided for rating child's 'cognitive actions' and parent's mediating interactions. Yields descriptions of child's functioning, parent's current repertory, and suggestions for intervention

Instrument	Author (country)	Population	Domain/content	Procedure	Evidence
Dynamic Assessment of the Level of Internalization of Problem-Solving Activity	Karpov & Gindis (USA)	Children 6 to 7 years of age	Analogical reasoning using shapes and figures cut from construction paper	The child is taught to solve problems at the simplest, visual-motor level and tested for transfer to higher levels	Findings from a series of Russian studies provide evidence for discriminant validity, intra-individual cross-domain consistency, and predictive validity
Dynomath (English)	Gerber (USA)	Secondary students with learning disabilities	Multidigit multiplication, simple multiplication retrieval and spatial-procedural knowledge	Series of prompts contingent upon errors, following principles of 'intelligent tutoring'	Computerized assessment of speed and accuracy. Computer generated report regarding individual's profile regarding retrieval speed and accuracy, time utilized, errors made, and prompts required. Evidence regarding test–retest reliability and face validity
Evaluacion del Potencial de Aprendizaje (EPA) (Spanish)	Fernandez-Ballesteros & Calero (Spain)	Ages 10 years through adult with average or below ability	Based on Raven Matrices. Training uses 68 matrix problems on 132 slides (stimulus and response slides), some from Budoff's research	Structured training procedure with items parallel to Raven. Provides dialogue aimed at generalization, incorporating feedback, elicited verbalization, and strategy analysis. Two training sessions between pretest and posttest	Scores for pretest, posttest, and gain leading to gainer/non-gainer classification and error analysis. Evidence provided regarding effectiveness of training, reliability, and predictive validity
Learning Potential Test for Ethnic Minorities (LEM) (Dutch)	Hessels (The Netherlands)	Ages 5 through 8 years; focus on minorities	Classification, word–object association, recognition and naming, number series, syllable recall and figurative analogies	Train-within-test model; incorporates repetition, non-verbal feedback or demonstration	Assesses extent of benefit from help. High reliability, minimized bias, satisfactory construct validity, good short term predictive validity
Learning Potential Test of Inductive Reasoning (LIR) (Dutch)	Resing (The Netherlands)	Children ages 7 and 8 years	Inductive reasoning through verbal analogy and visual exclusion. Intended to supplement intelligence test	Graduated hints based upon research literature task analysis of cognitive components necessary for task solution. Involves six training sessions between pre-post testing	Rubric regarding amount (number of hints) of help needed during training to criterion for each session. Scores also for posttests, training time, type of hints, child's justifications for solutions. Preliminary norms available, with more in preparation. High internal consistency. Evidence supporting construct, discriminant, and predictive validity

(continued)

Table 1. Continued

Test	Author(s)	Population	Content	Intervention	Properties
Leipzig Learning Test (LLT) (German)	Guthke & Beckmann (Germany)	End of first grade	Puzzles; classification tasks	Graduated hints	Good discriminant and concurrent validity; satisfactory reliability
Mindladder: Computer Assisted Modifiability Enhancement Techniques (CAMET) (English)	Jensen (USA)	Students in primary grades through college	Computerized presentation and record keeping. Wide range of reasoning and academic skills, including matrices, reading, associated recall. Functions as both an assessment and training program	Mediations provided by assessor in response to needs of learner, for example provision of feedback, strategies, and promotion of meaning	Graphs regarding time spent, retention, and performance efficiency. Information added to 150 item inventory regarding intellective and non-intellective dimensions. Preliminary research shows positive effects of program involvement on achievement
Swanson–Cognitive Processing Test (S-CPT) (English)	Swanson (USA)	Ages 4,5 through adult	Eleven subtests assessing working memory	Standardized prompts	Normed. Yields initial, gain, and maintenance scores. High internal reliability; good discriminant validity
Testing the Limits (English/German)	Carlson & Wiedl (USA/Germany)	Children and adults with range of learning difficulties. Also, series of studies with schizophrenics	Template of dynamic format on pre-existing tests. With schizophrenic participants, used Wisconsin Card Sorting Test	Emphasis on verbalization of task solution by learner and elaborated feedback by assessor	Series of studies documented effectiveness of the two interventions on learning outcome. With schizophrenic patients, studies show differential ability to profit from intervention that informs rehabilitation planning

brain as well. The challenges of establishing the reliabilities and validities of these approaches are increasingly being addressed, with a substantial body of research literature available addressing these issues.

References

Budoff, M. (1987). Measures for assessing learning potential. In Lidz, C.S. (Ed.), *Dynamic Assessment: An Interactional Approach to Evaluating Learning Potential* (pp. 173–195). New York: Guilford.

Campione, J.C. & Brown, A.L. (1987). Linking dynamic assessment with school achievement. In Lidz, C.S. (Ed.), *Dynamic Assessment: An Interactional Approach to Evaluating Learning Potential* (pp. 82–115). New York: Guilford.

Carlson, J.S. (Ed.) (1995). *European Contributions to Dynamic Assessment*. London: JAI Press Ltd.

Feuerstein, R., Rand, Y. & Hoffman, M. (1979). *Dynamic Assessment of Retarded Performers*. Baltimore: University Park Press.

Grigorenko, E.L. & Sternberg, R. (1998). Dynamic testing. *Psychological Bulletin, 124,* 75–111.

Gupta, R.M. & Coxhead, P. (Eds.) (1986). *Cultural Diversity and Learning Efficiency: Recent Developments in Assessment*. New York: St. Martin's Press.

Guthke, J. (1992). Learning tests: the concept, main research findings, problems and trends. *Learning and Individual Differences, 4,* 137–151.

Guthke, J., Beckmann, J.F. & Stein, H. (1995). Recent research evidence on the validity of learning tests. In Carlson, J.S. (Ed.), *Advances in Cognition and Educational Practice*, Vol. 3. Greenwich, CT: JAI.

Guthke, J. & Wiedl, K.H. (1996). *Dynamisches Testen*. Goettingen: Hogrefe.

Hamers, J.H.M., Sijtsma, K. & Ruijssenaars, A.J.J.M. (Eds.) (1993). *Learning Potential Assessment: Theoretical, Methodological, and Practical Issues*. Amsterdam: Swets & Zeitlinger.

Haywood, H.C. & Tzuriel, D. (Eds.) (1992). *Interactional Assessment*. New York: Springer-Verlag.

Lidz, C.S. (Ed.) (1987). *Dynamic Assessment: An Interactional Approach to Evaluating Learning Potential*. New York: Guilford.

Lidz, C.S. (1991). *Practitioner's Guide to Dynamic Assessment*. New York: Guilford.

Lidz, C.S. (1997). Dynamic assessment approaches. In Flanagan, D.P., Genshaft, J.L. & Harrison, P.L. (Eds.), *Contemporary Approaches to Assessment of Intelligence*. New York: Guilford.

Lidz, C.S. & Elliott, J.G. (Eds.) (2000). *Dynamic Assessment: Prevailing Models and Practices*. Oxford: Elsevier.

Vygotsky, L.S. (1978). *Mind in Society: The Development of Higher Psychological Processes*. Cole, M., John-Steiner, V., Scribner, S. & Souberman, E. (Eds.). Cambridge, MA: Harvard University Press.

Carol S. Lidz

RELATED ENTRIES

APPLIED FIELDS: EDUCATION, APPLIED FIELDS: CLINICAL, APPLIED FIELDS: GERONTOLOGY, INTELLIGENCE ASSESSMENT (GENERAL), COGNITIVE PLASTICITY, MENTAL RETARDATION, CHILDREN WITH DISABILITIES, LEARNING DISABILITIES

E EATING DISORDERS

INTRODUCTION

Anorexia nervosa (AN), bulimia nervosa (BN) and binge eating disorder (BED) are complex disorders in which a great variety of factors are implicated. Due to this complexity, a great diversity of instruments is required to collect the data needed to complete the initial assessment, to design the treatment plan, and to evaluate the outcomes. The aim of the initial assessment must be to gather information not only about weight and eating behaviour, but also about all the factors that are related to the onset, course and maintenance of the disorder. It is necessary to have in mind that a variety of professionals may collaborate in the care of these patients. Different levels of assessment are needed to complete the evaluation of eating disorders (see Table 1). First of all, a full physical examination should be preformed and laboratory analysis should be determined before the psychological assessment begins. For making treatment decisions, it is very important to know the patient's nutritional state, vital signs, physical and sexual growth and development, the cardiovascular system, evidence of dehydration, lanugo, salivary gland enlargement, etc. This knowledge is especially important in AN patients with great weight loss or in BN patients with a high frequency of vomiting. Then, attention must be paid to weight and the history of the eating disorder, the eating behaviour, binge eating and compensatory behaviours such as vomiting, misuse of laxatives or

diuretics, fasting and/or excessive exercise. More specific factors like body image, cognitive concerns, emotional state and comorbility with other disorders, especially affective and anxiety disorders, obsessive-compulsive disorder, personality disturbance and substance abuse, should be analysed too. It is very important to remember that these eating disorder patients frequently deny their problem. In consequence, it will be necessary to gather information from other family members and from different instruments on the same topics to validate the data. To reach all these goals, a great variety of instruments are required. A full review of these instruments can be found in Allison (1995), Rosen and Srebnik (1990) and Saldaña (1994).

BODY WEIGHT ASSESSMENT

Information on a patient's weight is very important especially in AN patients in which diagnostic criteria are related with underweight. There are several indexes, which allow us to know if a person is normal weight, underweight or overweight. Commonly accepted indexes are the index of relative weight (RWI) and the Quetelet index or Body Mass Index (BMI). Both of them are used for diagnostic criteria, the former in the DSM-IV (APA, 1994) and the last in the ICD-10 (WHO, 1992). However, the most recommended index is the BMI which can be calculated by the following formula [BMI = Weight (in kg)/height (in m)^2]. A BMI

Table 1. Levels of eating disorders assessment

Levels of assessment	Goals	Ways of assessment
First level	To make treatment decisions: hospitalization, day-care treatment, and outpatient treatment	Complete physical examination. Body weight assessment (Body Mass Index)
Second level	To establish good rapport and to develop therapeutic relationship with the patient To assess: • History of eating disorder • Eating behaviour and eating habits • Compensatory behaviours • Emotional states while eating • Worries about food and eating • Physical activity	1 Clinical interview 2 Semi-structured interviews: • Eating Disorders Examination (EDE) • Yale–Brown–Cornell Eating Disorders Scale (YBC-EDS) • Structured Interview for Anorexic and Bulimic Disorders (SIAB) 3 Self-report questionnaires: • Eating Attitudes Test (EAT-40, EAT-26) • Eating Disorders Inventory 2 (EDI-2) • Eating Disorders Examination Self-Report Questionnaire (EDE-Q) • Questionnaire of Eating and Weight Patterns (QEWP) 4 Self-monitoring records 5 Family interview
Third level	To differentiate between the features of eating disorder patients and those of the body dysmorphic disorder To assess: • Body image dissatisfaction • Body image disturbance • Worries about weight and figure • Desire to lose weight	1 Interviews • Shape concern and weight concern EDE subscales • Body image and slimness ideal SIAB subscale 2 Self-report questionnaires • Body Shape Questionnaire (BSQ) • Body dissatisfaction EDI subscale • Cuestionario de Influencia del Modelo Estético Corporal (CIMEC)
Fourth level	To assess other disorders comorbility: affective and anxiety disorders, obsessive-compulsive disorder, personality disturbance and/or substance abuse	1 Clinical interview 2 Semi-structured interviews 3 Self-report questionnaires

346

between 20 and 25 represents normal weight, a value above 25 overweight, between 18 and 20 mild underweight and below 17 severe underweight. In the ICD-10, a BMI below 17.5 is the diagnostic criteria for AN. BMI is a good index that not only informs about patients' weight but also on their nutritional status.

ASSESSMENT OF EATING HABITS AND COMPENSATORY BEHAVIOURS

The assessment of these important factors should be done through different instruments. Interviews, self-report questionnaires and self-monitoring records that are completed by patients.

Interviews

First, interviews are used to establish a good rapport and develop a therapeutic relationship with the patient, and to gather information about the principal features of eating disorders. For clinical purpose, clinicians can develop an interview to assess which is the eating pattern of the patient. The questions must permit knowledge of the type of food, quantity and frequency of eating, eating style, restrained eating and fasting. Also, it is necessary to ask about forbidden food and level of anxiety that provokes eating those forbidden food, binge eating episodes, feeling of loss of control while eating, nutritional knowledge and attitudes towards eating. Type and frequency of compensatory behaviours, such as vomiting, misuse of diuretic and/or laxatives, excess of physical activity and fasting, must be assessed too. However, several semi-structured or standardized interviews have been developed for clinical and research purposes. They permit assessment of the eating habits and compensatory behaviours of patients with eating disorders in addition to the associated psychopathology. The interviews used more frequently are the Eating Disorder Examination (EDE; Cooper & Fairburn, 1987), the Yale–Brown–Cornell Eating Disorders Scale (YBC-EDS; Mazure et al., 1994; Sunday et al., 1995), or the Structured Interview for Anorexic and Bulimic Disorders (SIAB; Fitcher et al., 1991). These instruments – even though they are different – measure the features of the eating

disorders, and they have helped to increase the reliability in the assessment of symptoms. Special training is needed to correctly use these interviews.

The EDE is a semi-structured interview developed to assess eating disorder psychopathology. The aim of the last version of this interview (EDE-12.0; Fairburn & Cooper, 1993) is to measure, through 22 items, the presence and severity of eating and compensatory behaviours during the most recent 4-week period (28 days) and in the last 3 months. In addition, the EDE-12.0 assesses the associated disturbances of the subject in cognitions and attitudes towards weight, food and body image. The EDE-12.0 has four subscales, Restraint, Shape Concern, Weight Concern, and Eating Concern, and provides operational DSM-IV diagnosis. The scales score range from 0 (no pathology) to 6 (extreme severity of pathology). Several studies have evidenced the interrater reliability and validity of the EDE. Recently, Rizvi et al. (2000) have provided data showing test–retest reliability of this instrument. One important advantage of the EDE is that it permits gathering of extent information about binge eating behaviour.

The YBC-EDS is a semi-structured, clinician-administered interview. It includes a 65-item symptom checklist plus 19 questions, covering eighteen general categories of rituals and preoccupations related to eating disorders. This interview has been found to be reliable and valid when measuring type and severity of eating disorder symptomatology.

Finally, the SIAB assesses a wide range of symptoms that are frequent in different types of eating disorders. The third revision of the SIAB (Fichter et al., 1998) permits assessment of eating disorders following DSM-IV and ICD-10. The SIAB contains six subscales: (1) body image and slimness ideal, (2) general psychopathology and social integration, (3) sexuality, (4) bulimic symptoms, (5) measures to counteract weight gain, substance abuse, fasting, and (6) atypical binges. This interview has showed good internal consistency for five of their six components and its interrater reliability is also good (ranging from 0.86 to 0.96).

Self-Report Questionnaires

Although it is not possible to confirm a diagnosis through these instruments, they offer several advantages: they permit validation of data gathered through the interview, they are less time consuming and they can be used at community studies for screening purposes. The following are the most recommended self-report instruments. Most of them are used in Europe, America and Australia and have been adapted to different languages.

The Eating Attitudes Test (EAT-40; Garner & Garfinkel, 1979), and its brief 26-item version (EAT-26; Garner et al., 1982), is a self-report that permits assessment of symptoms and concerns characteristic of eating disorders. Patients answer in a 6-point scale (from never to always). The EAT permits, through three scales (oral control, diet and bulimia), discrimination of BN and AN. Both forms of the EAT (EAT-40 and EAT-26) have good psychometric properties. There is a general agreement about the use of these self-reports for screening purposes.

The Eating Disorders Inventory 2 (EDI-2) is the more recent version of the Garner et al. (1983) self-report for eating disorders. It was developed to assess the behavioural and cognitive characteristics of anorexia and bulimia nervosa. Three of its eight subscales have a special value for the diagnosis of BN: drive for thickness, bulimia and body dissatisfaction. The remaining five subscales are related to secondary symptoms of the disorder.

The Eating Disorders Examination Self-Report Questionnaire (EDE-Q; Fairburn & Beglin, 1994) is a 41-item self-report instrument adapted from the EDE; it contains the same four subscales as the EDE. It may be an alternative to clinical interviews and has shown a high predictive value to detect eating disorder cases. The EDE-Q has good psychometric properties because it has showed excellent internal consistency, test–retest reliability, and concurrent validity in several studies with community and clinical populations.

Finally, the Questionnaire of Eating and Weight Patterns (QEWP; Spitzer et al., 1992, 1993) was developed exclusively for the identification of binge-eating disorder (BED) patients. It consists of 13 items that focus directly on the behavioural criteria of BED, such as the amount of food eaten, the duration of eating episodes, and the experience of loss of control while eating. The QEWP scores and classifies

respondents with BED and BN. Its psychometric properties are promising; it correlates moderately with BED diagnoses based on structured interview.

Self-Monitoring Records

The primary goal of the self-monitoring records is to complete the data gathered by interviews and self-reports. The information that a subject provides through the daily record of her/his eating behaviour will be of great value to decide the treatment plan and to assess recovery. Clinicians have to ask patients to record their daily food intake and the variety of food that they eat. If patients inform about binge–purge episodes, they have to record the frequency, duration and time of day the binge–purge sequence occurs. The affect and cognition associated with the sequence (before, during and after the binge episode), and the type of compensatory behaviours used, including excessive physical activity, must be recorded too.

Self-monitoring data present many reliability problems. It is necessary to train patients to record their behaviour; however, training is not sufficient to avoid the frequent mistakes that patients commit. They forget to record behaviours that from their point of view are not considered relevant, they underestimate or overestimate the amount of food eaten in a binge. Also they estimate imprecisely the time they spend practising physical activity or they hide how many laxatives they have used. In spite of that, self-monitoring is of great value at initial assessment, during treatment, and post-treatment assessment.

ASSESSMENT OF BODY IMAGE

The assessment of body image requires a differentiation between the features of eating disorder patients and those related to the body dysmorphic disorder. For the purpose of this review, we will only mention the two principal categories that form the focus of the assessment of body image in eating disorder patients. First, the assessment of the feelings and attitudes towards the own body image, and second, the perception and estimation about silhouette and figure. There are several instruments that allow us to know the degree of body dissatisfaction and disturbance that the subject experiences as a consequence of her/his negative body image, and the subject's perception of the body, silhouette and figure. Research has shown inconsistent results on the perceptual component of the body image construct. In some studies, patients with eating disorders seemed to overestimate their body sizes, while other studies have not met differences between normal samples and eating disorder samples. Treatment outcomes have shown no differences between the studies in which patients are trained to correctly estimate their body size, and those studies where training was not done. Due to these inconsistencies, we will only analyse some of the instruments related to feelings and attitudes towards body image.

Interviews

They are a direct way to know about a subject's attitudes and emotions toward her/his body image. Self-reports do not permit evaluation of the details of this kind of information. The interviews we mentioned before, EDE and SIAB, contain questions related to the assessment of this area. For example, two EDE subscales (shape concern and weight concern) are related to worries about silhouette and weight. Also one SIAB scale (body image and slimness ideal) assesses these concerns.

Self-Report Questionnaires

One can expect that this area is easy to assess through self-reports; however, there are so many questionnaires related to body image evaluation, which confirms the complexity of the topic assessment. The Body Shape Questionnaire (BSQ; Cooper et al., 1987) was developed to rate the degree of body dissatisfaction in eating disorder patients. It has 34 items rated in a 6-point scale, and measures attitudes towards body image: body dissatisfaction, fear of becoming fat, low self-esteem due to the appearance and desire to lose weight, and weight and figure preoccupations. The BSQ has very good psychometric properties, and permits discrimination between normal samples, those worried about their body image and eating disorder patients.

From a cultural perspective, Toro et al. (1994) have developed the *Cuestionario de Influencia del Modelo Estético Corporal* (CIMEC), which measures the importance given by the subject to the aesthetic body model proposed by social signs (movies, magazines, advertisements, etc.). The CIMEC has 26 items; it has good psychometric properties and a high prediction value between normal and anorexic samples.

Finally, some of the questionnaires developed to assess eating disorder contain subscales to assess body image disturbance. This is the EDI case, which includes the body dissatisfaction subscale. The nine items of this subscale rate the beliefs about body size. The body dissatisfaction subscale has showed internal consistency indexes between 0.90 and 0.91 and has proved a good concurrent validity with the BSQ.

FUTURE PERSPECTIVES

During the last two decades, research has contributed to the advancement in the eating disorder assessment. However, we would like to point out some of the topics that, in our opinion, have to be investigated during this first decade of the new millennium. First, it is necessary to develop sensible instruments to discriminate the subtypes of AN and BN, full eating disorders syndrome vs. partial syndrome, and the non-purgative subtypes of BN and BED. Second, it will be important too to develop and validate new instruments related to different phases of the eating disorder patients' treatment, especially in AN subjects. For instance, it should be possible to measure readiness to recover in AN, and motivational issues relevant to eating disorders. Recently, Rieger et al. (2000) have presented the Anorexia Nervosa Stages of Changes Questionnaire, that may be the first step on this new area of research. Other topics that should be studied are the behavioural and psychological features of patients, which facilitates one to pass from their nutritional rehabilitation to their psychological treatment, etc. Finally, it is very important to come to a certain agreement about the criteria employed to measure treatment outcome, and to develop and validate a unique instrument that could be extensively used by researchers and clinicians.

CONCLUSIONS

As we have shown all through this entry, assessment of eating disorders is a complex task, that requires the employment of different kinds of instruments. To gather all the necessary information, several health professionals have to work together at this task. It is also important to know that there are different levels of assessment, as shown in Table 1, in which those professionals have to take part to make treatment decisions. The results of the complete physical examination plus the information obtained through the interview, self-report questionnaires and self-monitoring records will allow a good picture of the patient's state to be drawn. However, it will be of great significance to combine these data with the experience and the clinical judgement of the clinician.

During the last two decades, much has been done on eating disorders assessment, especially in the development of sensitive instruments to detect the idiosyncratic characteristics of these disorders. This is particularly true with those instruments developed for initial assessment. However, in our opinion, clinicians and researchers have to arrive to a consensus to determine the specific instruments to employ at each level of assessment. Likewise, time has come to spend great efforts in other relevant topics of eating disorders. Motivational factors in general, progress during treatment, criteria of recovery, and specific instruments to assess treatment outcomes could be some of those topics.

References

Allison, D.B. (1995). *Handbook of Assessment Methods for Eating Disorders and Weight-Related Problems*. London: Sage.

American Psychiatric Association (1994). *Diagnostic and Statistical Manual of Mental Disorders* (4th ed.). Washington, DC: American Psychiatric Association.

Cooper, Z. & Fairburn, C.G. (1987). The eating disorder examination: a semi-structured interview for the assessment of the specific psychopathology of eating disorders. *International Journal of Eating Disorders*, 6, 1–8.

Cooper, P.J., Taylor, M.J., Cooper, Z. & Faiburn, C.G. (1987). The development and validation of the Body Shape Questionnaire. *International Journal of Eating Disorders*, 6, 485–494.

Fairburn, C.G. & Beglin, S.J. (1994). The assessment of eating disorders: interview or self-report questionnaire? *International Journal of Eating Disorders*, 16, 363–370.

Fitcher, M.M., Elton, M., Engel, K., Meyer, A.-E., Mall, H. & Poustka, F. (1991). Structured interview for anorexia and bulimia nervosa (SIAB): development of a new instrument for the assessment of eating disorders. *International Journal of Eating Disorders*, 10, 571–592.

Fichter, M.M., Herpertz, S., Quadflieg, N. & Herpertz-Dahlmann, B. (1998). Structured interview for anorexic and bulimic disorders for DSM-IV and ICD-10: updated (third) revision. *International Journal of Eating Disorders*, 24, 227–249.

Garner, D.M. & Garfinkel, P.E. (1979). The eating attitudes test: an index of the symptoms of anorexia nervosa. *Psychological Medicine*, 9, 273–279.

Garner, D.M., Olmstead, M.P., Bohr, Y. & Garfinkel, P.E. (1982). The eating attitudes test: psychometric features and clinical correlates. *Psychological Medicine*, 12, 871–878.

Garner, D.M., Olmstead, M.P. & Polivy, J. (1983). Development and validation of a multidimensional eating disorder inventory for anorexia nervosa and bulimia. *International Journal of Eating Disorders*, 2, 15–34.

Mazure, C.M., Halmi, K.A., Sunday, S.R., Romano, S.J. & Einhorn, A.N. (1994). Yale–Brown–Cornell eating disorder scale: development, use, reliability and validity. *Journal of Psychiatric Research*, 28, 425–445.

Rieger, E., Touyz, S., Schotte, D., Beumont, P., Russell, J., Clarke, S., Kohn, M. & Griffiths, R. (2000). Development of an instrument to assess readiness to recover in anorexia nervosa. *International Journal of Eating Disorders*, 28, 387–396.

Rizvi, S.L., Paterson, C.B., Crow, S.J. & Agras, W.S. (2000). Test–retest reliability of the eating disorder examination. *International Journal of Eating Disorders*, 28, 311–316.

Rosen, J.C. & Srebnik, D. (1990). The assessment of eating disorders. In McReynolds, P., Rosen, J.C. & Chelune, G. (Eds.), *Advances in Psychological Assessment*, Vol. 7 (pp. 229–259). New York: Plenum Press.

Saldaña, C. (1994). Evaluación de Trastornos Del Comportamiento Alimentario. In R. Fernández-Ballesteros (Ed.), *Evaluación Conductual hoy. Un Enfoque Para el Cambio en Psicología Clínica y de la Salud* (pp. 537–570). Madrid: Pirámide.

Spitzer, R.L., Devlin, M., Walsh, B.T., Hasin, D., Wing, R.R., Marcus, M.D., Stunkard, A., Wadden, T., Yanovski, S., Agras, S., Mitchell, J. & Nonas, C. (1992). Binge eating disorder: a multisite field trial of the diagnostic criteria. *International Journal of Eating Disorders*, 12, 191–204.

Spitzer, R.L., Yanovski, S., Wadden, T., Wing, R.R., Marcus, M.D., Stunkard, A., Devlin, M., Mitchell, J., Hasin, D. & Horne, R.L. (1993). Binge eating disorder: its further validation in a multisite study.

International Journal of Eating Disorders, 13, 137–153.

Sunday, S.R., Halmi, K.A. & Einhorn, A.N. (1995). The Yale–Brown–Cornell eating disorder scale: a new scale to assess eating disorders symptomatology. *International Journal of Eating Disorders, 18*, 237–245.

Toro, J., Salamero, M. & Martínez, E. (1994). Assessment of sociocultural influences on the aesthetic body shape model in anorexia nervosa, *Acta Psychiatrica Scandinavia, 89*, 147–151.

World Health Organization (1992). *The ICD-10 Classification of Mental and Behavioral Disorders.* Geneva: World Health Organization.

Carmina Saldaña

RELATED ENTRIES

APPLIED FIELDS: CLINICAL, APPLIED FIELDS: HEALTH

E EMOTIONAL INTELLIGENCE

INTRODUCTION

In a 1961 book of literary criticism, Van Ghent noted that certain characters within Jane Austen's *Pride and Prejudice* possessed 'emotional intelligence' (EI) in comparison with others (1961: 103). She referred to EI as '... emotionally informed intelligence – or shall we say, that intelligence which informs the emotions ...' (Van Ghent, 1961: 107). At roughly the same time, the term EI began to appear in psychological and medical articles, dissertations, and within books. The term was typically mentioned in passing, and not described or explained in any formal sense. Still, the term 'emotional intelligence' was too intriguing to disappear while, at the same time, too self-contradictory to be clearly useful as a scientific concept.

In 1990, two articles were published that first employed the EI label for a clearly specified set of findings in the scientific literature. The theoretical article, 'Emotional Intelligence', made the case that a coherent intelligence existed that was concerned with the emotions (Salovey & Mayer, 1990). Emotional intelligence was said to involve the ability to reason with emotions, and the capacity of emotions to enhance intelligence. Evidence for EI was collected from the areas of clinical psychology, artificial intelligence, aesthetics, and non-verbal perception. A pattern was present, it was argued, that indicated a heretofore overlooked human ability. The other, empirical, article provided a demonstration that emotional intelligence could

be measured as an ability (Mayer, DiPaolo & Salovey, 1990). Precursor measures in the area of non-verbal behaviour had mostly failed at identifying any meaningful, consistent individual differences (Buck, 1984). The 1990 article reported new measurement procedures by which consistency was greatly improved.

Emotional intelligence would probably thereafter have evolved slowly if it had not been for the science journalist Daniel Goleman, who was working on a book about social and emotional learning. Goleman entitled his book 'Emotional Intelligence', to reflect the work mentioned above. At the same time, he defined EI very broadly, in part, probably, so that the concept would cover the large number of studies he discussed. His lively popularization became an international best-seller and generated popular interest in the idea, and ultimately, further scientific interest in it as well.

The popularization, and the media reports about it, were accompanied by sensationalistic claims for the predictive power of emotional intelligence that had not been present in the scientific literature. 'Compared to IQ and expertise,' wrote Goleman of EI (1998: 31), 'emotional competence mattered *twice* as much.' At least some of the early scientific literature, and some popular rejoinders, as well, seemed aimed at debunking those unsupported (and, to serious researchers, embarrassing) claims (Davies, Stankov & Roberts, 1998; Newsome, Day & Catano, 2000).

Additional popular books and tests were hurriedly produced so as to capitalize on the faddish interest surrounding emotional intelligence. Most of these further altered the definition of emotional intelligence until it no longer bore any specific relationship to either emotion, intelligence, or their combination. Capitalizing on the media attention was alluring, however, and so tests that were originally designed to measure empathy, well-being, alexithymia, and optimism were said to measure emotional intelligence – or even renamed as emotional intelligence measures, despite the fact that their content could hardly be distinguished from many other general tests of personality. Later on, these theories and tests became known as 'mixed models' of EI because they mixed in a seemingly haphazard collection of whatever the authors thought would predict success – from 'diversity tolerance' to 'conscientiousness'. Work on the original, ability model of emotional intelligence also progressed. The current status of these theories can be illustrated with a consideration of the measurements available. These will be examined next.

TESTS AND OTHER MEASUREMENT DEVICES

Today, there have developed four approaches to measure emotional intelligence: self-report (focused and mixed), observer report, and ability testing (see Table 1). These will be dealt with in turn.

Self-Report

A number of self-report measures of EI exist. One relatively focused scale of emotional intelligence is the 33-item measure by Schutte and her colleagues (Schutte et al., 1998). Like other scales in this area, this one asks questions on the order of 'How accurately do you perceive your emotions?' and 'How empathic are you?'. Although the scale is self-report, it attempts to gauge ability at EI.

Self-report scales of mixed-model (i.e. popular) conceptions of EI are fairly numerous. For example, the Bar-On EQi was originally labelled a measure of well-being (Bar-On, 1997). In

Table 1.   Four approaches to measuring emotional intelligence

	Self-report		Observer report Mixed-model	Focused ability measure
	Focused	Mixed-model		
Relevant test	Emotional Intelligence Scale (Newsome et al., 2000)	Emotional Quotient Inventory (Bar-On, 1997)	Emotional Competencies Inventory (Boyatzis et al., 2000)	Mayer–Salovey–Caruso Emotional Intelligence Test (MSCEIT V. 2) (Mayer et al., in press)*
Representative subscales of the test	Overall emotional intelligence (no subscales)*	Emotional Self-Awareness* Interpersonal Relationships* Problem Solving* Stress Tolerance* Happiness*	Emotional Self-Awareness* Self-Control* Achievement Orientation* Empathy* Leadership*	*Perceiving Emotions *Using Emotions to facilitate thought *Understanding Emotions *Managing Emotions
Full test reliability	$\alpha = 0.90$	$r = 0.85$ (test–retest)	(No overall scale score reported)	$\alpha = 0.92$
Subscale reliabilities	No subscales	$\alpha = 0.69$–0.86	$\alpha = 0.73$–0.91	$\alpha = 0.73$–0.89 (for branch scales)
Scale arrangement is factor valid	Yes	No, but alternative factor analyses are provided	Partially	Yes

*Psychometric data for the MSCEIT V. 2 may change slightly as the manual is still undergoing modification as of this writing.

addition, its scales bear close resemblances to other personality scales. For example, the EQi and the California Psychological Inventory (CPI) both have subscales of empathy, independence, and flexibility. Other subscales indicate overlap between the two tests as well. For example, the EQi measures self-actualization, reality testing, and impulse control, whereas the CPI measures self-acceptance, intellectual efficiency, and self-control. Current empirical findings indicate that such 'new' mixed-model scales of EI are largely reordered versions of pre-existing personality scales (e.g. Newsome et al., 2000).

Self-report scales, whether focused or mixed, suffer from several drawbacks. First, intelligence refers to the capacity to problem-solve. For that reason, the most valid way to assess the concept is through ability testing. Moreover, people are generally poor judges of their abilities, and this is likely to be the case in the area of emotional intelligence too. For example, self-estimates of cognitive intelligence are almost unrelated to actual measured intelligence (Paulus, Lysy & Yik, 1998). To further complicate matters, both focused and mixed-model self-report measures of EI correlate very highly with scales of positive affect and attitude (e.g. $r = 0.60$ and higher) – although they possess some modest independent variance (Bar-On, 1997; Newsome et al., 2000). That is, when people feel happy, optimistic, and confident, they report they understand their emotions, whereas when they feel bad, they report being confused about their emotion. Thus, there is a confound in these measures which often is not dealt with in interpreting what they might or might not predict.

Observer-Rating Assessments

Boyatzis, Goleman, and Rhee (2000) have introduced an observer-rating scale of EI for a corporate audience. This measure asks informants to rate a target individual on their EI. Much of the data concerning the scale is proprietary (i.e. owned and kept confidential by the consulting firm Hay/McBer). Hence, other than scale reliabilities and some sketchy information about factor analyses, little is known of its properties. In general, observer ratings suffer from the same difficulties as self-ratings: that is,

high emotional intelligence may be difficult to gauge, or even 'over the heads' of many raters. In addition, there is evidence that the ECI also correlates highly with pre-existing personality measures (Murensky, 2000).

Ability Testing

The two major ability measures in the area are both based on a revised model of EI that divides it into four areas or branches (Mayer, Salovey & Caruso, 2000):

Emotional Perception and Expression

The capacity to perceive emotions in oneself and others, as well as in aesthetics; the ability to express emotion accurately.

Emotional Facilitation of Thought

The ability to use emotions to facilitate and inform thinking.

Emotional Understanding

The ability to understand the meanings of emotions, their likely transitions, blends, and progressions.

Emotional Management

The capacity to manage or regulate emotions for personal and social growth.

Two tests, the Multifactor Emotional Intelligence Scale (MEIS) and the more recently developed Mayer–Salovey–Caruso Emotional Intelligence Scale (MSCEIT), were designed to measure the four-branch model described above (Mayer, Caruso & Salovey, 1999; Mayer, Salovey & Caruso, 2002). The first, exploratory, EI ability tests had focused on emotional perception (Mayer et al., 1990). A typical test question asked people to identify the emotional content of a photograph of a face, or an abstract design. Thus, a test-taker might look at a face and be asked 'How much anger is present in the face' and answer on a five-point scale, where 1 is anchored by 'no anger' and 5 is anchored by 'much anger'. Several criteria were explored for identifying the correct answer on such a test. Most commonly, correct answers are identified by studying the endorsements of a group of general test-takers, and then weighting answers according to what is most commonly chosen by the group. Alternatively, one can use the endorsements of emotions experts rather than average test-takers. These methods generally converge (Mayer et al., 1999).

Items measuring the emotional facilitation of thought take two forms. Some such items ask people to integrate emotions with other sensations, as in: 'How "hot" is envy?' – to which test takers might answer on a Likert scale anchored by: '1: extremely cold' or '5: extremely hot'. Other such items ask people what mood might be best to enter into when thinking of new career directions. To answer this question, participants might choose from among four alternatives such as: *happy*, *angry*, *envious* or *calm*.

To gauge their understanding of emotions, participants are asked to choose the best definitions of emotion terms, or, for other items, to identify which two emotions might blend together to form a third. For example, they may indicate that *dislike* and *disgust* blend together to form *contempt*.

Finally, emotion management tasks ask people to read vignettes and respond in ways that will bring about specific emotions or moods. For example, participants might select what actions might preserve a person's happy mood.

The best factor structure for EI is still a matter of some dispute, and, given the nature of factor analysis, is likely to remain so for a while. One group of researchers argue that EI forms a global g, which they refer to as g_{ei}, and that it can be further broken down into the four factors representing the four-branch model of EI (perception, facilitation, understanding, and management; Mayer et al., 1999). Others have argued for two factors (Ciarrochi, Chan & Caputi, 2000). Factor analysis is a matter of preference and it is possible that either of these are viable interpretations.

Full-scale ability measures of EI are just a few years old, and yet a fair amount is already known about their predictive validity. Such EI measures are fairly distinct from measures of general intelligence and from self-report measures of

empathy (correlating with both at about the $r = 0.35$ level) (Ciarrochi et al., 2000; Mayer et al., 1999). More generally, they are distinct from a variety of general personality measures such as the Big Five, and other tests. That is, ability tests of EI appear to measure a new psychological construct that was not measured in applied settings before. There has been a focus on examining EI in children and college students, and there, mounting evidence indicates that they predict a lowered degree of violence and problem behaviour (Formica, 1998; Rubin, 1999; Trinidad & Johnson, 2002).

FUTURE PERSPECTIVES

Self-report and rater-report scales of EI overlap substantially with existing measures of personality. The ease of use of such scales makes it unlikely they will disappear soon, but their ease of use must be balanced against the difficulty of interpreting exactly what they are measuring that is new, and the rationale behind whatever conception of EI they employ. Ability scales of EI increasingly appear established and validated as measures of a new construct. A few remaining measurement controversies involve EI's factor structure, and the best criteria for correct answers. Researchers are now examining what EI, measured as an ability, predicts. If it does, indeed, predict lower levels of violence and problem behaviour among school children then it may be of considerable importance to assess. It might well make similar predictions of lower problem behaviours in adults, as well. Moreover, if the relationship is causal, then it may make sense to teach emotional knowledge to those who lack it (Elias et al., 1997).

CONCLUSIONS

Emotional intelligence is a promising new type of intelligence for which sound ability-based measures now exist. The attribute – measured as an ability – is distinct from earlier discovered intelligences, as well as from earlier-measured motivation- and emotion-related personality traits. Early research with such scales suggest that they may be of value for predicting lowered tendencies (among those higher in emotional intelligence) toward problem behaviours such as alcohol and drug abuse, and lowered levels of interpersonal violence. Further research is needed to more fully explore these relationships and understand the causal factors and directions involved.

Acknowledgements

I would like to acknowledge the contributions of two colleagues to this entry. Tracey Martin drew my attention to Van Ghent's 1960 mention of emotional intelligence. Steve Hein edited an early draft of the entry. My thanks to them both.

References

Bar-On, R. (1997). *Bar-On Emotional Quotient Inventory: Technical Manual.* Toronto, Canada: Multi-Health Systems.

Boyatzis, R.E., Goleman, D. & Rhee, K.S. (2000). Clustering competence in emotional intelligence. In Bar-On, R. & Parker, J.D.A. (Eds.), *The Handbook of Emotional Intelligence* (pp. 343–362). San Francisco: Jossey-Bass.

Buck, R. (1984). *The Communication of Emotion.* New York: Guilford Press.

Ciarrochi, J.V., Chan, A.Y. & Caputi, P. (2000). A critical evaluation of the emotional intelligence concept. *Personality and Individual Differences, 28,* 539–561.

Davies, M., Stankov, L. & Roberts, R.D. (1998). Emotional intelligence: in search of an elusive construct. *Journal of Personality and Social Psychology, 75,* 989–1015.

Elias, M.J., Zins, J.E., Weissberg, R.P., Frey, K.S., Greenberg, M.T., Haynes, N.M., Kessler, R., Schwab-Stone, M.E. & Shriver, T.P. (1997). *Promoting Social and Emotional Learning: Guidelines for Educators.* Alexandria, VA: Association for Supervision and Curriculum Development.

Formica, S. (1998). Description of the socio-emotional life space: life qualities and activities related to emotional intelligence. Unpublished Senior Honours Thesis, University of New Hampshire, Durham, NH.

Goleman, D. (1998). *Working with Emotional Intelligence.* New York: Bantam.

Mayer, J.D., Caruso, D.R. & Salovey, P. (1999). Emotional intelligence meets traditional standards for an intelligence. *Intelligence, 27,* 267–298.

Mayer, J.D., DiPaolo, M.T. & Salovey, P. (1990). Perceiving affective content in ambiguous visual stimuli: a component of emotional intelligence. *Journal of Personality Assessment, 54,* 772–781.

Mayer, J.D., Salovey, P. & Caruso, D.R. (2000). Models of emotional intelligence. In Sternberg, R.J. (Ed.), *Handbook of Intelligence* (pp. 396–420). Cambridge, England: Cambridge University Press.

Mayer, J.D., Salovey, P. & Caruso, D.R. (2002). *Manual for the MSCEIT (Mayer–Salovey–Caruso Emotional Intelligence Test).* Toronto, Canada: MHS Publishers.

Murensky, C.L. (2000). The relationships between emotional intelligence, personality, critical thinking ability and organizational leadership performance at upper levels of management. *Dissertation Abstracts International: Section B: The Sciences & Engineering, 61(2-B),* 1121 (US: Univ Microfilms International ISSN/ISBN: 0419–4217).

Newsome, S., Day, A.L. & Catano, V.M. (2000). Assessing the predictive validity of emotional intelligence. *Personality and Individual Differences, 29,* 1005–1016.

Paulus, D.L., Lysy, D.C. & Yik, M.S.M. (1998). Self-report measures of intelligence: are they useful as proxy IQ tests? *Journal of Personality Psychology, 66,* 525–554.

Rubin, M.M. (1999). Emotional intelligence and its role in mitigating aggression: a correlational study of the relationship between emotional intelligence and aggression in urban adolescents. Unpublished Dissertation, Immaculata College, Immaculata, Pennsylvania.

Salovey, P. & Mayer, J.D. (1990). Emotional intelligence. *Imagination, Cognition, and Personality, 9,* 185–211.

Schutte, N.S., Malouff, J.M., Hall, L.E., Haggerty, D.J., Cooper, J.T., Golden, C.J. & Dornheim, L. (1998). Development and validation of a measure of emotional intelligence. *Personality and Individual Differences, 25,* 167–177.

Trinidad, D.R. & Johnson, C.A. (2002). The association between emotional intelligence and early adolescent tobacco and alcohol use. *Personality and Individual Differences, 32,* 95–105.

Van Ghent, D. (1961). *The English Novel: Form and Function.* New York: Harper & Row Publishers.

John D. Mayer

RELATED ENTRIES

INTELLIGENCE ASSESSMENT (GENERAL), PROSOCIAL BEHAVIOUR, SOCIAL COMPETENCE, EMOTIONS

EMOTIONS

CONCEPTUAL ISSUES

Psychologists distinguish among several inter-related constructs that are each associated with the everyday use of the word 'emotion'. The presumably most fundamental concept is that of 'affect'. Affect has been characterized as the first stage of an organism's reaction to stimuli, an experiential process that precedes and is possibly independent of those processes labelled as 'cognitive' (Zajonc, 2000). Affect is a process in which subjective, evaluative information is derived from the flow of perception. Affects can be consciously experienced as 'feelings', and are often described in terms of pleasure, displeasure, and degree of activation. Affective feelings are thought to play a key role in the judgements, preferences, and behavioural action patterns critical for survival.

Affect is closely linked to 'mood', which is most often conceptualized as a sustained affective experience. Mood can be thought of as a comparatively stable affective state that is not necessarily aroused by a particular event. Researchers have found that mood is correlated with particular personality traits, an association which may contribute to the stability of over-arching affective dispositions throughout life.

What most psychologists refer to as 'emotions' are feeling states that are both briefer and more intense than moods. A necessary component of emotion assessment is the measurement of affect, its fundamental ingredient. Emotion assessment quite often also involves measuring cognitive, physiological, and behavioural response domains (see Figure 1).

THE DESCRIPTION OF AFFECT

Some theorists posit that affect is not a cognitive process per se, but is better conceptualized as a rather primitive and irreducible psychological experience. Nevertheless, cognitive representations of affective experience are made. One fruitful approach to the measurement of affect has thus been to consider the interaction of affect with its cognitive representation. One assumption underlying this approach is that everyday language – especially emotion-related words – is replete with affective meanings that can be described along two or more dimensions.

The dimensional perspective offers a simple yet powerful measurement strategy that enables the scalar representation of phenomena that are clearly experienced but not fully captured with language. Different interpretations have been provided for the mathematical solutions used to derive affect dimensions. For example, in his analyses of emotion-related words, Russell (1979) proposed two bipolar dimensions to describe affective experience: a valence dimension anchored at either end by strong pleasure and displeasure, and an arousal or activation dimension ranging from low to high levels of arousal (*cf.* Watson & Tellegen, 1985). As these dimensions were specified to be uncorrelated, they can be represented in a two-dimensional, Cartesian space. The resulting circumplex model of emotion-related words is applicable across various languages, and provides researchers and practitioners alike with a way to measure and represent the affective feeling states and associated behaviours.

Commonly used self-report measures of affective experience include the Affect Circumplex (Larsen & Diener, 1992), the PANAS (Watson, Clark & Tellegen, 1988), and the Self-Assessment Manikin (SAM; Lang, Bradley & Cuthbert, 1995). Measures are also available to assess comparatively trait-like components of affect, including intensity (e.g. Bachorowski & Braaten, 1994) and expressivity (Kring, Smith & Neale, 1994). These and other measures can be used, for instance, in detailed examinations of the structure of consciously perceived affective experience, and to monitor change in response to therapeutic intervention.

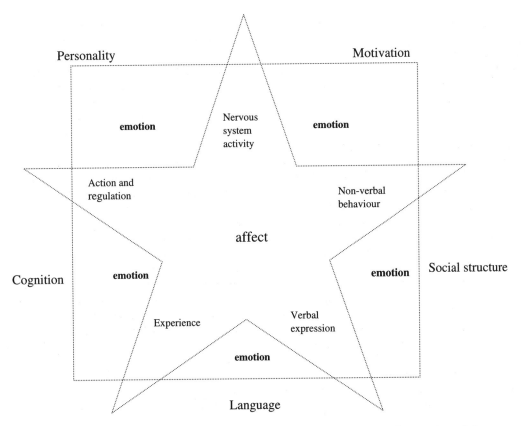

Figure 1.   A conceptual map for assessment strategies on emotion and affect. The position of the categories does not exclude other possible combinations. Personality, motivation, social structure, language and cognition are related issues that should be taken into account in any assessment strategy. The figure represents emotion as an object that overlaps with and is grounded in affect. Affect and emotion can be described through different sets of variables using both dimensional and categorical approaches.

CATEGORICAL APPROACHES

Dimensional approaches to affective experience are challenged by perspectives that treat emotions as discrete phenomena that arise from activity in specific neural pathways and that have characteristic experiential, expressive, and behavioural consequences. The resulting 'affect programmes' are held to have high adaptive value, or to have at least had adaptive value during evolutionary history. A classic example of this approach relies on the construct of 'basic emotions' (e.g. Ekman, 1992). Although there is debate about what is meant by an emotion being 'basic', common to this perspective is the belief that a small number of emotions account for a large proportion of emotional experience.

Basic emotions are brief, rapid, and involuntary. Lists of these emotions differ, but typically include at least anger, fear, sadness, disgust, surprise, and joy. Basic emotions are often assessed by choosing the one of seven or so words that best describes individuals' reactions to a given situation. These responses might then be used to identify emotion-specific physiological patterns, or to anchor particular kinds of behavioural responses to experienced emotion. Some investigators have used this perspective to study perceptions of expressive reactions in efforts to demonstrate commonalities in basic-emotion processes across cultures.

FACIAL AND VOCAL EXPRESSIONS OF EMOTION

By far, the most widely examined aspect of expressive behaviour is activity in the facial musculature. Electromyography provides an objective yet somewhat intrusive means of describing both visible and non-perceptible isolated facial movements through the detection of aggregated action potentials from underlying muscles (see Wagner, 1997). Comparatively unintrusive methods involve coding observable changes in facial musculature activity. Popular coding systems from a categorical perspective are Izard's MAX and AFFEX (Izard, 1979; Izard & Dougherty, 1980) and Ekman and Friesen's FAST (Ekman, Friesen & Tomkins, 1971) and FACS (Ekman & Friesen, 1978). MAX, AFFEX, and FAST systems enable coders to make global judgements of different facial configurations. The time-intensive FACS is a comparatively micro-level measurement tool used to code the activity of 'action units', which are highly specific regions of the facial musculature. Facial coding systems that rely on a dimensional approach to emotion expression are also available (Kring & Sloan, 1991). Dimensional systems involve less training and are less time-intensive than those systems that code for discrete expressions.

There is as yet no firm evidence that prototypic expressions of basic emotion are necessarily produced during even intense emotional experiences. Recent findings have given rise to a lively debate about the ways in which facial expressions are linked to emotion, and particularly about the roles of social context and self-regulation in emotion-related expressions (Russell & Fernández-Dols, 1997).

Although receiving substantially less attention than that given to facial expression, vocal expression is another expressive behaviour linked to emotional experience. Most empirical studies have studied the acoustics of stock phrases produced by individuals asked to speak as if they were experiencing particular emotional states. While providing suggestive data, it is unclear whether outcomes obtained with these strategies generalize to naturally occurring instances of emotion-expression through the vocal channel. More informative work will necessarily involve studying the vocal acoustics produced during naturally occurring emotional states.

Measurement of emotion-related vocal expression involves acoustic analysis. The most commonly measured acoustic cues are those associated with the fundamental frequency (F_0)

of speech, which corresponds to the rate of vocal-fold vibration and is perceived as vocal pitch. F_0 has been shown, for instance, to be relatively high during the experience of fear, anger, and joy, but to be comparatively low during the experience of sadness (see Johnstone & Scherer, 2000). Other promising measures include those associated with the filtering properties of the vocal tract.

Given well-established connections between speech acoustics and various aspects of vocal anatomy and physiology, researchers have been able to make fairly detailed predictions about vocal changes in response to particular emotional states. As exemplified by the work of Scherer (e.g. Scherer, 1986), most investigators have relied on basic-emotion frameworks to shape their thinking about vocal expression of emotion. However, the most parsimonious account of the available data is that expression in the vocal channel is associated with arousal, and to a lesser extent the valence of experienced emotion (Bachorowski, 1999).

LAY DESCRIPTIONS OF BASIC EMOTIONS

Some investigators have explored the associations between lay descriptions of basic-emotion experiences and their cognitive, behavioural, and somatic consequences. This approach assumes that individuals can provide fairly accurate retrospective reports about the cognitive and behavioural concomitants of emotional events. Retrospective studies of this nature may also be useful for understanding how individuals encode and remember emotional events. A different perspective has led some investigators to pursue the core meaning of basic-emotion words either through the 'semantic primitives' thought to occur in all languages (e.g. 'want', 'bad', 'cause'; Wiertzbicka, 1995), or through the over-arching dimensions used to summarize emotion words in different languages (Frijda, 1986).

Overall, studying the everyday language of emotions has provided insights concerning the universals of emotion-related experience, but has also led to debate about the validity of the conclusions being drawn. Two pivotal concerns are the extent to which individuals' introspective accounts provide veridical descriptions of their emotional experiences, and the extent to which meaning varies from culture to culture, thereby dooming to failure the search for universal descriptions of emotions (Shweder, 1991).

BASIC EMOTIONS AND NERVOUS SYSTEM ACTIVITY

A number of investigators have attempted to identify the associations between basic emotions and highly specific patterns of autonomous nervous system (ANS) activity. For instance, Levenson et al. (1990) provided data to indicate that anger, fear, and sadness, but not disgust or surprise, are associated with heart rate acceleration, whereas skin conductance increases are associated with fear and disgust but not happiness and surprise. These kinds of results are used to support the hypothesis that discrete emotional experiences are associated with specific patterns of ANS activity. Others have taken a different stance, arguing that valence and arousal dimensions provide a better account of ANS responding than do discrete emotions (e.g. Lang, Greenwald, Bradley & Hamm, 1993). Outcomes from a recent meta-analysis indicate that the latter interpretation is more consistent with the available evidence (Cacioppo, Bernston, Larsen, Poehlmann & Ito, 2000).

Given rapid technological advances, investigators have become increasingly focused on identifying the neural processes involved in the perceptual and experiential components of emotions. Central nervous system (CNS) patterns of emotion-related activation have been examined through the use of electroencephalography (EEG) for some time. This tool has been especially useful for testing hypotheses concerning activity in lateralized approach- and withdrawal-related emotion systems. For example, and consistent with hypotheses concerning approach-related motivation deficits in depression, both currently depressed and remitted individuals are more likely to show relative left frontal hypoactivation when compared to non-depressed controls (e.g. Henriques & Davidson, 1990).

More recently, a variety of neuroimaging techniques have become available. A crucial assumption underlying imaging methods is that the brain regions involved in a given perceptual or behavioural task are more active than uninvolved regions. For instance, capitalizing on the assumption that functional activity is associated with increase in blood supply, positron emission tomography (PET) techniques can be used to measure regional blood flow. Using a much different technology, functional magnetic resonance imaging (fMRI) also capitalizes on haemodynamic responses in response to stimulus or task demands. These and other techniques have given scientists an opportunity to identify the neural substrates underlying both normal and disturbed emotional processes.

EMOTIONS AS PROCESSES

Well-deserved attention has recently been given to the construct of 'emotion regulation', itself a set of processes used to shape emotional experience and expression. Empirical work has shown that emotion-regulation strategies such as reappraisal, occurring early in the emotion-generative process, and suppression, occurring relatively late in the emotion-generative process, have functionally different effects on emotion experience, memory, and physiological responding (Gross, 2001). This kind of work underscores the fact that emotional processes are inherently plastic, varying with both individual differences and situational constraints. The conceptually related construct of 'emotional intelligence' highlights the role of individual differences in emotion perception, experience, and expression (Mayer, Caruso & Salovey, 2000). Although a systematic approach to the measurement of emotional regulation involves a number of pragmatic difficulties and conceptual ambiguities, self-report inventories for this purpose are available (e.g. Gross & John, 2002).

FUTURE PERSPECTIVES AND CONCLUSIONS

There are many avenues to assessing emotion, including self-report, facial expression, vocal expression, and measures of central and peripheral physiology. The choice of measures is typically dictated not only by pragmatic constraints, but also by the theoretical perspective held by individual investigators. Further advances in emotion assessment will likely require some sort of rapprochement between current theoretical dichotomies. Of these, distinctions between categorical and dimensional perspectives, and between approaches that treat emotion-related expressions as veridical readouts of internal states versus those that approach these signals as strictly social displays, are two of the most salient areas of debate. Rather than being antithetical, outcomes from some empirical studies have shown there is clear merit in giving explicit attention to both perspectives. These kinds of results indicate that further elucidation of emotional processes – including their assessment – will benefit from inclusive measurement strategies.

References

Bachorowski, J.-A. (1999). Vocal expression and perception of emotion. *Current Directions in Psychological Science*, 8, 53–57.

Bachorowski, J.-A. & Braaten, E.B. (1994). Emotional intensity: measurement and theoretical implications. *Personality and Individual Differences*, 17, 191–200.

Cacioppo, J.T., Bernston, G.G., Larsen, J.T., Poehlmann, K.M. & Ito, T. AS. (2000). The psychophysiology of emotion. In Lewis, M. & Haviland-Jones, J.M. (Eds.), *Handbook of Emotions* (2nd ed.). New York: Guilford.

Ekman, P. (1992). An argument for basic emotions. *Cognition and Emotion*, 6, 169–200.

Ekman, P. & Friesen, W.V. (1978). *The Facial Action Coding System*. Palo Alto, CA: Consulting Psychologists Press.

Ekman, P., Friesen, W.V. & Tomkins, S.S. (1971). Facial affect scoring technique: a first validity study. *Semiotica*, 3, 37–38.

Frijda, N.H. (1986). *The Emotions*. Cambridge: Cambridge University Press.

Gross, J.J. (2001). Emotion regulation in adulthood: timing is everything. *Current Directions in Psychological Science*, 10, 214–219.

Gross, J.J. & John, O.P. (2002). Measuring individual differences in emotion regulation: the emotion regulation questionnaire. Manuscript in preparation.

Henriques, J.B. & Davidson, R.J. (1990). Regional brain electrical asymmetries discriminate between previously depressed subjects and healthy controls. *Journal of Abnormal Psychology*, 99, 22–31.

Izard, C.E. (1979). *The Maximally Discriminative Facial Movement Coding System (MAX)*. Newark, DE: University of Delaware Office of Instructional Technology.

Izard, C.E. & Dougherty, L.M. (1980). *A System for Identifying Affect Expressions by Wholistic Judgments*. Newark, DE: Instructional Resources Center.

Johnstone, T. & Scherer, K.R. (2000). Vocal communication of emotion. In Lewis, M. & Haviland-Jones, J.M. (Eds.), *Handbook of Emotions* (2nd edn., pp. 220–235). New York: Guilford.

Kring, A.M. & Sloan, D. (1991). The facial expression coding system (FACES): a user's guide. Unpublished manuscript.

Kring, A.M., Smith, D.A. & Neale, J.M. (1994). Individual differences in dispositional expressiveness: development and validation of the emotional expressivity scale. *Journal of Personality and Social Psychology*, 66, 934–949.

Lang, P.J., Bradley, M.M. & Cuthbert, B.N. (1995). *International Affective Picture System (IAPS): Technical Manual and Affective Ratings*. Gainesville, FL: The Center for Research in Psychophysiology, University of Florida.

Lang, P.J., Greenwald, M.K., Bradley, M.M. & Hamm, A.O. (1993). Looking at pictures: affective, facial, visceral, and behavioural reactions. *Psychophysiology*, 30, 261–273.

Larsen, R.J. & Diener, E. (1992). Promises and problems with the circumplex model of emotion. In Clark, M.S. (Ed.), *Review of Personality and Social Psychology: Emotion*, Vol. 13 (pp. 25–59). Newbury Park, CA: Sage.

Levenson, R.W., Ekman, P. & Friesen, W.V. (1990). Voluntary facial action generates emotion-specific autonomic nervous system activity. *Psychophysiology*, 27, 363–384.

Mayer, J.D., Caruso, D. & Salovey, P. (2000). Emotional intelligence meets traditional standards for intelligence. *Intelligence*, 27, 267–298.

Russell, J.A. (1979). Affective space is bipolar. *Journal of Personality and Social Psychology*, 37, 345–356.

Russell, J.A. & Fernández-Dols, J.M. (1997). What does a facial expression mean? In Russell, J.A. & Fernández-Dols, J.M. (Eds.), *The Psychology of Facial Expression* (pp. 3–30). New York: Cambridge University Press.

Scherer, K.R. (1986). Vocal affect expression: a review and model for future research. *Psychological Bulletin*, 99, 143–165.

Shweder, R.A. (1991). *Thinking Through Cultures: Expeditions in Cultural Psychology*. Cambridge, MA: Harvard University Press.

Wagner, H.L. (1997). Methods for the study of facial behavior. In Russell, J.A. & Fernández-Dols, J.M. (Eds.), *The Psychology of Facial Expression* (pp. 31–54). New York: Cambridge University Press.

Watson, D., Clark, L.A. & Tellegen, A. (1988). Development and validation of brief measures of positive and negative affect: the panas scales. *Journal of Personality and Social Psychology*, *54*, 1063–1070.

Watson, D. & Tellegen, A. (1985). Toward a consensual structure of mood. *Psychological Bulletin*, *98*, 219–235.

Wiertzbicka, A. (1995). Everyday conceptions of emotion: a semantic perspective. In Russell, J.A., Fernández-Dols, J.M., Manstead, A.S.R. & Wellenkamp, J.C. (Eds.), *Everyday Conceptions of Emotion: An Introduction to the Psychology, Anthropology and Linguistics of Emotion* (pp. 17–47). Dordrecht, NL: Kluwer Academic Publishers.

Zajonc, R.B. (2000). Feeling and thinking. In Forgas, J.P. (Ed.), *Feeling and Thinking* (pp. 31–58). New York: Cambridge University Press.

José-Miguel Fernández-Dols and
Jo-Anne Bachorowski

RELATED ENTRIES

Personality Assessment (General), Attitudes, Applied Fields: Psychophysiology

EMPOWERMENT

INTRODUCTION

Empowerment is both a multilevel (individual, group, organizational, community) and a multidimensional (intrapersonal, social, behavioural, organizational and community) construct. It has been defined as a process through which people, organizations and communities gain mastery over their own affairs. Empowerment is a construct that links individual competencies, existing helping systems and proactive behaviours to matters of social policy and social change. The individual experience of empowerment includes a combination of self-acceptance and self-confidence, social and political understanding and the ability to play an assertive role in controlling resources and decisions in one's community. Psychological empowerment can be described therefore as the connection between a sense of personal competence, a desire for, and a willingness to take, action in the public domain (Zimmerman & Rappaport, 1988).

In the last decades the concept of empowerment has been widely used cross-culturally in five different domains: politics, adult education, health, management and organizational and community psychology (Piccardo, 1995). In this entry, I will briefly describe how the construct of empowerment has been applied in different fields, and how it has been defined and assessed at the individual, group, organizational and community levels.

In politics, the construct was first proposed in the context of the civil rights and women's liberation movements of the 1960s. It meant giving more legal, political and economic power to people who had less access to valued resources. Since then, empowerment has become one of the main aims of all intervention programmes carried out in developing countries or in disadvantaged areas of rich nations. Empowerment has become a key concept also in the environmental movement and in many projects aimed at fostering the rights of oppressed groups (Francescato, 2000; Human, 1990).

In the field of adult education, empowerment has become a cornerstone in lifelong learning projects, aimed at favouring personal growth and at increasing active participation of trainees in defining training goals and processes. Empowering in education means shifting the power from teacher to trainees, so these can make the choices that are more relevant to their emancipation (Bruscaglioni, 1994).

In the health field, empowerment has been used to indicate the process by which patients become less dependent on doctors, acquire the skills and knowledge necessary to take care of their health, and become aware of the social and environmental factors impinging on their individual well-being. (Hess, 1984; McWhirter, 1991; Pasini & Francescato, 2001; Wilkinson, 1996).

In management and organizational psychology empowerment has been used to promote a shift in organizational values, moving away from bureaucratic paternalistic culture and promoting an entrepreneurial-emancipatory environment which allows workers to participate more in decision making, and to share risks and rewards (Putnam, 1991; Piccardo, 1995).

In community psychology, empowerment is a value orientation for working in the community, that directs attention to promoting wellness instead of preventing illness, identify strengths instead of cataloguing risk factors and enhance assets instead of solving problems. According to Zimmerman (2000) empowerment is a continuous variable, a developmental construct that can change over time, and it is context and population specific. Finally, empowerment is an individual-level construct when one is concerned with intrapersonal and behavioural variables, an organizational-level construct when one is concerned with resource mobilization and participatory opportunities and a community-level construct when sociopolitical structures and social change are involved. Three concepts can be applied across levels of analysis to understand empowered processes and outcomes for individuals, groups, organizations and communities: control, critical awareness and participation. Control refers to perceived or actual capacity to influence decisions. Critical awareness refers to understanding how the power structures operate, how decisions are made, causal agents influenced and resources mobilized. Participation refers to taking action promoting desired outcomes.

The variegated characteristics of the empowerment construct make measurement difficult, in fact most existing tools assess primarily individual empowerment and only a very few group organizational or community empowerment.

ASSESSING INDIVIDUAL EMPOWERMENT

Several scales have been constructed to measure empowerment at the individual's level. Zimmerman and Rappaport (1988) used eleven indices of empowerment representing personality, cognitive and motivational measures, and examined in three studies the relationship between empowerment and participation in community activities and organizations. In each study, individuals reporting a greater amount of participation scored higher on indices of empowerment. Building on Zimmerman and Rappaport's indices and adapting them to an Italian context, Francescato and Perugini (1997)

constructed a 'Scala Di Empowerment' (SE) and tested it on 1568 men and women, aged 17 to 70.

Confirmatory factor analyses were conducted to evaluate the internal structure of the scale and the reliability of its score. Results provided evidence for convergent and discriminant validity for 3 subscales: political engagement, leadership and self-efficacy. Further studies (Francescato & Burattini, 1997; Francescato et al., 2000) showed that men were generally more empowered than women, with the exception of women holding political office or working in unions or police, that young people become more empowered after an experience in tutoring young children and taking part in other community projects, confirming the link already found in American studies between empowerment and participation.

Akey et al. (2000) have validated a Psychological Empowerment Scale (PES) using 293 SS. The results of the confirmatory factor analysis showed four subscales underlying the PES: (1) attitudes of control and competence, (2) cognitive appraisals of critical skills and knowledge, (3) formal participation in organization and (4) informal participation in social systems and relationships.

Qualitative tools can also be used to assess individual empowerment. Francescato et al. (2001) have used personal narratives to assess individual empowerment. Using 172 life stories it was found that one could assess levels of locus of control, self-esteem, self-efficacy, resilience, self-awareness and action motivation, and these were related to levels of empowerment measured by scales (SE). Kieffer (1984) has used interviews on life experiences to assess individual empowerment. Self-control and acquired responsibility through concrete life experiences were correlated with psychological empowerment.

ASSESSING GROUP EMPOWERMENT

Narratives have been used by Gone et al. (1999) and Mankowski and Rappaport (2000) to both assess and promote group empowerment in various settings. Rappaport suggests that community psychologists should help transform personal and community tales of terrors into tales of joy. Francescato et al. (2000) have used movie scripts to measure the empowerment level of various groups within an organization or a community. For instance, asking students, teachers, staff and parents to write a script about their schools allows one to detect patterns of hopefulness or helplessness, preferred solutions to problems, locus of control for each group and similarities and differences among groups. Movie scripts have also been used to evaluate the effect of empowerment training programmes with students from 240 high schools.

ASSESSING ORGANIZATIONAL EMPOWERMENT

Zimmerman (2000) distinguishes between empowering organizations that provide opportunities for its members to gain control over their lives, and empowered organizations which are successful in their mission and can influence community decisions.

Several authors have attempted to measure some single aspects of organizational empowerment. Florin and Wandersman (1990) have constructed organizational level measures of incentive and cost management and examined their relation to organizational viability and empowerment. Many organizational consultants and industrial psychologists have constructed scales that measure organizational variables that are related to empowerment (Moos & Lemke, 1984; Spaltro, 1977; Muchinsky, 2000). We lack, however, a complex measure of organizational empowerment. An attempt in this direction has been made by Francescato and Tancredi (1992). They have created a tool called multidimensional organizational analysis that involves people on all hierarchical levels of an organization. Together they analyse their organizational functioning across four dimensions (structural-strategic, functional, psychoenvironmental and cultural). Weak and strong points are outlined for each dimension and organizational empowerment levels are measured accordingly. Different narratives and preferred visions of the future are then formulated and organization members negotiate change priorities. This tool can be used both to make organizations more empowering and empowered (Francescato & Morganti, 1997).

ASSESSING COMMUNITY EMPOWERMENT

Again, at the community level of analysis, empowerment can be conceptualized as empowering or empowered or both. An empowering community provides residents with opportunities to exert control, develop and practise skills, and participate in community policy making. An empowered community is one that initiates effort to improve community life, has good links with regional, national and international policy making bodies.

In Italy, Martini and Sequi (1988), Francescato, Leone and Traversi (1993), Francescato (2000), and, in Austria, Ehmayer et al. (2000), have developed a methodology called 'community profiling' to both assess and promote community empowerment. Strong and weak points are diagnosed for seven profiles: territorial, demographic, economic, service, institutional, anthropological and psychological. Techniques of data gathering vary from profile to profile, and include walks, drawings, movie scripts, narratives, jokes for the more subjective profiles and a series of hard indicators for the first five profiles.

FUTURE PERSPECTIVES AND CONCLUSIONS

At the individual level, empowerment can be assessed reliably through both qualitative and quantitative data. However, only a few prevalently qualitative methods have been developed to assess empowerment at the group, organizational and community level. Moreover, since empowerment is used to measure both a process of empowering, and an outcome (empowered individuals, organizations, etc.), we need to develop better tools to assess both aspects of the construct.

References

Akey, T.M., Marquis, J.G. & Ross, M.E. (June 2000). Validation of scores on the psychological empowerment scale: a measure of empowerment for parents of children with a disability. *Educational and Psychological Measurement*, 60(3), 419–438.

Bruscaglioni, M. (1994). *La Società Liberata*. Milano: Angeli.

Ehmayer, C., Reinfeldt, S. & Gstotter, S. (2000). Agenda 21 as a concept for sustainable development. Paper presented at the III panel of experts, May 11–13th, Vienna.

Florin, P. & Wandersman, A. (1990). An introduction to citizen participation, voluntary organisations and community development: insights for empowerment through research. *American Journal of Community Psychology*, 18(1), 41–53.

Francescato, D. (2000). Community psychology intervention strategies to enhance participation in projects promoting sustainable development and quality of life. *Gemeinde Psychologie Rundbrief*, 2(6), 49–57.

Francescato, D. & Burattini, M. (Eds.) (1997). *Empowerment e Contesti Psicoambientali di Donne e Uomini Oggi*. Roma: Arcane.

Francescato, D., Leone, L. & Traversi, M. (1993). *Oltre La Psicoterapia*. Roma: Carocci.

Francescato, D. & Morganti, M. (1997). People first: strategies of empowerment in work organisations. *Analise Psicologica*, 15(3), 405–417.

Francescato, D. & Perugini, M. (1997). Definizione Delle Dimensioni Fattoriali Del Questionario e Validazione Della Scala Di Empowerment. In Francescato, D. & Burattini E.M. (Eds.), *Empowerment e Contesti Psicoambientali di Donne e Uomini Oggi* (pp. 47–61). Roma: Arcane.

Francescato, D. & Tancredi, M. (1992). Methodologies of organisational change: the need for an integrated approach. In Hosking, D.M. & Anderson, N. (Eds.), *Organisational Change and Innovation: Psychological Perspectives and Practices in Europe* (pp. 129–146). London: Routledge.

Francescato, D., Tomai, M., Burattini, M. & Rosa, V. (2000). Affective education as a strategy for primary and secondary prevention in underprivileged schools and communities of Italy. *Curriculum and Teaching*, 15(2), 103–111.

Francescato, D., Tomai, M. & Ghirelli, G. (2001). *Fondamenti di Psicologia di Comunità*. Roma: Carocci.

Gone, J.P., Miller, P.J. & Rappaport, J. (1999). Conceptual narrative as normatively oriented: the suitability of past personal narrative for the study of cultural identity. *Culture and Psychology*, 5(1), 371–398.

Hess, R. (1984). Thoughts on empowerment. *Prevention in Human Services*, 3(2), 227–230.

Human, L. (1990). Empowerment through development: the role of affirmative action and management development in the demise of apartheid. *Management, Education and Development*, 4(2), 273–286.

Kieffer, C.H. (1984). Citizen empowerment: a developmental perspective. *Prevention in Human Services*, 3(1), 9–36.

Mankowski, E.S. & Rappaport, J. (2000). Narratives, concepts and analysis in spiritually-based communities. *Journal of Community Psychology*, 28(5), 479–493.

Martini, R. & Sequi, R. (1988). *II Lavoro Nella Comunità*. Roma: Carocci.

McWhirter, E. (1991). Empowerment in counseling. *Journal of Counseling and Development*, 69(3), 222–227.

Moos, R.H. & Lemke, S. (1984). *Multiphasic Environmental Assessment Procedures*. Palo Alto: Stanford University Press.

Muchinsky, P.M. (2000). *Psychology Applied to Work*. Belmont, Ca.: Wadsworth.

Pasini, W. & Francescato, D. (2001). *Le Courage de Changer*. Paris: Editions Odile Jacob.

Piccardo, C. (1995). *Empowerment*. Milano: Cortina.

Putnam, A.O. (1991). Empowerment in search of a viable paradigm. *Performance Improvement Quarterly*, 4(2), 4–11.

Spaltro, E. (1977). *Il Check-up Organizzativo*. Milano: ISEDI.

Wilkinson, R. (1996). *Unhealthy Societies: The Afflictions of Inequalities*. London: Routledge.

Zimmerman, M.C. (2000). Empowerment and community participation: a review for the next millennium. In Ornelas, J. (Ed.), *Actas II Congressu Europeu de Psicologia Comunitaria* (pp. 17–42). Lisboa: ISPA.

Zimmerman, M.C. & Rappaport, J. (1988). Citizen participation, perceived control and psychological empowerment. *American Journal of Community Psychology*, 16(5), 725–750.

Donata Francescato

RELATED ENTRIES

Personality Assessment (General), Self-Efficacy

ENVIRONMENTAL ATTITUDES AND VALUES

INTRODUCTION

The emergence of societal awareness of environmental problems was quickly followed by efforts to assess individuals' concerns about environmental quality. Over a thousand published articles reporting empirical investigations of environmental attitudes, beliefs, values, etc. have been published in the past few decades. These studies have employed a huge variety of differing techniques to assess aspects of individuals' concern for the state of the environment, or 'environmental concern', leading some observers to see the literature as hopelessly disorganized (Heberlein, 1981: 242). The goal of this entry is to clarify the conceptual foundations of environmental concern and review major assessment techniques employed to measure it.

CONCEPTUAL AMBIGUITIES: 'ENVIRONMENT' AS AN ATTITUDE OBJECT

Heberlein (1981: 242) noted that, 'The great difficulty with even thinking about environmental attitudes is the ambiguity of the object itself', and the situation has been exacerbated by the changing nature of environmental problems. Air and water pollution were salient in the 1960s and 1970s; toxic wastes, energy shortages, acid rain, and hazardous technologies emerged in the 1970s and 1980s; followed by deforestation, biodiversity, ozone depletion and climate change in the 1990s. Overall, the problems have become less localized and visible, making their awareness more dependent on media and other information sources than on first-hand experience. These trends make the assessment of environmental attitudes even more challenging than Heberlein suggested. Yet, it is possible to provide an overview of empirical research on 'environmental concern', the term typically used in the empirical literature (Dunlap & Jones, 2002).

CLARIFYING THE MEANING OF 'ENVIRONMENTAL CONCERN'

Environmental concern refers to the degree to which people are aware of environmental problems and support efforts to solve them and/or indicate a willingness to contribute personally to their solution. Researchers investigating environmental concern must inevitably choose from a wide range of environmental issues or substantive topics and from the numerous ways in which concern over these issues/topics can be expressed by respondents. Consequently, environmental concern is a construct consisting of two

conceptual components: 'environmental topics' and 'expressions of concern' (Dunlap & Jones, 2002; Gray, 1985).

The environmental component represents the substantive content of environmental concern, and is operationalized by the particular topic (e.g. acid rain) or set of topics (e.g. pollution) or broad topic (e.g. environmental degradation) chosen by the researcher from the potential pool of environmental issues. The concern component represents the way in which environmental concern is operationalized via the particular manner employed by the researcher to elicit people's expressions of concern about environmental issues (Dunlap & Jones, 2002).

The Environmental Component

The environmental component varies considerably in empirical studies because the potential pool of environmental phenomena is vast. For example, we can treat the phenomena that constitute the biophysical environment – atmosphere (air), hydrosphere (water), lithosphere (land), flora (plants) and fauna (animals) – as comprising a biophysical facet. Or, we can distinguish among different outcomes of human activities on the biophysical environment, such as resource depletion versus conservation, pollution generation versus abatement, and development versus preservation, and treat these elements as a biophysical facet. Each represents a way of organizing the enormously complex universe of biophysical properties into a manageable set of elements that comprise conceptually meaningful facets which can be employed in measures of 'environmental concern' (see Dunlap & Jones, 2002 on facet theory).

Several other facets such as the spatial (local to global) and temporal (past, current, and future) dimensions of environmental problems have also been found useful in representing important properties of such problems (Dunlap & Jones, 2002: 488). The resulting complexity of the environmental component helps account for the huge diversity in existing measures of environmental concern. Studies of environmental concern often fail to consider these important features, and inconsistent findings stem from the many ways biophysical, spatial, temporal, and other facets of the environmental component are haphazardly combined in measures of environmental concern.

The Concern Component

The second major source of variation in environmental concern research stems from the ways in which investigators conceptualize the 'concern' component of the construct. Two major approaches exist: the first is based on efforts to examine policy relevant aspects of environmental problems, and the second applies various forms of attitude theory when examining individuals' assessment of these problems.

The 'policy' approach is used in studies that conceptualize the concern component based on the investigator's understanding of environmental problems and their policy implications. Although not grounded in attitude theory, these studies have nonetheless yielded important insights into the public's concern for environmental quality by assessing perceptions of the seriousness of environmental problems; their major causes; support for various solutions; pro-environmental behaviours; etc. Use of such items is common in studies of public opinion toward environmental issues, but in in-depth surveys as well.

The 'theoretical' approach is used in studies that conceptualize the concern component based on the investigator's theoretical knowledge of the nature of beliefs, attitudes, intentions, and behaviours and their theoretical and empirical relationships. Although fewer in number, these studies of environmental concern draw explicitly on various forms of attitude theory. They typically conceptualize the concern component in terms of the classical tripartite conceptualization of 'attitude' as consisting of affective, cognitive and conative dimensions (Gray, 1985).

The cognitive expression of environmental concern is usually treated as the beliefs and/or knowledge an individual has about environmental problems. The affective expression of concern involves an emotive and evaluative element which is synonymous with a narrow conceptualization of attitude and tap personal feelings or evaluations (good–bad, like–dislike, etc.) about environmental issues. The conative expressions of concern reflect a readiness to perform, or a commitment to support, a variety of actions that can potentially impact environmental quality. Some researchers also include a behavioural

expression of concern representing the actual or reported pro-environmental actions (Dunlap & Jones, 2002).

Summary Typology

Given the diverse ways in which both the environment and concern components of the construct 'environmental concern' can be conceptualized, it is not surprising that one finds enormous diversity among existing assessments of individuals' levels of concern for environmental quality. A typology of efforts to conceptualize and measure environmental concern can be developed by dichotomizing attempts to conceptualize/measure both the environment and concern components. First, studies can focus on a single environmental issue or substantive topic (the preferred term) or on multiple topics; second, studies can focus on a single expression of concern or on multiple expressions.

Putting these two together yields a four-fold typology of potential measuring instruments: (1) Multiple-topic, multiple-expression instruments that examine phenomena such as beliefs, attitudes, intentions, and behaviours concerning various environmental topics; (2) Multiple-topic, single-expression instruments that measure beliefs, attitudes, intentions, *or* behaviours across a range of substantive topics; (3) Single-topic, multiple-expression instruments that measure beliefs, attitudes, intentions, and behaviours toward specific topics such as population or air or water pollution; and (4) Single-topic, single-expression instruments that measure beliefs, attitudes, intentions, *or* behaviours concerning a specific topic like global warming. The next section briefly reviews examples of these varying techniques.

SELECTIVE REVIEW OF EXISTING MEASURES

Maloney et al.'s (1975) early effort to develop a measuring instrument for environmental concern grounded in attitude theory remains the most comprehensive assessment technique available. It includes multi-item measures of ecological knowledge, affect, verbal commitment, and actual commitment. While each measure thus focuses on a single expression of environmental concern the items within them cover a wide range of environmental topics, making the overall instrument a multiple topic/multiple expression assessment technique. A more recent example of this technique, also based on attitude theory, is Kaiser et al.'s (1999) effort to measure environmental knowledge, behaviours, and attitudes.

Other researchers have developed similarly broad assessment techniques based more on a policy approach, developing measures that focus on key issues and topics but are not designed explicitly to tap the cognitive, evaluative, and conative components of attitudes. Van Liere and Dunlap (1981) include measures of support for environmental regulations, support for environmental spending, and reported pro-environment behaviours as well as measures of attitudes toward pollution, resources, and population. The overall instrument thus represents a multiple topic/multiple expression assessment technique. More recently Klineberg et al. (1998) have used a similar assessment strategy, measuring environmental-economic tradeoffs, perceived seriousness of pollution, pro-environmental behaviours, and ecological worldview.

The above efforts achieve reasonably comprehensive coverage of both environmental topics and expressions of concern via the use of multiple-topic, multi-item measures, but Weigel and Weigel (1978) achieve the same thing with a single measure. Their widely used scale includes items tapping a range of topics and reflecting cognitive, evaluative and conative expressions of concern.

One finds examples of multiple topic/single expression measures of environmental concern in two ways. First, individual measures within the Maloney et al. (1975) and Kaiser et al. (1999) instruments represent good examples, as each includes items tapping a single expression (or attitudinal component) but several environmental topics. Second, several researchers have developed individual measures that cover a range of topics but employ a single expression of concern. Examples include numerous efforts to develop measures of pro-environmental behaviours (e.g. Seguin et al., 1998).

Similarly, single topic/multiple expression measures can be found within the instruments developed by Van Liere and Dunlap (1981) and Klineberg et al. (1998) – represented, e.g., by the pollution scales in each – as well as in studies that have developed single measures such as McCutcheon's (1974) early population control scale.

Finally, good examples of single topic/single expression measures are rare, because sets of items focused on a single topic often encompass both the cognitive and evaluative dimensions of attitudes. However, Bord et al.'s (2000) recent study of global warming includes measures of both knowledge about the causes of global warming and support for governmental action to combat global warming.

ADDITIONAL COMPLEXITIES AND MEASURES

Asssessments of environmental concern are even more varied than noted above because of additional sources of variation (Dunlap & Jones, 2002). For example, some measures achieve broad coverage of environmental phenomena via items that tap a wide variety of environmental topics, as exemplified by the Weigel and Weigel (1978) scale. Others achieve broad coverage by including items focusing on 'environmental' problems, quality and protection (e.g. Guagnano & Markee, 1995). The latter approach has the advantage of avoiding the use of specific environmental topics that become dated as new issues emerge, a problem with the Maloney et al. (1975) and Weigel and Weigel (1978) measures.

The continual emergence of new environmental problems reinforces the idea that modern societies are causing major 'ecological deterioration', and has made measures assessing the overall relationship between humans and the environment popular. Indeed, the earliest such measure, Dunlap and Van Liere's (1978) 'New Environmental Paradigm Scale', has become the most widely used measure of environmental concern. The original NEP Scale and a recent revision (Dunlap et al., 2000) assess beliefs about the balance of nature, limits to growth, and anthropocentrism (representing a multiple topic/ single expression measure) and are widely regarded as measures of environmental/ecological 'consciousness'. Similar measures are beginning to appear, most notably Thompson and Barton's (1994) measures of 'ecocentric' and 'anthropocentric' attitudes.

Table 1.   Well-established and widely used measures of environmental concern

1	Maloney, Ward and Braucht's (1975) 'Ecology Scale' Consists of four subscales measuring 'Verbal Commitment', 'Actual Commitment', 'Affect', and 'Knowledge'. Each found to be internally consistent and possessing face and known-group validity.
2	Weigel and Weigel's (1978) 'Environmental Concern Scale' Consists of 16 items focusing on the cognitive, affective, and conative aspects of several environmental topics. Found to be internally consistent and possessing test–retest reliability, known-group and predictive validity.
3	Dunlap and Van Liere's (1978) 'New Environmental Paradigm Scale' (revised in Dunlap et al., 2000) Consists of 12 items focusing on cognitions about the balance of nature, limits to growth, and anthropocentrism. Found to be internally consistent and possessing known-group validity.

CHOOSING AN INSTRUMENT

There is an endless variety of approaches to assessing individuals' concern for environmental quality stemming from the wide range of potential ways of conceptualizing and measuring the two components of environmental concern. Unfortunately, the vast majority of available instruments have never been used in replications, and only three have been widely used and their validity and reliability established. These are the Maloney et al. (1975), Weigel and Weigel (1978) and Dunlap and Van Liere (1978) measures (see Table 1). All are becoming dated, and only the last has been updated (Dunlap et al., 2000). Nonetheless, the first two represent good examples of theoretically grounded and psycho-metrically robust measures whose content in terms of environmental topics can be updated, and they should therefore be consulted at least until newer assessment techniques such as Kaiser et al.'s (1999) become widely replicated and validated.

FUTURE PERSPECTIVES AND CONCLUSIONS

Researchers interested in assessing environmental attitudes should carefully specify the environmental phenomena under investigation, and then decide on which aspects of concern they wish to measure (attitudes, beliefs, behavioural intentions, etc.), before choosing items and designing measuring instruments. They should also consider using existing measures that have been found to possess validity and reliability whenever possible, as replications are crucial in building a solid knowledge base regarding environmental concern.

References

Bord, R.J., O'Connor, R.E. & Fisher, A. (2000). In what sense does the public need to understand global climate change? *Public Understanding of Science*, 9, 205–218.

Dunlap, R.E. & Jones, R.E. (2002). Environmental concern: conceptual and measurement issues. In Dunlap, R.E. & Michelson, W. (Eds.), *Handbook of Environmental Sociology*. Westport, CT: Greenwood Press.

Dunlap, R.E. & Van Liere, K.D. (1978). The new environmental paradigm: a proposed measuring instrument and preliminary results. *Journal of Environmental Education*, 9, 10–19.

Dunlap, R.E., Van Liere, K.D., Mertig, A.G. & Jones, R.E. (2000). Measuring endorsement of the new ecological paradigm: a revised NEP scale. *Journal of Social Issues*, 56, 425–442.

Gray, D. (1985). *Ecological Beliefs and Behaviours*. Westport, CT: Greenwood Press.

Guagnano, G.A. & Markee, N. (1995). Regional differences in the sociodemographic determinants of environmental concern. *Population and Environment: A Journal of Interdisciplinary Studies*, 17, 135–149.

Heberlein, T.A. (1981). Environmental attitudes. *Zeitschrift fur Umweltpolitik*, 2, 241–270.

Kaiser, F.G., Wölfing, S. & Fuhrer, U. (1999). Environmental attitude and ecological behaviour. *Journal of Environmental Psychology*, 19, 1–19.

Klineberg, S.L., McKeever, M. & Rothenbach, B. (1998). Demographic predictors of environmental concern: it does make a difference how it's measured. *Social Science Quarterly*, 79, 734–753.

Maloney, M.P., Ward, M.P. & Braucht, G.N. (1975). Psychology in action: a revised scale for the measurement of ecological attitudes and knowledge. *American Psychologist*, 30, 787–790.

McCutcheon, L.E. (1974). Development and validation of a scale to measure attitude toward population control. *Psychological Reports*, 34, 1235–1242.

Seguin, C., Pelletier, L.G. & Hunsley, J. (1998). Toward a model of environmental activism. *Environment and Behaviour*, 30, 628–652.

Thompson, S.C. & Barton, M.A. (1994). Ecocentric and anthropocentric attitudes toward the environment. *Journal of Environmental Psychology*, 14, 149–157.

Van Liere, K.D. & Dunlap, R.E. (1981). Environmental concern: does it make a difference how it's measured? *Environment and Behaviour*, 13, 651–676.

Weigel, R. & Weigel, J. (1978). Environmental concern: the development of a measure. *Environment and Behaviour*, 10, 3–15.

Riley E. Dunlap and Robert Emmet Jones

RELATED ENTRIES

ATTITUDES

EQUIPMENT FOR ASSESSING BASIC PROCESSES

INTRODUCTION

Cognitive processes as information processing, reasoning, and the awareness of subjective experiences are unobservable. Usually the objects of cognitive research are reconstructions derived from controlled observations of settings, instructions and stimuli as well as from responses such as motor reactions, decisions, kinds of trials in problem solving and verbal reports (Monsell & Driver, 2000). The main goal is to describe sequences of steps in cognitive functioning with respect to genetic, skilled and actual causes of the occurrence of responses and their chaining.

GENERAL REMARKS ON MEASURES IN COGNITIVE RESEARCH

Cognitive behaviour is *setting*-dependent. Effects of bodily position (unusual or rotated views) are observed for recognition effects and for the extent of optical illusions. Certain environmental circumstances in a study phase (classroom setting, weightlessness) might be part of elaboration and associative chaining.

Instructions on how to deal with a target stimulus can be given in a multitude of ways. Mostly they act as a cue to prime certain associations in preparing how target information should be processed. The simplest kind of cues are so-called peripheral cues which are close to the target in space and time. Symbolic or exogenous cues are more remote from the stimulus features;

mostly verbal instructions are used in these cases. Effectiveness of instruction is often strengthened by a training phase up to a compliance criterion.

Stimuli are certain changes in the environment, affecting one or more senses. Because cognitive research is mostly based on assumptions on a sequence of cognitive operations (mental chronometry), a precise control of stimulation is needed, such as time relation to cues, onset, extent and comprehensibility. Standardized stimulation needs suitable devices, such as monitors, earphones, or skin stimulators.

Experiments are often designed to measure knowledge or ability, or to measure concomitants (such as emotional, psychophysiological, or neurological processes), or to measure time up to the correct response. Sometimes, frequency or types of errors or the ways of responding are assessed. To avoid uncontrolled influences by chance, reaction is usually restricted by instruction. Choice reactions can be restricted by forced choice and can be realized between two or more alternatives.

An elementary decision is to decide dichotomously as between confirmative or non-confirmative (signal detection theory – SDT). In this case, four response classes are considered (hits, misses, correct rejections and false alarms), usually according to fixed criteria (right or wrong). To evaluate performance in SDT paradigms, a large number of responses and special procedures are required (Snodgrass & Corwin, 1988). Most of cognitive research is done by the use of certain materials for testing failures and errors. Apart from psychophysiological methods of error processing, evaluation and back propagation of failures (e.g. automatic feedback presentation by PC) is commonly used in research on concept formation.

Responding is most restrictive in so-called go–no go paradigms. An often-used example is the odd ball paradigm. Here, usually two classes of stimuli are presented for go–no go in a time series, instances of one class with a low frequency.

Responses can be realized by verbal or by non-verbal output, e.g. movements. In both cases, special equipments for response detection are used, especially in time-critical designs. Motor responses such as writing, drawing, or marking with a cross are often required. Sometimes one has to move a joystick, to press a handle or a key, or has simply to move a finger. In measuring reaction times, movement detection and evaluation are serious problems.

Special equipment is needed to measure reactions accompanying desired responses, such as *eye movements*, psychophysiological or neurological events, indicating global or side aspects of information processing (e.g. Furedy & Ben-Shakhar, 1991). Moreover, studies using biomedical indicators have to be appropriately designed. Physiological responses such as *electrodermal responses* or the BOLD-response in *functional Magnetic Resonance Imaging* (fMRI) need time to abate before the next stimulation. Sometimes a number of responses have to be aggregated to assess noisy parameters, such as event-related potentials or EEG background activity, or in long-lasting physiological measures, such as *Positron Emission Tomography* (PET).

ASSESSMENT PRACTICES IN SPECIAL AREAS OF COGNITIVE PSYCHOLOGY

Measurement in Topographic Research and Hemispheric Interaction

A great part of research in cognitive neuropsychology is done in biomedical settings and in animal experiments. This is to find out principles of the functional brain architecture to get a theoretical frame for the architecture of cognition. One of the main goals is the functional specialization of certain brain areas as revealed by deep recording or stimulation techniques.

Apart from the microscopic functional architecture, cognitive processes do not always affect both hemispheres. Differences in cognitive performance (as global vs. routinized verbal processing) depend sometimes on the involvement of one or both hemispheres. Manipulation of hemispheric stimulation can be done by lateralized visual probes or *dichotic tasks* (simultaneous stimulation of both ears by different stimuli). Reaction times in right or left handed responses reveal direct processing in one hemisphere or callosal relay to the contralateral side (*cf.* Zaidel, 1983). This can be interpreted as topographically specialized and often time requiring processing.

Perception, Attention, and Imagery

Sensory mechanisms and encoding processes are usually a domain of psychophysics and psychoneurological cooperation. To stimulate particular areas, certain patterns of stimuli are used (such as an animated checkerboard for area V5). Trickier are questions concerning attention, because they are closely related to cortical self-regulation of activity. Exogenous or automatic attention can be analysed only with respect to interacting processes in lower (e.g. thalamic) levels, i.e. with respect to concurrent environmental information. Here, short time (tachistoscopic) presentations are required as well as the exact control of a stimulus onset asynchrony (SOA) (*cf.* Pesce Anzeneder & Bösel, 1998). Endogenous or concept driven attention and phenomena of active perception (as revealed by familiarity ratings) are closely related to backpropagations and re-entries from higher level processing (such as from the associative areas of the working memory), with respect to intentions, instructions and memory standards (*cf.* Bösel, 2001). Apart from performance data, parameters of electroencephalography (event-related potentials, slow EEG rhythmicity, gamma waves for binding phenomena) are used to indicate particular changes of significance in feature processing.

Imagery can be seen as brain activity without sensory stimulation, but often localized in the same areas. In agreement with the neurological assumptions on automatic and endogenous attention, reasons for imagery under instruction, in drug action, in psychopathology, or in dreaming are frequently analysed by the use of biomedical methods (Transmagnetic Stimulation [TMS], neurochemical alterations).

Priming, Working Memory, Long Term Memory

Recognition tests can be done in the form of familiarity tests (such as lexical decision) or in n-back paradigms. *Recall* is mostly tested by free or choiced naming. To evaluate recall performance and understanding of complex facts as, for example, empathy performance in the social field, special arrangements such as the Sally-and-Anne-experiment are required, and formal aspects of the report have to be considered. Short term memory span has to be assessed by an item set presented within a short time interval as well as with respect to a short retention interval between learning and test. It is assumed that encoding complex information needs time, which can be tested by encoding speed. Because chunking capacity is a predictor of consolidation, some particular test materials are used as well in testing short term memory as in testing long term memory, e.g. character sets or arrangements of block-tapping. The product of memory span times encoding speed reveals capacity of short term memory. Testing *learning and re-learning* performance needs study trials with respect to learning criteria. Testing of implicit memory requires decisions on features, such as of artificial brain scans, or lexical decisions on character strings fixed on so-called artificial grammars. An experimental manipulation of attention and re-learning performance can be done by variation of minor attended additional stimuli, as realized in double tasks paradigms (where performance is measured with respect to a receiver–operator-curve ROC) or by minimal changes of instruction in repeating learning trials (such as done in testimony experiments or to increase the memory set). Particular inventories are used to assess variables of personality assumed to influence cognitive performance, such as intelligence (for example measured by Progressive Matrices).

Categorical Thinking, Decision-Making, and Language

Assessment in testing categorical thinking depends on the chosen theoretical model and the intended field of application. Models of categorical thinking are often based on processing simulation programmes, such as in LISREL or in parallel distributed processing systems (PDP). For instance, in reading disabilities, models of artificial intelligence (AI) are used to explain the aetiology of psychopathology (Plaut & Shallice, 1993). Models of decision-making in AI use expert systems and fuzzy set algorithms.

For testing basic neuropsychological abilities, more simple questionnaires or particular materials are often required, such as the Clock Test or the Token Test. Special equipment is needed for auditory or visual stepwise presentation in sentence comprehension. Phonograms or time-spectrograms are used to detect onset and other formal parameters of verbal responses, such as sentence accent and prosodic components.

Voluntary Action and Problem Solving

In the early times of experimental psychology, timing was done by watching harmonic motions, e.g. of a tuning fork. By the use of such methods, difficult time measures are possible up to now, such as watching rotating lines on an oscilloscope to measure the onset of a voluntary action (Libet et al., 1983). Most parts of problem solving research (such as the use of the Tower of Hanoi) can be understood as investigation of the features of working memory as enumerated by Norman and Shallice (1986).

In applied fields, sometimes choice reaction apparatus are used, up to simulations of real work settings with the opportunity to particularly control stimuli and responses, even by registration of certain biological data.

THE MINIMAL COGNITIVE LABORATORY

The careful investigation of verbal and behavioural data is a basal requirement, even recommended in preparation of experiments or examinations requiring neuropsychological methods. This kind of investigation could be done in a minimal cognitive lab with features as follows.

The rooms for cognitive assessment have to be free of noisy air, light or sound contaminations. Stimulus presentation, procedure control, and response registration should be done with the aid of a computer. The monitor should not be too inert (as in the case of most flat screens) and have highest monitor frequencies. Hardware features as graphic and sound cards should match the requirements of the task. Software systems are available for a lot of cognitive paradigms; an experimental run time system for self-fixed experiments is usually required. A crucial point is equipment for detection of the exact time of stimulus onset and response, because of the unpredictable timing when using a windows standard socket. Programming language and operating system should have real time features. Further, a package of statistical routines is required. Technical personnel should be trained for PC hardware and software administration as well as for checking experimental settings, such as times for image change and response registration.

FUTURE PERSPECTIVES AND CONCLUSIONS

As true as in other psychological fields, cognitive measurement requires reliable prediction of certain cognitive functions, i.e. undisturbed occurrence and valid detection. To ensure this requirement, clear conditions, simple responses, and short time arrangements are attended. In this way, often plain behaviour such as cued recognition or sentence comprehension is known to be influenced by a number of factors causing alternative sequences of particular processes.

As a consequence, it is necessary to make the predictions more precise and to extend the control of variables in the cognitive field, including acquisition of supportive variables. Apart from ocular movements or vegetative responses, both brain imaging and brain potentials are valuable methods for detecting cognitive components as well as the time course of cognitive processing.

Further research requires an improvement in resolution and pattern analysis with regard to topography and time, and a sophisticated combination of methods in cognitive research. This will advance our knowledge on how processing units indicated by different methods interact in causing cognitive phenomena.

References

Bösel, R.M. (2001). *Denken [Thinking]*. Göttingen: Hogrefe.

Furedy, J. & Ben-Shakhar, G. (1991). The role of deception, intention to deceive, and motivation to avoid detection in the psychophysiological detection of guilty knowledge. *Psychophysiology*, 28, 163–167.

Libet, B., Gleason, C.A., Wright, E.W. & Pearl, D.K. (1983). Time of conscious intention to act in relation to onset of cerebral activities (readiness-potential): the unconscious initiation of a freely voluntary act. *Brain*, 106, 623–642.

Monsell, S. & Driver, J. (Eds.) (2000). *Control of Cognitive Processes. Attention and Performance XVIII*. Cambridge, MA: MIT Press.

Norman, D.A. & Shallice, T. (1986). Attention to action: willed and automatic control of behaviour. In Davidson, R.J., Schwartz, G.E. & Shapiro, D. (Eds.), *Consciousness and Self-Regulation* (pp. 1–18). New York: Plenum.

Pesce Anzeneder, C. & Bösel, R.M. (1998). Modulation of the spatial extent of the attentional focus in high-level volleyball players. *The European Journal of Cognitive Psychology*, 10, 247–267.

Plaut, D.C. & Shallice, T. (1993). Deep dyslexia: a case study of connectionist neuropsychology. *Cognitive Neuropsychology*, 10, 377–500.

Snodgrass, J.G. & Corwin, J. (1988). Pragmatics of measuring recognition memory: applications to dementia and amnesia. *Journal of Experimental Psychology: General*, 117, 34–50.

Zaidel, E. (1983). Disconnection syndrome as a model for laterality in the normal brain. In Hellige, J.B. (Ed.), *Cerebral Hemisphere Asymmetry* (pp. 95–151). New York: Praeger.

Rainer M. Bösel

RELATED ENTRIES

Brain Activity Measurement, Cognitive Processes: Current Status, Psychophysiological Equipment and Measurements, Theoretical Perspective: Cognitive, Applied Fields: Psychophysiology

ETHICS

INTRODUCTION

Wherever people live and work together, they evaluate their own actions and those of others as good or bad, justified or unjustified, fair or unfair, and they ascribe to others and to themselves in particular situations the responsibility for doing what should be done and not doing what should not be done. The entirety of the rules that these evaluations follow in everyday life is characterized as morality. Anyone publicly violating them incurs the disdain of the others. Insofar as people acknowledge the existence of moral rules, they also judge themselves before their own conscience. Moral rules therefore have a high status in subjective experiencing, thinking, and acting. Morality, however, can also be misused in order to give others a bad conscience. It can likewise be employed as a weapon to question the privileges of others or to defend one's own privileges. Finally, it can be used to create solidarity with others.

Moral rules can also find their way into national laws. But not all national laws have a moral basis. Whoever can be shown to have violated national laws must usually reckon with sanctions of the state, such as fines or prison terms. Finally, in addition to the rules of morality and the laws of the state, there are standards or norms, such as those of associations or professional organizations (American Educational Research Association, American Psychological Association, and National Council on Measurement in Education, 1999; International Test Commission, 2000). These prescribe how the members of these organizations are to conduct themselves during the performance of their professional activities. Anyone who can be demonstrated to have violated these rules is threatened in the worst instance with expulsion from the professional organization, which in some countries can have legal consequences, namely, one can be prohibited from carrying out one's professional activities.

In the following, the term 'ethics' will be elucidated and the two main fields of ethics will be introduced. Then the main participants in the assessment process will be introduced and their ethically justifiable responsibilities and rights will be worked out against the backdrop of fundamental theories of normative ethics. This will then be followed by a presentation of the positions taken by the critics of normative ethics. In conclusion, the practical implications of professional codes of behaviour will be shown.

ETHICS AND ITS BRANCHES

Ethics is a discipline of scientific philosophy (Frankena, 1963). It is concerned with evaluations. It is divided into two branches – meta-ethics and normative ethics. Meta-ethics examines the language of evaluation, the meaning of the evaluative terms, of evaluative standards and of their logical implications. A core insight of meta-ethics, which is called the Humean Law after the Scottish philosopher, states that no normative statement can logically follow solely from a descriptive statement: no findings, for example, on a person's intelligence, permit, in and of themselves, a statement concerning the moral value of that person and of that person's dignity. Normative ethics examines the moral rules of groups and societies, national laws or standards of voluntary organizations. These norms are rationally examined on the basis of universal principles. The object of normative ethics is thus the rational examination of norms and the universally binding justification of principles.

A STAKEHOLDER ANALYSIS

In order to be able to determine the ethical responsibility and obligatory duties of the people involved in psychological assessment, it will be necessary in the following subsections to go into the question of the most important actors, the so-called stakeholders (Lindsay, 1996; Airaksinen, 1998; Carroll & Buchholtz, 1999), and their interests.

The Stakeholders

Scientific Psychology

Psychological science is in competition with other sciences for the distribution of resources and reputation. It develops universal standards of professional competence and provides for the education and training of future psychologists. Like all other sciences, psychological science is involved in the social construction of reality. It creates social realities by means of its constructs (such as the intelligence construct; Johnson, 1998). The social importance of these constructs is substantiated by the prestige of the science and of the profession. The modification and further development of assessment constructs rests in the hands of the sciences. It thus has an influence on the social consequences that result from the spread of their constructs and methods.

Test Developers

Persons or small groups develop the procedures of psychological assessment for scientific purposes or for a fee on behalf of a commercial client. Considerable costs are often involved in the development and validation of assessment procedures. The developers, however, if they are working commercially, have an interest in low development costs and a broad, long-term application of their procedures, hence the professional quality of the procedures developed and the financial investment to be spent developing them are frequently stuck together in a reciprocal trade-off relationship.

Distributors

The publishing companies and the distributors of assessment procedures are interested in their broad and long-term application. The lower the costs of development are, the lower the prices can be for the assessment procedures being offered, and the more widely they can be marketed. The scientific reputation of procedures likewise contributes in a positive way to their marketability. The distributors therefore like to market products with a scientific reputation. They have no genuine interest, however, in selling particular assessment procedures only to one particular profession or in limiting it at all to members of particular professions, since that would reduce the size of the potential market.

Professional Associations

The professional psychological associations represent the interests of working psychologists. They try to strengthen their position in the competition with other professions in society. One of their strategies is to develop competency profiles with exclusive status. A part of this is also the claim that, as a profession, on the basis of education, training and professional competence, their members have the exclusive right to use particular assessment procedures. To achieve this objective, they can try to ensure that the customers of psychological assessment, the persons analysed and the public, as well as governmental bodies, have confidence in their professional competence and their observance of particular standards. To do this they develop codes of conduct for their members.

Customers

The customers of psychological assessment can be businesses or organizations, schools or universities, other professions (e.g. physicians), courts, particular state institutions, scientific institutes, etc., to name only those that are most important. They are interested in their commission being carried out in a reliable, valid, and quiet fashion, with no unpleasant side-effects for themselves, the customer. Often customers have a limited understanding of psychological assessment and their assessment objectives are not sufficiently specified. The assessment findings are nevertheless frequently used by customers as the basis for making a decision.

Assessors

The psychological assessor draws up the overall concrete assessment plan. In general, this person works on his or her own responsibility without instructions from anyone else. To carry out the assessment plan, and to evaluate and communicate the results, this person may make use of assistants who follow his or her instructions. As a rule, the psychological assessor is assigned the responsibility for their selection and activity. He or she strives to fulfil his or her contracts to the satisfaction of his or her customers so that he or she will be entrusted with new tasks to perform. Generally, he or she earns at least a part of his or her livelihood through this activity. In so doing, he or she finds himself competing with members of other professions or other non-professional suppliers. The parameters of the competition could be the following: costs, side-effects, quiet performance, loyalty to the customer, reputation, and acceptance by those affected. Often, membership in professional organizations is a prerequisite for practising certain activities.

Examinees

Persons are often the object of psychological assessment – however, this is not always the case. Workplaces, machines, animals, medicines or programmes, for example, can also be examined. If persons are being examined, their participation can be voluntary or involuntary. In either case, the circumstances of the examination itself are usually connected with a high degree of power asymmetry to the disadvantage of the examinees. Moreover, as a result of the standardized procedure the possibilities for reaction on the part of the examinees are often drastically limited. The examination can occur partially or completely announced, unannounced, or falsely announced. The affected person may or may not be informed of the results. Finally, the affected person, depending on the case and situation, may or may not have any influence on the examination's consequences. The assessment process can also have a considerable impact on the individual's current well-being, self-concept, self-esteem and respect from others, as well as future professional and social chances. The examinees often react to the examination with a reduced willingness to cooperate as well as deliberate withholding and filtering of information.

Coaching

To improve the individual examinee's chances of doing well on the examination, there exists coaching. This comprises either people or

literature that, on the basis of alleged or actual professional or insider knowledge and for a fee, prepares the future examinee for the assessment procedure.

Legal Guardians

In the event that the examinee is unable or is not permitted to make his or her own decisions (children, the elderly, the handicapped, prisoners), other persons or courts give permission for the examination and evaluate the potential consequences for the examinee.

The State

Frequently, the state not only acts as the customer of psychological assessment, such as in school and court, but also directly regulates the assessment process and the evaluation of its results by means of orders and prohibitions.

The Public in General

Finally, in the public in general, there exist certain expectations and moral notions about how assessment procedures should be conducted and what consequences they should have and for whom. These notions are transported and formed by the mass media. If the assessment practice supposedly or in fact deviates from these expectations and moral guidelines, and this becomes known to the public in general, the affected assessor, the institution that has commissioned him, his or her professional association, as well as the governmental regulatory authorities are placed under a considerable amount of pressure to justify themselves. If the actors involved are unable to give a satisfactory justification, they lose their public legitimation. Yet, because the other actors are essentially dependent upon public legitimation, they often develop so-called legitimation facades. In their external self-portrayal they demonstrate a high degree of conformity to public expectations, which frequently, however, do not correspond with actual practice (Haney & Madaus, 1991). This, however, is not a peculiarity of the assessment process, but can be observed in all actors who require public support for their work.

The Ethically Justifiable Responsibilities of Stakeholders

As this stakeholder analysis shows, a complicated tangle of interests and expectations, which must be assessed and evaluated in terms of their ethical justification, are woven around psychological assessment. An overview of the central theories of normative ethics is provided by Velasquez (1998: 67–163; more exhaustively in Chadwick, 1998).

In accordance with the contractarian approach, all of the implicit or explicit contractual relations of the actors involved can be examined as to whether or not they had arisen voluntarily, as to whether the contractual partners had beforehand received a true and accurate disclosure of all of the relevant facts of the matter, and as to whether any unethical performance or consideration had been contractually agreed upon. In this sense, one can understand the so-called ethical codes of many professional psychological organizations. They make clear what professional psychologists expect of the other actors in the assessment process and describe explicitly their own ethical commitments.

The contractarian approach, however, is not fundamental in terms of ethics. In the first place, not all of the relationships in the assessment process are voluntary contractual relationships and, secondly, although in the contractarian approach it is a precondition that nothing unethical may be agreed upon, the contractarian approach cannot itself determine these unethical facts. The relationship between wards and their guardians cannot be based on contractual principles, but must be based on principles of care. Accordingly, the person whose duty it is to give assistance has to act in the best long-term interests of the person in his care. Following the theory of fundamental human rights, the relationships between the actors should also be examined as to whether they are compatible with the fundamental human rights of individuals; in other words, dignity, freedom, life, privacy, rational self-determination, as well as physical and emotional integrity.

Good reasons, however, can also be given for limiting basic rights, such as personal freedom or the voluntary nature of an assessment. Rule-utilitarianism demands that this does not occur arbitrarily, but only according to certain well-justified rules. What, however, is a well-justified rule? Discourse ethics (Habermas, 1990) answers as follows: every legitimate norm for the regulation of the relationships among various stakeholders must meet the condition that the consequences and side-effects that in each case result or can be expected to result from its universal observance for the satisfaction of the interests of each stakeholder can be accepted by all affected parties (and such effects preferred to the known alternative regulatory possibilities).

According to this view, individual stakeholders (e.g. professional groups) cannot one-sidedly establish standards that can rightly claim to be ethical standards (Ladd, 1991). Thus, in a democratic state in which the rule of law prevails, it is the parliament that often assumes the task, after the various stakeholders have been heard, of passing laws that bring into balance the interests and basic rights of individuals as well as the public interest. To prevent any misunderstandings, it should be pointed out that this does not mean that every legal regulation of duties in the assessment process is ethically justified. It simply means that in a state in which the rule of law prevails, the parliament is the actor that has the best chances of moderating a rational discourse among stakeholders.

CRITICISM OF NORMATIVE ETHICS

The critics of normative ethics are of the opinion that a universally binding justification of ethical principles is impossible. Instead, they say, the acceptance of these principles is based on a frequently implicit decision which is not susceptible to further rational justification (Weber, 1949). This commitment to ultimate principles or values – as in communitarianism (Moon, 1998), a recently much-discussed variant of the so-called decisionism in normative ethics – is based on the anchoring of people in particular communities. From this point of view, the values and ideals of psychological assessment are also merely group standards that can, but need not, be accepted, such as rationality, empirical support for assertions, impartiality, openness to revisions, and the acknowledgment of limits to one's own competence. They are directed against a magical way of viewing the world (e.g. astrology, tarot, palmistry or pendulums), the unexamined clinging to traditions (because it has 'always been' done like that, it will also be done like that in the future) and habits (e.g. the decisive private job interview with the boss), political claims to power and personal or political wishful thinking. Because of this value basis, psychological assessment is frequently attacked politically by groups with other value bases. In the former Soviet Union at the time of Stalinism there was even a general ban on the use of psychological tests.

In defending normative ethics against the reproach of decisionism, it has been pointed out by discourse ethics (Habermas, 1990) that any person who argues that there are no universally binding ethical principles has already contradicted himself, because anyone who argues, in doing so, acknowledges that he wants, solely on the basis of an understanding of his arguments, to move his interlocutor to accept his own position. He has thus, however, already accepted the principle of discourse ethics, according to which a norm is only valid if it has been accepted by a consensus arrived at through free and rational argumentation.

FUTURE PERSPECTIVES

Laws and codes of conduct must necessarily be formulated in a universally applicable way, because it ought to be possible to subsume under them as many groups of cases as possible and because they ought to provide a regulation as well for facts and circumstances that were not yet known at the time the standards were promulgated. The American Psychological Association (APA) therefore did not just adopt a code of conduct, but published and continued to develop an extensive systematic collection of concrete cases (Eyde et al., 1993) to illustrate the application of this code. Moreover, this collection of cases has been drawn up in such a way that it can be used in the education and training of future psychological assessors. This approach is highly commendable since no rule contains its own conditions of application. In order to apply rules sensibly, one also needs to be aware of the circumstances and the relevant limiting conditions. To guarantee the observance of its code of conduct, the APA set up a professional tribunal as well and passed rules of procedure for it

(Ethics Committee of the American Psychological Association, 1996).

In order to attain an ethically justifiable practice of psychological assessment, the following steps are therefore necessary: development of legal and professional standards in the dialogue by all and for all of the stakeholders participating in the assessment process, collection and documentation of typical sample cases, training of the persons involved and in particular of beginners, as well as the establishment of legal and professional procedures to monitor the observance of standards in individual cases.

References

Airaksinen, T. (1998). Professional ethics. In R. Chadwick (Ed.), *Encyclopedia of Applied Ethics*, Vol. 3 (pp. 671–682). San Diego, CA: Academic Press.

American Educational Research Association, American Psychological Association, and National Council on Measurement in Education (Eds.) (1999). *Standards for Educational and Psychological Testing*. Washington, DC: American Educational Research Association.

Carroll, A.B. & Buchholtz, A.K. (1999). *Business & Society. Ethics and Stakeholder Management* (4th ed.). Cincinnati, OH: South-Western College Publishing.

Chadwick, R. (Ed.) (1998). *Encyclopedia of Applied Ethics*, 4 Vols. San Diego, CA: Academic Press.

Ethics Committee of the American Psychological Association (1996). Rules and procedures. *American Psychologist*, 51(5), 529–548.

Eyde, L.D. et al. (1993). *Responsible Test Use. Case Studies for Assessing Human Behaviour*. Washington, DC: American Psychological Association.

Frankena, W.K. (1963). *Ethics*. Englewood Cliffs, NJ: Prentice Hall.

Habermas, J. (1990). Discourse ethics – notes on a program of philosophical justification, In Habermas, J. (Ed.), *Moral Conscienciousness and Communicative Action* (pp. 117–194). Cambridge, MA: MIT Press.

Haney, W. & Madaus, G. (1991). The evolution of ethical and technical standards for testing. In Hambleton, R.K. & Zaal, J.N. (Eds.), *Advances in Educational and Psychological Testing: Theory and Applications* (pp. 395–425). Boston: Kluwer Academic Press.

International Test Commission (2000). *International Guidelines for Test Use*. http://cwis.kub.n1/~fsw_1/itc/.

Johnson, E. (1998). Intelligence testing. In Chadwick, R. (Ed.), *Encyclopedia of Applied Ethics*, Vol. 2 (pp. 711–723). San Diego, CA: Academic Press.

Ladd, J. (1991). The quest for a code of professional ethics: an intellectual and moral confusion. In Johnson, D.G. (Ed.), *Ethical Issues in Engineering* (pp. 130–136). Englewood Cliffs, NJ: Prentice Hall.

Lindsay, G. (1996). Psychology as an ethical discipline and profession. *European Psychologist*, *1*(2), 79–88.

Moon, J.D. (1998). Communitarianism. In Chadwick, R. (Ed.), *Encyclopedia of Applied Ethics*, Vol. 1 (pp. 551–561). San Diego, CA: Academic Press.

Velasquez, M.G. (1998). *Business Ethics* (4th edn.), Upper Saddle River, NJ: Prentice Hall.

Weber, M. (1949). *The Methodology of the Social Sciences*. Glencoe, Ill: Free Press.

Gerhard Blickle

RELATED ENTRIES

EVALUABILITY ASSESSMENT

INTRODUCTION

Programme evaluation is a common practice in public and private organizations in the western world. It is an essential step, and the final one when actions are carried out to solve a social problem. Rossi and Freeman (1993) defined programme evaluation as *the systematic application of social research procedures for assessing the conceptualization, design, implementation, and utility of social interventions programs* (Rossi & Freeman, 1993: 5).

However, before evaluating a programme, we must inquire about the need for the evaluation. Wholey (Wholey, Scanlon, Duffy, Fukumoto & Vogt, 1970; Wholey, 1983, 1987) described this question as evaluability assessment.

The concept of evaluability assessment emerged in the context of the problems Wholey and his colleagues experienced when they were working at the Urban Institute of Washington in the early 1970s. These problems were of two main types. First, stakeholders' resistance to co-operate in the evaluation, and second, the limited use of evaluation outcomes for the improvement of the programmes (Wholey et al., 1970). In short, evaluation was difficult due to stakeholders' resistance and was not useful because its outcomes did not help to bring about changes in the social interventions.

Subsequently, Wholey (1983, 1987) developed the concept further, identifying four problematic areas that increase the difficulty of programme evaluation. Such areas are:

1   A lack of definition of the problem addressed, the programme intervention, the expected outcomes of the programme, and/or the expected impact on the problem.
2   A lack of a clear logic of testable assumptions linking expenditure of programme resources, the implementation of the programme, the expected outcomes (to be caused by that programme), and the resulting impact.
3   A lack of agreement on the evaluation's priorities and its intended uses.
4   The inability to make decisions on the basis of evaluation information.

Wholey himself established concrete problems to identify the evaluability assessment process associated with these four areas. Such problems are poor programme definition, misjudgement to implement the programme, lack of establishing realistic objectives, and contradictory presence of non-expected effects. In this regard, we can use the definition reached by the author:

Evaluability assessment is a diagnostic and prescriptive tool that can be used to determine the extent to which any of these four problems exists and to help ensure that such problems are solved before decisions are made to proceed with any further evaluation. (Wholey, 1987: 78)

EVALUABILITY ASSESSMENT: USES

Smith (1989) identified two steps in the carrying out of evaluability assessment, and three possible uses of it, depending on moments and objectives. According to the steps, firstly, evaluability makes a contribution to the guarantees and technical credibility of the programme. Secondly, evaluability assessment determines the plausibility and feasibility of the programme and its evaluation. In conclusion, the two old problems that Wholey and his team pointed out are discussed: the knowledge of the easiness and feasibility of the evaluation and the knowledge of the utility of the evaluative process.

As regards the uses of evaluability assessment, the first of them should be its use as a summative tool or as a preliminary step in evaluating the effectiveness or the programme's impact. The second use is as a formative tool to decide what can be changed to make the programme more evaluable. The third use is as a planning tool to define objectives, identify actions for attaining those objectives and find the appropriate resources for implementing such actions.

Smith (1989) arrived at a wide and comprehensive definition of this process:

Evaluability assessment is a diagnostic and prescriptive tool for improving programs and making evaluations more useful. (Smith, 1989: 1)

In accordance with this definition, Smith (1989) attempts to answer several questions about the programme, for example: (a) What is it? What are its components? (b) Why do it? What are its expected outcomes? (c) How does it start? What is the logical first step, second step, etc? (d) How did someone else do it? The answers to these questions lead to making decisions about whether or not to carry out the programme evaluation. In brief, evaluability assessment attempts to answer the following question: 'To what extent can a programme be evaluated?'

However, where do we draw the line between programmes that can be evaluated and those that cannot? Some authors have tried to establish a sequence of criteria to indicate such limits (Rutman, 1980; Muscatello, 1988; Fernández-Ballesteros & Hernández, 1995).

EVALUABILITY CRITERIA

Berk and Rossi (1990) defined the existence of four evaluability criteria:

An impact assessment is impossible without well-formulated program objectives (...) A second criterion for evaluability is that program content be well specified (...) A program's impact may be estimated only if it is possible to credibly approximate what would have happened to the targeted recipients in the absence of the program (...) Finally, effectiveness evaluations are often the most difficult kinds of evaluations, requiring highly trained personnel and, sometimes, large sums of money. (Berk & Rossi, 1990: 72–73)

Even though the authors did not explicitly say so, it would seem that these criteria have different weights. Thus, it has been considered that a programme that fails to specify its objectives in a clear way cannot be evaluated. (Weiss, 1972; House, 1980; Rutman, 1980)

EVALUABILITY ASSESSMENT INSTRUMENTS

Shadish (1986) stresses the need to answer questions about the programme before the beginning of the programme evaluation: what are the concerning dimensions in the evaluative process, to which precision have such dimensions been defined in the planning, design, and implementation of the programme? The specification of such dimensions and their precision are relevant criteria on which to base a decision about whether or not to evaluate a programme.

Muscatello (1988) developed a sequence of evaluability dimensions from a formal and rational perspective. Such dimensions are: Completion Time, Costs of Materials, Staff Costs, Resistance, Programme Purpose, Programme Maturity, Programme Definition, Measurement Validity, Measurement Reliability, Administrative Constraints, Political Constraints, and Legal Constraints. The judgement on each of these areas is made by means of a 5-point scale. Although Muscatello did not show empirical data, his proposal is useful to organize the gathered information in the evaluability assessment.

Fernández-Ballesteros and Hernández (1995) developed an assessment device: the 'Listado de Cuestiones Relevantes en Evaluación de

Programas' (LCREP: 'Programme Evaluation Relevant Questions Form'; Fernández-Ballesteros & Hernández, 1995). The LCREP is a 53-item questionnaire with a Yes/No/Do not know format. Each item is related to one out of twelve dimensions. Eight of these theoretically relevant dimensions are linked to the policy cycle (*Need assessment*, *Objectives established*, *Programme quality*, *Programme definition*, *Implementation level*, *Design feasibility*, *Quality of data collected*, and *Context information*) and four of them are related to potential evaluation constraints (*Acceptability*, *Evaluator implications*, *Purposes for evaluation*, and *Costs*). Three scores can be obtained from the LCREP. First, Direct score: the number of total items answered 'Yes' or 'No' in the expected way (0–53). Second, Rating scale scores: each dimension can be assessed by means of a 5-point rating scale. Third, Weighted scores: using rational criteria, each item is weighted. Evaluators should have a basic but adequate knowledge of the policy cycle and the evaluation context before they administer the LCREP.

Several studies have been carried out to obtain the inter-judge agreement using the LCREP (Fernández-Ballesteros et al, 1989; Fernández-Ballesteros, 1992). Prior to the evaluation of five programmes, six evaluators responded to the LCREP individually for each programme after examining documents about the programmes and conducting interviews with the client, policy-makers, managers, and other stakeholders. Authors obtained significant correlations (phi coefficient) item-by-item in 86.6% of the comparisons ($p < 0.005$). Nevertheless, using the rating scale scores only 26% of the comparisons were significant ($p < 0.01$). Finally, there were strong relationships (Kendall W Test) between dimensions scores (weighted scores and rating scale scores) throughout the programmes. 'Purposes and evaluation' and 'Costs' were the dimensions with least agreement. 'Programme quality', 'Programme definition', 'Implementation level' and 'Quality of data collected' were the most consistent dimensions.

The LCREP appears to be potentially useful: (1) in order to help the evaluator make a rational decision about whether or not the programme should be evaluated, (2) as a tool in planning programme evaluation, (3) in order to assess potential sources of problems that may be relevant during the evaluation process, and (4) to guide the evaluator through the first stage of the evaluation process.

FUTURE PERSPECTIVES AND CONCLUSIONS

Evaluability assessment should be the first step in programme evaluation. Accordingly, evaluability assessment must be incorporated into programme planning and design as an evaluation strategy. Moreover, the shortcomings of programme planning mentioned by Wholey could be overcome if evaluability assessment were used as a guide for programme design. Hence, the development of evaluability assessment instruments would be improved. The final goal of evaluability assessment should be to improve evaluations and increase their reliability and usefulness.

References

Berk, R.A. & Rossi, P.H. (1990). *Thinking About Program Evaluation*. Newbury Park, CA: Sage.

Fernández-Ballesteros, R. (1992). A model for planning evaluation research. In Mayne, J., Bemelmans-Videc, M.L., Hudson, J. & Conner, R. (Eds.), *Advancing Public Policy Evaluation*. Amsterdam: North-Holland.

Fernández-Ballesteros, R. & Hernández, J.M. (1995). Listado de Cuestiones Relevantes en Evaluación de Programas (LCREP). In Fernández-Ballesteros, R. (Ed.), *Evaluación de Programas: Una Guía Práctica en Ámbitos Sociales, Educativos y de Salud*. Madrid: Síntesis.

Fernández-Ballesteros, R., Hernández, J.M., Montorio, I., Llorente, G., Izal, M. & Guerrero, M.A. (1989). Evaluability assessment of social programmes and services. Annual Meeting of the American Evaluation Association: New Perspectives from International and Cross-Cultural Evaluation. San Francisco.

House, E.R. (1980). *Evaluating with Validity*. Beverly Hills, CA: Sage.

Muscatello, D.B. (1988). Developing an agenda that works: the right choice at the right time. In McLaughlin, J.A., Weber, L.J., Covert, R.W. & Ingle, R.B. (Eds.), *Evaluation Utilization. New Directions for Program Evaluation*, No. 39. San Francisco: Jossey Bass.

Rossi, P.H. & Freeman, H.E. (1993). *Evaluation. A Systematic Approach*. Newbury Park, CA: Sage.

Rutman, L. (1980). *Planning Useful Evaluations: Evaluability Assessment*. Beverly Hills, CA: Sage.

Shadish, W.R. (1986). Sources of evaluation practice: needs, purposes, questions, and technology. In Bickman, L. & Weatherford, D.L. (Eds.), *Evaluating*

Early Intervention Programs for Severely Handicapped Children and their Families. Austin, TX: Pro-Ed.

Smith, M.F. (1989). *Evaluability Assessment. A Practical Approach*. Boston: Kluwer.

Weiss, C.H. (1972). *Evaluation Research: Methods of Assessing Program Effectiveness*. Englewood Cliffs, NJ: Prentice Hall.

Wholey, J.S. (1983). *Evaluation and Effective Public Management*. Boston: Little, Brown.

Wholey, J.S. (1987): Evaluability assessment: developing program theory. In Bickman, L. (Ed.), *Using Program Theory in Evaluation. New Directions for Program Evaluation*, No. 33. San Francisco: Jossey Bass.

Wholey, J.S., Scanlon, J.W., Duffy, H.B., Fukumoto, J.S. & Vogt, L.M. (1970). *Federal Evaluation Policy: Analyzing the Effects of Public Programs*. Washington, DC: The Urban Institute.

José Manuel Hernández

RELATED ENTRIES

EVALUATION: PROGRAMME EVALUATION (GENERAL)

INTRODUCTION

The relation between psychological assessment and programme evaluation is a reciprocal one: a great many programme evaluations, especially in the educational and mental health fields, use some kind of psychological test, or other psychological methodology such as focus groups, in order to gather data; and, on the other hand, any systematic use of psychological assessment is a programme and hence a candidate for programme evaluation. For example, the use of test-based, simulation-based, or explicit psychological assessment by a clinician in the hiring or promoting process needs to be, and has occasionally been, evaluated seriously, since the impact on the bottom line (and other matters) is in fact quite variable, despite the intuition of many psychologists that it will be positive. Of course, any other changes in procedures at an organization, such as its treatment of customers, or new hires, or minorities, are also good subjects for evaluation, which often yields surprising and potentially useful results. What follows provides coverage of some of the major developments in the field of programme evaluation across the past few decades, during which the national association (American Evaluation Association) has gone from zero to more than 3000 members, and the number of analogous associations in other countries from zero to about 30. It only sketches the details of the actual process of programme evaluation, which is extremely complex in many cases.

PERSPECTIVE ON PROGRAMME EVALUATION

Evaluation can be defined, following the dictionaries, as the systematic determination of merit, worth, or significance (hereafter, m/w/s).[1] Programmes are just one type of target for this process (all targets for evaluation are known as evaluands; when a person or their work – two different though related matters – is being evaluated, the term evaluee is often used). Programme evaluation is thus best understood as one branch of the *applied field* of evaluation: other examples of evaluation that are relevant to readers of this work includes personnel assessment itself, product evaluation (e.g. of test instruments, Scantron alternatives, focus group software), policy studies (e.g. of legislation for controlling drug abuse or programmes claimed to reduce obesity), performance evaluation (e.g. the SAT), and proposal evaluation (e.g. at NSF or NIH) are some others. There are in all about 20 named fields of applied evaluation, many of them outside science but entirely disciplined, e.g. the jurisprudence of appellate courts; others are without significant validity, e.g. aesthetic evaluation of modern art; yet others have partial validity, e.g. literary criticism, where in some genres the plot has to avoid inconsistency.

Two branches of applied evaluation are relatively novel as studies, although ancient practices, and of great importance: (i) meta-evaluation (the evaluation of evaluations), and (ii) intradisciplinary evaluation (the evaluation of methodological entities within a discipline, e.g. data, experimental designs, interpretations). The first of these is important because it demonstrates the self-referent nature of evaluation and, taken seriously, is the field leading to an answer to The Question That Must Be Answered, namely who evaluates the evaluator? The second is important because it makes a farce out of the doctrine of value-free science, since this kind of evaluation, no different in its logic from any other kind, is part of what every psychologist (and other scientist) has been taught for longer than there has been a doctrine of value-free science. To put it bluntly, the difference between science and pseudo-science is the difference between good evidence, good data, good hypotheses, good inferences, etc., and their bad counterparts, which is of course an evaluative difference. Hence, the idea that there was something scientifically improper about evaluation is absurd.

The existence of intradisciplinary evaluation also shows that evaluation skill does not transfer readily between applied fields, since social science PhDs, who originated the value-free doctrine, could not recognize its inconsistency with their own practice. Thus, there were and are sophisticated evaluators who denied the legitimacy of evaluation, hence lacked any skill at meta-evaluation. Meta-analysis, by the way, is quite different: it is the synthesizing of multiple studies of the same or closely related phenomena; the studies might be, but usually are not, themselves evaluative, i.e. their conclusions are typically about descriptive or causal matters, not about merit/worth/significance.

The valid fields or parts of applied fields that make up the widespread disciplined practice of evaluation are characterized by the same underlying logic, and the study of that logic constitutes the *logical theory of evaluation* (sometimes also seen as part of the philosophy of evaluation), a study that has only emerged in quite recent years, whereas the modern phase of programme evaluation – i.e. the period when something like an autonomous applied discipline emerged – began to bloom in the 1960s, much later than the applied field of personnel assessment or product evaluation.

There are also *empirical theories of evaluation*, which are also often referred to as theories of evaluation. For example, there are theories about the circumstances under which the results of (programme) evaluations are influential in policy making, and theories about the personalities or backgrounds of evaluators that use certain models of evaluation.

Programme evaluation is not a simple extension of applied psychology, although it uses many of the tools developed in applied psychology, perhaps most obviously because it necessarily involves combining the results of observation, measurement, and calculation with multiple relevant values, usually starting with needs assessment. Not only the combinatorial process but the latter process, needs assessment are research tasks for which psychologists get little or no training. In fact, competent performance of programme evaluation requires many further skills (more on this below), although it can, and often must, use many of the same ones as well. Of course, as one would expect in such a new field, some of the practice in the field is far from competent by reasonable professional standards, although it is moving in that direction and often performed by those with strong credentials in related fields – sociology, economics, and accounting, as well as management and psychology. There is indeed a set of professional standards, in terms of which such judgements can be made: it was first formulated and published 20 years ago by a committee representing half a dozen professional societies, and since then even more widely endorsed (*The Program Evaluation Standards*, 1994).

In (logical) evaluation theory it is argued that the discipline of evaluation is of a particular kind, a transdiscipline. These are distinctive in that they not only have an autonomous study area and several applied fields, but one of their most important functions is to provide tools for use in some or all other disciplines. Statistics is a transdiscipline that immediately springs to the mind of an applied psychologist, and perhaps measurement would also qualify; in many other areas such as engineering, design is the or a key transdiscipline, and in all areas, logic qualifies. The latest candidate is 'informing science' which is essentially the art or science of presentation, i.e. the organization of knowledge for use and understanding.

PRECURSORS OF PROGRAMME EVALUATION THEORY

Now the transdisciplinary theory of evaluation did not explode into a theoretical vacuum, despite the taboo on the legitimacy of the subject expressed in the widely accepted doctrine of value-free social science. Every field of applied evaluation, e.g. product and programme evaluation, had developed a proto-theory in response to the practical necessity for optimal distribution of resources, e.g. money, scholarships, places in the freshman class, support for the needy. We long ago learnt that looking critically at our own practices, while often reviled as idle theorizing by practitioners, is a major force towards improving practice. Since random distribution of scarce resources does not maximize the return from the relevant investment, evaluation of the alternative distribution approaches is a survival characteristic in the worlds of business, ecosystems, and personal affairs. It was inevitable that there be some attention to developing general principles of good practice, the embryo of most theories. In personnel assessment, these theories included views about the importance and testability of character, skills, dispositions, abilities, nature/nurture, personality, etc. In programme evaluation, they were much more like conventional theories, as we shall see in a moment.

The most serious problem for developing any general accounts, however, was that the social sciences were acting out the century-long farce of the value-free doctrine, although every person in the social sciences was not only evaluating, with some degree of competence, student work, candidates for jobs, papers for journals, and previous work for emulation, extension, or refutation, but also, in their own research, the quality of data, experimental designs, and instruments. Hence, those who might be seen as the most qualified candidates for developing a theory of evaluation were effectively banned from working on that job site. Unfortunately, this meant that the infant evaluation theories, developed by practitioners for their own domains, were reinventing the wheel, repeatedly getting trapped in the same fallacies, etc. What was needed was at least one good theory of one field of evaluation, and some kind of theory of evaluation as a whole.

In the event, it was the field of education rather than the social sciences that first drew attention to the possibility of a highly disciplined study under the heading of (educational) programme evaluation. Tyler deserves some of the first credit, but he was quickly joined and improved on by Stufflebeam, Cronbach, Provus, Stake, Wolf, and a number of others. An excellent account of this

process is given in Worthen, Sanders, and Fitzpatrick (1996). The first general theories of programme evaluation turned up here, often implicit in the theories of educational programme evaluation, along with improvements in standard practice. The US was the centre of much of this early activity, but Scandinavia and the UK were active at about the same time if rarely on the same scale.

EARLY THEORIES OF PROGRAMME EVALUATION

The first of these theories sprang out of the early practice of evaluation, which reflected the need of legislators and programme managers for feedback on the success of their programmes. Thus they identified programme evaluation with whether the programme did what it was supposed to do. This is still a popular substitute for serious programme evaluation, though it's only what serious evaluators would now call programme monitoring. In midstream and at the end of a programme (if it had one), the key questions were 'On Time? On Task? On Budget?' Good questions indeed, and crucial for managers, but not the real core of serious evaluation. However, they became the basis for one of the first 'evaluation models', the Discrepancy Model, due to Malcolm Provus (1967). The methodology of this approach involved three steps: identifying programme goals, converting them into testable claims, and then doing an empirical study to discover the extent to which these goals (educational, social, fiscal, etc.) had been met; the report simply focused on that issue. This approach was and is particularly attractive to social scientists who were brought up on the value-free doctrine because it avoids making any value judgements at all, by merely using those of the client, and converting the evaluation into an empirical exercise. We gradually came to see that this omitted too much of importance to count as serious determination of the m/w/s of the programme. During the programme's run, it should be seen as monitoring; at the end, it is no more than an accountability exercise, both of them worthy but limited undertakings.

To begin the list of shortcomings, there was the explicit rejection of any study of the inevitable and often crucially important unanticipated effects of the programme (side-effects) or of the unanticipated impactees (side-impacts). These were quite often so serious that they led to programmes being cancelled; more rarely they saved programmes that were not achieving their goals, but doing something else that was valuable instead. Then there were crucial issues about whether the programme actually met the needs of the targeted population, or just what someone *thought* were the needs. And there were proper questions about the ethicality of the way the programme operated, e.g. about sexism or racism in its personnel policies; and about the legality of its operation; and about the adequacy of the scientific basis for its justification. And more questions about cost then come up when you're simply looking at the programme's spending vs. its budget; for example, problems about the non-money costs of the programme (morale, time, space, expertise, etc.) and little matters such as whether there exist other and better or cheaper ways to produce the same results.

Eventually, the core of programme evaluation came to be seen as centred on five factors: Outcomes, Process, Costs, Comparisons, and Generalizability (which includes exportability, durability, transferability, etc., and is close to what Don Campbell called external validity). Now, the interpretation and application of these checkpoints is quite complex, as can, for example, be seen from the lengthy discussion of just one of them in the best monographs on cost analysis (e.g. Levin & McEwan, 2001). To the treatment of each must be added the complex further topic of synthesizing them, first with the relevant values, and eventually into an overall conclusion, as is often necessary, e.g. in ranking candidates for jobs or admissions, or programmes for funding. We'll spell out a little more of this process in a moment, but first it is time to look at the underlying theory of evaluation, which provides an essential clarification of the key concepts.

As these further relevant dimensions of evaluation emerged from practice and reflection on practice, other models of programme evaluation began to emerge. Some of these were checklist models, e.g. Stufflebeam and Scriven (2001), some focused on particular processes, e.g. transactional, adversary, empowerment, or the theoretical foundations of the programme. A good survey of this complex developmental process is provided by Worthen, Sanders and Fitzpatrick (1996).

A GENERAL THEORY OF EVALUATION

It was not until the late 1980s that the idea of a general, i.e. all-encompassing, discipline of evaluation was put forward (Scriven, 1991). Earlier efforts at a general theory of values or valuation by philosophers under the heading of axiology or deontic logic did not lead to any significant payoff for practice. The general theory of evaluation involves a small set of concepts, and some principles involving them, described below. What it does not cover, of course (since it is a theoretical discipline), is the extremely complex field of evaluation methodology and praxis, with which every evaluation practitioner is necessarily involved – people doing psychological assessment as well as those doing programme evaluation – and the empirical theories of evaluation, including the psychology of evaluation, the sociology of the profession and its clients, and its economics. The intensely practical nature of programme evaluation affected the development of theories of programme evaluation in what might be thought of this second phase of their development, the phase that went beyond mere local generalizations.

THE LOGIC OF EVALUATION

Serious evaluation is, as indicated above, the attempt to determine m/w/s in as systematic and objective a way as is possible. (m/w/s are roughly the same, respectively, as quality, value, and importance.) There are at least forty other terms in the language that are approximately equivalent to or involve these, at least in some contexts: evaluation is a deeply rooted part of human life and thought. The first conceptual point to make is that merit/quality does not, whereas worth/value does (in the most common usage), involve bringing in costs. Significance/importance involves bringing in a large number of contextual considerations, which differ hugely as between, e.g., discussions of what should count as significant events in Einstein's life vs. significant progress on a doctoral dissertation. This is not a sign of fatal imprecision, just of the high context-dependence of practical language, as used by scientists as well as citizens.

These three properties are the ones with which evaluation is concerned. What are the logical and practical processes in which they are involved, i.e. how are they applied? There are four important types of systematic evaluation process that come into every applied field of evaluation: grading, ranking, scoring, and apportioning (a.k.a. allocating, distributing). All are part of common practices, but rarely defined precisely. In programme evaluation, as in personnel evaluation, one must try to clarify which of these is the required type of conclusion before designing an evaluation to reach that type of conclusion. All too often, clients – and sometimes evaluators – think that a particular test or study is going to yield grades (criterion-referencing) when at most it can yield ranks (norm-referencing).

There are also four 'natural types' of value claim that cross-cut the four processes, again familiar ones. These are (i) personal preferences ('X likes A'); (ii) market values, a hypothetical construct from group preferences ('This house is worth US$600,000'); (iii) contextually evaluative claims, which are intrinsically factual but in context evaluative (e.g. 'This drug abuse programme is very appealing to Native Americans, but not to Hispanics'); and (iv) the essentially evaluative claim, where the claim has a factual or logical foundation other than personal or group preferences. For example, such a claim might refer to a human need, e.g. 'Daily amounts of X units of Vitamin C are good for your health'; to the results of testing, e.g. 'Kathy is a better 400 m. runner than Joan'; or to mathematical standards, e.g. 'The right answer to the question asking for the square root of 81 is 9.' This is a type of claim which every one of us was taught to use as part of the language, as in 'It's very bad to say mean things about other people without good reason' (or, '... to conclude that causation has been established when all you have is evidence of correlation.') The claim that evaluation can lead to objective conclusions refers to this fourth type of value claim and is itself an essentially (a.k.a. intrinsically, definitionally) evaluative claim. Much of the scepticism about the legitimacy of evaluation was based on confusing type (i) with type (iv): but preference claims are not claims of intersubjective, testable, value. Of course, in some areas, e.g. wine-tasting or art criticism, many of what are put forward as objective evaluations are, in fact, nothing more than dressed-up preference claims; but one does not judge a field by its incompetents or physics would be in a sorry state.

With that basic conceptual primer under our belts, we are in a position to understand that the aim of programme evaluation is to establish type (iv) truths about the m/w/s of programmes with the same degree of scientific objectivity as truths about their causation. It's on balance a little harder because type (iv) claims usually include plenty of causal claims, whereas the reverse is not true (at least not in the same way). The five core dimensions of programme performance (process, outcomes, costs, comparisons, generalizability) are matched up to the values and standards from about a dozen sources that have substantial relevance and objectivity; and the integration of these five sub-evaluations, if required, is then done using a procedure called qualitative weight and sum. The sources of value, not all of substantial importance for every evaluation (but all must be checked to see if this is true), include: (i) needs of the impacted population, via a needs assessment; (ii) criteria of merit for entities of this type, from definitions, standard usage, and expert practice; (iii) legal and (iv) ethical requirements; (v) descriptive accuracy requirements (the 'index of implementation'); (vi) personal and organizational goals; (vii) professional standards, (viii) logical (e.g. consistency) requirements, (ix) legislative, (x) scientific, (xi) market, (xii) expert judgement, (xiii) historical/traditional/cultural standards. How can any of these value standards be objective? Well, the easy ones are matters of law, logic, science, and descriptive accuracy (is this evaluand an example of what it claims to be, e.g. Sloan's Reading to Write?). The ethics to use is normally the ethics embodied in our constitution and Bill of Rights, but in other cultures it will be somewhat different (this does not imply accepting ethical relativism). The needs assessment is a special part of evaluation, and a long way from wants assessment because needs are objectively determinable states of the individual and/or society, not mere wants; the need for children to imbibe vitamins is a good example of the difference, and cases from education or law enforcement illustrate the same point. Needs in those areas may be less easily determined but that's a measurement problem, not an essential problem with evaluation; the need for a child to learn to read, in our society, is no harder to demonstrate than the need for vitamins.

The reader will see that serious programme evaluation is a complex business, of which the measurement and observation components are important but not the major part. They are just partners with the value analysis and combinatorial procedures. Beyond that cognitive content, it is also important to realize that, as with psychotherapy, the book learning is only part of good practice: various management, negotiating, and people skills are also involved, to a degree that varies, depending on the project and its context, from almost nothing to almost everything. Some enthusiasts argue that programme evaluation skill is essentially and necessarily a matter of people skills, but this is simply false. Much important programme evaluation is done as part of the routine work of the offices of legislative analysts and philanthropic foundations, by people sitting at their desks and studying data and reports. Of course, there is plenty of room and need for people skills in the broad domain of programme evaluation, just as there is room for them in the broad domain of statistics or game theory, without any need to suppose that either domain lacks solid logical foundations. At the moment, however, too much time is spent arguing about procedural matters such as the extent to which the staff of a programme under evaluation should take an active part in the evaluation. Those are interesting matters, but secondary to the question of the correct core logic for identifying the needed data and combinatorial procedures. The problem at the moment is that all the people skills in the world are no substitute for the getting the logic right, and that is still uncommon. For example, the standard 'commonsense' procedure for combining performance scores and weights to determine the most meritorious of several evaluands, which consists of allocating numerical values to the weights and standardizing the scores on a numerical scale (the so-called quantitative weight and sum approach), is in fact invalid. It presupposes an interval scale for the weights which is highly unrealistic. (A more detailed discussion of this will be found in Scriven, 1991.)

FUTURE PERSPECTIVES AND CONCLUSIONS

Evaluative conclusions, like explanatory and causal ones, can sometimes be mere matters of skilled observation (as when a chess master judges a move to be brilliant or injudicious), but in the case of programme evaluation they are much more likely to be matters of very complex inference. We have now reached the point where we know what the premises have to be – data about performance on certain specifiable dimensions, and values data of certain specifiable types – and it is now known how to get this data and how to combine the two types in order to get the required kind of conclusion. But there is still a long way to go in getting this into the formal training courses and standard practice of evaluators. Even identifying the dimensions along which performance is to be measured, i.e. the criteria of merit, is a special skill that has not yet been well attended to in most training programmes for evaluators; and the synthesis procedure, including weighting and resolving conflicts between competing values, requires new techniques that are hardly known in the evaluation community. We may look forward to increasing attention to these matters as evaluation matures.

We should also expect increasing payoffs from the application of the logic of evaluation to intradisciplinary evaluation in applied psychology. Of course, the 30-year history of the significance test controversy (Morrison, 1970) and the 20-year boom in meta-analysis illustrate how this has long been a latent theme in psychology, but there are many more opportunities and needs for it. An example is provided in Scriven (2001).

Beyond that, there are huge areas in the other disciplines, from history to economics, where intradisciplinary as well as programme evaluation have a high degree of applicability. And we should expect to see the fundamental principles trickling down into undergraduate and pre-college education, for evaluation is part of everyone's life, and changing the way in which people make choices between jobs or major purchase options offers a great deal of room for substantial improvement in the quality of life.

In the end, however, the greatest effect of programme evaluation, and evaluation theory in general, is that it will force social scientists and especially psychologists to treat ethics itself as a complex element in social science. This is a long overdue epiphany for psychology and an inevitable consequence of two forces: the work on game theory, decision theory, and evolutionary psychology, on the one hand, which forces one to see the underlying rationale of ethics; and doing serious programme evaluation, on the other, which forces one to deal with ethics in the particular. In the long run, then, the future of psychology will be massively changed by the necessity for dealing with programme evaluation, and hence ethics, as an essential element in any serious attempt to make applied psychology useful.

Note

1   Amusingly, the great 20 volume Oxford English Dictionary (2nd ed.) (Oxford University Press, 1989), the doyen of them all, mistakenly reports that evaluation simply means determining real estate taxes. (I have registered a complaint, and had it accepted for the third edition; and its little brother, the Shorter Oxford a mere two volumes, has it more or less right.)

References

Levin, H.M. & McEwan, P.J. (2001). *Cost-Effectiveness Analysis: Methods and Applications.* Thousand Oaks, CA: Sage.

Morrison, D.E. (1970). *The Significance Test Controversy: A Reader.* Amsterdam: Walter de Gruyter.
Provus, M. (1967). *Discrepancy Evaluation.* McCutchan.
Scriven, M. (1991). *Evaluation Thesaurus* (4th ed.). Newbury Park, CA: Sage.
Scriven, M. (2001). Assessing six assumptions about assessment. In Henry, I., Braun, D.E. & Wiley, M. (Eds.), *The Role of Constructs in Psychological and Educational Measurement.* Hillsdale, NJ: Lawrence Erlbaum Associates.
Stufflebeam, D. & Scriven, M. (2001). http://www.wmich.edu/evalctr/checklists/
Worthen, B.R., Sanders, J.R. & Fitzpatrick, J.L. (1996). *Program Evaluation.* London: Addison Wesley Longman.
The Joint Committee on Standards for Educational Evaluation (1994). *The Program Evaluation Standards* (2nd ed.). Thousand Oaks, CA: Sage.

Michael Scriven

RELATED ENTRIES

Evaluation in Higher Education, Evaluability Assessment, Needs Assessment, Outcome Assessment/Treatment Assessment, Outcome Evaluation in Neuropsychological Rehabilitation, Goal Attainment Scaling (GAS), Total Quality Management

EVALUATION IN HIGHER EDUCATION

INTRODUCTION

Although there are many different approaches to programme evaluation in higher education, there is nonetheless a general agreement regarding its main objective. Programme evaluation in higher education is the systematic process of obtaining relevant information which is then used to make decisions in regard to different university domains (i.e. research, services, teaching, departments, programmes, etc.). This decision-making process should be based on scientific methodology according to valid and reliable data. In addition, and under the premises of utility, feasibility, propriety, and accuracy, the results obtained should enable institutions to improve practices in order to achieve excellence in their activities and processes (Volkwein et al., 1995).

The implementation of programme evaluation in higher education is difficult for three reasons. First, due to the peculiar characteristics of university context, there is a low degree of institutional autonomy in decision-making, coupled with inefficient communication systems. Second, it is difficult to define programme evaluation in this complex context. Critical groups with different interests (researchers, administrative staff, teachers, students, etc.) have different evaluation objectives, which are not always measurable; it is sometimes difficult to determine who controls the evaluation process. Third, faculty or staff in units being evaluated are often fearful because evaluation can imply cutting back on resources (Ruby, 1990). These difficulties have brought about the need to develop procedures to obtain a continuous flow of relevant and useful information with regard to university input, context, resources, processes, and results.

MAIN EVALUATION PRACTICES IN HIGHER EDUCATION

It is difficult to find an evaluation of the whole university; usually, evaluations are applied to specific faculties, departments, or programmes. The following four evaluation practices can be complementary and can even be used at the same time:

- Accreditation, which involves state or regional licensing of qualified colleges and universities to carry out their activities. Usually it is specific to studies and/or programmes. Through this process, predefined standards or criteria of performance are verified within institutions of higher learning.
- Self-studies, involving a process of evaluation through an institution's internal audience with the aim of moving towards a process of self-improvement. These studies stimulate self-observation as well as the detection of weaknesses within the system.
- Formalization of systems of indicators through the operationalization of the institutional objectives, processes, resources, contexts and results into observable quantitative or qualitative variables. By measuring these variables, information is obtained which allows for the assessment of the evaluated areas (Oakes, 1986; Chacón, Pérez-Gil, Holgado & Lara, 2001).
- 'Peer review', in which a group of recognized experts in the field of university evaluation is asked to judge the merits of the institution under evaluation (Frazer, 1997).

In practice, a combination of the above evaluation practices are used. Thus, it is often found that an institution may use the peer review process while at the same time indicators are set up and viewed to counteract any possible subjectivity on the part of the peer reviewers. This mixture of evaluative practices implies that there is a high degree of flexibility in the application of different strategies and measurement instruments for obtaining data. The main measurement instruments used in these mixed evaluative practices are interviews, the analysis of written documents, application of systems of categories and field formats, as well as the use of semi-standard and standard evaluation instruments (Porter, 1991).

All of these approximations and alternative approaches to evaluation in higher education are framed within a global concept of institutional evaluation. Therefore, evaluation in higher education implies a global assessment of its educational, research, and management processes. When considering programme evaluation in higher education from this global perspective, and taking into account the low degree of institutional autonomy in decision-making, coupled with inefficient communication systems, the need for commitment on the part of the different parties involved in the evaluation process becomes paramount.

MAIN THEORETICAL EVALUATION MODELS IN HIGHER EDUCATION

The United States is the country which has traditionally most frequently used programme evaluation in higher education. The predominant programme evaluation model used in the United States is accreditation.

Although receiving public funding depends on accreditation, the process of accreditation in universities in the United States is voluntary. Programme evaluation in the United States does not always end with accreditation. The different stages of the accreditation process are as follows (Kells, 1988):

(a) Self-study/evaluation of the curricula/ programmes offered by the university (although usually not all university programmes have to be accredited).
(b) The institution is visited by a group of experts which writes up a report according to given standards.
(c) The evaluated institution is allowed to comment on the report made by the technical accreditation committee.
(d) According to the results of the report, the accreditation committee grants the corresponding licence.

The programme evaluation model in higher education followed by most European countries is that used in the Netherlands. Their main difference is that the European model does not end with the accreditation of a university or a programme. But, nowadays there is a tendency to implement the accreditation system in European universities, at least in certain university areas (i.e. health programmes that gives doctors licences, counselling, psychology programmes, or education programmes that give teachers licences). As seen in Figure 1, six stages can be clearly delineated in the model from the Netherlands:

(a) Internal evaluation: different types of data (statistics, opinions, input, process, and results indicators) are gathered and integrated into a global evaluation report by an internal evaluation committee.

(b) External evaluation: an external evaluation committee revises the internal evaluation report and then visits the institution being evaluated.

(c) Self-evaluation report: a final report is made based on the findings of the internal evaluation and the external evaluation committee. This report is then published and public notification is given.

(d) Meta-evaluation: in order to validate the process of evaluation and to provide a context for improvement plans, a large-scale analysis of the process of evaluation is carried out.

(e) Improvement project: different quality improvement activities are proposed in order to increase the quality of input, processes, and results of the evaluated institution.

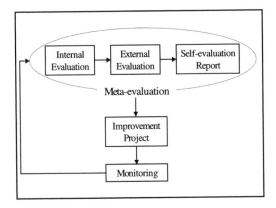

Figure 1. Evaluation model of higher education in the Netherlands.

(f) Follow-up and evaluation of the improvement project: the degree of implementation of the proposed improvement activities is evaluated, thus initiating a process of continuous evaluation of quality in higher education.

VIEWPOINTS OF QUALITY IN PROGRAMME EVALUATION IN HIGHER EDUCATION

As we have previously stated, the concept of quality as an evaluative reference is normally used to judge the different areas in higher education, and based on this judgement, actions are taken (Segers & Dochy, 1996; Chacón, Pérez-Gil, Holgado & Lara, 2001). There are three principal viewpoints of quality applied to programme evaluation in higher education.

First, the European Foundation for Quality Management (EFQM) focuses on eight areas in which to evaluate quality.

(a) Leadership: university authorities' commitment to transmitting a culture of quality management.

(b) Planning and strategy: how continuous improvement objectives are defined in order to subsequently translate them into concrete actions.

(c) Personnel management: the degree of personnel participation found in achieving improvements, in planning and in the development of human potential, in the process of assigning responsibility, in decision making, and in communication.

(d) Resources: identification, selection, use and maintenance of the available resources used to promote higher levels of quality.

(e) Processes: how to identify, evaluate, and improve key processes.

(f) Satisfaction level of the involved parties.

(g) Impact on society: to what extent are the demands, needs, and expectations of society met.

(h) Results/objectives achievement.

This European model has been standardized for education according to the rules of the International Standardization Organization (ISO). See also 'Total Quality Management' entry for a more extensive description of this model.

The other two models of quality evaluation delineate additional domains of quality. The Japanese evaluation model includes the following domains: policies and planning; organization and control; education and quality control implementation; quality information recording, transmission and use of quality information; analysis; standardization; quality control guarantee; results; and future planning. On the other hand, the American model of quality evaluation emphasizes leadership; information and analysis; quality planning; management and development of human resources; quality management in processes; operational results; and quality and client satisfaction.

In summary, quality evaluation of higher education should include different interrelated domains. Following the classic Stufflebeam's CIPP model, the evaluation of quality in education, research, and services in higher education should include the analysis of interrelated elements from context, input, processes, and products, all of which are considered as components from the same system. In addition, quality evaluation must strive to achieve the following conditions: obtaining comparable results; be feasible, be realistic and accepted by different audiences; be flexible; allow continuous evaluation; be oriented towards clients' demands; be oriented towards continuous improvements; be useful to the institution; and obtaining weighted quality domains (Benson, Hinn & Lloyd, 2001).

FUTURE PERSPECTIVES

Programme evaluation in higher education is going to be one of the most important applied areas of evaluation in the 21st century because evaluation will become a useful tool in developing cost-effective measures and in analysing the effectiveness of resources invested in higher education (Desautels, 1997).

Evaluation in higher education will be focused on international studies in order to compare quality evaluation and management systems between different countries (Brennan & Shah, 2000). These studies will be complementary to meta-studies of the evaluation processes in higher education in order to analyse their feasibility (Yorke, 1998).

Education and research will continue to be the most important domains evaluated in higher education, but quality management excellence will also play an important role (Heck, Johnsrud & Rosser, 2000). In addition, needs assessment in society will be in increasing demand in order to develop university services that respond to societal demands (Broadfoot, 1998).

CONCLUSIONS

The conceptualization of higher education has undergone huge changes. Currently, universities are considered to be complex systems requiring a large-scale analysis in order to respond to societal needs. Programme evaluation in higher education plays a key role in coordinating the interests of universities, social agents, and governments.

The concept of university quality has become the evaluative criteria of merit to make decisions regarding different university domains. In summary, programme evaluation in higher education endeavours to implement continuous improvement systems based on the systematic collection of data from the different university domains.

References

Benson, A., Hinn, M. & Lloyd, C. (2001). *Visions of Quality: How Evaluators Define, Understand and Represent Program Quality*. Amsterdam: JAI Press.

Brennan, J. & Shah, T. (2000). Quality assessment and institutional changes: experiences from 14 countries. *Higher Education*, 40(3), 331–349.

Broadfoot, P. (1998). Quality standards and control in higher education: what price life-long learning? *International Studies in Sociology of Education*, 8(2), 155–179.

Chacón, S., Pérez-Gil, J.A., Holgado, F.P. & Lara, A. (2001). Evaluation of quality in higher education: content validity. *Psicothema*, 13(2), 294–301.

Desautels, L.D. (1997). Evaluation as an essential component of 'value-for-money'. In Chelimsky, E. & Shadish, W.R. (Eds.), *Evaluation for the 21st Century: A Handbook* (pp. 72–79). London: Sage Publications.

Frazer, M. (1997). Report on the modalities of external evaluation of higher education in Europe: 1995–1997. *Higher Education in Europe*, XXII(3), 349–401.

Heck, R.H., Johnsrud, L.K. & Rosser, V.J. (2000). Administrative effectiveness in higher education: improving assessment procedures. *Research in Higher Education*, 41(6), 663–684.

Kells, H.R. (1988). *Self-Study Processes*. New York: Macmillan.

Oakes, J. (1986). *Educational Indicators: A Guide for Policymakers*. Wisconsin: Center for Policy Research in Education.

Porter, A.C. (1991). Creating a system of school process indicators. *Educational Evaluation and Policy Analysis*, 13(1), 13–29.

Ruby, A. (1990). The Australian national project on indicators in education. *International Journal of Educational Research*, 14(4), 401–408.

Segers, M. & Dochy, F. (1996). Quality assurance in higher education: theoretical considerations and empirical evidence. *Studies in Educational Evaluation*, 22, 115–137.

Volkwein, J., Farmer, D., Fernández, T., Hernández, D., Lee, M., Nettles, M. & Gerald, W.P. (1995).

Framework for Outcomes Assessment. Albany: Commission on Higher Education.

Yorke, M. (1998). The management of assessment in higher education. *Assessment and Evaluation in Higher Education*, 23(2), 101–116.

Salvador Chacón Moscoso and
Francisco Pablo Holgado Tello

RELATED ENTRIES

APPLIED FIELDS: EDUCATION, EVALUATION: PROGRAMME EVALUATION (GENERAL), TOTAL QUALITY MANAGEMENT

EXECUTIVE FUNCTIONS DISORDERS

INTRODUCTION

Executive functions are those which regulate, control and direct human behaviour. Mental activity and human behaviour would not be possible without a system to control, organize and direct them. The executive system ensures that the different cognitive and emotional subsystems function in a coordinated way as they activate and deactivate the different functional circuits implicated in any human activity. The concept of executive function can be studied in Luria's (1966) *Higher Cortical Function in Man*, which was popularized in neuropsychology by Lezak (1976) and further developed by Fuster (1980) and Stuss and Benson (1986).

According to Lezak (1995: 42), executive functions are those abilities which allow an individual to function with independence, with a set goal, and with self-sufficient behaviour in a satisfactory manner. As long as the executive functions are intact, an individual may lose important cognitive abilities yet continue to be independent, constructively self-sufficient and productive. However, and no matter the state of the cognitive functions, should the executive functions become impaired, one is no longer able to care for oneself, to work for oneself or others, nor to maintain normal social relationships.

Executive functions are to be considered as different from the cognitive functions. The latter specifically refer to the reception and generation of information or to the stimulation received from any of the senses. Cognitive functions are attention, perception, language, memory, mental images, or higher motor functions. Executive functions are concerned with the organization of cognition and emotion and, when necessary, in their timing. Thus, cognitive impairment will especially affect the functional area involved, while executive impairment will affect the controlling functions and will therefore be reflected in a more general way in the individual's behaviour.

The anterior part of the brain is of extraordinary importance in the coordination and integration of the cognitive activity carried out in the posterior part of the brain. This is especially so with regard to the components of anticipation, initiating activity and even for decision-making. The frontal cortex is at the highest level within the hierarchy of the neural structures dedicated to the representation and performance of the activities of the organism. There are three prefrontal functions that ensure the integrity and purpose of all the novel and complex sequences of goal-directed behaviour. Two are chiefly based in the dorsolateral cortex (preparatory set and working memory) and the other in the orbital cortex (inhibitory control). The prefrontal cortex is the anatomical basis of these control functions, especially when active control is required during the process of learning a new activity. Once the activity becomes routine, the active control is carried out by another brain area and not necessarily by the prefrontal cortex (León-Carrión & Barroso y Martín, 1997; Shallice, 1982).

A revision of the specialized literature concerning problem solving, planning, prospective, control and performance associates these functions with the frontal lobe due to how these functions are affected when injury is incurred in this area of the brain, and especially in the prefrontal areas (León-Carrión, 1997; Lezak, 1995).

The classic tests that have most commonly been used to assess these functions are the *Stroop Test* (Stroop, 1935; León-Carrión, 1998), sorting tasks such as the *Wisconsin Card Sorting Test* (Grant & Berg, 1948), category tasks such as the *Category Test* (Halstead, 1947), problem solving tasks such as in the different versions of the *Tower of Hanoi* (Anzai & Simon, 1979; León-Carrión et al., 1991; and León-Carrión, 1998) or maze tests such as the *Porteus Maze Test* (Porteus, 1959). A good set of clinical frontal tasks for frontal lobe deficits are those from *Luria/Christensen's Neuropsychological Investigation* (Christensen, 1975).

Currently, neuropsychologists specialized in clinical practice affirm that highly structured tests are not sufficiently sensitive to be able to detect deficits that are observed when evaluating goal directed behaviour. Given that this ability is best evaluated with the use of loosely structured tests in which the subject must work actively in order to discover their rules and principles, their use is encouraged by clinical neuropsychologists (León-Carrión, 1995).

THE STROOP TEST

The Stroop Test is of interest in evaluating resistance to cognitive interference. The test is based on the Stroop effect and consists of asking the subject to respond to only one of the parts of which the stimulus is made up, inhibiting the response to the other part. The subject is shown the name of a colour written in a colour different from the colour named and asked to say the name of the colour in which the word is written. For example, the subject may be shown the word RED written in green and the subject must respond by saying GREEN. The subject must therefore inhibit the reading process and activate the colour recognition process.

Some consider this to be a divided attention test. It is considered to measure the ability and speed with which the frontal lobes inhibit and activate. The different specialists who have presented the most relevant research done with this test agree that the different mechanisms of divided attention, the functioning of activation/inhibition mechanisms, and the functioning of the neurocognitive interference mechanism can be studied with it. Different authors have shown with neuroimaging techniques that the right frontal regions, in particular the right anterior cingulate gyrus (zones 23, 24, 32) and the right orbital zones (10 and 47), are involved during the Stroop Test (Bench et al., 1983; Pardo et al., 1990).

There are several different pen and pencil versions of the classic *Stroop Words and Colours Test*, which was originally designed to study perceptive interference. However, a computerized adaptation of this classic is included in the Seville Neuropsychological Battery (BNS) (León-Carrión, 1998). Eight subtests are used in the BNS to observe the following described mechanisms: (1) identification of monochromatic colours; (2) identification of blocks of colour; (3) identification of colour ignoring content (both eyes); (4) identification of content ignoring colour (both eyes); (5) identification of colour ignoring content (left eye); (6) identification of content ignoring colour (left eye); (7) identification of colour ignoring content (right eye); (8) identification of content ignoring colour (right eye).

THE WISCONSIN CARD SORTING TEST

The purpose of this test is to measure the capacity of abstract thought, concept formation, and cognitive flexibility, all components of executive function associated with the frontal lobe. Both the computerized and manual versions present subjects with four stimulus cards whose figures are different from the others based on criteria of form, colour or number of elements presented on the card. With the four cards displayed before him/her, the subject is shown one card at a time and must match it according to one of three different criteria of which s/he is not previously informed. After a pre-determined number of consecutive successful matches, the matching criteria is changed without informing the subject, who is then obliged to change his/her matching strategies in order to achieve successful matches under the new criteria.

Clinical experience with this test has shown that subjects with frontal deficits generally exhibit large numbers of errors of perseveration and great difficulty in changing criteria, especially patients with left dorsolateral frontal lesions. The test requires the ability to recognize changes in conditions, and cognitive flexibility, in order to learn from experience and received information.

THE TOWER OF HANOI–SEVILLE

In following with the principle of using loosely structured tests, together with ease of correction and interpretation, the BNS has incorporated a computerized version of the *Tower of Hanoi*. Due to the modifications made, in this version the test receives the name of Tower of Hanoi–Seville (León-Carrión et al., 1991; León-Carrión, 1998). The trial consists of a transformation problem in which a final goal must be achieved by carrying out a series of non-routine movements in which ordered planning strategies and complex problem solving abilities must be applied. Subjects must establish a plan and then carry it out and reach the correct solution. This plan must include a global solution that is divided into various sub-solutions that are sequenced over a period of time in order to achieve the main objective. All of these planning abilities directed towards solving a complex problem are seriously affected in lesions affecting the frontal lobe after sustaining traumatic brain injury and can be observed in this task (Barroso y Martín et al., 1999).

The task consists of three parallel pegs that are numbered 1, 2 and 3 from left to right. There are discs of different sizes and colours (from 3 to 5, chosen by the tester) on peg number 1. These discs form a pyramid with the largest at the bottom and the smallest at the top. The goal of the task is to move the different discs by pressing the number key on the computer that corresponds to the number on the peg until a tower is formed that is the same as the original tower on peg number 3. In the Seville version of the Tower of Hanoi, two different types of administration can be observed, A and B. The difference between the two is that one allows the subject to be informed of the

principles and rules of the task while the other does not. Administration type A best describes problem solving functioning given that the subject must discover the rules and principles of the task in order to correctly solve it.

CATEGORY TEST

The Category Test is included in the Halstead–Reitan Battery (Halstead, 1947) and according to its authors evaluates concept formation. The purpose is to determine a subject's ability to make use of both positive and negative information in such a way as to serve as a basis to modify activity or behaviour in order to correctly solve a problem or task. The original test consists of 208 stimuli displayed on a screen and a response panel related to the stimuli. The subject must mark the correct response associated with the stimulus being displayed. A sound will indicate whether the subject has chosen a correct or incorrect response. The test is divided into seven groups, each one of which must be completed. The sound is the feedback which guides the subject towards improved performance. Subjects with frontal lesions generally persevere in their errors and exhibit difficulties in finding the keys to the correct responses, as well as in making spontaneous cognitive changes in problem solving strategies.

OTHER TESTS FOR EXECUTIVE FUNCTIONING ASSESSMENT

One of the sub-tests of the *Halstead/Reitan Battery*, the Trail Making Test in part B, is considered to be a good indicator of the mental control associated with executive functioning. In this test, the subject must alternately join circled numbers to circled letters scattered over a sheet of paper, following a numeric and alphabetic sequence. Another test that is good for indicating frontal functioning is the *Porteus Maze Test*. Results with this test show that subjects with frontal lesions tend to become lost in the mazes and/or unable to find the exit, or have great difficulty in finding it. From a qualitative point of view, the *Luria/Christensen* tasks can be used for frontal lesions, especially the following: tapping rhythm, alternating figures or verbal regulation of motor movement.

FUTURE PERSPECTIVES AND CONCLUSIONS

The complex evaluation of all of the components of executive functioning is an important challenge to be addressed during the coming years. Conjoining neuroimaging, cognitive and behavioural testing will be an invaluable aid to neuropsychologists in achieving more complete and integrative instruments. The search for a frontal lobe battery has not as yet come to an end, although the theoretical aspects regarding executive functions are becoming more firmly established and current tests afford useful information both for diagnosis and rehabilitation.

References

Anzai, Y. & Simon, H.A. (1979). The theory of learning by doing. *Psychological Review*, 86, 124–140.

Barroso y Martín, J.M., León-Carrión, J. & Murillo, F. (1999). Funcionamiento ejecutivo y capacidad para la resolución de problemas en pacientes con traumatismos craneoencefálicos. *Revista Española de Neuropsicología*, 1(1), 3–20.

Bench, C.J., Frith, C.D., Grasby, P.M., Friston, K.J., Pulesu, E., Frackowiak, R.S., Benton, A.L., Hamsher, K. deS., Varney, N.R. & Spreen, O. (1983). *Contributions to Neuropsychological Assessment*. New York: Oxford University Press.

Christensen, Anne-Lise (1975). *Luria's Neuropsychological Investigation*. Copenhagen: Munksgaard.

Fuster, J.M. (1980). *The Prefrontal Cortex*. New York: Raven.

Grant, D.A. & Berg, E.A. (1948). A behavioural analysis of the degree of reinforcement and ease of shifting to new responses in a Weigl-type card sorting problem. *Journal of Experimental Psychology*, 38, 404–411.

Halstead, W.C. (1947). *Brain and Intelligence*. Chicago: University of Chicago Press.

León-Carrión, J. (1995). *Manual de Neuropsicología Humana [Handbook of Human Neuropsychology]*. Madrid: Siglo XXI Editores.

León-Carrión, J. (1997). *Neuropsychological Rehabilitation: Fundamentals, Directions, and Innovations*. del Ray Beach, FL: St. Lucie Press.

León-Carrión, J. (1998). *Sevilla Neuropsychological Test Battery*. Madrid: TEA Ediciones (American version distributed by HDA, Houston).

León-Carrión, J. & Barroso y Martín (1997). *Neuropsicología del Pensamiento: Lóbulo Frontal y Control Ejecutivo*. Sevilla: Kronos.

León-Carrión, J., Morales, M., Forastero, P., Domínguez-Morales, M.R., Murillo, F., Jiménez-Baco, R. & Gordon, P. (1991). The computerized Tower of Hanoi: a new form of administration and suggestions for interpretation. *Perceptual and Motor Skills*, 73, 63–66.

Lezak, M.D. (1976). *Neuropsychological Assessment* (1st ed.). New York: Oxford University Press.

Lezak, M.D. (1995). *Neuropsychological Assessment*. (3rd ed.). New York: Oxford University Press.

Luria, A.R. (1966). *Higher Cortical Function in Man*. New York: Basic Books.

Pardo, J.V., Pardo, P.S., Janer, K.W. and Raicle, M.E. (1990). The anterior cingulate cortex mediates processing selection in the Stroop attentional conflict paradigm. *Proc. Natl. Acad. Sci. USA*, 87, 256–259.

Porteus, S.D. (1959). *The Maze Test and Clinical Psychology*. Palo Alto, CA: Pacific Books.

Shallice, T. (1982). Specific impairments of planning. *Philosophical Transactions of the Royal Society of London*, 298, 199–209.

Stroop, J.R. (1935). Studies of interference in serial verbal reactions. *Journal of Experimental Psychology*, 18, 643–662.

Stuss, D.T. & Benson, D.F. (1986). *The Frontal Lobes*. New York: Raven Press.

José León-Carrión

RELATED ENTRIES

APPLIED FIELDS: NEUROPSYCHOLOGY, VOLUNTARY MOVEMENT, NEUROPSYCHOLOGICAL TEST BATTERIES

E XPLANATION

INTRODUCTION

Psychological assessment serves several functions: classification, explanation, prediction, and decision aid. Classification means the assignment of the single case to be assessed to an element or category of a classification system, as shown by, for example, the DSM or the ICD. Prediction aims at an answer to the question of what will happen in the future, if the single case concerned is treated in specific ways. And decision aid means supporting the selection of an optimal treatment for the single case, i.e. a treatment with the highest benefit or utility in the respective case. Finally, explanation as the topic of this entry is, generally spoken, a statement or account which makes what is to be explained clearer than it was before and promotes its understanding. What is to be explained in psychological assessment are the problems or disorders which occur in the single case concerned. If explanation is at stake, the assessment process can be construed as setting up and testing case-related idiographic hypotheses (Fernández-Ballesteros et al., 2001) which refer to the causes, reasons or conditions which brought about the problems or disorders. The well-confirmed idiographic hypotheses which hopefully come out at the end of such an assessment process make up the explanation or are at least an important part of it.

TYPES OF PSYCHOLOGICAL EXPLANATIONS

Explanations in psychological assessment can be of very different types. Bunge and Ardila (1987) distinguish the following ones for psychology in general: *Tautological explanations* refer to basic capabilities or mental faculties of a person (e.g.: Person p is able to imitate another person because of p's vicarious capability). *Teleological explanations* refer to goals or purposes of a person (e.g.: Person p studied law in order to become a lawyer). *Mentalist explanations* refer to mental events of a person (e.g.: Person p developed a perversion because p suffered from an intrapsychic conflict between id and superego). *Metaphorical explanations* refer to analogies with physical or social processes, or with animals or machines (e.g.: In person p aggressive energy accumulates like heat in a steam boiler). *Genetic explanations* refer to the genetic endowment of a person (e.g.: Person p shows a high musical intelligence because p comes from a family of conductors and composers). *Developmental explanations* refer to stages or levels of biological or psychological development or to events in a person's past (e.g.: Person p suffers from social phobia because p was often rejected by his or her social environment in his or her childhood). *Environmental explanations* refer to external conditions and factors influencing a

person (e.g.: The phobic symptoms of p are weakened because p is massively exposed to the threatening stimuli). *Evolutionary explanations* refer to the survival value of a behaviour or behaviour tendency of a person, its selective advantages or disadvantages (e.g.: Person p has a high pain threshold under duress because of its survival value). *Physiological explanations* refer to physiological, especially neurophysiological and endocrinological, processes and mechanisms of a person (e.g.: The depressive person p experienced an elevation of her or his mood because p took a cyclic antidepressant which increased the chemical neurotransmitter serotonin). *Mixed explanations* are combinations of two or more of the above mentioned types of explanation. Many explanations occurring in psychology are not pure cases of one type, but combinations of at least two types, i.e. they are mixed explanations. Especially in psychological assessment, mixed explanations are not an exception but the rule, since one-sided explanations usually provide only a partial answer to the problem concerned.

In the examples of the different types of psychological explanations, the relation term 'because' occurs. It links that which is to be explained to that which explains. A characterization of this relation is provided by the so-called *models of explanation*.

MODELS OF EXPLANATION

If explanation as a goal of psychological assessment is considered, the case formulation as the result of the respective assessment process can be conceived of as an explanation. This underlines the fundamental similarities between the process of psychological assessment in which idiographic hypotheses are tested and the process of scientific research in which the test of more general hypotheses is at stake. In both cases, explanation is an important goal. In reconstructing explanatory efforts in science, many different models of scientific explanation have been construed, especially in philosophy of science (*cf.* Salmon, 1989). Each model attempts to answer at least two questions: (1) What is (the structure of) an explanation? and (2) What is a good (proper, appropriate, adequate) explanation? Some answers to these questions which are especially important to psychological assessment will be briefly outlined.

The Deductive-Nomological Model of Explanation

According to this classical view, an explanation is an *argument* which shows that the phenomenon to be explained can be inferred from certain other facts by means of specified general laws. This type of argument may be schematized as a deductive inference of the following form (*cf.* Hempel, 1965):

$$
\text{(D-NE)} \quad
\begin{array}{ll}
L_1, L_2, \ldots, L_r & \text{General laws} \\
C_1, C_2, \ldots, C_k & \text{Statements of} \\
 & \text{antecedent} \\
 & \text{conditions} \\
\hline
E & \text{Description of} \\
 & \text{the empirical} \\
 & \text{phenomenon to be} \\
 & \text{explained}
\end{array}
$$

E as the description of the phenomenon to be explained is called the *explanandum (sentence)*. The statements of antecedent conditions, which make assertions about particular facts, and the general laws together form the *explanans*, i.e. that which explains. Explanations of this kind are called explanations by deductive subsumption under general laws, or *deductive-nomological explanations*.

In an application to the domain of psychological assessment, the following correspondences would hold (*cf.* Westmeyer, 1972): the *explanandum* would be the description of the problem or disorder to be explained in the course of the assessment process; the *explanans* would be the case formulation, i.e. the set of confirmed case-related idiographic hypotheses; and the nomological hypotheses would be part of the knowledge base of psychological assessment.

D-NE gives an answer to the question, 'What is (the structure of) an explanation?' A comparison between this structure and the one underlying the examples of the different types of psychological explanations reveals that most of the latter are stated in an elliptical form, viz. 'E because of C'.

The component C refers only to a subset of the antecedent conditions $C_1, C_2, \ldots, C_k$ that are required for a proper explanation of the explanandum E, and the general laws, if there are any at all, are totally omitted in the examples. Thus, explanations of the form 'E because of C' do not count as proper explanations.

To give an answer to the second question, i.e. 'What is a proper explanation?', requires the formulation of *conditions of adequacy*. In the case of the model of deductive-nomological explanation, there are four such conditions (*cf.* Hempel, 1965):

(R1) The explanandum must be a logical consequence of the explanans, i.e. the explanandum must be logically deducible from the information contained in the explanans.

(R2) The explanans must contain general assumptions or hypotheses, and these must actually be required for the derivation of the explanandum.

(R3) The explanans must have empirical content, i.e. it must be capable, at least in principle, of test by experiment or observation.

(R4) The sentences constituting the explanans must be well confirmed.

In an application of D-NE to psychological assessment, these conditions of adequacy would become evaluation criteria for the products of explanatory efforts in the course of an assessment process. But there are good reasons not to rely too much on this model of explanation. It is not easy to find convincing examples of deductive-nomological explanations in psychological assessment that display the proper structure and satisfy the conditions R1 to R4 because universal deterministic laws, as they are required by the model, are hard to find in this domain.

The Statistical-Relevance Model of Probabilistic Explanation

Whereas genuine nomological laws in psychology in general and psychological assessment in particular are an exception, if they exist at all, statements which describe *statistical regularities* between events are the rule. The knowledge base of psychological assessment is made up of statements of this kind. They refer to information about conditional probabilities, differences in central tendencies, correlations, factor structures, etc. '85% of the persons who have a panic disorder and who undergo an exposure therapy experience relief from their symptoms' is an example.

If extended information about conditional probabilities is available, Salmon's (1989) *statistical-relevance model of probabilistic explanation* can be applied. An explanation of an event according to this model is an assemblage of factors that are statistically relevant to the occurence of the event to be explained, accompanied by an associated probability distribution. For a concrete example, see Salmon and Salmon (1979). Although this model has already been applied to the domain of psychological assessment (*cf.* Westmeyer, 1975), it is still too ambitious and requires more knowledge than is available in most cases of psychological assessment. Especially the probability distribution as the probabilistic equivalent to the nomological hypotheses in the deductive-nomological case goes well beyond the knowledge base of psychological assessment at the time being. But there is another model of explanation better suited to what psychological assessment demands and what it has to offer.

The Model of Aleatory Explanations

A more recent model of causal explanations of specific events is the model of aleatory explanation (see Table 1) introduced by Humphreys

Table 1. The canonical form for causal explanations of specific events (*cf.* Humphreys, 1989, pp. 286 ff.)

Request for explanation:
What is the explanation of Y in S at t?

Appropriate explanation:
Y in S at t [occurs, was present] because of Φ
despite Ψ.

Notes:
'Y' is a term referring to a property or change in property.
'S' is a term referring to a system.
't' is a term referring to a time.
'Φ' is a (non-empty) list of terms referring to contributing causes of Y.
'Ψ' is a (possibly empty) list of terms referring to counteracting causes of Y.

(1989). He agrees with Salmon that causal explanations are possible within the realm of chancy, or aleatory, phenomena. But in his model, in contrast to Salmon's, no probability value is assigned to an explanation. The demands on the knowledge base are much lower than in Salmon's model.

What is required for a proper explanation of a specific event Y in S at t are two lists of causes of Y, i.e. a list of *contributing* and a list of *counteracting causes*. In Humphreys' model, for something to be a cause it must invariantly produce its effect. But causes in this model are probabilistic causes, and they produce changes in the value of the *chance* of the effect. A contributing cause of Y produces an increase, a counteracting cause of Y a decrease in the value of the chance of Y.

This model seems to be applicable in various contexts within psychology. It takes account of the fact that psychological phenomena are usually the result of multiple causal influences. And it does not presuppose the existence of complete lists of all influences which, positively or negatively, affect a given outcome. Aleatory explanations are conjunctive. They can be improved by including additional probabilistic causes which may come up in further research.

In an application of this model to the domain of psychological assessment, the selected problem or disorder to be explained can be expressed as a property or a change in property of the single case concerned, i.e. the term 'Y' in Humphreys' model refers to the selected problem or disorder. The term 'S' refers to the single case concerned, and the term 't' to the time at/during which the problem or disorder occurs/is present in the single case concerned. The list 'Φ' in Humphreys' model refers to the set of positive diagnostic findings relative to the selected problem, whereas the list 'Ψ' refers to the set of negative diagnostic findings relative to the selected problem Φ and Ψ together constitute the case formulation.

A diagnostic finding is called a *positive diagnostic finding* relative to Y, if it refers to something which makes the occurrence of Y more probable (i.e. if it refers to a contributing cause of Y); it is called a *negative diagnostic finding* relative to Y, if it refers to something which makes the occurrence of Y less probable (i.e. if it refers to a counteracting cause of Y).

The ascription of these properties to diagnostic findings is part of the knowledge base of psychological assessment.

This model has already been applied to explanations within a theory of social interaction in small groups (Westmeyer, 1996) and has been recommended as an adequate framework for explanatory efforts in psychological assessment in general (*cf.* Westmeyer & Hageboeck, 1992).

FUTURES PERSPECTIVES AND CONCLUSIONS

Explanatory efforts in psychological assessment should rely on realistic and well established models of scientific explanation. These models provide answers to important questions such as: What is the structure of a case formulation, and how to differentiate an adequate case formulation from an inadequate one? Answers to these basic questions are rarely given in traditional discourses in psychological assessment. A profound discussion of these issues with regard to the models introduced in this entry could promote theory and practice of psychological assessment alike.

REFERENCES

Bunge, M. & Ardila, R. (1987). *Philosophy of Psychology*. New York: Springer-Verlag.

Fernández-Ballesteros, R., De Bruyn, E.E.J., Godoy, A., Hornke, L.F., Ter Laak, J., Vizcarro, C., Westhoff, K., Westmeyer, H. & Zaccagnini, J.L. (2001). Guidelines for the assessment process (GAP): a proposal for discussion. *European Journal of Psychological Assessment*, 17(3), 178–191.

Hempel, C.G. (1965). *Aspects of Scientific Explanation*. New York: The Free Press.

Humphreys, P.W. (1989). Scientific explanation: the causes, some of the causes, and nothing but the causes. In Kitcher, P. & Salmon, W.C. (Eds.), *Minnesota Studies in the Philosophy of Science, Vol. XIII: Scientific Explanation*. pp. 283–306. Minneapolis, MN: University of Minnesota Press.

Kitcher, P. & Salmon, W.C. (Eds.) (1989). *Minnesota Studies in the Philosophy of Science, Vol. XIII: Scientific Explanation*. Minneapolis, MN: University of Minnesota Press.

Salmon, W.C. (1989). Four decades of scientific explanation. In Kitcher, P. & Salmon, W.C. (Eds.), *Minnesota Studies in the Philosophy of Science, Vol. XIII: Scientific Explanation*. (pp. 3–219). Minneapolis, MN: University of Minnesota Press.

Salmon, W.C. and Salmon, M.H. (1979). Alternative models of scientific explanation. *American Anthropologist*, 81, 61–74.

Westmeyer, H. (1972). *Logik der Diagnostik [The Logic of Assessment]*. Stuttgart: Kohlhammer.

Westmeyer, H. (1975). The diagnostic process as a statistical-causal analysis. *Theory and Decision*, 6, 57–86.

Westmeyer, H. (1996). A concept of explanation for social interaction models. In Hegselmann, R., Mueller, U. & Troitzsch, K.G. (Eds.), *Modelling and Simulation in the Social Sciences from the Philosophy of Science Point of View* (pp. 169–181). Dordrecht, NL: Kluwer.

Westmeyer, H. & Hageboeck, J. (1992). Computer-assisted assessment: a normative perspective. *European Journal of Psychological Assessment*, 8, 1–16.

Hans Westmeyer

RELATED ENTRIES

CLASSIFICATION, DECISION, PREDICTION (GENERAL)

F FACTOR ANALYSIS: CONFIRMATORY

INTRODUCTION

Fundamental to the factor analytic model is that some variables of theoretical interest cannot be directly observed; these unobserved variables are termed *latent variables*, or *factors*. Although latent variables cannot be directly observed, information related to them can be obtained indirectly by noting their effects on observed variables believed to represent them. The oldest and best-known statistical procedure for investigating relations between sets of observed and latent variables is that of factor analysis. In using this approach to data analyses, researchers examine the covariation among a set of observed variables in order to gather information on the latent constructs (or factors) that underlie them. Because factor analysis is concerned with the extent to which the observed variables are generated by the underlying latent constructs, strength of the regression paths from the factors to the observed variables (i.e. the factor loadings) are of primary interest.

There are two basic types of factor analyses: exploratory factor analysis (EFA) and confirmatory factor analysis (CFA). EFA is most appropriately used when the links between the observed variables and their underlying factors are unknown or uncertain. It is considered to be exploratory in the sense that the researcher has no prior knowledge that the observed variables do, indeed, measure the intended factors. In contrast, CFA is appropriately used when the researcher

has some knowledge of the underlying latent variable structure. Based on theory and/or empirical research, he or she postulates relations between the observed measures and the underlying factors a priori, and then tests this hypothesized structure statistically. More specifically, the CFA approach examines the extent to which a highly constrained *a priori* factor structure is consistent with the sample data.

Of the two factor analytic approaches, CFA is by far the more rigorous procedure. Indeed, it enables the researcher to overcome many limitations associated with the EFA model; these are as follows: first, whereas the EFA model assumes that all common factors are either correlated, or that they are uncorrelated, the CFA model makes no such assumptions. Rather, the researcher specifies, a priori, only those factor correlations that are considered to be substantively meaningful. Second, with the EFA model, all observed variables are directly influenced by all common factors. With CFA, each factor influences only those observed variables with which it is purported to be linked. Third, although each observed variable has associated with it a unique factor that comprises random as well as systematic error, the EFA model is incapable of taking this measurement error into account. The CFA model, on the other hand, allows for the quantification of this measurement error. Fourth, whereas in EFA the unique factors are assumed to be uncorrelated, in CFA specified covariation among particular uniquenesses can be tapped. Finally, provided with a malfitting model in

EFA, there is no mechanism for identifying which areas of the model are contributing most to the misfit. In CFA, on the other hand, the researcher is guided to a more appropriately specified model via indices of misfit provided by the statistical program.

Given the a priori knowledge of a factor structure and the testing of this factor structure based on the analysis of covariance structures, CFA belongs to a class of methodology known as *structural equation modelling* (SEM). The term structural equation modelling conveys two important notions: (a) that structural relations can be modelled pictorially to enable a clearer conceptualization of the theory under study, and (b) that the causal processes under study are represented by a series of structural (i.e. regression) equations. The hypothesized model can then be tested statistically in a simultaneous analysis of the entire system of variables to determine the extent to which it is consistent with the data. If goodness-of-fit is adequate, the model argues for the plausibility of postulated relations among variables; if it is inadequate, the tenability of such relations is rejected.

To assist the reader in better conceptualizing the CFA model, a more paradigmatic explanation of the procedure will be presented next. Consistent with the two aspects of SEM noted above, the graphical specification of an hypothesized CFA model will be described, and then this specification will be summarized in terms of its structural equations.

GRAPHICAL SPECIFICATION OF THE MODEL

CFA models are schematically portrayed as path diagrams through the incorporation of four geometric symbols: a circle (or ellipse) representing unobserved latent factors; a square (or rectangle) representing observed variables; a single-headed arrow ($\rightarrow$) representing the impact of one variable on another; and a double-headed arrow ($\leftrightarrow$) representing covariance between pairs of variables. In building a CFA model, researchers use these symbols within the framework of three basic configurations, each of which represents an important component in the analytic process. We turn now to the CFA model presented in Figure 1, which represents the postulated 3-factor structure

of burnout as tapped by items comprising the Maslach Burnout Inventory (MBI: Maslach & Jackson, 1986).

Based on the geometric configurations noted above, decomposition of this CFA model conveys the following information: (a) there are three factors, as indicated by the three ellipses labelled Emotional Exhaustion (F1), Depersonalization (F2), and Personal Accomplishment (F3); (b) the three factors are intercorrelated, as indicated by the two-headed arrows; (c) there are 22 observed variables, as indicated by the 22 rectangles (ITEM1–ITEM22): each represents one item from the MBI; (d) the observed variables load on the factors in the following pattern: items 1, 2, 3, 6, 8, 13, 14, 16, and 20 load on Factor 1; items 5, 10, 11, 15, and 22 load on Factor 2; and items 4, 7, 9, 12, 17, 18, 19, and 21 load on Factor 3; (e) each observed variable loads on one and only one factor; and (f) errors of measurement associated with each observed variable (err1–err22) are uncorrelated.

In summary, a more formal description of the CFA model in Figure 1 argues that: (a) responses to the MBI are explained by three factors; (b) each item has a non-zero loading on the burnout factor it was designed to measure (termed 'target loadings'), and zero loadings on all other factors (termed 'non-target loadings'); (c) the three factors are correlated; and (d) measurement error terms are uncorrelated.

STRUCTURAL EQUATION SPECIFICATION OF THE MODEL

CFA models can also be represented by a series of regression (i.e. structural) equations. Because (a) regression equations represent the influence of one or more variables on another, and (b) this influence, conventionally in SEM, is symbolized by a single-headed arrow pointing *from* the variable of influence *to* the variable of interest, we can think of each equation as summarizing the impact of all relevant variables in the model (observed and unobserved) on one specific variable (observed or unobserved). Thus, one relatively simple approach to formulating these equations is to note each variable that has one or more arrows pointing towards it, and then record the summation of all such influences for each of these dependent variables. Turning again to Figure 1, we see that there are 22 variables with arrows pointing

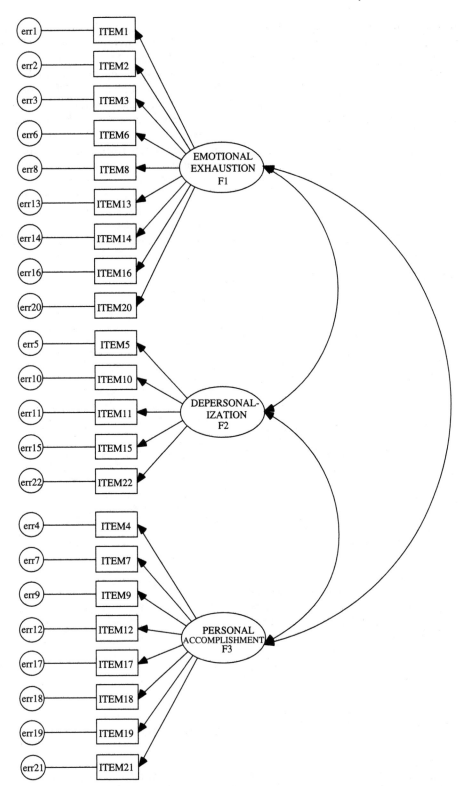

Figure 1.   Example of a hypothesized CFA model.

towards them; all represent observed variables (ITEM1–ITEM22). Accordingly, these regression functions can be summarized in terms of 22 separate equations as follows:

$$ITEM1 = F1 + err1$$

$$ITEM2 = F1 + err2$$

$$ITEM3 = F1 + err3$$

M

$$ITEM20 = F1 + err20$$
$$ITEM5 = F2 + err5$$
$$ITEM10 = F2 + err10$$

M

$$ITEM22 = F2 + err22$$
$$ITEM4 = F3 + err4$$
$$ITEM7 = F3 + err7$$

N

$$ITEM21 = F3 + err21$$

Although, in principle, there is a one-to-one correspondence between the schematic presentation of a model, and its translation into a set of structural equations, it is important to note that neither one of these representations tells the whole story; some parameters critical to the estimation of the model are not explicitly shown and thus may not be obvious to the novice CFA analyst. For example, in both the schematic model (see Figure 1) and the linear structural equations cited above, there is no indication that the factor variances are parameters in the model. Indeed, such parameters are essential to all structural equation models and therefore must be included in the model specification. Likewise, it is equally important to draw your attention to the specified non-existence of certain parameters in a model. For example, in Figure 1, we detect no curved arrow between err1 and err2, which suggests the lack of covariance between the error terms associated with the observed variables ITEM1 and ITEM2.

FUTURE PERSPECTIVES AND CONCLUSIONS

It is important to note that only issues related to the specification of CFA models have been included here. Indeed, any testing of these models requires additional procedures that bear on model identification, model estimation, and assessment of model fit, as well as possible model respecification and re-estimation. However, given the complex nature of these topics, their related discussion extends well beyond the limits of the present entry. Nonetheless, for a thorough explanation of these topics, together with their application to several different CFA models based on the EQS (Bentler, 2000), LISREL (Jöreskog & Sörbom, 1996), and AMOS (Arbuckle, 1999) statistical packages, respectively, readers are referred to Byrne (1994, 1998, 2001a). For a comparison of these three popular programs, see Byrne (2001b).

References

Arbuckle, J.L. (1999). *Amos 4.0* [Computer software]. Chicago, IL: Smallwaters.

Bentler, P.M. (2000). *EQS 6 Structural Equations Program Manual*. Encino, CA: Multivariate Software Inc.

Byrne, B.M. (1994). *Structural Equation Modelling with EQS and EQS/Windows: Basic Concepts, Applications, and Programming*. Thousand Oaks, CA: Sage.

Byrne, B.M. (1998). *Structural Equation Modelling with Lisrel, Prelis, and Simplis: Basic Concepts, Applications, and Programming*. Mahwah, NJ: Erlbaum.

Byrne, B.M. (2001a). *Structural Equation Modelling with Amos: Basic Concepts, Applications, and Programming*. Mahwah, NJ: Erlbaum.

Byrne, B.M. (2001b). Structural equation modelling with AMOS, EQS, and LISREL: comparative approaches to testing for the factorial validity of a measuring instrument. *International Journal of Testing*, 1(1), 55–86.

Jöreskog, K.G. & Sörbom, D. (1996). *LISREL 8: User's Reference Guide*. Chicago, IL: Scientific Software International.

Maslach, C. & Jackson, S.E. (1986). *Maslach Burnout Inventory Manual* (2nd ed.). Palo Alto, CA: Consulting Psychologists Press.

Barbara M. Byrne

RELATED ENTRIES

Factor Analysis: Exploratory, Validity: Construct, Theoretical Perspective: Psychometrics, Multidimensional Item Response Theory

FACTOR ANALYSIS: EXPLORATORY

INTRODUCTION

Exploratory Factor Analysis (EFA) has long been a central technique in psychological research, as a powerful tool for reducing the complexity in a set of data. Its key idea is that the variability in a large sample of observed variables is dependent upon a restricted number of non-observable 'latent' constructs. This entry addresses key issues in EFA, such as: aims of EFA, basic equations, factor extraction and rotation, number of factors in a factor solution, factor measurement and replicability, assumptions, future perspectives.

AIMS OF EXPLORATORY FACTOR ANALYSIS

Exploratory Factor Analysis (EFA) has long been a central technique that has been widely used, since the beginning of the 20th century, in different fields of psychological research such as the study of mental abilities, of personality traits, of values and of beliefs, and the development of psychological tests (see Cattell, 1978; Comrey & Lee, 1992; Harman, 1976; McDonald, 1985). Its key idea is that the variability in a large sample of observed variables is dependent upon the action of a much-restricted number of non-observable 'latent' constructs. The aims of EFA are twofold: to reduce the dimensionality of the original set of variables, and to identify major latent dimensions (the factors) that explain the correlations among the observed variables. The starting point of an EFA is a matrix ($\mathbf{R}$) of correlation coefficients (usually Pearson coefficients). The end is a matrix ($\mathbf{A}$) that contains the correlations among the factors and the observed variables (called 'factor loadings'): this is a rectangular matrix containing as many rows as the observed variables, and as many columns as the latent factors.

BASIC EQUATIONS

The basic idea of EFA is that a standard score on a variable can be expressed as a weighted sum of the latent factors, so that the following specification equation holds:

$$z_{ik} = a_{i1}F_{1k} + a_{i2}F_{2k} + \cdots + a_{ip}F_{pk} \\ + a_{is}S_{ik} + a_{ie}E_{ik}$$

where z_{ik} is the standard score for a person k on the variable i; a_{i1} to a_{ip}, a_{is} and a_{ie} are the loadings on, respectively, the common factors F, the specific factor S and the error factor E; F_{1k} to F_{pk}, S_{ik} and E_{ik} are the standard scores of person k on, respectively, the common factors F, the specific factor S and the error factor E. While the common factors represent the variance that each variable shares with the other variables, the specific and error factors represent sources of variance that are unique for each variable.

The equation above is a basis for 'decomposing' the $\mathbf{R}$ matrix into the product of two other matrices, the matrix of factor loadings ($\mathbf{A}$) and its transpose ($\mathbf{A}'$), so that $\mathbf{R} = \mathbf{AA}'$ (this is called the *fundamental equation* of Factor Analysis). The key idea here is that the original correlation matrix can be 'reproduced' from the factor solution. From this decomposition it is possible to derive the following equation, which relates the variance of a standardized variable z_i to the factor loadings:

$$\mathrm{Var}(z_i) = 1 = a_{i1}^2 + a_{i2}^2 + \cdots + a_{ip}^2 + a_{is}^2 + a_{ie}^2$$

In sum, the total variance of a standard variable can be divided into a part that each variable shares with the other variables and that is explained by the p common factors (this part is called *communality*, and is equal to the sum of squared loadings for the variable on the common factors, $h_{ii}^2 = a_{i1}^2 + a_{i2}^2 + \cdots + a_{ip}^2$) and a part that is explained by the specific and the error factors (the combination of these two components is called *uniqueness*, $u_{ii}^2 = a_{is}^2 + a_{ie}^2$).

FACTOR EXTRACTION

EFA is mainly interested in estimating *common variance*. The unique variance is derived a posteriori, once the loadings on the common factors is estimated by means of several methods that have been developed to this aim. A set of methods, as Principal Axes Factor Analysis (PAF) and Principal Components Analysis (PCA), aims at maximizing the variance of the original variables explained by the latent factors. The most important difference between PAF and PCA regards the content of the principal diagonal of the **R** matrix that is analysed. Where in PCA the diagonal of **R** contains all ones (i.e. the total variance of each standardized variable), in PAF the diagonal of **R** contains an estimate of the communality (usually the square of the multiple correlation of each variable with all the other variables).

Other methods (like the MinRes and the Minimum Residuals) use a Least Squares (LS) approach to identify the factor loadings in matrix **A** so that the squared values of the matrix subtraction ($\mathbf{R} - \mathbf{AA}'$) are minimal (these values are called 'residuals', while the matrix **R*** obtained from the matrix multiplication **AA**' is called 'reproduced' correlation matrix). Another method (the Maximum Likelihood method, ML) estimates population values for **A** in order to maximize the probability of observing the sample correlation matrix **R**.

Other methods that solve the equality $\mathbf{R} = \mathbf{AA}'$ have been developed and are available in the major statistical software packages. All these methods are usually referred to as methods of factor '*extraction*', and estimate factor loadings under the condition that factors must be *uncorrelated* among each other.

A major difference between PCA and all other factor extraction techniques is that PCA analyses all the variance of the observed variance, while the other methods analyse only common variance. Accordingly, while PCA reproduces the complete **R** matrix, the other methods reproduce the correlation matrix **R** with communalities in the principal diagonal.

The numerical process that leads to factor analysis solution implies a series of operations on the correlation matrix **R**. The products of these operations are always the 'eigenvalues' and the 'eigenvectors' of the **R** matrix. Both eigenvalues and eigenvectors are necessary to decompose the correlation matrix. The former, in particular, summarize the variance of the observed variables explained by each latent factor. For each factor, the sum, across the corresponding column, of squared loadings contained in matrix **A** is equal to the 'eigenvalue' associated to that factor: this quantity, divided by the number of observed variables, is equal to the proportion of variance of the observed variables explained by that factor.

FACTOR ROTATION

Once factors are extracted, they must be interpreted. The more a variable is correlated with a factor (i.e. the higher is its *loading* on that factor), the more important is the interpretation of this factor. However, the initial factor solution is not always adequate for factor interpretation. To facilitate factor interpretation a 'rotational' procedure is usually applied after the extraction. In this procedure a *simple structure* is pursued. The *simple structure* criterion has been developed by Thurstone and states that, for being maximally interpretable, a solution with p common factors must have the following features: (a) each row of the matrix **A** must have at least one value equal to zero; (b) each column of **A** must have at least p zeros; (c) for every pair of columns in **A**, there must be at least p observed variables with a zero value in one column, and a non-zero value in the other; (d) if $p > 3$, then for every pair of columns in **A** the proportion of observed variables with zeros in both columns must be large; (e) for every pair of columns in **A**, the proportion of observed variables with non-zero values in both columns must be small. These five criteria can be used to guide the analyst in finding, among all possible transformations of

A, the one that maximizes a solution's interpretability.

Once factors are rotated the total variance they are explaining is distributed across the new rotated factors, whose loadings are usually different from those of the unrotated factors. The sums by column of squared loadings on the rotated factors are not more equal to the eigenvalues of **R**: indeed, when divided by the number of observed variables, they represent the proportion of variance explained by the rotated factors. However, the rotation process does not influence variable communalities that remain the same in both rotated and unrotated solutions.

Factor rotation evidences an important issue in EFA: there are infinite ways to rotate the original unrotated factors, and there is an infinite set of values that can be found for **A**. Each one of this set reproduces equally well the original correlation matrix **R** (i.e. if **B** is the new rotated factor matrix derived from a rotation of the factors in **A**, then $\mathbf{R} = \mathbf{BB'}$). Then, all rotations fit the data equally well than the initial non-rotated solution. This problem is usually referred to as 'factor indeterminacy'.

In rotation factors may be left uncorrelated (like in orthogonal rotations such as Varimax or Tandem Criteria) or may be allowed to correlate (like in oblique rotation such as Promax and Oblimin). When an oblique rotation is performed, because factors are correlated, there are two different matrices that summarize the relation among observed variables and latent factors: the pattern matrix (**P**) containing the regression weights of the variables on the factors, and the structure matrix (**S**) containing the correlations among variables and factors. While the pattern matrix contains the coefficients summarizing the direct effect of the factors on the variables, the structure matrix contains the coefficients summarizing the total effect (i.e. direct plus indirect) of the factors on the variables. The structure matrix is obtainable from the pattern by post-multiplying the latter by the factor correlation matrix Φ (i.e. $\mathbf{S} = \mathbf{P}\Phi$). In oblique factor rotation the proportion of variance explained by the rotated factors is obtained by first multiplying the Pattern and Structure matrices element by element, then by summing across columns the resulting products, and finally by dividing the resulting sums by the number of observed variables.

IDENTIFYING, MEASURING AND GENERALIZING FACTORS

Several methods have been proposed to identify the number of factors to be extracted, although none of them offers a definitive solution. The 'mineigen' criterion extracts all factors whose corresponding eigenvalue is greater than 1. This method tends to overestimate the number of factors when the variables are many, and to underestimate it when the variables are few. In the 'scree test' method the eigenvalues are plotted, where a straight line is drawn through the latter smaller values: the larger values that are separated from the smaller do not fall on the line and correspond to the factors to retain. This method can be used for obtaining a first idea of the number of factors but is subject to strong idiosyncratic interpretation. When the LS and ML methods of extraction are used it is possible to use a test of fit (based on the chi-square distribution) that examines whether the difference among the observed (**R**) and the reproduced ($\mathbf{R^*} = \mathbf{AA'}$) correlation matrices is statistically significant. Then, one can extract new factors until this difference becomes non-significant. This test, however, is strongly dependent on sample size. New promising methods for determining the number of factors have been proposed, based on the generalizability of a factor solution. Only those factors that can be replicated across samples should be considered.

Once a factor solution has been defined and interpreted, the researcher may want to 'measure' the latent factors for each subject. Several methods have been proposed for estimating subjects' scores on the latent factors; the more frequently used are based on a regression approach.

Several indices, moreover, have been proposed for comparing factor solutions across different samples. In this regard, indices of factor invariance or factor congruence (such as the Tucker coefficient) assess the 'resemblance' of separate factor solutions derived from the same variables on different samples. These indices, however, are mainly of practical utility, and must be used with caution since they cannot be tested for statistical significance.

ASSUMPTIONS UNDERLYING EFA

There are several assumptions underlying the EFA model. Variables must be at least at the interval level and must follow the multivariate normal distribution (this is particularly crucial in ML extraction), relations among the variables must be linear, the number of subjects must be much higher than the number of variables, the sampling scheme must be the simple random sampling. For a correct application of EFA, correlations in **R** must be different from 0. This can be tested using the Bartlett test of sphericity (that must be statistically significant) and the Kaiser–Meyer–Olkin test of sampling adequacy (that must give values higher at least than 0.6): otherwise factor analysis is not recommended.

If EFA assumptions cannot be met, conclusions drawn from the results of an EFA may be taken with caution. This represents an important limitation for the technique. Generally, EFA results are influenced by the set of variables used: accordingly, variables must be used that has been carefully chosen to measure the domains of interest. In particular, at least 3 variables (i.e. 'markers') for each hypothesized factor must be provided, and a similar number of variables per factor is highly recommended. Another limitation of EFA derives from the indeterminacy problem: the factor solution is not identifiable, and the statistical significance of the factor loadings cannot be tested.

Assumptions violation may no longer be important if one utilizes appropriate methods that were developed for analysing dichotomous, ordinal and non-normal variables, as well as methods for non-linear factor analysis. Also identification and hypothesis testing are no longer a problem if one conducts EFA within the context of Confirmatory Factor Analysis using Jöreskog's restricted EFA approach (Jöreskog & Sörbom, 1979).

FUTURE PERSPECTIVES AND CONCLUSIONS

EFA has been mainly used to explore the dimensionality of a set of variables by finding the smallest number of interpretable factors needed to explain the correlations among them. Its exploratory essence lies in the fact that it places no structure on the relationships between the observed variables and the factors, but only specifies the number of factors. Recently, new methods for Confirmatory Factor Analysis were proposed and used to overcome many of the limitations of EFA. Accordingly, there is the tendency to consider EFA as an 'old style' method of data analysis and to prefer more 'advanced' techniques such as CFA. However, EFA may still be considered as a useful instrument, especially in test building, and in research on personality and intelligence, not only to identify the number of factors but also to: (a) determine the quality of a measurement instrument; (b) identify variables that are poor factor indicators; (c) identify factors that are poorly measured. For these reasons EFA may be considered as an essential preliminary step to CFA if not a valid alternative at all, especially in the first steps of a research and when the number of observed variables to analyse is high.

The vitality of EFA is furthermore well testified by recent developments that highlighted the possibility of using this technique: (a) in multilevel-data structures (*multilevel EFA*, see Hox, 2000); (b) in multivariate time series (*dynamic factor analysis*, see Hershberger, 1998); (c) in the analysis of non-linear relations and multidimensional item response models (see McDonald, 1999); (d) in the analysis of dichotomous and ordinal data (see Muthén & Muthén, 1998). All these expand the potentiality of EFA and prefigure interesting future developments.

References

Cattell, R.B. (1978). *The Scientific Use of Factor Analysis*. New York: Plenum Press.
Comrey, A.L. & Lee, H.B. (1992). *A First Course in Factor Analysis* (2nd ed.). Hillsdale, NJ: Lawrence Erlbaum Associates.
Harman, H.H. (1976). *Modern Factor Analysis* (3rd ed.). Chicago: University of Chicago Press.
Hershberger, S.L. (1998). Dynamic factor analysis. In Marcoulides, G.A. (Ed.), *Modern Methods for Business Research* (pp. 217–249). Mahwah, NJ: Lawrence Erlbaum Associates.
Hox, J.J. (2000). Multilevel analysis of grouped and longitudinal data. In Little, T.D., Schnabel, K.U.

& Baumert, J. (Eds.), *Modelling Longitudinal and Multilevel Data* (pp. 15–32). Mahwah, NJ: Lawrence Erlbaum Associates.

Jöreskog, K.G. & Sörbom, D. (1979). *Advances in Factor Analysis and Structural Equation Models.* Cambridge, MA: Abt Books.

McDonald, R.P. (1985). *Factor Analysis and Related Methods.* Hillsdale, NJ: Lawrence Erlbaum Associates.

McDonald, R.P. (1999). *Test Theory. A Unified Treatment.* Mahwah, NJ: Lawrence Erlbaum Associates.

Muthen, L.K. & Muthen, B.O. (1998). *MPLUS. User's Guide.* Los Angeles, CA: StatModel.

Claudio Barbaranelli

RELATED ENTRIES

F AMILY

INTRODUCTION

Research of the past three decades has repeatedly implicated the family in the aetiology, course, treatment, and prevention of most psychopathological disorders. Equally important, there is increasing recognition that family influences play a key role in a range of major social problems, which although not achieving psychiatric status, are critical to the physical and psychological welfare of millions. Further, studies of normative family transitions such as marriage, childbirth, ageing, and death are of increasing interest in both the development and prevention of psychopathology. Regardless of disciplinary identification, theoretical orientation, or substantive focus, all family researchers must ultimately select, revise, or develop measurement procedures that operationalize the family constructs they wish to investigate.

In pursuing this goal, the investigator soon encounters a tremendous number of instrument choices spanning a range of constructs and applications, what L'Abate (1994) has called an 'embarrassment of riches'. To address this plethora of choices, the present entry will present a general schema for classifying available family assessment procedures including examples and references to particular instruments that represent different techniques as well as brief discussion of related methodological issues.

CLASSIFYING FAMILY ASSESSMENT PROCEDURES

In considering the breadth of family assessment procedures, three organizing dimensions are particularly helpful: (a) the method of data collection used (report or observational procedures); (b) the unit that is the focus of assessment (i.e. the number of family members); and (c) the major constructs that an instrument attempts to measure. These dimensions guide assessment decisions, implementation, and eventual interpretation.

Method of Data Collection

Methods of data collection include (a) self-reports of family members and (b) direct observation of families during actual interactions. The key feature of the self-report approach is that the participant is asked for his/her perceptions of family events. There are many advantages to report methods, including the strong face validity, convenience, and modest cost for administration and scoring. Also, given the possibility of a large sample base, normative data may be available to which individual protocols can be related. Further, there is greater access to 'private' family data which cannot be reasonably obtained by other procedures (e.g. the nature of sexual interactions, or members' unexpressed dissatisfaction). Most importantly, self-report procedures capture members' cognitions and attributions about relationships and events, data that are increasingly viewed as essential to the goals of understanding and predicting family processes and outcomes. Notwithstanding these benefits, self-report procedures are, in the end, an individual's own perception of self and other, perceptions that can be inaccurate, biased, and at times seriously distorted. Furthermore, the researcher must reconcile the inevitable inconsistencies that are found in reports from different family members. Finally, most self-report data provide little in the way of the fine-grained details of moment to moment, day-to-day interactions between family members, data that are of great importance to researchers interested in the analysis of actual family processes which are only available through observation.

In contrast, observational procedures inform us most directly about actual interchanges among family members. Under the best of circumstances, such procedures provide highly detailed information regarding streams of behaviour that characterize the family 'in operation'. Specific coding systems can be applied to these interactions allowing for precise measurement of aspects of family processes and patterns of interaction. These results provide a critical foundation for an empirically based theory of family interaction with consequent links to the disorders of children and adults. Even so, direct observation strategies involving the use of complex coding procedures are costly and labour intensive, and require a significant commitment of time and resources in order to collect, collate, and analyse complex interaction data. Furthermore, there are methodological issues associated with these measures including subject reactivity to being observed and the meaningfulness of highly specific behavioural codes as indices of the larger dimensions and constructs of relevance to family experience.

In considering the unique features and methodological limitations of self-report and observational procedures, neither method appears *generally* more valuable, useful, or defensible. Rather, the two strategies are complementary and therefore necessary for full elucidation of the relationship between family interaction and psychopathology.

Within each data collection approach are important subgroups. Self-report procedures include objective tests such as the Family Environment Scale (FES) and the Family Assessment Measure (FAM-III) that tap various aspects of family functioning. Examples of structured interviews are the McMaster Structured Interview of Family Functioning (McSIFF), the Camberwell Family Interview Schedule (CFIS) and the UCLA Parent Interview for assessing expressed emotion; and the Family Ritual Interview developed by Wolin and his colleagues to investigate the preservation of rituals in families of alcoholics. Other instruments are behaviourally focused, such as the marital and parental versions of the Areas of Change Questionnaire (ACQ), Child Report of Parent Behaviour Inventory (CRPBI), or the Quality of Relationships Inventory (QRI). (For references, see Jacob & Tennenbaum, 1988 and Grotevant & Carlson, 1989.)

Instruments using observational procedures can be further subdivided into laboratory and naturalistic settings. Laboratory procedures frequently use structured tasks or games to produce measures of family attributes or performance. For example, the Revealed Differences Technique (Strodtbeck, 1951) determines family power characteristics by considering the relative predominance of one member's individual choices over others in joint rankings of family activities and functions. Another laboratory procedure involves the assessment of actual interactions among family members using personally relevant and/or previously conflictual topics (e.g. Jacob, Seilhamer & Rushe, 1989). These discussions are recorded (using video or audio tape) and then assessed by various means: detailed, multicomponent coding systems that preserve the ordering of behaviour over time; ratings of the total interaction along general/global dimensions of interest; and the recording of members' psychophysiological or physical responses during the ongoing interactions (Weiss & Summers, 1983).

In contrast, naturalistic observations involve the observation and assessment of family interaction in the home setting. Methods for collecting data in natural contexts include audiotaping and videotaping that is similarly subjected to coding. Researchers have used video taping in the home at random or specified times of the day, and have used daily diaries updated at preset times or beepers to signal family members at unplanned times to record details of current daily events. All the above methods yield naturalistic observational data of day-to-day family experiences which characterize family attributes.

Unit of Assessment

This second dimension specifies the unit of assessment and involves a focus on individuals, relationships between two or more members (dyads, triads, etc.), the whole family, or the interface between the family and extrafamilial environment.

Individual assessments represent the most basic level of family characterization, and have included traditional tests of personality or psychopathology. These instruments provide important data regarding the psychiatric and psychosocial status of the individual members. For example, the measurement of Communication Deviance is based upon analysis of each parent's individual Rorschach responses (see Jacob & Tennenbaum, 1988).

A second level of family assessment focuses on dyadic descriptions; that is, on marital, parent–child, and child–sibling relationships. In contrast with the assessment of individuals, relationship assessments provide information about dyadic status and functioning. By far, the most extensive group of dyadic assessment measures has concerned marital relationships (Spanier & Thompson, 1982), whereas procedures for assessing parent–child and child–sibling relationships have been more limited (Jacob et al., 2000).

Further, the family can be assessed as a whole; that is, across all family members to characterize the family in general or as a totality. For example, assessments can be obtained via self-report procedures concerning an individual's perceptions/descriptions of his/her family; alternatively, laboratory procedures may be used to observe the family's performance on a structured task which can then be coded and analysed to identify patterns among family members. In addition, projective methods are available that address the family as a unit such as conjoint family drawings and a consensus version of the Thematic Apperception Test (Jacob & Tennenbaum, 1988).

Finally, several assessment procedures provide information about extrafamilial variables and their impact on family functioning. Measures of social support and social networks (Anderson, 1982), for example, are based on the recognition that the family system can vary in its permeability. Instrument development in this area has focused largely on family adaptation and utilization of extrafamilial resources associated with specific stressors, such as chronic illness, divorce, or death (see Buehler, 1990; Conoley & Werth, 1995). Examples of instruments that evaluate community and extended family supports are the Feetham Family Functioning Survey (FFFS) and the Family Inventory of Resources for Management (FIRM).

The critical issue for each level of assessment is correspondence across different members' reports, an issue with a long history in family studies (Jacob & Windle, 1999). Although early work on this topic indicated low to moderate correlations between different informants, recent work has provided a clearer and more encouraging view. Cook and Goldstein (1993), for example, examined the correspondence among three members' reports (mother, father, child) on the same dyadic relationships (mother to child negativity, and father to child negativity). Using a latent variable approach, the investigators were able to determine the degree to which each member's reports represented a 'unique perspective' versus a 'common perspective' shared by that of other family members, and demonstrated significant 'common' experience across family members.

Constructs Assessed

The third dimension specifies the variables of interest. How one conceptualizes and examines the relationship between family influences and childhood or adult disorders will vary in relation to one's theoretical model. Given the past four decades of theoretical and empirical effort, a wide range of family constructs have been presented as relevant to understanding the family–psychopathology complex. Thus, family assessment instruments often include a variety of subscales purporting to assess various concepts of a particular theoretical model. However, seldom has a convincing case been made for the statistical independence of the component scales (especially in self-report methods). Specifically, significant correlation between component scales demonstrates redundance and suggests that different scales may be measuring the same underlying factor. It appears that relationships may be differentiated along but a few orthogonal dimensions, a conclusion which has received considerable support from a range of theory and research in the domain of interpersonal processes (see Jacob & Tennenbaum, 1988). As well, recent work by the authors (Jacob & Windle, 1999; Gondoli & Jacob, 1993) indicate that score variance is best captured by three general factors (affect, control, and activity) rather than by the many dimensions that these instruments purport to measure. Four sets of constructs have received consistent support in the literature: affect, control, communication, and family systems properties.

Affect

The primacy of the affective bond as a determinant of relationship satisfaction and individual outcome has been emphasized across a broad range of disciplines and types of interpersonal relationships. From early studies of infant attachment and group process to investigations of marital dissatisfaction and patterns of childhood socialization, the importance of a supportive and nurturing affective relationship has been repeatedly underscored. Clearly, the affective relationship characterizing the parent–child and marital dyads has received most emphasis by theorists and clinicians.

Control

As with the affective dimension, interpersonal influence/control has been of major importance in conceptualizations of a wide range of relationships (see Jacob & Tennenbaum, 1988). In adult relationships, the most common descriptors have been power, influence, and dominance. In parent–child relationships, the literature has focused on strategies, techniques, and styles of parenting behaviour with an emphasis on those processes by which parents attempt to control and shape the behaviour of their offspring during early childhood and adolescence. Similar to assessments of affect, the measurement of influence and control strategies at a general family level or with regard to parent–child or marital dyads has received most attention,

whereas child–sibling relationships have received minimal attention.

Communication

In the family literature relevant to psychopathology, several models of communication have been of interest. First, certain types of communication distortions are related to the development and perpetuation of cognitive disorders in children. This line of research began with family theories of schizophrenia which emphasized the role of communication distortion in development of a child's cognitive disturbances. Key concepts included the notions of double bind, transactional thought disorder, and, more recently, communication deviance.

Second, investigators soon broadened the meaning of double bind communications, and integrated it into a rapidly developing literature on non-verbal communication which focused on family communication with disturbed but non-psychotic samples (see review by Jacob & Lessin, 1982). In exploring the relationship between verbal and non-verbal communication channels, particular interest has focused on the conditions under which channel inconsistency occurs (i.e. non-redundant information emerges) and the consequent impact of such inconsistent messages on receivers.

A third communication focus has involved studies of family problem solving in dysfunctional family units and the development of treatment programmes aimed at enhancing those 'communication skills' thought to be most relevant to the effective and satisfactory resolution of conflict (Brown et al., 1997).

Systems Properties

Attention is here directed toward general properties and principles of family systems that characterize relationships within the family as well as with extrafamilial systems. Included in this domain of processes would be such characteristics as system flexibility and adaptability, and the family's ability to change patterns of control and affect in response to changing needs of members and in response to situational stresses imposed on the family (Jacob & Tennenbaum, 1988). Related processes such as boundary permeability, subsystem relationships, and alliance structures have also been emphasized in the application of systems perspectives to the diagnosis and treatment of family dysfunction. Vuchinich, Emery, and Cassidy (1988) based an observational study of third-party interventions in dyadic interactions on the contention that additional family members often become involved in what begins as a dyadic conflict. In their observations of videotaped dinners in the home, they found specific effects for child gender (girls are more likely to intervene than boys), parents' behaviour (they are usually on opposing sides), and role ascriptions (fathers use authority, mothers use mediation, children use distraction). Other theorists have highlighted the family's use of time and space as well as amount of interaction that occurs within different family subsystems as relevant to understanding the nature of functional versus dysfunctional family systems (Steinglass, 1979).

FUTURE PERSPECTIVES AND CONCLUSIONS

As can be gleaned from the foregoing overview, the family assessment domain is characterized by a great diversity of instruments that span a range of data collection methods, assessment foci, target populations, and constructs. And although our evaluation of the field is generally positive and optimistic, it is tempered by the recognition that much work remains to be done to address and expand upon current limitations. Most importantly, future assessment efforts can be profitably directed toward clarification of five major research areas: instrument dimensionality, correspondence across different family members, correspondence across different family subsystems, correspondence across different methods, and undeveloped assessment targets and concepts. As an aid to understanding the potential relevance of work in each of these theoretical areas, Table 1 suggests several key questions that should be answerable through future research efforts.

In addition, recent societal changes suggest a number of newly emerging topics for future study including issues related to dual career families, divorce, single parenting, stepparent families, lesbian and gay families, cultural differences of minority populations, homeless families, the impact of chronic illness upon family functioning, and family stresses related to the care of the

Table 1. Future research directions

Research topic	Questions to address
Instrument dimensionality	(a) How many dimensions best characterize report-based and observation-based measures of family functioning?
	(b) Is instrument dimensionality similar across different family subsystems?
Correspondence across different family members	(a) To what degree do different family members describe family functioning in a similar fashion?
	(b) Does correspondence across different family members vary as a function of family subsystem assessed?
Correspondence across different family subsystems	(a) To what degree is there similarity in the description of different family subsystems?
	(b) Under what conditions are cross-system similarities maximized?
Correspondence across different methods	(a) Is there convergent and discriminate validity of key family constructs assessed by different methods?
	(b) Does correspondence across methods vary in relation to construct assessed and subsystem assessed?
Undeveloped assessment targets and concepts	(a) How can key family systems concepts be operationalized and measured?
	(b) What methods appear best suited for describing such complex processes?
	(c) Can such constructs be differentiated from the general family dimensions of affect, engagement, and control?

elderly. The reader is referred to recent reviews that include further discussion and abstracts of existing instruments for special needs populations (see Buehler, 1990; Conoley & Werth, 1995). Further, there are many available handbooks and reviews that catalogue existing measures (often according to constructs of interest or levels of family subsystems). The reader is referred to the following publications for detailed presentations of the development and psychometric properties of specific instruments, further appreciation of the diversity and breadth of family assessment methods, and in depth discussion of the complex methodological issues in family assessment research: Jacob and Windle, 1999; Jacob, 1987; Bray, 1995; Grotevant and Carlson, 1989; and Jacob and Tennenbaum (1988).

References

Anderson, C. (1982). The community connection: the impact of social networks on family and individual functioning. In Walsh, F. (Ed.), *Normal Family Processes* (1st ed., pp: 425–445). New York: Guilford Press.

Bray, J.H. (Ed.) (1995). Methodological advances in family psychology: special section. *Journal of Family Psychology*, 9(2), 107–185.

Brown, T.L., Swenson, C.C., Cunningham, P.B., Henggeler, S.W., Schoenwald, S.K. & Rowland, M.D. (1997). Multisystemic treatment of violent and chronic juvenile offenders: bridging the gap between research and practice. Special issue: assertive community treatment. *Administration & Policy in Mental Health*, 25(2), 221–238.

Buehler, C. (1990). Adjustment. In Touliatos, J., Perlmutter, B.F. & Straus, M.A. (Eds.), *Handbook of Family Measurement Techniques* (pp. 493–516). Newbury Park, CA: Sage Publications.

Conoley, J.C. & Werth, E.B. (Eds.) (1995). *Family Assessment*. Lincoln, NE: Buros Institute of Mental Measurements, University of Nebraska-Lincoln.

Cook, W. & Goldstein, M. (1993). Multiple perspectives on family relationships: a latent variable model. *Child Development*, 64, 1377–1388.

Gondoli, D. & Jacob, T. (1993). Factor structure within and across three family assessment procedures. *Journal of Family Psychology*, 6, 278–289.

Grotevant, H. & Carlson, C. (1989). *Family Assessment*. New York: Guilford Press.

Jacob, T. (1987). *Family Interaction and Psychopathology: Theories, Methods, and Findings*. New York: John Wiley.

Jacob, T. & Lessin, S. (1982). Inconsistent communication in family interaction. *Clinical Psychology Review*, 2, 295–309.

Jacob, T., Moser, R.P., Windle, M., Loeber, R. & Stouthamer-Loeber, M. (2000). A new measure of parenting practices involving preadolescent and adolescent-aged children. *Behaviour Modification*, 24, 611–634.

Jacob, T., Seilhamer, R.A. & Rushe, R. (1989). Alcoholism and family interaction: an experimental paradigm. *American Journal of Drug and Alcohol Abuse*, 15(1), 73–91.

Jacob, T. & Tennenbaum, D.L. (Eds.) (1988). *Family Assessment: Rationale, Methods, and Future Directions*. New York: Plenum Press.

Jacob, T. & Windle, M. (1999). Family assessment: instrument dimensionality and correspondence across family reporters. *Journal of Family Psychology*, 13(3), 339–354.

L'Abate, L. (1994). *Family Evaluation: A Psychological Approach*. Thousand Oaks, CA: Sage Publications.

Spanier, G.B. & Thompson, L. (1982). A confirmatory analysis of the dyadic adjustment scale. *Journal of Marriage and the Family*, 44, 731–738.

Steinglass, P. (1979). The home observation assessment method (HOAM): real-time naturalistic observation of families in their homes. *Family Process*, 18, 337–354.

Strodtbeck, F.L. (1951). Husband–wife interaction over revealed differences. *American Sociological Review*, 16, 468–473.

Vuchinich, S., Emery, R.E. & Cassidy, J. (1988). Family members as third parties in dyadic family conflict: strategies, alliances, and outcomes. *Child Development*, 59, 1293–1302.

Weiss, R.L. & Summers, K.J. (1983). The Marital Interaction Coding System – III. In Filsinger, E. (Ed.), *Marriage and Family Assessment: A Sourcebook for Family Therapy*. Beverly Hills, CA: Sage Publications.

Theodore Jacob and Jon Randolph Haber

RELATED ENTRIES

APPLIED FIELDS: CLINICAL, CAREGIVER BURDEN, CHILD CUSTODY, COUPLE ASSESSMENT IN CLINICAL SETTINGS, SOCIAL NETWORKS, SOCIAL RESOURCES

FIELD SURVEY: PROTOCOLS DEVELOPMENT

INTRODUCTION

Survey research is the methodological field within the social sciences concerned with the systematic collection and analysis of information from a subset of individuals or groups of persons chosen randomly from a population. Technically speaking it involves the following steps: (1) question wording, (2) structuring of the questionnaire, (3) sampling, (4) interviewing, (5) coding, (6) reporting.

TYPES OF SURVEYS

There are three main types of surveys, depending on how information is collected: face-to-face, mail, and telephone surveys. Each of these collection methods presents advantages and disadvantages (Groves, 1979; Backstrom & Hursh, 1986). The face-to-face method is the most efficient method for interviewing people from difficult-to-reach groups. Another advantage is that the researcher has more control over respondents. This allows for longer interviews and increases the probability that the interview will be completed. Face-to-face interviews also allow for the use of visual aids. Their biggest disadvantage is their cost and the fact in large cities it is often difficult to get access to where people live. Telephone surveys can avoid this problem; moreover, they are much cheaper: with current computer programs, a single person can randomly select respondents, interview them, and code the answers directly into the computer (Saris, 1991). The drawback of this method is that interviewers have less control over respondents than in face-to-face interviews. This sets limits on the duration of interviews. The cheapest survey method is the mail survey. It is particularly suited for topics that are not very complex. Its main drawbacks are the very low response rate, which can introduce bias in the results, and the absolute

lack of control over the person who fills out the questionnaire.

COMPARISON WITH OTHER DATA-GATHERING METHODS

Compared to ethnographic and experimental methods, survey research presents advantages in terms of external validity (ability to extrapolate survey results to the target population) and disadvantages in terms of internal validity (ability to draw causal conclusions from observed associations) (Cook & Campbell, 1972; Kish, 1987). Indeed, the correct implementation of probability sampling methods allows estimation with a given margin of error confidence, of intervals of varying precision for common statistics, like the mean or percentages, for a particular population. This sort of inferential precision is not possible with experimental and ethnographic methods. On the other hand, the general lack of randomization in the assignment of treatments differentiates survey research from experimental research, but not from ethnographic research, and complicates the process of attaching causal meaning to measured associations. The use of statistical controls in survey data analysis mitigates this problem but, since the number of potential statistical controls is infinite, this makes the statistical conclusions of survey research highly sensitive to the theoretical soundness that guides the selection of control variables and which thus determines the inclusion of particular questions in a questionnaire.

Another threat to the internal validity of survey research is that surveys are generally cross-sectional, which raises the problem of determining the causal order characterizing a particular association. Panel surveys and retrospective questions in cross-sectional surveys reduce this problem, but only at the cost of complex and not always easy to estimate statistical models in the case of Panel studies and lower reliability of the answers when one relies on retrospective information.

The comments above refer to the pros and cons of survey research as a method. There are, however, better and worse surveys, and this depends on the quality of the questions (Foddy, 1993; Schuman & Presser, 1980; Payne, 1951), how well the questionnaire is structured (Backstrom & Hursh, 1986), the quality of the sampling (Kalton, 1983; Kish, 1965), how well the interviews are conducted (Cannell et al., 1977; Converse & Schuman, 1974; Guenzel et al., 1983), and how accurate the coding of the interviews is.

QUESTION BUILDING

In order to ensure the quality of the questions, researchers must have a very clear idea about the information that they intend to collect. Moreover, the questions need to be short and devoid of grammatical complexity; they should also include simple and unambiguous words to ensure that they are understood the same way by respondents with very different social backgrounds. Loaded words or expressions must be avoided too.

When researchers design questionnaires they must weigh the advantages and disadvantages of closed- and open-ended questions. The prevalence of closed-ended questions is one of the main distinguishing features of survey methods when compared with more ethnographic techniques, such as the semi-structured interview. One main reason why closed-ended questions are preferred in survey research is that they are easy to code and therefore more appropriate for a method, one of whose main characteristics is the collection of information from large numbers of people that is then analysed statistically. Nevertheless, a few open-ended questions in survey research can make the interview more interesting to respondents, for they allow them to express themselves with their own words. Moreover, they provide qualitative information that may spice-up the final report. Finally, they can be used when the researcher is not sure about what answers to expect to a particular question. This goal is generally better served, however, by using open-ended questions at the pretest stage that are then transformed into closed-ended questions in the final version of the questionnaire.

Closed-ended questions involve two elements: the question proper and the answer-set. The structure and wording of the answer-set is as important for the quality of a survey as the question itself. Number of choices, order of answer options, balance among the different choices, and realism in the answer options are contextual factors that may influence the information one collects. For instance, in face-to-face interviews a long list of choices may result in higher percentages of respondents choosing the last options presented to them, whereas it may have the opposite effect in a mail survey, where the choices are read by the respondents. Neutral options (e.g. Neither...Or, DK, or Undecided) create special problems, since their inclusion in the middle of a list leads to higher percentages choosing the option than when included at the end of a list.

QUESTIONNAIRE STRUCTURE

There is no standard structure for a survey questionnaire. Manuals, however, often recommend the following sequence of sections: (1) Introduction, (2) Warm-up, (3) Topic 1, (4) Topic 2, ... (n) Topic n, ($n + 1$) Socio-demographic. Researchers must take into account that question order matters. Previous questions may involuntarily condition the answers to later questions, because of people's tendency to appear consistent or because of narrowing the type of factors respondents consider when answering general questions. These problems arise in General...Specific or Specific...General sequences of questions respectively.

Sampling

Survey research, compared to other research methods, is particularly strong with respect to external validity. This is because it relies on random selection methods. There are two main types of sampling: probabilistic – where the selection probabilities are or can be known – and non-probabilistic – where the selection probabilities cannot be ascertained. Only the former allow for the use of statistical procedures to infer population parameters from the sample results. Different factors influence the degree of precision of the population estimates obtained from a survey. The sample size is the most important factor, to such an extent that 1200 interviews, regardless of the size of the target population, can already provide a high degree of precision. Beyond this, different sampling designs can also affect precision. Stratified sampling, for instance, which consists in sampling within categories of theoretically relevant variables such that the proportion of interviews in each category matches the population distribution, leads to more precise estimates. Cluster sampling, on the other hand, which consists in sampling within a number of clusters (e.g. counties, provinces, electoral districts), randomly selected from the total number of clusters of a particular type in the population, tends to diminish the level of precision of the estimates. Many surveys involve multiple stages and include both stratified and cluster methods.

Interviewing

The interview stage of a survey is as important as the other stages. Like in an experiment, the reliability of the results is largely a measure of how well the environment conditions have been controlled for. All respondents to a survey should be exposed to the same type of stimuli from the interviewers, in order for the researcher to be able to rule out non-random interviewer effects from the explanation of the statistical results. This goal can be approached through detailed and clear instructions in the questionnaire and in the survey codebook about, for instance, the flow of the interview (e.g. skip patterns), the meaning of particular words or phrases, probing questions, and reactions to queries by the respondents. Also, interviewers should receive specialized training. Familiarity with the questionnaire, strict adherence to the text of the questionnaire, slow interviewing pace, indifference to the respondent's occasional interruption during the reading of a question, opaqueness about the interviewer's own feelings with respect to the questions being asked and the respondent's answers, the ability to reassure respondents about the value of their answers, are some of the skills that interviewers learn during their training.

Coding

The final stage in a survey, before the statistical analysis can proceed, is the coding phase or transfer of information from the written questionnaires to a computer database. To minimize errors coders must be trained and, most importantly, computer programs need to be developed that detect the input of erroneous codes, the transgression of particular skip patterns during the interview, or inconsistencies between answers to different questions.

FUTURE PERSPECTIVES AND CONCLUSIONS

Survey research is now a mature discipline and one may therefore expect few revolutionary developments. In the future, research may still offer new insights on the effects of question wording and order and about the effects of the structure of a questionnaire. In the field of sampling, researchers and institutions are experimenting with better designs for measuring both cross-sectional and time-dependent processes (e.g. rolling samples) and for sampling from small but difficult to reach populations. Just as computer-assisted telephone interviewing have radically transformed the comparative costs and benefits of this mode of survey data collection, the development of the internet poses a challenge to survey researchers; it opens the door to a new type of collecting survey information, which will surely present advantages and disadvantages with respect to face-to-face, telephone, and mail surveys.

In sum, survey research is an established methodology in the social sciences whose main comparative virtue is that of allowing us to generalize from small samples to large populations. Surveys can vary in quality, however, dependent on the data-collection method, the quality of the questionnaire, the sampling method used, the qualifications and training of the interviewers, and the way the collected information is coded.

References

Backstrom, C. & Hursh, G. (1986). *Survey Research*. Chicago: Northwestern University Press.

Cannell, C.F., Marquis, K.H. & Laurent A. (1977). *A Summary of Research Studies of Interviewing Methodology*. Rockville, MD: Health Resources Administration, National Center for Health Statistics.

Converse, J.M. & Schuman, H. (1974). *Conversations at Random: Survey Research as Interviewers See It*. New York: Wiley.

Cook, T., & Campbell, D. (1972). *Quasi-Experiments*. Boston: Houghton Miffin.

Foddy, W. (1993). *Constructing Questions for Interviews and Questionnaires*. Cambridge: Cambridge University Press.

Groves, R.M. (1979). *Surveys by Telephone: A National Comparison with Personal Interviews*. New York: Academic Press.

Guenzel, P.J., Berckmans, T.R. & Cannell, C.F. (1983). *General Interviewing Techniques: A Self-Instructional Workshop for Telephone and Personal Interviewer Techniques*. Ann Arbor, MI: ISR, Survey Research Center.

Kalton, G. (1983). *Introduction to Survey Sampling*. Newbury Park, CA: Sage.

Kish, L. (1965). *Survey Sampling*. New York: Wiley.

Kish, L. (1987). *Statistical Design for Research*. New York: Wiley.

Payne, S.L. (1951). *The Art of Asking Questions*. Princeton: Princeton University Press.

Saris, W.E. (1991). *Computer-Assisted Interviewing*. Newbury Park, CA: Sage.

Schuman, H. & Presser, S. (1980). *Questions and Answers in Attitude Surveys: Experiments in Question Form, Wording, and Context*. New York: Academic Press.

Juan Díez Medrano

RELATED ENTRIES

FLUID AND CRYSTALLIZED INTELLIGENCE

INTRODUCTION

Original Theory

The concept of fluid (g_f) and crystallized (g_c) intelligence was originally developed by Cattell and Horn (for example, Cattell, 1987, 1998; Horn, 1988). Horn (1988: 660) gives the following description of g_f: 'The g_f abilities are indicative of skills of perceiving relationships among stimulus patterns, drawing inferences from relationships and comprehending implications. The factor is a fallible indicator of reasoning of several kinds, abstracting, and problem solving, when these qualities are acquired outside the acculturational process ...' Horn (1988: 658) also provides a description of g_c: 'The measured factor is a fallible indicator of the extent to which an individual has incorporated, through systematic influences of acculturation, the knowledge and sophistication that can be referred to as the intelligence of a culture.'

Ability Structure

g_f and g_c are usually conceived as second-order or second-stratum factors in hierarchical factor analysis (*cf.* Cattell, 1987). 'Historical' $g_{f(b)}$ forms the third-stratum factor at the top of the hierarchy, while primaries corresponding to Thurstone's primary mental abilities are located at the bottom of the hierarchy. g_f and g_c are further embedded in a broader theoretical framework comprising second-order factors for visualization, fluency, and cognitive speed, and so-called *provincial factors* located between the primary and secondary level, which cannot be directly demonstrated through factor analysis (Cattell, 1987, 1998).

Dynamic Aspects

It is assumed that there is initially (perhaps two or three years after maturational shaping from birth) a single relation-perceiving ability. This ability is not tied to any specific habits or sensory, motor, or memory area, and is therefore termed 'fluid' intelligence, g_f (Cattell, 1987). Complex abilities representing g_c (reading, arithmetic, and abstract reasoning) are subsequently acquired through learning and thus through the investment of g_f. g_f has been found to increase in early life, reaching a peak at around 18–20 years, and then to slowly decrease. In contrast, g_c has been found to increase up to the age of 60 years.

FURTHER DEVELOPMENTS

Several models of intelligence integrate aspects of g_f and g_c. Gustafsson (1984) proposed a model including g_f and g_c as second-order factors, where g_f was identical to general intelligence. Ackerman (1996) presented an integrative theory of adult intellectual development, focusing on intelligence-as-process representing g_f-type abilities, and intelligence-as-knowledge representing g_c-type abilities. Baltes et al. (1998) integrated g_f and g_c in the developmental concept of the mechanics (close to g_f) and pragmatics (close to g_c) of intelligence. In Woodcock (1998), g_f represents high complexity information processing, whereas g_c is a component of declarative and procedural knowledge. Important evidence for g_f and g_c was presented in Carroll's (1993) monumental review and analysis in the domain of human abilities. The model comprises g_f and g_c, but the structure presented by Carroll differs from that presented in Cattell (1987, 1998) in that visual and auditory perception occur as second-order factors like g_f and g_c and not as provincial factors. Apart from the integrative models of intelligence listed above, a great deal of research has related g_f and g_c to very different theoretical approaches. g_f has been related to cognitive correlates, for example, by Kyllonen and Christal (1990), who found a strong relationship between reasoning measures, which they also consider to be measures of g_f, and working memory. Correlations between processing speed and g_f have been interpreted within the mental speed framework (for example, Rabbitt, 1996).

Stelzl et al. (1995) investigated the effects of schooling on g_f and g_c. They found substantial schooling effects on both g_c and g_f. The schooling effect observed on g_f is in conflict with the assumption that the development of g_f is primarily based on biological processes of neural growth and maturation, and that it is not influenced by formal education.

CRITERION VALIDITIES

Criterion validities with job performance as criterion are mostly reported for general intelligence, but not for g_f and g_c. It is therefore difficult to evaluate the extent to which the substantial predictive validities of general intelligence for job performance reported in Schmidt and Hunter (1998) can be attributed to g_f and g_c. However, job-related knowledge has some incremental validity when used with a measure of general intelligence as a predictor for job performance (Schmidt & Hunter, 1998). This may indicate that g_c is also important for the prediction of job performance. Further criterion validities for g_f and g_c are available for general and school achievement. Mitchell and Lawson (1988) reported that g_f was a powerful predictor of performance in a biological achievement test. Cattell (1987) reported substantial correlations between measures of g_f and g_c and school performance (for example, spelling, word meanings, arithmetic).

TESTS FOR g_f AND g_c

In the following, the most important tests of g_f and g_c are briefly presented (see Table 1). The Culture Fair Intelligence Test (CFT; Cattell, 1957) was primarily conceived for the measurement of g_f. In the CFT tests, the measurement of g_f is based on figural material (matrices, topologies). Because Raven's (1983) Advanced and Standard Progressive Matrices are based exclusively on matrices, they are often used for the measurement of g_f.

In the fourth edition of the Stanford–Binet Intelligence Scale, Thorndike et al. (1985) proposed measuring g_c by scales for verbal and numeric reasoning, and measuring g_f by a scale for abstract/visual reasoning. According to Kaufman and Kaufman (1997) the scales of the Kaufman Adolescent and Adult Intelligence Test (Kaufman & Kaufman, 1993) could also be used for the measurement of g_f and g_c, despite the fact that the test initially had another theoretical background.

The Wechsler Adult Intelligence Scale – Revised (Wechsler, 1981) has also been used to measure g_f and g_c. It has been assumed that the verbal part of the WAIS-R measures g_c and that the non-verbal part measures g_f (Grégoire, 1993). Amthauer et al. (2001) and Beauducel et al. (2001) suggest that g_f cannot simply be reduced to figural abilities and that g_c cannot simply be

Table 1. Tests for the measurement of g_f and g_c

Authors	Test	Measures	
Cattell, 1957	The IPAT Culture Fair Intelligence Scales 1, 2, and 3. Champaign, Illinois: Institute for Personality and Ability Testing.	g_f	
Raven, 1983	The Standard Progressive Matrices, 1938–83. New York: Psychological Corporation.	g_f	
Thorndike, Hagen & Sattler, 1985	Technical Manual: Stanford–Binet Intelligence Scale. Chicago: Riverside.	g_f	g_c
Kaufman & Kaufman, 1993	The Kaufman Adolescent and Adult/ Intelligence Test (KAIT) Manual. Circle Pines, MN: American Guidance Service.	g_f	g_c
Wechsler, 1981	Wechsler Adult Intelligence Scale – Revised. San Antonio, TX: Psychological Corporation.	g_f	g_c
Amthauer et al., 2001	Test for intelligence structure, 2000 R. Göttingen: Hogrefe.	g_f	g_c
Woodcock & Johnson, 1989	Woodcock–Johnson Psycho-Educational Battery-Revised. Chicago: Riverside.	g_f	g_c
Flanagan & McGrew, 1997	A cross-battery approach to assessing and interpreting cognitive abilities	g_f	g_c

reduced to verbal abilities. Even though figural abilities may be less influenced by acculturation than verbal abilities, it should not be assumed that figural abilities are pure measures of g_f. Beauducel et al. (2001) show that the contamination of g_f with figural abilities and of g_c with verbal abilities can be reduced by means of a faceted conceptualization of g_f and g_c, comprising a facet for the differentiation between g_f and g_c and another facet for the types of content (verbal, numerical, figural).

Flanagan and McGrew (1997) suggest that there is a problem of construct underrepresentation in the measurement of g_f and g_c, which means that g_f and g_c cannot generally be measured accurately with convenient single tests. Therefore, they recommend an improvement of the measurement of g_f and g_c by means of their 'cross-battery approach'. The cross-battery approach integrates a number of different tests, including the Woodcock–Johnson Psycho-Educational Battery – Revised and the Kaufman Adolescent and Adult Intelligence Test (see Table 1).

FUTURE PERSPECTIVES

Since g_f and g_c have been related to the domain of social intelligence (Lee et al., 2000) it could be expected that the g_f–g_c differentiation will be further extended beyond the domain of academic intelligence. Cattell (1987) already reports a loading of a test of mechanical knowledge on g_c which could indicate some relation to the domain of practical intelligence (see also Heidrich & Denney, 1994). Thus, the g_f–g_c differentiation could serve as a heuristic for future research within the broad field beyond academic intelligence.

CONCLUSIONS

The multitude of theoretical approaches relating to g_f and g_c demonstrates the importance of these concepts. However, with regard to the measurement of g_f and g_c, this multitude has produced considerable variations. Since there was already some degree of variability in the measurement of g_f and g_c, there has been a temptation to use only a single type of task for the measurement of g_f, and another single task for the measurement of g_c. Such construct underrepresentation may be avoided by the development of broad test batteries for the measurement of g_f and g_c, as in Amthauer et al. (2001), or by the combination of different test batteries, as in Flanagan and McGrew (1997). Of course, new theoretical developments (for example, Ackerman, 1996; Woodcock, 1998) will probably lead to further improvements in the measurement of g_f and g_c in the future.

References

Ackerman, P.L. (1996). A theory of adult intellectual development: process, personality, interests, and knowledge. *Intelligence, 22*, 227–257.

Amthauer, R., Brocke, B., Liepmann, D. & Beauducel, A. (2001). *Iutelliceuz-Struktur-Test 2000R(I.S.T 2000R)*. Göttingen: Hogrefe.

Baltes, P.B., Lindenberger, U. & Staudinger, U.M. (1998). Life-span theory in developmental psychology. In Damon, (Ed.), & Lerner, R.M. (Vol. Ed.), *Handbook of Child Psychology: Theoretical Models of Human Development*, Vol. 1 (5th ed., pp. 1029–1143). New York: Wiley.

Beauducel, A., Brocke, B. & Liepmann, D. (2001). Perspectives on fluid and crystallized intelligence: facets for verbal, numerical, and figural intelligence. *Personality and Individual Differences, 30*, 977–994.

Carroll, J.B. (1993). *Human Cognitive Abilities. A Survey of Factor-Analytic Studies*. Cambridge: Cambridge University Press.

Cattell, R.B. (1957). *The IPAT Culture Fair Intelligence Scale*. Champaign, IL: Institute for Personality Testing.

Cattell, R.B. (1987). *Intelligence: Its Structure, Growth, and Action*. Amsterdam: Elsevier Science Publishers B.V.

Cattell, R.B. (1998). Where is intelligence? Some answers from the triadic theory. In McArdle, J.J. & Woodcock, R.W. (Eds.), *Human Cognitive Abilities in Theory and Practice* (pp. 29–38). Mahwah, NJ: Lawrence Erlbaum Associates.

Flanagan, D.P. & McGrew, K.S. (1997). A cross-battery approach to assessing and interpreting cognitive abilities: narrowing the gap between practice and cognitive science. In Flanagan, D.P., Genshaft, J.L. & Harrison, P.L. (Eds.), *Contemporary Intellectual Assessment. Theories, Tests, and Issues* (pp. 314–325). New York: The Guilford Press.

Grégoire, J. (1993). Intelligence et vieillissement au WAIS-R [Measuring intelligence and aging using the WAIS-R]. *L'Année Psychologique, 93*, 379–400.

Gustafsson, J.-E. (1984). A unifying model for the structure of intellectual abilities. *Intelligence, 8*, 179–203.

Heidrich, S.M. & Denney, N.W. (1994). Does social problem solving differ from other types of problem solving during adult years? *Experimental Aging Research, 20*, 105–126.

Horn, J. (1988). Thinking about human abilities. In Nesselroade, J.R. & Cattell, R.B. (Eds.), *Handbook of Multivariate Experimental Psychology* (2nd ed., pp. 645–685). New York: Plenum Press.

Kaufman, A.S. & Kaufman, N.L. (1993). *Manual for Kaufman Adolescent and Adult Intelligence Test (KAIT)*, Circles Pines, MN: American Guidance Service, Inc.

Kaufman, A.S. & Kaufman, N.L. (1997). The Kaufman adolescent and adult intelligence test. In Flanagan, D.P., Genshaft, J.L. & Harrison, P.L. (Eds.), *Contemporary Intellectual Assessment. Theories, Tests, and Issues* (pp. 207–229). New York: The Guilford Press.

Kyllonen, P.C. & Christal, R.E. (1990). Reasoning ability is (little more than) working-memory capacity? *Intelligence, 14*, 389–433.

Lee, J.-E., Wong, C.-M.T., Day, J.D., Maxwell, S.E. & Thorpe, P. (2000). Social and academic intelligences: a multitrait–multimethod study of their crystallized and fluid characteristics. *Personality and Individual Differences, 29*, 539–553.

Mitchell, A. & Lawson, A.E. (1988). Predicting genetics achievement in nonmajors' college biology. *Journal of Research in Science Teaching, 25*, 23–37.

Rabbitt, P. (1996). Do individual differences in speed reflect 'global' or 'local' differences in mental abilities? *Intelligence, 22*, 69–88.

Raven, J.C. (1983). *The Standard Progressive Matrices, 1938–83*. New York: Psychological Corporation.

Schmidt, F.L. & Hunter, J.E. (1998). The validity and utility of selection methods in personnel psychology. Practical and theoretical implications of 85 years of research findings. *Psychological Bulletin, 124*, 262–274.

Stelzl, I., Merz, F., Ehlers, T. & Remer, H. (1995). The effect of schooling on the development of fluid and crystallized intelligence: a quasi-experimental study. *Intelligence, 21*, 279–296.

Thorndike R.L., Hagen, E.P. & Sattler, J.M. (1985), *Stanford–Binet Intelligence Scale* (4th ed.), Chicago: Riverside Publications.

Wechsler, D. (1981). *Manual for the Wechsler Adult Intelligence Scale – Revised*. New York: Psychological Corporation.

Woodcock, R.W. (1998). Extending g_f-g_c theory into practice. In McArdle, J.J. & Woodcock, R.W. (Eds.), *Human Cognitive Abilities in Theory and Practice* (pp. 137–156). Mahwah, NJ: Lawrence Erlbaum Associates.

Woodcock. R.W. & Johnson, M.B. (1989). Woodcock–Johnson Psycho-Educational Battery – Revised. Allen, TX: DLM Teaching Resources.

André Beauducel

RELATED ENTRIES

FORMATS FOR ASSESSMENT

INTRODUCTION

Psychological and educational assessments today come in many forms: they vary on the basis of the item type or types that are included, the physical means by which items are presented to test-takers and responses are supplied, and the manner in which items and test forms are assembled. In this way, the format of an assessment is the end result of numerous psychometric and practical considerations about the nature of the ability being evaluated and the appropriate and the most feasible ways to gather such information. By separating formats for assessment into several component parts, the layers of decisions that must be made in the process of test creation emerge and the full range of possibilities for test creation and use likewise become more readily apparent. The three component parts that constitute the format of an assessment are (1) methods of delivery and response collection, (2) test algorithm, and (3) item type. The remainder of this entry will focus on each component in turn and how they relate to each other and test purpose in defining the format of an assessment.

METHODS OF DELIVERY AND RESPONSE COLLECTION

The choice of delivery and response modes for assessment is central in the process of test development, as this refers to the physical means or medium by which items are presented to test-takers and how test-takers in turn provide answers. There are four methods by which a test can be presented and responded to/recorded: using pencil and paper, oral, by physically carrying out a behaviour or series of behaviours, or via electronic media such as computers or other audio/video devices. Of course, two or more delivery modes could be used in a single assessment; for example, a classroom teacher might read item stems aloud while students write answers on their papers.

Many educational assessments administered to students on a large scale are implemented as paper-and-pencil instruments for both item delivery and response collection. This builds flexibility into the test administration because many test-takers can be evaluated at once, they can work at their own pace, and answer sheets can be gathered for scoring at the convenience of the administrator. On the negative side, the paper-and-pencil format may not be the most flexible mode of delivery and response collection for all constructs.

Indeed, certain constructs of interest to psychologists and educators are better suited to assessment by oral or physical/behavioural means, especially with regard to test-takers' responses. These modes of assessment allow for the administrator to evaluate a test-taker in a more one-on-one setting, which the examinee may be more comfortable with and this may lead to more valid assessment. Completing an assessment by a series of behaviours could include the use of role-playing exercises, while an oral assessment might be along the lines of a psychological interview or thesis defence. By these two methods test-takers can demonstrate competency in areas that paper-and-pencil tests cannot readily assess, but in both methods practical considerations such as economic and time costs as well as psychometric complexity of scoring are factors that must be taken to account.

The fourth assessment format involves the use of electronic media to present items to examinees and/or to record their responses. Computers are one important route for test delivery and response collection (this is made promising by the escalating power of desktop computers as well as their increasing graphical and audio capabilities), but other forms of video and audio data transmission represent means by which assessment can take place as well.

These four methods of assessment provide test developers with a number of options for creating test instruments. In evaluating the different delivery and response collection methods for use in an assessment, however, particularly in terms of the nature of the response, it is important to recognize that each of these methods is more appropriate in some situations than others, dependent on the nature of the construct and how it can best be measured given concerns for validity and reliability and real-world constraints such as time and cost.

TEST ALGORITHM

The format of an assessment also refers to how the test form is assembled and the way in which items are sequenced for presentation to test-takers. Thissen and Mislevy (2000) describe test algorithms as a matter of three questions: how to start (what is the first item?), how to continue (after a response, what is the next item?), and how to stop (when is the test over?). The three basic test algorithms are linear, multi-stage, and fully adaptive, and a number of variations of each exist. These test algorithms are described and their strengths and weaknesses are highlighted in Table 1.

In a linear test algorithm, the ordering or inclusion of items may change across forms of

the test but not within a form. A test-taker starts with item one, proceeds to the next sequentially numbered items, and then goes on through to the last presented item (Thissen & Mislevy, 2000). Each test-taker who receives the same form of the test sees the same items in the same order. Different forms of the same test can also be created such that items are scrambled across forms or so that different items appear on different forms. These different 'versions' of the same test can be equated to each other statistically to ensure that all examinees receive comparably difficult tests, and when this is the case the forms are referred to as parallel. Nearly all paper-and-pencil tests are presented as a single linear form or with multiple linear forms that are parallel.

A second family of test algorithms is known as multi-stage testing (MST). The basic principle behind MST is sequential or adaptive testing, where the responses a test-taker provides to a given set of items determine the next set of items to be presented (Thissen & Mislevy, 2000). Each set of items is referred to as a stage. An examinee is presented a set of items, and the examinee's ability is estimated based on his or her responses to that stage. The examinee then progresses to the second stage of testing and is presented with a new set of items dependent on the estimated ability level. The difficulty level of any one stage is conditional on the test-taker's

Table 1. Continuum of test algorithms

	Variations	Comments	References
Linear	Single form Multiple parallel forms Linear-on-the-fly	Examinees can review items Inefficient for individuals	Thissen & Mislevy (2000)
Multi-stage	Two-stage	Stages tailored to examinee ability	Luecht & Nungester (2000)
	Flexilevel Stratified-adaptive Fixed-branching	2 to n stages Can be paper and pencil or computerized, depending on level of complexity	Thissen & Mislevy (2000)
	Variable-branching Testlet-based adaptive Computer-adaptive sequential testing	Potential for shorter test	
Fully adaptive		As many branching decisions as items on the test Items tailored to examinee ability Potential for shorter test	van der Linden & Pashley (2000)

performance on the previous stage, and stages are chained in this manner, from a minimum of two up to as many stages as the test user deems necessary given the test purpose. Different MST algorithms basically vary by the number of stages, the number of items per stage, and how examinees pass through stages (Patsula, 1999).

The third basic test algorithm is the fully adaptive test, where the examinee's response to one item determines the item that will follow it. In a sense, a fully adaptive test can be viewed as the limiting case of a MST where only one item appears at each stage and the number of items administered is identical to the number of stages in the test. Fully adaptive tests administered by computers are particularly useful in cases where a high degree of measurement precision is required, as these tests can be programmed to cease only when a pre-specified standard error of measurement is reached. Fully adaptive tests can also shorten the length of a test because only those items are administered that are judged as suitable for estimating ability. Items that are judged as too easy or too hard in relation to the candidate's ability level need not be administered as they provide very little information in the ability estimation process.

The emergence of these different test algorithms and their variations has provided test developers with a measure of freedom in the test creation process; the standard no longer is a single form or multiple parallel forms. By the same token, many of these algorithms are largely confined to the realm of computer-based tests, as in most cases only computers can process test-takers' responses fast enough to take advantage of the adaptive-type algorithms.

ITEM TYPE

In developing an assessment, the third essential element of format is item type, and in this regard test developers have a substantial number of options to select from. Without getting into specifics of content or constructs, these item types at a basic level vary from one another in one other important way – they vary in terms of the nature of the response that test-takers are expected to provide.

Responses to test items can take many different forms, such as the selection of one of several alternatives on a multiple-choice item, the development of an extended essay, or the acting out of driving skills in a road test. Clearly, these responses range along one significant dimension, in that with some item types (termed *selected-response* or *closed-product*) test-takers choose one of several pre-defined answer choices, while on others (*constructed-response* or *open-product*) answers are uniquely synthesized and expressed by each individual taking the test (Osterlind, 1998). As noted by Osterlind and Merz (1994), differentiating between item types based on the nature of response using a rigid classification system is not as useful as thinking about items in terms of whether more or fewer answers can be judged as acceptable. In this way, each different item type imaginable can be described as located somewhere on a continuum of more to less restrictive responses.

Some examples of item types that are familiar include the standard multiple-choice format (and its variations such as matching, k-type, true–false, and multiple true–false), fill-in/grid-in, and essays. Among the constructed-response item types are performance tasks, which are assessments that aim to align as closely as possible with the ability of interest to maintain a high degree of realism with an emphasis on doing (Hambleton, 1996). Some performance task formats are laboratory experiments, interviews, discussions, performances, exhibitions, oral reports and presentations, and portfolios. Additionally, recent advances in desktop computing have facilitated the emergence of a number of novel test item types that are primarily being researched and used in computer-based testing (reviewed in Zenisky & Sireci, in press), such as items where examinees are prompted to generate examples or hypotheses, edit onscreen passages, manipulate graphics or items onscreen using the computer mouse, interact with the computer in simulation activities, sort or order items according to various attributes, or type in numerical expressions. Research into emerging item types (e.g. Bennett, Morley & Quardt, 2000; Bennett et al., 1999; Bennett & Rock, 1995; Bennett & Sebrechts, 1997; Martinez & Bennett, 1992) is in response to test users who are increasingly interested in assessing new constructs as well as familiar constructs in new ways.

These latter item types in particular introduce another important component of item types: the incorporation of multimedia. While a number of item types are largely text- or language-based, many other assessments incorporate still graphics and images into the stem as a matter of routine. Furthermore, one emerging area of interest for assessment concerns the use of other media in item stems as assessment developers continue to explore and integrate audio, video, and computerized-interactive options (Parshall, Davey & Pashley, 2000). The extent to which different media are featured in item stems is not always directly related to item type, as whether an item type is selected-response, constructed-response, or performance assessment does not mean it will have more or less media complexity in the stem. For example, a short video in the prompt could be followed by a series of multiple-choice questions or an essay or a graphical modelling-type item.

In considering various item formats for use in psychological assessments, accepted standards of validity and reliability must be met, but it is also important to keep in mind additional practical constraints such as the amount of reasonable or available testing time, the time to score and scoring costs, and the development costs. Some of the free-response formats (such as oral presentations, portfolios, demonstrations, and essays) require substantial time commitments in terms of the amount of time that it will take examinees to complete and the time required to evaluate the finished product or performance. Test developers must try to balance many factors such as time to develop a test, the cost of development and scoring, the time required by candidates to complete the test, while at the same time retaining sufficiently high levels of reliability and validity to justify the use of the test.

FUTURE PERSPECTIVES AND CONCLUSIONS

Given the various delivery and response collection methods, a variety of test algorithms, and many item types, test developers have an assortment of choices to make in crafting a coherent final product known as the test instrument. The format of an assessment is the end product of many decisions about what a test needs to look like in order to accomplish a specific purpose. How test-takers will be presented test items and what item types can be used to evaluate a construct are issues that test developers must consider from numerous angles in order to ensure quality measurement.

References

Bennett, R.E., Morley, M. & Quardt, D. (2000). Three response types for broadening the conception of mathematical problem solving in computerized tests. *Applied Psychological Measurement*, 24(4), 294–309.

Bennett, R.E., Morley, M., Quardt, D. & Rock, D.A. (1999, September). *Graphical Modelling: A New Response Type for Measuring the Qualitative Component of Mathematical Reasoning* (ETS Research Report No. 99-21). Princeton, NJ: Educational Testing Service.

Bennett, R.E. & Rock, D.A. (1995). Generalizability, validity, and examinee perceptions of a computer-delivered formulating-hypotheses test. *Journal of Educational Measurement*, 32, 19–36.

Bennett, R.E. & Sebrechts, M.M. (1997). A computer-based task for measuring the representational component of quantitative proficiency. *Journal of Educational Measurement*, 34(1), 64–77.

Hambleton, R.K. (1996). Advances in assessment models, methods, and practices. In Berliner, D.C. & Calfee, R.C. (Eds.), *Handbook of Educational Psychology* (pp. 899–925). New York: Simon & Schuster/Macmillan.

Luecht, R.M. & Nungester, R.J. (2000). Computer-adaptive sequential testing. In van der Linden, W.J. & Glas, C.A.W. (Eds.), *Computerized Adaptive Testing: Theory and Practice* (pp. 117–128). Boston, MA: Kluwer Academic Publishers.

Martinez, M.E. & Bennett, R.E. (1992). A review of automatically scorable constructed-response item types for large-scale assessment. *Journal of Educational Measurement*, 5(2), 151–169.

Osterlind, S.J. (1998). *Constructing Test Items: Multiple-Choice, Constructed-Response, Performance, and Other Formats*. Boston: Kluwer Academic Publishers.

Osterlind, S.J. & Merz, W.R. (1994). Building a taxonomy for constructed-response test items. *Educational Assessment*, 2(2), 133–147.

Parshall, C.G., Davey, T. & Pashley, P. (2000). Innovative item types for computerized testing. In van der Linden, W.J. & Glas, C. (Eds.), *Computerized Adaptive Testing: Theory and Practice* (pp. 129–148). Boston, MA: Kluwer Academic Publishers.

Patsula, L.N. (1999). A comparison of computerized-adaptive testing and multi-stage testing. Unpublished doctoral dissertation, University of Massachusetts, Amherst.

Thissen, D. & Mislevy, R.J. (2000). Testing algorithms. In Wainer, H. et al. (Eds.), *Computerized Adaptive Testing: A Primer* (2nd ed.). Mahwah, NJ: Lawrence Erlbaum Associates.

van der Linden, W.J. & Pashley, P.J. (2000). Item selection and ability estimation in adaptive testing. In van der Linden, W.J. & Glas, C.A.W. (Eds.), *Computerized Adaptive Testing: Theory and Practice* (pp. 1–24). Boston, MA: Kluwer Academic Publishers.

Zenisky, A.L. & Sireci, S.G. (in press). Technological innovations in large-scale assessment. *Applied Measurement in Education.*

April L. Zenisky and Ronald K. Hambleton

RELATED ENTRIES

APPLIED FIELDS: EDUCATION, ACHIEVEMENT TESTING, CRITERION-REFERENCED TESTING: METHODS AND PROCEDURES, NORM-REFERENCED TESTING: METHODS AND PROCEDURES, PERFORMANCE

GENERALIZABILITY THEORY

Everyone who works in any field of science is well acquainted with the notion that whatever measure we take of whatever phenomenon, that measure is inherently affected by random error. Indeed, reliability issues are recognized as of capital importance in any scientific endeavour, as well as in psychology. Over the years, the classical test theory of measurement has been the solid ground for almost all of psychological testing. The aim of this entry is to describe generalizability theory (Brennan, 2001; Cronbach, Gleser, Nanda & Rajaratnam, 1972), which represents a more precise and complete model of the composition of an observed measure, and to show some of its advantages relative to classical test theory.

According to classical test theory, an observed score is composed of the sum of two components: the unknown true score and the random error. The central point of classical test theory is that error is randomly and independently distributed, and is uncorrelated with true score, as well as with true scores and errors on subsequent measurements.

The classical test theory only takes a unitary error term into account, even though errors actually come from multiple sources. This means that reliability assessment must rest on multiple procedures and indicators (for example, test–retest, split-half, Cronbach's alpha), each one accounting for a different error source. Thus, a high test–retest reliability means that we can trust that measure independently of the occasion when it is measured, but it tells us nothing about whether we can trust that measure independently of the system (human being or instrument) which actually makes the measurement. Consequently, multiple reliabilities exist within classical test theory, for instance across occasions, across raters, across items, and so forth. This represents a major limit of the classical approach to reliability, as it cannot account for multiple error sources. Far more importantly, classical theory of reliability cannot account for the interaction among different sources of error. For instance, neither Cronbach's alpha nor test–retest reliabilities are useful when consistency across items changes across occasions.

Generalizability theory represents a more general approach to the assessment of the reliability of a score. It defines a score as a sample from the universe of all the admissible observations, characterized by one or more conditions of measurement. Here, the true score is defined as the universe score, that is the average of all the observations in the universe of admissible observations, and errors are defined by the conditions of measurement. Items, raters, occasions, tests, and so forth, are examples of the conditions of measurement, and each one accounts for part of the variability of the observed scores. Generalizability theory is designed to estimate the multiple components of the obtained score variability, and to use them to explore the effects of different sources of measurement error. Consequently, it allows the investigation of several sources of variation simultaneously, and the estimation of the error in generalizing an observed result to the universe defined by each of them. Generalizability theory was developed in the context of dependability of behavioural measurements. Nevertheless, the model is rather general and may as well apply to other reliability issues.

Generalizability theory is founded upon the statistical model of the analysis of variance (ANOVA). In ANOVA, the total variance is partitioned according to the independent variables in the design. Similarly, generalizability theory uses the ANOVA model to estimate the variance components associated with the sources of variation that affect the score under investigation. In other words, the sources of variation define a model of the score, and specify which error source (by itself or combined with others) affects the measure and how much it does. In generalizability theory, sources of variation other than the object of measurement are defined as *facets*, while groupings within a facet are defined as *conditions* (factors and levels represent their analogues in factorial ANOVA). Facets may be considered as either random or fixed, likewise factors in ANOVA. Conditions within a random facet are considered as randomly sampled from the universe of conditions that define that facet. Specifying a facet as random allows the researcher to generalize to all the conditions within that facet, including those not explicitly included in the design. For instance, items of a test may be regarded as conditions within a random facet, since researchers are not usually interested to those particular items, but consider them as a sample drawn from the population of items that measure the same theoretical construct. Specifying a facet as fixed, instead, implies that all the conditions within that facet have been included in the model, or that the researcher is willing to generalize only to the conditions included in the design. Individuals enter as a source of variation in all the generalizability theory models, usually as the object of measurement. This means that the variance associated with the individuals represents actual differences among persons, whereas the variance associated with the facets reflects error.

The main focus of generalizability theory is upon the components of variance associated with the object of measurement, with the facets and their interactions, and with the residual. It should be noted that the components of variance are the variances of the hypothesized components of the score under investigation, and they are not the same as the mean squares in ANOVA. The component of variance associated with a facet reflects how much that facet contributes to the error in the score. In more analytical terms, the variance of a score is decomposed into its components. For a simple two-facets crossed design, for instance, Persons × Raters × Occasions, we have:

$$\sigma^2(X_{pro}) = \sigma_p^2 + \sigma_r^2 + \sigma_o^2 + \sigma_t^2 \\ + \sigma_{pr}^2 + \sigma_{po}^2 + \sigma_{ro}^2 + \sigma_{pro,e}^2$$

where X_{pro} represents the observed rating of a person (p) by a rater (r) on an occasion (o). In this example, the observed score is composed of the sum of the components of variance due to the object of measurement (individuals, σ_p^2), to the conditions of measurements (raters and occasions, σ_r^2 and σ_o^2), to the interactions between facets and between facets and individuals (σ_{ro}^2, σ_{po}^2, σ_{pr}^2), and finally to the residual ($\sigma_{pro,e}^2$). It should be noted that in these models the residual is confounded with the higher order interaction. As it can be seen, the main advantage of generalizability theory is that it allows the estimation of the components of variance for multiple facets and their interactions. In other words, it becomes possible not only to estimate how much a facet contributes to the error in the score by itself, but also if the contribution of that facet increases or decreases when it is associated with other facets (Shavelson, Webb & Rowley, 1989; Shavelson & Webb, 1991). Furthermore, the comparison of the size of each component suggests the relative ranking of error sources. For instance, if the component of variance associated with a given facet was small compared to others, then that facet contributes to a small extent to the variability of the observed score, thus it is not a major source of error.

Of course, the interpretation of the estimated components of variance depends on the goal of the study. When generalizability theory is applied to psychological testing, individuals are usually the object of interest. Variation among individuals represents real differences and is referred to as the estimated universe score variance. Instead, variations associated with the facets and their interactions represent the errors that affect the score. However, in other situations the object of measurement may change. For instance, experimental manipulation may be the object of interest in psychophysiological studies. In these cases, individual differences would be usually considered as measurement error. Cardinet, Tourneur and Allal (1976) proposed a principle of symmetry in order to enable generalizability theory to address the situation in which the object of measurement changes. The principle simply states that any facet in the design may be regarded as the object of measurement. Variance components may be computed regardless of the measurement design, since their meaning is defined only after a decision is made about the object of measurement.

One of the most important issues regarding generalizability theory concerns how to estimate the components of variance. Fisher (1925) proposed the 'analysis of variance' method of estimation, also called 'Expected Mean Squares' (EMS) method. Here, the sums of squares are equated to their expected values, obtaining a set of linear equations. In the simple case of a single facet $p \times i$ design we have:

$$\left\{ \begin{array}{l} E(MS_p) = \sigma_{pi,e}^2 + n_i \sigma_p^2 \\ E(MS_i) = \sigma_{pi,e}^2 + n_p \sigma_i^2 \\ E(MS_{pi,e}) = \sigma_{pi,e}^2 \end{array} \right\}$$

where n_p and n_i are the number of levels in p and i, respectively. These equations have to be solved to obtain estimates of each component of variance. Replacing the expected mean squares with the corresponding observed mean squares and replacing each σ^2 with the estimate σ^{*2} we have:

$$\left\{ \begin{array}{l} MS_p = \sigma_{pi,e}^{*2} + n_i \sigma_p^{*2} \\ MS_i = \sigma_{pi,e}^{*2} + n_p \sigma_i^{*2} \\ MS_{pi,e} = \sigma_{pi,e}^{*2} \end{array} \right\}$$

These equations can be easily solved using simple algebra.

The EMS method is very simple and gives unbiased estimates. Nevertheless it may give negative estimates of components of variance.

This is quite disturbing, of course, since a component of variance is by definition a non-negative quantity. Negative estimates may be due to an erroneous measurement model or to sampling error. In the former case, usually when the negative estimates are large, a different definition of the measurement model is needed. For instance, other facets should be included into the model. In the latter case, usually when the sample size or the number of conditions within one or more facets are smaller than needed, the relative magnitude of the negative estimates is normally close to zero. Cronbach, Gleser, Nanda and Rajaratnam (1972) proposed to solve this problem by setting the negative estimates to zero, and using this value to compute the other variance component estimates. A different approach was proposed by Brennan (2001), who suggested setting the negative estimates to zero, but to use the original negative values to compute the other variance components. As Shavelson and Webb (1991) pointed out, the first approach gets rid of an impossible result at the cost of producing biased estimates of the variance components. The second approach uses the negative variance component estimates, but returns unbiased estimates. Both are commonly used as well as unsatisfying approaches. An alternative that avoids the problem of the negative estimates is to use estimation methods that make them impossible, such as maximum likelihood, restricted maximum likelihood and Bayesian estimation.

A feature of the ML method is that in estimating variance components it does not take into account the degrees of freedom that are involved in estimating fixed effects. This characteristic is overcome by restricted (or residual) maximum likelihood estimation (REML). Generally speaking, in REML the estimation of variance components is based on residuals computed after fitting the fixed effects part of the model by ordinary least squares. REML estimates of variance components are closer to the true parameters than EMS estimates. However, with balanced data sets and normal distributions, REML and EMS methods perform similarly. Interested readers may refer to Searle, Casella and McCulloch (1992) for a discussion on estimating variance components.

The estimated components of variance are further used within generalizability theory in order to compute generalizability coefficients. They are analogous to the reliability coefficients in classical test theory. Generalizability theory distinguishes between decisions based on the relative standing of an individual and decisions based on the absolute value of a score. This is a rather important point because the error term that enters into the generalizability coefficients changes according to the nature of the decision the research is willing to make. Error term in relative decisions (σ^2_{rel}) arises from all the non-zero variance components associated with the rank ordering of individuals. Hence, variance components associated with the interaction of persons with each facet (or combination of facets) define the error term. For instance, in a person (p) by rater (r) by occasion (o) design the error term would be:

$$\sigma^2_{rel} = \frac{\sigma^2_{pr}}{n_r} + \frac{\sigma^2_{po}}{n_o} + \frac{\sigma^2_{pro,e}}{n_r n_o}$$

where n_r and n_o are the numbers of raters and occasions.

Instead, error term in absolute decisions (σ^2_{abs}) arises from all the components associated with the score, except the component associated with the object of measurement. That is:

$$\sigma^2_{abs} = \frac{\sigma^2_r}{n_r} + \frac{\sigma^2_o}{n_o} + \frac{\sigma^2_{ro}}{n_r n_o} + \frac{\sigma^2_{pr}}{n_r} + \frac{\sigma^2_{po}}{n_o} + \frac{\sigma^2_{pro,e}}{n_r n_o}$$

In generalizability theory, the generalizability coefficient E^2_p is the ratio of the universe score variance to the expected observed score variance; that is:

$$E\rho^2_{rel} = \frac{\sigma^2_p}{\left(\sigma^2_p + \sigma^2_{rel}\right)}$$

A reliability coefficient can be also defined for absolute decisions. Brennan and Kane (1977) called this coefficient an index of dependability and used the symbol ϕ (phi):

$$\phi = \frac{\sigma^2_p}{\left(\sigma^2_p + \sigma^2_{abs}\right)}$$

On the basis of this sketch of generalizability theory given above, it is clear that it provides a more complete picture of the sources of variability that affect an observed score. The exact meaning of the results of a generalizability study depends of course on the nature of the problem the study addresses. For example, consider a simplified study in which some ability is measured on a number of persons by two tests forms, each one composed of a number of items. This would be a $p \times t \times i$ crossed design. In a generalizability study on these hypothetical data, variance components associated with Persons, Tests, Items, Persons by Tests, Persons by Items, Items by Tests, and Persons by Tests by Items, the last interaction, confounded with Residual, would be estimated.

Depending on the relative amounts of the variance components associated with those sources, different conclusions would be drawn. If the component of variance associated with Persons was large and those associated with the other sources were small, then one could infer that the measure is highly reliable independently of the form of the test and the items. In this case, both generalizability coefficient and dependability index would be large, because both relative and absolute errors would be small. However, if the components of variance associated with both Persons and Test were large, then one should infer that the absolute scores of individuals depend on the particular form of the test that was administered. The generalizability coefficient would be still high, because the relative ranking of individuals would remain unaffected by the test form, but the dependability index would be low, because the absolute scores would not be independent of the test form.

In this case, classical test theory would only have provided a high reliability coefficient, if measured with parallel forms. On the other hand, if the components of variance associated with Persons and Persons by Test interaction were large, relative to the others, then one should conclude that also the relative ranking of individuals depends on the particular test form, and both generalizability coefficient and dependability index would be small.

More interesting to a researcher would be the pattern of results concerning the combined effect of Test and Items facets. Indeed, if the component of variance associated with the Test by Items interaction was large compared to the other sources of variability, then one should infer that individual score depends on both the form of the test and on the particular items which have been administered. In this case, individuals may behave consistently on each form and on each item, when separately considered, but still individual scores would be affected by a relevant source of error, which would go undetected with classical test theory.

Generalizability theory also distinguishes between generalizability studies (such as those described above) and decision studies. Generalizability studies provide an estimate of the variance components associated with the sources of measurement error. Decision studies are used to select the number of conditions of each facet that minimizes error for a specific purpose, much like the Spearman–Brown formula in the classical test theory.

Generalizability theory is perhaps the most complete measurement model currently available to researchers. As such, it is applicable to any scientific field in which a multifaceted perspective on measurement errors is important. Both SPSS and Statistica statistical packages include modules that estimate the components of variance in a variety of designs, whereas the GENOVA software program (Crick & Brennan, 1982) performs univariate generalizability analyses for balanced designs. Recently, other modules (urGENOVA and mGENOVA) have been added to deal with unbalanced designs and multivariate analyses.

FUTURE PERSPECTIVES AND CONCLUSIONS

Until recently, generalizability theory has been mostly applied in educational psychology, and mostly to address issues regarding the reliability of different proficiency tools. It has been also applied to other fields of investigation, such as psychophysiological (e.g. Strube, 2000), observational and longitudinal studies, albeit rather sparsely. Nevertheless, in recent years the interest toward this model has grown up to a large extent. In the near future, it is likely that the perspective the generalizability theory acknowledges will spread more consistently to other scientific fields, and develop as a standard

method in psychometrics. Also, the model underlying the generalizability theory was proved useful to address reliability issues in experimental as well as in observational studies (e.g. Di Nocera, Ferlazzo & Borghi, 2001), and in the near future it will likely contribute to make the reliability of results from psychological experiments more carefully addressed by investigators.

References

Brennan, R.L. (2001). *Generalizability Theory*. New York: Springer-Verlag.

Brennan, R.L. & Kane, M.T. (1977). An index of dependability for mastery tests. *Journal of Educational Measurement*, 14, 277–289.

Cardinet, J., Tourneur, Y. & Allal, L. (1976). The symmetry of generalizability theory: applications to educational measurement. *Journal of Educational Measurement*, 13, 119–135.

Crick, J.E. & Brennan, R.L. (1982). *GENOVA: A Generalized Analysis of Variance System*. Iowa City: ACT.

Cronbach, L.J., Gleser, G.C., Nanda, H. & Rajaratnam, N. (1972). *The Dependability of Behavioural Measurements: Theory of Generalizability of Scores and Profiles*. New York: John Wiley & Sons.

Di Nocera, F., Ferlazzo, F. & Borghi, V. (2001). G Theory and the reliability of psychophysiological measures: a tutorial. *Psychophysiology*, 38, 796–806.

Fisher, R.A. (1925). *Statistical Methods for Research Workers*. London: Oliver & Boyd.

Searle, S.R., Casella, G. & McCulloch, C.E. (1992). *Variance Components*. New York: John Wiley & Sons.

Shavelson, R.J. & Webb, N.M. (1991). *Generalizability Theory: A Primer*. London: Sage.

Shavelson, R.J., Webb, N.M. & Rowley, G.L. (1989). Generalizability theory. *American Psychologist*, 44, 922–932.

Strube, M.J. (2000). Psychometrics. In Cacioppo, J.T., Tassinary, L.G. & Berntson, G.G. (Eds.), *Handbook of Psychophysiology*. Cambridge: Cambridge University Press.

Fabio Ferlazzo

RELATED ENTRIES

CLASSICAL AND MODERN ITEM ANALYSIS, RELIABILITY, VALIDITY (GENERAL)

G GIFTEDNESS

INTRODUCTION

The assessment of giftedness has it roots in the study of individual differences which has focused on the constructs of intelligence, creativity, and motivation. Although broad definitions of giftedness have emerged, the most extensive body of research on assessment concentrates on intelligence. Unfortunately, the construct of intelligence is enigmatic and models of intelligence range from unidimensional to multidimensional. Of course, the identification of giftedness should not be based solely on an intelligence test, but also on the basis of the social and cultural context. To assess the construct of giftedness, valid and reliable measures of domain specific knowledge, speed, and metacognition are necessary. Alternative assessment procedures, such as Sternberg's Triarchic model or dynamic assessment, should also be considered.

DEFINITION OF GIFTEDNESS

There is no agreed upon definition of giftedness or talent that dominates the field. Sternberg and Davidson (1986) edited a collection of 17 conceptualizations of giftedness. The range in conceptualizations was diverse, but the majority concentrated on the psychological aspects of giftedness. The psychological aspects emphasized constructs of intelligence, creativity, and motivation. Renzulli (1978) suggested that giftedness is an interaction of three clusters of traits: above-average general or specific abilities, task commitment, and creativity.

Feldhusen and Jarwan's (1993) review of definitions of giftedness and talent fell into six categories: psychometric definitions, trait definitions, definitions focused on social needs, education-oriented definitions, special talent definitions, and multi-dimensional definitions. These categories were not mutually exclusive.

Often, giftedness and talent are used interchangeably. However, the two concepts can be differentiated (Gagne, Belanger & Motard, 1993). Giftedness is above average competence in a human ability, whereas talent is above average performance in a particular field. Giftedness refers to human aptitudes such as intelligence or creative abilities, whereas talent is demonstrated in a human activity such as mathematics, literature, or music.

PSYCHOLOGICAL CHARACTERISTICS

Theoretically, the study of giftedness is related to the psychology of individual differences. Constructs of intelligence and creativity, and to some extent motivation, have provided the psychological foundations for the assessment of giftedness. The empirical rigour of most of this research, however, is poor. However, by far the greatest body of empirical research on the assessment of giftedness is related to intelligence. Unfortunately, intelligence is an enigmatic concept. For example, is intelligence the same as verbal ability, analytic thinking, academic aptitude, strategy thinking, or just the ability to problem solve? Further, models of intelligence range from unidimensional, such as Spearman's g, to a three dimensional or multidimensional model according to Sternberg's (1985) Triarchic theory, or Guilford's 120 components.

In one of the classic longitudinal studies in the field, Terman (1925) investigated the various characteristics of individuals with high IQ (those with IQ scores at 140 and above). Using a 1916 edition of the Stanford–Binet, Terman and colleagues identified over 1500 children whose IQs of 140 or over placed them in the top 1% in the United States. He found that gifted individuals were of average socioeconomic status and physical characteristics, but scored above average on a variety of psychological characteristics.

Sternberg and Davidson's (1986) review outlined a number of cognitive abilities of which gifted individuals are exceptional: they have high general intelligence and specific ability in an area of expertise, and they can easily conceive of high order relations. Many of these characteristics are in an area we call metacognition.

Metacognition, or thinking about one's own thinking, is an important component of giftedness. Alexander, Carr, and Schwanenflugel (1995) reviewed the literature on giftedness and metacognition in the areas of factual knowledge about thinking strategies, the use of strategies, and cognitive monitoring. They found that gifted students showed better performance than other students in only some aspects (factual knowledge about metacognition and transfer of strategies). Swanson (1992) compared intellectually gifted children to high, average, and low average IQ children on problem solving tasks and a metacognitive questionnaire. Gifted children performed better on problem solving tasks and scored higher for information on a questionnaire related to attributions and strategy use.

Davidson (1986) compared gifted students on mathematical and verbal insight problems. Comparing information and combining novel encoding were considered measures of insight. The gifted scored better than the non-gifted sample on insight problems and they also employed more selective encoding.

In terms of cognitive differences, Rogers' (1986) comprehensive review concluded that gifted children and adults generally differ in degree and not kind of cognition.

SOCIAL/EMOTIONAL

Janos and Robinson (1985) concluded that the intellectually gifted, at least of moderate notice or ability, are often precocious or advanced in their social adjustments. Contrary to outdated stereotypes, gifted students are typically socially and emotionally well adjusted. Extremely gifted individuals have more social and emotional adjustment problems than those who are moderately gifted. There is some conflict in the literature on whether gifted children vary in self-esteem (see Olszewski-Kubilius et al., 1988, for a review). Some studies using global measures of self-esteem show that the gifted score higher on these measures whereas other studies suggest there are no differences between the groups. Olszewski-Kubilius et al. reviewed some studies showing that gifted younger students generally score higher on measures of locus of control than comparison students. Benbow, Arjmand, and Walberg (1991) investigated educational achievement in a sample of mathematically precocious youth. They found that motivation, as measured by the quantity of academic activities participated in, was an important predictor of educational achievement and aspiration at age 23, followed by the variables related to quality of instruction and home environment.

CULTURAL/SOCIAL CONTEXT

Many psychologists who have studied intelligence believe that it is in the 'eye of the beholder' and therefore intelligence is largely or wholly culturally defined. Different cultural views have concrete effects on children's performance in the schools. For example, Okagaki and Sternberg (1993) assessed parents' and teachers' conceptions of intelligence among a variety of ethnic groups in San Jose, California. Included among others were Cambodians, Laotians, Mexicans (first generation), Mexican-Americans (second generation), and Anglos. They found that different groups placed different emphases on cognitive versus social competence aspects of intelligence. Teachers, however, emphasized cognitive over social aspects of intelligence.

Giftedness includes cultural values and therefore the opportunities to use those gifts. For example, chess prodigies appear in cultures where chess is appreciated and available to the child. Thus individuals from diverse ethnic backgrounds may display certain gifts and talent in areas particularly valued by members of the culture, but not necessarily members of the other cultural groups.

ASSESSMENT TECHNIQUES

Intelligence Testing

Klausmeier, Mishra, and Maker (1987) surveyed psychologists to determine how giftedness was identified. The majority relied on intelligence tests, primarily the Wechsler scales, followed by the Stanford–Binet, and the Kaufman Abilities Scale for Children (K-ABC). Very few used tests

Table 1.   Summary of some important standardized instruments to assess intellectual giftedness

I Traditional measures
  A The Wechsler Tests (e.g. WISC-III)
  B Stanford–Binet Intelligence Scale
  C Kaufman Assessment Battery for Children
II Alternative measures
  A Sternberg Triarchic Abilities Test
  B Swanson–Cognitive Processing Test

Table 2.   System of categories with the gifted and talented populations

Label	SD	IQ equivalent	% of general population	Ratio
Basic	+ 1	112–115	15–20%	1 in 5 or 6
Moderate	+ 2	125–130	2–4%	1 in 35
High	+ 3	140–145	0.1–0.3%	1 in 600
Extreme	+ 4	155–160	0.002%	1 in 50,000

of creativity or achievement. The Wechsler series yield two primary factors: a verbal and a performance factor. The verbal and performance factored together yield what is known as a Full-Scale score, determined by professionals to reflect *g* (general intelligence). Table 1 provides a summary of some standardized traditional intelligence and alternative measures (to be discussed) to measure intellectual giftedness.

How far from the average a person's abilities should be before the labels of gifted or talented are applied is unclear. Some psychologists use Full-Scale IQ score at or above 120 as a cutoff score for identifying giftedness. This practice is questionable, however, because it obscures performance on individual subtests.

Subgroups of giftedness have been proposed. Gagne et al. (1993) have provided a continuum of differentiation that varies from a 'base of giftedness' to extremely gifted. As shown in Table 2, the cutoff scores on IQ tests vary from 1 standard deviation to 4 standard deviations with the prevalence in the population varying from 1 in 5 to 1 in 50,000. Conventional approaches rely on 1 standard deviation as a cutoff score from giftedness.

Criticisms

Some argue that intelligence tests are discriminatory, while others argue that they are valid predictors of school performance. Several authors argue that the identification of giftedness should not be based solely on intelligence tests, but takes into consideration expertise in a particular area. Thus, for example, if one is attempting to identify gifted writers, common sense would suggest having writing samples evaluated by an authority in that particular area. Others assume that intelligence should be defined the way the individuals are viewed in different cultures, ethnic or social backgrounds.

Alternatives

Additional arguments against traditional intelligence testing are: (a) traditional intelligence tests are more concerned with the product rather than the processes of learning, and (b) traditional testing does not address responsiveness of an individual to instruction. These criticisms have led to alternative techniques for measuring learning potential, discussed below.

Triarchic Model

One emerging model to assess giftedness is based on Sternberg's (1985) Triarchic theory. The model consists of three parts. The first relates to the internal world of the individual and specific mental mechanisms that lead to a more intelligent or less intelligent mediator. It focuses on three types of mental processes in planning what things to do, in learning how to do things, and actually doing them (referred to as meta-components, performance components, and knowledge acquisition components). The second part of the model focuses on tasks or situations that involve novelty or optimizing mental processes. Particular emphasis is given to insight and selective coding. The third part focuses on the external world of the individual and specifies three kinds of acts: environmental adaptation, environmental selection, and environmental shaping. The latter part of the theory emphasizes the role of environmental context in determining what constitutes intelligent behaviour in a given situation. Sternberg indicates that different individuals may be more or less intelligent through different patterns of abilities. However, he views mental representations and processes underlying intelligence as constant across individuals (the internal role), but the intelligent use of these processes in everyday life is not constant and may vary from person to person and culture to culture. External world, or context, varies both within and between cultures. The interaction of the internal with the external world is mediated by experience.

No existing test measures all of the different abilities in the Triarchic Model. Within this model, however, two instruments have emerged: the *Sternberg Triarchic Abilities Test* (STAT) based on a strict theory and the *Cognitive Abilities Survey* based on a rather loose notion of a theory. The STAT has been tested in upper elementary and high school populations. Subtests focus on analytical, creative, and practical abilities in verbal, quantitative, figural, and essay domains. The Cognitive Abilities Survey has nine subtests focusing on arithmetic, proverbs, practical maths, and other examples of real world problems.

Dynamic Assessment

Underachievement is one of many complicating factors in assessing the psychological characteristics of gifted individuals. Within this context, several authors suggest that traditional intelligence underestimates general ability (e.g. see Grigorenko & Sternberg, 1998, for a review). An alternative or supplement to traditional assessment is to measure an individual's performance when given examiner assistance. Procedures that modify performance, via examiner assistance, to understand learning potential, are called dynamic assessment. The examiner attempts to move the student from failure to success by modifying the format, providing more trials, providing information on successful strategies, or offering increasingly more direct cues, hints, or prompts. Thus, 'potential' for learning new information (or accessing previously presented information) is measured in terms of the distance, difference between, and/or change from unassisted performance to a performance level with assistance. In this context, giftedness may be defined as those individuals whose performance supersedes others (e.g. as predetermined by cutoff score at 1 standard deviation above the mean) under dynamic testing conditions. This would require a standardized dynamic processing test, such as the S-Cognitive Processing Test (Swanson, 1995). Unlike traditional testing procedures, score changes due to examiner intervention are not viewed as threatening task

validity. Limitations are that a number of dynamic assessment procedures provide minimal psychometric information.

Expert/Novice Strategies

Ericson and Lehmann (1996) provide a model with application to the assessment of giftedness. They review research showing large individual differences and varied performance associated with experts within a particular field. Experts are those with exceptional performance that reflects acquired abilities to store specific types of information in long-term memory. For example, those precocious in mathematics may also be precocious in their ability to remember numbers or those with expertise in a literary domain (e.g. writing) are accompanied by high vocabulary or quick retrieval of lexical information.

In one of the few subgrouping studies on expertise and giftedness, Swanson, O'Connor, and Carter (1991) compared High and Average IQ 4th and 5th grade children on measures of problem solving, strategy knowledge, creativity, academic achievement, and attributions. Subgroups were determined through a hierarchical cluster analysis for strategies for problem solving. One subgroup was designated as a prototype of gifted intelligence based on their sophisticated heuristic and strategy use. However, this gifted prototype excelled only on measures of attribution and mathematical achievement.

Speed

Another alternative assessment is reaction time or speed of information processing. Speed of memory retrieval is considered by some as an adequate measure of intelligence (Jensen, 1993). Such approaches place no emphasis on previous learning or acquired knowledge, yet these particular processes are strongly related to IQ measures.

Nomination

Numerous other techniques have been used to identify gifted people. Some are related to nominating techniques by parents, teachers, and peers on such questions as who has the most leadership ability, who has the most original ideas, and so on. Teacher nomination is not necessarily the most reliable one, because sometimes a gifted child might have misbehaviour in the class.

FUTURE PERSPECTIVES AND CONCLUSIONS

Several definitions, whether they are psychologically based or educationally driven, have moved away from equating giftedness with intelligence as defined by general IQ tests. Unfortunately, these alternative approaches are less reliable and more open to judgement. Emerging approaches broaden assessment to suggest that expert performance be observed as well as responsiveness to dynamic testing conditions. One of the most comprehensive empirically based alternative models to assess giftedness is outlined by Sternberg (e.g. Sternberg, Ferrari, Clinkenbeard & Grigorenko, 1996). The model focuses on the internal role of the individual, the individual experience, and the external world of the individual.

References

Alexander, J., Carr, M. & Schwanenflugel, P. (1995). Development of metacognition gifted children: directions for future research. *Developmental Review*, 15, 1–37.

Benbow, C.P., Arjmand, O. & Walberg, H.J. (1991). Educational productivity predictors among mathematically talented students. *Journal of Educational Research*, 84, 215–223.

Davidson, J.E (1986). The role of insight in giftedness. In Sternberg, R.J. & Davidson, J.E. (Eds.), *Conceptions of Giftedness* (pp. 201–222). New York: Cambridge University Press.

Ericson, K.A. & Lehmann, A.C. (1996). Expert and exceptional performance: evidence for a maximal adaptation to task constraints. *Annual Review of Psychology*, 47, 273–305.

Feldhusen, J.F. Jarwin, F. (1993). Identification of gifted and talented youth for educational programs. In Mouris, F.J. & Passoud A.H. (Eds.), *International Handbook of Research and Development of Giftedness and Talent* (pp. 233–251). Oxford: Pergamon Press.

Gagne, F., Belanger, J. & Motard, D. (1993). Popular estimates of the prevalence of giftedness and talent. *Roeper Review*, 16, 96–98.

Grigorenko, E.L. & Sternberg, R.J. (1998). Dynamic testing. *Psychological Bulletin*, 124, 75–111.

Janos, P.M. & Robinson, N.M. (1985). Psychosocial development in intellectually gifted children. In Horwitz, F.D. & Obrien, M. (Eds.), *The Gifted and Talented: Developmental Perspectives* (pp. 149–195). Washington DC: American Psychological Association.

Jensen, A. (1993). Why is reaction time correlated with psychometric g? *Current Directions in Psychological Science*, 2, 53–56.

Klausmeier, K.L., Mishra, S.P. & Maker, C.J. (1987). Identification of gifted learners: a national survey of assessment practices and training needs of school psychologists. *Gifted Child Quarterly*, 31, 135–137.

Okagaki, L. & Sternberg, R.J. (1993). Parental beliefs and children's school performance, *Child Development*, 64, 35–56.

Olszewski-Kubilius, P.M., Kulieke, M.J. & Krasney, N. (1988). Personality dimensions of gifted adolescents: a review of the empirical literature. *Gifted Child Quarterly*, 32, 347–352.

Renzulli, J.S. (1978). What makes giftedness? Reexamining a definition. *Phi Delta Kappa*, 60, 180–184.

Rogers, K.B. (1986). Do the gifted think and learn differently? A review of recent research and its implications for instruction. *Journal of Education for the Gifted*, 10, 17–39.

Sternberg, R.J. (1985). *Beyond IQ: A Triarchic Theory of Human Intelligence*. New York: Cambridge University Press.

Sternberg, R.J. & Davidson, J.E. (1986). Cognitive development in the gifted and talented. In Horwitz, F.D. & Obrien, M. (Eds.), *The Gifted and Talented: Developmental Perspectives* (pp. 37–74). Washington DC: American Psychological Association.

Sternberg, R.J., Ferrari, M., Clinkenbeard, P. & Grigorenko, E.L. (1996). Identification, instruction, and assessment of gifted children: a construct validation of a triarchic model. *Gifted Child Quarterly*, 40, 129–137.

Swanson, H.L. (1992). The relationship between metacognition and problem solving in gifted children. *Roeper Review*, 15, 43–47.

Swanson, H.L. (1995). *Swanson–Cognitive Processing Test: A Dynamic Testing Approach*. Austin, TX: Pro-Ed.

Swanson, H.L., O'Connor, J.E. & Carter, K.R. (1991). Problem solving subgroups as a measure of intellectual giftedness. *British Journal of Educational Psychology*, 61, 55–72.

Terman, L.M. (1925). Genetic studies of genius. *Mental and Physical Characteristics of a Thousand Gifted Children*, Vol. 1. Stanford, CA: Stanford Press.

H. Lee Swanson

RELATED ENTRIES

Applied Fields: Education, Creativity

G GOAL ATTAINMENT SCALING (GAS)

INTRODUCTION

This entry will provide a brief summary of background, major psychometric issues, implementation aids, and current developments of Goal Attainment Scaling (GAS).

BACKGROUND

Goal Attainment Scaling (Kiresuk & Sherman, 1968) is an individualized treatment outcome measure that was developed and first applied in the mental health department of the Hennepin County Medical Center, a major metropolitan teaching hospital in Minneapolis, Minnesota. Although initially used to measure inpatient, outpatient, and day treatment patient outcomes, the method was also applied to programme evaluation of administrative divisions. Since its inception, GAS has been applied to a wide range of human service interventions in addition to mental health. The initial research was funded by the National Institutes of Mental Health for the purpose of demonstrating the method, comparing mental health treatments, and developing related knowledge and technology to bring about improved evaluation and thereby reform of publicly funded mental health.

Unlike many goal setting methods commonly found in industry and service delivery (which specified only the intended goal or target), GAS provided for the assessment of a range of expected outcomes and a resulting quantitative summary score.

Early publications (Sherman et al., 1974) dealt with the psychometric properties of the Goal Attainment Score. Later, in the mid-1970s, Smith and Cardillo of the Ioannis A. Lougaris Veterans Administration Medical Center in Reno, Nevada, provided standardization of the method and clarified its psychometric status. GAS is best understood as a measure of change rather than immediate status as is the case with standardized measures (Kiresuk, Smith & Cardillo, 1994).

Widespread utilization of the method led to the accumulation of several hundred articles, brief reviews and chapters in evaluation textbooks, translations, many dissertations, and several hundred miscellaneous documents. Our current database contains 142 dissertations, and the total number of publications is about one thousand. It is important to note, however, that GAS has taken many forms and goal setting is referred to in several contexts. The relationship of many of these publications to the standards of application recommended in the Goal Attainment textbook has not been determined. The best source of information regarding GAS at this time is the 1994 textbook where one can find the history of the method, the details of its implementation and quality control, detailed discussion of reliability and validity, and scoring aids. The findings reported in this entry are all treated at length in that volume.

The essential idiographic concept of GAS is that individuals receiving any form of intervention should be judged according to their unique capacities, aspirations, and their abilities to achieve these aspirations. Standardized measures, i.e. personality scales, mental health scales, achievement scores, level of functioning scales, etc., compare an individual relative to the performance of particular populations. However, these measures do not deal with how an individual SHOULD or COULD perform relative to these standards. GAS is not appropriate if one requires a needs assessment, the absolute level of either adjustment or functioning of clients or students at the beginning or end of a treatment programme. The method is appropriate if one wants to know about the degree of change brought about by a programme or treatment, in which case the efficiency of GAS can exceed that of standardized measures with similar content.

Another factor driving the invention of GAS is the selection of relevant content for clients having a wide range of socio-economic, educational, age, racial, and cultural population characteristics. What may be perceived as a therapeutic achievement by the therapist and as a crucial change by the patient may never be taken into account in the organization's prescribed assessment of progress when that assessment relies entirely on standardized symptom scales.

THE BASIC PROCEDURE

The minimum requirements for GAS are (a) the specification of five plausible and scorable levels of outcome, (b) definitions of the levels consistent with the definitions originally proposed by Kiresuk and Sherman (1968), and (c) prespecification of the criteria for scoring at each level. Prespecification requires that the criteria for scoring at each of the five levels of a scale must be stated at the time the scale is constructed and not at the time of follow-up.

There are no restrictions on the types of goals that can be set (e.g. behavioural, affective, cognitive, standard scale scores, invented content) provided that a sufficiently skilled follow-up interviewer will be able to observe, elicit, document, or infer the client's level of attainment at the time of the follow-up interview. Tables 1 and 2 provide examples of Follow-up Guides for an adult medical patient and a child behavioural disorder.

Follow-Up Requirements

In all formal research or programme evaluation the follow-up interview and goal scoring should be conducted by a person who has not been directly involved in the client's treatment and has no personal investment in the outcome score. However, many therapists use the method as part of the treatment process rather than for treatment comparisons, and score the Follow-up Guide themselves. A treatment facilitation effect has been demonstrated in several studies.

Content Areas

The 1994 GAS textbook provides a wide range of examples of patient and organizational Follow-up Guides including: special education & learning disabilities, social services, diabetes, geriatric medicine, medical education, neurological handicaps, rehabilitation, marriage and family counselling, rape counselling, child abuse, crisis intervention, corrections, chemical abuse, Native American diabetic education, problem pregnancy.

For patient populations (such as geriatric patients) that have common characteristics, the process of goal specification is aided by providing content that had been found to be relevant and quality controlled for these special populations.

Table 1.   Goal attainment follow-up guide

Level of attainment	Scale 1 Control of hypertension	Scale 2 Control of congestive heart failure	Scale 3 Control of diabetes
− 2 Much less than expected	Cerebrovascular accident	Congestive heart failure	Diabetic acidosis in last 2 weeks
− 1 Somewhat less than expected	Diastolic pressure 105 or higher	Three or more severe symptoms: Dyspnea on exertion, shortness of breath, angina 4 or more per day, nocturnal dyspnea	Blood glucose level maintained at more than 158
0 Expected level of outcome	Diastolic pressure within 100–104	Dyspnea on exertion, shortness of breath, angina 2–3 times per day	Blood glucose maintained between 120–158 in last 2 weeks of treatment with medication
+ 1 Somewhat more than expected	Diastolic pressure within 95–99	Dyspnea on exertion, shortness of breath only when exercising, angina once a day	Blood glucose within normal limits in last 2 weeks with medication
+2 Much more than expected	Diastolic pressure 94 or less	Dyspnea on exertion, shortness of breath only when exercising, no angina	Within normal limits by diet alone (no medication)

Comments

Table 2. Goal attainment follow-up guide

Level of attainment	Scale 1 Eating behaviour	Scale 2 Tantrums	Scale 3 Dressing skills
− 2 Much less than expected	Eats alone with close supervision	5 or more tantrums per day in last 3 days	Parents dress child completely
− 1 Somewhat less than expected	Eats alone with no supervision	3 or 4 tantrums per day in last 3 days	Parents do most of dressing (pull pants up, shirt down, etc.)
0 Expected level of outcome	Eats at table with other children with special supervision	1 or 2 tantrums per day in last 3 days	Child puts clothes on with exception of shoes and socks; does no buttoning, tying, or zipping
+ 1 Somewhat more than expected	Eats at table with other children with little or no supervision	No more than 2 tantrums total in last 3 days	Also puts on shoes and socks with no tying, zipping, or buttoning
+ 2 Much more than expected	Eats with family with no supervision	No tantrums in last 3 or more days	Child ties, buttons, zips, and snaps all clothes

Comments

In addition, these scales can take on the properties of standardized scales as well (Smith et al., 1998).

Calculating the Score

In the original publication (1968), a comprehensive formula was presented which would convert the outcome levels indicated in the Follow-up Guide into a Goal Attainment Score, with a mean of 50 and standard deviation of 10. Since that time, this formula has been greatly simplified because weighting of the scales is no longer recommended and a reasonably accurate estimate of the average intercorrelation of the scale scores has been determined. A simple alternative is to sum the scale scores, note the number of scales that are summed, and use tables to find the T-score corresponding to a given sum for a given number of scales. The textbook provides tables for follow-up guides having one to eight scales. Examples appear in Table 3.

PSYCHOMETRIC PROPERTIES

Scale Characteristics

A properly constructed Goal Attainment scale is at least ordinal in character: that is, a higher attainment level on a scale always represents a better or more successful outcome than a lower level of attainment. Generally, it has been found that Follow-up Guide constructors produce Goal Attainment Scores that have symmetrical or approximately normal distribution with a mean of about 50.00 and a standard deviation of about 10.00.

Reliability

In the Minneapolis study (involving multiple goal setters and follow-up occurring at different times) the intraclass reliability coefficient was 0.57.

In two studies at the Reno VAH (involving therapist-set goals and multiple follow-ups conducted at the same time) an intraclass average of 0.97 was obtained.

The corresponding intraclass values for the Psychiatric Status Rating Scale and for the Brief Psychiatric Rating Scale were 0.82 and 0.90 respectively.

In the Reno study, Product-Moment Correlations for GAS ratings averaged 0.97, for the Psychiatric Status Rating Scale 0.86, and for the Brief Psychiatric Rating Scale 0.94.

Validity

Concurrent validity studies indicate that the correlation between the GAS score and rated degree of improvement on several different measures typically falls between $r = 0.40$ and $r = 0.50$. The agreement among change measures

Table 3. Conversions key for follow-up guides having four scored scales

Sum of scale scores	Average scale score	T-score
Conversion key for follow-up guides having four scored scales		
−8	−2.00	20.98
−7	−1.75	24.61
−6	−1.50	29.24
−5	−1.25	31.86
−4	−1.00	35.49
−3	−0.75	39.12
−2	−0.50	42.75
−1	−0.25	46.37
0	0	50.00
+1	+0.25	53.63
+2	+0.50	57.25
+3	+0.75	60.88
+4	+1.00	64.51
+5	+1.25	68.14
+6	+1.50	71.76
+7	+1.75	75.39
+8	+2.00	79.02
Conversion key for follow-up guides having five scored scales		
−10	−2.00	19.85
−9	−1.80	22.86
−8	−1.60	25.88
−7	−1.40	28.89
−6	−1.20	31.91
−5	−1.00	34.92
−4	−0.80	37.94
−3	−0.60	40.95
−2	−0.40	43.97
−1	−0.20	46.98
0	0	50.00
+1	+0.20	53.02
+2	+0.40	56.03
+3	+0.60	59.05
+4	+0.80	62.02
+5	+1.00	65.08
+6	+1.20	68.09
+7	+1.40	71.11
+8	+1.60	74.12
+9	+1.80	77.14
+10	+2.00	80.15

is largely effected by content similarities. For instance, when the mental health treatment goals were not represented at all in the Brief Psychiatric Rating Scale, then there was no significant relationship between the GAS score and Brief Psychiatric Rating Scale scores. However, as content of the two measurements became more similar (i.e. as goals were more adequately represented by the scales of the Brief Psychiatric

Rating Scale) the correlation between the GAS score and the posttreatment Brief Psychiatric Rating Scale score increased to 0.644. The same trend occurred for the correlation between the GAS score and true change on the Brief Psychiatric Rating Scale, increasing to 0.923. By including all the items in standard scales regardless of their relevance to particular clients, one is only adding error to the estimates of treatment related improvement.

There are a number of studies reported in the 1994 textbook which indicate the ability of the Goal Attainment Score to detect treatment differences.

FUTURE PERSPECTIVES AND CONCLUSIONS

The current and probable future of GAS lies in its application (along with other measures) in many areas of service delivery and in many countries. Early efforts have demonstrated that individualized outcome measures *can* be developed and used. There appears to be the nucleus of like-minded service providers and evaluators that have an affinity for understanding their interventions and their clients through the process of individualized goal setting, finding the method self-evident and facilitative of the treatment process (Gordon et al., 2000; Malec, 1999; Zaza et al., 1999). The Internet will greatly influence communication among GAS users. Current and future exchange of information regarding references and experiences with GAS can be facilitated by e-mail (thomas@kiresuk.com) and via the World Wide Web at http://www.kiresuk.com

References

Gordon, J., Rockwood, K. & Powell, C. (2000). Assessing patients' views of clinical changes. *JAMA: Journal of the American Medical Association*, 283(14), 1824–1825.

Kiresuk, T.J. & Sherman, R.E. (1968). Goal attainment scaling: a general method for evaluating comprehensive community mental health programs. *Community Mental Health Journal*, 4(6), 443–453.

Kiresuk, T.J., Smith, A.E. & Cardillo, J.E. (1994). *Goal Attainment Scaling: Applications, Theory, and Measurement*. Hillsdale, NJ, US: Lawrence Erlbaum Associates, Inc.

Malec, J.F. (1999). Goal attainment scaling in rehabilitation. *Neuropsychological Rehabilitation*, 9(3–4), 253–275.

Sherman, R.E. et al. (1974). Program evaluation project report, 1969–1973. Chapter Four: an examination of the reliability of the Kiresuk–Sherman goal attainment score by means of components of variance. Program Evaluation Resource Center: Minneapolis.

Smith, A., Cardillo, J.E., Smith, S.C. & Amezaga, A.M., Jr. (1998). Improvement scaling (rehabilitation version). A new approach to measuring progress of patients in achieving their individual rehabilitation goals. *Medical Care*, 36(3), 333–347.

Zaza, C., Stolee, P. & Prkachin, K. (1999). The application of goal attainment scaling in chronic pain settings. *Journal of Pain & Symptom Management*, 17(1), 55–64.

Website and e-mail addresses: http://www.kiresuk.com kires001@tc.umn.edu

Thomas J. Kiresuk

RELATED ENTRIES

APPLIED FIELDS: CLINICAL, APPLIED FIELDS: HEALTH, EVALUATION: PROGRAMME EVALUATION (GENERAL), OUTCOME ASSESSMENT/TREATMENT ASSESSMENT

H HEALTH

INTRODUCTION

Most lay people say that their health is more important than anything else. Though people value health, few question what it means. When asked, people define health in many ways depending on sociodemographic factors, on behaviour or personal factors, and on their culture. For example, common descriptions of health may include references to not being ill, absence of disease, behavioural functioning, role functioning, physical fitness, energy and vitality, emotional well-being, and social relationships. Even answers to the salutation 'how are you?' can be considered a general index of health or well-being (Feinstein, 1987).

Experts also define health in many ways and there is no right or wrong definition of health. However, few would disagree with the notion that health is a important dimension of quality of life. Healthcare professionals strive to help people achieve longer and better lives through interventions aimed to save lives, ameliorate suffering, improve functioning, and protect from disease. Ware (1987) indicated that the goal of healthcare is to maximize the health component of quality of life, which could be operationalized as returning patients to normal lives. Although health status and quality of life are used interchangeably (Bowling, 2001), quality of life in reference to health should be termed health-related quality of life. That is, health-related quality of life (HrQL) is the quality of life as it is

affected by health. It represents the impact of a person's health on his/her ability to lead a normal or fulfilling life. Chronic disease affects and is affected by broader aspects of people's lives and it is impossible to separate disease from an individual's personal and social context. No illness exists in a vacuum. Using health assessments instruments or HrQL measures ensure that treatment and evaluations focus on the patient rather than the disease. These instruments complement the traditional focus on disease outcomes (objective, clinical, or biological measures of disease) by assessing variables such as the need for healthcare, the quality of service, and the effectiveness or cost utility of treatments and interventions. Outcomes are defined as the change in health status that results from health interventions, or the deliberate decision not to intervene. An HrQL outcome has come to mean the extent to which a change in a patient's functioning and well-being meets that patient's needs or expectations.

Definitions of Health

Most definitions of health cluster around one of two views: health as the absence of illness and infirmity (freedom from disease, dysfunction, and disability), or health as a positive well-being (a state of equilibrium, adaptation, harmony, and wholeness). The World Health Organization (WHO) emphasizes the importance of defining health in terms of positive states and defines health as a 'state of complete physical, mental and social well-being and not merely the absence of disease or infirmity' (WHO, 1948). Two additional themes that emerge from the many definitions of health are (1) that premature mortality is undesirable, and (2) that quality of life is important. Thus, healthcare practices are concerned not only with the avoidance of death but also with the prevention and riddance of conditions that reduce quality of life.

Health is frequently conceptualized as a multi-dimensional construct that includes at least six dimensions (Bruess & Richardson, 1992): *Physical health* (efficient bodily functioning, resistance to disease, and physical fitness), *Mental health* (the ability to cope, grow in awareness and consciousness, and grow emotionally and develop to our fullest potential), *Emotional health* (the ability to control emotions and express them comfortably and appropriately), *Social health* (good relations with others, a supportive culture, and successful adaptation to the environment), *Occupational health* (feelings of comfort and accomplishment related to one's daily tasks), and *Spiritual health* (the ability to discover and articulate a personal purpose in life, learn how to experience love, peace, and fulfilment, and how to help oneself and others achieve full potential). Thus, any comprehensive health assessment should include measures of physical, mental, social, and role functioning along with global indicators of general health and quality of life perceptions (Ware, 1995).

A Concept of Health as a Personal Resource

Health can be conceptualized as a dynamic and empowering resource that improves quality of life and lengthens quantity of life. The attainment of health is not 'the' goal itself, but a tool or state that allows an individual to develop physical, psychological, social, and spiritual resources to function in his or her environment. Health is the ability to have and reach goals, meet personal needs, perform daily activities, fulfil role obligations, and cope with everyday problems. We also favour the view that health is not an *all-or-none* state. As a multifaceted resource, an individual may have both poor physical health and good psychological health. Moreover, poor and good health may co-occur within the same dimension

of health. For example, at the psychological level, a person may lack confidence but report being otherwise happy. If health and ill-health are not binary opposites, health and ill-health may, and most likely do, co-exist in all people. Health occurs in the presence of ill-health rather than in its absence (Buetow & Kerse, 2001).

Although a personal resource, health is also a socio-ecological product, whose effective promotion and successful attainment depends on the participation all those within the social milieu. The Ottawa Charter for Health Promotion stated that 'health is created and lived by people within the settings of their everyday life; where they learn, work, plan and love. Health is created by caring for oneself and others, by being able to take decisions and have control over one's life circumstances, and by ensuring that the society one lives in creates conditions that allow the attainment of health by all its members' (WHO, 1986). Thus, pro-health investments and responsibilities should be extended beyond the narrow spectrum of healthcare organisms and professionals. Growing out of this recognition that daily-living environments impact the health and well-being of their members are the well-known Healthy Cities movement and the more recent initiative 'health promoting universities' (Tsouros et al., 1998; Reig et al., 2001). These settings-based programmes aspire to: (1) provide with healthy working and living environments, (2) integrate health-promoting initiatives into the daily activities of those living within specific settings, and (3) reach out and incorporate these initiatives into the larger community.

HEALTH ASSESSMENT

One of the important developments in the healthcare field has been the recognition of the centrality of the patient's point of view in monitoring the quality of healthcare outcomes (Ware, 1992). Thus, health assessment, or the use of standardized procedures that quantify an individual's health, should in most cases include measurements of the person's subjective feelings of health, behavioural functioning, and well-being (HrQL). Subjective health assessments often complement objective measurements and contribute to develop a more complete picture of the person's health status, effects of a disease, and the effectiveness of healthcare interventions.

Perhaps the most important step in the health assessment process is the selection of appropriate measurement instruments, which should be guided by clearly conceptualized and operationalized definitions of health. Health assessment strategies may vary along a continuum from completely quantitative (e.g. cost-effectiveness) to qualitative methodologies (e.g. unstructured interviews), with many variations in between. It should be noted that theoretical and technical advances in test construction, design, international adaptation, and methods for self-administered questionnaires have contributed to important improvements within the health assessment field and that subjective, self-report inventories are not necessarily less valid or useful than instruments that measure more easily quantifiable data. General heath surveys have many valuable applications, including (a) monitoring the health of the general population, (b) evaluating healthcare policies, (c) evaluating clinical trials of alternative treatments, (d) designing systems for monitoring and improving healthcare outcomes, and (e) guiding treatment in clinical practice.

Most health assessment instruments can be grouped into three categories: Generic, Disease-specific, Domain-specific measures (Bowling, 1997; Bowling, 2001). Generic measures are useful when the purpose of the assessment is to cover basic relevant variables to make outcome comparisons between different diseases and conditions, or across different populations or reference groups, or to obtain norms about the health status of the general, 'healthy' population. However, when the investigator or practitioner is interested in a particular component or domain of health, domain-specific instruments are called for. A domain-specific measure is used when the area covered is of particular relevance to the study and its hypotheses, and where generic and disease-specific instruments neglect that area. Finally, disease-specific measures are used when disease-related outcomes for a specific illness or disease are the focus of study. The advantage of disease-specific measures is that they contain items highly relevant to specific medical conditions and are more likely to detect medical or quality of life changes within specific patient populations. Table 1 presents some of the

Table 1. Some examples of health status assessment instruments and health related quality of life measures

Generic measures
The Nottingham Health Profile
The Dartmund COOP Function Charts/
 The COOP-WONCA Charts
SF-36

Disease-specific/Condition-specific/
 Diagnostic-specific measures
Guyatt's Chronic Heart Failure
 Questionnaire (CHQ)
The EORTC Quality of Life Questionnaire
SmithKline Beecham Quality of Life Scale (SBQOL)
Stanford Arthritis Center Health Assessment
 Questionnaire (HAQ)
St George's Respiratory Questionnaire
Disease-specific measures of quality of life: Stroke
Kidney Disease Quality of Life Questionnaire
 (KDQoLQ)

Domain-specific measures
Goldberg's Health Assessment Questionnaire
The Mini-Mental State Examination
The McGill Pain Questionnaire
The Index of Independence in Activities of
 Daily Living
The Life Satisfaction Index
The Social Adjustment Scale
Rotter's Internal-External Locus of Control Scale

Note: For a more detailed description of these and other instruments see Bowling, 1997, 2001; McDowell & Newell, 1996; Salek, 1998; Stewart & Ware, 1992; Streiner & Norman, 1989.

best known health-assessment instruments classified under each of the three categories described above.

The universal and psychometrically perfect instrument does not exist. It would be deceiving to imagine that one set of questions could suit all health conditions, all individuals, and all applications. Increasingly, authors are calling for efforts to foster a science of health assessment that integrates the fields of psychometrics, clinimetrics, and econometrics. This vision sees health assessment as a clinical and policy-making guiding tool whose function would be to give practical solutions such as the selection of specific clinical interventions or the allocation of public funding to different healthcare initiatives. Ultimately, such an effort would improve the welfare of patients, and would pressure healthcare professionals to include HrQL outcome assessments in the routine of their clinical interventions.

Table 2.   COOP chart system. Nine scales, each of which is used to measure different dimensions of a person's behavioural functioning and well-being

Concept	Definitional strategy
Physical fitness	Shows a person's physical endurance
Feelings	Shows a person's emotional health
Daily activities	Shows the difficulty a person may have accomplishing daily tasks at home or work
Social activities	Shows the extent to which physical or emotional health interferes with a person's social activities
Pain	Shows the level of pain a person may be experiencing
Overall health	Shows the level of a person's overall health/well-being
Health change	Shows if change in a person's health has occurred
Social support	Shows the number of people an individual can turn to for help
Quality of life	Shows how a person does and feels about his/her life in general

Most health status instruments measure deviations away from a state of health, with health conceptualized as the absence of illness and disease. Whereas this narrow conceptualization of health can be appropriate when measuring health status in severely ill populations, general population surveys should include multidimensional, HrQL assessments that sample the individual's functioning across various domains of human activity (Bowling, 2001). The COOP Charts are a good example of the multidimensional approach to HrQL assessment (see Table 2).

Advances in Health Assessment or Health-Related Quality of Life

HrQL as an outcome measure redirects attention towards the impact of the health conditions and healthcare interventions on the patient's behavioural functioning and lifestyle. HrQL has become an industry in itself (Bowling, 2001). These measures should assess the complete range of normal activities that could potentially be affected by the medical condition and treatment under study. Findings obtained through applied investigations reveal the following conclusions:

- HrQL instruments provide important information to investigators and healthcare professionals, as well as to the patients and their significant others. Important benefits include aid in the identification and prioritization of problem areas, improvements in the communication and relationship between all interested parties (i.e. patients, their families and healthcare personnel), facilitation of the client's participation in

clinical decisions, and better detection of treatment-induced changes in the patient.
- Many HrQL instruments have good psychometric properties and their designs and formats make them amenable to both research and clinical settings.
- HrQL measures have contributed to the realization that there is not a direct correspondence between objective functioning and an individual's HrQL, nor between perceptions of patients, health professionals, or even others with similar disabilities. Health assessments as seen by the patients themselves, their healthcare providers, and those close to the patients are often uncorrelated.
- Patients may rate their health or quality of life highly despite having obvious medical problems. For example, patients may show significant improvement in HrQL scores that do not correlate with accompanying changes in objective measures of disease or physical functioning.
- Patients' priorities may change during the course of their disease or even near the end of their life.
- Patients may change their internal standards, values, or health and quality of life conceptualization as they respond and adapt to their situation. These have come to be known as the 'response shift'.
- Patients tend to rate their own health and quality of life as being better than the patients' own relatives and friends.
- Healthcare professionals may find it difficult to accept patients' positive ratings of health and quality of life.

- Healthcare professionals and informal caregivers can provide valid and useful information on concrete, observable aspects of health and quality of life, for patients who, as a result of age, cognitive impairment, communication deficits, severe distress, or because the measures are too burdensome, are unable to complete the HrQL measures themselves.

Testing the validity and usefulness of new and existing HrQL instruments continues to be an important endeavour within the health assessment field. Investigators are interested in checking whether all relevant concepts are represented in the measure or set of measures under investigation (content validity). Also important is to test whether the measure of interest correlates with a 'gold standard' measure of that concept (criterion validity), or with related variables in theoretically congruent ways (construct validity). Researchers are also interested in learning the meaning of specific scores and score-change values (interpretability of scale scores), and whether a particular measure adds substantial information above and beyond other measures and sources of information (incremental validity). Finally, researchers also examine systematic response biases and evaluate whether the psychometric properties generalize across populations (generalization validity).

FUTURE PERSPECTIVES

Fortunately, we have today many standardized health assessment instruments of sound psychometric properties, with simple well-organized formats that make them user friendly and attractive to the average person. However, more research might be needed to further refine their formats and designs to make them more valid to underserved and special populations such as psychiatric patients and individuals with perceptual or attentional deficits. Of special attention is the area of investigation invested in promoting the development and validation of instruments across culturally and ethnically diverse populations.

Individualized measurement is an area of particular relevance that will need further development. These instruments ask the same questions to all patients but allow them to specify their own responses. Current examples include the *Patient Generated Index*, the *Schedule for the Evaluation of the Individualised Quality of Life*, and the *Disease Repercussion Profile*. Developing new measures and refining existing ones to simplify weighing systems, facilitate data analysis, or combine short individualized measures with key-disease and treatment-outcome measures are advances to seek in the future.

Utilization of new technologies is already a highly adopted and accepted practice by researchers and clinicians. Today's potent computers facilitate the storage of huge data sets, and accelerate the process of data analysis and results presentation. The administration of questionnaires through the Internet has great potential for improving health assessment strategies because electronic administrations may facilitate data collection tasks, improve the accuracy and efficiency of data scoring and data analysis, and provide the scientific and lay communities with rapid access to the results and their implications. Thus, future areas of inquiry will include the validation of the Internet approach to data collection.

Of increasing interest is the area of clinical utility. In particular, it will be important to determine whether instruments are appropriate, valid, and useful in the clinical setting and, if not, whether new instruments should be developed. Clinical interpretations, the practical meaning of results obtained with HrQL instruments, continue to be ambiguous. Future research should answer the questions: what constitutes an important change in health or HrQL score? To whom is the change important?

Training in the use of health assessments is something that is generally lacking in undergraduate and postgraduate education. Proxies or informal caregivers would also benefit from specific education and training in the function and use of HrQL instruments. Here we are talking not only about ensuring that training and education occur and reach those involved in the direct care of patients, but also about the process of creating and testing effective instruction methods. A related area is that of public dissemination of scientific knowledge. Informing the public at large of the findings associated with treatment-outcome evaluations may foster social involvement with the potential for increasing accountability and the quality of care among healthcare professionals.

Last but not least, further development and refining of theoretical models of health should be at the forefront of the health assessment field. Outcome results need to be accompanied by an understanding of how they came about and how they may generalize or be specific to certain circumstances. Thus, theoretically driven research with clearly formulated, falsifiable hypotheses should continue to be the guiding principle.

CONCLUSIONS

Health is a personal resource that allows us to live a normal life and health problems represent a threat to our ability to carry out our daily-living activities. Currently, there are many health assessment instruments with good psychometric properties that are being used successfully within research and clinical settings. The great majority of these instruments belong to the area of study known as health-related quality of life (HrQL). HrQL measures are designed to assess people's own perspectives of the impact health and healthcare interventions have in their lives, and thus enable them to part take in research clinical decisions. Although comprehensive, reliable, and valid measures are available, further development of health assessment methodologies is needed. We must strive for a better understanding of how to interpret and use this information for clinical use and to develop better models for integrating health assessment data into a general model of health outcome.

References

Bowling, A. (1997). *Measuring Health. A Review of Quality of Life Measurement Scales*. Buckingham: Open University Press.

Bowling, A. (2001). *Measuring Disease. A Review of Disease Specific Quality of Life Measurement Scales*. Buckingham: Open University Press.

Bruess, C. & Richardson, G. (1992). *Decisions for Health*. Dubuque: Wm. C. Brown Publishers.

Buetow, S.A. & Kerse, N.M. (2001). Does reported health promotion activity neglect people with ill-health? *Health Promotion International*, 16, 73–78.

Feinstein, A.R. (1987). *Clinimetrics*. New Haven, Connecticut: Yale University Press.

McDowell, I. & Newell, C. (1996). *Measuring Health. A Guide to Rating Scales and Questionnaires* (2nd ed.). New York: Oxford University Press.

Reig, A., Cabrero, J., Ferrer, R. & Richart, M. (2001). *La calidad de vida y el estado de salud de los estudiantes universitarios [Quality of Life and Health Status in University Students]*. Alicante: Universidad de Alicante.

Salek, Sam (1998). *Compendium of Quality of Life Instruments*, 5 Vols. Chichester: John Wiley & Sons.

Stewart, A.L. & Ware, J.E., Jr. (Eds.) (1992). *Measuring Functioning and Well-Being. The Medical Outcomes Study Approach*. Durham and London: Duke University Press.

Streiner, D.L. & Norman, G.R. (1989). *Health Measurement Scales: A Practical Guide to Their Development and Use*. New York: Oxford University Press.

Tsouros, A.D., Dowding, G., Thompson, J. & Dooris, M. (Eds.) (1998). *Health Promoting Universities. Concept, Experience and Framework for Action*. Copenhagen: World Health Organization. Regional Office for Europe.

Ware, J.E., Jr. (1987). Standards for validating health measures: definition and content. *Journal of Chronic Diseases*, 40, 473–480.

Ware, J.E., Jr. (1992). Measures for a new era of health assessment. In Stewart, A.L. & Ware, J.E. (Eds.) (1992). *Measuring Functioning and Well-Being. The Medical Outcomes Study Aproach* (pp. 3–11). Durham and London: Duke University Press.

Ware, J.E., Jr. (1995). The status of health assessment 1994. *Annual Review of Public Health*, 16, 327–354.

World Health Organization (WHO) (1948). World Health Organization Constitution. In *Basic Documents*. Geneva: World Health Organization.

World Health Organization (WHO) (1986). *Ottawa Charter for Health Promotion. An International Conference on Health Promotion, November 1986*. WHO Regional Office for Europe, Copenhagen, Denmark.

Abilio Reig-Ferrer and
Antonio Cepeda-Benito

RELATED ENTRIES

APPLIED FIELDS: HEALTH, QUALITY OF LIFE, INTERVIEW IN BEHAVIOURAL AND HEALTH SETTINGS

HISTORY OF PSYCHOLOGICAL ASSESSMENT

INTRODUCTION

Assessment was introduced in psychology as part of the scientific methodology applied to the study of mental and behavioural processes. Evaluation, both in quantitative and qualitative terms, was needed in order to fulfil the scientific aspiration to determine, measure and evaluate all phenomena involved in that research, and turning into a measurable form those elements not yet quantified (Pearson).

The ways to carry out assessment very soon diverged, as dimensions and elements to be considered by psychologists increased very rapidly and related to different aspects of their object of study. Research concentrated at an early moment on individuals, but soon after social and group aspects gained salience. At the turn of the century, psychologists became progressively engaged in practical affairs. They needed to know not only who the person was and how his/her mind was working, but also what capacities and abilities could be employed as a means to reach personal aims. Individual assessment had to be completed with group and collective measures (Anastasi and Urbina, 1997).

The development of assessment techniques clearly parallels the history of psychological science (Carpintero, 1996). Types of evaluation have been adapted to the idiosyncratic kind of phenomena to be studied (normal vs. abnormal, individual vs. group dimensions, abilities vs. performance...). Only some crucial points will be included in what follows.

ASSESSMENT IN PRE-WUNDTIAN TIMES

Popular non-scientific techniques for assessing individuals have been employed since ancient times. Astrology, chiromancy and some similar procedures have spread out all over the world, as the need for knowing who the other is represents a basic and pungent one. But they will not be considered here.

A first scientific view on the subject may be related to early Greek medicine, and its Hippocratic school of thought. Reworked by Galen (2nd century A.D.), the doctrine that body constitution, conceived as the result of a combination of humours – yellow bile, black bile, blood and phlegm – caused the psychological qualities of the person lasted for a millennium or more. People could then be categorized into a fourfold system of temperaments (melancholic, choleric, phlegmatic and sanguine), predisposing them to experience different types of emotional reactions and to exhibit different personality styles (Fernández-Ballesteros, 1980).

In the Renaissance, the Spanish physician Juan Huarte (c.1530–1589) built a complete theory of vocational guidance based on Galenic ideas of temperament and body constitution, and on a rough 'professiography' of his own. He first claimed in his *The Trial of Wits* (1575) for an adjustment of the person's qualities to the requirements of each profession – theology, medicine, law, army and politics. He is usually credited as the 'Father' of the psychology of individual differences.

The doctrine of humours, variously reinterpreted, was still alive in the 20th century. I. Pavlov (1849–1936) redefined these temperaments in terms of dynamic properties of the nervous system as conceived by his own doctrine (nervous speed, strength and excitation–inhibition balance).

Some other approaches were developed in modern times, which were also based on natural science. Phrenology, created by the Austrian physician F.J. Gall (1758–1828), admitted that mental faculties were directly related to the relative volume of brain centres, whose size could be estimated through skull examination. Phrenologists (G. Combe, J.G. Spurzheim, M. Cubí and others) made personality diagnoses of normal and abnormal people. Influential among lay people and strongly criticized by philosophers and scientists, they in fact paved the way for the building of a scientific psychology.

The momentous importance of individual differences clearly appeared after the discovery of the so-called 'personal equation' characterizing the operation of individuals when registering events. The German astronomer F.W. Bessel (1784–1846), and the Dutch physiologist F.C. Donders (1818–1889), elaborated the 'reaction-time' concept that in the long run became the basis for mental chronometry, an essential methodology for the study of mental activity.

The theory of evolution (1859), by C. Darwin (1809–1882), marked a turning point in the issue. It stressed the variability of somatic and mental characteristics in individuals, which would enable best-endowed individuals to cope with environmental challenges, while less capable ones would not survive. Such 'natural selection' was a means of the evolution. Based on evolutionary grounds, a functional assessment of potentialities and abilities of organisms to face different types of situations was considered to provide with useful predictive knowledge of future behaviour in certain settings. So the basis of mental assessment had been laid.

PSYCHOLOGICAL ASSESSMENT IN MODERN TIMES

While scientific psychology is generally viewed as born under German W. Wundt's efforts in 1879, Englishman Francis Galton (1822–1911), a versatile genius, is usually conceived as the founder of psychological assessment. Influenced by Darwinism, he became interested in the study of differences among individuals, and worked out useful methods and designs (such as the study of twins), and statistical concepts and measures. He also established in London (1884) a laboratory for testing individuals, and devised some instruments (e.g. the Galton Whistle or the rating scale) for that purpose.

Differences among mental patients became the main focus of interest for some nineteenth century psychiatrists. German Emil Kraepelin (1856–1926) and Italian Giulio Cesare Ferrari (1868–1932) devised various mental proofs to test on dimensions like sensory discrimination, reaction time or mental association in order to arrive at a diagnosis. But it was in the US where the technical

concept of 'mental test' was introduced with its modern significance. This was done (1890) by J. McKeen Cattell (1860–1944), a former student of Wundt and Galton who tested sensory and motor abilities among college students. Soon after, J. Jastrow (1863–1944) administered a test battery to general people at the Chicago International Fair (1893). The testing movement had yet begun (McReynolds, 1968).

During the same time, educational authorities facing school problems asked psychologists for help. In Germany, H. Ebbinghaus (1850–1909) devised some tests for assessing school children on learning and retention (1897). But it was Frenchman A. Binet (1857–1911) who with his collaborator V. Henri made an epoch-making contribution, the metric scale for intelligence (1905), a worldwide test for assessing intellectual abilities, allowing the determination of the relative position of a child (his 'mental age') among a certain population. Evaluation and comparisons between individuals became then possible. German W. Stern (1871–1938), whose pioneer book (*Ueber Psychologie der individuellen Differenzen*, 1900) set the field for the followers, coined the idea of the Intelligence Quotient (IQ), conceived as the ratio of mental age to chronological age (times 100).

The Binet scale soon received a lot of attention by practitioners from all over the world (R.M. Yerkes [1876–1956], F. Kulhmann [1876–1941], O. Decroly [1871–1932], H. Goddard [1866–1957], W. Stern, among others). Some independent measures implemented by other people (like the Maze test of G.S. Porteus [1915] or the Kohs' Block-design test [1923]) were largely overshadowed by the success of the Binet–Simon scale.

Tests paved the way for an in-depth study of mental abilities and their structure. In the United Kingdom, C.E. Spearman (1863–1945), another student of Galton, working on correlation scores from different tests, set the basis for 'factor analysis', and considered that intelligence test scores resulted from two main components ('two-factor' theory): a general ability (*g* factor) for knowledge and various specific abilities related to each tested dimension. Abilities in every individual appeared then, forming a structure whose order had to be discovered.

Quantitative studies on intelligence benefited from large testing programmes carried out in various countries. The US Army carried out a noteworthy programme during World War I

(1917–18) in which over one and a half million people were tested with two parallel proofs – the Army Alpha for literate and the Army Beta for illiterate people [A. Otis and R.M. Yerkes]. It proved to be very effective in placing in the right place thousands of young soldiers entering the army, a result that strongly backed the usefulness of psychological methods in applied questions.

More and more, intelligence was seen as a general ability based on hereditary grounds, stable through ages, and easy to be measured with scales that were improved day after day. American L.M. Terman (1877–1956) assumed its distribution to be normal in a population. Also, the stability of mental measures along the lifetime was soon established. In the US, D. Wechsler (1896–1981) added a scale for adult testing, and considered adolescent scores as good estimates for adult ones. Such results stimulated further developments in other fields and new testing instruments were created for practical purposes. Musical talent was appreciated by the Seashore's proof; child development was evaluated through a battery of scales devised by A. Gesell (1880–1961) in the US, and by Ch. Bühler (1893–1974) in Austria; some other specific aptitudes, such as the mechanical ones, were evaluated through some tests created by McQuarry (1925) and many others. In the field of personality, US psychologist Robert S. Woodworth (1869–1962) created a 'Personal data sheet' (1918), the first personality inventory, to provide psychologists with an instrument to screen out neurotic tendencies and emotional aspects of personality among soldiers. Moral honesty, self-control and personal character were studied by two US psychologists, H. Hartshorne and H. May (1925), that created a large test battery with situations where deceit was more or less feasible, and defined moral traits through covariation of results.

The study of personality was enriched with new qualitative, non-quantitative, approaches. First, Swiss psychiatrist Hermann Rorschach (1884–1922) created an inkblot projective test, that proved very useful to detect psychopathological tendencies among patients in the clinic. Individuals were supposed to 'project' out the conflicts and forces acting in their minds through their responses to inkblots. While psychometric approaches offered some insights on mental structure, projective tests threw new light on mental dynamics.

Applied psychology has been one of the fields that largely stimulated the creation of new assessment techniques. These were required in order to formulate adequate predictions of the performance of individuals in real settings. A widely accepted principle was 'the right man in the right place'. Test situations had to be evaluated according to the predictive (valid) knowledge obtained through them. The need for efficacy oriented the work of many research groups all over the world.

The German psychologist H. Muensterberg (1863–1916), a former student of Wundt, became the leader of the field in the US until World War I, then as a German-born person was ostracized there and he soon died. He devised tests for attention, memory, speed response and accuracy. Under his influence, applied psychology rapidly developed in Germany and in other European countries. H. Tramm, W. Moede, K. Piorkowsky, in Germany; A. Gemelli in Italy; E. Mira in Spain; J.M. Lahy and H. Piéron in France; E. Claparède in Switzerland, C.S. Myers in Great Britain; O. Christiaens in Belgium, founded testing centres and devised instruments with which mental diagnosis and evaluation in different settings became possible, so that practical decisions could be taken.

The spreading of tests, procedures and instruments in different countries raised technical problems of communication among groups. Questions on vocabulary, test adaptation and score equivalence demanded cooperative work, and mainly through the efforts of Swiss E. Claparède (1873–1941) an international society (*Société internationale de psychotechnique*, then turned into the now existing IAAP) was established in 1920 to enhance practical research under common standards.

Some basic problems also appeared. For instance, psychotechnologists had to differentiate between innate and learned abilities, to compare the effectiveness of one-session against continuous assessing procedures, or to differentiate selection from vocational guidance techniques, among other questions.

In what concerns the innate-learned opposition, intelligence tests became strongly questioned. Was it an inborn quality, or could it be learned from experience? In the US,

H.H. Goddard (1866–1957), a Binet follower, tried to compare the achievements and life records of both legitimated and illegitimated lines flowing from one common ancestor – the former characterized by the respect to law and middle class morality, the other full of immoral or criminal individualities. He concluded from here (1912) the hereditary nature of mental traits. Not only intellectual but also moral qualities were supposed to be based on an inherited nature. As a consequence, US federal law regulating immigration excluded from it all the 'persons of constitutional psychopathic inferiority'.

Different races and cultures were also compared on the basis of their performance on intelligence tests. Data from the Army Alpha and Beta tests were studied and reanalysed. Significant differences on IQ among people from various ethnical origins were supposed to be found (Brigham, 1923). Among other pungent results, intellectual weakness of Negro Americans seemed to be firmly established on those grounds. Democracy was criticized by some groups on the grounds of offering political equality to unequally mentally endowed people. Racist arguments seemed to flow from psychological data. In Europe, data obtained by H. English and others suggested strong correlation between economic level and IQ, so pointing to non-inborn factors in intelligence scores. The discussion was deeply affected by political prejudices and attitudes. Voices then rose against IQ on political grounds. In the US, the journalist W. Lippmann (1899–1974) strongly criticized (1922) the testing procedures for taking scores as true 'things' instead of rough estimates of variable qualities in subjects. In other countries, reaction took place later. In Russia, then under the Soviet regime, a ban for all testing activities was imposed by the Communist Party's Central Committee, considering them as reactionary and anti-egalitarian techniques (1936).

Opposition to mental measurement also grew from theoretical grounds. Behaviourism, that largely dominated US psychology (between the 1920s and 1960s), banned all mentalistic concepts from its system, especially from its clinical topics. Psychology should only deal with behavioural facts and laws, and each individual should be tested in definite settings, in order to establish those precise S-R associations causing his/her behaviour. Adaptive or maladaptive habits substituted old personality traits, and were evaluated in order to permit their change under application of 'behaviour modification' procedures. New instruments based on observational procedures were developed, employing sampling recording of target behaviours; they substituted the traditional tests and questionnaires.

Notwithstanding, some classical tests continued to be successfully developed. During World War II, a new Army General Classification Test (AGCT, 1947) was administered to millions of US soldiers, and proved to be a useful instrument, largely employed in social studies of intelligence. At the other hand, in clinical grounds mental concepts were kept alive. C.G. Jung's associative test (1905) to explore the conflicts of mind through word associations represents a pioneer effort. Projective proofs were developed after the Rorschach model: H. Murray (1893–1988) created the TAT (Thematic Apperception Test, 1935) to explore needs and drives through the analysis of short stories; diagnoses based on the peculiarities of motor responses were offered by A. Luria (1902–1977); knowledge through drawings (L. Bender, F. Goodenough, K. Machover); and E. Mira-Lopez (1896–1964) with his PMK test, and so on. Comparison of 'answer profiles' with those coming from criterion groups of psychiatric patients were employed in MMPI (Hathaway & McKinley, 1943); comparison of performances with those of criterion groups is at the core of Luria's neurological test. All these explorations reflected psychologists' efforts to create qualitative ways of assessing psychological traits. (A basic source of information on testing devices is O.K. Buros' *Mental Measurement Yearbook*, that appears on a periodical rate since 1938). A related theoretical discussion rose between pros and cons of both 'clinical' and 'statistical' approaches to knowledge. L.J. Cronbach also pointed to a 'harder' and more basic opposition between 'experimental' and 'correlational' methodologies in psychology.

CONTEMPORARY PROBLEMS

The decline of behaviourism and the rise of the new cognitive model since the 1960s brought with them a renewed attention on mental processes as causing open behaviour (Silva, 1993). The 'computer metaphor of mind' largely inspired the new view, and great attention was paid to the ways and manners of mental information processing (IP) by individuals. Under its influence, the assessment process turned to be viewed mostly as a process of problem-solving and decision-making, in which measurements and analysis are employed as means for answering questions related to the characteristics of a certain target involved in a psychological intervention. As a result, it may be said that 'any type of psychological task involves assessment at some stage' (Fernández-Ballesteros, 1999).

The field has grown enormously in recent times. Now it includes not only the study of individuals and groups, but also of environmental characteristics and traits, and of the efficacy of intervention programmes. Both quantitative and qualitative standardized procedures are offering a detailed knowledge that permits not only objective classifications but also some well-controlled practical interventions (Matarazzo, 1992).

Present day psychological assessment is multifaceted and covers old and new topics. Among them are included the evaluation of a variety of dimensions – intelligence and aptitudes, personality, emotionality, motivation, attitudes and values etc. – that may well serve for theoretical or practical purposes in different areas (health, education, clinical practice, organizational work etc.) and perspectives.

The growing variety of theoretical constructs, and the technical advances in detection and measurement procedures, impulsed great developments in the field. For instance, the recent 'Big Five' factor model of personality (McCrae & Costa, 1990), that integrates many previous findings, has brought new vitality to that area. At the other hand, some mathematical developments paved the way for current 'Item response theory', which stresses the significance of responses to single items in order to evaluate a certain trait in an individual. Under its influence, some tailor-made proofs have been developed, in which an arborescent group of items are administered in an idiosyncratic way to individuals, according to their own traits and problems.

As it has been noted, contemporary societies are more and more interested in questions related to ageing, multiethnic characteristics, quality of life and its global distribution and inequalities, and other topics that demand the creation of new instruments for standardized measurement-enabling comparisons.

Recent progress in neurological and neuropsychological techniques (brain imaging, gene interventions and therapies etc.) is improving the knowledge of brain-behaviour dimensions and interactions. At the same time, computer assisted testing has largely developed, enabling researchers to operate with larger and faster volumes of information to be employed in assessment process. New instruments have been elaborated for these machines, that shorten the time for evaluation, permit comparisons with enormous amounts of data, and combine clinical and statistical approaches to the study of the individual (e.g. Krug, 1993).

The field, as a whole, is growing in parallel with that of scientific psychology in general, and both are facing the challenges of present-day societies.

FUTURE PERSPECTIVES AND CONCLUSIONS

As phenomena to be studied are changing, according both to variations of the theoretical points of view and to the emergence of new social needs, the field of assessment is in continuous evolution.

Some basic questions are at present demanding sound solutions.

(a) Assessment procedures are poorly regulated. Norms regulating adaptation and construction of instruments, scientific requirements to be fulfilled by technicians, and ethical standards protecting subjects under study are in need of a general consensus that will guide evaluation carried out in developed societies.

(b) Instruments employed into a wide range of cultures are scarce, and cross-cultural comparisons are a difficult task to be carried out, in many sorts of psychological dimensions. Wide acceptance of some models in western countries – as the mentioned Five Factors Model in personality – is a goal to be reached in other dimensions, in order to implement broad theoretical constructs well measured through widely spread out devices. Meta-analysis techniques have spread out in literature, trying to introduce normalization among the immense variety of empirical studies.

(c) An in-depth knowledge of the person–situation interactions cannot rely only on tests and psychometric devices, but need also to integrate holistic and qualitative information to mere quantitative measures. Theoretical models offering coherent integration of those dimensions are to be built as a means for enlarging our body of knowledge.

(d) Psychological models of man will include more and more gene-based knowledge of the biological basis of organisms. Evaluation of individuals will rely more and more both on genetic engineering and on a socio-historical approach to group mentalities.

Given the basic connections mediating psychological theory and evaluative processes, a continuous interaction between both lines of thought may be predicted for the coming future.

References

Anastasi, A. & Urbina, S. (1997). *Psychological Testing* (7th ed.). New York: Prentice Hall.

Brigham, C. (1923). *A Study of American Intelligence*, Princeton: Princeton University Press.

Carpintero, H. (1996). *Historia de las ideas Psicológicas*. Madrid: Pirámide.

Fernández-Ballesteros, R. (1980). *Psicodiagnóstico. Concepto y Metodología*. Madrid: Cincel-Kapelusz.

Fernández-Ballesteros, R. (1999). Psychological assessment: future challenges and progresses. *European Psychologist*, 4(4), 248–262.

Hathaway, S.R. & McKinley, J.C. (1943). *The Minnesota Multiphasic Personality Inventory*. New York: Psychological Corporation.

Krug, S.E. (1993). *Psychware Sourcebook* (4th ed.). Champaign, Ill: Metritech.

Matarazzo, J.D. (1992). Psychological testing and assessment in the 21st century. *American Psychologist*, 47, 1007–1018.

McCrae, R.R. & Costa, P.T. (1990) *Personality in Adulthood*. New York: Guilford Press.

McReynolds, P. (Ed.) (1968). *Advances in Psychological Assessment*, Vol. I–V. Palo Alto: Science and Behaviour Books.

Silva, F. (1993). *Psychometric Foundations and Behavioural Assessment*. London: Sage.

Heliodoro Carpintero

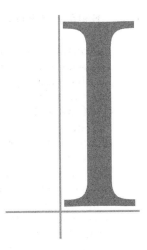

I IDENTITY DISORDERS

INTRODUCTION

This entry describes Erikson's concept of identity and important elaborations made by later researchers. It also overviews currently used measures of identity derived from Erikson's work. Various identity disorders linked with arrested development of the self are also addressed, along with current instruments used for assessment purposes. New directions for research on the relationship between identity development and psychopathology are suggested in conclusion.

IDENTITY DEFINED

Erikson (1963) defined identity as a sense of self-sameness and continuity, which enables one to express biological capacities and psychological needs and interests within a social context. Identity formation is the process of finding meaningful vocational directions, outlets for the expression of ideological values, and satisfying forms of sexual expression in a wider social milieu.

Issues of identity, according to Erikson (1963), generally come to the fore during adolescence, though they may continue to be revised and modified throughout adult life. Erikson has described an eight-stage sequence of psychosocial tasks requiring resolution for optimal personality development over the lifespan; he sees the task of finding some resolution to 'Identity vs. Role

Confusion' as central to adolescence. To Erikson, identity is something an individual possesses to a greater or lesser degree; one can assess an individual's identity as lying on a continuum somewhere between the poles of identity achievement and role confusion.

Elaborations on Identity

James Marcia (1966; Marcia et al., 1993) has operationalized and empirically elaborated Erikson's construct of identity by identifying different styles by which adolescents engage in forming their identities. The *identity achieved* and *foreclosed* individuals have both formed reasonably firm identity-defining commitments. However, the identity achieved has made such commitments on his or her own terms following a time of active exploration and experimentation, while the foreclosed individual has made commitments based on identifications with significant others, without significant exploration of alternative possibilities. *Moratorium* and *diffuse* individuals have not made identity-defining commitments; however, moratoriums are very much in the process of actively exploring possibilities, while diffusions are not. Identity-diffuse individuals may or may not have previously engaged in identity exploration, but are unable to form, or uninterested in forming, identity-defining commitments. These four identity statuses have consistently been associated with different clusters of personality variables, antecedent family conditions, and developmental patterns of movement over time.

IDENTITY STATUS ASSESSMENT

The Identity Status Interview (Marcia et al., 1993) assigns an overall ego identity status to an individual based on the ways in which he or she has explored (or not) and made commitments (or not) to identity-defining vocational, ideological, and sexual roles and values. The most commonly used paper-and-pencil measure of ego identity status is the Extended Objective Measure of Ego Identity Status – II (Adams, Bennion & Huh, 1989). This instrument assigns an identity status within each of eight identity domains, and provides ways of deriving an overall identity status assessment. Both measures have consistently shown good indices of reliability and validity.

Whether identity in general or each identity status in particular represents a unitary construct is an issue for further research. Preliminary research on the identity diffusion status with patient samples has suggested that identity diffusion can be divided into at least four facets: 'role absorption', 'painful incoherence', 'inconsistency', and 'lack of commitment' (Wilkinson-Ryan & Westen, 2000). The diffusion identity status may thus reflect any one of a variety of underlying identity disorders.

IDENTITY DISORDERS

A developmental prerequisite for optimal identity formation is the development of a stable sense of self. By and large, early disturbances in the development of a child's sense of self arise from a history of parental empathic failures and the child's consequent inability to create inner representations of these attachment figures. Failures by the child to establish basic trust and secure attachment to a caretaker as well as parental failure to optimally frustrate the child's grandiose sense of self are likely to create developmental deficits (Erikson, 1963). The lack of a secure base may lead the individual to avoid the exploration and experimentation necessary for future identity achievement, and may result in identity diffusion (Kroger, 2000). In some cases then, a state of identity diffusion could indicate a

fragmented self, feelings of emptiness, gender dysphoria, and a susceptibility to external influences. These circumstances may also create a vulnerability to dysfunctional impulse regulation typical of, for example, bulimic symptoms, suicide attempts and substance abuse. Other manifestations of identity diffusion might be the antisocial, paranoid and schizoid personality disorders and, in particular, the borderline personality disorder (Akhtar & Samuel, 1996). The latter will be reviewed in more detail below.

Gender Identity Disorder

Gender identity development normally takes place during the first 2–3 years of childhood. As children progress developmentally into adolescence, they attain a sense of certainty about their gender and their gender roles. Developing a sense of gender identity is usually an unconscious process, while more conscious considerations are involved in developing gender role behaviours. Normally, the adolescent operates within a rather wide range of culturally acceptable gender role behaviours.

In childhood and adolescence, some transitory cross-gender behaviours may occur as experimentations in the search for a sense of identity. However, a small number of individuals will develop a Gender Identity Disorder (GID), a more fundamental disturbance in gender identity preference. Here, cross-gender behaviours may be more stereotypical, and indicate an emotional identification with the opposite sex and a corresponding marked discomfort with one's own sex, primary and secondary sex characteristics, as well as gender role. One way of understanding individuals with GID is that they are identity diffuse, and that there is considerable anxiety and insecurity about the self (Akhtar & Samuel, 1996). Such feelings may develop from attachment difficulties, parental intolerance of cross-sex behaviours, as well as the same sex parent's inability to function as a role model (Zucker & Bradley, 1995).

Several projective and behavioural assessment methods have been developed with large samples to identify those children with GID (see Zucker & Bradley, 1995 for an overview). These measures have generally shown good discriminant validity and reliability. For adolescents and adults, however, psychometrically sound assessment methods for GID are lacking.

Dissociative Identity Disorder

Individuals with a Dissociative Identity Disorder (DIS) typically feel confused about the stability of their identity. They may feel as though they are playing roles, rather than experiencing themselves as consistent persons. In some cases, two or more distinct identities or personality states alternate, determining the individual's behaviour. DIS is also characterized by a marked dissociative amnesia, sometimes for basic personal information. DIS may be a psychological defence against painful or traumatic experiences (see Steinberg, 2000 for a review). The amnesia as well as alexithymia, denial, and an array of symptoms such as anxiety, depression, psychosis, and substance abuse complicate assessment of DIS. Recent empirical evidence indicates blurred boundaries between DIS, conversion, and somatization (e.g. Spitzer et al., 1999; Saxe et al., 1994). This blurring may challenge the current definition of DIS as a separate diagnosis, and revitalize the psychodynamic conceptions of hysteria. A sharp rise in the prevalence of DIS, particularly in the United States, may indicate previous professional neglect of the disorder. However, it may also serve as an example of how increased public attention and professional interest in a particular syndrome may give rise to such syndromes as culturally specific means to express general psychological distress or discomfort.

Indeed, the choice of self-report versus interview based assessment methods may also account for some of the variation in the prevalence figures. Among self-report measures, the Dissociative Experience Scale (DES) is a psychometrically sound screening tool (Dubester & Braun, 1995), though it captures a rather wide range of dissociative symptoms. However, recent research (Waller & Putnam, 1996) has identified a subset of 8 items from the DES that may identify DIS more precisely. Among interview measures, the DSM-IV based structured interview (Steinberg, 2000) has shown good reliability and discriminant validity (see Steinberg, 2000 for a review).

Personality Disorders

One aspect of understanding the aetiology of personality disorders is as a consequence of developmentally early deficits in the formation of the self, in affect regulation, as well as an imbalance between separation and individuation processes. Thus, the individual may not be able to integrate positive and negative representations of the self and of others. In adolescence and early adulthood, an identity disturbance manifested as a sense of self-incoherence and lack of commitment are prominent clinical features of the borderline personality disorder (Wilkinson-Ryan & Westen, 2000). In this disorder, the subjective experience of impaired identity may be more salient than in the other forms of personality disorders because the extremely poor integration creates a sense of inner emptiness and a hypersensitivity to external circumstances.

FUTURE PERSPECTIVES

Recent theoretical and empirical work has begun to differentiate forms of identity diffusion that may enable a more refined understanding of selected identity disorders (Marcia, 1989; Wilkinson-Ryan & Westen, 2000). For example, Marcia (1989) contrasts the pathological form of identity diffusion, characteristic of the borderline personality disorder (self-fragmentation), from the culturally adaptive, carefree, developmental, and disturbed (as per Erikson's schizoid loner) forms of identity diffusion. A fruitful line of future research may lie in identifying possible intrapsychic differences across these various diffusion groups in order to best determine possible intervention or treatment options. Another line of research investigates possible intrapsychic predictors of developmental arrest among both foreclosed and diffuse individuals (see Kroger, 2000 for a review). Future research on the more pathological forms of identity diffusion might begin to address the roles and functions of transitional objects that could facilitate further identity development during adolescent and adult life.

CONCLUSIONS

Erikson's (1963) theoretical writings on identity have been reviewed, and Marcia's elaborations of Erikson's fifth psychosocial task of adolescence, 'Identity vs. Role Confusion', have been described. Marcia's four identity statuses have been presented, along with measures currently used to assess identity status. The diffusion identity status has been associated with distinct forms of developmental arrest. More pathological forms of identity difficulties have been reviewed, including gender identity disorders, dissociative identity disorders, and personality disorders. Promising directions for future research lie in understanding the relationship between psycho-social identity development and intrapsychic forms of developmental arrest.

References

Adams, G.R., Bennion, L. & Huh, K. (1989). *Objective Measure of Ego Identity Status: A Reference Manual.* Unpublished manuscript, University of Guelph.

Akhtar, S. & Samuel, S. (1996). The concept of identity. *Harvard Review of Psychiatry, 3,* 254–267.

Dubester, K.A. & Braun, B.G. (1995). Psychometric properties of the dissociative experience scale. *Journal of Nervous and Mental Disease, 183,* 231–235.

Erikson, E.H. (1963). *Childhood and Society.* New York: Norton.

Kroger, J. (2000). *Identity Development: Adolescence Through Adulthood.* Newbury Park, CA: Sage, Inc.

Marcia, J.E. (1966). Development and validation of ego identity status. *Journal of Personality and Social Psychology, 3,* 551–558.

Marcia, J.E. (1989). Identity diffusion differentiated. In Luszez, M.A. & Nettelback, T. (Eds.), *Psychological Development: Perspectives Across the Life-Span.* North-Holland: Elsevier Science Publishers.

Marcia, J.E., Waterman, A.S., Matteson, D.R., Archer, S.L. & Orlofsky, J.L. (1993). *Ego Identity: A Handbook for Psychosocial Research.* New York: Springer-Verlag.

Saxe, G.N., Chinman, G., Berkowitz, R., Hall, K., Lieberg, G., Schwartz, J. & van der Kolk, B. (1994). Somatization in patients with dissociative disorders. *American Journal of Psychiatry, 151,* 1329–1334.

Spitzer, C., Spelberg, B., Grabe, H.J., Mundt, B. & Freyberger, H. (1999). Dissociative experiences and psychopathology in conversion disorders. *Journal of Psychosomatic Research, 46,* 291–294.

Steinberg, M. (2000). Advantages in the clinical assessment of dissociation. *Bulletin of the Menninger Clinic, 64,* 146–163.

Waller, N.G. & Putnam, F.W. (1996). Types of dissociation and dissociative types. *Psychological Methods, 1,* 300–321.

Wilkinson-Ryan, T. & Westen, D. (2000). Identity disturbance in borderline personality disorder: an empirical investigation. *American Journal of Psychiatry, 157,* 528–541.

Zucker, K.J. & Bradley, S.J. (1995). *Gender Identity Disorder and Psychosexual Problems in Children and Adolescents.* New York: Guilford.

Jane Kroger and Jan H. Rosenvinge

RELATED ENTRIES

Applied Fields: Clinical

IDIOGRAPHIC METHODS

INTRODUCTION

Idiographic methods of psychological assessment are techniques designed to capture the unique and potentially idiosyncratic qualities of the individual. The assessor seeks to identify the constellation of psychological attributes that best characterizes the particular individual who is the target of assessment.

The idea of idiographic assessment can be contrasted with that of nomothetic assessment. Nomothetic methods (from the Greek for 'law', *nomos,* referring here to the search for universal scientific laws) characterize individuals via a fixed set of psychological variables and assessment procedures; that is, variables and procedures that do not change from one person to the next. In nomothetic assessment, a primary goal is to describe individuals in relation to the population at large; for example, people may be ranked on interindividual-difference dimensions. In contrast, idiographic methods (from the Greek *idios*, referring to personal, private, and distinct characteristics) employ psychological constructs and assessment procedures that may vary from one person to the next. The primary aim is to describe qualities of the individual and the within-person organization among these qualities. In idiographic assessment, describing the individual with fidelity is the paramount task, whereas characterizing the individual's standing with respect to the population at large is of secondary importance.

This entry discusses the rationale behind idiographic assessment and reviews specific idiographic techniques. The focus primarily is on assessment in personality and clinical psychology. Personality psychologists have devoted particular attention to idiographic methods, spurred by Allport's (1937) highlighting of the organized qualities of the unique individual. Clinical psychologists' need to understand individual clients in depth inherently motivates idiographic methods in this field; indeed, although this entry focuses on quantitative idiographic assessment techniques, one should note that clinical case studies also constitute idiographic methods.

RATIONALE FOR IDIOGRAPHIC ASSESSMENT

To the extent that qualities of human nature are universal, idiographic methods might seem unnecessary. In principle, assessing universal aspects of psychological variation might be sufficient to characterize individual persons. There are, however, three reasons for adopting idiographic methods.

One is simply that assessors may desire more detailed information than is provided by nomothetic techniques. Describing individuals within a universal system of individual differences is only a first step in capturing the features of individual persons, who possess unique qualities that may require more detailed, individual-focused assessment techniques to be fully revealed.

A second reason for adopting idiographic methods involves predictive utility. The assessor may wish to predict a particular behavioural outcome, yet may know that established nomothetic methods already have proven to have little predictive value in the domain under investigation. This might occur, for example, if individuals tend to display criterion behaviours only in highly specific contexts that vary idiosyncratically from one person to the next. In such cases, pragmatic considerations motivate the use of idiographic techniques.

A third reason is not merely pragmatic, but conceptual. Theoretical considerations may suggest that standard nomothetic assessments do not adequately represent the psychological qualities in which the assessor is interested. Nomothetic assessments typically describe people according to individual-difference dimensions, where those dimensions commonly are statistical factors identified in analyses of the population at large. The factors, then, are statistical properties of populations, not of individuals. On purely statistical grounds, one cannot assume that group-level statistical parameters necessarily will capture the qualities of each individual in the group. Person-centred rather than population-based methods thus may be required to capture psychological qualities at the level of the individual.

IDIOGRAPHIC METHODS AND GENERAL LAWS

It is sometimes thought that idiographic methods conflict with the search for general psychological laws. Idiographic methods are sensitive to individual idiosyncracy, whereas scientific practices pursue generalizable principles. Idiographic methods might appear antithetical to nomothetic science. Such a conclusion, however, is unwarranted on various grounds.

Idiographic methods can complement the pursuit of generalizable knowledge. The careful analysis of multiple individual cases provides particularly strong support for generalizable conclusions if a particular finding proves replicable at the level of the individual case. Further, understanding of some phenomena might require idiographic techniques. For example, personality psychologists seek to understand the coherent within-person organization among distinct personality systems (Cervone & Shoda, 1999). This task inherently requires idiographic, person-centred assessments in addition to nomothetic, variable-centred techniques.

Idiographic and nomothetic procedures can be combined to yield generalizable conclusions. One might assess individuals idiographically, but aggregate findings across individuals help to identify general patterns. For example, idiographic assessments of cross-situational consistency in psychological response reveal patterns of consistency that often are idiosyncratic; people display personality consistency across relatively unique sets of social contexts. In the aggregate, however, consistency is lawfully related to individuals' beliefs about the self and social contexts (Cervone, 1997).

Another path from idiographic assessment to generalizable conclusions is to assess multiple variables at the level of the individual and then to employ statistical techniques that identify subgroups of individuals who are relatively homogeneous with respect to these variables, and thus constitute a qualitatively distinct class of persons. Research on temperament provides an example. Kagan and colleagues (Woodward, Lenzenweger, Kagan, Snidman & Arcus, 2000) obtain multiple measures of behavioural reactivity in infants and analyse them via statistical techniques designed to identify classes, or taxa, that may not be evident in simple frequency distributions. Results suggest that approximately 10% of infants possess a highly reactive biological temperament that differs qualitatively from the population at large.

IDIOGRAPHIC ASSESSMENT TECHNIQUES

The utility of idiographic methods can be illustrated by considering a series of psychological phenomena for which they have proven to be illuminating.

Behavioural Tendencies

Personality psychologists often wish to assess overt behavioural tendencies; that is, surface-level tendencies to display one versus another type of behaviour. A primary tool for assessing behavioural tendencies idiographically is 'P-technique' factor analyses, in which one studies a given individual over a large number of occasions to determine the primary dimensions along which the individual's actions vary. This contrasts with traditional R-factor analysis, where numerous individuals are assessed once and interindividual-difference dimensions are obtained. Importantly, idiographic within-person dimensions identified via P-factor methods may fail to correspond with nomothetic interindividual-difference factors. P-factor analyses of global dispositional tendencies assessed over multiple occasions have been found to correspond to a canonical five-factor model of interindividual-differences in only a small minority of cases (Borkenau & Ostendorf, 1998). P-technique factor analyses make the broader point that idiographic methods can be conducted with the same statistical rigour that typifies nomothetic assessment.

In addition to studying global dispositional tendencies, another idiographic method is to plot individuals' behavioural tendencies as a function of social contexts. Investigators construct dispositional profiles that represent the contingent relations between situational contexts and action tendencies. People's tendencies are found to vary in idiosyncrasy, yet the variations are temporally stable and thus constitute an enduring 'behavioural signature' of the individual (Mischel & Shoda, 1995).

Affective Tendencies

Idiographic methods also have been employed constructively in the study of affective tendencies, where they can help to resolve questions about the structure of affective experience. One key question is whether the tendencies to experience positive and negative affect are independent dimensions or bi-polar opposites. Nomothetic techniques have been used in efforts to obtain a general answer to this question. Idiographic analyses, however, have shed new light on the issue.

In this work, individuals rate their emotional experiences daily for more than two months (Feldman, 1995). P-factor findings indicate that people vary in the degree to which their tendencies to experience positive and negative affect covary; there is, then, no generalizable answer to the question of independence versus bipolarity. The covariation of positive and negative affectivity varies considerably across persons, with idiographic positive/negative affectivity correlations ranging from -0.72 to 0.21 (Feldman, 1995).

Idiographic methods also indicate that people differ not only in their average affective experience, but in the way their moods vary over time. Time-series analyses of daily reports of affective experience reveal that individuals differ in the frequency with which their mood shifts (Larsen, 1987).

Developmental Change

Idiographic methods have been used to study developmental change. Investigators recognize that group-level analyses may fail to represent developmental patterns experienced by individuals. A group may, on average, display stability with respect to a psychological characteristic, yet many individuals may change significantly.

An important intraindividual technique in the study of development is individual growth modelling, a statistical method that yields estimate magnitudes of both group-level and within-person change. The method has been applied fruitfully to the study of stability and change in self-reported extraversion in a large population of US men (Mroczek & Spiro, 2000). At the group level, results indicated that levels of extraversion were stable over time. At the individual level, however, there was evidence for change. Findings revealed statistically significant person-to-person variability in intraindividual change; in other words, many individual persons changed significantly in their levels of extraversion, despite the fact that the group, in the aggregate, was stable. Analyses of self-reported neuroticism similarly indicated significant individual differences in patterns of change over time (Mroczek & Spiro, 2000). These idiographic findings are important to personality theory. Based on nomothetic data, some theorists have contended that personality is stable across adulthood; these idiographic analyses, however, violate this contention, and thus compel investigators to develop personality theories that can embrace both stability and dynamic change in personality across the life course (Caprara & Cervone, 2000).

Knowledge and Belief Systems

Idiographic methods also have informed the study of knowledge and belief systems in personality functioning (Cervone, Shadel & Jencius, 2001). Investigators generally recognize that nomothetic systems are inadequate to capture the potential idiosyncrasy of people's beliefs, the way those beliefs are organized, and the contexts in which those beliefs come into play. They thus assess belief systems idiographically.

Kelly's (1955) Role Construct Repertory test (REP test) is a classic technique here. In some respects, the REP test is nomothetic. The assessor's goal is always to identify the ideas, or constructs, people use to understand their world, and the testing procedure always asks test takers to indicate how a set of target persons is similar or different from one another. The content of test items, however, varies idiographically. Test takers provide a personalized list of individuals of importance to them. This unique list then comprises the target persons employed in the test. The method thus uncovers the constructs individuals use to interpret the unique people and circumstances of their daily life.

An advance in representing the content of individuals' belief systems is HICLAS, a hierarchical classification procedure that can be used to identify idiographic groupings or 'families' of self-with-other representations. In the typical procedure (see, e.g., Ogilvie et al., 1998), participants first generate sets of 'targets' (usually significant others) that are important in their life and a set of 'features' (personal characteristics) that characterize themselves. They then indicate which features characterize their behaviour toward each target. The HICLAS algorithm provides an idiographic representation of target–feature clusters; that is, groupings of personal characteristics displayed in particular interpersonal settings.

Multidimensional statistical techniques such as cluster analysis or multidimensional scaling also have been employed to represent the pattern of interconnections in individuals' belief systems. Research reveals that representations obtained using different sources of data, such as spontaneous descriptions versus more structured techniques, converge (Hart et al., 1995), supporting the reliability of multidimensional idiographic methods.

Clinical Assessment

In clinical psychology, idiographic methods are important not only to the question of assessing individuals with fidelity, as noted above. They also bear on the issue of relating research to clinical practice. Ideally, clinical practice would employ treatments that are empirically validated. In trying to apply empirically supported interventions to individual clients, however, practising clinicians face a problem. The empirical evidence generally consists of outcome studies demonstrating statistically significant group-level effects, with interventions being beneficial compared to control treatments. Such effects commonly are based on large, heterogeneous samples of persons, with the same intervention applied to all persons and treatment effects summarized as average responses to the intervention. The empirical data, in other words, are nomothetic. The problem is determining whether these nomothetic effects can inform the treatment of individual clients, many of whom may differ from the research sample in ways important to their recovery. Although some judge that this problem is intractable, others suggest that improved research designs might better inform treatment of the individual case (Erwin, 1999).

Investigators have begun to seek such improvements via novel idiographic methods. For example, the Articulated Thoughts in Simulated Situations paradigm (ATSS; Davidson et al., 1997) exposes individuals in the laboratory to a relevant situation (i.e. a social criticism situation in order to elicit social anxiety) and instructs them to speak aloud their thoughts and feelings at periodic intervals during exposure to the simulated situation. These responses are then coded for content and structure by trained raters who are unaware of the circumstances of the data collection which could potentially bias their codes. The ATSS procedure has two main implications for idiographic assessment (Davidson et al., 1997). First, open-ended responses are collected from individuals; no predetermined set of questions is asked which might bias subject responses and no assumptions are made about the content or structure of the individual's cognitions. Second, the data can be reliably coded so as to reveal not only idiosyncratic cognitive content that is prompted by particular contextual stimuli, but also differences in the underlying structure and organization of those cognitions.

Research with addictive behaviours, such as nicotine dependence, also has employed idiographic methods to uncover individual differences in the structure and content of clinically relevant cognition, including cognitive factors that regulate

the execution of coping strategies that contribute to clinical success (Shadel, Niaura & Abrams, 2000). In this work, clinical assessments combine open-ended measures of multiple aspects of self-concept with individualized assessments of the social contexts in which these concepts come into play. Although treatments have yet to capitalize fully on these idiographic methods, these techniques promise to yield findings that might truly inform treatment of the individual case.

FUTURE PERSPECTIVES AND CONCLUSIONS

Idiographic methods have come of age and would appear to have a bright future. Advances in the area reflect an interplay of supply and demand. Increasingly, theories require assessment techniques that provide portraits of the structure and organization of psychological variables at the level of the individual (Cervone et al., 2001). The methods of assessment and statistical analysis reviewed here have begun to meet those needs.

Work in this area could productively progress along a number of paths. Future research should aim to enhance the psychometric reliability and validity of idiographic methods. Empirical work should further test theoretical assumptions about individual personality functioning and development that traditionally have been based on nomothetic methods. Finally, idiographic assessments might better capitalize on a broad range of data sources, including those yielded by narrative and ethnographic techniques.

References

Allport, G.W. (1937). *Personality: A Psychological Interpretation*. New York: Holt.

Borkenau, P. & Ostendorf, F. (1998). The Big Five as states: how useful is the five-factor model to describe intraindividual variations over time? *Journal of Research in Personality*, 32, 202–221.

Caprara, G.V. & Cervone, D. (2000). Personality: determinants, dynamics, and potentials. New York: Cambridge University Press.

Cervone, D. (1997). Social-cognitive mechanisms and personality coherence: self-knowledge, situational beliefs, and cross-situational coherence in perceived self-efficacy. *Psychological Science*, 8, 43–50.

Cervone, D., Shadel, W.G. & Jencius, S. (2001). Social-cognitive theory of personality assessment. *Personality and Social Psychology Review*, 5, 33–51

Cervone, D. & Shoda, Y. (Eds.) (1999). *The Coherence of Personality: Social-Cognitive Bases of*

Consistency, Variability, and Organization. New York: Guilford.

Davidson, G., Vogel, R. & Coffman, S. (1997). Think-aloud approaches to cognitive assessment and the articulated thoughts in simulated situations paradigm. *Journal of Consulting and Clinical Psychology, 65*, 950–958.

Erwin, E. (1999). How valuable are psychotherapy experiments? The idiographic problem. *Journal of Clinical Psychology, 55*(12), 1519–1530.

Feldman, L.A. (1995). Valence focus and arousal focus: individual differences in the structure of affective experience. *Journal of Personality and Social Psychology, 69*, 153–166.

Hart, D., Stinson, C., Field, N., Ewert, M. & Horowitz, M. (1995). A semantic space approach to representations of self and other in pathological grief. *Psychological Science, 6*, 96–100.

Kelly, G. (1955). *The Psychology of Personal Constructs*. New York: Norton.

Larsen, R.J. (1987). The stability of mood variability: a spectral analytic approach to daily mood assessments. *Journal of Personality and Social Psychology, 52*, 1195–1204.

Mischel, W. & Shoda, Y. (1995). A cognitive–affective system theory of personality: reconceptualizing situations, dispositions, dynamics, and invariance in personality structure. *Psychological Review, 102*, 246–286.

Mroczek, D.K. & Spiro, A. III (2000). Modelling intraindividual change in personality traits: findings from the normative aging study. Unpublished manuscript, Fordham University.

Ogilvie, D.M., Fleming, C.J. & Pennell, G. (1998). Self-with-other representations. In Barone, D.F., Hersen, M. & Van Hasselt, V.B. (Eds.), *Advanced Personality* (pp. 353–375). New York: Plenum.

Shadel, W.G., Niaura, R. & Abrams, D.B. (2000). An idiographic approach to understanding personality structure and individual differences among smokers. *Cognitive Therapy and Research, 24*, 345–359.

Woodward, S.A., Lenzenweger, M.F., Kagan, J., Snidman, N. & Arcus, D. (2000). Taxonic structure of infant reactivity: evidence from a taxometric perspective. *Psychological Science, 4*, 296–301.

Select Bibliography

Cacioppo, J., von Hippel, W. & Ernst, J. (1997). Mapping cognitive structures and processes through verbal content: the thought-listing technique. *Journal of Consulting and Clinical Psychology, 65*, 928–940.

Cairns, R.B., Bergman, L.R. & Kagan, J. (Eds.) (1998). *Methods and Models for Studying the Individual*. Thousand Oaks, CA: Sage.

Cattell, R.B. (1946). *Description and Measurement of Personality*. New York: World Books.

De Boeck, P. & Rosenberg, S. (1988). Hierarchical classes: model and data analysis. *Psychometrika, 53*, 361–381.

Haynes, S.N., Kaholokula, J.K. & Nelson, K. (1999). The idiographic application of nomothetic, empirically based treatments. *Clinical-Psychology: Science-and-Practice, 6*(4), 456–461.

Levine, F.M., Sandeen, E., Murphy, C.M. (1992). The therapist's dilemma: using nomothetic information to answer idiographic questions. *Psychotherapy, 29*(3), 410–415.

McCrae, R.R. & Costa, P.T. (1996). Toward a new generation of personality theories: theoretical contexts for the five-factor model. In Wiggins, J.S. (Ed.), *The Five-Factor Model of Personality. Theoretical Perspectives* (pp. 51–87). New York: Guilford.

Meehl, P. (1992). Factors and taxa, traits and types, differences of degree and differences in kind. *Journal of Personality, 60*, 117–174.

Rogosa, D., Brandt, D. & Zimowski, M. (1982). A growth curve approach to the measurement of change. *Psychological Bulletin, 92*, 726–748.

Daniel Cervone and William G. Shadel

RELATED ENTRIES

PERSONALITY ASSESSMENT (GENERAL), QUALITATIVE METHODS, SUBJECTIVE METHODS

INSTRUCTIONAL STRATEGIES

INTRODUCTION

Teaching, or instruction, has been defined as 'anything that is done to facilitate purposeful learning' (Reigeluth, 2000: 20). The assessment of teaching, then, needs to be referred to the process it aims to stimulate, i.e. learning, and the actions which may be taken to foster it. A variety of theories of learning have been proposed among which cognitive constructivist theories have been prevalent for some decades now. Important differences can be found among them, which come along significant differences in instructional theories. However, for brevity purposes we shall focus here on their common points. The main assumptions of constructivist theories hold that knowledge cannot be passed on from one mind to the other but needs instead integrating new information with existing knowledge and has to be constructed through experience. It could then be concluded that teaching consists of organizing experiences which facilitate and demand knowledge construction. Different theories emphasize either the cognitive processes of skill and knowledge acquisition, the social processes which support the growth of individual knowledge or the specific features of the learning tasks or environments which help learning to occur. In fact, a combination of these elements is present in most current theories of learning and should be taken into account in instructional theory.

Next, we shall review some approaches which suggest relevant variables in teaching around which assessment might take place, then discuss some general rules of assessment and finally mention some assessment methods.

Constructivist theories highlight different paths that teachers may use to stimulate students' learning. If we consider the richness of these theories together with the dramatic sociocultural and technological changes affecting teaching and learning in modern societies, the resulting picture is quite complex. As a result, good teaching may adopt different forms depending on context, learner characteristics and content knowledge.

To enhance significant cognitive activity different strategies have been suggested such as structuring and signalling materials in a way which fosters students' structuring, elaboration and organization of information (Mayer, 2000). Performance and error analyses have also been proposed as a means to help overcome misunderstandings, and giving appropriate and timely feedback also stands out as a crucial activity to promote understanding. Worked examples have been shown to be helpful to understanding and, finally, alternative assessment, including self-assessment, seems to be a powerful method to foster higher thinking abilities.

It is generally accepted that social exchanges stimulate learning and conceptual change and strengthen motivation and emotional support. Two kinds of social interactions are relevant: *teacher–learner interaction* and close observation along task performance will allow assessing students' prior knowledge, diagnose their state of knowledge and give appropriate feedback. *Students' interaction with other students* in cooperative or collaborative tasks will also help them elaborate and refine their knowledge and keep their motivation high.

Finally, the design of tasks or environments which stimulate learning is another hallmark of good teaching (Jonassen & Land, 2000). The main assumption is that learning is promoted through problem solving so that features of tasks and environments created with this purpose need to be analysed in detail. The common features of good learning environments seem to be authenticity, complexity and variety. Scaffolding along tasks is needed and can be assisted by computerized systems such as expert tutors (Collins, Brown & Newman, 1989).

Gilbert and Gibbs (1998) discuss some models of teacher training which are interesting for the topic of assessment in that they point to important outcome measures. *Developmental models* describe a shift in the professional development of teachers from attention on *self* to *skills* and then to *students*. *Conceptual change models* describe different intentions in teaching, from transmitting information to students, having their students acquire the concepts of the discipline through different methods, helping students develop their own conception or aiming at students changing their conception. Models based on *reflection* emphasize the flexible use of a broad repertoire of teaching methods to adapt to the needs of the different contexts, students and goals they may be faced with. *Student learning models*, in congruence with recent attention on learning, rather than teaching, focus on the approach students take for learning and on learning outcomes. Finally, *behavioural models* assume good teaching can be identified by overt behaviours in the classroom.

GENERAL ASSESSMENT RULES

Some general rules should be followed in planning the assessment process. Considering the complex and varying behaviours which constitute good teaching, it is easy to realize that no assessment method, in isolation, will give us a comprehensive account. To get a reasonably complete picture it will be necessary to combine some of them and triangulate the perceptions of different sources of information. Sources of information as well as the methods selected should be appropriate to the context and the aims of assessment. These might be account-ability or improving teaching; with this second goal, both measurement and feedback need to be non-judgemental and confidential, with a clear contract on by whom, what, how and when will the assessment be carried out and how will it be used. It may be argued that knowing these details in advance may allow teachers to prepare, thus making assessment less representative of real behaviour. This risk, however, needs to be upraised against the possibility that surprise might cause unrepresen-tatively poor performance. Assessment is fre-quently used as a crucial element of teachers' professional development and, with this end, it should be remembered that criticism is hard to take, while building on positive aspects may result in significant positive effects on performance.

Evaluation of teaching might focus on factors which foster learning or on the results achieved by learners. The target of assessment might then be *process* measures which describe how teaching is performed and experienced, or *result* measures, the first being richer to improve teaching. These two approaches are related to the two main goals of assessment and, in combination, provide a complete picture.

Next we shall discuss the main sources of information and some widely used assessment methods. Assessment may cover all the way from course proposal to peer observations and discus-sion of class and assessment practice to student feedback and outcome. Along this way, different sources of information will be relevant. A crucial decision in assessment planning will be the selection of sources and methods to gather information.

ASSESSMENT OF THE TEACHING PROCESS

Teacher Measures

Teachers are a valuable source of information about their own practice and intentions but their reflection should be supported in some structured way.

Self-monitoring, diaries or *interviews* structured after different models of teaching are used to explore relevant aspects of teaching and also may have an impact on the ability to reflect on their practice. Interviews may be carried out together with videotapes of teaching so that recall is anchored and communication facilitated. The best asset of these procedures is the quality of the information and the communication between teacher and assessor which is established, while the most outstanding difficulty has to do with the time needed for in-depth interviewing.

Schedules and inventories are also used, such as the *Approaches to Teaching Inventory* (Prosser & Trigwell, 1999), which reflects the intentions of teaching (teacher focused or information transmission vs. student focused and conceptual change) and strategy used.

The *Teaching Methods Inventory* (Gilbert & Gibbs, 1998) was created to describe the variety of methods teachers use and includes an open section where they can add to the existing list any additional practice they adopt. The rationale is that the variety of methods used to suit different situations and purposes will reflect the ability of teachers to flexibly adapt to different needs. The specificity of the information required makes it difficult to give a distorted picture of what is actually done.

Portfolio assessment has proven a robust method whereby teachers may collect evidence on their progress which can be used for self-development as well as for external purposes (Seldin, 1991).

Student Measures

Self-report: a number of schedules have been developed to gain information from students' experience in a structured way. They are com-monly used in many universities to get feedback from students. In spite of some criticism that students may be too sensible to some surface aspects of teacher behaviour, at least the better researched instruments have been shown to have good correlations with other measures of teaching quality and outcome, thus allowing a convenient and economical means to gather information. However, evidence of their shortcomings advise they should not be used in isolation. A comparison of the content of the best known questionnaires might be interesting. The *Students' Evaluations of Educational Quality* (Marsh, 1982) explores the amount of learning, instructor enthusiasm, organization of course, facilitation of group interaction, quality of personal relationship and width of contents. The instrument developed by Entwistle, Thompson and Tait (1992) covers presentation, level and structure, objectives, concern and friendliness, supporting learning, feedback, assessment, pace, workload and difficulty. The *Course Experience Questionnaire* (Ramsden, 1991) includes questions on good teaching, clear goals, workload, assessment and independence.

Peers and External Examiners

It is easy to see the value of having experts judge the adequacy of course planning, goals, content, sources and teaching methods from the standpoint of a given discipline or a degree. This is carried out by peers or professional staff, inspectors or superiors, usually via direct observations or structured rating scales both in natural and contrived situations. Teaching might be videotaped to facilitate discussion and feedback. A number of procedures have been developed to adapt to different contexts and goals of assessment (Brown, Jones & Rawnsley, 1993).

ASSESSMENT OF OUTCOME

Outcome is the most clear criteria of good teaching, although it is influenced by other variables. Two approaches might be followed, centred on the resulting learning or on learning processes adopted by students. Some confusion may arise around outcomes depending on how learning is defined; different approaches have privileged measurement of competences, results on traditional tests or integrated competent performance. Other indicators such as success rate or students enrolling in similar courses have

also been used. Strategies or approaches to learning have been documented to be related to teachers' practices and to correlate with different outcomes (see entry on 'Learning Strategies').

FUTURE PERSPECTIVES

Following the current trend to consider teaching as instrumental for learning it is of paramount importance to arrive at a clear definition of learning outcomes. Sound methods to measure learning are needed to estimate effectiveness of teaching. The challenge is to reflect in this definition the main facets of learning and not only superficial features.

References

Brown, S., Jones, G. & Rawnsley, S. (1993). *Observing Teaching*. Birmingham: SEDA Publications.

Collins, A., Brown, J.S. & Newman, S.E. (1989). Cognitive apprenticeship: teaching the crafts of reading, writing and mathematics. In Resnick, L.B. (Ed.), *Knowing, Learning and Instruction: Essays in Honor of Robert Glaser*. Hillsdale, NJ: Lawrence Erlbaum Associates.

Entwistle, N., Thompson, S. & Tait, H. (1992). Guidelines for promoting effective learning in higher education. Edinburgh: Centre for Research on Learning and Instruction.

Gilbert, A.K. & Gibbs, G. (1998). A proposal for a collaborative international research programme to identify the impact of initial training on university teaching. Higher Education Research and Development Society of Australasia. Wellington: NZ.

Jonassen, D.H. & Land, S. (Eds.) (2000). *Theoretical Foundations of Learning Environments*. London: Lawrence Erlbaum Associates.

Marsh, H.W. (1982). SEEQ: a reliable, valid and useful instrument for collecting students' evaluations of university teaching. *British Journal of Educational Psychology, 52*, 77–95.

Mayer, R.H. (2000). Designing instruction for constructivist learning. In Reigeluth, C.M. (Ed.), *Instructional-Design Theories and Models. A New Paradigm for Instructional Theory*, Vol. II (pp. 141–159). London: Lawrence Erlbaum Associates.

Prosser, M. & Trigwell, K. (1999). *Understanding Learning and Teaching*. Buckinham: SRHE & Open University Press.

Ramsden, P. (1991). A performance indicator of teaching quality in higher education: the course experience questionnaire. *Studies in Higher Education, 16*, 129–150.

Reigeluth, C.M. (2000). What is instructional-design theory and how is it changing? In Reigeluth, C.M. (Ed.), *Instructional-Design Theories and Models.*

A New Paradigm for Instructional Theory, Vol. II (pp. 5–29). London: Lawrence Erlbaum Associates.

Seldin, P. (1991). *The Teaching Portfolio*. Bolton, MA: Anker.

Carmen Vizcarro Guarch

RELATED ENTRIES

RELATED ENTRIES

APPLIED FIELDS: EDUCATION, THEORETICAL PERSPECTIVE: COGNITIVE, LEARNING STRATEGIES

I INTELLIGENCE ASSESSMENT (GENERAL)

INTRODUCTION

The assessment of intelligence via the conventional IQ test has tremendous potential for great use and great abuse. IQ tests can be used to categorize people into oblivion and misinterpreted to support a wide variety of racist and sexist ideologies. But they can also be used to examine and treat children once simply called 'stupid'. This entry will briefly touch on the history of intelligence assessment and then focus on the Wechsler Scales, the most-used tests of cognitive development, the Stanford–Binet IV, the descendant of the first major test of cognitive development, and then describe more recent tests of cognitive development, such as the Kaufman tests, the Woodcock–Johnson, the Differential Ability Scales, and the Cognitive Assessment System. Although theory played little or no role in the original Stanford–Binet and the Wechsler scales, the more recent tests have generally been theory-driven with Horn's model of intelligence (1989) and Luria's (1980) neuropsychological approach being the most influential. The uses for IQ tests in contemporary society are decidedly practical: *identification* (of mental retardation, learning disabilities, other cognitive disorders, giftedness), *placement* (gifted and other specialized programmes), and as a *cognitive adjunct* to a clinical evaluation whose main focus is on personality or neuropsychological evaluation. Yet, the introduction of theory into test development (e.g. Kaufman & Kaufman, 1983; Woodcock & Johnson, 1989) and test interpretation (Kaufman, 1994) has provided an important foundation for helping examiners optimize these practical applications of IQ tests.

HISTORY OF INTELLIGENCE ASSESSMENT

The assessment of intelligence was conceived in a theoretical void and born into a theoretical vacuum. During the last half of the nineteenth century, first Sir Francis Galton in England (1883) and then Alfred Binet in France (Binet & Henri, 1895) took turns in developing the leading intelligence tests of the day. Galton, who was interested in men of genius and in eugenics, developed his test from a vague, simplistic theory that people take in information through their senses, so the most intelligent people must have the best developed senses. His test included a series of sensory, motor, and reaction-time tasks, all of which produced reliable, consistent results (Galton, the half-cousin of Charles Darwin, was strictly a scientist, and accuracy was essential), but none of which proved to be valid as measures of the construct of intelligence (Kaufman, 2000). Alfred Binet, with the assistance of the Minister of Public Instruction in Paris (who was eager to separate mentally retarded from normal children in the classroom), published the first 'real' intelligence test in 1905. Like Galton's test, Binet's instrument had only a vague tie to theory (in this case, the notion that intelligence was a single, global ability that people possessed in different amounts). In a stance antithetical to Galton's, Binet declared that because intelligence is complex, so, too, must be its measurement. He conceptualized intelligence as one's ability to demonstrate memory, judgement, reasoning, and social comprehension, and he and his colleagues developed tasks to measure these aspects of global intelligence. Binet's contributions included his focus on language abilities (rather than the non-verbal skills measured by Galton) and his introduction of the mental age concept, derived from his use of age levels, ranging from 3 to 13 years, in his revised 1908 scale (mental age was the highest age level at which the child had success; the Intelligence Quotient, or IQ, became the ratio of the child's mental age to chronological age, multiplied by 100). In 1916, Lewis Terman of Stanford University translated and adapted the Binet–Simon scales in the US to produce the Stanford–Binet (Terman, 1916).

Nearly coinciding with the Stanford–Binet's birth was a second great influence on the development of IQ tests in the US: America's entry into World War I in 1917. Practical concerns superseded theoretical issues. Large numbers of recruits needed to be tested quickly, leading to the development of a group IQ test, the Army Alpha. Immigrants who spoke English poorly or not at all had to be evaluated with non-verbal measures, spearheading the construction of the non-verbal group test, the Army Beta.

The next great contributor to IQ test development was David Wechsler. While awaiting induction into the US Army in 1917, Wechsler obtained a job with E.G. Boring that required him to score thousands of Army Alpha exams. After induction he was trained to administer individual tests of intelligence such as the new Stanford–Binet. These clinical experiences paved the way for his Wechsler series of scales. Wechsler borrowed liberally from the Stanford–Binet and Army Alpha to develop his Verbal Scale and from the Army Beta and Army Performance Scale Examination to develop his non-verbal Performance Scale. His creativity came not from his choice of tasks, all of which were already developed and validated, but from his insistence that *everyone* should be evaluated on *both* verbal and non-verbal scales, and that profiles of scores on a variety of mental tasks should be provided for each individual to supplement the global or aggregate measure of intelligence.

THE WECHSLER SCALES

While Wechsler (1974) defined intelligence as being a person's capacity to understand and cope with his or her environment, his tests were not predicated on this definition. Tasks developed were not designed from well-researched concepts exemplifying his definition. In fact virtually all of his tasks were adapted from other existing tests. Wechsler did not give credence to one task above another, but believed that this global entity called intelligence could be ferreted out by probing a person with as many different kinds of mental tasks as one can conjure up. Wechsler did not believe in a cognitive hierarchy for his tasks, and he did not believe that each task was equally effective. He felt that each task was necessary for the fuller appraisal of intelligence. All of his scales yields IQs with a mean of 100 and standard deviation (SD) of 15, as well as subtest scaled scores with mean = 10 and SD = 3.

Wechsler Primary and Preschool Intelligence Scale – Revised (WPPSI-R)

The WPPSI-R (Wechsler, 1989) is an intelligence test for children aged 3 years, 0 months through to 7 years, 3 months. The WPPSI-R emphasizes intelligence as a global capacity (and, therefore, provides a Full Scale IQ) but has Verbal and Performance scales as two methods of assessing this global capacity. The Verbal IQ measures children's ability to understand language and express themselves verbally, whereas the Performance IQ assesses cognitive functioning non-verbally via spatial reasoning and visual–motor coordination.

Wechsler Intelligence Scale for Children – Third Edition (WISC-III)

The WISC-III (Wechsler, 1991) is geared for children aged 6 years, 0 months through to 16 years, 11 months. In addition to yielding Verbal, Performance, and Full Scale IQs and scaled scores on 13 subtests, the WISC-III offers standard scores (Indexes with mean = 100 and SD = 15) on four separate factors: Verbal Comprehension (VC), Freedom from Distractibility (FD), Perceptual Organization (PO), and Processing Speed (PS). The first two factors are composed of Verbal subtests and the last two comprise Performance subtests. The VC and PO factors provide the familiar distinction between verbal and non-verbal intelligence, respectively. The FD factor is extremely susceptible to the influences of distractibility and is dependent for success on attention, concentration, memory, sequencing ability, and numerical facility.

Wechsler Adult Intelligence Scale – Third Edition (WAIS-III)

The newest member of the Wechsler family of tests is the WAIS-III (Psychological Corporation, 1997; Wechsler, 1997), for adults of ages 16 to 89 years. Its lineage includes the original Wechsler–Bellevue Intelligence Scale, Form II, WAIS, and WAIS-R. The WAIS-III, the first Wechsler adult scale to be normed with a carefully stratified sample above the age of 74, was formatted to be similar to the WISC-III, i.e. it includes Verbal, Performance, and Full Scale IQs and Indexes on four factors: three factors with the same names as WISC-III factors – VC, PO, and PS – and the fourth factor is called Working Memory. The latter factor resembles the WISC-III Freedom from Distractibility factor, but includes a new subtest (Letter–Number Sequencing). This new task draws from cognitive research and theory on working memory (e.g. Woltz, 1988). Another theoretical advance in the WAIS-III concerns a new subtest, Matrix Reasoning (solving complex abstract analogies), which is a measure of the kind of fluid intelligence that Horn (1989) uses to exemplify his fluid construct.

THE STANFORD–BINET: FOURTH EDITION (BINET-IV)

Like its predecessors, the Binet IV (Thorndike, Hagen & Sattler, 1986) is based largely on the principle of a general ability factor, 'g', rather than on separate abilities, and the scale provides a continuous appraisal of cognitive development from ages two through to young adult. Unlike its previous versions, however, the Binet-IV has a decided theoretical basis for its structure, based on a three-level hierarchical model of the structure of cognitive abilities. Unfortunately, the theoretical basis of the Binet-IV was not supported very well by empirical, factor-analytic investigations. Despite the presentation of ample evidence of internal consistency and concurrent

validity for its scores, the substantial problems with construct validity, data collection method, and other difficulties with the Binet-IV led one reviewer to recommend that the battery be laid to rest (Reynolds, 1987): 'To the S-B IV, *Requiescat in pace*' (p. 141).

WOODCOCK–JOHNSON PSYCHO-EDUCATIONAL BATTERY – THIRD EDITION: TESTS OF COGNITIVE ABILITY (WJ III)

The original Woodcock–Johnson Psycho-Educational Battery: Tests of Cognitive Ability (WJ; Woodcock & Johnson, 1977) made a major contribution to test development because of its inclusion of a diversity of novel tasks that represented the first major departure from subtests originally developed by Binet or by World War I psychologists. The WJ, however, was developed from an entirely practical perspective, with no apparent emphasis on theory. All that changed with the publication of the WJ-R (Woodcock & Johnson, 1989), an expanded and reformulated test battery that is rooted firmly in Horn's modified g_f–g_c psychometric theory of intelligence, as is its recent successor, the third edition of the WJ (WJ III; Woodcock, McGrew & Mather, 2000).

The WJ III, for ages 2 to 90+ years and composed of Cognitive and Achievement sections, is undoubtedly the most comprehensive test battery available for clinical assessment. The WJ III Cognitive battery (like the WJ-R) is based on Horn's (1989) expansion of the fluid/crystallized model of intelligence and measures seven separate abilities: Long-Term Retrieval, Short-Term Memory, Processing Speed, Auditory Processing, Visual Processing, Comprehension-Knowledge and Fluid Reasoning. An eighth ability, Quantitative Ability, is measured by several subtests on the Achievement portion of the WJ III.

KAUFMAN ASSESSMENT BATTERY FOR CHILDREN (K-ABC)

The K-ABC (Kaufman & Kaufman, 1983) is a battery of tests measuring intelligence and achievement of children of ages 2 through to 12 years. The K-ABC intelligence scales are based on a theoretical framework of Sequential and Simultaneous information processing, which relates to *how* children solve problems rather than *what* type of problems they must solve (e.g. verbal or non-verbal). The Sequential and Simultaneous framework for the K-ABC stems from an updated version of a variety of theories (Lichtenberger, Broadbooks & Kaufman, 2000). The Sequential and Simultaneous theory was primarily developed from two lines of theory: the information processing approach of Luria (1980), derived from his neurophysiological observations, plus empirical research conducted on Luria's model (Das, Naglieri & Kirby, 1994); and the cerebral specialization work of Sperry and other researchers (e.g. Sperry, 1974).

KAUFMAN ADOLESCENT AND ADULT INTELLIGENCE TEST (KAIT)

The Kaufman Adolescent and Adult Intelligence Test (KAIT) (Kaufman & Kaufman, 1993) is an individually administered intelligence test for individuals between the ages of 11 and more than 85 years. It provides Fluid, Crystallized, and Composite IQs. It includes a Core Battery of six subtests (three Fluid and three Crystallized) and an Expanded Battery that also includes alternate Fluid and Crystallized subtests plus measures of delayed recall of information learned earlier in the evaluation during two of the Core subtests.

DIFFERENTIAL ABILITIES SCALES (DAS)

The DAS was developed by Elliott (1990) and is an individually administered battery of 17 cognitive and achievement tests for use with individuals aged 2 through to 17 years. The DAS Cognitive Battery has a preschool level and a school-age level. The school-age level includes reading, mathematics, and spelling achievement tests that are referred to as 'screeners'. The same sample of subjects was used to develop the norms for the Cognitive and Achievement Batteries; therefore, intra- and inter-comparisons of the two domains are possible. The DAS is not based on a specific theory of intelligence. Instead, the test's structure is based on tradition and statistical analysis. Elliott (1990) described his approach to

the development of the DAS as 'eclectic' and credited the work of researchers such as Cattell, Horn, Das, Jensen, Thurstone, Vernon, and Spearman.

COGNITIVE ASSESSMENT SYSTEM (CAS)

The Das–Naglieri Cognitive Assessment System (CAS; Naglieri & Das, 1997), for ages 5 to 17 years, is based on, and developed according to, the Planning, Attention, Simultaneous, and Successive (PASS) theory of intelligence. The PASS theory is a multidimensional view of ability that is the result of the merging of contemporary theoretical and applied psychology (see summaries by Das, Naglieri & Kirby, 1994). According to this theory, human cognitive functioning includes four components: planning processes that provide cognitive control, utilization of processes and knowledge, intentionality and self-regulation to achieve a desired goal; attentional processes that provide focused, selective cognitive activity over time; and simultaneous and successive information processes that are the two forms of operating on information.

FUTURE PERSPECTIVES AND CONCLUSIONS

The unchanging nature of IQ tests has begun to thaw. For the first three-quarters of a century, from Binet's 1905 scale until to about 1980, there was the Binet and there was the Wechsler and that was about it. Then came a series of tests that included novel tasks and an attempt to link theory to IQ assessment. Today, clinicians have more choice than ever before and these choices include a pick of theory – namely Horn–Cattell g_f-g_c, expanded Horn g_f-g_c, and Luria PASS.

The critics of IQ tests abound, especially among popular and influential theorists such as Sternberg (e.g. Sternberg & Kaufman, 1998), and these critics must be heard. It is partly because of the critics that the developers of IQ tests have constantly striven to improve the existing measures and to attempt to bring more theory and research into the development of new tests and the revision of old ones. Tests that are powerful psychometric tools that have a solid research history, and that are clinically and neuropsychologically relevant, are valuable if used *intelligently* by highly trained examiners. Clinicians who employ the intelligent testing philosophy as outlined in Kaufman (1994) can make a meaningful difference in a client's life when interpreting the results of a test profile in the context of clinical observations during the test session, background information about the client, research findings, and theoretical models. The array of instruments described in this entry, as well as others not included because of space constraints, can each serve quite well as the IQ test of choice for clinical evaluation. Perhaps when some of the highly respected theories of intelligence are translated into individual tests of intelligence it will be time to abandon existing instruments. But the test developers who attempt to translate the theories necessarily must be well versed in the clinical, neuropsychological, and psychometric aspects of assessment; otherwise, the perfect theory-based test will prove to be an imperfect clinical tool.

And what of the future? There has been considerable progress during the past two decades in providing options for clinicians apart from the Wechsler and Binet, and several of these options have impressive theoretical foundations. Yet progress has not been as rapid as most would wish. By their very nature, test publishers are conservative, investing their money in proven ventures rather than speculating on new ideas for measuring intelligence. Progress will likely continue to be controlled as the twenty-first century unfolds.

Eventually, new and improved high-tech instruments will be available that meet the rigours of psychometric quality and the demands of practical necessity. Hopefully those tests will not abandon theory but will embrace it, continuing the trend in the development of IQ tests that began in the early 1980s and has continued to the present. But none of the excellent instruments that are now available for clinical assessment of intelligence – Wechsler or otherwise – should be left for dead until there is something of value to replace them.

References

Binet, A. & Henri, V. (1895). La psychologie individuelle. *L'Année Psychologique, 2,* 411–465.

Das, J.P., Naglieri, J.A. & Kirby, J.R. (1994). *Assessment of Cognitive Processes: The PASS Theory of Intelligence.* Boston, MA: Allyn & Bacon.

Elliott, C.D. (1990). *Differential Ability Scales (DAS) Administration and Scoring Manual.* San Antonio, TX: Psychological Corporation.

Galton, F. (1883). *Inquiries into Human Faculty and its Development.* London: Macmillan.

Horn, J.L. (1989). Cognitive diversity: a framework of learning. In Ackerman, P.L., Sternberg, R.J. & Glaser, R. (Eds.), *Learning and Individual Differences* (pp. 61–116). New York: Freeman.

Kaufman, A.S. (1994). *Intelligent Testing with the WISC-III.* New York: John Wiley.

Kaufman, A.S. (2000). Tests of intelligence. In Sternberg, R.J. (Ed.), *Handbook of Intelligence* (pp. 445–476). New York: Cambridge University Press.

Kaufman, A.S. & Kaufman, N.L. (1983). *Administration and Scoring Manual for Kaufman Assessment Battery for Children (K-ABC).* Circle Pines, MN: American Guidance Service.

Kaufman, A.S. & Kaufman, N.L. (1993). *Manual for Kaufman Adolescent & Adult Intelligence Test (KAIT).* Circle Pines, MN: American Guidance Service, Inc.

Lichtenberger, E.O., Broadbooks, D.A. & Kaufman, A.S. (2000). *Essentials of Cognitive Assessment with the KAIT and Other Kaufman Tests.* New York: Wiley.

Luria, A.R. (1980). *Higher Cortical Functions in Man* (2nd ed.). New York: Basic Books.

Naglieri, J.A. & Das, J.P. (1997). *Das–Naglieri Cognitive Assessment System.* Chicago: Riverside.

Psychological Corporation (1997). *WAIS-III and WMS-III Technical Manual.* San Antonio, TX: The Psychological Corporation.

Reynolds, C.R. (1987). Playing IQ roulette with the Stanford-Binet (4th ed.). *Measurement and Evaluation in Counselling and Development, 20,* 139–141.

Sperry, R.W. (1974). Lateralization in the surgically separated hemispheres. In Schmitt, F.O. & Worden, F.G. (Eds.), *The Neurosciences: Third Study Program.* Cambridge, MA: MIT Press.

Sternberg, R.J. & Kaufman, J.C. (1998). Human abilities. *Annual Review of Psychology, 49,* 479–502.

Terman, L.M. (1916). *The Measurement of Intelligence.* Boston, MA: Houghton-Mifflin.

Thorndike, R.L., Hagen, E.P. & Sattler, J.M. (1986). *Technical Manual for the Stanford–Binet Intelligence Scale* (4th ed.). Chicago, IL: Riverside.

Wechsler, D. (1974). *Manual for the Wechsler Intelligence Scale for Children – Revised (WISC-R).* San Antonio, TX: The Psychological Corporation.

Wechsler, D. (1989). *Manual for the Wechsler Preschool and Primary Scale of Intelligence – Revised (WPPSI-R).* San Antonio, TX: The Psychological Corporation.

Wechsler, D. (1991). *Manual for the Wechsler Intelligence Scale for Children – Third Edition (WISC-III).* San Antonio, TX: The Psychological Corporation.

Wechsler, D. (1997). *Manual for the Wechsler Adult Intelligence Scale – Third Edition (WAIS-III).* San Antonio, TX: The Psychological Corporation.

Woltz, D.J. (1988). An investigation of the role of working memory in procedural skill acquisition. *Journal of Experimental Psychology: General,* 117, 319–331.

Woodcock, R.W & Johnson, M.B. (1977). *Woodcock–Johnson Psycho-Educational Battery.* Allen, TX: DLM/Teaching Resources.

Woodcock, R.W. & Johnson, M.B. (1989). *Woodcock–Johnson Psycho-Educational Battery – Revised.* Chicago, IL: Riverside.

Woodcock, R.W., McGrew, K.S. & Mather, N. (2000). *Woodcock-Johnson Psycho-Educational Battery – Third Edition (WJ III).* Chicago, IL: Riverside.

James C. Kaufman and Alan S. Kaufman

RELATED ENTRIES

COGNITIVE ABILITY: G FACTORS, DEVELOPMENT: INTELLIGENCE/COGNITIVE, COGNITIVE ABILITY: MULTIPLE COGNITIVE ABILITIES, FLUID AND CRYSTALLIZED INTELLIGENCE

I INTELLIGENCE ASSESSMENT THROUGH COHORT AND TIME

INTELLIGENCE: MODELS OF STRUCTURE AND THEORIES OF DEVELOPMENT

Intelligence measurement and theories of intelligence are represented in this encyclopedia by several entries. This corresponds to the importance and relevance that cognition, cognitive abilities, and intelligence have in the Western societies and consequently in psychological research since its beginning some 100 years ago. There exist hundreds of definitions of intelligence and cognitive abilities in philosophy and psychology, and in every day life. Most of them include a core of key concepts such as comprehension, judgement, reasonable thinking, but also successful adaptation to natural, cultural, societal circumstances and challenges in an efficient and practical manner, and finally productive and creative mental energy. As Schaie (1996) argued, in the scientific study of intelligence there is a hierarchy leading from information processing (speed, accuracy, mechanisms, strategies), through products measured in tests of intelligence to practical every day intelligence, and finally to wisdom.

This entry is devoted to the special aspect of development and change of intelligence through time (i.e. through ages), and through cohorts. Development and change are driven by environmental determinants (such as culture, generation, social and educational systems, family conditions and constellations etc.), by genetic determinants (including processes of maturation, growth, and ageing of the organism) and by interactions of influences from both. The entire human age span (or life time) should be included in studying these phenomena. A major task of this type of research is to identify the peaks in intellectual performance as well as to describe and to explain the rate and patterns of change and decline.

Schaie (1996) identified at least four theoretical positions which influenced paradigms of empirical research in intelligence and development of cognitive abilities and functions: unidimensional conceptions (such as those of Spearman, Binet and Simon – g-factor), the multidimensional concepts leading from Thorndike to Wechsler (multiple cognitive abilities), the multiple dimensions approach by Thurstone (primary mental abilities) leading to an expansion by Guilford and to the hierarchization by Cattell (fluid and crystallized intelligence), and finally the stage theoretical Piagetian approach (multiple cognitive abilities). There are some attempts to expand the Piagetian approach beyond childhood and adolescence to adulthood, middle age, and old age. However, the majority of research concerning change, growth, decline and development of intelligence across the lifespan is based on the psychometric assessment of intelligence (i.e. Spearman, Thurstone, Cattell tradition and paradigm).

The Cattellian theory of fluid (g_f) and crystallized (g_c) intelligence (including the theory of investment from fluid intelligence into crystallized over the lifespan) was important to the lifespan oriented research, since the g_f- and g_c-components (but various others within this Cattellian system as well) differed in their time/age/cohort trajectories in terms of gains and losses and in types of more or less accelerated decline. Closely related to the Cattellian view Baltes and his co-workers built a slightly different two-component model of lifespan intellectual development: on the one hand fluid mechanics, i.e. intelligence as basic information processing (reasoning, spatial orientation, perceptual speed etc.), which is content-poor, universal, biological and genetically predisposed, and characterized by a declining trajectory (i.e. after 25/30 years of age) similar to g_f, and on the other hand crystallized pragmatics (verbal knowledge, semantic memory, some facets of mathematical ability), i.e. intelligence of cultural acquired knowledge, which is content-rich, culture dependent and experience based, and characterized by a trajectory similar to g_c (stable, beyond 25/30 years of age even increasing, smoothly declining in very old age) (Baltes, 1997).

INTELLIGENCE: LATENT CONSTRUCTS

Research and theories of intelligence have been developed synchronously and in reciprocal interaction with factor analysis methodology and its refinement and its sophistication (compare Spearman, Thurstone, Guilford, Cattell, Eysenck, Vernon, Burt, Horn, just to name a few of the scientists). The reason is that behavioural scientists who investigate phenomena such as intellectual abilities are rarely interested in single reponses to specific intelligence tasks or items (observed variables). Instead, such responses are treated as one of many possible indicators of the respondent's location to an unobservable, theoretically defined, or at least empirically abstracted scientific construct, such as verbal intelligence (latent variable). Consequently, change and development are described in terms of underlying ability dimensions

as well, i.e. research is not too much concerned with age differences and age changes in specific measures but rather with differences and changes of underlying (latent) concepts and constructs. The primary mental abilities or g_c, g_f or pragmatics, mechanics, etc. are located on the latent variable level of the first or even respectively second order of abstraction.

TIME: LONGITUDINAL ORIENTATION

Descriptions of change and development (whether in observed or in latent variables) needs time-oriented designs, i.e. longitudinal observations and data, at least if the question is, how intelligence changes within individuals and/or what the conditions and antecedents of intraindividual changes, of interindividual differences and of interindividual differences in individual developmental trajectories.

Cross-sectional data are not relevant to these before-mentioned questions. Longitudinal designs and data are considered the *via regia* for conducting this type of research. However, the longitudinal study implies certain problems: sample comparability over time, selection and non-random selectivity processes. From a longitudinal perspective the attrition process of the sample, reflecting time-dependent biological, sociodemographic and psychological processes, reduces the generalizability of results, unless this selection process is mirroring the selectivity within the population; otherwise the generalizability can be maintained. However, it remains with the researcher to prove that there is no biasing selection effect working in the sample. Taking all these possible influences into account has an impact already on the sampling scheme and sampling plan, particularly with regard to disproportional sampling of these strata, which are expected to suffer extensively from an attrition process.

Of course, the longitudinal orientation offers a lot of advantages as well. A essential aim of a longitudinal study is, e.g., to extend the knowledge about the reciprocal relation between changes in various domains of psychological and physical functioning, i.e. the determination of structure of changes (Rudinger, Andres & Rietz, 1994). But also a simple description of interlaced series of changes (e.g. of cognitive functioning and biochemical parameters as in the case of Alzheimer's disease) would follow from this paradigm in an interdisciplinary way. In the modern view in the longitudinal paradigm it is assumed that the extent, direction, and sequence of development are connected to stability and change of the whole person–environment system.

STABILITY, INVARIANCE, AND CHANGE

In addition to change and variability, stability has proved to be a central concept in the description of development. The multivariate developmental situation can mean stability or differences either between or within subjects over time. An excellent discussion of the various meanings of stability can be found already in Wohlwill (1973); for example, stability as predictability, as invariance, as regularity, as consensus, as the constancy of the relative positions within a group, and as the preservation of individual differences. The numerous attempts to establish developmental functions and growth curves, expecially in the area of cognitive functions (stability as regularity and predictability), make clear the importance of this concept.

This seems to be an anomaly in the study of behaviour change and development over time – that in many instances stability has been empha- sized rather than lability as a target concern.

To explain this in more detail, for reasons of simplification, the Wohlwillian taxonomy will be reduced to three types of across-time change which may occur: structural, normative, and level. The latter two types of changes (stability) can only be examined if the structure of a concept that has repeatedly been measured did not change across time.

Structural Invariance

Structural invariance refers to the degree of continuity in the nature of the phenomenon under investigation. Two types of invariance need to be considered: (1) invariance across multiple age groups or cohorts, such as are usually found in cross-sectional studies or cohort comparisons, and (2) invariance across time for the same individuals measured longitudinally. For exam- ple, an intelligence construct may be considered

structurally invariant when it is characterized by the same dimension, and when there is a persistent pattern of relationships among its component attributes across time (McArdle, 1996; Schaie, Maitland, Willis & Intrieri, 1998). This issue has received much interest especially in relation to the across-time develop- ment of cognitive abilities. The generally accepted criterion for structural invariance is that the factor structure of the concept of interest is the same at each wave of the study. Thus, if a particular concept consists of two related factors at one occasion with three items loading on each factor, a 'similar' structure should be obtained for follow-up measurement of this concept. If not, development has been discontinuous; the terms 'structural', 'qualitative', or 'configural' change have been used when referring to this issue.

Only when factorial invariance has been demonstrated can one assume that quantitative comparisons of differences in developmental trajectories truly reflect changes in the underlying constructs; based on factorial invariance one should compare estimated factor scores on the latent constructs. Factorial invariance involves the same relative magnitude of factor loadings of variables on factors (i.e. measurement equivalence, metric invariance) as well as the same degree of relations between the factors (i.e. structural invariance). The degree of relation between (oblique) factors can range from zero to one in correlational terms. The emergence of qualitatively new structures can be mirrored by relations between factors changing from one measurement point to another. Differentiation can be indicated by weaker and weaker relations across time, and dedifferentiation by increasing relations across time. The differentiation–dedifferentiation hypoth- esis suggests differentiation of dimensions of human behaviour during the growth stage, and dedifferentiation or reintegration as individuals age (Carroll, 1993; Reinert, 1970). Structural equation models can be specified that are suitable for statistical tests of most of the previously mentioned invariance assumptions (Rudinger, Andres & Rietz, 1994; Schaie & Hertzog, 1985).

Normative (Interindividual) Stability

Normative stability refers to the persistence of individual ranks or differences on an attribute of interest (i.e. stability of interindividual differences). It is usually measured as the correlation between the measures of this attribute across time for a group of individuals (such correlations are sometimes referred to as 'autocorrelations'). Strong positive autocorrelations indicate that persons who received low (high) scores in relation to other members of this group at one wave of a study retained similar relative positions in a follow-up wave. Stability of the relative positions is reflected by parallel or monotonically ordered individual trajectories, and change by crossing individual trajectories (growth curves). In the case of monotonicity and crossing of the trajectories the variances of the measures in the sample can change as well across time (or remain stable) (Rudinger & Rietz, 2001).

Conversely, weak autocorrelations suggest that the relative position of the person in the study has changed strongly across time.

It is only meaningful to compare individual ranks on an attribute of interest across time if the meaning of this attribute has remained unchanged. So, in order to be able to say that a concept is normatively stable, the assumption that this is structurally invariant must be satisfied.

Level Stability/Quantitative Constancy

Level stability or 'quantitative' stability refers to persistence in the magnitude of a phenomenon across time. Level stability can be measured in terms of (the absence of) change in group means across occasions, such as when there is no change in average intellectual performance. Level stability can also be assessed at the individual level, by examining within-subject across-time scores in an IQ test. Like normative stability, the examination of level stability presumes that the concepts to be compared are structurally invariant across time.

In empirical research, investigations initially attend to the means. Analyses of differences or changes in means by *t*-tests, (M)ANOVA or non-parametric counterparts seem very simple and easily interpretable. In Structural Equation Modelling by contrast the basic analysis starts with variances and covariances. The analysis of mean structures in SEM is a non-standard procedure. One of the first explicit Latent

Growth Curve (LGC) models for analysing co/variances and mean structures as well in a longitudinal context was published by McArdle (1986). For recent developments see McArdle (1998) and Rudinger and Rietz (2001).

Stability, Invariance and Change in Latent Variables

The different features – level and its statistical counterpart the mean, interindividual differences in variables under study or variability among individuals' respective variances, and relative positions of subjects within their reference group across time (normative stability), respectively the autocorrelation/test–retest correlation – are distinct and independent facets of change.

In addition to means, variances, and individual slopes of the trajectories across time as a further aspect, it has to be taken into account whether stability or change is located on the observed or on the latent level. Increasing variances of the observed variables across time could indicate a 'real' fan-spread change on the latent level (i.e. growing variances of the latent variables across time) or could indicate decreasing reliability across time, i.e. increasing error variances over time. It is possible that behind every facet of change in the observed world the same or a different process of change is hidden in the latent world, i.e. on the level of constructs.

These considerations provide additional reasons why Structural Equation Modelling (SEM) – explicitly differentiating between observed and latent variables – is extremely useful for the analysis of stability, variability, and change in the context of longitudinal data. In terms of SEM the definition of stability refers to the structural model, specifying the relations hypothesized within a set of theoretical concepts. Stability is 'operationalized' as the correlation of latent variables adjacent in time. Stability in this sense mirrors the consistency of interindividual differences at the level of latent constructs and refers to theoretical assumptions about the time-bound process.

Hypothesized relations of theoretical concepts to a set of measured variables (measurement model) serve the estimation of reliability, which describes the quality of measurement of the phenomena under study.

COHORT EFFECTS

Levels and forms of age gradients in intellectual abilities are shaped, to varying degrees, by history-graded systems of influence, such as enduring differences between people born at different points in historical time (cohort effects), specific influences of historical events across chronological age (period effects), or generalized and enduring shifts in the environment affections of individuals of all ages and subsequent cohorts (general environmental change). Discrimination among these varieties of environmental change is not easy.

The 'General Developmental Model' (Schaie, 1965)

These three sources of different influences reflect the three components of Schaie's (1965) 'general developmental model'. The general developmental model characterizes the developmental status of a given behaviour to be a function of three components A, C, and T. In this context, age (A) refers to the number of years from birth to the chronological point at which the organism is observed or measured. Cohort (C) denotes a group of individuals who enter the environment at the same point in time (usually but not necessarily at birth), and time of measurement (T; sometimes called period P) indicates the temporal occasion on which a given individual or group of individuals is observed or measured.

Like Cohort, Age and Period are not of much intrinsic interest to researchers: they are usually measured because they present convenient and readily measurable indicators of more basic 'underlying' concepts (A, T, P, C as proxy variables). For example, cohort Age may represent concepts such as maturation and biological or intellectual development (for birth cohorts), vocational career phase (for labour market cohorts), etc. Similarly, the meaning of the Period concept is much wider than its simple measurement suggests. It refers to all events relevant to the issue of concern that have occurred between the waves of the study.

The rather diffuse and imprecise measurement of the concepts that underlie the Age, Period, and Cohort variables pose the problem that the effects of these variables can rarely be interpreted unambiguously unless they are broken down to concrete possible impact variables.

Further, the three components are confounded in the sense that once two of them are specified, then the third is known (linear dependency). Nevertheless, each of the three components may be of theoretical interest in the developmental sciences. If there exist some assumptions about cohort, period and/or age effects, which imply constraints in the model set up for analysis, some statistical solutions of the confounding problem are available (Erdfelder, Rietz & Rudinger, 1996).

The Cohort Variables

The Cohort variable must be theoretically distinguished from the two related concepts (A, T/P). In cohort analysis, Age is measured as the amount of time elapsed since the cohort was constituted. The second related concept is T or P. Operationally, this refers to the moment of observation. The different age groups represent necessarily different cohorts, which differ in social and historical experiences like educational systems, professional and vocational trainings, historical changes in health services, etc. Cohort is just a proxy variable for a set of theoretical intermitting influences and determinants.

It is a well-known fact in medicine, sociology, and psychology that belonging to a cohort is a co-determinant factor of health, life-style and thus for the development of modes of experience and behaviour. Cohort membership influences also the formation of attitudes, convictions and values. The cohort variable indicates at least three points:

- the weakness of explanation by simple, generally valid and universal laws of development ('differential gerontology' is the more appropriate approach)
- the untenability of purely person-oriented, intra-organismic models of development, and
- the necessity of interdisciplines (sociology, economics, educational and political sciences, demographics, epidemiology) as the description and explanation of cohort differences exceed the psychological domain.

Cohort Sequential Studies

The basic cross-sectional study (comparing different groups at one point in time) and the basic longitudinal study (following one cohort across time) are simple subsets of the general model. Using Baltes's (1968) terminology, a cross-sectional sequence usually involves the replication of a cross-sectional study so that the same age range of interest is assessed for at least two time periods, obtaining the estimate for each age level across multiple cohorts, where each sample is measured only once. By contrast, the longitudinal sequence represents the measurement of at least two cohorts over the same age range. Here also, estimates from each cohort are obtained at two or more points in time. The critical difference between the two approaches is that the longitudinal sequence permits the evaluation of intra-individual age change and inter-individual differences in rate of change, information about which cannot be obtained from cross-sectional sequences.

Developmental psychologists often find the cohort-sequential design of greatest interest because it explicitly differentiates intra-individual age changes within cohorts from inter-individual differences between cohorts (Schaie & Baltes, 1975). This design also permits a check of consistency of age functions over successive cohorts, thereby offering greater external validity than would be provided by a single-cohort longitudinal design.

In a typical longitudinal study, repeated measures are taken of the same subjects at different times. Another possibility is to use the same research design but with independent samples at each point on the longitudinal time scale. The independent sample procedure, used conjointly with the repeated-measurement procedure, permits estimation of the effects of experimental mortality and of instrumentation (practice) effects. The independent samples are initially drawn at each occasion; hence, they reflect the likely composition of the single sample the repeated-measurement study would have had if no subjects had been lost between testing – and, of course, if the subjects had not had any practice on the test instruments.

Cohort Effects on Intelligence

There have been marked generational shifts in levels of performance on tests of mental abilities (Schaie, 1996). Empirical findings suggest that later-born cohorts are generally advantaged when compared with earlier-born cohorts at the same

ages. This phenomenon has been explained by increased educational opportunities and improved life-styles, including nutrition and the conquest of childhood disease, which have enabled successive generations to reach ever higher ability asymptotes.

Studies with cohort-sequential designs allow three kinds of comparisons across age: cross-sectional, longitudinal, and independent-sample, same-cohort comparisons.

Intellectual ageing as a multidimensional process in normal community-dwelling populations has been studied most intensively in the Seattle Longitudinal Study (SLS; Schaie, 1996). The principal variables in this study, which was extended thus for over a 35-year period, were five measures of psychological competence known as primary mental abilities (Thurstone & Thurstone, 1949): Verbal Meaning, Space, Reasoning, Number, and Word Fluency (the ability to recall words according to a lexical rule). During the last two test occasions, five multiple marked abilities were assessed at the factor level: Inductive Reasoning, Spatial Orientation, Perceptual Speed, Verbal Ability, and Verbal Memory.

A number of recent short-term longitudinal studies confirm that age changing in cognitive functions is a rather slow process.

Although by age 60 virtually every subject had declined on one ability, few individuals showed global decline. Virtually no one showed universal decline on all abilities monitored, even by the 80s.

Significant reductions in psychological competence occur in most persons as the 80s and 90s are reached. However, even at such advanced ages, competent behaviour can be expected by many persons in familiar circumstances. Much of the observed loss occurs in highly challenging, complex, or stressful situations. The often-voiced hope that the more able are also more resistant to intellectual decline remains generally unsupported. There are tremendous individual differences in level and rate of change. But those who start out at high levels remain advantaged even after suffering some decline, i.e. inter-individual stability.

Due to substantial cohort differences age-comparative (cross-sectional) studies show greater age differences than do longitudinal data. Typically, ages of peak performance occur earlier (for later-born cohorts), and modest age differences are found by the early 50s for some and by the 60s for most dimensions of intelligence. Because of the slowing in the rate of positive cohort differences, age difference profiles have begun to converge somewhat more with the age changes from longitudinal studies.

FUTURE PERSPECTIVES

From research on the development of intelligence over the lifespan a couple of very interesting and intriguing topics have been derived (e.g. Baltes, Dittmann-Kohli & Dixon, 1984).

These are still here today and in the future the following ones will be:

1 Multidimensionality, the notion that intelligence is composed of multiple mental abilities, each with potentially distinct structural, functional, and developmental properties.
2 Multidirectionality, signifying that there are multiple distinct change patterns associated with these abilities.
3 Inter-individual variability, a conception reflecting the observed differences in the life-course change patterns of individuals.
4 Intra-individual plasticity, which indicates that, in general, throughout the life course individual behavioural patterns are modifiable.

While there is support for each of these, it is also the case that it would be possible to emphasize the converse principles of unidimensionality, unidirectionality, inter-individual stability, and intra-individual constancy from an examination of the present research body. Future research should clarify which of the mentioned perspectives is the appropriate and most plausible one.

CONCLUSIONS

Presenting a conclusion one can refer to Brody (1992) quoting the following statements:

1 There are secular increases in intelligence. These changes are not attributable to genetic influences.
2 Even the most ardent proponent of genetic influences on intelligence believes that there are environmental influences on the phenotype of intelligence.

3 (...) that genetic factors may be more important determiners of adult IQ than of IQ in childhood. This implies that the IQ index is not a measure of the same construct at different points of a person's life. If it were, the determinants of the construct would not change.
4 The content of intelligence tests changes over the life span. Items used to assess intelligence in 4 year old children are not the same as items used to assess intelligence in adults. In this respect, IQ is not like height, which increases but can be assessed by the same instruments at different times in a person's life. The means of assessing intelligence are not constant over the lifespan and hence the increase in intelligence is indexed by different instruments.
5 It has been argued that there are age-related changes in the biological basis of fluid intelligence over the lifespan. Therefore, some components of intelligence may be influenced by age-related changes in the biological basis of test performance.
6 While IQ test scores are stable, the test–retest correlation is less than perfect. IQ is only relatively fixed or unchanging. As the time between administrations increases, the test–retest stability of IQ decreases.
7 The intellectual skills that a person develops depend crucially on a person's 'cultural experiences'.

References

Baltes, P.B. (1968). Longitudinal and cross-sectional sequences in the study of age and generation effects. *Human Development, 11,* 145–171.

Baltes, P.B. (1997). On the incomplete architecture of human ontogeny: selection, optimization, and compensation as foundation of developmental theory. *American Psychologist, 52,* 366–380.

Baltes, P.B., Dittmann-Kohli, F. & Dixon, R.A. (1984). New perspectives on the development of intelligence in adulthood: toward a dual-process conception and a model of selective optimization with compensation. In Baltes, P.B. & Brim, O.G. Jr. (Eds.), *Lifespan Development and Behaviour* (pp. 33–76). New York: Academic Press.

Brody, N. (1992). *Intelligence.* San Diego: Academic Press.

Carroll, J.B. (1993). *Human Cognitive Abilities.* Cambridge: Cambridge University Press.

Erdfelder, E., Rietz, C. & Rudinger, G. (1996). Methoden der Entwicklungspsychologie [Methods of developmental psychology]. In Erdfelder, E., Mausfeld, R., Meiser, T. & Rudinger, G. (Eds.), *Handbuchdes Quantitative Methoden* [Handbook of Quantitative Methods] (pp. 539–550). Weinheim: PVU.

McArdle, J.J. (1986). Latent variable growth within behaviour genetic models. *Behaviour Genetics, 16,* 163–200.

McArdle, J.J. (1996). Current directions in structural factor analysis. *Current Directions in Psychological Science, 5*(1), 11–18.

McArdle, J.J. (1998). Modelling longitudinal data by latent growth curves methods. In Marcoulides, G.A. (Ed.), *Modern Methods for Business Research. Methodology for Business and Management* (pp. 359–406). Mahwah: Erlbaum.

Reinert, G. (1970). Comparative factor analytic studies of intelligence throughout the human life span. In Goulet, L.R. & Baltes, P.B. (Eds.), *Life-Span Development and Behaviour* (pp. 476–484). New York: Academic Press.

Rudinger, G., Andres, J. & Rietz, C. (1994). Structural equation models for studying intellectual development. In Magnusson, D., Bergman, L.R., Rudinger, G. & Törestad, B. (Eds.), *Problems and Methods in Longitudinal Research: Stability and Change* (pp. 274–307). Cambridge: Cambridge University Press.

Rudinger, G. & Rietz, C. (2001). Structural equation modelling in longitudinal research on aging. In Birren, J.E. & Schaie, K.W. (Eds.), *Handbook of the Psychology of Aging* (pp. 29–52). San Diego, CA: Academic Press.

Schaie, K.W. (1965). A general model for the study of developmental problems. *Psychological Bulletin, 64,* 92–107.

Schaie, K.W. (1996). *Intellectual Development in Adulthood: The Seattle Longitudinal Study.* Cambridge: Cambridge University Press.

Schaie, K.W. & Baltes, P.B. (1975). On sequential strategies in developmental research: description or explanation? *Human Development, 18,* 383–390.

Schaie, K.W. & Hertzog, C. (1985). Measurement in psychology of adulthood and aging. In Birren, J.E. & Schaie, K.W. (Eds.), *Handbook of the Psychology of Aging* (2nd ed., pp. 59–69). New York: Van Nostrand-Reinhold.

Schaie, K.W., Maitland, S.B., Willis, S.L. & Intrieri, R.C. (1998). Longitudinal invariance of adult psychometric ability factor structures across 7 years. *Psychology and Aging, 13*(1), 8–20.

Thurstone, L.L. & Thurstone, T.G. (1949). *Examiner Manual for the SRA Primary Mental Abilities.* Chicago: Science Research Associates.

Wohlwill, J.F. (1973). *The Study of Behavioural Development.* New York: Academic Press.

Georg Rudinger and Christian Rietz

RELATED ENTRIES

Intelligence Assessment (General), Personality Assessment Through Longitudinal Designs, Cognitive Decline/Impairment, Development: Intelligence/Cognitive, Cognitive Ability: Multiple Cognitive Abilities

I INTEREST

INTRODUCTION

This entry briefly summarizes highlights of what is known currently about the assessment of interests including its underlying scientific basis. The history of the measurement of interests is briefly described. Structural issues are discussed and alternative ways to measure interests, including some of the currently used measures of interests, are briefly reviewed.

NATURE OF INTERESTS

Although they have been studied most comprehensively as they relate to *occupational* choices, interests identify aspects of a person that constitute enduring individual difference variables (Crites, 1999). Interests affect a number of life choices and activities in which people are likely to invest time, energy and attention; they appear to influence *both* work and life satisfaction (Super, 1940; Super & Crites, 1962).

The definition of the term 'interests' that will be used here is the following:

Interests are relatively stable psychological characteristics of people which identify the personal evaluation (subjective attributions of 'goodness' or 'badness', judged degree of personal fit or misfit) attached to particular groups of occupational or leisure activity clusters.

Occupational interests, the primary focus of this entry, have been studied since the early 1900s, were initially approached primarily as a useful dimension for predicting such issues as occupational choice and career satisfaction rather than as psychological dimensions of interest in their own right.

Interests, as measured by such early measures as Strong's 1927 *Vocational Interest Blank* (SVIB; Strong, 1943) and Kuder's *Preference Record – Personal* (Kuder, 1948; Kuder and Zytowski, 1991), were found to be markedly reliable and to predict well the college and occupational choices. The reason for this consistency partly attests to the psychometric excellence of the early measures but also to the nature of the underlying construct. Recent evidence (e.g. Gottfredson, 1999) points to a strong heritability component to occupational interests, perhaps as much as 50%. Such data would help explain the strong reliability of occupational interests and their limited susceptibility to change efforts.

Contemporary interest theory, largely based on, or deriving from, the prolific empirical and theoretical work of John L. Holland and his associates (e.g. Holland, 1997), reduced complex interest measures that typically had focused on individual items or item clusters in predicting career choices to six primary factors, which Holland has labelled 'occupational personality' types. These groupings were also used to describe the occupational environments in which people work, essentially collections of people in particular occupational settings sharing similar patterns.

Holland's six 'RIASEC' interest types (realistic, investigative, artistic, social, enterprising, and conventional; Holland, 1997) are now popularly used throughout the world to measure occupational interests. The interest 'types' have

demonstrated both structural consistency and the ability to predict occupations likely to be found motivating and enjoyable (see Holland, 1997, for a comprehensive review). The interest types seem markedly resilient across ethnic groups, cultures and genders (Day & Rounds, 1998). Although the theory is described as being a six-factor one, in assessment practice individuals are typically classified on the basis of their three most highly endorsed vocational interest scales rather than just one, so that, in individual difference terms, 120 possible combinations of the three highest endorsed interest patterns are possible.

More recent work has sought to refine Holland's constructs, generally to encompass a smaller number of underlying structural dimensions of interests. Some of this research has identified two underlying poles, concerns with people vs. things and with data vs. ideas. Other underlying structural factors have also been suggested, e.g. gender-specificity of occupations and their perceived prestige, and alternative shapes of hexagons or geometric figures have been suggested to portray the relationship among the types. No theory or structure has yet displaced Holland's, either methodologically or in terms of practical measurement.

Less robust have been issues of the occupational environments and the bases for matching individuals to occupations and occupational settings. Alternative, sometimes derivative or expansionary, formulations (e.g. Dawis, 1996) have been offered to Holland's. This may be partly influenced by the stretch in trying to translate literally an individual difference variable into an organizational level one. Clearly many factors other than the interest composition of the employees combine to determine an organizational environment and therefore the fit between person and environment.

RELATIONSHIP OF INTERESTS TO PERSONALITY, VALUES, AND ABILITIES

Recent research has addressed the important questions of the relationship of vocational interests to other individual difference domains, most notably to personality and abilities. These efforts have proved more productive with relationship to personality than to abilities. Research shows strong overlap between the RIASEC types and conceptually related personality dimensions (e.g. social and enterprising interests to extraversion and agreeableness; openness to agreeableness) (Holland, 1997). Interests and values have similarly long been jointly considered but the constructs overlap and interests appear to be superior in predicting occupational outcomes (Holland, 1997).

Concerning the relationship of interests and abilities, there is less research and less basis on which to draw conclusions. Although the topic has been studied for many years (e.g. Gottfredson, 1986), there is surprisingly little that can yet be concluded with confidence. Similar structures do appear to characterize both interests and abilities (Ackerman, 1996; Lowman, 1991; Prediger, 1999) but, due to minimally overlapping variance between the two constructs, it remains important to measure interests and abilities separately (Lowman, 1991).

CONTEMPORARY MEASUREMENT OF INTERESTS

By the 1940s considerable progress had been made in refining the measurement of interests, especially with the advent of the Strong Vocational Interest Blank (Strong, 1943). For many years the SVIB dominated the field of interest measurement. Both this and Kuder's measure (Kuder, 1948), also very popular, in different versions, have now outlived their authors and continue to be used in the contemporary measurements of interests. Like the SVIB, the early Kuder has been updated and now carries a different name, the Kuder Occupational Interest Survey (KOIS; Diamond & Zytowski, 2000).

The Strong, now called the Strong Interest Inventory (SII; Donnay & Borgen, 1996), remains a very widely used and highly regarded measure of occupational interests. The SII uses a variety of item types to gather information on interests including queries about interest in specific occupations and non-occupational interests as well. It incorporates the six Holland types and a number of other dimensions also of interest to vocational counsellors such as personal styles, akin to personality variables. Its normative

base is excellent with a general norm sample of 18,951 (Harmon, Hansen, Borgen & Hammer, 1994). It has also been very responsive to the needs for ethnic diversity in the normative base. The RIASEC scales are incorporated into the test, which additionally includes test taking orientation (validity) indicators, specific occupational scales, and personality and educational predictors.

With the movement to Holland's (1997) theory-based occupational interest approach, newer instruments have also become very popular. These include two widely used measures of Holland's, the Vocational Preference Inventory (VPI; Holland, 1985) and the Self-Directed Search (SDS; Holland, Fritzsche & Powell, 1994; Spokane & Catalano, 2000). The VPI consists solely of occupational titles which respondents are asked to endorse or not as they appeal to the individual. The VPI measures the six Holland scores and several other related scales including validity, or test taking orientation, indicators (Infrequency and Acquiescence scales); a Masculinity–Femininity scale, and measures of Status and Self Control.

The SDS, also developed by Holland and his colleagues, is self-administered and scored. It is meant to simulate a career counselling experience and asks questions across a range of types of items, including occupational and activity preferences and self-ratings of abilities and competencies. Its summary scales include only the six RIASEC scores although a summary page provides scores for each of the component scales on the tests.

More recently, the Campbell Interest and Skill Survey® (CISS; Campbell, 1994; Hansen & Neuman, 1999) was published, a test authored by one of the major researchers in occupational interests. This instrument combined a number of psychometrically valuable techniques, well-grounded theory, and the measurement of both interests and self-assessed abilities. It includes seven orientation scales (influencing, organizing, helping, creating, analysing, producing, and adventuring), which generally correspond to Holland's typology except for having two realistic analogues ('producing' and 'adventuring'). The test also encompasses 29 basic interest and skill scales (clusters of occupations and skills, such as mathematics and science grouped with 'write computer programs ... perform lab

Table 1. Comparison of psychometric and other characteristics of four major psychological measures of occupational interests

	SII[a]	CISS[b]	VPI[c]	SDS[d]
Coefficient alphas for RIASEC scales	0.90–0.94	0.75–0.90	0.81–0.91	0.90–0.94
Test–retest reliabilities for RIASEC scales	0.74–0.92	0.69–0.91	0.45–0.92	0.76–0.89
Subcategory: National norm				
Samples	Yes	Yes?	No	No
Validity indicators	Yes	Yes	Yes	No
Extensiveness of supporting validity evidence	High	High	High	Moderate

[a]*Source*: General Reference Sample, Harmon et al. (1994).
[b]*Source*: Campbell (1994).
[c]*Source*: Holland (1985).
[d]*Source*: Holland, Fritzsche & Powell (1994).

research' and sample occupations such as chemist and computer programmer). The test also incorporates normative data for 58 occupational samples. Two additional scales, academic focus and extraversion, identify basic academic and personality orientations.

A number of other measures can also be classified as interest related even though they do not measure interests per se. These include measures of career indecision and vocational identity. Increasingly also, researchers and practitioners have turned their attention to the computerization of interest assessment (e.g. Carson & Cartwright, 1997).

No single measure of occupational interests can be declared universally superior for use in all circumstances and with all populations. The relative merits and limitations of each measure among those most commonly used are counterbalanced by those of the others. The SII includes one of the most impressive normative bases and one that is regularly updated; the SDS lends itself to self-administration, scoring and interpretation; the CISS explicitly tries to measure self-ratings of competencies, etc. All of these approaches have value and all measures in one way or another incorporate Holland's factors. Still, more research is needed examining the shared variance across these measures and whether it practically matters, in the measurement of interests, which measure was used. In the meantime, practitioners need carefully to choose measures of interests relevant for the particular assessment population and task at hand. Interpretation of interests should be done in the context of the client's understanding of self and in association with other variables (see Lowman, 1991).

FUTURE PERSPECTIVES AND CONCLUSIONS

The measurement of interests is alive and vibrant at the turn of the century. As one of the most stable variables identified in the 20th century, the measurement of interests is well-established and a thriving commercial enterprise. Emerging theories, particularly those pointing to a simpler structure underlying the ones popularly used today, will undoubtedly generate their own measuring instruments. The next decades will benefit from refinements in the inter-domain models which seek, more complexly, to examine the relationships across domains, especially of the relationships of properly measured abilities and interests.

References

Ackerman, P.L. (1996). A theory of adult intellectual development: process, personality, interests, and knowledge. *Intelligence*, 22, 227–257.

Campbell, D.P. (1994). *Campbell Interest and Skill Survey Manual*. Minneapolis, MN: National Computer Systems.

Carson, A.D. & Cartwright, G. (1997). Fifth-generation computer-assisted career guidance systems. *Career Planning and Adult Development Journal*, 13, 19–40.

Crites, J.O. (1999). Operational definitions of vocational interests. In Savickas, M.L. & Spokane, A.R. (Eds.), *Vocational Interests: Meaning, Measurement, and Counselling Use* (pp. 163–170). Palo Alto, CA: Davies-Black Publishing.

Dawis, R.V. (1996). The theory of work adjustment and person–environment-correspondence counselling. In Brown, D. & Brooks, L. (Eds.), *Career Choice and Development* (3rd ed.) (pp. 75–120). San Francisco: Jossey-Bass.

Day, S.X. & Rounds, J. (1998). Universality of vocational interest structure among racial and ethnic minorities. *American Psychologist, 53,* 728–736.

Diamond, E.E. & Zytowski, D.G. (2000). The Kuder occupational interest survey. In Watkins, C.E. Jr. & Campbell, V.L. (Eds.), *Testing and Assessment in Counselling Practice, Contemporary Topics in Vocational Psychology* (2nd ed., pp. 263–294). Mahwah, NJ: Lawrence Erlbaum.

Donnay, D.A.C. & Borgen, F.H. (1996). Validity, structure, and content of the 1994 Strong interest inventory. *Journal of Counselling Psychology, 43,* 275–291.

Gottfredson, L.S. (1986). Occupational aptitude patterns map: development and implications for a theory of job aptitude requirements [Monograph]. *Journal of Vocational Behaviour, 29,* 254–291.

Gottfredson, L.S. (1999). The nature and nurture of vocational interests. In Savickas, M.L. & Spokane, A.R. (Eds.), *Vocational Interests: Meaning, Measurement, and Counselling Use* (pp. 57–85). Palo Alto, CA: Davies-Black Publishing.

Hansen, J.-I.C. & Neuman, J.L. (1999). Evidence of concurrent prediction of the *Campbell interest and skill survey* (CISS) for college major selection. *Journal of Career Assessment, 7,* 239–247.

Harmon, L.W., Hansen, J.I.C., Borgen, F.H. & Hammer, A.L. (1994). *Strong Interest Inventory: Applications and Technical Guide.* Palo Alto, CA: Consulting Psychologists Press.

Holland, J.L. (1985). *Vocational Preference Inventory Manual.* Odessa FL: Psychological Assessment Resources.

Holland, J.L. (1997). *Making Vocational Choices: A Theory of Vocational Personalities and Work Environments* (3rd ed.). Odessa, FL: Psychological Assessment Resources.

Holland, J.L., Fritzsche, B.A. & Powell, A.B. (1994). *The Self-Directed Search Technical Manual.* Odessa, FL: Psychological Assessment Resources.

Kuder, G.F. (1948). *Kuder Preference Record – Personal.* Chicago: Science Research Associates.

Kuder, F. & Zytowski, D.G. (1991). *Kuder DD/PC: User's Guide.* Monterey, CA: CTB Macmillan/McGraw-Hill.

Lowman, R.L. (1991). *The Clinical Practice of Career Assessment: Interests, Abilities, and Personality.* Washington, DC: American Psychological Association.

Prediger, D.J. (1999). Integrating interests and abilities for career exploration: general considerations. In Savickas, M.L., Spokane, A.R. & Arnold, R. (Eds.), *Vocational Interests: Meaning, Measurement, and Counselling Use* (pp. 295–325). Palo Alto, CA: Davies-Black Publishing.

Spokane, A.R. & Catalano, M. (2000). The self-directed search: a theory-driven array of self-guiding career interventions. In Watkins, C.E. Jr. & Campbell, V.L. (Eds.), *Testing and Assessment in Counselling Practice, Contemporary Topics in Vocational Psychology* (2nd ed., pp. 339–370). Mahwah, NJ: Lawrence Erlbaum.

Strong, E.K. (1943). *Vocational Interests of Men and Women.* Palo Alto, CA: Stanford University Press.

Super, D.E. (1940). *Avocational Interest Patterns: A Study in the Psychology of Avocations.* Palo Alto, CA: Stanford University Press.

Super, D.E. & Crites, J.O. (1962). *Appraising Vocational Fitness by Means of Psychological Tests* (rev. ed.). New York: Harper & Brothers.

Rodney L. Lowman

RELATED ENTRIES

PERSONALITY ASSESSMENT (GENERAL), ATTITUDES, EMOTIONS, ENVIRONMENTAL ATTITUDES AND VALUES, SELF-REPORT QUESTIONNAIRES, PERSONNEL SELECTION, ASSESSMENT IN, APPLIED FIELDS: EDUCATION, APPLIED FIELDS: WORK AND INDUSTRY

INTERVIEW (GENERAL)

INTRODUCTION

The interview can be defined as the assessment or research instrument that precedes any type of intervention to decision-making process, adopting an interactive format, given the very nature of the instrument and because it is part of the assessment-intervention continuum (see entry on 'Interview in Behavioural and Health Settings').

It was recognized in the 1970s as the most widespread assessment instrument in applied psychology, regardless of the assessor's theoretical frame of reference (Kanfer & Grimm, 1977; Haynes, 1978). This can be confirmed by examining any applied field.

In the 1980s there was particular concern over the need to adapt the instrument to the area of social services (Chandler, 1989), and since the 1990s there has been a tendency to employ interviews directed towards specific populations and objectives: selection of subjects for positions with well-defined requirements; alleged child victims of physical or sexual abuse; the elderly; abused women; depressed patients; and experts, whose knowledge can be represented using physical devices. In the case of experts, the aim may be didactic or to provide a support tool for decision-making.

In addition, the interview usually constitutes the first contact with patients, clients, applicants or research participants. It is the fundamental unit of connection between the psychologist or counsellor and the person or persons looking for help, advice or a job, or in need of psychological assessment. It requires, at least, the presence of two persons who interact; one of these would be the expert in charge of leading the interactive process.

As an interactive process, the interview has aroused considerable attention in relation to the study of its three components: interviewer, interviewee and information.

Different lines of research have coincided in dealing with aspects and variables of the complex sequences of interactive behaviour: the simultaneous processing of verbal and non-verbal signals (see: De Paulo, 1980; Rosenthal, 1981; Zuckerman and Driver, 1985); the significance and perception of roles of the participants in interactive situations (see: Zebrowitz, 1990); the effect of appearance, physical characteristics, sex, etc., widely studied during the second half of the twentieth century; the basic skills an interviewer should possess in order to manage all the formal aspects (see: Matarazzo & Wiens, 1972) and verbal aspects, considered by the long tradition that began with the pioneering studies on verbal conditioning (Greenspoon, 1955; Taffel, 1955; Verplank, 1955); and finally, the management of information in interactive situations (Hart, 1989; Márquez & Muñoz, 1994).

There was a progressive growth in expectations that the interview, as an essential assessment technique, could provide professionals with valid, reliable and accurate information.

In general terms, the guarantees of information obtained via the interview are closely linked to the type of interview (according to the degree of structuredness), its objectives and the context of its application. Thus, in personnel selection, as well as in mental health or learning disabilities classifications, the professional aims to maximize certain achievements considered as reference criteria: job success, number of abilities for successful learning, presence of symptoms. He or she obtains a record of the outcome and compares it with the prediction suggested by the interview: predictive validity is being assessed. In other situations, data-collection methods may already be in use, so that the user tries to determine whether the new data provided by the interview agrees with the information already obtained, in order to assess concurrent validity. The relationship between content and construct validity is examined in order to assess whether the information gathered using the interview gives a fair measure of performance in some important sets of tasks or behaviours, and to evaluate whether such information reflects basic principles, concepts and assumptions held by the theoretical model employed. Reliability studies give information about the consistency throughout a series of assessments using interviews. An inaccurate interview cannot be a good predictor. The interviewer usually wishes to know the person's position with regard to certain general or specific variables (criteria); the information gathered from responses or narratives elicited by interview questions or topics is considered representative of the client's position or placement in relation to these criteria.

In sum, the quality, utility and guarantees of the results of an interview depend on the skills of the interviewer, the type of interview used and its suitability with regard to objectives, group differences and cultural differences.

BASIC SKILLS

Effective listening skills constitute the foundation of a valid interview. A professional interviewer actively listens to a client in an effort to evaluate and understand his or her problems, concerns and expectations, and, where appropriate, to be an instrument of change that enables the client to reduce personal distress and worries.

The ability to conduct effective interviews depends on a consideration of the following aspects:

1   How to focus on what clients or participants (children, adolescents, professors, students,

older adults, job applicants) are communicating.

2 How to develop positive relationships with those people.

3 How to accurately evaluate subjects' responses to the type of interview being used.

4 How to efficiently obtain valid and reliable information about the individuals related to criteria or categories used by the interviewer.

The skills and resources to be managed are quite numerous, and their coordination complex, but some subsets have been more widely studied and have constituted priority objectives of training programmes. A large proportion of these derive from the work carried out in the 1970s by Matarrazo and Wiens (see: Matarazzo & Wiens, 1972; Wiens, 1976).

The basic skills are defined in terms of the following variables:

1 Duration of interviewer verbalizations: measure of the distribution of total time consumed in an interview. The use of this variable permits the management of time in favour of the interviewee, who is the source of information, and at the same time it is a potential indicator of the interviewer's effectiveness in different phases of the interview (introduction phase, opening, central body and closing phase).

2 Interviewer interruptions: this is a variable on whose management (inhibition or voluntary production of interruptions) depend positive effects such as reducing the frequency of verbalizations irrelevant to the purpose of the interview or observing samples of subject behaviour with regard to this type of interactive activity.

3 Inter-verbalization latencies: measure of the time interval in which absence of verbal communication can be observed. Management of this variable is related to quantity of information gathered, insofar as the end of the interviewee's verbalization and the interviewer's verbalization are sufficiently separated in time to guarantee that the former has not been interrupted or that there has been no partial inhibition of what s/he was trying to say.

4 Emission of reinforcements without semantic verbal content: the emission of reinforcements requires that the interviewer learns to use them with a specific contingency relationship in relation to stimuli (verbal emissions) that are equally specific, thus leading to an increase in their frequency and to an effect on the emotional relationship.

5 Eye contact: this variable was already referred to by Argyle (1969) as a regulatory function of communication processes. It influences the empathy perceived by interviewees and can be used in a similar way to the emission of reinforcements without semantic content.

Other highly relevant aspects have been stressed from various perspectives, important among which is the Rogerian approach (Rogers, 1969). The following are some of the several factors that make the process of becoming an effective interviewer difficult:

1 The importance of knowing yourself.

2 The ability to set up an environment that is conducive to the purpose of the interview.

3 The competence to efficiently evaluate how individuals are relating to the interviewer and the ability to prioritize information.

4 The acquisition of sufficient practice through specific training experience that allows professionals to master the interview situation.

5 The understanding of practical, ethical and legal implications pertinent to confidentiality.

6 The ability to take into account the fact that many social and cultural differences can potentially affect the interview; every client or person is part of a particular subculture with associated behaviour patterns and social norms.

TYPE AND STRUCTURE OF INTERVIEW

Two types of interview are commonly identified, depending on the role (directivity/non-directivity) adopted by the interviewer:

• Non-directive: applied when the interviewer adopts a passive, silent and expectant attitude to the potential provision of information by the interviewee.

- Directive: with regard to the objectives for action decided by the interviewer (explanations, suggestions, advice, urging), or according to the nature of the interview itself, in the sense that the information units on which it is proposed to work are more or less predetermined; this latter aspect is an indicator of the structure of the interview.

According to the structure of the interview the reference is the structured/non-structured continuum, and in this sense, interviews tend to be classified in the following way:

- Structured: when the questions followed by the interviewer have been predetermined pending specific and precise responses, structured in some kind of response-alternatives format, with the object either of exploring specific aspects, or of making inter-subject comparisons.
- Semi-structured: using an interview format with structured questions, as defined above, but with the expectation of open responses.
- Non-structured: in which both questions and answers are open.

Research has developed different models to describe the temporal and substantive structure of that which occurs during the interview as a global process. The following events and tasks take place in an interview:

1 Introduction phase: begins with the individual's first contact with the interviewer.
2 Opening: starts when the professional first makes an open-ended inquiry into the client's or participant's condition.
3 Body: focuses on information gathering. The type of information to be gathered depends on the purpose of the interview. The administration of tests and projective techniques is included here.
4 Closing phase: introduces a shift from information gathering to prepare individuals for an effective end.

These different phases correspond to some extent to the needs identified for fulfilling the general requirements of many types of interview (Ivey, 1993):

1 Establishing rapport and structuring
2 Gathering information, defining the problem and identifying assets
3 Setting goals

4 Exploring alternatives and confronting client incongruities
5 Encouraging generalization of ideas and skills to situations of daily life

Obviously, guarantees of the information gathered, according to the level of structuring of the interview, are a separate matter.

GUARANTEES OF THE INTERVIEW

There has been considerable insistence on the need to establish the scientific guarantees of the interview, both in classical psychometric terms (reliability, validity) and with regard to universes of generalization (Cronbach, Glesser, Nanda & Rajaratnam, 1972), given the complexity of the interactive process of elicitation of information from the interviewee by the interviewer (see: Cannel & Kahn, 1968).

Results on the reliability and validity of the information obtained in an interview suggest the use of structured interviews, and hence the increase in the use of questionnaires for identifying and delimiting specific problems within equally specific contexts: for example, autobiographical questionnaires (Lazarus, 1971), interview patterns whose aim is to identify the existence of behavioural excesses such as the consumption of psychoactive substances (Marlat, 1976), scales for assessing children to be completed by parents (Holland, 1970), psychiatric interviews (Endicott & Spitzer, 1978), etc. This type of interview permits the relatively straightforward study and establishment of reliability and validity indicators. Other types of interview rely necessarily on partial, more or less objective indicators, which allow the formulation of judgements on the quality of the information collected.

A first objective that should be considered is that of obtaining the relevant information required. Relevant information can be defined as the subset of information obtained referring to previously defined objectives to be studied. The relevance of the information is indicated by: (a) the prescriptions marked by the theoretical model the clinician adopts; (b) the profile of the job position or the profile of the tasks to be carried out by successful candidates; or (c) the model represented by the system or tool with which it is attempted to simulate the handling of expert knowledge.

The aspects that appear to be most directly related to the maximization of relevant information obtained in an interview are empathy, management of reinforcements (verbal and non-verbal) and control of formal variables, in the sense defined above (Matarazzo, Saslow, Wiens, Weitman & Allen, 1964).

In order to optimize reliability and validity in an interview, sampling strategies and recognition strategies are used, rather than open questions. An undesirable effect of the use of open questions are responses of a general or highly summarized nature; these responses are subject to reinterpretation and incorrect or ill-fitting interpretations on the part of the interviewer. Even though open and ambiguous questions are those most frequently used in the initial stages of the interview process, they would appear to be less frequent when what is sought is concrete and specific information. In this case it seems clear that the most suitable approach is to use sampling strategies; that is, the exploration of the subject's behaviour over time and across different situations (Fernández-Ballesteros & Maciá, 1992). Once the interviewee's different action alternatives have been determined, it is possible, subsequent to the interview, to present him/her with these alternatives so that s/he can consider in which situations s/he would apply them, thus allowing the checking of the information previously obtained. This corresponds to the use of recognition strategies.

ETHICAL ISSUES

Clients entrust interviewers with private information. In this sense, the professional is a kind of confidant. There are legal and ethical limits to confidentiality. Although every client (clinical, educational, forensic) is asked to be open and honest, there is some information that the interviewer cannot keep secret. Psychologists' associations, counsellors and social workers follow ethical guidelines pertinent to confidentiality.

A professional may disclose information in situations such as:

1   When the client's permission is given.
2   The client is suicidal and there is real danger.

3   The client is a child and there is evidence suggesting that s/he is being abused or neglected.
4   The professional has been ordered by a court to provide information about the client.
5   Professionals have evidence to believe that the client is abusing a minor.

It is nearly always appropriate to inform clients, at the onset of the interviewing process, of the legal limits of confidentiality.

INTERVIEWS WITH PERSONS OF DIFFERENT AGES AND SPECIAL SETTINGS

Working with children requires special considerations (see: Hodges, 1993). Interviewers that work with them frequently end up making some errors:

- They may believe they are fully capable of understanding children because they were children once.
- They may experience children as not yet fully part of the human world.

To interview children effectively there are educational and attitudinal requirements; psychologists must be especially attuned to the skills, training and knowledge of applied aspects of child development, as well as the use of tools and resources (arts and crafts).

Interviewing children and adolescents presents many challenges: their language skills are less well developed than those of most adults, they are most often brought to the interview by others (it is usually their parents who bring them), etc.

The relevant context of an interview usually includes the child's family situation, his or her school context and, if the young person is employed, the employer may be involved (see entry on 'Interview in Child and Family Settings'). A child welfare agency, other social agencies, the police, the courts or the neighbourhood community may be involved in the child's life. Other professionals, teachers or parents must be interviewed at the beginning of the assessment, and they must be informed of the results of the interviewing process. Information may be passed on, at least, to the police, the referring professional, guardians, courts, probation officers or lawyers (see: Barker, 1990).

Interviewing more than one individual is a challenging endeavour. Working with couples, parents, groups and families requires focusing on relationships. Specific assessment techniques have been developed to facilitate data-gathering with couples and families, such as the Family Environment Scale, the Family Genogram or the Marital Satisfaction Inventory.

Interviewing older adults is often associated with some type of assessment: cognitive functioning, emotional status, need for resources, social support networks, etc. The way in which the ageing process is conceptualized determines the use of particular assessment and intervention approaches. A reasonable interview approach related to an elderly individual must ameliorate cultural and professional ageism and take into account diverse areas of daily life and internal and external antecedents for the worries or needs expressed.

In the field of Industrial and Organizational Psychology, interviews are not among the assessment techniques that receive most emphasis (see: Vodanovich & Piotrowski, 1999 and entry on 'Interview in Work and Organizational Settings'). Most common in this field are assessment centres and honesty tests, followed by an assortment of personality, aptitude and vocational measures.

Selection is based on the knowledge of what to look for in the applicant. In interviewing to evaluate a person for a job we need to know what abilities and personality traits are necessary for success (see: Rumsey & Harris, 1994).

Many companies have developed job descriptions as a result of job evaluation programmes, but most job descriptions tell us what must be done rather than what abilities or personality styles are required. All the information obtained from preliminary interviews, application forms and aptitude tests is combined with that related to the individual's background, in order to make the final decision: information on experience, mental ability, motivation, maturity and self-control.

Interview validity, in the field of Industrial and Organizational Psychology, increases as structuredness increases. Meta-analyses of interview reliability show that inter-rater reliability is higher when interviews incorporate multiple ratings, interviewer training, and standardization of questions and response evaluation.

More dynamic models are needed to evaluate suitability for the organization, including personality characteristics and personal values. It is important that interviews incorporate BIODATA, biographical information related to cultural socialization, preference for group attachments and achievement-oriented pursuits.

Personnel selection is moving from focusing on the goals of the user (employer) toward the needs and goals of the applicants. Important research (Smith, 1994; Messick, 1995) related to Standards for Psychological and Educational Assessment suggests treating the validity of interviews as a unified concept that must incorporate the notion of consequences. It is necessary to distinguish between universals (characteristics required for success in virtually all jobs) and occupationals (characteristics required for a subset of a single job).

FUTURE PERSPECTIVES AND CONCLUSIONS

Most clinical and educational assessments have emphasized deficits; new developments are necessary in relation to the use of interviews to evaluate factors such as adaptation, personal competence, quality of life, hope, psychological well-being and intra-personal strengths.

Some problems related to interviewing throughout the lifespan and interviews carried out in different applied settings remain to be investigated.

The current multicultural global society requires that professionals take into account, during the interviewing process, the impact of cultural values expressed through dimensions of discourse strategies as well as in specific semiotic issues (meaning systems).

References

Argyle, M. (1969). *Social Interaction*. London: Methuen.

Barker, P. (1990). *Clinical Interviews with Children and Adolescents*. New York: W.W. Norton & Company.

Cannel, C.F. & Kahn, R.L. (1968). Interviewing. In Lindzey, G. & Aronson, E. (Eds.), *The Handbook of Social Psychology*. New York: Addison-Wesley.

Chandler, M.H.H. (1989). Teaching interview techniques utilizing all instructional videotape. *Educational Gerontology*, 15, 377–383.

Cronbach, L.J., Glesser, G.C., Nanda, H. & Rajaratnam, N. (1972). *The Dependability of Behavioral Measurements Theory of Generalizability for Scores and Profiles*. New York: Wiley.

De Paulo, B.M. (1980). *Successes at Detecting Deception: Liability or Skill?* Conference C.H.P. Science Academy, New York.

Endicott, J. & Spitzer, R.L. (1978). A diagnostic interview: the schedule for affective disorders and schizophrenia. *Archives of General Psychiatry, 33,* 837–847.

Fernández-Ballesteros, R. & Maciá, A. (1992). Garantías científicas y éticas de la evaluación psicológica. In Fernández-Ballesteros, R. (Ed.), *Introducción a la evaluación psicológica.* Madrid: Pirámide.

Greenspoon, J. (1955). The reinforcing effect of tow spoken sounds on the frequency of tow responses. *American Journal of Psychology, 68,* 409–416.

Hart, A. (1989). *Knowledge Acquisition for Expert Systems.* Worcester: Biling & Son.

Haynes, S.N. (1978). *Principles of Behavioural Assessment.* New York: Gardner Press.

Hodges, K. (1993). Structured interviews for assessing children. *Journal of Child Psychology, 34,* 49–68.

Holland, C.J. (1970). An interview guide for behavioural counseling with parents. *Behaviour Therapy, 1,* 70–79.

Ivey, A.E. (1993). *Intentional Interviewing and Counselling.* Pacific Grove: Brooks/Cole.

Kanfer, F.H. & Grimm, E.G. (1977). Behavioural analysis: selecting target behaviours in the interview. *Behaviour Modification, 1,* 7–28.

Lazarus, A.A. (1971). *Behaviour Therapy and Beyond.* New York: McGraw Hill.

Marlat, A.G. (1976). The drinking profile: a questionnaire for the behavioral assessment of alcoholism. In Mash, E.J. & Terdal, L.G. (Eds.), *Behavior Therapy Assessment.* New York: Springer.

Márquez, M.O. & Muñoz, M.D. (1994). In La Entrevista, P., Adarraga, P. & Zaccagnini, J.L. (Eds.), *Psicología e Inteligencia Artificial.* Madrid: Trotta.

Matarazzo, J.D., Saslow, G., Wiens, A.N., Weitman, M. & Allen, B.V. (1964). Interviewer head-nodding and interviewer speech duration. *Psychotherapy, 1,* 54–63.

Matarazzo, J.D. & Wiens, A.N. (1972). *The Interview: Research on its Anatomy and Structure.* Chicago: Aldine-Atherton.

Messick, S. (1995). Validity of psychological assessment. *American Psychologist, 50,* 741–749.

Rogers, C. (1969). *Psicoterapia Centrada en el Cliente: Práctica, Implicaciones y teoría.* Buenos Aires: Paidós.

Rosenthal, R. (1981). Conducting judgement studies. In Scherer, K.R. & Ekman, P. (Eds.), *Handbook of Methods in Nonverbal Behavior Research.* London: Cambridge University Press.

Rumsey, M. & Harris, W.C. (Eds.), (1994). *Personnel Selection and Classification,* Hillsdale, N.J: Erlbaum.

Smith, M. (1994). A theory of the validity of predictors in selection. *Journal of Occupational Organizational Psychology, 67,* 13–31.

Sommers-Flanagan, R. & Sommers-Flanagan, J. (1999). *Clinical Interviewing.* New York: J. Wiley and sons.

Taffel, C. (1955). Anxiety and the conditioning of verbal behavior. *Journal of Abnormal and Social Psychology, 51,* 496–501.

Uerplanck, W. (1955). The control of the content of conversation: reinforcement of statements of opinion. *Journal of Abnormal and Social Psychology, 51,* 668–676.

Vodanovich, S. & Piotrowski, C. (1999). Training in personnel selection assessment: survey of graduate I/O programs. *Journal of Instructional Psychology, 23,* 201–242.

Wiens, A.N. (1976). The assessment interview. In Wiener, I.B. (Ed), *Clinical Methods in Psychology.* New York: Wiley.

Zebrowitz, L.A. (1990). *Social Perception.* London: Open University Press.

Zuckerman, M. & Driver, R.E. (1985). Telling lies: verbal and nonverbal correlates of deception. In Siegman, A.W. & Feldstein, S. (Eds.), *Multichannel Integrations of Nonverbal Behavior.* New York: LEA.

María Martina Casullo and María Oliva Márquez

RELATED ENTRIES

I INTERVIEW IN BEHAVIOURAL AND HEALTH SETTINGS

INTRODUCTION

The concept *interview* within a psychological assessment context is employed with two different meanings: as an information tool and, in a broader sense, as the professional interaction between client and psychologist. In this study, we will employ the concept to talk about the procedure to gather information both in clinical and health contexts. In both cases, the interview is the most used tool when a verbal interaction takes place between a professional and a client (or clients). The interview has a main goal: to obtain the maximum information possible in order to develop a functional analysis. This analysis will provide the basis to understand and to modify the problem when necessary. On the other hand, the interview, in addition to the use of questionnaires, is the only procedure available currently to obtain information on a client's cognitive responses, verbal-cognitive in this case (thoughts, attributions, belief system, etc.). Furthermore, it constitutes an economical tool to assess psycho-physiological responses (throbbing, muscular tension, etc.). Also, the interview is cheaper than the use of psycho-physiological devices, even though it is an indirect method (assessing the subjective perception that the client has).

In spite of its usefulness and popularity, only a few studies have analysed its reliability and validity. However, these studies obtained discouraging results (Hay, Angle & Nelson, 1979; Felton & Nelson, 1984).

DEFINITION

A clinical interview can be defined as the procedure followed by a professional (psychologist-interviewer) in a conversation with one person or more (clients) with the goal of getting desired information. Accordingly, it can be stressed that the basic interview characteristics within an assessment procedure are the following:

- An interaction between two or more people.
- A two-way route verbal communication.
- Some goals previously established by the interviewer who controls the procedure and withdraws the information from the interviewee.

In sum, the main goal of the interview as an assessment tool is to obtain information in order to build the behaviour-problem's functional analysis. In order to reach this goal, there should be followed several steps (Table 1). First, the problem description should be pursued in the most objective way available (behavioural, cognitive and psycho-physiologic responses). Secondly, the quantitative parameters that define the problem

Table 1.   General interview guidance

1   Behaviour-problem delimitation
- Problem identification
- Problem description (behavioural, cognitive and psycho-physiologic responses)
- Description of the last incident
2   Behaviour-problem parameters
- Frequency (maximum and minimum)
- Intensity (maximum and minimum)
- Duration (maximum and minimum)
- Recent frequency, duration or intensity of the behaviour-problem
3   Behaviour-problem determinants
- Description of the situation/context in which the problem occurs
- What does the client do when the behaviour-problem starts and finishes?
- How do surrounding people react when the problem starts and when it finishes?
4   History of the behaviour-problem from its start
- When was the problem first displayed and under what characteristics and parameters?
- Evolution of the problem through its start until today
- Differences and similarities between then and now
5   Impact of the behaviour-problem
- How does the problem affect the client's life?
- How does the problem affect other people around?
- Client's motivation to solve the problem
6   Expectations and goals
- Causal attributions
- Personal or professional actions and intervention to solve the problem
- Results obtained in the past
- Recent expectations to solve the problem
- What does the client expect?

should be specified and, thereinafter, delimitated antecedent and consequent elements in order to establish the behaviour functionality (antecedent stimuli, conditioned and/or discriminative and consequent stimuli and reinforcements). Once the fundamental aspects of the problem are assessed for current incidents, the history and the evolution of the problem should be inquired, as well as its impact in the client's life.

The interview should be displayed in a directing but flexible way. It should have an initial-facilitating phase (exploratory); an intermediate phase for clarification and specification; and a final phase focused on solving doubts and assuring congruency on the obtained data with the client. It is important to take into account that the interview is essentially an active interaction process between two or more people. Regardless of the goal of gathering information, the interview itself may also have therapeutic effects on the client. Therefore, it is critical to assure that the communication process is effective as a critical aspect to develop positive boundaries with clients. That is to say, when the treatment includes behavioural aspects, it is essential that the client is ready to accomplish the prescribed assignments to solve the problem. Therefore, a good communication and comprehension between professional and client should be maximized. Professional skills such as the ability of providing information, offering confidence, showing comprehension, operating management and, in sum, displaying basic technical and social abilities (therapeutic skills) are critical in order to develop an interview within a clinical or health assessment.

The language used by the professional during the interview has to be culturally adapted to the interviewee. As time goes by, the interviewee will acquire a behavioural language through a modelling and moulding process. Thus, the client will facilitate the required information with precision.

Another important aspect during the development of the interview is to collect the obtained information. Recording the information with an audiovisual device would be the best technique because it may allow registering of either verbal or non-verbal content. Another frequently used alternative is taking notes simultaneously while the client speaks. However, this method to collect information is somewhat problematic because it can impede and jeopardize the communication

fluency. In addition, the professional may also lose important pieces both of verbal and non-verbal contents.

The client's role during the interview should be active and collaborative, even though it is the psychologist's responsibility to reach these goals by using his/her therapeutic skills (communication and operating management).

The interview completion requires a summary of the obtained information in order to guarantee its veracity according to the client's judgement. Eventually, it is usually required to complete the information with other evaluation procedures, especially questionnaires and the use of direct observation when possible within clinical and health assessment contexts.

FUTURE PERSPECTIVES

There was an attempt to outline the utility of the interview as a behavioural evaluation procedure during the 60s. In spite of the efforts accomplished to systematize the interview (Haynes, 1978; Linehan, 1977) during the 70s, it was not until the 90s that the importance of developing more investigation to identify the relative efficiency of the various components, procedures and strategies of the behavioural interview was taken into account. Recent discoveries led to a change that will affect both the evaluation and the therapy, in relation to the importance of verbal exchanges within a behavioural clinical context. From this perspective, investigations on verbal behaviour, especially from an operative conditioning perspective, represent one of the most fruitful lines on scientific psychology (Hayes, 1989). Taking in account that the interview is essentially a verbal exchange (regardless of the importance of non-verbal communication acts), studies focused on verbal behaviour are of high interest.

CONCLUSIONS

The interview is the most employed assessment procedure. However, its psychometrical properties have not been specified yet neither has the most effective method to carry it out. The main goal is to obtain relevant information on the behavioural sequence (what constitutes the problem to study and solve) in order to develop a functional analysis. Being an interpersonal exchange of communication, it is not appropriate to neglect the importance of the communication proficiency (therapeutic skills) as well as the therapeutic effects that, independently of the assessment goal, may occur during the communicative exchange. The psychological interview is mainly directing, being the interviewer responsible to evoke relevant information in order to assess the problem.

References

Felton, J. & Nelson, R. (1984). Inter-assessor agreement on hypothesized controlling variables and treatment proposal. *Behavioral Assessment, 6,* 199–208.

Hay, L.R., Angle, H.V. & Nelson, R.O. (1979). The reliability of problem identification in the behavioral interview. *Behavioral Assessment, 1,* 107–118.

Hayes, S.C. (1989). *Rule-Governed Behavior: Cognitions, Contingencies, and Instructional Control.* New York: Plenum Press.

Haynes, S. (1978). *Principles of Behavioral Assessment.* New York: Gardner.

Linehan, M.M. (1977). Issues in behavioural interview. In Cone, J.D. & Hawkins, R.P. (Eds.) *Behavioral Assessment: New Directions in Clinical Psychology.* New York: Brunel-Mazel.

María Xesús Froján Parga

RELATED ENTRIES

APPLIED FIELDS: CLINICAL, APPLIED FIELDS: HEALTH, THEORETICAL PERSPECTIVE: BEHAVIOURAL, THEORETICAL PERSPECTIVE: COGNITIVE-BEHAVIOURAL, INTERVIEW (GENERAL), INTERVIEW IN CHILD AND FAMILY SETTINGS, BEHAVIOURAL ASSESSMENT TECHNIQUES

INTERVIEW IN CHILD AND FAMILY SETTINGS

INTRODUCTION

Interview can be defined as a system of communication, typically dyadic, aimed at acquiring information. The interview is a basic tool in many social sciences, including psychology. In every field of child psychology, from basic research to professional practice, sooner or later one will be faced with the task of discovering what a child thinks, feels or knows. Nevertheless, the validity of the interview (and more generally the use of verbal protocols; see Praetorious & Duncan, 1988) is continually debated, especially with children (Bruck & Ceci, 1996).

Interviewing is dangerously similar to everyday conversations. In fact, asking and answering are basic human activities (Flammer, 1981), which take place in the most varied occasions: a dialogue between friends, a school exam, a medical interrogation, a police questioning, and so on. In each of these situations, the communicative exchange is set by implicit, yet powerful rules (Schenkein, 1978). Some of these regulative factors apply to every dialogue, such as the need of turn taking, or the looks which signal the onset and the end of the verbal exchange; other rules, such as the degree of interpersonal distance, vary from one culture to another; still others, such as the degree of politeness required or the reciprocity of roles, depend on the characteristics of the partners and the content of the dialogue. We apply all these non-written rules based on tacit assumptions about speakers' roles and aims, and children more than anyone else do it unknowingly. It is hence clear that the first step towards interviewing well is to know the nature of this particular kind of verbal exchange, and to make it clear to the interviewees.

INVESTIGATIVE AND CLINICAL INTERVIEWS

Psychological interviews can be grouped in two broad classes, each roughly associated with some general characteristics. In the first class – investigative interviews – we can include all the interviews aimed exclusively at discovering some respondent's mental contents, for research or forensic purposes. The second class comprises all kinds of clinical interviews, in which the need of obtaining useful information for the diagnosis is intertwined with that of establishing a therapeutic alliance. Investigative interviews are associated with: the interviewer as a main beneficiary of the obtained information; a strategy of non-interference with the interviewee's ideas and feelings; a preference for standardized formats. Clinical interviews are associated with: the interviewee as a main beneficiary of the given information; a legitimate intervention in the interviewee's ideas and feelings; a preference for highly flexible formats.

In practice, psychological interviews often escape such a clear-cut classification. For instance, with young children the maximum of possible standardization can be a list of contents to be orderly followed since it is necessary to adapt the actual phrasing to the child's language, attention span and tolerance for the interview situation as a whole.

Investigative interview techniques were first developed in the context of research about cognitive development. Piaget (1926) explained how it is possible to use interview as reliable sources for studying children's ideas, but he also outlined how easy it is to come up with useless answers. Children can answer randomly, if poorly motivated, tired, bored; or they can produce myths and fantasies, if they treat the interview as play; or they can parrot the interviewer's suggestions. Piaget's generalized guidelines on how to conduct valid interviews were incorporated in the research paradigm stemming from his work. Only recently, however, systematic studies have become common, especially under the pressure of the increasing number of child witnesses in legal cases of abuse or controversial parental custody (Pool & Lamb, 1998). In fact, legal court and psychological research are among the few situations in which children can be irreplaceable sources of information.

Clinical interviews with children and parents are an integral part of child psychoanalytic and psychiatric treatment (A. Freud, 1966; Winnicott, 1971; Sullivan, 1954; Rutter, Taylor & Hersov, 1994). In these contexts, three categories of patients can be distinguished: co-operative patients, who openly talk about their problems; 'resistant' patients, who conceal part of their problems; and patients unaware of their problems (Othmer & Othmer, 1994); accordingly, the interviewer is forced to use more direct questions to obtain relevant information. It is also clear that children belong more frequently to the third category, as they are often unaware that communicating certain experiences could help solve their problems; hence more guidance is needed when children are interviewed for diagnostic purposes. Moreover, it is always necessary to validate the information so obtained with data from other sources, usually parents and sometimes other figures (other relatives, teachers) (AA.VV., 1997). Direct observation during play sessions, or in everyday settings (e.g. school), is recommended with young children.

ESTABLISHING SETTINGS

In both investigative and clinical interviews, the first methodological precaution is to create an appropriate setting. The ambience should be pleasant and stimulating, but not too rich with distracting objects; it should be equipped for videotaping if testimony has to be collected. Some simple toys for symbolic play and materials for drawing and moulding should be at hand, depending on the child's age.

Children are often unaware of the reasons for their having been brought to the consultation, or (worse) they are led to believe that some unpleasant medical procedure would take place. In a simple and encouraging way, the interviewer must explain the aim of the questions, guarantee confidentiality and reaffirm the child's right to not answer. In the case of legal interviews, some authors also recommend ascertaining whether the child can distinguish between truth and lying (McGough, 1994), but the best ways to reach this goal are still a question of debate (Pool & Lamb, 1998). Instead, it has been experimentally demonstrated that children provide a larger proportion of correct answers about a previously witnessed event if they are told in advance that the adult does not know what happened and that they can answer 'I don't know' when appropriate (Mulder & Vrij, 1996). Another useful practice, in the preliminary phase of forensic interviews, is to enhance the remembering of past events with the instructions provided by the 'Cognitive Interview' (Geiselman, Saywitz & Bornstein, 1993).

BUILDING A RELATIONSHIP AND BEGINNING THE INTERVIEW

A familiarization phase with the child is always necessary. For instance, in a clinical setting, it is not always opportune to begin the interview talking about symptoms. Talking for a while about neutral matters helps the child to develop a sense of self-assurance and trust (Angold, 1994), while the interviewer can appraise the child's communicative abilities. With young children playing or drawing can help break the ice. In forensic interviews, the child can be asked to talk about a recent, non-related event (Pool & Lamb, 1998). In clinical consultations, when the child or the adolescent arrives accompanied by parents, who will be also interviewed, it is necessary to give complete assurance that his/her point of view is important and will be respected as much as that of the adults.

STRUCTURING THE INTERVIEW

Some clinicians point to the advantages of open, non-directive interviews ('client-centred', Rogers, 1945, 1951) while others claim superior merit for structured interviews in one or another of their numerous formats (many of which are listed in AA.VV., 1997). It has been noted, however, that no interview can be really 'non-directive': it is sufficient for the clinician to smile or take notes to reinforce some answers (Cox & Rutter, 1985). It is better to manage explicitly the situation than to risk selectively distorting the child's answers under the influence of those 'confirmatory biases' widely documented by social psychology and inevitably as much present in the interviewer's as in anyone else's.

The choice of a structured interview does not necessarily imply abandoning personal initiative. This can be true for highly structured interviews ('respondent-based') but not for semi-structured interviews ('interviewer-based') (Angold, 1994) in which a series of key questions are listed, some of which can be omitted, while others can be

elaborated in depth. In diagnostic settings, the course of the interview will depend on two key factors: the subject's age (see Barker, 1990) and the 'decisional tree' adopted by the clinician (analytical examples in Harrison & Eth, 1998). Investigative interviews can be highly structured when they are conducted for research purposes (but not necessarily so, *cf.* Lumbelli, 1993), and less structured in forensic contexts.

ASKING QUESTIONS

Questions are 'open' when they allow for a wide range of answers, and 'closed' if they admit only yes or no answers or allow for choosing between a few, ready-made options (multiple choice questions). The principal merit of open questions is that they reduce the interviewer influence. Interviewers should be aware that materials derived from interviews are rarely 'spontaneous'. When based on children's reflections about topics they had not considered before, answers are, at best, genuine, but 'provoked' (Piaget, 1926). Open questions are widely used in the legal field, to obtain narrative accounts of allegations. Young children, however, are not very productive in answering open questions, and resorting to closed questions in order to cover all relevant aspects is almost inevitable. Besides a correct setting, productivity can be enhanced by techniques such as mirroring (Rogers, 1945) or non-specific verbal prompts such as 'tell me all that you have seen' or 'all you have heard' (Elichsberger & Roebers, 2001).

EVALUATING ANSWERS

In clinical assessment, the conclusions drawn from an interview should be always conceived as hypotheses, verification of which relies on the continuing therapeutic process. The situation is different with investigative interviews, where the validity of the protocol should be in itself evident enough to be used as a proof. Methods of content analysis for evaluating protocols have been developed (Steller & Koehnken, 1989), based on the assumption that truthful narratives of events are different from inventions or biased descriptions (Undeutsch, 1982). Recent studies

(Orbach & Lamb, 2001) have shown that leading questions generate more contradictions than open, non-leading questions. Contradictions, then, can be used as indices of a poor interview and not only (or not always) of the interviewee's uncertainty or reticence.

AVOIDING ERRORS

Conversation in everyday contexts is a robust communicative tool, since participants can go back over unclear subjects in order to achieve reciprocal understanding. Adults capitalize on this when talking with children, often using new terms or complex linguistic forms (double negatives, passive verbs, subordinates) as occasions for linguistic apprenticeship (Wertsch, 1985). In an interview, instead, difficult or obscure forms should be carefully avoided, especially with young children. Misunderstandings that are easily remedied in everyday situations can create serious problems in an interview. For instance, if one includes two questions in a single utterance, children usually answer only one, and it can even be impossible to detect which one they have actually responded to (Walker & Hunt, 1998).

Some conversational styles are also sources of error in interviews. With children it is common to use rhetorical questions that are in fact orders ('would you please get up?') or suggestions ('it's a nice toy, isn't it?'). Not only should this kind of leading question be avoided, but it is also necessary to make clear to the child that there are no 'right answers' to guess. It is also safer to avoid repeating the same question, a way of talking which is often used in everyday life as a strong suggestion to change answer, and in fact has been found to elicit contradictions from young interviewees.

When it becomes necessary to resort to closed questions, multiple choice questions which allow a 'content' answer should be preferred to those eliciting yes–no alternatives, to avoid the effect of any subjective bias towards answering always yes (or always no) in case of doubt.

And above all, one should be aware that memorizing this list of errors, or a series of good practices, does not transform anybody by magic into an expert interviewer (Sternberg et al., 2001). On the contrary, only a long apprenticeship joined with deep intellectual honesty and a vibrant interpersonal sensitivity can help a person acquire the difficult art of interviewing children.

FUTURE PERSPECTIVES AND CONCLUSIONS

The interview is undoubtedly one of the most important psychological tools, and it promises to be employed in the future as much as it has been used during a century of psychological research practice. Perhaps the interview will become even more necessary, if the present popularity of cognitive theories does not decline, since these theories almost invariably require discovering the subject's perspective. The recognition that young children are most competent knowers than they were previously thought to be is another factor which has increased the population of potential interviewees, and this trend is likely to continue. The difficulty of avoiding suggestions and other mistakes while verbally interacting with preschoolers has led psychologists to refine the interviewing techniques, taking into account memory and language problems, as well as social roles as sources of bias. These advances will be beneficial for interviewing other 'special populations' such as immigrant adults with limited linguistic skills, or mentally retarded people. Most important, a new wave of experimental research on the interview has begun, which is especially concerned with the validity of interviews in forensic settings. It would be important if this effort of refinement and validation were to be developed to cover still other aspects of interviewing and extended to a wider variety of fields of application, including diagnostic and clinical. Finally, how to teach interviewing to psychology students and young practitioners is a question that requires special attention indeed: no instrument can be fully appreciated without those people capable of using it at its best.

References

AA.VV. (1997). Practice parameters for the psychiatric assessment of children and adolescents [AACAP Official Action]. *Journal of the American Academy* of *Child and Adolescent Psychiatry*, 36(10) *Supplement*, 4–20.

Angold, A. (1994). Clinical interviewing with children and adolescents. In Rutter, M., Taylor, E. & Hersov, L. (Eds.), *Childhood and Adolescent Psychiatry: Modern Approaches* (3rd ed., pp. 51–63). Oxford: Blackwell.

Barker, P. (1990). *Clinical Interviews with Children and Adolescents*. New York: Norton.

Bruck, M. & Ceci, S.J. (1996). Issues in the scientific validation of interviews with young children. Commentary. In Steward, M.S. & Steward, D.S. (Eds.), *Interviewing Young Children about Body Touch and Handling. Monographs of the SSRCD*, Serial 248, 61(4–5), 204–222.

Cox, A. & Rutter, M. (1985). Diagnostic appraisal and interviewing. In Rutter, M. & Hersov, L. (Eds.), *Child and Adolescent Psychiatry: Modern Approaches* (2nd ed., pp. 233–248). Oxford: Blackwell.

Elichsberger, H.B. & Roebers, C.M. (2001). Improving young children's narratives about an observed event: the effect of nonspecific verbal prompts. *International Journal of Behavioural Development*, 25(2), 160–166.

Flammer, A. (1981). Towards a theory of question asking. *Psychological Research*, 43, 407–420.

Freud, A. (1966). *Normality and Pathology in Children*. London: Hogarth.

Geiselman, R.E., Saywitz, K. & Bornstein, G.K. (1993). Cognitive questioning techniques for child victims and witnesses of crime. In Goodman, G. & Bottoms, B. (Eds.), *Child Victims, Child Witnesses*. New York: Guilford.

Harrison, S.I. & Eth, S. (Eds.) (1998). Clinical assessment and intervention planning. In Noshpitz, J.D. (Ed.), *Handbook of Child and Adolescent Psychiatry*, Vol. 5. New York: Wiley.

Lumbelli, L. (1993). L'intervista dentro l'esperimento [The interview within the experiment]. *Eta' Evolutiva*, 46, 39–53.

McGough, L.S. (1994). *Child Witnesses: Fragile Voices in the American Legal System*. New Haven, CT: Yale University Press.

Mulder, M.R. & Vrij, A. (1996). Explaining conversation rules to children: an intervention study to facilitate accurate responses. *Child Abuse and Neglect*, 7, 623–631.

Orbach, Y. & Lamb, M.E. (2001). The relationship between within-interview contradictions and eliciting interviewer utterances. *Child Abuse and Neglect*, 25, 323–333.

Othmer, E. & Othmer, S.C. (1994). *The Clinical Interview Using DSM-IV. Fundamentals*, Vol. 1. Washington, DC: American Psychological Association.

Piaget, J. (1926). *La representation du monde chez l'enfant*. Paris: Alcan (English translation 1929. *The Child's Conception of the World*. London: Routledge & Kegan Paul).

Pool, D.A. & Lamb, M.E. (1998). *Investigative Interviews of Children. A Guide for Helping Professionals*. Washington, DC: American Psychological Association.

Praetorius, N. & Duncan, K.D. (1988). Verbal reports: a problem in research design. In Goldstein, L.P., Andersen, H.B & Olsen, S.E. (Eds.), *Tasks, Errors and Mental Models* (pp. 1239–1314). London: Taylor.

Rogers, C.R. (1945). The non directive method as a technique in social research. *American Journal of Sociology*, 50, 279–283.

Rogers, C.R. (1951). *Client-Centered Therapy*. New York: Houghton-Mifflin.

Rutter, M., Taylor, E. & Hersov, L. (Eds.) (1994). *Child and Adolescent Psychiatry: Modern Approaches* (3rd ed.). Oxford: Blackwell.

Schenkein, J. (Ed.) (1978). *Studies in the Organization of Conversational Interactions*. New York: Academic Press.

Steller, M. & Koehnken, G. (1989). Criteria-based content analysis. In Raskin, D. (Ed.), *Psychological Methods in Criminal Investigation and Evidence* (pp. 217–245). New York: Springer.

Sternberg, K.J., Lamb, M.E., Davies, G.M. & Westcott, H. (2001). The memorandum of good practice: theory versus application. *Child Abuse and Neglect*, 25, 669–681.

Sullivan, H.S. (1954). *The Psychiatric Interview*. New York: Norton.

Undeutsch, U. (1982). Statement reality analysis. In Trankell, A. (Ed.), *Reconstructing the Past* (pp. 27–56). Stockholm: Norstedt & Soners.

Walker, N.E. & Hunt, J.S. (1998). Interviewing child victim-witness: how you ask is what you get. In Thompson, C.P., Herrman, D.J., Read, D., Bruce, D., Payne, D.G. & Toglia, M.P. (Eds.), *Eyewitness Memory*. Mahwah, NJ: Erlbaum.

Wertsch, J.V. (Ed.) (1985). *Culture, Communication and Cognition: Vygotskian Perspectives*. Cambridge: Cambridge University Press.

Winnicott, D.W. (1971). *Therapeutic Consultation in Child Psychiatry*. London: Hogarth.

Anna Silvia Bombi

RELATED ENTRIES

Applied Fields: Clinical, Applied Fields: Education, Interview (General), Family, Child Custody

INTERVIEW IN WORK AND ORGANIZATIONAL SETTINGS

INTRODUCTION

This entry describes the central results of research on the selection interview. After a definition of the interview in psychological assessment main features of selection interviews are described. Prerequisites of psychological interviews are given and the central developments in the area of the selection interview are summarized. Then the results of meta-analyses on reliability and validity of selection interviews are presented. Finally conclusions and future perspectives on selection interviews are given.

DEFINITION

A psychological interview is a kind of conversation between one or more interviewers and one or more interviewees which follows implicit and explicit rules and aims at gathering information for the description, explanation or prediction of individual behaviour or the relationship between people, or at gathering information about the conditions that change or stabilize individual behaviour or the relationship between people.

FEATURES OF SELECTION INTERVIEWS

Most frequently, one person interviews another. A group of interviewers interviewing one applicant is called a panel or a board. A psychological interview has the following three sections: (a) planning, (b) realizing, and (c) summarizing. Rules for realizing the interview are very often agreed at the beginning of a psychological interview. These rules relate for example to aims, duration, themes, recording and summarizing of the psychological interview. In addition, both interview partners behave according to implicit rules for a conversation. All conceptions of psychological interviews which lead to psychometrically acceptable interview results have an explicit planning in common. Thus, these interviews are (at least partially) structured or completely standardized. In partially structured interviews the questions are prepared; in structured interviews, the sequence of questions is also prescribed. In standardized interviews, furthermore, explicit rules are given concerning all relevant conditions for realizing and summarizing the interview.

PREREQUISITES

In all fields of applied psychology, the abilities of interviewers have been initially overestimated and the complexity of planning, realizing and summarizing an interview have been systematically underestimated. If interviewers want to arrive at satisfying decisions, i.e. not to regret later the low procedural quality in these decisions, the following prerequisites must be fulfilled. They (a) need to plan an interview systematically and to base it on empirically well founded research results, (b) must be well trained individually in realizing an interview, and (c) must summarize, after individual training, the results of an interview according to explicit rules.

DEVELOPMENTS

In the last five decades there has been an increasing tendency to structure selection interviews. In addition to this, a growing number of selection interviews are founded on basic theoretical notions. The Situational Interview (Latham et al., 1980) is based on goal setting theory and its basic assumption is that people behave according to their goals. In contrast to this interview conception, the (Patterned) Behaviour Description Interview (Janz, 1982) is, like the Experience-Based Interview (Pulakos & Schmitt, 1995), based on the assessment prediction rule that the best predictor of future behaviour is past behaviour. In traditional selection interviews, personality traits were assessed. This, however, did not prove to be very useful. More valid information results from selection interviews based on a requirement profile derived from an empirical job analysis. Selection interviews of the 'third generation', e.g. Schuler's (e.g. 1989) Multimodal Interview, combine all these measures relatively successfully.

RELIABILITY AND VALIDITY OF SELECTION INTERVIEWS

Reliability

Because reliability defines the upper limit of validity, Conway et al. (1995) published a meta-analysis on the reliability of the selection interview. Interview reliability is higher for panel interviews than for individual interviews, higher for trained interviewers than for untrained interviewers, and higher for highly structured interviews than for those with a lower degree of structuring. Structure was operationalized by three dimensions: standardization of questions, standardization of response evaluations (global rating vs. multiple-dimension ratings vs. ratings for each answer) and standardization of method for combining ratings (subjective vs. mechanical). Conway et al. (1995: 573–574) found that 'Estimates of upper limits of validity were 0.67 for highly structured interviews, 0.56 for moderately structured interviews, and only 0.34 for interviews with low structure. These upper limits represent the highest validities that could be achieved with a perfectly reliable criterion.' McDaniel et al. (1994: 604) reported higher mean reliability coefficients: 0.68 for unstructured interviews and 0.84 for structured interviews.

Validity

Hunter and Hunter's (1984) often cited meta-analysis found a validity coefficient of 0.14 for the selection interview. In contrast to this, later meta-analyses based on many more studies and people revealed that the 'received doctrine' of interview invalidity is false (Wiesner & Cronshaw, 1988). Structured selection interviews were found to have higher validity than unstructured interviews (Wiesner & Cronshaw, 1988; McDaniel et al., 1994; Huffcutt & Arthur, 1994). Furthermore, Huffcutt and Arthur (1994: 184) found that 'Interviews, particularly when structured, can reach levels of validity that are comparable to those of mental ability tests. Although validity does increase through much of the range of structure, there is a point at which additional structure yields no incremental validity. Thus, results suggested a ceiling effect for structure.' Mental ability tests are usually seen as the predictors with the highest validity. Structured selection interviews in particular can be as valid as mental ability tests (Huffcutt & Arthur, 1994). Contrary to widespread opinion, the results of a meta-analysis indicate that individual interviews are more valid than board interviews whether they are structured or not (McDaniel et al., 1994). The use of job-analytic information for the preparation of an interview yields higher validity coefficients (Wiesner & Cronshaw, 1988), which also accords with the data of Conway et al. (1995). Contrary to a variety of earlier studies, Wiesner and Cronshaw (1988) in their meta-analysis did not find any moderating effect of the sex and race of rater or ratee.

Reliability of Criteria

Validity of selection interviews can be evaluated by the application of criteria like success in training, job performance or tenure. These criteria are more reliable than psychiatrists' diagnoses, but they are far from being perfect in reliability and validity, which must be taken into account in meta-analyses. In meta-analyses, the lack of reliability in estimates of these criteria is used for assessing the true validity of selection interviews. Recent studies on the reliability of these criteria show, however, that they are better than estimated (e.g. Rothstein, 1990). This allows the conclusion that validity of selection interviews is underestimated by the meta-analyses.

Incremental Validity

There is a widespread opinion that selection interviews mainly assess verbal intelligence. The studies of Campion et al. (1994) and Schuler et al. (1995), however, indicate that selection interviews can have incremental validity beyond that of cognitive tests, i.e. a correlation remains between interview data and criteria even when intelligence has been held constant. Both studies used carefully prepared interview guides based on an empirical job analysis, and standardized questions of the situational interview type as well as questions of the behaviour description type. Additionally, the interviewers had to evaluate as well as combine the answers according to explicit rules.

FUTURE PERSPECTIVES AND CONCLUSIONS

After ten years of meta-analytical work, we can state that a well structured selection interview based on empirical job analysis can measure highly reliable predictors which cannot be measured by tests. There are a lot of hints on the potential influence which interindividual differences of interviewers and interviewees can have on the selection interview result (for an overview see Graves, 1993), but these differences seem to be of no practical influence in highly structured interviews (Pulakos et al., 1996).

The following question must still be answered: what constructs can be assessed only by interviews or more efficiently by interviews than by other methods? (See Conway et al., 1995; Pulakos & Schmitt, 1995; Roth & Campion, 1992; Schuler, 1989).

References

Campion, M.A., Campion, J.E. & Hudson, J.P. (1994). Structured interviewing: a note on incremental validity and alternative question types. *Journal of Applied Psychology*, 79, 998–1002.

Conway, J.M., Jako, R.A. & Goodman, D.F. (1995). A meta-analysis of interrater and internal consistency reliability of selection interviews. *Journal of Applied Psychology*, 80, 565–579.

Graves, L.M. (1993). Sources of individual differences in interviewer effectiveness: a model and implications for future research. *Journal of Organizational Behavior*, 14, 349–370.

Huffcutt, A.I. & Arthur, W. Jr. (1994). Hunter and Hunter (1984) revisited: interview validity for entry-level jobs. *Journal of Applied Psychology*, 79, 184–190.

Hunter, J.E. & Hunter, R.F. (1984). Validity and utility of alternative predictors of job performance. *Psychological Bulletin*, 96, 72–98.

Janz, T. (1982). The patterned behavior description interview versus unstructured interviews. *Journal of Applied Psychology*, 67, 577–580.

Latham, G.P., Saari, L.M., Pursell, E.D. & McDaniel, M.A. (1980). The situational interview. *Journal of Applied Psychology*, 65, 422–427.

McDaniel, M.A., Whetzel, D.L., Schmidt, F.L. & Maurer, S.D. (1994). The validity of employment interviews: a comprehensive review and meta-analysis. *Journal of Applied Psychology*, 79, 599–616.

Pulakos, E.D. & Schmitt, N. (1995). Experience-based and situational interview questions: studies of validity. *Personnel Psychology*, 48, 289–308.

Pulakos, E.D., Schmitt, N., Whitney, D. & Smith, M. (1996). Individual differences in interviewer ratings: the impact of standardization, consensus discussion, and sampling error on the validity of a structured interview. *Personnel Psychology*, 49, 85–102.

Roth, P.L. & Campion, J.E. (1992). An analysis of the predictive power of the panel interview and pre-employment tests. *Journal of Occupational and Organizational Psychology*, 65, 51–60.

Rothstein, H.R. (1990). Interrater reliability of job performance ratings: growth to asymptote level with increasing opportunity to observe. *Journal of Applied Psychology*, 75, 322–327.

Schuler, H. (1989). Construct validity of a multimodal employment interview. In Fallon, B.J., Pfister, H.P. & Brebner, J. (Eds.), *Advances in Industrial Organizational Psychology* (pp. 343–354). Amsterdam: North-Holland, Elsevier.

Schuler, H., Moser, K., Diemand, A. & Funke, U. (1995). Validität eines Einstellungsinterviews zur Prognose des Ausbildungserfolgs. *Zeitschrift für Pädagogische Psychologie*, 9, 45–54.

Wiesner, W.H. & Cronshaw, S.F. (1988). A meta-analytic investigation of the impact of interview format and degree of structure on the validity of the employment interview. *Journal of Occupational Psychology*, 61, 275–290.

Karl Westhoff

RELATED ENTRIES

APPLIED FIELDS: ORGANIZATIONS, APPLIED FIELDS: WORK AND INDUSTRY, PERSONNEL SELECTION, ASSESSMENT IN, CENTRE (ASSESSMENT CENTRES), INTERVIEW (GENERAL)

IRRATIONAL BELIEFS

INTRODUCTION

Cognitive-behavioural assessment is a technique used to test the thought processes which define many psychological disorders. A major component of cognitive-behavioural assessment is the measurement of irrational thoughts and beliefs. The tests of irrational thinking developed thus far have grown out of the work of American clinical psychologists Albert Ellis and Aaron Beck.

IRRATIONAL BELIEFS IN CLINICAL PSYCHOLOGY

Albert Ellis developed rational-emotive therapy (RET), now known as rational-emotive-behaviour therapy (REBT), during the 1950s as a result of his discontent with the efficacy of psychoanalysis (Ellis, 1962). The main hypothesis of REBT is that beliefs about events are the most important cause of appropriate or self-defeating emotions and behaviours. REBT is based on the ABC model of psychopathology, in which unpleasant activating environmental events (A) do not cause undesirable emotional and behavioural consequences (C); instead they are caused by the irrational beliefs (B) held about the event.

Irrational beliefs are beliefs by which external events are interpreted which are absolutistic and self-defeating observations. They are self-statements, unlikely to find empirical support, that reflect unspoken assumptions about what is necessary to lead a meaningful life. In a person holding irrational beliefs, inevitable setbacks will lead to inappropriate negative behaviours and emotions. Rorer (1989: 484), in describing the absolutistic nature of these beliefs, referred to them as 'beliefs that the world or someone or something in it should be different than it, she, or he is, because one wants it to be'. One very common irrational belief noted by Ellis is that people believe they must be completely competent in everything they do.

When an inevitable error is committed, it becomes catastrophic because it is a violation of the belief in personal perfection.

Another version of the ABC model was provided by Beck (1976). According to Beck's theory, numerous disorders are caused and maintained by negative thinking styles and negative beliefs that people have about themselves, their current circumstances, and the future. Included among these cognitive errors are assuming excessive personal causality for negative events, and thinking of the worst believing that it is most likely to happen. These cognitive errors, referred to as distortions, guide the interpretation of new experiences and increase vulnerability to psychopathology.

The theories of both Ellis and Beck describe the logic of people with behaviour disorders as faulty in that they make exaggerated negative inferences about what happens to them. However, recent research suggests that for REBT, demandingness, thinking that someone or some circumstance must be a certain way rather than preferring that something be a certain way, is the main quality of all irrational beliefs. It is in this way that the theories of Ellis and Beck differ; for REBT disorders occur if beliefs are demanding rather than preferential (McDermut, Haaga & Bilek, 1997).

The aim of REBT is to eliminate self-defeating beliefs via cognitive restructuring. Therapists forcefully dispute clients' irrational beliefs by questioning the evidence for the belief. The eventual goal is the integrating of cognitive, affective, and behavioural processes in order to bring about the desired therapeutic result. As in the case of REBT, the goal of Beck's cognitive therapy (CT) is to alter systematic errors in logic or misinterpretations about events which predispose an individual to develop pathological behaviours. Consequently, accurate assessment of irrational beliefs is essential for treatment. Perhaps more importantly, as REBT and CT are receiving increasing empirical scrutiny, valid measures of irrationality are necessary to furnish evidence of their scientific status.

EARLY MEASURES BASED ON THE ELLIS MODEL

Initially, assessment of irrational thinking was conducted via clinical interviews, which owing to problems with replication, are not appropriate for research purposes. The first objective measures were based on Ellis' (1962) original list of 11 specific irrational ideas. Nearly all tests of irrational beliefs are in the form of questionnaires.

Irrational Beliefs Test (IBT)

Jones (1968) developed the 100-item IBT which requires subjects to indicate their level of agreement or disagreement with each of the 100 items on a 5-point scale (such as 'I frequently worry about things over which I have no control'). Half of the items indicate the presence of a particular irrational belief, the other half its absence.

Adult Irrational Ideas Inventory (AII)

The AII (Fox & Davies, 1971) is a 60-item scale for adults based on an earlier version for children developed by Zingle (1965). The response mode is a four-point Likert scale, from 'strongly agree' to 'strongly disagree'. Item statements were presented so that strong agreement was sometimes very irrational and sometimes very rational.

Self-Inventory

The Self-Inventory (Plutchik, 1976) is a 45-item scale in the form of simple statements that can be answered 'Yes' or 'No' in terms of self-descriptions. The Self-Inventory was designed as both a therapeutic screening and evaluation index, and a research instrument. A German questionnaire, the *Fragebogens Irrationaler Einstellungen* or FIE (Joorman, 1998), includes translations of items used in the Self-Inventory.

Rational Behaviour Inventory (RBI)

Developed by Shorkey and Whiteman (1977), the 38-item RBI was designed as an instrument for treatment planning and assessment of REBT clients. The answers range, on a 5-point Likert scale, from 'strongly agree' to 'strongly disagree'.

There are 11 rationality factors plus a total score; the higher the score, the more rational the person is.

Idea Inventory

The Idea Inventory (Kassinove, 1977) is a 33-item 3-point Likert scale, with each of Ellis' 11 irrational beliefs measured by three items. All items are presented as an irrational idea; consequently any disagreement represents rational thinking. The questionnaire results in a total irrationality score plus scores on each individual belief.

Articulated Thoughts in Simulated Situations (ATSS)

ATSS (Davison, Robins & Johnson, 1983) is unlike the questionnaire format of previous measures of irrationality in that it provides a constant analysis of participants' thoughts while they imagine themselves in four negative or stressful scenarios. Narrated events are presented via audiotape; respondents vividly imagine that the events are happening to them. The respondents' thoughts are taped and later evaluated for irrationality.

SECOND GENERATION MEASURES BASED ON THE ELLIS MODEL

Despite their widespread use, subsequent research has questioned the discriminant validity of many of these early measures in that they appear to be confounding irrational beliefs with negative affect. More recent measures have been designed to maximize discriminant validity by excluding items consisting of emotional statements.

Belief Scale (BS)

Malouff and Schutte (1986) created the 20-item BS, with the intention of devising a scale which was shorter and which had more construct validity than previous measures (no items asked about anxiety reactions). Respondents indicate the degree to which they agree with 20 statements on a 5-point Likert scale ranging from 'strongly disagree' to 'agree strongly'.

General Attitude and Belief Scale (GABS)

Burgess (1986) developed a 96-item measure of irrationality which excluded items referring to behavioural or emotional consequences. Bernard (1990) established a 55-item version of the test (on a 5-point scale), which provides a total irrationality score, six irrationality subscales, and one rationality subscale. The GABS was again shortened to form the 26-item shortened GABS or SGABS (Lindner, Kirkby, Wertheim & Birch, 1999).

Survey of Personal Beliefs (SPB)

The SPB (Demaria, Kassinove & Dill, 1989) is a 50-item self-report scale scored on a 5-point Likert format. It was created as a measure of irrational beliefs free of affectively worded items. Further, the test items reflect more recent conceptualizations of irrational beliefs. The SBP assesses Ellis' four core irrational beliefs of awfulizing, demandingness, low frustration tolerance, and self/other rating (shoulds) as well as providing a total rationality score.

Irrational Beliefs Inventory (IBI)

This 50-item scale developed by Koopmans, Sanderman, Timmerman, and Emmelkamp (1994) is based on the item pool of the IBT and the RBI. The IBI, answered via a 5-point scale, consists of five subscales plus a total irrationality score. The IBI is distinguishable from negative affect in that it measures cognitions rather than anxiety or depression.

BECK'S COGNITIVE MODEL

Central themes of Beck's cognitive model of psychopathology are dysfunctional attitudes (shoulds and musts) and cognitive errors in response to negative life experiences. These errors are interpretations and predictions which are not justified by the information provided. Beck's model led to the development of measures designed to assess these negative thinking styles and dysfunctional beliefs.

Dysfunctional Attitude Scale (DAS)

The DAS (Weissman, 1979) is a 100-item measure, answered on a 7-point Likert scale from 'totally agree' to 'totally disagree'. It identifies beliefs that might interact with a stressor to produce psychopathology. The short form devised by Dyck (1992) comprises 56 items representing 8 subscales. This form provides an indication of the general level of dysfunctional thinking as well as specific types of dysfunctional thought represented by the individual subscales. Lower scores represent greater maladaptive thinking.

General Cognitive Error Questionnaire (CEQ)

The General CEQ (Lefebvre, 1980) was designed to measure cognitive errors or distortions related to general life experiences. The General CEQ consists of 24 short vignettes followed by a dysphoric cognition about that vignette. Vignettes were categorized according to four cognitive errors identified by Beck, including catastrophizing and personalizing. Respondents are asked to rate how similar the cognition is to the thought they would have had. The 5-point rating scale ranges from 'almost exactly like I would think' to 'not at all like I would think'.

FUTURE PERSPECTIVES AND CONCLUSIONS

Many early measures of irrationality remain in use. The IBT and RBI remain popular tests and are frequently cited in the research literature. This is despite criticisms that the questionnaire versions are dated (they reflect Ellis' earlier theories of irrational thinking), and because they do not measure irrational beliefs independently of the affect they were theorized to cause. Second generation tests based on the Ellis model are recognized as having higher discriminant validity because they do not refer to affect in their items. The DAS and CEQ based on Beck's model are regarded as valid measures of irrationality and continue to be cited frequently as well.

REBT and CT are based on theories which are continuously evolving due to rigorous research on the role of irrationality in behaviour disorders.

Both have shown that they are receptive to research findings. Similarly, as theory changes, the measures of irrationality have changed as well. The SPB (Demaria et al., 1989) reflects changes in REBT from 11 irrational beliefs to 4 core ideas. Newer measures will continue to be created to further test the thesis that there is a relationship between behaviour and irrational beliefs. These measures will have enhanced content validity by aligning item content with theoretical changes.

There are several areas of future concern in which irrational beliefs assessment will play a key role. They include: (1) discovering if specific types of irrational thinking are associated with specific disorders; (2) paying particular attention to the evaluation of change in irrationality due to treatment; (3) studying the effect of cultural influences in the development of irrational beliefs; and (4) determining if rational training prevents psychological disorders.

References

Beck, A.T. (1976). *Cognitive Therapy and the Emotional Disorders*. New York: International Universities Press.

Bernard, M.E. (1990). Validation of general attitude and belief scale. Presented at the World Congress on Mental Health Counselling, Keystone, Colorado.

Burgess, P. (1986). Belief systems and emotional disturbance: evaluation of the rational emotive model. Doctoral Dissertation, University of Melbourne, Australia.

Davison, G.C., Robins, C. & Johnson, M.K. (1983). Articulated thoughts during simulated situations: a paradigm for studying cognition in emotion and behavior. *Cognitive Therapy and Research*, 7, 17–40.

Demaria, T.P., Kassinove, H. & Dill, C.A. (1989). Psychometric properties of the survey of personal beliefs: a rational-emotive measure of irrational thinking. *Journal of Personality Assessment*, 53, 329–341.

Dyck, M.J. (1992). Subscales of the dysfunctional attitudes scale. *British Journal of Clinical Psychology*, 31, 333–335.

Ellis, A. (1962). *Reason and Emotion in Psychotherapy*. New York: Lyle-Stuart.

Fox, E.E. & Davies, R.L. (1971). Test your rationality. *Rational Living*, 5, 23–25.

Jones, R. (1968). A factored measure of Ellis irrational beliefs system with personality maladjustment correlates. Doctoral Dissertation, Texas Technological College.

Joorman, J. (1998). Eine überprüfung der Konstruktvalidität des Fragebogens Irrationaler Einstellungen (FIE). *Diagnostica*, 44, 201–208.

Kassinove, H. (1977). Developmental trends in rational thinking: implications for rational-emotive school health programs. *Journal of Community Psychology*, 5, 266–274.

Koopmans, P.C., Sanderman, R., Timmerman, I. & Emmelkamp, P.M.G. (1994). The irrational beliefs inventory (IBI): development and psychometric evaluation. *European Journal of Psychological Assessment*, 10, 15–27.

Lefebvre, M.F. (1980). Cognitive distortion in depressed psychiatric and low back pain patients. Doctoral Dissertation, University of Vermont, Burlington.

Lindner, H., Kirkby, R., Wertheim, E. & Birch, P. (1999). A brief assessment of irrational thinking: the shortened general attitude and belief scale. *Cognitive Therapy and Research*, 23, 651–663.

Malouff, J.M. & Schutte, N.S. (1986). Development and validation of a measure of irrational belief. *Journal of Consulting and Clinical Psychology*, 54, 860–862.

McDermut, J.F., Haaga, D.A.F. & Bilek, L.A. (1997). Cognitive bias and irrational beliefs in major depression and dysphoria. *Cognitive Therapy and Research*, 21, 459–476.

Plutchik, R. (1976). The self-inventory: a measure of irrational attitudes and behavior. *Rational Living*, 11, 31–33.

Rorer, L.G. (1989). Rational-emotive theory: I. an integrated psychological and philosophical basis. *Cognitive Therapy and Research*, 13, 475–492.

Shorkey, C.T. & Whiteman, V.L. (1977). Development of the Rational Behavior Inventory: initial validity and reliability. *Educational and Psychological Measurement*, 37, 527–534.

Weissman, A.N. (1979). The Dysfunctional Attitude Scale: a validation study. Doctoral Dissertation, University of Pennsylvania, Philadelphia.

Zingle, H.W. (1965). A rational therapy approach to counselling underachievers. Doctoral Dissertation, University of Alberta.

K. Robert Bridges

RELATED ENTRIES

I ITEM BANKING

INTRODUCTION

Item banks are used in a variety of contexts ranging from individual classrooms, schools, districts, state or other governmental units, to large scale computer-based testing programs. Typically, the purpose of developing an item bank is to assist, improve, and automate the test assembly process. In developing an item bank, a number of decisions about two factors need to be considered. These factors are the design of the bank and the methods for maintaining and refreshing it once it has been created.

Designing an item bank is analogous to creating a database. At the simplest level, the designer must decide what data elements to store and then how to structure the data in order to facilitate data extraction and reporting, test assembly, and possibly even test administration functions. For item banks these functions are realized through item selection and test assembly processes. Item selection and test assembly processes can be placed into two broad categories: one in which human intervention is heavily relied upon and another in which automation is heavily relied upon (e.g. through the use of computerized algorithms). Each of these approaches place differing requirements on an item bank. Ultimately, if a bank is to be used to assist humans in the assembly process, the challenges of building the bank are less difficult to meet. This is in contrast to the context in which tests must be administered directly from a bank without human intervention, requiring full automation of the test assembly process.

A typical item bank contains four classes of information about each item: (a) the actual item text and associated graphical or stimulus material, (b) some classification information about the item characterizing its non-statistical properties such as relevance to educational standards, cognitive processes required to produce a successful solution and content, (c) some form of statistical and performance data about the item, and (d) some representation of the history of an item's use.

BANK DESIGN

Most automated test assembly algorithms rely on item statistics that have been placed on a common scale. Although transformations of the proportion correct (Gulliksen, 1950) and biserial correlations can be used, the most popular of these are based on Item Response Theory (IRT, Lord, 1980). In fact, the majority of literature on the topic of item banking has focused on methods and procedures for developing and maintaining an IRT scale. The interested reader might find the December 1996 volume of *Applied Psychological Measurement*, a special issue dedicated to item banking, helpful, and papers by Rudner (1998) and Flaugher (2000).

For traditional paper-and-pencil tests, assembled in advance of test administration, the amount of item classification data stored is relatively small. Although by no means incomplete, the data elements stored tend to be the minimum set required to guide a human assembly of a test with the added assumption that the test will be reviewed and revised before use. For a Quantitative measure, this might include:

(a) Math Content – Arithmetic, Algebra, Geometry, or Calculus
(b) Level of Context – Pure Math or Word Problem
(c) Response Format – Multiple Choice, Short Answer, or Numeric Entry
(d) Correct Answer

A number of features tend not to be stored. These include many aspects of the item's content that only became an issue with respect to other items assembled into a single test. For example, in a Verbal measure, the fact that a reading passage is about the works of Charles Dickens is typically not a feature that is stored or even explicitly considered. If two passages about Dickens are selected in a draft assembly, a human reviewer would note this and one of the passages would be replaced. As a second example, two Analogy items might rely on the test taker knowing the definition of 'inflammable'. It is generally considered unacceptable practice to include multiple items in the same test that rely on specific vocabulary. Here again, key vocabulary is not typically an attribute that is stored for each item. Other types of interactions between items rely on global human impressions rather than extensive item classifications. For example, it might be found that a test is well within statistical specifications, but that a test reviewer has the impression that this collection of items is unusually time consuming to complete.

As test assembly becomes dynamic and performed in real time during a test administration it becomes necessary to codify, at the item level, every aspect of a form that should be controlled. This requires a priori specification of every item property of concern. While this seems relatively intuitive for the examples above, when extended to controlling the number of references about medical conditions, colours, boats, etc. in a test, it becomes apparent that the complexity and richness of the classification scheme is the key to the success of item bank development.

Historically, these item properties and their interactions with each other have been evaluated by having a human actually perform all pairwise comparisons and identify those items that should not appear in the same test. This avoids the need to delineate all of the specific features that would be of concern and to identify whether each item does or does not have the feature. While a viable, albeit time consuming, practice when banks contain hundreds of items, this practice becomes untenable when banks include thousands of items. Every addition to the bank requires a redefinition of the lists of items that should not appear together. Thus, as the bank becomes large, management of these lists becomes intractable and the information becomes stored in a classification scheme as a list of features that the item does or does not have.

With on-demand testing, it has become necessary for the lag between uses of an item to become smaller. Most testing programmes simply don't have the resources to have a new test or pool in the field every day. This introduces a number of security concerns. Way, Steffen and Anderson (1998) detail one method for mitigating the potential risks of this practice. The core idea is to reuse items only when necessary and then restrict use, to the degree possible, to items that were seen by fewer test takers than other items. The implications of any such plan for an item bank is that it is now necessary to track the complete history of usage for every item. That includes any pool to which the item has been assigned, the administration period of that pool, and the number of test takers delivered the item during that administration period.

BANK MAINTENANCE/ REFRESHMENT

There are a number of commercially available software packages that perform all of the functions described above, including the IRT calibration/scaling functions (e.g. CAT Builder [2001], FastTEST [2001]). However, the effective use of an item bank requires careful consideration of a number of issues that software cannot address. This includes deciding how often to augment or refresh the bank, what types of items to write, when items should be retired, what kinds of content and statistical reviews should precede an item's entry into the bank, how many items should be included in the bank, and an item tryout/calibration plan so that new items can be screened, calibrated, and scaled.

Performance standards for including items in the bank can take a variety of forms. For paper-and-pencil testing programmes, these criteria typically involve some classical item analysis statistics (Henrysson, 1971). The proportion correct cannot be too high or too low, some minimum level of item-total score correlation is required as well as empirical verification that there is only a single correct response. For IRT-based programmes, this is usually done with some form of model-data fit statistic (Kingston & Dorans, 1985; Thissen, Steinberg & Fitzpatrick, 1989). Adaptive testing programmes also add criteria about the magnitude of the parameters themselves. For example, with maximum information item selection, items with discrimination parameters that are low (e.g. less than 0.40) have virtually no chance of being selected for administration. Thus, if resources allow, these items might be discarded. More recently, computer-based testing programs have begun to incorporate criteria for item latencies into the item screening process. Based on item tryout data, it is possible to identify items that require inordinately more time to answer than other items that have similar content and statistical characteristics. These items are actually discarded, thus reducing the risk that tests that appear parallel to the assembly algorithm are differentially speeded.

On-demand pool-based testing programmes have been exploring the issues of minimum bank size for several years. The concerns focus mainly on security issues. Unfortunately, definitive answers have yet to appear in the literature; we simply do not know how often an item can be administered before its subsequent performance is altered.

Refreshing a bank is conceptually straightforward. The goal is to create at least as many new items as are retired. The difficulty is anticipating which items will be retired. For linear paper-and-pencil testing programmes this is relatively easy since items in a test form are retired as a unit, and specifications are constant across forms. However, for adaptive testing programmes, items are not used equally. In order to obtain desired levels of measurement precision with fewer items, adaptive algorithms seek to deliver highly informative items at higher rates than in paper-and-pencil tests. Additionally, high and low performing test takers are administered a greater number of items with extreme difficulty than typically appear in a single paper-and-pencil test. In order to avoid administering the same items to all of these examinees, large numbers of items of extreme (high and low) difficulty are needed. These tend to be the most challenging items to develop.

FUTURE PERSPECTIVES AND CONCLUSIONS

An item bank can be a powerful support tool for test development activities. However, the creation of an item bank is not an activity to be undertaken lightly. It is important to keep in mind that item banks are developed to support a test assembly algorithm. The constraints imposed by an algorithm should influence, if not determine, the decisions made about the design and maintenance of the item bank. Clearly, more research on topics such as the optimal design of item banks, item selection, and the maintenance of item banks can be expected in the coming years.

References

CAT Builder [Computer Software] (2001). St. Paul, MN: Assessment Systems Corporation.

FastTEST Professional 1.5 [Computer Software] (2001). Evanston, IL: Computer Adaptive Technologies.

Flaugher, R. (2000). Item pools. In Wainer, H. et al. (Eds.), *Computerized Adaptive Testing: A Primer* (2nd ed., pp. 37–60). Hillsdale, NJ: Erlbaum.

Gulliksen, H. (1950). *Theory of Mental Tests*. New York: John Wiley & Sons.

Henrysson, S. (1971). Gathering, analyzing, and using data on test items. In Thorndike, R.L. *Educational Measurement* (2nd ed., pp. 130–159). Washington, DC: American Council on Education.

Kingston, N.M. & Dorans, N.J. (1985). The analysis of item ability regressions: an exploratory IRT model fit tool. *Applied Psychological Measurement*, 9, 281–288.

Lord, F.M. (1980). *Applications of Item Response Theory to Practical Testing Problems*. Hillsdale, NJ: Erlbaum.

Rudner, L. (1998). Item banking. *Practical Assessment, Research and Evaluation*, 6(4), special issue.

Thissen, D., Steinberg, L. & Fitzpatrick, A.R. (1989). Multiple choice models: the distractors are part of the item. *Journal of Educational Measurement*, 26, 161–176.

Way, W.D., Steffen, M. & Anderson, G.S. (1998, September). Developing, maintaining, and renewing the item inventory to support computer-based testing. Invited Paper Presented at the Colloquium. Computer-Based Testing: Building the Foundation for Future Assessments, Philadelphia.

Manfred Steffen and Martha Stocking

RELATED ENTRIES

ACHIEVEMENT TESTING, ADAPTIVE AND TAILORED TESTING, COMPUTER-BASED TESTING, CRITERION-REFERENCED TESTING. METHODS AND PROCEDURES, ITEM RESPONSE THEORY: MODELS AND FEATURES

ITEM BIAS

INTRODUCTION

Methods for detecting differential item function-ing (DIF) and item bias typically are used in the process of developing new measures, adapting existing measures, or validating test score inferences. DIF methods allow one to judge whether items (and ultimately the test they constitute) are functioning in the same manner in various groups of examinees. In broad terms, this is a matter of measurement invariance; that is, is the test performing in the same manner for each group of examinees? What follows is a brief introduction to DIF and item bias, including the context in which DIF methods arose. The goal is to provide some organizing principles that allow one to catalogue and then contrast the various DIF detection methods. This entry will end with a discussion of current and future directions for DIF.

CONTEXT IN WHICH DIF METHODS AROSE

Concerns about item bias emerged within the context of test bias and high-stakes decision-making involving achievement, aptitude, certifica-tion, and licensure tests in which matters of fairness and equity were paramount. Historically, concerns about test bias have centred around differential performance by groups based on gender or race. If the average test scores for such groups (e.g. men vs. women, Blacks vs. Whites) were found to be different, then the question arose as to whether the difference reflected bias in the test. Given that a test is comprised of items, questions soon emerged about which specific items might be the source of such bias.

Given this context, many of the early item bias methods focused on (a) comparisons of only two groups of examinees, (b) terminology such as 'focal' and 'reference' groups to denote minority and majority groups, respectively, and (c) binary

(rather than polytomous) scored items. Due to the highly politicized environment in which item bias was being examined, two inter-related changes occurred. First, the expression 'item bias' was replaced by the more palatable term 'differential item functioning' or DIF in many descriptions. DIF was the statistical term that was used to simply describe the situation in which persons from one group answered an item correctly more often than equally knowledgeable persons from another group. Second, the introduction of the term 'differential item functioning' allowed one to distinguish item impact from item bias. Item impact described the situation in which DIF exists because there were true differences between the groups in the underlying ability of interest being measured by the item. Item bias described the situations in which there is DIF because of some characteristic of the test item or testing situation that is not relevant to the underlying ability of interest (and hence the test purpose).

Traditionally, consumers of DIF methodology and technology have been educational and psychological measurement specialists. As a result, research has primarily focused on devel-oping sophisticated statistical methods for detect-ing or 'flagging' DIF items rather than on refining methods to distinguish item bias from item impact and providing explanations for why DIF was occurring. Although this is changing as increasing numbers of non-measurement specia-lists become interested in exploring DIF and item bias in tests, it has become apparent that much of the statistical terminology and software being used is not very accessible to many researchers.

FRAMEWORKS FOR CONSIDERING DIF

At least three frameworks for thinking about DIF have evolved in the literature: (1) modelling item responses via contingency tables and/or regres-sion models, (2) item response theory, and

(3) multidimensional models. Although these frameworks may be seen as inter-related, they are freestanding. Each framework provides useful organizing principles for describing DIF and developing methods for detecting DIF in items.

MODELLING ITEM RESPONSES VIA CONTINGENCY TABLES AND/OR REGRESSION MODELS

A statistical implication of the definition of DIF (i.e. persons from one group answering an item correctly more often than equally knowledgeable persons from another group) is that one needs to match the groups on the ability of interest prior to examining whether there is a group effect. That is, the definition of DIF implies that after conditioning on (i.e. statistically controlling for) the differences in item responses that are due to the ability being measured, the groups still differ. Thus, within this framework, one is interested in stating a probability model that allows one to study the main effects of group differences (termed 'uniform DIF') and the interaction of group by ability (termed 'non-uniform DIF') after statistically matching on the test score.

This class of DIF methods, in essence, consists of conditional methods in that they study the effect of the grouping variable(s) and the interaction term(s) over-and-above (i.e. while conditioning on) the total score. In this sense, they share a lot in common with analysis of covariance (ANCOVA) or attribute-by-treatment interaction (ATI) methods. Building on this similarity, it is important to recognize that nearly all DIF methods are applied in what would be called an observational or quasi-experimental study design and so one must keep in mind all of the commonly known caveats around making causal claims of grouping variable effects in observational studies involving intact groups.

This framework for DIF has resulted in two broad classes of DIF detection methods: Mantel–Haenszel (MH) and logistic regression (LogR) approaches. The MH class of methods (Holland & Thayer, 1988) treats the DIF detection problem as one involving, in essence, three-way contingency tables. The three dimensions of the contingency table involve (a) whether one gets an item correct or incorrect, (b) group membership, while conditioning on (c) the total score discretized into a number of category score bins. The LogR class of methods (Swaminathan & Rogers, 1990) entails conducting a regression analysis (in the most common case, a logistic regression analysis as the scores are binary) for each item wherein one tests the statistical effect of the grouping variable(s) and the interaction of the grouping variable and the total score after conditioning on the total score. One clear contrast between the MH and LogR methods is that one needs to discretize the conditioning variable in the MH methods whereas one does not have to do so with the LogR methods. The MH assumes no interaction (like ANCOVA) whereas the LogR allows for an interaction (like ATI methods).

ITEM RESPONSE THEORY

Referring back to the definition of DIF in the previous section, one can approach DIF from an item response theory (IRT) framework. In this case, one considers two item characteristic curves (ICCs) of the same item but computed from two groups. In the IRT context, if the items exhibit DIF, then the ICCs will be identifiably different for the groups. The ICCs can be identifiably different in two common ways. First, the curves can differ only in terms of their threshold (i.e. difficulty) parameter and hence the curves are displaced by a shift in their location on the theta continuum of variation. Second, the ICCs may differ not only on difficulty but also on discrimination (and/or guessing) and hence the curves may be seen to intersect. Within this context, the former represents uniform DIF (i.e. a main effect of group) whereas the latter represents non-uniform DIF (i.e. an interaction of group by ability).

In its essence, the IRT approach is focused on determining the area between the curves (or, equivalently, comparing the IRT parameters) of the two groups. It is noteworthy that, unlike the contingency table or regression modelling methods, the IRT approach does not match the groups by conditioning on the total score. That is, the question of 'matching' only comes up if one computes the difference function between the groups conditionally (as in MH or LogR). Comparing the IRT parameter estimates or ICCs is an unconditional analysis because it implicitly assumes that the ability distribution has been 'integrated out'. The mathematical expression 'integrated out' is commonly used in some DIF literature and is used in the sense that one computes the area between the ICCs *across the distribution* of the continuum of variation, theta.

A problem occurs in the IRT context because it is a latent variable modelling approach. Because the scale for theta in any IRT model is arbitrary, one must set it during calibration. How is this resolved? Computing algorithms like BILOG (and other such 2PL/3PL varieties of calibration software) set the mean of the ability distribution at zero. Some Rasch calibration software typically set the mean of the item difficulties at zero whereas others fix a single item parameter estimate, much like one does in confirmatory factor analysis to fix the scale of the latent variable.

The issue that arises in DIF is that if the two groups have different ability distributions, then the scales for the groups will be arbitrarily different. This is a problem because, in the case of DIF, one wants the two groups on the same scale or metric. If the two groups are not on the same metric, any DIF results will be impossible to interpret. This matter of a common metric is important to highlight because, in several recent studies, some Rasch analysts have ignored this matter and computed the difference between the item difficulty parameter for the two groups with a t-statistic, falsely relying on Rasch invariance claims to justify the computation and incorrectly ignoring the need for a common metric.

Because it is also relevant to the multidimensional framework that follows, more detail is provided on how to establish a common metric. In many IRT applications, one way to do this is to estimate the item parameters for a subset of items common to each group and use these item parameters to estimate abilities on the common metric. Then, one recalibrates the items, one at a time, for each group using this common metric. The most appropriate way of doing the DIF analysis is to leave the item(s) of concern out of the calibration, estimate the abilities on the common metric (without being influenced by the response patterns of the item(s) of concern), and then do the separate calibration of just the studied item using the uncontaminated ability estimates as fixed values that 'anchor' the scale.

The most common IRT methods for DIF include: signed area tests (which only focus on uniform DIF), unsigned area tests (which allow for non-uniform DIF), and nested model testing via a likelihood ratio test, which is most easily conducted for uniform DIF. In addition, one can approach this via non-parametric IRT using the software TestGraf (Ramsay, 2001). An advantage of non-parametric IRT is that it provides a graphical method and needs far fewer items and subjects than other IRT approaches.

MULTIDIMENSIONAL MODELS

There has been a longstanding framework for DIF based on the dimensionality of items. This framework begins with the assumption that all tests are, to some extent, multidimensional. The informal rationale has been that there is typically one primary dimension of interest in a test but there may also be other dimensions within that test that produce construct-irrelevant variance. For example, in a problem-based test of mathematics, the test will consist of some primary dimension that reflects mathematics ability as well as some other dimensions that may reflect other secondary abilities such as reading comprehension or verbal abilities. These other dimensions are often correlated with the primary dimension. As part of this informal rationale, it was not uncommon to think of DIF as arising from dimensions other than those of primary interest in the test. Ackerman (1992) provides a thorough discussion of the basis for the multidimensional framework.

Stout and his colleagues (e.g. Shealy & Stout, 1993) formalized some of this thinking and introduced a new DIF test statistic, simultaneous item bias test (SIBTEST) based on their framework. The multidimensional approach to DIF, as implemented in SIBTEST, allows for a variety of scenarios that comprise differential dimensionality as the source for DIF. Because this method involves a type of factor analysis, it requires the analyst to study sets (or bundles) of items, rather than individual items, for DIF.

Because the multidimensional framework, like IRT, is a latent variable approach, it must be noted that the above discussion regarding the importance of a common metric and how one establishes a common metric using subsets of items also applies to the multidimensional approach. This similarity is often overlooked in the literature.

A FINAL COMMENT ON THE THREE FRAMEWORKS

Although the three frameworks are freestanding, as a set they have provided a powerful lens for describing DIF, developing statistical methods for detecting DIF, and thinking about the sources of DIF. As a final layer to cataloguing and contrasting the various DIF methods, the first framework described above can be seen to use observed score methods (because MH and LogR generally condition on the observed total score) whereas the latter two frameworks are latent variable approaches.

CONFIRMATORY VERSUS EXPLORATORY METHODS

Each of the above sets of methods could be used in a confirmatory or exploratory manner. That is, as has been noted by the proponents of the multidimensional approaches to DIF detection, the conventional manner in which one investigates DIF is to individually examine all items on a test for DIF and then, if the results suggest DIF, those items are further studied by content specialists and others to ascertain possible reasons for the observed DIF and determine whether item impact or bias is present. Given that such DIF studies usually occur in the context of observational (rather than experimental) studies, the sources or causes of DIF may be difficult to establish. Thus, the conventional approach is an inductive or exploratory approach to investigating DIF.

Alternatively, one could approach the DIF detection issue from a more theory-based and hypothetico-deductive strategy. That is, one would consult (with the aid of a content specialist) the relevant literature and determine whether any predictions (i.e. scientific hypotheses) can be made for where and why and for who DIF may be present. Once this has been accomplished, one then goes about testing the predictions using any of the DIF detection methods. The attractiveness of this strategy

for many is the hope that a theory-based approach will provide an explanation for why DIF would be present (i.e. from a multidimensional framework, the literature would identify the secondary dimension(s)) and whether the DIF reflects item impact or bias. Of course, the confirmatory (i.e. theory-based) strategy is most fruitful when the content literature is well developed.

FUTURE PERSPECTIVES

The direction and focus of DIF research has been shaped by its origins in test bias and high-stakes decision-making involving achievement, aptitude, certification, and licensure tests. Current directions in DIF research find their inspiration from considering many testing situations outside of test bias, per se. Today, in addition to matters of bias, DIF technology is used to help answer a variety of basic research and applied measurement questions wherein one wants to compare item performance between or among groups when taking into account the ability distribution. At this point, applications of DIF have more in common with the uses of ANCOVA or ATI than test bias per se.

This broader application has been the impetus for a variety of current and future directions in DIF development, such as test translation and cross-cultural adaptation. Many novel applications of DIF occur because previous studies of group differences compared differences in mean performance without taking into account the underlying ability continuum. An example of such an application in language testing would be a study of the effect of background variables such as discipline of study, culture, and hobbies on item performance.

Moving beyond the traditional bias context has demanded developments for DIF detection in polytomous, graded-response, and rating scale (e.g. Likert) items. Furthermore, because DIF methods are being used increasingly by non-measurement specialists, it has been necessary to develop more user-friendly software and more accessible descriptions of the statistical techniques as well as more accessible and useful measures of DIF effect size for both the binary and polytomous cases.

Finally, ongoing research is focusing on complex data situations wherein one has students nested within classrooms, classrooms nested within larger school organizations, and a myriad of contextual variables at each level that are potentially related to DIF. New methods are being developed to study the contextual variables while remaining true to the complex data structure with random coefficient models and generalized estimating equations.

CONCLUSIONS

It is important to note that in this entry we have focused on 'internal' methods for studying potential item bias, i.e. within the test or measure itself. It is important for the reader to note that there is also a class of methods for studying potential item bias wherein we have a predictor and criterion relationship in the testing context. For example, in some industrial and organizational contexts, one has a test that is meant to predict some criterion behaviour. Item (or, in fact, test level) bias then focuses on whether the criterion and predictor relationship is the same for the various groups of interest.

References

Ackerman, T. (1992). A didactic explanation of item bias, item impact, and item validity from a multi-dimensional perspective. *Journal of Educational Measurement, 29,* 67–91.

Holland, P.W. & Thayer, D.T. (1988). Differential item functioning and the Mantel–Haenszel procedure. In Wainer, H. & Braun, H.I. (Eds.), *Test Validity* (pp. 129–145). Hillsdale, NJ: Lawrence Erlbaum.

Ramsay, J.O. (2001). *TestGraf: A Program for the Graphical Analysis of Multiple-Choice Test and Questionnaire Data* [software and manual]. McGill University, Montreal, Canada.

Shealy, R. & Stout, W.F. (1993). A model-based standardization approach that separates true bias/DIF from group ability differences and detects test bias/DTF as well as item bias/DIF. *Psychometrika, 58,* 159–194.

Swaminathan, H. & Rogers, H.J. (1990). Detecting differential item functioning using logistic regression procedures. *Journal of Educational Measurement, 27,* 361–370.

Bruno D. Zumbo and Anita M. Hubley

RELATED ENTRIES

Achievement Testing, Criterion-Referenced Testing: Methods and Procedures, Assessor's Bias

ITEM RESPONSE THEORY: MODELS AND FEATURES

INTRODUCTION

Educational and psychological testing has been undergoing major changes in recent years. Demands for new psychological measures, increased interest in diagnostic assessment, the influence of cognitive psychology on testing, introduction of new test item formats, and the role of computers in test administration, scoring, and score interpretations are five of many changes taking place in testing practices today.

Less well known among psychologists is the fact that the basic psychometric theory for developing educational and psychological tests and evaluating tests and test scores is changing too and these changes should make the construction and evaluation of tests and the interpretation of test scores easier and potentially more valid.

Psychologists have seen occasional references to the Rasch model, the three-parameter logistic model, latent trait theory, item response theory, latent ability, item characteristic curves, computer adaptive testing, etc. in popular psychological testing texts, test manuals, and journals (see, for example, Anastasi, 1989). These new psychometric terms are associated with modern test theory, known as 'item response theory'. The purposes of this entry are (1) to describe some of the shortcomings of classical test theory, models, and methods, (2) to introduce item response theory and related concepts and models, and (3) to identify some of the advantages of item response theory and associated methods for psychologists.

SHORTCOMINGS OF CLASSICAL TEST THEORY AND METHODS

Classical test theory has provided the statistical underpinnings for both educational and psychological tests. While popular psychological testing books such as those of Thorndike and Hagen, Anastasi, and Cronbach do not provide the relevant theory and derivations, all of the popular measurement formulas and approaches for constructing tests, evaluating tests, and interpreting scores that appear in these books (e.g. Spearman–Brown formula, standard error of measurement, corrections for score range restrictions) are derived from the classical test model.

Despite the usefulness of classical test theory and models in psychometric methods, shortcomings in the basic theory underlying psychological testing and measurement procedures for test construction have been recognized for over 50 years (see Gulliksen, 1950). One such shortcoming is that classical item statistics – item difficulty and item discrimination – depend on the particular examinee samples from which they were obtained. A consequence of this dependence on a specific sample of examinees is that these item statistics are only useful when constructing tests for examinee populations that are similar to the sample of examinees from which the item statistics were obtained. Unfortunately, one cannot always be sure that the population of examinees for whom a test is intended is similar to the sample of examinees used in obtaining item statistics. Preferable would be statistics for test items which are

independent of the particular sample of examinees in which they are obtained. 'Invariant item statistics over samples' is the goal.

Not only are popular classical item statistics used in test development samples dependent, but so are other important test statistics such as test reliability and validity. Test reliability is higher when estimated in heterogeneous samples of examinees rather than in more homogeneous samples of examinees. Correction factors are often used to adjust reliability estimates for this problem but the fact is that the dependence of reliability indices on the choice of examinee sample is troublesome. Again, test statistics independent of examinee samples would be valuable.

A second shortcoming of classical test theory is that comparisons of examinees on the test score scale are limited to situations where examinees are administered the same (or parallel) tests. The seriousness of this shortcoming is clear when it is recognized that examinees often take different forms of a test or even different sections within a test. For example, one medical board requires candidates to take a 'core section' and then three of six additional sections of the test. Examinees are compared using scores based on a test consisting of the core and three optional sections. Since the sections are not equally difficult and there are twenty different combinations of three sections possible, comparisons among candidates become difficult. In fact, it is *not* fair to require the same passing score for candidates who have been administered tests that differ, perhaps substantially, in difficulty. When several forms of a test that vary in difficulty are used, examinee scores across non-parallel forms are *not* comparable unless one makes use of equating procedures, which are often quite complex.

There are many situations where the use of non-equivalent tests are of interest. Out-of-level achievement testing in schools is one example. More effective administration of a battery of aptitude tests by adapting the battery to the examinee's ability is another. Starting examinees at different points in an intelligence test based on some prior information about the examinee is another example. But these examples create a problem at some point and that is examinees who have taken different forms of the test needed to be compared to each other, or to a norm group who took a different version of the test. As test scores are sample dependent (test scores depend on the set of items administered), they are not an adequate basis for score reporting or using norms tables, when examinees are administered tests that are non-equivalent in difficulty.

A computer-adaptive test (CAT) is another excellent example of the problem of item dependent scores. A CAT is a test administered by a computer, where the items administered are dependent on the candidate's performance on previous items: perform well and the computer selects harder items; perform poorly and the computer selects easier items. But, again, the non-equivalence of test forms makes comparisons among examinees or comparisons of examinees' test scores to passing scores difficult without the use of complex equating methods. Other short-comings of classical test models have been described by Hambleton and Swaminathan (1985) and Hambleton, Swaminathan, and Rogers (1991).

What is needed, if the goal is to tailor or adapt the administration of tests to examinees, is an approach to ability estimation which is not test dependent. The influence of the particular items on the test administered to the examinee needs to be accounted for.

ITEM RESPONSE THEORY

Frederic Lord and Harold Gulliksen from the Educational Testing Service in Princeton, New Jersey, and many other psychometricians in the 1940s and 1950s, were interested in producing a psychometric theory by which to assess examinees in a way which did not depend directly on the *particular* items which were included in a test. The idea was that an examinee may score high on an easy test or lower on a hard test, but there is a more fundamental ability that the examinee brings to any given testing situation which does not change as a function of the sample of items administered. It is that more fundamental characteristic of the examinee which is usually of interest to the psychologist and it is that more fundamental characteristic, referred to as a 'latent variable', which is of interest in modern test theory. This construct of interest is more fundamental than test score because ability unlike test score does not change with the

particular choice of items in a test. It could change, however, over time, because of instruction, life changes, experiences, etc.

Ability is the term used by psychometricians to describe the construct measured by a test. It might be verbal or numerical ability, intelligence, creativity, or mathematics achievement. It might also be self-esteem, achievement motivation, or attitudes about school. The label 'ability' is used to describe whatever construct validation studies have shown that a test measures.

Item response theory (IRT) purports to overcome the shortcomings of classical test theory by providing a reporting scale on which examinee ability (the construct measured by the test) is independent of the particular choice of test items administered. What began in the 1940s and 1950s as a goal of psychometricians, became reality beginning in the 1960s and 1970s. By the early 1970s, the theory was developing nicely, computer software was available, and applications of IRT were beginning to appear. Today, IRT is well developed and being used by test publishers, large testing agencies, test developers, and researchers to address technical problems such as the design of tests, the study of item bias, equating test scores, and computer-adaptive testing.

IRT, in its basic form, postulates that (1) underlying examinee performance on a test is a single ability or trait, and (2) the relationship between the probability that an examinee will provide a correct answer (or agree to a statement, in the case of a personality or attitude survey) and the examinee's ability can be described by a *mono-tonically* increasing curve. We would expect examinees with more ability to have a higher probability of providing a correct answer than those with less ability so this feature is highly desirable. Or in the case of (say) an instrument measuring student attitudes towards a topic, we would expect those persons with very positive attitudes to agree with a statement more frequently than those persons with less positive attitudes.

The curve representing the relationship between the probability of a correct response and ability is called an 'item characteristic curve' (ICC). Figure 1 shows the item characteristic curve for the three-parameter logistic model which can be applied to test items scored 0 or 1. Each item in the model is described by three parameters: the c-parameter is the probability of

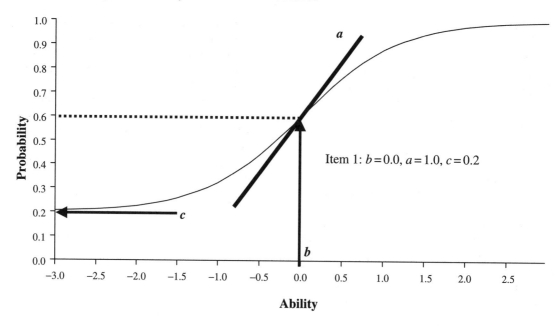

Figure 1.   A typical item characteristic curve for the three-parameter logistic model.

low-performing examinees answering an item correctly by guessing (0.20 is a typical value), the b-parameter is the point on the ability continuum where an examinee has a probability of $(1 + c)/2$ of giving a correct answer (this parameter corresponds to item difficulty in the classical test model), and the a-parameter is proportional to the slope of the curve at the point b on the ability continuum (this parameter corresponds to item discrimination in the classical test model). The particular values of the item parameters for any item determine the exact shape of the ICC. The choice of IRT model dictates the mathematical form of the ICCs and the number of item parameters in the model. With highly discriminating items, the kind of item a test developer wants, the ICCs are very steep; for easy items, the ICCs are shifted to the left end of the ability scale, and for hard items, the ICCs are shifted to the right end. It is typical to scale ability scores to a mean of zero and a standard deviation of one in research work. For score reporting, a more convenient scale is used – one without decimals and negatives.

ICCs for dichotomously scored items (e.g. correct/incorrect or true/false) are typically described by one, two, or three parameters. The number of parameters identifies the IRT model. With the popular Rasch model, or one-parameter

model, items are described by a single item parameter, called the 'item difficulty statistic'. This would mean that all of the test items would have the same shape, but the items could vary in their difficulty. With the two- and three-parameter models, items have more degrees of freedom for fitting data – but with improved fit and flexibility, come complications in parameter estimation.

Figure 2 highlights another attractive feature of IRT models. It is the concept of 'item information'. Here, the contribution an item makes to the precision of ability estimation at each ability level can be determined. The item shown in Figure 2 will be most effective for estimating ability of examinees in the interval, say, between about −0.50 and 1.0. The sum of the item information curves for items selected in a test produces the test information curve which indicates the precision of ability estimation at each point along the ability continuum.

Within an IRT measurement system, ability estimates for an examinee obtained from tests which vary in difficulty will be the same, except for the usual measurement errors. Some samples of items are more useful for assessing ability, and therefore the corresponding errors associated with ability estimation will be smaller. But the ability parameter being estimated is the same

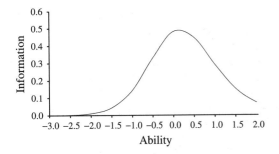

Figure 2. The item information curve corresponding to the item characteristic curve shown in Figure 1.

across items unlike in classical test theory where the person parameter of interest, true score, is test dependent. This invariance feature in the ability parameter is obtained by incorporating information about the items into the ability estimation process. Sample invariant ability estimates are of immense value in testing because tests can be matched to the ability level of examinees to minimize errors of measurement and maximize test appropriateness, while at the same time, comparisons in ability scores can be made because the ability estimates are *not* test dependent.

The concept that ability and item parameters do not change as a result of different samples of persons and items is known as *ability parameter invariance* and *item parameter invariance*, respectively. In theory, this is because when the item parameters are estimated, ability estimates are used in the item parameter estimation process (which is not the case in classical test theory). Also, when examinees' abilities are estimated, item parameter estimates are incorporated in that process (again, this is not the case in classical test theory). Both ability estimates and item statistics are reported on the same scale, so they look different from classical test scores and item statistics. Finally, IRT provides a direct way to estimate measurement error at each ability estimate (score level). In classical test theory, it is common to report a single estimate of error, known as the standard error of measurement, and apply that error to all examinees. Clearly, such an approach is less satisfactory than producing an error estimate at each ability score level.

IRT models (e.g. the one-, two-, and three-parameter logistic models) provide both invariant item statistics and ability estimates. Both features

are of considerable value to test developers because they open up new directions for assessment such as adaptively administered tests and item banking. Of course, the feature of *invariance* will not always be present. Item and ability parameter invariance will be obtained when there is (at least) a reasonable fit between the chosen IRT model and the test data. Not surprisingly, then, considerable importance is attached to determining the fit of an IRT model to the test data. This point is addressed briefly in the next section.

There are IRT models to handle nominal, ordinal and equal-interval educational and psychological data: one-, two-, and three-parameter normal ogive and logistic models; partial credit and graded response models; multidimensional normal ogive and logistic models; cognitive component models; rating scale model; nominal response model; and many more. There are at least 50 IRT models in the measurement literature (see, for example, van der Linden & Hambleton, 1997).

MODEL FIT AND IRT SOFTWARE

Details on item and ability parameter estimation can be found in Embretson and Reise (2000) and Hambleton, Swaminathan, and Rogers (1991). As for IRT software, Assessment Systems Corporation has provided a great service to the measurement profession by collecting books and software from many of the publishers and making them available through their own catalogue (see www.assess.com). In addition, they publish the MicroCAT System and IRT parameter estimation software (e.g. ASCAL, RASCAL). Some of the Rasch model and its extensions software (e.g. FACETS and BIGSTEP) can be obtained from MESA at the University of Chicago. Other publishers of software include Scientific Software (e.g. MULTILOG, PARSCALE) and Computer Adaptive Technologies (CAT), Inc.

Figure 3 shows an example of how model fit at the item level can be addressed. The item characteristic curve is estimated and assumed to be correct. For intervals along the ability continuum (denoted 1, 2, 3, 4, 5, 6 and 7 in the figure) the actual item performance of examinees in each interval is calculated. A comparison is made between the actual item

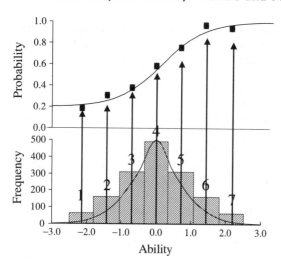

Figure 3. Assessing model fit.

performance and the predictions assuming the model to be true, and when the differences between actual item performance and predictions assuming the model to be true are small, as they are in Figure 3, the model is considered to fit the available data. Normally, what is desired in these model fit studies are differences (called 'item residuals') to be small and randomly distributed around the ICC. Of course the process must be repeated for each item, and there are many other analyses that are often carried out to investigate model fit including studies to assess the assumption of unidimensionality, and checks on item and ability parameter invariance. Statistical tests are also available.

FUTURE PERSPECTIVES AND CONCLUSIONS

Presently, item response models, especially the one- and three-parameter logistic models for analysing 0–1 data, are receiving increasing use from testing agencies. Other models not discussed here are models for handling polytomous response data and multidimensional data (see, for example, van der Linden & Hambleton, 1997). Measurement specialists are also exploring the uses of IRT in preparing computerized banks of test questions and in computer-administered and computer-adaptive tests.

The various applications have been sufficiently successful that researchers in the IRT field have shifted their attention from a consideration of IRT model advantages and disadvantages in relation to classical test theory to consideration of such IRT technical problems as goodness-of-fit investigations, model selection, parameter estimation, and steps for carrying out particular applications. Certainly some issues and technical problems remain to be solved in the IRT field, but it would seem that item response model technology is more than adequate at this time to serve a variety of uses in the testing field. Useful introductory references include Embretson and Reise (2000), Hambleton, Swaminathan, and Rogers (1991) and Wright and Stone (1979). For more advanced material, Hambleton and Swaminathan (1985) and van der Linden and Hambleton (1997) may be suitable.

References

Anastasi, A. (1989). *Psychological Testing* (6th ed.). New York: Macmillan.

Embretson, S.E. & Reise, S.P. (2000). *Item Response Theory for Psychologists*. Mahwah, NJ: Lawrence Erlbaum Associates, Publishers.

Gulliksen, H. (1950). *Theory of Mental Tests*. New York: Wiley.

Hambleton, R.K. & Swaminathan, H. (1985). *Item Response Theory: Principles and Applications*. Boston: Kluwer Academic Publishers.

Hambleton, R.K., Swaminathan, H. & Rogers, H.J. (1991). *Fundamentals of Item Response Theory*. Newbury Park, CA: Sage Publications.

van der Linden, W.J. & Hambleton, R.K. (Eds.) (1997). *Handbook of Modern Item Response Theory*. New York: Springer-Verlag.

Wright, B.D. & Stone, M.H. (1979). *Best Test Design*. Chicago: MESA.

Ronald K. Hambleton and Michael Jodoin

RELATED ENTRIES

Adaptive and Tailored Testing, Automated Test Assembly Systems, Classical Test Theory, Computer-Based Testing, Multidimensional Item Response Theory.

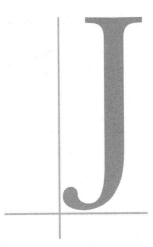

J

JOB CHARACTERISTICS

Motivation and achievement at work is an interactive phenomenon it results from the intricate interplay between characteristics of the job and characteristics of the person. The nature of job characteristics, though, is changing at a much faster pace than personality variables. Job changes are related to changing organizational designs and structures, caused by environmental pressures, such as the increased globalization, rapid technological changes and tougher competition. The increased reliance on autonomous but temporary teams leaves fewer clearly defined job positions. Consequently, the area of research on job characteristics has become more challenging than ever. There is a strong need for conceptualizing dimensions of job characteristics which are universal and stable in a period of transition, filled with both a lot of uncertainty and arising opportunities.

INTRODUCTION

Two broad orientations and theoretical preconceptions may be distinguished when describing job characteristics. The first orientation is job-oriented and yields information about job outputs, guidelines, job contexts and tasks. Examples for this approach, which are provided in the section about tests, are the *Job Diagnostic Survey* (JDS), and *Functional Job Analysis* (FJA).

The second orientation is worker oriented and yields information about aptitudes, abilities, critical incidents, behaviours and personality traits needed for succeeding in a particular job. Examples given in the section about tests are the *Position Analysis Questionnaire* (PAQ), the *Holland Position Classification Inventory* (PCI) and critical incident techniques like *Behavioural Expectation Scales* (BES).

Both approaches are complementary. Thus, job-oriented information can be used for drawing inferences about worker characteristics, and worker-oriented information can be used for gaining insights about jobs. The former has been demonstrated by Gottfredson (1997): job complexity is increasing with technological change and globalization. It follows, that intelligence or general mental abilities must be increasingly critical for success, which is indeed the case. The latter has been illustrated by the work of Holland (1997). His theory began with a worker-oriented, personality test approach, but over the years has moved toward an ecological, job-oriented perspective. Gottfredson and Holland (1996) classified all occupations in the *Dictionary of Occupational Titles*, which is based on FJA, in terms of a personality typology. Thus, jobs may also be described as 'personality niches' that elicit, develop and reward basic patterns of interests, competencies and behaviours (Gottfredson & Richards, 1999).

JOB CHARACTERISTICS IN A CHANGING ECONOMY

Jobs are the building blocks of organizations (Ghorpade, 1988). If organizations have to change, job characteristics must also change. In fact, technological changes and globalization tend to affect jobs first, which consequently become the building blocks of organizational change (see Figure 1).

In times of rapid changes, the following questions arise: what will change in job requirements? Can new performance patterns be foreseen or already perceived? Which job characteristic dimensions will be or will remain useful? The differentiation of job-oriented and worker-oriented approaches will be of heuristic value to gain some answers to these questions.

A Worker-Oriented Approach to Job Characteristics

Holland's theory (1997) provides a parallel way of describing people and environments since environmental profiles are characterized in ways analogous to personality profiles. The six environmental models are described in Table 1.

It is predicted that occupations will reflect particular patterns of job characteristics and rewards depending on which of the Holland environmental models they most resemble. It is further predicted that workers will be attracted to environments which closely match their personality. Thus, people are motivated to create congruence between their personality type and their working environment. It should be mentioned, however, that job choices are often also based on choices by significant others, driven by market forces, risk considerations, and are by no means so deliberate and conscious as the Holland model suggests.

Will the Holland model provide a useful description of a job characteristics dimension as well as the interaction of person and environment in the future? It can be expected that one of the most pervasive influences of technological innovations and globalization on job characteristics from a worker-oriented perspective may be sketched as follows: jobs will be less consistent

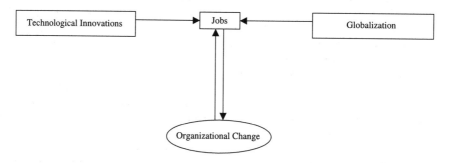

Figure 1.   Jobs as building blocks of change.

Table 1.   The six environmental models in Holland's theory (see Holland, 1997: 43–48)

Environment	Demands, values and competencies
Realistic	Using machines and tools; technical competencies; rewards people for having traditional values
Investigative	Symbolic, systematic, and creative investigations; scientific and mathematical competencies; rewards people to be complex, abstract and independent
Artistic	Create art forms or products; creativity; rewards people for enjoying ambiguous, free, unsystemized activities
Social	Inform, train, develop, cure others; empathy; rewards people for seeing the world in flexible ways
Enterprising	Selling or leading others; dominance and speaking abilities; rewards people for striving for power and status
Conventional	Ordered and systematic manipulation of data; clerical competencies; rewards people for being dependable and conformist

and differentiated in terms of the personality types they demand. Thus, job environments will represent more diverse demands and rewards, and the gap between the highest and lowest of the six job aspects described in Table 1 will decrease.

This is illustrated by the increased reliance on autonomous but temporary teams and fewer clearly defined job positions in the new economy. For example, many jobs today are organized around the 'cross-functional team' where technicians, computer experts, scientists, marketing specialists and human resource managers closely work together to create new business solutions. Consequently, no single type as described in Table 1 suffices to describe all demands, values and competencies needed in a 'cross-functional team'. Thus, jobs in the new economy will probably be more undifferentiated and thus less narrow concerning the involved personality traits than traditional jobs. They will stimulate and afford a wider range of behaviours, beliefs, and competencies on the one hand, but also provide more ambiguous guidance (Weinert, 2001). In an extreme case, a 'cross-functional team' may demand and reward all six Holland environments at close points in time and may actually ask for all six personality types. Nevertheless, differentiation will remain a valid job characteristics dimension. Undifferentiated job environments which demand, for example, Artistic, Enterprising, and Investigative competencies at neighbouring points in time will be a challenge both for job-analysis as well as for personnel selection.

Job environments in the new economy may function like a melting pot for diverse personality traits and behaviours in organizations. This is unlikely, though, for another trait – intelligence. Already in the past the major distinction among jobs has been their general intellectual complexity level (Gottfredson, 1997). This is shown by factor analysis of job analysis data revealing that the first factor obtained is the mental complexity of the work required from workers to perform. For example, attributes loading highly on this factor are the PAQ factors *using various information sources*, and *communicating judgements*. Also high-level information-processing activities according to FJA – like compiling, planning, reasoning and decision making – are highly correlated with patterns of intelligence. There is strong evidence that technological change as well as globalization

both make jobs increasingly intelligence-loaded. Jobs become more and more enriched by content-diverse mental tasks involving learning, problem solving, and information processing, which is the essence of intelligence.

Where the old industrial economy rewarded mass production of standardized products for large markets, the new post-industrial economy rewards the timely customization and delivery of high-quality, convenient products for increasingly specialized markets. Where the old economy broke work in to narrow, routinized, and closely supervised tasks, the new economy increasingly requires workers to work in cross-functional teams, gather information, make decisions, and undertake diverse, changing, and challenging sets of tasks in a fast-changing and dynamic global market. (Gottfredson, 1997: 121)

From a worker oriented view of job analysis, thus, general mental ability as a highly general information-processing capacity has been one of the most critical personality characteristics for being successful in a wide range of jobs, and will be increasingly so. Over the decades, strong evidence has accumulated that there appear to be minimum IQ patterns that increase steadily with job level and rise constantly with time. It can be expected that jobs will uniformly demand higher general mental ability on the one hand and more diverse social competencies, traits, and values on the other hand.

A Job-Oriented Approach to Job Characteristics

A job-oriented approach is devoted to the content of jobs. An example is the research concerning the Job Characteristic Model (JCM) of Hackman and Oldham (1976, 1980). This job design theory identifies five core job characteristics: task identity, task significance, skill variety, feedback from the job and from agents and autonomy. According to Hackman and Oldham, these job characteristics give rise to three psychological states (feelings of meaningfulness of the work, knowledge of results achieved and responsibility for one's own work outcomes) which in turn affect personal work outcomes of the job incumbent like general satisfaction and internal motivation. Thus, the JCM is devoted to the motivational capacity of a job.

All five job characteristics can be combined to create an index of overall job complexity, and as has been argued above, technological innovations as well as globalization increases complexity of jobs. Advanced manufacturing technology makes it possible for workers to produce large parts of or even whole products (task identity), and often demands cross-functional manufacturing solutions (skill variety). Skill variety is also increased since people will often not remain in one job or area of speciality for a long period of time (Weinert, 2001). 'Boundaryless' career principles like protean careers and career ownership will result in greater autonomy in the job. 'High involvement work teams' coordinate schedule, and distribute the work on their own, giving the individual a large amount of responsibility and independence. Tougher competition between organizations for talented employees results in more feedback from agents, as is indicated by the increasing use of '360-Degree-Feedbacks' in many organizations. It seems like an open question, though, if changing organizational designs and structures as reaction to increasingly specialized markets will also lead to more task significance.

While the five core job characteristics identified by JCM are clearly of relevance also in the new economy, it has been criticized because of its limitation for advanced manufacturing technology. Jackson et al. (1993) have proposed a set of other job characteristics as significant determinants of employee well-being and performance which are listed in Table 2.

Another important job characteristic is production uncertainty which may be defined as the degree to which a qualified incumbent faces unexpected problems in the course of job performance (Wright & Cordery, 1999). As mentioned above, contemporary work systems are increasingly characterized by instability and unpredictability. Uncertainty should receive explicit treatment as a variable within job analysis since it may moderate the impact of other job

characteristics on personal work outcomes. For example, affective well-being seems to decline under more traditional job designs as uncertainty increases, but seems to increase under empowered job designs (Wright & Cordery, 1999).

The JCM may also be criticized because of its individualistic bias. Cross-cultural research suggests that social interdependence is an attribute with significant motivating potential especially in collectivistic cultures (Marcus & Kitayama, 1991). Job attributes which effect a response of experiencing responsibility for the work of others are increasingly important also in countries with an individualistic background, but have yet received too little attention. Van der Vegt et al. (1998) distinguished between initiated task interdependence, received task interdependence, and outcome interdependence, and report substantial and combined effects of the three social interdependence dimensions on personal work outcomes of individual team members. Note that the three social interdependence dimensions affect personal work outcomes via *responsibility of others work*, a variable originally not included in the JCM.

In sum, the JCM will remain at the core of interest of job analysis. It should be supplemented, though, by job characteristics which reflect ongoing technological change (like problem-solving demand) and globalization (outcome interdependence).

TESTS

The function of job analysis is to clarify job responsibilities, to develop selection systems and to identify training needs. A large array of instruments is available today to meet these functions. Table 3 provides a brief overview over some frequently used tests and procedures.

Table 2. Job characteristics which are significant especially for advanced manufacturing technology (see Jackson et al., 1993)

Job characteristic	Description
Timing control	Opportunity to determine the scheduling of his or her work behaviour
Method control	Individual choice in how to carry out given tasks
Monitoring demand	The extent of passive monitoring required
Problem-solving demand	Cognitive processing required to prevent or recover errors
Production responsibility	The cost of errors in terms of lost output and damage to equipment

Table 3. Frequently used tests and procedures in job analysis and some of their advantages and disadvantages

Test/procedure	Advantages	Disadvantages
Position Analysis Questionnaire (PAQ, McCormick, Jeanneret & Mecham, 1972)	Gives an understanding of cognitive job components	Provides little information regarding the non-cognitive characteristics that are fundamental to perform
Holland Position Classification Inventory (PCI, Gottfredson & Holland, 1991)	Assigns scores to a job for each of the six Holland dimensions (Realistic, Investigative, Artistic, Social, Enterprising, and Conventional).	The six dimensions may be too broad for the definition of specific jobs
Behaviour Expectation Scales (BES, Smith & Kendall, 1963)	Offers a customized way of strategic job analysis; may have highly motivating effects on incumbents	Is time consuming; problems with transferability between different organizations or departments
Job Diagnostic Survey (JDS, Hackman & Oldham, 1975)	Offers an operationalization of the job characteristic model	May not be valid in societies and organizations with a collectivistic/interdependent background

Probably the most frequently used instrument of a worker-oriented job analysis is the PAQ (McCormick, Jeanneret & Mecham, 1972). The PAQ primarily measures information-processing demands of the worker in the job and gives us an understanding of cognitive job components. It provides little information, though, regarding the non-cognitive characteristics that are fundamental to perform.

The latter is addressed more directly by the recently developed PCI (Gottfredson & Holland, 1991), which is an application of Holland's theoretical formulations in classifying jobs. The PCI is designed to assign scores to a job for each of the six Holland dimensions (Realistic, Investigative, Artistic, Social, Enterprising, and Conventional). Respondents are asked to indicate what people have to do in their job, what are the personal characteristics and skills exercised, and what personal values are expressed. Maurer and Tarulli (1997) were able to show that the PCI yields expected correlations between traditional job analysis variables and the Holland constructs. For example, *variety* and *autonomy* were positively related to the Investigative and Artistic dimensions and negatively related to the Conventional construct. De Fruyt and Mervielde (1999) demonstrated the fruitfulness of the PCI environmental typology also from the perspective of the Big Five model of personality description.

Worker-oriented approaches to describing job characteristics will remain influential, because personality characteristics like intelligence, extraversion or conscientiousness have a strong genetic component and will be important for jobs at any time in human evolution. As has been mentioned above, though, it can be expected that workers will have to exercise a wider range of personal characteristics in the new economy. The PCI could be too undifferentiated to describe most of these personal characteristics fundamental to perform in the future.

Job-oriented approaches also face a problem: we need to do job analysis for jobs which do not exist yet (Schneider & Konz, 1989). Thus, in times when new jobs can be created almost overnight many practitioners need a flexible method of designing their own strategic job analysis. Behavioural Expectation Scales provide this flexibility since they are developed through an iterative procedure that results in scaled expectations of independent performance behaviours.

This technique, which involves three distinct steps, has been first reported by Smith and Kendall (1963). In the first step, behavioural episodes or critical incidents are generated which illustrate job performance dimensions. This first phase has been proven to be an excellent way of worker-oriented job analysis, especially if many organizational perspectives (managers, peers, subordinates, clients) are involved in the process of defining and clarifying success-critical behaviours for the job. The first phase of constructing BES is a meaningful job analysis for incumbents because they uniquely understand the jargon and situations used in the content of behavioural anchors. It also holds a high motivational potential, since it may be considered as an 'empowered' form of job analysis in the eyes of subordinates.

Also, the second and third phase may be considered as part of a job analysis. In the second step, the behavioural incidents are retranslated into performance dimensions. Incidents are retained only if they are reliably placed in the dimension for which they were generated. Needless to say all three phases are done by different people (around 10 per step). The third phase scales each remaining incident according to the level of performance it represents. In this last step, different perspectives between superiors and subordinates arise reflecting different perceptions of the job. However, only those incidents make up the final BES where inter-rater-agreement is at least 80% in the second and third step. This procedure results in worker-oriented job scales with excellent reliability and very high face validity and, thus, a common 'reference system' for all incumbents. A very advantageous side effect of BES is the motivation superiors and subordinates gain by constructing this common 'reference system'.

Another future-oriented job analysis process is an instrument based on the JCM (Hackman & Oldham, 1975). The JDS is designed to assess the motivational capacity of jobs. It contains items measuring the extent to which workers feel the characteristics are present in their job and statements about job characteristics on which workers must agree or disagree. There is considerable evidence that variations in the job characteristics measured by the JDS exert an influence on people's feelings and motivation at work. Job significance (the combined effect of task identity, task significance and skill variety) is positively correlated with meaningfulness of work. Feedback positively influences knowledge of results. Autonomy is positively associated with responsibility for own work (Van der Vegt et al., 1998). These job characteristics are also positively correlated with empowerment conceptualized as a gestalt of autonomy, competence, meaningfulness and impact (Gagné et al., 1997). Wright and Cordery (1999) showed that job characteristics leading to higher job control may positively influence intrinsic motivation and job satisfaction only under conditions of high production uncertainty.

Functional job analysis (FJA) has been in the forefront of analysing job characteristics since the 1930s. It will remain influential since it is based on a very simple theory: FJA systems are based on the notion that job situations call for some involvement on the part of the worker with data, people and things which are expressed through sets of common functions or activities. FJA currently consists of three systems: The Department of Labour system, Sydney Fine's Functional Job Analysis and the Job Information Matrix Systems (Ghorpade, 1988). All job analyses consist of defining functions of the job and placing them within the hierarchy of complexity. Figure 2 shows the hierarchy of worker functions in the Job Information Matrix Systems with the most complex function at the top and the least complex at the bottom.

FUTURE PERSPECTIVES

The area of research on job characteristics has become more challenging than ever in a rapidly changing economy. We often do job analysis for jobs which do not exist yet. This forces practitioners to conceptualize dimensions of job characteristics which are universal and stable, and which consequently hold the promise to be relevant also in the future. A worker-oriented job analysis seems to be adequate since personality variables are highly stable and will clarify job responsibilities also in the future. It has been noted, though, that there is no well-researched method for identifying personality characteristics for *specific* jobs. The Big-Five approach as well as the Holland types must be considered as too general to be linked to valid personality predictors of specific job performance. Five to six personality factors are sufficient only to define *job families*. In the future, we need to define job characteristics in terms of more specific personality descriptions as provided, for example, by the CPI.

There also is a strong need for more research on the universality and stability of job-oriented dimensions of job characteristics. For example, research concerning the JCM must demonstrate that the core job characteristics unfold their motivational capacity also in collectivistic societies and organizations. Since about 70% of the world's population comes from collectivistic societies this seems like a rather important question. A related topic is the following: some

Increasing complexity

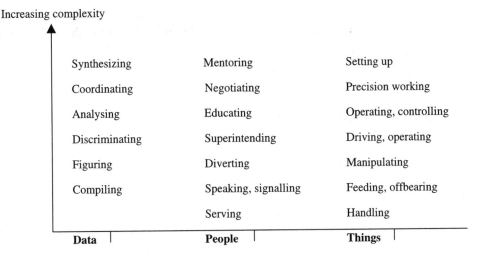

Data	People	Things
Synthesizing	Mentoring	Setting up
Coordinating	Negotiating	Precision working
Analysing	Educating	Operating, controlling
Discriminating	Superintending	Driving, operating
Figuring	Diverting	Manipulating
Compiling	Speaking, signalling	Feeding, offbearing
	Serving	Handling

Figure 2.   Worker functions (see Ghorpade, 1988: 237–254).

authors have suggested that the inclusion of non-task factors as independent variables in the JCM have important effects in many jobs which primarily consist of dealing with other people. For example, a study by Landeweerd and Boumans (1994) indicates that variables like job satisfaction, health complaints, and experienced significance of nurses can be better predicted if the JCM includes work dimensions like social-emotional leadership of the head nurse and patient attending. Since in post-industrial societies a rising percentage of jobs are in the customer service, the measurement of social relationships and interdependence as part of the job characteristics is of increasing importance.

CONCLUSIONS

Psychological job analysis will be able to prove its significance for the future if it becomes truly interdisciplinary. At a basic level, this means to fully appreciate that motivation and achievement at work is an interactive phenomena, which results from the intricate interplay between characteristics of the job and characteristics of the person. At a more general level, this also means to acknowledge influences of technological changes, globalization effects, migration and even demographic factors. Thus, research on job characteristics really seems to provide an exciting laboratory for related disciplines like psychology, sociology, business administration and job engineering.

References

De Fruyt, F. & Mervielde, I. (1999). RIASEC types and Big Five traits as predictors of employment status and nature of employment. *Personnel Psychology*, 52, 701–727.

Gagné, M., Senécal, C.B. & Koestner, R. (1997). Proximal job characteristics, feelings of empowerment, and intrinsic motivation: a multidimensional model. *Journal of Applied Social Psychology*, 27(14), 1222–1240.

Ghorpade, J. (1988). *Job Analysis. A Handbook for the Human Resource Manager*. Englewood Cliffs, NJ: Prentice-Hall.

Gottfredson, L.S. (1997). Why *g* matters: the complexity of everyday life. *Intelligence*, 24, 79–132.

Gottfredson, G.D. & Holland, J.L. (1991). *Position Classification Inventory Professional Manual*. Odessa, FL: Psychological Assessment Resources.

Gottfredson, G.D. & Holland, J.L. (1996). *Dictionary of Holland Occupational Codes*. Odessa, FL: Psychological Assessment Resources.

Gottfredson, L.S. & Richards, J.M. (1999). The meaning and measurement of environments in Holland's theory. *Journal of Vocational Behaviour*, 55(1), 57–73.

Hackman, J.R. & Oldham, G.R. (1975). Development of the job diagnostic survey. *Journal of Applied Psychology*, 60, 159–170.

Hackman, J.R. & Oldham, G.R. (1976). Motivation through the design of work: test of a theory. *Organizational Behaviour and Human Performance*, 16, 250–279.

Hackman, J.R. & Oldham, G.R. (1980). *Work Redesign*. Reading, MA: Addison Wesley.

Holland, J.L. (1997). *Making Vocational Choices: A Theory of Vocational Personalities and Work Environments*. Englewood Cliffs, NJ: Prentice-Hall.

Jackson, P.R., Wall, T.D., Martin, R. & Davids, K. (1993). New measures of job control, cognitive demand, and production responsibility. *Journal of Applied Psychology, 78*(5), 753–762.

Landeweerd, J.A. & Boumans, N.P.G. (1994). The effect of work dimensions and need for autonomy on nurses' work satisfaction and health. *Journal of Occupational and Organizational Psychology, 67*(3), 207–217.

Markus, H.M. & Kitayama, S. (1991). Culture and the self: implications for cognition, emotion and motivation. *Psychological Review, 98*, 224–253.

Maurer, T.J. & Tarulli, B.A. (1997). Managerial work, job analysis, and Holland's RIASEC vocational environment dimensions. *Journal of Vocational Behaviour, 50*(3), 365–381.

McCormick, E.J., Jeanneret, P.R. & Mecham, R.C. (1972). A study of job characteristics and job dimensions as based on the position analysis questionnaire (PAQ). *Journal of Applied Psychology, 56*, 347–368.

Schneider, B. & Konz, A.M. (1989). Strategic job analysis. *Human Resource Management, 28*(1), 51–63.

Smith, P.C. & Kendall, L.M. (1963). Retranslation of expectations: an approach to the construction of unambiguous anchors for rating scales. *Journal of Applied Psychology, 47*, 149–155.

Van der Vegt, G., Emans, B. & Van De Vliert, E. (1998). Motivating effects of task and outcome interdependence in work teams. *Group & Organization Management, 23*(2), 124–143.

Weinert, A.B. (2001). The psychology of career development. In Smelser, N.J. & Baltes, P.B. (Eds.), *The International Encyclopedia of the Social & Behavioural Sciences. 3*, 1471–1476. New York: Elsevier Science.

Wright, B.M. & Cordery, J.L. (1999). Production uncertainty as contextual moderator of employee reactions to job design. *Journal of Applied Psychology, 84*(3), 456–463.

David Scheffer

RELATED ENTRIES

J | JOB STRESS

INTRODUCTION

Job Stress Assessment (JSA) stands for methods claiming to capture stress in occupational settings. Consequently, JSA deals with phenomena occurring at work, like drop in performance and productivity, psychological and somatic complaints as well as health disorders attributed to work conditions. These phenomena are conceived as the result of a process called stress which is induced by stressors and leads to strain (stress reactions).

ASSESSMENT APPROACHES AND MODELS

Basic Common Assumptions of Stress Models

In the history of stress research (see e.g. Appley & Trumbell, 1986) some approaches focused on physiological and behavioural response patterns as stress reactions (e.g. Cannon, Mason, Selye, Levi, Frankenhaeuser, Ursin) and some identified and differentiated stressors (e.g. Dohrenwend). Others promoted the modelling of the mediating stress process between stressors and strain as an interactional or even transactional process indicating the individual coping behaviour in a given situation (Lazarus, Cox, McGrath).

There is agreement that JSA should consider all aspects mentioned below (see e.g. Cox & Griffiths, 1999; Chmiel, 2000; Schabracqu et al., 1996): characteristics of the job in relation to the individual and situational resources, mentioned as demand–resource discrepancies (stressors), the efficiency of compensatory regulation (coping), motivational patterns of conflict and negative emotions (strain) and long term effects on health (disorders).

There are two mainstreams of approaches with different topics and methods (Gaillard, 1993): the 'experimental' approach on the background of cognitive and physiological psychology focuses on mental load, whereas the 'correlational' approach of social and health psychology concentrates on affective well-being, complaints and psychosomatic disorders. Therefore, we differentiate between mental load models corresponding with the 'experimental' approach and health models related to the 'correlational' approach.

Mental Load Models

These models are dealing with the imbalance between task demands and individual resources and the coping behaviour resulting from it. They either focus on effort-regulation (Hockey, 1997; Sanders, 1983; see Gaillard, 1993), problem solving (Hockey, 1997; Schönpflug in Appley & Trumbell, 1986) or multiple level hierarchy of regulatory control (Frese & Zapf, 1994; see Semmer in Schabracqu et al., 1996). The models differ with respect to the sort of job and personal characteristics. Sanders' cognitive energetics model considers task variables and energetic resources, while Hockey's compensatory control model, just like Schönpflug's economic approach, relates task and environmental variables to the management of effort and performance regulation. Various types of data are obtained: performance data (reaction time, errors), self-assessment data (subjective load measures) and physiological data of different systems, e.g. the cardiovascular system, the adrenocortical (cortisol) and adrenomedullar system (adrenaline, noradrenaline) and, recently, the immune system. The methods are from the same type when dealing with workload assessment (see Tattersdal in Chmiel, 2000). The action-oriented approach is methodologically somewhat different, however, describing performance patterns to fulfil task-related goals under limiting conditions (Semmer in Schabracqu et al., 1996).

Health Models

These models consider job features and their influences on job-related health (see Le Blanc et al., 2000 for the following references). They are mainly based on observational, interview and questionnaire data. According to the early Michigan Model (Kahn et al., 1964) psychological stressors develop from an imbalance between job characteristics and job expectancies which are related to individual resources. Stressors such as role conflict, role ambiguity and role overload lead to strains as precursors of psychosomatic complaints and psychosomatic diseases. Recent models assume patterns of job variables as predictably (linear, curvilinear) related to strain and mental health, e.g. the person–environment (P-E) fit model of French et al. (1982), Warr's vitamin model (1994), the job demand-control model of Karasek (1979), the demand control–support model by Johnson (1989) and the effort–reward imbalance model by Siegrist (1996).

OBJECTIVES AND MEASUREMENT INSTRUMENTS

JSA refers to the objectives listed below. Due to different mainstreams of approaches ranging from epidemiology to psychophysiology different types of instruments are deployed. For overviews (inclusively all references below) see Hurrell, Nelson and Simmons (1998), Dunckel (1999), Fahrenberg and Myrtek (2001).

Measuring Discrepancies between Demands and Resources

Measures of discrepancies between demands and resources can refer to job contents, working conditions, employment conditions or social relations at work. Within each category we can describe discrepancies between demands and resources. For instance, with regard to working conditions the following discrepancies can be described: the discrepancy between the demand at a given *time of day* and *energetic resources* (e.g. shift work, sleep deprivation, jet lag); between *time on task* and *capability of sustaining effort* (e.g. fatigue after long driving); between the *time pattern* of demand and *performing capability* (e.g. time pressure).

There are methodological aspects concerning the type of measurement which should be used:

- *Analytic–synthetic aspect*: Only feeble attempts have been made in measuring demand–resource discrepancies analytically so that measures for both, demands and resources, are considered. Instead, research is dominated by 'synthetic' job stressor measures which get their status by means of implicit assumptions about discrepancies.

- *Objective–subjective aspect*: By means of most job stressor measures, those conditions are identified as stressful which are perceived as aversive or which even have high incidence of strain. Consequently, it is controversially discussed how measures precisely separate antecendents (stressors) from consequences (appraisal, strain) (see Kasl, 1998). Objections are raised against self-report measures especially if they focus on transactional appraisal rather than on work. It seems that the more specifically we study a job the more input is made to get objective or even analytically derived measures.
- *Demand–resource aspect*: Sometimes job stressor measures are either conceived in terms of work-demand (e.g. time pressure) or in terms of resources (e.g. temporal degree of freedom). It remains indistinct whether the same phenomenon is measured.
- *Stressor–moderator aspect*: Often job variables are categorized into stressors (e.g. time pressure) and moderators (e.g. type A personality, low social support). The distinction, however, only makes sense for testable models, e.g. when hypotheses on intermediate processes between stimulus and the final response can be studied. From a demand–resource discrepancy perspective, the moderator-variables belong to resources (individual, situational). Consequently, if there are different sources of discrepancies the pattern of those should be regarded.

Analytical Approaches

- *Laboratory job simulation studies* are suitable to identify demand–resource discrepancies analytically, e.g. the simulation of an office job (Schönpflug; see Chmiel, 2000) allows determination of the demand–resource discrepancy by measuring the number of task operations per time and the capacity of working memory under the influence of situational capacity limiting conditions (noise, negative feedback).
- *Job surveys* may be analytically designed if a theory gives criteria explicitly for the evaluation of discrepancies as models like the action theory does (TDS; Semmer in Schabracqu et al., 1996).

Observational Job Stressor Measures

Observational methods for job analyses are based on observation of job processes and interviews with job incumbents and supervisors (see Dunckel, 1998). Deployed methods are:

- PAQ – Position Analysis Questionnaire (Mecham, McCormick & Jeanneret; see Hurrell et al., 1998): stressors like repetitive work, shift work, physical discomfort, vigilant tasks, worker autonomy etc. Adaptations in non-English speaking countries, e.g. the German FAT and AET (see Dunckel, 1999), also new developments, e.g. the German TAI (see Dunckel, 1999).
- TBS – activity evaluation system (Hacker et al., 1995; see Dunckel, 1999), an instrument based on action theory: temporal and procedural degree of freedom etc. (26 scales [s]).
- ISTA – instrument for stress-related task analysis, observational version in analogy to a self-report version with the intention to apply both, objective and subjective, measures (German: see Dunckel, 1999): task complexity, task variability etc. (19s).

Self-Report Measures

Most methods are based on self-reports of employees (see review by Hurrell, Nelson & Simmons, 1998).

- SDS – Stress Diagnostic Survey (Ivancevich & Matteson, 1984): role demands, workload, time pressure, task demands, etc. (15s).
- WES – Work Environment Scale (Moos, 1981) assesses the perception of work climate: work pressure, control, task orientation, peer cohesion, etc. (10s).
- JCQ – Job Content Questionnaire (Karasek, 1985); refers to Karasek's model: psychological job demand (workload and role conflict), skill utilization, job decision latitude (3s).
- OSInv – Occupational Stress Inventory (Osipow & Davis, 1988): role overload, role insufficiency, role ambiguity, role

boundary, responsibility, physical environment (6s).

- OSInd – Occupational Stress Index (Cooper, Sloan & Williams, 1988): job and organizational characteristics (6s); revision: PMI – Pressure Management Index (Williams & Cooper, 1998).
- GJSQ – Generic Job Stress Questionnaire (Hurrell & McLaney, 1988): workload, responsibility, role demands, etc. (13s).
- JSS – Job Stress Survey (Spielberger, 1994): Severity and frequency for job pressure and organizational support (2s).
- JDS – Job Diagnostic Survey (Hackman & Oldham, 1975): feedback, task significance, task variety, task identity, interaction with coworkers, autonomy (6s).
- ISTA (see above).

Measuring Efficiency of Compensatory Regulation

The stress process develops when the applied coping strategies are inefficient in managing the discrepancies between demand and resources. Costs of performance protection may be additional regulation expenditure (effort, time, strategies), new problems and demands (e.g. not in time), changed goals, reduced aspiration levels, and negative external feedback.

Laboratory Work Simulation Studies

Well controlled experimental studies are needed to describe processes related to compensatory control and its efficiency. Examples are laboratory work simulation experiments on performance and suboptimal energetic resources and on resource management under stress (e.g. Hockey in Chmiel, 2000). Usually, the costs of compensatory control in protecting performance are studied in experimental settings by measuring the following behavioural patterns:

- *Performance measures* focus on secondary performance decrements (selective impairment of low-priority task components, neglect of subsidiary activities, attentional narrowing) and strategy changes (shift to simpler procedures).
- *Subjective and physiological measures of regulatory costs* indicate increase of effort

(e.g. SWAT – subjective work load assessment; TLX – task load index: see Chmiel, 2000; heart rate variability) and fatigue (e.g. eye-lid parameters: see Backs & Boucsein, 2000).

- *Behavioural measures* relate to post-task preference for low-effort activities, risky decision making etc.

Analyses in Occupational Settings

Some of the self-report job stressor instruments include measures of coping, e.g. OSInd: coping strategies. Occasionally, self-report measures of coping strategies are obtained (e.g. in form of diaries) in field studies focusing on transactional processes. However, elaborated methods are not available. Attempts to incorporate scales of coping have not been successful due to unsufficient reliability.

Motivational Pattern of Conflict and Negative Emotions

As a consequence of inefficient coping, a motivational pattern results which is characterized through the hopelessness of reaching goals, the conflict between goals, e.g. the ambivalence to engage sufficiently in coping, a state of emotional tension and job dissatisfaction, and low competence to regulate negative emotions. Epidemiologists use questionnaires and interviews. Psychophysiologists study physiological response patterns.

Self-Report Measures

Some examples of a large variety of self-report measures follow (for a review see Hurrell et al., 1998):

- Emotional tension (tense, anxious, worried, non-calm, -relaxed, -contented)
  - STAI – State–Trait–Anxiety Inventory (Spielberger et al., 1970)
  - Index of job-related anxiety (Caplan et al., 1975) on the basis of STAI
- Fatigue (fatigued, tired, weary, non-alert, -energetic, -lively)
  - Subscale of many mood adjective check lists (e.g. ADCL by Thayer)

- Other mood aspects, like depression, anger-hostility etc.

  - Adjective check lists: POMS – Profile of mood states (McNair et al., 1971), and similar versions

- Physiological complaints

  - Symptom lists, like the GHQ and SCL (see below), CMI – Cornell Medical Index (Brodenan et al., 1949), FBL – Freiburg complaints list (see Fahrenberg & Myrtek, 2001)

- Job dissatisfaction: subscales in JCQ, ISTA.

Physiological Response Measures

Measurement procedures for the following physiological systems can be found in, e.g., Backs and Boucsein (2000) or Fahrenberg and Myrtek (2001).

- Cardiovascular activity: e.g. blood pressure, heart rate variability, emotional heart rate
- Hormonal activity: catecholamines (noradrenaline, adrenaline) in blood or urine, cortisol in serum and saliva
- Immunological indices: immunoglobulines and cytokines.

Measuring Long Term Effects on Health

Research is focused on chronic states of mental and somatic disorders. Special interest refers to the burnout syndrome: 'a state of physical, emotional and mental exhaustion caused by long term involvement in emotionally demanding situations' (Pines & Aronson, 1988). With respect to diseases emphasis has been placed on coronary heart disease. However, also diseases of other systems have been studied, e.g. the respiratory system and the gastro-intestinal system. Nowadays diseases of the immune system are of increasing interest.

Self-Report Measures

Examples of frequently used self-report measures are (for a review, see Hurrell et al., 1998):

- SCL – Symptom-Distress Checklist (Derogatis, 1977): somatization, hostility,

phobic anxiety, depression, paranoid ideation, etc. (9s).
- GHQ – General Health Questionnaire (Goldberg, 1978): (4–8s).
- BM – Burnout Measure: physical, emotional and mental exhaustion (Pines & Aronson, 1988) (3s).
- MBI – Maslach Burnout Inventory (Maslach & Jackson, 1986): emotional exhaustion, depersonalization, personal accomplishment (3s).

Objective Measures

These measures include parameters of physiological response patterns (see above) and behavioural indices, like stress-related absenteeism, consumption of drugs, alcohol and nicotine.

Summary

Table 1 gives a summarized overview of typical and frequently used JSA measures mentioned above.

METHODOLOGICAL PERSPECTIVES

Combined Field and Laboratory Studies

A combination of field and laboratory studies may be an efficient methodology to improve our knowledge about job stress and the methodology of testing hypotheses. Field studies describe phenomena of a certain type of job stress and laboratory studies test the assumed interrelations between stressors and strains. Examples are provided by studies on office workers (e.g. see Schönpflug in Appley & Trumbell, 1986).

Analysis of Causal and Temporal Sequences

Experimental research is explicitly concerned with detecting causal and temporal sequences between stressors and strains. Correlational survey studies referring to the wide range between stressors and health problems often confine to causal and temporal interpretations. There are, however, testing procedures and statistical methods available which allow such

Table 1.   Job stress assessment: summarized overview of measures with regard to objectives

Objectives	Measures			
	Registration	Observation	Self-report	Combined measures
Discrepancies: demands–resources (stressors)	R within AM	PAQ, TBS,	SDS, WES, JCQ, OSInv, OSInd, GJSQ, JSS, JDS	ISTA: O-S
Efficiency: compensatory regulation (coping)	TM: secondary task efficiency and strategy BM: post-task preferences PM: Indices of effort and fatigue		Effort: SWAT, TLX Coping: OSInd	
Motivational pattern of conflict and negative emotions (strain)	PM: response pattern		Tension: STAI Fatigue: ADCL Mood: POMS Complaints: GHQ, SCL, FBL Job dissatisfaction: JCQ, ISTA	
Long term effects on health (disorders)	BM: absenteeism PM: response pattern		GHQ, SCL; BM, MBI	
Combined objectives	AM		AM	AM

Abbreviations: R – Registration, O – Observation, S – Self-report, AM – Ambulatory monitoring, BM – Behavioural measures, TM – Task-performance measures, PM – Physiological measures

interpretations to be tested (e.g. Frese, 1985). As long as job stress assessment is to a large extent based upon subjective reports, causal and temporal sequence conclusions cannot be drawn unless method variance due to response sets and styles (e.g. negative affectivity bias) is tested. Analytical research designs and data analysing methods, e.g. using structural equation models, are available.

Ambulatory Monitoring as a Bridge between Surveys and Laboratory Testing

Today and even more in the future, portable equipment and enhanced methodology does and will allow objective real life assessment of job conditions as well as behavioural and physiological activity (see Fahrenberg & Myrtek, 1996, 2001). These objective measures become less expensive and difficult to obtain in comparison to the so far cheaper, more easily available and more convenient self-report measures. By means of ambulatory monitoring it is possible to study the processes at work more directly as by means of surveys. In comparison to laboratory studies

they have the advantage of greater external validity. Furthermore, longitudinal studies are more feasible to design. Exactly these are needed to study the development from strain to diseases. Finally, ambulatory monitoring may bring together the two approaches, mental load and health models.

FUTURE PERSPECTIVES AND CONCLUSIONS

So far, job stress assessment comprises models and methods belonging to a wide range of approaches like epidemiology and psychophysiology, correlational and experimental methodology, micro-level and macro-level analysis. We should enhance interaction and communication between the approaches. Models and methods for job stress assessment have to be referred to a more ecological and concrete context of occupational jobs. Both will improve the more stress will be longitudinally studied as the process between demand–resource discrepancies and disorders.

References

Appley, M.H. & Trumbell, R. (Eds.) (1986). *Dynamics of Stress. Physiological, Psychological and Social Perspectives*. New York: Plenum.

Backs, R.W. & Boucsein, W. (Eds.) (2000) *Engineering Psychophysiology*. London: Erlbaum.

Chmiel, N. (Ed.) (2000). *Work and Organizational Psychology*. Oxford: Blackwell.

Cox, T. & Griffiths, A. (1999). The nature and measurement of work stress: theory and practice. In Wilson, J.R. & Corlett, E.N. (Eds.) (1999). *Evaluation of Human Work*. London: Taylor and Francis.

Dunckel, H. (Ed.) (1999). *Handbuch Psychologischer Arbeitsanalyseverfahren*. Zürich: vdf Hochschulverlag.

Fahrenberg, J. & Myrtek, M. (Eds.) (1996). *Ambulatory Assessment: Computer-Assisted Psychological and Psychophysiological Methods in Monitoring and Field Studies*. Seattle: Hogrefe & Huber.

Fahrenberg, J. & Myrtek, M. (Eds.) (2001). *Progress in Ambulatory Assessment*. Seattle: Hogrefe & Huber.

Frese, M. (1985). Stress at work and psychosomatic complaints: a causal interpretation. *Journal of Applied Psychology*, 70, 314–328.

Gaillard, A.W.K. (1993). Comparing the concepts of mental load and stress. *Ergonomics*, 9, 991–1005.

Hockey, G.R.J. (1997). Compensatory control in the regulation of human performance under stress and high work load: a cognitive-energetical framework. *Biological Psychology*, 45, 73–93.

Hurrell, J.J., Nelson, D.L. & Simmons, B.L. (1998). Measuring job stressors and strains: where we have been, where we are, and where we need to go. *Journal of Occupational Health Psychology*, 3, 368–389.

Kasl, S.V. (1998). Measuring job stressors and studying the health impact of the work environment: an epidemiological commentary. *Journal of Occupational Health Psychology*, 3, 390–401.

Le Blanc, P., Jonge, J.de & Schaufeli, W. (2000). Job stress and health. In Chmiel, N. (Ed.), *Work and Organizational Psychology* (pp. 149–177). Oxford: Blackwell.

Schabracqu, M.J., Winnubst, J.A.M. & Cooper, C.L. (Eds.) (1996). *Handbook of Work and Health Psychology*. New York: Wiley.

Günter Debus and Maike Oppe

RELATED ENTRIES

APPLIED FIELDS: WORK AND INDUSTRY, STRESS, RISK AND PREVENTION IN WORK AND ORGANIZATIONAL SETTINGS, BURNOUT ASSESSMENT, CAREGIVER BURDEN

L LANDSCAPES AND NATURAL ENVIRONMENTS

INTRODUCTION

As commonly used in behavioural research, 'natural environment' refers to a large outdoor area with little or no apparent evidence of human presence or intervention (Pitt & Zube, 1987). In contrast, 'landscape' refers to a view over or into an area of land, or the area and landforms encompassed by a view (Daniel, 2001). Although research and practical efforts may focus on a landscape as the visual aspect of a natural environment, definitions of landscape often eschew the human exclusion criterion typically used in defining a natural environment. Landscape designations such as 'cultural', 'pastoral', and 'natural' imply varying degrees of human involvement.

In line with these definitions, most landscape assessment work treats the person as a viewer, whereas assessments concerning natural environments commonly treat people as visitors seeking an appropriate setting for outdoor recreation activities, including but not limited to viewing scenery. Work in both areas serves descriptive and evaluative purposes (Craik & Feimer, 1987). Whether relying on experts, technical devices, and/or perceptual capabilities of an appropriate panel of human observers, descriptive assessments characterize landscapes and natural/recreational settings in terms of physical or other attributes that are grounded in some conception of environmental quality, such as scenic beauty.

Evaluative assessments document observer responses to landscapes or natural/recreational settings using criterion variables that reflect on an underlying conception of environmental quality, such as ratings of scenic beauty or the importance of escape from stressors. Together, descriptive and evaluative assessments can provide a basis for predicting public responses to changes in the environment.

Pressing concerns about human impacts on the possibilities for realizing valued outcomes drive much of the assessment work on landscape and natural environments. Human activities can add to scenic and other amenity values, or they can diminish or destroy them. Recent decades have seen demand for buildable land, natural resources, and infrastructure increase alongside demand for outdoor recreation. Environmental policies in many countries now direct environmental managers to weigh the demands of competing uses and users. To fulfil this responsibility, managers need information on how users experience and evaluate not only environments as they now exist, but also environmental changes associated with different management alternatives.

APPROACHES AND THEORIES

Daniel and Vining (1983; see also Daniel, 2001) overview several landscape assessment approaches. Ecological and formal aesthetic approaches rely on biologists and other experts to classify landscapes using ecological or formal attributes as a basis for scenic quality judgements. For example, a landscape architect applying the Visual Management System (USDA, 1974) would render an area's features (e.g. rock outcroppings, lakes, streams, vegetation) in terms of form, line, colour and texture. He or she would then assign the area to one of three scenic quality categories according to the diversity of its formal attributes. When joined with other information, such as the number and type of users, the classification would support decisions about the suitability of activities that would alter the formal attributes of the landscape, such as timber cutting. Problems with expert approaches include the uncertain validity of chosen attributes as indicators of visual quality; potential disagreement by experts on landscape classifications; lack of sensitivity to variations in visual quality given broad quality categories; and lack of public input despite differences between expert and public aesthetic preferences.

In contrast, a psychophysical approach relies on public input (Daniel & Vining, 1983). For landscapes viewed on-site or with the aid of surrogates, observers provide judgements of scenic beauty, preference, naturalness or some other variable. They do so using rankings, paired comparisons, a rating scale, or some other method. The objective is to then develop a mathematical model that relates their judgements to practically meaningful physical variables on one or more scales (e.g. land use type; number of trees of a given diameter per unit area; amount of grass covered surface per unit area; presence of water features). With accurate and reliable psychophysical models comprising variables that they regularly monitor, managers can estimate visual quality impacts of environmental changes without having to survey new samples from an affected public. Relatively reliable and sensitive assessments are claimed for this public perception-based approach. Daniel and Boster's (1976) Scenic Beauty Estimation procedure is a widely used example.

Daniel and Vining (1983) associate theorizing on the visual experience of landscape with a second type of public perception-based approach to landscape assessment, the psychological. Like the psychophysical approach, the psychological approaches locate scenic quality in the meeting between person and environment, not in either alone. In contrast to the psychophysical approach, they have a basic research interest in affective, cognitive, and behavioural processes that mediate the relationship between environment and scenic beauty or preference judgements. Their utility for environmental management, however, still requires linking the psychological variables they comprise to specific physical referents.

Several theories propose that aesthetic and evaluative responses to landscapes originate in an evolved capacity to rapidly evaluate environmental conditions according to their relevance for survival. For example, Kaplan and Kaplan (1989) assert that an evolved evaluative capacity serves ongoing needs for making sense of and acquiring information from the environment. When viewing a scene, order perceived among visual elements (coherence) serves understanding, whereas their number and diversity (complexity) serve information acquisition. The visual array also enables inferences about staying oriented (legibility) and acquiring new information (mystery) when going further into the environment. In several studies guided by this theory, some participants have used rating scales to indicate how much they liked each of a sample of scenes while others have rated each scene in terms of one or more of the informational predictors (e.g. a single item for coherence: 'How well the scene "hangs together". How easy is it to organize and structure the scene?'). Regression analyses then treat the scenes as cases (for a review of such studies, see Kaplan & Kaplan, 1989).

North American, European and Asian samples consistently prefer scenes of natural landscapes over urban scenes (Ulrich, 1993). Although this general finding may reflect adaptedness to the (natural) environments of human evolution, theorists accept that learning processes also shape preferences, as through repeated pairing of beneficial experience with natural environments. Interweaving evolutionary with cultural and personal explanations for aesthetic responses to landscapes, various syntheses converge on the theme of the preferred natural landscape as the visual aspect of a setting for beneficial experience (e.g. Appleton, 1996).

This theme echoes in assessments for outdoor recreation management, exemplified by the research carried out for land management agencies in the USA. Driver and Bruns (1999) describe the management of outdoor recreation areas as a production process that starts with the recreationist's desires, expectations, and preferences; proceeds through the recreationist's interactions with the (managed) environment; generates recreation opportunities; and ultimately results in psychological benefits, among other outputs. Management efforts have over time encompassed successive aspects of this process, each of which implies particular assessment needs. Activity-based management has focused on supplying opportunities to perform particular activities, but without considering the psychological dimensions of recreation opportunities or recreation quality. Experience-based management (EBM) extended the focus to the psychological experiences sought in recreation. Net benefits-based management extends EBM by encompassing the full range of recreation benefits (and costs) over a longer term. To support these management approaches, researchers have assessed motives for, satisfaction with, and benefits from recreation experiences. They have developed various measures for these purposes, such as the Experience Preference Scales (e.g. Manfredo et al., 1996). Work in this area has also considered how desired outcomes relate to environmental attributes such as level of development (e.g. Williams & Knopf, 1985), as well as the acceptability of varying numbers of other recreationists (e.g. Manning et al., 1999) and levels of human-induced change in the recreation environment (e.g. Hollenhorst & Gardner, 1994).

Reviewing a multidisciplinary array of studies on outdoor recreation motives, Knopf (1987) considers what they tell us about recreation in natural settings versus recreation activities in general. The motive studies do commonly attest to a desire to experience nature per se. Stress reduction also recurs as a potent motivation. The desire to escape stress appears to covary with crowding and other stressful conditions in recreationists' everyday environments.

As important benefits of nature recreation, stress recovery and other forms of psychological restoration will remain a concern for outdoor recreation managers. Their efforts can benefit from developing theory and research on restorative environments, which extend from studies of landscape perception and outdoor recreation. One theory views psychophysiological stress recovery as a form of change supported by natural scenes with particular stimulus properties (e.g. moderate complexity) and contents (e.g. water) (Ulrich, 1993). Attention restoration theory (Kaplan & Kaplan, 1989) attributes renewal of a depleted attentional capacity to psychological distance from routine mental contents (being away); immersion in a coherent environment of sufficient scope to sustain exploration (extent); effortless attention engaged while making sense of and exploring the environment (fascination); and congruence between personal inclinations, environment demands, and environmental supports for intended activities (compatibility). Hartig et al. (1997) have published initial measures of these four factors, but further work is needed.

These theories guide a growing number of field and laboratory studies on the restorative values of natural, urban and other environments (e.g. Hartig et al., 1991). Experiments have consistently documented relatively beneficial affective, cognitive, and/or physiological changes in natural versus urban environments following stressful or demanding experiences. However, these studies have used severely limited samples of environments.

GENERAL METHODOLOGICAL CONCERNS

Assessment involves sampling from the environment to represent variation in relevant visual or recreational attributes. Relevance has to do with what people see and use, not necessarily the full range of physical or ecological variation. In landscape assessment, sampling takes into consideration the vantage points from which observers view the landscape. As a given vantage point offers numerous views that may vary widely in their character, sampling also considers viewing direction and visual angle. Additional concerns relate to the dynamic character of the landscape; visibility, the quality of light, the presence and colour of vegetation, and other visual attributes change with the time of day, season of the year, and atmospheric conditions. Beyond such variables, Hull and Revell (1989) note that the scenes people select for viewing vary with their purposes, the meanings they attach to landscape features, their speed of movement, their emotional state, and the presence of scenic features that command attention. Such concerns, in particular the activity pursued, also hold when assessing the recreational quality of outdoor settings.

Constraints on environmental sampling relate to the method used to present environments to the people who provide descriptive judgements or evaluative responses. Respondents may not always be available on-site, and even when they are, evaluations of future conditions present a problem. Given the costs involved in transporting people to multiple field locations or a need to represent possible changes in the environment, assessments frequently use visual surrogates or simulations to depict the environment. These represent a landscape or recreation setting in its current condition or, through the manipulation of images, how it might appear, as with different timber cutting alternatives. Presentation methods have evolved substantially, and emerging virtual reality (VR) technologies can help to reduce sampling constraints grounded in the use of static images such as photographs (Orland et al., 2001).

The validity of a given presentation method rests in part on the equivalence of an observer's response to the visual surrogate vis-à-vis the place portrayed. Although high correlations or a lack of significant differences between field and photo-based ratings have often been taken as evidence of validity, Palmer and Hoffman (2001) note reasons to question these approaches to establishing response equivalence. For example, a large correlation between ratings obtained on-site and with a surrogate indicates similarity in a pattern of responses, but not whether the absolute levels of the rated variable are the same in the two conditions.

FUTURE PERSPECTIVES AND CONCLUSIONS

Population will continue to increase in the coming years, and with it competition between commodity and non-commodity uses of landscapes and natural environments. This will drive further demand for information on the visual and recreational values of landscapes and natural environments. Improved environmental sampling and representation methods will aid the acquisition and application of such information. In the broadest sense, assessments concerning landscapes and natural environments will continue to play a role in sociocultural evolution by informing decisions that weigh multiple demands placed on the natural environment (Craik & Feimer, 1987).

References

Appleton, J. (1996). *The Experience of Landscape* (revised ed.). London: Wiley.

Craik, K.H. & Feimer, N.R. (1987). Environmental assessment. In Stokols, D. & Altman, I. (Eds.), *Handbook of Environmental Psychology*, Vol. 2 (pp. 891–918). New York: Wiley.

Daniel, T.C. (2001). Whither scenic beauty? Visual landscape quality assessment in the 21st century. *Landscape and Urban Planning, 54*, 267–281.

Daniel, T.C. & Boster, R.S. (1976). *Measuring Landscape Aesthetics: The Scenic Beauty Estimation Method* (USDA Forest Service Research Paper RM-167). Ft. Collins, CO: Rocky Mountain Forest and Range Experiment Station.

Daniel, T.C. & Vining, J. (1983). Assessment of landscape quality. In Altman, I. & Wohlwill, J.F. (Eds.), *Behaviour and the Natural Environment* (pp. 39–84). New York: Plenum Press.

Driver, B.L. & Bruns, D.H. (1999). Concepts and uses of the benefits approach to leisure. In Jackson, E.L. & Burton, T.L. (Eds.), *Leisure Studies: Prospects for the 21st Century* (pp. 349–369). State College, PA: Venture Publishing.

Hartig, T., Korpela, K., Evans, G.W. & Gärling, T. (1997). A measure of restorative quality in environments. *Scandinavian Housing and Planning Research, 14*, 175–194.

Hartig, T., Mang, M. & Evans, G.W. (1991). Restorative effects of natural environment experiences. *Environment and Behaviour, 23*, 3–26.

Hollenhorst, S. & Gardner, L. (1994). The indicator performance estimate approach to determining acceptable wilderness conditions. *Environmental Management, 18*, 901–906.

Hull, R.B. & Revell, G.R.B. (1989). Issues in sampling landscapes for visual quality assessments. *Landscape and Urban Planning, 17*, 323–330.

Kaplan, R. & Kaplan, S. (1989). *The Experience of Nature: A Psychological Perspective*. New York: Cambridge University Press.

Knopf, R.C. (1987). Human behaviour, cognition, and affect in the natural environment. In Stokols, D. & Altman, I. (Eds.), *Handbook of Environmental Psychology*, Vol. 1 (pp. 783–825). New York: Wiley.

Manfredo, M.J., Driver, B.L. & Tarrant, M.A. (1996). Measuring leisure motivation: a meta-analysis of the recreation experience preference scales. *Journal of Leisure Research*, 28, 188–213.

Manning, R.E., Valliere, W.A., Wang, B. & Jacobi, C. (1999). Crowding norms: alternative measurement approaches. *Leisure Sciences*, 21, 97–115.

Orland, B., Budthimedhee, K. & Uusitalo, J. (2001). Considering virtual worlds as representations of landscape realities and as tools for landscape planning. *Landscape and Urban Planning*, 54, 139–148.

Palmer, J.F. & Hoffman, R.E. (2001). Rating reliability and representation validity in scenic landscape assessments. *Landscape and Urban Planning*, 54, 149–161.

Pitt, D.G. & Zube, E.H. (1987). Management of natural environments. In Stokols, D. & Altman, I. (Eds.), *Handbook of Environmental Psychology*, Vol. 2 (pp. 1009–1042). New York: Wiley.

Ulrich, R.S. (1993). Biophilia, biophobia, and natural landscapes. In Kellert, S. & Wilson, E.O. (Eds.), *The Biophilia Hypothesis* (pp. 73–137). Washington, DC: Island Press.

USDA Forest Service (1974). *National Forest Landscape Management*, Vol. 2 (Agriculture Handbook 462). Washington, DC: US Government Printing Office.

Williams, D.R. & Knopf, R.C. (1985). In search of the primitive-urban continuum: the dimensional structure of outdoor recreation settings. *Environment and Behaviour*, 17, 351–370.

Terry Hartig

RELATED ENTRIES

Observational Methods (General), Person/Situation (Environment) Assessment, Theoretical Perspective: Behavioural, Unobtrusive Measures

L LANGUAGE (GENERAL)

INTRODUCTION

The practice of language assessment, both in children and adult populations, has been undertaken from various perspectives, and its evolution mirrors to some extent the development of Psychology as a scientific discipline from the first decades of the twentieth century. In this regard, there are two most influential lines of thought, generally known as the *psychometric* and the *cognitive* approaches. Since there are a number of background theoretical issues concerning the nature of language as an object of scientific inquiry that have an important bearing on either approach to language assessment, we will begin by briefly addressing these theoretical issues. This will lead us to describe the main strategies used for language assessment purposes, and to review the main components or processing levels of language and the tasks that are used in adult language assessment for each component, together with the major variables that should be taken into account in the assessment process. Finally, we will review some problems, both

theoretical and methodological, that assessment procedures have to face.

THEORETICAL BACKGROUND

Language is a very peculiar object of study. It is both a declarative body of knowledge possessed by adult competent speakers, and a set of procedures (or abilities) by which such knowledge is put to use in a variety of ways in linguistic activities. Furthermore, language can be viewed primarily as a means of communication among conspecifics (human language being the most developed and sophisticated code), but also as a means of representing and conveying thoughts and intentions, as a symbolic tool or device relating sound and meaning. In this regard, the psychological study of language is at least a twofold enterprise, for it must address (1) a wide array of information types and processing levels involved in understanding and speaking (which in principle can be selectively impaired); and (2) the intimate connection between the speakers' linguistic knowledge and abilities, on the one hand, and their cognitive and communicative capacities at large, of which linguistic skills are but a subset.

The *psychometric* approach to language assessment (e.g. Burt, 1940; Carroll, 1941; Hakstian & Cattell, 1978; Thurstone, 1938; Vernon, 1950) views language as a set of performance skills that rest on a number of underlying, more or less permanent, abilities. Although this view of language seems to parallel the competence–performance distinction proposed by Chomsky (1965), it does not carry any commitment to a rule-based account of linguistic competence or an information-processing view of the cognitive operations underlying linguistic performance. Rather, it defines 'verbal' (as opposed to 'linguistic') abilities in crudely operational terms; that is, as a direct reflection of the subject's performance in a number of standardized linguistic tasks. Language, more properly called 'verbal ability', is thus seen as a factor (or number of factors) of intelligence along which subjects may show quantitative variations. Verbal intelligence is alternatively viewed as a unitary ability, or as a set of distinct factors (e.g. 'verbal comprehension', 'verbal fluency', etc.) that can be independently evaluated. From this perspective, the targets of language assessment, or the components of verbal ability, are defined by crossing the main modalities of language use (spoken vs. written language) with the major linguistic tasks (comprehension and production), rendering the four basic language skills, namely listening, speaking, reading and writing.

The *cognitive* approach to language assessment entertains an entirely different conception of linguistic abilities. Language is seen as a cognitive faculty; that is, as a set of mental processes that operate on linguistic representations by means of a system of abstract rules that are mentally represented (as declarative but largely unconscious knowledge) (Clark & Clark, 1977; Chomsky, 1957, 1965; Fodor, 1983; Fodor, Bever & Garrett, 1974; Levelt, 1989; Pinker, 1994). Basic linguistic competence is by assumption equal to all healthy adults, who can in turn differ in their processing skills. Accordingly, language assessment procedures are theory-governed: processing models in various linguistic domains or components guide the elaboration of assessment tasks and materials. These domains are individuated in terms of the kinds of linguistic information each one of them is supposed to process. The emerging picture of the language faculty consists of a set of autonomous processing components (or levels) – acoustic, phonological, lexical, syntactic, semantic – working in a coordinated fashion to perform complex linguistic tasks (e.g. word, sentence and discourse comprehension and production).

As for cross-modal differences in language processing, no particular assumption is made about the relative autonomy of processing modalities; it is claimed at most that the processes subserving language performance may be modality-specific at the periphery, due to specific input–output constraints, but are most likely to share the same central processing mechanisms. Moreover, the cognitive approach to the study of language views the language faculty as a (partially) autonomous processing device (or module) itself with regard to other cognitive abilities or faculties (e.g. visual perception, auditory perception, motor control, musical processing, etc.), though it may make use of a common pool of processing resources in terms of attention, working memory, etc.

Since both psychometric and cognitive approaches see language simultaneously as a *unitary* and a *multiple* ability, the psychological assessment of language could provide two kinds of information: (1) information about the subject's *general* capacity to communicate by means of well-formed linguistic messages, both spoken and written; and (2) detailed information of the various components of linguistic knowledge and processes involved in the performance of language tasks, either to evaluate the level of proficiency attained in each of these components, or to ascertain the nature and possible causes of language impairments.

The assessment procedures intended to measure the level of language proficiency have been mostly used in educational settings, as a tool either in the teaching of a second or foreign language, or in the diagnosis and rehabilitation of children with language development disabilities (see entry on 'Development: Language'). On the other hand, the assessment procedures employed in the diagnosis and rehabilitation of adult language impairments (see Kremin, in this volume) have normally developed from neuropsychological studies with brain injured patients.

LANGUAGE ASSESSMENT METHODS

From a methodological standpoint, language assessment is roughly based on three different strategies: (1) the application of *standardized tests*; (2) the *analysis of samples of speech*; and (3) the use of *experimental tasks*.

Standardized tests for language assessment are sets of highly structured tasks intended to assess subjects' knowledge of various linguistic components and their ability to carry out the processes underlying the comprehension and production of spoken/written language. In a few cases, these tests were designed to assess one particular component of linguistic knowledge or modality (e.g. 'The Token Test', de Renzi & Vignolo, 1962; 'The Object and Action Naming Battery'; Druks & Masterson, 2000), whereas in most others (e.g. 'The Boston Diagnostic Aphasia Examination'; BDAE; Goodglass & Kaplan, 1972) they include subtests that address several components of language in spoken/written modalities: phonology/orthography, lexicon (including word form and word meaning), and syntax.

As Tables 1 and 2 show, a wide variety of linguistic tasks have been developed so far. A range of different variables are thought to influence subjects' performance in these tasks, according to the results from psycholinguistic research.

In many classical neuropsychological batteries, such as the BDAE, the assessment is based on a small number of tasks with a few items in each, which makes it somewhat difficult to manipulate and control the relevant variables that influence linguistic performance, and might bring incorrect generalizations about the processing capabilities or limitations of the subjects examined.[1] In contrast, neuropsychological batteries following a cognitive approach (e.g. PALPA; Kay, Lesser & Coltheart, 1992) provide different tasks and item lists for the evaluation of particular linguistic components, allowing a more detailed and controlled assessment of the subjects' preserved and impaired abilities (while demanding a careful selection of tests on the part of the examiner).[2]

Analysis of speech samples: The need to exert close control over the variables involved in language performance, together with the influence of Chomskyan linguistics on many areas of psycholinguistic research, have strongly biased the structure and contents of standardized language tests, which are mostly restricted to the assessment of phonological, lexical and morphosyntactic domains. However, the increasing interest of linguists and psychologists in pragmatics from the late 1970s has broadened the scope of psycholinguistic research to cover the comprehension and production of complex texts, discourses and conversations.

The evaluation of *text and discourse processing* is intended to provide information about the subject's ability to understand and use broader linguistic units comprising several interrelated sentences with complex and coherent meanings. The *analysis of conversation*, in turn, reveals the subject's capacity to produce and interpret relevant messages that are tuned to the listener's informational demands, to comply with the implicit rules regulating turn taking in conversational exchanges, to properly convey communicative intentions, etc. (see 'Communicative Language Abilities' in this volume).

Discourse and conversation analyses require the recording of spontaneous (or elicited) linguistic samples: narratives elicited by pictures where the examiner controls for the content and complexity of the information expressed; story-recall texts that allow the researcher to manipulate the content and linguistic complexity of stories; conversational discourse about topics with different degrees of relevance for participants, with familiar and unfamiliar partners, etc. Once the speech samples have been transcribed (or the texts are written), a host of techniques and measures can be used to describe how subjects organize and relate their ideas across sentences (see Table 3).[3]

Discourse and conversation analysis techniques have been extensively used to examine the patterns of preserved and impaired discourse behaviour in clinical populations and normal adults. These techniques provide *qualitative* information about the subjects' ability to organize their linguistic productions, thus revealing the complex relationships between language, social context and cognitive and communicative abilities. However, given the absence of normative data, the

Table 1.   Tasks used in the assessment of spoken language, and relevant factors to be controlled

Components of linguistic knowledge and processing	Tasks	Relevant factors
Phonology	Phoneme discrimination (minimal pairs) Non-word repetition Phonological phrasing Judgements on rhymes	Acoustic/phonological similarity Length of sequence Phonemic context
Lexicon Word form	Identification of spelled words Repetition of words and non-words Word–picture matching Picture naming Identification/naming of real objects (body parts, furniture, etc.) Auditory lexical decision task	Words vs. non-words Word frequency Familiarity Imageability Abstractness Word length Grammatical class of words (open/closed) Morphology
Word meaning	Naming from definitions Synonymity judgements Semantic association/discrimination Semantic classification Generation of exemplars from categories Questions about word knowledge	Distractors (response choices) Homophones Age-of-acquisition
Syntax	Acting-out tasks Spoken sentence–pictures matching Comprehension of verbs and adjectives Comprehension of prepositions and adverbs Comprehension of arguments in sentences Elicited production of sentences Elicited production of changes in verbal inflection Sentence repetition Grammaticality judgements	Length of sentence (number of words) Grammatical structure of sentences (active/passive, empty categories, locatives, reversible/non-reversible, etc.) Type of referents (animate/inanimate, abstract/concrete, etc.) Prosodic variations Knowledge of vocabulary

interpretation of results yielded by these techniques requires the examiner to possess an extensive knowledge of the psychological processes involved in these activities, which lie at the border between language and reasoning.

Experimental tasks: A recent methodological development in the assessment of language involves the use in clinical contexts of experimental procedures originally devised for psycholinguistic research. The justifying assumption is that both normal and impaired language processes are affected by the same sorts of variables. In neurologically intact subjects, the influence of these variables can only be detected with very sensitive measures such as reaction

time, whereas in impaired subjects these variables may prevent the responses altogether. Therefore, both error rates and reaction times can be taken as appropriate measures for patients with language deficits and normal unimpaired subjects alike.

Although experimental procedures are still seldom used for clinical purposes at large, there is an increasing trend to employ computer-based tasks in the presentation of stimuli and the recording of time-locked responses from patients with language impairments. One well-known example is the use of *priming techniques*, which have been extensively used in Experimental Psychology. In semantic priming studies, for

Table 2. Tasks used in the assessment of reading and writing abilities, and relevant factors to be controlled

Activity	Linguistic component	Tasks	Relevant factors*
Reading	Phonology/ Ortography Lexicon Syntax/ Semantics Discourse	Discrimination/identification of letters Matching letter names (sounds) and orthographic representation Matching allographic representations of letters and words Visual lexical decision task Reading of words Reading of non-words Matching spoken and written words (multiple choice tests) Synonymity judgements with written words Cloze tests (with/without multiple choice tests) Questions about written sentences (open questions, true/false questions, or multiple choice tests) Summarization tasks	(Only for cloze tests) Grammatical/semantic dependence (within-clause, across-clause, across-sentence, extra-textual) (Only for text comprehension tests) Discourse genre (narrative vs. expository texts) Conceptual organization of ideas in text
Writing	Phonology Lexicon Syntax Discourse	Writing letters and numbers by dictation Writing words and non-words by dictation Copy of allographs Writing spelled words Writing names from pictures Writing sentences by dictation Narrative writing (e.g. description of pictures)	Regular vs. arbitrary orthography of words (Allograph copying tasks) Common nouns vs. proper names

*Only specific factors for the visual modality are included here, that have *not* been previously listed in Table 1.

Table 3. Parameters for language assessment that can be obtained through the analysis of discourses, texts and conversations

Spoken discourse/Written texts	Cohesion devices (syntactic, lexical and semantic relations that link linguistic items across sentences) Local and global coherence of ideas Hierarchical organization of ideas and propositions Narrative/expository schemata (global macrostructure)
Conversations	Turn-taking mechanics Conversational breakdowns and repairs Pragmatic functions (directives, responses to directives, comments and representatives, expressives, requests for objects, actions and clarification, etc.) Topic manipulation

instance, subjects are presented with a target stimulus (e.g. a written word to be identified or pronounced) preceded by a semantically related prime (e.g. *doctor* immediately followed by *nurse*). In normal speakers, the prior presentation of the prime facilitates the recognition or naming of the target word. In contrast, brain injured patients and patients affected by Alzheimer-type dementia appear to be unaffected by the semantic relationship between both words, which seems to show that there is a functional disconnection of the lexical and semantic systems in such patients.

FUTURE PERSPECTIVES AND CONCLUSIONS

The functional complexity of human language raises a host of problems and challenges for assessment. First of all, the examiner is bound to gather detailed information about a huge number of relatively autonomous linguistic components and processing systems, which are influenced by a range of different variables. This makes it advisable to combine different tasks and procedures in the evaluation of every single component. In addition, it makes it necessary to acknowledge the close connection between some linguistic processes and other non-linguistic domains of information processing in humans, which nonetheless play a prominent role in linguistic performance (e.g. conceptual knowledge, attentional and working memory resources – whose demands are sharply increased as linguistic units become more complex, etc.).

Language assessment, as well as the clinical (and theoretical) interpretation of its outcomes, must be driven by theoretical models and by the conceptual distinctions they propose. A particular case in point is the distinction between *implicit* vs. *explicit* forms of information retrieval (see 'Memory (General)' in this volume). The observation that jargon aphasics are incapable of making semantic similarity judgements (an *explicit* task) while showing semantic priming effects (an *implicit* task) may serve as an illustration of the need to find out whether the deficits shown by a patient only affect strategic/conscious language processes or also interfere in automatic/non-conscious processes.

Another problem that commonly arises when assessing language deficits is the issue of whether selective impairments should be seen as caused by a disruption of the subject's *store* of information within a specific component of the language system (e.g. the phonological input lexicon, the semantic system), or by a trouble with *accessing* otherwise intact information within that particular component. This problem is further complicated by the fact that performance deficits can arise as a consequence of a loss of processing resources: therefore, a shrinking of the working memory span could be claimed to underlie some language impairments which were traditionally interpreted as affecting *specific* kinds of linguistic information (e.g. bound morphemes and closed-class words) in children language impairments and adult agrammatic aphasia. A useful strategy to clarify this issue involves the joint application of specific tests intended to sort out the possible underlying causes of the deficit (e.g. the use of general and language working memory tests alongside standard sentence processing measures, like sentence–picture matching).

A final question that deserves some attention is the assumption of a modular architecture for the language processing system. This can be seen both as a theoretical claim and as an empirical issue. Assessment procedures inevitably take for granted that linguistic abilities form a relatively closed set, but it is in the interest of researchers and practitioners to clarify the pattern of associations and dissociations between the different components of the language faculty, and between the language faculty as a whole and other related cognitive abilities. More importantly for assessment purposes is the need to define in a psychologically plausible fashion the nature of the internal components of the language faculty.

The traditional view that these components should be distinguished in terms of complex behavioural tasks (i.e. listening or spoken comprehension, reading, spoken production and writing) bluntly contradicts the assumptions of the cognitive view of the language system, which views the architecture of the language faculty as a set of processing devices individuated by information types (phonological processing, word recognition and selection, syntactic processing, semantic and pragmatic processing) rather than tasks or modalities. The overcoming of these theoretical differences is currently pursued by cognitive psychologists and neuropsychologists of language within the broad framework of the Cognitive Neurosciences (Gazzaniga, 1995, 2000). Undoubtedly, this new framework brings the promise of future payoffs for language assessment endeavours.

Notes

1 For instance, the auditory discrimination task in the BDAE includes only 6 words with widely different frequencies of use ('chair', 'key', 'glove', 'feather', 'chaise-longue' and 'cactus'). As Byng et al. (1990) pointed out, if a patient responds correctly to two of these items (2/6), it turns out that she will have a very defective auditory discrimination. However, the correctly identified items might be those with highest frequency names (say, 'chair' and 'key'), in which case this patient might have a normal auditory discrimination for high frequency and an impaired discrimination for medium and low frequency items.

2 In classical neuropsychological batteries, the examiner has to go through a closed catalogue of tests to be applied as a whole.

3 The analysis of speech samples can also be used to gather information about the morphosyntactic features of the subject's discourse, by examining its grammatical structure, errors, etc.

References

Burt, C. (1940). *The Factors of the Mind*. London: University of London Press.

Byng, S., Kay, J., Edmundson, A. & Scott, C. (1990). Aphasia test reconsidered. *Aphasiology, 4*, 67–91.

Carroll, J.B. (1941). A factor analysis of verbal abilities. *Psychometrika, 6*, 279–307.

Clark, H.H. & Clark, E.V. (1977). *Psychology and Language: An Introduction to Psycholinguistics*. New York: Harcourt, Brace and Jovanovich.

Chomsky, N. (1957). *Syntactic Structures*. The Hague: Mouton.

Chomsky, N. (1965). *Aspects of the Theory of Syntax*. Cambridge, MA: The MIT Press.

de Renzi, E. & Vignolo, L. (1962). The Token Test: a sensitive test to detect receptive disturbances in aphasics. *Brain, 85*, 665–678.

Druks, J. & Masterson, J. (2000). *An Object and Action Naming Battery*. Hove, UK: Psychology Press.

Fodor, J.A. (1983). *The Modularity of Mind*. Cambridge, MA: The MIT Press.

Fodor, J.A., Bever, T.G. & Garrett, M.F. (1974). *The Psychology of Language: An Introduction to Psycholinguistic and Generative Grammar*. New York: McGraw Hill.

Gazzaniga, M.S. (Ed.) (1995). *The Cognitive Neurosciences*. Cambridge, MA: The MIT Press.

Gazzaniga, M.S. (Ed.) (2000). *The Cognitive Neurosciences* (2nd ed.). Cambridge, MA: The MIT Press.

Goodglass, H. & Kaplan, E. (1972). *Boston Diagnostic Aphasia Examination*. Philadelphia: LEA & Febiger.

Hakstian, A.R. & Cattell, R.B. (1978). Higher-stratum ability structure on a basis of twenty primary abilities. *Journal of Educational Psychology, 70*, 657–669.

Kay, J., Lesser, R. & Coltheart, M. (1992). *PALPA: Psycholinguistic Assessment of Language Processing in Aphasia*. Hove, UK: Erlbaum.

Levelt, W.J.M. (1989). *Speaking: From Intention to Articulation*. Cambridge, MA: The MIT Press.

Pinker, S. (1994). *The Language Instinct: How the Mind Creates Language*. New York: William Morrow and Company.

Thurstone, L.L. (1938). Primary mental abilities. *Psychometric Monographs, 1*, 121. Chicago: Chicago University Press.

Vernon, P.E. (1950). *The Structure of Human Abilities*. London: Methuen.

José Manuel Igoa and Mercedes Belinchón

RELATED ENTRIES

Theoretical Perspective: Cognitive, Development: Language, Communicative Language Abilities, Testing in the Second Language in Minorities, Applied Fields: Neuropsychology, Neuropsychological Test Batteries

L LATENT CLASS ANALYSIS

INTRODUCTION

Latent class analysis is a statistical tool for classifying objects or individuals according to their values on a set of observed, i.e. manifest, variables. Like cluster analysis, it is aimed at identifying clusters of individuals or objects that are in some sense 'similar'. In order to separate to the terminology of cluster analysis, the groups of individuals are called 'classes' or 'latent classes' in latent class analysis (LCA) instead of clusters.

Unlike cluster analysis, the grouping is not done by means of some measure of similarity or distance between each pair of objects to be classified. There is also no need to define some criterion of cluster distance (or similarity), nor to select one of the various cluster algorithms (e.g. agglomerative, centroid method, etc.). In contrast, latent class analysis classifies objects according to their probabilities of the values of all observed variables (feature patterns of the objects). This distinction allows for two significant indications of cluster analysis or latent class analysis, respectively.

First, cluster analysis is to be preferred for small numbers of objects to be classified, LCA for large numbers of objects, say $N = 50$ or $N = 100$ be the criterion of applying one or the other. This is because in LCA the probability distributions of all manifest variables have to be parameterized (and estimated) for each latent class (which requires large numbers of observations), whereas in cluster analysis each object has to be measured according to its distance to each other object (which is more tractable for smaller sets of objects).

Second, LCA is better suited for categorical or ordinal data (where each manifest variable has a small number of values, e.g. yes–no responses or rating scale responses to some questionnaire items), whereas cluster analysis is better suited for metric variables (where some distance measure between the objects, like the Euclidean distance, is unproblematic).

But there is a third difference between cluster analysis and LCA that is significant for specifying submodels and extended models: cluster analysis is aimed at identifying a manifest classification, i.e. each object is assigned to one and only one group or cluster (which is also true for some borderline cases, that have the same distance to two or more clusters and may, therefore, be assigned to a single cluster only with high uncertainty). LCA, in contrast, assumes a latent grouping variable, so that each object belongs to each latent class with a certain (assignment) probability. This distinction may be regarded as a more academic distinction, but it has enormous practical implications.

The most prominent of them is the possibilty of defining specific statistical models for each latent class. Whereas cluster analysis can only clump together objects that are more or less similar, LCA is capable of identifying classes of objects that can be described by different statistical models. Latent class analysis belongs to the family of (discrete) mixture distribution models, whereas cluster analysis does not. But before going into the details of different variants of LCA, a brief introduction to the assumptions and ideas of LCA is given.

THE MODEL AND ITS HISTORY

The concept of LCA has been developed 50 years ago by Paul Lazarsfeld (1950) who considered it as part of the more general framework of latent structure analysis. The idea of latent structure analysis was based on the distinction between manifest and latent variables. While manifest variables can be directly observed, like socioeconomic variables, item responses in a questionnaire or some codification of observed behaviour, latent variables cannot be observed or measured by means of a yardstick. The notions of a disposition, hypothetical construct, or intervening variable, incorporate the idea that theories in psychology or sociology usually are built on the basis of latent variables like intelligence or socioeconomic status, but all that can be assessed are manifest indicators like income and success or failure in an intelligence task (Lazarsfeld & Henry, 1968).

The insight that manifest variables have to be linked to latent constructs was not new at that time, since the methodology of factor analysis was well developed and often applied in various fields of research. However, there are three significant distinctions between factor analysis and the ideas of latent structure analysis. Factor analysis applies to metric or quantitative manifest variables, factor analysis introduces metric or quantitative latent variables (the 'factors'), and factor analysis does this on the basis of the correlations among the manifest variables, i.e. only considers the bivariate associations of the observed variables. Latent structure analysis, in contrast, has been developed on grounds of the philosophy that observable variables in sociology and psychology usually are categorical, i.e. nominal or ordinal, that also the latent variable needs not to be metric but should be conceptualized as a categorical variable, and that it is insufficient to only consider bivariate associations when working with many manifest variables, among which interactions among three or more variables may exist.

The paradigm of latent structure analysis is the principle of local independence, which means that the observed associations of the manifest variables are caused by a latent construct or a latent variable. If this latent variable is held constant, the associations between the observed variables vanish. For example, income, level of education, and the brand of the owned car are associated in any representative sample. If it is true that the socioeconomic status can be described by three levels only, i.e. lower, middle, and upper class, then the associations between income, education, and brand of car are not given, when only persons of the same class are investigated. This is to say that the criterion of identifying latent classes is the absence of associations between the observed variables within each class.

Local independence means that all observed variables are independent for the same locus of the latent variable. It is a rather fundamental principle in statistical analysis and a powerful tool for constructing models. Latent class analysis is the basic model of this family of local independence models. It simply assumes that the probability of observing a pattern of indicators x, y, and z, given a latent class A, is the product of the probabilities of each single indicator, given that class:

$$P(x, y, z|A) = P(x|A) * P(y|A) * P(z|A)$$

The second assumption is that these classes (say A, B, and C) are mutually exclusive and have proportions in the population that sum to unity:

$$P(A) + P(B) + P(C) = 1.$$

Then, the model of latent class analysis is defined as:

$$P(x, y, z) = P(A) * P(x, y, z|A) + PB)$$
$$* P(x, y, z|B) + P(C) * P(x, y, z|C)$$

Although the basic structure of this model seems to be rather simple, it could not be applied for a long period of time, since no algorithms for estimating its parameters were available. Only the work of Leo Goodman (1974) made an application of the model to realistic sets of data possible. Goodman's algorithm later turned out as a special case of the nowadays famous EM-algorithm described by Dempster, Laird and Rubin (1977). Today, some excellent software products are available for estimating the model parameters and applying the model to large sets of data (e.g. WINMIRA, Davier, 2000; LATENT GOLD, Vermunt & Magidson, 2000; the GIBBS-sampler, Hoijtink & Molenaar, 1997; PANMARK, van de Pol, Langeheine & de Jong, 1996).

These software products cover many more models than the simple basic model of LCA as described before. WINMIRA is specialized to so-called mixed Rasch models, i.e. latent class models where the Rasch model (Rasch, 1960, 1980 [2nd ed.]) holds within each latent class, but with different item difficulty parameters between the classes (Rost, 1990, 1991, 1996). Another feature of WINMIRA are latent class models for ordinal data (Rost, 1988a and b). Other programs have their own advantages and some very powerful LCA programs exist that are not commercially distributed but have to be requested from the authors (Linear Logistic LCA, Formann, 1992a and b; or LAT, Haberman, 1979).

APPLICATIONS IN PSYCHOLOGICAL ASSESSMENT

Although the field of possible applications in psychological assessment is by far larger than the number of applications available in the literature, its number is high enough to not be listed and commented here. A collection of different applications is provided in the book by Rost and Langeheine (1997), which is now available from the Internet (www.ipn.uni-kiel.de).

As an example for a typical latent class analysis in the field of psychological assessment, the analysis of social needs in a study of environmental behaviour is described in the following (Gresele, 2000).

Each five items for assessing the social need for affiliation, conformity, influence and approval have been constructed on the basis of existing questionnaires on social needs. Two items aimed at assessing the need for approval had to be removed due to failures of item construction. The remaining 18 items were analysed by means of LCA and revealed 4 latent classes that can be interpreted as social need types. Figure 1 shows the response profiles of the 4 types on the 18 items of the questionnaire. Since the response format was a 4-point rating scale, the ordinate of this figure ranges from 0 to 3, indicating the mean (expected) response of the types on the items of the questionnaire.

Only one profile is low on the items of affiliation, giving reason to call them the *introverts*. In fact, they have an intermediate need for conformity, the lowest need for influence, and a relative low need for approval, which fits to the interpretation of this type as the introverts. This class (no. 4) covers 21 per cent of the students.

The profile of class one (27%) shows lowest values on the approval items, i.e. these students are independent of approval or *self-determined*. These students have intermediate needs for conformity and influence (which underlines their

self-determination) but are high on the affiliation items.

High on influence but low on conformity is the profile of the *leader* type (class 2; 27%). These students are not oriented at the norm of their peer group, but they are themselves opinion leaders. Of course, they are high on affiliation and have a high need for approval, which they strive for by leading and influencing others.

As compared to the leaders, class 3 (26%) has a stronger need for conformity but a lower one for influence. Their needs for affiliation and approval are relatively high, so that this type can be identified as the *sociables*.

This example is to illustrate that the assessment of psychological variables by means of latent class analysis needs no assumption of dimensionality of the items and goes beyond the pairwise correlations of the item responses. The analysis considers the entire pattern of item responses and identifies groups of individuals that have similar response patterns in terms of response probabilities. Hence, latent class analysis can be seen as the qualitative counterpart to quantitative item response theory: it assesses latent types instead of latent traits (Langeheine & Rost, 1988).

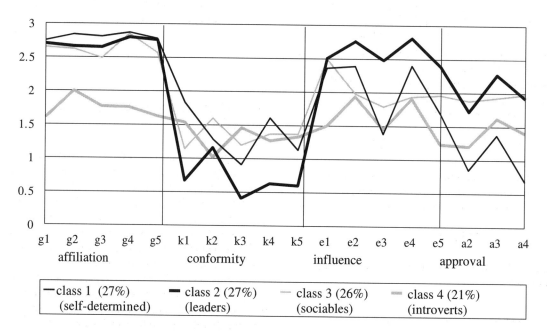

Figure 1.   Social need profiles.

FUTURE PERSPECTIVES

Models based on the idea of latent class analysis constitute a growing field of methodological research. Many kinds of statistical models, like factor analysis or linear structural equation models, are going to be generalized to discrete mixture models. It certainly will become a standard for statistical data analysis to first try to unmix given data before applying some model to the entire population. The consequence for psychological assessment may be that the assessment of types of individuals will turn to be a focus of research and diagnosis, additionally to that of trait analyses.

CONCLUSIONS

Latent class analysis is only the basic model of a growing type of statistical models, that are better labelled as discrete mixture models. As a probabilistic model based on the concept of local independence, LCA parallels the models of item response theory. Moreover, latent class models may be applied when latent trait models fail to fit the data (Rost, in press).

References

Davier, M. von (2000). WINMIRA – a program system for analyses with the Rasch model, with the latent class analysis and with the mixed Rasch model. program.

Dempster, A.P., Laird, N.M. & Rubin, D.B. (1977). Maximum likelihood estimation from incomplete data via the EM-algorithm. *Journal of the Royal Statistical Society*, 39, 1–22.

Formann, A.K. (1992a). Latent class models with order restrictions. *Methodika*, VI, 131–149.

Formann, A.K. (1992b). Linear logistic latent class analysis for polytomous data. *Journal of the American Statistical Association*, 87, 476–486.

Goodman, L.A. (1974). Exploratory latent structure analysis using both identifiable and unidentifiable models. *Biometrika*, 61(2), 215–231.

Gresele, C. (2000). *Die Bedeutung sozialer Bedürfnisse und sozialer Situationen bei der Erklärung des Umwelthandelns*. Hamburg: Kovač.

Haberman, S.J. (1979). *Analysis of Qualitative Data*, Vol. 2: *New Developments*. New York: Academic Press.

Hoijtink, H. & Molenaar, I.W. (1997). A multi-dimensional item response model: constrained latent class analysis using the Gibbs sampler and posterior predictive checks. *Psychometrika*, 62, 171–189.

Langeheine, R. & Rost, J. (1988). *Latent Trait and Latent Class Models*. New York: Plenum.

Lazarsfeld, P.F. (1950). The logical and mathematical foundation of latent structure analysis. In Stouffer, S.A., Guttman, L., Suchman, E.A., Lazarsfeld, P.F., Star, S.A. & Clausen, J.A. (Eds.), *Studies in Social Psychology in World War II*, Vol. IV (pp. 362–412). Princeton/NJ: Princeton University Press.

Lazarsfeld, P.F. & Henry, N.W. (1968). *Latent Structure Analysis*. Boston: Houghton Mifflin Co.

Rasch, G. (1960). *Probabilistic Models for Some Intelligence and Attainment Tests*. Copenhagen: Nielsen & Lydiche (Expanded Edition, Chicago, University of Chicago Press, 1980).

Rost, J. (1988a). Measuring attitudes with a threshold model drawing on a traditional scaling concept. *Applied Psychological Measurement*, 12(4), 397–409.

Rost, J. (1988b). Rating scale analysis with latent class models. *Psychometrika*, 53(3), 327–348.

Rost, J. (1990). Rasch models in latent classes: an integration of two approaches to item analysis. *Applied Psychological Measurement*, 14(3), 271–282.

Rost, J. (1991). A logistic mixture distribution model for polychotomous item responses. *British Journal of Mathematical and Statistical Psychology*, 44, 75–92.

Rost, J. (1996). *Lehrbuch Testtheorie, Testkonstruktion*. Bern: Huber.

Rost, J. (in press). When personality questionnaires fail to be unidimensional. To be published in *Psychologische Beiträge*.

Rost, J. & Langeheine, R. (1997). *Applications of Latent Trait and Latent Class Models in the Social Sciences*. Münster: Waxmann.

Van de Pol, F., Langeheine, R. & de Jong, W. (1996). *PANMARK User Manual: PANel Analysis Using MARKov Chains*. Voorburg: Netherlands Central Bureau of Statistics.

Vermunt, J.K. & Magidson, J. (2000). *LATENT GOLD: A Breakthrough in Latent Class/Mixture Modelling*.

Jürgen Rost

RELATED ENTRIES

LEADERSHIP IN ORGANIZATIONAL SETTINGS

INTRODUCTION

From an organizational standpoint one major element that sets apart successful from unsuccessful organizations is leadership, which should be dynamic and effective.

Leadership can be seen as the activity to influence others to willingly achieve specified objectives; it is clearly dependent on individual behaviours and a set of attributes which characterize a leader.

Peter F. Drucker referred to business leaders as the basic and scarcest resource of any enterprise. Therefore, it should not be a surprise that organizations are looking at the selection process for candidates (Drucker, 1954).

Trying to respond to the question of how to assess leadership at the individual level, several tools have been developed and tested during the last decades.

The entry on 'Leadership Personality' in this Encyclopedia, by Robert Hogan and Robert Tett, includes a complete summary of outside and inside assessment methods, with demonstrated validity for predicting leadership personality.

Leadership assessment at the organizational level should focus on extending the evaluation of the individual, looking at the effectiveness of the organization as a whole (Bennis & Nanus, 1985; Burns, 1978).

This entry is intended to review the concept of leadership and what attributes the followers expect from their leaders and supervisors. It will summarize the way existing tools, like Total Quality Management, are being used in the assessment process of organizational leadership.

Extending the basic traits of leadership to the entire organization, we shall cover in detail organizational leadership assessment, from a Total Quality Management standpoint (Bradford & Cohen, 1984). We shall discuss, as well, some other assessment instruments available today.

Whenever individuals attempt to affect the behaviour of other people without using a coercive form of power, we describe it as leadership.

Specifically, 'leadership is an attempt at influencing the activities of followers to willingly cooperate through the communication process toward the attainment of some goal or goals' (Fleishman and Hunt, 1973).

This definition suggests that the ability to influence other people is essential to leadership and, consequently, all relationships can involve it. Besides that, communication appears to be of critical importance for this purpose.

On the other hand, the definition includes the attainment of goals. Leadership effectiveness at the individual, group or organizational level is measured by the accomplishment of one or a combination of goals.

In a hierarchically structured organization, the managers and supervisors may direct, instruct or command, but unless followers have the choice to follow or not follow, there is no leadership.

There is a clear distinction between managing and leading: the latter emphasizes 'get others to want to do' versus get others to do.

Managers get subordinates to do through objective setting and the classical management functions (planning, organizing, directing and controlling). Leaders get followers to want to do, by inspiring a vision, modelling the way, innovating, developing their people and always setting the example (see Cleveland, 1985).

LEADERSHIP CHARACTERISTICS

Much of the early work on leadership focused on identifying the traits of effective leaders. Most research was designed to identify intellectual, emotional, physical and other personal traits of successful leaders: intelligence, personality, physical characteristics or supervisory ability were investigated. In this way, a number of trait theories emerged (Gibson, Ivancevich & Donnelly, 1988).

On the other hand, the word 'charismatic' frequently comes up in discussions of leadership. For example, people might think that some leaders have charisma and other leaders don't. Leaders don't have charisma; followers give leaders charisma. We have all seen that phenomenon with elected officials. They are often carried into office because of their charisma, but when their actions do not gain general approval, they may lose their charisma overnight. 'Charisma' has become such an overused and misused term that it is almost useless as a descriptor of leaders. Bernard Bass, professor of organizational behaviour at the State University of New York, has done extensive research on charisma (Bass, 1985).

Other people have investigated the expectations that followers have of leaders, to determine the extent to which their perceptions of leadership matched what leaders themselves said they did. One of these studies was sponsored by the American Management Association (Kouzes & Posner, 1987; Kanter, 1983).

As a result, more than 225 different values, traits and characteristics were identified, but reduced afterwards to 15 by classification. The most frequent responses, in order of mention, were (1) integrity, (2) competence and (3) leadership.

In a follow-up study, the four top characteristics of superior leaders were, by order of importance, honesty, competency, forward-looking and inspiring.

The above mentioned studies suggest the effective leadership traits which should be ideally found in leaders.

LEADERSHIP PRACTICES

Kouzes and Posner (1987) have discovered that the ordinary executives who convinced others to join them on pioneering journeys followed the path of a three-phase strategy. They refer to it as the VIP – vision–involvement–persistence – model of leadership.

Looking deeper into this dynamic VIP process, five fundamental practices were identified that enabled leaders to get extraordinary things done: (1) challenging the process, (2) inspiring a shared vision, (3) enabling others to act, (4) modelling the way and (5) encouraging the heart.

1 Challenging the process involves questioning what is done regularly in order to find new ideas and innovate. Leaders may challenge the process by searching for opportunities, experimenting and taking risks.

2 Leaders should constantly look for the future, imagining what it will be like when they have arrived at their final destinations. This activity should be shared with their people. They should envisage the future and commit others in the process.

3 Enabling others to act means leading activities to get the collaboration of the people, by building teams and empowering. They regularly foster cooperation, delegate and empower their people.

4 Modelling the way involves directing the course of action and practising what you preach. Setting the example and planning small wins are ways to model the way.

5 Encouraging the heart means recognizing and celebrating what is done successfully by the employees.

The above mentioned commitments of leadership are very deeply analysed by Kouzes and Posner (1987).

MODELLING ORGANIZATIONAL LEADERSHIP ASSESSMENT

Many models for organizational assessment have been developed. For detailed information see the entry on 'Total Quality Management' in this Encyclopedia, where several are mentioned and the EFQM (European Foundation for Quality Management) Model is analysed in detail.

A number of behavioural commitments support leadership practices. Adoption of the process of self-assessment is the EFQM's recommended strategy for improving performance (EFQM, 2000).

Self-assessment is a comprehensive, systematic and regular review of an organization's activities and results referenced against the EFQM Model. Today, many organizations are using the Model for this purpose, determining their strengths and areas subject to improvement (Peters & Austin, 1985).

Organizations carry out this cycle of evaluating and taking action repeatedly, so that they can achieve a sustained improvement. The most advanced have integrated self-assessment in the regular organization's planning cycle.

The evaluation is valid for the different criteria (enablers and results) implied in the Model. The first criterion is specifically leadership. The contribution of leadership to the business is measured by the overall results of the organization, but leadership is evaluated in terms of the specific attributes of its leaders (Kanter, 1983).

The criterion on leadership responds to the definition previously written and includes the different practices which have been covered in this entry.

The assessment reviews how the leaders demonstrate their commitment and how actively they drive improvement activities, implicating people, customers, suppliers and external organizations (Watson, 1963).

Examples of these areas are: the way they develop values and expectations and act as role models of these values; how they prioritize, fund, organize and support improvement activities within the organization; how they manage relationships with customers, suppliers and other external organizations; how they demonstrate business knowledge and get involved in education activities; how they communicate with their subordinates, listening, informing and reviewing the effectiveness of their leadership. On the other hand, how they recognize and celebrate people successes.

Being an 'enabler' criterion of the Model, leadership is assessed as a combination of the following two items.

On one hand, the approach used by the leaders in meeting their responsibilities is assessed looking at a number of attributes: has the approach a good base? Is the approach systematic? Has it preventive mechanisms? Is it reviewed against its effectiveness and changed accordingly for permanent improvement? Is it integrated in the normal business operations?

Trained assessors judge on a percentage scale how much each of those criteria are met. In this way an average percentage of performance is obtained for the leaders in the organization.

On the other hand, deployment of those attributes has to be assessed by answering the following questions: to what extent are the preceding activities extended within the organization? Do they relate with only the top of the institution or are they spread overall? Are they extended to all functions and areas of the business, or do they concentrate only in a single part of the organization?

Deployment is then assessed with another percentage, which in fact is an average of the perception the assessor has on the number of managers practising leadership at the level of the approach assessed, as opposed to the total number of executives, managers and supervisors existing in the organization.

The mean of the 'approach' and the 'deployment' is the end result of the organizational leadership assessment.

ASSESSMENT INSTRUMENTS AND TOOLS

Traditionally, interviewing techniques, group sessions and role play have been used in several ways to assess leadership capacities and potentials. Some corporations have developed direct assessment methods by asking employees by means of questionnaires what they think about their leaders.

IBM, for example, developed in the 1980s an instrument which was made available to all management levels, to assess leadership styles and behaviours by means of opinions of their employees; it was called MAP (Management Activity Profile). It helped managers to put in place improvement techniques for achieving a better leadership profile.

Assessment centre techniques, which were pioneered by Douglas Bray and his associates at the American Telephone and Telegraph Company in the mid-1950s, became very popular as evaluation techniques, in general terms, but could be used for leadership assessment purposes as well. The foundation of this technique is a series of situational exercises in which candidates for several managerial programmes take part over a certain period of time (two to three days) while being observed and rated; role playing and case analysis are part of the exercise.

However, one of the potential problems of the assessment centre evaluation procedure is that it is so pressure-packed. Outstanding employees who have contributed to the organization may simply not perform well in the centre. Another problem involves the feelings of individuals who receive mediocre or poor evaluations. Basing promotion decisions or identification of individuals with high potential on the results of a single assessment centre experience is questionable. It may have potential benefits and potential problems.

Kouzes and Posner (1987: 309) developed a 'Leadership Practices Inventory', based on a survey. It consists of thirty-eight open-ended questions which were tested with several populations. The outcome of these procedures resulted in thirty statements (six statements for measuring each of the five leadership practices); there are two forms – self and other – which differ only in whether the behaviour described is the respondent's (self) or that of another specific person (other).

Quite a number of instruments have been developed for assessing leadership: for example, Ohio State University initiated studies in 1945, attempting to identify various dimensions of leader behaviour (Stogdill & Coons, 1957). To gather data about the behaviour of leaders, they developed the Leader Behaviour Description Questionnaire, an instrument designed to describe how leaders carry out their activities; although the major emphasis in the Ohio State leadership studies was on observed behaviour, the staff did develop the Leader Opinion Questionnaire, to gather data about the self-perceptions that leaders have about their own leadership style.

FUTURE PERSPECTIVES AND CONCLUSIONS

Organizations are using several procedures for assessing their leaders, as well as other management activities, looking at results as a consequence of 'enablers'.

The domain of the leaders is the future. Their unique legacy is creating valued institutions that survive over time.

The most significant contributions leaders may make is not to today's operational bottom-line activities but to long-term development of people and organizations who prosper and grow.

References

Bass, B.M. (1985). *Leadership and Performance Beyond Expectations*. New York: Free Press.

Bennis, W. & Nanus, B. (1985). *Leaders: The Strategies for Taking Charge*. New York: Harper & Row.

Bradford, D.L. & Cohen, A.R. (1984). *Managing for Excellence*. New York: Wiley.

Burns, J.M. (1978). *Leadership*. New York: Harper & Row.

Cleveland, H. (1985). *The Knowledge Executive: Leadership in an Information Society*. New York: Truman Talley Books/Dutton.

Drucker, P.F. (1954). *The Practice of Management*. New York: Harper & Row.

EFQM (2000). *Small and Medium Sized Enterprises: Application*. Brussels: Foundation for Quality Management.

Fleishman, E.A. & Hunt, J.G. (1973). Twenty years of consideration and structure. *Current Developments in the Study of Leadership*. Carbondale, Southern Illinois: University Press.

Gibson, J.L., Ivancevich, J.M. & Donnelly, J.H. (1988). *Organizations: Behaviour, Structure, Processes*. BPI/Irwin: Homewood.

Kanter, R.M. (1983). *The Change Masters: Innovation for Productivity in the American Corporation*. New York: Simon & Schuster.

Kouzes, J.M. & Posner, B.Z. (1987). *The Leadership Challenge*. San Francisco: Jossey-Bass Inc., Publishers.

Mintzberg, H. (1973). *The Nature of Managerial Work*. New York: Harper & Row.

Peters, T.J. & Austin, N.K. (1985). *A Passion for Excellence*. New York: Random House.

Stogdill, R.M. & Coons, A. (Eds.) (1957). *Leader Behaviour: Its Description and Measurement*. Research Monograph No. 88. Bureau of Business Research: Ohio State University.

Watson, T.J. Jr. (1963). *A Business and its Beliefs*. New York: McGraw Hill.

Francisco Fernández Ballesteros

RELATED ENTRIES

APPLIED FIELDS: ORGANIZATIONS, APPLIED FIELDS: WORK AND INDUSTRY, LEADERSHIP PERSONALITY, TOTAL QUALITY MANAGEMENT

L|EADERSHIP PERSONALITY

INTRODUCTION

Common sense suggests that leadership is the most important topic in the social, behavioural, and organizational sciences. A trip through the business section of any bookstore will also reveal that it is the most popular – based on the number of books written on the topic (well over 7000). The literature on leadership falls into two discrete categories. The first, and by far the largest, contains books designed for the popular or mass market. This vast literature contains nuggets of wisdom and flashes of insights from entrepreneurs, military officers, historians, business school professors, and consultants; however, it is not systematic, empirical, or verifiable, and it lacks an assessment base. In short, it is not a foundation on which to build a reliable understanding of leadership; it is entertaining rather than deeply informative.

The second literature, and by far the smaller of the two, comes from the empirical tradition of Academia. This tradition has the critically important characteristic of adhering to the standards of intellectual accountability that normally prevail in empirical research – publicly available data, standardized analytical methods, peer review, etc. By definition, then, the empirical tradition is more informative about leadership, at least in principle, than the vast collection of opinions contained in the literature designed for mass markets. But the empirical tradition suffers from four problems that limit its utility. First, it typically defines leadership in terms of the persons who happen to be in charge of the organizational unit being studied. But many, if not most, people who are in charge of organizational units attain their status for political reasons rather than because they have demonstrated significant leadership. In addition, by defining leadership operationally, the empirical tradition avoids the question of what leadership really is. Second, by defining leadership operationally, the empirical literature doesn't converge – because the characteristics of

persons in charge of one organizational unit are typically different from the characteristics of persons in charge of a different unit, and it is nearly impossible to compare leadership (defined in this way) across organizations. Third, the empirical tradition has been strongly influenced by behaviourism, and as a result largely ignores the relationship between personality and leadership – from a behaviourist perspective, circumstances are more important than personality as an influence on leadership. And fourth, the empirical tradition has largely ignored the links between leadership and organizational effectiveness – arguing that effectiveness is too hard to define.

We believe that some attention to these definitional and conceptual issues will substantially clarify the assessment of leadership.

Leadership Defined

Data and common sense indicate that people are naturally selfish; nonetheless, all significant human achievement is the result of collective effort. Consequently, leadership should be defined in terms of the ability to persuade people to set aside their personal concerns and support a larger agenda – at least for a while. Leadership differs from management – subordinates respond to leaders because they want to, they respond to managers because they are paid to. Good managers, nonetheless, are often able leaders and vice versa.

Leadership and Organizational Effectiveness

All real world groups compete with other groups for desired resources – money, land, energy, food, loyal supporters, official patronage, league championships. Because leadership is a resource for a group, affecting its ability to attain its goals, leadership should be evaluated in terms of the effectiveness of the leader's team: Did it win the prize, the goal, the race, or the war?

Sometimes a good leader's team loses because it is overmatched, and sometimes a bad leader's team wins because it has superior resources; nonetheless, leadership and organizational effectiveness are co-dependent.

Leadership and Personality

To clarify the links between leadership and personality, we need first to define personality. Personality has two definitions, they are quite distinct, and they concern personality from the inside and from the outside. Personality from the inside, which we call identity, is composed of a person's values, goals, aspirations, and self-image; identity can be assessed by asking a person about his/her goals, aspirations, and self-image. Leadership assessment from the inside consists of assessing the identities of leaders and comparing them with the identities of non-leaders.

Leadership from the outside, which we call reputation, is composed of the images and evaluations of a person, as held by those people with whom that person interacts. Leadership reputation is assessed using observer ratings from whatever source a researcher might prefer. This would include assessment centre ratings and 360 feedback evaluations. Relevant research questions here include whom to ask to provide ratings, what rating dimensions should be used, and how leaders differ from non-leaders in terms of these ratings. The bottom line of this discussion is that leadership needs to be assessed from the inside and from the outside.

ASSESSING LEADERSHIP FROM THE INSIDE

As noted above, personality from the inside concerns a person's values, motives, and self-image – identity. Various methods and instruments are available to assess leadership from the inside and many of them yield valid results. For example, Sparks (1990) reports on research conducted at EXXON in the 1950s, designed to identify managerial talent. Using a combination of measures of cognitive ability, personality, biodata, and interviews, in a sample of 443 managers, and a composite success criterion

(salary, level, and rated effectiveness), Sparks reports a cross-validated multiple R of 0.70. Howard and Bray (1990) report roughly comparable results using multiple methods in a longitudinal study at AT&T. Thus, it is possible to predict leadership performance using measures of identity, and in many cases with an admirable degree of validity.

The most robust procedures for assessing leadership from the inside fall into four categories: (A) projective measures of personality; (B) objective measures of personality; (C) specialized measures of personality; and (D) mixed measures of personality.

Projective Measures

McClelland (1975) and his associates have used the Thematic Apperception Test (TAT) to study leadership in a wide variety of organizations and countries. They report reasonable validity coefficients with scores for 'socialized power' (desiring power in order to bring about organizational change, not self-aggrandizement) and leadership performance.

Objective Measures

Objective measures of personality with demonstrated validity for predicting leadership fall naturally into four sub-groups. The best-known exemplars of the first group are the 16 PF (Cattell & Eber, 1961), and the Guilford–Zimmerman Temperament Survey (Guilford & Zimmerman, 1956). These inventories were constructed using internal consistency indices and factor analysis; the goal was to define reproducible factors, and predictive validity was a side issue. The second group contains objective measures of personality developed in an empirical manner and designed to maximize validity. The best-known example of this approach is the California Psychological Inventory (CPI; Gough, 1987); the well-respected CPI is widely used in management consulting around the world. The third group of measures concerns values and occupational interests. The best known of these is the Myers–Briggs Type Indicator (MBTI; McCaulley, 1990); the MBTI is not well regarded by many psychometricians, but McCaulley provides clear data that a pattern of MBTI scores typifies executives world wide. A second important measure in this category is the Campbell Work Orientations Surveys (Campbell, 1990); Campbell shows that his inventory of values, interests, and preferences predicts a wide variety of leadership outcomes. The final category of objective personality measures contains inventories based on the Five-Factor Model (FFM; Wiggins, 1996). A substantial body of research shows that: (a) most existing measures of personality can be reconfigured in terms of the FFM, and (b) measures of normal personality based on the FFM are also robust predictors of leadership (cf. Hogan & Hogan, 1995). The FFM is the new paradigm for measures of normal personality, although there is strong resistance to this notion among some personality researchers (e.g. Block, 1995).

Specialized Measures of Personality

There are far too many specialized measures of personality, used to predict leadership, to cover responsibly here. There are thousands of individual scales, the best known of which concern authoritarianism, machiavellianism, self-monitoring, and dogmatism; these measures predict specific aspects of leader performance. Recent developments in theory and research suggest that these specific scales can be placed in the larger context of the FFM. Two recent special measures are important here – Emotional Intelligence (EQ) and Transformational leadership. The measurement base for the EQ movement (Goleman, 1995) is ad hoc and not well regarded by measurement experts. Nonetheless, a mounting body of evidence indicates that the ad hoc dimensions of EQ (self-awareness, self-management, social awareness, and social skill, as identified by Goleman) can be reliably measured and predict leadership performance fairly well.

The transformational leadership movement begins with Sigmund Freud and Max Weber, who argued that successful leaders have charisma, the ability to attract and develop a following. Robert House (1977) turned Weber's list of charismatic traits into a rating scale, and showed that the scale predicted leadership performance. House's results, combined with

Burns' (1978) book, created a surge of interest in charismatic leadership, now termed neo-charismatic or transformational leadership, around which a substantial body of empiricism has developed, much of it based on a measure called the Multifactor Leadership Questionnaire (MLQ; Bass & Avolio, 1991). The results of this movement can be summarized in terms of six points. First, there is considerable consensus regarding the components of transformational leadership – the key components include integrity, conviction, commitment, vision, optimism, openness to new ideas, and consideration of and concern for subordinates. Transformational leadership is contrasted with transactional leadership, which emphasizes goals, accountability, performance management, and compensation. Second, these characteristics – which are desired by subordinates regardless of cultural context – resemble the components of EQ. Third, transformational leadership as a gestalt suggests that: (a) there is a moral component to leadership; (b) leadership depends on the ability to develop a relationship with subordinates; and (c) there is one best way to behave as a leader. Fourth, considerable data support these claims. Fifth, transformational leadership (and EQ) is clearly related to personality. Consequently, sixth, transformational leadership seems to be a syndrome of normal personality and should be captured by components of the FFM.

Mixed Measures of Personality

Several leadership assessment procedures combine measures of leadership from the inside with measures of leadership from the outside, and form a bridge to the next section of this entry. The two best known and thoroughly validated of these mixed measures are the Managerial Practices Survey (MPQ; Yukl, Wall & Lepsinger, 1990), and the Leadership Practices Inventory (Posner & Kouzes, 1990). The MPQ is better regarded by academic researchers; it asks a manager to evaluate him/herself in terms of 11 categories of managerial behaviour; then subordinates evaluate the manager using the same categories. The Leadership Practices Inventory is based on a critical incidents survey of experienced managers ('What did you do when you were at your best?'); the dimensions of this assessment line up with the model of transformational leadership discussed in the preceding subsection.

ASSESSING LEADERSHIP FROM THE OUTSIDE

Subjective ratings of others' reputation as leaders began the 1950s using: (a) on-the-job behavioural description; and (b) assessment centres. Researchers at Ohio State University analysed 1800 behavioural descriptors and developed the Leader Behaviour Description Questionnaire (LBDQ; Stogdill & Coons, 1957) and the Supervisory Behaviour Description Questionnaire (SBDQ; Fleishman, 1957) which contained two broad dimensions: Consideration and Initiating Structure. Researchers at the University of Michigan created scales of leader Support, Goal Emphasis, Work Facilitation, and Interaction Facilitation (Bowers & Seashore, 1966). More recent on-the-job leadership rating scales are psychometrically improved, broader in scope, and use multiple rating sources. For example, *The Profilor* (Hezlett, Ronnkvist, Holt & Hazucha, 1997) assesses 38 managerial and leadership competencies using multisource ratings. A growing number of 360-degree measures of leader and managerial behaviour are available for use in developmental feedback (London & Smither, 1995).

The second major source of leadership ratings from the outside is the assessment centre. Originally developed in World War II to select officers and spies (Murray & Mackinnon, 1946), modern assessment centres use job simulations (e.g. in-basket exercise, leaderless group discussion) to evaluate leadership potential. The advantage of assessment centres over on-the-job ratings include control of situational factors and better assessor training and accountability. Assessment centres are valid predictors of leadership (Gaugler, Rosenthal, Thornton & Bentson, 1987), but there are many questions about what they measure (e.g. Bycio, Alvares & Hahn, 1987; Sackett & Dreher, 1982). Specifically, measures of such themes as planning and organizing, and interpersonal skills, correlate higher within exercises than individually between exercises. Nonetheless, assessment centres are a major source of data on leader and managerial behaviour.

FUTURE PERSPECTIVES AND CONCLUSIONS

Leadership assessment is intimately linked to leadership research. Key findings include the following.

Leadership is multidimensional. Leadership has often been conceptualized in terms of dichotomies; for example, Consideration and Initiating Structure, participative and autocratic styles, and person- and task-orientation. But leadership is a more nuanced concept, composed of an array of narrower facets. More specific leadership assessment allows (a) greater precision in developmental feedback and matching people to jobs; (b) richer conceptual frameworks for comparing alternative leadership perspectives; and (c) stronger tests of nomological networks guiding validation efforts (Tett, Guterman, Bleier & Murphy, 2000). A multidimensional approach also requires lengthy testing time for high fidelity data, and poses logistic problems in multisource feedback systems (Graddick & Lane, 1998).

Leadership is an evolving construct. Leadership assessment tools may need to be updated or replaced to reflect changes in the meaning of leadership as research progresses over time.

Leadership means different things to different people. Agreement among peer, subordinate, and supervisor ratings in multisource systems is moderate at best on most dimensions (Conway & Huffcutt, 1997; Dalessio, 1998; Harris & Schaubroeck, 1988). Validation efforts need to be sensitive to the diverse and sometimes competing values others hold about a given leader's role (Butterfield & Bartol, 1977), and to differences between raters in opportunity to observe leader performance.

Leadership assessment is a cognitive process and needs to be treated as such (Brown & Lord, 2001). Person perception holds promise as a framework for studying leadership reputation (Lord, De Vader & Alliger, 1986; Mount & Scullen, 2001; Sessa, 2001). Greater attention needs to be given to the mental processes by which individuals form judgements of themselves and others as leaders (Church, 1997).

Leadership effectiveness depends on the context. Skills required in higher level leadership roles typically are different from those required at lower levels (Silzer, 1998). Leadership succession planning requires identifying the demands expected in future leadership roles.

Leader promotion can entail an assessment paradox. Despite the greater importance of leadership at higher levels, assessing senior leaders poses unique challenges due to greater ambiguity of the leader's role, increased political use of appraisal results, and reduced accountability for not undergoing appraisal (Gioia & Longenecker, 1994; Graddick & Lane, 1998; Longenecker & Gioia, 1992).

Responsible leadership assessment requires commitment from upper management that results will be used for stated purposes. Using developmental feedback data for promotion decisions can undermine assessment goals. Special efforts are needed to ensure adherence to stated purposes and confidentiality of results (Silzer, 1998).

References

Bass, B.M. & Avolio, B.J. (1991). *The Multifactor Leadership Questionnaire*. Palo Alto, CA: Consulting Psychologists Press.

Block, J. (1995). A contrarian view of the five-factor approach to personality description. *Psychological Bulletin, 117*, 187–215.

Bowers, D. & Seashore, S. (1966). Predicting organizational effectiveness with a four-factor theory of leadership. *Administrative Science, 11*, 238–263.

Brown, D.J. & Lord, R.G. (2001). Leadership and perceiver cognition: moving beyond first order constructs. In London, M. (Ed.), *How People Evaluate Others in Organizations*. Mahwah, NJ: Lawrence Erlbaum Associates.

Burns, J.M. (1978). *Leadership*. New York: Harper & Row.

Butterfield, D.A. & Bartol, K.M. (1977). Evaluators of leader behaviour: a missing element in leadership theory. In Hunt, J.G. & Larson, L.L. (Eds.), *Leadership: The Cutting Edge*. Carbondale, IL: Southern Illinois University Press.

Bycio, P., Alvares, K.M. & Hahn, J. (1987). Situational specificity in assessment center ratings: a confirmatory factor analysis. *Journal of Applied Psychology, 72*, 463–474.

Campbell, D.P. (1990). The Campbell work orientation surveys. In Clark, K.E. & Clark, M.B. (Eds.), *Measures of Leadership*. West Orange, NJ: Leadership Library of America.

Cattell, R.B. & Eber, H.W. (1961). *The Sixteen Personality Factor Questionnaire* (3rd ed.). Champaign, IL: IPAT.

Church, A.H. (1997). Do you see what I see? An exploration of congruence in ratings from multiple perspectives. *Journal of Applied Social Psychology, 27*, 983–1020.

Conway, J.M. & Huffcutt, A.I. (1997). Psychometric properties of multisource performance ratings: a meta-analysis of subordinate, supervisor, peer, and self-ratings. *Human Performance, 10*, 331–360.

Dalessio, A.T. (1998). Using multisource feedback for employee development and personnel decisions. In Smither, J.W. (Ed.), *Performance Appraisal: State of the Art in Practice*. San Francisco: Jossey-Bass.

Fleishman, E.A. (1957). A leader behaviour description for industry. In Stogdill, R.M. & Coons, A.E. (Eds.), *Leader Behaviour: Its Description and Measurement*. Columbus, OH: Ohio State University.

Gaugler, B.B., Rosenthal, D.B., Thornton III, G.C. & Bentson, C. (1987). Meta-analysis of assessment center validity [Monograph]. *Journal of Applied Psychology, 72*, 493–511.

Gioia, D.A. & Longenecker, C.O. (1994). The politics of the executive appraisal. *Organizational Dynamics*, 47–57.

Goleman, D. (1995). *Emotional Intelligence*. New York: Bantam.

Gough, H.G. (1987). *California Psychological Inventory: Administrator's Guide*. Palo Alto, CA: Consulting Psychologists Press.

Graddick, M.M. & Lane, P. (1998). Evaluating executive performance. In Smither, J.W. (Ed.), *Performance Appraisal: State of the Art in Practice*. San Francisco: Jossey-Bass.

Guilford, J.P. & Zimmerman, W.S. (1956). Fourteen dimensions of temperament. *Psychological Monographs, 70*, 417.

Harris, M.M. & Schaubroeck, J. (1988). A meta-analysis of self-supervisor, self-peer, and peer-supervisor ratings. *Personnel Psychology, 41*, 43–62.

Hezlett, S.A., Ronnkvist, A.M., Holt, K.E. & Hazucha, J.F. (1997). *The Profilor Technical Summary*. Minneapolis, MN: Personnel Decisions, Inc.

Hogan, R. & Hogan, J. (1995). *Hogan Personality Inventory Manual*. Tulsa, OK: Hogan Assessment Systems.

House, R.J. (1977). A 1976 theory of charismatic leadership. In Hunt, J.G. & Larson, L.L. (Eds.), *Leadership* (pp. 189–207). Carbondale, IL: Southern Illinois University Press.

Howard, A. & Bray, D.W. (1990). Prediction of managerial success over long periods of time. In Clark, K.E. & Clark, M.B. (Eds.), *Measures of Leadership*. West Orange, NJ: Leadership Library of America.

London, M. & Smither, J. (1995). Can multi-source feedback change perceptions of goal accomplishment, self evaluations, and performance related outcomes? Theory-based applications and directions for research. *Personnel Psychology, 48*, 803–839.

Longenecker, C.O. & Gioia, D.A. (1992). The executive appraisal paradox. *Academy of Management Executive, 6*, 18–28.

Lord, R.G., De Vader, C.L. & Alliger, G.M. (1986). A meta-analysis of the relation between personality traits and leadership perceptions: an application of validity generalization procedures. *Journal of Applied Psychology, 71*, 402–410.

McCaulley, M.H. (1990). The Myers–Briggs Type Indicator and leadership. In Clark, K.E. & Clark, M.B. (Eds.), *Measures of Leadership*. West Orange, NJ: Leadership Library of America.

McClelland, D.C. (1975). *Power*. New York: Irvington.

Mount, M.K. & Scullen, S.E. (2001). Multisource feedback ratings: What do they really measure? In London, M. (Ed.), *How People Evaluate Others in Organizations*. Mahwah, NJ: Lawrence Erlbaum Associates.

Murray, H.A. & Mackinnon, D.W. (1946). Assessment of OSS personnel. *Journal of Consulting Psychology, 10*, 76–80.

Posner, B.Z. & Kouzes, J.M. (1990) Leadership practices. In Clark, K.E. & Clark, M.B. (Eds.), *Measures of Leadership*. West Orange, NJ: Leadership Library of America.

Sackett, P.R. & Dreher, G.F. (1982). Constructs and assessment center dimensions: some troubling empirical findings. *Journal of Applied Psychology, 67*, 401–410.

Sessa, V.I. (2001). Executive promotion and selection. In London, M. (Ed.), *How People Evaluate Others in Organizations*. Mahwah, NJ: Lawrence Erlbaum Associates.

Silzer, R. (1998). Shaping organizational leadership: the ripple effect of assessment. In Jeanneret, R. &

Silzer, R. (Eds.), *Individual Psychological Assessment*. San Francisco: Jossey-Bass.

Sparks, C.P. (1990). Testing for management potential. In Clark, K.E. & Clark, M.B. (Eds.), *Measures of Leadership*. West Orange, NJ: Leadership Library of America.

Stogdill, R.M. & Coons, A.E. (1957). *Leader Behaviour: Its Description and Measurement*. Columbus, OH: Ohio State University.

Tett, R.P., Guterman, H.A., Bleier, A. & Murphy, P.J. (2000). Development and content validation of a 'hyperdimensional' taxonomy of managerial competence. *Human Performance, 13*, 205–251.

Wiggins, J.S. (1996). *The Five-Factor Model*. New York: Guilford.

Yukl, G., Wall, S. & Lepsinger, R. (1990). Preliminary report on validation of the Managerial Practices Survey. In Clark, K.E. (Ed.), *Measures of Leadership*. West Orange, NJ: Leadership Library of America.

Robert Hogan and Robert Tett

RELATED ENTRIES

PERSONALITY ASSESSMENT (GENERAL), LEADERSHIP IN ORGANIZATIONAL SETTINGS

L LEARNING DISABILITIES

INTRODUCTION

The number of individuals classified with learning disabilities (LD) has increased dramatically over the last twenty years. This is because the classification of LD is based on the context of school learning. Consequently, considerable latitude exists among psychologists in defining LD. This latitude is reflected in social/political issues as well as non-operational definitions of LD (see Swanson, 1989, for a review).

The purpose of this entry is to bring some commonality to the assessment of LD. We address this problem by providing an operational definition of LD that will be useful in diagnostic assessment. Directions for future diagnostic research are also provided.

DEFINITION

Several definitions refer to LD as reflecting a heterogeneous group of individuals with 'intrinsic' disorders that are manifested by specific difficulties in the acquisition and use of listening, speaking, reading, writing, reasoning, or mathematical abilities (see Hammill, 1990, for a review). Most definitions assume that learning difficulties in such individuals are (a) *not* due to inadequate opportunity to learn, general intelligence, or to significant physical or emotional disorders, but to *basic* disorders in specific psychological processes, (b) these specific psychological processing deficits are a reflection of neurological, constitutional, and/or biological factors, and (c) there is a psychological processing deficit that depresses only a limited aspect of academic or contextually appropriate behaviour.

Thus, to assess individuals with potential LD, efforts are made to determine: (a) normal intelligence, (b) below normal achievement in isolated academic skills, (c) below normal performance in specific psychological processes (i.e. phonological awareness, working memory) and (d) adequate opportunity to learn (documentation that optimal instruction has been presented but deficits in isolated processes remain).

ASSESSMENT ISSUES

Traditionally, the assessment of individuals with LD has been directed towards (1) isolating *specific* learning problems, (2) establishing a significant *discrepancy* between IQ and achievement, and (3) demonstrating that *responsiveness* to instruction varies from those of other handicapping conditions. The literature notes problems in each of these areas (e.g. Aaron, 1997; Fletcher et al., 1994).

Specificity

Current efforts have been made to define individuals with LD as having problems in specific *primary* academic areas (word recognition, word reading fluency, arithmetic calculation) rather than problems in high-order or more complex academic domains (e.g. reading comprehension, problem solving). Although conceptually the notion of specificity is critical to the assessment of LD (Stanovich, 1986), it has not been established that the specific psychological processes that separate individuals with potential LD are different from other individuals who suffer similar academic problems. For example, Siegel (1992) found few differences in performance between dyslexics (individuals with LD in word recognition) and low achievers on language, spelling, and memory measures.

Discrepancy

Poor performance in individuals with LD in specific academic areas is unexpected based on their average intelligence. Identification of

this unexpected outcome has relied primarily on uncovering a discrepancy between achievement and intellectual ability. These discrepancies are quantified using: (a) mathematical formulas that emphasize current achievement, IQ, or mental age; (b) standard score discrepancies; and/or (c) regression formulas that account for the effects of scores regressing toward the mean (e.g. Kavale & Forness, 1994). A discrepancy of at least 1 standard deviation in one academic domain when compared to IQ is considered by some to reflect LD.

Unfortunately, several statistical flaws are inherent in many discrepancy formulas (e.g. Reynolds, 1981). For example, the regression formulas, in many cases, are dependent on the types of tests used. In other words, it is plausible that a student could be given a different battery of tests resulting in a different classification decision using the same formula but with different tests.

Responsiveness

Efforts are made by psychologists to distinguish individuals with LD from other general handicapping conditions, such as mental retardation, visual, and hearing impairments. Further specification is made that bilingual, socioeconomic status, and conventional instructional opportunity do not adequately account for depressed achievement scores. Such specification allows one to infer that the learning problems are intrinsic to the individual. Unfortunately, traditional assessment procedures seldom provide information that assesses the stability and/or durability of these intrinsic psychological processing deficits under instructional conditions. If an individual with LD has an inability to remember specific aspects of language (phonological information), then documentation must be provided when they have been systematically exposed to such instruction.

Some literature suggests that LD individuals are less responsive to intervention than individuals with similar primary academic levels but without LD (Swanson & Hoskyn, 1998, 1999) and these academic problems persist into adulthood (e.g. Bruck, 1992). However, differential responsiveness to instruction has not been directly tested under well-controlled experimental conditions.

CLASSIFICATION RESEARCH

The implicit assumption for using discrepancy scores in the classification of LD is that individuals who experience reading, writing and/ or maths difficulties, unaccompanied by a low IQ, are distinct in cognitive processing from slow or low achievers. This assumption is equivocal.

A plethora of studies have compared children with discrepancies between IQ and reading with non-discrepancy defined poor achievers (i.e. children whose IQ scores are in the same low range as their reading scores) and found that these groups are more similar in processing difficulties than different (e.g. Shaywitz et al., 1992; Stanovich & Siegel, 1994). As a result, some researchers have advocated abandoning the concept of discrepancy between IQ and achievement measures. In the area of reading deficits, some have even suggested dropping the requirement of average intelligence, in favour of a view where children with reading problems are best conceptualized as existing at the extreme end of a continuum from poor to good readers (e.g. Stanovich & Siegel, 1994). In addition, some researchers have argued that IQ is irrelevant to the definition of reading disabilities and that poor readers share similar cognitive deficits, irrespective of general cognitive abilities (Siegel, 1992).

In a major synthesis of the literature, Hoskyn and Swanson (2000) calculated effect sizes across studies to determine if LD readers and low achievers (LA) share common cognitive deficits. The characteristics of the sample are shown in Table 1. The most common standardized measures of intelligence were from the Wechsler Intelligence Tests (75% of the studies) and the most common measures of word recognition were from the Wide Range Achievement Test or the Woodcock Reading Mastery Test (57% of the studies). Table 2 shows the comparisons between the groups. Positive effect sizes favour children with LD in reading (reading disabled – RD). Effect sizes around 0.80 are considered substantial, those around 0.60 are moderate, and those below 0.20 are marginal.

Table 1. Age and psychometric characteristics of children with RD and low achievers (LA)

Variable	RD group mean	RD group SD	LA group mean	LA group SD
Age	111.05	33.34	110.92	33.48
Word recognition	79.82	5.75	84.09	5.72
Verbal intelligence	99.46	4.79	83.64	4.91

SD = standard deviation.

Table 2. Magnitude of effect size by category of dependent measure

Category of dependent measure	K	Mean effect size	SD
Phonological processing			
Speech-related phonological processing	34	0.27	0.5
Pseudo-word reading	18	0.29	0.39
Real-word phonetic analysis	26	−0.02	0.52
Automaticity (Naming speed)	55	0.05	0.45
Spelling	8	0.19	0.43
Memory	59	0.12	0.89
Syntactical knowledge	11	0.87	0.24
Lexical knowledge	17	0.55	0.63
Visual spatial reasoning			
Visual-motor skills	9	0.15	0.8
Spatial ability	37	0.36	0.67

K = number of studies.

The important results were that although the RD and LA groups share deficits in phonological processing and automaticity (naming speed), the RD group's performance was superior to the LA group on measures of syntactical knowledge, lexical knowledge, and spatial ability. Another important finding was that cognitive difference between the two ability groups becomes less ostensible after age 12.

BEST OPERATIONAL DEFINITION TO DATE

The majority of classification research in the last 10 years has focused on primary deficits in reading or mathematics. This research defines LD as those individuals with IQ scores equal to or above a Full Scale IQ score of 85 and reading subtest scores equal to or below the 16th percentile and/or arithmetic subtest score equal to or below the 16th percentile. The most commonly used intelligence tests are the Wechsler measures, and achievement tests include measures of word recognition or identification (i.e. Wide Range Achievement Test, Woodcock Reading Mastery Test, Kaufman Test of Educational Achievement, Peabody Individual Test) and arithmetic calculation (all the aforementioned tests that include arithmetic measures and the Key Math Test). This definition captures two high incidence disorders within LD: reading (word recognition), and arithmetic (computation, written work).

DIRECTIONS FOR FUTURE RESEARCH

Because the validity of defining LD is undermined by the use of discrepancy classification procedures, further research is necessary to classify such individuals. Several means of advancing the classification literature are as follows:

Choose Measures of Construct Integrity

Although current assessments use the WISC III (or WISC-R) and standardized achievement (e.g. reading) tests to determine discrepancy scores, this is not an argument for conceptual integrity

(also see Kavale & Forness, 1994: 41, for a discussion of this issue). Neither a theoretical rationale nor empirical evidence is available to substantiate the claim that IQ tests, e.g. WISC III, capture the construct of 'potential'. Quite simply, it is not the case that individuals with comparable IQ scores on the WISC III have the same potential. In addition, a difference between an intelligence score on the Wechsler test and a serious performance deficit on the Wide Range Achievement Test (or any other achievement test) in the area of reading is not a valid test of a discrepancy model. Neither test fits into a theoretical framework of intelligence nor reading. Advances in testing LD are better served if classification is grounded in theory.

Ensure Independence among Measures

Discrepancy scores (or discrepancy defined groups) are correlated with their component parts, and therefore the discrepancy measure will relate significantly to other variables correlated with the component parts (Cronbach & Furby, 1970). When discrepancy scores are correlated with their component parts, there is a greater than chance tendency for them to be correlated with other variables which are associated with those component parts.

An example of the above rule is as follows. When (a) reading recognition is part of the discrepancy score, and (b) when low reading ability groups are comparable on reading recognition performance, then performance is comparable between discrepancy and non-discrepancy groups on processes (phonological awareness) related to reading. Thus, the discrepancy group is little more than a surrogate of the poor reading group. This circularity in findings has been recognized in the literature for some time (Cronbach & Gleser, 1953).

Direction of Outcomes must be Consequential in Performance

For example, *Child A* who has a high reading score, but low intelligence score, should reflect a different 'set of' or 'level of' processes when compared to *Child B* who has a high IQ score but low reading score. If individuals are identified by use of a discrepancy, assessment must address or determine if direction is consequential on cognitive performance. If the direction is unimportant, those measures used to determine a discrepancy should be removed from the discrepancy formula.

Measures Related to Discrepancy Scores are Only Valid if Assessed on Something above and beyond their Components and Correlates

Most researchers recognize the reliability problems with discrepancy scores, but few recognize that the use of discrepancy scores implies that it accomplishes something beyond their component parts. Responsiveness to instruction seems to be a missing test in the majority studies comparing discrepancy and non-discrepancy groups. There is some suggestive research based on meta-analysis that groups with discrepancies are less responsive to general interventions than those whose IQ and reading scores are at the same low level (Swanson & Hoskyn, 1999).

FUTURE PERSPECTIVES AND CONCLUSIONS

This entry has reviewed some of the common assumptions related to definitions of LD. We also review evidence on the validity of classifications based on a discrepancy between IQ and achievement. Future approaches to defining LD will rely on cut-off scores on standardized measures

above a certain criterion of general intelligence measures (e.g. standard score > 85) and cut-off scores below a certain criterion (standard score < 85) on primary academic domains (e.g. reading and mathematics). Table 3 provides a list of some common standardized measures used to assess learning disabilities.

Acknowledgement

This entry was supported, in part, by Grant No. H023E0014 for the US Department of Education and Peloy Endowment Funds to the author.

References

Aaron, P.G. (1997). The impending demise of the discrepancy formula. *Review of Educational Research*, 67, 461–502.

Bruck, M. (1992). Persistence of dyslexics' phonological awareness deficits. *Developmental Psychology*, 28, 874–886.

Cronbach, L. & Furby, L. (1970). How we should measure 'change' – or should we? *Psychological Bulletin*, 74, 68–80.

Cronbach, L. & Gleser, G.C. (1953). Assessing similarity between profiles. *Psychological Bulletin*, 50, 456–473.

Fletcher, J.M., Shaywitz, S.E., Shankweiler, D.P, Katz, L., Liberman, I.Y., Stuebing, K.K., Francis, D.J., Fowler, A.E. & Shaywitz, B.A. (1994). Cognitive profiles of reading disability: comparisons of discrepancy and low achievement definitions. *Journal of Educational Psychology*, 86(1), 6–23.

Hammill, D. (1990). On defining learning disabilities: an emerging consensus. *Journal of Learning Disabilities*, 23, 74–84.

Hoskyn, M. & Swanson, H.L. (2000). Cognitive processing of low achievers and children with reading disabilities: a selective review of the published literature. *School Psychology Review*, 29, 102–119.

Kavale, S. & Forness, S.R. (1994). Learning disabilities and intelligence: an uneasy alliance. In Scruggs, T. & Mastropieri, M. (Eds.), *Advances in Learning and Behavioural Disabilities*, Vol. 8 (pp. 1–64). Greenwich, CT: JAI Press.

Reynolds, C.R. (1981). The fallacy of two years below grade level for age as a diagnostic criterion for reading disorders. *Journal of School Psychology*, 11, 250–258.

Shaywitz, B.A., Fletcher, J.M., Holahan, J.M. & Shaywitz, S.E. (1992). Discrepancy compared to low achievement definitions of reading disability: results from the Connecticut longitudinal

Table 3. Some standardized measures used to diagnose learning disabilities

I *Intelligence*
   A Wechsler tests (e.g. WISC-III)
   B Raven progressive matrices test

II *Achievement*
   A Woodcock reading mastery test
   B Wide range achievement test
   C Woodcock psychoeducational inventory
      (Achievement Clusters)
   D Test of written language

III *Cognitive processes*
   A Comprehensive test of phonological processing
   B Test of word reading efficiency
   C Swanson–cognitive processing test

study. *Journal of Learning Disabilities, 25*(10), 639–648.

Siegel, L.S. (1992). An evaluation of the discrepancy definition of dyslexia. *Journal of Learning Disabilities, 25*(10), 618–629.

Stanovich, K.E. (1986). Matthew effects in reading: some consequences of individual differences in the acquisition of literacy. *Reading Research Quarterly, 21,* 360–407.

Stanovich, K.E. & Siegel, L.S. (1994). Phenotypic performance profile of children with reading disabilities: a regression-based test of the phono-logical-core variable-difference model. *Journal of Educational Psychology, 1,* 24–53.

Swanson, H.L. (1989). Operational definition: an overview. *Learning Disability Quarterly, 14,* 242–254.

Swanson, H.L. & Hoskyn, M. (1998). Experimental intervention research on students with learning disabilities: a meta-analysis of treatment outcomes. *Review of Educational Research, 68,* 277–321.

Swanson, H.L. & Hoskyn, M. (1999). Definition × treatment interactions for students with learning disabilities. *School Psychology Review, 28,* 644–658.

H. Lee Swanson

RELATED ENTRIES

APPLIED FIELDS: CLINICAL, APPLIED FIELDS: EDUCATION, MENTAL RETARDATION, DYNAMIC ASSESSMENT, LEARNING STRATEGIES, CHILDREN WITH DISABILITIES

L LEARNING STRATEGIES

INTRODUCTION

Students differ in the approach they take to learning and in the cognitive processes they engage in when performing academic tasks, and these differences are of interest because they correlate with differences in the quality of academic outcome. The basic idea is to identify the features of more successful learning as well as the best ways to develop them. There has been much confusion and different meanings associated with the term learning strategies (LS) as well as different terms to describe similar processes. This discussion will take as a starting point the arguments of van Dijk and Kintsch (1983) regarding strategies of discourse comprehension. According to them, a strategy is 'the idea of an agent about the way to act in order to reach a goal (in the most effective way)' (p. 64), or, in other words, '... a global representation of the means of reaching (a) goal. This overall means will dominate a number of lower level, more detailed decisions and actions' (p. 65). It is not a detailed planning, since sequences of actions, complex informations

and circumstances interact to produce a given result, but 'merely a global instruction for such necessary choice to be made along the path of the course of action' (p. 65). Related to strategies, and contrasted to mere actions, they describe a *move* as 'any action that is accomplished with the intention of bringing about a state of affairs that ... will (probably) lead to a desired goal' (p. 66). Thus, 'a strategy is defined as a cognitive unit dominating only the moves of an action sequence and not each action' (p. 66). It is also interesting to keep in mind that in 'complex problems part of these strategies may be consciously intended and, yet, part of them will also be more or less automatized' (p. 70). Finally, they describe a tactic as a system of strategies.

In the field of LS, two sources of differences among students can be distinguished which might be understood in the light of these concepts. *Approaches to learning* dominate, give meaning and a style to most of the activities a student carries out; in terms of the above discussion, they might be taken as tactics students may adopt when learning. On the other hand, *strategies* have to do with more discrete, yet complex activities such as the way they address an academic reading or set out to write an essay.

The goals students with opposing approaches pursue in learning differ in important ways; students with a *deep approach* try to learn and to change their perception of reality, while those with a *surface approach* try to comply with academic demands, pass exams or take learning as a means to get a better job. Approaches to learning have been documented to be related to teachers' practices (see entry on 'Instructional Strategies') and to correlate with different ways of performing academic tasks and with outcomes measured in various ways (Ramsden, 1992). They act at the intentional level and permeate lower level strategies. *Approaches to learning* have been summarized (Ramsden, 1992) as shown in Table 1.

LS have been defined as different ways of processing information (Weinstein & Mayer, 1986) and are often used coherently with the two main approaches (deep vs. surface). It is interesting to remember they are units complex enough to entail different moves and decisions and may comprise more or less automatized components but are by definition selected among other alternatives, thus flexibly and deliberately applied to reach specific goals. Weinstein and Mayer offer a taxonomy of LS which has become a classic and includes 6 categories of *cognitive strategies*, in fact 3 types of strategies carried out in basic (learning of isolated facts) or complex (learning of integrated bodies of knowledge) tasks. These strategies are: *Repetition*, *Elaboration* and *Organization*. These cognitive strategies are complemented by 2 categories of support

strategies: *affective* (anxiety and motivational) and *metacognitive*, having to do with planning, monitoring and reviewing.

Thus LS embrace a wide range of moves and processes from the cognitive, affective, social and metacognitive levels which interact with each other. A student with good learning strategies will be able to formulate clear task objectives, select the right cognitive activities to reach a given learning goal, learn in a self-regulated way, look out for support when needed, be able to apply the acquired knowledge to solve problems and succesfully monitor and orchestrate the whole process, thus resulting in enhanced abilities to continue learning autonomously throughout life.

ASSESSMENT METHODS

Approaches to Learning

To assess them, a number of instruments have been developed. *Interviews* with students have been used from a phenomenographic ethnographic approach, with the purpose of understanding how learning is approached and experienced (Marton, Hounsel & Entwistle, 1984). Their main difficulty is the high costs of in-depth interviews, but they are fundamental in a qualitative approach to students' experience which might then lead to more structured devices.

Various *self-report measures* have also been developed. Among the best known is the *Approaches to Study Inventory* (ASI, Entwistle & Ramsden, 1983). Its 64 items basically cover three orientations to learning (meaning, reproducing and achieving) with their corresponding

Table 1. Summary of approaches to learning

Deep approach	Surface approach

Intention to understand.
  Student maintains structure of task.
Focus on 'what is signified'
Relate previous knowledge to new knowledge
Relate knowledge from different courses
Relate theoretical ideas to everyday experience
Relate and distinguish evidence and argument
Organize and structure content into a coherent
  whole Internal emphasis
	Intention only to complete task requirements.
	  Student distorts task structure.
	Focus on 'the signs'
	Memorize information for assessment
	Associate facts and concepts unreflectively
	Knowledge cut off from everyday reality
	Fail to distinguish principles from examples
	Focus on unrelated parts of the task
	Treat the task as an external imposition
	External emphasis: demands of assessment

approaches (deep, surface, strategic) and two styles of learning (comprehension and operation) with their corresponding pathologies (globetrotting and improvidence). The *Module Experience Questionnaire* (MEQ, Ramsden, 1992) combines with scales related to teaching, deep vs. surface approaches to learning.

Learning Strategies

Self-Report: General

These self-reports consist of a list of characteristic activities students do or do not usually engage in when performing academic activities. So, they refer to what they do *generally*, not in a specific task; but it is easy to see that they can significantly change from one task or knowledge domain to another. In spite of these limitations, these procedures are an economic and quick way of assessment which can be used for screening in a first phase of work. However, they should be supplemented with more specific devices such as specific reports or observations (or both) in order to fully understand the functioning of a student.

Many of these questionnaires do not derive from an explicit theoretical framework: items have generally been selected through rational or empirical approaches, but often the overall theoretical framework is not made explicit. Thus the number of scales and items widely differ and it is often difficult to compare them. Among those with best foundations we shall mention (Zimmerman & Palmer, 1988).

The *Learning and Study Strategies Inventory* (LASSI, Weinstein et al., 1988) includes 77 items distributed in 10 scales: Attitude, Motivation, Time Management, Anxiety, Concentration, Information Processing, Selecting Main Ideas, Study Aids, Self Testing and Test Strategies.

The *Motivated Strategies for Learning Questionaire* (MSLQ, Pintrich, Smith, García & McKeachie, 1991) is comprised of 81 items distributed in 15 scales: 6 related to aspects of motivation (Value, Expectancy and Affect) and 9 to Learning Strategies: Cognitive (Rehearsal, Elaboration, Organization and Critical Thinking), Metacognitive and Resource Management (Time and Study Environment, Effort, Peer Learning and Help-seeking).

The *Inventario De Estrategias de Aprendizaje* (IDEA, Vizcarro, Bermejo, del Castillo & Aragonés, 1996) has 153 items distributed in 14 scales (plus Sincerity): Attention, Establishing Connections, Knowledge Representation, Oral & Written Expression, Assertivity with Teacher, Motivation-Effort, Perception of Control, Non-Repetitive Learning, Taking Examinations, Work Management, Metacognition, Physical & Environmental Conditions and Reflective Learning.

Self-Report: Specific

These devices ask for the subject's report through interviews or think aloud protocols while or immediately after performing a given task (reading, problem solving, written composition, etc.). Typical *interview* questions include: 'How does a good reader go about reading?' Or 'Did you look back while reading?'

Think aloud protocols may take two forms: asking the subject to report the operations he/she is performing along a task or at specific moments (for instance, in reading, after each paragraph or at given marks in the text). These reports may also take place after completing the task, supported by audio or video recordings to stimulate recall.

Observation

This method of data collection may be used to register some open features of strategic behaviour, traces or results of behaviour. An example of the first kind is observing task centred behaviour or search for information of external sources. As traces of behaviour, underlining book or note taking are typical in situational tests of study or reading behaviour. Finally, a synthesis elaborated after reading or number of correct answers to open or closed questions are frequently used as a measure of quality of outcome of reading or studying, that is, as a criterion.

Recently, some simulations and electronic environments allow a continuous registration of the work done by a student and the paths followed when performing a task, thus making possible a detailed follow-up and analysis of the strategies used in task completion.

More informal data may take place in classroom observations of the process of academic performance. These informal observations are usually complemented by the dialogue between teacher and student whereby the goals and reasons of a given strategy may be thoroughly explored. In fact, observation methods should be complemented by in-depth questioning regarding the reasons behind a given strategy or the extent of its use to gather a more precise picture.

FUTURE PERSPECTIVES AND CONCLUSIONS

One limitation of focusing on learning approaches or strategies is that we might forget about contextual demands, with which they are necessarily related. While there is not much discussion on the existence of different approaches and strategies which correlate with different levels of achievement, a crucial question is how to help students develop more effective ways of learning. Independent study skills programmes have been developed trying to teach broad LS which can be applied to any subject matter. However, other findings show strategies acquired in this way are difficult to generalize to new situations and effective LS can only be acquired along with specific content knowledge, that is through quality teaching in specific domains. The challenge, then, is to train teachers so that they are able to help students develop the appropriate strategies within their subject framework. A mid-way solution might be to help students acquire general LS which teachers will then develop in their own class-rooms and subjects. A good definition and assessment of LS are required as well as the ability of teachers to observe and model the best strategies.

References

Entwistle, N.J. & Ramsden, P. (1983). *Understanding Student Learning*. London: Croom Helm.
Marton, F., Hounsel, D. & Entwistle, N. (1984). *The Experience of Learning*. Edinburgh: Scottish Academic Press.
Pintrich, P.R., Smith, D.A.F., García, T. & McKeachie, W.J. (1991). *A Manual for the Use of the Motivated Strategies for Learning Questionnaire*. University of Michigan, Ann Arbor: NCRIPTL Technical Report.
Ramsden, P. (1992). *Learning to Teach in Higher Education*. London: Routledge.
van Dijk, T.A. & Kintsch, W. (1983). *Strategies of Discourse Comprehension*. London: Academic Press.
Vizcarro, C., Bermejo, I., del Castillo, M. & Aragonés, C. (1996). Development of an inventory to measure learning strategies. In Birenbaum, M. & Dochy, F. (Eds.), *Alternatives in Assessment of Achievements, Learning Processes and Prior Knowledge* (pp. 341–361). Boston: Kluwer.
Weinstein, C.E. & Mayer, R.E. (1986). The teaching of learning strategies. In Wittrock, M.C. (Ed.), *Handbook of Research on Teaching* (pp. 315–327). New York: Macmillan.
Weinstein, C.E., Zimmerman, S.A. & Palmer, D.R. (1988). Assessing learning strategies: the design and development of the LASSI. In Weinstein, C.E., Goetz, E.T. & Alexander, P. (Eds.), *Learning and Study Strategies* (pp. 25–40). San Diego, CA: Academic Press.

Carmen Vizcarro Guarch

RELATED ENTRIES

APPLIED FIELDS: EDUCATION, THEORETICAL PERSPECTIVE: COGNITIVE, INSTRUCTIONAL STRATEGIES

LIFE EVENTS

INTRODUCTION

Although it is long established that stress is related to ill health and psychological distress, there remains ambiguity about the dimensions of stress involved in this process, specifically the types of stressors that have more deleterious effects on health. To study the naturalistic stress process, the field requires valid and reliable measures of *life events*, to use in conjunction with measures of vulnerability to stress. A *life events scale* is a comprehensive list of external events and situations (stressors) that are hypothesized to place demands that exceed the capacity of the average individual to adapt. Sample items in life events scales include recent divorce or separation, the death of a close family member, a job loss, moving, and the onset of a health problem.

Two types of life events assessment dominate the literature; exposure to out-of-the-ordinary events that have the capacity to change the patterns of life or arouse very unpleasant feelings (*life events*) and exposure to relatively minor, less emotionally arousing events whose effects disperse in a day or two (*hassles*). These measures often, but not always, take the *environmental* perspective on stress (e.g. Cohen, Kessler & Gordon, 1995), which tends to view events as triggers for disease. Life events measures differ to the extent to which they include self-reports of perceived stressfulness and threat posed by events (*appraisals*) and enduring or recurrent difficulties in an area of life (*chronic stressors*). The dimension of appraisal incorporates more fully the *psychological* perspective on stress (e.g. Lazarus, 1999). These variations in life event assessment have developed in response to different types of research questions, the outcome of interest in the investigation, and the period of time over which a particular event is thought to have impact, whether a few hours, or many years.

LIFE EVENTS

There are two general methods of life events assessment, checklist measures (Turner & Wheaton, 1995) and personal interview measures (Wethington, Brown & Kessler, 1995). Interview measures incorporate qualitative probes that specify the characteristics of life events theorized to produce physical or psychological stress, the severity of the occurrence (the threat), and the timing of life events in relationship to the outcome. Some checklist measures use standardized probes to assess perceived severity, appraised threat, and timing of the event. Both checklist and interview measures can assess chronic stressors as well as acute or discrete life events.

A typical checklist measure consists of a series of yes/no questions, asking participants to report if any situation like the one described has occurred over a past period of time (e.g. one month, a year). Checklist measures may rely on respondent self-report to rate event severity and threat, or may assign average ('normative') severity ratings developed by investigators. Either method results in a summary score of the estimated stressfulness of events experienced over a period of time.

Checklist measures are popular, inexpensive, and easy to administer. They also yield consistent relationships with physical health outcomes, which is a property that makes them useful for exploratory studies (Turner & Wheaton, 1995). The Social Readjustment Rating Scale (SRSS: Holmes & Rahe, 1967) is the ancestor of many checklist measures in current use. The SRSS included both positive and negative events because its developers believed that change *per se* was associated with changes in health status. Over time, checklists have moved toward including only negative or undesirable events, based on repeated findings that undesirable events are more predictive of severe health problems than positive events. Special measures have been developed for other populations, including adolescents and ageing adults (Turner & Wheaton, 1995).

Despite their popularity, checklist measures have been criticized on the grounds of reliability and validity. These criticisms include inadequate or generalized severity ratings, lack of comprehensiveness across different life domains and the experiences of special populations, and fall-off in reporting more distant rather than more recent events (Herbert & Cohen, 1996).

The early development of personal interview methods that use qualitative probes was driven by a perspective that assumes social and environmental changes (and anticipations of those changes) threatening the most strongly held *emotional commitments* are the basis of severe stress. This perspective also asserts that severe stress threatens health, rather than minor stress, distinguishing it from measures of hassles, or daily events (e.g. Lazarus & Folkman, 1984).

Interview measures are more often used if research requires one or more of the following: (1) more precise severity ratings, that are less contaminated by respondent appraisal; (2) the relative timing of exposure and disease onset; and (3) establishing that stressors are 'independent' of respondent illness or behaviour. Promoters of interview methods also claim that they are more reliable and valid than checklist measures, although it is probably more accurate to assert that they measure different phenomena. Their expense rules them out for exploratory, low budget studies.

The purpose of the interview probing is to gather enough information to rate the objective long-term contextual threat or severity of situations. The rating of event severity is the major aim of personal interview methods, as the experience of a very severely threatening situation is hypothesized to pose a risk for illness. Rating the degree of severity and threat for objective situations has been documented over several decades in dictionaries available for researchers. Events may also occur because of the pre-existence of a physical or mental disorder. If that pre-existing disorder is as well the major outcome of the research study, interpretive difficulties arise. Rating routines for most personal interview measures of stressor exposure include an assessment of whether a situation is (1) known to be related to an actual disorder the respondent reports (e.g. getting fired because of drinking), or (2) hypothetically related to symptomatology (e.g. events involving interpersonal conflict). The Life Events and Difficulty Schedule (LEDS: Brown & Harris, 1978) is the best-known and best-documented interview method. Many interview measures use LEDS or LEDS-like rating schemes.

The LEDS has experienced criticism for its rating and interview methods. Wethington, Brown, and Kessler (1995) discuss these criticisms extensively. The most persistent criticism is that ratings of 'threat' include contexts many researchers would like to measure separately as modifiers of the impact of stressors on health. Specifically, there is a long-standing controversy over whether LEDS ratings of contextual threat cloud the distinction between event severity and the individual's vulnerability to a stressor (Tennant, Bebbington & Hurry, 1981).

All interview and checklist measures aim to be comprehensive across types of stressors. They vary, however, in whether they include comprehensive assessment of chronic stressors as well as discrete events. This distinction is important for investigators, because chronic stress assessment is apt to be more important for some health outcomes (e.g. physical precursors to heart disease) in comparison to others (e.g. onset of depression).

Measures of life events also differ in whether they include or exclude appraisal. Many checklist and interview measures of life events for the most part aim to exclude appraisal from stressor exposure assessment. Those that exclude appraisal do so because of concerns that stressor appraisal may be confounded with the health and psychological outcomes that stressor exposure is hypothesized to predict (Monroe & Kelly, 1995). Indeed, researchers have speculated that some stressor appraisals are 'caused' by underlying, persistent mood disturbance, rather than vice-versa (Stone, Kessler & Haythornthwaite, 1991).

HASSLES

Early hassles assessment relied on diary methods of collection, where respondents were asked to keep records of small events occurring over a given period of time, usually a 24-hour or 1-week period. Researchers have taken two approaches to measurement: open-ended questions which asked respondents to describe bothersome events of the day; and structured questions, simple yes or no response questions modelled on life events checklists (Eckenrode & Bolger, 1995).

Current hassle scales share the strengths and weaknesses of related approaches to the assessment of major life events and chronic stressors. One of the most persistent has been that diary methods of data collection, relying on written self-report, confound objective events with psychological appraisal processes (Eckenrode & Bolger, 1995). Hassle measures assume participants respond to the questions in a relatively neutral and uniform way (Schwartz & Stone, 1993). A second persistent criticism is that the self-report of hassles is confounded with coping. The argument here is that when a respondent copes successfully with small hassles, such as overloads or interruptions, he or she is less likely to either (1) remember the occurrence, or (2) interpret the situation as a stressor (Aspinwall & Taylor, 1997).

A third criticism is that methods of data collection for hassles are too time-consuming and expensive to use in large-scale surveys of the population, particularly on a daily basis. Most research on daily events has been conducted in small, discrete, relatively homogeneous samples (Stone et al., 1991; Eckenrode & Bolger, 1995). Such samples limit the generalizability of findings. Almeida and colleagues (Almeida, Wethington & Kessler, 2002) have recently completed a national study of hassles, developing a telephone interview measure of hassles. Future work on life events and hassles assessment will lead to more refinements in assessment.

References

Almeida, D.M., Wethington, E. & Kessler, R.C. (2002). The daily inventory of stressful experiences (DISE): an investigator-based approach for measuring daily stressors. *Assessment, 9*, 41–55.

Aspinwall, L.G. & Taylor, S.E. (1997). A stitch in time: self-regulation and proactive coping. *Psychological Bulletin, 121*, 417–436.

Brown, G.W. & Harris, T.O. (1978). *Social Origins of Depression: A Study of Depressive Disorder in Women.* New York: Free Press.

Cohen, S., Kessler, R.C. & Gordon, L.U. (1995). Strategies for measuring stress and its relationship to psychological disorders. In Cohen, S., Kessler, R.C. & Gordon, L.U. (Eds.), *Measuring Stress: A Guide for Health and Social Scientists* (pp. 3–26). New York: Oxford University Press.

Eckenrode, J. & Bolger, N. (1995). Daily and within-day event measurement. In Cohen, S., Kessler, R.C. & Gordon, L.U. (Eds.), *Measuring Stress: A Guide for Health and Social Scientists* (pp. 80–101). New York: Oxford University Press.

Herbert, T.B. & Cohen, S. (1996). Measurement issues in research on psychosocial stress. In Kaplan, H.B. (Ed.), *Psychosocial Stress: Perspectives on Structure, Theory, Life-Course, and Methods* (pp. 295–332). New York: Academic.

Holmes, T.H. & Rahe, R.H. (1967). The social readjustment rating scale. *Journal of Psychosomatic Research, 11*, 213–218.

Lazarus, R.S. (1999). *Stress and Emotion.* New York: Springer Publishing.

Lazarus, R.S. & Folkman, S. (1984). *Stress, Appraisal, and Coping.* New York: Springer Publishing.

Monroe, E. & Kelly, J.M. (1995). Measurement of stress appraisal. In Cohen, S., Kessler, R.C. & Gordon, L.U. (Eds.), *Measuring Stress: A Guide for Health and Social Scientists* (pp. 122–147). New York: Oxford University Press.

Schwartz, J.E. & Stone, A.A. (1993). Coping with daily work problems: contributions of problem content, appraisals, and person factors. *Work and Stress, 1*, 47–62.

Stone, A.A., Kessler, R.C. & Haythornthwaite, J.A. (1991). Measuring daily events and experiences: methodological considerations. *Journal of Personality, 59*, 575–607.

Tennant, C., Bebbington, P. & Hurry, J. (1981). The role of life events in depressive illness: is there a substantial causal relation? *Psychological Medicine, 11*, 379–389.

Turner, R.J. & Wheaton, B. (1995). Checklist measurement of stressful life events. In Cohen, S., Kessler, R.C. & Gordon, L.U. (Eds.), *Measuring Stress: A Guide for Health and Social Scientists* (pp. 29–58). New York: Oxford University Press.

Wethington, E., Brown, G.W. & Kessler, R.C. (1995). Interview measurement of stressful life events. In Cohen, S., Kessler, R.C. & Gordon, L.U. (Eds.), *Measuring Stress: A Guide for Health and Social Scientists* (pp. 59–79). New York: Oxford University Press.

Elaine Wethington

RELATED ENTRIES

Applied Fields: Clinical, Applied Fields: Health, Stress, Job Stress, Health

L LOCUS OF CONTROL

INTRODUCTION

Locus of control (LOC) is an individual's expectancy about the typical source (locus) of reinforcement. Does reinforcement originate within an individual ('When something good happens to me, it is because I worked for it') or from outside ('I have no influence on what the government does')? In the former case, we have an *internal* LOC, whereas in the latter case, we have an *external* LOC.

I provide a brief overview of the LOC construct and how it has been measured with self-report questionnaires. This task is daunting. LOC has been one of the most frequently investigated individual differences, and LOC measures have been used in thousands of empirical investigations. I have relied here on several earlier and more extensive reviews (Lefcourt, 1991; MacDonald, 1973).

In addition to its own popularity, the LOC construct has inspired related lines of research into generalized expectancies about the sources of good and bad events – notions like explanatory style, helplessness, hope, illusory control, John Henryism, secondary control, self-efficacy, and so on (Peterson, 1999). Those who work within these other traditions may not always cite LOC as the intellectual parent of their constructs, or they may insist that their own approaches are distinct. Regardless, there is considerable overlap – theoretically and empirically – between LOC and its offspring.

SOCIAL LEARNING THEORY AND LOCUS OF CONTROL RESEARCH

Rotter (1954) introduced locus of control in his social learning theory to make sense of people's varying reactions to success and failure. A radical learning theory, one that does not look within an individual to explain behaviour, would predict that success (reinforcement) should always result in continued responses, whereas failure (punishment or extinction) should never do so. This prediction proves to be wrong. In some cases, success does not produce perseverance, and in other cases, failure does not produce passivity.

Rotter therefore proposed that people's behaviour is influenced not just by reinforcement or punishment but also by their expectancies about the link between responses and outcomes. It is only when expectancies are congruent with what happens that success and failure have effects. People who do not expect that efforts and actions produce reinforcement will not have their response tendencies changed by occasional reward. And those who do expect that efforts and actions produce reinforcement will not be dissuaded from future responding by occasional lack of reward.

According to Rotter (1966), expectancies about a given situation are shaped by the features of that situation and by experiences in similar situations. These experiences accumulate and produce generalized expectancies. So, LOC is abstracted from past experiences, but it also determines future learning and thus can have a life of its own. LOC is psychologically interesting because it is *not* always redundant with reality.

Lefcourt (1991: 415) summarized what early researchers learned about the correlates of LOC:

> An internal locus of control was associated with a more active pursuit of valued goals, as would be manifested in social action ... information seeking ... alertness ... autonomous decision making ... and a sense of well-being. Those who were assumed to have a more external locus of control were often found to be depressed ... anxious ... and less able to cope with stressful life experiences.

These findings are consistent with the role assigned to LOC in social learning theory. However, other findings seemed contrary. Either LOC was not associated with the active pursuit of goals, or the magnitudes of correlations were surprisingly low.

In response, Rotter (1975) wrote a cautionary article about 'misconceptions and misuses' of the LOC construct. First, he urged researchers to take into account the reinforcement value of goals. Those with an internal locus of control may not participate in a political protest, for example, if they do not agree with the cause.

Second, he reminded researchers that LOC refers to *generalized* expectancies, and it should not be surprising that LOC plays a small role in explaining behaviour in situations in which specific expectancies are well-established. For instance, an internal LOC predicts good grades early in a student's academic career but less so as the student learns what is involved in doing well.

A third point made by Rotter (1975) is that researchers may inadvertently fall into a 'good guy–bad guy' way of thinking about LOC, assuming that internals only do good things and that externals only do bad things. So, 'internals should be more liberal, more socially skilled, better adjusted, more efficient' (p. 60). There is no reason to make these assumptions, and if they are used as hypotheses, they will not yield consistently confirming data. To have 'good' consequences, an individual's LOC must be congruent with the causal texture of given situations, and there are settings in which a realistic external LOC is more useful than an unrealistic internal LOC.

Rotter (1975) also touched upon two methodological issues that have guided subsequent researchers as they developed additional LOC measures. The first issue concerns domain-specific LOC measures. Consistent with social learning theory, expectancies about a given sphere of activity – such as academics – should better predict behaviour in that domain than expectancies about other spheres. Accordingly, recent years have seen the development of dozens of domain-specific LOC measures.

The second issue is the dimensionality of LOC. Rotter's (1966) original LOC measure, described in the next section, conceptualized the construct as unidimensional, an assumption apparently supported by factor analyses. However, Rotter (1975) pointed out that such findings are not incompatible with the possibility that there are subtypes of internality or externality and that there may be good reasons to identify these. Subsequent researchers have thus unpacked LOC.

REPRESENTATIVE MEASURES OF LOCUS OF CONTROL

Space does not permit discussion of all extant LOC measures, or even a listing of them by name. My strategy is to focus on three representative measures (see Table 1).

Rotter's (1966) own *IE* (Internal–External) *Locus of Control Scale* was one of the first measures of LOC and is still widely used. It presents respondents with pairs of statements, one exemplifying internal LOC and the other external LOC. Respondents choose one statement in each pair, and the number of external choices is ascertained. The content of the items ranges widely. In the process of scale development, candidate items were discarded if they were linked to social desirability. Factor analyses implied that the resulting scale was unidimensional. Subsequent studies, however, cast doubt on both the independence of the measure from social desirability and its unidimensionality. Indices of internal consistency and test–retest reliability are nonetheless satisfactory. Validity

Table 1.   Representative LOC measures

IE Locus of Control Scale (Rotter, 1966)

Purpose: to measure general LOC
Format: 23 forced-choice items
Internal consistency: $\alpha = 0.70$
Test–retest reliability: $r = 0.50$–0.70
Validity evidence: see text

IAR Questionnaire (Crandall et al., 1965)

Purpose: to measure LOC of children in
    academic domains, separately
    for success and failure
format: 34 forced-choice items, half for success
    and half for failure
Internal consistencies: $\alpha = 0.55$ for subscales,
    0.70 overall
Test–retest reliability: $r = 0.70$
Validity evidence: internality scores predict grades,
    achievement test scores, and amount of time
    spent pursuing 'intellectual' activities

IPC Scales (Levenson, 1981)

Purpose: to measure internal, powerful others,
    and chance LOC
Format: 24 Likert 6-point scale items, 8 items
    per subscale
Internal consistencies: $\alpha = 0.60$–0.90 for subscales
Test–retest reliability: $r = 0.60$–0.80
Validity evidence: subscales show differential
    correlates with types of political activism, types of
    psychopathology,
    length of internment among prisoners, and
    retrospective reports of parental behaviour

has been established in a variety of ways, including known-groups' strategies. Individuals who arguably have an external LOC because of the circumstances of their lives – such as prisoners – score toward the external end of the scale.

Crandall, Katkovsky, and Crandall's (1965) *IAR* (Intellectual Achievement Responsibility) *Questionnaire* was one of the first domain-specific measures. The IAR Questionnaire measures LOC with respect to academic outcomes and is suitable for grade school and high school students. Like Rotter's measure, the IAR Questionnaire uses a forced-choice format. However, it distinguishes between success experiences and failure experiences. Another feature of the IAR Questionnaire is that it renders externality in terms of 'other people' as opposed to chance or fate. The IAR Questionnaire is consistent and reliable, and it has accrued good validity evidence.

Among a number of multidimensional LOC measures, Levenson's (1981) *IPC* (Internality, Powerful Others, and Chance) *Scales* have become particularly well-known. This measure distinguishes two types of externality: the belief that powerful others control reinforcement and the belief that chance is the locus of control. Three subscales therefore comprise the measure. Each is measured with statements presented in a Likert format. Levenson (1981) reported factor analyses supporting the independence of these three factors, although appreciate that these subscales are not orthogonal. Internality is negatively correlated with both externality subscales, which in turn are positively correlated with one another. Again, this measure is consistent, reliable, and valid.

FUTURE PERSPECTIVES

Several lines of current research seem fruitful. The first are studies of domain-specific LOC that investigate generalized expectancies with respect to health (e.g. Wallston, Wallston, Kaplan & Maides, 1976) and religiosity (e.g. Jackson & Coursey, 1988). Next are studies that investigate LOC cross-culturally. In light of arguments that personal control is a culture-bound construct, such investigations are important because they suggest boundary conditions to LOC as typically construed as well as discover additional expectancies that influence behaviour (Weisz, Rothbaum & Blackburn, 1984). A third line of work attempts to discern the developmental precursors of LOC and may lead to interventions that cultivate appropriate expectancies. Finally, the links between LOC and its numerous cognates deserve not only theoretical speculation but also earnest empirical inquiry.

CONCLUSIONS

LOC has long been a central topic of investigation by psychologists and will continue to be. LOC researchers have not always followed the good advice offered by Rotter (1975) about the meaning and measurement of LOC, and contemporary investigators who study cognates of LOC have certainly not heeded the analogous advice vis-à-vis their own constructs. The most important conclusion that I can offer is to echo Rotter's admonition that researchers should keep theory in mind as they design and interpret studies.

References

Crandall, V.C., Katkovsky, W. & Crandall, V.J. (1965). Children's beliefs in their own control of reinforcement in intellectual-academic achievement situations. *Child Development*, 36, 91–109.

Jackson, L.E. & Coursey, R.D. (1988). The relationship of God control and internal locus of control to intrinsic religious motivation, coping, and purpose in life. *Journal for the Scientific Study of Religion*, 27, 399–410.

Lefcourt, H.M. (1991). Locus of control. In Robinson, J.P., Shaver, P.R. & Wrightsman, L.S. (Eds.), *Measures of Personality and Social Psychological Attitudes* (pp. 413–499). San Diego: Academic Press.

Levenson, H. (1981). Differentiating among internality, powerful others, and chance. In Lefcourt, H.M. (Ed.), *Research with the Locus of Control Construct*, Vol. 1 (pp. 15–63). New York: Academic Press.

MacDonald, A.P. (1973). Internal–external locus of control. In Robinson, J.P. & Shaver, P.R. (Eds.), *Measures of Social Psychological Attitudes* (Rev. ed., pp. 169–243). Ann Arbor, MI: Institute for Social Research.

Peterson, C. (1999). Personal control and well-being. In Kahneman, D., Diener, E. & Schwarz, N. (Eds.), *Well-Being: The Foundations of Hedonic Psychology* (pp. 288–301). New York: Russell Sage.

Rotter, J.B. (1954). *Social Learning and Clinical Psychology*. Englewood Cliffs, NJ: Prentice-Hall.

Rotter, J.B. (1966). Generalized expectancies for internal versus external control of reinforcement. *Psychological Monographs*, 81 (1, Whole No. 609).

Rotter, J.B. (1975). Some problems and misconceptions related to the construct of internal versus external reinforcement. *Journal of Consulting and Clinical Psychology*, 43, 56–67.

Wallston, B.S., Wallston, K.A., Kaplan, G.D & Maides, S.A. (1976). Development and validation of the Health Locus of Control (HLC) Scale. *Journal of Consulting and Clinical Psychology*, 44, 580–585.

Weisz, J.R., Rothbaum, F.M. & Blackburn, T.C. (1984). Standing out and standing in: the psychology of control in America and Japan. *American Psychologist*, 39, 955–969.

Christopher Peterson

RELATED ENTRIES

Personality Assessment (General), Cognitive Styles, Attributional Styles, Theoretical Perspective: Cognitive